Get Connected.

Interactive Presentations

Connect Accounting's **Interactive Presentations** teach each chapter's core learning objectives and concepts through an engaging, hands-on presentation, bringing the text content to life. Interactive Presentations harness the full power of technology to truly engage and appeal to all learning styles. Interactive Presentations are ideal in all class formats—online, face-to-face, or hybrid.

Intelligent Response Technology

Intelligent Response Technology (IRT) is Connect Accounting's new student interface for end-of-chapter assessment content. Intelligent Response Technology provides a general journal application that looks and feels more like what you would find in a general ledger software package, improves answer acceptance to reduce student frustration with formatting issues (such as rounding), and, for select questions, provides an expanded table that guides students through the process of solving the problem.

view transaction list	view general journal

Journal Entry Worksheet

1 2 3 4 5 6 7

Two-thirds of the work related to $12,000 cash received in advance is performed this period.

Transaction	General Journal	Debit	Credit
a.	Unearned fee revenue	12,000	
	fe		12,000
	Fee revenue		
	Unearned fee revenue		

*Enter debits before credits

done	clear transaction	record transaction

Get Engaged.

eBooks

Connect Plus includes a media-rich eBook that allows you to share your notes with your students. Your students can insert and review their own notes, highlight the text, search for specific information, and interact with media resources. Using an eBook with Connect Plus gives your students a complete digital solution that allows them to access their materials from any computer.

Lecture Capture

Make your classes available anytime, anywhere. With simple, one-click recording, students can search for a word or phrase and be taken to the exact place in your lecture that they need to review.

Fundamentals of
FINANCIAL ACCOUNTING

Fourth Edition

FRED PHILLIPS
University of Saskatchewan

ROBERT LIBBY
Cornell University

PATRICIA A. LIBBY
Ithaca College

McGraw-Hill
Irwin

FUNDAMENTALS OF FINANCIAL ACCOUNTING, FOURTH EDITION

Published by McGraw-Hill/Irwin, a business unit of The McGraw-Hill Companies, Inc., 1221 Avenue of the Americas, New York, NY, 10020. Copyright © 2013 by The McGraw-Hill Companies, Inc. All rights reserved. Printed in the United States of America. Previous editions © 2011, 2008, and 2006. No part of this publication may be reproduced or distributed in any form or by any means, or stored in a database or retrieval system, without the prior written consent of The McGraw-Hill Companies, Inc., including, but not limited to, in any network or other electronic storage or transmission, or broadcast for distance learning.

Some ancillaries, including electronic and print components, may not be available to customers outside the United States.

This book is printed on acid-free paper.

1 2 3 4 5 6 7 8 9 0 DOW/DOW 1 0 9 8 7 6 5 4 3 2

ISBN   978-0-07-802537-2
MHID   0-07-802537-0

Senior Vice President, Products & Markets: *Kurt L. Strand*
Vice President, General Manager, Products & Markets: *Brent Gordon*
Vice President, Content Production & Technology Services: *Kimberly Meriwether David*
Director: *Tim Vertovec*
Executive Director of Development: *Ann Torbert*
Executive Brand Manager: *James Heine*
Development Editor: *Rebecca Mann*
Director of Digital Content: *Patricia Plumb*
Senior Marketing Manager: *Kathleen Klehr*
Manager, Content Production: *Mary Conzachi*
Content Project Manager: *Bruce Gin*
Senior Buyer: *Carol A. Bielski*
Senior Designer: *Matt Diamond*
Cover Designer: *Gino Cieslik*
Interior Designer: *Laurie Entringer*
Senior Content Licensing Specialist: *Jeremy Cheshareck*
Photo Researcher: *Editorial Image, LLC*
Typeface: *10.5/12 Goudy*
Compositor: *Laserwords Private Limited*
Printer: *R. R. Donnelley*
Cover Photos: *PS3 Controller, Soda Can: © Corbis. Pizza: Getty Images. North Face:
© Danita Delimont/Alamy. Roller Coaster: © Robin Smith/Stone/Getty Images.*

All credits appearing on page or at the end of the book are considered to be an extension of the copyright page.

Library of Congress Cataloging-in-Publication Data

Phillips, Fred.
    Fundamentals of financial accounting / Fred Phillips, Robert Libby,
Patricia A. Libby.—4th ed.
        p. cm.
    Includes index.
    ISBN 978-0-07-802537-2 (alk. paper)—ISBN 0-07-802537-0 (alk. paper)
    1. Accounting. I. Libby, Robert. II. Libby, Patricia A. III. Title.
HF5636.P545 2013
657—dc23

                                                                2012026231

The Internet addresses listed in the text were accurate at the time of publication. The inclusion of a website does not indicate an endorsement by the authors or McGraw-Hill, and McGraw-Hill does not guarantee the accuracy of the information presented at these sites.

www.mhhe.com

Dedication

I dedicate this book to the best teachers I've ever had: my Mom and
Dad, Barb, Harrison, and Daniel
FRED PHILLIPS

Herman and Doris Hargenrater, Laura Libby, Oscar and Selma Libby
PATRICIA AND ROBERT LIBBY

Fred Phillips

Fred Phillips is a professor and the George C. Baxter Chartered Accountants of Saskatchewan Scholar at the University of Saskatchewan, where he teaches introductory financial accounting. He also has taught introductory accounting at the University of Texas at Austin and the University of Manitoba. Fred has an undergraduate accounting degree, a professional accounting designation, and a PhD from the University of Texas at Austin. He previously worked as an audit manager at KPMG.

Fred's main career interest is accounting education. He has been recognized with more than 20 awards, as chosen by his students and peers. In 2006, Fred was awarded the title Master Teacher at the University of Saskatchewan. In 2011, he was admitted to the 3M National Teaching Fellowship, the highest honor for undergraduate teaching in Canada. In the same year, he won a national competition for an instructional case that is integrated throughout assignment materials in Chapters 5–12 of this textbook. In 2012, Fred received the L. S. Rosen Outstanding Educator Award, the American Accounting Association's Innovation in Auditing and Assurance Education Award, and the American Accounting Association's Award for Outstanding Research in Accounting Education. His peer-reviewed publications include education-focused research and instructional cases in *Issues in Accounting Education*, as well as professional judgment studies in *Journal of Accounting Research* and *Organizational Behavior and Human Decision Processes*, among others. Fred is a current member of the Teaching, Curriculum, & Learning and Two-Year College sections of the American Accounting Association. In his spare time, he likes to work out, drink iced cappuccinos, and relax with his family.

Robert Libby

Robert Libby is the David A. Thomas Professor of Accounting at Cornell University, where he teaches the introductory financial accounting course. He previously taught at the University of Illinois, Pennsylvania State University, the University of Texas at Austin, the University of Chicago, and the University of Michigan. He received his BS from Pennsylvania State University and his MAS and PhD from the University of Illinois; he is also a CPA.

Bob is a widely published author and researcher specializing in behavioral accounting. He was selected as the AAA Outstanding Educator in 2000, received the AAA Outstanding Service Award in 2006, and received the AAA Notable Contributions to the

Literature Award in 1985 and 1996. He is the only person to have received all three of the Association's highest awards for teaching, service, and research. He has published numerous articles in *The Accounting Review*; *Journal of Accounting Research*; *Accounting, Organizations, and Society*; and other accounting journals. He has held a variety of offices including vice president in the American Accounting Association and is a member of the American Institute of CPAs and the editorial boards of *The Accounting Review*; *Accounting, Organizations, and Society*; and *Journal of Accounting Literature*.

Patricia A. Libby

Patricia Libby is associate professor of accounting at Ithaca College, where she teaches the undergraduate financial accounting course. She previously taught graduate and undergraduate financial accounting at Eastern Michigan University and the University of Texas. Before entering academe, she was an auditor with Price Waterhouse (now PricewaterhouseCoopers) and a financial administrator at the University of Chicago. She is also faculty advisor to Beta Alpha Psi and Ithaca College Accounting Association.

She received her BS from Pennsylvania State University, her MBA from DePaul University, and her PhD from the University of Michigan; she is also a CPA.

Pat conducts research on using cases in the introductory course and other parts of the accounting curriculum. She has published articles in *The Accounting Review, Issues in Accounting Education*, and *The Michigan CPA*.

Focused on Financial Accounting in the Context of Real Business

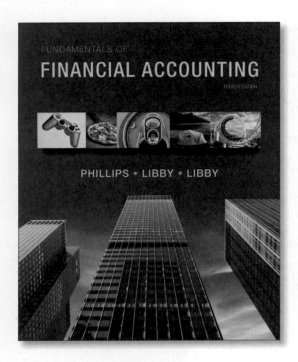

One of the most widely used introductory accounting textbooks, Phillips/Libby/Libby *Fundamentals of Financial Accounting* focuses on three key attributes.

Engaging Writing. *Fundamentals of Financial Accounting* introduces students to financial accounting using an appropriate mix of conversational wording, clear and concise presentations, and everyday examples. It does this without ever sacrificing its rigor or the concepts that are important to grasping financial accounting. Students can feel comfortable as they are introduced to the world of financial accounting.

Relevant Focus Companies. Each chapter of *Fundamentals of Financial Accounting* makes financial accounting come alive by using a real company whose products and services are popular with students. Students learn financial accounting concepts through the use of examples from such companies as **American Eagle** (clothing), **Activision** (video games), and **Under Armour** (sportswear).

Proven Pedagogy. The authors' approach to introducing the accounting cycle and using visual aids throughout the textbook has been tested in peer-reviewed, published research studies. One of these award-winning studies has shown that the accounting cycle approach used in this textbook yields learning gains that outpace approaches used in other textbooks by a significant margin. The current edition of this textbook also integrates an award-winning continuing case in the assignment materials for Chapters 5–12. This continuing case enables your students to learn key accounting judgments that affect business decisions in the workplace. Through ongoing research and development of innovative material, the authors are committed to helping your students succeed in accounting.

> *Practical, applicable to both accounting and non-accounting majors and a very thorough financial accounting textbook.*
>
> —Ronald Premuroso, *University of Montana*
>
> *Students should find the use of companies from their generation, as examples, interesting.*
>
> —Diane Marker, *University of Toledo*

> *This book is an easy and informative book. It contains many examples that would appeal to students which in turn makes them more likely to read. . . . Your problems are outstanding and it makes it so helpful when you include similar problems to allow the professor to be able to go through one and assign another that is almost identical, but uses different numbers. Overall, it is one of the best books I have seen or reviewed. The authors have done an outstanding job with this text! . . . It beats out all other books I have seen thus far.*
>
> —Stephen Benner, *Eastern Illinois University*

Dedicated to Student Motivation and Success

The accounting world is encountering new challenges and *Fundamentals of Financial Accounting* aims to help instructors and students take them in stride. Instructors will find some important features in the fourth edition that will give students the tools and information necessary to help them succeed. Based on the feedback and advice from several financial accounting faculty, the most significant of these include:

- The **entrepreneurial focus company introduced in Chapter 1 extends through Chapters 2, 3, and 4,** allowing students to see how a business plan (Chapter 1) leads to accounting decisions that affect the balance sheet (Chapter 2), and income statement (Chapter 3), and adjustments made prior to evaluating the financial results (Chapter 4). Students emerge from the first four chapters with a solid understanding of how the accounting process plays a pivotal role in business.

- Recognizing the presence of International Financial Reporting Standards (IFRS) in more than 100 countries worldwide and within foreign-owned companies in the United States, we integrate selected IFRS topics in appropriate chapters at a level suitable for introductory financial accounting. We summarize these topics at the end of the last chapter in the book (in chapter supplement 13B) and we tie this summary to specific references in each chapter. To support discussions and analyses involving IFRS, we include questions and exercises in **end-of-chapter assignments** that specifically focus on IFRS.

> *Spotlight on the World is the **best introduction to IFRS** that I have seen in any introductory textbook.*
>
> —Betty David, *Francis Marion University*

- To further engage students and provide instructors material for in-class discussion, we integrate **Spotlight features** in each chapter, focusing on business decisions, ethics, internal controls, financial reporting, and the world (IFRS). Key Spotlights are supported by 4-minute videos that are scripted specifically for this textbook.

> *I like how Phillips/Libby/Libby **separates balance sheet transactions and income statement transactions into two chapters.** This really gives us a chance to **explore the accounting process cycle by diving into** the details of transaction analysis, recording a transaction, and summarizing in the ledgers.*
>
> —Ryan Enlow, *University of Nevada, Las Vegas*

> *Phillips/Libby/Libby 3e introduces all of the financial statements in the first chapter, then utilizes debits and credits combined with increases and decreases for transactions affecting the balance sheet, and then reinforces the methodology when presenting the transactions affecting the income statement in Chapter 3. This area is the toughest for students and requires the most practice. Phillips understands this and expertly navigates through the two statements and demonstrates how the two interconnect and depend upon each other, setting the stage for an easier adjustment and closing process ahead.*
>
> —Margaret Costello Lambert, *Oakland Community College*

Real Companies Bring Accounting Concepts to Life

Not all students learn financial accounting with ease. With so many distractions these days, it is difficult to keep both majors and non-majors focused on the big picture. The authors of *Fundamentals of Financial Accounting* understand the challenges instructors face and the need for a financial accounting text that is relevant, easy to read, and current.

Fundamentals of Financial Accounting responds by using **carefully chosen focus companies that students not only recognize but are familiar with because they have visited or used their products.** From companies like the local pizza restaurant to the world's most familiar businesses, each chapter features the business and accounting concepts underlying prominent companies such as Walmart, Activision, Cedar Fair, American Eagle, National Beverage, Under Armour, and General Mills.

Through crisp, clear, and engaging writing, the financial decisions these companies make and the financial statements they use come alive for students and they are able to see the big picture of how accounting relates to the real world—their world.

From **Concepts** to **Comprehension**–
Reinforcement Is Key

Whether you're presenting, discussing, or problem solving, you want materials that will motivate students and hold their interest. Motivating today's students requires materials that connect them with the workplace and encourage them to think about course topics before, during, and after class. *Fundamentals of Financial Accounting* offers students many tools to help reinforce the concepts discussed throughout the text.

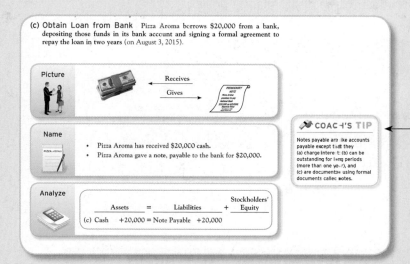

Coach's Tips

Every student needs encouragement and Coach's Tips are just one way *Fundamentals of Financial Accounting* fulfills that need. Coach's Tips appear throughout the text and in selected end-of-chapter problems to offer tips, advice, and suggestions.

How's it going?
Self-Study Practice

Research shows that students learn best when they are actively engaged in the learning process. This active learning feature engages the student, provides interactivity, and promotes efficient learning. These quizzes ask students to pause at strategic points throughout each chapter to ensure they understand key points before moving ahead.

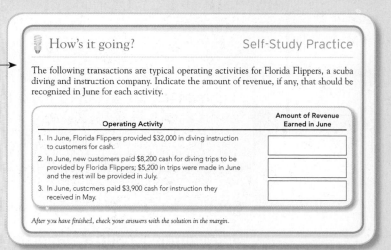

> " I really liked the discussions on **fraud, SOX, and IFRS.** These are important topics which really must be addressed. [Chapter 5] does a **great job in addressing timely topics**—why financial statements have failed in the past and how we are addressing weaknesses of the statements, and what to anticipate in the future. **Your discussion on IFRS was great.**
>
> —Linda K. Whitten, *Skyline College*

Videos Put the Spotlight on Issues in Financial Accounting

Spotlight Features

Each chapter includes Spotlight features focusing on business decisions, ethics, internal controls, financial reporting, and the world (IFRS). These features are designed to further engage students and provide instructors with material for in-class discussion. New for this edition, these features illustrate the effects of the global financial crisis.

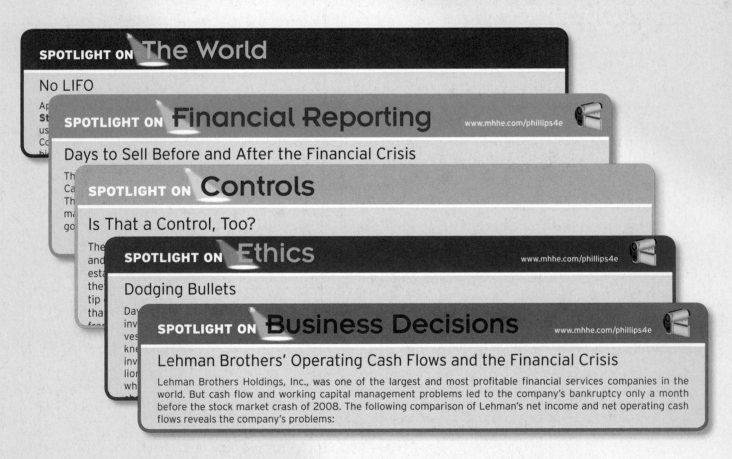

SPOTLIGHT ON The World

No LIFO

SPOTLIGHT ON Financial Reporting   www.mhhe.com/phillips4e

Days to Sell Before and After the Financial Crisis

SPOTLIGHT ON Controls

Is That a Control, Too?

SPOTLIGHT ON Ethics   www.mhhe.com/phillips4e

Dodging Bullets

SPOTLIGHT ON Business Decisions   www.mhhe.com/phillips4e

Lehman Brothers' Operating Cash Flows and the Financial Crisis

Lehman Brothers Holdings, Inc., was one of the largest and most profitable financial services companies in the world. But cash flow and working capital management problems led to the company's bankruptcy only a month before the stock market crash of 2008. The following comparison of Lehman's net income and net operating cash flows reveals the company's problems:

- **Spotlight on the World**—highlights significant impacts of IFRS.

- Spotlight on Financial Reporting—connects chapter topics with real-world disclosures provided in the financial statements of our focus companies and other contrast companies.

- **Spotlight on Controls**—highlights applications of internal control principles in the workplace.

- **Spotlight on Ethics**—emphasizes ethical issues faced in business and the importance of acting responsibly.

- **Spotlight on Business Decisions**—helps students develop strong decision-making skills by illustrating the relevance of accounting in real-world decision making and the lessons learned from the global economic crisis.

Videos

Selected **Spotlight on Ethics, Financial Reporting,** and **Business Decisions** features are brought to life in 2-5 minute newsmagazine-style videos, which are available in McGraw-Hill *Connect Accounting*. These investigative videos written by Fred Phillips tie to specific topics in *Fundamentals of Financial Accounting*. Bring business and accounting into your classroom in a way that is sure to engage students and get them talking about the stories in your textbook. Instructors can assign students to watch the videos and answer questions regarding the content in Connect.

Chapter	Video Title	Video Description
Chapter 3 (page 97)	Time Is Money	In 2000-01, Computer Associates violated the time period assumption in order to present a picture of smooth, steady growth. This video illustrates the effect of shifting sales from one period to another and asks students to discuss its impact.
Chapter 4 (page 167)	Anatomy of a Business Failure	Circuit City once was a leading electronics retailer. But, as this video demonstrates, the company's financial problems led to a free-fall in the company's stock price. This video walks students through the series of events that ultimately ended when Circuit City liquidated in January 2009.
Chapter 6 (page 263)	Granny Does Time	After twelve years of honest bookkeeping, a grandmother begins embezzling from her employer by writing checks to herself, recording them as inventory purchases, and then destroying them when preparing the bank reconciliation. This is a must-see video for future business owners and financial advisers because it underscores the importance of internal controls over cash and inventory.
NEW! Chapter 6 (page 271)	Financial Crisis Erodes Margins	Discusses the decline and recovery of gross profit percentage at Nike, Puma, and Adidas before and after the 2008-09 financial crisis.
Chapter 7 (page 316)	Dodging Bullets	Body armor made by DHB Industries in 2004-05 for the U.S. Marines and local police departments did not meet quality standards. Knowing the impact of an inventory write-down, DHB tried to conceal its problems. By telling these events, this video invites students to consider how fraudulent actions may put innocent people in harm's way.
NEW! Chapter 7 (page 321)	Financial Crisis Slows Inventory	Discusses the decline and recovery of inventory turnover at Caterpillar before and after the 2008-09 financial crisis.
Chapter 8 (page 367)	Resetting the Clock	This video describes how a credit manager at MCI used his knowledge of the allowance method to avoid recording $70 million in bad debts. The video shows students how small initial missteps led the credit manager to redirect his genuine ambition into criminal actions, which ended in a prison sentence and personal ruin.
NEW! Chapter 8 (page 369)	Financial Crisis Delays Collections	Discusses the decline and recovery of receivables turnover at K·Swiss before and after the 2008-09 financial crisis.
Chapter 9 (page 400)	Simple Violations, Serious Consequences	This video describes how the simple act of capitalizing expenses enabled WorldCom to mislead financial statement users. Students are invited to consider the judgment inherent in many seemingly simple accounting decisions.
NEW! Chapter 12 (page 566)	Financial Crisis Cuts Cash Flows	Discusses the disparity between net income and operating cash flows at Lehman Brothers, immediately preceding the 2008-09 financial crisis.

I thought the coverage on fraud and SOX was very good. Also, the inclusion of GAAP vs. IFRS. The information presented was easy to read and understand.

—Victoria White, *Ivy Tech Community College of Indiana-Evansville*

Practice and Review Materials

To effectively evaluate and guide student success with the appropriate feedback, you need homework & test materials that are easy to use and tied to the chapter discussions.

> *The end of chapter problems and exercises are ample, diverse (in terms of rigor) and congruent with the material covered in the chapter.*
>
> –Brian Nagle, *Duquesne University*

Each chapter of *Fundamentals of Financial Accounting* is followed by an extensive variety of end-of-chapter material that applies and integrates topics presented in the chapter. We have retained many of the popular items from prior editions and added new types of end-of-chapter materials including a Homework Helper, multiple-perspective discussion questions, comprehensive problems, and continuing cases.

Chapter Summary

Each chapter concludes with an end-of-chapter summary, organized by chapter learning objective, that revisits the learning objectives from the beginning of the chapter.

Key Terms

Includes key terms, definitions, and page references. Full definitions for all key terms are found in the back of the text.

Homework Helper

Immediately precedes each chapter's homework materials, highlighting subtleties discussed in the chapter and providing practice advice so that students can avoid common pitfalls when completing homework.

HOMEWORK HELPER

Multistep Income Statement Format (heading omitted)

Sales Revenue	$100,000
Less: Sales Returns and Allowances	(2,500)
Sales Discounts	(1,500)
Net Sales	96,000
Cost of Goods Sold	55,000
Gross Profit	41,000
Selling, General, and Administrative Expenses	21,000
Income from Operations	20,000
Other Revenue (Expenses)	5,000
Income before Income Tax Expense	25,000
Income Tax Expense	10,000
Net Income	$ 15,000

Reported Externally / Reported Internally

Alternative terms

- Gross profit is also called gross margin or margin.

Helpful reminders

- When preparing a bank reconciliation, your goals are to determine which transactions the bank has not yet processed and which transactions your company has not yet processed. You will record transactions correctly processed by the bank but not yet processed by your company.
- Sales Returns have two components: (1) an adjustment to the selling price (record a contra-revenue and a decrease in Cash or Accounts Receivable) and (2) return of goods previously recorded as sold (record an increase in Inventory and a decrease in Cost of Goods Sold). Sales Allowances involve only the first component, because no goods are returned to the seller.

Build Confidence and Success

PRACTICE MATERIAL

QUESTIONS (⊕ Symbol indicates questions that require analysis from more than one perspective.)

1. Define the following:
   a. Asset
   b. Current asset
   c. Liability
   d. Current liability
   e. Contributed capital
   f. Retained earnings
2. Define a transaction and give an example of each of the two types of events that are considered transactions.
3. For accounting purposes, what is an account? Explain why accounts are used in an accounting system.
4. What is the basic accounting equation?
5. Explain what *debit* and *credit* mean.
6. Briefly explain what is meant by *transaction analysis*. What are the two principles underlying transaction analysis?

7. What two different accounting equalities must be maintained in transaction analysis?
8. What is a journal entry? What is the typical format of a journal entry?
9. What is a T-account? What is its purpose?
10. Explain the cost principle.
11. To obtain financing for her hair salon, Valeri asked you to prepare a balance sheet for her business. When she sees it, she is disappointed that the assets exclude a value for her list of loyal customers. What can you tell her to explain why this "asset" has been excluded? Knowing this, what should she tell her banker when they meet next week? ⊕

MULTIPLE CHOICE

1. Which of the following is not an asset?
   a. Cash

5. The T-account is used to summarize which of the following?

Multi-perspective Discussion Questions

Each chapter includes 10–20 questions that ask students to explain and discuss terms and concepts presented in the chapter. Selected questions, denoted with an icon, are designed to help students begin developing critical thinking skills. These questions are ideal for sparking debate at the beginning of class or when transitioning between or reviewing topics.

Multiple-Choice Questions

Each chapter includes 10 multiple-choice questions that let students practice basic concepts. Solutions for these questions are provided in the back of the text.

Mini-Exercises

These assignments illustrate and apply a single learning objective from the chapter.

Exercises

These additional assignments illustrate and apply single and multiple learning objectives from the chapter.

Problems (Coached, Group A, and Group B)

Each chapter includes three problem sets to help students develop decision-making skills. Coached problems include question-specific tips to assist students who need a little help getting started. Groups A and B are similar problems but without the coaching.

 ## Level-up Questions

In each chapter, particularly challenging questions, designated by the level-up icon, require students to combine multiple concepts to advance to the next level of accounting knowledge.

Comprehensive Problems

Selected chapters include problems that cover topics from earlier chapters to refresh, reinforce, and build an integrative understanding of the course material. These are a great resource for helping students stay up-to-date throughout the course.

Skills Development Cases

Each chapter offers cases designed to help students develop analytical, critical thinking, and technology skills. These cases are ideal for individual assignments, class discussions, and group projects.

 Encourage your students to find financial information in an actual annual report. The first case of every chapter presents, in multiple-choice format, an opportunity to connect your students with real-world financial reporting.

Chapters 5–12 present a continuing case involving Wiki Art Gallery. This case depicts a setting in which accounting information is used for determining a company's selling price. By examining accounting decisions, again in an easy-to-use multiple-choice format, students can learn that not all numbers are what they appear at first glance.

Continuing Cases

In Chapter 1, students are introduced to Nicole's Getaway Spa (NGS). In the following chapters, this continuing case is extended to encompass each new topic.

In Chapter 5, assignment material for a second continuing case (Wiki Art Gallery) is introduced. As with NGS, this case extends through the following chapters, but with an eye to developing the critical thinking skills valued by accounting professionals.

CONTINUING CASE

CC1-1 Financial Statements for a Business Plan

Nicole Mackisey is thinking of forming her own spa business, Nicole's Getaway Spa (NGS). Nicole expects that she and two family members will each contribute $10,000 to the business and receive 1,000 shares each. Nicole forecasts the following amounts for the first year of operations, ending December 31, 2013: Cash on hand and in the bank, $2,150; amounts due from customers from spa treatments, $1,780; building and equipment, $70,000; amounts owed to beauty supply outlets for spa equipment, $4,660; notes payable to a local bank for $38,870. Cash dividends of $2,000 will be paid to the stockholders during the year. Nicole also forecasts that first year sales revenues will be $40,000; wages will be $24,000; the cost of supplies used up will be $7,000; selling and administrative expenses will be $5,000; and income taxes will be $1,600.

Required:

1. Based on Nicole's estimates, prepare a (forecasted) income statement for Nicole's Getaway Spa for the year ended December 31, 2013.
2. Prepare a (forecasted) statement of retained earnings for Nicole's Getaway Spa for the year ended December 31, 2013.

A PROVEN TEACHING AND LEARNING METHODOLOGY

Compressed Coverage (Other textbooks)	**Step-by-Step Coverage** (Phillips/Libby/Libby)
Overview of F/S and Users	Overview of F/S and Users
F/S, Ratios, and Conceptual Framework	B/S Transactions with Accounting Equation, Journal Entries, and T-accounts
B/S and I/S Transactions with Accounting Equation, Journal Entries, and T-accounts	B/S and I/S Transactions with Accounting Equation, Journal Entries, and T-accounts
Adjustments, Closing Entries, F/S Preparation	Adjustments, Closing Entries, F/S Preparation

Faculty agree the accounting cycle is the most critical concept to learn and master for students studying financial accounting. The approach to this topic in Phillips/Libby/Libby is based on the belief that students struggle with the accounting cycle when transaction analysis is covered in one chapter. If students are exposed to the accounting equation, journal entries, and T-accounts for both balance sheet and income statement accounts in a single chapter, many are left behind and are unable to grasp material in the next chapter, which typically covers adjustments and financial statement preparation.

The accompanying graphic shows how, unlike other textbooks, the Phillips/Libby/Libby approach spreads transaction analysis coverage over two chapters so that students have the time to master the material. In Chapter 2 of *Fundamentals of Financial Accounting*, students are exposed to the accounting equation and transaction analysis for transactions that affect only balance sheet accounts. This provides students with the opportunity to learn the basic structure and tools used in accounting in a simpler setting. In Chapter 3, students are exposed to more complex transactions that affect both balance sheet and income statement accounts. As a result of this progressive approach to transaction analysis, students learn more, as documented in peer-reviewed research.* We have also seen that our approach prepares students to learn adjustments, financial statement preparation, and more advanced topics.

---

*Phillips, F., and L. Heiser, "A Field Experiment Examining the Effects of Accounting Equation Emphasis and Transaction Scope on Students Learning to Journalize," *Issues in Accounting Education,* 26: 681–699, 2011.

What's New in the Fourth Edition?

In response to the feedback and guidance from numerous financial accounting faculty, *Fundamentals of Financial Accounting*, 4e, includes several important changes, including new focus companies, new chapter openers, more than 50 **new** end-of-chapter assignments, and refinements and updates to over 500 remaining questions, exercises, problems, and cases. Several new features are introduced in this edition, including new Spotlight discussions highlighting the effects of the global financial crisis, new annual report cases featuring easy-to-use multiple-choice question formats, new comprehensive problems (spanning multiple chapters), and new critical thinking case questions (again in multiple-choice format).

CHAPTER 1
Focus Company: Pizza Aroma

- Updated IFRS map in Spotlight on the World
- Revised illustrative financial statements and discussion including reference to required statement of comprehensive income
- **New** chapter supplement to explain relevance of accounting to non-majors
- Revisions to end-of-chapter material: Streamlined account names to correspond to standardized chart of accounts for hypothetical companies; updated numerical data for 100 percent of real-world companies; revised annual report case to multiple-choice format

CHAPTER 2
Focus Company: Pizza Aroma

- Refocused discussion on the balance sheet, and its relationship to financing, investing, and select operating activities
- **New** Spotlight on Financial Reporting about the importance of meeting deadlines
- Updated data for contrast company (Papa John's)
- **New** Spotlight on Financial Reporting comparing current ratios before and after the 2008-09 financial crisis
- Revisions to end-of-chapter material: Streamlined account names to correspond to standardized chart of accounts for hypothetical companies; updated numerical data for 100 percent of real-world companies; revised annual report case to multiple-choice format; **new** challenging "level-up" exercises

CHAPTER 3
Focus Company: Pizza Aroma

- **New** discussion on the income statement, and evaluating net profit margin

- **New** Spotlight on Financial Reporting comparing net profit margin ratios before and after the 2008-09 financial crisis
- Revisions to end-of-chapter material: Streamlined account names to correspond to standardized chart of accounts for hypothetical companies; updated numerical data for 100 percent of real-world companies; revised exercises to include transaction analysis and determination of income effects; revised annual report case to multiple-choice format; **new** challenging "level-up" exercises and problems

CHAPTER 4
Focus Company: Pizza Aroma

- **New** self-study practice focused on reasons for adjustments
- **New** illustration of adjustments in Exhibit 4.3
- **New** discussion to tie adjusted financial results to preliminary net profit margin from Chapter 3
- Revisions to end-of-chapter material: Streamlined account names to correspond to standardized chart of accounts for hypothetical companies; updated numerical data for 100 percent of real-world companies; revised exercises to encourage reflection on income effects of adjustments; revised annual report case to multiple-choice format; **new** challenging "level-up" exercises and continuing problems

CHAPTER 5
Focus Company: Activision Blizzard

- **New** illustration of financial statement users/uses in Exhibit 5.1
- Updated information regarding focus company and IFRS contrast company
- Revisions to end-of-chapter material: Streamlined account names to correspond to standardized chart of accounts for hypothetical companies; updated numerical data for 100 percent of real-world companies; revised annual report case to multiple-choice format; new comprehensive problem; **new** "level-up" critical thinking case (in multiple-choice format)

CHAPTER 6

Focus Company: Walmart

- **New** illustration of service and merchandising operations in Exhibit 6.1
- **New** illustration of cash receipt controls in Exhibit 6.2
- Updated information regarding focus company and contrast companies
- **New** Spotlight on Financial Reporting comparing gross profit percentages before and after the 2008–09 financial crisis
- Revisions to end-of-chapter material: Expanded demonstration case; streamlined account names to correspond to standardized chart of accounts for hypothetical companies; updated numerical data for 100 percent of real-world companies; revised annual report case to multiple-choice format; **new** comprehensive problem; **new** "level-up" exercise and critical thinking case (multiple-choice format)

CHAPTER 7

Focus Company: American Eagle Outfitters

- **New** illustration of FIFO and LIFO effects when costs are rising or declining
- **New** Spotlight on Financial Reporting discussing effect of $485 million Playbook® write-down on Research in Motion's stock price
- Updated information regarding focus company and contrast companies
- **New** Spotlight on Financial Reporting comparing days to sell before and after the 2008–09 financial crisis
- Revisions to end-of-chapter material: Streamlined account names to correspond to standardized chart of accounts for hypothetical companies; updated numerical data for 100 percent of real-world companies; revised annual report case to multiple-choice format; **new** "level-up" comprehensive problems (Chapters 6 and 7 and Chapters 2 and 7) and critical thinking case (multiple-choice format)

CHAPTER 8

Focus Company: VF Corporation

- **New** focus company (maker of North Face jackets, JanSport backpacks, Wrangler jeans)
- Updated Spotlight on Business Decisions tracking Target's bad debts before and after the 2008–09 financial crisis

- Updated discussion to incorporate changes from new revenue standard (footnoted future reclassification of bad debts from expense to contra revenue)
- Revised summary of T-accounts affected by the allowance method
- Updated information regarding focus company and contrast companies
- **New** Spotlight on Financial Reporting comparing days to collect before and after the 2008–09 financial crisis
- Revisions to end-of-chapter material: Streamlined account names to correspond to standardized chart of accounts for hypothetical companies; updated numerical data for 100 percent of real-world companies; revised annual report case to multiple-choice format; revised "level-up" comprehensive problem (Chapters 6 and 8) and **new** critical thinking case (multiple-choice format)

CHAPTER 9

Focus Company: Cedar Fair

- Updated Spotlight on the World example involving componentization
- **New** bar chart illustrations of depreciation method effects
- Cite authoritative support for including disposal gains/losses in operating income
- Updated information regarding focus company and contrast companies
- **New** Spotlight on Financial Reporting comparing fixed asset turnover before and after the 2008–09 financial crisis
- Revisions to end-of-chapter material: Streamlined account names to correspond to standardized chart of accounts for hypothetical companies; updated numerical data for 100 percent of real-world companies; revised annual report case to multiple-choice format; revised comprehensive problem (Chapters 4, 8, and 9) and **new** critical thinking case (multiple-choice format)

CHAPTER 10

Focus Company: General Mills

- Revised illustration of contingent liability accounting in Exhibit 10.9
- Updated information regarding focus company
- Revisions to end-of-chapter material: Streamlined account names to correspond to standardized chart of accounts

for hypothetical companies; updated numerical data for 100 percent of real-world companies; revised annual report case to multiple-choice format; **new** comprehensive problem (Chapters 9 and 10) and "level-up" critical thinking case (multiple-choice format)

CHAPTER 11

Focus Company: National Beverage

- **New** chapter opener comparing National Beverage stock price growth to PepsiCo and Coca-Cola
- Brief discussion of Accumulated Other Comprehensive Income in Stockholders' Equity
- Revised illustration of authorized, issued, outstanding, and treasury stock in Exhibit 11.4
- Revised Spotlight on Business Decisions to relate National Beverage's dividend policy to governmental politics
- Updated information regarding focus company
- Revisions to end-of-chapter material: Streamlined account names to correspond to standardized chart of accounts for hypothetical companies; updated numerical data for 100 percent of real-world companies; revised annual report case to multiple-choice format; **new** "level-up" critical thinking case (multiple-choice format)

CHAPTER 12

Focus Company: Under Armour

- **New** discussion to tie cash flow patterns to stages of corporate lifecycle (deleted discussion of cash flow ratios)
- **New** Spotlight on Business Decisions showing disparity between net income and operating cash flows prior to Lehman Brothers' collapse
- **New** Supplement 12B demonstrating use of T-account approach to preparing an indirect method statement of cash flows
- **New** demonstration case illustrating preparation of indirect method SCF from comparative balance sheet and income statement information

- Updated information regarding focus company
- Revisions to end-of-chapter material: Updated numerical data for 100 percent of real-world companies; revised annual report case to multiple-choice format; **new** "level-up" critical thinking case (multiple-choice format)

CHAPTER 13

Focus Company: Lowe's

- Updated information regarding focus company and contrast company (Home Depot), including all narrative interpreting and comparing financial results
- Expanded demonstration case to illustrate horizontal and vertical analyses
- Revisions to end-of-chapter material: Updated numerical data for 100 percent of real-world companies; revised annual report case to multiple-choice format

APPENDIXES A AND B

- Updated annual report excerpts for The Home Depot and Lowe's

APPENDIX C

- **New** exercise involving present value calculations of bond prices at par, discount, and premium

APPENDIX D

Focus Company: Washington Post

- Updated information regarding focus company
- Simplified accounting for passive investments by directly adjusting the investment account to fair value
- **New** Spotlight on Financial Reporting discussing Level 1, 2, and 3 fair values
- Revisions to end-of-chapter material: Updated all exercises and problems to reflect simplified accounting for passive investments

Leading Technology Extends
Learning Beyond the Classroom

McGraw-Hill *Connect Accounting*
LESS MANAGING. MORE TEACHING. GREATER LEARNING.

McGraw-Hill *CONNECT ACCOUNTING*

is an online assignment and assessment solution that connects students with the tools and resources needed to achieve success through faster learning, more efficient studying, and higher retention of knowledge.

Online Assignments

Connect Accounting helps students learn more efficiently by providing feedback and practice material when they need it, where they need it. *Connect* grades homework automatically and gives immediate feedback on any questions students may have missed.

Intelligent Response Technology (IRT)

IRT is a redesigned student interface for our end-of-chapter assessment content. The benefits include improved answer acceptance to reduce students' frustration with formatting issues (such as rounding); and a general journal application that looks and feels more like what you would find in a general ledger software package. Also, select questions have been redesigned to test students' knowledge more fully. They now include tables for students to work through rather than requiring that all calculations be done offline.

LearnSmart

LearnSmart adaptive self-study technology within *Connect Accounting* helps students make the best use of their study time. LearnSmart provides a seamless combination of practice, assessment, and remediation for every concept in the textbook. LearnSmart's intelligent software adapts to students by supplying questions on a new concept when they are ready to learn it. With LearnSmart, students will spend less time on topics they understand and practice more on those they have yet to master.

Interactive Presentations

The interactive presentations provide engaging narratives of all chapter learning objectives in an interactive online format. The presentations are tied specifically to *Fundamentals of Financial Accounting*, 4e. They follow the structure of the text and are organized to match the learning objectives within each chapter. While the interactive presentations are not meant to replace the textbook in this course, they provide additional explanation and enhancement of material from the text chapter, allowing students to learn, study, and practice with instant feedback at their own pace.

Guided Examples

The Guided Examples in *Connect Accounting* provide a narrated, animated, step-by-step walk-through of select exercises similar to those assigned. These short presentations provide reinforcement when students need it most.

Student Resource Library

The *Connect Accounting* Student Study Center gives students access to additional resources such as recorded lectures, online practice materials, an eBook, and more.

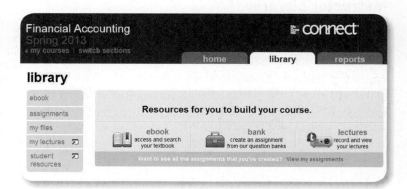

McGRAW-HILL *CONNECT ACCOUNTING* FEATURES

Connect Accounting offers a number of powerful tools and features to make managing assignments easier, so faculty can spend more time teaching.

Simple Assignment Management and Smart Grading

With *Connect Accounting,* creating assignments is easier than ever, so instructors can spend more time teaching and less time managing.

- Create and deliver assignments easily with selectable end-of-chapter questions and test bank items.
- Go paperless with the eBook and online submission and grading of student assignments.
- Have assignments scored automatically, giving students immediate feedback on their work and side-by-side comparisons with correct answers.
- Access and review each response; manually change grades or leave comments for students to review.
- Reinforce classroom concepts with practice tests and instant quizzes.

Student Reporting

Connect Accounting keeps instructors informed about how each student, section, and class is performing, allowing for more productive use of lecture and office hours. The progress-tracking function enables you to:

- View scored work immediately and track individual or group performance with assignment and grade reports.
- Access an instant view of student or class performance relative to learning objectives.
- Collect data and generate reports required by many accreditation organizations, such as AACSB and AICPA.

Instructor Library

The *Connect Accounting* Instructor Library is a repository for additional resources to improve student engagement in and out of class. You can select and use any asset that enhances your lecture. The *Connect Accounting* Instructor Library includes access to the eBook version of the text, videos, slide presentations, Solutions Manual, Instructor's Manual and Test Bank. The *Connect Accounting* Instructor Library also allows you to upload your own files.

McGraw-Hill *Connect Plus Accounting*

McGraw-Hill reinvents the textbook learning experience for the modern student with *Connect Plus Accounting*. A seamless integration of an eBook and *Connect Accounting*, *Connect Accounting Plus Accounting* provides all of the *Connect Accounting* features plus the following:

- An integrated, media-rich eBook, allowing for anytime, anywhere access to the textbook.
- Media-rich capabilities like embedded audio/visual presentations, highlighting, and sharing notes.
- Dynamic links between the problems or questions you assign to your students and the location in the eBook where that concept is covered.
- A powerful search function to pinpoint and connect key concepts for review.

In short, *Connect Plus Accounting* offers students powerful tools and features that optimize their time and energy, enabling them to focus on learning.

For more information about *Connect Plus Accounting*, go to **www.mcgrawhillconnect.com**, or contact your local McGraw-Hill sales representative.

Tegrity Campus: Lectures 24/7

Tegrity Campus is a service that makes class time available 24/7 by automatically capturing every lecture. With a simple one-click start-and-stop process, you capture all computer screens and corresponding audio in a format that is easily searchable, frame by frame. Students can replay any part of any class with easy-to-use browser-based viewing on a PC, Mac, or iPod, or other mobile device.

Educators know that the more students can see, hear, and experience class resources, the better they learn. In fact, studies prove it. Tegrity Campus's unique search feature helps students efficiently find what they need, when they need it, across an entire semester of class recordings. Help turn your students' study time into learning moments immediately supported by your lecture. With Tegrity Campus, you also increase intent listening and class participation by easing students' concerns about note-taking. Tegrity Campus will make it more likely you will see students' faces, not the tops of their heads.

To learn more about Tegrity, watch a 2-minute Flash demo at **http://tegritycampus.mhhe.com**.

> *Students like the flexibility that Connect offers. It has made a major difference in the student athletes' participation and performance. They can complete their work and catch up on lectures anytime and anywhere.*
>
> —Professor Lisa McKinney, McKinney, M.T.A., CPA, University of Alabama

McGraw-Hill Campus

McGraw-Hill Campus™ is a new one-stop teaching and learning experience available to users of any learning management system. This institutional service allows faculty and students to enjoy single sign-on (SSO) access to all McGraw-Hill Higher Education materials, including the award winning McGraw-Hill *Connect* platform, from directly within the institution's website. McGraw-Hill Campus provides faculty with instant access to teaching materials (e.g., eTextbooks, test banks, PowerPoint slides, animations, and learning objects), allowing them to browse, search, and use any ancillary content in our vast library. Students enjoy SSO access to a variety of free products (e.g., quizzes, flash cards, narrated presentations) and subscription-based products (e.g., McGraw-Hill *Connect*). With McGraw-Hill Campus, faculty and students will never need to create another account to access McGraw-Hill products and services.

Dramatically Increase Student Success and Retention

"**Students using ALEKS* performed significantly better** than those who had not on the exams that tested the underlying financial accounting material. **I spent far less office-hour time tutoring students** on financial accounting material. ALEKS provides a great way for educators teaching the introduction to accounting course to address the functional competencies (AICPA, 1999, 2000) of financial accounting in both an efficient and effective manner."

– *Ryan J. Baxter and Jay C. Thibodeau, Bentley University, MA*
Issues in Accounting Education: Nov 2011, Vol. 26, No. 4

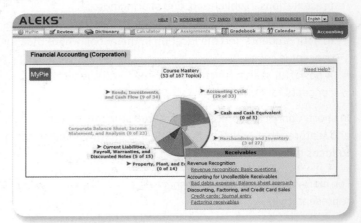

ALEKS: A Superior, Student-Friendly Accounting Experience:

- **Artificial Intelligence** Fills Knowledge Gaps
- **Cycle of Learning & Assessment** Increases Learning Momentum & Engages Students
- **Customizable Curriculum** Aligns with Your Course Syllabi and Textbooks
- **Dynamic, Automated Reports** Monitor Detailed Student & Class Progress

To learn more, visit: www.aleks.com/highered/business

CourseSmart

Learn Smart. Choose Smart.

CourseSmart is a way for faculty to find and review eTextbooks. It's also a great option for students who are interested in accessing their course materials digitally and saving money.

CourseSmart offers thousands of the most commonly adopted textbooks across hundreds of courses from a wide variety of higher education publishers. It is the only place for faculty to review and compare the full text of a textbook online, providing immediate access without the environmental impact of requesting a print exam copy.

With the CourseSmart eTextbook, students can save up to 45 percent off the cost of a print book, reduce their impact on the environment, and access powerful Web tools for learning. CourseSmart is an online eTextbook, which means users access and view their textbook online when connected to the Internet. Students can also print sections of the book for maximum portability. CourseSmart eTextbooks are available in one standard online reader with full text search, notes and highlighting, and email tools for sharing notes between classmates. For more information on CourseSmart, go to **www.coursesmart.com**.

*ALEKS is a registered trademark of ALEKS Corporation.

Tools to Support Teaching

Access to the instructor's key text ancillary materials at your fingertips. You can find all of the instructor ancillaries available in *Connect Accounting*: PowerPoint slides, Solutions Manual, Instructor's Resource Manual, Test Bank and Computerized Test Bank, Solutions to Excel templates, text exhibits, and more.

☑ Presentation Slides

Completely customized PowerPoint presentations for use in your classroom. Available on the Instructor CD-ROM.

☑ Animated PowerPoint exhibits and exercises

These aren't the typical set of PowerPoint slides that accompany most textbooks. These slides allow you to present key chapter topics and build solutions to popular end-of-chapter exercises one step at a time. Walk students through each stage in the thinking process.

☑ Solutions Manual

Prepared by Fred Phillips. Provides solutions to end-of-chapter questions, mini-exercises, exercises, problems, and cases. Available on the Instructor CD-ROM and text website.

☑ Test Bank

Prepared by Gabrielle Serrano, at Elgin Community College. Available on the Instructor CD-ROM and password protected Instructor site, this comprehensive Test Bank includes more than 1,500 true/false, multiple choice, problems, and matching questions, each tagged by learning objective, topic area, difficulty level, and AACSB, Bloom's, and AICPA categories.

☑ Instructor's Resource Manual

Prepared by Jeannie Folk at College of DuPage. Includes overviews of chapter topics and resources to help you prepare for class. It describes the ready-to-use resources that support the text (including synchrosummaries) and presents other enrichment resources, including innovative active learning exercises that you can use in class. This manual is a must-read for any instructor interested in improving teaching evaluations. Available on the Instructor CD-ROM and text website.

☑ Instructor Excel Templates

Solutions to the student Excel Templates used to solve selected end-of-chapter exercises and problems. These assignments are designated by the Excel icon. Available on the text website.

☑ EZ Test Online

McGraw-Hill's EZ Test Online is a flexible and easy-to-use electronic testing program that allows instructors to create tests from book-specific items. EZ Test Online accommodates a wide range of question types and allows instructors to add their own questions. Multiple versions of the test can be created and any test can be exported for use with course management systems such as BlackBoard/WebCT. EZ Test Online gives instructors a place to easily administer exams and quizzes online. The program is available for Windows and Macintosh environments.

ASSURANCE OF LEARNING READY

Many educational institutions today are focused on the notion of *assurance of learning,* an important element of some accreditation standards. *Fundamentals of Financial Accounting* is designed specifically to support your assurance of learning initiatives with a simple, yet powerful solution.

Each test bank question for *Fundamentals of Financial Accounting* maps to a specific chapter learning objective listed in the text. You can use our test bank software, EZ Test and EZ Test Online, or *Connect Accounting* to easily query for learning outcomes/objectives that directly relate to the learning objectives for your course. You can then use the reporting features of EZ Test or *Connect Accounting* to aggregate student results in a similar fashion, making the collection and presentation of assurance of learning data simple and easy.

AACSB STATEMENT

The McGraw-Hill Companies is a proud corporate member of AACSB International. Understanding the importance and value of AACSB accreditation, *Fundamentals of Financial Accounting* recognizes the curricula guidelines detailed in the AACSB standards for business accreditation by connecting selected questions in the test bank to the six general knowledge and skill guidelines in the AACSB standards.

The statements contained in *Fundamentals of Financial Accounting* are provided only as a guide for the users of this textbook. The AACSB leaves content coverage and assessment within the purview of individual schools, the mission of the school, and the faculty. While *Fundamentals of Financial Accounting* and the teaching package make no claim of any specific AACSB qualification or evaluation, within the Test Bank to accompany *Fundamentals of Financial Accounting* we have labeled selected questions according to the six general knowledge and skill areas.

Tools to Support Learning

☑ Online Learning Center

www.mhhe.com/phillips4e
The Online Learning Center includes multiple choice quizzes, Excel templates, and PowerPoint presentations.

☑ Student PowerPoint Presentations

Selected presentation slides reproduced in student version. Presentation Slides are located on the text's Online Learning Center.

☑ Check Figures

This tool provides answers to select problems and cases. Check Figures are located on the text's Online Learning Center.

☑ Excel Templates

Available on the Online Learning Center www.mhhe.com/phillips4e. These templates are tied to selected end-of-chapter material. These assignments are designated by the Excel icon.

☑ McGraw-Hill's Connect Accounting

See page xviii.

☑ LearnSmart

See page xviii.

McGraw-Hill Customer Experience Group Contact Information

At McGraw-Hill, we understand that getting the most from new technology can be challenging. That's why our services don't stop after you purchase our products. You can contact our Product Specialists 24 hours a day to get product training online. Or you can search the knowledge bank of Frequently Asked Questions on our support website. For Customer Support, call **800-331-5094,** or visit **www.mhhe.com/support.** One of our Technical Support Analysts will be able to assist you in a timely fashion.

Acknowledgments

We are deeply indebted to the following individuals who helped develop, critique, and shape the extensive ancillary package:

James Aitken, *Central Michigan University;*
Muriel Anderson, *SUNY-Buffalo;*
Linda Chase, *Baldwin-Wallace College;*
Betty David, *Francis Marion University;*
Jeannie Folk, *College of DuPage;*
Laurie Larson, *Valencia Community College;*
Nancy Lynch, *West Virginia University;*
Darla Karnes; *Southern Illinois University;*
Sara Melendy; *Gonzaga University;*
Debra L. Schmidt, *Cerritos College;*
Gabrielle Serrano, *Elgin Community College;*
Jack Terry, *ComSource Associates, Inc.;*
Beth Woods, *Accuracy Counts;*

We also received invaluable input and support from present and former colleagues and students, in particular Jocelyn Allard, Anders Bergstrom, Shari Boyd, Kara Chase, Shana M. Clor, Nicole Dewan, Erin Ferguson, Aaron Ferrara, Sarah Guina, Robin Harrington, Lee Harris, Blair Healy, Candice Heidt, Devon Hennig, Carrie Hordichuk, Lorraine Hurst, Jennifer Johnson, Nancy Kirzinger, Paul Knepper, Deborah Loran, Nicole Mackisey, Diana Mark, Roger Martin, Jason Matshes, Jennifer Millard, Kimberley Olfert, Ryan Olson, David Pooler, Jessica Pothier, Nick Purich, Emery Salahub, Bailey Schergevitch, Marie Tait, and Kory Wickenhauser.

Last, we thank the extraordinary efforts of a talented group of individuals at McGraw-Hill/Irwin who made all of this come together. We would especially like to thank our director, Tim Vertovec, Rebecca Mann, our development editor; Kathleen Klehr, our senior marketing manager; Mary Conzachi, our lead project manager; Matt Diamond, our designer; Carol Bielski, our buyer; Bruce Gin, our content project manager; Jeremy Cheshareck, our photo research coordinator; David Tietz, our photo researcher; and Marcy Lunetta, our permissions researcher.

We also want to recognize the valuable input of all those who helped guide our developmental decisions for the past four editions.

Debora Constable, *Georgia Perimeter College*
Robert Conway, *University of Wisconsin-Platteville*
John Cooper, *Wentworth Institute of Technology*
Anthony Copa, *Anoka-Ramsey Community College*
Meg Costello Lambert, *Oakland Community College*
Sue Counte, *Saint Louis Community College-Meramec-Kirkwood*
Rich Criscione, *Moorehead State University*
John Critchett, *Madonna University*
Marcia Croteau, *University Maryland-Baltimore County*
Stephen Crow, *California State University Sacramento*
Kathy Crusto-Way, *Tarrant Community College*
Karl Dahlberg, *Rutgers University*
Laurie Dahlin, *Worcester State College*
Roger Daniels, *College of Charleston*
Dori Danko, *Grand Valley State University*
Betty David, *Francis Marion University*
David Davis, *Tallahassee Community College*
Jan Kyle Davison, *Jefferson Davis Community College*
David Deeds, *University of Northern Iowa*
John E. Delaney, *Southwestern University*
Jamie Doran, *Muhlenberg College*
Norris Dorsey, *California State University, Northridge*
Joanne Duke, *San Francisco State University*
Jeff Edwards, *Portland Community College*
Craig R. Ehlen, *University of Southern Indiana*
Susan Eldridge, *University of Nebraska at Omaha*
Ryan Enlow, *University of Nevada, Las Vegas*
Steven Ernest, *Baton Rouge Community College*
Ann Escaro, *McHenry County College*
Janice Fergusson, *University of South Carolina*
Linda Flaming, *Monmouth University*
Lou Fowler, *Missouri Western State University*
Harlan Fuller, *Illinois State University*
Lisa Gillespie, *Loyola University-Chicago*
Mark Gleason, *Metropolitan State University*
Mariana Grau-Nathan, *Houston Community College*
Barbara Gregorio, *Nassau Community College*
Tony Greig, *Purdue University*
Ronald Guidry, *University of Louisiana-Monroe*
Geoffrey Gurka, *Mesa State College*
Abo-El-Yazeed Habib, *Minnesota State University*
Laurie Hagberg, *Trident Technical College*
Heidi Hansel, *Kirkwood Community College*
Coby Harmon, *University of California-Santa Barbara*
Betty S. Harper, *Middle Tennessee State University*

Phillip Harper, *Middle Tennessee State University*
Candice S. Heino, *Anoka Ramsey Community College*
Joshua Herbold, *University of Montana*
George Heyman, *Oakton Community College*
Traci Hodges, *University of Missouri-St. Louis*
Anita Hope, *Tarrant County College*
Robert Hurt, *California Polytechnic Pomona*
Laura Ilcisin, *University of Nebraska-Omaha*
Sharon Jackson, *Sanford University*
Carolyn Johnson, *Northern Oklahoma College*
Shondra Johnson, *Bradley University*
Derek Johnston, *Colorado State University*
David Juriga, *Saint Louis Community College at Forest Park*
John Karayan, *California Polytechnic Pomona*
Catherine Katagiri, *College of Saint Rose*
Ann Kelley, *Providence College*
Ann Kelly, *Georgia Southern University*
Janice Kerber, *Durham Tech Community College*
Tim Kizirian, *California State University-Chico*
April Klein, *New York University*
Janice L. Klimek, *Central Missouri State University*
Christine Kloezeman, *Glendale Community College*
Trevor Knox, *Muhlenberg College*
Mark Kohlbeck, *Florida Atlantic University*
Dennis L. Kovach, *Community College of Allegheny*
Cynthia Krom, *Marist College*
Terrie Kroshus, *Inver Hills Community College*
Christy Land, *Catawba Valley Community College*
Phillips Landers, *Pennsylvania College of Technology*
Joe Larkin, *Saint Joseph's University*
Laurie Larson, *Valencia Community College*
Daniel Law, *Gonzaga University*
G. Suzanne Lay, *Mesa State College*
Ron Lazer, *University of Houston-Houston*
Chuo-Hsuan Lee, *SUNY Plattsburgh*
Xu Li, *University of Texas, Dallas*
Betsy Lin, *Montclair State University*
Joseph Lipari, *Montclair State University*
Chao-Shin Liu, *University of Notre Dame*
Julie Lockhart, *Western Washington University*
Claudia Lubaski, *Lorain County Community College*
Joseph Lupino, *Saint Mary's College of California*
Mostafa Maksy, *Northeastern Illinois University*
Diane Marker, *University of Toledo*
Angie Martin, *Tarrant County College*

James Martin, *Washburn University*
Peter Martino, *Johnson & Wales University*
Dawn Massey, *Fairfield University*
Christian Mastilak, *Xavier University*
Maureen McBeth, *College of DuPage*
Florence McGovern, *Bergen Community College*
Noel McKeon, *Florida Community College*
Lisa McKinney, *University of Alabama*
Jeffrey McMillan, *Clemson University*
Shaen McMurtrie, *Northern Oklahoma College*
Chris McNamara, *Finger Lakes Community College*
Kevin McNelis, *New Mexico State University*
Barbara Merino, *University of North Texas*
Tony Mifsud, *Catawba Valley Community College*
Paul Mihalek, *Central Connecticut State University*
Paulette Miller, *Collin County Community College*
Tim Mills, *Eastern Illinois University*
Susan Minke, *Indiana University/Purdue University-Ft Wayne*
Birendra Mishra, *University of California, Riverside*
Syed M. Moiz, *Marian College*
Dennis Moore, *Worcester State College*
Charles Moores, *University of Nevada, Las Vegas*
Tommy Moores, *University of Nevada, Las Vegas*
Arabian Morgan, *Orange Coast College*
Judy Morse, *Providence College*
Michelle Moshier, *University at Albany*
Gerald Motl, *Xavier University*
Matt Muller, *Adirondack Community College*
Johnna Murray, *University of Missouri-St. Louis*
Brian Nagle, *Duquesne University*
Presha Neidermeyer, *West Virginia University*
Barbara Norris, *Johnson & Wales University*
Adel M. Novin, *Clayton College & State University*
Thomas Nunamaker, *Washington State University*
Ron O'Brien, *Fayetteville Technical Community College*
Emeka Ofobike, *University of Akron*
Janet O'Tousa, *University of Notre Dame*
Jo-Ann Pacenta, *Pennsylvania College of Technology*
Susanna Pendergast, *Western Illinois University*
Viola Persia, *Stony Brook University*
Jan Pitera, *Broome Community College*
Duane Ponko, *Indiana University of Pennsylvania*
Todd Pull, *Georgia Perimeter College*
Mary Prater, *Clemson University*
Ronald Premuroso, *University of Montana*

Elizabeth Rabe, *Bacone College*
Kris Raman, *University of Northern Texas*
Rama Ramamurthy, *Ohio State University*
Richard Rand, *Tennessee Tech University*
Alan Ransom, *Cypress College*
Tommy Raulston, *Midwestern State University*
Donald Raux, *Siena College*
Aaron Reeves, *Saint Louis Community College-Forest Park*
Patrick Reihing, *Nassau Community College*
Gayle Richardson, *Bakersfield College*
Joanne Rockness, *University of North Carolina-Wilmington*
Carol Rogers, *Central New Mexico Community College*
Mark Ross, *Western Kentucky University*
Eric Rothenburg, *Kingsborough Community College*
Ann Rowell, *Central Piedmont Community College*
John Rude, *Bloomsburg University of Pennsylvania*
Karen Russom, *North Harris College*
Huldah A. Ryan, *Iona College*
Bob Sanborn, *SUNY-Buffalo*
Amy Santos, *Manatee Community College*
Marguerite Savage, *Elgin Community College*
Albert Schepanski, *University of Iowa*
Lydia Schleifer, *Clemson University*
Arnie Schneider, *Georgia Institute of Technology*
Henry Schulman, *Grossmont College*
Ann E. Selk, *University Wisconsin-Green Bay*
Gabrielle Serrano, *Elgin Community College*
Ted Skekel, *University of Texas-San Antonio*
John Smigla, *Robert Morris University*
Talitha Smith, *Auburn University*
Virginia Smith, *Saint Mary's College of California*
Karen Sneary, *Northwestern Oklahoma*
Nancy Snow, *University of Toledo*
Barb Squires, *Corning Community College*
James Stekelberg, *Clackamas Community College*
Ross Stewart, *Seattle Pacific University*
Dennis Stovall, *Grand Valley State University*
Stephen Strand, *Southern Maine Community College*
Arlene Strawn, *Tallahassee Community College*
Gloria Stuart, *Georgia Southern University*
Aida Sy, *Baruch College*
Albert Taccone, *Cuyamaca College*
Robert Taylor, *Mayland Community College*
Steve Teeter, *Utah Valley State*
Denise Teixeira, *Chemeketa Community College*

Advice on Working in Teams

Accounting information is always created and shared with others, making teamwork an important skill to develop. Our research finds that, whether you select your own teammates or your instructor assigns them to you, taking certain steps can improve your chances of your team being successful.* We share four of our key observations below.

1. Know what you want. Talk with your teammates about the quality of work your team aspires to produce and the amount of commitment to reach that goal. Define the general rules by which the team will work. How will the team determine who does what? How often will you meet, and for how long? How will you keep in touch between meetings? Spending a few minutes at the start to put these "rules" in writing can save you much frustration and disappointment later.

2. Plan how to get there. Team projects can feel overwhelming at first, and you may be tempted to quickly split-up the work so that everyone can get started on it. Do not do this. Take time to identify (a) the specific steps needed to complete the project, (b) the skills required at each step, and (c) the strengths of each team member. Two benefits of being in a team are that you do not have to be an expert in everything and you do not have to do it all yourself. So assign work to team members based on their strengths and workload, ensuring that everyone gets to do their fair share. Our research shows that teams earn better grades when everyone participates in a meaningful way.

3. Work as a team. Teams are more than just groups of people. To be a team, you must be committed to the same goal and be willing to "step up" when you can. Teams can accomplish much when working as a single unit, but not without the individual effort made by team members. Our research shows that the highest project grades are earned when team members work together bringing their skills and abilities to bear on each task.

4. Build the team. Teams rarely are perfect when they first start. It takes time to build the trust that is needed when relying on others. Help each other along by scheduling times to review each other's work and to give constructive feedback on how it can be improved. As a team, assess the whole team's performance and the openness of its communications. Do this often, and small difficulties will be less likely to turn into big problems.

---

*S. Hilton, and F. Phillips. Instructor-assigned and Student-selected Groups: A View from Inside. *Issues in Accounting Education,* 25, pp. 15-33, 2010.

Advice on Using Your Textbook

What does it take to do well in your Financial Accounting course? Our research finds that the way you read and use your textbook can have a major impact on your course performance.* The following graphic summarizes our primary findings, which suggest four things you can do to improve your chances of earning a good grade.

1. **Read the chapters to learn rather than just to get through them.** Learning doesn't miraculously occur just because your eyes have skimmed all the assigned lines of the textbook. You have to think and focus while reading to sink the material into your understanding and memory. Use the text's learning objectives to focus on what's really important in the chapters.

2. **Don't be discouraged if you initially find some material challenging to learn.** At one time or another, both the best and weakest students describe themselves as "confused" and "having a good grasp of the material," "anxious" and "confident," and "overwhelmed" and "comfortable." The simple fact is that, for anyone, learning new material can be challenging and initially confusing. Success does not depend as much on whether you become confused as it does on what you do when you become confused.

3. **Clear up confusion as it arises.** A key difference between the most and least successful students is how they respond to

difficulty and confusion. When successful students are confused or unsure, they immediately try to enhance their understanding through rereading, self-testing, and seeking outside help if necessary. In contrast, unsuccessful students try to reduce anxiety by delaying further reading or by resorting to memorizing without understanding. Aim to clear up confusion when it arises because accounting in particular is a subject for which your understanding of later material depends on your understanding of earlier material.

4. **Think of reading as the initial stage of studying.** Abandon the idea that "studying" only occurs during the final hours before an exam. By initially reading with the same intensity that occurs when later reviewing for an exam, you can create extra time for practicing exercises and problems. This combination of concentrated reading and extensive practice is likely to contribute to better learning and superior exam scores.

*B.J. Phillips, and F. Phillips, "Sink or Skim: Textbook Reading Behaviors of Introductory Accounting Students," *Issues in Accounting Education* 22, pp. 21–44, 2007.

BRIEF CONTENTS

CHAPTER 1 2
Business Decisions and Financial Accounting

CHAPTER 2 44
The Balance Sheet

CHAPTER 3 92
The Income Statement

CHAPTER 4 144
Adjustments, Financial Statements, and Financial Results

CHAPTER 5 202
Financial Reporting and Analysis

CHAPTER 6 248
Internal Control, Cash, and Merchandise Sales

CHAPTER 7 304
Inventories and Cost of Goods Sold

CHAPTER 8 354
Receivables, Bad Debt Expense, and Interest Revenue

CHAPTER 9 396
Long-Lived Tangible and Intangible Assets

CHAPTER 10 446
Liabilities

CHAPTER 11 500
Stockholders' Equity

CHAPTER 12 548
Statement of Cash Flows

CHAPTER 13 606
Measuring and Evaluating Financial Performance

APPENDIX A A1
Excerpts from the Fiscal 2010 Annual Report of The Home Depot, Inc.

APPENDIX B B1
Excerpts from the Fiscal 2010 Annual Report of Lowe's Companies, Inc.

APPENDIX C C1
Present and Future Value Concepts

APPENDIX D D1
Investments in Other Corporations

GLOSSARY G1

CONTENTS

CHAPTER 1
Business Decisions and Financial Accounting 2
PIZZA AROMA 3

Understand the Business 4
  Organizational Forms 4
  Accounting for Business Decisions 5
Study the Accounting Methods 7
  The Basic Accounting Equation 7
  Financial Statements 9
Evaluate the Results 17
  Using Financial Statements 17
  Useful Financial Information 17
Supplement 1A: Careers That Depend on Accounting Knowledge 20
Review the Chapter 21
  Demonstration Case 21
  Chapter Summary 23
  Key Terms 24
  Homework Helper 24
Practice Material 25
  Questions 25
  Multiple Choice 25
  Mini-Exercises 26
  Exercises 31
  Coached Problems 36
  Group A Problems 37
  Group B Problems 39
  Skills Development Cases 40
  Continuing Case: Financial Statements for a Business Plan 43

CHAPTER 2
The Balance Sheet 44
PIZZA AROMA 45

Understand the Business 46
  Building a Balance Sheet 46
  Financing, Investing, and Operating Activities 46
  Transactions and Other Activities 48
Study the Accounting Methods 49
  Step 1: Analyze Transactions 49
  Steps 2 and 3: Record and Summarize 54
  The Debit/Credit Framework 56

  Preparing a Balance Sheet 63
Evaluate the Results 64
  Assessing the Ability to Pay 64
  Balance Sheet Concepts and Values 65
Review the Chapter 68
  Demonstration Case 68
  Chapter Summary 70
  Key Terms 71
  Homework Helper 71
Practice Material 72
  Questions 72
  Multiple Choice 72
  Mini-Exercises 73
  Exercises 78
  Coached Problems 83
  Group A Problems 85
  Group B Problems 87
  Skills Development Cases 89
  Continuing Case: Accounting for the Establishment of a Business 91

CHAPTER 3
The Income Statement 92
PIZZA AROMA 93

Understand the Business 94
  Operating Activities 94
  Income Statement Accounts 95
Study the Accounting Methods 97
  Cash Basis Accounting 97
  Accrual Basis Accounting 98
  The Expanded Accounting Equation 102
  Unadjusted Trial Balance 108
  Review of Revenues and Expenses 110
Evaluate the Results 111
  Net Profit Margin 111
  Income Statement Limitations 112
Review the Chapter 113
  Demonstration Case A 113
  Demonstration Case B 114
  Chapter Summary 117
  Key Terms 118
  Homework Helper 118
Practice Material 119

Questions   119
Multiple Choice   120
Mini-Exercises   120
Exercises   126
Coached Problems   133
Group A Problems   135
Group B Problems   137
Comprehensive Problem   139
Skills Development Cases   140
Continuing Case: Accounting for Business Operations   142

CHAPTER 4

**Adjustments, Financial Statements,
and Financial Results**   144
PIZZA AROMA   145

Understand the Business   146
Why Adjustments Are Needed   146
Study the Accounting Methods   148
Making Required Adjustments   148
Preparing an Adjusted Trial Balance and the Financial Statements   158
Closing Temporary Accounts   162
Evaluate the Results   166
Adjusted Financial Results   166
Review the Chapter   167
Demonstration Case   167
Chapter Summary   173
Key Terms   174
Homework Helper   174
Practice Material   174
Questions   174
Multiple Choice   175
Mini-Exercises   176
Exercises   180
Coached Problems   188
Group A Problems   190
Group B Problems   192
Comprehensive Problems   194
Skills Development Cases   199
Continuing Case: Adjusting the Accounting Records   201

CHAPTER 5

Financial Reporting and Analysis   202
ACTIVISION   203

Understand the Business   204
The Needs of Financial Statement Users   204
The Financial Reporting Environment   205
Study the Accounting Methods   209

Financial Reporting in t.
Globalization and Internat,
Standards (IFRS)   216
Evaluate the Results   219
Economic Crisis   219
Comparison to Common Benchmarks
Financial Statement Ratio Analysis   220
Review the Chapter   225
Demonstration Case   225
Chapter Summary   227
Key Terms   228
Homework Helper   229
Practice Material   229
Questions   229
Multiple Choice   229
Mini-Exercises   230
Exercises   234
Coached Problems   237
Group A Problems   239
Group B Problems   240
Comprehensive Problems   242
Skills Development Cases   243
Continuing Case 5-1: Evaluating the Impact of Typical Transactions   246
Continuing Case 5-2: Wiki Art Gallery (WAG)   247

CHAPTER 6

Internal Control, Cash, and Merchandise Sales   248
WALMART   249

Understand the Business   250
Operating Cycles   250
Internal Control   251
Study the Accounting Methods   253
Controlling and Reporting Cash   253
Controlling and Reporting Merchandise Sales   263
Evaluate the Results   269
Gross Profit Analysis   269
Review the Chapter   272
Demonstration Case A: Bank Reconciliation   272
Demonstration Case B: Merchandise Sales   273
Chapter Summary   274
Key Terms   276
Homework Helper   276
Practice Material   277
Questions   277
Multiple Choice   277
Mini-Exercises   278
Exercises   282
Coached Problems   288

roblems 291

up B Problems 295

    Skills Development Cases 299

    Continuing Case 6-1: Accounting for Merchandising Operations 302

    Continuing Case 6-2: Wiki Art Gallery (WAG) 303

CHAPTER 7

Inventories and Cost of Goods Sold 304

AMERICAN EAGLE OUTFITTERS 305

Understand the Business 306

    Inventory Management Decisions 306

    Types of Inventory 306

Study the Accounting Methods 307

    Balance Sheet and Income Statement Reporting 307

    Inventory Costing Methods 309

    Lower of Cost or Market 314

    Recording Inventory Transactions 315

Evaluate the Results 318

    Inventory Turnover Analysis 318

Supplement 7A: FIFO, LIFO, and Weighted Average in a Perpetual Inventory System 321

Supplement 7B: The Effects of Errors in Ending Inventory 324

Supplement 7C: Recording Inventory Transactions in a Periodic System 325

Review the Chapter 327

    Demonstration Case 327

    Chapter Summary 328

    Key Terms 329

    Homework Helper 330

Practice Material 330

    Questions 330

    Multiple Choice 331

    Mini-Exercises 331

    Exercises 334

    Coached Problems 341

    Group A Problems 344

    Group B Problems 346

    Comprehensive Problems 349

    Skills Development Cases 351

    Continuing Case 7-1: Accounting for Changing Inventory Costs 352

    Continuing Case 7-2: Wiki Art Gallery (WAG) 353

CHAPTER 8

Receivables, Bad Debt Expense, and Interest Revenue 354

VF Corporation 355

Understand the Business 356

    Pros and Cons of Extending Credit 356

Study the Accounting Methods 357

    Accounts Receivable and Bad Debts 357

    Methods for Estimating Bad Debts 361

    Notes Receivable and Interest Revenue 364

    Recording Notes Receivable and Interest Revenue 365

Evaluate the Results 368

    Receivables Turnover Analysis 368

Supplement 8A: Direct Write-Off Method 371

Review the Chapter 371

    Demonstration Case A: Bad Debts 371

    Demonstration Case B: Notes Receivable 373

    Chapter Summary 374

    Key Terms 375

    Homework Helper 375

Practice Material 375

    Questions 375

    Multiple Choice 376

    Mini-Exercises 376

    Exercises 379

    Coached Problems 383

    Group A Problems 385

    Group B Problems 388

    Comprehensive Problem 390

    Skills Development Cases 391

    Continuing Case 8-1: Accounting for Receivables and Uncollectible Accounts 394

    Continuing Case 8-2: Wiki Art Gallery (WAG) 394

CHAPTER 9

Long-Lived Tangible and Intangible Assets 396

CEDAR FAIR 397

Understand the Business 398

    Definition and Classification 398

Study the Accounting Methods 399

    Tangible Assets 399

    Intangible Assets 413

Evaluate the Results 416

    Turnover Analysis 416

    Impact of Depreciation Differences 418

Supplement 9A: Natural Resources 420

Supplement 9B: Changes in Depreciation 421

Review the Chapter 422

    Demonstration Case 422

    Chapter Summary 424

    Key Terms 426

    Homework Helper 426

Practice Material 427

    Questions 427

    Multiple Choice 427

    Mini-Exercises 428

Exercises   431
Coached Problems   435
Group A Problems   437
Group B Problems   439
Comprehensive Problem   441
Skills Development Cases   441
Continuing Case 9-1: Accounting for the Use and Disposal
of Long-Lived Assets   444
Continuing Case 9-2: Wiki Art Gallery (WAG)   445

CHAPTER 10

Liabilities   446
GENERAL MILLS   447

Understand the Business   448
The Role of Liabilities   448
Study the Accounting Methods   449
Measuring Liabilities   449
Current Liabilities   449
Long-Term Liabilities   456
Contingent Liabilities   463
Evaluate the Results   464
Quick Ratio   464
Times Interest Earned Ratio   465
**Supplement 10A: Straight-Line Method of
Amortization**   466
**Supplement 10B: Effective-Interest Method of
Amortization**   467
**Supplement 10C: Simplified Effective-Interest
Amortization**   471
Review the Chapter   475
Demonstration Case A: Accrued Liabilities
and Unearned Revenue   475
Demonstration Case B: Notes Payable
and Accrued Interest   476
Demonstration Case C: Bonds Payable   477
Chapter Summary   478
Key Terms   479
Homework Helper   479
Practice Material   480
Questions   480
Multiple Choice   480
Mini-Exercises   481
Exercises   483
Coached Problems   487
Group A Problems   491
Group B Problems   493
Comprehensive Problems   496
Skills Development Cases   497
Continuing Case 10-1: Accounting for
Debt Financing   499
Continuing Case 10-2: Wiki Art Gallery (WAG)   499

CHAPTER 11

Stockholders' Equity   500
NATIONAL BEVERAGE CORP.   501

Understand the Business   502
Corporate Ownership   502
Equity versus Debt Financing   503
Study the Accounting Methods   504
Common Stock Transactions   504
Stock Dividends and Stock Splits   511
Preferred Stock   514
Retained Earnings   516
Evaluate the Results   516
Earnings per Share (EPS)   517
Return on Equity (ROE)   518
Price/Earnings (P/E) Ratio   519
**Supplement 11A: Owners' Equity for Other Forms
of Business**   519
Review the Chapter   523
Demonstration Case A: Stock Issuance and
Repurchases   523
Demonstration Case B: Cash and Stock Dividends   524
Chapter Summary   525
Key Terms   526
Homework Helper   526
Practice Material   527
Questions   527
Multiple Choice   527
Mini-Exercises   528
Exercises   530
Coached Problems   536
Group A Problems   538
Group B Problems   540
Comprehensive Problem   543
Skills Development Cases   543
Continuing Case 11-1: Accounting for Equity
Financing   545
Continuing Case 11-2: Wiki Art Gallery (WAG)   546

CHAPTER 12

Statement of Cash Flows   548
UNDER ARMOUR, INC.   549

Understand the Business   550
Business Activities and Cash Flows   550
Classifying Cash Flows   551
Study the Accounting Methods   554
Relationship to Other Financial Statements   554
Preparing the Statement of Cash Flows   555
Evaluate the Results   564
Evaluating Cash Flows   565
Operating Cash Flows Revisited (Direct Method)   567

Supplement 12A: Reporting Disposals of Property, Plant, and Equipment (Indirect Method)   571

Supplement 12B: T-Account Approach (Indirect Method)   572

Supplement 12C: Spreadsheet Approach (Indirect Method)   574

Review the Chapter   576

Demonstration Case A: Indirect Method   576

Demonstration Case B: Direct Method   577

Chapter Summary   578

Key Terms   579

Homework Helper   579

Practice Material   580

Questions   580

Multiple Choice   581

Mini-Exercises   582

Exercises   585

Coached Problems   594

Group A Problems   597

Group B Problems   600

Skills Development Cases   602

Continuing Case 12-1: Accounting for Cash Flows   605

Continuing Case 12-2: Wiki Art Gallery (WAG)   605

CHAPTER 13

Measuring and Evaluating Financial Performance   606

LOWE'S   607

Understand the Business   608

Horizontal, Vertical, and Ratio Analyses   608

Study the Accounting Methods   609

Horizontal (Trend) Computations   609

Vertical (Common Size) Computations   611

Ratio Computations   612

Evaluate the Results   614

Interpreting Horizontal and Vertical Analyses   614

Interpreting Ratio Analyses   615

Underlying Accounting Decisions and Concepts   620

Supplement 13A: Nonrecurring and Other Special Items   622

Supplement 13B: Reviewing and Contrasting IFRS and GAAP   623

Review the Chapter   625

Demonstration Case   625

Chapter Summary   626

Key Terms   627

Homework Helper   627

Practice Material   627

Questions   627

Multiple Choice   628

Mini-Exercises   629

Exercises   630

Coached Problems   635

Group A Problems   639

Group B Problems   643

Skills Development Cases   646

Continuing Case: Evaluating Profitability, Liquidity, and Solvency   648

APPENDIX A

Excerpts from the Fiscal 2010 Annual Report of The Home Depot Inc.   A1

APPENDIX B

Excerpts from the Fiscal 2010 Annual Report of Lowe's Companies, Inc.   B1

APPENDIX C

Present and Future Value Concepts   C1

Computing Future and Present Values of a Single Amount   C2

Future Value of a Single Amount   C2

Present Value of a Single Amount   C3

Computing Future and Present Values of an Annuity   C4

Future Value of an Annuity   C5

Present Value of an Annuity   C5

Interest Rates and Interest Periods   C6

Accounting Applications of Present Values   C6

Present Value Computations Using Excel   C11

Key Terms   C18

Practice Material   C18

Questions   C18

Multiple Choice   C18

Mini-Exercises   C19

Exercises   C19

Coached Problem   C21

Group A Problem   C21

Group B Problem   C21

APPENDIX D on OLC at www.mhhe.com/phillips4e

Investments in Other Corporations   D1

An Overview   D1

Reasons Companies Invest   D1

Identifying Investment Types and Accounting Methods   D2

Accounting for Passive Investments   D3

   Debt Investments Held to Maturity: Amortized
Cost Method   D3

   Available-for-Sale Securities: Fair Value Method   D5

   Comparison of Available-for-Sale and Trading
Securities   D8

Accounting for Influential Investments   D10

   Investments for Significant Influence: Equity Method   D10

   Investments with Controlling Interests: Consolidated
Statements   D13

   Demonstration Case A: Trading Securities   D15

   Demonstration Case B: Available-for-Sale Securities   D16

   Demonstration Case C: Equity Method   D17

   Key Terms   D17

Practice Material   D17

   Questions   D17

   Multiple Choice   D18

   Mini-Exercises   D18

   Exercises   D20

   Coached Problems   D21

   Group A Problems   D22

**SOLUTIONS TO MULTIPLE CHOICE
QUESTIONS**   Q1

GLOSSARY   G1

PHOTO CREDITS   PC1

INDEX   I.1

In Action: Video Guides for Selected Self-Study Practice

Use the camera on your web-enabled smartphone or tablet to scan the Quick Response (QR) code you see below to access guided tutorial videos.

Getting started with QR codes is easy:

1. Use your smartphone to download any two-dimensional or QR-enabled barcode reader from your provider's marketplace.
2. Focus your smartphone's camera on the code below.
3. From the list that appears, select the tutorial you'd like to see.

These tutorial videos illustrate the thought processes applicable to just a sample of topics, including how to analyze transactions, adjust accounts, account for inventory and receivables, and prepare a statement of cash flows. Additional guided tutorials are available for select exercises in McGraw-Hill *Connect Accounting*.

fundamentals of
FINANCIAL ACCOUNTING

www.mhhe.com/phillips4e

Business Decisions and Financial Accounting

YOUR LEARNING OBJECTIVES

Understand the business

LO 1-1   Describe various organizational forms and business decision makers.

Study the accounting methods

LO 1-2   Describe the purpose, structure, and content of the four basic financial statements.

Evaluate the results

LO 1-3   Explain how financial statements are used by decision makers.

LO 1-4   Describe factors that contribute to useful financial information.

Review the chapter

THAT WAS THEN

If you think accounting is far removed from your personal life, you might be in for a surprise. Your ordinary life experiences, especially as a student, actually prepare you well to learn accounting.

FOCUS COMPANY: Pizza Aroma, Ithaca, NY

Welcome to the world of business and financial accounting. One of our goals for this book is to help you see the role that accounting plays in helping people turn their good ideas into successful businesses. The founder of FedEx first introduced his ideas about a nationwide transportation business in a college essay. With the help of accounting, FedEx has become a multibillion dollar business. Perhaps the only thing stopping you from doing this is that you don't feel you know what's involved in starting and running a business. We're here to help with that.

Another important goal for us is to explain topics in ways that you can relate to. We want you to see that your personal life experiences help you to learn accounting. Often, we will explain topics in the context of a real business. For example, in the first four chapters, you will learn the steps that one person took to start his own business and turn his dream into reality. By reading about his experiences, you'll gain a realistic understanding of how accounting is a key part of all businesses. So, let's get started.

About two decades ago, Mauricio Rosa brought his young family from El Salvador to America to build a better life. While working in several New York pizza restaurants, he perfected a gourmet pizza concept. Thinking gourmet pizza would be a great addition to the local restaurant scene, Mauricio decided to start his own pizza business. Although eager to get started, Mauricio had several questions and decisions to consider. He contacted Laurie Hensley, a local CPA (certified public accountant) to ask her advice. As you will read in this chapter, Laurie met with Mauricio in June to help him understand what's involved in starting a business and monitoring its success. He eventually started a business, called Pizza Aroma, which actually exists—at 128 S. Cayuga St. in Ithaca, NY.

THIS IS NOW

This chapter focuses on the key financial reports that business people rely on when evaluating a company's performance.

3

Understand the business	Study the accounting methods	Evaluate the results	Review the chapter
• Organizational forms • Accounting for business decisions	• The basic accounting equation • Financial statements	• Using financial statements • Useful financial information	• Demonstration case • Chapter summary • Key terms • Homework helper • Practice material

Understand the Business

 "Mauricio, we should start by talking about how you want to organize your business."

"Well, I'm opening a gourmet pizza restaurant. What else do I need to know?"

ORGANIZATIONAL FORMS

Learning Objective 1-1
Describe various organizational forms and business decision makers.

Laurie outlined three primary ways businesses can be organized: sole proprietorship, partnership, and corporation.

Sole Proprietorship

This is a form of business owned (and usually operated) by one individual. It is the easiest form of business to start because it doesn't require any special legal maneuvers. Just get a business license and you're good to go. A sole proprietorship is considered a part of the owner's life, with all profits (or losses) becoming part of the taxable income of the owner, and the owner being personally liable for all debts of the business.

Partnership

A partnership is similar to a sole proprietorship, except that profits, taxes, and legal liability are the responsibility of two or more owners instead of just one. It is slightly more expensive to form than a sole proprietorship because a lawyer typically is needed to draw up a partnership agreement, which describes how profits are shared between partners and how that would change if new partners are added or existing partners leave. The key advantage of a partnership over a sole proprietorship is that it typically has more resources available to it, which can fuel the business's growth.

Corporation

Unlike sole proprietorships and partnerships, a corporation is a separate entity from both a legal and accounting perspective. This means that a corporation, not its owners, is legally responsible for its own taxes and debts. Thus, owners cannot lose more than their investment in the corporation, which is a major advantage to the owners. Two disadvantages of incorporation are that the legal fees for creating a corporation can be high and income taxes must be paid by both the corporation and its owners.

Corporations can raise large amounts of money for growth because they divide ownership of the corporation into shares that can be sold to new owners. A share of the corporation's ownership is indicated on a legal document called a stock certificate. The owners of a company's stock (stockholders) can buy and sell stock privately or publicly on a stock exchange if the company has legally registered to do so. Most corporations start out as private companies and will apply to become public companies ("go public") if they need a lot of financing, which they obtain from selling new stock certificates to investors. Some big-name corporations, like Cargill and Chick-Fil-A, haven't gone public because they get enough financing from private sources, but many that you are familiar with (and most examples in this book) are public companies.

Other

Other organizational forms exist, such as a limited liability company (LLC), which combines characteristics of a partnership and a corporation. We focus on corporations.

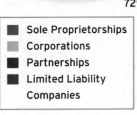

Percentage of Organizational Forms in the U.S.

4% 6%
18%
72%

- ■ Sole Proprietorships
- ■ Corporations
- ■ Partnerships
- ■ Limited Liability Companies

Source: IRS.gov.

"I'm interested in limiting my legal liability and getting some financing by selling ownership shares to investors, so I will create a private corporation called Pizza Aroma, Inc. What's next?"

ACCOUNTING FOR BUSINESS DECISIONS

Most companies exist to earn profits for their stockholders. They earn profits by selling goods or services to customers for more than they cost to produce. Mauricio's company will be successful if it is able to make pizzas at a cost of $2 and sell them for $9. To know just how successful his company is, Mauricio will need to establish and maintain a good system of financial recordkeeping—an accounting system. **Accounting** is an information system designed by an organization to capture (analyze, record, and summarize) the activities affecting its financial condition and performance and then report the results to decision makers, both inside and outside the organization. It's such a key part of business that business people typically talk about their companies using accounting terms, which is why they often call it the "language of business."

Every organization needs accountants to assist in reporting financial information for decision making and to help its owners understand the financial effects of those business decisions. Mauricio can get this help in one of two ways. He can hire an accountant to work as an employee of his business (a **private accountant**) or he can contract with someone like Laurie who provides advice to a variety of businesses (a **public accountant**). Because Mauricio's business is small, he doesn't yet need a full-time accountant. Instead, he agrees that Pizza Aroma will pay fees to Laurie for basic services. She'll help him to set up an accounting system and advise him on key business decisions.

> **YOU SHOULD KNOW**
>
> **Accounting:** A system of analyzing, recording, and summarizing the results of a business's activities and then reporting the results to decision makers.

"How will an accounting system help me run my business?"

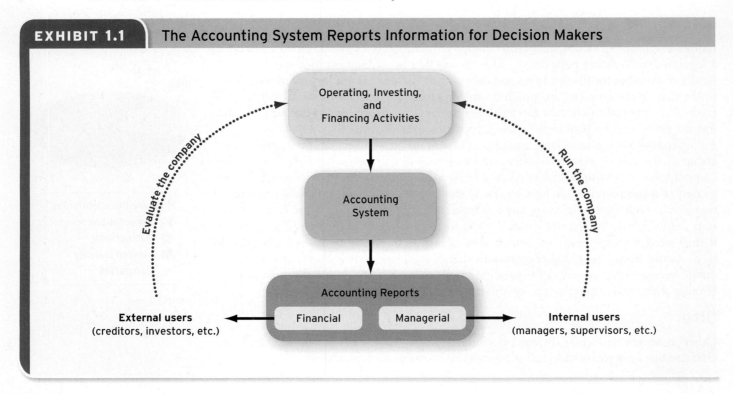

EXHIBIT 1.1   The Accounting System Reports Information for Decision Makers

The main goal of an accounting system is to capture information about the operating, investing, and financing activities of a company so that it can be reported to decision makers, both inside and outside the business. Exhibit 1.1 illustrates this role and shows that this information can be presented in two kinds of reports. **Managerial accounting reports** include detailed financial plans and continually updated reports about the operating performance of the company. These reports are made available only to the company's employees (internal users) so that they can make business decisions related to production, marketing, human resources, and finance. For example, managerial accounting reports are needed when determining whether to build, buy, or rent a building; whether to continue or discontinue making particular products; how much to pay employees; and how much to borrow. As manager of a restaurant, Mauricio will regularly need managerial accounting reports to monitor the quantity of supplies on hand, evaluate the various costs associated with making and selling his gourmet pizza, and assess the productivity of his employees.

 "Others outside your business will need financial information about your restaurant. For example, where will the money come from to start your business?"

"My wife and I will probably contribute $30,000 from personal savings. But I'll still need to ask the bank for a $20,000 loan to buy equipment. What will the bank want to know?"

Laurie described **financial accounting reports,** called **financial statements**, which are prepared periodically to provide information to people not employed by the business. These external financial statement users aren't given access to detailed internal records of the company, so they rely extensively on the financial statements. Creditors and investors are the two primary external user groups, but other external users also find the information helpful.

- **Creditors**—anyone to whom money is owed.
  - **Banks** use financial statements to evaluate the risk that they will not be repaid the money they've loaned to a company. Because banks are taking a risk when they loan money to a company, they want periodic financial reports from the company so they can keep an eye on how the business is doing and intervene if it looks like the company will have trouble repaying the loan.
  - **Suppliers** also want to be sure a business can pay them for the goods or services they deliver. They usually check the business's credit standing and may also ask for its financial statements before entering into significant business relationships.
- **Investors**
  - **Stockholders** are a major external user group. Both existing and future stockholders rely on financial statements to evaluate whether the company is financially secure and likely to be a profitable investment.
- **Other external users**
  - Certain **customers** use financial statements to judge the company's ability to provide service on its products and honor warranties.
  - Various local, state, and federal **governments** also collect taxes based on information used to prepare the financial statements.

In Pizza Aroma's case, the bank will be the main external user. Mauricio will be expected to prepare financial statements to obtain the loan and then regularly provide updated financial reports until the loan is repaid. If the company's stock is ever sold to other investors, these stockholders will rely on financial statements to estimate the value of their shares and determine whether to buy, sell, or hold Pizza Aroma stock.

While Mauricio understood everything Laurie had told him up to this point, he had another major concern.

"I want to sound intelligent when I talk to my banker, but I don't know much about accounting."

 "This is a common concern for new business owners, so let's start with the most basic thing you need to know about accounting."

Study the Accounting Methods

THE BASIC ACCOUNTING EQUATION

One of the central concepts to understanding financial reports is that **what a company owns must equal what a company owes to its creditors and stockholders.** In accounting, there are special names for the items a company owns (assets) and the claims on these items by creditors (liabilities) and stockholders (equity), as shown below.

Learning Objective 1-2
Describe the purpose, structure, and content of the four basic financial statements.

Resources Owned . . .	=	Resources Owed . . .	
by the **company**		to **creditors**	to **stockholders**
Assets	**=**	**Liabilities**	**+** **Stockholders' Equity**

The relationship between assets (A), liabilities (L), and stockholders' equity (SE) is known as the **basic accounting equation**. The business itself, not the stockholders who own the business, is viewed as owning the assets and owing the liabilities. This is called the **separate entity assumption**, which requires that a business's financial reports include only the activities of the business and not those of its stockholders.

The elements of the basic accounting equation are fundamental to reading and understanding financial statements, so let's look at each in detail.

Assets

An **asset** is an economic resource presently controlled by the company; it has measurable value and is expected to benefit the company by producing cash inflows or reducing cash outflows in the future. For Pizza Aroma, assets include things like cash, supplies, cookware, and equipment such as tables, chairs, and pizza ovens.

Liabilities

Liabilities are measurable amounts that the company owes to creditors. If Pizza Aroma borrows from a bank, it would owe a liability called a Note Payable. This particular name is used because banks require borrowers to sign a legal document called a *note*, which describes details about the company's promise to repay the bank. Pizza Aroma is likely to also owe suppliers for ingredients and other supplies delivered to Pizza Aroma. When a company buys goods from another company, it usually does so on credit by promising to pay for them at a later date. The amount owed is called an Account Payable because purchases made using credit are said to be "on account." Pizza Aroma could also owe wages to employees (Wages Payable) and taxes to governments (Taxes Payable). From a legal perspective, creditors have priority over stockholders. Thus, if a company goes out of business, liabilities must be paid before any amounts are paid to stockholders.

Stockholders' Equity

Stockholders' equity represents the owners' claims on the business. These claims arise for two reasons.

Stockholders' Equity

Contributed Capital
(paid in by stockholders)

Retained Earnings
(earned by the company)

1. First, the owners have a claim on amounts they contributed directly to the company in exchange for its stock (Contributed Capital).

2. Second, the owners have a claim on amounts the company has earned through profitable business operations (Retained Earnings).

The second item listed above is particularly important because a business can survive only if it is profitable. It will be profitable if the total amount earned from selling goods and services is greater than the costs incurred to generate those sales. Theoretically, these profits belong to the company's owners, so they increase stockholders' equity. Through these profits, owners can get more money back from the company than they paid in (a return on their investment).

Given the importance of a company's profits, accounting systems separately track the two components of profit: revenues and expenses.

Revenues Revenues are earned by selling goods or services to customers. For Pizza Aroma, revenues are measured at the amount the company charges its customers for pizza.

Expenses Expenses are all costs of doing business that are necessary to earn revenues. For Pizza Aroma, these include advertising, utilities, rent, wages, insurance, repairs, and supplies used in making pizza. Expenses are said to be incurred to generate revenues. The word *incurred* means that the activities giving rise to a cost (e.g., running an ad, using electricity) have occurred in the period in which the related revenues have been generated.

Net Income   Although *profit* is used in casual conversation, the preferred term in accounting is *net income*. Net income is calculated as revenues minus expenses. For Pizza Aroma to be profitable, its revenues must be greater than its expenses. (If revenues are less than expenses, the company would have a net loss, but for now we'll optimistically assume that Pizza Aroma is going to earn a profit.) **By generating net income, a company increases its stockholders' equity,** as illustrated below. This net income can be left in the company to accumulate (with earnings that have been retained from prior years) or it can be paid out to the company's stockholders for their own personal use (called *dividends*).

Dividends   A company's profits are accumulated in Retained Earnings until a decision is made to distribute them to stockholders in what is called a dividend. The simplest type of dividend, and the most common for a small business like Pizza Aroma, is a dividend paid in cash. **Dividends are not an expense incurred to generate earnings.** Rather, dividends are a distribution of earnings. They are determined at the discretion of the company's stockholders. If Mauricio wanted, he could choose to leave all the profits in Pizza Aroma by never declaring a dividend.

"Okay, I think I get it, but can you tell me how all those items relate to each other and where they are reported in the financial statements?"

FINANCIAL STATEMENTS

Assets, liabilities, stockholders' equity, revenues, expenses, and dividends appear in different reports that collectively are called financial statements. The term *financial statements* refers to four accounting reports, typically prepared in the following order:

1. Income Statement
2. Statement of Retained Earnings
3. Balance Sheet
4. Statement of Cash Flows

Financial statements can be prepared at any time during the year, although they are most commonly prepared monthly, every three months (quarterly reports), and at the end of the year (annual reports). Companies are allowed to choose a calendar or fiscal year-end. A calendar year is a 12-month period ending on December 31, and a fiscal year is a 12-month period ending on a day other than December 31. The toy maker Mattel uses a calendar year-end because this is the start of its slow business period. The only U.S. professional sports team operating as a public company—Green Bay Packers Inc.—has chosen a fiscal year-end of March 31, after the season ends.

The Income Statement

The first financial statement prepared is the **income statement** (also called the statement of operations). Laurie gives Mauricio Exhibit 1.2 to show what Pizza Aroma's income statement might look like for the month ended September 30, assuming he is able to open his restaurant on September 1. The heading of the income statement identifies who, what, and when: the name of the business, the title of the report, and the time period covered by the financial statement. Larger businesses with thousands or millions of dollars in revenues and expenses add a fourth line under the date to indicate if the numbers reported are rounded to the nearest thousand or million. For international companies, this fourth line also reports the currency used in the report. An international company based in the United States, like Papa John's, will translate any foreign currency into U.S. dollars—basically assuming all its business was done in U.S. dollars. This is the **unit of measure assumption**. We see it in the reporting currency used by Nestlé (Swiss franc), LEGO (Danish krone), and Adidas (euro). Companies with complex activities report a statement of comprehensive income that shows net income as well as gains and losses relating to pensions, certain investments, and foreign currency translations. Appendix D of this text illustrates this expanded reporting.

EXHIBIT 1.2 | Income Statement

PIZZA AROMA, INC.
Income Statement (Projected)
For the Month Ended September 30, 2013

		Explanation
		Who: Name of the business
		What: Title of the statement
		When: Accounting period
Revenues		
Pizza Revenue	$ 12,000	Revenue earned from the sale and delivery of pizza to customers
Total Revenues	12,000	**Total amount earned during September**
Expenses		
Supplies Expense	5,000	Cost of pizza ingredients used up in September
Wages Expense	2,000	Cost of employee wages for work done in September
Rent Expense	1,500	Cost of rent for the month of September
Utilities Expense	600	Cost of utilities used in September
Insurance Expense	300	Cost of insurance coverage for September
Advertising Expense	100	Cost of advertising done in September
Income Tax Expense	500	Cost of taxes on September's income
Total Expenses	10,000	**Total expenses incurred in September to generate revenues**
Net Income	$ 2,000	**Difference between total revenues and total expenses**

Notice that an income statement for Pizza Aroma would have three major captions—revenues, expenses, and net income—corresponding to the equation for the income statement (Revenues − Expenses = Net Income). Individual types of revenues and expenses would be reported under the revenue and expense headings. These **accounts**, as they are called, are typical for most businesses, whether small or big. Notice that each major caption has an underlined subtotal, and the "bottom line" amount for net income has a double underline to highlight it. Finally, a dollar sign appears at the top and bottom of the column of numbers.

When listing the accounts on the income statement, revenues are on top, usually with the largest, most relevant revenue listed first. Then expenses are subtracted, again from largest to smallest, except that Income Tax Expense is the last expense listed. Net Income is the difference between total revenues and total expenses. Other income statement formats are possible, as explained in Chapters 5 and 6.

"So, does the $2,000 of Net Income mean I'll have that much more cash?"

 "No. Net income is a measure of how much better off your business is, not how much cash you made."

Laurie's point is one of the key ideas of the income statement. It's quite common for a business to provide goods or services to customers in one month, but not collect cash from them until a later month. Similarly, expenses for the current month's activities may actually be paid in a different month. You'll have a chance to learn this in more detail later, but it's worth trying to understand from the beginning that revenues don't necessarily equal cash coming in during the month and expenses don't always equal cash going out during the month.

Mauricio seemed disappointed to see only $2,000 of projected net income for the first month. Laurie reassured him that it's typical for new businesses like Pizza Aroma to initially struggle to generate a profit because they have lots of expenses related to advertising and employee training but relatively little revenues because they haven't yet built a loyal customer base.[1] Pizza Aroma's net income will likely increase in the future after the business becomes well known. By selling more pizza, revenues will increase without a major increase in expenses, except for the cost of ingredients and supplies that will be used in making the additional pizzas. Expenses like employee wages and rent will likely not increase all that much.

"I guess that's not so bad. It does make me want to watch my expenses and try to boost my pizza sales quickly. What about the amount Pizza Aroma owes to the bank? Should we talk about the balance sheet?"

 "Before we look at that, I want to show you the next statement that connects the income statement to the balance sheet, so you'll understand the relationships between the reports."

The Statement of Retained Earnings

Pizza Aroma will report a **statement of retained earnings**, as shown in Exhibit 1.3. A more comprehensive statement of stockholders' equity that explains changes in all stockholders' equity accounts is provided by large corporations. But for Pizza Aroma, most changes in stockholders' equity relate to generating and distributing earnings, so a statement of retained earnings is just as good as a full-blown statement of stockholders' equity. The heading in Exhibit 1.3 identifies the name of the company, the title of the report, and the accounting period. The statement starts with the Retained Earnings balance at the beginning of the period. Remember that retained earnings are the profits that have accumulated in the company over time. Because this is a new business, there aren't any accumulated profits yet so the beginning balance is $0. Next, the statement adds Net Income and subtracts any Dividends for the current period, to arrive at Retained Earnings at the end of

---

[1] In fact, 50 percent of all new businesses fail or close within the first six years of opening. Not many start out with a positive net income in the first month. For more information on small business failures, see Brian Headd, "Redefining Business Success: Distinguishing between Closure and Failures," *Small Business Economics*, 21: 51–61, 2003.

EXHIBIT 1.3   Statement of Retained Earnings   PIZZA AROMA

PIZZA AROMA, INC. Statement of Retained Earnings (Projected) For the Month Ended September 30, 2013		Explanation Who: Name of the business What: Title of the statement When: Accounting period
Retained Earnings, September 1, 2013	$ 0	Last period's ending Retained Earnings balance
Add: Net Income	2,000	Reported on the income statement (Exhibit 1.2)
Subtract: Dividends	(1,000)	Distributions to stockholders in the current period
Retained Earnings, September 30, 2013	$1,000	This period's ending Retained Earnings balance

the period.[2] Again, a dollar sign is used at the top and bottom of the column of numbers and a double underline appears at the bottom.

The Balance Sheet

The next financial report is the **balance sheet**. It is also known as the statement of financial position. The balance sheet's purpose is to report the amount of a business's assets, liabilities, and stockholders' equity at a specific point in time. Exhibit 1.4 presents Pizza Aroma's projected balance sheet. Think of the balance sheet as a picture or screen capture of Pizza Aroma's resources and claims to resources at the end of the day on September 30, 2013.

EXHIBIT 1.4   Balance Sheet   PIZZA AROMA

PIZZA AROMA, INC. Balance Sheet (Projected) At September 30, 2013		Explanation Who: Name of the business What: Title of the statement When: Point in time
Assets		Resources controlled by the company
Cash	$14,000	Amount of cash on hand and in the business's bank account
Accounts Receivable	1,000	Pizza Aroma's right to collect from customers for prior credit sales
Supplies	3,000	Cost of food and paper supplies on hand
Equipment	40,000	Cost of ovens, tables, etc.
Total Assets	$58,000	Total amount of the company's resources
Liabilities and Stockholders' Equity		Claims on the company's resources
Liabilities		Creditors' claims on the company's resources
Accounts Payable	$ 7,000	Amount owed to suppliers for prior credit purchases (on account)
Note Payable	20,000	Amount of loan owed to the bank (for promissory note)
Total Liabilities	27,000	Total claims on the resources by creditors
Stockholders' Equity		Stockholders' claims on the company's resources
Contributed Capital	30,000	Amount stockholders contributed for company stock
Retained Earnings	1,000	Total earnings retained in the business (Exhibit 1.3)
Total Stockholders' Equity	31,000	Total claims on the company's resources by stockholders
Total Liabilities and Stockholders' Equity	$58,000	Total claims on the company's resources

---

[2]For companies that have a net loss (expenses exceed revenues), the statement of retained earnings would subtract the net loss rather than add net income.

Notice again that the heading specifically identifies the name of the company and title of the statement. Unlike the other financial reports the balance sheet is presented for a point in time (at September 30, 2013, in this case). The assets are listed in order of how soon they are to be used or turned into cash. Likewise, liabilities are listed in order of how soon each is to be paid or settled.

The balance sheet first lists the assets of the business, which for Pizza Aroma total $58,000. The second section lists the business's liabilities and stockholders' equity balances, also totaling $58,000. The balance sheet "balances" because the resources equal the claims to the resources. The basic accounting equation (also called the balance sheet equation) reflects the business's financial position at September 30, 2013:

Assets	=	Liabilities	+	Stockholders' Equity
$58,000	=	$27,000	+	$31,000

Cash is the first asset reported on the balance sheet. The $14,000 would represent the total amount of cash on hand and in Pizza Aroma's bank account. The $1,000 reported as Accounts Receivable would represent Pizza Aroma's right to collect from customers for sales made on credit. Pizza Aroma intends to allow local colleges to buy pizza for college events on account by running a tab that Pizza Aroma sends as a bill after the deliveries are made. The $3,000 reported for Supplies indicates the cost of pizza supplies on hand at the balance sheet date. The same is true for the $40,000 of Equipment. According to the **cost principle** of accounting, assets are initially reported on the balance sheet based on their original cost to the company.

Under liabilities, Laurie includes $7,000 of Accounts Payable as the amount Pizza Aroma owes suppliers for food and paper supplies purchased on account. The Note Payable is the written promise to repay the loan from the bank. As with all liabilities, these are financial obligations of the business arising from past business activities.

Finally, within stockholders' equity, Contributed Capital reflects the dollar amount of the company's stock given when Mauricio and his wife contribute $30,000 to the company. Retained Earnings reports the earnings expected to be retained in the company as of September 30, 2013. It matches the ending amount of Retained Earnings on the statement of retained earnings (Exhibit 1.3).

COACH'S TIP

Any account name containing *receivable* is an asset and any containing *payable* is a liability.

"Besides monitoring my revenues and expenses, it looks like I need to make sure I have enough assets to pay my liabilities."

 "Sharp observation! Your creditors are most interested in your ability to pay cash to them in the future. However, not all assets can be easily turned into cash and not all revenues and expenses are received or paid in cash. So, there is one more important financial statement."

The Statement of Cash Flows

Pizza Aroma's projected income statement (back in Exhibit 1.2) shows a positive net income of $2,000. However, net income is not necessarily equal to cash because revenues are reported when earned and expenses when incurred regardless of when cash is received or paid. The fourth financial report of interest to external users, then, is the **statement of cash flows**. It includes only those activities that result in cash changing hands. Exhibit 1.5 shows Pizza Aroma's projected statement of cash flows for the month ended September 30, 2013.

YOU SHOULD KNOW

Statement of cash flows: Reports the operating, investing, and financing activities that caused increases and decreases in cash during the period.

EXHIBIT 1.5	Statement of Cash Flows	PIZZA AROMA

Explanation

PIZZA AROMA, INC.
Statement of Cash Flows (Projected)
For the Month Ended September 30, 2013

Who: Name of the entity
What: Title of the statement
When: Accounting period

Cash Flows from Operating Activities		**Activities directly related to earning income**
Cash received from customers	$11,000	Amount of cash received from customers
Cash paid to employees and suppliers	(6,000)	Amount of cash paid to employees and suppliers of goods/services
Cash Provided by Operating Activities	5,000	Cash inflows minus outflows ($11,000 − $6,000)
Cash Flows from (Used in) Investing Activities		**Activities related to the sale/purchase of productive assets**
Cash used to buy equipment	(40,000)	Amount of cash spent on equipment
Cash from (Used in) Investing Activities	(40,000)	
Cash Flows from Financing Activities		**Activities involving investors and banks**
Capital contributed by stockholders	30,000	Amount of cash received from owners
Cash dividends paid to stockholders	(1,000)	Amount of cash paid to owners
Cash borrowed from the bank	20,000	Amount of cash received from the bank
Cash Provided by Financing Activities	49,000	Cash inflows minus outflows ($30,000 − $1,000 + $20,000)
Change in Cash	14,000	Sum of three categories of cash flows ($5,000 − $40,000 + $49,000)
Beginning Cash, September 1, 2013	0	Cash balance at the beginning of the accounting period
Ending Cash, September 30, 2013	$14,000	Cash balance reported on the balance sheet (Exhibit 1.4)

> **COACH'S TIP**
>
> Parentheses are used on the statement of cash flows to indicate negative cash flows (outflows rather than inflows).

The statement of cash flows is divided into three types of activities:

1. **Operating:** These activities are directly related to running the business to earn profit. They include buying supplies, making pizza, serving food to customers, cleaning the store, buying advertising, renting a building, repairing ovens, and obtaining insurance coverage.

2. **Investing:** These activities involve buying and selling productive resources with long lives (such as buildings, land, equipment, and tools), purchasing investments, and lending to others. As Exhibit 1.5 shows, Pizza Aroma expects to purchase equipment for $40,000 cash.

3. **Financing:** Any borrowing from banks, repaying bank loans, receiving contributions from stockholders, or paying dividends to stockholders are considered financing activities.

Pizza Aroma's statement of cash flows is typical of a new start-up business or a business in expansion. The negative number for investing cash flows occurs because the company needs to buy a significant amount of equipment. The bank will be interested in watching how the cash flows reported on this statement change in the future to assess Pizza Aroma's ability to make cash payments on the loan.

Notes to the Financial Statements

The four basic financial statements are not complete without notes to help financial statement users understand how the amounts were derived and what other information may affect their decisions. We'll talk about notes in more detail in later chapters.

"How does the whole picture fit together?"

Relationships among the Financial Statements

Exhibit 1.6 shows how the four basic financial statements connect to one another. The arrows show that:

1 Net Income, from the income statement, is a component in determining ending Retained Earnings on the statement of retained earnings.

2 Ending Retained Earnings from the statement of retained earnings is then reported on the balance sheet.

3 The Cash on the balance sheet is equal to the ending Cash reported on the statement of cash flows.

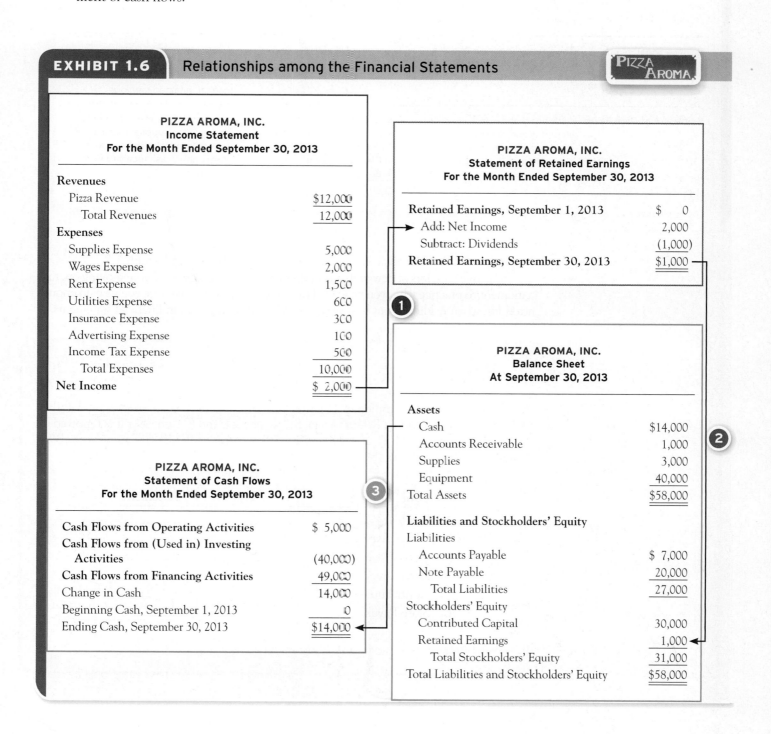

EXHIBIT 1.6 | Relationships among the Financial Statements

PIZZA AROMA, INC.
Income Statement
For the Month Ended September 30, 2013

Revenues	
Pizza Revenue	$12,000
Total Revenues	12,000
Expenses	
Supplies Expense	5,000
Wages Expense	2,000
Rent Expense	1,500
Utilities Expense	600
Insurance Expense	300
Advertising Expense	100
Income Tax Expense	500
Total Expenses	10,000
Net Income	$ 2,000

PIZZA AROMA, INC.
Statement of Retained Earnings
For the Month Ended September 30, 2013

Retained Earnings, September 1, 2013	$ 0
Add: Net Income	2,000
Subtract: Dividends	(1,000)
Retained Earnings, September 30, 2013	$1,000

PIZZA AROMA, INC.
Statement of Cash Flows
For the Month Ended September 30, 2013

Cash Flows from Operating Activities	$ 5,000
Cash Flows from (Used in) Investing Activities	(40,000)
Cash Flows from Financing Activities	49,000
Change in Cash	14,000
Beginning Cash, September 1, 2013	0
Ending Cash, September 30, 2013	$14,000

PIZZA AROMA, INC.
Balance Sheet
At September 30, 2013

Assets	
Cash	$14,000
Accounts Receivable	1,000
Supplies	3,000
Equipment	40,000
Total Assets	$58,000
Liabilities and Stockholders' Equity	
Liabilities	
Accounts Payable	$ 7,000
Note Payable	20,000
Total Liabilities	27,000
Stockholders' Equity	
Contributed Capital	30,000
Retained Earnings	1,000
Total Stockholders' Equity	31,000
Total Liabilities and Stockholders' Equity	$58,000

EXHIBIT 1.7	Summary of Four Basic Financial Statements

Financial Statement	Purpose: To report . . .	Structure	Examples of Content
Income Statement	The financial performance of the business *during the current accounting period.*	Revenues − Expenses = Net Income	Sales revenue, wages expense, supplies expense, rent expense
Statement of Retained Earnings	The accumulation of earnings retained in the business *during the current accounting period* with that of prior periods.	Beginning Retained Earnings + Net Income (this period) − Dividends (this period) = Ending Retained Earnings	Net income is from the income statement. Dividends are amounts distributed this period.
Balance Sheet	The financial position of a business *at a point in time.*	Liabilities Assets = + Stockholders' Equity	Cash, receivables, supplies, equipment, accounts payable, notes payable, contributed capital, retained earnings
Statement of Cash Flows	Activities that caused increases and decreases in cash *during the current accounting period.*	+/− Operating Cash Flows +/− Investing Cash Flows +/− Financing Cash Flows = Change in Cash + Beginning Cash = Ending Cash	Cash collected from customers, cash paid to suppliers, cash paid for equipment, cash borrowed from banks, cash received from issuing stock

A summary of the four basic financial statements is presented in Exhibit 1.7.

You have seen lots of new and important material in this section. Before moving on, take a moment to practice what you've read. This is the best way to make sure you've paid enough attention when reading about how business activities are reported in financial statements.

 How's it going? Self-Study Practice

In the space provided, indicate: (1) the type of account (A = asset, L = liability, SE = stockholders' equity, R = revenue, E = expense), and (2) whether it is reported on the income statement (I/S), statement of retained earnings (SRE), balance sheet (B/S), or statement of cash flows (SCF).

Account Title	Type	Statement
1. Land	_____	_____
2. Wages Expense	_____	_____
3. Accounts Receivable	_____	_____
4. Rent Revenue	_____	_____
5. Contributed Capital	_____	_____
6. Note Payable	_____	_____

After you have finished, check your answers with the solution in the margin.

Solution to Self-Study Practice

	Type	Statement
1.	A	B/S
2.	E	I/S
3.	A	B/S
4.	R	I/S
5.	SE	B/S
6.	L	B/S

"So, you've just seen how your financial statements should look in one month and how they relate. Are you feeling okay with all this?"

"It actually makes me anxious to get started. What will my external users look for?"

Evaluate the Results

USING FINANCIAL STATEMENTS

Learning Objective 1-3
Explain how financial statements are used by decision makers.

The financial statements are a key source of information when external users, like creditors and investors, make decisions concerning a company. As you will see throughout this course, the amounts reported in the financial statements can be used to calculate percentages and ratios that reveal important insights about a company's performance. For now, however, let's consider how creditors and investors might gain valuable information simply by reading the dollar amounts reported in each financial statement.

- Creditors are mainly interested in assessing:
  1. **Is the company generating enough cash to make payments on its loan?** Answers to this question will come from the statement of cash flows. In particular, creditors would be interested in seeing whether operating activities are producing positive cash flows. Pizza Aroma's expected net inflow of $5,000 cash from operating activities is very good for a new business. Find it in Exhibit 1.5.
  2. **Does the company have enough assets to cover its liabilities?** Answers to this question will come from comparing assets and liabilities reported on the balance sheet. Pizza Aroma is expected to own slightly more than twice what it owes to creditors at September 30 (total assets of $58,000 versus total liabilities of $27,000). With $14,000 in Cash, Pizza Aroma would be able to immediately pay all of its Accounts Payable and part of its Note Payable if needed.

- **Investors expect a return on their contributions to a company.** The return may be immediate (through dividends) or long-term (through selling stock certificates at a price higher than their original cost). Dividends and higher stock prices are more likely if a company is profitable. As a result, investors look closely at the income statement (and statement of retained earnings) for information about the company's ability to generate profits (and distribute dividends).

"I've heard a lot about 'cooking the books.' How do users know the information they're getting is useful and can be trusted?"

USEFUL FINANCIAL INFORMATION

Learning Objective 1-4
Describe factors that contribute to useful financial information.

Laurie indicated that useful financial information arises when businesses apply generally accepted accounting principles in an ethical business environment.

Generally Accepted Accounting Principles

As it turns out, the system of financial statement reporting in use today has a long history—all the way back to a publication in 1494 by an Italian monk and mathematician, Luca Pacioli. Currently, the Financial Accounting Standards Board (FASB) has the primary responsibility for setting the underlying rules of accounting in the U.S. As a group, these rules are called **Generally Accepted Accounting Principles**, or **GAAP** for short (pronounced like the name of the clothing store).

The accounting rules in the United States are similar, for the most part, to those used elsewhere in the world, but some important differences exist. The FASB is working alongside the International Accounting Standards Board (IASB) to eliminate these differences so that investors can more easily compare the financial statements of companies from different countries. Throughout this course, we'll use a pullout feature called Spotlight on the World to alert you to important differences.

SPOTLIGHT ON The World

The accounting rules developed by the IASB are called **International Financial Reporting Standards**, or **IFRS** for short. As the map indicates, accounting bodies in many countries already require or permit the use of IFRS (dark green), or plan to converge with IFRS in the near future (blue). The plans for converging U.S. GAAP with IFRS are discussed in Chapter 5.

The main goal of GAAP and IFRS is to ensure companies produce financial information that is useful to existing and potential investors, lenders, and other creditors **in making decisions** about providing resources to the companies. For financial information to be judged useful, it must possess two fundamental characteristics: **relevance** and **faithful representation.** Information is relevant if it makes a difference in decision making and it is a faithful representation if it fully depicts the economic substance of business activities. The usefulness of financial information is enhanced when it is (i) comparable (to prior periods and other companies), (ii) verifiable, (iii) timely, and (iv) understandable. To achieve these broad objectives, the

EXHIBIT 1.8	Key Concepts for External Financial Reporting

Objective of External Financial Reporting
To provide useful financial information to external users for decision making
- It must be relevant and a faithful representation of the business
- It is more useful if it is comparable, verifiable, timely, and understandable

Elements to Be Measured and Reported
- Assets, Liabilities, Stockholders' Equity, Revenues, Expenses, Dividends

Concepts for Measuring and Reporting Information
- **Assumptions:** Unit of Measure, Separate Entity, Going Concern, Time Period
- **Principles:**   Cost, Revenue Recognition, Expense Recognition, Full Disclosure

FASB and IASB have developed a framework that outlines the financial elements to be measured and reported as well as various concepts for measuring and reporting financial information. Laurie summarized these elements and concepts for Mauricio, highlighting in red the concepts briefly introduced already (see Exhibit 1.8). (The remaining concepts will be introduced in later chapters and all will be reviewed in the final chapter.)

> **"Who is responsible for ensuring that businesses follow GAAP?"**

Laurie told Mauricio that a company's managers have primary responsibility for following GAAP. To provide additional assurance, some private companies and all public companies hire independent auditors to scrutinize their financial records. Following rules approved by the Public Company Accounting Oversight Board (PCAOB) and other accounting bodies, these auditors report whether, beyond reasonable doubt, the financial statements represent what they claim to represent and whether they comply with GAAP. In a sense, GAAP are to auditors and accountants what the criminal code is to lawyers and the public. The Securities and Exchange Commission (SEC) is the government agency that oversees stock exchanges and financial reporting by public companies in the U.S.

> **"Overall, users expect information that is truthful, and this assumes that the company is following strong ethical business and accounting practices."**

Ethical Conduct

Ethics refers to the standards of conduct for judging right from wrong, honest from dishonest, and fair from unfair. Intentional financial misreporting is both unethical and illegal. As you will see throughout this course, some accounting and business issues have clear answers that are either right or wrong. However, many situations require accountants, auditors, and managers to weigh the pros and cons of alternatives before making final decisions. To help ensure these decisions are made in a professional and ethical manner, the American Institute of Certified Public Accountants (AICPA) requires that all its members adhere to a **Code of Professional Conduct.** Despite this code of conduct, some individuals have been involved in accounting scandals and fraud.

In response to frauds, the government introduced new laws through the **Sarbanes-Oxley Act**. The Act requires top managers of public companies to sign a report certifying their responsibilities for the financial statements, maintain an audited system of **internal controls** to ensure accuracy in the accounting reports, and maintain an independent committee to oversee top management and ensure that they cooperate with auditors. As a result of the act, corporate executives face severe consequences—20 years in prison and $5 million in fines—if they are found guilty of committing accounting fraud.

Ethical conduct is just as important for small private businesses as it is for large public companies. Laurie's advice to Mauricio and to all managers is to strive to create an ethical environment and establish a strong system of checks and controls inside the company. Do not tolerate blatant acts of fraud, such as employees making up false expenses for reimbursement, punching in a time card belonging to a fellow employee who will be late for work, or copying someone's ideas and claiming them as his or her own. Also be aware that not all ethical dilemmas are clear-cut. Some situations will require you to weigh

Accounting Scandals

Accounting scandals are driven by greed and the fear of personal or business failure. Initially, some people may appear to benefit from fraudulent reporting. In the long run, however, fraud harms most individuals and organizations. When it is uncovered, the corporation's stock price drops dramatically. In one case involving MicroStrategy, the stock price dropped 65 percent in a single day of trading, from $243 to $86 per share. Creditors are also harmed by fraud. As a result of a fraud at WorldCom, creditors recovered only 42 percent of what they were owed. They lost $36 billion. Innocent employees also are harmed by fraud. At Enron, 5,600 employees lost their jobs and many lost all of their retirement savings. The auditing firm Arthur Andersen, which once employed 28,000 people, went out of business after becoming entangled in the WorldCom and Enron frauds.

one moral principle (e.g., honesty) against another (e.g., loyalty). Advise your employees that, when faced with an ethical dilemma, they should follow a three-step process:

1. **Identify who will be affected by the situation**—both those who will appear to benefit (often the manager or employee) and those who will be harmed (other employees, the company's reputation, owners, creditors, and the public in general).

2. **Identify and evaluate the alternative courses of action.**

3. **Choose the alternative that is the most ethical**—and that you would be proud to have reported in the news.

Often, there is no one right answer to ethical dilemmas and hard choices will need to be made. In the end, however, following strong ethical practices is a key factor in business success and in ensuring good financial reporting.

Epilogue for Pizza Aroma

Mauricio got going quickly and, in August, created a corporation called Pizza Aroma, Inc. Things didn't turn out exactly as he had planned, but his dream-turned-business has been successful. Pizza Aroma has received the "Best Pizza" award several years in a row in the *Ithaca Times* readers' poll.

The next three chapters will take you step by step through the financing, investing, and operating decisions that occurred at Pizza Aroma during its first month of business. We will look at the way accountants collect data about business activities and process it to construct the financial statements. The key to success in this course is to **practice** the skills that are presented in this text. It is very difficult to learn accounting without doing the assignments and keeping up with the reading.

SUPPLEMENT 1A   CAREERS THAT DEPEND ON ACCOUNTING KNOWLEDGE

Accounting knowledge can make the difference in your ability to land a dream job, whether you hope to work in production and operations management, human resources, finance, or marketing. Exhibit 1S.1 displays nonaccounting jobs that could be available to you at the world's leading companies and explains how accounting knowledge can be vital to these positions. If, instead, you have your eyes set on an accounting career, see page 547 for further information.

EXHIBIT 1S.1	Accounting Knowledge Can Benefit All Majors

Production and Operations Management

Production Manager, Nintendo: Figure out how to make a $250 3DS for $100.71.

Outsourcing Specialist, Apple: Coordinate more than 20 suppliers of parts for the next iPad, at the same total cost as legacy iPads.

Human Resources

Compensation Analyst, Google: Develop affordable, attractive global pay programs.

Labor Relations Manager, NBA Players' Union: Assist in salary renegotiations involving the $58 million salary cap and 57% revenue sharing guarantee.

Accounting

Finance

Investment Analyst, Goldman Sachs: Assess value of investing $50 million in Facebook.

Financial Analyst, Target Corporation: Help credit card segment reduce the number of days awaiting collections from customers.

Marketing

Brand Manager, H. J. Heinz Company: Set prices to achieve 5% annual sales growth.

Customer Business Developer, Procter & Gamble: Collaborate with accounting to enhance customer profits and cash flows.

Sources: http://techland.time.com/2011/03/29/the-incredibly-cheap-100-nintendo-3ds, http://blogs.forbes.com/johnray/2011/03/11/isuppli-teardown-of-the-ipad-2-investor-edition/, http://www.isuppli.com/Teardowns/News/Pages/iPad-2-Carries-Bill-of-Materials-of-$326-60-IHS-iSuppli-Teardown-Analysis-Shows.aspx, http://www.nytimes.com/2011/05/25/sports/basketball/players-accuse-nba-of-failing-to-bargain-in-good-faith.html?_r=1&ref=nationallaborrelationsboard.

REVIEW THE CHAPTER

DEMONSTRATION CASE

The introductory case presented here reviews the items reported on the income statement, statement of retained earnings, and balance sheet, using the financial statements of Under Armour, Inc.—a public company founded in 1996 by a former University of Maryland football player to develop, market, and distribute athletic apparel and gear. Following is a list of items and amounts (in thousands of U.S. dollars) adapted from Under Armour, Inc.'s financial statements for the quarter ended March 31, 2011.

Accounts Payable	$ 88,678	Other Expenses	$ 1,089
Accounts Receivable	163,385	Other Liabilities	70,197
Cash	110,844	Property and Equipment	80,298
Contributed Capital	240,643	Retained Earnings, March 31, 2011	284,532
Dividends	0	Retained Earnings, January 1, 2011	272,393
General and Administrative Expenses	123,909	Sales Revenues	312,699
Income Tax Expense	7,914	Total Assets	691,710
Inventories	243,614	Total Expenses	300,560
Net Income	12,139	Total Liabilities	166,535
Notes Payable	7,660	Total Liabilities and Stockholders' Equity	691,710
Operating Expenses	167,648	Total Revenues	312,699
Other Assets	83,569	Total Stockholders' Equity	525,175

Required:

1. Prepare an Income Statement, Statement of Retained Earnings, and a Balance Sheet for the quarter, following the formats in Exhibits 1.2, 1.3, and 1.4.

2. Describe the content of these three statements.

3. Name the other statement that Under Armour would include in its financial statements.

4. Did financing for Under Armour's assets come primarily from liabilities or stockholders' equity?

5. Explain why Under Armour would subject its statements to an independent audit.

Suggested Solution

1. The first step to reach a solution is to distinguish accounts as belonging to the income statement (revenues and expenses), statement of retained earnings (retained earnings and dividends), and balance sheet (assets, liabilities, and stockholders' equity). Organize the accounts in proper format and follow the flow from one to another (as shown by the following arrows).

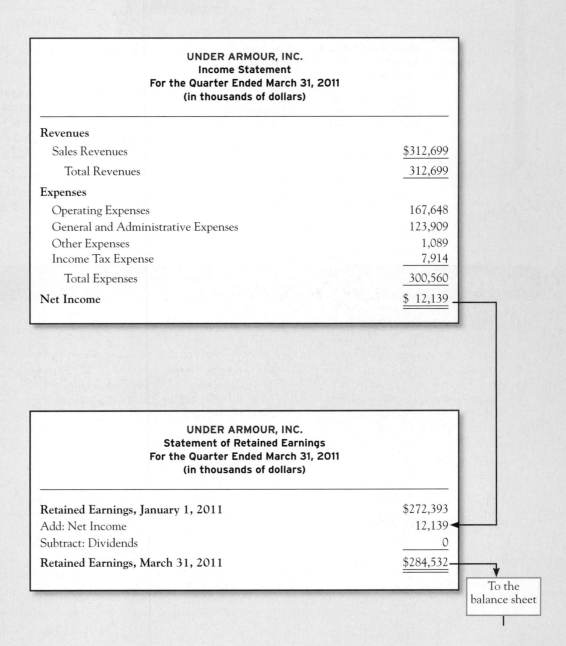

UNDER ARMOUR, INC.
Income Statement
For the Quarter Ended March 31, 2011
(in thousands of dollars)

Revenues	
Sales Revenues	$312,699
Total Revenues	312,699
Expenses	
Operating Expenses	167,648
General and Administrative Expenses	123,909
Other Expenses	1,089
Income Tax Expense	7,914
Total Expenses	300,560
Net Income	$ 12,139

UNDER ARMOUR, INC.
Statement of Retained Earnings
For the Quarter Ended March 31, 2011
(in thousands of dollars)

Retained Earnings, January 1, 2011	$272,393
Add: Net Income	12,139
Subtract: Dividends	0
Retained Earnings, March 31, 2011	$284,532

To the balance sheet

UNDER ARMOUR, INC.
Balance Sheet
At March 31, 2011
(in thousands of dollars)

Assets	
Cash	$110,844
Accounts Receivable	163,385
Inventories	248,614
Property and Equipment	80,298
Other Assets	88,569
Total Assets	$691,710
Liabilities	
Accounts Payable	$88,678
Notes Payable	7,660
Other Liabilities	70,197
Total Liabilities	166,535
Stockholders' Equity	
Contributed Capital	240,643
Retained Earnings	284,532
Total Stockholders' Equity	525,175
Total Liabilities and Stockholders' Equity	$691,710

From the statement of retained earnings

2. The income statement reports the most common measure of financial performance for a business: net income (revenues minus expenses during the accounting period). The statement of retained earnings links the net income number from the income statement to the end-of-period retained earnings balance on the balance sheet. The balance sheet reports the amount of assets, liabilities, and stockholders' equity of a business at a point in time.

3. Under Armour would also present a statement of cash flows.

4. The balance sheet indicates that financing for Under Armour's assets is provided primarily from stockholders' equity ($525,175) rather than liabilities ($166,535).

5. Like all public companies, Under Armour will subject its financial statements to an audit because it is required by the SEC to have an independent audit. Also, an audit will give users greater confidence in the accuracy of financial statement information because the people who audited the statements are required to meet professional standards of ethics and competence.

CHAPTER SUMMARY

Describe various organizational forms and business decision makers. p. 4   LO 1-1

- Sole proprietorships are owned by one individual, are relatively inexpensive to form, and are not treated legally as separate from their owners. Thus, all profits or losses become part of the taxable income to the owner who is also responsible personally for all debts of the business.

- Partnerships are businesses legally similar to proprietorships, but with two or more owners.

- Corporations are separate legal entities (thus, corporations pay taxes) that issue shares of stock to investors (stockholders) and are more costly to establish. Stockholders cannot be held liable for more than their investment in the corporation. Private corporations issue stock to a few individuals while public corporations issue stock in the stock market.

- Business decision makers include creditors (banks, suppliers), investors (stockholders), customers, governments, and other external users.

LO 1-2   **Describe the purpose, structure, and content of the four basic financial statements. p. 7**

- The *income statement* reports the net amount that a business earned (net income) over a period of time by subtracting the costs of running the business (expenses) from the total amount earned (revenues).

- The *statement of retained earnings* explains changes in the Retained Earnings account over a period of time by considering increases (from net income) and decreases (from dividends to stockholders).

- The *balance sheet* reports what the business owns (reported as assets) at a particular point in time and how much of the financing for these assets came from creditors (reported as liabilities) and stockholders (reported as stockholders' equity).

- The *statement of cash flows* explains changes in the cash account over a period of time by reporting inflows and outflows of cash from the business's operating, investing, and financing activities.

LO 1-3   **Explain how financial statements are used by decision makers. p. 17**

- Creditors are mainly interested in assessing whether the company: (1) is generating enough cash to make payments on its loan, and (2) has enough assets to cover its liabilities. Answers to these questions are indicated by the statement of cash flows and the balance sheet.

- Investors look closely at the income statement for information about a company's ability to generate profits, and at the statement of retained earnings for information about a company's dividend distributions.

LO 1-4   **Describe factors that contribute to useful financial information. p. 17**

- Companies generate useful financial information by applying Generally Accepted Accounting Principles (GAAP) or International Financial Reporting Standards (IFRS) in an ethical business environment.

- To be useful, information must be relevant and a faithful representation of reality. Information is more useful when it is comparable, verifiable, timely, and understandable.

KEY TERMS

Accounting p. 5

Accounts p. 10

Balance Sheet p. 12

Basic Accounting Equation p. 8

Financial Statements p. 6

Generally Accepted Accounting
  Principles (GAAP) p. 18

Income Statement p. 10

International Financial Reporting
  Standards (IFRS) p. 18

Sarbanes-Oxley Act (SOX) p. 19

Separate Entity Assumption p. 8

Statement of Cash Flows p. 13

Statement of Retained Earnings p. 11

Unit of Measure Assumption p. 10

See complete definitions in the glossary in the back of this text.

HOMEWORK HELPER

Alternative terms

- The balance sheet also can be called the statement of financial position.
- The income statement also can be called the statement of operations.
- Net Income also can be called Net Earnings.

Helpful reminders

- The balance in each account is reported once and only once in either the balance sheet, income statement, or statement of retained earnings.

Frequent mistakes

- Dividends are not expenses. Dividends relate to distributing (not generating) earnings. Consequently, a company's dividends are reported on its statement of retained earnings (not its income statement).

PRACTICE MATERIAL

QUESTIONS (⊖ Symbol indicates questions that require analysis from more than one perspective.)

1. Define *accounting*.

2. Valeri is opening a hair salon but she does not know what business form it should take. What can you tell her about the advantages and disadvantages of operating as a sole proprietorship versus a corporation? ⊖

3. Briefly distinguish financial accounting from managerial accounting.

4. The accounting process generates financial reports for both internal and external users. Describe some of the specific groups of internal and external users.

5. Explain what the separate entity assumption means when it says a business is treated as separate from its owners for accounting purposes.

6. List the three main types of business activities on the statement of cash flows and give an example of each.

7. What information should be included in the heading of each of the four primary financial statements?

8. What are the purposes of (*a*) the balance sheet, (*b*) the income statement, (*c*) the statement of retained earnings, and (*d*) the statement of cash flows?

9. Explain why the income statement, statement of retained earnings, and statement of cash flows would be dated "For the Year Ended December 31, 2012," whereas the balance sheet would be dated "At December 31, 2012."

10. Briefly explain the difference between *net income* and *net loss*.

11. Describe the basic accounting equation that provides the structure for the balance sheet. Define the three major components reported on the balance sheet.

12. Describe the equation that provides the structure for the income statement. Explain the three major items reported on the income statement.

13. Describe the equation that provides the structure for the statement of retained earnings. Explain the four major items reported on the statement of retained earnings.

14. Describe the equation that provides the structure for the statement of cash flows. Explain the three major types of activities reported on the statement.

15. Briefly describe the organization that is responsible for developing accounting measurement rules (Generally Accepted Accounting Principles) in the United States.

16. What is the main goal for accounting rules in the United States and around the world? What characteristics must financial information possess to reach that goal?

17. Briefly define what an ethical dilemma is and describe the steps to consider when evaluating ethical dilemmas.

18. In what ways might accounting frauds be similar to cases of academic dishonesty?

MULTIPLE CHOICE

1. Which of the following is *not* one of the four basic financial statements?
   a. The balance sheet
   b. The audit report
   c. The income statement
   d. The statement of cash flows

2. Which of the following is true regarding the income statement?
   a. The income statement is sometimes called the statement of operations.
   b. The income statement reports revenues, expenses, and liabilities.
   c. The income statement only reports revenue for which cash was received at the point of sale.
   d. The income statement reports the financial position of a business at a particular point in time.

3. Which of the following is false regarding the balance sheet?
   a. The accounts shown on a balance sheet represent the basic accounting equation for a particular business.
   b. The retained earnings balance shown on the balance sheet must agree with the ending retained earnings balance shown on the statement of retained earnings.

   c. The balance sheet summarizes the net changes in specific account balances over a period of time.
   d. The balance sheet reports the amount of assets, liabilities, and stockholders' equity of a business at a point in time.

4. Which of the following regarding retained earnings is false?
   a. Retained earnings is increased by net income.
   b. Retained earnings is a component of stockholders' equity on the balance sheet.
   c. Retained earnings is an asset on the balance sheet.
   d. Retained earnings represents earnings not distributed to stockholders in the form of dividends.

5. Which of the following is *not* one of the items required to be shown in the heading of a financial statement?
   a. The financial statement preparer's name.
   b. The title of the financial statement.
   c. The financial reporting date or period.
   d. The name of the business entity.

6. Which of the following statements regarding the statement of cash flows is false?
   a. The statement of cash flows separates cash inflows and outflows into three major categories: operating, investing, and financing.

b. The ending cash balance shown on the statement of cash flows must agree with the amount shown on the balance sheet at the end of the same period.

c. The total increase or decrease in cash shown on the statement of cash flows must agree with the "bottom line" (net income or net loss) reported on the income statement.

d. The statement of cash flows covers a period of time.

7. Which of the following regarding GAAP is true?

a. GAAP is an abbreviation for generally applied accounting principles.

b. Changes in GAAP always affect the amount of income reported by a company.

c. GAAP is the abbreviation for generally accepted accounting principles.

d. Changes to GAAP must be approved by the Senate Finance Committee.

8. Which of the following is true?

a. FASB creates SEC.
b. GAAP creates FASB.
c. SEC creates CPA.
d. FASB creates GAAP.

9. Which of the following would *not* be a goal of external users reading a company's financial statements?

a. Understanding the current financial state of the company.

b. Assessing the company's contribution to social and environmental policies.

c. Predicting the company's future financial performance.

d. Evaluating the company's ability to generate cash from sales.

10. Which of the following is *not* required by the Sarbanes-Oxley Act?

a. Top managers of public companies must sign a report certifying their responsibilities for the financial statements.

b. Public companies must maintain an audited system of internal control to ensure accuracy in accounting reports.

c. Public companies must maintain an independent committee to meet with the company's independent auditors.

d. Top managers of public companies must be members of the American Institute of Certified Public Accountants.

> For answers to the Multiple-Choice Questions **see page Q1** located in the last section of the book.

MINI-EXERCISES

Mc Graw Hill **connect** | ACCOUNTING

LO 1-4   **M1-1 Identifying Definitions with Abbreviations**

The following is a list of important abbreviations used in the chapter. These abbreviations also are used widely in business. For each abbreviation, give the full designation. The first one is an example.

Abbreviation	Full Designation
1. CPA	Certified Public Accountant
2. GAAP	_____
3. FASB	_____
4. SEC	_____
5. IFRS	_____

LO 1-1, 1-2, 1-4   **M1-2 Matching Definitions with Terms or Abbreviations**

Match each definition with its related term or abbreviation by entering the appropriate letter in the space provided.

Term or Abbreviation	Definition
_____ 1. SEC	A. A system that collects and processes financial information about an organization and reports that information to decision makers.
_____ 2. Investing activities	
_____ 3. Private company	B. Measurement of information about a business in the monetary unit (dollars or other national currency).
_____ 4. Corporation	
_____ 5. Accounting	C. An unincorporated business owned by two or more persons.
_____ 6. Partnership	
_____ 7. FASB	D. A company that sells shares of its stock privately and is not required to release its financial statements to the public.
_____ 8. Financing activities	
_____ 9. Unit of measure	

_____ 10. GAAP

_____ 11. Public company

_____ 12. Operating activities

E. An incorporated business that issues shares of stock as evidence of ownership.

F. Buying and selling productive resources with long lives.

G. Transactions with lenders (borrowing and repaying cash) and stockholders (selling company stock and paying dividends).

H. Activities directly related to running the business to earn profit.

I. Securities and Exchange Commission.

J. Financial Accounting Standards Board.

K. A company that has its stock bought and sold by investors on established stock exchanges.

L. Generally accepted accounting principles.

M1-3 Matching Definitions with Terms

LO 1-2, 1-4

Match each definition with its related term by entering the appropriate letter in the space provided.

Term	Definition
_____ 1. Relevance	A. The financial reports of a business are assumed to include the results of only that business's activities.
_____ 2. Faithful Representation	
_____ 3. Comparability	B. The resources owned by a business.
_____ 4. Separate Entity	C. Financial information that can be compared across businesses because similar accounting methods have been applied.
_____ 5. Assets	
_____ 6. Liabilities	
_____ 7. Stockholders' Equity	D. The total amounts invested and reinvested in the business by its owners.
_____ 8. Revenues	
_____ 9. Expenses	E. The costs of business necessary to earn revenues.
_____ 10. Unit of Measure	F. A feature of financial information that allows it to influence a decision.
	G. Earned by selling goods or services to customers.
	H. The amounts owed by the business.
	I. Financial information that depicts the economic substance of business activities.
	J. The assumption that states that results of business activities should be reported in an appropriate monetary unit.

M1-4 Matching Financial Statement Items to Balance Sheet and Income Statement Categories

LO 1-2

According to its annual report, "Procter & Gamble markets a broad range of laundry, cleaning, paper, beauty care, health care, food and beverage products in more than 180 countries around the world, with leading brands including Tide, Ariel, Crest, Crisco, Vicks and Max Factor." The following are items taken from its recent balance sheet and income statement. For each item, indicate: (1) the type of account (A = asset, L = liability, SE = stockholders' equity, R = revenue, E = expense), and (2) whether it is reported on the income statement (I/S) or balance sheet (B/S).

P&G

1. Accounts Payable

2. Accounts Receivable

3. Cash

4. Income Tax Expense

5. Selling and Administrative Expenses

6. Sales Revenue

7. Notes Payable

8. Retained Earnings

LO 1-2   **M1-5** **Matching Financial Statement Items to Balance Sheet and Income Statement Categories**

For each item, indicate: (1) the type of account (A = asset, L = liability, SE = stockholders' equity, R = revenue, E = expense), and (2) whether it is reported on the income statement (I/S) or balance sheet (B/S).

1. Accounts Receivable
2. Sales Revenue
3. Equipment
4. Supplies Expense
5. Cash
6. Advertising Expense
7. Accounts Payable
8. Retained Earnings

LO 1-2   **M1-6** **Matching Financial Statement Items to Balance Sheet and Income Statement Categories**

Tootsie Roll Industries manufactures and sells more than 64 million Tootsie Rolls and 20 million Tootsie Roll Pops each day. The following items were listed on Tootsie Roll's recent income statement and balance sheet. For each item, indicate: (1) the type of account (A = asset, L = liability, SE = stockholders' equity, R = revenue, E = expense), and (2) whether it is reported on the income statement (I/S) or balance sheet (B/S).

1. Accounts Receivable
2. Selling and Administrative Expenses
3. Cash
4. Equipment
5. Advertising Expense
6. Sales Revenue
7. Notes Payable
8. Retained Earnings
9. Accounts Payable

LO 1-2   **M1-7** **Matching Financial Statement Items to Balance Sheet and Income Statement Categories**

General Mills is a manufacturer of food products, such as Lucky Charms cereal, Pillsbury crescent rolls, and Green Giant vegetables. The following items were presented in the company's financial statements. For each item, indicate: (1) the type of account (A = asset, L = liability, SE = stockholders' equity, R = revenue, E = expense), and (2) whether it is reported on the income statement (I/S) or balance sheet (B/S).

1. Accounts Payable
2. Contributed Capital
3. Equipment
4. Accounts Receivable
5. Notes Payable
6. Cash
7. Retained Earnings
8. Selling and Administrative Expenses
9. Sales Revenue
10. Supplies

LO 1-2   **M1-8** **Matching Financial Statement Items to the Four Basic Financial Statements**

Prior to being acquired in November 2007 by Luxottica Group—an Italian eyewear company—Oakley, Inc., reported the following items in its financial statements. For each item, indicate: (1) the type of account (A = asset, L = liability, SE = stockholders' equity, R = revenue, E = expense, D = dividend), and (2) whether it is reported on the income statement (I/S), statement of retained earnings (SRE), and/or balance sheet (B/S).

1. Dividends
2. Contributed Capital
3. Sales Revenue
4. Equipment
5. Cash
6. Long-term Debt
7. Accounts Payable
8. Retained Earnings, Beginning of Year

LO 1-2   **M1-9** **Matching Financial Statement Items to the Four Basic Financial Statements**

Match each element with its financial statement by entering the appropriate letter in the space provided.

Element	Financial Statement
_____ 1. Cash Flows from Financing Activities	A. Balance Sheet
_____ 2. Expenses	B. Income Statement
_____ 3. Cash Flows from Investing Activities	C. Statement of Retained Earnings
_____ 4. Assets	D. Statement of Cash Flows
_____ 5. Dividends	
_____ 6. Revenues	
_____ 7. Cash Flows from Operating Activities	
_____ 8. Liabilities	

M1-10 Reporting Amounts on the Statement of Cash Flows

LO 1-2

Learning which items belong in each cash flow statement category is an important first step in understanding their meaning. Use a letter to mark each item in the following list as a cash flow from Operating, Investing, or Financing activities. **Put parentheses around the letter if it is a cash *outflow* and use no parentheses if it's an *inflow*.**

_____ 1. Cash paid for dividends   _____ 4. Cash paid to employees

_____ 2. Cash collected from customers   _____ 5. Cash paid to purchase equipment

_____ 3. Cash received when signing a note   _____ 6. Cash received from issuing stock

M1-11 Reporting Amounts on the Statement of Cash Flows

LO 1-2

Learning which items belong in each category of the statement of cash flows is an important first step in understanding their meaning. Use a letter to mark each item in the following list as a cash flow from Operating, Investing, or Financing activities. **Put parentheses around the letter if it is a cash *outflow* and use no parentheses if it's an *inflow*.**

_____ 1. Cash paid to purchase land   _____ 4. Cash paid for dividends

_____ 2. Cash collected from clients   _____ 5. Cash paid to suppliers

_____ 3. Cash received from selling equipment   _____ 6. Cash received from issuing stock

M1-12 Preparing a Statement of Retained Earnings

LO 1-2

Stone Culture Corporation was organized on January 1, 2012. For its first two years of operations, it reported the following:

Net Income for 2012	$40,000	Dividends for 2013	$ 20,000
Net Income for 2013	45,000	Total assets at the end of 2012	125,000
Dividends for 2012	15,000	Total assets at the end of 2013	242,000

On the basis of the data given, prepare a statement of retained earnings for 2012 (its first year of operations) and 2013.

M1-13 Relationships among Financial Statements

LO 1-2

Apple, Inc.
Google, Inc.
Intel Corp.

Items from the income statement, statement of retained earnings, and balance sheet are listed below in alphabetical order. For the companies shown in each column, solve for the missing amounts.

   TIP: Use Exhibit 1.6 to identify relations among the items, then solve for amounts.

	Apple, Inc.	Google, Inc.	Intel Corp.
Contributed Capital	$11	$18	$17
Dividends	0	0	4
Net Income	(a)	(d)	(g)
Retained Earnings, Beginning of Year	23	20	26
Retained Earnings, End of Year	(b)	(e)	(h)
Total Assets	(c)	(f)	(i)
Total Expenses	51	20	33
Total Liabilities	27	12	13
Total Revenues	65	29	44

LO 1-2   **M1-14 Relationships among Financial Statements**

Items from the income statement, statement of retained earnings, and balance sheet are listed below in alphabetical order. For the companies shown in each column, solve for the missing amounts.

	Amazin' Corp.	Best Tech, Inc.	Colossal Corp.
Contributed Capital	$ 5	$15	$100
Dividends	10	5	50
Net Income	(a)	(d)	(g)
Retained Earnings, Beginning of Year	30	0	200
Retained Earnings, End of Year	(b)	(e)	(h)
Total Assets	(c)	(f)	(i)
Total Expenses	75	30	200
Total Liabilities	30	30	350
Total Revenues	100	50	300

LO 1-2

Electronic Arts, Inc.

M1-15 Relationships among Financial Statements

Items from the 2011 income statement, statement of retained earnings, and balance sheet of Electronic Arts, Inc., are listed below in alphabetical order. Solve for the missing amounts, and explain whether the company was profitable.

> **TIP:** Use Exhibit 1.6 to identify relations among the items, then work backward to solve for amounts.

	Electronic Arts, Inc.
Contributed Capital	$2,430
Dividends	0
Net Income (Loss)	(a)
Retained Earnings, Beginning of Year	370
Retained Earnings, End of Year	(b)
Total Assets	4,900
Total Expenses	(c)
Total Liabilities	2,400
Total Revenues	3,600

LO 1-2, 1-3   **M1-16 Preparing an Income Statement, Statement of Retained Earnings, and Balance Sheet**

The following information was reported in the December 31, 2010, financial statements of Southwest Airlines, Inc. (listed alphabetically, amounts in millions).

Accounts Payable	$1,602	Other Assets	$ 909
Accounts Receivable	195	Other Liabilities	1,703
Aircraft Fuel Expense	3,620	Other Expenses	2,340
Cash	3,538	Other Revenue	615
Contributed Capital	838	Property and Equipment	10,578
Dividends	31	Repairs and Maintenance Expense	751
Income Tax Expense	287	Retained Earnings (as of December 31)	5,399
Interest Expense	136	Salaries Expense	3,704
Landing Fees Expense	807	Supplies	243
Notes Payable	5,921	Ticket Revenues	11,489

1. Prepare an income statement for the year ended December 31, 2010.
2. Prepare a statement of retained earnings for the year ended December 31, 2010.
   TIP: Assume the balance in retained earnings was $4,971 (million) at January 1, 2010.
3. Prepare a balance sheet at December 31, 2010.
4. Using the balance sheet, indicate whether the total assets of Southwest Airlines at the end of the year were financed primarily by liabilities or stockholders' equity.

EXERCISES

LO 1-2

E1-1 Reporting Amounts on the Four Basic Financial Statements

Using the following table and the equations underlying each of the four basic financial statements, show (a) that the balance sheet is in balance, (b) that net income is properly calculated, (c) what caused changes in the retained earnings account, and (d) what caused changes in the cash account.

Assets	$18,200	Beginning Retained Earnings	$3,500
Liabilities	13,750	Ending Retained Earnings	4,300
Stockholders' Equity	4,450	Cash Flows from Operating Activities	1,600
Revenue	10,500	Cash Flows from Investing Activities	(1,000)
Expenses	9,200	Cash Flows from Financing Activities	(900)
Net Income	1,300	Beginning Cash	1,000
Dividends	500	Ending Cash	700

LO 1-2

E1-2 Reporting Amounts on the Four Basic Financial Statements

Using the following table and the equations underlying each of the four basic financial statements, show (a) that the balance sheet is in balance, (b) that net income is properly calculated, (c) what caused changes in the retained earnings account, and (d) what caused changes in the cash account.

Assets	$79,500	Beginning Retained Earnings	$20,500
Liabilities	18,500	Ending Retained Earnings	28,750
Stockholders' Equity	61,000	Cash Flows from Operating Activities	15,700
Revenue	32,100	Cash Flows from Investing Activities	(7,200)
Expenses	18,950	Cash Flows from Financing Activities	(5,300)
Net Income	13,150	Beginning Cash	3,200
Dividends	4,900	Ending Cash	6,400

LO 1-2, 1-3

DSW, Inc.

E1-3 Preparing a Balance Sheet

DSW, Inc., is a designer shoe warehouse, selling some of the most luxurious and fashionable shoes at prices that people can actually afford. Its balance sheet, at January 29, 2011, contained the following (listed alphabetically, amounts in thousands).

Accounts Payable	$149,722	Other Liabilities	$122,822
Accounts Receivable	12,514	Property, Plant, and Equipment	210,391
Cash	93,617	Retained Earnings	326,382
Contributed Capital	314,382	Total Assets	1,008,897
Notes Payable	95,589	Total Liabilities and Stockholders' Equity	?
Other Assets	692,375		

Required:

1. Prepare the balance sheet as of January 29, 2011, solving for the missing amount.
2. As of January 29, did most of the financing for assets come from creditors or stockholders?

LO 1-2, 1-3   **E1-4 Completing a Balance Sheet and Inferring Net Income**

Ken Young and Kim Sherwood organized Reader Direct as a corporation; each contributed $49,000 cash to start the business and received 4,000 shares of stock. The store completed its first year of operations on December 31, 2012. On that date, the following financial items for the year were determined: cash on hand and in the bank, $47,500; amounts due from customers from sales of books, $26,900; property and equipment, $48,000; amounts owed to publishers for books purchased, $8,000; one-year note payable to a local bank for $2,850. No dividends were declared or paid to the stockholders during the year.

Required:

1. Complete the following balance sheet at December 31, 2012.

Assets		Liabilities and Stockholders' Equity	
Cash	$_____	**Liabilities**	
Accounts Receivable	_____	Accounts Payable	$_____
Property and Equipment	_____	Note Payable	_____
		Total Liabilities	_____
		Stockholders' Equity	
		Contributed Capital	_____
		Retained Earnings	13,550
		Total Stockholders' Equity	_____
Total Assets	$_____	Total Liabilities and Stockholders' Equity	$_____

2. Using the retained earnings equation and an opening balance of $0, work backwards to compute the amount of net income for the year ended December 31, 2012.
3. As of December 31, 2012, did most of the financing for assets come from creditors or stockholders?
4. Assuming that Reader Direct generates net income of $3,000 and pays dividends of $2,000 in 2013, what would be the ending Retained Earnings balance at December 31, 2013?

LO 1-2   **E1-5 Labeling and Classifying Business Transactions**

K·Swiss Inc.   The following items relate to business transactions involving K·Swiss Inc.

a. Coins and currency
b. Amounts K·Swiss owes to suppliers of watches
c. Amounts K·Swiss can collect from customers
d. Amounts owed to bank for loan to buy building
e. Property on which buildings will be built
f. Amounts distributed from profits to stockholders
g. Amounts earned by K·Swiss by selling watches
h. Unused paper in K·Swiss head office
i. Cost of paper used up during month
j. Amounts contributed to K·Swiss by stockholders

Required:

1. Identify an appropriate label (account name) for each item as it would be reported in the company's financial statements.

2. Classify each item as an asset (A), liability (L), stockholders' equity (SE), revenue (R), or expense (E).

E1-6 Preparing an Income Statement and Inferring Missing Values

LO 1-2, 1-3

Cinemark Holdings, Inc.

Cinemark Holdings, Inc. operates movies and food concession counters throughout the United States. Its income statement for the quarter ended March 31, 2011, reported the following (listed alphabetically in thousands):

Admissions Revenue	$311,692	Net Income	?
Concessions Expenses	23,282	Other Expenses	$24,265
Concessions Revenue	146,681	Other Revenues	24,763
Film Rental Expenses	165,153	Rent Expense	66,426
General and Administrative Expenses	179,047	Total Expenses	?

Required:

1. Solve for the missing amounts and prepare an income statement for the quarter ended March 31, 2011.

2. What are Cinemark's main source of revenue and two biggest expenses?

E1-7 Preparing an Income Statement

LO 1-2

Home Realty, Incorporated, has been operating for three years and is owned by three investors. J. Doe owns 60 percent of the total outstanding stock of 9,000 shares and is the managing executive in charge. On December 31, 2012, the following financial items for the entire year were determined: sales revenue, $166,000; wages expense, $97,000; interest expense, $6,300; advertising expenses, $9,025; and income tax expense, $18,500. Also during the year, the company declared and paid the owners dividends amounting to $12,000. Prepare the company's income statement.

E1-8 Inferring Values Using the Income Statement and Balance Sheet Equations

LO 1-2

Review the chapter explanations of the income statement and the balance sheet equations. Apply these equations in each of the following independent cases to compute the two missing amounts for each case. Assume that it is the end of the first full year of operations for the company.

   TIP: First identify the numerical relations among the columns using the balance sheet and income statement equations. Then compute the missing amounts.

Independent Cases	Total Revenues	Total Expenses	Net Income (Loss)	Total Assets	Total Liabilities	Stockholders' Equity
A	$110,000	$82,000	$	$150,000	$70,000	$
B		80,000	12,000	112,000		70,000
C	80,000	86,000		104,000	26,000	
D	50,000		20,000		22,000	77,000
E		81,000	(6,000)		73,000	28,000

LO 1-2, 1-3   **E1-9 Preparing an Income Statement and Balance Sheet**

Five individuals organized Miami Music Corporation on January 1, 2012. At the end of January 31, 2012, the following monthly financial data are available:

Total Revenues	$131,000
Operating Expenses	90,500
Cash	30,800
Accounts Receivable	25,300
Supplies	40,700
Accounts Payable	25,700
Contributed Capital	30,600

No dividends were declared or paid during January.

Required:

1. Complete the following income statement and balance sheet for the month of January.

MIAMI MUSIC CORPORATION
Income Statement
For the Month Ended January 31, 2012

Total Revenues	$_____
Operating Expenses	_____
Net Income	$_____

MIAMI MUSIC CORPORATION
Balance Sheet
At January 31, 2012

Assets	
Cash	$_____
Accounts Receivable	_____
Supplies	_____
Total Assets	$_____
Liabilities	
Accounts Payable	$_____
Total Liabilities	_____
Stockholders' Equity	
Contributed Capital	_____
Retained Earnings	_____
Total Stockholders' Equity	_____
Total Liabilities and Stockholders' Equity	$_____

2. Did Miami Music Corporation generate a profit? How can you tell?

3. Discuss whether Miami Music Corporation will be able to pay its liabilities. Consider the relationship between total assets and total liabilities.

E1-10 Analyzing and Interpreting an Income Statement   LO 1-2, 1-3

Three individuals organized Pest Away Corporation on January 1, 2012, to provide insect exter-
mination services. The company paid dividends of $10,000 during the year. At the end of 2012,
the following income statement was prepared:

PEST AWAY CORPORATION
Income Statement
For the Year Ended December 31, 2012

Revenues		
Service Revenue	$192,000	
Sales Revenue	24,000	
Total Revenues		$216,000
Expenses		
Supplies Expense	$ 76,000	
Salaries and Wages Expense	33,000	
Advertising Expense	22,000	
Other Expenses	46,000	
Total Expenses		177,000
Net Income		$ 39,000

Required:

1. What was the amount of average monthly revenue?

2. What was the average amount of monthly salaries and wages expense?

3. Explain why advertising is reported as an expense.

4. Explain why the dividends are not reported as an expense.

5. Can you determine how much cash the company had on December 31, 2012? Answer yes or
    no, and explain your reasoning.

E1-11 Matching Cash Flow Statement Items to Business Activity Categories   LO 1-2

Tech Data Corporation is a leading distributor of computer peripherals and network solutions.   Tech Data Corporation
The following items were taken from its recent cash flow statement. Mark each item in the following list with a letter to indicate whether it is a cash flow from Operating, Investing, or Financing
activities. **Put parentheses around the letter if it is a cash** *outflow* **and use no parentheses if it's
an** *inflow.*

_____ 1. Cash paid to suppliers and employees

_____ 2. Cash received from customers

_____ 3. Cash received from borrowing long-term debt

_____ 4. Cash received from issuing stock

_____ 5. Cash paid to purchase equipment

E1-12 Matching Cash Flow Statement Items to Business Activity Categories   LO 1-2

The Coca-Cola Company is one of the world's leading manufacturers, marketers, and distributors   Coca-Cola Company
of nonalcoholic beverage concentrates and syrups, producing more than 500 beverage brands.
Mark each item in the following list with a letter to indicate whether it is a cash flow from Operating, Investing, or Financing activities. **Put parentheses around the letter if it is a cash** *outflow*
and use no parentheses if it's an *inflow.*

_____ 1. Purchases of equipment

_____ 2. Cash received from customers

____ 3. Cash received from issuing stock

____ 4. Cash paid to suppliers and employees

____ 5. Cash paid on notes payable

____ 6. Cash received from selling equipment

COACHED PROBLEMS

LO 1-2   **CP1-1 Preparing an Income Statement, Statement of Retained Earnings, and Balance Sheet**

Assume that you are the president of Nuclear Company. At the end of the first year of operations (December 31, 2012), the following financial data for the company are available:

Accounts Payable	$30,000
Accounts Receivable	59,500
Cash	12,000
Contributed Capital	62,280
Dividends	200
Equipment	36,000
Notes Payable	1,470
Operating Expenses	57,200
Other Expenses	8,850
Sales Revenue	88,000
Supplies	8,000

Required:

1. Prepare an income statement for the year ended December 31, 2012.
   TIP: Begin by classifying each account as asset, liability, stockholders' equity, revenue, or expense. Each account is reported on only one financial statement.
2. Prepare a statement of retained earnings for the year ended December 31, 2012.
   TIP: Because this is the first year of operations, the beginning balance in Retained Earnings will be zero.
3. Prepare a balance sheet at December 31, 2012.
   TIP: The balance sheet includes the ending balance from the statement of retained earnings.

LO 1-3   **CP1-2 Interpreting the Financial Statements**

Refer to CP1-1.

Required:

1. Evaluate whether the company was profitable.
2. Evaluate whether the company could have paid a greater amount for dividends.
3. Evaluate whether the company is financed mainly by creditors or stockholders.
4. Determine the amount of cash increase or decrease that would be shown in the statement of cash flows.

LO 1-2   **CP1-3 Reporting Amounts on the Four Basic Financial Statements**

Life Time Fitness   Life Time Fitness, Inc., reported the following information for the nine-month period ended September 30, 2010. Items are listed alphabetically, and are in thousands of dollars.

Accounts Payable	$ 36,389	Notes Payable	$ 631,746
Accounts Receivable	5,453	Operating Expenses	424,940
Advertising Expense	18,940	Other Assets	101,054
Cash (January 1, 2010)	6,282	Other Liabilities	190,004
Cash (September 30, 2010)	33,502	Property and Equipment	1,546,749
Contributed Capital	406,043	Rent Payable	31,455
General and Administrative Expense	32,606	Retained Earnings (January 1, 2010)	343,789
Income Tax Expense	42,156	Service Revenue	689,171
Interest Expense	107,431	Supplies	15,766

Other cash flow information:

Cash received from issuing common stock	$ 3,660
Cash paid to purchase equipment	101,088
Cash paid to suppliers and employees	541,597
Repayments of borrowings	38,067
Cash received from customers	687,744
Cash received from borrowings	13,939
Cash received from sale of long-term assets	2,629
Dividends paid to stockholders	0

Required:

Prepare the four basic financial statements for the nine months ended September 30, 2010.

TIP: Prepare the four statements in the following order:

a. Income statement
b. Statement of retained earnings
c. Balance sheet
d. Statement of cash flows

CP1-4 Evaluating Financial Statements

Refer to CP1-3.

LO 1-3

Life Time Fitness

Required:

1. Did Life Time Fitness rely more on creditors or stockholders for its financing at September 30, 2010? What is your information source?
2. Was the stockholders' equity at September 30, 2010, comprised primarily of contributions made by stockholders directly to the company, amounts earned and retained through profitable business operations, or approximately equal amounts of both? What is your information source?

GROUP A PROBLEMS

PA1-1 Preparing an Income Statement, Statement of Retained Earnings, and Balance Sheet

LO 1-2

Assume that you are the president of High Power Corporation. At the end of the first year of operations (December 31, 2013), the following financial data for the company are available:

Accounts Payable	$32,100
Accounts Receivable	9,550
Cash	13,300
Contributed Capital	59,090
Dividends	1,950
Equipment	86,000
Notes Payable	1,160
Operating Expenses	58,700
Other Expenses	7,850
Sales Revenue	90,000
Supplies	5,000

Required:

1. Prepare an income statement for the year ended December 31, 2013.
2. Prepare a statement of retained earnings for the year ended December 31, 2013.
3. Prepare a balance sheet at December 31, 2013.

LO 1-3

PA1-2 Interpreting the Financial Statements

Refer to PA1-1.

Required:

1. Evaluate whether the company was profitable.
2. Evaluate whether the company could have paid a greater amount for dividends.
3. Evaluate whether the company is financed mainly by creditors or stockholders.
4. Determine the amount of cash increase or decrease that would be shown in the statement of cash flows.

LO 1-2

PA1-3 Reporting Amounts on the Four Basic Financial Statements

Coinstar, Inc.

The following information for the year ended December 31, 2010 was reported by Coinstar, Inc.—a company that began as a student project and now is known for its Redbox DVD rental kiosks. Amounts are in millions of dollars.

Accounts Payable	$ 270	Notes Payable	$ 377
Accounts Receivable	26	Other Assets	460
Cash (balance on December 31, 2009)	146	Other Liabilities	95
Cash (balance on December 31, 2010)	183	Other Revenues	1
Contributed Capital	341	Prepaid Rent	28
Dividends	—	Property and Equipment	445
General and Administrative Expenses	129	Retained Earnings (beginning)	51
Inventories	140	Service Revenue	1,436
Kiosk Expenses	1,001	Utilities Expense	251
Legal Expenses	5	Wages Payable	97

Other cash flow information:	
Cash outflows for other financing activities	$ 11
Cash paid for kiosk operations	887
Cash paid to suppliers and employees	238
Repayments of borrowings	111
Cash received from customers	1,430
Cash received from sale of long-term assets	27
Cash paid to purchase long-term assets	173
Dividends paid in cash	0

Required:

Prepare the four basic financial statements for 2010.

PA1-4 Evaluating Financial Statements

Refer to PA1-3.

LO 1-3

Coinstar, Inc.

Required:

1. Did Coinstar rely more on creditors or stockholders for its financing at December 31, 2010? What is your information source?
2. Did the retained earnings at December 31, 2010, arise primarily from current year earnings, earnings retained from prior years, or approximately equal amounts of both? What is your information source?

GROUP B PROBLEMS

PB1-1 Preparing an Income Statement and Balance Sheet

LO 1-2

Assume that you are the president of APEC Aerospace Corporation. At the end of the first year of operations (December 31, 2012), the following financial data for the company are available:

Accounts Payable	$35,130
Accounts Receivable	9,500
Cash	15,900
Contributed Capital	10,000
Dividends	1,100
Equipment	86,000
Notes Payable	57,220
Operating Expenses	60,000
Other Expenses	8,850
Sales Revenue	94,000
Supplies	9,000

Required:

1. Prepare an income statement for the year ended December 31, 2012.
2. Prepare a statement of retained earnings for the year ended December 31, 2012.
3. Prepare a balance sheet at December 31, 2012.

PB1-2 Interpreting the Financial Statements

LO 1-3

Refer to PB1-1.

Required:

1. Evaluate whether the company was profitable.
2. Evaluate whether the company could have paid a greater amount for dividends.
3. Evaluate whether the company is financed mainly by creditors or stockholders.
4. Determine the amount of cash increase or decrease that would be shown in the statement of cash flows.

PB1-3 Reporting Amounts on the Four Basic Financial Statements

LO 1-2

Cheese Factory Incorporated reported the following information for the fiscal year ended December 31, 2012.

Accounts Payable	$ 35,000	Other Liabilities	$ 110,000
Accounts Receivable	15,000	Property and Equipment	755,000
Cash (balance on January 1, 2012)	75,000	Prepaid Rent	50,000
Cash (balance on December 31, 2012)	80,000	Retained Earnings (beginning)	410,000
Contributed Capital	100,000	Sales Revenue	1,660,000
Dividends	10,000	Supplies	25,000
General and Administrative Expenses	95,000	Utilities Expense	530,000
Notes Payable	30,000	Wages Expense	540,000
Operating Expenses	415,000	Wages Payable	170,000

Other cash flow information:	
Additional investments by stockholders	$ 34,000
Cash paid to purchase equipment	40,000
Cash paid to suppliers and employees	1,490,000
Repayments of borrowings	155,000
Cash received from customers	1,661,000
Cash received from borrowings	5,000
Dividends paid in cash	10,000

Required:

Prepare the four basic financial statements for the fiscal year ended December 31, 2012.

PB1-4 Evaluating Financial Statements

Refer to PB1-3.

Required:

1. Did Cheese Factory's cash balance increase or decrease during the year ended December 31, 2012? What is your information source?

2. What would Cheese Factory's 2012 net income have been had it given a 10 percent wage increase to all employees on January 1, 2012? What is your information source?

SKILLS DEVELOPMENT CASES

LO 1-1, 1-2, 1-3

S1-1 Finding Financial Information

Refer to the financial statements of The Home Depot for the 2010 fiscal year in Appendix A at the end of this book, or download the annual report from the *Cases* section of the text's Web site at www.mhhe.com/phillips4e. (Note: The Home Depot's 2010 fiscal year runs from January 31, 2010, to January 30, 2011.)

Required:

1. What amount of net income was reported (in millions) for the year ended January 30, 2011?
   a. $67,997
   b. $14,995
   c. $5,273
   d. $3,338

2. What amount of sales revenue (in millions) was earned for the year ended January 30, 2011?
   a. $67,997
   b. $14,995
   c. $5,273
   d. $3,338

3. What was the cost (in millions) of the company's inventory on January 30, 2011?
    a. $44,693
    b. $25,060
    c. $10,625
    d. $10,188

4. How much cash (in millions) does The Home Depot have on January 30, 2011?
    a. $14,995
    b. $1,421
    c. $878
    d. $545

S1-2 Comparing Financial Information

LO 1-1, 1-2, 1-3

Lowe's

Refer to the 2010 fiscal year-end financial statements of The Home Depot in Appendix A and Lowe's in Appendix B at the end of this book, or download the annual reports from the *Cases* section of the text's Web site at www.mhhe.com/phillips4e. (Note: The Home Depot's 2010 fiscal year runs from January 31, 2010, to January 30, 2011. Lowe's 2010 fiscal year runs from January 30, 2010, to January 28, 2011.)

Required:

1. Was Lowe's net income for the year ended January 28, 2011, greater (or less) than The Home Depot's?
2. Was Lowe's sales revenue for the year ended January 28, 2011, greater (or less) than The Home Depot's?
3. Did Lowe's have more (or less) inventories than The Home Depot at the end of January 2011?
4. Did Lowe's have more (or less) cash than The Home Depot at the end of January 2011?
5. The Home Depot's stock is traded on the New York Stock Exchange under the symbol HD. What kind of company does this make The Home Depot? Is Lowe's the same type of business organization as The Home Depot? How can you tell?
6. Why might The Home Depot and Lowe's choose such odd dates to end their fiscal years?
7. On an overall basis, was Lowe's or The Home Depot more successful in the 2010 fiscal year?

S1-3 Internet-Based Team Research: Examining an Annual Report

LO 1-1, 1-2, 1-3

Reuters

As a team, select an industry to analyze. Reuters provides lists of industries and their makeup at www.reuters.com/finance/industries. Each group member should access the annual report (or Form 10-K filed with the SEC) for one publicly traded company in the industry, with each member selecting a different company. In addition to the company's own Web site, a great source is the SEC's Electronic Data Gathering, Analysis, and Retrieval (EDGAR) service. This free source is available by going to the "Filings" section of www.sec.gov and clicking on "Search for Company Filings" and then "Company or fund name."

Required:

1. On an individual basis, each team member should write a short report that lists the following information:
    a. What type of business organization is it?
    b. What types of products or services does it sell?
    c. On what day of the year does its fiscal year end?
    d. For how many years does it present complete balance sheets? Income statements? Cash flow statements?
    e. Are its financial statements audited by independent CPAs? If so, by whom?
    f. Did its total assets increase or decrease over the last year?
    g. Did its net income increase or decrease over the last year?

2. Then, as a team, write a short report comparing and contrasting your companies using these attributes. Discuss any patterns across the companies that you as a team observe. Provide potential explanations for any differences discovered.

LO 1-2, 1-3, 1-4

Adelphia Communications

S1-4 Ethical Decision Making: A Real-Life Example

Complete this case involving Adelphia Communications, available online at www.mhhe.com/phillips4e. By completing the requirements of this case, which ask you to explain how accounting concepts apply to Adelphia's business, you will learn the challenges and importance of distinguishing between personal and business activities when accounting for a family-owned business.

LO 1-4

S1-5 Ethical Decision Making: A Mini-Case

You are one of three stockholders who own and operate Mary's Maid Service. The company has been operating for seven years. One of the other stockholders has always prepared the company's annual financial statements. Recently, you proposed that the statements be audited each year because it would benefit the stockholders. The stockholder who prepares the statements proposed that his uncle, who has a lot of financial experience, can do the job at little cost. The other stockholder remained silent.

Required:

1. What position would you take on the proposal? Justify your response in writing.
2. What would you recommend? Give the basis for your recommendation.

LO 1-2, 1-3, 1-4

S1-6 Critical Thinking: Developing a Balance Sheet and Income Statement

On September 30, Ashley and Jason started arguing about who is better off. Jason said he was better off because he owned a PlayStation console that he bought last year for $250. He figures that, if needed, he could sell it to a friend for $180. Ashley argued that she was better off because she had $1,000 cash in her bank account and a piece of art that she bought two years ago for $800 but could now probably sell for $1,400. Jason countered that Ashley still owed $250 on a loan and that Jason's dad promised to buy him a Porsche if he does really well in his accounting class. Jason said he had $6,000 cash in his bank account right now because he just received a $4,800 student loan. Ashley knows that Jason also owes a tuition installment of $800 for this term.

Ashley and Jason met again in early November. They asked how each other was doing. Ashley claimed that she'd become much more successful than Jason. She had a part-time job, where she earned $1,500 per month. Jason laughed at Ashley because he had won $1,950 on a lottery ticket he bought in October, and that was merely for the "work" of standing in line for a minute. It was just what he needed because his apartment costs $800 each month. Ashley, on the other hand, pays $470 for her share of the rent. Both Ashley and Jason have other normal living costs that total $950 each month.

1. Prepare a financial report that compares what Ashley and Jason each own and owe on September 30. Make a list of any decisions you had to make when preparing your report.
2. In a written report, identify and justify which of the two characters is better off. If you were a creditor, to whom would you rather lend money?
3. Prepare a report that compares what Ashley and Jason each earned during October. Make a list of any decisions you had to make when preparing your report.
4. In a written report, identify and justify which of the two characters is more successful. If you were a creditor considering a three-year loan to one of these characters, to whom would you rather lend money?

LO 1-2

Electronic Arts Inc.

S1-7 Preparing an Income Statement and Balance Sheet

Complete this case involving Electronic Arts, available online at www.mhhe.com/phillips4e. By completing this case, you will learn to use a spreadsheet to prepare a balance sheet and income statement. Detailed advice, including a screen capture, is included in the case to help you set up and complete the spreadsheet.

CONTINUING CASE

CC1-1 Financial Statements for a Business Plan

LO 1-2, 1-3

Nicole Mackisey is thinking of forming her own spa business, Nicole's Getaway Spa (NGS). Nicole expects that she and two family members will each contribute $10,000 to the business and receive 1,000 shares each. Nicole forecasts the following amounts for the first year of operations, ending December 31, 2013: Cash on hand and in the bank, $2,150; amounts due from customers from spa treatments, $1,780; building and equipment, $70,000; amounts owed to beauty supply outlets for spa equipment, $4,660; notes payable to a local bank for $38,870. Cash dividends of $2,000 will be paid to the stockholders during the year. Nicole also forecasts that first year sales revenues will be $40,000; wages will be $24,000; the cost of supplies used up will be $7,000; selling and administrative expenses will be $5,000; and income taxes will be $1,600.

Required:

1. Based on Nicole's estimates, prepare a (forecasted) income statement for Nicole's Getaway Spa for the year ended December 31, 2013.
2. Prepare a (forecasted) statement of retained earnings for Nicole's Getaway Spa for the year ended December 31, 2013.
3. Prepare a (forecasted) balance sheet for Nicole's Getaway Spa at December 31, 2013.
4. As of December 31, 2013, would most of the financing for assets come from creditors or stockholders?

The Balance Sheet

YOUR LEARNING OBJECTIVES

Understand the business

LO 2-1   Identify financial effects of common business activities that affect the balance sheet.

Study the accounting methods

LO 2-2   Apply transaction analysis to accounting transactions.

LO 2-3   Use journal entries and T-accounts to show how transactions affect the balance sheet.

LO 2-4   Prepare a classified balance sheet.

Evaluate the results

LO 2-5   Interpret the balance sheet using the current ratio and an understanding of related concepts.

Review the chapter

THAT WAS THEN

In the previous chapter, you were introduced to the four main financial statements: the balance sheet, income statement, statement of retained earnings, and statement of cash flows.

FOCUS COMPANY: Pizza Aroma, Ithaca, NY

I n Chapter 1 you heard about Mauricio Rosa's plans for starting a pizza company in New York. Mauricio's local CPA, Laurie Hensley, advised him that all businesses, big and small, need systems for gathering and organizing financial information. Just as FedEx must have a way to monitor and evaluate its use of $18.7 billion in delivery equipment,[1] smaller companies like Pizza Aroma, Inc., must track the financial results of their activities. With Laurie's help, Mauricio will implement an accounting system to do this for Pizza Aroma. This system will provide the financial information that he needs to manage the company and to report its results to others interested in his business.

The focus in this chapter is on the activities that occurred during August, when Mauricio was establishing Pizza Aroma, long before it could open its doors to customers. You will learn how these activities are captured in an accounting system, leading to the assets, liabilities, and stockholders' equity that are reported in a balance sheet. Later, in Chapter 3, you will learn about the operating activities that occur after a business opens its doors to customers and begins generating the revenues and expenses that are reported in an income statement. Your introduction to the accounting system will conclude in Chapter 4, where you will learn about the steps needed to adjust the accounting records before finalizing and evaluating a company's financial results.

THIS IS NOW

This chapter focuses on just the balance sheet and the accounting system used to produce it.

---

[1]http://annualreport.ir.fedex.com/files/FedEx_Annual_Report_2011_Financials.pdf.

Understand the business	**Study the accounting methods**	**Evaluate the results**	**Review the chapter**
• Building a balance sheet • Financing, investing, and operating activities • Transactions and other activities	• Step 1: Analyze transactions • Steps 2 and 3: Record and summarize • The debit/credit framework • Preparing a balance sheet	• Assessing the ability to pay • Balance sheet concepts and values	• Demonstration case • Chapter summary • Key terms • Homework helper • Practice material

Understand the Business

BUILDING A BALANCE SHEET

After meeting with Laurie, Mauricio understood that before he could open his restaurant, he would first have to establish the business. This would involve acquiring **assets** that Pizza Aroma would use for many months or years to come. The assets would be owned by Pizza Aroma, but creditors would have a claim to those assets equal to the amount of **liabilities** that the company owes. As owners of Pizza Aroma, Mauricio and his wife also would have a claim on the company's assets (**stockholders' equity**), but their claim would be secondary to creditors' claims. Mauricio remembered that the balance sheet was structured like the basic accounting equation (A = L + SE), but it was only by accounting for Pizza Aroma's actual activities that he truly learned how a balance sheet was built.

FINANCING, INVESTING, AND OPERATING ACTIVITIES

A key activity for any start-up company, such as Pizza Aroma, is to obtain **financing**. Two sources of financing are available to businesses: equity and debt. Equity refers to financing a business obtains through owners' contributions and reinvestments of profit. Debt refers to financing the business obtains through loans. A business is obligated to repay debt financing, but it is not obligated to repay its equity financing.

Like most small business owners, Mauricio and his wife used their personal savings to make an initial cash contribution to the company. They decided to contribute $50,000, which is more than they had originally planned, but by relying more on equity financing, the company wouldn't require quite as much debt financing. When a corporation receives cash contributions from its owners like this, it gives documents called stock certificates to the owners as evidence of their ownership.

Mauricio had determined that Pizza Aroma would need additional money to become established so, on behalf of the company, he applied for a loan from a bank. Soon after the loan was approved, Pizza Aroma received $20,000 cash in exchange for its promise to repay the loan in two years. The terms for repaying the loan were described in detail on a legal document called a promissory note. Pizza Aroma's initial financing activities are pictured in Exhibit 2.1.

EXHIBIT 2.1 Financing Activities

Issue stock
The business receives $50,000 cash.
The business gives stock certificates.

Obtain loan
The business receives $20,000 cash.
The business gives a promissory note.

After obtaining initial financing, a company will start **investing** in assets that will be used later when the business opens. In the case of Pizza Aroma, Mauricio first spent $42,000 cash by writing company checks to buy and install restaurant booths, cash registers, and other equipment. The company also needed to buy **operating** assets, such as cookware and related items like pizza pans, pizza cutters, serving plates, cutlery, drink glasses, napkin holders, and cheese and spice shakers. These items could be purchased with cash, but that would be inconvenient and inefficient. Instead, businesses typically buy goods or services from others on credit, by promising to pay within 30 days of the purchase. Pizza Aroma bought $630 of these items on credit, as indicated by the supplier's bill (or "invoice"). These examples are pictured in Exhibit 2.2.

EXHIBIT 2.2 Investing and Operating Activities

Purchase equipment
The business receives equipment.
The business gives checks for $42,000.

Purchase cookware
The business receives kitchen cookware.
The business gives a promise to pay $630.

By carefully reading Exhibits 2.1 and 2.2, you will see three features that will be important for understanding how accounting works.

1. The company always **documents** its activities. Stock certificates, promissory notes, checks, and invoices indicate the nature of the underlying business activity.

2. The company always **receives** something and **gives** something. This is a basic feature of all business activities. A business enters into an exchange either to earn a profit immediately or to obtain resources that will allow it to earn a profit later. This is the fundamental idea of business: to create value through exchange. Any exchange that affects the company's assets, liabilities, or stockholders' equity must be captured in and reported by the accounting system. Because the accounting system captures both what is received and what is given, it is often referred to as a "double-entry" system.

3. Each exchange is analyzed to determine a dollar amount that represents the value of items given and received. This value is called the **cost** and is used to measure the financial effects of the exchange, as required by the **cost principle**.

> **YOU SHOULD KNOW**
>
> **Cost principle:** Assets and liabilities should be initially recorded at their original cost to the company.

As illustrated in Exhibit 2.3, these three features are key inputs into the process used, when accounting for business activities. After each activity is documented, accountants assign names to the items exchanged and then analyze their financial effects on the accounting equation. The ultimate goal is to capture these financial effects so that they can be reported in the financial statements for use by decision makers inside and outside the company. Take a moment right now to read Exhibit 2.3.

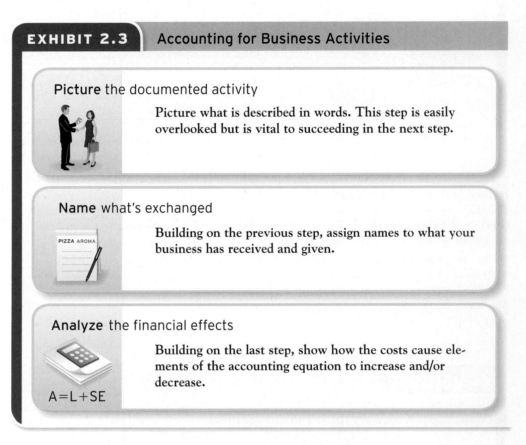

EXHIBIT 2.3 Accounting for Business Activities

Picture the documented activity

Picture what is described in words. This step is easily overlooked but is vital to succeeding in the next step.

Name what's exchanged

Building on the previous step, assign names to what your business has received and given.

Analyze the financial effects

Building on the last step, show how the costs cause elements of the accounting equation to increase and/or decrease.

A = L + SE

TRANSACTIONS AND OTHER ACTIVITIES

Business activities that affect the basic accounting equation (A = L + SE) are called **transactions**. Transactions are of special importance because they are the only activities that enter the financial accounting system. Transactions include two types of events:

1. **External exchanges:** These are exchanges involving assets, liabilities, and/or stockholders' equity that you can see between the company and someone else. When Starbucks sells you a Frappuccino®, it is exchanging an icy taste of heaven for your cash, so Starbucks would record this in its accounting system.

2. **Internal events:** These events do not involve exchanges with others outside the business, but rather occur within the company itself. For example, when the company Red Bull combines sugar, water, taurine, and caffeine, something magical happens: these ingredients turn into Red Bull Energy Drink. This internal event is a transaction because it has a direct financial effect whereby some assets (supplies of sugar, etc.) are used up to create a different asset (an inventory of Red Bull drinks).

During the first month of business, some important activities that occur will not be captured by the accounting system because they are not transactions. For example, Mauricio signed a contract on behalf of Pizza Aroma to rent restaurant space in a building. This activity was not a transaction because no assets or services were exchanged at that time. The landlord exchanged a promise to rent the building for Pizza Aroma's promise to pay rent, but **an exchange of only promises is not an accounting transaction.**

For this same reason, Pizza Aroma's accounting system did not capture other activities such as placing orders with suppliers or promising to hire employees. Documents were created to indicate that these activities occurred, but they were appropriately excluded from the accounting records because these were not transactions. Later, when these promises result in actually receiving or giving an asset or service, they will become transactions to be captured by the accounting system.

Study the Accounting Methods

A systematic accounting process is used to capture and report the financial effects of a company's activities. This process includes three basic steps:

 Analyze ⟶ Record ⟶ Summarize

Learning Objective 2-2
Apply transaction analysis to accounting transactions.

STEP 1: ANALYZE TRANSACTIONS

The process in Exhibit 2.3 is commonly referred to as transaction analysis, which involves determining whether a transaction exists and, if it does, analyzing its impact on the accounting equation. Two simple ideas are used when analyzing transactions:

1. **Duality of effects.** It's a fancy name, but the idea is simple. Every transaction has at least two effects on the basic accounting equation. To remember this, just think of expressions like "give and receive" or "push and pull" or, if you're a closet scientist, Newton's third law of motion.

2. **A = L + SE.** You know this already, right? Well, just remember that the dollar amount for assets must always equal the total of liabilities plus stockholders' equity for every accounting transaction. If it doesn't, then you are missing something and you should go back to the first (duality of effects) idea.

As part of transaction analysis, a name is given to each item exchanged. Accountants refer to these names as account titles. To ensure account titles are used consistently, every company establishes a **chart of accounts**—a list that designates a name and reference number that the company will use when accounting for each item it exchanges. A partial chart of accounts for Pizza Aroma is shown in Exhibit 2.4. (The chart of accounts shown in Chapter 2 includes only balance sheet accounts. Chapter 3 will expand this to include additional assets and liabilities as well as revenue and expense accounts.) **A more comprehensive chart of accounts to use when completing homework assignments is presented in the Homework Helper on page 71.**

YOU SHOULD KNOW

Chart of accounts: A summary of all account names (and corresponding account numbers) used to record financial results in the accounting system.

EXHIBIT 2.4	Pizza Aroma's (Partial) Chart of Accounts	
Account Number	**Account Name**	**Description**
101	Cash	— Dollar amount of coins, paper money, funds in bank
113	Cookware	— Cost of cutlery, pizza pans, dishes, etc.
135	Equipment	— Cost of pizza ovens, restaurant booths, dishwashers, etc.
201	Accounts Payable	— Owed to suppliers for goods or services bought on credit
222	Note Payable	— Owed to lenders, as per terms of promissory note
301	Contributed Capital	— Stock issued for contributions made to the company
310	Retained Earnings	— Accumulated earnings (not yet distributed as dividends)

The chart of accounts is tailored to each company's business, so although some account titles are common across all companies (Cash, Accounts Payable), others may be used only by that particular company (Cookware). Depending on the company, you may see a liability for a bank loan called a Note Payable or a Loan Payable.[2]

The best way to learn how to account for business activities is to work through examples. So skim the names and descriptions in Exhibit 2.4 one more time and then let's look more closely at Pizza Aroma's business activities.

(a) Issue Stock to Owners   Mauricio Rosa incorporates Pizza Aroma, Inc., on August 1. The company issues stock to Mauricio and his wife as evidence of their contribution of $50,000 cash, which is deposited in the company's bank account.

COACH'S TIP

Analyze transactions from the standpoint of the business, not its owners.

Notice that in the accounting equation table above, we included a reference (a) so that we can refer back to the original transaction description if needed. You too should use transaction letters (or numbers or dates) as references in your homework problems. The goal of transaction analysis is to identify the specific accounts affected, the dollar amount of the change in the accounts, and the direction of this change ($+$ or $-$) on the accounting equation category. In example (a), an asset (Cash) increases by $50,000, which equals the increase in the stockholders' equity account (Contributed Capital).

(b) Invest in Equipment   Pizza Aroma pays $42,000 cash to buy restaurant booths and other equipment.

---

[2]The account names you see in the financial statements of most large businesses are actually aggregations of several specific accounts. For example, Papa John's International—a competitor of Pizza Aroma—keeps separate accounts for land, buildings, and equipment but combines them into one title on its balance sheet called Property and Equipment.

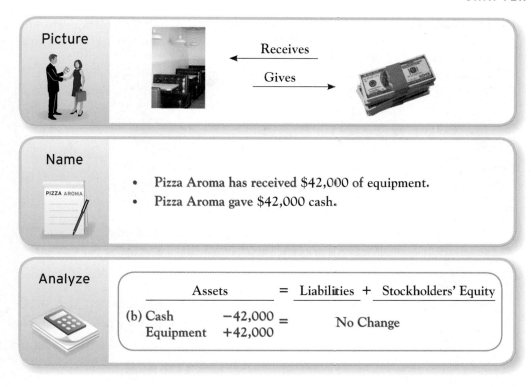

Picture	
Name	• Pizza Aroma has received $42,000 of equipment. • Pizza Aroma gave $42,000 cash.
Analyze	**Assets** = **Liabilities** + **Stockholders' Equity** (b) Cash −42,000 = No Change Equipment +42,000

Notice that even though transaction (b) did not affect liabilities or stockholders' equity, the accounting equation remained in balance because the decrease in one asset (Cash) was offset by the increase in another asset (Equipment). **The accounting equation must always "balance" (be equal) for each transaction.**

(c) Obtain Loan from Bank Pizza Aroma borrows $20,000 from a bank, depositing those funds in its bank account and signing a formal agreement to repay the loan in two years (on August 3, 2015).

Picture	
Name	• Pizza Aroma has received $20,000 cash. • Pizza Aroma gave a note, payable to the bank for $20,000.
Analyze	**Assets** = **Liabilities** + **Stockholders' Equity** (c) Cash +20,000 = Note Payable +20,000

COACH'S TIP

Notes payable are like accounts payable except that they (a) charge interest, (b) can be outstanding for long periods (more than one year), and (c) are documented using formal documents called notes.

(d) Invest in Equipment Pizza Aroma purchases $18,000 in pizza ovens and other restaurant equipment, paying $16,000 in cash and giving an informal promise to pay $2,000 at the end of the month.

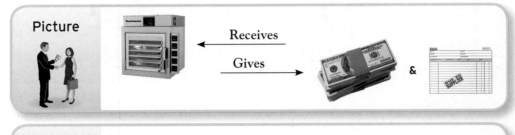

Picture

Receives

Gives &

Name

PIZZA AROMA

- Pizza Aroma has received $18,000 of equipment.
- Pizza Aroma gave $16,000 cash and a promise to pay $2,000 on account.

Analyze

Assets	=	Liabilities	+	Stockholders' Equity
(d) Cash −16,000	=	Accounts Payable +2,000		
Equipment +18,000				

If you ever run into a transaction that you have no idea how to analyze, try to break it down. Rather than trying to solve it all at once, begin by looking just for what is received. Another strategy is to look for any cash exchanged because by getting a handle on that part of the transaction, the other parts often become easier to see. Always be sure to summarize the effects in terms of the accounting equation, because it must balance if you've detected all the accounts affected by the transaction.

(e) Order Cookware Pizza Aroma orders $630 of pans, dishes, and other cookware. None have been received yet.

Picture

Promise of Future Delivery	**Receives**
	Gives → Promise to Pay for Purchase

Name

PIZZA AROMA

- An exchange of only promises is not a transaction.
- This does not affect the accounting equation.

Analyze

Assets	=	Liabilities	+	Stockholders' Equity
(e) No Change	=	No Change		

Not all documented business activities are considered accounting transactions. As shown in (e), Pizza Aroma and the supplier have documented the order, but it involves an exchange of only promises, so it is not an accounting transaction.

(f) Pay Supplier   Pizza Aroma pays $2,000 to the equipment supplier in (d).

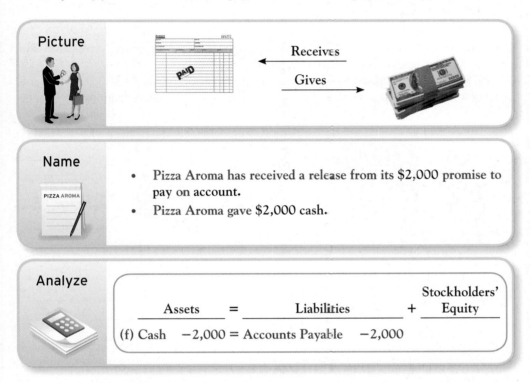

Name

- Pizza Aroma has received a release from its $2,000 promise to pay on account.
- Pizza Aroma gave $2,000 cash.

Analyze

	Assets	=	Liabilities	+	Stockholders' Equity
(f) Cash	−2,000	=	Accounts Payable	−2,000	

In (f), Pizza Aroma fulfills its liability by paying the amount owed to a supplier. Thus, the Accounts Payable is decreased because, in exchange for its payment to the supplier, Pizza Aroma receives a release from its original promise to pay the supplier.

(g) Receive Cookware   Pizza Aroma receives $630 of the cookware ordered in (e) and promises to pay for it next month.

Name

- Pizza Aroma has received cookware costing $630.
- Pizza Aroma gave a promise to pay $630 on account.

Analyze

	Assets	=	Liabilities	+	Stockholders' Equity
(g) Cookware	+630	=	Accounts Payable	+630	

As we said, the best way to learn accounting is to do examples, so try the following practice question. (Cover the answers in the margin with your thumb until you're done.)

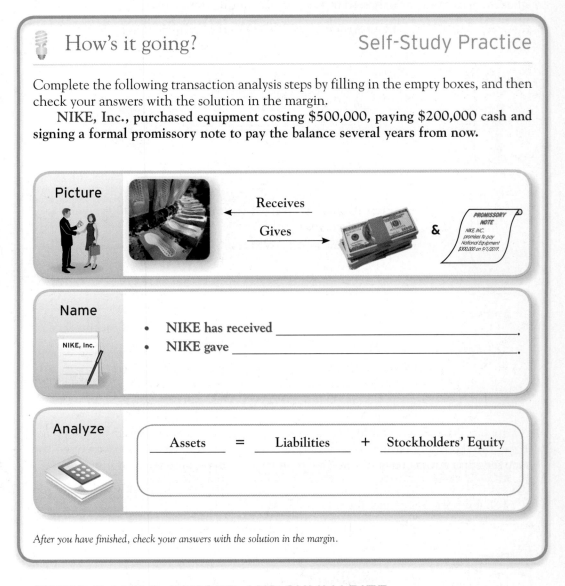

How's it going?   Self-Study Practice

Complete the following transaction analysis steps by filling in the empty boxes, and then check your answers with the solution in the margin.

NIKE, Inc., purchased equipment costing $500,000, paying $200,000 cash and signing a formal promissory note to pay the balance several years from now.

Picture

Receives
Gives
&
PROMISSORY NOTE
NIKE INC. promises to pay National Equipment $300,000 on 9/1/2019.

Name

NIKE, Inc.

- NIKE has received _____.
- NIKE gave _____.

Analyze

Assets   =   Liabilities   +   Stockholders' Equity

After you have finished, check your answers with the solution in the margin.

Solution to Self-Study Practice

NIKE has received equipment costing $500,000.
NIKE gave $200,000 cash and a $300,000 note.

Assets		=	Liabilities	+	Stockholders' Equity
Cash	−200,000	=	Note		
Equipment	+500,000		Payable +300,000		

STEPS 2 AND 3: RECORD AND SUMMARIZE

In the previous section, you learned how to analyze transactions, which ended with an understanding of the financial effects of each transaction on a company's asset, liability, and stockholders' equity accounts. In an academic setting, we have encouraged you to write down these accounting equation effects. In the workplace, an accountant would not actually capture the effects in this way. Instead, after determining the financial effects of a transaction, an accountant would capture the effects through two additional steps: recording and summarizing.

One way to record and summarize the financial effects of transactions would be to enter your understanding of their effects into a spreadsheet like the one shown in Exhibit 2.5. By summing each spreadsheet column, you could compute new balances at the end of each month and report them on a balance sheet.

A spreadsheet makes it easy to see the individual impact of each transaction and how transactions combine with beginning balances to yield ending balances, but it is impractical for most large organizations to use. Just imagine how big a spreadsheet would have to be to handle millions of transactions affecting hundreds of accounts. Rather than create a ginormous spreadsheet, a more manageable system is used.

| EXHIBIT 2.5 | Using a Spreadsheet to Record and Summarize Transactions |

Exhibit 2.5.xlsx - Microsoft Excel

Home   Insert   Page Layout   Formulas   Data   Review   View

		Assets			=	Liabilities		+	Stockholders' Equity
						Accounts Payable	Notes Payable		Contributed Capital
		Cash	Cookware	Equipment					
3	Beginning	0	0	0	=	0	0		0
4	(a)	+50,000			=				+50,000
5	(b)	-42,000		+42,000	=				
6	(c)	+20,000			=		+20,000		
7	(d)	-16,000		+18,000	=	-2,000			
8	(e)		no change		=		no change		
9	(f)	-2,000			=	-2,000			
10	(g)		+630		=	+630			
11	Ending	10,000	630	60,000	=	630	20,000	+	50,000

Exhibit 2.5

Ready   100%

Most companies record and summarize the financial effects of transactions with computerized accounting systems, which can handle a large number of transactions. These systems follow a cycle, called **the accounting cycle, which is repeated day after day, month after month, and year after year.** As shown in Exhibit 2.6, a three-step analyze-record-summarize process is applied to **daily transactions** and is then followed by **adjustments and closing processes at the end of the accounting period.** Our focus in Chapter 2 is on applying the three-step process during the period to activities that affect only balance sheet accounts. After you've become comfortable with this process, you will learn (in Chapter 3) to apply this process to operating activities that affect both balance sheet and income statement accounts. In Chapter 4, you will learn how the process is applied at the end of the accounting period, when the accounting records are adjusted and closed.

The three-step process of analyzing, recording, and summarizing is a lot like what you do as a student when attending class, taking notes, and preparing for exams. Day

| EXHIBIT 2.6 | Elements of the Accounting Process |

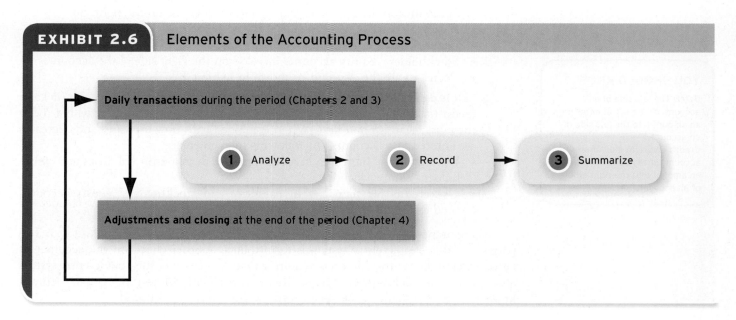

after day, you analyze what is said in class and you record important points in a notebook, which is kind of like an academic diary or journal. Later, when preparing for exams, you copy your notes to summary sheets, which you then use to study for the exams. The same ideas are used in the accounting cycle. Transactions are analyzed, and their financial effects are entered into **journals** each day they occur. Later, these journal entries are summarized in **ledger** accounts that keep track of the financial effects on each account. To make this process as efficient as possible, journals and ledger accounts share the same underlying framework discussed in the following section.

THE DEBIT/CREDIT FRAMEWORK

The framework used for journals and ledger accounts was created more than 500 years ago, yet it continues to exist in accounting systems today. Although computers now perform many routine accounting tasks involving journals and ledger accounts, most computerized systems still require you to know how these accounting records work. To understand this framework, think of the accounting equation (A = L + SE) as an old-fashioned weight scale that tips at the equals sign. Assets—like Cash and Equipment—are put on the left side of the scale and liabilities and stockholders' equity accounts are put on the right. Likewise, each individual account has two sides, with one side used for increases and the other for decreases, similar to what is shown in Exhibit 2.7.

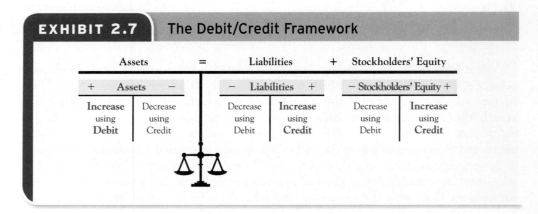

EXHIBIT 2.7 | **The Debit/Credit Framework**

Take special note of two important rules illustrated in Exhibit 2.7:

1. **Accounts increase on the same side as they appear in A = L + SE.** Accounts on the left side of the accounting equation increase on the left side of the account and accounts on the right side of the equation increase on the right. So
   - **Assets increase on the left** side of the account.
   - **Liabilities increase on the right** side of the account.
   - **Stockholders' equity accounts increase on the right** side of the account.
   - Decreases are the opposite, as shown in Exhibit 2.7.

2. **Left is debit (*dr*), right is credit (*cr*).** The terms (and abbreviations) **debit** (*dr*) and **credit** (*cr*) come from Latin words that had meaning back in the day, but today they just mean *left* and *right*. When combined with how increases and decreases are entered into accounts, the following rules emerge:
   - **Use debits for increases in assets** (and for decreases in liabilities and stockholders' equity accounts).
   - **Use credits for increases in liabilities and stockholders' equity** accounts (and for decreases in assets).

Accountants didn't dream up this debit/credit framework just to confuse you. The purpose of this double-entry system is to introduce another check on the accuracy of accounting numbers. In addition to requiring that A = L + SE, the double-entry system also requires that **debits = credits.** If either of these relationships is not equal, then you know for sure that you've made an error that will need to be corrected.

Step 1: Analyzing Transactions

The debit/credit framework does not change this first step of the accounting process. Continue to use the approach shown in Exhibit 2.3 to determine the financial effects of transactions, which you will learn to enter into the accounting system in step 2.

Step 2: Recording Journal Entries

The financial effects of transactions are entered into a journal using a debits-equal-credits format, as shown in Exhibit 2.8. When looking at these **journal entries**, as they are called, notice the following:

- A date is included for each transaction.
- Debits appear first (on top). Credits are written below the debits and are indented to the right (both the words and the amounts). The order of the debited accounts or credited accounts doesn't matter, as long as for each journal entry debits are on top and credits are on the bottom and indented.
- Total debits equal total credits for each transaction (for example, see the entry on August 5 where $18,000 = $16,000 + $2,000).
- Dollar signs are not used because the journal is understood to be a record of financial effects.
- The reference column (Ref.) will be used later (in step 3) to indicate when the journal entry has been summarized in the ledger accounts.
- A brief explanation of the transaction is written below the debits and credits.
- The line after the explanation is left blank before writing the next journal entry.

EXHIBIT 2.8	Formal Journal Page

	General Journal			Page G1
Date	Account Titles and Explanation	Ref.	Debit	Credit
2013				
Aug. 1	Cash		50,000	
	Contributed Capital			50,000
	(Financing from stockholders.)			
Aug. 2	Equipment		42,000	
	Cash			42,000
	(Bought equipment using cash.)			
Aug. 5	**Equipment**		**18,000**	
	Cash			**16,000**
	Accounts Payable			**2,000**
	(Bought equipment using cash and credit.)			

When writing journal entries in this course, we'll make a few minor changes to the formal entries, which should make it easier for you to learn the most important aspects of recording journal entries. The way we would show the journal entry for August 5 is:

(d) *dr* **Equipment** (+A) 18,000
         cr **Cash** (−A) 16,000
         cr **Accounts Payable** (+L)................................... 2,000

The main differences between our simplified format and a formal journal entry are:

- When a date is not given, use some form of reference for each transaction, such as (d), to identify the event.
- Omit the reference column and transaction explanation to simplify the entry.
- Indicate whether you are debiting (dr) or crediting (cr) each account. This will help to reinforce the debit/credit framework from Exhibit 2.7. Plus, it will make it easier to interpret journal entries when indents aren't clear (sometimes an issue in handwritten homework).
- Include the appropriate account type (A, L, or SE) along with the direction of the effect (+ or −) next to each account title to clarify the effects of the transaction on each account. Again, this will reinforce the debit/credit framework and help you to determine whether the accounting equation has remained in balance.

Step 3: Summarizing in Ledger Accounts

By themselves, journal entries show the effects of transactions, but they do not provide account balances. That's why ledger accounts are needed. After journal entries have been recorded (in step 2), their dollar amounts are copied ("posted") to each ledger account affected by the transaction, so that account balances can be computed. In most computerized accounting systems, this happens automatically. In homework assignments, you'll have to do it yourself, so Exhibit 2.9 shows you how this is done using the journal entry for August 5. If account numbers are provided, keep track of the posting of journal entries to general ledger accounts by writing the account number in the Ref. column of the journal and the journal page number in the Ref. column of the ledger.

As we did earlier for journal entries, we will use a simplified format for ledger accounts to make it easier to focus on their main features. The simplified version of a ledger account is called a **T-account**. Each T-account represents the debit and credit

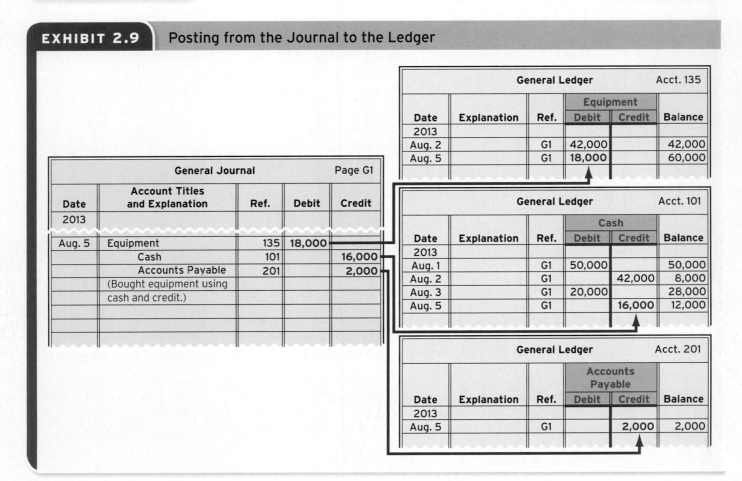

EXHIBIT 2.9 | **Posting from the Journal to the Ledger**

General Ledger   Acct. 135

Date	Explanation	Ref.	Equipment Debit	Equipment Credit	Balance
2013					
Aug. 2		G1	42,000		42,000
Aug. 5		G1	18,000		60,000

General Journal   Page G1

Date	Account Titles and Explanation	Ref.	Debit	Credit
2013				
Aug. 5	Equipment	135	18,000	
	Cash	101		16,000
	Accounts Payable	201		2,000
	(Bought equipment using cash and credit.)			

General Ledger   Acct. 101

Date	Explanation	Ref.	Cash Debit	Cash Credit	Balance
2013					
Aug. 1		G1	50,000		50,000
Aug. 2		G1		42,000	8,000
Aug. 3		G1	20,000		28,000
Aug. 5		G1		16,000	12,000

General Ledger   Acct. 201

Date	Explanation	Ref.	Accounts Payable Debit	Accounts Payable Credit	Balance
2013					
Aug. 5		G1		2,000	2,000

columns of a ledger account. Exhibit 2.10 shows the T-accounts for Pizza Aroma's Equipment, Cash, and Accounts Payable, based on transactions (a) through (d) on pages 50–52. It also shows how an individual journal entry's effects would be summarized in these T-accounts. The debit to Equipment in the journal entry is copied into the debit (left) side of its T-account. The credits to Cash and Accounts Payable are copied into the credit (right) side of those T-accounts. (If you've forgotten why the transaction is recorded this way, take a quick look back at Exhibit 2.7 on page 56 or the graphic to the right.)

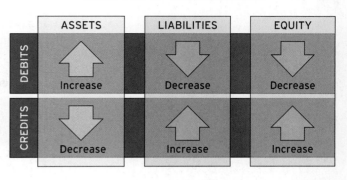

	ASSETS	LIABILITIES	EQUITY
DEBITS	Increase	Decrease	Decrease
CREDITS	Decrease	Increase	Increase

EXHIBIT 2.10   **Posting from a Simplified Journal Entry to T-Accounts**

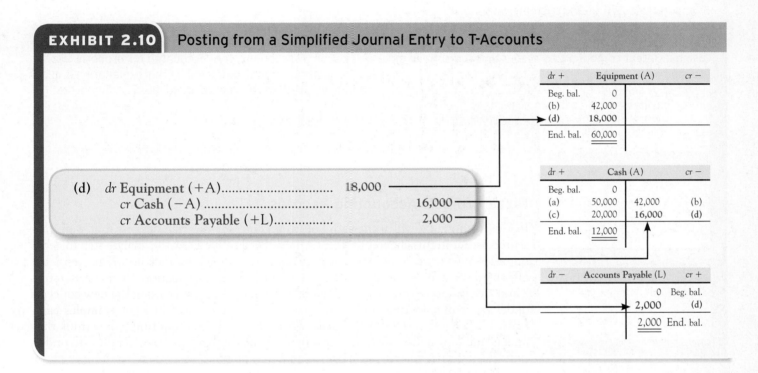

		Equipment (A)	
dr +			cr −
Beg. bal.	0		
(b)	42,000		
(d)	18,000		
End. bal.	60,000		

(d)   dr Equipment (+A)............... 18,000
  cr Cash (−A) 16,000
  cr Accounts Payable (+L)........ 2,000

		Cash (A)		
dr +				cr −
Beg. bal.	0			
(a)	50,000	42,000	(b)	
(c)	20,000	16,000	(d)	
End. bal.	12,000			

		Accounts Payable (L)		
dr −				cr +
		0	Beg. bal.	
		2,000	(d)	
		2,000	End. bal.	

In Exhibit 2.10, notice the following:

- Every account starts with a beginning balance, usually on the side where increases are summarized. For balance sheet accounts, the ending balance from the prior period is the beginning balance for the current period. Because Pizza Aroma is in its first month of business, the beginning balance in each account is zero in this example.
- Dollar signs are not needed.
- Each amount is accompanied by a reference to the related journal entry, which makes it easy to trace back to the original transaction should errors occur.
- To find ending account balances, express the T-accounts as equations:

	Equipment	Cash	Accounts Payable
Beginning balance	0	0	0
Add: "+" side	42,000	+50,000	+2,000
	18,000	+20,000	
Subtract: "−" side		−42,000	
		−16,000	
Ending balance	60,000	12,000	2,000

Knowing how to use T-accounts in this way will help you answer homework questions that involve solving for missing values in accounts.

- The ending balance is double underlined to distinguish it from transactions and symbolize the final result of a computation. The ending balance is shown on the side that has the greater total dollar amount.

SPOTLIGHT ON Financial Reporting

The Ultimate Irony: Teacher Late with Report

K12, Inc., claims to be the leader in computer-based instruction for grades K through 12, yet it couldn't get its own computerized accounting systems working in time to meet an important financial reporting deadline. K12 admitted that it was struggling with "the integration of diverse accounting systems," and that it would be about a month late releasing its annual report. The company explained that it had recently acquired several other companies that were using different computerized accounting systems. To ensure all of the transactions were accounted for properly, K12 needed extra time to conduct a thorough review of its systems. Investors weren't comforted by this explanation and reacted by selling their shares of K12, causing a drop in the company's stock price. Meeting deadlines is as important in the business world as it is in academics.

Source: K12, Inc., "K12 Inc. Releases Selected Preliminary FY 2011 Financial Data and Announces Delay in Filing Annual Report," press release, 2011, www.sec.gov.

Pizza Aroma's Accounting Records

In this section, we will work with you to account for the transactions that were presented earlier in this chapter for Pizza Aroma. Because we show the analyze step in detail on pages 49–54, we do not show it in detail here. Instead, we pick up where step 1 left off—with the effects of each transaction on the accounting equation. By reviewing steps 2 and 3 of the accounting cycle in detail, you will get to practice using the new concepts of debits, credits, journal entries, and T-accounts. **Study the following examples carefully.** The biggest mistake people make when first learning accounting is they think they understand how it all works without actually going through enough examples. To understand accounting, you have to practice, practice, practice, as if you're learning to play a new sport or a musical instrument.

(a) Issue Stock to Owners   Mauricio Rosa incorporates Pizza Aroma, Inc., on August 1. The company issues stock to Mauricio and his wife as evidence of their contribution of $50,000 cash, which is deposited in the company's bank account.

① Analyze

	Assets	=	Liabilities	+	Stockholders' Equity	
(a) Cash	+50,000	=			Contributed Capital	+50,000

② Record

(a)	dr Cash (+A)...	50,000	
	cr Contributed Capital (+SE)		50,000

③ Summarize

dr +	Cash (A)	cr −		dr −	Contributed Capital (SE)	cr +
Beg. bal.	0				0	Beg. bal.
(a)	50,000				50,000	(a)

(b) Invest in Equipment   Pizza Aroma pays $42,000 cash to buy restaurant booths and other equipment.

1 Analyze

	Assets	=	Liabilities	+	Stockholders' Equity
(b) Cash	−42,000				
Equipment	+42,000				

2 Record

(b)	dr Equipment (+A)...	42,000	
	cr Cash (−A)..		42,000

3 Summarize

dr +	Cash (A)		cr −		dr +	Equipment (A)		cr −
Beg. bal.	0				Beg. bal.	0		
(a)	50,000	42,000	(b)		(b)	42,000		

(c) Obtain Loan from Bank   Pizza Aroma borrows $20,000 from a bank, depositing those funds in its bank account and signing a formal agreement to repay the loan in two years (on August 3, 2015).

1 Analyze

	Assets		=	Liabilities		+	Stockholders' Equity
(c) Cash	+20,000		=	Note Payable	+20,000		

2 Record

(c)	dr Cash (+A)...	20,000	
	cr Note Payable (+L).....................................		20,000

3 Summarize

dr +	Cash (A)		cr −		dr −	Note Payable (L)		cr +
Beg. bal.	0						0	Beg. bal.
(a)	50,000	42,000	(b)				20,000	(c)
(c)	20,000							

(d) Invest in Equipment   Pizza Aroma purchases $18,000 in pizza ovens and other restaurant equipment, paying $16,000 in cash and giving an informal promise to pay $2,000 at the end of the month.

1 Analyze

	Assets		=	Liabilities		+	Stockholders' Equity
(d) Cash	−16,000		=	Accounts Payable	+2,000		
Equipment	+18,000						

2 Record

(d)	dr Equipment (+A)........	18,000	
	cr Cash (−A).............		16,000
	cr Accounts Payable (+L)..		2,000

3 Summarize

dr +	Cash (A)	cr −		dr +	Equipment (A) cr −		dr − Accounts Payable (L) cr +	
Beg. bal.	0			Beg. bal.	0			0 Beg. bal.
(a)	50,000	42,000	(b)	(b)	42,000		2,000	(d)
(c)	20,000	16,000	(d)	(d)	18,000			

(e) Order Cookware   Pizza Aroma orders $630 of pans, dishes and other cookware. None have been received yet. Because this event involves the exchange of only promises, it is not considered a transaction. No journal entry is needed.

(f) Pay Supplier   Pizza Aroma pays $2,000 to the equipment supplier in (d).

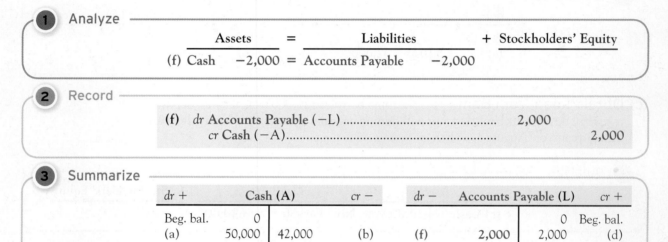

1 Analyze

	Assets	=	Liabilities	+ Stockholders' Equity
(f) Cash	−2,000	=	Accounts Payable −2,000	

2 Record

(f)   dr Accounts Payable (−L) 2,000
     cr Cash (−A)..   2,000

3 Summarize

dr +	Cash (A)	cr −		dr −	Accounts Payable (L)	cr +	
Beg. bal.	0					0 Beg. bal.	
(a)	50,000	42,000	(b)	(f)	2,000	2,000	(d)
(c)	20,000	16,000	(d)				
		2,000	(f)				

(g) Receive Cookware   Pizza Aroma receives $630 of the cookware ordered in (e) and promises to pay for it next month.

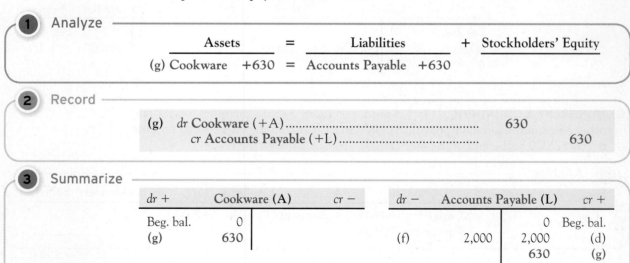

1 Analyze

	Assets	=	Liabilities	+ Stockholders' Equity
(g) Cookware	+630	=	Accounts Payable +630	

2 Record

(g)   dr Cookware (+A).. 630
     cr Accounts Payable (+L)..   630

3 Summarize

dr +	Cookware (A)	cr −		dr −	Accounts Payable (L)	cr +	
Beg. bal.	0					0 Beg. bal.	
(g)	630			(f)	2,000	2,000	(d)
						630	(g)

Exhibit 2.11 summarizes the journal entries and T-accounts affected by events (a) through (g) for Pizza Aroma. It also reports the ending balances for each account.

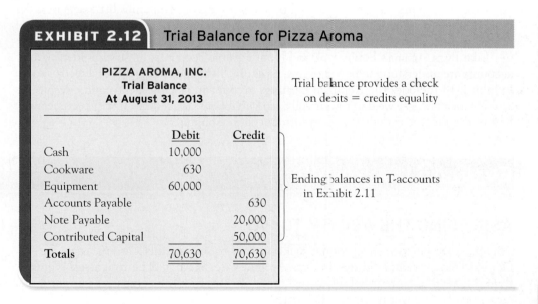

EXHIBIT 2.11 | Journal Entries and T-Accounts for Pizza Aroma

| | Assets | = | Liabilities | + | Stockholders' Equity |

Journal Entries

(a) *dr* Cash (+A)................................... 50,000
    cr Contributed Capital (+SE).....   50,000

(b) *dr* Equipment (+A)......................... 42,000
    cr Cash (−A)   42,000

(c) *dr* Cash (+A)................................... 20,000
    cr Note Payable (+L)   20,000

(d) *dr* Equipment (+A)......................... 18,000
    cr Cash (−A)   16,000
    cr Accounts Payable (+L)   2,000

(e) Not a transaction.

(f) *dr* Accounts Payable (−L)............... 2,000
    cr Cash (−A)   2,000

(g) *dr* Cookware (+A)........................... 630
    cr Accounts Payable (+L)   630

Cash (A)

Beg. bal.	0		
(a)	50,000	42,000	(b)
(c)	20,000	16,000	(d)
		2,000	(f)
End. bal.	10,000		

Cookware (A)

Beg. bal.	0		
(g)	630		
End. bal.	630		

Equipment (A)

Beg. bal.	0		
(b)	42,000		
(d)	18,000		
End. bal.	60,000		

Accounts Payable (L)

		0	Beg. bal.
(f)	2,000	2,000	(d)
		630	(g)
		630	End. bal.

Note Payable (L)

	0	Beg. bal.
	20,000	(c)
	20,000	End. bal.

Contributed Capital (SE)

	0	Beg. bal.
	50,000	(a)
	50,000	End. bal.

PREPARING A BALANCE SHEET

Using the ending amount from each T-account, you could now prepare a balance sheet. Before you do this, however, it's a good idea to check that the accounting records are in balance by determining whether debits = credits. If total debits don't equal total credits, the balance sheet will not balance. The equality of debits and credits can be checked by preparing an internal accounting report called the trial balance, shown in Exhibit 2.12. Fortunately the column totals are equal, so the Pizza Aroma balance sheet can be prepared and shown to Mauricio.

EXHIBIT 2.12 | Trial Balance for Pizza Aroma

PIZZA AROMA, INC.
Trial Balance
At August 31, 2013

	Debit	Credit
Cash	10,000	
Cookware	630	
Equipment	60,000	
Accounts Payable		630
Note Payable		20,000
Contributed Capital		50,000
Totals	**70,630**	**70,630**

Trial balance provides a check on debits = credits equality

Ending balances in T-accounts in Exhibit 2.11

Exhibit 2.13 shows Pizza Aroma's balance sheet based on the transactions in this chapter. The balance sheet is prepared by taking the ending balances for each account and grouping them as assets, liabilities, and stockholders' equity in balance sheet format. We've used a balance sheet format in Exhibit 2.13 called the **classified balance sheet**.

EXHIBIT 2.13   Classified Balance Sheet

PIZZA AROMA

PIZZA AROMA, INC. Balance Sheet At August 31, 2013		Explanation of Classification
Assets		
Current Assets		Current assets will be used up or turned into cash within 12 months.
Cash	$10,000	Cash in the company's bank account will be used up before August 31, 2014.
Cookware	630	Pizza pans and dishes will likely be used up or replaced before August 31, 2014.
Total Current Assets	10,630	
Equipment	60,000	Ovens and restaurant booths will be used for many years.
Total Assets	$70,630	
Liabilities and Stockholders' Equity		
Current Liabilities		Current liabilities will be paid or fulfilled within 12 months.
Accounts Payable	$ 630	Amounts owed to suppliers are usually paid within one or two months.
Total Current Liabilities	630	
Note Payable	20,000	The promissory note is not required to be repaid until August 3, 2015.
Total Liabilities	20,630	
Stockholders' Equity		
Contributed Capital	50,000	
Retained Earnings	0	Stockholders' equity accounts are not classified as current or noncurrent.
Total Stockholders' Equity	50,000	
Total Liabilities and Stockholders' Equity	$70,630	

YOU SHOULD KNOW

Current assets: To be used up or converted into cash within 12 months of the balance sheet date.
Current liabilities: Debts and obligations that will be paid, settled, or fulfilled within 12 months of the balance sheet date.
Noncurrent (or long-term): Assets and liabilities that do not meet the definition of current.

A classified balance sheet contains subcategories for assets and liabilities labeled *current*. **Current assets** are assets the business will use up or turn into cash within 12 months of the balance sheet date. **Current liabilities** are debts and other obligations that will be paid or fulfilled within 12 months of the balance sheet date. In our example, Accounts Payable is the only current liability. The other liability—Note Payable—is expected to be paid in two years, so it is considered **noncurrent**. Most companies list assets in order of liquidity (how soon they will be used up or turned into cash) and liabilities in order of maturity (how soon they will be paid in cash or fulfilled by providing a service).

Like Pizza Aroma's Equipment and Note Payable accounts, its stockholders' equity accounts are understood to be long-term in nature, although they are not labeled as such. Exhibit 2.13 includes the Retained Earnings account in stockholders' equity despite its zero balance because we don't want you to forget about this account. It will become a key link to the income statement, when introduced in Chapter 3.

Evaluate the Results

Learning Objective 2-5
Interpret the balance sheet using the current ratio and an understanding of related concepts.

ASSESSING THE ABILITY TO PAY

The classified balance sheet format makes it easy to see whether current assets are sufficient to pay current liabilities. In Pizza Aroma's case, $10,630 of current assets is greater than the $630 of current liabilities, making it obvious that the company's current assets are sufficient to cover its current liabilities.

The only problem with looking at total dollar amounts is the difficulty in comparing across companies. It's far easier to express the relationship as a ratio, by dividing current assets by current liabilities. This calculation is known as the current ratio. It is used to evaluate liquidity, which is the ability to pay liabilities as they come due in the short run. Generally speaking, a high current ratio suggests good liquidity. Pizza Aroma's current ratio ($10,630 ÷ $630 = 16.9) is unusually high. Current ratios typically vary from 1.0 to 2.0. Recently, Papa John's current ratio was 0.97, as shown below.

Accounting Decision Tools

Name of Measure	Formula	What It Tells You
Current ratio	$$\frac{\text{Current Assets}}{\text{Current Liabilities}}$$	• Whether current assets are sufficient to pay current liabilities • A higher ratio means better ability to pay

SPOTLIGHT ON Financial Reporting

Papa John's is a significantly larger company than Pizza Aroma, but the structure of the balance sheet and its account titles are quite similar. Its current ratio is typical of many large companies.

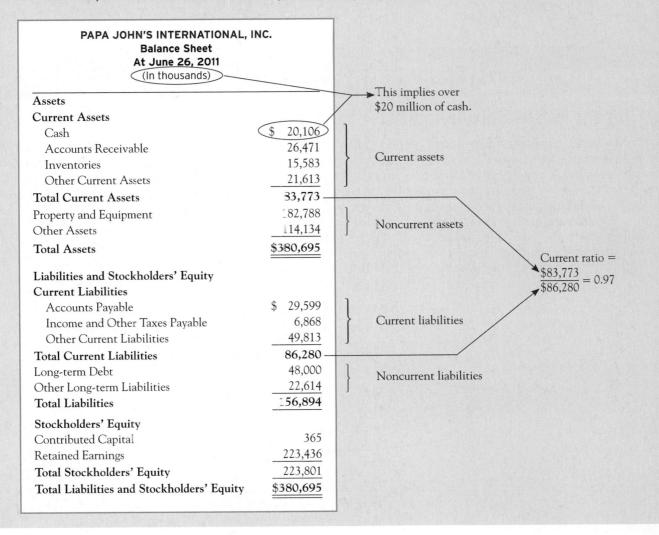

PAPA JOHN'S INTERNATIONAL, INC.
Balance Sheet
At June 26, 2011
(In thousands)

This implies over $20 million of cash.

Assets		
Current Assets		
Cash	$ 20,106	
Accounts Receivable	26,471	Current assets
Inventories	15,583	
Other Current Assets	21,613	
Total Current Assets	83,773	
Property and Equipment	182,788	Noncurrent assets
Other Assets	114,134	
Total Assets	**$380,695**	
Liabilities and Stockholders' Equity		
Current Liabilities		
Accounts Payable	$ 29,599	
Income and Other Taxes Payable	6,868	Current liabilities
Other Current Liabilities	49,813	
Total Current Liabilities	86,280	
Long-term Debt	48,000	Noncurrent liabilities
Other Long-term Liabilities	22,614	
Total Liabilities	156,894	
Stockholders' Equity		
Contributed Capital	365	
Retained Earnings	223,436	
Total Stockholders' Equity	223,801	
Total Liabilities and Stockholders' Equity	**$380,695**	

Current ratio = $$\frac{\$83,773}{\$86,280} = 0.97$$

BALANCE SHEET CONCEPTS AND VALUES

The purpose of a balance sheet is to report what a company owns and owes, but not necessarily what the company is worth. Some people mistakenly believe that the balance sheet reports a company's current value. To them, this isn't a crazy idea because the balance sheet lists a company's assets and liabilities, so the net difference between the two must be the company's worth. In fact, *net worth* is a term that many accountants and analysts use when referring to stockholders' equity. So why is it wrong to think that the balance sheet reports a company's current value?

The answer comes from knowing that accounting is based on recording and reporting transactions, which affects: (1) what is (and is not) recorded, and (2) the amounts assigned to recorded items.

1. **What is (and is not) recorded?**
   - Measurable exchanges, such as a purchase of ovens, are recorded. Pizza Aroma's gourmet pizza recipes, on the other hand, were not acquired in an exchange, so they are not listed on the balance sheet.

2. **What amounts are assigned to recorded items?**
   - Following the cost principle, assets and liabilities are first recorded at the amounts that were measurable at the time transactions occurred. Later, if an asset's value increases, the increase is generally not recorded under GAAP. However, if an asset's value falls, it is generally reported at that lower value. This conservatism is followed when doubt exists about the amount at which to report assets and liabilities (and revenues and expenses).

SPOTLIGHT ON Financial Reporting

Current Ratios Before and After the Financial Crisis in Fall 2008

During 2008, companies experienced a crisis unlike anything since the Great Depression of the 1930s. Financial institutions, such as Lehman Brothers, had collapsed or were on the verge of collapse. Consequently, banks became ultra-conservative and stopped lending to one another, which severely limited the amount of cash available to lend to businesses. The best way for a company to survive this credit crisis was to have a strong balance sheet, which meant having lots of cash and other current assets relative to the amount of liabilities owed.

The following graph shows the current ratios of three large pizza companies before and after the financial crisis. Notice how both Papa John's and Domino's Pizza significantly increased their ratios of current assets to current liabilities soon after the financial crisis began in the fall of 2008. California Pizza Kitchen did not follow this same path. After four years of declining financial results, California Pizza was sold to a private company in 2011.

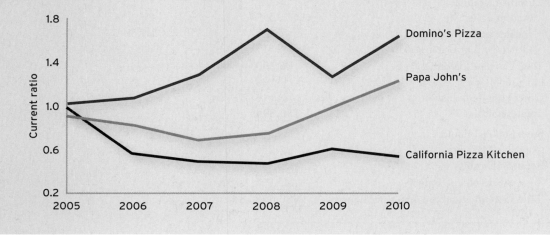

Summary of the Accounting Cycle

To show that the accounting process explained in this chapter can apply to any business, Exhibit 2.14 illustrates it for a fictitious construction company.

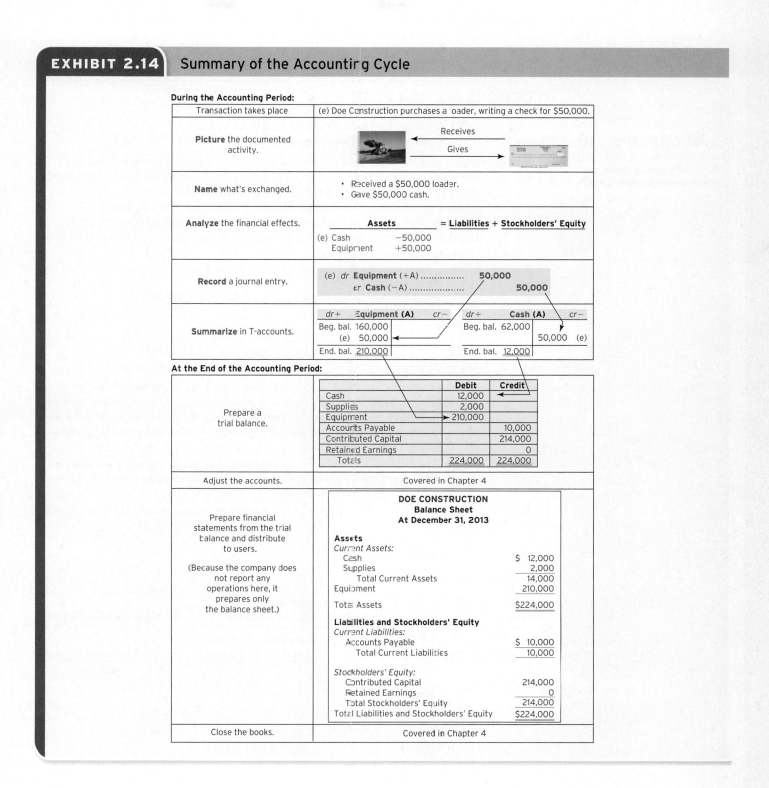

EXHIBIT 2.14 | Summary of the Accounting Cycle

During the Accounting Period:

Transaction takes place	(e) Doe Construction purchases a loader, writing a check for $50,000.
Picture the documented activity.	Receives ← Gives →
Name what's exchanged.	• Received a $50,000 loader. • Gave $50,000 cash.
Analyze the financial effects.	**Assets** = **Liabilities + Stockholders' Equity** (e) Cash −50,000 Equipment +50,000
Record a journal entry.	(e) dr Equipment (+A) .... 50,000 cr Cash (−A) 50,000
Summarize in T-accounts.	dr+ Equipment (A) cr− / dr+ Cash (A) cr− Beg. bal. 160,000 / Beg. bal. 62,000 (e) 50,000 / 50,000 (e) End. bal. 210,000 / End. bal. 12,000

At the End of the Accounting Period:

		Debit	Credit
Prepare a trial balance.	Cash	12,000	
	Supplies	2,000	
	Equipment	210,000	
	Accounts Payable		10,000
	Contributed Capital		214,000
	Retained Earnings		0
	Totals	224,000	224,000

Adjust the accounts.	Covered in Chapter 4

Prepare financial statements from the trial balance and distribute to users. (Because the company does not report any operations here, it prepares only the balance sheet.)	**DOE CONSTRUCTION** **Balance Sheet** **At December 31, 2013** **Assets** *Current Assets:* Cash $ 12,000 Supplies 2,000 Total Current Assets 14,000 Equipment 210,000 Total Assets $224,000 **Liabilities and Stockholders' Equity** *Current Liabilities:* Accounts Payable $ 10,000 Total Current Liabilities 10,000 *Stockholders' Equity:* Contributed Capital 214,000 Retained Earnings 0 Total Stockholders' Equity 214,000 Total Liabilities and Stockholders' Equity $224,000
Close the books.	Covered in Chapter 4

REVIEW THE CHAPTER

This section provides a chance to solidify your understanding of key points. It's worth your time to work through the following demonstration case, scan the chapter summary, test your understanding of key terms, and then practice, practice, practice.

DEMONSTRATION CASE

COACH'S TIP

For possible account names, see the Homework Helper on page 71.

On April 1, 2013, three college students started Goodbye Grass Corporation (GGC). A summary of GGC's transactions completed through April 30, 2013, follows:

a. Issued shares of stock to the three investors in exchange for cash contributions totaling $9,000.
b. Acquired rakes and other hand tools (equipment) for $600, paying the hardware store $200 cash and agreeing informally to pay the balance in three months.
c. Ordered lawn mowers and edgers costing $4,000 from XYZ Lawn Supply, Inc.
d. Purchased four acres of land for the future site of a storage garage. Paid cash, $5,000.
e. Received the mowers and edgers that had been ordered and signed a promissory note to pay XYZ Lawn Supply in full in 60 days.
f. Sold for $1,250 one acre of land to the city for a park and accepted a note from the city indicating payment will be received by GGC in six months.
g. One of the owners borrowed $3,000 from a local bank for personal use.

Required:

1. Analyze each event to determine its effects on the accounting equation.
2. Prepare journal entries to record transactions listed above (omit explanations).
3. Set up T-accounts for Cash, Note Receivable (from the city), Equipment (hand tools and mowing equipment), Land, Accounts Payable (to hardware store), Note Payable (to equipment supply company), and Contributed Capital. Indicate the beginning balances of $0 in each T-account, and then summarize the effects of each journal entry in the appropriate T-accounts. Determine the ending balance in each account.
4. Use the amounts in the T-accounts, developed in requirement 3, to prepare a classified balance sheet for Goodbye Grass Corporation at April 30, 2013. Show the balances for all assets, liabilities, and stockholders' equity accounts.
5. As of April 30, 2013, has financing for GGC's assets come primarily from liabilities or stockholders' equity?

Suggested Solution

1. Analyze transactions:

		Assets			=	Liabilities		+	Stockholders' Equity
	Cash	Note Receivable	Equipment	Land	=	Accounts Payable	Note Payable		Contributed Capital
(a)	+9,000				=				+9,000
(b)	−200		+600		=	+400			
(c)		No change*			=		No change		
(d)	−5,000			+5,000	=		No change		
(e)			+4,000		=		+4,000		
(f)	+1,250			−1,250	=		No change		
(g)		No change*			=		No change		

*Event (c) is not considered a transaction because it involves only the exchange of promises. Event (g) is not considered a transaction of the company because the separate entity assumption (from Chapter 1) states that transactions of the owners are separate from transactions of the business.

2. Record journal entries:

a. *dr* Cash (+A) 9,000
       cr Contributed Capital (+SE) 9,000

b. *dr* Equipment (+A) 600
       cr Cash (−A) 200
       cr Accounts Payable (+L) 400

c. This is not an accounting transaction, so a journal entry is not needed.

d. *dr* Land (+A) 5,000
       cr Cash (−A) 5,000

e. *dr* Equipment (+A) 4,000
       cr Note Payable (+L) 4,000

f. *dr* Note Receivable (+A) 1,250
       cr Land (−A) 1,250

g. This is not a transaction of the business, so a journal entry is not needed.

3. Summarize journal entries in T-accounts:

| Assets | = | Liabilities | + | Stockholders' Equity |

Cash (A)

Beg. bal.	0	200	(b)
(a)	9,000	5,000	(d)
End. bal.	3,800		

Equipment (A)

Beg. bal.	0	
(b)	600	
(e)	4,000	
End. bal.	4,600	

Accounts Payable (L)

	0	Beg. bal.
	400	(b)
	400	End. bal.

Contributed Capital (SE)

	0	Beg. bal.
	9,000	(a)
	9,000	End. bal.

Note Receivable (A)

Beg. bal.	0	
(f)	1,250	
End. bal.	1,250	

Land (A)

Beg. bal.	0		
(d)	5,000	1,250	(f)
End. bal.	3,750		

Note Payable (L)

	0	Beg. bal.
	4,000	(e)
	4,000	End. bal.

4. Prepare a classified balance sheet from the T-accounts:

GOODBYE GRASS CORPORATION
Balance Sheet
At April 30, 2013

Assets		Liabilities	
Current Assets		Current Liabilities	
Cash	$ 3,800	Accounts Payable	$ 400
Note Receivable	1,250	Note Payable	4,000
Total Current Assets	5,050	Total Current Liabilities	4,400
Equipment	4,600		
Land	3,750	**Stockholders' Equity**	
		Contributed Capital	9,000
		Retained Earnings	0
		Total Stockholders' Equity	9,000
Total Assets	$13,400	Total Liabilities and Stockholders' Equity	$13,400

5. The primary source of financing for GGC's assets (totaling $13,400) has come from stockholders' equity ($9,000) rather than liabilities ($4,400).

CHAPTER SUMMARY

LO 2-1 **Identify financial effects of common business activities that affect the balance sheet. p. 46**

- Financing activities involve debt transactions with lenders (e.g., Notes Payable) or equity transactions with investors (e.g., Contributed Capital).

- Investing activities involve buying and selling long-term assets (e.g., Buildings, Equipment).

- Operating activities involve day-to-day transactions with suppliers, employees, and customers, and typically affect current assets and current liabilities.

LO 2-2 **Apply transaction analysis to accounting transactions. p. 49**

- Transactions include external exchanges and internal events.

- Transaction analysis is based on the duality of effects and the basic accounting equation. *Duality of effects* means that every transaction affects at least two accounts.

- Transaction analysis follows a systematic approach of picturing the documented business activity; naming the assets, liabilities, or stockholders' equity that are exchanged; and analyzing the financial effects on the basic accounting equation.

LO 2-3 **Use journal entries and T-accounts to show how transactions affect the balance sheet. p. 56**

- Debit means left and credit means right.

- Debits increase assets and decrease liabilities and stockholders' equity.

- Credits decrease assets and increase liabilities and stockholders' equity.

- Journal entries express, in debits-equal-credits form, the effects of a transaction on various asset, liability, and stockholders' equity accounts. Journal entries are used to record financial information in the accounting system, which is later summarized by accounts in the ledger (T-accounts).

- T-accounts are a simplified version of the ledger, which summarizes transaction effects for each account. T-accounts show increases on the left (debit) side for assets, which are on the left side of the accounting equation. T-accounts show increases on the right (credit) side for liabilities and stockholders' equity, which are on the right side of the accounting equation.

LO 2-4 **Prepare a classified balance sheet. p. 63**

- A *classified balance sheet* separately classifies assets as current if they will be used up or turned into cash within one year. Liabilities are classified as current if they will be paid, settled, or fulfilled within one year.

LO 2-5 **Interpret the balance sheet using the current ratio and an understanding of related concepts. p. 64**

- The current ratio divides current assets by current liabilities to determine the extent to which current assets are likely to be sufficient for paying current liabilities.

- Because accounting is transaction-based, the balance sheet does not necessarily represent the current value of a business.

- Some assets are not recorded because they do not arise from transactions.

- The amounts recorded for assets and liabilities may not represent current values because under the cost principle they generally are recorded at cost, using the exchange amounts established at the time of the initial transaction.

Accounting Decision Tools		
Name of Measure	**Formula**	**What It Tells You**
Current ratio	$\dfrac{\text{Current Assets}}{\text{Current Liabilities}}$	• Whether current assets are sufficient to pay current liabilities • A higher ratio means better ability to pay

KEY TERMS

Assets p. 46

Chart of Accounts p. 49

Classified Balance Sheet p. 63

Cost Principle p. 47

Current Assets p. 64

Current Liabilities p. 64

Debits and Credits p. 56

Journal p. 56

Journal Entry p. 57

Ledger p. 56

Liabilities p. 46

Noncurrent p. 64

Stockholders' Equity p. 46

T-account p. 58

Transaction p. 48

See complete definitions in the glossary in the back of this text.

HOMEWORK HELPER

Account Name	Description
Assets	
Cash	Includes cash in the bank and in the cash register
Accounts Receivable	The right to collect from customers for prior sales on credit
Interest Receivable	The right to collect interest from others
Inventories	Goods on hand that are being held for resale
Supplies	Items on hand that will be used to make goods or provide services
Prepaid Insurance	Amount paid to obtain insurance covering future periods
Prepaid Rent	Amount paid for rent relating to future periods
Notes Receivable	The right to collect from others under a formal agreement ("note")
Land	Cost of land to be used by the business
Buildings	Cost of buildings the business will use for operations
Equipment	Cost of equipment used to produce goods or provide services
Intangible Assets	Trademarks, brand names, goodwill, and other assets that lack a physical presence
Liabilities	
Accounts Payable	Amounts owed to suppliers for goods or services bought on credit
Wages Payable	Amounts owed to employees for salaries, wages, and bonuses
Accrued Liabilities	Amounts owed to others for advertising, utilities, interest, etc.
Unearned Revenues	Amounts (customer deposits) received in advance of providing goods or services to customers
Notes Payable	Amounts borrowed from lenders; involves signing a promissory note
Interest Payable	Amount due on loans as the cost of borrowing
Bonds Payable	Amounts borrowed from lenders; involves issuance of bonds
Other Liabilities	A variety of liabilities with smaller balances
Stockholders' Equity	
Contributed Capital	Amount of cash (or other property) contributed in exchange for the company's stock
Retained Earnings	Amount of accumulated earnings not distributed as dividends

> **COACH'S TIP**
>
> Read this chart of accounts but don't memorize it. Also, don't try to force this chart of accounts on all problems. Account names vary from company to company.

Alternative terms

- Stockholders' equity also can be called shareholders' equity.
- The balance sheet also can be called the statement of financial position.

Helpful reminders

- It's easier to account for a transaction if you can accurately determine how it might affect Cash before determining its impact on other account(s).
- The word *pay* and the expression *purchase with cash* both imply a reduction in Cash.

Frequent mistakes

- When accounting for transactions, avoid thinking of yourself as the customer, investor, or creditor. Instead, put yourself in the position of the company you're accounting for.
- Stockholders' is plural; stockholder's is singular.

PRACTICE MATERIAL

QUESTIONS   (⊖ Symbol indicates questions that require analysis from more than one perspective.)

1. Define the following:
   a. Asset
   b. Current asset
   c. Liability
   d. Current liability
   e. Contributed capital
   f. Retained earnings

2. Define a transaction and give an example of each of the two types of events that are considered transactions.

3. For accounting purposes, what is an account? Explain why accounts are used in an accounting system.

4. What is the basic accounting equation?

5. Explain what *debit* and *credit* mean.

6. Briefly explain what is meant by *transaction analysis*. What are the two principles underlying transaction analysis?

7. What two different accounting equalities must be maintained in transaction analysis?

8. What is a journal entry? What is the typical format of a journal entry?

9. What is a T-account? What is its purpose?

10. Explain the cost principle.

11. To obtain financing for her hair salon, Valeri asked you to prepare a balance sheet for her business. When she sees it, she is disappointed that the assets exclude a value for her list of loyal customers. What can you tell her to explain why this "asset" has been excluded? Knowing this, what should she tell her banker when they meet next week? ⊖

MULTIPLE CHOICE

1. Which of the following is not an asset?
   a. Cash
   b. Land
   c. Equipment
   d. Contributed capital

2. Which of the following statements describe transactions that would be recorded in the accounting system?
   a. An exchange of an asset for a promise to pay.
   b. An exchange of a promise for another promise.
   c. Both of the above.
   d. None of the above.

3. Total assets on a balance sheet prepared on any date must agree with which of the following?
   a. The sum of total liabilities and net income as shown on the income statement.
   b. The sum of total liabilities and contributed capital.
   c. The sum of total liabilities and retained earnings.
   d. The sum of total liabilities and contributed capital and retained earnings.

4. The *duality of effects* can best be described as follows:
   a. When a transaction is recorded in the accounting system, at least two effects on the basic accounting equation will result.
   b. When an exchange takes place between two parties, both parties must record the transaction.
   c. When a transaction is recorded, both the balance sheet and the income statement must be impacted.
   d. When a transaction is recorded, one account will always increase and one account will always decrease.

5. The T-account is used to summarize which of the following?
   a. Increases and decreases to a single account in the accounting system.
   b. Debits and credits to a single account in the accounting system.
   c. Changes in specific account balances over a time period.
   d. All of the above describe how T-accounts are used by accountants.

6. Which of the following describes how assets are listed on the balance sheet?
   a. In alphabetical order.
   b. In order of magnitude, lowest value to highest value.
   c. In the order they will be used up or turned into cash.
   d. From least current to most current.

7. A company was recently formed with $50,000 cash contributed to the company by stockholders. The company then borrowed $20,000 from a bank and bought $10,000 of supplies on account. The company also purchased $50,000 of equipment by paying $20,000 in cash and issuing a note for the remainder. What is the amount of total assets to be reported on the balance sheet?
   a. $110,000
   b. $100,000
   c. $90,000
   d. None of the above

8. Which of the following statements would be considered true regarding debits and credits?

   a. In any given transaction, the total dollar amount of the debits and the total dollar amount of the credits must be equal.

   b. Debits decrease certain accounts and credits decrease certain accounts.

   c. Liabilities and stockholders' equity accounts usually end in credit balances, while assets usually end in debit balances.

   d. All of the above.

9. Which of the following statements would be considered true regarding the balance sheet?

   a. One cannot determine the true current value of a company by reviewing just its balance sheet.

   b. The balance sheet reports assets only if they have been acquired through identifiable transactions.

   c. A balance sheet shows only the ending balances, in a summarized format, of balance sheet accounts in the accounting system as of a particular date.

   d. All of the above.

10. If a publicly traded company is trying to maximize its perceived value to decision makers external to the corporation, the company is most likely to report too small a value for which of the following on its balance sheet?

    a. Assets
    b. Liabilities
    c. Retained earnings
    d. Contributed capital

For answers to the Multiple-Choice Questions **see page Q1** located in the last section of the book.

MINI-EXERCISES

M2-1 Identifying Increase and Decrease Effects on Balance Sheet Accounts   LO 2-3

Complete the following table by entering either the word *increases* or *decreases* in each column.

	Debit	Credit
Assets		
Liabilities		
Stockholders' Equity		

M2-2 Identifying Debit and Credit Effects on Balance Sheet Accounts   LO 2-3

Complete the following table by entering either the word *debit* or *credit* in each column.

	Increase	Decrease
Assets		
Liabilities		
Stockholders' Equity		

M2-3 Matching Terms with Definitions   LO 2-2, 2-3, 2-5

Match each term with its related definition by entering the appropriate letter in the space provided. There should be only one definition per term. (That is, there are more definitions than terms.)

Term		Definition
____ 1. Journal entry	A.	An exchange or event that has a direct and measurable financial effect.
____ 2. A = L + SE; Debits = Credits	B.	Four periodic financial statements.
____ 3. Transaction	C.	The two equalities in accounting that aid in providing accuracy.
____ 4. Liabilities		
____ 5. Assets	D.	The results of transaction analysis in debits-equal-credits format.
____ 6. Income statement, balance sheet, statement of retained earnings, and statement of cash flows	E.	The account that is debited when money is borrowed from a bank.
	F.	A resource owned by a business, with measurable value and expected future benefits.
	G.	Cumulative earnings of a company that are not distributed to the owners.
	H.	Every transaction has at least two effects.
	I.	Amounts presently owed by a business.
	J.	Assigning dollar amounts to transactions.

LO 2-1, 2-4 **M2-4 Classifying Accounts on a Balance Sheet**

The following are a few of the accounts of Aim Delivery Corporation:

_____ 1. Wages Payable   _____ 8. Income Taxes Payable

_____ 2. Accounts Payable   _____ 9. Equipment

_____ 3. Accounts Receivable   _____ 10. Notes Payable (due in six months)

_____ 4. Buildings   _____ 11. Retained Earnings

_____ 5. Cash   _____ 12. Supplies

_____ 6. Contributed Capital   _____ 13. Utilities Payable

_____ 7. Land

In the space provided, classify each as it would be reported on a balance sheet. Use the following code:

      CA = Current Asset   CL = Current Liability   SE = Stockholders' Equity
      NCA = Noncurrent Asset   NCL = Noncurrent Liability

LO 2-1, 2-3, 2-4 **M2-5 Identifying Accounts on a Classified Balance Sheet and Their Normal Debit or Credit Balances**

According to a recent report of Hasbro, Inc., the company is "a worldwide leader in children's and family games and toys." Hasbro produces products under several brands including Tonka, Milton Bradley, Playskool, and Parker Brothers. The following are several of the accounts from a recent balance sheet:

1. Accounts Receivable   6. Property, Plant, and Equipment
2. Short-term Bank Loan   7. Retained Earnings
3. Contributed Capital   8. Accounts Payable
4. Long-term Debt   9. Cash
5. Income Taxes Payable

Required:

1. Indicate how each account normally should be categorized on a classified balance sheet. Use CA for current asset, NCA for noncurrent asset, CL for current liability, NCL for noncurrent liability, and SE for stockholders' equity.
2. Indicate whether the account normally has a debit or credit balance.

LO 2-1, 2-3, 2-4 **M2-6 Identifying Accounts on a Classified Balance Sheet and Their Normal Debit or Credit Balances**

Netflix, Inc.

Netflix, Inc., is the world's leading Internet subscription service for movies and TV shows, with more than 20 million members. The following are several of the accounts included in a recent balance sheet:

1. Accrued Liabilities   5. Long-term Debt
2. Prepaid Rent   6. Property and Equipment
3. Cash   7. Retained Earnings
4. Contributed Capital   8. Accounts Payable

Required:

1. Indicate how each account normally should be categorized on a classified balance sheet. Use CA for current asset, NCA for noncurrent asset, CL for current liability, NCL for noncurrent liability, and SE for stockholders' equity.
2. Indicate whether the account normally has a debit or credit balance.

LO 2-2 **M2-7 Identifying Events as Accounting Transactions**

TORO.

Do the following events result in a recordable transaction for The Toro Company? Answer yes or no for each.

____ 1. Toro purchased robotic manufacturing equipment that it paid for by signing a note payable.

____ 2. Toro's president purchased stock in another company for his own portfolio.

____ 3. The company lent $550 to an employee.

____ 4. Toro ordered supplies from Office Max to be delivered next week.

____ 5. Six investors in Toro sold their stock to another investor.

____ 6. The company borrowed $2,500,000 from a local bank.

M2-8 Identifying Events as Accounting Transactions

LO 2-2

With 116 locations in 16 states, Half Price Books is the country's favorite new and used bookstore chain. Do the following events result in a recordable transaction for Half Price Books? Answer yes or no for each.

____ 1. Half Price Books bought an old Laundromat in Dallas.

____ 2. The privately held company issued stock to new investors.

____ 3. The company signed an agreement to rent store space in Columbia Plaza near Cleveland.

____ 4. The company paid for renovations to prepare its Seattle store for operations.

____ 5. The vice president of the company spoke at a literacy luncheon in Indiana, which contributed to building the company's reputation as a responsible company.

M2-9 Determining Financial Statement Effects of Several Transactions

LO 2-2

For each of the following transactions of Spotlighter, Inc., for the month of January 2013, indicate the accounts, amounts, and direction of the effects on the accounting equation. A sample is provided.

a. (Sample) Borrowed $3,940 from a local bank on a note due in six months.
b. Received $4,630 cash from investors and issued stock to them.
c. Purchased $1000 in equipment, paying $200 cash and promising the rest on a note due in one year.
d. Paid $300 cash for supplies.
e. Bought and received $700 of supplies on account.

Assets		=	Liabilities	+	Stockholders' Equity
a. *Sample:*	Cash	+3,940	Notes Payable (short-term) +3,940		

M2-10 Preparing Journal Entries

LO 2-3

For each of the transactions in M2-9 (including the sample), write the journal entry using the format shown in this chapter (omit explanations).

M2-11 Posting to T-Accounts

LO 2-3

For each of the transactions in M2-9 (including the sample) post the effects to the appropriate T-accounts and determine ending account balances.

Cash (A)	Supplies (A)	Equipment (A)

Accounts Payable (L)	Notes Payable (L)	Contributed Capital (SE)

LO 2-4 **M2-12 Reporting a Classified Balance Sheet**

Given the transactions in M2-9 (including the sample), prepare a classified balance sheet for Spotlighter, Inc., as of January 31, 2013.

LO 2-3 **M2-13 Identifying Transactions and Preparing Journal Entries**

J.K. Builders was incorporated on July 1, 2013. Prepare journal entries for the following events from the first month of business. If the event is not a transaction, write "no transaction."

a. Received $70,000 cash invested by owners and issued stock.
b. Bought an unused field from a local farmer by paying $60,000 cash. As a construction site for smaller projects, it is estimated to be worth $65,000 to J.K. Builders.
c. A lumber supplier delivered lumber supplies to J.K. Builders for future use. The lumber supplies would have normally sold for $10,000, but the supplier gave J.K. Builders a 10 percent discount. J.K. Builders has not yet received a bill from the supplier.
d. Borrowed $25,000 from the bank with a plan to use the funds to build a small workshop in August. The loan must be repaid in two years.
e. One of the owners sold $10,000 worth of his stock to another shareholder for $11,000.

LO 2-3 **M2-14 Determining Financial Statement Effects of Transactions**

Analyze the accounting equation effects of the transactions in M2-13 using the format shown in the chapter, and compute total assets, total liabilities, and total stockholders' equity.

LO 2-3 **M2-15 Identifying Transactions and Preparing Journal Entries**

Joel Henry founded Bookmart.com at the beginning of August, which sells new and used books online. He is passionate about books, but does not have a lot of accounting experience. Help Joel by preparing journal entries for the following events. If the event is not a transaction, write "no transaction."

a. The company purchased equipment for $4,000 cash. The equipment is expected to be used for 10 or more years.
b. Joel's business bought $7,000 worth of books from a publisher. The company will pay the publisher within 45–60 days.
c. Joel's friend Sam lent $4,000 to the business. Sam had Joel write a note promising that bookmart.com would repay the $4,000 in four months. Because they are good friends, Sam is not going to charge Joel interest.
d. The company paid $1,500 cash for books purchased on account earlier in the month.
e. Bookmart.com repaid the $4,000 loan established in (c).

LO 2-3 **M2-16 Determining Financial Statement Effects of Transactions**

Analyze the accounting equation effects of the transactions in M2-15 using the format shown in the chapter, and compute total assets, total liabilities, and total stockholders' equity.

LO 2-3 **M2-17 Identifying Transactions and Preparing Journal Entries**

Sweet Shop Co. is a chain of candy stores that has been in operation for the past ten years. Prepare journal entries for the following events, which occurred at the end of the most recent year. If the event is not a transaction, write "no transaction."

a. Ordered and received $12,000 worth of cotton candy machines from Candy Makers Inc., which Sweet Shop Co. will pay for in 45 days.
b. Sent a check for $6,000 to Candy Makers Inc., for the cotton candy machines from (a).
c. Received $400 from customers who bought candy on account in previous months.
d. To help raise funds for store upgrades estimated to cost $20,000, Sweet Shop Co. issued 1,000 shares for $15 each to existing stockholders.
e. Sweet Shop Co. bought ice cream trucks for $60,000 total, paying $10,000 cash and signing a long-term note for $50,000.

LO 2-3 **M2-18 Determining Financial Statement Effects of Transactions**

Analyze the accounting equation effects of the transactions in M2-17 using the format shown in the chapter, and compute total assets, total liabilities, and total stockholders' equity.

LO 2-3 **M2-19 Identifying Transactions and Preparing Journal Entries**

Katy Williams is the manager of Blue Light Arcade. The company provides entertainment for parties and special events. Prepare journal entries for the following events relating to the year ended December 31. If the event is not a transaction, write "no transaction."

a. Blue Light Arcade received $50 cash on account for a birthday party held two months ago.
b. Agreed to hire a new employee at a monthly salary of $3,000. The employee starts work next month.
c. Paid $2,000 for a table top hockey game purchased last month on account.
d. Repaid a $5,000 bank loan that had been outstanding for six months. (Ignore interest.)
e. The company purchased an air hockey table for $2,200, paying $1,000 cash and signing a short-term note for $1,200.

M2-20 Determining Financial Statement Effects of Transactions

LO 2-3

Analyze the accounting equation effects of the transactions in M2-19 using the format shown in the chapter, and compute total assets, total liabilities, and total stockholders' equity.

M2-21 Ordering Current Assets and Current Liabilities within a Classified Balance Sheet

LO 2-4

Charlie's Crispy Chicken (CCC) operates a fast-food restaurant. When accounting for its first year of business, CCC created several accounts. Using the following descriptions, prepare a classified balance sheet at September 30, 2013. Are CCC's current assets sufficient to be converted into cash to cover its current liabilities? How can you tell?

Account Name	Balance	Description
Accounts Payable	$ 2,000	Payment is due in 30 days
Cash	1,800	Includes cash in register and in bank account
Contributed Capital	30,000	Stock issued in exchange for owners' contributions
Food Ingredients	400	Includes frozen chicken, french fries, beverages, etc.
Kitchen Equipment	13,000	Includes deep fryers, microwaves, dishwasher, etc.
Land	18,900	Held for future site of new restaurant
Note Payable	25,000	Payment is due in 2019
Restaurant Booths	25,000	Likely to be used through 2023
Retained Earnings	3,000	Total earnings through September 30, 2013
Supplies	1,400	Includes serving trays, condiment dispensers, etc.
Utilities Payable	300	Payment is due in 30–45 days
Wages Payable	200	Payment is due in 7 days

M2-22 Preparing a Classified Balance Sheet

LO 2-4, 2-5

The following accounts are taken from the financial statements of Trump Entertainment Resorts, Inc., at its December 31, 2010, year-end. (Amounts are in thousands.)

TRUMP
ENTERTAINMENT RESORTS
MARINA   PLAZA   TAJ MAHAL

Operating Expenses	$ 117,995
Salaries Payable	24,338
Interest Expense	21,078
Accounts Payable	40,862
Other Current Liabilities	74,248
Food and Beverage Revenue	46,775
Cash	85,585
Accounts Receivable	26,094
Other Current Assets	129,343
Equipment	463,988
Long-term Note Payable	366,752
Contributed Capital	11
Retained Earnings	198,799

Required:

1. Prepare a classified balance sheet at December 31, 2010
   TIP: This exercise requires you to remember material from Chapter 1. (Some of the above accounts are not reported on the balance sheet.)

2. Using the balance sheet, indicate whether the total assets of Trump Entertainment Resorts, Inc., at the end of the year were financed primarily by liabilities or stockholders' equity.

3. Were the current assets sufficient to cover the current liabilities at December 31, 2010? How can you tell?

LO 2-5

M2-23 Calculating and Interpreting the Current Ratio

The balance sheet of Mister Ribs Restaurant reports current assets of $30,000 and current liabilities of $15,000. Calculate and interpret the current ratio. Does it appear likely that Mister Ribs will be able to pay its current liabilities as they come due in the next year?

LO 2-5

M2-24 Evaluating the Impact of Transactions on the Current Ratio

Refer to M2-23. Evaluate whether the current ratio of Mister Ribs Restaurant will increase or decrease as a result of the following transactions.

a. Paid $2,000 cash for a new oven.
b. Received a $2,000 cash contribution from the company's main stockholder.
c. Borrowed $5,000 cash from a bank, issuing a note that must be repaid in three years.
d. Purchased $500 of napkins, paper cups, and other disposable supplies on account.

LO 2-5

M2-25 Analyzing the Impact of Transactions on the Current Ratio

BSO, Inc., has current assets of $1,000,000 and current liabilities of $500,000, resulting in a current ratio of 2.0. For each of the following transactions, determine whether the current ratio will increase, decrease, or remain the same.

a. Purchased $20,000 of supplies on credit.
b. Paid Accounts Payable in the amount of $50,000.
c. Recorded $100,000 of cash contributed by a stockholder.
d. Borrowed $250,000 from a local bank, to be repaid in 90 days.

EXERCISES

LO 2-1, 2-2, 2-3, 2-5

E2-1 Matching Terms with Definitions

Match each term with its related definition by entering the appropriate letter in the space provided. There should be only one definition per term (that is, there are more definitions than terms).

Term	Definition
_____ 1. Transaction	A. Economic resources to be used or turned into cash within one year.
_____ 2. Separate Entity Assumption	
_____ 3. Balance Sheet	B. Reports assets, liabilities, and stockholders' equity.
_____ 4. Liabilities	C. Decrease assets; increase liabilities and stockholders' equity.
_____ 5. Assets = Liabilities + Stockholders' Equity	D. Increase assets; decrease liabilities and stockholders' equity.
_____ 6. Current Assets	E. An exchange or event that has a direct and measurable financial effect.
_____ 7. Notes Payable	F. Accounts for a business separate from its owners.
_____ 8. Duality of Effects	G. The principle that assets should be recorded at their original cost to the company.
_____ 9. Retained Earnings	H. A standardized format used to accumulate data about each item reported on financial statements.
_____ 10. Debit	I. The basic accounting equation.
	J. The two equalities in accounting that aid in providing accuracy.
	K. The account credited when money is borrowed from a bank using a promissory note.
	L. Cumulative earnings of a company that are not distributed to the owners.
	M. Every transaction has at least two effects.
	N. Amounts presently owed by the business.

E2-2 Identifying Account Titles

The following are independent situations.

a. A company orders and receives 10 personal computers for office use for which it signs a note promising to pay $25,000 within three months.

b. A company purchases for $21,000 cash a new delivery truck that has a list ("sticker") price of $24,000.

c. A women's clothing retailer orders 30 new display stands for $300 each for future delivery.

d. A new company is formed and issues 100 shares of stock for $12 per share to investors.

e. A company purchases a piece of land for $50,000 cash. An appraiser for the buyer valued the land at $52,500.

f. The owner of a local company uses a personal check to buy a $10,000 car for personal use. Answer from the company's point of view.

g. A company borrows $2,000 from a local bank and signs a six-month note for the loan.

h. A company pays $1,500 owed on its ten-year note payable (ignore interest).

Required:

1. Indicate titles of the appropriate accounts, if any, affected in each of the preceding events. Consider what the company gives and receives.

2. At what amount would you record the delivery truck in b? The piece of land in e? What measurement principle are you applying?

3. What reasoning did you apply in c? For f, what accounting concept did you apply?

E2-3 Classifying Accounts and Their Usual Balances

As described in a recent annual report, Digital Diversions, Inc , (DDI) designs, develops, and distributes videogames for computers and advanced game systems. DDI has been operating for only one full year.

Required:

For each of the following accounts from DDI's recent balance sheet, complete the following table. Indicate whether the account is classified as a current asset (CA), noncurrent asset (NCA), current liability (CL), noncurrent liability (NCL), or stockholders' equity (SE), and whether the account usually has a debit (dr) or credit (cr) balance.

Account	Balance Sheet Classification	Debit or Credit Balance
1. Land		
2. Retained Earnings		
3. Notes Payable (due in three years)		
4. Accounts Receivable		
5. Supplies		
6. Contributed Capital		
7. Equipment		
8. Accounts Payable		
9. Cash		
10. Income Taxes Payable		

E2-4 Determining Financial Statement Effects of Several Transactions

The following events occurred for Favata Company:

a. Received $10,000 cash from owners and issued stock to them.

b. Borrowed $7,000 cash from a bank and signed a note due later this year.

c. Bought and received $800 of equipment on account.

d. Purchased land for $12,000; paid $1,000 in cash and signed a long-term note for $11,000.

e. Purchased $3,000 of equipment, paid $1,000 in cash and charged the rest on account.

Required:

For each of the events (a) through (e), perform transaction analysis and indicate the account, amount, and direction of the effect (+ for increase and − for decrease) on the accounting equation.

Check that the accounting equation remains in balance after each transaction. Use the following headings:

Event	Assets	=	Liabilities	+	Stockholders' Equity

LO 2-1, 2-2, 2-5

E2-5 Determining Financial Statement Effects of Several Transactions

NIKE, Inc.

NIKE, Inc., with headquarters in Beaverton, Oregon, is one of the world's leading manufacturers of athletic shoes and sports apparel. The following activities occurred during a recent year. The amounts are presented in millions of dollars.

a. Purchased $216 in equipment; paid by signing a $5 long-term note and fulfilling the rest with cash.
b. Issued $21 in additional stock for cash contributions made by stockholders.
c. Several NIKE investors sold their own stock to other investors on the stock exchange for $110 per share of stock.

Required:

1. For each of these events, perform transaction analysis and indicate the account, amount (in millions), and direction of the effect on the accounting equation. Check that the accounting equation remains in balance after each transaction. Use the following headings:

Event	Assets	=	Liabilities	+	Stockholders' Equity

2. Explain your response to transaction (c).
3. Did these transactions change the extent to which NIKE relied on creditors versus stockholders for financing? Explain.

LO 2-3

E2-6 Recording Journal Entries

Refer to E2-4.

Required:

For each of the events in E2-4, prepare journal entries, checking that debits equal credits.

LO 2-3, 2-5

E2-7 Recording Journal Entries

Refer to E2-5.

Required:

1. For each of the events in E2-5, prepare journal entries, checking that debits equal credits.
2. Explain your response to event (c).

LO 2-2, 2-3, 2-5

E2-8 Analyzing the Effects of Transactions in T-Accounts

Mulkeen Service Company, Inc., was incorporated by Conor Mulkeen and five other managers. The following activities occurred during the year:

a. Received $60,000 cash from the managers; each was issued 1,000 shares of stock.
b. Purchased equipment for use in the business at a cost of $12,000; one-fourth was paid in cash and the company signed a note for the balance (due in six months).
c. Signed an agreement with a cleaning service to pay it $120 per week for cleaning the corporate offices, beginning next year.
d. Conor Mulkeen borrowed $10,000 for personal use from a local bank, signing a one-year note.

Required:

1. Create T-accounts for the following accounts: Cash, Equipment, Note Payable, and Contributed Capital. Beginning balances are zero. For each of the above transactions, record its effects in the appropriate T-accounts. Include referencing and totals for each T-account.
2. Using the balances in the T-accounts, fill in the following amounts for the accounting equation:

Assets $_____ = Liabilities $_____ + Stockholders' Equity $_____

3. Explain your response to events (c) and (d).

E2-9 Inferring Investing and Financing Transactions and Preparing a Balance Sheet   LO 2-1, 2-2, 2-4

Home Comfort Furniture Company completed four transactions with the dollar effects indicated in the following schedule:

	Assets		=	Liabilities	+	Stockholders' Equity
	Cash	Equipment		Notes Payable		Contributed Capital
Beginning	$ 0	$ 0	=	$ 0		$ 0
(1)	+12,000		=			+12,000
(2)	+50,000		=	+50,000		
(3)	−4,000	+12,000	=	+8,000		
(4)	+4,000		=	+4,000		
Ending	$____	$____	=	$____		$____

Required:

1. Write a brief explanation of transactions 1 through 4. Explain any assumptions that you made.
2. Compute the ending balance in each account.
3. Has most of the financing for Home Comfort's investments in assets come from liabilities or stockholders' equity?

E2-10 Analyzing Accounting Equation Effects, Recording Journal Entries, and Summarizing Financial Statement Impact   LO 2-2, 2-3, 2-4

Rawlco Communications operates 15 radio stations throughout the West. The following events are representative of those occurring during September 2012.

a. Placed an order for office supplies costing $2,000. Supplier intends to deliver later in the month.
b. Purchased equipment that cost $30,000; paid $10,000 cash and signed a promissory note to pay $20,000 in one month.
c. Negotiated and signed a one-year bank loan, and then deposited $5,000 cash in the company's checking account.
d. Hired a new finance manager on the last day of the month.
e. Received an investment of $10,000 cash from the company's owners, in exchange for issuing shares.
f. Supplies (ordered in a) were received, along with a bill for $2,000.

Required:

1. Indicate the specific account, amount, and direction of effects for each transaction on the radio station's accounting equation. If an event is not considered a transaction, explain why.
2. Prepare journal entries to record each transaction.
3. Rawlco began the month with $220,000 in total assets. What total assets would be reported on the balance sheet after events a–f?

E2-11 Recording Journal Entries and Preparing a Classified Balance Sheet   LO 2-1, 2-3, 2-5

Assume Down.com was organized on May 1, 2013 to compete with Despair.com—a company that sells de-motivational posters and office products. The following events occurred during the first month of Down.com's operations.

:-(®

a. Received $60,000 cash from the investors who organized Down.com Corporation.
b. Borrowed $20,000 cash and signed a note due in two years.
c. Ordered equipment costing $16,000.
d. Purchased $9,000 in equipment, paying $2,000 in cash and signing a six-month note for the balance.
e. Received the equipment ordered in (c), paid for half of it, and put the rest on account.

Required:

1. Summarize the financial effects of items (*a*)–(*e*) in a table or spreadsheet similar to Exhibit 2.5.
2. Prepare journal entries for each transaction. Be sure to use referencing and categorize each account as an asset (A), liability (L), or stockholders' equity (SE). If a transaction does not require a journal entry, explain the reason.
3. Prepare a classified balance sheet at May 31, 2013. Include Retained Earnings with a balance of zero.

LO 2-2, 2-3, 2-4   **E2-12 Analyzing the Effects of Transactions Using T-Accounts; Preparing and Interpreting a Balance Sheet**

Laser Delivery Services, Inc., (LDS) was incorporated in 2013. The following transactions occurred during the year:

a. Received $40,000 cash from organizers in exchange for stock in the new company.
b. Purchased land for $12,000, signing a two-year note (ignore interest).
c. Bought two used delivery trucks at the start of the year at a cost of $10,000 each; paid $2,000 cash and signed a note due in three years for $18,000 (ignore interest).
d. Paid $2,000 cash to a truck repair shop for a new motor, which increased the cost of one of the trucks.
e. Stockholder Jonah Lee paid $300,000 cash for a house for his personal use.

Required:

1. Analyze each item for its effects on the accounting equation of LDS, for the year ended December 31, 2013.
   TIP: Transaction (*a*) is presented below as an example.

	Assets	=	Liabilities	+	Stockholders' Equity	
(a) Cash	+40,000	=			Contributed Capital	+40,000

   TIP: The new motor in transaction (*d*) is treated as an increase to the cost of the truck.
2. Record the effects of each item using a journal entry.
   TIP: Use the simplified journal entry format shown in the demonstration case on page 68.
3. Summarize the effects of the journal entries by account, using the T-account format shown in the chapter.
4. Prepare a classified balance sheet for LDS at the end of 2013.
5. Using the balance sheet, indicate whether LDS's assets at the end of the year were financed primarily by liabilities or stockholders' equity.

LO 2-1, 2-2, 2-3   **E2-13 Explaining the Effects of Transactions on Balance Sheet Accounts Using T-Accounts**

Heavey and Lovas Furniture Repair Service, a company with two stockholders, began operations on June 1, 2013. The following T-accounts indicate the activities for the month of June.

	Cash (A)		
(*a*)	17,000	10,000	(*b*)
		1,500	(*c*)

	Supplies (A)	
(*c*)	1,500	

	Building (A)	
(*b*)	50,000	

Notes Payable (L)		
	40,000	(*b*)

Contributed Capital (SE)		
	17,000	(*a*)

Required:

For each of the events (*a*)–(*c*), explain what transaction resulted in the indicated increases and/or decreases in the T-accounts.

LO 2-1, 2-5   **E2-14 Calculating and Evaluating the Current Ratio**

Volcom, Inc., is a clothing designer, marketer, and distributor, known widely for its motto of "youth against establishment." The company reported the following in recent balance sheets (amounts in thousands).

	March 31, 2011	December 31, 2010
Assets		
Current Assets:		
Cash	$ 81,453	$ 80,300
Accounts Receivable	73,165	66,542
Inventories	29,971	41,449
Other Current Assets	26,211	26,480
Total Current Assets	210,800	214,771
Property, Equipment, and Other Long-term Assets	44,484	42,788
Total Assets	$255,284	$257,559
Liabilities and Stockholders' Equity		
Current Liabilities:		
Accounts Payable	$ 15,217	$ 22,902
Other Current Liabilities	13,630	16,181
Income Taxes Payable	94	131
Total Current Liabilities	28,941	39,214
Long-term Liabilities	1,380	1,387
Stockholders' Equity	224,963	216,958
Total Liabilities and Stockholders' Equity	$ 255,284	$ 257,559

Required:

1. Calculate the current ratio at March 31, 2011 and December 31, 2010.

2. Did the company's current ratio increase or decrease? What does this imply about the company's ability to pay its current liabilities as they come due?

3. What would Volcom's current ratio have been if, on March 31, 2011, the company were to have paid down $10,000 of its Accounts Payable? Does paying down Accounts Payable in this case increase or decrease the current ratio?

4. Are the company's total assets financed primarily by liabilities or stockholders' equity at March 31, 2011?

E2-15 Analyzing and Recording Transactions, and Preparing and Evaluating a Balance Sheet

LO 2-2, 2-3, 2-4, 2-5

Business Sim Corp. (BSC) issued 1,000 shares to Kelly in exchange for $12,000. BSC borrowed $30,000 from the bank, promising to repay it in two years. BSC paid $35,000 for computer equipment with check number 101 and signed a note for $5,000 due in six months. BSC received $900 of supplies purchased on account. BSC's loan contains a clause ("covenant") that requires BSC to maintain a ratio of current assets to current liabilities of at least 1.3.

Required:

1. Identify the transactions and analyze their accounting equation effects, using the format shown in the chapter.

2. Prepare journal entries for the transactions described above, and post them to T-accounts.

3. Assuming BSC entered into no other activities during its first year ended September 30, 2013, prepare the company's classified balance sheet. Include a balance of zero in Retained Earnings.

4. Determine and explain whether BSC is complying with or violating its loan covenant.

COACHED PROBLEMS

CP2-1 Determining Financial Statement Effects of Various Transactions

LO 2-2, 2-5

Ag Bio Tech (ABT) was organized on January 1, 2013, by four friends. Each organizer invested $10,000 in the company and, in turn, was issued 8,000 shares of common stock. To date, they are the only stockholders. During the first month (January 2013), the company had the following five events:

a. Collected a total of $40,000 from the organizers and, in turn, issued the shares of stock.
b. Purchased a building for $65,000, equipment for $16,000, and three acres of land for $18,000; paid $13,000 in cash and signed a note for the balance, which is due to be paid in 15 years.
c. One stockholder reported to the company that 500 shares of his ABT stock had been sold and transferred to another stockholder for $5,000 cash.
d. Purchased supplies for $3,000 cash.
e. Sold one acre of land for $6,000 cash to another company.

Required:

1. Was ABT organized as a partnership or corporation? Explain the basis for your answer.
2. During the first month, the records of the company were inadequate. You were asked to prepare a summary of the preceding transactions. To develop a quick assessment of their economic effects on ABT, you have decided to complete the spreadsheet that follows and to use plus (+) for increases and minus (−) for decreases for each account.
   TIP: Transaction (a) is presented below as an example.

	Assets					=	Liabilities	+	Stockholders' Equity	
	Cash	Supplies	Land	Building	Equipment =		Notes Payable		Contributed Capital	Retained Earnings
(a)	+40,000								+40,000	

3. Did you include the transaction between the two stockholders—event (c)—in the spreadsheet? Why?
   TIP: Think about whether this event caused ABT to receive or give up anything.
4. Based only on the completed spreadsheet, provide the following amounts (show computations):
   a. Total assets at the end of the month.
   b. Total liabilities at the end of the month.
   c. Total stockholders' equity at the end of the month.
   d. Cash balance at the end of the month.
   e. Total current assets at the end of the month.
5. As of January 31, 2013, has the financing for ABT's investment in assets primarily come from liabilities or stockholders' equity?

LO 2-2, 2-3, 2-4, 2-5 **CP2-2 Recording Transactions (in a Journal and T-Accounts); Preparing and Interpreting the Balance Sheet**

Athletic Performance Company (APC) was incorporated as a private company on June 1, 2013. The company's accounts included the following at July 1, 2013:

Accounts Payable	$ 4,000	Land	$90,000
Building	200,000	Notes Payable	17,000
Cash	16,000	Retained Earnings	0
Contributed Capital	308,000	Supplies	5,000
Equipment	18,000		

During the month of July, the company had the following activities:

a. Issued 2,000 shares of stock for $200,000 cash.
b. Borrowed $30,000 cash from a local bank, payable June 30, 2015.
c. Bought a building for $141,000; paid $41,000 in cash and signed a three-year note for the balance.
d. Paid cash for equipment that cost $100,000.
e. Purchased supplies for $10,000 on account.

Required:

1. Analyze transactions (a)–(e) to determine their effects on the accounting equation. Use a spreadsheet format with a column for each account, enter the July 1, 2013, amounts in the first line under the account headings, and calculate ending balances.

TIP: You won't need new accounts to record the transactions described above, so have a quick look at the ones listed before you begin.

TIP: In transaction (c), three different accounts are affected.

2. Record the transaction effects determined in requirement 1 using journal entries.

3. Summarize the journal entry effects from requirement 2 using T-accounts.

   TIP: Create a T-account for each account listed above. Enter the July 1, 2013, balances as the month's beginning balances.

4. Prepare a classified balance sheet at July 31, 2013.

5. As of July 31, 2013, has the financing for APC's investment in assets primarily come from liabilities or stockholders' equity?

CP2-3 Recording Transactions (in a Journal and T-Accounts); Preparing and Interpreting the Balance Sheet   **LO 2-2, 2-3, 2-4, 2-5**

Performance Plastics Company (PPC) has been operating for three years. The December 31, 2013, account balances are:

Cash	$ 35,000	Buildings	$120,000
Accounts Receivable	5,000	Land	30,000
Inventory	40,000	Accounts Payable	37,000
Supplies	5,000	Notes Payable (due 2017)	80,000
Notes Receivable (due 2016)	2,000	Contributed Capital	150,000
Equipment	80,000	Retained Earnings	50,000

During the year 2014, the company had the following summarized activities:

a. Purchased equipment that cost $21,000; paid $5,000 cash and signed a two-year note for the balance.

b. Issued an additional 2,000 shares of stock for $20,000 cash.

c. Borrowed $50,000 cash from a local bank, payable June 30, 2016.

d. Purchased supplies for $4,000 cash.

e. Built an addition to the factory buildings for $41,000; paid $12,000 in cash and signed a three-year note for the balance.

f. Hired a new president to start January 1, 2015. The contract was for $95,000 for each full year worked.

Required:

1. Analyze transactions (a)–(f) to determine their effects on the accounting equation.

   TIP: You won't need new accounts to record the transactions described above, so have a quick look at the ones listed in the beginning of this question before you begin.

   TIP: In transaction (e), three different accounts are affected.

   TIP: In transaction (f), consider whether PPC owes anything to its new president for the year ended December 31, 2014.

2. Record the transaction effects determined in requirement 1 using journal entries.

3. Summarize the journal entry effects from requirement 2 using T-accounts.

   TIP: Create a T-account for each account listed above. Enter the December 31, 2013, balances as the 2014 beginning balances.

4. Explain your response to event (f).

5. Prepare a classified balance sheet at December 31, 2014.

6. As of December 31, 2014, has the financing for PPC's investment in assets primarily come from liabilities or stockholders' equity?

GROUP A PROBLEMS

PA2-1 Determining Financial Statement Effects of Various Transactions   **LO 2-2, 2-5**

Mallard Incorporated (MI) is a small manufacturing company that makes model trains to sell to toy stores. It has a small service department that repairs customers' trains for a fee. The company has been in business for five years. At the end of the most recent year, 2012, the accounting records reflected total assets of $500,000 and total liabilities of $200,000. During the current year, 2013, the following summarized events occurred:

a.   Issued additional shares of stock for $100,000 cash.
b.   Borrowed $120,000 cash from the bank and signed a 10-year note.
c.   Built an addition on the buildings for $200,000 and paid cash to the contractor.
d.   Purchased equipment for the new addition for $30,000, paying $3,000 in cash and signing a note due in six months for the balance.
e.   Returned a $3,000 piece of equipment, from (d), because it proved to be defective; received a reduction of the note payable.
f.   Purchased a delivery truck (equipment) for $10,000; paid $7,000 cash and signed a nine-month note for the remainder.
g.   A stockholder sold $5,000 of his stock in Mallard Incorporated to his neighbor.

Required:

1.   Complete the spreadsheet that follows, using plus (+) for increases and minus (−) for decreases for each account. The first transaction is used as an example.

	Assets			=	Liabilities	+	Stockholders' Equity	
							Contributed	Retained
	Cash	Equipment	Buildings	=	Notes Payable		Capital	Earnings
(a)	+100,000						+100,000	

2.   Did you include event (g) in the spreadsheet? Why or why not?
3.   Based on beginning balances plus the completed spreadsheet, provide the following amounts (show computations):
   a.   Total assets at the end of the year.
   b.   Total liabilities at the end of the year.
   c.   Total stockholders' equity at the end of the year.
4.   As of December 31, 2013, has the financing for MI's investment in assets primarily come from liabilities or stockholders' equity?

LO 2-2, 2-3, 2-4, 2-5   **PA2-2 Recording Transactions (in a Journal and T-Accounts); Preparing and Interpreting the Balance Sheet**

Deliberate Speed Corporation (DSC) was incorporated as a private company on June 1, 2013. The company's accounts included the following at June 30, 2013:

Accounts Payable	$ 20,000	Land	$200,000
Buildings	100,000	Notes Payable (long-term)	2,000
Cash	36,000	Retained Earnings	259,000
Contributed Capital	180,000	Supplies	7,000
Equipment	118,000		

During the month of July, the company had the following activities:

a.   Issued 4,000 shares of stock for $400,000 cash.
b.   Borrowed $100,000 cash from a local bank, payable June 30, 2015.
c.   Bought a building for $182,000; paid $82,000 in cash and signed a three-year note for the balance.
d.   Paid cash for equipment that cost $200,000.
e.   Purchased supplies for $30,000 on account.

Required:

1.   Analyze transactions (a)–(e) to determine their effects on the accounting equation.
2.   Record the transaction effects determined in requirement 1 using a journal entry format.
3.   Summarize the journal entry effects from requirement 2 using T-accounts.
4.   Prepare a classified balance sheet at July 31, 2013.
5.   As of July 31, 2013, has the financing for DSC's investment in assets primarily come from liabilities or stockholders' equity?

PA2-3 Recording Transactions (in a Journal and T-Accounts); Preparing and Interpreting the Balance Sheet

LO 2-2, 2-3, 2-4, 2-5

ETHAN
ALLEN

Ethan Allen Interiors, Inc., is a leading manufacturer and retailer of home furnishings in 291 retail stores in the United States and abroad. The following is adapted from Ethan Allen's balance sheet as of March 31, 2011. Dollars are in millions.

Cash	$ 71	Accounts Payable	$ 23
Accounts Receivable	20	Wages Payable	114
Inventories	135	Long-term Debt	173
Other Current Assets	30	Other Noncurrent Liabilities	31
Property, Plant, and Equipment	295	Contributed Capital	236
Other Noncurrent Assets	66	Retained Earnings	40

Assume that the following events occurred in the quarter ended June 30. Dollars are in millions.

a. Paid $2 cash for an additional "other asset."
b. Issued additional shares of stock for $2 in cash.
c. Purchased property, plant, and equipment; paid $2 in cash and signed a note to pay the remaining $9 in two years.
d. Sold, at cost, other assets for $1 cash.
e. Conducted negotiations to purchase a sawmill, which is expected to cost $36.

Required:

1. Analyze transactions (a)–(e) to determine their effects on the accounting equation. Use the format shown in the demonstration case on page 68.
2. Record the transaction effects determined in requirement 1 using journal entries.
3. Summarize the journal entry effects from requirement 2 using T-accounts. Use the March 2011 ending balances as the beginning balances for the April–June 2011 quarter.
4. Explain your response to event (e).
5. Prepare a classified balance sheet at June 30, 2011.
6. As of June 30, 2011, has the financing for Ethan Allen's investment in assets primarily come from liabilities or stockholders' equity?

GROUP B PROBLEMS

PB2-1 Determining Financial Statement Effects of Various Transactions

LO 2-2, 2-5

Swish Watch Corporation manufactures, sells, and services expensive, ugly watches. The company has been in business for three years. At the end of the most recent year, 2012, the accounting records reported total assets of $2,255,000 and total liabilities of $1,780,000. During the current year, 2013, the following summarized events occurred:

a. Issued additional shares of stock for $109,000 cash.
b. Borrowed $186,000 cash from the bank and signed a 10-year note.
c. A stockholder sold $5,000 of his stock in Swish Watch Corporation to another investor.
d. Built an addition on the factory buildings for $200,000 and paid cash to the contractor.
e. Purchased equipment for the new addition for $44,000, paying $12,000 in cash and signing a six-month note for the balance.
f. Returned a $4,000 piece of equipment, from (e), because it proved to be defective; received a cash refund.

Required:

1. Complete the spreadsheet that follows, using plus (+) for increases and minus (−) for decreases for each account. The first transaction is used as an example.

	Assets			=	Liabilities	+	Stockholders' Equity	
	Cash	Equipment	Buildings	=	Notes Payable		Contributed Capital	Retained Earnings
(a)	+109,000						+109,000	

2. Did you include event (c) in the spreadsheet? Why?

3. Based on beginning balances plus the completed spreadsheet, provide the following amounts (show computations):

   a. Total assets at the end of the year.
   b. Total liabilities at the end of the year.
   c. Total stockholders' equity at the end of the year.

4. As of December 31, 2013, has the financing for Swish Watch Corporation's investment in assets primarily come from liabilities or stockholders' equity?

LO 2-2, 2-3, 2-4, 2-5   **PB2-2 Recording Transactions (in a Journal and T-Accounts); Preparing and Interpreting the Balance Sheet**

Bearings & Brakes Corporation (B&B) was incorporated as a private company on June 1, 2013. The company's accounts included the following at June 30, 2013:

Accounts Payable	$ 50,000	Land	$444,000
Buildings	500,000	Notes Payable	5,000
Cash	90,000	Retained Earnings	966,000
Contributed Capital	170,000	Supplies	9,000
Equipment	148,000		

During the month of July, the company had the following activities:

a. Issued 6,000 shares of stock for $600,000 cash.
b. Borrowed $60,000 cash from a local bank, payable June 30, 2015.
c. Bought a building for $166,000; paid $66,000 in cash and signed a three-year note for the balance.
d. Paid cash for equipment that cost $90,000.
e. Purchased supplies for $90,000 on account.

Required:

1. Analyze transactions (a)–(e) to determine their effects on the accounting equation. Use the format shown in the demonstration case on page 68.

2. Record the transaction effects determined in requirement 1 using a journal entry format.

3. Summarize the journal entry effects from requirement 2 using T-accounts.

4. Prepare a classified balance sheet at July 31, 2013.

5. As of July 31, 2013, has the financing for B&B's investment in assets primarily come from liabilities or stockholders' equity?

LO 2-2, 2-3, 2-4, 2-5   **PB2-3 Recording Transactions (in a Journal and T-Accounts); Preparing and Interpreting the Balance Sheet**

Starbucks

Starbucks is a coffee company—a big coffee company. During a 10-year period, the number of Starbucks locations grew from 165 to over 8,800 stores in 50 countries. The following is adapted from Starbucks's annual report for the year ended September 30, 2010, and dollars are reported in thousands.

Cash	$ 1,164,000	Accounts Payable	$ 282,600
Accounts Receivable	302,700	Short-term Bank Loans	1,496,500
Inventories	543,300	Long-term Debt	549,400
Other Current Assets	746,400	Other Noncurrent Liabilities	375,100
Property, Plant, and Equipment	2,416,500	Contributed Capital	211,100
Other Noncurrent Assets	1,213,000	Retained Earnings	3,471,200

Assume that the following events occurred in the following quarter, which ended December 31, 2010. Dollars are in thousands.

a. Paid $10,000 cash for additional other long-term assets.
b. Issued additional shares of stock for $5,100 in cash.
c. Purchased property, plant, and equipment; paid $11,200 in cash and signed additional long-term loans for $9,500.
d. Sold, at cost, other long-term assets for $6,000 cash.
e. Conducted negotiations to purchase a coffee farm, which is expected to cost $8,400.

Required:

1. Analyze transactions (*a*)–(*e*) to determine their effects on the accounting equation. Use the format shown in the demonstration case on page 68.

2. Record the transaction effects determined in requirement 1 using journal entries.

3. Summarize the journal entry effects from requirement 2 using T-accounts. Use the September 2010 ending balances (reported above) as the beginning balances for the October–December 2010 quarter.

4. Explain your response to event (*e*).

5. Prepare a classified balance sheet at December 31, 2010.

6. As of December 31, 2010, has the financing for the investment in assets made by Starbucks primarily come from liabilities or stockholders' equity?

SKILLS DEVELOPMENT CASES

S2-1 **Finding and Analyzing Financial Information**

|ACCOUNTING   LO 2-1, 2-4, 2-5

Refer to the financial statements of The Home Depot in Appendix A at the end of this book, or download the annual report from the *Cases* section of the text's Web site at www.mhhe.com/phillips4e.

Required:

1. On what dates did the company's fiscal year end in 2011 and 2010?

Current	Prior
a. January 31, 2011	January 31, 2010
b. January 31, 2011	February 1, 2010
c. January 30, 2011	January 31, 2010
d. January 30, 2011	February 1, 2010

2. Which of the following are the amounts in the company's accounting equation ($A = L + SE$) for the year ended in January 2011?
   a. $40,877 = $21,484 + $19,393
   b. $40,125 = $21,236 + $18,889
   c. $67,997 = $64,659 + $3,338
   d. $25,060 = $10,122 + $14,938

3. What is the company's current ratio at the end of the January 2011 reporting period?
   a. 1.99
   b. 1.64
   c. 0.75
   d. 1.33

4. What does the company's current ratio in requirement 3 indicate?
   a. The company has nearly two dollars of current assets for every dollar of liabilities due in the next year.
   b. The company has less than one dollar of current assets for every dollar of liabilities due in the next year.
   c. The company has between one and two dollars of current assets for every dollar of liabilities due in the next year.
   d. The current ratio does not indicate a company's ability to fulfill liabilities due in the next year.

Lowe's

S2-2 Finding and Analyzing Financial Information

Refer to the financial statements of The Home Depot in Appendix A and Lowe's in Appendix B at the end of this book, or download the annual reports from the *Cases* section of the text's Web site at www.mhhe.com/phillips4e.

Required:

1. Use the company's balance sheet to determine the amounts in the accounting equation (A = L + SE). Is Lowe's or The Home Depot larger in terms of total assets?

2. Does Lowe's have more or less current liabilities than The Home Depot at the end of January 2011? Which company has a larger current ratio?

3. On the balance sheet, Lowe's reports inventories of $8,321,000,000. Does this amount represent the expected selling price? Why or why not?

4. Has financing for Lowe's investment in assets primarily come from liabilities or stockholders' equity at January 28, 2011? Thinking back to Chapter 1, what does this imply about the risk assumed by Lowe's investors, relative to those investing in The Home Depot?

S2-3 Team Research, Financial Analysis, Technology, and Communication: Examining the Balance Sheet

As a team, select an industry to analyze. Using your Web browser, each team member should access the annual report or 10-K for one publicly traded company in the industry, with each member selecting a different company. (See S1-3 in Chapter 1 for a description of possible resources for these tasks.)

Required:

1. On an individual basis, each team member should write a short report that lists the following information.
   a. The date of the balance sheet.
   b. The major noncurrent asset accounts and any significant changes in them.
   c. The major noncurrent liability accounts and any significant changes in them.
   d. Any significant changes in total stockholders' equity.
   e. Whether financing for the investment in assets primarily comes from liabilities or stockholders' equity.

2. Then, as a team, write a short report comparing and contrasting your companies using the above dimensions. Discuss any similarities across the companies that you as a team observe, and provide potential explanations for any differences discovered.

S2-4 Ethical Reasoning, Critical Thinking, and Communication: A Real-Life Fraud

In the world of financial fraud, a "Ponzi scheme" is famous. Here is the story behind how the scam got its name. Charles Ponzi started the Security Exchange Company on December 26, 1919. He thought he had discovered a way to purchase American stamps in a foreign country at significantly lower amounts than they were worth in the United States. He claimed his idea was so successful that anyone who gave money to his company would be repaid their original loan plus 50 percent interest within 90 days. Friends and family quickly offered their money to Ponzi and they were handsomely rewarded, being repaid their original loan and the 50 percent interest within just 45 days. Thanks to an article in *The New York Times*, word spread quickly about Ponzi's business, attracting thousands of people seeking a similar payback. He might have had a successful business had his idea actually worked. The problem, however, was that it didn't. The 50 percent interest paid to early investors did not come from the profits of a successful underlying business idea (which didn't even exist) but instead was obtained fraudulently from funds contributed by later lenders. Eventually, the Ponzi scheme collapsed on August 10, 1920, after an auditor examined his accounting records.

Required:

1. Assume that on December 27, 1919, Ponzi's first three lenders provided his company with $5,000 each. Use the basic accounting equation to show the effects of these transactions on December 27, 1919.

2. If the first two lenders are repaid their original loan amounts plus the 50 percent interest promised to them, how much cash is left in Ponzi's business to repay the third lender? Given what you discovered, how was it possible for Ponzi's company to remain in "business" for over eight months?

3. Who was harmed by Ponzi's scheme?

Epilogue: After taking in nearly $15 million from 40,000 people. Ponzi's company failed with just $1.5 million in total assets. Ponzi spent four years in prison before jumping bail, to become involved in fraudulently selling swampland in Florida. We're not kidding. In December 2008, Bernard Madoff was arrested for using a modern-day Ponzi scheme to defraud investors of $65,000,000,000. On June 29, 2009, he was sentenced to 150 years in prison.

S2-5 Ethical Reasoning, Critical Thinking, and Communication: A Mini-Case

LO 2-1, 2-5

You work as an accountant for a small land development company that desperately needs additional financing to continue in business. The president of your company is meeting with the manager of a local bank at the end of the month to try to obtain this financing. The president has approached you with two ideas to improve the company's reported financial position. First, he claims that because a big part of the company's value comes from its knowledgeable and dedicated employees, you should report their "Intellectual Abilities" as an asset on the balance sheet. Second, he claims that by reporting the company's land on the balance sheet at its cost, rather than the much higher amount that real estate appraisers say it's really worth, the company is understating the true value of its assets.

Required:

1. Thinking back to Chapter 1, why do you think the president is so concerned with the amount of assets reported on the balance sheet?
2. What accounting concept introduced in Chapter 2 relates to the president's first suggestion to report "Intellectual Abilities" as an asset?
3. What accounting concept introduced in Chapter 2 relates to the president's second suggestion to report the land's current value?
4. Who might be hurt by the president's suggestions, if you were to do as he asks? What should you do?

S2-6 Financial Analysis and Critical Thinking: Evaluating the Reliability of a Balance Sheet

LO 2-1, 2-4, 2-5

Complete this case, available online at www.mhhe.com/phillips4e, which involves identifying flaws in a company's balance sheet.

S2-7 Using Technology to Analyze Transactions and Prepare a Balance Sheet

LO 2-2

Complete this case involving Elizabeth Arden, available online at www.mhhe.com/phillips4e. By completing this case, you will learn to use a spreadsheet to capture the accounting equation effects of basic transactions.

Elizabeth Arden, Inc.

CONTINUING CASE

CC2-1 Accounting for the Establishment of a Business

LO 2-1, 2-2, 2-3, 2-4, 2-5

Nicole has decided that she is going to start her business Nicole's Getaway Spa (NGS). A lot has to be done when starting a new business. Here are some transactions that have occurred prior to April 30, 2013.

a. Received $80,000 cash when issuing 8,000 new shares.
b. Purchased some land by paying $2,000 cash and signing a note payable for $7,000 due in 2016.
c. Hired a new aesthetician for a salary of $1,000 a month, starting next month.
d. NGS purchased a company car for $18,000 cash (list price of $21,000) to assist in running errands for the business.
e. Bought and received $1,000 in supplies for the spa on credit.
f. Paid $350 of the amount owed in (e).
g. Nicole sold 100 of her own personal shares to Raea Gooding for $300.

Required:

1. For each of the events, prepare journal entries if a transaction exists, checking that debits equal credits. If a transaction does not exist explain why there is no transaction.
2. Assuming that the beginning balances in each of the accounts are zero, complete T-accounts to summarize the transactions (a)–(g).
3. Prepare a classified balance sheet at April 30, 2013, using the information given in the transactions.
4. Calculate the current ratio at April 30, 2013. What does this ratio indicate about the ability of NGS to pay its current liabilities?

CHAPTER

3

The Income Statement

YOUR LEARNING OBJECTIVES

Understand the business

LO 3-1 Describe common operating transactions and select appropriate income statement account titles.

Study the accounting methods

LO 3-2 Explain and apply the revenue and expense recognition principles.

LO 3-3 Analyze, record, and summarize the effects of operating transactions using the accounting equation, journal entries, and T-accounts.

LO 3-4 Prepare an unadjusted trial balance.

Evaluate the results

LO 3-5 Evaluate net profit margin, but beware of income statement limitations.

Review the chapter

THAT WAS THEN

In the previous chapter, you learned how to analyze, record, and summarize the effects of transactions on balance sheet accounts.

FOCUS COMPANY: Pizza Aroma, Ithaca, NY

I n Chapter 2, Mauricio Rosa, owner-manager of Pizza Aroma, established his new gourmet pizza business. Using money he had contributed plus a loan from the bank, he purchased the ovens, restaurant booths, and other equipment he needed to run the business. His next step is to draw customers into the restaurant and provide them with the service that will keep them coming back. These day-to-day **operating activities will determine whether Pizza Aroma makes a profit.**

The first goal of this chapter is to help you understand common operating activities and see how an income statement indicates whether a business generated a profit (or loss). Then, we'll show how the transaction analysis approach from Chapter 2 can be used to analyze and record transactions affecting the income statement. Finally, at the end of the chapter, we will highlight some uses and limitations of the income statement.

THIS IS NOW

This chapter focuses on analyzing, recording, and summarizing the effects of operating transactions on balance sheet and income statement accounts.

Understand the business	Study the accounting methods	Evaluate the results	Review the chapter
• Operating activities • Income statement accounts	• Cash basis accounting • Accrual basis accounting • The expanded accounting equation • Unadjusted trial balance • Review of revenues and expenses	• Net profit margin • Income statement limitations	• Demonstration cases • Chapter summary • Key terms • Homework helper • Practice material

Understand the Business

OPERATING ACTIVITIES

Learning Objective 3-1
Describe common operating transactions and select appropriate income statement account titles.

Operating activities are the day-to-day functions involved in running a business. Unlike the investing and financing activities in Chapter 2 that occur infrequently and typically produce long-lasting effects, operating activities occur regularly and often have a shorter duration of effect. Operating activities include buying goods and services from suppliers and employees and selling goods and services to customers and then collecting cash from them. The period from buying goods and services through to collecting cash from customers is known as the operating cycle. Exhibit 3.1 illustrates the operating cycle for Pizza Aroma.

EXHIBIT 3.1 | Typical Operating Cycle Activities

4 COLLECT CASH FROM CUSTOMERS.
The business receives $50 cash.
The business gives up right to collect $50.

1 BUY GOODS AND SERVICES.
The business receives $30 of pizza supplies.
The business gives a promise to pay $30.

3 SELL GOODS AND SERVICES.
The business receives right to collect $50.
The business gives pizzas at a price of $50.

2 PAY CASH TO SUPPLIERS.
The business receives release from $30 promise.
The business gives $30 cash.

Although most businesses have the same steps in their operating cycles, the length of time for each step varies from company to company. For example, Pizza Aroma usually collects cash from restaurant customers within minutes of making a sale, whereas the breakfast cereal company Kellogg's might wait several weeks to collect on sales it makes to grocery stores.

To be successful, Mauricio must closely monitor Pizza Aroma's operating activities. **Operating activities are the primary source of revenues and expenses** and, thus, can determine whether a company earns a profit (or incurs a loss). Although Mauricio may intuitively sense how his business is doing, a more reliable management approach is to evaluate the revenues and expenses reported on the income statement. Mauricio takes a quick look at the income statement Laurie had prepared (Exhibit 3.2) based on the operating activities that were expected for Pizza Aroma (in Chapter 1). This projected income statement will provide a benchmark for him to evaluate actual results.

EXHIBIT 3.2	Income Statement		

PIZZA AROMA

		Explanation
PIZZA AROMA, INC. **Income Statement (Projected)** **For the Month Ended September 30, 2013**		Who: Name of the business What: Title of the statement When: Accounting period
Revenues		
Pizza Revenue	$12,000	Revenue from sale/delivery of pizza to customers in September
Total Revenues	12,000	**Total revenues earned during September**
Expenses		
Supplies Expense	5,000	Cost of pizza ingredients used-up in September
Wages Expense	2,000	Cost of employee wages for work done in September
Rent Expense	1,500	Cost of rent for the month of September
Utilities Expense	600	Cost of utilities used in September
Insurance Expense	300	Cost of insurance coverage for September
Advertising Expense	100	Cost of advertising done in September
Income Tax Expense	500	Cost of taxes on September's income
Total Expenses	10,000	**Total expenses incurred in September to generate revenues**
Net Income	$ 2,000	**Difference between total revenues and total expenses**

INCOME STATEMENT ACCOUNTS

The income statement summarizes the financial impact of operating activities undertaken by the company during the accounting period. It includes three main sections: revenues, expenses, and net income.

Revenues

Revenues are the amounts a business charges its customers when it provides goods or services. If Pizza Aroma sells 1,200 pizzas in September and charges $10 per pizza, Pizza Revenue would total $12,000. The amount of revenue earned during the period is the first thing reported in the body of the income statement.

Expenses

Expenses are costs of operating the business, incurred to generate revenues in the period covered by the income statement. Expenses are reported when the company uses something, like space in a building, supplies for providing services, or the efforts of employees. Basically, whenever a business uses up its resources to generate revenues during the period,

> **YOU SHOULD KNOW**
>
> **Revenues:** Amounts earned by selling goods or services to customers.
> **Expenses:** Costs of business necessary to earn revenues.

it reports an expense, regardless of whether or not payment for the resources has occurred. Expenses are reported in the body of the income statement after revenues. Some of Pizza Aroma's typical expenses are listed in the income statement shown in Exhibit 3.2.

Net Income

Net income is a total that is calculated by subtracting expenses from revenues; it is not an account like Pizza Revenue or Wages Expense. Because it is a total, net income summarizes the overall impact of revenues and expenses in a single number. It is called a net loss if expenses are greater than revenues, and net income if revenues are greater than expenses. **Net income indicates the amount by which stockholders' equity increases as a result of a company's profitable operations.** For this reason, net income (or loss) is a closely watched measure of a company's success.

Exhibit 3.2 shows how revenues, expenses, and net income would be reported in Pizza Aroma's income statement. Each account title describes the specific type of revenue or expense arising from the business's particular operations. This is true for all companies. Pizza Aroma reports "Pizza Revenue," but Netflix reports "Movie Subscription Revenue." Google reports "Traffic Acquisition Expenses" and Southwest Airlines reports "Landing Fee Expenses." You'll become more comfortable with various account titles as this course progresses, but to keep things simple right now we'll stick to common types of revenues and expenses.

The income statement in Exhibit 3.2 is for the month ended September 30, 2013. As it turns out, September 30, 2013, is a Monday. There is nothing particularly special about this date—it's just the last day of the month. By dividing the company's long life into meaningful and shorter chunks of time, Mauricio can measure and evaluate Pizza Aroma's financial performance on a timely basis. This is known in accounting as the **time period assumption**. If net income is low in the current month, Mauricio will find out about it quickly and be able to take steps to become more profitable in the following month.

Notice that the income statement reports the financial effects of business activities that occurred during just the current period. They relate only to the current period and do not have a lingering financial impact beyond the end of the current period. This is a key distinction between the income statement and the balance sheet. **The revenues and expenses on an income statement report the financial impact of activities in just the current period whereas items on a balance sheet will continue to have a financial impact beyond the end of the current period. Balance sheet accounts are considered permanent, whereas income statement accounts are considered temporary.** Another way people describe this difference is that **the balance sheet takes stock of what exists at a point in time whereas the income statement depicts a flow of what happened over a period of time.**

How's it going? — Self-Study Practice

For each item listed below, indicate whether the company should report it on the income statement this period (yes/no). If yes, indicate an appropriate account title for the item described.

Description	Yes/No	Account Title
1. Bank of America charges customers a monthly service fee.	_____	_____
2. Target buys a new building to use as a retail store.	_____	_____
3. Dell pays to deliver computers to customers.	_____	_____
4. Pizza Hut buys supplies to be used next month.	_____	_____
5. Abercrombie pays this week's wages to employees.	_____	_____

After you have finished, check your answers with the solution in the margin.

Solution to Self-Study Practice

	Yes/No	Account Title
1.	Yes	Service Fee Revenue
2.	No	(a building is an asset not an expense)
3.	Yes	Delivery Expense
4.	No	(supplies are assets until used up)
5.	Yes	Salaries and Wages Expense

35 Days Hath September?

It seems some managers—specifically those at Computer Associates (CA)—haven't learned the **time period assumption.** CA was charged with financial statement fraud for improperly recording 35 days of sales in September—a month that has only 30 days. To make it look like managers had met their September sales targets, CA included the first five days of sales from October in its September income statement. This accounting fraud led managers to be paid bonuses they hadn't earned and tricked investors into thinking CA was a successful company. When the truth was revealed later, CA's stockholders quickly abandoned the company, causing its stock price to fall 43 percent in a single day. CA ultimately paid stockholders $225 million to make up for its bad accounting and agreed to ensure all inappropriate management bonuses were paid back to the company. In addition, several marketing and accounting personnel were sent to jail. Proper revenue reporting is obviously a very serious matter.

Study the Accounting Methods

CASH BASIS ACCOUNTING

What's a good way to determine whether you're doing well financially? Many people simply look at the balance in their bank accounts to gauge their financial performance. If the over-all balance increased this month, they take that as a sign that they've done a good job of managing their finances. If it has gone down, that's a clue they need to tame their spending next month. The reason that the change in your bank balance tends to give a decent measure of financial performance is that your cash flows (in and out) occur close in time to the activities that cause those cash flows. Reporting your income on this basis, called **cash basis accounting**, is fine for managing personal finances, but not for running a business.

> **YOU SHOULD KNOW**
>
> **Cash basis accounting:** Reports revenues when cash is received and expenses when cash is paid; not allowed under GAAP.

Cash basis accounting doesn't measure financial performance very well when transactions are conducted using credit rather than cash. Credit often introduces a significant delay between the time an activity occurs and the time it impacts a bank account balance. If you are paid for work once a month, for example, the results of your hard work don't show up until the end of the month. Similarly, if you go crazy with your credit card at the mall, these transactions won't affect your bank balance until you pay the bill the following month.

Because most companies use credit for their transactions, cash basis accounting is not likely to correspond to the business activities that actually occur during a given period. Imagine if Pizza Aroma paid its employees to cater a party in one month but didn't receive its customer's payment for these services until the following month. Under cash basis accounting, Pizza Aroma would report expenses in Month 1 but wouldn't report revenue until it received the payment from its customer in Month 2. This leads to a rather distorted view of the company's financial performance, as shown in Exhibit 3.3.

EXHIBIT 3.3	Cash Basis Can Distort Reported Profits

MONTH 1		MONTH 2	
(No cash received, but **cash is paid**)		(No cash paid, but **cash is received**)	
Revenues	$ 0	Revenues	$15,000
Expenses	10,000	Expenses	0
Net Income (Loss)	$ (10,000)	Net Income	$15,000

Under cash basis accounting, the company would report a net loss in Month 1 and a huge net income in Month 2, when the truth is the business activities generate revenue of $15,000, expenses of $10,000, and net income of $5,000, all of which relate to the activities that occurred in Month 1 when the party was catered. A better method of accounting is needed—one that reports the revenues and related expenses during the same period.

ACCRUAL BASIS ACCOUNTING

An alternative method of accounting would be to report revenues and expenses when services are provided, regardless of when cash is received or paid. This approach, called **accrual basis accounting**, produces a better measure of the profits arising from the company's activities. As shown in Exhibit 3.4, accrual accounting would require that Pizza Aroma report all its revenues, expenses, and net income in the period the catering service occurs (Month 1). In the following month, Pizza Aroma doesn't cater any parties, so it does not report revenues and expenses.

EXHIBIT 3.4	Accrual Basis Relates Profit to Underlying Activities

MONTH 1 (No cash received, but **service is provided**)		**MONTH 2** (Cash is received, but **no service is provided**)	
Revenues	$15,000	Revenues	$ 0
Expenses	10,000	Expenses	0
Net Income	$ 5,000	Net Income	$ 0

According to GAAP and IFRS, the accrual basis is the only acceptable method for external reporting of income. The cash basis can be used internally by some small companies, but GAAP and IFRS do not allow it for external reporting. The "rule of accrual" is that the financial effects of business activities are measured and reported when the activities actually occur, not when the cash related to them is received or paid. That is, **revenues are recognized when they are earned and expenses when they are incurred.** The two basic accounting principles that determine when revenues and expenses are recognized under accrual basis accounting are called the revenue recognition and expense recognition principles.

Revenue Recognition Principle

According to the **revenue recognition principle, revenues should be recognized when they are earned.** The word *recognized* means revenues are measured and recorded in the accounting system. The word *earned* means the company has fulfilled its obligation to the customer by doing what it promised to do. For most businesses, these conditions are met at the point of delivery of goods or services.

All companies expect to receive cash in exchange for providing goods and services, but the timing of cash receipts does not dictate when revenues are recognized. Instead, the key factor in determining when to recognize revenue is whether the company has provided goods or services to customers during the accounting period. Regardless of the length of the period (month, quarter, or year), cash can be received (1) in the same period the goods or services are provided, (2) in a period before the goods or services are provided, or (3) in a period after the goods or services are provided, as shown on the timeline in Exhibit 3.5. Let's see how to handle each of these cases.

 1 **Cash is received in the same period the goods or services are provided.** This is a common occurrence for Pizza Aroma. Pizza Aroma earns revenue by delivering pizza to the customer as ordered. Within minutes of delivery, Pizza Aroma receives cash from the customer.

EXHIBIT 3.5   Timing of Reporting Revenue versus Cash Receipts

2 ▷ **Cash is received in a period before goods or services are provided.** This situation occurs when Pizza Aroma receives cash for gift cards that customers can use to pay for pizza in the future. Pizza Aroma will record the cash received, but since it hasn't delivered pizza for these customers, no revenue is recorded yet. Instead, Pizza Aroma has an obligation to accept the gift card as payment for pizza in the future. This obligation is a liability called **Unearned Revenue**, and it is recorded on the balance sheet equal in amount to the cash received for the gift card. Businesses that routinely receive cash before delivering goods or services include airlines, magazine publishers, and insurance companies.

3 ▷ **Cash is to be received in a period after goods or services are provided.** This situation typically arises when a company sells to a customer on account. Selling on account means that the company provides goods or services to a customer not for cash, but instead for the right to collect cash in the future. This right is an asset called Accounts Receivable. Thus, if Pizza Aroma delivers pizza sold on account to a college organization in September, it will report Pizza Revenue on the September income statement. Accounts Receivable will be reported on the balance sheet, until Pizza Aroma receives the customer's payment. When the payment is received, Pizza Aroma will increase its Cash account and decrease its Accounts Receivable account. No additional revenue is reported when the customer's payment is received because the revenue was already recorded when the pizza was delivered.

> **YOU SHOULD KNOW**
> **Unearned Revenue:** A liability representing a company's obligation to provide goods or services to customers in the future.

SPOTLIGHT ON Financial Reporting

Revenue Recognition Policy

Every company reports its revenue recognition policy in its notes to the financial statements. Pizza Aroma follows the same revenue recognition policy as Papa John's which explains its policy as follows.

> **Papa John's International Inc.**
>
> Restaurant sales are recognized as revenues when the products are delivered to or carried out by customers.

PIZZA
PAPA JOHNS®
Better Ingredients.
Better Pizza.

It's worthwhile making sure you understand what sparks the recording of revenues because, in the next section, you'll see that this also triggers the recording of expenses. To ensure that you have a handle on this, spend a minute on the following Self-Study Practice.

💡 How's it going?   Self-Study Practice

The following transactions are typical operating activities for Florida Flippers, a scuba diving and instruction company. Indicate the amount of revenue, if any, that should be recognized in June for each activity.

Operating Activity	Amount of Revenue Earned in June
1. In June, Florida Flippers provided $32,000 in diving instruction to customers for cash.	
2. In June, new customers paid $8,200 cash for diving trips to be provided by Florida Flippers; $5,200 in trips were made in June and the rest will be provided in July.	
3. In June, customers paid $3,900 cash for instruction they received in May.	

After you have finished, check your answers with the solution in the margin.

Expense Recognition Principle ("Matching")

The business activities that generate revenues also create expenses. **Under accrual basis accounting, expenses are recognized in the same period as the revenues to which they relate**, not necessarily the period in which cash is paid for them. For example, for Pizza Aroma to deliver pizza in September, it must rent space in a building and have its employees work that month. Under accrual basis accounting, Pizza Aroma would report rent expense and wages expense in September, even if the rent were paid in August and the wages were paid in October. This is what accountants call the **expense recognition principle (or "matching")**: record expenses in the same period as the revenues with which they can be reasonably associated. If an expense cannot be directly associated with revenues, it is recorded in the period that the underlying business activity occurs. For example, because it's not clear how or when advertising affects revenue, advertising expense is simply reported in the period that ads are run. Notice that it is the timing of the underlying business activities, not the cash payments, that dictates when expenses are recognized. Cash payments may occur (1) at the same time as, (2) before, or (3) after the related expenses are incurred to generate revenue, as shown in Exhibit 3.6.

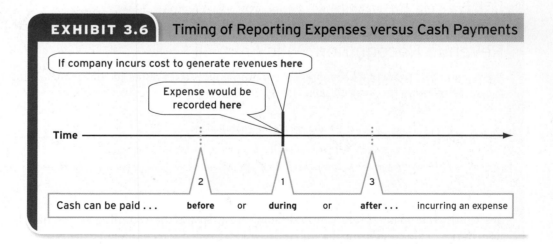

EXHIBIT 3.6   Timing of Reporting Expenses versus Cash Payments

1 ▷ **Cash is paid at the same time that the expense is incurred to generate revenue.** Although this isn't as common in business as in your personal life, expenses are sometimes paid for in the period that they arise. For example, Pizza Aroma could spend $50 cash for balloons to celebrate its grand opening this month. It would report this cost on this month's income statement because the balloons were used for an activity occurring this month. In other words, the benefits of incurring the cost are entirely used up in the current accounting period.

2 ▷ **Cash is paid before the expense is incurred to generate revenue.** It is common for businesses to pay for something that provides benefits only in future periods. For example, Pizza Aroma might buy paper napkins now but not use them until next month. Under the expense recognition principle, the expense from using these supplies (Supplies Expense) is reported next month, when the supplies are used to earn revenue, not in the current month, when the supplies were purchased. This month, the supplies represent an asset (Supplies). Similar situations arise when a company prepays rent or insurance this month and uses up these assets in a later month.

3 ▷ **Cash is paid after the cost is incurred to generate revenue.** Although rent is paid and supplies are purchased before they are used, many costs are paid after receiving and using goods or services. For example, Pizza Aroma uses electricity to heat the ovens and light the restaurant this month but does not pay for its electricity usage until next month. Because the cost of the electricity relates to revenues earned now, it represents an expense that will be reported on this month's income statement. Because the cost has not yet been paid at the end of the month, the balance sheet reports a corresponding liability called Accounts Payable. Similar situations arise when employees work in the current period but are not paid their wages until the following period. This period's wages are reported as Wages Expense on the income statement and any unpaid wages are reported as Wages Payable on the balance sheet.

It's time for you to practice determining which costs should be reported as expenses on an income statement prepared using accrual basis accounting. As you work through the next Self-Study Practice, feel free to glance at Exhibit 3.6 for help.

COACH'S TIP

Promises exchanged for promises are not considered transactions, as you learned in Chapter 2. Here, a service has been received in exchange for a promise (of future payment), so it is considered a transaction.

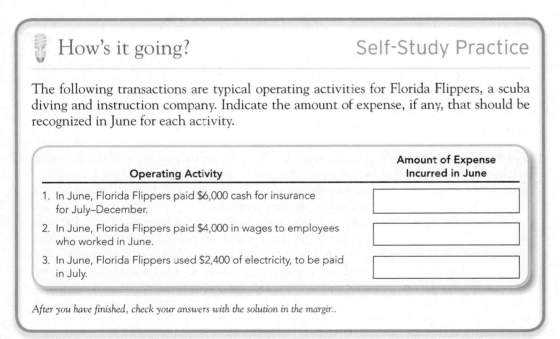

💡 How's it going?   Self-Study Practice

The following transactions are typical operating activities for Florida Flippers, a scuba diving and instruction company. Indicate the amount of expense, if any, that should be recognized in June for each activity.

Operating Activity	Amount of Expense Incurred in June
1. In June, Florida Flippers paid $6,000 cash for insurance for July–December.	
2. In June, Florida Flippers paid $4,000 in wages to employees who worked in June.	
3. In June, Florida Flippers used $2,400 of electricity, to be paid in July.	

After you have finished, check your answers with the solution in the margin.

Solution to Self-Study Practice

1. No expense in June for the $6,000 payment; the $6,000 will be reported as an asset called Prepaid Insurance until used up in July–December.

2. $4,000.

3. $2,400; this cost relates to business activities in June, so the $2,400 is reported as an expense in June (a corresponding liability is reported on the balance sheet).

THE EXPANDED ACCOUNTING EQUATION

When we introduced the basic accounting equation in Chapter 2, we didn't mention how to account for the income statement effects of operating activities. You already had enough to learn, relating to the effects of business activities on assets, liabilities, and contributed capital. The time has now come for you to learn how to analyze, record, and summarize the effects of activities affecting the income statement. To do this, you first need to know how the debit/credit framework works with revenues and expenses.

Let's start with the basic accounting equation from Chapter 2. Assets equal liabilities plus stockholders' equity, or A = L + SE. For now, focus on the stockholders' equity category. As you already know from Chapters 1 and 2, stockholders' equity represents stockholders' claims on the company, which come from either (1) **Contributed Capital**, given to the company by stockholders in exchange for stock, or (2) **Retained Earnings**, generated by the company itself through profitable operations. Retained Earnings is the part that expands to include revenues and expenses, as shown in Exhibit 3.7.

EXHIBIT 3.7   The Expanded Debit/Credit Framework

Take a moment to look at how Exhibit 3.7 encourages you to **think of revenues and expenses as subcategories within retained earnings.** They are shown this way because revenues and expenses eventually flow into Retained Earnings, but they aren't initially recorded there. Instead, each revenue and expense is accumulated in a separate account, making it easier to identify the amount to report for each item on the income statement. At the end of each accounting year, these separate revenue and expense accounts are transferred to (or "closed") into Retained Earnings through a process we'll demonstrate in Chapter 4. For now, just focus on learning how revenues and expenses are recorded to indicate increases and decreases in the company's earnings, with corresponding effects recorded in the company's asset and/or liability accounts.

Because revenue and expense accounts are subcategories of Retained Earnings, they are affected by debits and credits in the same way as all stockholders' equity accounts. You already know that increases in stockholders' equity are recorded on the right side. You also know that revenues increase net income, which increases the stockholders' equity account Retained Earnings. So putting these ideas together should lead to the conclusion that **revenues are recorded on the right (credit).** Here's the logic again: Increases in stockholders' equity are on the right, revenues increase stockholders' equity, so revenues are recorded on the right (credit). Decreases in stockholders' equity are recorded on the left side, so to show that expenses decrease net income and retained earnings, **expenses are recorded on the left (debit).** Exhibit 3.7 summarizes these effects.

Transaction Analysis, Recording, and Summarizing

To learn how to use your new knowledge of the revenue and expense recognition principles, the expanded accounting equation, and the debit/credit framework, you'll need lots of practice. The best place to start is by reading our analysis of the following examples, which involve Pizza Aroma's operating activities during September.

(a) Provide Services for Cash In September, Pizza Aroma delivered pizza to customers for $15,000 cash. These activities qualify as accounting transactions because Pizza Aroma received cash and delivered pizza, which generates revenues. The increase in Cash (an asset) must be recorded (with a debit) along with the revenue (which, as a subcategory of stockholders' equity, is recorded with a credit). To indicate that the pizza deliveries increase revenue, which ultimately increases stockholders' equity, we use the notation (+R, +SE) in the journal entry. The increase in Cash is summarized in the Cash T-account, which carried a debit balance of $10,000 forward from the end of August (Chapter 2). The revenues earned are recorded in a new account called Pizza Revenue, which has a beginning balance of zero because the company began operating only this month.

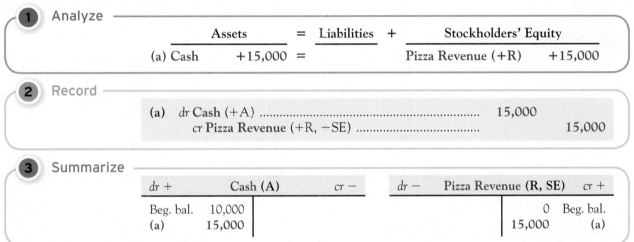

1 Analyze

	Assets	=	Liabilities	+	Stockholders' Equity	
(a) Cash	+15,000	=			Pizza Revenue (+R)	+15,000

2 Record

(a)	dr Cash (+A)	15,000	
	cr Pizza Revenue (+R, −SE)		15,000

3 Summarize

dr +	Cash (A)	cr −		dr −	Pizza Revenue (R, SE)	cr +
Beg. bal.	10,000				0	Beg. bal.
(a)	15,000				15,000	(a)

(b) Receive Cash for Future Services Pizza Aroma issued three $100 gift cards at the beginning of September. Pizza Aroma receives cash but gives only gift cards, which creates an obligation to accept the gift cards as payment for pizzas in the future. This obligation is recorded as a liability called Unearned Revenue.

> **COACH'S TIP**
>
> The word *unearned* in the Unearned Revenue account means the company hasn't done everything it was paid to do. It has a liability to do the work or return the cash.

1 Analyze

	Assets	=	Liabilities		+ Stockholders' Equity
(b) Cash	+300	=	Unearned Revenue	+300	

2 Record

(b)	dr Cash (+A)	300	
	cr Unearned Revenue (+L)		300

3 Summarize

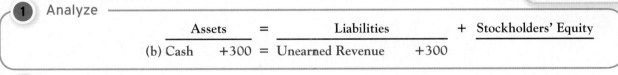

dr +	Cash (A)	cr −		dr −	Unearned Revenue (L)	cr +
Beg. bal.	10,000				0	Beg. bal.
(a)	15,000				300	(b)
(b)	300					

(c) Provide Services on Credit   Pizza Aroma delivers $500 of pizza to a college organization, billing this customer on account. Once again, this is another instance where revenues are recorded based on whether the work has been done, not whether cash has been received. Because the pizza has been delivered, Pizza Aroma has earned revenue and now has the right to collect $500 from the college organization. The right to collect money is an asset called Accounts Receivable. Use a debit to increase this asset, and a credit to increase revenue.

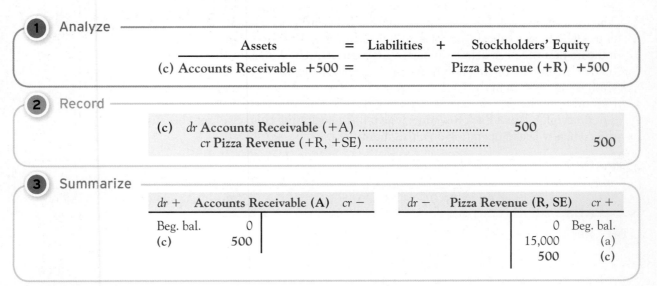

1 Analyze

	Assets	=	Liabilities	+	Stockholders' Equity
(c) Accounts Receivable	+500	=			Pizza Revenue (+R) +500

2 Record

(c)	dr Accounts Receivable (+A)	500	
	cr Pizza Revenue (+R, +SE)		500

3 Summarize

dr +	Accounts Receivable (A)	cr −		dr −	Pizza Revenue (R, SE)	cr +
Beg. bal.	0				0	Beg. bal.
(c)	500				15,000	(a)
					500	(c)

(d) Receive Payment on Account   Pizza Aroma received a $300 check from the college organization, as partial payment of its account balance. This transaction does not involve additional pizza deliveries, so no additional revenue is generated. Instead, the receipt of cash reduces the amount that Pizza Aroma can collect from this customer in the future, so it causes a decrease in Accounts Receivable.

1 Analyze

	Assets		=	Liabilities	+	Stockholders' Equity
(d) Cash		+300	=			
Accounts Receivable		−300				

2 Record

(d)	dr Cash (+A)	300	
	cr Accounts Receivable (−A).................................		300

3 Summarize

dr +	Cash (A)	cr −		dr +	Accounts Receivable (A)	cr −
Beg. bal.	10,000			Beg. bal.	0	
(a)	15,000			(c)	500	300	(d)
(b)	300					
(d)	300					

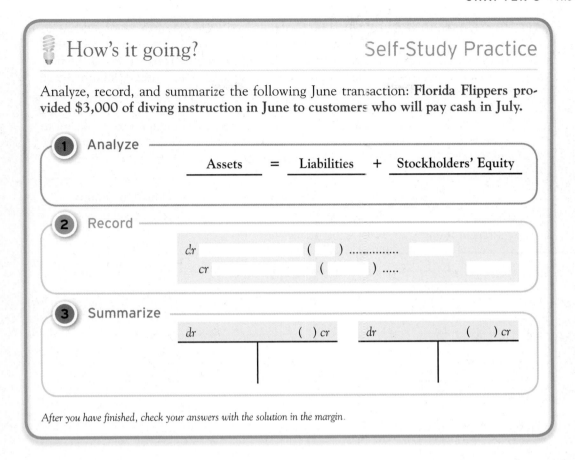

💡 How's it going?   Self-Study Practice

Analyze, record, and summarize the following June transaction: **Florida Flippers provided $3,000 of diving instruction in June to customers who will pay cash in July.**

1 Analyze

Assets	=	Liabilities	+	Stockholders' Equity

2 Record

dr _____ (___) .... _____
  cr _____ (___) ..... _____

3 Summarize

dr   ( ) cr   dr   ( ) cr

After you have finished, check your answers with the solution in the margin.

Solution to Self-Study Practice

1.

Assets	=	Liabilities	+	Stockholders' Equity
Accts. Receivable+3,000 =				Diving Revenue (+R) +3,000

2. dr Accounts Receivable (+A).......... 3,000
   cr Diving Revenue (+R, +SE)...... 3,000

3.

dr +	Accts. Rec. (A)	cr −		dr −	Diving Revenue (R, SE)	cr +
(June)	3,000				3,000	(June)

(e) Pay Cash to Employees   Pizza Aroma wrote checks to employees, totaling **$8,100 for wages related to hours worked in September.** The expense recognition principle requires that all expenses that relate to revenues earned in the current period be recorded in the current period. Because this transaction involves using the efforts of employees to make and deliver pizza, it represents an expense. We show (+E,−SE) because as expenses increase, net income decreases, which causes stockholders' equity to decrease.

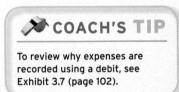

🔨 **COACH'S TIP**

To review why expenses are recorded using a debit, see Exhibit 3.7 (page 102).

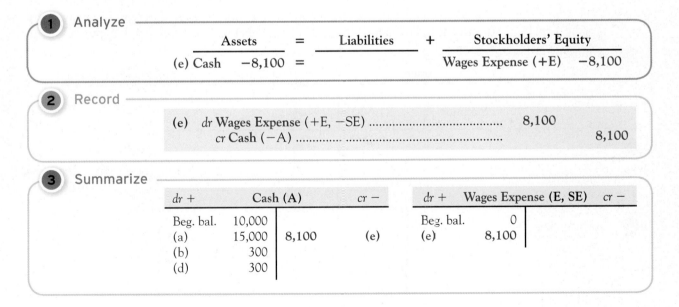

1 Analyze

	Assets	=	Liabilities	+	Stockholders' Equity	
(e) Cash	−8,100	=			Wages Expense (+E)	−8,100

2 Record

(e) dr Wages Expense (+E, −SE) 8,100
      cr Cash (−A) 8,100

3 Summarize

dr +	Cash (A)		cr −		dr +	Wages Expense (E, SE)	cr −
Beg. bal.	10,000				Beg. bal.	0	
(a)	15,000	8,100	(e)		(e)	8,100	
(b)	300						
(d)	300						

(f) Pay Cash in Advance
On September 1, Pizza Aroma paid **$7,200 in advance for September, October, and November rent.** This transaction involves paying for the right to use the rented building for three months following the payment. This payment provides an economic resource to Pizza Aroma (building space for three months), so it will be initially reported as an asset called Prepaid Rent. Each month, when the rented space has been used, Pizza Aroma will reduce Prepaid Rent and show the amount used up as Rent Expense. The adjustment needed to report September's share of the total rent expense (1/3 × $7,200 = $2,400) will be covered in Chapter 4. For now, we will record just the $7,200 rent prepayment.

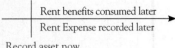

Pay rent now

Rent benefits consumed later

Rent Expense recorded later

Record asset now
(Prepaid Rent)

1 Analyze

	Assets	=	Liabilities	+	Stockholders' Equity
(f) Cash	−7,200				
Prepaid Rent	+7,200				

2 Record

(f)	dr Prepaid Rent (+A)	7,200	
	cr Cash (−A)		7,200

3 Summarize

dr +	Cash (A)		cr −		dr +	Prepaid Rent (A)	cr −
Beg. bal.	10,000				Beg. bal.	0	
(a)	15,000	8,100	(e)		(f)	7,200	
(b)	300	7,200	(f)				
(d)	300						

Prepayments for insurance, advertising, and other time-based services would be analyzed and recorded in a similar manner.

(g) Pay Cash in Advance
On September 2, Pizza Aroma wrote a check for **$1,600 for pizza sauce, dough, cheese, and paper products.** This transaction provides another example of a prepayment that is initially recorded as an asset. The supplies are an asset because they can be used to make and sell pizza in the future. Later, when that happens and the supplies have been used up, Pizza Aroma will reduce the Supplies account balance and report the amount used up as Supplies Expense. The adjustment to be made at the end of September will be covered in Chapter 4.

1 Analyze

	Assets	=	Liabilities	+	Stockholders' Equity
(g) Cash	−1,600				
Supplies	+1,600				

2 Record

(g)	dr Supplies (+A)	1,600	
	cr Cash (−A)		1,600

3 Summarize

dr +	Cash (A)		cr −		dr +	Supplies (A)	cr −
Beg. bal.	10,000				Beg. bal.	0	
(a)	15,000	8,100	(e)		(g)	1,600	
(b)	300	7,200	(f)				
(d)	300	1,600	(g)				

(h) Incur Cost to Be Paid Later Pizza Aroma received a bill for $400 for running a newspaper ad in September. The bill will be paid in October. This cost was incurred for September advertising services, so according to the expense recognition principle it should be recorded as an expense in September. Rather than pay cash for this expense, Pizza Aroma gave a promise to pay, which increases the liability called Accounts Payable.

COACH'S TIP

The beginning balance in Accounts Payable is carried forward from the previous month's activities discussed in Chapter 2.

1 Analyze

Assets	=	Liabilities	+	Stockholders' Equity
(h)		Accounts Payable +400		Advertising Expense (+E) −400

2 Record

(h) dr Advertising Expense (−E, −SE) 400
     cr Accounts Payable (+L) 400

3 Summarize

dr −	Accounts Payable (L)	cr +
	630	Beg. bal.
	400	(h)

dr +	Advertising Exp. (E, SE)	cr −
Beg. bal.	0	
(h)	400	

(i) Pay Cash for Expenses Pizza Aroma received and paid bills totaling $600 for September utilities services. Just like transaction (e), the cash payment and expense occurred during the same period.

1 Analyze

Assets	=	Liabilities	+	Stockholders' Equity
(i) Cash −600 =				Utilities Expense (+E) −600

2 Record

(i) dr Utilities Expense (+E, −SE) 600
     cr Cash (−A) 600

3 Summarize

dr +	Cash (A)		cr −
Beg. bal.	10,000		
(a)	15,000	8,100	(e)
(b)	300	7,200	(f)
(d)	300	1,600	(g)
		600	(i)

dr +	Utilities Expense (E, SE)	cr −
Beg. bal.	0	
(i)	600	

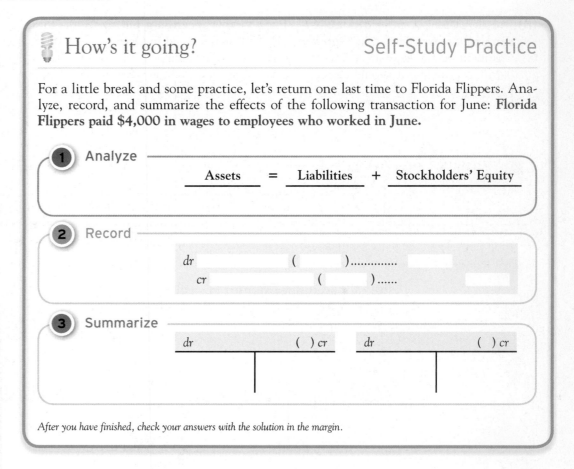

Calculating Account Balances After entering ("posting") the effects of each journal entry into the T-accounts, we can now calculate the ending balances. In Exhibit 3.8, we have included all the T-accounts for Pizza Aroma (from this chapter as well as Chapter 2). You've heard it before, but we'll just remind you that the ending balance in each account is the amount by which the total of the increase (+) side exceeds the total of the decrease (−) side.

UNADJUSTED TRIAL BALANCE

Learning Objective 3-4
Prepare an unadjusted trial balance.

After summarizing journal entries in the various accounts and then calculating ending balances for each account, you should check that the total recorded debits equal the total recorded credits. It's easy to make mistakes when you're doing the recording and summarizing steps by hand. Typical mistakes involve (a) forgetting to post both sides of a journal entry, (b) posting a debit in the credit column (or vice versa), (c) recording the wrong amount, or (d) miscalculating the ending account balance. The best way to ensure your accounts are "in balance" is to prepare a **trial balance**, like the one in Exhibit 3.9. A trial balance is an internal report used to determine whether total debits equal total credits. Also, as you will see in Chapter 4, it's a great tool to use when preparing the financial statements. Typically, a trial balance lists every account name in one column (usually in the order of assets, liabilities, stockholders' equity, revenues, and expenses). The ending balances obtained from the ledgers (T-accounts) are listed in the appropriate debit or credit column.

YOU SHOULD KNOW

Trial balance: An internal report that lists all accounts and their balances to check on the equality of total recorded debits and total recorded credits.

If your trial balance indicates that total debits don't equal total credits, you will experience a sickening feeling in your stomach because this means you've made an error somewhere in preparing or posting the journal entries to the T-accounts. Don't panic or start randomly changing numbers. The first thing to do when you find yourself in a

EXHIBIT 3.8   T-Accounts for Pizza Aroma

Assets				=	Liabilities			+	Stockholders' Equity		

Assets

dr +	Cash (A)		cr −
Beg. bal.	10,000		
(a)	15,000	8,100	(e)
(b)	300	7,200	(f)
(d)	300	1,600	(g)
		600	(i)
End. bal.	8,100		

dr +	Accounts Receivable (A)		cr −
Beg. bal.	0		
(c)	500	300	(d)
End. bal.	200		

dr +	Supplies (A)		cr −
Beg. bal.	0		
(g)	1,600		
End. bal.	1,600		

dr +	Prepaid Rent (A)		cr −
Beg. bal.	0		
(f)	7,200		
End. bal.	7,200		

dr +	Cookware (A)		cr −
Beg. bal.	630		

dr +	Equipment (A)		cr −
Beg. bal.	60,000		

Liabilities

dr −	Accounts Payable (L)		cr +
		630	Beg. bal.
		400	(h)
		1,030	End. bal.

dr −	Unearned Revenue (L)		cr +
		0	Beg. bal.
		300	(b)
		300	End. bal.

dr −	Note Payable (L)		cr +
		20,000	Beg. bal.

Stockholders' Equity

dr −	Contributed Capital (SE)		cr +
		50,000	Beg. bal.

dr −	Retained Earnings (SE)		cr +
		0	Beg. bal.

dr −	Pizza Revenue (R, SE)		cr +
		0	Beg. bal.
		15,000	(a)
		500	(c)
		15,500	End. bal.

dr +	Wages Expense (E, SE)		cr −
Beg. bal.	0		
(e)	8,100		
End. bal.	8,100		

dr +	Utilities Expense (E, SE)		cr −
Beg. bal.	0		
(i)	600		
End. bal.	600		

dr +	Advertising Expense (E, SE)		cr −
Beg. bal.	0		
(h)	400		
End. bal.	400		

> Beginning balances in this exhibit (September 1) are the ending balances in Exhibit 2.12 (August 31).

hole is stop digging. Calmly look at the difference between total debits and credits and consult the Homework Helper section on page 118 for tips on how to find the error causing that difference.

Be aware that even if total debits equal total credits, it's still possible that you've made an error. For example, if you accidentally debit an asset rather than an expense or credit Accounts Payable instead of Unearned Revenue, total debits would still equal total credits. So if the trial balance doesn't balance, you know you've made an error for sure. If the trial balance does balance, it's still possible that you've made a mistake.

If you haven't already scanned the trial balance in Exhibit 3.9 (on the next page), take a moment to do it now. Notice that the title says **unadjusted** trial balance. It is called this because several adjustments will have to be made at the end of the accounting period to update the accounts. For example, some of the benefits of Prepaid Rent were used up in September, but this wasn't recorded yet. If you're really sharp, you'll also have noticed that income taxes haven't been calculated and recorded yet. Although it's possible to prepare preliminary financial statements using the numbers on the unadjusted

EXHIBIT 3.9 | Sample Unadjusted Trial Balance

PIZZA AROMA, INC.
Unadjusted Trial Balance
At September 30, 2013

Account Name	Debits	Credits
Cash	$ 8,100	
Accounts Receivable	200	
Supplies	1,600	
Prepaid Rent	7,200	
Cookware	630	
Equipment	60,000	
Accounts Payable		$ 1,030
Unearned Revenue		300
Note Payable		20,000
Contributed Capital		50,000
Retained Earnings		0
Pizza Revenue		15,500
Wages Expense	8,100	
Utilities Expense	600	
Advertising Expense	400	
Totals	$86,830	$86,830

Balance sheet accounts }

Income statement accounts }

COACH'S TIP

A trial balance is prepared by simply listing and summing the T-account balances.

trial balance, most companies don't. They wait until after the final adjustments are made. These adjustments will ensure the revenues and expenses are up to date and complete, so that the (adjusted) net income number will provide a good indication about whether the company was profitable during the period. Don't worry about how to make the end-of-period adjustments yet. We'll spend most of Chapter 4 on that. For now, just realize that the accounts still have to be adjusted before we can prepare financial statements that follow GAAP or IFRS.

REVIEW OF REVENUES AND EXPENSES

Up to this point of the chapter, you've analyzed some transactions—nine actually—that involve operating activities. While this is a good introduction, it doesn't quite prepare you for the variety of operating activities that most companies engage in. What you really need is a general summary of everything you've learned about revenues, expenses, and journal entries, and then lots of practice applying it to a broad range of activities. Let's start with revenues.

Remember that revenues are recorded when the business fulfills its promise to provide goods or services to customers, which is not necessarily the same time that cash is received. Because of this, we look at three cases, where cash is received (1) before the revenue is earned by delivering goods or services, (2) in the same period in which the revenue is earned, and (3) after the period in which the revenue is earned. The journal entries for these situations are shown in the following panels.

These three panels correspond to the revenue transactions for Pizza Aroma analyzed earlier in this chapter, but they can be applied to any business. We use a generic label "_____ Revenue" with the expectation that you will fill in the blank with whatever type of revenue you are recording. That is, when accounting for revenue from delivering pizza, you should use an account name like Pizza Revenue. A more complete list of account names is provided in the Homework Helper section on page 118.

Let's look at a similar summary for expenses now. Under accrual accounting, expenses are recorded when incurred (by using up the economic benefits of acquired items). Expenses are not necessarily incurred at the same time that cash is paid. Because of this, we look at three cases, where cash is paid (1) before the expense is incurred, (2) in the same period in which the expense is incurred, and (3) after the expense is incurred. The corresponding journal entries are summarized in the following panels.

Again, we use generic labels like "Prepaid _____" and "_____ Expense" with the expectation that you will fill in the blank with whatever type of item you are recording (e.g., Prepaid Rent, Rent Expense, Prepaid Insurance, Insurance Expense).

Evaluate the Results

NET PROFIT MARGIN

Learning Objective 3-5
Evaluate net profit margin, but beware of income statement limitations.

The income statement provides the main measure of a company's operating performance. The key thing to look for is whether net income is positive (revenues exceed expenses). Beyond that, it's useful to consider whether revenues are growing faster than expenses. If so, the company's net income will be increasing.

Currently, Pizza Aroma's accounting records report revenues of $15,500 and expenses of $8,100, $600, and $400, suggesting a net income of $6,400. This $6,400 of net income is about 41.3% of the $15,500 of revenues ($6,400 ÷ 15,500 = 0.413). This **net profit margin,** as it is called, implies that Pizza Aroma earned 41.3 cents of net income from each dollar of pizza revenue. But Laurie cautions Mauricio that these measures are preliminary and will change when the accounting records are adjusted at the end of September. The adjustment process is the main topic of Chapter 4.

Accounting Decision Tools

Name of Measure	Formula	What It Tells You
Net profit margin	$\dfrac{\text{Net Income}}{\text{Total Revenue}}$	• How much profit from each dollar of revenue • A higher ratio means better performance

As Mauricio realized, a good accountant like Laurie monitors how well other companies are doing. She was able to advise Mauricio that pizza companies usually have low net profit margins because their ingredients are relatively expensive. For example, as shown below, Papa John's net profit margin has been around 5%, except during the financial crisis when it was 3%.

SPOTLIGHT ON Financial Reporting

Net Profit Margin Before and After the Financial Crisis

The following graph indicates the net profit margins of three dominant pizza companies: Papa John's, Domino's Pizza, and California Pizza Kitchen. The graph shows a significant decline in net profit margin leading into the financial crisis of 2008, with a good recovery in 2009 for two of the companies. Unfortunately, California Pizza Kitchen was unable to reverse its declining profit margin and was sold to a private company in 2011.

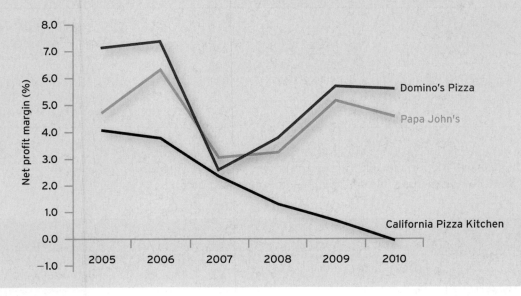

INCOME STATEMENT LIMITATIONS

Although an income statement is useful for assessing a company's performance, it does have some limitations that lead to common misconceptions. One of the most common is that some people think net income equals the amount of cash generated by the business during the period. While this is the way many of us think about our own income, it's not the way companies recognize revenues and expenses on the income statement when using accrual basis accounting.

A second, related misconception is that a company's net income represents the change in the company's value during the period. While a company's net income is one source of value to the company, many other determinants of its value are not included in the income statement. A good example is the increase in the value of Pizza Aroma's name as it grows its reputation for making great pizza.

A third common misconception is that the measurement of income involves only counting. Proper counting is critical to income measurement, but estimation also plays a role. For example, Pizza Aroma's equipment will not last forever. Instead, it will be "used up" over time to generate the company's revenue. It should therefore be expensed over the period in which it is used. Doing so requires an estimate of the period over which each category of equipment will be used. We will discuss this particular example in Chapter 4; many other estimates affecting income measurement will arise in later chapters.

REVIEW THE CHAPTER

DEMONSTRATION CASE A

Carnival Corporation

1. From the following list of balance sheet and income statement account balances for Carnival Corporation, prepare an income statement for the year ended November 30, 2010. (Amounts are reported in millions of U.S. dollars.)

2. Explain what the results suggest about the cruise ship company's operating performance. For the same period last year, net income was $1,790 (in millions of U.S. dollars) and net profit margin was 13.3 percent.

Transportation Expenses	$2,272	Wage Expenses	$1,611	Selling Expenses	$1,614
Passenger Ticket Revenue	11,084	Fuel Expenses	1,622	Prepaid Expenses	247
Onboard Revenue	3,385	Accounts Payable	503	Ship Expenses	3,448
Food Expenses	1,343	Income Tax Expense	581	Unearned Revenue	2,805

Suggested Solution

1. Income Statement

CARNIVAL CORPORATION Income Statement For the Year Ended November 30, 2010 (amounts in millions of U.S. dollars)	
Revenues	
Passenger Ticket Revenue	$11,084
Onboard Revenue	3,385
Total Revenues	14,469
Expenses	
Ship Expenses	3,448
Transportation Expenses	2,272
Selling Expenses	1,614
Fuel Expenses	1,622
Wage Expenses	1,611
Food Expenses	1,343
Income Tax Expense	581
Total Expenses	12,491
Net Income	$ 1,978

COACH'S TIP

Prepaid Expenses of $247 is excluded from the income statement because it is an asset on the balance sheet. Accounts Payable of $503 and Unearned Revenue of $2,805 are excluded from the income statement because they are liabilities on the balance sheet.

2. The net income of $1,978 (million) indicates that Carnival Corporation was profitable, meaning that the revenues it earned were greater than the expenses it incurred. Its net profit margin was 13.7 percent of total revenues ($1,978 ÷ $14,469 = 0.137). This is a positive sign. It is an improvement over the net income of $1,790 (million) and net profit margin of 13.3 percent reported in the prior year.

DEMONSTRATION CASE B

This case is a continuation of the Goodbye Grass Corporation case introduced in Chapter 2. The company was established and property and equipment were purchased. The balance sheet at April 30, 2013, based on only the investing and financing activities (from Chapter 2) is as follows:

GOODBYE GRASS CORPORATION
Balance Sheet
At April 30, 2013

Assets		Liabilities	
Current Assets		Current Liabilities	
Cash	$ 3,800	Accounts Payable	$ 400
Note Receivable	1,250	Note Payable	4,000
Total Current Assets	5,050	Total Current Liabilities	4,400
Equipment	4,600	**Stockholders' Equity**	
Land	3,750	Contributed Capital	9,000
		Retained Earnings	0
		Total Stockholders' Equity	9,000
Total Assets	$13,400	Total Liabilities and Stockholders' Equity	$13,400

The following activities also occurred during April 2013:

a. Purchased and used gasoline for mowers and edgers, paying $90 in cash at a local gas station.
b. In early April, received $1,600 cash from the city in advance for lawn maintenance service for April through July ($400 each month). The entire amount is to be recorded as Unearned Revenue.
c. In early April, purchased $300 of insurance covering six months, April through September. The entire payment is to be recorded as Prepaid Insurance.
d. Mowed lawns for residential customers who are billed every two weeks. A total of $5,200 of service was billed and is to be recorded in April.
e. Residential customers paid $3,500 on their accounts.
f. Paid wages every two weeks. Total cash paid in April was $3,900.
g. Received a bill for $320 from the local gas station for additional gasoline purchased on account and used in April.
h. Paid $100 on accounts payable.

Required:

1. Analyze activities (a)–(h) with the goal of indicating their effects on the basic accounting equation (Assets = Liabilities + Stockholders' Equity), using the format shown in the chapter.
2. Prepare journal entries to record the transactions identified among activities (a)–(h).
   TIP: Treat insurance (in c) in the same manner as Pizza Aroma's rent in transaction (f) on page 106.
3. Summarize the effects of each transaction in the appropriate T-accounts. Before entering these effects, set up T-accounts for Cash, Accounts Receivable, Note Receivable, Prepaid Insurance, Equipment, Land, Accounts Payable, Unearned Revenue, Note Payable, Contributed Capital, Retained Earnings, Mowing Revenue, Wages Expense, and Fuel Expense.

The beginning balance in each T-account should be the amount shown on the balance sheet above or $0 if the account does not appear on the above balance sheet. After posting the journal entries to the T-accounts, compute ending balances for each of the T-accounts.

4. Use the amounts in the T-accounts to prepare an unadjusted trial balance for Goodbye Grass Corporation at April 30, 2013.

After completing the above requirements, check your answers with the following solution.

Suggested Solution

1. Transaction analysis:

	Assets		=	Liabilities		+	Stockholders' Equity	
a.	Cash	−90	=				Fuel Expense (+E)	−90
b.	Cash	+1,600	=	Unearned Revenue	+1,600			
c.	Cash	−300	=				No change	
	Prepaid Insurance	+300						
d.	Accounts Receivable	+5,200	=				Mowing Revenue (+R)	+5,200
e.	Cash	+3,500	=				No change	
	Accounts Receivable	−3,500						
f.	Cash	−3,900	=				Wages Expense (+E)	−3,900
g.	No change		=	Accounts Payable	+320		Fuel Expense (+E)	−320
h.	Cash	−100	=	Accounts Payable	−100			

2. Journal entries:

    a. dr **Fuel Expense** (+E, −SE) 90
          cr **Cash** (−A) 90

    b. dr **Cash** (+A) 1,600
          cr **Unearned Revenue** (+L) 1,600

    c. dr **Prepaid Insurance** (+A) 300
          cr **Cash** (−A) 300

    d. dr **Accounts Receivable** (+A) 5,200
          cr **Mowing Revenue** (+R, +SE) 5,200

    e. dr **Cash** (+A) 3,500
          cr **Accounts Receivable** (−A) 3,500

    f. dr **Wages Expense** (+E, −SE) 3,900
          cr **Cash** (−A) 3,900

    g. dr **Fuel Expense** (+E, −SE) 320
          cr **Accounts Payable** (+L) 320

    h. dr **Accounts Payable** (−L) 100
          cr **Cash** (−A) 100

3. T-Accounts:

	Assets	=	Liabilities	+	Stockholders' Equity

dr +   Cash (A)   cr −

Beg. bal.	3,800		
(b)	1,600	90	(a)
(e)	3,500	300	(c)
		3,900	(f)
		100	(h)
End. bal.	4,510		

dr + Accounts Receivable (A) cr −

Beg. bal.	0		
(d)	5,200	3,500	(e)
End. bal.	1,700		

dr + Note Receivable (A) cr −

Beg. bal.	1,250	
End. bal.	1,250	

dr + Prepaid Insurance (A) cr −

Beg. bal.	0	
(c)	300	
End. Bal.	300	

dr +   Equipment (A)   cr −

Beg. bal.	4,600	
End. bal.	4,600	

dr +   Land (A)   cr −

Beg. bal.	3,750	
End. bal.	3,750	

dr − Accounts Payable (L) cr +

		400	Beg. bal.
(h)	100	320	(g)
		620	End. bal.

dr − Unearned Revenue (L) cr +

		0	Beg. bal.
		1,600	(b)
		1,600	End. bal.

dr −   Note Payable (L)   cr +

		4,000	Beg. bal.
		4,000	End. bal.

dr +   Wages Expense (E)   cr −

Beg. bal.	0	
(f)	3,900	
End. bal.	3,900	

dr +   Fuel Expense (E)   cr −

Beg. bal.	0	
(a)	90	
(g)	320	
End. bal.	410	

dr − Contributed Capital (SE) cr +

		9,000	Beg. bal.
		9,000	End. bal.

dr − Retained Earnings (SE) cr +

		0	Beg. bal.
		0	End. bal.

dr − Mowing Revenue (R) cr +

		0	Beg. bal.
		5,200	(d)
		5,200	End. bal.

4. Unadjusted trial balance:

GOODBYE GRASS CORPORATION
Unadjusted Trial Balance
At April 30, 2013

Account Name	Debits	Credits
Cash	$ 4,510	
Accounts Receivable	1,700	
Note Receivable	1,250	
Prepaid Insurance	300	
Equipment	4,600	
Land	3,750	
Accounts Payable		$ 620
Unearned Revenue		1,600
Note Payable		4,000
Contributed Capital		9,000
Retained Earnings		0
Mowing Revenue		5,200
Wages Expense	3,900	
Fuel Expense	410	
Totals	$20,420	$20,420

CHAPTER SUMMARY

Describe common operating transactions and select appropriate income statement account titles. p. 94

LO 3-1

- The income statement reports the results of transactions that affect net income, which includes

  Revenues—amounts charged to customers for sales of goods or services provided.

  Expenses—costs of business activities undertaken to earn revenues.

- See Exhibit 3.2 on page 95 for basic income statement format.

Explain and apply the revenue and expense recognition principles. p. 98

LO 3-2

- The two key concepts underlying accrual basis accounting and the income statement are

  Revenue recognition principle—recognize revenues when they are earned by providing goods or services, regardless of when cash is received.

  Expense recognition principle ("matching")—recognize expenses when they are incurred in generating revenue, regardless of when cash is paid.

Analyze, record, and summarize the effects of operating transactions using the accounting equation, journal entries, and T-accounts. p. 102

LO 3-3

- The expanded transaction analysis model includes revenues and expenses as subcategories of Retained Earnings. Increases, decreases, and normal account balances (*dr* or *cr*) are shown below.

Prepare an unadjusted trial balance. p. 108

LO 3-4

- The unadjusted trial balance is a list of all accounts and their unadjusted balances, and is used to check on the equality of recorded debits and credits.

Evaluate net profit margin, but beware of income statement limitations. p. 111

LO 3-5

- Net profit margin expresses net income as a percentage of total revenues.
- The income statement indicates whether the company is profitable, but this might not explain whether cash increased or decreased.
- The income statement does not directly measure the change in value of a company during the period.
- Estimation plays a key role when measuring income.

Accounting Decision Tools		
Name of Measure	**Formula**	**What It Tells You**
Net profit margin	$\dfrac{\text{Net Income}}{\text{Total Revenue}}$	• How much profit from each dollar of revenue • A higher ratio means better performance

KEY TERMS

Accrual Basis Accounting p. 98

Cash Basis Accounting p. 97

Expenses p. 95

Expense Recognition Principle
    ("Matching") p. 100

Net Income p. 96

Net Profit Margin p. 112

Revenue Recognition Principle p. 98

Revenues p. 95

Time Period Assumption p. 96

Trial Balance p. 108

Unearned Revenue p. 99

See complete definitions in the glossary in the back of this text.

HOMEWORK HELPER

Account Name	Description
Revenues	
Sales	Arise from delivering products in the ordinary course of business
Service Revenues	Arise from providing services in the ordinary course of business
Rental Revenues	Amounts earned by renting out company property
Interest Revenues	Amounts earned on savings and loans to others
Dividend Revenues	Dividends earned from investing in other companies
Fees Earned	Fees that the company charges its customers

Account Name	Description
Expenses	
Cost of Goods Sold	Cost of products sold in the ordinary course of business
Repairs & Maintenance Expense	Cost of routine maintenance and upkeep of buildings/equipment
Advertising Expense	Cost of advertising services obtained during the period
Depreciation Expense	Cost of plant and equipment used up during the period
Insurance Expense	Cost of insurance coverage for the current period
Salaries and Wages Expense	Cost of employees' salaries and wages for the period
Rent Expense	Cost of rent for the period
Supplies Expense	Cost of supplies used up during the period
Delivery Expense	Cost of transportation to deliver goods to customers
Utilities Expense	Cost of power, light, heat, Internet, and telephone for the period
Amortization Expense	Cost of intangible assets used up or expired during the period
Interest Expense	Interest charged on outstanding debts owed during the period
Income Tax Expense	Taxes charged on net income reported for the period

Alternative terms

- Net income also can be called net earnings or net profit.

- Prepaid Rent and Prepaid Insurance can be called Prepaid Expenses, which is reported as a current asset on the balance sheet.

- The income statement may also be called the statement of comprehensive income, statement of earnings, or statement of operations.

Helpful reminders

- To properly understand why Prepaid Expenses is an asset and Unearned Revenue is a liability, emphasize the first word (prepaid and unearned).

- If the trial balance doesn't balance, look at the difference between total debits and total credits. If it is . . .

  - **The same as** one of your T-account balances, you probably forgot to include the account in your trial balance.

- **Twice the amount of an account balance,** you may have included it in the wrong column of the trial balance.
- **Twice the amount of a transaction,** you may have posted a debit as a credit or a credit as a debit in your T-accounts.
- **Evenly divisible by 9,** you may have reversed the order of two digits in a number (a transposition error) or left a zero off the end of a number.
- **Evenly divisible by 3,** you may have hit the key above or below the one you intended to hit (like a 9 instead of a 6) on your numeric keypad.

Frequent mistakes

- Accrual is <u>not</u> spelled accural.

PRACTICE MATERIAL

QUESTIONS (⊖ Symbol indicates questions that require analysis from more than one perspective.)

1. Show the income statement equation and define each element.

2. When accounting was developed in the 14th and 15th centuries, some businesses had very short lives. For instance, a business might have been created for a ship to sail from Europe to North America and return with furs and other goods. After the goods were delivered and profits were distributed among those who financed the shipment, the business ceased to exist. In more recent centuries, businesses began to experience longer lives. Identify the accounting concept that is needed when accounting for businesses with long lives. Explain what this concept means and why it is necessary for modern-day accounting. ⊖

3. Define *accrual basis accounting* and contrast it with *cash basis accounting*.

4. Why is it appropriate to use cash basis accounting in your personal life but not in the business world? ⊖

5. What does it mean to *recognize* an accounting transaction?

6. When is revenue typically recognized under accrual basis accounting?

7. Explain the expense recognition principle ("matching").

8. Explain why stockholders' equity is increased by revenues and decreased by expenses.

9. Explain why revenues are recorded as credits and expenses as debits.

10. Complete the following table by entering either *debit* or *credit* in each cell:

Item	Increase	Decrease
Revenues		
Expenses		

11. Complete the following table by entering either *increase* or *decrease* in each cell:

Item	Debit	Credit
Revenues		
Expenses		

12. What basic characteristic distinguishes items reported on the income statement from items reported on the balance sheet?

13. Which of the four basic accounting reports indicates that it is appropriate to consider revenues and expenses as sub-categories of retained earnings? Explain.

14. What is the difference between Accounts Receivable and Revenue?

15. What is the difference between Accounts Payable for advertising and Advertising Expense?

16. For each of the following situations, indicate whether it represents an accounting error and explain why it is or is not an error. Also state whether a trial balance would indicate that an error exists for each situation. ⊖
   a. Cash received from a customer was debited to Accounts Receivable and credited to Cash.
   b. Revenue was recognized when a customer purchased a gift card for future use.
   c. An expense was recorded as an asset.
   d. The debit side of a journal entry was recorded in the accounts, but the credit side was not.
   e. A company shareholder purchased a new car, but this was not recorded by the company.

17. What are three limitations of the income statement that often lead to misconceptions?

MULTIPLE CHOICE

1. Which of the following items is not a specific account in a company's accounting records?

   a. Accounts Receivable   **c.** Sales Revenue
   b. Net Income   **d.** Unearned Revenue

2. Which of the following accounts normally has a debit balance?

   a. Unearned Revenue   **c.** Retained Earnings
   b. Rent Expense   **d.** Sales Revenue

3. The expense recognition principle ("matching") controls

   a. Where on the income statement expenses should be presented.
   b. When revenues are recognized on the income statement.
   c. The ordering of current assets and current liabilities on the balance sheet.
   d. When costs are recognized as expenses on the income statement.

4. When should companies that sell gift cards to customers report revenue?

   a. When the gift card is issued and cash is received.
   b. When the gift card is used by the customer.
   c. At the end of the year in which the gift card is issued.
   d. None of the above.

5. If a company incorrectly records a payment as an asset, rather than as an expense, how will this error affect net income in the current period?

   a. Net income will be too high.
   b. Net income will be too low.
   c. Net income will not be affected by this error.
   d. It's a mystery; nobody really knows.

6. When should a company report the cost of an insurance policy as an expense?

   a. When the company first signs the policy.
   b. When the company pays for the policy.
   c. When the company receives the benefits from the policy over its period of coverage.
   d. When the company receives payments from the insurance company for its insurance claims.

7. When expenses exceed revenues in a given period,

   a. Stockholders' equity will not be impacted.
   b. Stockholders' equity will be increased.
   c. Stockholders' equity will be decreased.
   d. One cannot determine the impact on stockholders' equity without information about the specific revenues and expenses.

8. Which account is *least* likely to be debited when revenue is recorded?

   a. Accounts Payable
   b. Accounts Receivable
   c. Cash
   d. Unearned Revenue

9. Webby Corporation reported the following amounts on its income statement: service revenues, $32,500; utilities expense, $300; net income, $1,600; and income tax expense, $900. If the only other amount reported on the income statement was for selling expenses, what amount would it be?

   a. $2,200   **c.** $30,000
   b. $29,700   **d.** $30,900

10. Which of the following is the entry to be recorded by a law firm when it receives a payment from a new client that will be earned when services are provided in the future?

   a. *Debit* Accounts Receivable; *credit* Legal Services Revenue.
   b. *Debit* Unearned Revenue; *credit* Legal Services Revenue.
   c. *Debit* Cash; *credit* Unearned Revenue.
   d. *Debit* Unearned Revenue; *credit* Cash.

> For answers to the Multiple-Choice Questions **see page Q1** located in the last section of the book.

MINI-EXERCISES

LO 3-2   **M3-1 Reporting Cash Basis versus Accrual Basis Income**

Mostert Music Company had the following transactions in March:

a. Sold music lessons to customers for $10,000; received $6,000 in cash and the rest on account.

b. Paid $600 in wages for the month.

c. Received a $200 bill for utilities that will be paid in April.

d. Received $1,000 from customers as deposits on music lessons to be given in April.

Complete the following statements for March:

Cash Basis Income Statement		Accrual Basis Income Statement	
Revenues		Revenues	
Cash Sales	$	Sales	$
Customer Deposits			
Expenses		Expenses	
Wages Paid		Wages Expense	
		Utilities Expense	
Cash Income	$	Net Income	$

M3-2 Identifying Accrual Basis Revenues

LO 3-2

The following transactions are July 2013 activities of Bill's Extreme Bowling, Inc., which operates several bowling centers. If revenue is to be recognized in July, indicate the amount. If revenue is not to be recognized in July, explain why.

Activity	Amount or Explanation
a. Bill's collected $12,000 from customers for services related to games played in July.	
b. Bill's billed a customer for $250 for a party held at the center on the last day of July. The bill is to be paid in August.	
c. The men's and women's bowling leagues gave Bill's advance payments totaling $1,500 for the fall season that starts in September.	
d. Bill's received $1,000 from credit sales made to customers last month (in June).	

M3-3 Identifying Accrual Basis Expenses

LO 3-2

The following transactions are July 2013 activities of Bill's Extreme Bowling, Inc., which operates several bowling centers. If an expense is to be recognized in July, indicate the amount. If an expense is not to be recognized in July, explain why.

Activity	Amount or Explanation
e. Bill's paid $1,500 to plumbers for repairing a broken pipe in the restrooms.	
f. Bill's paid $2,000 for the June electricity bill and received the July bill for $2,500, which will be paid in August.	
g. Bill's paid $5,475 to employees for work in July.	

M3-4 Recording Accrual Basis Revenues

LO 3-3

For each of the transactions in M3-2, write the journal entry using the format shown in the chapter.

M3-5 Recording Accrual Basis Expenses

LO 3-3

For each of the transactions in M3-3, write the journal entry using the format shown in the chapter.

M3-6 Determining the Accounting Equation Effects of Operating Activities Involving Revenues

LO 3-2, 3-3

The following transactions are July 2013 activities of Bill's Extreme Bowling, Inc., which operates several bowling centers. For each of the following transactions, complete the spreadsheet, indicating the amount and effect (+ for increase and − for decrease) of each transaction under the accrual basis. Write NE if there is no effect. Include revenues as a subcategory of stockholders' equity, as shown for the first transaction, which is provided as an example.

Transaction	Assets	Liabilities	Stockholders' Equity
a. Bill's collected $12,000 from customers for services related to games played in July.	+12,000	NE	Service Revenue (+R) + 12,000
b. Bill's billed a customer for $250 for a party held at the center on the last day of July. The bill is to be paid in August.			
c. The men's and women's bowling leagues gave Bill's advance payments totaling $1,500 for the fall season that starts in September.			
d. Bill's received $1,000 from credit sales made to customers last month (in June).			

LO 3-2, 3-3 **M3-7 Determining the Accounting Equation Effects of Operating Activities Involving Expenses**

The following transactions are July 2013 activities of Bill's Extreme Bowling, Inc., which operates several bowling centers. For each of the following transactions, complete the spreadsheet, indicating the amount and effect (+ for increase and − for decrease) of each transaction under the accrual basis. Write NE if there is no effect. Include expenses as a subcategory of stockholders' equity, as shown for the first transaction, which is provided as an example.

Transaction	Assets	Liabilities	Stockholders' Equity
e. Bill's paid $1,500 to plumbers for repairing a broken pipe in the restrooms.	−1,500	NE	Repairs Expense (+E) −1,500
f. Bill's paid $2,000 for the June electricity bill and received the July bill for $2,500, which will be paid in August.			
g. Bill's paid $5,475 to employees for work in July.			

LO 3-1 **M3-8 Preparing an Income Statement**

Given the transactions in M3-6 and M3-7 (including the examples), prepare an income statement for Bill's Extreme Bowling, Inc., for the month ended July 31, 2013. (This income statement would be considered "preliminary" because it uses unadjusted balances.)

LO 3-2 **M3-9 Identifying Accrual Basis Revenues**

The following transactions are February 2013 activities of Swing Hard Incorporated, which offers indoor golfing lessons in the northeastern United States. If revenue is to be recognized in February, indicate the amount. If revenue is not to be recognized in February, explain why.

Activity	Amount or Explanation
a. Swing Hard collected $15,000 from customers for lesson services given in February.	
b. Swing Hard sold a gift card for golf lessons for $150 cash in February.	
c. Swing Hard received $4,000 from services provided on account to customers in January.	
d. Swing Hard collected $2,250 in advance payments for services to start in June.	
e. Swing Hard bills a customer $125 for services provided between February 25 and February 28. The bill is to be paid in March.	

M3-10 Identifying Accrual Basis Expenses LO 3-2

The following transactions are February 2013 activities of Swing Hard Incorporated, which offers indoor golfing lessons in the northeastern United States. If an expense is to be recognized in February, indicate the amount. If an expense is not to be recognized in February, explain why.

Activity	Amount or Explanation
f. Swing Hard paid $4,750 to its golf instructors for the month of February.	
g. Swing Hard paid $1,750 for electricity used in the month of January.	
h. Swing Hard received an electricity bill for $800 for the month of February, to be paid in March.	

M3-11 Recording Accrual Basis Revenues LO 3-3

For each of the transactions in M3-9, write the journal entry using the format shown in the chapter.

M3-12 Recording Accrual Basis Expenses LO 3-3

For each of the transactions in M3-10, write the journal entry using the format shown in the chapter.

M3-13 Preparing Accrual Basis Journal Entries for Business Activities LO 3-3

Quick Cleaners, Inc., (QCI) has been in business for several years. It specializes in cleaning houses, but has some small business clients as well. Prepare journal entries for the following transactions, which occurred during a recent month, and determine QCI's preliminary net income.

a. Issued $25,000 of QCI stock for cash.
b. Incurred $600 of utilities costs this month and will pay them next month.
c. Paid wages for the current month, totaling $2,000.
d. Performed cleaning services on account worth $2,800.
e. Some of Quick Cleaners' equipment was repaired at a total cost of $150. The company paid the full amount immediately.

M3-14 Preparing Accrual Basis Journal Entries for Business Activities LO 3-3

Junktrader is an online company that specializes in matching buyers and sellers of used items. Buyers and sellers can purchase a membership with Junktrader, which provides them advance notice of potentially attractive offers. Prepare journal entries for the following transactions, which occurred during a recent month, and determine Junktrader's preliminary net income.

a. Junktrader provided online advertising services for another company for $200 on account.
b. On the last day of the month, Junktrader paid $50 cash to run an ad promoting the company's services. The ad ran that day in the local newspaper.
c. Received $200 cash in membership fees for the month from new members.
d. Received an electricity bill for $85, for usage this month. The bill will be paid next month.
e. Billed a customer $180 for helping sell some junk. Junktrader expects to receive the customer's payment by the end of next month.

M3-15 Preparing Accrual Basis Journal Entries for Business Activities LO 3-3

An international children's charity collects donations, which are used to buy clothing and toys for children in need. The charity records donations of cash and other items as Donations Revenue when received. Prepare journal entries for the following transactions, which occurred during a recent month, and determine the charity's preliminary net income.

a. Received $4,000 in cash and checks from a door-to-door campaign.
b. Paid $2,000 cash for employee wages this month.
c. Paid $1,000 cash on a short-term loan from the bank (ignore interest).
d. Bought $3,000 worth of new toy supplies from a large toy manufacturer, paying $1,000 cash and signing a short-term note for $2,000.
e. The manufacturer generously donated an additional $2,500 of toy supplies.

LO 3-3   **M3-16 Preparing Accrual Basis Journal Entries for Business Activities**

An auto-body repair shop has been in business for 23 years. Prepare journal entries for the following transactions, which occurred during a recent month, and determine the auto-body shop's preliminary net income.

a. Signed a long-term note and received a $150,000 loan from a local bank.
b. Billed a customer $2,000 for repair services just completed. Payment is expected in 45 days.
c. Wrote a check for $600 of rent for the current month.
d. Received $450 cash from a customer for work done the same day.
e. The company incurred $400 in advertising costs for the current month and is planning to pay these costs next month.

LO 3-2, 3-3   **M3-17 Determining the Accounting Equation Effects of Operating Activities Involving Revenues**

The following transactions are February 2013 activities of Swing Hard Incorporated, which offers golfing lessons in the northeastern United States. For each of the following transactions, complete the spreadsheet, indicating the amount and effect (+ for increase and − for decrease) of each transaction under the accrual basis. Write NE if there is no effect. Include revenues as a subcategory of stockholders' equity, as shown for the first transaction, which is provided as an example.

Transaction	Assets	Liabilities	Stockholders' Equity
a. Swing Hard collected $15,000 from customers for lesson services provided in February.	+15,000	NE	Service Revenue (+R) +15,000
b. Swing Hard sold a gift card for golf lessons for $150 cash in February.			
c. Swing Hard received $4,000 from credit sales made to customers in January.			
d. Swing Hard collected $2,250 in advance payments for golf lessons to start in June.			
e. Swing Hard billed a customer $125 for services provided between February 25 thru February 28. The bill is to be paid in March.			

LO 3-2, 3-3   **M3-18 Determining the Accounting Equation Effects of Operating Activities Involving Expenses**

The following transactions are February 2013 activities of Swing Hard Incorporated, which offers golfing lessons in the northeastern United States. For each of the following transactions, complete the spreadsheet, indicating the amount and effect (+ for increase and − for decrease) of each transaction under the accrual basis. Write NE if there is no effect. Include expenses as a subcategory of stockholders' equity, as shown for the first transaction, which is provided as an example.

Transaction	Assets	Liabilities	Stockholders' Equity
f. Swing Hard paid $4,750 for wages to its golf instructors for the month of February.	−4,750	NE	Wages Expense (+E) −4,750
g. Swing Hard paid $1,750 for electricity used in the month of January.			
h. Swing Hard received an electricity bill for $800 for the month of February, to be paid in March.			

LO 3-1   **M3-19 Preparing an Income Statement**

Given the transactions in M3-17 and M3-18 (including the examples), prepare an income statement for Swing Hard Incorporated for the month ended February 28, 2013. (This income statement would be considered "preliminary" because it uses unadjusted balances.)

M3-20 Preparing Financial Statements from a Trial Balance (Dividends Included)

The following accounts are taken from Equilibrium Riding, Inc., a company that specializes in occupational therapy and horseback riding lessons, as of December 31, 2013.

EQUILIBRIUM RIDING, INC.
Unadjusted Trial Balance
At December 31, 2013

Account Name	Debits	Credits
Cash	$ 59,750	
Accounts Receivable	3,300	
Prepaid Insurance	4,700	
Equipment	64,600	
Land	23,000	
Accounts Payable		$ 29,230
Unearned Revenue		1,500
Long-term Notes Payable		74,000
Contributed Capital		5,000
Retained Earnings		14,500
Dividends	0	
Therapy Revenue		25,200
Lesson Revenue		10,500
Wages Expense	3,900	
Repairs and Maintenance Expense	410	
Other Expenses	270	
Totals	$159,930	$159,930

Required:

Using the unadjusted trial balance provided, create a classified Balance Sheet, Statement of Retained Earnings, and Income Statement for Equilibrium Riding, Inc., for the year ended December 31, 2013. (These financial statements would be considered "preliminary" because they use unadjusted balances.)

> **TIP:** Create the Income Statement first, followed by the Statement of Retained Earnings, and finally the classified Balance Sheet. Follow the formats presented in Exhibits 1.2, 1.3, and 2.13.

M3-21 Preparing an Income Statement

The following accounts are taken from the December 31, 2010, financial statements of Time Warner, Inc. (Amounts are in millions.)

Service Revenue	$ 9,028
Other Revenues	14,749
Salaries Expense	6,126
Cash	3,663
Accounts Receivable	6,413
Interest Expense	1,178
Accounts Payable	7,733
Advertising Revenue	5,682
Long-term Debt	15,523
Other Expenses	3,213
Unearned Revenue	884
Equipment	3,874
Income Tax Expense	1,348
Operating Expense	15,023

Required:

Prepare an Income Statement for the year ended December 31, 2010.

> **TIP:** Some of the above accounts are not reported on the income statement.
> **TIP:** List expenses in order of size except for income taxes, which should be listed last.

EXERCISES

LO 3-1   E3-1 Matching Definitions with Terms

Match each definition with its related term by entering the appropriate letter in the space provided.

Term	Definition
____ 1. Expenses	A. A liability account used to record the obligation to provide future services or return cash that has been received, before revenues have been earned.
____ 2. Unearned Revenue	
____ 3. Prepaid Expenses	B. Costs that result when a company sacrifices resources to generate revenues in the current period.
____ 4. Revenues	
	C. A type of asset account used to record the benefits obtained, when cash is paid before expenses are incurred.
	D. The amount charged to customers for providing goods or services.

LO 3-1   E3-2 Matching Definitions with Terms

Match each definition with its related term by entering the appropriate letter in the space provided.

Term	Definition
____ 1. Accrual basis accounting	A. Record expenses when incurred in earning revenue.
____ 2. Expense recognition principle	B. Record revenues when earned, not necessarily when cash is received.
____ 3. Revenue recognition principle	
____ 4. Cash basis accounting	C. Record revenues when received and expenses when paid.
	D. Record revenues when earned and expenses when incurred.

LO 3-1, 3-2   E3-3 Identifying Accrual Basis Revenues

Apple

AT&T
American Airlines

According to the revenue recognition principle, revenues should be recognized when they are earned, which happens when the company performs acts promised to the customer. For most businesses, this condition is met at the point of delivery of goods or services. The following transactions occurred in September 2013:

a. A customer paid $10 cash for 10 song files from Apple's iTunes store. Answer from Apple's standpoint.

b. Home Depot provided a carpet installation for $2,000 cash. A comparable installation from other companies costs $3,000.

c. AT&T is scheduled to install digital cable at 1,000 Austin area homes next week. The installation charge is $100 per home. The terms require payment within 30 days of installation. Answer from AT&T's standpoint.

d. AT&T completed the installations described in (c). Answer from AT&T's standpoint.

e. AT&T received payment from customers for the installations described in (c). Answer from AT&T's standpoint.

f. A customer purchased a ticket from American Airlines in September for $500 cash to travel in December. Answer from American Airlines' standpoint.

Required:

For each of the transactions, if revenue is to be recognized in September, indicate the amount. If revenue is not to be recognized in September, explain why.

E3-4 Identifying Accrual Basis Revenues

According to the revenue recognition principle, revenues should be recognized when they are earned, which happens when the company performs acts promised to the customer. For most businesses, this condition is met at the point of delivery of goods or services. The following transactions occurred in September 2013:

a. Gillespie Enterprises Inc. issued $26 million in new common stock.
b. Cal State University received $20,000,000 cash for 80,000 five-game season football tickets. None of the games have been played.
c. Cal State played the first football game referred to in (b).
d. Hall Construction Company signed a contract with a customer for the construction of a new $500,000 warehouse. At the signing, Hall received a check for $50,000 as a deposit to be applied against amounts earned during the first phase of construction. Answer from Hall's standpoint.
e. A popular snowboarding magazine company received a total of $1,800 today from subscribers. The subscriptions begin in the next fiscal year. Answer from the magazine company's standpoint.
f. T-Mobile sold a $100 cell phone plan for service in September to a customer who charged the sale on his credit card. Answer from the standpoint of T-Mobile.

Required:

For each of the transactions, if revenue is to be recognized in September, indicate the amount. If revenue is not to be recognized in September, explain why.

E3-5 Identifying Accrual Basis Expenses

Under accrual basis accounting, expenses are recognized when incurred, which means the activity giving rise to the expense has occurred. Assume the following transactions occurred in January 2013:

a. Dell paid its computer service technicians $90,000 in salary for work done in January 2013. Answer from Dell's standpoint.
b. At the beginning of January, Turner Construction Company paid $3,000 in rent for February–April 2013.
c. McGraw-Hill Education—publisher of this textbook—used $3,000 worth of electricity and natural gas in January for which it has not yet been billed.
d. Pooler Company received and paid in January a $1,500 invoice from a consulting firm for services received in January.
e. The campus bookstore received consulting services at a cost of $5,000. The terms indicate that payment is due within 30 days of the consultation.
f. Schergevitch Incorporated had its delivery van repaired in January for $280 and charged the amount on account.

Required:

For each of the transactions, if an expense is to be recognized in January, indicate the amount. If an expense is not to be recognized in January, indicate why.

E3-6 Identifying Accrual Basis Expenses

Under accrual basis accounting, expenses are recognized when incurred. The following transactions occurred in January 2013:

a. American Express paid its salespersons $3,500 in commissions related to December sales of financial advisory services. Answer from American Express's standpoint.
b. On January 31, American Express determined that it will pay its salespersons $4,200 in commissions related to January sales. The payment will be made in early February. Answer from American Express's standpoint.
c. The city of Omaha hired Waste Management, Inc., to provide trash collection services beginning January 1. The city paid $12 million for the entire year. Answer from the city's standpoint.
d. The University of Florida paid $10,000 in advance for refundable airline tickets to fly the baseball team to a tournament in California. The first game will be played in March. Answer from the university's standpoint.

LO 3-1, 3-2
T-Mobile

LO 3-1, 3-2

Dell

LO 3-1, 3-2
American Express
Waste Management, Inc.

e. A Houston Community College employee worked eight hours, at $15 per hour, on January 31; payday is not until February 3. Answer from the college's point of view.
f. Wang Company paid $3,600 for a fire insurance policy on January 1. The policy covers 12 months beginning on January 1. Answer from Wang's point of view.
g. Ziegler Company, a farm equipment company, received a phone bill for $230 of January calls. The bill has not been paid to date.

Required:

For each of the transactions, if an expense is to be recognized in January, indicate the amount. If an expense is not to be recognized in January, indicate why.

LO 3-2, 3-3   **E3-7 Determining Accounting Equation Effects and Net Income**

The following transactions occurred during a recent year:

a. Paid wages of $1,000 for the current period (example).
b. Borrowed $5,000 cash from local bank using a short-term note.
c. Purchased $2,000 of equipment on credit.
d. Earned $400 of sales revenue, collected cash.
e. Received $800 of utilities services, on credit.
f. Earned $1,700 of service revenue, on credit.
g. Paid $300 cash on account to a supplier.
h. Incurred $70 of travel expenses, paid cash.
i. Earned $400 of service revenue, collected half in cash, balance on credit.
j. Collected $100 cash from customers on account.
k. Incurred $300 of advertising costs, paid half in cash, balance on credit.

Required:

For each of the transactions, complete the table below, indicating the account, amount, and direction of the effect (+ for increase and − for decrease) of each transaction under the accrual basis. Write NE if there is no effect. Include revenues and expenses as subcategories of stockholders' equity, as shown for the first transaction, which is provided as an example. Also, determine the company's preliminary net income.

Transaction	Assets	=	Liabilities	+	Stockholders' Equity
(a) (example)	Cash −1,000		NE		Wages Expense (+E) −1,000

LO 3-2, 3-3   **E3-8 Determining Accounting Equation Effects and Net Income**

WOLVERINE ⌒

Wolverine World Wide, Inc., manufactures military, work, sport, and casual footwear and leather accessories under a variety of brand names, such as Caterpillar, Hush Puppies, Wolverine, and Steve Madden. The following transactions occurred during a recent month.

a. Made cash sales of $49,000 (example).
b. Purchased $3,000 of additional supplies on account.
c. Borrowed $58,000 on long-term notes.
d. Purchased $18,600 in additional equipment, paying in cash.
e. Incurred $27,000 in selling expenses, paying two-thirds in cash and owing the rest on account.
f. Paid $4,700 in rent for this month, and $4,700 for next month.

Required:

For each of the transactions, complete the table below, indicating the account, amount, and direction of the effect (+ for increase and − for decrease) of each transaction under the accrual basis. Write NE if there is no effect. Include revenues and expenses as subcategories of stockholders' equity, as shown for the first transaction, which is provided as an example. Also, determine the company's preliminary net income.

Transaction	Assets	Liabilities	Stockholders' Equity
(a) (example)	Cash +49,000	NE	Sales Revenue (+R) +49,000

E3-9 Recording Journal Entries and Determining Net Income

LO 3-2, 3-3

Sysco, formed in 1969, is America's largest marketer and distributor of food service products, serving nearly 250,000 restaurants, hotels, schools, hospitals, and other institutions. The following transactions are typical of those that occurred in a recent year, but the amounts are simplified.

Sysco

a. Borrowed $80,000 from a bank, signing a short-term note payable.
b. Provided $100,000 in service to customers, with $95,000 on account and the rest received in cash.
c. Purchased equipment for $130,000 in cash.
d. Paid employee wages of $1,000.
e. Received $410 on account from a customer.
f. Paid $4,000 cash for travel costs during the year.
g. Paid $8,200 cash on accounts payable.
h. Incurred $20,000 in utility expenses during the year, of which $15,000 was paid in cash and the rest owed on account.

Required:

For each of the transactions, prepare accrual basis journal entries and determine whether the accounting equation remains in balance and debits equal credits after each entry. Also, calculate the company's preliminary net income.

E3-10 Recording Journal Entries and Determining Net Income

LO 3-2, 3-3

Greek Peak is a ski resort in upstate New York. The company sells lift tickets, ski lessons, and ski equipment. It operates several restaurants and rents townhouses to vacationing skiers. The following hypothetical December 2013 transactions are typical of those that occur at the resort.

Greek Peak

a. Borrowed $500,000 from the bank on December 1, signing a note payable, due in six months.
b. Purchased a new snowplow for $20,000 cash on December 31.
c. Purchased ski supplies for $10,000 on account.
d. Incurred $22,000 in routine maintenance expenses for the chairlifts; paid cash.
e. Received $72,000 for season passes (beginning in the new year).
f. Daily lift passes were sold this month for a total of $76,000 cash.
g. Received a $320 deposit on a townhouse to be rented for five days in January 2014.
h. Paid half the charges incurred on account in (c).
i. Paid $18,000 in wages to employees for the month of December.

Required:

Prepare accrual basis journal entries for each transaction. Be sure to categorize each account as an Asset (A), Liability (L), Stockholders' Equity (SE), Revenue (R), or Expense (E), and check that debits equal credits for each journal entry. Also, calculate the company's preliminary net income.

E3-11 Recording Journal Entries and Determining Net Income

LO 3-2, 3-3

Rowland & Sons Air Transport Service, Inc., has been in operation for three years. The following transactions occurred in February 2013:

Feb. 1	Paid $200 for rent of hangar space in February.
Feb. 4	Received customer payment of $800 to ship several items to Philadelphia next month.
Feb. 7	Flew cargo from Denver to Dallas; the customer paid in full ($900 cash).
Feb. 10	Paid pilot $1,200 in wages for flying in February.
Feb. 14	Paid $100 for an advertisement run in the local paper on February 14.
Feb. 18	Flew cargo for two customers from Dallas to Albuquerque for $1,700; one customer paid $500 cash and the other asked to be billed $1,200.
Feb. 25	Purchased on account $1,350 in supplies for future use on the planes.

Required:

Prepare accrual basis journal entries for each transaction. Be sure to categorize each account as an Asset (A), Liability (L), Stockholders' Equity (SE), Revenue (R), or Expense (E). Also, calculate the company's preliminary net income.

E3-12 Recording and Posting Accrual Basis Journal Entries

Ricky's Piano Rebuilding Company has been operating for one year (2012). At the start of 2013, its income statement accounts had zero balances and its balance sheet account balances were as follows:

Cash	$ 6,000	Accounts Payable	$ 8,000
Accounts Receivable	25,000	Unearned Revenue (deposits)	3,200
Supplies	1,200	Notes Payable	40,000
Equipment	8,000	Contributed Capital	8,000
Land	6,000	Retained Earnings	9,000
Building	22,000		

Required:

1. Create T-accounts for the balance sheet accounts and for these additional accounts: Service Revenue, Rent Revenue, Wages Expense, and Utilities Expense. Enter the beginning balances.

2. Prepare journal entries for the following January 2013 transactions, using the letter of each transaction as a reference:

   a. Received a $500 deposit from a customer who wanted her piano rebuilt in February.
   b. Rented a part of the building to a bicycle repair shop; $300 rent received for January.
   c. Delivered five rebuilt pianos to customers who paid $14,500 in cash.
   d. Delivered two rebuilt pianos to customers for $7,000 charged on account.
   e. Received $6,000 from customers as payment on their accounts.
   f. Received an electric and gas utility bill for $350 for January services to be paid in February.
   g. Ordered $800 in supplies.
   h. Paid $1,700 on account in January.
   i. Paid $10,000 in wages to employees in January for work done this month.
   j. Received and paid cash for the supplies in (g).

3. Post the journal entries to the T-accounts. Show the unadjusted ending balances in the T-accounts.

E3-13 Preparing an Unadjusted Trial Balance

Refer to E3-12.

Required:

Use the balances in the completed T-accounts in E3-12 to prepare an unadjusted trial balance at the end of January 2013.

E3-14 Analyzing Transactions from Seller and Buyer Perspectives

Over-the-Top Technologies (OTT) operates a computer repair and web consulting business. News Now (NN) publishes a local newspaper. The two companies entered into the following transactions.

   a. NN billed OTT for $500 of advertising services provided this month on account.
   b. OTT repaired some of NN's equipment this month, for $135 on account.
   c. NN collected $500 cash from OTT for the advertising services provided in (a).
   d. NN paid $60 cash to OTT for OTT advertising NN's online newspaper this month on OTT's Web site.
   e. OTT and NN signed a promissory note, documenting OTT's $1,000 cash loan to NN this month with repayment to occur in six months.

Required:

Show the journal entries that OTT and NN would record for items (a)–(e). Use a two-part table, with the left side showing OTT's journal entries and the right side showing NN's journal entries.

E3-15 Inferring Transactions and Computing Effects Using T-Accounts

A company's accounting records included the following accounts.

Accounts Receivable (A)			Prepaid Rent (A)			Unearned Revenue (L)		
1/1	313		1/1	25			240	1/1
	2,573	a		43	b	c	328	
12/31	295		12/31	26			253	12/31

Required:

1. For each T-account, describe the typical transactions that cause it to increase and decrease.

2. Express each T-account in equation format (Beginning + Increase Side − Decrease Side = Ending) and then solve for the missing amounts. For example, the Accounts Receivable T-account can be expressed as: $313 + 2{,}573 - a = 295$. By rearranging the equation, you can solve for $313 + 2{,}573 - 295 = a$.

E3-16 Determining Accounting Equation Effects of Several Transactions

In January 2013, Tongo, Inc., a branding consultant, had the following transactions. Indicate the accounts, amounts, and direction of the effects on the accounting equation under the accrual basis. A sample is provided.

a. (Sample) Received $9,500 cash for consulting services rendered in January.
b. Issued stock to investors for $10,000 cash.
c. Purchased $12,000 of equipment, paying 25 percent in cash and owing the rest on a note due in 2 years.
d. Received $7,500 cash for consulting services to be performed in February.
e. Bought $1,000 of supplies on account.
f. Received utility bill for January for $1,250, due February 15.
g. Consulted for customers in January for fees totaling $15,900, due in February.
h. Received $12,000 cash for consulting services rendered in December.
i. Paid $500 toward supplies purchased in (e).

	Assets	=	Liabilities	+	Stockholders' Equity	
a. Cash	+9,500 =				Service Revenue (+R)	+9,500

E3-17 Preparing Journal Entries

For each of the transactions in E3-16 (including the sample), write the journal entry using the format shown in this chapter.

E3-18 Posting to T-Accounts

For each of the transactions in E3-16 (including the sample), post the effects to the appropriate T-accounts and determine ending account balances. Beginning account balances have been given. The sample transaction has been posted as an example.

Cash (A)			Accounts Payable (L)			Contributed Capital (SE)	
1/1/13	10,000			5,000	1/1/13		12,000 1/1/13
a.	9,500						

Accounts Receivable (A)			Unearned Revenue (L)			Retained Earnings (SE)	
1/1/13	12,500			2,500	1/1/13		8,800 1/1/13

Supplies (A)				Note Payable (L)				Service Revenues (R)	
1/1/13	800					0	1/1/13		0 1/1/13
									9,500 a.

Equipment (A)				Utilities Expense (E)	
1/1/13	5,000			1/1/13	0

LO 3-4 **E3-19 Creating an Unadjusted Trial Balance**

Based on the transactions posted to T-accounts in E3-18, create an unadjusted trial balance for Tongo, Inc., for the month ended January 31, 2013. Distinguish the balance sheet and income statement accounts as shown in Exhibit 3.9.

LO 3-3 **E3-20 Inferring Transactions and Creating Financial Statements**

An analysis of transactions made during July 2013 by NepCo, an Internet service provider, during its first month of operations is shown below. Increases and decreases affecting revenues and expenses are explained.

	Assets				=	Liabilities	+	Stockholders' Equity	
	Cash	Accounts Receivable	Supplies	Equipment		Accounts Payable		Contributed Capital	Retained Earnings
(a)	+11,000							+11,000	
(b)						+710			−710 Utilities expense
(c)		+5,000							+5,000 Service revenue
(d)	−6,000			+10,000		+4,000			
(e)	+1,000								+1,000 Service revenue
(f)			+550			+550			
(g)	−3,000					−3,000			
(h)	−2,000								−2,000 Wage expense
(i)	−750								−750 Rent expense
(j)	+1,500	−1,500							
	1,750	3,500	550	10,000		2,260		11,000	2,540

Required:

1. Describe the business activities that led to the accounting equation effects for each transaction shown above.

2. Prepare an income statement and a statement of retained earnings for July, and a classified balance sheet as of July 31, 2013. (These financial statements would be considered "preliminary" because they use unadjusted balances.)

LO 3-3 **E3-21 Determining the Effects of Various Transactions**

EZ Reader was founded in January 2013 to provide text reading and recording services. Selected transactions for EZ Reader's first month of business are as follows:

a. Issued stock to investors for $50,000 cash.
b. Billed customers $10,500 for services performed in January.
c. Purchased equipment for $24,500 for use in the business. Paid in cash.
d. Purchased $2,400 of supplies on account.
e. Received $7,500 cash from customers billed in transaction (b).
f. Used $1,500 in utilities, which will be paid in February.
g. Paid employees $3,500 cash for work done in January.
h. Paid $1,200 cash toward supplies purchased in transaction (d).

Required:

For each transaction, give (a) the name of the account being debited or credited, (b) the basic account type (A, L, SE, R, E), (c) whether the account is increased (+) or decreased (−) due to the transaction, and (d) whether the account normally holds a debit or credit balance. Transaction (a) has been given as an example. Also, calculate the company's preliminary net income.

	Debit Side of Journal Entry			
	Account Name	Account Type	Direction of Change	Normal Balance
(a)	Cash	A	+	Debit

	Credit Side of Journal Entry			
	Account Name	Account Type	Direction of Change	Normal Balance
	Contributed Capital	SE	+	Credit

COACHED PROBLEMS

|ACCOUNTING

LO 3-1, 3-2, 3-3

CP3-1 Recording Nonquantitative Journal Entries

The following list includes a series of accounts for B-ball Corporation, which has been operating for three years. These accounts are listed alphabetically and numbered for identification. Following the accounts is a series of transactions. For each transaction, indicate the account(s) that should be debited and credited by entering the appropriate account number(s) to the right of each transaction. If no journal entry is needed, write *none* after the transaction. The first transaction is used as an example.

> **TIP:** In transaction (h), remember what the expense recognition principle says.
> **TIP:** Think of transaction (j) as two transactions: (1) incur expenses and liability and (2) pay part of the liability.

Account No.	Account Title	Account No.	Account Title
1	Accounts Payable	8	Note Payable
2	Accounts Receivable	9	Prepaid Insurance
3	Cash	10	Rent Expense
4	Contributed Capital	11	Service Revenue
5	Equipment	12	Supplies Expense
6	Income Tax Expense	13	Supplies
7	Income Tax Payable		

Transactions	Debit	Credit
a. Example: Purchased equipment for use in the business; paid one-third cash and signed a note payable for the balance.	5	3, 8
b. Issued stock to new investors.	——	——
c. Collected cash for services performed this period.	——	——
d. Paid cash for rent this period.	——	——
e. Performed services this period on credit.	——	——
f. Collected cash on accounts receivable for services performed last period.	——	——
g. Paid cash on accounts payable for expenses incurred last period.	——	——
h. Purchased supplies to be used later; paid cash.	——	——
i. Used some of the supplies for operations.	——	——
j. Paid three-fourths of the income tax expense for the year; the balance will be paid next year.	——	——
k. On the last day of the current period, paid cash for an insurance policy covering the next two years.	——	——

LO 3-2, 3-3   **CP3-2 Recording Journal Entries**

Ryan Olson organized a new company, MeToo, Inc. The company provides networking management services on social network sites. You have been hired to record the following transactions.

a. May 1: Issued 1,000 shares of stock to investors for $30 per share.

b. May 15: Borrowed $50,000 from the bank to provide additional funding to begin operations; the note is due in two years.

c. May 31: Paid $2,400 for a one-year fire insurance policy with coverage starting June 1.

> **TIP:** For convenience, simply record the full amount of the payment as an asset (Prepaid Insurance). At the end of June, this account will be adjusted to its proper balance. We will study this adjustment process in Chapter 4, so just leave it as Prepaid Insurance for now.

d. June 3: Purchased furniture for the store for $15,000 on account. The amount is due within 30 days.

e. June 5: Placed advertisements in local college newspapers for a total of $250 cash.

f. June 9: Sold services for $400 cash.

g. June 14: Made full payment for the furniture purchased on account on June 3.

Required:

For each of the transactions, prepare journal entries. Be sure to categorize each account as an asset (A), liability (L), stockholders' equity (SE), revenue (R), or expense (E).

LO 3-1, 3-2, 3-3, 3-4   **CP3-3 Analyzing the Effects of Transactions Using T-Accounts, Preparing an Unadjusted Trial Balance, and Determining Net Income**

Barbara Jones opened Barb's Book Business on February 1, 2013. You have been hired to maintain the company's financial records. The following transactions occurred in February 2013, the first month of operations.

a. Received shareholders' cash contributions totaling $16,000 to form the corporation; issued stock.

b. Paid $2,400 cash for three months' rent for office space.

> **TIP:** For convenience, simply record the full amount of the payment as an asset (Prepaid Rent). At the end of the month, this account will be adjusted to its proper balance. We will study this adjustment process in Chapter 4, so just leave it as Prepaid Rent for now.

c. Purchased supplies for $300 cash.

d. Signed a promissory note, payable in two years; deposited $10,000 in the company's bank account.

e. Used the money from (d) to purchase equipment for $7,500 and other noncurrent assets for $2,500.

f. Placed an advertisement in the local paper for $425 cash.

g. Made sales totaling $1,800; $1,525 was in cash and the rest on accounts receivable.

h. Incurred and paid employee wages of $420.

i. Collected accounts receivable of $50 from customers.

j. Repaired one of the computers for $120 cash.

> **TIP:** Most repairs involve costs that do *not* provide additional future economic benefits.

Required:

1. Set up appropriate T-accounts for Cash, Accounts Receivable, Supplies, Prepaid Rent, Equipment, Other Noncurrent Assets, Notes Payable, Contributed Capital, Service Revenue, Advertising Expense, Wages Expense, and Repair Expense. All accounts begin with zero balances because this is the first month of operations.

> **TIP:** When preparing the T-accounts, you might find it useful to group them by type: assets, liabilities, stockholders' equity, revenues, and expenses.

2. Record in the T-accounts the effects of each transaction for Barb's Book Business in February, referencing each transaction in the accounts with the transaction letter. Show the unadjusted ending balances in the T-accounts.

3. Prepare an unadjusted trial balance at the end of February.

4. Refer to the revenues and expenses shown on the unadjusted trial balance. Based on this information, calculate preliminary net income and write a short memo to Barbara offering your opinion on the results of operations during the first month of business.

CP3-4 **Analyzing, Journalizing, and Interpreting Business Activities**

Lakewood Tennis Club (LTC) operates an indoor tennis facility. The company charges a $150 annual membership fee plus a member rental rate of $20 per court per hour. LTC's fiscal year end is August 31. LTC's revenue recognition policy is described in its financial statement notes as follows:

> *Revenue Recognition*—LTC earns revenue from two sources. Annual membership fees are earned by providing twelve months of services to members, so they are reported as membership revenue as they are earned over that 12-month period. Court rental fees are earned by renting courts each day, so they are reported as service revenue as courts are used by members.

On August 31, 10 new members joined and paid the annual membership fee in cash. The memberships do not begin until September 1. For the week ended September 11, LTC provided 190 court-hours of rental services for members, and collected its fees in cash. On September 13, LTC purchased and received tennis balls and other supplies. The regular retail price was $220, but LTC negotiated a lower amount ($200) that is to be paid in October. On September 15, LTC paid $1,500 to employees for the hours they worked from September 1–15. For the two weeks ended September 25, LTC provided 360 court-hours for members, and collected its fees in cash. On September 26, LTC's courts were used for a member's birthday party. LTC expects the member to pay the special event booking fee of $210 on Saturday, October 2. On September 27, LTC wrote a $300 check to an advertising company to prepare advertising flyers that will be inserted in local newspapers on October 1. On September 29, LTC received $210 on account for the member's birthday party that was held on September 26. On September 30, LTC submitted its electricity and natural gas meter readings online. According to the suppliers' Web sites, the total charges for the month will be $300. This amount will be paid on October 17 through a preauthorized online payment.

Required:

1. Indicate the accounting equation effects of the August and September events, using a table similar to the one shown for Demonstration Case B on page 114. Reference each transaction by date.

2. Prepare journal entries to record the August and September events described above. Reference each transaction by date.

3. Using your answer to requirement 1 or 2, calculate LTC's preliminary net income for September. Is LTC profitable, based on its preliminary net income?

4. Identify at least two adjustments that LTC will be required to make before it can prepare a final income statement for September.

   TIP: Scan the accounts used to answer requirements 1 and 2, looking for amounts that are no longer accurate at September 30.

GROUP A PROBLEMS

PA3-1 **Recording Nonquantitative Journal Entries**

The following is a series of accounts for Dewan & Allard, Incorporated, which has been operating for two years. The accounts are listed alphabetically and numbered for identification. Following the accounts is a series of transactions. For each transaction, indicate the account(s) that should be debited and credited by entering the appropriate account number(s) to the right of each transaction. If no journal entry is needed, write *none* after the transaction. The first transaction is given as an example.

Account No.	Account Title	Account No.	Account Title
1	Accounts Payable	9	Land
2	Accounts Receivable	10	Note Payable
3	Advertising Expense	11	Prepaid Insurance
4	Buildings	12	Service Revenue
5	Cash	13	Supplies Expense
6	Contributed Capital	14	Supplies
7	Income Tax Expense	15	Wages Expense
8	Income Tax Payable		

	Transactions	Debit	Credit
a.	Example: Issued stock to new investors.	5	6
b.	Performed services for customers this period on credit.	___	___
c.	Purchased on credit but did not use supplies this period.	___	___
d.	Prepaid a fire insurance policy this period to cover the next 12 months.	___	___
e.	Purchased a building this period by making a 20 percent cash down payment and signing a note payable for the balance.	___	___
f.	Collected cash for services that had been provided and recorded in the prior year.	___	___
g.	Paid cash for wages that had been incurred this period.	___	___
h.	Paid cash for supplies that had been purchased on accounts payable in the prior period.	___	___
i.	Paid cash for advertising expense incurred in the current period.	___	___
j.	Incurred advertising expenses this period to be paid next period.	___	___
k.	Received cash for services rendered this period.	___	___
l.	Used supplies on hand to clean the offices.	___	___
m.	Recorded income taxes for this period to be paid at the beginning of the next period.	___	___
n.	This period a shareholder sold some shares of her stock to another person for an amount above the original issuance price.	___	___

LO 3-2, 3-3

PA3-2 Recording Journal Entries

Diana Mark is the president of ServicePro, Inc., a company that provides temporary employees for not-for-profit companies. ServicePro has been operating for five years; its revenues are increasing with each passing year. You have been hired to help Diana in analyzing the following transactions for the first two weeks of April 2013:

April 2	Purchased office supplies for $500 on account.
April 5	Billed the local United Way office $3,000 for temporary services provided.
April 8	Paid $250 for supplies purchased and recorded on account last period.
April 8	Placed an advertisement in the local paper for $400 cash.
April 9	Purchased new equipment for the office costing $2,300 cash.
April 10	Paid employee wages of $1,200, which were incurred in April.
April 11	Received $1,000 on account from the local United Way office billed on April 5.
April 12	Purchased land as the site of a future office for $10,000. The land value was appraised as $11,000. Paid $2,000 down and signed a long-term note payable for the balance.
April 13	Issued 2,000 additional shares of stock for $40 per share in anticipation of building a new office.
April 14	Billed Family & Children's Services $2,000 for services rendered this month.
April 15	Received the April utilities bill for $300 to be paid next month.

Required:

For each of the transactions, prepare journal entries. Be sure to categorize each account as an asset (A), liability (L), stockholders' equity (SE), revenue (R), or expense (E).

LO 3-1, 3-2, 3-3, 3-4

PA3-3 Analyzing the Effects of Transactions Using T-Accounts, Preparing an Unadjusted Trial Balance, and Determining Net Income

Spicewood Stables, Inc., was established in Dripping Springs, Texas, on April 1, 2013. The company provides stables, care for animals, and grounds for riding and showing horses. You have been hired as the new Assistant Controller. The following transactions for April 2013 are provided for your review.

a. Received contributions from five investors of $200,000 in cash ($40,000 each).
b. Built a barn and other buildings for $142,000. The company paid half the amount in cash on April 1 and signed a three-year note payable for the balance.
c. Provided $16,000 in animal care services for customers, all on credit.
d. Rented stables to customers who cared for their own animals; received cash of $13,000.
e. Received from a customer $1,500 to board her horse in May, June, and July (record as Unearned Revenue).
f. Purchased hay and feed supplies on account for $3,000.
g. Paid $800 in cash for water utilities incurred in the month.
h. Paid $1,700 on accounts payable for previous purchases.
i. Received $1,000 from customers on accounts receivable.
j. Paid $4,000 in wages to employees who worked during the month.
k. At the end of the month, prepaid a two-year insurance policy for $3,600.
l. Received an electric utility bill for $1,200 for usage in April; the bill will be paid next month.

Required:

1. Set up appropriate T-accounts. All accounts begin with zero balances.
2. Record in the T-accounts the effects of each transaction for Spicewood Stables in April, referencing each transaction in the accounts with the transaction letter. Show the unadjusted ending balances in the T-accounts.
3. Prepare an unadjusted trial balance as of April 30, 2013.
4. Refer to the revenues and expenses shown on the unadjusted trial balance. Based on this information, calculate preliminary net income and write a short memo to the five owners offering your opinion on the results of operations during the first month of business.

PA3-4 Analyzing, Journalizing, and Interpreting Business Activities

LO 3-3, 3-5

On September 1, Pat Hopkins established Ona Cloud Corporation (OCC) as a provider of cloud computing services. Pat contributed $10,000 for 1,000 shares of OCC. On September 8, OCC borrowed $30,000 from a bank, promising to repay the bank in two years. On September 10, OCC wrote a check for $20,000 to acquire computer equipment. On September 15, OCC received $1,000 of supplies purchased on account and, on September 16, paid $1,500 for September rent. Through September 22, OCC billed its customers for $8,000 of services, of which OCC collected $6,000 in cash. On September 28, OCC paid $200 for Internet and phone service this month. On September 29, OCC paid wages of $4,000 for the month. Finally, on September 30, OCC submitted its electricity meter reading online and determined that the total charges for the month will be $300. This amount will be paid on October 14 through a preauthorized online payment.

Required:

1. Indicate the accounting equation effects of the September events, using a table similar to the one shown for Demonstration Case B on page 114. Reference each transaction by date.
2. Prepare journal entries to record the September events described above. Reference each transaction by date.
3. Using your answer to requirement 1 or 2, calculate OCC's preliminary net income for September. Is OCC profitable, based on its preliminary net income?
4. Identify at least two adjustments that OCC will be required to make before it can prepare a final income statement for September.

GROUP B PROBLEMS

PB3-1 Recording Nonquantitative Journal Entries

LO 3-1, 3-2, 3-3

Abercrombie & Fitch

Abercrombie & Fitch Co. is a specialty retailer of casual apparel. The following is a series of accounts for Abercrombie. The accounts are listed alphabetically and numbered for identification. Following the accounts is a series of transactions. For each transaction, indicate the account(s) that should be debited and credited by entering the appropriate account number(s) to the right of each transaction. If no journal entry is needed, write *none* after the transaction. The first transaction is given as an example.

Account No.	Account Title	Account No.	Account Title
1	Accounts Payable	7	Prepaid Rent
2	Accounts Receivable	8	Rent Expense
3	Cash	9	Supplies Expense
4	Contributed Capital	10	Supplies
5	Equipment	11	Unearned Revenue
6	Interest Revenue	12	Wages Expense

Transactions	Debit	Credit
a. Example: Incurred wages expense; paid cash.	12	3
b. Collected cash on account.	___	___
c. Used up supplies (cash register tapes, etc.) this period.	___	___
d. Sold gift certificates to customers; none redeemed this period.	___	___
e. Purchased equipment, paying part in cash and charging the balance on account.	___	___
f. Paid cash to suppliers on account.	___	___
g. Issued additional stock for cash.	___	___
h. Paid rent to landlords for next month's use of mall space.	___	___
i. Earned and received cash for interest on investments.	___	___

LO 3-2, 3-3

PB3-2 Recording Journal Entries

Robin Harrington established Time Definite Delivery on January 1, 2013. The following transactions occurred during the company's most recent quarter.

a. Issued stock for $80,000.
b. Provided delivery service to customers, receiving $72,000 in accounts receivable and $16,000 in cash.
c. Purchased equipment costing $82,000 and signed a long-term note for the full amount.
d. Incurred repair costs of $3,000 on account.
e. Collected $65,000 from customers on account.
f. Borrowed $90,000 by signing a long-term note.
g. Prepaid $74,400 cash to rent equipment next quarter.
h. Paid employees $38,000 for work done during the quarter.
i. Purchased (with cash) and used $49,000 in fuel for delivery equipment.
j. Paid $2,000 on accounts payable.
k. Ordered, but haven't yet received, $700 in supplies.

Required:

For each of the transactions, prepare journal entries. Be sure to categorize each account as an asset (A), liability (L), stockholders' equity (SE), revenue (R), or expense (E).

LO 3-1, 3-2, 3-3, 3-4

PB3-3 Analyzing the Effects of Transactions Using T-Accounts and Preparing an Unadjusted Trial Balance

Jessica Pothier opened FunFlatables on June 1, 2013. The company rents out moon walks and inflatable slides for parties and corporate events. The company also has obtained the use of an abandoned ice rink located in a local shopping mall, where its rental products are displayed and available for casual hourly rental by mall patrons. The following transactions occurred during the first month of operations.

a. Jessica contributed $50,000 cash to the company in exchange for its stock.
b. Purchased inflatable rides and inflation equipment, paying $20,000 cash.
c. Received $5,000 cash from casual hourly rentals at the mall.
d. Rented rides and equipment to customers for $10,000. Received cash of $2,000 and the rest is due from customers.
e. Received $2,500 from a large corporate customer as a deposit on a party booking for July 4.
f. Began to prepare for the July 4 party by purchasing various party supplies on account for $600.
g. Paid $6,000 in cash for renting the mall space this month.
h. Prepaid next month's mall space rental charge of $6,000.

i. Received $1,000 from customers on accounts receivable.
j. Paid $4,000 in wages to employees for work done during the month.
k. Paid $1,000 for running a television ad this month.

Required:

1. Set up appropriate T-accounts. All accounts begin with zero balances.
2. Record in the T-accounts the effects of each transaction for FunFlatables in June, referencing each transaction in the accounts with the transaction letter. Show the unadjusted ending balances in the T-accounts.
3. Prepare an unadjusted trial balance for the end of June 2013.
4. Refer to the revenues and expenses shown on the unadjusted trial balance to calculate preliminary net income and write a short memo to Jessica offering your opinion on the results of operations during the first month of business.

PB3-4 Analyzing, Journalizing, and Interpreting Business Activities

LO 3-3, 3-5

The following items present a sample of business activities involving Dry Cleaner Corporation (DCC) for the year ended December 31, 2013. DCC provides cleaning services for individual customers and for employees of several large companies in the city.

Dec 1:   DCC's owner paid $10,000 cash to acquire 200 DCC shares directly from DCC.

Dec 7:   DCC ordered cleaning supplies at a total cost of $2,000. The supplies are expected to be received in early January 2014.

Dec 17: Customers paid $200 cash to DCC to obtain DCC gift cards that they could use to obtain future cleaning services at no additional cost.

Dec 21: DCC ran advertising in the local newspaper today at a total cost of $500. DCC is not required to pay for the advertising until January 21, 2014.

Dec 22: DCC paid $1,000 to the landlord for January 2014 rent.

Dec 23: DCC's owner sold 20 of his own DSS shares to a private investor, at a selling price of $1,200.

Dec 28: DCC paid in full for the advertising run in the local newspaper on December 21.

Dec 29: The cleaning supplies ordered on December 7 were received today. DCC does not have to pay for these supplies until January 29.

Dec 31: Today, DCC completed cleaning services for several large companies at a total price of $2,000. The companies are expected to pay for the services by January 31, 2014.

Required:

1. Indicate the accounting equation effects of each item, using a table similar to the one shown for Demonstration Case B on page 114. Reference each item by date.
2. Prepare journal entries to record each item. Reference each item by date. If a journal entry is not required, explain.
3. Identify at least two adjustments that DCC will be required to make before it can prepare a final income statement for December.

COMPREHENSIVE PROBLEM

C3-1 Analyzing, Recording, and Posting, and
Preparing and Evaluating Financial Statements (Chapters 1-3)

|ACCOUNTING   LO 3-2, 3-3, 3-4, 3-5

Vanishing Games Corporation (VGC) operates a massively multiplayer online game, charging players a monthly subscription of $15. At the start of 2013, VGC's income statement accounts had zero balances and its balance sheet account balances were as follows:

Cash	$1,500,000	Accounts Payable	$ 108,000
Accounts Receivable	150,000	Unearned Revenue	73,500
Supplies	14,700	Notes Payable (due 2016)	60,000
Equipment	874,500	Contributed Capital	2,500,000
Land	1,200,000	Retained Earnings	1,419,700
Building	422,000		

In addition to the above accounts, VGC's chart of accounts includes the following: Subscription Revenue, Licensing Revenue, Wages Expense, Advertising Expense, and Utilities Expense.

Required:

1. Analyze the effect of the January 2013 transactions (shown below) on the accounting equation, using the format shown in this chapter's Demonstration Case B.

   a. Received $50,000 cash from customers for subscriptions that had already been earned in 2012.
   b. Received $25,000 cash from Electronic Arts, Inc., for licensing revenue earned in the month of January 2013.
   c. Purchased 10 new computer servers for $33,500; paid $10,000 cash and signed a three-year note for the remainder owed.
   d. Paid $10,000 for an Internet advertisement run on Yahoo! in January 2013.
   e. Sold 15,000 monthly subscriptions at $15 each for services provided during the month of January 2013. Half was collected in cash and half was sold on account.
   f. Received an electric and gas utility bill for $5,350 for January 2013 utility services. The bill will be paid in February.
   g. Paid $378,000 in wages to employees for work done in January 2013.
   h. Purchased $3,000 of supplies on account.
   i. Paid $3,000 cash to the supplier in (h).

2. Prepare journal entries for the January 2013 transactions listed in requirement 1, using the letter of each transaction as a reference.

3. Create T-accounts, enter the beginning balances shown above, post the journal entries to the T-accounts, and show the unadjusted ending balances in the T-accounts.

4. Prepare an unadjusted trial balance as of January 31, 2013.

5. Prepare an Income Statement for the month ended January 31, 2013, using unadjusted balances from requirement 4.

6. Prepare a Statement of Retained Earnings for the month ended January 31, 2013, using the beginning balance given above and the net income from requirement 5. Assume VGC has no dividends.

7. Prepare a classified Balance Sheet at January 31, 2013, using your response to requirement 6.

8. Why does the income statement total not equal the change in cash?

SKILLS DEVELOPMENT CASES

S3-1 Finding Financial Information

Refer to the financial statements of The Home Depot in Appendix A at the end of this book, or download the annual report from the *Cases* section of the text's Web site at www.mhhe.com/phillips4e.

Required:

1. How much did The Home Depot's sales revenue increase or decrease in the year ended January 30, 2011?
   a. Decreased $5,112 (million)
   b. Decreased $401 (million)
   c. Increased $1,821 (million)
   d. Increased $677 (million)

2. What is the largest expense on the income statement, and how much did it change from the previous year?
   a. Cost of Sales, which decreased $3,534 (million)
   b. Cost of Sales, which increased $929 (million)
   c. Selling, General and Administrative Expenses, which decreased $53 (million)
   d. Selling, General and Administrative Expenses, which increased $1,944 (million)

3. Which of the following was The Home Depot's net profit margin in the year ended January 30, 2011?
   a. 34.3%
   b. 7.8%
   c. 4.9%
   d. 4.0%

S3-2 **Comparing Financial Information**

LO 3-1

Refer to the financial statements of The Home Depot in Appendix A and Lowe's in Appendix B at the end of this book, or download the annual reports from the *Cases* section of the text's Web site at www.mhhe.com/phillips4e.

Lowe's

Required:

1. Did Lowe's sales revenues increase or decrease in the year ended January 28, 2011, as compared to the previous year? By how much? Calculate this change as a percentage of the previous year's sales revenues. Is the trend in Lowe's sales revenues more or less favorable than The Home Depot's?

2. State the amount of the largest expense on the income statement of Lowe's for the year ended January 28, 2011, and describe the transaction represented by the expense. Did this expense increase or decrease and by what percentage, as compared to the previous year? Is the trend in Lowe's largest expense more or less favorable than the trend for The Home Depot's largest expense?

S3-3 **Internet-Based Team Research: Examining the Income Statement**

LO 3-1, 3-5

As a team, select an industry to analyze. Using your Web browser, each team member should access the annual report or 10-K for one publicly traded company in the industry, with each member selecting a different company. (See S1-3 in Chapter 1 for a description of possible resources for these tasks.)

Required:

1. On an individual basis, each team member should write a short report that lists the following information:
   a. The major revenue and expense accounts on the most recent income statement.
   b. Description of how the company has followed the conditions of the revenue recognition principle.
   c. The percentage of revenues that go to covering expenses, and that are in excess of expenses (in other words, net profit margin expressed as a percentage).

2. Then, as a team, write a short report comparing and contrasting your companies using these attributes. Discuss any patterns across the companies that you as a team observe. Provide potential explanations for any differences discovered.

S3-4 **Ethical Decision Making: A Real-Life Example**

LO 3-1, 3-2, 3-3, 3-5

Read the following excerpt from an article in *Fortune* magazine and answer the questions that appear below.

> Forget about fraud. Companies don't need to lie, cheat, and steal to fool investors. Clever managers have always had, and continue to have, access to perfectly legal tricks to help make their balance sheets and income statements look better than they really are—tricks that even today won't jeopardize their ability to swear to the SEC that their books are on the up and up . . . One of the most controversial of all number games—the one that got WorldCom in trouble—is to capitalize expenses. That can have a tremendous impact on the bottom line.

1. When a company incurs a cost, its accountants have to decide whether to record the cost as an asset or expense. When costs are recorded as an asset, they are said to be *capitalized*. This builds on ideas first presented in Chapter 2, where you learned that it was appropriate to record costs as assets, provided that they possess certain characteristics. What are those characteristics?

2. The author of the article argues that even with clear rules like those referenced in question 1 above, accounting still allows managers to use "tricks" like *capitalizing expenses*. What do you suppose the author means by the expression *capitalizing expenses*?

3. Suppose that, in the current year, a company inappropriately records a cost as an asset when it should be recorded as an expense. What is the effect of this accounting decision on the current year's net income? What is the effect of this accounting decision on the following year's net income?

4. Later in the article (not shown) the author says that the videogame industry is one where companies frequently capitalize software development costs as assets. These costs include wages paid to programmers, fees paid to graphic designers, and amounts paid to game testers. Evaluate whether software development costs are likely to possess the main characteristics possessed by all assets. Can you think of a situation where software development costs might not possess these main characteristics?

5. Do you think it is always easy and straightforward to determine whether costs should be capitalized or expensed? Do you think it is always easy and straightforward to determine whether a manager is acting ethically or unethically? Give examples to illustrate your views.

LO 3-1, 3-2, 3-5

S3-5 Ethical Decision Making: A Mini-Case

Mike Lynch is the manager of an upstate New York regional office for an insurance company. As the regional manager, his pay package includes a base salary, commissions, and a bonus, when the region sells new policies in excess of its quota. Mike has been under enormous pressure lately, stemming largely from two factors. First, he is experiencing mounting personal debt due to a family member's illness. Second, compounding his worries, the region's sales of new insurance policies have dipped below the normal quota for the first time in years.

You have been working for Mike for two years, and like everyone else in the office, you consider yourself lucky to work for such a supportive boss. You also feel great sympathy for his personal problems over the last few months. In your position as accountant for the regional office, you are only too aware of the drop in new policy sales and the impact this will have on the manager's bonus. While you are working on the year-end financial statements, Mike stops by your office.

Mike asks you to change the manner in which you have accounted for a new property insurance policy for a large local business. A check for the premium, substantial in amount, came in the mail on December 31, the last day of the reporting year. The premium covers a period beginning on January 5. You deposited the check and correctly debited Cash and credited Unearned Revenue. Mike says, "Hey, we have the money this year, so why not count the revenue this year? I never did understand why you accountants are so picky about these things anyway. I'd like you to change the way you've recorded the transaction. I want you to credit a revenue account. And anyway, I've done favors for you in the past, and I am asking for such a small thing in return." With that, he leaves your office.

Required:

How should you handle this situation? What are the ethical implications of Mike's request? Who are the parties who would be helped or harmed if you went along with the request? If you fail to comply with his request, how will you explain your position to him? Justify your answers in writing.

LO 3-1, 3-2, 3-4

S3-6 Critical Thinking: Analyzing Changes in Accounts and Preparing an Unadjusted Trial Balance

Complete this case, available online at www.mhhe.com/phillips4e. By completing this case, you will learn to identify changes in spreadsheet values and infer the underlying transactions responsible for those changes.

LO 3-2, 3-3, 3-4

S3-7 Analyzing Transactions and Preparing an Unadjusted Trial Balance

Complete this case, available online at www.mhhe.com/phillips4e. By completing this case, you will learn to use a spreadsheet to capture transactions and use cell linking to prepare an end-of-period trial balance.

CONTINUING CASE

McGraw Hill connect

LO 3-2, 3-3, 3-5

CC3-1 Accounting for Business Operations

|ACCOUNTING

Starting in May 2013, Nicole has decided that she has everything that she needs to open her doors to customers. To keep up with competition, Nicole has added gift certificates and has started to advertise her company more to keep her business going in the long term. Here is a sample of some transactions that occurred in the month of May at Nicole's Getaway Spa (NGS).

May 1	Paid $3,000 cash for an insurance policy that covers the period from June 1 until May 31 next year.
May 4	Ordered five new massage tables from Spa Supplies Unlimited for $250 each for future delivery.
May 7	Provided $860 of spa services to customers on account.
May 10	Received spa supplies purchased for $800 on account to use at Nicole's Getaway Spa.
May 13	Received a bill for $60 for running an advertisement in the newspaper in May. The bill was paid in cash.
May 16	Paid one-quarter of the amount owed from May 10.
May 19	Issued $1,900 of gift certificates to customers for cash.
May 20	Obtained financing from the bank by signing a $5,000 two-year note payable.
May 22	Received two of the massage tables ordered on May 4 and paid the full amount in cash.
May 25	Paid $500 cash for utility bills for services received and billed in May.

Required:

1. For each of the transactions prepare journal entries, using the date of the transaction as the reference.
2. Calculate NGS's preliminary net income and net profit margin for the month.
3. Which of the following best describes the adjustment(s) that will have to be made before the income statement is finalized?

    a. Record supplies used up in May.
    b. Record income taxes on May's net income.
    c. All of the above.
    d. None of the above.

Adjustments, Financial Statements, and Financial Results

YOUR LEARNING OBJECTIVES

Understand the business

LO 4-1   Explain why adjustments are needed.

Study the accounting methods

LO 4-2   Prepare adjustments needed at the end of the period.

LO 4-3   Prepare an adjusted trial balance.

LO 4-4   Prepare financial statements.

LO 4-5   Explain the closing process.

Evaluate the results

LO 4-6   Explain how adjustments affect financial results.

Review the chapter

THAT WAS THEN

In the previous chapter, you learned how to analyze, record, and summarize the effects of operating transactions on balance sheet and income statement accounts.

FOCUS COMPANY: PIZZA AROMA, Ithaca, NY

In Chapter 3, you saw that Pizza Aroma sold a lot of pizza during its first month of operations—more than owner-manager Mauricio Rosa had expected. Mauricio was very curious to know how the business performed, so he computed net income based on the company's unadjusted balances. When he saw that $15 500 of revenues had led to net income of $6,400 (a net profit margin of 41.3 percent), Mauricio was very excited.

Mauricio's CPA, Laurie Hensley, cautioned him that, because he had been using unadjusted amounts in his computations, his results were not meaningful. She emphasized that under accrual accounting, adjustments need to be made at the end of an accounting period to (1) update amounts already recorded in the accounting records and (2) include events that had occurred but had not yet been recorded. These adjustments ensure that the recognition of revenues and expenses occurs in the proper period, and that assets and liabilities are reported at appropriate amounts.

In the first section of this chapter, we'll help you to understand why adjustments are a necessary part of accrual basis accounting. In the second part of the chapter, we'll show you how to determine what adjustments are needed and how they are recorded and summarized in the accounting system. This second section concludes with the final steps involved in the accounting cycle. In the third part of this chapter, you will learn the importance of adjustments for external financial statement users and, as always, the final section provides lots of opportunities for you to review and work with the material presented in this chapter.

THIS IS NOW

This chapter concludes the accounting cycle by focusing on adjustments, financial statement preparation, and the closing process.

ORGANIZATION OF THE CHAPTER

Understand the business	**Study the accounting methods**	**Evaluate the results**	**Review the chapter**
• Why adjustments are needed	• Making required adjustments • Preparing an adjusted trial balance and the financial statements • Closing temporary accounts	• Adjusted financial statements	• Demonstration case • Chapter summary • Key terms • Homework helper • Practice material

Understand the Business

WHY ADJUSTMENTS ARE NEEDED

Accounting systems are designed to record most recurring daily transactions, particularly any involving cash. As cash is received or paid, it is recorded in the accounting system. This focus on cash works well, especially when cash receipts and payments occur in the same period as the activities that lead to revenues and expenses. However, as you learned in Chapter 3, cash is not always received in the period in which the company earns the related revenue; likewise, cash is not always paid in the period in which the company incurs the related expense. In these situations, **adjustments** are made to the accounting records at the end of the period to ensure assets and liabilities are reported at appropriate amounts. These adjustments also ensure the related revenues and expenses are reported in the proper period, as required by the revenue and expense recognition principles.

Adjustments involve both income statement and balance sheet accounts. They are needed to ensure

- **Revenues** are recorded when earned (the revenue recognition principle).
- **Expenses** are recorded in the same period as the revenues to which they relate (the expense recognition or "matching" principle).
- **Assets** are reported at amounts representing economic benefits that remain at the end of the current period.
- **Liabilities** are reported at amounts owed at the end of the current period that will require a future sacrifice of resources.

Companies wait until the **end of the accounting period** to adjust their accounts because daily adjustments would be costly and time consuming. In practice, almost every financial statement account could require adjustment. Rather than try to memorize an endless list of examples, you should instead focus on learning the general nature of adjustments and the process for determining them. In general, adjustments can be grouped into two categories: (1) deferrals, and (2) accruals.

1. Deferral Adjustments

The word *defer* means to postpone until later. In accounting, we say an expense or revenue has been deferred if we have postponed reporting it on the income statement until a later period. As you saw in Chapter 3, when Pizza Aroma pays its rent in advance, the expense is initially deferred as an asset on the balance sheet (in an account called Prepaid Rent). The adjustment part comes later, at the end of the month, when one month of the prepaid rent benefits have been used up. The deferral adjustment involves reducing Prepaid Rent on the balance sheet and increasing Rent Expense on the income statement.

Deferral adjustments also can involve revenues. For example, when GQ receives cash for subscriptions before it has delivered magazines to subscribers, this revenue is initially deferred as a liability on the balance sheet (in an account called Unearned Subscriptions Revenue). The liability indicates the company's obligation to deliver magazines in the future. Later, when the company delivers the magazines, thereby meeting its obligation and earning the revenue, a deferral adjustment is made to reduce Unearned Subscriptions Revenue on the balance sheet and increase Subscriptions Revenue on the income statement.

You should note two key ideas here.

1. **Deferral adjustments are used to decrease balance sheet accounts and increase corresponding income statement accounts.** Previously deferred amounts exist on the balance sheet because the company paid cash before incurring the expense or received cash before earning revenue. When revenues are earned (as defined by the revenue recognition principle) or expenses incurred (as defined by the expense recognition principle), the previously deferred amounts are adjusted and amounts are transferred to the income statement using a deferral adjustment.

2. **Each deferral adjustment involves one asset and one expense account, or one liability and one revenue account.** The left side of Exhibit 4.1 shows a partial list of accounts that commonly require deferral adjustments.

EXHIBIT 4.1   Examples of Accounts Affected by Adjustments

Deferral Adjustments			Accrual Adjustments		
Balance Sheet	**Income Statement**		**Balance Sheet**	**Income Statement**	
Assets: Supplies ————	Supplies Expense	Expenses	Assets: Interest Receivable ————	Interest Revenue	Revenues
Prepaid Rent ————	Rent Expense		Rent Receivable ————	Rent Revenue	
Prepaid Insurance ————	Insurance Expense				
Liabilities: Unearned Ticket Revenue ———	Ticket Sales Revenue	Revenues	Liabilities: Income Tax Payable ————	Income Tax Expense	Expenses
Unearned Subscriptions Revenue ————	Subscriptions Revenue		Wages Payable ————	Wages Expense	
			Interest Payable ————	Interest Expense	

2. Accrual Adjustments

Accrual adjustments are needed when a company has earned revenue or incurred an expense in the current period but has not yet recorded it because the related cash will not be received or paid until a later period. For example, Pizza Aroma will eventually pay taxes on the income it earns this period, so an accrual adjustment will be needed at the end of the month to record increases in its Income Tax Expense and Income Tax Payable accounts. This adjustment matches Income Tax Expense to the period in which the company earned the income that caused the income taxes. Likewise, if interest revenue

January 1   January 31   March 31

Earn interest

Adjustment needed

Cash received for interest

is earned on investments this month but not received in cash until a later month, an accrual adjustment is needed at the end of the current month to record increases in the company's Interest Revenue and Interest Receivable accounts.

You should note two key ideas here.

1. **Accrual adjustments are used to record revenue or expenses when they occur prior to receiving or paying cash, and to adjust corresponding balance sheet accounts.**

2. **Each accrual adjustment involves one asset and one revenue account, or one liability and one expense account.** Notice that this differs from deferral adjustments, which pair assets with expenses and liabilities with revenues. The right side of Exhibit 4.1 shows a partial list of accounts that require accrual adjustments.

 How's it going?   Self-Study Practice

Match each situation below to two applicable reasons that require an adjustment to be made.

___ 1. Brand Affinity Technologies received a bill for this month's celebrity advertising services, which it will pay next month.

___ 2. Concerts, for which Live Nation Entertainment had sold tickets last month, were performed this month.

___ 3. Chiquita Brands International used up some of the benefits of its banana harvesting and transportation equipment.

___ 4. International Flavors and Fragrances completed a project to develop a new scent for Hilton Hotels and will be paid next month.

A. Revenue has been earned.
B. Expense has been incurred.
C. Liability has been incurred.
D. Liability has been fulfilled.
E. Asset has been acquired.
F. Asset has been used up.

After you have finished, check your answers with the solutions in the margin.

Solution to Self-Study Practice
1. B, C
2. A, D
3. B, F
4. A, E

Study the Accounting Methods

MAKING REQUIRED ADJUSTMENTS

The process of making adjustments is similar to the process you learned in Chapters 2 and 3, when accounting for daily transactions. As shown in Exhibit 4.2, the main difference is that adjustments are made at the end of each accounting period immediately prior to preparing financial statements. Adjustments are not made on a daily basis because it's more efficient to do them all at once at the end of each period. After determining the necessary adjustments (in Step 1), they are recorded using **adjusting journal entries** (in Step 2) and then summarized in the accounts (in Step 3). An adjusted trial balance is prepared to ensure total debits still equal total credits after having posted the adjusting journal entries to the accounts. If the trial balance is in balance, the financial statements can be prepared and then distributed to interested users.

EXHIBIT 4.2	Month-end Adjustments as Part of the Accounting Cycle

Timing	① Analyze	② Record	③ Summarize
Daily	Transactions	Journal entries (JEs)	• Ledgers (T-accounts) • Unadjusted trial balance
Month-end	Adjustments	Adjusting journal entries (AJEs)	• Ledgers (T-accounts) • Adjusted trial balance • Financial statements

Adjustment Analysis, Recording, and Summarizing

The first step, Analyze, involves determining the necessary adjustments to make to the accounting records. To complete this step, you need to know the balance currently reported in each account, then determine what should be reported as the balance, and finally figure out the adjustment that will take you from the current (unadjusted) balance to the desired (adjusted) balance. Exhibit 4.3 illustrates this thinking process.

EXHIBIT 4.3	Analyzing Accounts to Determine Necessary Adjustments

Where are we now?
Current (unadjusted) balances

Adjustment

Where do we need to be?
Desired (adjusted) balances

The unadjusted trial balance is a key starting point for the adjustment process because it presents the unadjusted balances for every account, which will help you identify accounts that require adjustment. Exhibit 4.4 shows Pizza Aroma's unadjusted trial balance at the end of September. This trial balance is identical to Exhibit 3.9 on page 110, except we've included balances for all accounts in Pizza Aroma's chart of accounts, including those that currently have zero balances. Alongside the unadjusted trial balance, we've identified accounts requiring adjustment at the end of September.

In the remainder of this section, we show how to analyze, record, and summarize the required adjustments. Read these pages carefully. They contain the topics that people typically find the most challenging in this chapter.

Deferral Adjustments   Let's begin by looking at deferral adjustments, which are used to update amounts that have been previously deferred on the balance sheet.

(a) Supplies Used during the Period   Of the $1,600 in supplies received in early September, $400 remain on hand at September 30.

The supplies were initially recorded as an asset on September 2 (in Chapter 3), but some of them have now been used up as of September 30. The **expense recognition principle** requires an adjustment be made to report the cost of supplies used up this month as an expense (to match against revenues). To determine the cost of supplies used up, you

EXHIBIT 4.4	Unadjusted Trial Balance

PIZZA AROMA, INC.
Unadjusted Trial Balance
At September 30, 2013

Explanation of Adjustments Needed

Account Name	Debit	Credit	
Cash	$ 8,100		
Accounts Receivable	200		Increase for right to collect from Mauricio's friend for pizza delivery (see e).
Supplies	1,600		Decrease for supplies used up during September (see a).
Prepaid Rent	7,200		Decrease for prepaid September rent benefits now used up (see b).
Cookware	630		
Equipment	60,000		
Accumulated Depreciation		$ 0	Adjust for equipment benefits used up in September (see c).
Accounts Payable		1,030	
Unearned Revenue		300	Decrease for gift card obligations met in September (see d).
Wages Payable		0	Increase for September wages incurred but not yet paid (see f).
Income Tax Payable		0	Increase for tax owed on income generated in September (see h).
Interest Payable		0	Increase for interest owed on unpaid note in September (see g).
Note Payable		20,000	
Contributed Capital		50,000	
Retained Earnings		0	
Dividends Declared	0		
Pizza Revenue		15,500	Increase for revenues earned by delivering pizza to Mauricio's friend (see e).
Wages Expense	8,100		Increase for employees' September wages not yet recorded (see f).
Rent Expense	0		Increase for expense incurred for September rent (see b).
Supplies Expense	0		Increase for supplies used up in September (see a).
Depreciation Expense	0		Increase for expense incurred by using equipment in September (see c).
Utilities Expense	600		
Advertising Expense	400		
Interest Expense	0		Increase for September interest incurred on unpaid note (see g).
Income Tax Expense	0		Increase for taxes on income generated in September (see h).
Totals	$86,830	$86,830	

have to do a little calculating. If you had $1,600 of supplies available for use and only $400 are left at the end of the month, then the $1,200 difference must be the cost of supplies used this month. In accounting terms, you should reduce the asset (Supplies) by $1,200 and show this amount as an expense (Supplies Expense).

Where are we now?
Supplies	$1,600
Supplies Expense	0

Adjustment
Supplies	−1,200
Supplies Expense	+1,200

Where do we need to be?
Supplies	$400
Supplies Expense	1,200

The effects of this adjustment on the accounting equation are shown on page 151, along with the required adjusting journal entry (AJE) and the accounts affected by it.

1 Analyze

Assets	=	Liabilities	+	Stockholders' Equity
(a) Supplies −1,200	=			Supplies Expense (+E) −1,200

2 Record

(a) *dr* Supplies Expense (+E, −SE) 1,200
        cr Supplies (−A) 1,200

3 Summarize

dr +	Supplies (A)	*cr* −		*dr* +	Supplies Expense (E, SE)	*cr* −
Unadj. bal. 1,600				Unadj. bal. 0		
	1,200	AJE (a)		AJE (a) 1,200		
Adj. bal. 400				Adj. bal. 1,200		

COACH'S TIP

The notation "Supplies Expense (+E, − SE) − 1,200" implies that the increase in an expense causes a decrease in stockholders' equity (through its negative impact on net income and retained earnings). To review this point see Exhibit 3.7 on page 102.

The financial statement effects of this adjustment are pictured in Exhibit 4.5.

EXHIBIT 4.5 **Adjusting for Assets Used-up**

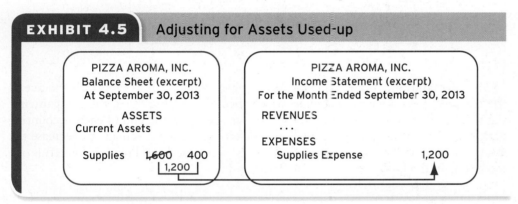

PIZZA AROMA, INC.
Balance Sheet (excerpt)
At September 30, 2013

ASSETS
Current Assets

Supplies 1,600 400
              1,200

PIZZA AROMA, INC.
Income Statement (excerpt)
For the Month Ended September 30, 2013

REVENUES
    ...

EXPENSES
    Supplies Expense   1,200

(b) Rent Benefits Expired during the Period   Three months of rent were prepaid on September 1 for $7,200, but one month has now expired, leaving only two months prepaid at September 30.

To picture how costs relate to various time periods, it's useful to draw a timeline like the one shown in Exhibit 4.6.

EXHIBIT 4.6 **Using a Timeline to Calculate Adjustments**

$1/3 \times \$7,200 = \$2,400$ expense used up as of September 30

$2/3 \times \$7,200 = \$4,800$ asset remains prepaid as of September 30

Prepaid $7,200

$2,400	$2,400	$2,400
September rent	October rent	November rent
September 1	September 30	October 31	November 30

Adjustment needed

The timeline in Exhibit 4.6 shows that the September prepayment of $7,200 represented three equal pieces of $2,400. The benefits of the first piece (pictured in red) have now expired, so they should be reported as an expense on the September income statement. Only two of the three months (2/3) remain prepaid on September 30. Thus, the $7,200 that was prepaid on September 1 needs to be adjusted on September 30 to $4,800 (2/3 × 7,200), which is the cost of the two remaining months of Prepaid Rent.

The preceding analysis has determined that an adjustment is needed to reduce Prepaid Rent by $2,400, from $7,200 to $4,800. Likewise, the adjustment needs to increase Rent Expense by $2,400. These effects are accounted for as follows:

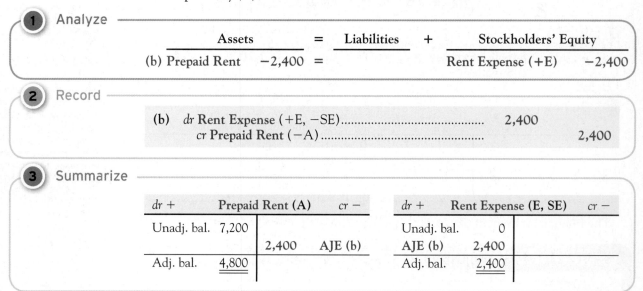

① Analyze

	Assets	=	Liabilities	+	Stockholders' Equity	
(b) Prepaid Rent	−2,400	=			Rent Expense (+E)	−2,400

② Record

(b)	dr Rent Expense (+E, −SE)...	2,400	
	cr Prepaid Rent (−A)...		2,400

③ Summarize

dr +	Prepaid Rent (A)	cr −		dr +	Rent Expense (E, SE)	cr −
Unadj. bal. 7,200				Unadj. bal. 0		
	2,400	AJE (b)		AJE (b) 2,400		
Adj. bal. 4,800				Adj. bal. 2,400		

Similar adjustments are made for other prepayments, such as Prepaid Insurance. If the company pays the cost of services in advance of receiving them, the company initially defers that cost as an asset on the balance sheet. At the end of each accounting period in which the services are used up, a deferral adjustment is made to decrease the asset and increase the related expense on the income statement. Practice doing this one more time in the following Self-Study Practice.

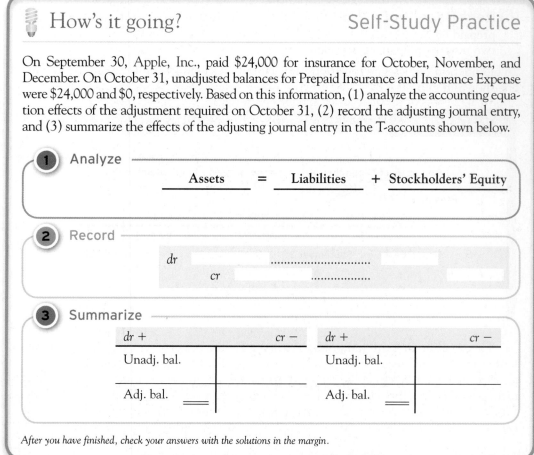

How's it going? Self-Study Practice

On September 30, Apple, Inc., paid $24,000 for insurance for October, November, and December. On October 31, unadjusted balances for Prepaid Insurance and Insurance Expense were $24,000 and $0, respectively. Based on this information, (1) analyze the accounting equation effects of the adjustment required on October 31, (2) record the adjusting journal entry, and (3) summarize the effects of the adjusting journal entry in the T-accounts shown below.

① Analyze

	Assets	=	Liabilities	+	Stockholders' Equity

② Record

dr	....	
cr	....	

③ Summarize

dr +		cr −		dr +		cr −
Unadj. bal.				Unadj. bal.		
Adj. bal.				Adj. bal.		

After you have finished, check your answers with the solutions in the margin.

Solution to Self-Study Practice

1.

	Assets	=	Liabilities	+	Stockholders' Equity	
	Prepaid Insurance −8,000	=			Insurance Expense (+E)	−8,000

2.

dr Insurance Expense (+E, −SE) 8,000
cr Prepaid Insurance (−A) 8,000

3.

dr +	Prepaid Insurance (A)	cr −		dr +	Insurance Expense (E, SE)	cr −
Unadj. bal. 24,000				Unadj. bal. 0		
	8,000	AJE		AJE 8,000		
Adj. bal. 16,000				Adj. bal. 8,000		

Notice that for events in (a), (b), and the Self-Study Practice, the deferral adjustments have two effects: (1) they reduce the **carrying value** of assets on the balance sheet, and (2) they transfer the amount of the reductions to related expense accounts on the income statement. This happens whether we're adjusting supplies, prepaid rent, or even long-term assets like buildings, vehicles, and equipment. When accounting for the use of long-term assets like buildings, vehicles, and equipment, there is one slight difference in how the carrying value is reduced, as we'll explain next.

(c) Depreciation Is Recorded for Use of Equipment
The restaurant equipment, which was estimated to last five years, has now been used for one month, representing an estimated expense of $1,000.

The expense recognition principle ("matching") indicates that when equipment is used to generate revenues in the current period, part of its cost should be transferred to an expense account in that period. This process is referred to as **depreciation**, so an income statement account named Depreciation Expense reports the cost of equipment use in the current period. On the balance sheet, we reduce the amount reported for equipment but we don't take the amount of depreciation directly out of the Equipment account. Rather, a **contra-account** is created to keep track of all the depreciation recorded against the equipment. This contra-account, named Accumulated Depreciation, is like a negative asset account that is subtracted from the Equipment account in the assets section of the balance sheet, as shown in Exhibit 4.7.

EXHIBIT 4.7 Reporting Accumulated Depreciation on the Balance Sheet

PIZZA AROMA, INC.
Balance Sheet (excerpt)
At September 30, 2013

Assets		
Equipment	$60,000	← Original cost of equipment
Less: Accumulated Depreciation	(1,000)	← Running total of depreciation recorded
Equipment, Net of Accumulated Depreciation	59,000	← Carrying value (or book value)

In our analyses below, we use a small "x" to indicate a contra-account, so the notation for a contra-account for an asset is "xA." An increase in a contra-asset account (+xA) decreases total assets on the balance sheet (−A).

1 Analyze

Assets	= Liabilities +	Stockholders' Equity
(c) Accumulated Depreciation (+xA) −1,000 =		Depreciation Expense (+E) −1,000

2 Record

(c) dr Depreciation Expense (+E, −SE)............................. 1,000
      cr Accumulated Depreciation (+xA, −A)................   1,000

3 Summarize

dr +	Equipment (A)	cr −
Unadj. bal.	60,000	
Adj. bal.	60,000	

dr −	Accumulated Depreciation (xA)	cr +
		0	Unadj. bal.
	1,000	AJE (c)
	1,000	Adj. bal.

dr +	Depreciation Expense (E, SE)	cr −
Unadj. bal.	0	
AJE (c)	1,000	
Adj. bal.	1,000	

There are four aspects of this example that you should note:

1. **Accumulated Depreciation is a balance sheet account and Depreciation Expense is an income statement account.** As a balance sheet account, Accumulated Depreciation will increase over time as it accumulates the depreciation of each period until the asset is no longer used. As an income statement account, Depreciation Expense will include only the depreciation of the current accounting year.

2. **By recording depreciation in Accumulated Depreciation, separate from the Equipment account, you can report both the original cost of equipment and a running total of the amount that has been depreciated.** This gives financial statement users a rough idea of how much of the asset's original cost (representing its original usefulness) has been used up as of the balance sheet date. In our example, approximately 1/60 ($1,000/$60,000) of the equipment's total usefulness has been used up as of September 30, 2013.

3. **The normal balance in a contra-account is always the opposite of the account it offsets.** Accumulated Depreciation is recorded with a credit because the account that it offsets, Equipment, is recorded with a debit.

4. **The amount of depreciation depends on the method used for determining it.** Depreciation methods (and their formulas) will be discussed in Chapter 9.

Just as deferral adjustments are used to record expenses incurred when assets are used up, they also are used to record the revenues earned when a company meets its obligation to provide goods or services to customers. For example, when American Airlines, Dow Jones, and T-Mobile receive cash in advance of providing flights, newspapers, and cell phone service, they initially increase (debit) Cash and increase (credit) a liability account called Unearned Revenue. Later, when they meet their obligations, a deferral adjustment is recorded, reducing the liability (with a debit) and reporting the revenue earned from these services (with a credit). Let's see how this idea applies to Pizza Aroma.

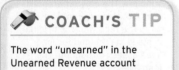

COACH'S TIP

The word "unearned" in the Unearned Revenue account means that the company hasn't done what it was paid to do. In other words, the company has an obligation (liability) to do the work or return the cash.

(d) Gift Cards Redeemed for Service   Pizza Aroma redeemed $160 of gift cards that customers used to pay for pizza.

The unadjusted trial balance reports $300 of Unearned Revenue, which represents Pizza Aroma's obligation to honor gift cards previously issued to customers. By accepting $160 of gift cards in exchange for pizza this month, Pizza Aroma has fulfilled a portion of its obligation and has earned additional revenue. Thus, a deferral adjustment is needed to reduce Unearned Revenue and increase Pizza Revenue.

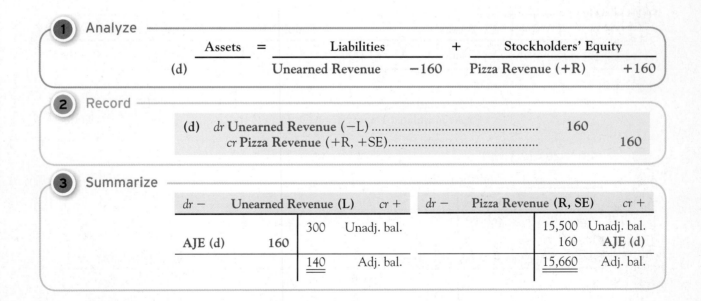

Accrual Adjustments Let's now look at common examples of accrual adjustments, which are adjustments that make the accounting records complete by including transactions that occurred but have not been recorded.

(e) Revenues Earned but Not Yet Recorded Pizza Aroma **provided $40 of Pizza to Mauricio's close friend on the last day of September, with payment to be received in October.**

Companies that regularly provide services on credit will design their accounting systems to record transactions like this on a daily basis. However, for a business like Pizza Aroma that does not typically extend credit to its customers, these kinds of events may require an accrual adjustment at month-end. Because these revenues and the right to collect them (Accounts Receivable) are earned in September, the **revenue recognition principle** indicates they should be recorded in September. The accrual adjustment will increase Accounts Receivable on the balance sheet and increase Pizza Revenue on the income statement.

1 Analyze

	Assets	= Liabilities +	Stockholders' Equity	
(e)	Accounts Receivable +40 =		Pizza Revenue (+R)	+40

2 Record

(e)	dr Accounts Receivable (+A)..	40	
	cr Pizza Revenue (+R, +SE)...		40

3 Summarize

dr +	Accounts Receivable (A)	cr −		dr −	Pizza Revenue (R, SE)	cr +
Unadj. bal.	200				15,500	Unadj. bal.
AJE (e)	40				160	AJE (d)
Adj. bal.	240				40	AJE (e)
					15,700	Adj. bal.

Other situations require accrual adjustments for revenue earned but not yet recorded. For example, interest on investments is earned daily but typically is received in cash on a yearly basis, so each month an accrual adjustment is made to increase Interest Receivable and Interest Revenue for amounts earned but not yet recorded. Also, if a company provides professional accounting, advertising, or legal services over two or more accounting periods, it typically will not receive cash or bill its customer until the services have been provided in full. Consequently, an adjustment is needed to record the portion of the total revenue that has been earned as of the end of the month.

(f) Wage Expense Incurred but Not Yet Recorded Pizza Aroma owes **$900 of wages to employees for work done in the last three days of September.**

Back in Chapter 3, Pizza Aroma paid employees $8,100 for work done through September 27 ($300 per day). As of September 30, three additional days of work have been completed at a cost of $900. Although this amount will not be paid until October, the expense relates to work done (and revenues generated) in September, so the **expense recognition principle ("matching")** requires an adjustment be made to accrue the $900 of additional wages incurred and owed by Pizza Aroma, as shown here.

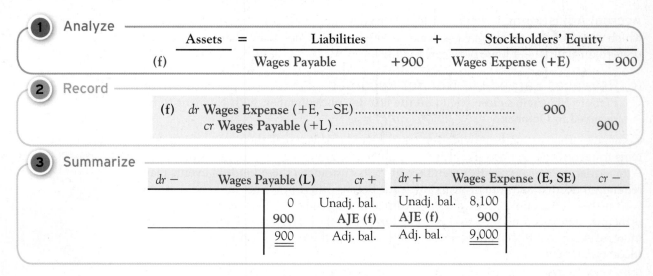

① Analyze

	Assets	=	Liabilities	+	Stockholders' Equity	
(f)			Wages Payable	+900	Wages Expense (+E)	−900

② Record

(f)	dr Wages Expense (+E, −SE)..	900	
	cr Wages Payable (+L)		900

③ Summarize

dr −	Wages Payable (L)	cr +		dr +	Wages Expense (E, SE)	cr −
	0	Unadj. bal.		Unadj. bal. 8,100		
	900	AJE (f)		AJE (f) 900		
	900	Adj. bal.		Adj. bal. 9,000		

When these $900 of wages are paid in cash the following month, Pizza Aroma will decrease Wages Payable (with a debit) and decrease Cash (with a credit).

(g) Interest Expense Incurred but Not Yet Recorded   Pizza Aroma has not paid or recorded the $100 interest that it owes for this month on its note payable to the bank.

As we saw in Exhibit 4.4, Pizza Aroma incurs interest each month on its unpaid note payable to the bank. An adjustment is needed to record the Interest Expense relating to September and, because this interest has not yet been paid, the adjustment also must record a liability called Interest Payable. Currently, the unadjusted trial balance shows $0 of Interest Payable and $0 of Interest Expense.

① Analyze

	Assets	=	Liabilities	+	Stockholders' Equity	
(g)			Interest Payable	+100	Interest Expense (+E)	−100

② Record

(g)	dr Interest Expense (+E, −SE)...	100	
	cr Interest Payable (+L)...		100

③ Summarize

dr −	Interest Payable (L)	cr +		dr +	Interest Expense (E, SE)	cr −
	0	Unadj. bal.		Unadj. bal. 0		
	100	AJE (g)		AJE (g) 100		
	100	Adj. bal.		Adj. bal. 100		

Accrual adjustments also may be required for other expenses, like property taxes and utilities, if incurred and owed during the current period (but not yet recorded). The adjusting journal entry required for each of these items would be identical to the one shown in (g), except that the word *interest* would be replaced with the particular type of cost incurred and the applicable amounts would be used. For purposes of our Pizza Aroma example, we'll assume the only remaining expense to record is the accrual of income taxes that are incurred this month but won't be paid until a later period.

(h) Income Taxes Incurred but Not Yet Recorded   Pizza Aroma pays income tax at an average rate equal to 40 percent of the company's income before taxes.

Just like you, a corporation is responsible for income tax when it generates more revenue than expenses in the current period. Income tax is calculated by multiplying (1) the company's adjusted income (before income taxes) by (2) the company's tax rate. To calculate adjusted income (before income tax), the following table starts with the unadjusted revenue and expense numbers from the unadjusted trial balance (Exhibit 4.4) and then includes the effects of adjustments to revenues and expenses. Multiply the adjusted income before income tax ($1,000) by the tax rate (40%) to get the amount of income tax ($400).

	Revenues		Expenses	
Unadjusted totals	$15,500		$ 9,100	← Calculated from Exhibit 4.4
				($9,100 = $8,100 + $600 + $400)
Adjustments: (a)			+ 1,200	
(b)			+ 2,400	
(c)			+ 1,000	
(d)	+	160		
(e)	+	40		
(f)			+ 900	
(g)			+ 100	
Adjusted totals	$ 15,700	−	$14,700	= $1,000 ← Adjusted income before income tax expense

 COACH'S TIP

Always calculate income tax expense after taking into account all revenue and expense adjustments.

The unadjusted trial balance shows that no income tax has been recorded (both Income Tax Payable and Income Tax Expense are $0). Because income was reported in September, the **expense recognition principle** requires that we record the $400 tax expense in September. The tax hasn't been paid yet, so a liability is recorded.

① Analyze

Assets	=	Liabilities	+	Stockholders' Equity
(h)		Income Tax Payable +400		Income Tax Expense (+E) −400

② Record

(h)	dr Income Tax Expense (+E, −SE)	400	
	cr Income Tax Payable (+L)		400

③ Summarize

dr −	Income Tax Payable (L)	cr +		dr + Income Tax Expense (E, SE)	cr −
		0 Unadj. bal.		Unadj. bal. 0	
	400	AJE (h)		AJE (h) 400	
		400 Adj. bal.		Adj. bal. 400	

 How's it going?   Self-Study Practice

Prior to accruing marketing expenses of $5 million, Pixar's adjusted income before income taxes was $245 million. Assuming the company's average tax rate was 40%, (1) analyze the effect of the required income tax adjustment on the accounting equation, and (2) prepare the adjusting journal entry, assuming that no amounts have been recorded yet for income taxes.

① Analyze

Assets	=	Liabilities	+	Stockholders' Equity

② Record

dr	....	
cr	....	

After you have finished, check your answers with the solution in the margin.

Additional Comments

There are three final points to learn before finishing this section. First, notice that none of the adjusting journal entries affected the Cash account. **Adjusting journal entries never involve cash.** Second, adjusting entries always include one balance sheet and one income statement account.

The third point doesn't relate to adjusting entries. Instead, it relates to dividends, which a corporation uses to distribute profits to stockholders as a return on their investment in the corporation. The decision to pay a dividend is made by the company's board of directors *after* profits have been generated, so **dividends are not expenses of the business.** Instead, they are a reduction of the retained earnings. Consequently, dividends are not reported on the income statement, but instead are subtracted on the Statement of Retained Earnings (as shown in Chapter 1). Dividends are recorded in their own special account called Dividends Declared. Because dividends reduce stockholders' equity, they are recorded with a debit just like all reductions in stockholders' equity. Now that we know Pizza Aroma has generated a profit for the month, we'll assume the company pays a dividend to stockholders. (Technically speaking, a dividend can occur any time during the year so it is typically recorded as a daily transaction when declared, rather than at the end of the period as an adjusting journal entry. But we'll show it here for convenience.)

(i) Dividend Declared and Paid   Pizza Aroma declares and pays a $500 cash dividend.

The dividend is recorded as a reduction in stockholders' equity in a special account called Dividends Declared. Because it reduces stockholders' equity, it is recorded as a debit. The corresponding reduction in Cash is recorded as a credit.

1 Analyze

	Assets	=	Liabilities	+	Stockholders' Equity	
(i) Cash	−500	=			Dividends Declared (+D)	−500

2 Record

(i)	*dr* Dividends Declared (+D, −SE)	500	
	cr Cash (−A)...		500

3 Summarize

dr +	Cash (A)	*cr* −		*dr* +	Dividends Declared (D, SE)	*cr* −
Unadj. bal. 8,100				Unadj. bal. 0		
	500	(i)		(i)	500	
Adj. bal. 7,600				Adj. bal. 500		

Exhibit 4.8 summarizes the work we've done to this point. Starting with the unadjusted trial balance prepared at the end of Chapter 3 (see the left side of Exhibit 4.8), we determined the journal entries that needed to be recorded at the end of this month (see the right side of Exhibit 4.8). Next, we posted journal entries (a) through (i) to the T-accounts, as summarized in Exhibit 4.9. Next we need to check that the accounting records are still in balance by using the adjusted T-account balances to prepare an adjusted trial balance. Assuming the trial balance shows that debits equal credits, we will finally be able to prepare the financial statements.

PREPARING AN ADJUSTED TRIAL BALANCE AND THE FINANCIAL STATEMENTS

Adjusted Trial Balance

An **adjusted trial balance** is prepared to check that the accounting records are still in balance, after having posted all adjusting entries to the T-accounts. To prepare an

EXHIBIT 4.8	Summary of Unadjusted Balances and Adjusting Journal Entries

PIZZA AROMA, INC.
Unadjusted Trial Balance
At September 30, 2013

Account Name	Debit	Credit
Cash	$ 8,100	
Accounts Receivable	200	
Supplies	1,600	
Prepaid Rent	7,200	
Cookware	630	
Equipment	60,000	
Accumulated Depreciation		$ 0
Accounts Payable		1,030
Unearned Revenue		300
Wages Payable		0
Income Tax Payable		0
Interest Payable		0
Note Payable		20,000
Contributed Capital		50,000
Retained Earnings		0
Dividends Declared	0	
Pizza Revenue		15,500
Wages Expense	8,100	
Rent Expense	0	
Supplies Expense	0	
Depreciation Expense	0	
Utilities Expense	600	
Advertising Expense	400	
Interest Expense	0	
Income Tax Expense	0	
Totals	$86,830	$86,830

PIZZA AROMA, INC.
General Journal

(a) dr Supplies Expense (+E, −SE) 1,200
    cr Supplies (−A) 1,200

(b) dr Rent Expense (+E, −SE) 2,400
    cr Prepaid Rent (−A) 2,400

(c) dr Depreciation Expense (+E, −SE) 1,000
    cr Accumulated Depreciation (+xA, −A) 1,000

(d) dr Unearned Revenue (−L) 160
    cr Pizza Revenue (+R, +SE) 160

(e) dr Accounts Receivable (+A) 40
    cr Pizza Revenue (+R, +SE) 40

(f) dr Wages Expense (+E, −SE) 900
    cr Wages Payable (+L) 900

(g) dr Interest Expense (+E, −SE) 100
    cr Interest Payable (+L) 100

(h) dr Income Tax Expense (+E, −SE) 400
    cr Income Tax Payable (+L) 400

(i) dr Dividends Declared (+D, −SE) 500
    cr Cash (−A) 500

> **Next step:** Post these adjusting journal entries as shown in Exhibit 4.9.

adjusted trial balance, just copy the adjusted T-account balances (Exhibit 4.9) into the debit or credit columns of the adjusted trial balance (left side of Exhibit 4.10).

List the accounts in the order they will appear in the balance sheet, statement of retained earnings, and income statement. As you can see in Exhibit 4.10, the trial balance proves that Pizza Aroma's accounting records are in balance (total debits = $89,270 = total credits), so the financial statements can be prepared. The balance for each account in the trial balance is reported only once on either the income statement, statement of retained earnings, or balance sheet. Typically, the income statement is prepared first because its final number, net income, flows into the statement of retained earnings, which then flows into the balance sheet. As you will see in later chapters of this book, the statement of cash flows and notes to the financial statements are prepared last because they include information obtained from the income statement, statement of retained earnings, and balance sheet (plus other sources).

Income Statement and Statement of Retained Earnings

Prepare the income statement by creating the usual heading (who, what, when) and listing the names and amounts for each revenue and expense account from the adjusted

> **Learning Objective 4-4**
> Prepare financial statements.

EXHIBIT 4.9 Pizza Aroma's Adjusted Accounts

Cash (A) — dr + / cr −

Unadj. bal.	8,100		
		500	(i)
Adj. bal.	7,600		

Accounts Receivable (A) — dr + / cr −

Unadj. bal.	200	
AJE (e)	40	
Adj. bal.	240	

Supplies (A) — dr + / cr −

Unadj. bal.	1,600		
		1,200	AJE (a)
Adj. bal.	400		

Prepaid Rent (A) — dr + / cr −

Unadj. bal.	7,200		
		2,400	AJE (b)
Adj. bal.	4,800		

Cookware (A) — dr + / cr −

Adj. bal.	630

Equipment (A) — dr + / cr −

Adj. bal.	60,000

Accumulated Depreciation (xA) — dr − / cr +

		0	Unadj. bal.
		1,000	AJE (c)
		1,000	Adj. bal.

Accounts Payable (L) — dr − / cr +

		1,030	Adj. bal.

Unearned Revenue (L) — dr − / cr +

		300	Unadj. bal.
AJE (d)	160		
		140	Adj. bal.

Wages Payable (L) — dr − / cr +

		0	Unadj. bal.
		900	AJE (f)
		900	Adj. bal.

Income Tax Payable (L) — dr − / cr +

		0	Unadj. bal.
		400	AJE (h)
		400	Adj. bal.

Interest Payable (L) — dr − / cr +

		0	Unadj. bal.
		100	AJE (g)
		100	Adj. bal.

Note Payable (L) — dr − / cr +

		20,000	Adj. bal.

Contributed Capital (SE) — dr − / cr +

		50,000	Adj. bal.

Retained Earnings (SE) — dr − / cr +

		0	Adj. bal.

Dividends Declared (D, SE) — dr + / cr −

Unadj. bal.	0	
(i)	500	
Adj. bal.	500	

Pizza Revenue (R, SE) — dr − / cr +

		15,500	Unadj. bal.
		160	AJE (d)
		40	AJE (e)
		15,700	Adj. bal.

Wages Expense (E, SE) — dr + / cr −

Unadj. bal.	8,100	
AJE (f)	900	
Adj. bal.	9,000	

Rent Expense (E, SE) — dr + / cr −

Unadj. bal.	0	
AJE (b)	2,400	
Adj. bal.	2,400	

Supplies Expense (E, SE) — dr + / cr −

Unadj. bal.	0	
AJE (a)	1,200	
Adj. bal.	1,200	

Depreciation Expense (E, SE) — dr + / cr −

Unadj. bal.	0	
AJE (c)	1,000	
Adj. bal.	1,000	

Utilities Expense (E, SE) — dr + / cr −

Adj. bal.	600

Advertising Expense (E, SE) — dr + / cr −

Adj. bal.	400

Interest Expense (E, SE) — dr + / cr −

Unadj. bal.	0	
AJE (g)	100	
Adj. bal.	100	

Income Tax Expense (E, SE) — dr + / cr −

Unadj. bal.	0	
AJE (h)	400	
Adj. bal.	400	

> **Next step:** Summarize these adjusted balances in an adjusted trial balance as shown in Exhibit 4.10.

trial balance, as shown in Exhibit 4.10. Notice that each major category of items on the income statement is subtotaled prior to computing net income for the period.

Account balances from the adjusted trial balance are also used in the statement of retained earnings, as shown in Exhibit 4.10. Notice that **the amount coming from the adjusted trial balance is the beginning-of-year balance for Retained Earnings.** This account balance doesn't yet include revenues, expenses, and dividends for the current period because they've been recorded in their own separate accounts. Eventually we will

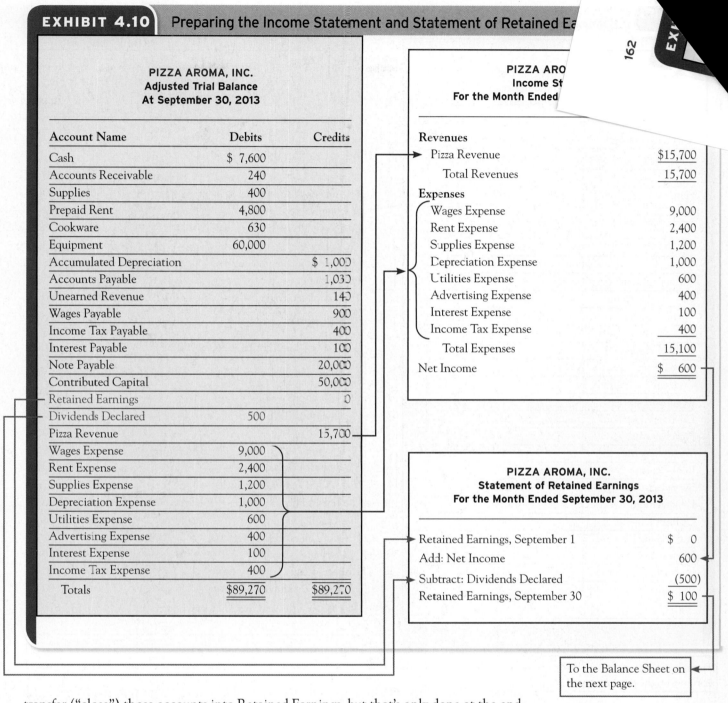

EXHIBIT 4.10 Preparing the Income Statement and Statement of Retained Ea...

PIZZA AROMA, INC.
Adjusted Trial Balance
At September 30, 2013

Account Name	Debits	Credits
Cash	$ 7,600	
Accounts Receivable	240	
Supplies	400	
Prepaid Rent	4,800	
Cookware	630	
Equipment	60,000	
Accumulated Depreciation		$ 1,000
Accounts Payable		1,030
Unearned Revenue		140
Wages Payable		900
Income Tax Payable		400
Interest Payable		100
Note Payable		20,000
Contributed Capital		50,000
Retained Earnings		0
Dividends Declared	500	
Pizza Revenue		15,700
Wages Expense	9,000	
Rent Expense	2,400	
Supplies Expense	1,200	
Depreciation Expense	1,000	
Utilities Expense	600	
Advertising Expense	400	
Interest Expense	100	
Income Tax Expense	400	
Totals	$89,270	$89,270

PIZZA ARO...
Income St...
For the Month Ended...

Revenues

Pizza Revenue	$15,700
Total Revenues	15,700

Expenses

Wages Expense	9,000
Rent Expense	2,400
Supplies Expense	1,200
Depreciation Expense	1,000
Utilities Expense	600
Advertising Expense	400
Interest Expense	100
Income Tax Expense	400
Total Expenses	15,100
Net Income	$ 600

PIZZA AROMA, INC.
Statement of Retained Earnings
For the Month Ended September 30, 2013

Retained Earnings, September 1	$ 0
Add: Net Income	600
Subtract: Dividends Declared	(500)
Retained Earnings, September 30	$ 100

To the Balance Sheet on the next page.

transfer ("close") those accounts into Retained Earnings, but that's only done at the end of the year. For now, the Retained Earnings account on the adjusted trial balance provides the opening amount on the statement of retained earnings. The amount for Net Income on the next line of the statement of retained earnings comes from the income statement, and the Dividends Declared number comes from the adjusted trial balance.

Balance Sheet

Like the other statements, the balance sheet is prepared from the adjusted trial balance, as shown in Exhibit 4.11. When preparing the balance sheet, watch out for three things. First, remember to classify assets as current if they will be turned into cash or used up within 12 months. Liabilities should be classified as current if they will be fulfilled (paid) within 12 months. Second, note that Accumulated Depreciation is subtracted from Equipment in the assets section. Third, get the Retained Earnings balance from the statement

COACH'S TIP

Dividends Declared is reported only on the statement of retained earnings.

HIBIT 4.11 **Preparing the Balance Sheet**

PIZZA AROMA

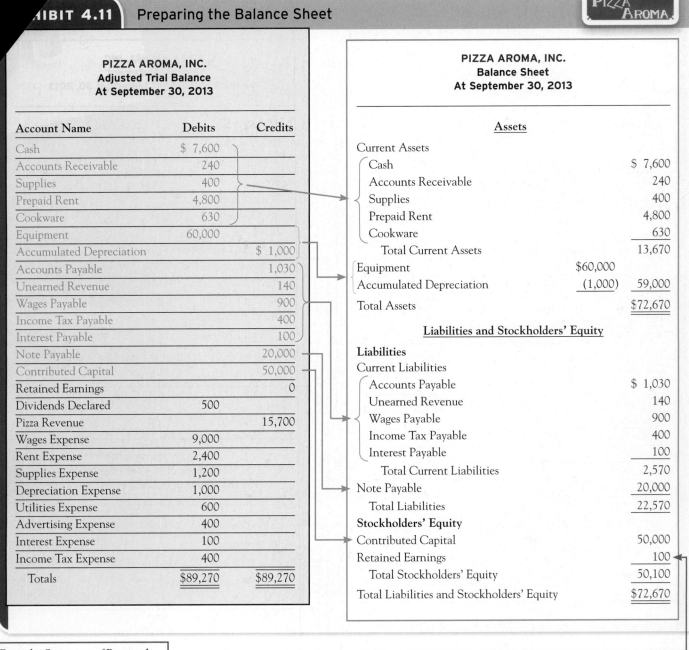

PIZZA AROMA, INC.
Adjusted Trial Balance
At September 30, 2013

Account Name	Debits	Credits
Cash	$ 7,600	
Accounts Receivable	240	
Supplies	400	
Prepaid Rent	4,800	
Cookware	630	
Equipment	60,000	
Accumulated Depreciation		$ 1,000
Accounts Payable		1,030
Unearned Revenue		140
Wages Payable		900
Income Tax Payable		400
Interest Payable		100
Note Payable		20,000
Contributed Capital		50,000
Retained Earnings		0
Dividends Declared	500	
Pizza Revenue		15,700
Wages Expense	9,000	
Rent Expense	2,400	
Supplies Expense	1,200	
Depreciation Expense	1,000	
Utilities Expense	600	
Advertising Expense	400	
Interest Expense	100	
Income Tax Expense	400	
Totals	$89,270	$89,270

PIZZA AROMA, INC.
Balance Sheet
At September 30, 2013

Assets

Current Assets		
Cash		$ 7,600
Accounts Receivable		240
Supplies		400
Prepaid Rent		4,800
Cookware		630
Total Current Assets		13,670
Equipment	$60,000	
Accumulated Depreciation	(1,000)	59,000
Total Assets		$72,670

Liabilities and Stockholders' Equity

Liabilities		
Current Liabilities		
Accounts Payable		$ 1,030
Unearned Revenue		140
Wages Payable		900
Income Tax Payable		400
Interest Payable		100
Total Current Liabilities		2,570
Note Payable		20,000
Total Liabilities		22,570
Stockholders' Equity		
Contributed Capital		50,000
Retained Earnings		100
Total Stockholders' Equity		50,100
Total Liabilities and Stockholders' Equity		$72,670

From the Statement of Retained Earnings on the previous page.

of retained earnings, not from the adjusted trial balance. (The adjusted trial balance still reports the period's opening Retained Earnings balance.)

Statement of Cash Flows and Notes

We don't want you to forget that the statement of cash flows (SCF) and notes to the financial statements must also be prepared as part of the financial statements. But you look a little tired, so we'll leave the SCF for Chapter 12 and we'll slide information about financial statement notes into each of the remaining chapters.

CLOSING TEMPORARY ACCOUNTS

Learning Objective 4-5
Explain the closing process.

The last step of the accounting cycle is referred to as the *closing process*. As shown in the first column in Exhibit 4.12, this step is performed only at the end of the year, after the financial statements have been prepared. The closing process cleans up the accounting records to get them ready to begin tracking the results in the following year. It's kind of like hitting the trip odometer on your car or the reset button on your Xbox.

EXHIBIT 4.12	Year-end Closing Concludes the Accounting Cycle

Timing	① Analyze ⟶	② Record ⟶	③ Summarize
Daily	Transactions	Journal entries (JEs)	• Ledgers (T-accounts) • Unadjusted trial balance
Month-end	Adjustments	Adjusting journal entries (AJEs)	• Ledgers (T-accounts) • Adjusted trial balance • Financial statements
Year-end	Closing	Closing journal entries (CJEs)	• Ledgers (T-accounts) • Post-closing trial balance

Closing Income Statement and Dividend Accounts

In Chapter 3, you learned to think of revenue and expense accounts as subcategories of Retained Earnings, which are used to track earnings-related transactions of the current year. Earlier in this chapter, you saw that the Dividends Declared account is similarly used to track dividends declared during the current year. At the end of each year, after all the year's transactions and adjustments are recorded, all revenue, expense, and dividends declared accounts are closed by moving their balances to their permanent home in Retained Earnings. The Retained Earnings account, like all other balance sheet accounts, is considered a **permanent account** because its ending balance from one year becomes its beginning balance for the following year. In contrast, revenues, expenses, and dividends declared are considered **temporary accounts** because they are used to track only the current year's results and then are closed before the next year's activities are recorded.

The closing process serves two purposes:

1. **Transfer net income (or loss) and dividends to Retained Earnings.** After the closing journal entries are prepared and posted, the balance in the Retained Earnings account will agree with the ending Retained Earnings balance on the statement of retained earnings and the balance sheet.

2. **Establish zero balances in all income statement and dividend accounts.** After the closing journal entries are prepared and posted, the balances in the temporary accounts are reset to zero to start accumulating next year's results.

Closing journal entries follow the usual debits-equal-credits format used for the transaction journal entries (in Chapters 2 and 3) and adjusting journal entries (shown earlier in this chapter). Because they're the last thing done during the year, they're posted immediately to the accounts. (Some computerized systems record and post closing journal entries automatically.) Two closing journal entries are needed:[1]

1. Debit each revenue account for the amount of its credit balance, credit each expense account for the amount of its debit balance, and record the difference in Retained Earnings. If you've done it right, **the amount credited to Retained Earnings should equal Net Income on the Income Statement.** (If the company has a net loss, Retained Earnings will be debited.)

2. Credit the Dividends Declared account for the amount of its debit balance and debit Retained Earnings for the same amount.

Exhibit 4.13 shows the closing process for Pizza Aroma (assuming, for sake of illustration, that it closes its books on the last day of September).

> **YOU SHOULD KNOW**
>
> **Permanent accounts:** Accounts that track financial results from year to year by carrying their ending balances into the next year. **Temporary accounts:** Accounts that track financial results for a limited period of time by having their balances zeroed out at the end of each accounting year.

---

[1]Some companies use a four-step process, by closing (1) revenue and (2) expense accounts to a special summary account, called (3) Income Summary, which then is closed to (4) Retained Earnings, along with Dividends Declared.

EXHIBIT 4.13   Analyzing, Preparing, and Summarizing the Closing Journal Entries

1 Analyze

The analysis step for closing the temporary accounts only requires that you identify, from the adjusted trial balance, the temporary accounts with debit balances (to be credited below) and the temporary accounts with credit balances (to be debited below).

2 Record

CJE 1. Close revenue and expense accounts:

dr Pizza Revenue (−R)	15,700	
cr Wages Expense (−E)		9,000
cr Rent Expense (−E)		2,400
cr Supplies Expense (−E)		1,200
cr Depreciation Expense (−E)		1,000
cr Utilities Expense (−E)		600
cr Advertising Expense (−E)		400
cr Interest Expense (−E)		100
cr Income Tax Expense (−E)		400
cr Retained Earnings (+SE)		600

CJE 2. Close the dividends declared account:

dr Retained Earnings (−SE)	500	
cr Dividends Declared (−D)		500

3 Summarize

dr −	Pizza Revenue (R, SE)		*cr* +
		15,700	Adj. bal.
CJE (1)	15,700		
		0	Closed bal.

dr +	Advertising Expense (E, SE)		*cr* −
Adj. bal.	400		
		400	CJE (1)
Closed bal.	0		

dr +	Wages Expense (E, SE)		*cr* −
Adj. bal.	9,000		
		9,000	CJE (1)
Closed bal.	0		

dr +	Interest Expense (E, SE)		*cr* −
Adj. bal.	100		
		100	CJE (1)
Closed bal.	0		

dr +	Rent Expense (E, SE)		*cr* −
Adj. bal.	2,400		
		2,400	CJE (1)
Closed bal.	0		

dr +	Income Tax Expense (E, SE)		*cr* −
Adj. bal.	400		
		400	CJE (1)
Closed bal.	0		

dr +	Supplies Expense (E, SE)		*cr* −
Adj. bal.	1,200		
		1,200	CJE (1)
Closed bal.	0		

dr +	Dividends Declared (D, SE)		*cr* −
Adj. bal.	500		
		500	CJE (2)
Closed bal.	0		

dr +	Depreciation Expense (E, SE)		*cr* −
Adj. bal.	1,000		
		1,000	CJE (1)
Closed bal.	0		

dr −	Retained Earnings (SE)		*cr* +
		0	Adj. bal.
CJE (2)	500	600	CJE (1)
		100	Closed bal.

dr +	Utilities Expense (E, SE)		*cr* −
Adj. bal.	600		
		600	CJE (1)
Closed bal.	0		

Post-Closing Trial Balance

After the closing journal entries are posted, all temporary accounts should have zero balances. These accounts will be ready for summarizing transactions recorded next year. The ending balance in Retained Earnings is now up to date (it matches the year-end amount on the statement of retained earnings and the balance sheet) and is carried forward as the beginning Retained Earnings balance for the next year. As the last step of the accounting cycle, you should prepare a **post-closing trial balance** (as shown in Exhibit 4.14). In this context, *post* means "after," so a post-closing trial balance is an "after-closing" trial balance that is prepared as a final check that total debits still equal total credits and that all temporary accounts have been closed.

EXHIBIT 4.14	Pizza Aroma's Post-Closing Trial Balance

PIZZA AROMA, INC.
Post-Closing Trial Balance
At September 30, 2013

Account Name	Debits	Credits
Cash	$ 7,600	
Accounts Receivable	240	
Supplies	400	
Prepaid Rent	4,800	
Cookware	630	
Equipment	60,000	
Accumulated Depreciation		$ 1,000
Accounts Payable		1,030
Unearned Revenue		140
Wages Payable		900
Income Tax Payable		400
Interest Payable		100
Note Payable		20,000
Contributed Capital		50,000
Retained Earnings		100
Dividends Declared	0	
Pizza Revenue		0
Wages Expense	0	
Rent Expense	0	
Supplies Expense	0	
Depreciation Expense	0	
Utilities Expense	0	
Advertising Expense	0	
Interest Expense	0	
Income Tax Expense	0	
Totals	$73,670	$73,670

COACH'S TIP

Total debits on the post-closing trial balance don't equal the total assets on the balance sheet because Accumulated Depreciation (a credit balance on the trial balance) is subtracted from assets on the Balance Sheet.

EXHIBIT 4.15   The Accounting Process

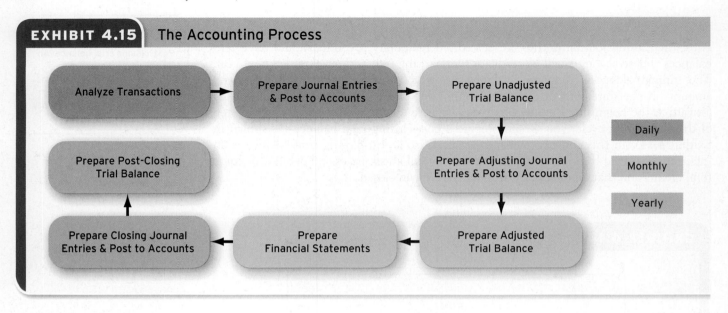

Now that we've completed the accounting cycle, it seems appropriate to summarize it one more time. Exhibit 4.12 (on page 163) showed one way to organize the various steps of the accounting cycle. Exhibit 4.15 presents the same ideas in a slightly different format. The steps in the coral, blue, and gold boxes are done daily, monthly, and yearly, respectively.

Evaluate the Results

ADJUSTED FINANCIAL RESULTS

Learning Objective 4-6
Explain how adjustments affect financial results.

Throughout this chapter, you learned various adjustments that must be made to the accounting records, when finalizing and preparing the financial statements. These adjustments help to ensure that all revenues and expenses are reported in the period in which they are earned and incurred. As a result of these adjustments, the financial statements present the best picture of whether the company's business activities were profitable that period and what economic resources the company owns and owes at the end of that period. Without these adjustments, the financial statements present an incomplete and misleading picture of the company's financial performance.

Pizza Aroma provides a good example of the extent to which unadjusted balances may change during the adjustment process. Chapter 3 ended with Mauricio believing that Pizza Aroma had earned a sizable profit (net income of $6,400 from revenue of $15,500, resulting in a net profit margin of 41.3%). After making the required adjustments in this chapter, the company's adjusted results indicated a much different picture (net income of $600 from revenue of $15,700, yielding a net profit margin of 3.8%). Consequently, Mauricio learned that he had much to improve upon in the upcoming months. He set a goal of attempting to increase the company's revenue by expanding his customer base, while at the same time trying to control expenses. He was well aware that even large companies go out of business if they fail to maintain revenues and control their expenses (as demonstrated in the following Spotlight on Financial Reporting).

Financial Crisis: Anatomy of a Business Failure

Until its bankruptcy in late 2008 and liquidation in early 2009, Circuit City was one of the largest electronics stores in the United States. However, Circuit City's inability to maintain sales and control expenses ultimately led to its demise. Notice how quickly the company's stock price fell as it reported deteriorating financial results.

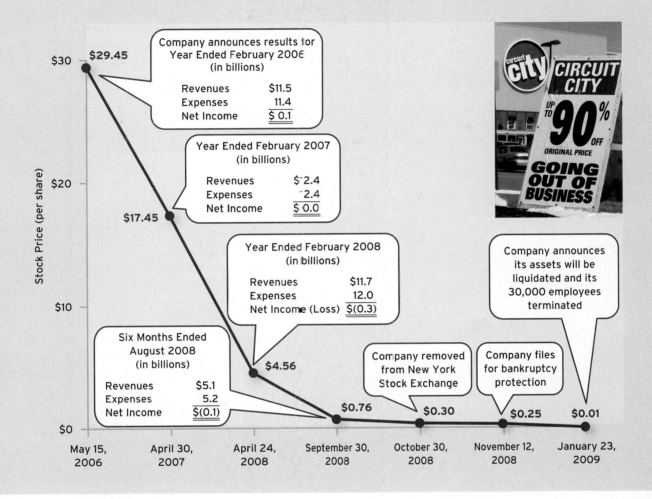

REVIEW THE CHAPTER

DEMONSTRATION CASE

We take our final look at the accounting activities of Goodbye Grass Corporation by illustrating the activities at the end of the accounting cycle: the adjustment process, financial statement preparation, and the closing process. No adjustments have been made to the accounts yet. Your starting point will be the following unadjusted trial balance dated April 30, 2013:

GOODBYE GRASS CORPORATION
Unadjusted Trial Balance
At April 30, 2013

Account Name	Debits	Credits
Cash	$ 4,510	
Accounts Receivable	1,700	
Note Receivable	1,250	
Interest Receivable	0	
Prepaid Insurance	300	
Equipment	4,600	
Accumulated Depreciation		$ 0
Land	3,750	
Accounts Payable		620
Unearned Revenue		1,600
Wages Payable		0
Interest Payable		0
Income Tax Payable		0
Note Payable		4,000
Contributed Capital		9,000
Retained Earnings		0
Mowing Revenue		5,200
Interest Revenue		0
Wages Expense	3,900	
Fuel Expense	410	
Insurance Expense	0	
Depreciation Expense	0	
Interest Expense	0	
Income Tax Expense	0	
Totals	$20,420	$20,420

By reviewing the unadjusted trial balance, you identify three deferral accounts (Prepaid Insurance, Equipment, and Unearned Revenue) that may need to be adjusted in addition to accruals that may be necessary relating to wages, income taxes, and interest on the Note Receivable and Note Payable. The following information is determined at the end of the accounting cycle:

Deferral Adjustments

a. One-fourth of the $1,600 cash received from the city at the beginning of April for future mowing service has been earned in April. The $1,600 in Unearned Revenue represents four months of service (April through July).

b. Insurance purchased at the beginning of April for $300 provides coverage for six months (April through September). The insurance coverage for April has now been used.
   TIP: Account for the expiry of prepaid insurance just like the expiry of prepaid rent.

c. Mowers, edgers, rakes, and hand tools (equipment) have been used in April to generate revenues. The company estimates $300 in depreciation each year.

Accrual Adjustments

d. Wages have been paid through April 28. Employees worked the last two days of April and will be paid in May. Wages amount to $200 per day.

e. Interest incurred and payable on the note payable is $45 for the month of April.

f. Interest earned and receivable on the note receivable is $10 for the month of April.

g. The estimated income tax rate for Goodbye Grass Corporation is 35 percent.

Required:

1. Analyze items (a)–(g) with the goal of identifying the effects of required adjustments on the basic accounting equation (Assets = Liabilities + Stockholders' Equity), using the format shown in the chapter.

2. Record the adjusting journal entries required at the end of April.

3. Summarize the effects of each adjusting journal entry in T-accounts for each account affected. Obtain beginning balances from the unadjusted trial balance, then post the adjusting journal entries from requirement 2, and calculate adjusted April 30 balances.

4. Prepare an adjusted trial balance to ensure debit and credit balances are equal, remembering to include all accounts in the trial balance (and not just the ones affected by the adjusting journal entries).

5. Prepare an income statement, statement of retained earnings, and classified balance sheet from the amounts in the adjusted trial balance.

6. Prepare the closing journal entries that would be required if Goodbye Grass Corporation's fiscal year ended April 30, 2013.

   After completing requirements 1–6, check your answers with the following solution.

Suggested Solution

1. Adjustment analysis:

   a. The unadjusted balances are $1,600 for Unearned Revenue and $5,200 for Mowing Revenue. One-fourth of the $1,600 has been earned in April ($400 = ¼ × $1,600), bringing total mowing revenues for the month to $5,600 ($5,200 + $400). Three-fourths of the $1,600 remain unearned at the end of April ($1,200 = ¾ × $1,600). To reach these desired balances, we need an adjustment that decreases Unearned Revenue by $400 and increases Mowing Revenue by $400.

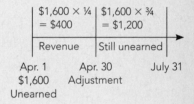

Assets	=	Liabilities	+	Stockholders' Equity
		Unearned Revenue −400		**Mowing Revenue (+R)** +400

   b. The unadjusted balances are $300 for Prepaid Insurance and $0 for Insurance Expense. One-sixth of the $300 has expired in April, resulting in an insurance expense for the month of $50 (= ⅙ × $300). Five of the six months of insurance coverage remain unused at the end of April ($250 = ⅚ × $300). To reach these desired balances, we need an adjustment that decreases Prepaid Insurance by $50 and increases Insurance Expense by $50.

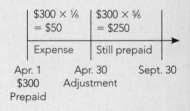

Assets	=	Liabilities	+	Stockholders' Equity
Prepaid Insurance −50				**Insurance Expense (+E)** −50

   c. The unadjusted balances are $0 for Accumulated Depreciation and $0 for Depreciation Expense. Yearly depreciation of $300 equals $25 for just one month ($300 × 1/12). To go from the unadjusted balances of $0 to the desired adjusted balances of $25, we increase the expense and contra-account balances by $25.

Assets	=	Liabilities	+	Stockholders' Equity
Accumulated Depreciation (+xA) −25				**Depreciation Expense (+E)** −25

   d. The unadjusted balances are $0 for Wages Payable and $3,900 for Wages Expense. Because the final two days of work done in April are unpaid, we need to record a liability for $400 (2 × $200). Total wages expense for the month should include the $3,900 paid for work from April 1–28 plus the $400 not yet paid for work on April 29 and 30. To reach these desired balances, we need an adjustment increasing Wages Payable by $400 and increasing Wages Expense by $400.

Assets	=	Liabilities	+	Stockholders' Equity
		Wages Payable +400		**Wages Expense (+E)** −400

   e. The unadjusted balances are $0 for Interest Payable and $0 for Interest Expense. Interest of $45 was incurred in April, so the adjustment needs to increase both accounts by $45.

Assets	=	Liabilities	+	Stockholders' Equity
		Interest Payable +45		**Interest Expense (+E)** −45

f. The unadjusted balances are $0 for Interest Receivable and $0 for Interest Revenue. Interest of $10 was earned in April, so the adjustment needs to increase both accounts by $10.

Assets	=	Liabilities	+	Stockholders' Equity	
Interest Receivable	+10			Interest Revenue (+R)	+10

g. The unadjusted balances are $0 for Income Tax Payable and $0 for Income Tax Expense. The amount of calculated income taxes will increase both of these accounts. Income taxes are calculated as 35% of adjusted income before tax for the month, as follows:

		Revenues	Expenses	
Unadjusted totals		$5,200	$4,310	← Calculated from unadjusted trial balance
Adjustments:	(a)	+ 400		($4,310 = $3,900 + $410)
	(b)		+ 50	
	(c)		+ 25	
	(d)		+ 400	
	(e)		+ 45	
	(f)	+ 10		
Adjusted totals		$5,610	− $4,830	= $780 Adjusted income before income tax
				× 35% Tax rate
				$273 **Income tax**

Assets	=	Liabilities	+	Stockholders' Equity	
		Income Tax Payable	+273	Income Tax Expense (+E)	−273

2. Adjusting journal entries:

  a. *dr* Unearned Revenue (−L)... 400

      cr Mowing Revenue (+R, +SE)...   400

  b. *dr* Insurance Expense (+E, −SE)... 50

      cr Prepaid Insurance (−A)..   50

  c. *dr* Depreciation Expense (+E, −SE)..................................... 25

      cr Accumulated Depreciation (+xA, −A).......................   25

  d. *dr* Wages Expense (+E, −SE)... 400

      cr Wages Payable (+L)   400

  e. *dr* Interest Expense (+E, −SE)... 45

      cr Interest Payable (+L)...   45

  f. *dr* Interest Receivable (+A)... 10

      cr Interest Revenue (+R, +SE)...   10

  g. *dr* Income Tax Expense (+E, −SE)..................................... 273

      cr Income Tax Payable (+L)   273

3. T-accounts affected by adjusting journal entries:*

dr +	Interest Receivable (A)	*cr* −
Beg. bal.	0	
(f)	10	
End. bal.	10	

dr −	Interest Payable (L)	*cr* +
	0	Beg. bal.
	45	(e)
	45	End. bal.

dr +	Insurance Expense (E)	*cr* −
Beg. bal.	0	
(b)	50	
End. bal.	50	

dr +	Prepaid Insurance (A)	*cr* −
Beg. bal.	300	
	50	(b)
End. bal.	250	

dr −	Income Tax Payable (L)	*cr* +
	0	Beg. bal.
	273	(g)
	273	End. bal.

dr +	Depreciation Expense (E)	*cr* −
Beg. bal.	0	
(c)	25	
End. bal.	25	

*See page 114 (Chapter 3) for balances of T-accounts not affected by adjusting journal entries.

dr –	Accumulated Depreciation (xA)	cr +
	0	Beg. bal.
	25	(c)
	25	End. bal.

dr –	Mowing Revenue (R, SE)	cr +
	5,200	Beg. bal.
	400	(a)
	5,600	End. bal.

dr +	Interest Expense (E, SE)	cr –
Beg. bal.	0	
(e)	45	
End. bal.	45	

dr –	Unearned Revenue (L)	cr +
	1,600	Beg. bal.
(a) 400		
	1,200	End. bal.

dr –	Interest Revenue (R, SE)	cr +
	0	Beg. bal.
	10	(f)
	10	End. bal.

dr +	Income Tax Expense (E, SE)	cr –
Beg. bal.	0	
(g)	273	
End. bal.	273	

dr –	Wages Payable (L)	cr +
	0	Beg. bal.
	400	(d)
	400	End. bal.

dr +	Wages Expense (E, SE)	cr –
Beg. bal.	3,900	
(d)	400	
End. bal.	4,300	

4. Adjusted trial balance:

GOODBYE GRASS CORPORATION
Adjusted Trial Balance
At April 30, 2013

Account Name	Debits	Credits	
Cash	$ 4,510		
Accounts Receivable	1,700		
Note Receivable	1,250		
Interest Receivable	10		
Prepaid Insurance	250		
Equipment	4,600		
Accumulated Depreciation		$ 25	
Land	3,750		To Balance Sheet
Accounts Payable		620	
Unearned Revenue		1,200	
Wages Payable		400	
Interest Payable		45	
Income Tax Payable		273	
Note Payable		4,000	
Contributed Capital		9,000	
Retained Earnings		0	To Statement of Retained Earnings
Mowing Revenue		5,600	
Interest Revenue		10	
Wages Expense	4,300		
Fuel Expense	410		
Insurance Expense	50		To Income Statement
Depreciation Expense	25		
Interest Expense	45		
Income Tax Expense	273		
Totals	$21,173	$21,173	

5. Income statement, statement of retained earnings, and balance sheet:

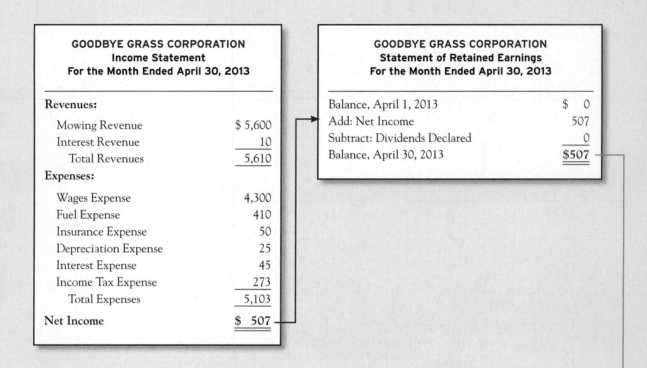

GOODBYE GRASS CORPORATION
Income Statement
For the Month Ended April 30, 2013

Revenues:	
Mowing Revenue	$ 5,600
Interest Revenue	10
Total Revenues	5,610
Expenses:	
Wages Expense	4,300
Fuel Expense	410
Insurance Expense	50
Depreciation Expense	25
Interest Expense	45
Income Tax Expense	273
Total Expenses	5,103
Net Income	$ 507

GOODBYE GRASS CORPORATION
Statement of Retained Earnings
For the Month Ended April 30, 2013

Balance, April 1, 2013	$ 0
Add: Net Income	507
Subtract: Dividends Declared	0
Balance, April 30, 2013	$507

GOODBYE GRASS CORPORATION
Balance Sheet
At April 30, 2013

Assets			Liabilities and Stockholders' Equity	
Current Assets:			Liabilities	
Cash		$ 4,510	Current Liabilities:	
Accounts Receivable		1,700	Accounts Payable	$ 620
Note Receivable		1,250	Unearned Revenue	1,200
Interest Receivable		10	Wages Payable	400
Prepaid Insurance		250	Interest Payable	45
Total Current Assets		7,720	Income Tax Payable	273
Equipment	$ 4,600		Note Payable	4,000
Less: Accumulated Depreciation	(25)		Total Current Liabilities	6,538
Equipment, Net		4,575	Stockholders' Equity	
			Contributed Capital	9,000
Land		3,750	Retained Earnings	507
Total Assets		$16,045	Total Liabilities and Stockholders' Equity	$16,045

6. Closing journal entry:

If Goodbye Grass Corporation had adopted an April 30 year-end, the company would require a journal entry to close its revenue and expense accounts into Retained Earnings. Because the company has not declared a dividend, a Dividends Declared account does not exist to be closed into Retained Earnings. The closing journal entry needed to close revenues and expenses into Retained Earnings is

dr Mowing Revenue (−R)	5,600	
dr Interest Revenue (−R)...	10	
cr Wages Expense (−E)...		4,300
cr Fuel Expense (−E)		410
cr Insurance Expense (−E)...		50
cr Depreciation Expense (−E)....................................		25
cr Interest Expense (−E)		45
cr Income Tax Expense (−E)......................................		273
cr Retained Earnings (+SE).......................................		507

CHAPTER SUMMARY

Explain why adjustments are needed. p. 146   LO 4-1

Adjustments are needed to ensure:

- Revenues are recorded when earned (the revenue recognition principle),

- Expenses are recorded when incurred to generate revenues (the expense recognition principle),

- Assets are reported at amounts representing the economic benefits that remain at the end of the current period, and

- Liabilities are reported at amounts owed at the end of the current period that will require a future sacrifice of resources.

Prepare adjustments needed at the end of the period. p. 148   LO 4-2

- The process for preparing adjustments includes
  1. Analyzing the unadjusted balances in balance sheet and income statement accounts, and calculating the amount of the adjustment needed, using a timeline where appropriate.
  2. Preparing an adjusting journal entry to make the adjustment.
  3. Summarizing the adjusting journal entry in the applicable ledger (T-accounts).

- Each adjusting journal entry affects one balance sheet and one income statement account.

Prepare an adjusted trial balance. p. 158   LO 4-3

An adjusted trial balance is a list of all accounts with their adjusted debit or credit balances indicated in the appropriate column to provide a check on the equality of the debits and credits.

Prepare financial statements. p. 159   LO 4-4

Adjusted account balances are used in preparing the following financial statements:

- Income Statement: Revenues − Expenses = Net Income.

- Statement of Retained Earnings: Beginning Retained Earnings + Net Income − Dividends Declared = Ending Retained Earnings.

- Balance Sheet: Assets = Liabilities + Stockholders' Equity.

- The statement of cash flows and notes to the financial statements are important components of adjusted financial statements, but they will be studied in later chapters.

Explain the closing process. p. 162   LO 4-5

- Closing journal entries are required to (*a*) transfer net income (or loss) and dividends declared into retained earnings, and (*b*) prepare all temporary accounts (revenues, expenses, dividends declared) for the following year by establishing zero balances in these accounts.

- Two closing journal entries are needed:
  1. Debit each revenue account for the amount of its balance, credit each expense account for the amount of its balance, and record the difference (equal to net income) in Retained Earnings.
  2. Credit the Dividends Declared account for the amount of its balance and debit Retained Earnings for the same amount.

LO 4-6   Explain how adjustments affect financial results. p. 166

Adjustments help ensure all revenues and expenses are reported in the period in which they are earned and incurred, as a result of a company's activities. Without these adjustments, the financial statements present an incomplete and potentially misleading picture of the company's financial performance.

KEY TERMS

Adjusted Trial Balance p. 158

Adjusting Journal
   Entries p. 148

Adjustments p. 146

Carrying Value (Net Book Value,
   Book Value) p. 153

Contra-Account p. 153

Depreciation p. 153

Permanent Accounts p. 163

Post-Closing Trial
   Balance p. 165

Temporary Accounts p. 163

See complete definitions in the glossary in the back of this text.

HOMEWORK HELPER

Alternative terms

- Accrued Liabilities is a generic account name that can include liabilities recorded using accrual adjustments for salaries, utilities, income taxes, and many other items.

Helpful reminders

- When determining each adjustment, draw timelines to picture where we are now, where we need to be, and the adjustment to get us there.
- Cash is never part of an accrual or deferral adjustment.
- The income statement is the temporary home for revenue and expense accounts, and their permanent home is Retained Earnings in the stockholders' equity section of the balance sheet.

Frequent mistakes

- Accumulated Depreciation and Depreciation Expense are not the same accounts. Accumulated Depreciation is a permanent, balance sheet account that accumulates each period of depreciation. Depreciation Expense is a temporary, income statement account that reports only the current period's depreciation.
- Dividends are not expenses, but rather are distributions to stockholders of the company's prior profits that have accumulated in Retained Earnings.
- The amount in Retained Earnings on an adjusted trial balance is not reported on the balance sheet; it is the beginning balance on the statement of retained earnings. The ending balance from the statement of retained earnings is reported on the balance sheet.

PRACTICE MATERIAL

QUESTIONS (⊖ Symbol indicates questions that require analysis from more than one perspective.)

1. Briefly explain the purposes of adjustments.

2. Explain the relationships between adjustments and the following Chapter 3 concepts: (*a*) the time period assumption, (*b*) the revenue recognition principle, and (*c*) the expense recognition principle.

3. List the two types of adjustments and give an example of an adjustment affecting revenues and expenses for each type.

4. Explain the effect of adjusting journal entries on cash.

5. What is a contra-asset? Give an example of one.

6. Explain the differences between depreciation expense and accumulated depreciation.

7. What is an adjusted trial balance? What is its purpose?

8. On December 31, a company makes a $9,000 payment for renting a warehouse in January, February, and March of the following year. Show the accounting equation effects of the transaction on December 31, as well as the adjustments required on January 31, February 28, and March 31.

9. Using the information in question 8, determine the amounts and accounts that will be reported on the January 31 balance sheet and the income statement for the month ended January 31.

10. Using the information in question 8, prepare the journal entry and adjusting journal entries to be made on December 31, January 31, February 28, and March 31.

11. What is the equation for each of the following statements: (*a*) income statement, (*b*) balance sheet, and (*c*) statement of retained earnings?

12. Explain how the financial statements in question 11 relate to each other.

13. What is the purpose of closing journal entries?

14. How do permanent accounts differ from temporary accounts?

15. Why are the income statement accounts closed but the balance sheet accounts are not?

16. Is Dividends Declared considered an asset, liability, or stockholders' equity account? Is it a permanent or temporary account? Does it normally have a debit or credit balance?

17. What is a post-closing trial balance? Is it a useful part of the accounting cycle? Explain.

18. The owner of a local business complains that the adjustments process consumes a lot of time and delays reporting month-end financial results. How would you convince her of the importance of this process? ●

MULTIPLE CHOICE

1. Which of the following accounts would not appear in a closing journal entry?

   a. Interest Revenue
   b. Accumulated Depreciation
   c. Retained Earnings
   d. Salary Expense

2. Which account is least likely to appear in an adjusting journal entry?

   a. Cash
   b. Interest Receivable
   c. Income Tax Expense
   d. Salaries Payable

3. When a concert promotions company collects cash for ticket sales two months in advance of the show date, which of the following accounts is recorded?

   a. Accrued Liability
   b. Accounts Receivable
   c. Prepaid Expense
   d. Unearned Revenue

4. On December 31, an adjustment is made to reduce unearned revenue and report (earned) revenue. How many accounts will be included in this adjusting journal entry?

   a. None
   b. One
   c. Two
   d. Three

5. An adjusting journal entry to recognize accrued salaries payable would cause which of the following?

   a. A decrease in assets and stockholders' equity.
   b. A decrease in assets and liabilities.
   c. An increase in expenses, liabilities, and stockholders' equity.
   d. An increase in expenses and liabilities and a decrease in stockholders' equity.

6. An adjusted trial balance

   a. Shows the ending balances in a debit and credit format before posting the adjusting journal entries.
   b. Is prepared after closing entries have been posted.

   c. Is a tool used by financial analysts to review the performance of publicly traded companies.
   d. Shows the ending balances resulting from the adjusting journal entries in a debit-and-credit format.

7. Company A has owned a building for several years. Which of the following statements regarding depreciation is false from an accounting perspective?

   a. Depreciation Expense for the year will equal Accumulated Depreciation.
   b. Depreciation is an estimated expense to be recorded each period during the building's life.
   c. As depreciation is recorded, stockholders' equity is reduced.
   d. As depreciation is recorded, total assets are reduced.

8. Which of the following trial balances is used as a source for preparing the income statement?

   a. Unadjusted trial balance
   b. Pre-adjusted trial balance
   c. Adjusted trial balance
   d. Post-closing trial balance

9. Assume the balance in Prepaid Insurance is $2,500 but it should be $1,500. The adjusting journal entry should include which of the following?

   a. Debit to Prepaid Insurance for $1,000.
   b. Credit to Insurance Expense for $1,000.
   c. Debit to Insurance Expense for $1,000.
   d. Debit to Insurance Expense for $1,500.

10. Assume a company receives a bill for $10,000 for advertising done during the current year. If this bill is not yet recorded at the end of the year, what will the adjusting journal entry include?

    a. Debit to Advertising Expense of $10,000.
    b. Credit to Advertising Expense of $10,000.
    c. Debit to Accrued Liabilities of $10,000.
    d. Need more information to determine.

> For answers to the Multiple-Choice Questions **see page Q1** located in the last section of the book.

MINI-EXERCISES

LO 4-1   M4-1 Understanding Concepts Related to Adjustments

Match each situation below to two applicable reasons that require an adjustment to be made.

Delta Airlines
GSD + M
Abercrombie
Tiger Woods Foundation

_____ 1. Delta Airlines provided flights this month for customers who paid cash last month for tickets.

_____ 2. GSD + M completed work on an advertising campaign that will be collected next month.

_____ 3. Abercrombie received a telephone bill for services this month, which must be paid next month.

_____ 4. The Tiger Woods Foundation used up some of the benefits of its 35,000 square foot building.

A. Revenue has been earned.
B. Expense has been incurred.
C. Liability has been incurred.
D. Liability has been fulfilled.
E. Asset has been acquired.
F. Asset has been used up.

LO 4-1   M4-2 Understanding Concepts Related to Adjustments

Match each situation below to two applicable reasons that require an adjustment to be made.

IBM
Apple, Inc.
Schutt Sports
Procter & Gamble

_____ 1. IBM completed a consulting project for the CDC to simulate the spread of contagious viruses and will be paid next month.

_____ 2. This month Apple, Inc. redeemed iTunes gift cards that had been issued last month.

_____ 3. Schutt Sports used up some of the benefits of its football helmet manufacturing equipment.

_____ 4. Procter & Gamble received a bill for this month's advertising services, which it will pay next month.

A. Revenue has been earned.
B. Expense has been incurred.
C. Liability has been incurred.
D. Liability has been fulfilled.
E. Asset has been acquired.
F. Asset has been used up.

LO 4-1, 4-2   M4-3 Matching Transactions with Type of Adjustment

Match each transaction with the type of adjustment that will be required, by entering the appropriate letter in the space provided.

	Transaction	Type of Adjustment
_____ 1.	Supplies for office use were purchased during the year for $500, of which $100 remained on hand (unused) at year-end.	A. Accrual adjustment
_____ 2.	Interest of $250 on a note receivable was earned at year-end, although collection of the interest is not due until the following year.	B. Deferral adjustment
_____ 3.	At year-end, wages payable of $3,600 had not been recorded or paid.	
_____ 4.	At year-end, one-half of a $2,000 advertising project had been completed for a client, but nothing had been billed or collected.	
_____ 5.	Redeemed a gift card for $600 of services.	

LO 4-2   M4-4 Recording Adjusting Journal Entries

Using the information in M4-3, prepare the adjusting journal entries required.

LO 4-2   M4-5 Determine Accounting Equation Effects of Deferral Adjustments

For each of the following transactions for the Sky Blue Corporation, give the accounting equation effects of the adjustments required at the end of the month on December 31, 2012:

a. Collected $2,400 rent for the period December 1, 2012, to February 28, 2013, which was credited to Unearned Revenue on December 1, 2012.

b. Paid $1,200 for a two-year insurance premium on December 1, 2012, and debited Prepaid Insurance for that amount.

c. Used a machine purchased on December 1, 2012, for $48,000. The company estimates *annual* depreciation of $4,800.

M4-6 Recording Adjusting Journal Entries

LO 4-2

Using the information in M4-5, prepare the adjusting journal entries required on December 31, 2012.

M4-7 Determining Accounting Equation Effects of Accrual Adjustments

LO 4-2

For each of the following transactions for New Idea Corporation, give the accounting equation effects of the adjustments required at the end of the month on December 31, 2013:

a. Received a $600 utility bill for electricity usage in December to be paid in January 2014.

b. Owed wages to 10 employees who worked three days at $100 each per day at the end of December. The company will pay employees at the end of the first week of January 2014.

c. On December 1, 2013, loaned money to an employee who agreed to repay the loan in one year along with $1,200 for one full year of interest. No interest has been recorded yet.

M4-8 Recording Adjusting Journal Entries

LO 4-2

Using the information in M4-7, prepare the adjusting journal entries required on December 31, 2013.

M4-9 Preparing Journal Entries for Deferral Transactions and Adjustments

LO 4-2

For each of the following independent situations, prepare journal entries to record the initial transaction on September 30 and the adjustment required on October 31.

a. Hockey Helpers paid $4,000 cash on September 30, to rent an arena for the months of October and November.

b. Super Stage Shows received $16,000 on September 30, for season tickets that admit patrons to a theatre event that will be held twice (on October 31 and November 30).

c. Risky Ventures paid $3,000 on September 30, for insurance coverage for the months of October, November, and December.

M4-10 Preparing Journal Entries for Deferral Transactions and Adjustments

LO 4-2

For each of the following independent situations, prepare journal entries to record the initial transaction on December 31 and the adjustment required on January 31.

a. Magnificent Magazines received $12,000 on December 31, 2013, for subscriptions to magazines that will be published and distributed in January through December 2014.

b. Walker Window Washing paid $1,200 cash for supplies on December 31, 2013. As of January 31, 2014, $200 of these supplies had been used up.

c. Indoor Raceway received $3,000 on December 31, 2013, from race participants for providing services for three races. One race is held January 31, 2014, and the other two will be held in March 2013.

M4-11 Preparing Journal Entries for Deferral and Accrual Adjustments

LO 4-2

Service Pro Corp (SPC) determined that its unadjusted net income was $10,000 for the year ended September 30, 2013. For the following transactions and events, show the September 30, 2013, adjusting entries that SPC would make.

a. Prepaid Insurance shows a balance of zero at September 30, but Insurance Expense shows a debit balance of $2,340, representing the cost of a three-year fire insurance policy that was purchased on September 1, 2013.

b. On August 31, 2011, Cash was debited and Service Revenue was credited for $1,500. The $1,500 related to fees for a three-month period beginning September 1, 2013.

c. The company's income tax rate is 20%. An income tax installment of $2,000 was paid for this year on September 1, at which time it was recorded in Prepaid Expenses.

M4-12 Reporting Adjusted Account Balances

LO 4-3, 4-4

Indicate whether each of the following accounts would be reported on the balance sheet (BS) or income statement (IS) of Home Repair Company. Further, if the account is reported on the balance sheet, indicate whether it would be classified with current assets (CA), noncurrent assets (NCA), current liabilities (CL), noncurrent liabilities (NCL), or stockholders' equity (SE). If the account is reported on the income statement, indicate whether it would be classified as revenue (R) or expense (E). Finally, for each account, indicate whether the company's accounting records would normally show a debit (*dr*) or credit (*cr*) balance.

Account	Financial Statement?	Classification?	Normal *dr* or *cr* Balance?
Interest Expense			
Prepaid Rent			
Unearned Revenue			
Retained Earnings			
Accumulated Depreciation			

LO 4-3

M4-13 Preparing an Adjusted Trial Balance

Macro Company has the following adjusted accounts and balances at year-end (June 30, 2013):

Accounts Payable	$ 300	Contributed Capital	$ 300	Salaries Expense	$ 660
Accounts Receivable	550	Depreciation Expense	110	Sales Revenue	3,600
Accrued Liabilities	150	Income Tax Expense	110	Supplies	710
Accumulated		Income Tax Payable	30	Rent Expense	400
Depreciation	250	Interest Expense	180	Retained Earnings	120
Administrative		Interest Revenue	50	Unearned Revenue	100
Expense	820	Land	200		
Buildings	1,400	Long-term Debt	1,300		
Cash	1,020	Prepaid Expenses	40		

Required:

Prepare an adjusted trial balance for Macro Company at June 30, 2013.

LO 4-4

M4-14 Reporting an Income Statement

The Sky Blue Corporation has the following adjusted trial balance at December 31, 2012.

	Debit	Credit
Cash	$ 1,230	
Accounts Receivable	2,000	
Prepaid Insurance	2,300	
Notes Receivable (long-term)	3,000	
Equipment	12,000	
Accumulated Depreciation		$ 2,600
Accounts Payable		1,600
Utilities Payable		3,820
Wages Payable		1,000
Income Taxes Payable		2,900
Unearned Revenue		600
Contributed Capital		2,400
Retained Earnings		1,000
Dividends Declared	300	
Sales Revenue		42,030
Rent Revenue		300
Wages Expense	21,600	
Depreciation Expense	1,300	
Utilities Expense	4,220	
Insurance Expense	1,400	
Rent Expense	6,000	
Income Tax Expense	2,900	
Total	$58,250	$58,250

Prepare an income statement for the year ended December 31, 2012. How much net income did the Sky Blue Corporation generate during 2012?

M4-15 Reporting a Statement of Retained Earnings   LO 4-4

Refer to M4-14. Prepare a statement of retained earnings for 2012.

M4-16 Reporting a Balance Sheet   LO 4-4

Refer to M4-14. Prepare a classified balance sheet at December 31, 2012. Are the Sky Blue Corporation's assets financed primarily by debt or equity?

M4-17 Recording Closing Journal Entries   LO 4-5

Refer to the adjusted trial balance in M4-14. Prepare closing journal entries on December 31, 2012.

M4-18 Preparing and Posting Adjusting Journal Entries   LO 4-2

At December 31, the unadjusted trial balance of H&R Tacks reports Supplies of $9,000 and Supplies Expense of $0. On December 31, supplies costing $7,700 are on hand. Prepare the adjusting journal entry on December 31. In separate T-accounts for each account, enter the unadjusted balances, post the adjusting journal entry, and report the adjusted balance.

M4-19 Preparing and Posting Adjusting Journal Entries   LO 4-2

At December 31, the unadjusted trial balance of H&R Tacks reports Equipment of $30,000 and zero balances in Accumulated Depreciation and Depreciation Expense. Depreciation for the period is estimated to be $6,000. Prepare the adjusting journal entry on December 31. In separate T-accounts for each account, enter the unadjusted balances, post the adjusting journal entry, and report the adjusted balance.

M4-20 Preparing and Posting Adjusting Journal Entries   LO 4-2

At December 31, the unadjusted trial balance of H&R Tacks reports Prepaid Insurance of $7,200 and Insurance Expense of $0. The insurance was purchased on July 1 and provides coverage for 24 months. Prepare the adjusting journal entry on December 31. In separate T-accounts for each account, enter the unadjusted balances, post the adjusting journal entry, and report the adjusted balance.

M4-21 Preparing and Posting Adjusting Journal Entries   LO 4-2

At December 31, the unadjusted trial balance of H&R Tacks reports Unearned Revenue of $5,000 and Service Revenues of $33,800. One-half of the unearned revenue has been earned as of December 31. Prepare the adjusting journal entry on December 31. In separate T-accounts for each account, enter the unadjusted balances, post the adjusting journal entry, and report the adjusted balance.

M4-22 Preparing and Posting Adjusting Journal Entries   LO 4-2

At December 31, the unadjusted trial balance of H&R Tacks reports Wages Payable of $0 and Wages Expense of $20,000. Employees have been paid for work done up to December 27, but the $1,200 they have earned for December 28–31 has not yet been paid or recorded. Prepare the adjusting journal entry on December 31. In separate T-accounts for each account, enter the unadjusted balances, post the adjusting journal entry, and report the adjusted balance.

M4-23 Preparing and Posting Adjusting Journal Entries   LO 4-2

At December 31, the unadjusted trial balance of H&R Tacks reports Interest Payable of $0 and Interest Expense of $0. Interest incurred and owed in December totals $500. Prepare the adjusting journal entry on December 31. In separate T-accounts for each account, enter the unadjusted balances, post the adjusting journal entry, and report the adjusted balance.

M4-24 Preparing and Posting Journal Entries for Dividends   LO 4-2

At December 31, the unadjusted trial balance of H&R Tacks reports Dividends Declared of $0 and Dividends Payable of $0. A $200 dividend was declared on December 27, with payment in cash to occur three weeks later. Prepare the required journal entry. In separate T-accounts for each account, enter the unadjusted balances, post the journal entry, and report the adjusted balance.

M4-25 Preparing an Adjusted Trial Balance   LO 4-3

The adjusted trial balance for PI Detectives reported the following account balances: Accounts Receivable $500; Supplies $9,000; Prepaid Insurance $7,200; Equipment $28,000; Accumulated

Depreciation $4,000; Accounts Payable $200; Unearned Revenue $5,000; Notes Payable $3,000; Contributed Capital $22,000; Retained Earnings $5,700; Dividends $3,000; Service Revenue $33,800; Wages Expense $20,000; and Depreciation Expense $1,000. Prepare an adjusted trial balance as of December 31, and solve for its missing Cash balance.

LO 4-2, 4-4, 4-5   **M4-26 Progression of Prepaid Expenses over Several Periods**

Midwest Manufacturing purchased a three-year insurance policy for $30,000 on January 2, 2012. Prepare any journal entries, adjusting journal entries, and closing journal entries required on January 2, 2012, December 31, 2012, and December 31, 2013. Summarize these entries in T-accounts for Prepaid insurance, Insurance Expense, Cash, and Retained Earnings. Assume the January 2, 2012, balances in these accounts were $0, $0, $90,000, and $80,000, respectively. Given only the entries for insurance, indicate what amounts would be reported for each of these accounts on the balance sheet and income statement prepared on December 31, 2012, and December 31, 2013.

EXERCISES

LO 4-3   **E4-1 Preparing an Adjusted Trial Balance from Adjusted Account Balances**

Gibson Consultants, Inc., provides marketing research for clients in the retail industry. The company had the following adjusted balances at December 31, 2012 (listed alphabetically):

Accounts Payable		Equipment		Other Assets		Service Revenue	
	86,830	323,040		145,000			2,564,200

Accounts Receivable		General and Administrative Expense		Other Expenses		Supplies	
225,400		320,050		188,000		12,200	

Accrued Liabilities		Income Taxes Payable		Other Revenue		Supplies Expense	
	25,650		2,030		20,800	42,590	

Accumulated Depreciation		Interest Expense		Prepaid Rent		Unearned Revenue	
	18,100	17,200		10,200			32,500

Cash		Land		Rent Expense		Utilities Expense	
173,000		60,000		152,080		25,230	

Contributed Capital		Notes Payable		Retained Earnings		Wages Expense	
	233,370		160,000		?	1,590,000	

Dividends Declared	
5,000	

Required:

1. Prepare an adjusted trial balance listing the accounts in proper order at December 31, 2012. Solve for the "?" in Retained Earnings.

2. Does the Retained Earnings balance determined in requirement 1 represent the balance at December 31, 2012, or December 31, 2011? Explain.

LO 4-1   **E4-2 Identifying Adjustments by Scanning a Trial Balance**

Coach, Inc.—the maker of handbags and other women's and men's accessories—was previously owned by Sara Lee Corporation until April 2001, when Coach was spun off as a separate company.

Assume the following were reported in Coach's adjusted trial balance and were used to prepare its June 28, 2010, year-end financial statements.

COACH INCORPORATED
Adjusted Trial Balance
At June 28, 2010
(millions of dollars)

	Debit	Credit
Cash	$ 596	
Accounts Receivable	109	
Inventories	363	
Prepaid Expenses	30	
Property and Equipment	1,033	
Accumulated Depreciation		$ 485
Other Assets	821	
Accounts Payable		106
Wages Payable		422
Income Taxes Payable		29
Other Current Liabilities		405
Contributed Capital		3
Retained Earnings		767
Sales Revenue		3,608
Cost of Sales	974	
Selling, General and Administrative Expenses	1,484	
Interest Revenue		2
Income Tax Expense	417	
	$5,827	$5,827

COACH

Required:

1. Based on the information in the trial balance, list two pairs of balance sheet and income statement accounts that likely required *deferral adjustments* as of June 28 (no computations are necessary).

2. Based on the information in the trial balance, list two pairs of balance sheet and income statement accounts that likely required *accrual adjustments* as of June 28 (no computations are necessary).

E4-3 Recording Initial Transactions and Subsequent Adjustments   LO 4-1, 4-2

During the month of September, the Texas Go-Kart Company had the following business activities:

a. On September 1, paid rent on the track facility for six months at a total cost of $12,000.
b. On September 1, received $60,000 for season tickets for 12-month admission to the race track.
c. On September 1, booked the race track for a private organization that will use the track one day per month for $2,000 each time, to be paid in the following month. The organization uses the track on September 30.
d. On September 1, hired a new manager at a monthly salary of $3,000, to be paid the first Monday following the end of the month.

Required:

First prepare the journal entry, if any, required to record each of the initial business activities on September 1. Then, prepare the adjusting journal entries, if any, required on September 30.

LO 4-1, 4-2   **E4-4 Determining Adjustments and Accounting Equation Effects**

Mobo, a wireless phone carrier, completed its first year of operations on December 31, 2012. All of the 2012 entries have been recorded, except for the following:

a.   At year-end, employees earned wages of $6,000, which will be paid on the next payroll date, January 6, 2013.

b.   At year-end, the company had earned interest revenue of $3,000. It will be collected March 1, 2013.

Required:

1.   What is the annual reporting period for this company?
2.   Identify whether each required adjustment is a deferral or an accrual.
3.   Show the accounting equation effects of each required adjustment, using the format shown in the demonstration case.
4.   Why are these adjustments needed?

LO 4-1, 4-2   **E4-5 Recording Adjusting Journal Entries**

Refer to E4-4.

Required:

Record the required adjusting journal entry for transactions (a) and (b).

LO 4-1, 4-2   **E4-6 Determining Adjustments and Accounting Equation Effects**

Fes Company is making adjusting journal entries for the year ended December 31, 2013. In developing information for the adjusting journal entries, you learned the following:

a.   A two-year insurance premium of $7,200 was paid on January 1, 2013, for coverage beginning on that date. As of December 31, 2013, the unadjusted balances were $7,200 for Prepaid Insurance and $0 for Insurance Expense.

b.   At December 31, 2013, you obtained the following data relating to supplies.

Unadjusted balance in Supplies on December 31, 2013	$15,000
Unadjusted balance in Supplies Expense on December 31, 2013	72,000
Supplies on hand, counted on December 31, 2013	10,000

Required:

1.   Of the $7,200 paid for insurance, what amount should be reported on the 2013 income statement as Insurance Expense? What amount should be reported on the December 31, 2013, balance sheet as Prepaid Insurance?

2.   What amount should be reported on the 2013 income statement as Supplies Expense? What amount should be reported on the December 31, 2013, balance sheet as Supplies?

3.   Using the format shown in the demonstration case, indicate the accounting equation effects of the adjustment required for (a) insurance and (b) supplies.

LO 4-1, 4-2   **E4-7 Recording Adjusting Journal Entries**

Refer to E4-6.

Required:

Prepare adjusting journal entries at December 31, 2013, for (a) insurance, and (b) supplies.

LO 4-1, 4-2, 4-6   **E4-8 Recording Typical Adjusting Journal Entries**

Jaworski's Ski Store is completing the accounting process for its first year ended December 31, 2013. The transactions during 2013 have been journalized and posted. The following data are available to determine adjusting journal entries:

a.   The unadjusted balance in Supplies was $850 at December 31, 2013. The unadjusted balance in Supplies Expense was $0 at December 31, 2013. A year-end count showed $100 of supplies on hand.

b. Wages earned by employees during December 2013, unpaid and unrecorded at December 31, 2013, amounted to $3,700. The last paychecks were issued December 28; the next payments will be made on January 6, 2014. The unadjusted balance in Wages Expense was $40,000 at December 31, 2013.

c. A portion of the store's basement is now being rented for $1,100 per month to K. Frey. On November 1, 2013, the store collected six months' rent in advance from Frey in the amount of $6,600. It was credited in full to Unearned Revenue when collected. The unadjusted balance in Rent Revenue was $0 at December 31, 2013.

d. The store purchased delivery equipment at the beginning of the year. The estimated depreciation for 2013 is $2,000, although none has been recorded yet.

e. On December 31, 2013, the unadjusted balance in Prepaid Insurance was $3,000. This was the amount paid in the middle of the year for a two-year insurance policy with coverage beginning on July 1, 2013. The unadjusted balance in Insurance Expense was $600, which was the cost of insurance from January 1 to June 30, 2013.

f. Jaworski's store did some ski repair work for Frey. At the end of December 31, 2013, Frey had not paid for work completed amounting to $750. This amount has not yet been recorded as Service Revenue. Collection is expected during January 2014.

Required:

For each situation, prepare the adjusting journal entry that Jaworski's should record at December 31, 2013.

E4-9 Determining Accounting Equation Effects of Typical Adjusting Journal Entries   LO 4-2, 4-6

Refer to E4-8.

Required:

For each of the transactions in E4-8, indicate the amount and direction of effects of the adjusting journal entry on the elements of the accounting equation. Using the following format, indicate + for increase, − for decrease, and NE for no effect. Include account names using the format shown for the following sample.

Transaction	Assets	Liabilities	Stockholders' Equity
a	Office Supplies −750	NE	Supplies Expense (+E) −750
etc.			

E4-10 Inferring Transactions from Accrual and Deferral Accounts   LO 4-1, 4-2

A company reported the following information.

Income Tax Payable			Wages Payable			Interest Payable		
	100	Beg. bal.		1,000	Beg. bal.		140	Beg. bal.
600	?	(a)	(b) ?	20,000		1,000	?	(c)
	80	End. bal.		1,200	End. bal.		150	End. bal.

Required:

1. For each account, describe the typical transactions that cause it to increase and decrease.

2. Express each T-account in equation format and then solve for the missing amounts for (a), (b), and (c). For example, the Interest Payable T-account can be expressed as: Beg. bal. (140) + increases (?) − decreases (1,000) = End. bal. (150). By rearranging the equation, you can solve for ? = 150 + 1,000 − 140.

E4-11 Reporting Depreciation   LO 4-4

The adjusted trial balance for Rowdy Profits Corporation reports that its equipment had cost $250,000. For the current year, the company has recorded $30,000 of depreciation, which brings the total depreciation to date to $150,000.

Balance Sheet	Income Statement
Assets	Revenues
Liabilities	Expenses
Stockholders' Equity	

Required:

Using the headings shown above, indicate the location and amounts that would be used to report the three items on the company's balance sheet and income statement.

LO 4-2, 4-5   **E4-12 Recording Transactions Including Adjusting and Closing Journal Entries**

The following accounts are used by Mouse Potato, Inc., a computer game maker.

Codes	Accounts	Codes	Accounts
A	Accounts Receivable	I	Note Payable
B	Accumulated Depreciation	J	Retained Earnings
C	Cash	K	Service Revenue
D	Depreciation Expense	L	Supplies
E	Equipment	M	Supplies Expense
F	Interest Expense	N	Unearned Revenue
G	Interest Payable	O	Wage Expense
H	Interest Revenue	P	Wages Payable

Required:

For each of the following independent situations, give the journal entry by entering the appropriate code(s) and amount(s). We've done the first one for you as an example.

		Debit		Credit	
	Independent Situations	Code	Amount	Code	Amount
a.	Accrued wages, unrecorded and unpaid at year-end, $400 (example).	O	400	P	400
b.	Service revenue collected in advance, $600.				
c.	At year-end, interest on note payable not yet recorded or paid, $220.				
d.	Depreciation expense for year, $1,000.				
e.	Service revenue earned but not yet collected at year-end, $1,000.				
f.	Balance in Supplies account, $400; supplies on hand at year-end, $150.				
g.	Adjusted balance at year-end in Service Revenue account, $75,000. Give the journal entry to close this one account at year-end.				

LO 4-2, 4-6   **E4-13 Analyzing the Effects of Adjusting Journal Entries on the Income Statement and Balance Sheet**

On December 31, 2012, Alan and Company prepared an income statement and balance sheet but failed to take into account four adjusting journal entries. The income statement, prepared on this incorrect basis, reported income before income tax of $30,000. The balance sheet (before the effect of income taxes) reflected total assets, $90,000; total liabilities, $40,000; and stockholders' equity, $50,000. The data for the four adjusting journal entries follow:

a. Depreciation of $8,000 for the year on equipment was not recorded.
b. Wages amounting to $17,000 for the last three days of December 2012 were not paid and not recorded (the next payroll will be on January 10, 2013).
c. Rent revenue of $4,800 was collected on December 1, 2012, for office space for the three-month period December 1, 2012, to February 28, 2013. The $4,800 was credited in full to Unearned Rent Revenue when collected.
d. Income taxes were not recorded. The income tax rate for the company is 30%.

Required:

Complete the following table to show the effects of the four adjusting journal entries (indicate deductions with parentheses):

Items	Net Income	Total Assets	Total Liabilities	Stockholders' Equity
Amounts reported	$30,000	$90,000	$40,000	$50,000
Effect of depreciation				
Effect of wages				
Effect of rent revenue				
Adjusted balances	6,600	82,000	55,400	26,600
Effect of income tax				
Correct amounts				

E4-14 Reporting an Adjusted Income Statement   LO 4-2, 4-4, 4-6

Dyer, Inc., completed its first year of operations on December 31, 2013. Because this is the end of the annual accounting period, the company bookkeeper prepared the following preliminary income statement:

Income Statement, 2013		
Rent Revenue		$114,000
Expenses:		
Salaries and Wages Expense	$28,500	
Repairs and Maintenance Expense	12,000	
Rent Expense	9,000	
Utilities Expense	4,000	
Travel Expense	3,000	
Other Expenses	1,000	
Total Expenses		57,500
Income		$ 56,500

You are an independent CPA hired by the company to audit the firm's accounting systems and financial statements. In your audit, you developed additional data as follows:

a. Wages for the last three days of December amounting to $310 were not recorded or paid.
b. The $400 telephone bill for December 2013 has not been recorded or paid.
c. Depreciation amounting to $23,000 for 2013, was not recorded.
d. Interest of $500 was not recorded on the note payable by Dyer, Inc.
e. The Rental Revenue account includes $4,000 of revenue to be earned in January 2014.
f. Supplies costing $600 were used during 2013, but this has not yet been recorded.
g. The income tax expense for 2013 is $7,000, but it won't actually be paid until 2014.

Required:

1. What adjusting journal entry for each item (*a*) through (*g*) should be recorded at December 31, 2013? If none is required, explain why.
2. Prepare, in proper form, an adjusted income statement for 2013.
3. Did the adjustments have a significant overall effect on the company's net income?

LO 4-2, 4-3   **E4-15 Recording Adjusting Entries and Preparing an Adjusted Trial Balance**

North Star prepared the following unadjusted trial balance at the end of its second year of operations ending December 31, 2012.

Account Titles	Debit	Credit
Cash	$12,000	
Accounts Receivable	6,000	
Prepaid Rent	2,400	
Equipment	21,000	
Accumulated Depreciation		$ 1,000
Accounts Payable		1,000
Utilities Payable		0
Income Tax Payable		0
Contributed Capital		24,800
Retained Earnings		2,100
Sales Revenue		50,000
Wages Expense	25,000	
Utilities Expense	12,500	
Rent Expense	0	
Depreciation Expense	0	
Income Tax Expense	0	
Totals	$78,900	$78,900

Other data not yet recorded at December 31, 2012:

a. Rent expired during 2012, $1,200.
b. Depreciation expense for 2012, $1,000.
c. Utilities payable, $9,000.
d. Income tax expense, $390.

Required:

1. Using the format shown in the demonstration case, indicate the accounting equation effects of each required adjustment.
2. Prepare the adjusting journal entries required at December 31, 2012.
3. Summarize the adjusting journal entries in T-accounts. After entering the beginning balances and computing the adjusted ending balances, prepare an adjusted trial balance as of December 31, 2012.
4. Compute the amount of net income using (*a*) the preliminary (unadjusted) numbers, and (*b*) the final (adjusted) numbers. Had the adjusting entries not been recorded, would net income have been overstated or understated, and by what amount?

LO 4-2, 4-3   **E4-16 Recording Four Adjusting Journal Entries and Preparing an Adjusted Trial Balance**

Mint Cleaning Inc. prepared the following unadjusted trial balance at the end of its second year of operations ending December 31, 2013. To simplify this exercise, the amounts given are in thousands of dollars.

Account Titles	Debit	Credit
Cash	$ 38	
Accounts Receivable	9	
Prepaid Insurance	6	
Equipment	80	
Accumulated Depreciation		$ 0
Accounts Payable		9
Contributed Capital		76
Retained Earnings		4
Sales Revenue		80
Administrative Expenses	26	
Wages Expense	10	
Totals	$169	$169

Other data not yet recorded at December 31, 2013:

a. Insurance expired during 2013, $5.
b. Depreciation expense for 2013, $4.
c. Wages payable, $7.
d. Income tax expense, $9.

Required:

1. Prepare the adjusting journal entries for 2013.
2. Using T-accounts, determine the adjusted balances in each account and prepare an adjusted trial balance as of December 31, 2013.
3. By what amount would net income have been understated or overstated had the adjusting journal entries not been recorded?

E4-17 Reporting an Income Statement, Statement of Retained Earnings,   LO 4-4
     and Balance Sheet

Refer to E4-16.

Required:

Using the adjusted balances in E4-16, prepare an income statement, statement of retained earnings, and balance sheet for 2013.

E4-18 Recording Closing Entries   LO 4-5

Refer to E4-16.

Required:

Using the adjusted balances in E4-16, give the closing journal entry for 2013. What is the purpose of "closing the books" at the end of the accounting period?

E4-19 Analyzing, Recording, and Summarizing Business Activities   LO 4-1, 4-2, 4-6
     and Adjustments

The following relates to a magazine company called My Style Mag (MSM). You will use your understanding of the relationships among: (1) business activities, (2) accounting equation effects, (3) journal entries, and (4) T-accounts, to complete a four-part table similar to the following. Prepare a separate table for each item (*a*)–(*f*) listed below.

(1)	(Description of the business activity.)		

(2)	Assets	=	Liabilities	+	Stockholders' Equity

(3)	Account Names	Debit	Credit

(4)		

Required:

For each item (*a*)–(*f*) listed below, use the information provided to prepare and complete a four-part table similar to that shown above. Items (*a*)–(*f*) are independent of one another.

a.

(1)	On January 22, 2012, MSM received $24,000 cash from customers for one-year subscriptions to the magazine for February 2012–January 2013.

b.

(3)	Account Names	Debit	Credit
Jan. 31	Utilities Expense (+E, −SE)	3,000	
	Accounts Payable (+L)		3,000

c.

(2)	Assets	=	Liabilities	+	Stockholders' Equity
Feb. 28			Unearned Revenue −2,000		Subscription Revenue (+R) +2,000

d.

(1)	On March 31, 2012, MSM recorded an adjusting entry for the month's depreciation of $10,000.

e.

(4)	Cash		Prepaid Rent

5,000	Apr. 1	Apr. 1	5,000

f.

(4)	Accounts Receivable		Advertising Revenue

Apr. 30	10,000		10,000	Apr. 30

COACHED PROBLEMS

LO 4-3, 4-5   **CP4-1 Preparing an Adjusted Trial Balance, Closing Journal Entry, and Post-Closing Trial Balance**

Building on its brand's success in boardsports, Volcom, Inc., has become a premium designer, marketer, and distributor of clothing and accessories for young men and women. The following is a list of accounts and amounts reported for the fiscal year ended December 31, 2010. The accounts have normal debit or credit balances and the dollars are rounded to the nearest thousand.

Accounts Payable	$ 22,902	Long-term Debt	$ 1,518
Accounts Receivable	66,542	Other Noncurrent Assets	42,616
Accrued Liabilities	16,181	Other Revenue	4,244
Accumulated Depreciation	21,496	Product Cost Expense	164,161
Cash	80,300	Property and Equipment	48,148
Contributed Capital	94,757	Retained Earnings	99,911
Income Tax Expense	10,540	Sales Revenue	321,414
Inventories	41,449	Selling, General, and Administrative Expenses	128,667

Required:

1. Prepare an adjusted trial balance at December 31, 2010. Is the Retained Earnings balance of $99,911 the amount that would be reported on the balance sheet as of December 31, 2010?

   TIP: Volcom, Inc., did not declare a dividend during 2010 but it did earn net income.

2. Prepare the closing entry required at December 31, 2010.

3. Prepare a post-closing trial balance at December 31, 2010.

CP4-2 Analyzing and Recording Adjusting Journal Entries

LO 4-1, 4-2

Jordan Company's annual accounting year ends on December 31. It is now December 31, 2012, and all of the 2012 entries have been made except for the following:

a. The company owes interest of $700 on a bank loan. The interest will be paid when the loan is repaid on September 30, 2013. No interest has been recorded.

b. On September 1, 2012, Jordan collected six months' rent of $4,800 on storage space. At that date, Jordan debited Cash and credited Unearned Revenue for $4,800.

c. The company earned service revenue of $3,300 on a special job that was completed December 29, 2012. Collection will be made during January 2013. No entry has been recorded.

d. On November 1, 2012, Jordan paid a one-year premium for property insurance of $4,200, for coverage starting on that date. Cash was credited and Prepaid Insurance was debited for this amount.

e. At December 31, 2012, wages earned by employees but not yet paid totaled $1,100. The employees will be paid on the next payroll date, January 15, 2013.

f. Depreciation of $1,000 must be recognized on a service truck purchased this year.

g. On December 27, 2012, the company received a tax bill of $400 from the city for 2012 property taxes on land. The tax bill is payable during January 2013.

h. The income before any of the adjustments or income taxes was $27,400. The company's income tax rate is 30%. Compute adjusted income based on (a) through (g) to determine and record income tax expense.

Required:

1. Determine the accounting equation effects of each required adjustment.

   TIP: In transaction (b), Jordan Company has met its obligation for four of the six months, thereby earning 4/6 of the rent collected.

   TIP: In transaction (d), two months of insurance coverage has now expired.

   TIP: Adjusted income based on (a) through (g) should be $30,000.

2. Give the adjusting journal entry required for each transaction at December 31, 2012.

CP4-3 Determining Accounting Equation Effects of Adjusting Journal Entries

LO 4-2, 4-6

Refer to CP4-2.

Required:

Indicate the effects (account, amount, and direction) of each adjusting journal entry. Use + for increase, − for decrease, and NE for no effect. Provide an appropriate account name for any revenue and expense effects.

TIP: The first transaction is done for you as an example.

Transaction	Assets	Liabilities	Stockholders' Equity
a	NE	Interest Payable +700	Interest Expense (+E) −700
b			
etc.			

LO 4-1, 4-2, 4-3, 4-6   **CP4-4 Identifying and Preparing Adjusting Journal Entries**

Golf Academy, Inc., provides private golf lessons. Its unadjusted trial balance at December 31, 2012, follows, along with information about selected accounts.

Account Names	Debit	Credit	Further Information
Cash	$ 31,900		As reported on December 31 bank statement.
Supplies	600		Based on count, only $200 of supplies still exist.
Unearned Revenue		$ 3,500	Of this amount, $3,000 was received for December lessons and $500 for January lessons.
Wages Payable		0	Employees were paid $1,000 for 10 days of work through December 28. They have not yet been paid for work on December 29 and 30.
Income Tax Payable		0	The company has paid last year's income tax but not this year's tax.
Interest Payable		0	The company has not paid the $100 of interest owed on its note payable for the current period.
Note Payable		12,000	This one-year note was taken out this year on December 1.
Contributed Capital		1,000	This amount was contributed to the company in prior years.
Retained Earnings		3,000	This is the balance reported at the end of last year.
Lesson Revenue		51,500	Most customers pay cash for lessons each time they are provided, but some customers pay in advance.
Wages Expense	36,100		Employees worked through December 30, but did not work on December 31.
Supplies Expense	2,400		This is the cost of supplies used through November 30.
Interest Expense	0		The company has not paid the $100 of interest owed on its note payable for the current period.
Income Tax Expense	0		The company has an average tax rate of 30%.
Totals	**$71,000**	**$71,000**	

Required:

1. Calculate the (preliminary) unadjusted net income for the year ended December 31, 2012.
2. Name the five pairs of balance sheet and income statement accounts that require adjustment.
3. Calculate the desired balances for each account listed in the unadjusted trial balance.
4. Prepare the adjusting journal entries that are required at December 31, 2012.
5. Calculate the adjusted net income that the company should report for the year ended December 31, 2012. By how much did the adjustments in requirement (4) cause net income to increase or decrease?

GROUP A PROBLEMS

LO 4-3, 4-5   **PA4-1 Preparing a Trial Balance, Closing Journal Entry, and Post-Closing Trial Balance**

Starbooks Corporation provides an online bookstore for electronic books. The following is a simplified list of accounts and amounts reported in its accounting records. The accounts have normal debit or credit balances and the dollars are rounded to the nearest thousand. Assume the year ended on September 30, 2012.

Accounts Payable	$ 221	Other Current Assets	$ 71
Accounts Receivable	191	Other Noncurrent Assets	461
Accrued Liabilities	354	Other Expenses	197
Accumulated Depreciation	300	Prepaid Expenses	94
Cash	307	Property and Equipment	2,142
Contributed Capital	151	Retained Earnings	1,445
Depreciation Expense	340	Selling Expenses	2,605
General and		Service Revenue	6,369
Administrative Expenses	357	Short-term Bank Loan	476
Income Tax Expense	302	Store Operating Expenses	2,166
Interest Revenue	92	Supplies	546
Long-term Debt	196	Unearned Revenue	175

Required:

1. Prepare an adjusted trial balance at September 30, 2012. Is the Retained Earnings balance of $1,445 the amount that would be reported on the balance sheet as of September 30, 2012?
2. Prepare the closing entry required at September 30, 2012.
3. Prepare a post-closing trial balance at September 30, 2012.

PA4-2 Analyzing and Recording Adjusting Journal Entries

LO 4-1, 4-2

Brokeback Towing Company is at the end of its accounting year, December 31, 2013. The following data that must be considered were developed from the company's records and related documents:

a. On July 1, 2013, a two-year insurance premium on equipment in the amount of $600 was paid and debited in full to Prepaid Insurance on that date. Coverage began on July 1.
b. At the end of 2013, the unadjusted balance in the Office Supplies account was $1,000. A physical count of supplies on December 31, 2013, indicated supplies costing $300 were still on hand.
c. On December 31, 2013, YY's Garage completed repairs on one of Brokeback's trucks at a cost of $800. The amount is not yet recorded. It will be paid during January 2014.
d. In December the 2013 property tax bill for $1,600 was received from the city. The taxes, which have not been recorded, will be paid on February 15, 2014.
e. On December 31, 2013, the company completed a contract for an out-of-state company for $7,950 payable by the customer within 30 days. No cash has been collected and no journal entry has been made for this transaction.
f. On July 1, 2013, the company purchased a new hauling van. Depreciation for July–December 2013, estimated to total $2,750, has not been recorded.
g. As of December 31, the company owes interest of $500 on a bank loan taken out on October 1, 2013. The interest will be paid when the loan is repaid on September 30, 2014. No interest has been recorded yet.
h. The income before any of the adjustments or income taxes was $30,000. The company's federal income tax rate is 30%. Compute adjusted income based on all of the preceding information, and then determine and record income tax expense

Required:

1. Give the adjusting journal entry required for each item at December 31, 2013.
2. Without the adjustments made in requirement 1, by what amount would Brokeback's net income have been understated or overstated?

PA4-3 Determining Accounting Equation Effects of Adjusting Journal Entries

LO 4-2, 4-4, 4-6

Refer to PA4-2.

Required:

Indicate the accounting equation effects (amount and direction) of each adjusting journal entry. Use + for increase, − for decrease, and NE for no effect. Provide an appropriate account name for any revenue and expense effects.

Transaction	Assets	Liabilities	Stockholders' Equity
a			
b			
etc.			

LO 4-1, 4-2, 4-3, 4-6   **PA4-4 Identifying and Preparing Adjusting Journal Entries**

Val's Hair Emporium operates a hair salon. Its unadjusted trial balance as of December 31, 2013, follows along with information about selected accounts.

Account Names	Debit	Credit	Further Information
Cash	$ 3,800		As reported on December 31 bank statement.
Supplies	4,300		Based on count, only $1,300 of supplies still exist.
Prepaid Rent	6,000		This amount was paid November 1 for rent through the end of January.
Accounts Payable		$ 1,500	This represents the total amount of bills received for supplies and utilities through December 15. Val estimates that the company has received $450 of utility services through December 31 for which it has not yet been billed.
Wages Payable		0	Stylists have not yet been paid $150 for their work on December 31.
Income Tax Payable		0	The company has paid last year's income taxes but not this year's taxes.
Contributed Capital		2,000	This amount was contributed to the company in prior years.
Retained Earnings		900	This is the balance reported at the end of last year.
Service Revenue		75,800	Customers pay cash when they receive services.
Wages Expense	29,100		This is the cost of stylist wages through December 30.
Utilities Expense	12,200		This is the cost of utilities through December 15.
Rent Expense	20,000		This year's rent was $2,000 per month.
Supplies Expense	4,800		This is the cost of supplies used through November 30.
Income Tax Expense	0		The company has an average tax rate of 30%.
Totals	**$80,200**	**$80,200**	

Required:

1. Calculate the (preliminary) unadjusted net income for the year ended December 31, 2013.
2. Name the five pairs of balance sheet and income statement accounts that require adjustment.
3. Calculate the desired balances for each account listed in the unadjusted trial balance.
4. Prepare the adjusting journal entries that are required at December 31, 2013.
5. Calculate the adjusted net income that the company should report for the year ended December 31, 2013. By how much did the adjustments in requirement (4) cause net income to increase or decrease?

GROUP B PROBLEMS

LO 4-3, 4-5   **PB4-1 Preparing a Trial Balance, Closing Journal Entry, and Post-Closing Trial Balance**

Regis Corporation

Regis Corporation operates hair salons under various brand names including Supercuts, Mia & Maxx, and Style America. The following is a simplified list of accounts and amounts (in millions) reported in the company's accounts for the year ended June 30, 2010.

Required:

1. Prepare an adjusted trial balance at June 30, 2010. Is the Retained Earnings balance of $297 the amount that would be reported on the balance sheet as of June 30, 2010?
2. Prepare the closing entry required at June 30, 2010.
3. Prepare a post-closing trial balance at June 30, 2010.

Accounts Payable	$ 54	Income Tax Expense	$ 26
Accounts Receivable	24	Interest Expense	54
Accrued Liabilities	156	Inventories	153
Accumulated Depreciation	632	Long-term Labilities	843
Cash	152	Other Current Assets	107
Contributed Capital	335	Other Noncurrent Assets	1,152
Cost of Operations	1,280	Property, Plant, and Equipment	983
Depreciation Expense	109	Retained Earnings	297
General and		Rent Expense	344
Administrative Expenses	291	Service Revenue	2,358

PB4-2 Recording Adjusting Journal Entries

LO 4-1, 4-2

Cactus Company's annual accounting year ends on June 30. It is June 30, 2013, and all of the 2013 entries except the following adjusting journal entries have been made:

a. The company earned service revenue of $2,000 on a special job that was completed June 29, 2013. Collection will be made during July 2013; no entry has been recorded.

b. On March 31, 2013, Cactus paid a six-month premium for property insurance in the amount of $3,200 for coverage starting on that date. Cash was credited and Prepaid Insurance was debited for this amount.

c. At June 30, 2013, wages of $900 were earned by employees but not yet paid. The employees will be paid on the next payroll date, which is July 15, 2013.

d. On June 1, 2013, Cactus collected two months' revenue of $450. At that date, Cactus debited Cash and credited Unearned Revenue for $450. One-half of it has now been earned but not yet recorded.

e. Depreciation of $1,500 must be recognized on a service truck purchased on July 1, 2012.

f. Cash of $4,200 was collected on May 1, 2013, for services to be rendered evenly over the next year beginning on May 1. Unearned Revenue was credited when the cash was received. Some of it has now been earned but not yet recorded.

g. The company owes interest of $600 on a bank loan taken out on February 1, 2013. The interest will be paid when the loan is repaid on January 31, 2014.

h. The income before any of the adjustments or income taxes was $31,675. The company's federal income tax rate is 30%. Compute adjusted income based on all of the preceding information, and then determine and record income tax expense.

Required:

1. Determine the accounting equation effects of each required adjustment.
2. Give the adjusting journal entry required for each transaction at June 30, 2013.

PB4-3 Determining Accounting Equation Effects of Adjusting Journal Entries

LO 4-2, 4-6

Refer to PB4-2.

Required:

Indicate the accounting equation effects (amount and direction) of each adjusting journal entry. Use + for increase, − for decrease, and NE for no effect. Provide an appropriate account name for any revenue and expense effects.

Transaction	Assets	Liabilities	Stockholders' Equity
a			
b			
c			
etc.			

PB4-4 Identifying and Preparing Adjusting Journal Entries

LO 4-1, 4-2, 4-3, 4-6

Learn to Play, Inc., is a one-person company that provides private piano lessons. Its unadjusted trial balance at December 31, 2013, follows along with information about selected accounts.

Account Names	Debit	Credit	Further Information
Cash	$ 23,800		As reported on December 31 bank statement.
Supplies	300		Based on count, only $200 of supplies still exist.
Unearned Revenue		$ 1,500	Of this amount, $500 was received for December lessons and $1,000 for January lessons.
Wages Payable		0	The employee was paid $500 for 10 days of work through December 29. She has not yet been paid for work on December 30 and 31.
Income Tax Payable		0	The company has paid last year's income taxes but not this year's taxes.
Interest Payable		0	The company has not paid the $100 of interest owed on its note payable for the current period.
Note Payable		12,000	This one-year note was taken out this year on December 1.
Contributed Capital		1,000	This amount was contributed to the company in prior years.
Retained Earnings		3,000	This is the balance reported at the end of last year.
Service Revenue		25,500	Most customers pay cash for lessons each time they are provided, but some customers paid in advance.
Wages Expense	18,100		The company's employee worked through December 31.
Supplies Expense	800		This is the cost of supplies used through November 30.
Interest Expense	0		The company has not paid the $100 of interest owed on its note payable for the current period.
Income Tax Expense	0		The company has an average tax rate of 30%.
Totals	**$43,000**	**$43,000**	

Required:

1. Calculate the (preliminary) unadjusted net income for the year ended December 31, 2013.
2. Name the five pairs of balance sheet and income statement accounts that require adjustment.
3. Calculate the desired balances for each account listed in the unadjusted trial balance.
4. Prepare the adjusting journal entries that are required at December 31, 2013.
5. Calculate the adjusted net income that the company should report for the year ended December 31, 2013. By how much did the adjustments in requirement (4) cause net income to increase or decrease?

COMPREHENSIVE PROBLEMS

LO 2-3, 3-3, 4-2, 4-3, 4-4

C4-1 From Recording Transactions to Preparing Accrual and Deferral Adjustments and Reporting Results on the Balance Sheet and Income Statement (Chapters 2, 3, and 4)

RunHeavy Corporation (RHC) is a corporation that manages a local rock band. RHC was formed with an investment of $10,000 cash, paid in by the leader of the band on January 3. On January 4, RHC purchased music equipment by paying $2,000 cash and signing an $8,000 promissory note payable in three years. On January 5, RHC booked the band for six concert events, at a price of $2,500 each. Of the six events, four were completed between January 10 and 20. On January 22, cash was collected for three of the four events. The other two bookings were for February concerts, but on January 24, RHC collected half of the $2,500 fee for one of them. On January 27, RHC paid $3,140 cash for the band's travel-related costs. On January 28, RHC paid its band members a total of $2,400 cash for wages for the first three events. As of January 31, the band members hadn't yet been paid wages for the fourth event completed in January, but they would be paid in February at the same rate as for the first three events. As of January 31, RHC has not yet recorded the $100 of monthly depreciation on the equipment. Also, RHC has not yet paid or recorded the $60 interest owed on the promissory note at January 31. RHC is subject to a 15% tax rate on the company's income before tax.

Required:

1. Prepare journal entries to record the transactions and adjustments needed on each of the dates indicated above.

2. Post the journal entries from requirement 1 to T-accounts, calculate ending balances, and prepare an adjusted trial balance.

3. Prepare a classified balance sheet and income statement as of and for the month ended January 31, 2013.

C4-2 **From Recording Transactions (Including Adjusting Journal Entries) to Preparing Financial Statements and Closing Journal Entries (Chapters 2, 3, and 4)**

LO 2-3, 3-3, 4-1, 4-2, 4-3, 4-4, 4-5, 4-6

Brothers Harry and Herman Hausyerday began operations of their machine shop (H & H Tool, Inc.) on January 1, 2010. The annual reporting period ends December 31. The trial balance on January 1, 2012, follows (the amounts are rounded to thousands of dollars to simplify):

Account Titles	Debit	Credit
Cash	$ 3	
Accounts Receivable	5	
Supplies	12	
Land	0	
Equipment	60	
Accumulated Depreciation		$ 6
Other Noncurrent Assets	4	
Accounts Payable		5
Notes Payable (short-term)		0
Wages Payable		0
Interest Payable		0
Income Tax Payable		0
Contributed Capital		65
Retained Earnings		8
Dividends Declared	0	
Service Revenue	0	
Wages Expense	0	
Depreciation Expense	0	
Income Tax Expense	0	
Interest Expense	0	
Supplies Expense	0	
Totals	$84	$84

Transactions during 2012 (summarized in thousands of dollars) follow:

a. Borrowed $12 cash on a six-month note payable dated March 1, 2012.
b. Purchased land for future building site, paid cash, $9.
c. Earned revenues for 2012, $160, including $40 on credit and $120 collected in cash.
d. Issued additional shares of stock for $3.
e. Recognized wages expense for 2012, $85 paid in cash.
f. Collected accounts receivable, $24.
g. Purchased other noncurrent assets, $10 cash.
h. Paid accounts payable, $13.
i. Purchased supplies on account for future use, $18.
j. Signed a $25 service contract to start February 1, 2013.
k. Declared and paid a cash dividend, $17.

Data for adjusting journal entries:

l. Supplies counted on December 31, 2012, $10.
m. Depreciation for the year on the equipment, $6.
n. Accrued interest of $1 on notes payable.
o. Wages earned not yet paid or recorded, $12.
p. Income tax for the year was $8. It will be paid in 2013.

Required:

1. Set up T-accounts for the accounts on the trial balance and enter beginning balances.
2. Record journal entries for transactions (a) through (k), and post them to the T-accounts.
3. Prepare an unadjusted trial balance.
4. Record and post the adjusting journal entries (l) through (p).
5. Prepare an adjusted trial balance.
6. Prepare an income statement, statement of retained earnings, and balance sheet.
7. Prepare and post the closing journal entries.
8. Prepare a post-closing trial balance.
9. How much net income did H & H Tool, Inc., generate during 2012? What was its net profit margin? Is the company financed primarily by liabilities or stockholders' equity? What is its current ratio?

LO 2-3, 3-3, 4-1, 4-2, 4-3, 4-4, 4-5, 4-6   **C4-3 From Recording Transactions (Including Adjusting Journal Entries) to Preparing Financial Statements and Closing Journal Entries (Chapters 2, 3, and 4)**

Drs. Glenn Feltham and Gary Entwistle began operations of their physical therapy clinic called Northland Physical Therapy on January 1, 2011. The annual reporting period ends December 31. The trial balance on January 1, 2012, was as follows (the amounts are rounded to thousands of dollars to simplify):

Account Titles	Debit	Credit
Cash	$ 7	
Accounts Receivable	3	
Supplies	3	
Equipment	8	
Accumulated Depreciation		$ 1
Other Noncurrent Assets	4	
Accounts Payable		5
Notes Payable		0
Wages Payable		0
Interest Payable		0
Income Taxes Payable		0
Unearned Revenue		0
Contributed Capital		15
Retained Earnings		4
Dividends Declared	0	
Service Revenue		0
Depreciation Expense	0	
Income Tax Expense	0	
Interest Expense	0	
Supplies Expense	0	
Totals	$25	$25

Transactions during 2012 (summarized in thousands of dollars) follow:

a. Borrowed $22 cash on July 1, 2012, signing a six-month note payable.
b. Purchased equipment for $25 cash on July 1, 2012.
c. Issued additional shares of stock for $5.

d. Earned revenues for 2012 of $55, including $8 on credit and $47 received in cash.
e. Recognized wages expense for 2012 of $30, paid in cash.
f. Purchased other noncurrent assets, $3 cash.
g. Collected accounts receivable, $9.
h. Purchased supplies on account for future use, $7.
i. Paid accounts payable, $10.
j. Received a $3 deposit from a hospital for a contract to start January 5, 2013.
k. Declared and paid a cash dividend, $4.

Data for adjusting journal entries:

l. Supplies of $3 were counted on December 31, 2012.
m. Depreciation for 2012, $4.
n. Accrued interest of $1 on notes payable.
o. Wages incurred not yet paid or recorded, $3.
p. Income tax expense for 2012 was $4, and will be paid in 2013.

Required:

1. Set up T-accounts for the accounts on the trial balance and enter beginning balances.
2. Record journal entries for transactions (a) through (k), and post them to the T-accounts.
3. Prepare an unadjusted trial balance.
4. Record and post the adjusting journal entries (l) through (p).
5. Prepare an adjusted trial balance.
6. Prepare an income statement, statement of retained earnings, and balance sheet.
7. Prepare and post the closing journal entries.
8. Prepare a post-closing trial balance.
9. How much net income did the physical therapy clinic generate during 2012? What was its net profit margin? Is the business financed primarily by liabilities or stockholders' equity? What is its current ratio?

C4-4 From Recording Transactions (Including Adjusting Journal Entries) to Preparing Financial Statements and Closing Journal Entries (Chapters 2, 3, and 4)   LO 2-3, 3-3, 4-1, 4-2, 4-3, 4-4, 4-5, 4-6

Alison and Chuck Renny began operations of their furniture repair shop (Lazy Sofa Furniture, Inc.) on January 1, 2011. The annual reporting period ends December 31. The trial balance on January 1, 2012, appears on the following page (amounts are rounded to thousands of dollars to simplify):
Transactions during 2012 (summarized in thousands of dollars) follow:

a. Borrowed $21 cash on July 1, 2012, signing a six-month note payable.
b. Purchased equipment for $18 cash on July 1, 2012.
c. Issued additional shares of stock for $5.
d. Earned revenues for 2012 in the amount of $65, including $9 on credit and $56 received in cash.
e. Recognized operating expenses for 2012, $35, including $7 on credit and $28 in cash.
f. Purchased additional equipment, $3 cash.
g. Collected accounts receivable, $8.
h. Paid accounts payable, $11.
i. Purchased on account supplies for future use, $10.
j. Received a $3 deposit on work to start January 15, 2013.
k. Declared and paid a cash dividend, $10.

Data for adjusting journal entries:

l. Supplies of $4 were counted on December 31, 2012.
m. Depreciation for 2012, $2.
n. Accrued interest on notes payable of $1.
o. Wages earned since the December 24 payroll not yet paid, $3.
p. Income tax for 2012 was $4, and will be paid in 2013.

Required:

1. Set up T-accounts for the accounts on the trial balance and enter beginning balances.
2. Record journal entries for transactions (a) through (k), and post them to the T-accounts. Note that Lazy Sofa classifies the cost of its wages and supplies used-up as "operating expenses."
3. Prepare an unadjusted trial balance.

Account Titles	Debit	Credit
Cash	$ 5	
Accounts Receivable	4	
Supplies	2	
Equipment	6	
Accumulated Depreciation		$ 0
Other Noncurrent Assets	9	
Accounts Payable		7
Notes Payable		0
Wages Payable		0
Interest Payable		0
Income Tax Payable		0
Unearned Revenue		0
Contributed Capital		15
Retained Earnings		4
Dividends Declared	0	
Service Revenue		0
Depreciation Expense	0	
Income Tax Expense	0	
Interest Expense	0	
Operating Expenses	0	
Totals	$26	$26

4. Record and post the adjusting journal entries (*l*) through (*p*).
5. Prepare an adjusted trial balance.
6. Prepare an income statement, statement of retained earnings, and balance sheet.
7. Prepare and post the closing journal entries.
8. Prepare a post-closing trial balance.
9. How much net income did Lazy Sofa Furniture, Inc., generate during 2012? Is the company financed primarily by liabilities or stockholders' equity?

LO 4-2, 4-4   **C4-5 From Recording Transactions to Preparing Accrual and Deferral Adjustments and Reporting Results on the Balance Sheet and Income Statement (Chapters 2, 3, and 4)**

House of Tutors, Incorporated, (HTI) is a company that runs a tutoring service for high school and university students. The company reported the following amounts in its post-closing trial balance, prepared at the end of its first fiscal year, at August 31, 2013.

Accounts Payable	$ 60	Equipment	$ 12,000
Accounts Receivable	220	Interest Payable	40
Accumulated Depreciation	1,200	Note Payable (long-term)	8,000
Cash	700	Retained Earnings	820
Contributed Capital	2,900	Supplies	100

The company encountered the following events during September 2013:

a. HTI provided 100 hours of regular hourly tutoring at the rate of $20 per hour, all of which was collected in cash.

b. HTI paid tutors at the hourly rate of $10 per hour. On September 28, HTI paid for 90 hours of tutor time and promised to pay the remaining hours worked.

c. HTI hosted an all-night review session on September 29 for people cramming for midterm exams, at a special price of $10 per attendee. Rather than collect cash at the time of the review session, HTI will send bills in October to the 75 people who attended the review session.

d. At the beginning of the night-long review session, HTI paid $200 cash to its tutors for wages. No additional wages will be paid for the review session.

e. HTI collected $200 cash on account from students who received tutoring during summer 2013.

f. HTI also collected $250 cash from a high school for a tutoring session to be held in October 2013.

g. HTI determined that depreciation for September should be $100.

h. On September 30, HTI declared and paid a $500 cash dividend.

i. Although HTI adjusted its accounts on August 31, it has not yet paid the $40 monthly interest owed on the promissory note, for either August or September. The note is due October 2016.

j. HTI has only $40 of supplies left at September 30.

k. HTI's income taxes are approximately 30% of income before tax.

Required:

1. Prepare HTI's journal entries and adjusting journal entries.

2. Prepare HTI's income statement and statement of retained earnings for the month ended September 30, 2013.

3. Prepare HTI's classified balance sheet at September 30, 2013.

SKILLS DEVELOPMENT CASES

S4-1 Finding Financial Information

LO 4-1, 4-6

Refer to the financial statements of The Home Depot in Appendix A at the end of this book, or download the annual report from the *Cases* section of the text's Web site at www.mhhe.com/phillips4e.

Required:

1. How much did The Home Depot owe for salaries and related expenses at January 30, 2011? Was this an increase or decrease from the previous year?

   a. $1,290 million (Increase)
   b. $1,290 million (Decrease)
   c. $1,263 million (Decrease)
   d. $1,263 million (Increase)

2. Refer to the Revenues note in the Summary of Significant Accounting Policies that follows The Home Depot's statements of cash flows. How does the company account for customer payments received in advance of providing services?

   a. Record the prepayment as revenue.
   b. The funds are deposited in the bank account and no entry is recorded.
   c. The funds are not deposited in the bank account, and no entry is recorded.
   d. The revenue is deferred until the goods or services are provided to the customer.

3. What adjusting journal entry must The Home Depot make when it provides services paid by gift card?

   a. *dr* Cash, *cr* Unearned Revenue
   b. *dr* Unearned Revenue, *cr* Service Revenue
   c. *dr* Service Revenue, *cr* Unearned Revenue
   d. *dr* Unearned Revenue, *cr* Cash

S4-2 Comparing Financial Information

LO 4-1, 4-6

Refer to the financial statements of The Home Depot in Appendix A and Lowe's in Appendix B at the end of this book, or download the annual reports from the *Cases* section of the text's Web site at www.mhhe.com/phillips4e.

Required:

1. Refer to the notes to the financial statements to determine how much The Home Depot and Lowe's each spent on advertising expenses in the year ended January 30, 2011 (fiscal 2010).

Lowe's

2. How much did The Home Depot and Lowe's each owe for salaries and wages at January 30, 2011? Provide one reason that would explain the difference between the two companies' accrued payroll liabilities.

LO 4-1, 4-4

S4-3 Internet-Based Team Research: Examining Deferrals and Accruals

As a team, select an industry to analyze. Using your Web browser, each team member should access the annual report or 10-K for one publicly traded company in the industry, with each member selecting a different company. (See S1-3 in Chapter 1 for a description of possible resources for these tasks.)

Required:

1. On an individual basis, each team member should write a short report listing the following:
    a. The company's total assets and total liabilities at the end of each year.
    b. The company's prepaid expenses and accrued liabilities at the end of each year.
    c. The percentage of prepaid expenses to total assets and the percentage of accrued liabilities to total liabilities.
    d. Describe and explain the types of accrued liabilities reported in the notes to the financial statements.
2. Discuss any patterns that you as a team observe. Then, as a team, write a short report comparing and contrasting your companies according to the preceding attributes. Provide potential explanations for any differences discovered.

LO 4-1, 4-2, 4-6

Safety-Kleen Corp.

S4-4 Ethical Decision Making: A Real-Life Example

On December 12, 2002, the SEC filed a lawsuit against four executives of Safety-Kleen Corp., one of the country's leading providers of industrial waste collection and disposal services. The primary issue was that the executives had directed others in the company to record improper adjustments, which had the effect of overstating net income during those periods. Complete this case by downloading, from www.mhhe.com/phillips4e, excerpts from the SEC's court documents and questions about adjustments related to Safety-Kleen's operating expenses and management bonuses.

LO 4-1, 4-2, 4-6

Coinstar, Inc.

S4-5 Ethical Decision Making: A Mini-Case

Assume you work as an assistant accountant in the head office of a DVD movie kiosk business, similar to Coinstar, Inc. With the increasing popularity of online movie rental operations, your company has struggled to meet its earnings targets for the year. It is important for the company to meet its earnings targets this year because the company is renegotiating a bank loan next month, and the terms of that loan are likely to depend on the company's reported financial success. Also, the company plans to issue more stock to the public in the upcoming year, to obtain funds for establishing its own presence in the online movie rental business. The chief financial officer (CFO) has approached you with a solution to the earnings dilemma. She proposes that the depreciation period for the stock of reusable DVDs be extended from 3 months to 15 months. She explains that by lengthening the depreciation period, a smaller amount of depreciation expense will be recorded in the current year, resulting in a higher net income. She claims that generally accepted accounting principles require estimates like this, so it wouldn't involve doing anything wrong.

Required:

Discuss the CFO's proposed solution. In your discussion, consider the following questions. Will the change in depreciation affect net income in the current year in the way that the CFO described? How will it affect net income in the following year? Is the CFO correct when she claims that the change in estimated depreciation is allowed by GAAP? Who relies on the video company's financial statements when making decisions? Why might their decisions be affected by the CFO's proposed solution? Is it possible that their decisions would not be affected? What should you do?

S4-6 Critical Thinking: Adjusting an Income Statement and Balance Sheet for Deferrals and Accruals

LO 4-1, 4-2, 4-4, 4-6

Complete this case, available online at www.mhhe.com/phillips4e. By completing this case, you will learn to identify misstatements and make adjustments to correct the financial statements.

S4-7 Aggregating Accounts on an Adjusted Trial Balance to Prepare an Income Statement, Statement of Retained Earnings, and Balance Sheet

LO 4-3, 4-4, 4-6

Escalade, Inc.

Complete this case involving Escalade, Inc., available online at www.mhhe.com/phillips4e. By completing this case, you will learn to use a spreadsheet to link account balances on an adjusted trial balance to produce aggregated amounts reported in an income statement, statement of retained earnings, and balance sheet.

CONTINUING CASE

CC4-1 Adjusting the Accounting Records

LO 4-1, 4-2

Assume it is now December 31, 2013, and Nicole has just completed her first year of operations at Nicole's Getaway Spa. After looking through her trial balance, she noticed that there are some items that have either not been recorded or are no longer up-to-date.

a. Nicole's Getaway Spa is renting its space at a cost of $600 per month. On September 1, 2013, Nicole paid eight months' rent in advance using cash. This prepayment was recorded in the account Prepaid Rent back in September.
b. The building, purchased at the beginning of the year for $47,000 cash, has estimated depreciation of $2,000 for 2013, but none has been recorded yet.
c. Wages to the support staff at Nicole's Getaway Spa have been paid up to December 26, 2013. The support staff worked both December 27 and 28 and will be paid on January 5, 2014. Wages amount to $1,000 per day. The spa was closed December 29–31.
d. The insurance policy, purchased on June 1 for $3,000 cash, provides coverage for 12 months. The insurance coverage since June has now been used up.
e. The unadjusted amount in the Spa Supplies account was $2,000 at December 31, 2013, for supplies purchased on account. A year-end count showed $700 of supplies remain on hand.
f. On the last day of December, a customer obtained spa services by using a $90 gift certificate that was purchased earlier in the month. Use of the gift certificate to pay for these services had not yet been recorded.

Required:

1. For each of the items listed above, identify whether an accrual adjustment, a deferral adjustment, or no adjustment is required.
2. For each of the deferral adjustments, prepare the initial journal entry that would have been recorded.
3. Prepare the adjusting journal entries that should be recorded for Nicole's Getaway Spa at December 31, 2013, assuming that the items have not been adjusted prior to December 31, 2013.

Financial Reporting and Analysis

YOUR LEARNING OBJECTIVES

Understand the business

LO 5-1   Explain the needs of financial statement users.

LO 5-2   Describe the environment for financial reporting, including the Sarbanes-Oxley Act.

Study the accounting methods

LO 5-3   Prepare a comparative balance sheet, multiple-step income statement, and statement of stockholders' equity.

LO 5-4   Describe other significant aspects of the financial reporting process, including external audits and the distribution of financial information.

LO 5-5   Explain the reasons for, and financial statement presentation effects of, adopting IFRS.

Evaluate the results

LO 5-6   Compare results to common benchmarks.

LO 5-7   Calculate and interpret the debt-to-assets, asset turnover, and net profit margin ratios.

Review the chapter

THAT WAS THEN

In the previous chapters, you learned about the accounting system that produces the basic financial statements.

FOCUS COMPANY: Activision

ACTIVISION®

A s you have seen in Chapters 1 through 4, accounting plays a vital role when establishing and operating a small business like Pizza Aroma. Chapter 5 will continue to broaden your understanding by looking at the role accounting plays in large public companies that carry out their business activities in many cities and countries throughout the world. As you will learn in this chapter, accounting is actually one of the most pressure-filled, fast-paced elements of business. In the past 10 years alone, the accounting world has tackled frauds and scandals, increasing regulation, globalization, and economic turmoil. The purposes of this chapter are to explain these four major topics and begin to equip you with tools that will help you use financial statement information.

In keeping with the theme that accounting can be useful and fun, we focus on an exciting company that is bringing smiles to people of all ages, whether they live in India, China, or Europe, or the home of its headquarters in Santa Monica, California. Activision started as a private company in 1979, went public in 1983, survived economic troubles in the late 1980s, and became known as Activision Blizzard in late 2008 when it merged with a European video game company (Vivendi Games) to create the world's largest video game company. Famous for its Call of Duty® video games and World of Warcraft® online role-playing game, Activision Blizzard provides an ideal background for learning about the role of accounting in business and the ways in which U.S. accounting rules are changing to become more comparable with those used in European countries and throughout the world.

www.activision.com

THIS IS NOW

This chapter describes the environment in which financial statements are used, and introduces common ratio analyses.

ORGANIZATION OF THE CHAPTER

Understand the business	Study the accounting methods	Evaluate the results	Review the chapter
• The needs of financial statement users • The financial reporting environment	• Financial reporting in the United States • Globalization and International Financial Reporting Standards (IFRS)	• Economic crisis • Comparison to common benchmarks • Financial statement ratio analysis	• Demonstration case • Chapter summary • Key terms • Homework helper • Practice material

Understand the Business

Learning Objective 5-1
Explain the needs of financial statement users.

THE NEEDS OF FINANCIAL STATEMENT USERS

Chapter 1 provided an overview of the many people who use financial statements to make decisions. A more detailed look at the main user groups is presented in Exhibit 5.1 and in the discussion that follows.

EXHIBIT 5.1 Users and Uses of Accounting Information

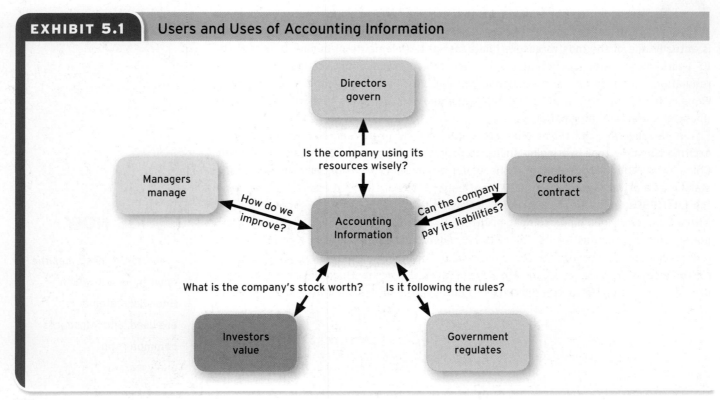

Managers

Managers at all levels of a company use accounting information to run the business. Based on sales and expense information for each game title, managers at Activision Blizzard decided to discontinue the company's popular but unprofitable Guitar Hero product line. When accounting information is used to manage the business, it is being used to fulfill a *management* function.

Directors

Directors is the short title used to describe members of the board of directors, who are elected by the company's stockholders to serve as their representatives. Directors oversee the managers of the company, with the primary goal of ensuring that management and financial decisions aim to benefit stockholders. Directors will use the financial statements to evaluate whether the Chief Executive Officer (CEO), Chief Financial Officer (CFO), and others have made wise decisions about the amount to invest in assets and have managed to generate sufficient sales and net income from those assets. When accounting information is used to oversee the business, it is being used in a *governance* role.

Creditors

All creditors use accounting information. Suppliers, for example, use it to decide whether to enter into contracts to supply other companies, based in part on whether those companies have sufficient assets to pay their liabilities. Bankers use financial statement information to evaluate (and sometimes limit) a company's activities by measuring the company's ability to satisfy certain financial targets, such as maintaining specific levels of assets or stockholders' equity. These **loan covenants** help to ensure the company will be able to repay loans owed to the bank. When accounting information is used to administer contract terms such as these, it is being used in a *contracting* role.

Investors

Investors (and their advisers) look to accounting information to help assess the financial strength of a business and, ultimately, to estimate its value. Part of this analysis involves forecasting the company's future revenues, expenses, and net income. Larger revenues and net income usually lead to higher prices for a company's stock. Activision's stock hit a three-year high when the company announced sales of its new *Skylander* toys were higher than expected. When accounting information is used to assess stock prices, it is being used in a *valuation* role.

Government

Several government agencies look closely at the financial statements prepared by companies. The Securities and Exchange Commission (SEC), for example, is responsible for the functioning of stock markets, so it keeps a close watch on the information that public companies report in financial statements. Also, the Internal Revenue Service (IRS) is interested in financial statements because the income statement provides a starting point for determining the amount of income taxes that should be paid by private and public corporations.

As Exhibit 5.1 indicates, many different groups use accounting information to make decisions. These decisions can affect employee bonuses, stock prices, and the interest paid on loans. All this attention to a company's financial results creates a high-pressure and potentially explosive environment, as discussed in the next section.

THE FINANCIAL REPORTING ENVIRONMENT

The accounting world was rocked in the last decade with scandal and fraud, leading to significant changes in the financial reporting environment. In this section, we describe what appears to have fueled the fraud and how accounting regulators have responded with changes that are likely to affect your future career.

Accounting Fraud

Three things have to exist for accounting fraud to occur. First, there must be an incentive for someone to commit the fraud. Second, an opportunity must exist to commit the fraud. Third, the person committing the fraud must be able to rationalize and conceal the fraud. Fraud investigators refer to these three elements as the *fraud triangle*, which is shown in Exhibit 5.2.

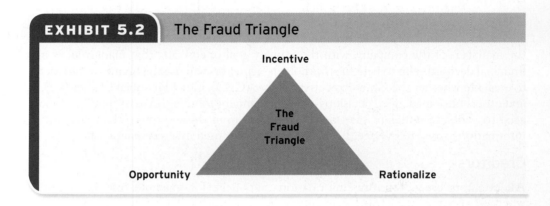

EXHIBIT 5.2 The Fraud Triangle

Incentive

The Fraud Triangle

Opportunity   Rationalize

Incentive to Commit Fraud   Financial misreporting is both unethical and illegal, so there must be enormous incentives driving some accountants and business managers to commit fraud. As shown in Exhibit 5.3, incentives can be divided into two categories: (1) creating business opportunities and (2) satisfying personal greed.

1. **Creating business opportunities.** Management is under constant pressure to produce pleasing financial results for at least three business reasons:
   * *Satisfy loan covenants.* As you learned earlier in this chapter, lenders rely on financial statements to determine whether a company has violated its loan covenants by failing to meet specific financial targets. If they are desperate, managers might overstate their company's financial condition to avoid violating loan covenants. Violating loan covenants can require the company to pay a higher interest rate, repay its loan balance right away, or be forced to put up extra collateral to secure its loan.
   * *Increase equity financing.* The amount of money obtained from issuing stock depends, in part, on the price of the stock when it is issued. An issuance of 100,000 shares will yield double the money if the stock price is $20 per share rather than $10 per share.
   * *Attract business partners.* By making the business appear more stable than it actually is, management can mislead suppliers and other companies into pursuing a business relationship with the company.

EXHIBIT 5.3 Possible Incentives for Committing Accounting Fraud

Creating Business Opportunities	Satisfying Personal Greed
• Satisfy loan covenants	• Enhance job security
• Increase equity financing	• Increase personal wealth
• Attract business partners	• Obtain bigger paycheck

2. **Satisfying personal greed.** By producing pleasing financial results, members of top management can benefit personally in three ways:
   - *Enhance job security.* The financial statements are a report card on both the company and the company's management. If top management reports strong financial results, they'll likely get to keep their high-paying jobs.
   - *Increase personal wealth.* Members of top management often own shares of their company's stock, so their personal shareholdings will be worth more (and their personal wealth will increase) if their company reports financial results that increase its stock price.
   - *Obtain a bigger paycheck.* Managers often receive cash bonuses based on the strength of their company's reported financial performance. A (former) CEO of video game company Take-Two Interactive once received a $3 million bonus after reporting increased profits. But he later had to return it and pay $1 million in additional fines after the SEC found he had manipulated Take-Two's profits.

Opportunity to Commit Fraud   As you saw in Chapters 2–4, financial statements are produced by an accounting system that involves analyzing, recording, and summarizing the results of business activities. Weaknesses in this system create an opportunity for fraudulent information to be entered into it, which increases the risk that the financial statements will be fraudulently misreported. To reduce this risk, certain procedures and policies can be put in place to help ensure that information entered into the accounting system and reported in the financial statements is accurate and complete. These internal controls, as they are called, can't completely eliminate the opportunity for fraud, but they can limit it if they operate effectively. You will learn about internal controls in detail in Chapter 6.

Rationalize and Conceal Fraud   For people to commit fraud and keep it secret, they have to feel "OK" with their actions. Most fraudsters achieve this through a sense of personal entitlement, which outweighs other moral principles, such as fairness, honesty, and concern for others. Many are said to be egotistical and possess an ability to lie or pressure others to look the other way.[1] It's not easy to counteract these undesirable traits, but recent changes in the financial reporting environment begin to do so, as we discuss in the next section.

The Sarbanes-Oxley Act

The **Sarbanes-Oxley (SOX) Act** is one of the most significant changes to the financial reporting environment in the United States since the Securities Acts were introduced in the 1930s. All companies that trade on U.S. stock exchanges must comply with requirements of SOX. The impact of SOX has been felt by nearly everyone in the business world. Whether you're an accounting major or not, you will likely be affected by SOX.

SOX was created in response to the many financial frauds and scandals occurring in the late 1990s and early 2000s. Confidence in the stock markets had been shaken by frauds involving Enron (now bankrupt) and WorldCom (now a part of Verizon), so the U.S. Congress passed the act in an attempt to improve the financial reporting environment and restore investor confidence. SOX introduced many new requirements. Some of the key changes are summarized in Exhibit 5.4.

Counteract Incentives for Committing Fraud   Those who willfully misrepresent financial results face stiff penalties, including fines of up to $5 million. Also,

> **YOU SHOULD KNOW**
> **Sarbanes-Oxley (SOX) Act:**
> A set of regulations passed by Congress in 2002 in an attempt to improve financial reporting and restore investor confidence.

---

[1]David T. Wolfe and Dana R. Hermanson, "The Fraud Diamond: Considering the Four Elements of Fraud," *The CPA Journal*, December 2004, pp. 38–41.

EXHIBIT 5.4   Significant Changes Introduced by the Sarbanes-Oxley (SOX) Act

Counteract Incentives
- Stiffer fines and prison terms

SOX

Reduce Opportunities
- Internal control report from management
- Stronger oversight by directors
- Internal control audit by external auditors

Encourage Honesty
- Anonymous tip lines
- Whistle-blower protection
- Code of ethics

maximum jail sentences are now 20 years, which can really add up because federal sentencing guidelines allow judges to declare consecutive jail terms for each violation.

Reduce Opportunities for Fraud   Of the three parts of the fraud triangle, this is the area in which business owners, managers, and accountants can do the most to reduce opportunities for fraud. Not surprisingly, then, it's also the area affected most by SOX. The main thrust of SOX, as it applies to this area, is to improve internal control over companies' financial reporting. SOX aims to achieve this in three ways:

1. Managers must review how well their company's internal controls worked during the year and issue a report that indicates whether the controls over financial reporting operated effectively. This requirement means that most marketing managers, for example, now have some accounting responsibilities such as determining whether their staff submit accurate sales and expense reports.

2. The company's board of directors is required to establish an audit committee of independent directors to oversee financial matters of the company. One of the primary functions of this committee is to communicate with external auditors and ensure they are able to effectively perform the work described below in 3.

3. The external auditors of large public companies must test the effectiveness of the company's internal controls and issue a report that gives an opinion about the company's internal controls over financial reporting. As was the case before SOX, the external auditors also must examine the company's financial statements and report whether they were presented fairly (no material misstatements) in accordance with GAAP.

Encourage Honesty in Employees   Admittedly, it's difficult for any law to achieve this, but some provisions of SOX should help honest employees confront those inclined to rationalize and conceal fraud. For example, companies must create tip lines that allow employees to secretly submit concerns about questionable accounting or auditing practices. Further, SOX grants legal protection to these whistle-blowers so they aren't retaliated against by those charged with fraud. If you tattle on your boss for submitting a fraudulent expense claim, you can't be fired for it. Finally, companies are required to adopt a code of ethics for their senior financial officers. Google begins its code with "Don't be evil" and then explains what this means in plain English.

How's it going? | Self-Study Practice

Identify whether each of the following increases (+) or decreases (−) the risk of fraud, arising from incentives (I), opportunities (O), or rationalizing/concealing (R).

	+/−	I/O/R
1. Enron was notorious for its "rank and yank" practice that involved ranking the financial performance of each business unit and then firing managers in the lowest 20%.		
2. Nintendo of America conducts pre-employment screening before hiring anyone.		
3. The H. J. Heinz Company board of directors is one of the strongest boards in America, according to Institutional Shareholder Services.		

After you have finished, check your answers with the solution in the margin.

SPOTLIGHT ON Ethics

You Can't Count That!

Most of the big accounting frauds involve uncertain judgments or complex accounting decisions that later are found to be inappropriate. However, some frauds have involved blatantly unethical acts. In one famous case, managers at Bausch & Lomb shipped as much as two years' worth of contact lenses to opticians who hadn't even ordered them. These shipments were counted as sales revenue, which led to overstated financial results and unwarranted bonuses. An investigation later found: (1) an environment of extreme pressure created incentives, (2) weak internal controls provided opportunities, and (3) unscrupulous managers rationalized the fraud.

Study the Accounting Methods

In the previous section, we discussed some of the *regulatory* changes made to improve the quality of publicly reported financial statements. In this section, we describe some of the *financial reporting* changes that publicly traded companies make to improve the quality and usefulness of their financial statements. We also describe how increasing globalization has created a need for common accounting rules worldwide, which has led to the emergence of International Financial Reporting Standards (IFRS).

> **Learning Objective 5-3**
> Prepare a comparative balance sheet, multiple-step income statement, and statement of stockholders' equity.

FINANCIAL REPORTING IN THE UNITED STATES

The good news is that the accounting and financial statement preparation processes that you learned in Chapters 1–4 for small, private companies continue to apply for even the largest, publicly traded corporations. To further improve the usefulness of financial statements for their external users, though, all public companies and some private companies take three additional steps: (1) enhance the financial statement format, (2) obtain an independent external audit, and (3) release additional financial information. Exhibit 5.5 presents a timeline showing how this financial reporting process typically occurs for a company that ends its year on December 31, 2013.

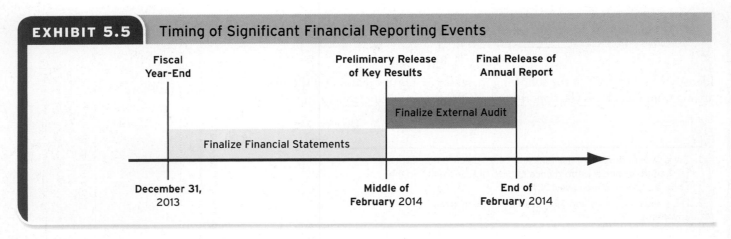

EXHIBIT 5.5   Timing of Significant Financial Reporting Events

Financial Statement Formatting

The financial statements shown in previous chapters provided a good introduction to their basic structure and content. However, in comparison to what you'll see in the corporate world, they were somewhat simplified. In this section, we show three enhancements that are intended to provide additional information for financial statement users: comparative financial statements, multiple-step income statements, and the statement of stockholders' equity.

> **YOU SHOULD KNOW**
>
> **Comparative financial statements:** Report numbers for two or more time periods.

Comparative Financial Statements   To make it easy for financial statement users to compare account balances from one period to the next, most companies report **comparative financial statements**. Comparative financial statements contain two or more columns of numbers, with each column representing the financial results for different time periods. For example, Activision's comparative balance sheets in Exhibit 5.6 show a big drop in Inventories after it stopped making all those plastic accessories for Guitar Hero. Note that the balance sheet is still classified, as introduced in Chapter 2. The only difference in a comparative balance sheet is that it uses separate columns to report different points in time.

Income statements also can be presented in a comparative format, often reporting three periods of results as shown in Exhibit 5.7. By including three columns, managers and accountants help reveal trends that persist over longer periods of time. For example, Exhibit 5.7 indicates that Activision has grown its revenues and net income each year since 2008. Activision says this success has come from focusing its marketing and production on fewer game titles.

> **YOU SHOULD KNOW**
>
> **Single-step income statement:** Reports net income by subtracting a single group of expenses from a single group of revenues.

Multiple-step Income Statements   If you look carefully at Exhibit 5.7, you'll notice the income statement format differs in another way from that used in earlier chapters. Earlier chapters used a format that contained a single grouping of revenues and a single grouping of expenses in what is typically called a **single-step income statement** format. Exhibit 5.7 presents a variation on the single-step income statement by displaying subtotals that indicate multiple steps before reaching Net Income at the bottom. **The purpose of these multiple steps is to display important measures of profit in addition to net income.** Exhibit 5.7 shows two new subtotals:

1. **Income (Loss) from Operations**—As an investor or creditor interested in Activision's long-term success, you probably care most about the company's ability to generate income from its core business activities like developing, making, and selling video games. Peripheral activities, like earning revenue from investments, aren't as important in the long-run because they're not the key reason Activision is in business (and they're not as likely to recur in the future). To make it easy for you to distinguish core and peripheral results, the top portion of the income statement reports revenues and expenses relating only to core activities, as shown in Exhibit 5.7. Public companies in the United States group their expenses by the type of business function (e.g., production, research, marketing, general operations) rather than by

EXHIBIT 5.6	Comparative Balance Sheet	ACTIVISION

ACTIVISION BLIZZARD, INC.
Balance Sheet
(in millions of U.S. dollars)

	December 31, 2010	December 31, 2009	Observations
Assets			
Current Assets:			
Cash	$ 2,812	$ 2,768	A comparative format reveals changes over time.
Short-term Investments	696	477	
Accounts Receivable	640	739	
Inventories	112	241	Activision cut its inventory in half by discontinuing games like Guitar Hero.
Other Current Assets	1,125	1,104	
Total Current Assets	5,385	5,329	
Property and Equipment, net	169	138	
Other Noncurrent Assets	720	1,121	
Goodwill	7,132	7,154	
Total Assets	$13,406	$13,742	
Liabilities and Stockholders' Equity			
Current Liabilities:			
Accounts Payable	$ 363	$ 302	Unearned Revenue relates to online services owed to customers who also purchased Wii, Xbox, and other console games.
Unearned Revenue	1,726	1,426	
Accrued and Other Liabilities	818	779	
Total Current Liabilities	2,907	2,507	
Other Noncurrent Liabilities	296	479	
Total Liabilities	3,203	2,986	
Stockholders' Equity:			
Contributed Capital	10,146	11,117	Changes in stockholders' equity accounts are shown in the Statement of Stockholders' Equity, as shown in Exhibit 5.8.
Retained Earnings (Accumulated Deficit)	57	(361)	
Total Stockholders' Equity	10,203	10,756	
Total Liabilities and Stockholders' Equity	$13,406	$13,742	

EXHIBIT 5.7	Income Statement with Multiple Steps	ACTIVISION

ACTIVISION BLIZZARD, INC.
Income Statement
(in millions of U.S. dollars)

	Year Ended December 31,			Observations
	2010	2009	2008	
Sales and Service Revenues	$4,447	$4,279	$3,026	
Expenses:				Core results—include revenues and expenses from the company's main business activities. Expenses are reported by function (e.g., production, research, marketing, general operations).
Production	2,126	2,307	1,839	
Research and Development	642	627	592	
Marketing and Sales	520	544	464	
General and Administrative	690	827	364	
Total Operating Expenses	3,978	4,305	3,259	
Income (Loss) from Operations	469	(26)	(233)	Peripheral results—include any revenues and expenses from activities other than the company's main business.
Revenue from Investments	23	18	46	
Income (Loss) before Income Tax	492	(8)	(187)	
Income Tax Expense (Recovery)	74	(121)	(80)	
Net Income (Loss)	$ 418	$ 113	$ (107)	

the nature of each expense (e.g., salaries, rent, supplies, electricity). After the core revenues and expenses, a multiple-step income statement presents a subtotal called Income from Operations. This is a useful measure, because in Activision's case, it reveals that the company's core business was generating losses prior to 2010. Revenue from Investments did contribute to net income so it is included in the income statement, but since it's not a core business activity for Activision it is shown after Income from Operations. Other companies, particularly financial institutions like Capital One and Bank of America, would consider Revenue from Investments a core business activity. But Activision is in business to generate profit from video game sales, not from interest on investments.

2. **Income (Loss) before Income Tax Expense**—This other new subtotal in Exhibit 5.7 indicates how much profit the company would have reported had there been no income taxes. This subtotal is useful because not all companies pay the same rate of tax. So, if you're trying to decide whether to invest in Pfizer or FedEx, which had effective tax rates in 2010 ranging from 12 to 36 percent, you might be interested in comparing their pretax levels of income. Of course, you will also care about Net Income, which is obtained by subtracting Income Tax Expense from Income before Income Tax Expense. Net Income is the same whether a single-step or multiple-step income statement is presented.

Statement of Stockholders' Equity   Previous chapters indicated that companies report a statement of retained earnings to show how net income increased and dividends decreased the retained earnings balance during the period. While this information is useful, it doesn't tell the full story because Retained Earnings is only one of the stockholders' equity accounts. Contributed Capital is another important stockholders' equity account whose balance increases and decreases during the accounting period. To show all the changes, public companies report a more comprehensive version of the statement of retained earnings called the statement of stockholders' equity. The statement of stockholders' equity has a column for each stockholders' equity account and shows the factors that increased and decreased these account balances during the period. Exhibit 5.8 shows a modified version of Activision's statement. Notice how the beginning and ending balances for each account correspond to the balance sheet (in Exhibit 5.6). From this statement, we can see that Activision issued and repurchased shares of its stock in 2010. But the biggest increase in stockholders' equity ($418 million) came from the company's own generation and retention of net income, returning the company to a positive balance in Retained Earnings.

EXHIBIT 5.8	Statement of Stockholders' Equity	ACTIVISION.

ACTIVISION BLIZZARD, INC.
Statement of Stockholders' Equity
For the Year Ended December 31, 2010
(in millions of U.S. dollars)

	Contributed Capital	Retained Earnings (Deficit)
Balances at December 31, 2009	$11,117	$ (361)
Net Income		418
Dividends Declared		(-0-)
Issued Shares of Stock	73	
Repurchased Shares of Stock	(1,044)	
Balances at December 31, 2010	$10,146	$ 57

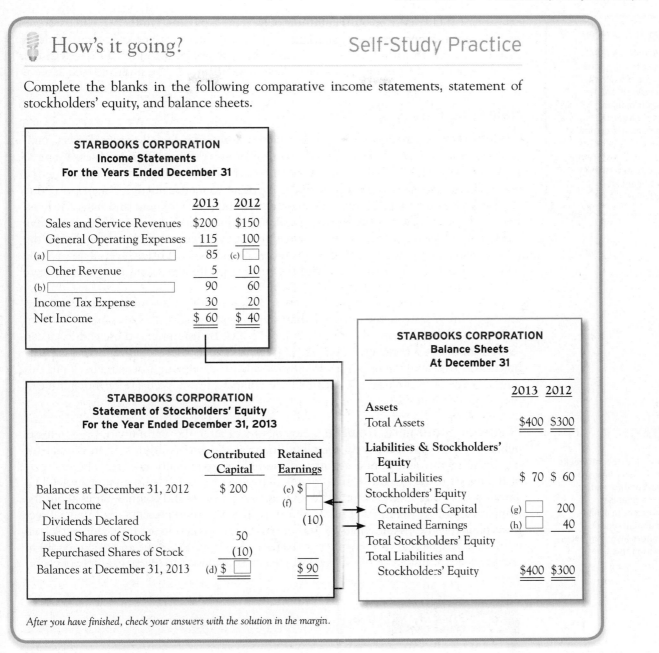

💡 How's it going?   Self-Study Practice

Complete the blanks in the following comparative income statements, statement of stockholders' equity, and balance sheets.

STARBOOKS CORPORATION
Income Statements
For the Years Ended December 31

	2013	2012
Sales and Service Revenues	$200	$150
General Operating Expenses	115	100
(a) ▭	85	(c) ▭
Other Revenue	5	10
(b) ▭	90	60
Income Tax Expense	30	20
Net Income	$ 60	$ 40

STARBOOKS CORPORATION
Statement of Stockholders' Equity
For the Year Ended December 31, 2013

	Contributed Capital	Retained Earnings
Balances at December 31, 2012	$ 200	(e) $ ▭
Net Income		(f) ▭
Dividends Declared		(10)
Issued Shares of Stock	50	
Repurchased Shares of Stock	(10)	
Balances at December 31, 2013	(d) $ ▭	$ 90

STARBOOKS CORPORATION
Balance Sheets
At December 31

	2013	2012
Assets		
Total Assets	$400	$300
Liabilities & Stockholders' Equity		
Total Liabilities	$ 70	$ 60
Stockholders' Equity		
Contributed Capital	(g) ▭	200
Retained Earnings	(h) ▭	40
Total Stockholders' Equity		
Total Liabilities and Stockholders' Equity	$400	$300

After you have finished, check your answers with the solution in the margin.

Solution to Self-Study Practice
(a) Income from Operations (b) Income before Income Tax Expense (c) 50 (d) 240
(e) 40 (from the balance sheet on December 31, 2012) (f) 60 (g) 240 (h) 90

Independent External Audit

To ensure that the financial statements, shown in the previous section, are prepared properly, the SEC requires all publicly traded companies to have their financial statements audited by external auditors. Many privately owned companies have their financial statements audited, too, often at the request of lenders or private investors. External audits are conducted by Certified Public Accountants (CPAs) who are independent of the company. These trained professionals examine the company's financial statements (and its accounting system) with the goal of detecting **material misstatements**. It is not practical for auditors to check every single business transaction to ensure it was accurately reported, so they can't be 100 percent sure they have caught *every* error. Instead, their audit provides *reasonable* assurance to financial statement users. After completing the audit, external auditors will attach a report to the financial statements that gives a pass/fail type of

Learning Objective 5-4
Describe other significant aspects of the financial reporting process, including external audits and the distribution of financial information.

YOU SHOULD KNOW

Material misstatements:
Large enough to influence the decisions of financial statement users.

opinion. An **unqualified audit opinion** represents a passing grade. See the example for The Home Depot on page A.1 at the back of this textbook. If the financial statements fail to follow GAAP, or if the auditors were not able to complete the tests needed to determine whether GAAP was followed, the auditors will issue a **qualified audit opinion**.

Releasing Financial Information

Preliminary Releases   To provide timely information for all external users, public companies announce annual (and quarterly) results through a press release sent to news agencies. This press release is issued three to five weeks after the accounting period ends. The press release typically includes key figures, management's discussion of the results, and attachments containing a condensed income statement and balance sheet. Exhibit 5.9 shows an excerpt from a typical press release for Activision. Notice that five weeks elapsed between the end of the company's year (December 31) and the date of the press release (February 9). During this time, Activision's accountants were busy making adjusting journal entries and finalizing the financial statements, and its managers were preparing an analysis and discussion of the results.

Many companies, including Activision, follow up the press release with a conference call broadcast on the Internet that allows analysts to grill the company's senior executives with questions about the financial results. By listening to these calls, you can learn a lot about a company's business strategy, its expectations for the future, and the key factors that analysts consider when they evaluate a company. You can check out this useful source of information by visiting each company's own Web site or the archive of conference calls at biz.yahoo.com/cc.

Financial Statement Release   Several weeks after the preliminary press release, public companies release their complete financial statements as part of an annual (or quarterly) report. The annual report is organized into two main sections. The first part of the report usually begins with a friendly letter to investors from the company's CEO. This is followed by glossy pictures of the company's products and commentaries about the company's positioning in its industry. The annual report then presents the financial section. The typical elements of an annual report's financial section are listed and explained in Exhibit 5.10, along with references to pages in Appendix A (at the end of this book) or online (at www.mhhe.com/phillips4e) where you should look to see an example of each.

EXHIBIT 5.9   Preliminary Release of Key Results

ACTIVISION BLIZZARD REPORTS DECEMBER QUARTER AND CALENDAR YEAR 2010 FINANCIAL RESULTS

SANTA MONICA, CA—February 9, 2011—Activision Blizzard, Inc. (Nasdaq: ATVI) today announced financial results for the calendar year and quarter ending December 31, 2010.

For calendar year 2010, Activision Blizzard's GAAP net revenues increased to $4.45 billion, as compared with $4.28 billion for 2009.

Robert Kotick, CEO of Activision Blizzard, stated, "Activision Blizzard's key franchises have larger audience bases than ever before. Notably, since **Call of Duty: Black Ops** was launched in November players have spent an average of 52 minutes per day playing online, roughly equivalent to the 55 minutes that the average user spends each day on Facebook."

Today at 4:30 p.m. EST, Activision Blizzard's management will host a conference call and Webcast to discuss the company's results for the quarter and year ended December 31, 2010, and management's outlook for 2011.

EXHIBIT 5.10 | Typical Elements of an Annual Report's Financial Section

Name of Financial Section	Information Presented	Example in Appendix A or Online
1. Summarized financial data	• key figures covering a period of 5 or 10 years.	Online
2. Management's discussion and analysis (MD&A)	• an honest and detailed analysis of the company's financial condition and operating results; a must-read for any serious financial statement user.	Online
3. Management's report on internal control	• statements that describe management's responsibility for ensuring adequate internal control over financial reporting and that report on the effectiveness of these controls during the year.	Online
4. Auditor's report	• the auditor's conclusion about whether GAAP was followed (and, for public companies, whether internal controls were effective).	p. A.3
5. Comparative financial statements	• a multi-year presentation of the four basic statements.	p. A.5
6. Financial statement notes	• further information about the financial statements; crucial to understanding the financial statement data.	p. A.9
7. Recent stock price data	• brief summary of highs and lows during the year.	Online
8. Unaudited quarterly data	• condensed summary of each quarter's results.	Online
9. Directors and officers	• a list of who's overseeing and running the company.	Online

A company's **quarterly** report is like a supercondensed version of its annual report. Following a short letter to stockholders and abbreviated discussion of the financial results, a quarterly report presents a condensed income statement for the quarter, a condensed balance sheet dated at the end of the quarter, and a condensed statement of cash flows. These condensed financial statements typically show less detail than the annual statements, often omitting items 4, 7, 8, and 9 in Exhibit 5.10. Quarterly financial statements are not audited, so they are labeled as unaudited. Obviously, with all these limitations, the quarterly reports aren't quite as informative as the annual reports, but they have the benefit of being released on a timelier basis (every three months rather than every year).

Securities and Exchange Commission (SEC) Filings To ensure sufficient, relevant information is available to investors, the SEC requires public companies to electronically file certain reports with the SEC, including an **annual report on Form 10-K, quarterly reports on Form 10-Q,** and **current event reports on Form 8-K.** (We wouldn't burden you with the details of the form numbers except that most people refer to them by number.) Several of these reports require release of additional information beyond that reported in quarterly or annual reports. In fact, many companies use these reports as substitutes for their glossy annual and quarterly reports. The additional information in the SEC filings can provide great insight about a company. For example, Activision's 2010 10-K describes 56 significant business risks that the company faces and outlines the business strategies for addressing those risks. The 8-K reports significant business events that occur between financial statement dates, such as the acquisition of another company (e.g., Activision's combination with Vivendi Games), a change in its year-end (from March 31 to December 31), or a change in auditor.

These filings are available to the public as soon as they are received by the SEC's Electronic Data Gathering and Retrieval service (EDGAR). As a result, most users can get all the details about a company's financial results in the SEC filings several weeks before the company's glossy reports are posted on the company's Web site. To find a company's SEC filings, click on "Search for Company Filings" at www.sec.gov.

SPOTLIGHT ON Financial Reporting

Speaking a New Language–XBRL (eXtensible Business Reporting Language)

Beginning in 2011, all public companies in the U.S. were required to file financial information in an interactive format called XBRL. This tagging system allows software applications to retrieve and compare financial data from a broad range of businesses, making comparisons far more efficient and reliable than in the past. Previously, you could never know whether investor information Web sites, like reuters.com/finance or Yahoo!Finance, had correctly entered financial information into their databases. Data error rates in some industries were as high as 34 percent but have fallen to near zero since XBRL was adopted.* For you, this means it just got a little easier to compare financial data (which should simplify some of the skills development cases at the end of this chapter). For further information, go to xbrl.org.

Yahoo! My Yahoo! Mail

YAHOO! FINANCE Sign In New User? Sign Up

Welcome [Sign In]

Yahoo! Finance

Enter symbol(s): e.g. YHOO, ^DJI [   ] [Go] Symbol Lookup | Finance Search

---

*Leone, M. "10-Ks, 8-Ks a Thing of the Past?" *CFO.com*, September 25, 2006. Retrieved March 6, 2012, from www.cfo.com/article.cfm/7960677/1/c_2984312.

Learning Objective 5-5
Explain the reasons for, and financial statement presentation effects of, adopting IFRS.

GLOBALIZATION AND INTERNATIONAL FINANCIAL REPORTING STANDARDS (IFRS)

It's become cliché but business really has gone global. Abercrombie operates stores in Sweden, and Swedish companies like IKEA and H&M are popular throughout the United States. Similar trends are occurring in the investing world, where shares of foreign companies Benetton and Toyota are traded on the New York Stock Exchange (NYSE). Until recently, investors struggled to compare the financial statements of companies like these because different countries used different accounting rules. This is in the process of changing as countries switch from national GAAP to **International Financial Reporting Standards** (abbreviated IFRS).

IFRS are developed by the International Accounting Standards Board (IASB), which is the international counterpart to the FASB in the United States. Over 100 countries including Australia, Canada, China, the European Union, South Africa, and New Zealand currently require or permit the use of IFRS, or a local version of IFRS. The United States has not yet switched to IFRS, but it is considering aligning U.S. accounting rules with IFRS. In 2007, the Securities and Exchange Commission (SEC) began moving in this direction by allowing foreign companies to issue stock in the United States without having to convert their IFRS-based accounting numbers to U.S. generally accepted accounting principles (GAAP). In 2008, the SEC announced a plan to allow some U.S. companies, to use IFRS in 2009. As of 2012, the SEC was still weighing its options. IFRS already is used in the United States by foreign-owned private companies such as Mack Trucks and Dreyer's Grand Ice Cream, to make it easy to combine their financial statements with their foreign owners' financial statements.

Although IFRS differ from GAAP, they do not dramatically alter what you have learned to this point in this course. IFRS use the same system of analyzing, recording, and summarizing the results of business activities that you learned in Chapters 1–4. The most significant differences between IFRS and GAAP relate to technical issues that are typically taught in intermediate and advanced accounting courses. For the topics discussed in this introductory course, differences between IFRS and GAAP are limited. One place where IFRS differ from GAAP is in the formatting of financial statements.

Formatting of Financial Statements

Although financial statements in the United States and other countries include the same items (assets, liabilities, revenues, expenses, etc.), a single, consistent format has not been mandated. Consequently, various formats have evolved over time, with those in the United States differing from those typically used internationally. You can gain a good understanding of the most common differences by reading Exhibit 5.11.

EXHIBIT 5.11	Financial Statement Presentation under GAAP and IFRS

	GAAP	IFRS
Financial Statement Titles • The financial statements report similar items but under different titles.	Balance sheet .... Income statement .... Statement of stockholders' equity ... Statement of cash flows	Statement of financial position Statement of comprehensive income Statement of shareholders' equity Statement of cash flows
Presentation of Expenses • Similar expenses are reported, but may be grouped in different ways.	Public companies categorize expenses by business **function** (e.g., production, research, marketing, general operations).	Companies can categorize expenses by either function **or nature** (e.g., salaries, rent, supplies, electricity).

Balance Sheet Order
• Similar accounts are shown, but differ in order of liquidity (for assets) and order of maturity (for liabilities).
	Assets
	  Current
	  Noncurrent
	Liabilities
	  Current
	  Noncurrent
	Stockholders' Equity
		Assets
		  Noncurrent
		  Current
		Shareholders' Equity
		Liabilities
		  Noncurrent
		  Current

Of the differences listed in Exhibit 5.11, balance sheet order is the most striking. Most companies that follow GAAP begin with current items whereas those that follow IFRS tend to begin with noncurrent items. Consistent with this, **assets are listed in decreasing order of liquidity under GAAP, but internationally they are usually listed in increasing order of liquidity.** IFRS similarly emphasize longer-term financing sources by listing equity before liabilities and, within liabilities by listing noncurrent liabilities before current liabilities (**decreasing time to maturity**).

Activision provides an ideal case for illustrating these differences because its balance sheet is prepared using GAAP, but its main stockholder (a European company named Vivendi) reports a statement of financial position based on IFRS. A side-by-side comparison is shown in Exhibit 5.12. As you can see, Vivendi is a larger company than Activision (one euro is equal to about $1.30 in U.S. dollars) and it reports its assets, liabilities, and stockholders' equity accounts in the typical IFRS order. But, despite these differences in appearance, the two companies are involved in the same sort of business activities, so the specific items on the financial statements are similar. It may take you a moment or two, but you should be able to find Cash, Short-term Investments, and so on, on both companies' financial statements. Locating this kind of information is the first step to evaluating the companies' financial results, as you will see in the next section.

EXHIBIT 5.12   Comparison of GAAP Balance Sheet to IFRS Statement of Financial Position

ACTIVISION, INC.
Balance Sheet
(in millions of U.S. dollars)

	December 31, 2010	December 31, 2009
Assets		
Current Assets:		
Cash	$ 2,812	$ 2,768
Short-term Investments	696	477
Accounts Receivable	640	739
Inventories	112	241
Other Current Assets	1,125	1,104
Total Current Assets	5,385	5,329
Property and Equipment, net	169	138
Other Noncurrent Assets	720	1,121
Goodwill	7,132	7,154
Total Assets	$13,406	$13,742
Liabilities and Stockholders' Equity		
Current Liabilities:		
Accounts Payable	$ 363	$ 302
Unearned Revenue	1,726	1,426
Accrued and Other Liabilities	818	779
Total Current Liabilities	2,907	2,507
Other Noncurrent Liabilities	296	479
Total Liabilities	3,203	2,986
Stockholders' Equity:		
Contributed Capital	10,146	11,117
Retained Earnings (Deficit)	57	(361)
Total Stockholders' Equity	10,203	10,756
Total Liabilities and Stockholders' Equity	$13,406	$13,742

Differences
← Title →

Order
← of →
Liquidity
(Decreasing vs. Increasing)

Time
← to →
Maturity
(Increasing vs. Decreasing)

VIVENDI
Statement of Financial Position
(in millions of euros)

	September 30, 2011	September 30, 2010
Assets		
Goodwill	€25,045	€25,131
Other Noncurrent Assets	8,919	13,344
Property and Equipment, net	8,538	7,586
Total Noncurrent Assets	42,502	46,061
Current Assets:		
Inventories	652	650
Other Current Assets	1,409	1,427
Accounts Receivable	6,158	6,079
Short-term Investments	387	745
Cash	2,420	2,435
Total Current Assets	11,026	11,336
Total Assets	€53,528	€57,397
Equity and Liabilities		
Stockholders' Equity:		
Contributed Capital	€17,471	€19,411
Retained Earnings and Other	3,881	8,427
Total Stockholders' Equity	21,352	27,838
Long-term Borrowings	10,381	9,160
Other Noncurrent Liabilities	2,770	4,069
Total Noncurrent Liabilities	13,151	13,229
Current Liabilities:		
Short-term Borrowings	5,752	2,936
Accounts Payable and Other	13,273	13,394
Total Current Liabilities	19,025	16,330
Total Liabilities	32,176	29,559
Total Stockholders' Equity and Liabilities	€53,528	€57,397

Evaluate the Results

ECONOMIC CRISIS

Beginning in late 2008 most businesses began to struggle financially, whether they were based in the United States, or China, or India, or Europe. Financing was tight and sales were lagging. In an effort to control expenses, companies cut back on workers through massive layoffs. The global economy started to recover in 2010, but then encountered another economic crisis, this time relating to financial concerns in Europe. Whether they will withstand this economic turmoil is still being determined, but by understanding how to read financial statements, you're in a better position to identify the companies that are likely to survive.

COMPARISON TO COMMON BENCHMARKS

If you're like most people, you probably find it hard to know whether Activision's $418 million in net income is a decent level of performance. It seems like a good number, but to interpret financial statement amounts, it's useful to have points of comparison, or benchmarks. Two commonly used benchmarks are

1. **Prior periods.** By comparing a company's current period results to its own results in prior periods, we can gain a sense of how the company's performance is changing over time. The trend is your friend. In Wall Street language, this comparison of the same company over a series of prior time periods is called **time-series analysis**.

2. **Competitors.** Although an analysis focused on one company is useful, it doesn't show what's happening in the industry. It's possible that the company is improving (good), but still hasn't caught up to others in the same industry (not so good). Or it could be that the company's performance is declining (bad), but it has avoided the severe financial problems others experienced (not so bad). To get this industrywide perspective, most analysts will compare competitors within a particular industry. The name for comparing across companies that compete in the same section of an industry is **cross-sectional analysis**.

In Exhibit 5.13, we present a time-series chart that compares Activision to itself on several key totals from the balance sheet and income statement. From the chart, we can see that Activision was virtually unchanged between 2009 and 2010. To assess Activision's

> **Learning Objective 5-6**
> Compare results to common benchmarks.

> **YOU SHOULD KNOW**
> **Time-series analysis:** Compares a company's results for one period to its own results over a series of time periods.
> **Cross-sectional analysis:** Compares the results of one company with those of others in the same section of the industry.

EXHIBIT 5.13 Time-Series Analysis Chart

standing in the video game industry, analysts also would compare Activision to competitors, such as Electronic Arts (maker of The Sims and Madden NFL).

In Exhibit 5.14, we present a cross-sectional chart that compares Activision to Electronic Arts (stock ticker symbol ERTS) based on its financial statement data for the fiscal period from April 1, 2010, to March 31, 2011.

COACH'S TIP

Average measures for each industry also can be used in cross-sectional analysis. Obtain these measures from the *Annual Statement Studies* published online by the Risk Management Association at statementstudies .org or by clicking on the ratios link in the stock section of reuters.com/finance.

| EXHIBIT 5.14 | Cross-Sectional Analysis of Video Game Competitors |

The bar chart in Exhibit 5.14 shows that Activision towers over Electronic Arts in every category. Given these mammoth differences in size, do analysts simply conclude that Activision is the winner and give them a pocketful of investment tokens? In a word, no. This means only that Activision is a bigger company. It says nothing about whether it's best at using the resources provided to it. In fact, as you will see in the next section, Electronic Arts actually outperformed Activision on at least one aspect of its business. To reach such a conclusion, analysts rely on financial statement ratio analysis.

FINANCIAL STATEMENT RATIO ANALYSIS

Learning Objective 5-7
Calculate and interpret the debt-to-assets, asset turnover, and net profit margin ratios.

The goal of ratio analysis is to get to the heart of how well a company performed given the resources it had available. By using ratios, you can take into account differences in company size and uncover results that aren't easily detected by looking at total dollar amounts. For example, as you will see below, ratios allow you to discover Electronic Arts reported lower sales than Activision, but it was more efficient than Activision in using its assets to generate sales.

A Basic Business Model

Before evaluating Activision's financial performance, it is useful to first consider what's involved in running a business. Most businesses can be broken down into four elements:

① **Obtain financing** from lenders and investors, which is used to invest in assets.

② **Invest in assets,** which are used to generate revenues.

③ **Generate revenues,** which lead to producing net income.

④ **Produce net income,** which is needed to comfort lenders, satisfy investors, and provide resources for future expansion.

From this description, a business model can be created, as shown in Exhibit 5.15. This business model includes the key financial measures analyzed earlier, including total liabilities (debt), stockholders' equity, assets, revenues, and net income. What's really useful about this business model is that it links one business element to another, so you aren't limited to looking at just total dollar amounts, as we did before. The business model in Exhibit 5.15 provides a framework for understanding three ratios that we introduce in the next section.

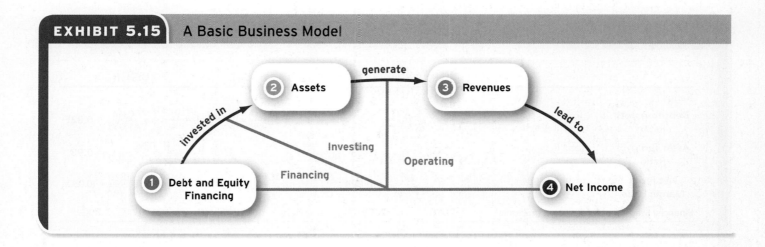

EXHIBIT 5.15 A Basic Business Model

Financial Statement Ratios

The business model in Exhibit 5.15 contains three links: (1) debt and equity financing is invested in assets, (2) assets are used to generate revenues, and (3) revenues lead to net income. Using these links, three key financial ratios can be created, as shown below.

Accounting Decision Tools		
Name of Measure	Formula	What It Tells You
1. Debt-to-assets ratio	$\dfrac{\text{Total Liabilities}}{\text{Total Assets}}$	• The percentage of assets financed by debt • A higher ratio means greater financing risk
2. Asset turnover ratio	$\dfrac{\text{Total Revenue}}{\text{Average Total Assets}}$	• How well assets are used to generate revenue • A higher ratio means greater efficiency
3. Net profit margin ratio	$\dfrac{\text{Net Income}}{\text{Total Revenue}}$	• How much profit is earned from each dollar of revenue • A higher ratio means better performance

These three ratios are calculated in the top panel of Exhibit 5.16, using relevant amounts (in the bottom panel) from the financial statements of Activision, Electronic Arts, and Ubisoft (a European company that makes Rayman and Assassin's Creed games). In addition to making it possible to compare companies of different sizes, **a benefit of** ratio analysis is that it enables comparisons between companies reporting in different currencies (dollars vs. euros).[2]

Note that to calculate average total assets in the bottom of the asset turnover ratio, you need amounts from two balance sheets. An average is needed in the asset turnover ratio so that the bottom part spans the entire year, just like the top part. In the following discussion, we explain the significance of each of the three ratios and provide examples of how you could conduct similar analyses with other companies.

EXHIBIT 5.16 | **Analysis of Video Game Companies**

Ratios		Activision Inc.		Electronic Arts Inc.		Ubisoft	
Debt-to-Assets Ratio	$\dfrac{\text{Total Liabilities}}{\text{Total Assets}}$	$\dfrac{\$3,203}{\$13,406} = 0.239$		$\dfrac{\$2,364}{\$4,928} = 0.480$		$\dfrac{€344}{€1,058} = 0.325$	
Asset Turnover Ratio	$\dfrac{\text{Total Revenue}}{\text{Average Total Assets}}$	$\dfrac{\$4,447}{(\$13,406 + \$13,472)/2} = 0.33$		$\dfrac{\$3,589}{(\$4,928 + \$4,646)/2} = 0.75$		$\dfrac{€1,039}{(€1,058 + €1,184)/2} = 0.93$	
Net Profit Margin Ratio	$\dfrac{\text{Net Income}}{\text{Total Revenue}}$	$\dfrac{\$418}{\$4,447} = 0.094$		$\dfrac{\$(276)}{\$3,589} = (0.077)$		$\dfrac{€(52)}{€1,039} = (0.050)$	
Financial Statement Information (millions)		**2010**	**2009**	**2010**	**2009**	**2010**	**2009**
Total assets		$13,406	$13,742	$4,928	$4,646	€1,058	€1,184
Total liabilities		3,203	2,986	2,364	1,917	344	422
Total stockholders' equity		10,203	10,756	2,564	2,729	714	762
Total revenue		4,447	4,279	3,589	3,654	1,039	871
Net income (loss)		418	113	(276)	(677)	(52)	(43)

YOU SHOULD KNOW

Debt-to-assets ratio: Indicates financing risk by computing the proportion of total assets financed by debt.

1. Debt-to-Assets Ratio   The **debt-to-assets ratio** compares total liabilities to total assets. It is usually calculated to three decimal places, and can be expressed as a percentage by multiplying by 100. This ratio indicates the proportion of total assets that are financed by debt. It's important to know how much debt is used to finance assets because debt has to be repaid whether or not a company is doing well financially. If assets are financed mainly by debt, rather than equity, then this ratio will be high, which would suggest the company has adopted a risky financing strategy. Ultimately, a company could be forced into bankruptcy if it took on more debt than it ever could repay. Exhibit 5.16 shows that, for all three companies, debt plays a small role in financing the companies' assets. Activision is the lowest, with a debt-to-assets ratio (0.239 or 23.9%) that is lower than either Electronic Arts (0.480 or 48.0%) or Ubisoft (0.325 or 32.5%). This means that the likelihood of Activision being able to repay its existing liabilities is very high, so the company has little financing risk.

YOU SHOULD KNOW

Asset turnover ratio: Indicates how well assets are being used to generate revenues by dividing total assets into total revenue.

2. Asset Turnover Ratio   The **asset turnover ratio** compares total revenue to average total assets. It is usually calculated to two decimal places and not expressed as a percentage. This ratio indicates the revenue generated per dollar invested in the assets of the business. The higher the ratio, the more efficiently the company

---

[2]Any differences in accounting methods, which are discussed in later chapters, can limit the ability to draw conclusions from ratio analysis. One of the goals in moving to IFRS is to eliminate cross-country differences and thereby improve comparability.

is utilizing its assets to generate revenue. Exhibit 5.16 shows that Activision is generating the lowest revenue per dollar invested in assets (as indicated by the ratio of 0.33). In contrast, Electronic Arts generated 75 cents (0.75) of revenue for each dollar of assets and Ubisoft generated nearly a dollar (0.93). Why is Activision's ratio so low compared to the others? Its asset base ballooned when it merged with Blizzard in 2008. The merger added billions of dollars of assets to its balance sheet at their 2008 market values.

3. Net Profit Margin Ratio

The **net profit margin ratio** measures the amount of net income (profit) generated from each dollar of revenue. It is usually calculated to three decimal places and can be expressed as a percentage by multiplying by 100. Net profit margin is a key ratio because it indicates how well a company has controlled its expenses. Although it's important for companies to generate lots of revenue, it's equally important to control expenses. A company generating tons of revenue will go bankrupt if its expenses are out of control. Exhibit 5.16 shows that Activision was the leader in controlling its expenses, generating a net profit margin of 0.094 (or 9.4%). In other words, each dollar in revenue produced $0.09 in profit. In its annual report, Activision explains it was able to attain its strong profit margin during difficult economic times by releasing fewer new game titles, which reduced production, marketing, and head office expenses. Both Electronic Arts and Ubisoft stumbled, as indicated by their negative net profit margins of (0.077) and (0.050). As world economies struggle, these kinds of financial results have become more typical. **A small negative net profit margin (NPM) does not usually cause a company to go out of business; however, large or repeating negative NPMs are definitely cause for concern.** Look back at the Circuit City spotlight on page 167 for an example of a company that failed within a year of reporting its first *negative* NPM.

Although it is useful to consider each of the ratios separately, it is even more informative to consider them together, to tell a "story" about the company's financial results. Based on the 2010 ratios in Exhibit 5.16, Activision appears to be a leader in its industry. Of the three companies, Activision relied the least on debt financing (debt-to-assets ratio of 0.239), and although it generated fewer sales for each dollar invested in assets (asset turnover ratio of 0.33), it was the only company to convert those sales into profit (NPM ratio of 0.094).

Many other financial statement ratios exist to assess profitability (the ability to generate income in the current period), liquidity (the ability to use current assets to pay liabilities), and solvency (the ability to repay lenders when debt matures). Rather than load you up with them all at once, we will introduce them gradually in Chapters 6–12, and then we'll summarize and apply them in a comprehensive analysis in Chapter 13.

 COACH'S TIP

Some analysts also compare net income to average total assets to compute a return on assets ratio. If this ratio is greater than the company's interest rate on bank loans, the company can increase its profits by using borrowed money to buy more assets that generate more revenue and net income, as suggested in Exhibit 5.15.

💡 How's it going?   Self-Study Practice

Vivendi owns a significant part of Activision Blizzard. In the twelve months ended September 30, 2011, Vivendi reported (in millions of euros) total revenues of €14,786 and net income of €1,122. Using this information and Exhibit 5.12, calculate ratios to indicate whether, relative to Activision, Vivendi has higher or lower levels of (a) financing risk, (b) asset efficiency, and (c) profitability.

After you have finished, check your answers with the solution in the margin.

Solution to Self-Study Practice

(a) Debt-to-assets ratio = 32,176/53,528 = 0.601
This indicates higher financing risk than Activision's 0.239.

(b) Asset turnover ratio = $\dfrac{14,786}{53,528 + 57,397} = 0.27$
This indicates lower asset efficiency than Activision's 0.33.

(c) Net profit margin ratio = 1,122/14,786 = 0.076
This indicates lower profitability than Activision's 0.094.

How Transactions Affect Ratios

To properly interpret financial statement ratios, you will find it useful to understand how they are affected by transactions. Apply the following three-step process to determine the impact of each transaction on a particular ratio:

1. **Analyze the transaction to determine its effects on the accounting equation,** just as you have learned to do in Chapters 2–4.

2. **Relate the effects in step 1 to the ratio's components,** to determine whether each component increases, decreases, or stays the same.

3. **Evaluate the combined impact of the effects in step 2 on the overall ratio.**

A ratio will increase if (a) its top number increases and the bottom number does not change, (b) its bottom number decreases and its top number does not change, or (c) the top number increases while the bottom number decreases. Changes in the opposite direction have the opposite effect.

When a transaction causes both the top and bottom numbers to change in the same direction, the overall impact on a ratio depends on whether the ratio is greater or less than 1.0 before the transaction. A useful approach for determining the impact of a transaction on a ratio in these cases is to assume some simple numbers for the ratio's starting point and then recalculate the ratio after taking into account the effects of the transaction. Exhibit 5.17 illustrates this approach.

EXHIBIT 5.17	Changes in Ratios Given Changes in Its Components

Situation	Before	Change	After
1. Ratio < 1	$\frac{5}{10}$	$\frac{+5}{+5}$	$\frac{10}{15}$
	= 0.50		= 0.67
2. Ratio > 1	$\frac{10}{5}$	$\frac{+5}{+5}$	$\frac{15}{10}$
	= 2.0		= 1.5

In the first situation, the $5 increases in the top and bottom of the ratio cause the overall ratio to increase from 0.50 to 0.67. In the second situation, the $5 increases cause the overall ratio to decrease from 2.0 to 1.5. These different outcomes occur because in situation (1), the increase has a greater proportionate effect on the top number than on the bottom, whereas in situation (2), the change has a greater proportionate effect on the bottom number than on the top.

For many situations, you will know whether a ratio is greater or less than one, as a result of understanding the relationship between the ratio's components. For example, **the debt-to-assets ratio is likely to be less than 1.0 because the balance sheet equation (A = L + SE) indicates that liabilities are less than assets.** Similarly, **the net profit margin ratio is less than 1.0 because the income statement equation (Revenues − Expenses = Net Income) implies that net income is less than revenues.** Only in a few cases (e.g., asset turnover ratio) will you need to know whether the ratio is greater or less than 1.0 to determine the impact of a transaction that causes both the top and bottom numbers of a ratio to change in the same direction.

REVIEW THE CHAPTER

DEMONSTRATION CASE

Some analysts claim the video game business is similar to the book business. In this demonstration case, we'll take a look at just how similar they are in terms of financial results by analyzing the financial statements of John Wiley & Sons—a company that publishes textbooks.

John Wiley & Sons

JOHN WILEY & SONS, INC.
Income Statement (modified)
(U.S. dollars in millions)
For the Years Ended April 30

	2010	2009
Total Sales Revenue	$1,699	$1,611
Cost of Sales	534	516
Operating and Administrative Expenses	872	840
Other Expenses	60	42
Income from Operations	233	213
Interest Expense	32	48
Income before Income Tax Expense	201	165
Income Tax Expense	57	36
Net Income	$ 144	$ 129

JOHN WILEY & SONS, INC.
Balance Sheet (modified)
(U.S. dollars in millions)
April 30

	2010	2009
Assets		
Current Assets	$ 486	$ 440
Other Assets	1,830	1,784
Total Assets	$2,316	$2,224
Liabilities and Stockholders' Equity		
Current Liabilities	$ 674	$ 597
Other Liabilities	920	1,113
Total Liabilities	1,594	1,710
Stockholders' Equity	722	514
Total Liabilities and Stockholders' Equity	$2,316	$2,224

Required:

1. Compute Wiley's debt-to-assets ratio at the end of the 2010 and 2009 fiscal years. How has Wiley changed its financing strategy from 2009 to 2010? Is this likely to be considered a riskier or safer strategy? How similar is the proportion of debt financing used by the book publisher to that used by the video game companies analyzed in Exhibit 5.16?

2. Compute Wiley's asset turnover ratio for 2010 and 2009. (In millions, Wiley's total assets at April 30, 2008, were $2,589.) Between 2009 and 2010, was there a change in Wiley's efficiency in using its assets to generate revenues? Does the book publisher generate more or less revenue from each dollar invested in assets than the video game companies analyzed in Exhibit 5.16?

3. Compute Wiley's net profit margin ratio for the 2010 and 2009 fiscal years. How has this aspect of Wiley's financial performance changed? Does the book publisher make more or less profit from each dollar of revenue than the video game companies analyzed in Exhibit 5.16?

4. In the aftermath of the 2001 Enron financial scandal, one of the biggest auditing firms in the world (Arthur Andersen) shut down. On April 15, 2002, John Wiley & Sons announced that KPMG would replace Arthur Andersen as the company's auditor. How would Wiley report this news to the SEC?

After completing requirements 1–4, check your answers with the following solution.

Suggested Solution

1. Debt-to-Assets Ratio = Total Liabilities ÷ Total Assets

	2010	2009
$\dfrac{\text{Total Liabilities}}{\text{Total Assets}}$	$\dfrac{\$1,594}{\$2,316} = 0.688$ or 68.8%	$\dfrac{\$1,710}{\$2,224} = 0.768$ or 76.8%

Wiley has moved toward a safer financing strategy in 2010, by relying less on debt (down from 76.8 percent in 2009 to 68.8 percent in 2010). Despite this change, Wiley still relies much more on debt than the video game companies in Exhibit 5.16, which financed less than 48 percent of their total assets using debt.

2. Asset Turnover Ratio = Total Revenue ÷ Average Total Assets

	2010	2009
$\dfrac{\text{Total Revenue}}{\text{Average Total Assets}}$	$\dfrac{\$1,699}{(\$2,316 + \$2,224)/2} = 0.75$	$\dfrac{\$1,611}{(\$2,224 + \$2,589)/2} = 0.67$

Wiley generated more revenue per dollar invested in assets in 2010 (0.75) than in 2009 (0.67). In comparison to the video game companies in Exhibit 5.16, it appears Wiley's assets are generating revenue with greater efficiency.

3. Net Profit Margin Ratio = Net Income ÷ Total Revenue

	2010	2009
$\dfrac{\text{Net Income}}{\text{Total Revenue}}$	$\dfrac{\$144}{\$1,699} = 0.085$ or 8.5%	$\dfrac{\$129}{\$1,611} = 0.08$ or 8.0%

Wiley has improved its net profit margin from 8.0 percent in 2009 to 8.5 percent in 2010. This means that, in 2010, Wiley made about 8.5 cents of profit for each dollar of revenue. These ratios are slightly lower than Activision's in 2010.

4. Form 8-K is used to report significant events such as this change in auditor.

CHAPTER SUMMARY

Explain the needs of financial statement users. p. 204   LO 5-1

- The main financial statement users are:

    Managers, who use accounting information to run the business.

    Directors, who use accounting information to oversee the business.

    Creditors, who use accounting information to administer business contracts.

    Investors, who use accounting information to value the business.

    Government, which uses accounting information to ensure compliance with regulations.

Describe the environment for financial reporting, including the Sarbanes-Oxley Act. p. 205   LO 5-2

- For someone to commit fraud, three things must exist: incentive, opportunity, and a rationalizing/concealing attitude.

- Incentives that motivate managers to misreport financial results include creating business opportunities (by satisfying loan covenants, increasing equity financing, and attracting business partners) and satisfying personal greed (enhancing job security, increasing personal wealth, and obtaining a bigger paycheck).

- The Sarbanes-Oxley (SOX) Act reduced the incentive to commit fraud by introducing stiffer penalties. It also limited opportunities by improving internal controls through management reporting, audit committee functioning, and external audit reporting. Finally, it attempted to support honest employees confronting those with questionable personalities.

Prepare a comparative balance sheet, multiple-step income statement, and statement of stockholders' equity. p. 209   LO 5-3

- Comparative financial statements include separate columns for each period's results. See Exhibit 5.6 (p. 211) for an example.

- A multiple-step income statement displays subtotals that indicate multiple steps before reaching Net Income at the bottom. See Exhibit 5.7 (p. 211) for an example.

- The statement of stockholders' equity, which replaces the statement of retained earnings, has columns for each stockholders' equity account and shows the factors that increased and decreased these account balances during the period. See Exhibit 5.8 (p. 212) for an example.

Describe other significant aspects of the financial reporting process, including external audits and the distribution of financial information. p. 213   LO 5-4

- Financial information can be distributed through press releases, SEC filings, investor information Web sites, and quarterly and annual reports.

- Press releases typically include key figures (sales revenues, net income), management's discussion of the results, and attachments containing a condensed income statement and balance sheet.

- Form 10-K is the SEC's version of the annual report, which includes the annual financial statements, auditor's report, management's discussion and analysis, stock price data, and other financial schedules. Form 10-Q is the SEC's version of the quarterly report, which includes the quarterly financial statements and management's discussion and analysis. Form 8-K is the SEC's form that companies use to report significant current events, such as changes in auditors, press releases issued, and acquisitions of other companies.

LO 5-5   **Explain the reasons for, and financial statement presentation effects of, adopting IFRS. p. 216**

- IFRS are intended to reduce or eliminate differences in accounting rules that have developed previously on a country-by-country basis.
- These improvements in comparability are needed as a result of increasing globalization in corporate operations and investing.
- IFRS introduce new financial statement titles, order of balance sheet accounts, and groupings of expenses, as summarized in Exhibit 5.11 (p. 217).

LO 5-6   **Compare results to common benchmarks. p. 219**

- Common benchmarks include: prior periods (used in time-series analysis) and competitors (used in cross-sectional analysis).

LO 5-7   **Calculate and interpret the debt-to-assets, asset turnover, and net profit margin ratios. p. 220**

- The debt-to-assets ratio is calculated by dividing total liabilities by total assets. It indicates the percentage of assets financed by debt, with a higher ratio indicating a riskier financing strategy.
- The asset turnover ratio is calculated by dividing total revenue for the period by average total assets held during the period. Average total assets usually is calculated by adding the beginning and ending total assets together and dividing by 2. The asset turnover ratio indicates how well assets are used to generate revenue, with a higher ratio indicating greater efficiency.
- The net profit margin ratio is calculated by dividing net income by total revenue. It indicates the ability to control expenses, with a higher ratio indicating better performance.

Accounting Decision Tools

Name of Measure	Formula	What It Tells You
1. Debt-to-assets ratio	$\dfrac{\text{Total Liabilities}}{\text{Total Assets}}$	• The percentage of assets financed by debt • A higher ratio means greater financing risk
2. Asset turnover ratio	$\dfrac{\text{Total Revenue}}{\text{Average Total Assets}}$	• How well assets are used to generate revenue • A higher ratio means greater efficiency
3. Net profit margin ratio	$\dfrac{\text{Net Income}}{\text{Total Revenue}}$	• How much profit is earned from each dollar of revenue • A higher ratio means better performance

KEY TERMS

Asset Turnover Ratio p. 222

Comparative Financial Statements p. 210

Cross-Sectional Analysis p. 219

Debt-to-Assets Ratio p. 222

Loan Covenants p. 205

International Financial Reporting
 Standards (IFRS) p. 216

Material Misstatements p. 213

Net Profit Margin Ratio p. 223

Qualified Audit Opinion p. 214

Sarbanes-Oxley (SOX) Act p. 207

Single-Step Income Statement p. 210

Time-Series Analysis p. 219

Unqualified Audit Opinion p. 214

See complete definitions in the glossary in the back of this text.

HOMEWORK HELPER

Alternative terms

- Under IFRS, the balance sheet is called the statement of financial position, and the income statement is called the statement of comprehensive income.

Helpful reminders

- If you're not sure how a transaction affects a particular ratio, assume simple numbers for the ratio's starting point (before the transaction) and then recalculate the ratio after taking into account the effects of the transaction.

Frequent mistakes

- Some students assume that a ratio does not change when its numerator and denominator change by the same amount. A ratio is likely to change even if both its top and bottom parts increase (or decrease) by an equal dollar amount. See Exhibit 5.17.

PRACTICE MATERIAL

QUESTIONS (⊖ Symbol indicates questions that require analysis from more than one perspective.)

1. Describe one way that each of the main financial statement user groups uses financial statement information.

2. What are the three points of the fraud triangle? Is fraud more or less likely to occur if one of these elements is missing?

3. Why would managers misrepresent the financial results of their companies? What are the incentives for doing this?

4. What aspect(s) of the Sarbanes-Oxley Act might counteract the incentive to commit fraud?

5. What aspect(s) of the Sarbanes-Oxley Act might reduce opportunities for fraud?

6. What aspect(s) of the Sarbanes-Oxley Act might allow honest employees to prevail?

7. What roles do auditors play in the financial reporting process?

8. In what ways are fraudulent financial reporting and academic dishonesty (e.g., cheating on exams) similar? Consider the three points of the fraud triangle.

9. Companies incur substantial costs to implement XBRL. What are some benefits of requiring companies to report interactive data in this format? ⊖

10. In what three ways might corporate financial statements in the United States differ from the examples shown in Chapters 1–4?

11. Switching to International Financial Reporting Standards (IFRS) will require companies to incur significant costs. What are the benefits of countries adopting IFRS? ⊖

12. In what three general ways might financial statements prepared using IFRS differ from those prepared using GAAP?

13. What two benchmarks are commonly used to interpret and evaluate amounts reported for specific financial statement items?

14. What is the goal of ratio analysis?

15. Explain the simple business model that starts with obtaining financing and then proceeds through other investing and operating decisions.

16. Why do some ratios use just the ending balance sheet amounts, whereas others use averages of the beginning and ending balances?

17. What are the key business activities that the debt-to-assets, asset turnover, and net profit margin ratios assess?

MULTIPLE CHOICE

1. If total assets increase but total liabilities remain the same, what is the impact on the debt-to-assets ratio?

   a. Increases.
   b. Decreases.
   c. Remains the same.
   d. Cannot be determined without additional information.

2. Costco and Sam's Club are two companies that offer low prices for items packaged in bulk. This strategy increases total sales volume but generates less profit for each dollar of sales. Which of the following ratios is improved by this strategy?

   a. Net profit margin.   c. Debt-to-assets.
   b. Asset turnover.   d. All of the above.

3. Which of the following would increase the net profit margin ratio in the current year?

   a. Increase the amount of research and development in the last month of the year.
   b. Decrease the amount of sales in the last month of the year.
   c. Postpone routine maintenance work that was to be done this year.
   d. All of the above.

4. The asset turnover ratio is directly affected by which of the following categories of business decisions?

   a. Operating and investing decisions.
   b. Operating and financing decisions.
   c. Investing and financing decisions.
   d. Operating, investing, and financing decisions.

5. Which of the following reports is filed annually with the SEC?

   a. Form 10-Q
   b. Form 10-K
   c. Form 8-K
   d. Press release

6. Which of the following describes the order in which assets are reported under IFRS?

   a. Increasing order of liquidity.
   b. Increasing time to maturity.
   c. Decreasing order of liquidity.
   d. Decreasing time to maturity.

7. Which of the following describes a time-series analysis of your academic performance?

   a. Counting the number of A's on your transcript.

   b. Comparing the number of A's you received this year to the number you received last year.
   c. Comparing the number of A's you received this year to the number your friend received.
   d. Counting the total number of A's given out to your class as a whole.

8. Which of the following is always included in an annual report but never in a quarterly report?

   a. Balance sheet.
   b. Income statement.
   c. Management's discussion and analysis.
   d. Auditor's report.

9. Which of the following transactions will increase the debt-to-assets ratio?

   a. The company issues stock to investors.
   b. The company uses cash to buy land.
   c. The company issues a note payable to buy machinery.
   d. None of the above.

10. What type of audit report does a company hope to include with its annual report?

    a. Conservative report
    b. Qualified report
    c. Comparable report
    d. Unqualified report

> For answers to the Multiple-Choice Questions **see page Q1** located in the last section of the book.

MINI-EXERCISES

Mc Graw Hill **connect** |ACCOUNTING

LO 5-1   **M5-1 Matching Players in the Financial Reporting Process with Their Definitions**

Match each player with the related definition by entering the appropriate letter in the space provided.

Players	Definitions
____ 1. Independent auditors	A. Investors and creditors (among others).
____ 2. External users	B. People who are elected by stockholders to oversee a company's management.
____ 3. Directors	C. CPAs who examine financial statements and attest to their fairness.

LO 5-2   **M5-2 Matching Sarbanes-Oxley (SOX) Requirements to the Fraud Triangle**

Match each of the following SOX requirements to the corresponding element of the fraud triangle by entering the appropriate letter in the space provided.

____ 1. Establish a tip line for employees to report questionable acts.	A. Incentive
____ 2. Increase maximum fines to $5 million.	B. Opportunity
____ 3. Require management to report on effectiveness of internal controls.	C. Rationalize
____ 4. Legislate whistle-blower protections.	
____ 5. Require an external auditors' report on internal control effectiveness.	

M5-3 Identifying the Sequence of Financial Reports and Disclosures

Indicate the order in which the following reports and disclosures are normally issued by public companies in any given year.

No.	Title
____	Form 10-K
____	Annual Report
____	Press release announcing annual earnings

M5-4 Preparing and Interpreting a Multiple-step Income Statement

Nutboy Theater Company reported the following single-step income statement. Prepare a multiple-step income statement that distinguishes the financial results of the local theater company's core and peripheral activities. Also, calculate the net profit margin using the company's core revenues and compare it to the 8 percent earned in 2012. In which year did the company generate more profit from each dollar of sales?

NUTBOY THEATER COMPANY
Income Statement
For the year ended December 31, 2013

Revenues	
Ticket Sales	$50,000
Concession Sales	2,500
Interest Revenue	200
Other Revenue	50
Total revenues	52,750
Expenses	
Salaries and Wage Expense	30,000
Advertising Expense	8,000
Utilities Expense	7,000
Income Tax Expense	2,500
Total Expenses	47,500
Net Income	$ 5,250

M5-5 Preparing a Statement of Stockholders' Equity

On December 31, 2011, WER Productions reported $100,000 of contributed capital and $20,000 of retained earnings. During 2012, the company had the following transactions. Prepare a statement of stockholders' equity for the year ended December 31, 2012.

a. Issued stock for $50,000.
b. Declared and paid a cash dividend of $5,000.
c. Reported total revenue of $120,000 and total expenses of $87,000.

M5-6 Determining the Accounting Equation Effects of Transactions

Complete the following table, indicating the sign and amount of the effect (+ for increase, − for decrease, and NE for no effect) of each transaction. Provide an account name for any revenue or expense transactions included in stockholders' equity. Consider each item independently.

a. Recorded services provided to a customer on account for $500.
b. Recorded $50 of supplies purchased from a supplier on account.
c. Recorded advertising services of $1,000 received but not yet paid for.

Transaction	Assets	Liabilities	Stockholders' Equity
a			
b			
c			

LO 5-7

M5-7 Determining the Effects of Transactions on Debt-to-Assets, Asset Turnover, and Net Profit Margin Ratios

Using the transactions in M5-6, complete the following table by indicating the sign of the effect (+ for increase, − for decrease, NE for no effect, and CD for cannot determine) of each transaction. Consider each item independently.

Transaction	Debt-to-Assets	Asset Turnover	Net Profit Margin
a			
b			
c			

LO 5-3

M5-8 Determining the Accounting Equation Effects of Transactions

Complete the following table, indicating the sign and amount of the effect (+ for increase, − for decrease, and NE for no effect) of each transaction. Provide an account name for any revenue or expense transactions included in stockholders' equity. Consider each item independently.

a. Issued 10,000 shares of stock for $90,000 cash.
b. Equipment costing $4,000 was purchased by issuing a long-term note payable.
c. Recorded depreciation of $1,000 on the equipment.

Transaction	Assets	Liabilities	Stockholders' Equity
a			
b			
c			

LO 5-7

M5-9 Determining the Effects of Transactions on Debt-to-Assets, Asset Turnover, and Net Profit Margin Ratios

Using the transactions in M5-8, complete the following table by indicating the sign of the effect (+ for increase, − for decrease, NE for no effect, and CD for cannot determine) of each transaction. Consider each item independently.

Transaction	Debt-to-Assets	Asset Turnover	Net Profit Margin
a			
b			
c			

LO 5-3

M5-10 Preparing Comparative Financial Statements

Complete the blanks in the following comparative income statements, statement of stockholders' equity, and balance sheets.

STARBOOKS CORPORATION
Income Statements
For the Years Ended December 31

	2013	2012
Sales and Service Revenues	$400	$300
General Operating Expenses	230	200
(a)	170	(c)
Other Revenue	10	20
(b)	180	120
Income Tax Expense	60	40
Net Income	$120	$ 80

STARBOOKS CORPORATION
Statement of Stockholders' Equity
For the Year Ended December 31, 2013

	Contributed Capital	Retained Earnings
Balances at December 31, 2012	$400	(e) $
Net Income		(f)
Dividends Declared		(20)
Issued Shares of Stock	100	
Repurchased Shares of Stock	(20)	
Balances at December 31, 2013	(d) $	$180

STARBOOKS CORPORATION
Balance Sheets
December 31

	2013	2012
Assets		
Total Assets	$800	$600
Liabilities & Stockholders' Equity		
Total Liabilities	$140	$120
Stockholders' Equity		
Contributed Capital	(g)	400
Retained Earnings	(h)	80
Total Stockholders' Equity		
Total Liabilities & Stockholders' Equity	$800	$600

M5-11 Preparing a Financial Statement under IFRS LO 5-5

Show how the balance sheet in M5-10 would be presented under International Financial Reporting Standards.

M5-12 Computing and Interpreting the Net Profit Margin Ratio LO 5-7

Happy's Golf Corporation recently reported the following December 31 amounts in its financial statements (in thousands):

	Prior Year	Current Year
Income from Operations	$ 1,700	$1,400
Net Income	850	700
Total Assets	10,000	9,000
Total Stockholders' Equity	8,000	7,500
Total Revenue	9,000	7,000

Compute the net profit margin ratio for the current and prior years. What do these analyses indicate?

M5-13 Computing and Interpreting the Debt-to-Assets Ratio LO 5-7

Using the data in M5-12, compute the debt-to-assets ratio for the current and prior years. What do these analyses indicate?

LO 5-7

M5-14 Computing and Interpreting the Asset Turnover Ratio

Using the data in M5-12, compute the asset turnover ratio for the current year. Assuming the asset turnover ratio in the prior year was 0.852, what does your analysis indicate?

LO 5-6, 5-7

Columbia Sportswear
Levi Strauss

M5-15 Computing and Interpreting Financial Ratios

Key financial data for Columbia Sportswear and Levi Strauss follow (amounts in millions). Using two ratios included in this chapter, compare their relative abilities to generate (a) sales from assets and (b) net income from sales. Which company appears more successful on each of the measures?

	Columbia Sportswear	Levi Strauss and Co.
Sales	$1,484	$4,326
Net Income	77	149
Total Assets, 2010	1,295	3,135
Total Assets, 2009	1,213	2,989

EXERCISES

LO 5-1, 5-4

E5-1 Matching Components of the Financial Reporting Process with Their Definitions

Match each component with the related definition by entering the appropriate letter in the space provided.

Components	Definitions
___ 1. Investor information Web site	A. Individual who purchases stock in companies for personal ownership or for pension funds or mutual funds.
___ 2. External auditor	
___ 3. Investor	B. Financial institution or supplier that lends money to the company.
___ 4. Creditor	
___ 5. SEC	C. Independent CPA who examines financial statements and attests to their fairness.
	D. Securities and Exchange Commission, which regulates financial disclosure requirements.
	E. Gathers, combines, and transmits financial and related information from various sources.

LO 5-4

E5-2 Matching Definitions with Information Releases Made by Public Companies

Following are the titles of various information releases. Match each definition with the related release by entering the appropriate letter in the space provided.

Information Release	Definitions
___ 1. Annual report	A. Comprehensive report containing the four basic financial statements and related notes, statements by management and auditors, and other descriptions of the company's activities.
___ 2. Form 8-K	
___ 3. Press release	
___ 4. Form 10-Q	B. Annual report filed by public companies with the SEC that contains detailed financial information.
___ 5. Quarterly report	
___ 6. Form 10-K	C. Quarterly report filed by public companies with the SEC that contains unaudited financial information.
	D. A company-prepared news announcement that is normally distributed to major news agencies.
	E. Brief unaudited report for the quarter, normally containing condensed income statement and balance sheet (unaudited).
	F. Report of special events (e.g., auditor changes, mergers and acquisitions) filed by public companies with the SEC.

E5-3 Finding Financial Information: Matching Information Items to Financial Reports

Following are information items included in various financial reports. Match each information item with the report(s) where it would most likely be found by entering the appropriate letter(s) in the space provided.

Information Item	Report
_____ 1. Summarized financial data for 5- or 10-year period.	A. Annual report
_____ 2. Initial announcement of hiring of new vice president for sales.	B. Form 8-K
_____ 3. Initial announcement of quarterly earnings.	C. Press release
_____ 4. Initial announcement of a change in auditors.	D. Form 10-Q
_____ 5. Complete quarterly income statement, balance sheet, and cash flow statement.	E. Quarterly report
_____ 6. The four basic financial statements for the year.	F. Form 10-K
_____ 7. Summarized income statement information for the quarter.	G. None of the above
_____ 8. Detailed discussion of the company's business risks and strategies.	
_____ 9. Detailed notes to financial statements.	

E5-4 Understanding the Financial Reporting Process

During the first half of 2010, Mad Catz Interactive, Inc., completed its fiscal year, filed reports with the SEC, and issued various reports to the public. Match each date in the table below with the related activity by entering the appropriate letter in the space provided.

Date Filed/Issued	Activity
_____ 1. March 31, 2010	A. Issued annual earnings press release
_____ 2. June 14, 2010	B. Filed Form 8-K announcing press release
_____ 3. June 14, 2010	C. Filed Form 10-K
_____ 4. June 15, 2010	D. Completed fiscal year

E5-5 Matching Events with Concepts

Following are accounting concepts covered in Chapters 1 through 5. Match each event (A–I) with its related concept (1–9) by entering the appropriate letter in the space provided. Use one letter for each blank.

Concepts	Events
_____ 1. Users of financial statements	A. Counted unused supplies at the end of the period and valued them in U.S. dollars.
_____ 2. Objective of financial statements	B. Analyzed the financial statements to assess the company's performance.
_____ 3. Faithful representation	C. Established an accounting policy that sales revenue shall be recognized only when services have been provided to the customer.
_____ 4. Comparability	D. Prepared and distributed financial statements that provide useful financial information for creditors and investors.
_____ 5. Separate entity	E. Established a policy not to include in the financial statements the personal financial affairs of the owners of the business.
_____ 6. Unit of measure	
_____ 7. Cost principle	F. Used the same accounting policies over several years to facilitate analysis.
_____ 8. Revenue recognition principle	G. Established policies to report the company's business activities in a way that depicts their economic substance.
_____ 9. Expense recognition principle	H. Adjusted the rent accounts to show the cost of rent used up in the current period.
	I. Acquired a vehicle for use in the business, reporting it at the agreed-upon purchase price rather than its higher sticker price.

LO 5-1, 5-4, 5-7
Atari Incorporated

E5-6 Understanding the Characteristics of Useful Financial Information and the Financial Reporting Process

Atari Incorporated began with $250 and an idea for a video game named Pong, eventually becoming a $28 million enterprise. Over the years, Atari has been owned by a variety of companies, including Time-Warner, Hasbro, and, most recently, Infogrames (a public company in France). Infogrames made the following announcement:

> On March 28, 2003, the Company announced that it has changed its fiscal year-end from June 30 to March 31. As a result of this change, the Company's fiscal year 2003 was a nine-month period. The Company believes that the March 31 year-end is consistent with more of its peers in the video game industry, allowing for more meaningful analysis and comparisons within the sector.

Required:

1. To which of the four factors that enhance the usefulness of information, introduced in Chapter 1, is the company referring?
   TIP: Rather than look for key words in the announcement, read it for meaning.
2. On what SEC form would the change in year-end be reported?
3. Since the 2003 fiscal period includes only nine months, will the debt-to-assets, asset turnover, and net profit margin ratios be meaningful in 2003? Explain your reasoning.

LO 5-1, 5-7

Better Ingredients.
Better Pizza.

E5-7 Analyzing and Interpreting Asset Turnover and Net Profit Margin Ratios

Papa John's is one of the fastest-growing pizza delivery and carry-out restaurant chains in the country. Presented here are selected income statement and balance sheet amounts (in millions).

	2010	2009
Total Revenues	$1,126	$1,079
Net Income	52	57
Total Assets, beginning of year	394	386
Total Assets, end of year	416	394

Required:

1. Compute the asset turnover and net profit margin ratios for 2010 and 2009.
2. Would analysts more likely increase or decrease their estimates of stock value on the basis of these changes? Explain by interpreting what the changes in these two ratios mean.

LO 5-1, 5-7

Ⓡ **RadioShack**

E5-8 Analyzing and Interpreting Asset Turnover and Net Profit Margin Ratios

RadioShack Corporation reported the following amounts (in millions) in its income statement and balance sheet.

	2010	2009	2008
Total Revenue	$4,473	$4,276	$4,225
Net Income	206	205	189
Total Assets	2,175	2,429	1,990
Total Liabilities	640	660	348

Required:

1. Compute the asset turnover and net profit margin ratios for 2010 and 2009.
2. Would analysts be more likely to increase or decrease their estimates of stock value on the basis of these changes? Explain what the changes in these two ratios mean.

3. Compute the debt-to-assets ratio for 2010 and 2009.
4. Would analysts be more likely to increase or decrease their estimates of RadioShack's ability to repay lenders on the basis of this change? Explain by interpreting what the change in this ratio means.

E5-9 Determining the Accounting Equation Effects of Transactions

LO 5-3

La-Z-Boy Incorporated

La-Z-Boy Incorporated is a furniture manufacturer. Listed here are typical aggregate transactions from the first quarter of a recent year (in millions). Complete the following table, indicating the sign (+ for increase, − for decrease, and NE for no effect) and amount of the effect of each transaction. Provide an account name for any revenue or expense transactions included in stockholders' equity. Consider each item independently.

a. Repaid $10 on a long-term note payable to a bank. (Interest was paid separately.)
b. Recorded collections of cash from customers who owed $32.

Transaction	Assets	Liabilities	Stockholders' Equity
a			
b			

E5-10 Determining the Effects of Transactions on Debt-to-Assets, Asset Turnover, and Net Profit Margin Ratios

LO 5-7

Using the transactions in E5-9, complete the following table by indicating the sign of the effect (+ for increase, − for decrease, NE for no effect, and CD for cannot determine) of each transaction. Consider each item independently.

Transaction	Debt-to-Assets	Asset Turnover	Net Profit Margin
a			
b			

E5-11 Finding Financial Statement Information

LO 5-3

Indicate whether each of the following would be reported on the balance sheet (B/S), income statement (I/S), or statement of stockholders' equity (SSE).

1. Insurance costs paid this year, to expire next year.
2. Insurance costs expired this year.
3. Insurance costs still owed.
4. Cost of equipment used up this accounting year.
5. Equipment book value (carrying value).
6. Amounts contributed by stockholders during the year.
7. Cost of supplies unused at the end of the year.
8. Cost of supplies used during the accounting year.
9. Amount of unpaid loans at end of year.
10. Dividends declared and paid during this year.

COACHED PROBLEMS

CP5-1 Determining the Accounting Equation Effects of Transactions

|ACCOUNTING LO 5-3

Yahoo! Inc. is a leading provider of Internet products and services. Listed here are representative transactions from 2010 (in millions). Complete the following table, indicating the sign (+ for increase, − for decrease, and NE for no effect) and amount of the effect of each transaction. Provide an account name for any revenue or expense transactions included in stockholders' equity.

Consider each item independently.

a. Recorded marketing revenues on account of $6,325.
b. Obtained $167 cash by issuing stock.
c. Incurred research and development expense of $1,080, which was paid in cash.

Transaction	Assets	Liabilities	Stockholders' Equity
a			
b			
c			

LO 5-7

CP5-2 Determining the Effects of Transactions on Debt-to-Assets, Asset Turnover, and Net Profit Margin Ratios

Using the transactions in CP5-1, complete the following table by indicating the sign of the effect (+ for increase, − for decrease, NE for no effect, and CD for cannot determine) of each transaction. Consider each item independently.

TIP: To determine the impact of a transaction on a ratio, try an example with numbers. For example, assume asset turnover ratios of 9/10 or 10/9 and see how an increase of 1 in the top and bottom numbers affects the ratios.

TIP: A = L + SE implies that total assets are almost always greater than total liabilities. This means that if assets and liabilities change by the same dollar amount, the impact on liabilities will be proportionally bigger than the impact on assets.

Transaction	Debt-to-Assets	Asset Turnover	Net Profit Margin
a			
b			
c			

LO 5-7

Best Buy Co. Inc.

CP5-3 Interpreting Debt-to-Assets, Asset Turnover, and Net Profit Margin Ratios

The following ratios for Best Buy Co. Inc. and its competitor GameStop Corp. were obtained from reuters.com/finance. Compare the two companies based on the following ratios:

Ratio	Best Buy	GameStop Corp.
Debt-to-assets	0.96	0.90
Asset turnover ratio	2.78	1.89
Net profit margin	2.71%	4.29%

Required:

1. Which company appears to rely more on debt financing? Describe the ratio that you used to reach this decision, and explain what the ratio means.
2. Which company appears to use its assets more efficiently? Describe the ratio that you used to reach this decision, and explain what the ratio means.
3. Which company appears to better control its expenses? Describe the ratio that you used to reach this decision, and explain what the ratio means.

LO 5-5, 5-6, 5-7

CP5-4 Preparing and Interpreting IFRS Financial Statements

H&M is a retail clothing company headquartered in Sweden with operations in 38 countries, including 208 stores in the United States. The company began its 2010 fiscal year with assets totaling 54,363 (in millions of Swedish krona) but ended the year (on November 30, 2010) with 59,182 in total assets. Account balances on November 30, 2010, are listed below (in millions of Swedish krona).

Accounts Payable	3,965	Long-term Liabilities	1,163
Accounts Receivable	3,711	Other Current Liabilities	4,506
Accrued Liabilities	5,376	Other Non-current Assets	2,717
Accumulated Depreciation	8,831	Prepaid Expenses	876
Buildings and Equipment	24,205	Profit for the Year (Net Income)	18,681
Contributed Capital	207	Retained Earnings, Dec. 1, 2009	25,284
Goodwill and Intangible Assets	64	Sales Revenue	235,449
Land	95	Stock-in-Trade (Inventory)	11,487
Liquid Funds (Cash)	24,858		

Required:

1. Prepare a statement of financial position at November 30, 2010, using Exhibit 5.12 as a guide.
   TIP: Not all of the accounts listed are reported on the Statement of Financial Position.

2. Use an appropriate ratio to compute H&M's financing risk. Compare H&M's ratio to the 0.158 reported for Volcom (a clothing company headquartered in California) on December 31, 2010. Which company appears more likely to pay its liabilities?

3. Use an appropriate ratio to compute the amount of profit H&M earns from each dollar of sales. Compare H&M's ratio to that of Volcom, which earned 6.9 cents of profit for each dollar of sales in the year ended December 31, 2010.

4. Use an appropriate ratio to compute H&M's efficiency at using assets to generate sales. Compare H&M's ratio to the 1.27 reported for Volcom for the year ended December 31, 2010.

GROUP A PROBLEMS

PA5-1 Determining the Accounting Equation Effects of Transactions

LO 5-3

Papa John's International began in the back of a tavern in Jeffersonville, Indiana, and has since become one of the largest pizza companies in America. Listed here are transactions that typically occur each year. Complete the following table, indicating the sign (+ for increase, − for decrease, and NE for no effect) and amount of the effect of each transaction. Provide an account name for any revenue or expense transactions included in stockholders' equity. Consider each item independently.

a. Repaid a long-term note payable of $80,000. (Interest was paid separately.)
b. Paid cash to purchase equipment costing $120,000.
c. Purchased additional equipment costing $20,000 by issuing a long-term note payable.
d. Recorded service revenues on account of $30,000.

Transaction	Assets	Liabilities	Stockholders' Equity
a			
etc.			

PA5-2 Determining the Effects of Transactions on Debt-to-Assets, Asset Turnover, and Net Profit Margin Ratios

LO 5-7

Using the transactions in PA5-1, complete the following table by indicating the sign of the effect (+ for increase, − for decrease, NE for no effect, and CD for cannot determine) of each transaction. Consider each item independently.

Transaction	Debt-to-Assets	Asset Turnover	Net Profit Margin
a			
etc.			

LO 5-7

Kohl's Corporation
Dillard's, Inc.

PA5-3 Interpreting Debt-to-Assets, Asset Turnover, and Net Profit Margin Ratios

The following ratios for Kohl's Corporation and its competitor Dillard's, Inc., were obtained from reuters.com/finance. Compare the two companies based on the following ratios:

Ratio	Kohl's	Dillard's
Debt-to-assets	0.96	0.98
Asset turnover ratio	1.39	1.40
Net profit margin	6.1%	4.9%

Required:

1. Which company appears to rely more on debt for financing? Describe the ratio that you used to reach this decision, and explain what the ratio means.
2. Which company appears to use its assets more efficiently? Describe the ratio that you used to reach this decision, and explain what the ratio means.
3. Which company appears to better control its expenses? Describe the ratio that you used to reach this decision, and explain what the ratio means.

LO 5-5, 5-6, 5-7

PA5-4 Preparing and Interpreting IFRS Financial Statements

Glücklich Golfspieler (GG) is a golf club company headquartered in Germany. The company began its 2013 fiscal year with assets totaling 10 million euro but ended the year (on December 31, 2013) with 13 million euro of total assets. Account balances on December 31, 2013, appear below (in thousands of euro).

Accounts Payable	1,000	Contributed Capital	400	Other Non-current Assets	400
Accounts Receivable	500	Goodwill and Intangible Assets	450	Prepaid Expenses	250
Accrued Liabilities	900	Inventory	2,500	Profit for the Year (Net Income)	4,000
Accumulated Depreciation	2,500	Land	100	Retained Earnings, Jan. 1, 2013	5,000
Buildings and Equipment	5,500	Notes Payable, due 2012	600	Sales Revenue	44,000
Cash	5,800	Other Long-term Liabilities	1,100		

Required:

1. Prepare a statement of financial position at December 31, 2013, using Exhibit 5.12 as a guide.
2. Use an appropriate ratio to compute GG's financing risk. Compare GG's ratio to the 0.20 reported for one of its close competitors. Which company appears more likely to pay its liabilities?
3. Use an appropriate ratio to compute the amount of profit GG earns from each euro of sales. Compare GG's ratio to its competitor, which had a ratio of 0.05. Which company is better able to control its expenses?
4. Use an appropriate ratio to compute GG's efficiency at using assets to generate sales. Compare GG's ratio to the 2.60 reported for its competitor. Which company is more efficient at using its assets to generate sales?

GROUP B PROBLEMS

LO 5-3

Regal Entertainment Group

PB5-1 Determining the Accounting Equation Effects of Transactions

Regal Entertainment Group is the largest movie company in the world, taking in over 20 percent of the box office receipts in the United States. Listed here are transactions that typically occur each quarter. Complete the following table, indicating the sign (+ for increase, − for decrease, and NE for no effect) and amount of the effect of each transaction. Provide an account name for any revenue or expense transactions included in stockholders' equity. Consider each item independently.

a. Paid cash to purchase equipment costing $30,000.
b. Declared and paid a cash dividend totaling $40,000.
c. Recorded depreciation on property and equipment totaling $78,000.
d. Recorded cash admissions revenues of $450,000.

Transaction	Assets	Liabilities	Stockholders' Equity
a			
etc.			

PB5-2 Determining the Effects of Transactions on Debt-to-Assets, Asset Turnover, and Net Profit Margin Ratios

LO 5-7

Using the transactions in PB5-1, complete the following table by indicating the sign of the effect (+ for increase, − for decrease, NE for no effect, and CD for cannot determine) of each transaction. Consider each item independently.

Transaction	Debt-to-Assets	Asset Turnover	Net Profit Margin
a			
etc.			

PB5-3 Interpreting Debt-to-Assets, Asset Turnover, and Net Profit Margin Ratios

LO 5-7

i'm lovin' it

YUM Brands, Inc.

The following ratios for McDonald's Corporation and its competitor YUM Brands, Inc., (the owner of KFC, Pizza Hut, and Taco Bell) were obtained from reuters.com/finance. Compare the two companies based on the following ratios:

Ratio	McDonald's	YUM
Debt-to-Assets	0.54	0.80
Asset Turnover Ratio	0.76	1.47
Net Profit Margin	20.55%	10.21%

Required:

1. Which company appears to rely more on debt than stockholders' equity for financing? Describe the ratio that you used to reach this decision, and explain what the ratio means.
2. Which company appears to use its assets more efficiently? Describe the ratio that you used to reach this decision, and explain what the ratio means.
3. Which company appears to better control its expenses? Describe the ratio that you used to reach this decision, and explain what the ratio means.

PB5-4 Preparing and Interpreting IFRS Financial Statements

LO 5-5, 5-6, 5-7

Latteria Limited (LL) is a dairy company headquartered in Italy. The company began its 2013 fiscal year with assets totaling 9 million euro but ended the year (on December 31, 2013) with 13 million euro of total assets. Account balances on December 31, 2013, appear below (in thousands of euro).

Accounts Payable	1,300	Cash	1,200	Prepaid Expenses	250
Accounts Receivable	500	Contributed Capital	400	Profit for the Year (Net Income)	2,200
Accrued Liabilities	600	Inventory	2,500	Retained Earnings, Jan. 1, 2013	6,800
Accumulated Depreciation	3,600	Land	5,550	Sales Revenue	22,000
Buildings and Equipment	6,600	Notes Payable, due 2015	1,700		

Required:

1. Prepare a statement of financial position at December 31, 2013, using Exhibit 5.12 as a guide.

2. Use an appropriate ratio to compute LL's financing risk. Compare LL's ratio to the 0.42 reported in a recent year for Saputo, Inc. (a dairy company based in Montreal, Canada). Which company appears more likely to pay its liabilities?

3. Use an appropriate ratio to compute the amount of profit LL earns from each euro of sales. Compare LL's ratio to Saputo, which had a ratio of 0.07. Which company is better able to control its expenses?

4. Use an appropriate ratio to compute LL's efficiency at using assets to generate sales. Compare LL's ratio to the 1.74 reported for Saputo. Which company is more efficient at using its assets to generate sales?

COMPREHENSIVE PROBLEMS

LO 4-2, 5-2, 5-4, 5-3, 5-7

C5-1 Adjusting and Interpreting Financial Statements (Chapters 4–5)

Biz Zing Inc. (BZI) provides life and work counseling to companies. At the end of 2012, BZI's total assets were $1,120. BZI's unadjusted trial balance includes the following for the twelve months ended December 31, 2013.

Accounts Receivable	$160	Note Payable, due 2016	$ 220
Accounts Payable	40	Prepaid Rent	240
Accumulated Depreciation	120	Rent Expense	120
Cash	420	Retained Earnings	215
Contributed Capital	320	Salaries Expense	750
Depreciation Expense	30	Salaries Payable	5
Equipment	300	Service Revenue	1,000
Income Tax Expense	20	Unearned Revenue	120
Income Tax Payable	0		

Other information:

a. Only six months of depreciation have been recorded so far.

b. BZI has provided services that fulfilled half of the $120 unearned revenue.

c. Until June 2013, BZI paid rent at the beginning of each month. On June 30, 2013, BZI paid for rent from July 1, 2013, through June 30, 2014. Prepaid Rent has not been adjusted since that payment was made.

d. Salaries Payable includes amounts owed to an employee as of June 30, 2013. At December 31, 2013, a total of $15 is owed to the employee.

e. BZI provided $150 of services in December 2013 that have not yet been billed or recorded.

f. During 2013, the company made an initial payment of $20 for income tax. The company's income tax rate is 20%.

Required:

1. Using the unadjusted balances, compute the (a) debt-to-assets, (b) asset turnover, and (c) net profit margin ratios.

2. Prepare the adjusting journal entries required at December 31, 2013.

3. Using properly adjusted balances, prepare a classified balance sheet and multiple step income statement at and for the year ended December 31, 2013.

4. Using the adjusted balances, compute the (a) debt-to-assets, (b) asset turnover, and (c) net profit margin ratios.

5. Compare answers in requirements 1 and 4. Did the adjustments cause BZI's financial statements to indicate (a) more or less financing risk, (b) more or less efficient use of assets in generating revenue, and (c) more or less profit from each dollar of revenue?

LO 3-5, 5-3, 5-6, 5-7

C5-2 Preparing and Interpreting Financial Statements (Chapters 3 and 5)

The December 31, 2013 and 2012 adjusted trial balances for Sportlife Gym Corporation are shown on the following page.

	2013		2012	
	Debit	Credit	Debit	Credit
Cash	$ 31,500		$ 30,000	
Accounts Receivable	2,500		2,000	
Supplies	13,000		13,000	
Prepaid Rent	3,000		3,000	
Equipment	350,000		350,000	
Accumulated Depreciation		$ 20,000		$ 10,000
Other Noncurrent Assets	20,000		12,000	
Accounts Payable		5,000		6,000
Unearned Revenue		72,000		80,000
Income Taxes Payable		13,000		14,000
Long-term Debt		10,000		200,000
Contributed Capital		214,000		50,000
Retained Earnings		50,000		19,400
Dividends Declared	5,000		0	
Membership Revenue		399,000		398,000
Coaching Revenue		11,000		10,000
Coaching and Assistants' Wages	221,000		219,400	
Management Salaries	100,000		100,000	
Facilities Rent Expense	12,000		12,000	
Depreciation Expense	10,000		10,000	
General Operating Expenses	6,150		7,700	
Interest Revenue		750		700
Interest Expense	600		15,000	
Income Tax Expense	20,000		14,000	
	$794,750	$794,750	$788,100	$788,100

Required:

1. Prepare a comparative income statement for 2013 and 2012, a statement of stockholders' equity for 2013, and a comparative classified balance sheet for 2010 and 2012. The income statement should distinguish the gym's core and peripheral results, and group expenses by function (coaching, facilities, and general management). The change in Contributed Capital was caused by the issuance of new stock in 2013.

2. Identify two balance sheet and two income statement accounts that changed significantly in 2013. What might be the cause of these changes?

3. Calculate and interpret the debt-to-assets, asset turnover, and net profit margin ratios in 2013 and 2012. Total assets were $400,000 on December 31, 2011.

C5-3 Preparing Financial Statements in a Typical European Format   LO 5-5

Refer to C5-2.

Required:

1. Prepare a comparative classified statement of financial position, as typically presented using IFRS.

2. Prepare a comparative statement of comprehensive income
   TIP: Use Exhibit 5.7 as a guide, except group expenses by nature (e.g., salaries and wages, rent, etc.) as outlined in Exhibit 5.11.

SKILLS DEVELOPMENT CASES

S5-1 Finding Financial Information |ACCOUNTING   LO 5-7

Refer to the financial statements of The Home Depot in Appendix A at the end of this book, or download the annual report from the *Cases* section of the text's Web site at www.mhhe.com/phillips4e.

Required:

1. Calculate the debt-to-assets ratio at January 30, 2011, and January 31, 2010. Based on these calculations, has The Home Depot's financing become more or less risky over these two years?
   a. 0.529 and 0.526 (less risky)
   b. 0.526 and 0.529 (more risky)
   c. 0.526 and 0.529 (less risky)
   d. 0.529 and 0.526 (more risky)

2. Calculate the asset turnover ratio for the January 2011 and 2010 year-ends. The Home Depot's total assets at the end of fiscal 2009 were $41,164 million.
   a. 1.68 and 1.61
   b. 5.00 and 4.80
   c. 1.69 and 1.62
   d. 1.69 and 4.80

3. Calculate the net profit margin ratio for 2010–2011 and 2009–2010.
   a. 4.9% and 4.0%
   b. 4.0% and 3.2%
   c. 4.3% and 4.9%
   d. 1.6% and 2.0%

LO 5-6, 5-7

Lowe's

S5-2 Comparing Financial Information

Refer to the financial statements of The Home Depot in Appendix A and Lowe's in Appendix B at the end of this book, or download the annual reports from the *Cases* section of the text's Web site at www.mhhe.com/phillips4e.

Required:

1. Calculate the debt-to-assets ratio for Lowe's at January 28, 2011. Based on this calculation, was Lowe's financing more or less risky than The Home Depot's at the end of January 2011?

2. Calculate the asset turnover ratio for Lowe's for the year ended January 30, 2011. Lowe's total assets at the end of fiscal 2009 were $33,005 million. Based on this calculation, did Lowe's use its assets more or less efficiently than The Home Depot in 2010–2011?

3. Calculate the net profit margin ratio for Lowe's for the year ended January 28, 2009. Based on this calculation, did Lowe's generate more or less profit per dollar of sales than The Home Depot in 2010–2011?

LO 5-6, 5-7

S5-3 Internet-Based Team Research: Examining an Annual Report

As a team, select an industry to analyze. Using your Web browser, each team member should access the annual report or 10-K for one publicly traded company in the industry, with each member selecting a different company (see S1-3 in Chapter 1 for a description of possible resources for these tasks).

Required:

1. On an individual basis, each team member should write a short report that incorporates the following:
   a. Calculate the debt-to-assets ratio at the end of the current and prior years, and explain any change between the two years.
   b. Calculate the asset turnover ratio at the end of the current and prior years and explain any change between the two years. (To calculate average assets for the prior year, you will need the total assets number for the beginning of the prior year. If this isn't reported in the summarized financial data section in the current annual report, you will need to get it from the prior year's annual report or 10-K.)
   c. Calculate the net profit margin ratio at the end of the current and prior years and explain any change between the two years.

2. Then, as a team, write a short report comparing and contrasting your companies using these attributes. Discuss any patterns across the companies that you observe as a team. Provide potential explanations for any differences discovered.

LO 5-1, 5-2, 5-7

S5-4 Ethical Decision Making: A Real-Life Example

Complete this case involving Aurora Foods, Inc., available online at www.mhhe.com/phillips4e. By completing this case, you will learn how the maker of Duncan Hines cake mixes fraudulently reported its financial statements and misstated its debt-to-assets, asset turnover, and net profit margin ratios.

S5-5 Ethical Decision Making: A Mini-Case

Assume you've been hired to replace an accounting clerk for a small public company. After your second month on the job, the chief financial officer (CFO) approached you directly with a "special project." The company had just finished installing a new production line earlier in the year, and the CFO wanted you to go through all of the company's expense accounts with the goal of finding any costs that might be related to the machinery's installation or to "tinkering with it" to get the line working just right. He said that the previous accounting clerk, whom you had replaced, didn't understand that these costs should have been recorded as part of the production line (an asset) rather than as expenses of the period. The CFO indicated that there was some urgency, as the company had to finalize its quarterly financial statements so they could be filed with the SEC. Also, the company was close to violating its loan covenants and it needed a few extra dollars of profit this quarter to ensure the bank didn't demand immediate repayment of the loan. As you thought about this situation, you tried to remember what Chapter 2 in your accounting textbook said regarding the key characteristics of assets.

Required:

1. Which of the three ratios discussed in this chapter (debt-to-assets, asset turnover, and net profit margin) are affected by the decision to record costs as an asset rather than an expense? Indicate whether each ratio will be higher or lower if costs are recorded as an asset rather than an expense.
2. Is there anything in the case that makes you uncomfortable with the work that you've been asked to do?
3. What should you do?

S5-6 Critical Thinking: Analyzing Income Statement-Based Executive Bonuses

Callaway Golf believes in tying executives' compensation to the company's performance as measured by accounting numbers. Suppose, in a recent year, Callaway had agreed to pay its executive officers bonuses if (a) asset turnover meets or exceeds 0.8, and (b) net profit margin meets or exceeds 5.0 percent. Their bonuses will be even larger, if asset turnover meets (or exceeds) 1.6 and net profit margin meets (or exceeds) 7.0 percent. Total assets were $855 (million) and $838 (million) at December 31, 2008 and 2007, respectively. For the year ended December 31, 2008, total revenue was $1,117 (million) and net income was $66 (million).

Required:

1. Use the preceding information to determine whether Callaway executives met the two bonus targets in 2008.
2. Explain why the bonus arrangement might be based on both asset turnover and net profit margin ratios, rather than just one of these two ratios.

S5-7 Computing, Charting, and Interpreting Time-Series and Cross-Sectional Analyses

Assume that *Candy Industry Magazine* has contracted you to write an article discussing the financial status of Hershey Foods Corporation over the last few years. The editor suggests that your article should also compare Hershey's recent financial performance to competitors like Tootsie Roll Industries and Rocky Mountain Chocolate Factory. You gather the following information from the 2010 10-Ks of the three companies.

Hershey Foods Corporation

Tootsie Roll Industries

(In millions of U.S. dollars)	Hershey Foods Corporation			Tootsie Roll Industries	Rocky Mountain Chocolate Factory
	2008	2009	2010	2010	2010
Total Liabilities	3,285	2,915	3,335	191	5
Total Assets	3,634	3,675	4,273	860	21
Sales Revenue	5,133	5,299	5,671	517	31
Net Income	311	436	510	54	4

Required:

Enter the above information into a spreadsheet and perform the following analyses:

1. *Time-series analysis:* Demonstrate the changes in Hershey's size over the three years by charting its total liabilities, total assets, sales revenues, and net income.

2. *Cross-sectional analysis:* Demonstrate the size of Hershey relative to Tootsie Roll and Rocky Mountain Chocolate Factory, by charting the three companies' total liabilities, total assets, sales revenues, and net income for 2010.

3. *Ratio analysis:* Compare the performance of Hershey relative to Tootsie Roll and Rocky Mountain Chocolate Factory, by computing the debt-to-assets and net profit margin ratios for 2010.

CONTINUING CASES

LO 3-3, 4-2, 5-7

CC5-1 Evaluating the Impact of Typical Transactions

After finishing her first year of operations, Nicole used the debt-to-assets, asset turnover, and net profit margin ratios to determine how effective she was in running the business. Listed here are a few company transactions from the past quarter that may have influenced these ratios.

a. Customers used $200 of gift certificates to pay for spa services.

b. Acquired, on account, equipment costing $320.

c. Recorded spa treatment revenues of $1,500 on account.

d. Incurred advertising expense of $40, paid in cash.

e. Accrued $750 for utility bills.

f. Received $50,000 cash from an investor in exchange for company shares.

g. Received $2,500 cash by signing a short-term note payable.

h. Recorded $1,800 in depreciation expense.

Required:

1. Complete the following table, indicating the effects (account, amount, and direction) of each transaction. Use + for increase, − for decrease, and NE for no effect.

Transaction	Assets	Liabilities	Stockholders' Equity
a			
etc.			

2. Complete the following table, indicating the sign (+ for increase, − for decrease, and NE for no effect) for each transaction. Assume that, prior to recording items (a)–(h), Nicole's Getaway Spa had more assets than liabilities, more revenues than net income, and more revenues than average assets.

Transaction	Debt-to-Assets	Asset Turnover	Net Profit Margin
a			
etc.			

CC5-2 Wiki Art Gallery (WAG)

Access the Wiki Art Gallery (WAG) instructional case in Connect, and read the case in sufficient depth to answer the following questions.

1. Which of the following statements uses the fraud triangle appropriately when identifying the risks of financial misreporting at Wiki Art Gallery (WAG)?

   a. Because Rob prepares WAG's financial statements, the incentive for misstating the financial results is heightened.

   b. Because WAG's financial statements are not audited, the opportunity for misstating the financial results is heightened.

   c. The risk of financial reporting fraud is heightened because Stephen has shown a tendency to rationalize and conceal misdeeds.

   d. The pending sale of WAG increases the opportunity for misstating the financial results.

2. Which of the following properly calculates and interprets the change in WAG's net profit margin?

   a. WAG's net profit margin increased from 0.35% in 2010 to 0.45% in 2011, suggesting an increase in WAG's ability to generate profits from revenues.

   b. WAG's net profit margin decreased from 3.5% in 2010 to 0.45% in 2011, suggesting a decrease in WAG's ability to generate profits from revenues.

   c. WAG's net profit margin increased from 3.5% in 2010 to 4.5% in 2011, suggesting an increase in WAG's ability to generate profits from revenues.

   d. WAG's net profit margin increased from 3.5% in 2010 to 45.0% in 2011, suggesting an increase in WAG's ability to generate profits from revenues.

3. Exhibit 1 of the case indicates that WAG violated its debt-to-assets loan covenant in May 2011. Which of the following events would have increased the risk of violating this loan covenant?

   a. The risk of violating the loan covenant would be increased when WAG paid cash to purchase artwork.

   b. The risk of violating the loan covenant would be increased when WAG used its cash to pay suppliers on account.

   c. The risk of violating the loan covenant would be increased when WAG used its cash to pay dividends to Rob.

   d. The risk of violating the loan covenant would be increased when WAG reduced the salary it paid to Rob.

Internal Control, Cash, and Merchandise Sales

YOUR LEARNING OBJECTIVES

Understand the business

LO 6-1   Distinguish among service, merchandising, and manufacturing operations.

LO 6-2   Explain common principles and limitations of internal control.

Study the accounting methods

LO 6-3   Apply internal control principles to cash receipts and payments.

LO 6-4   Perform the key control of reconciling cash to bank statements.

LO 6-5   Explain the use of a perpetual inventory system as a control.

LO 6-6   Analyze sales transactions under a perpetual inventory system.

Evaluate the results

LO 6-7   Analyze a merchandiser's multistep income statement.

Review the chapter

THAT WAS THEN

Earlier chapters have focused on companies whose operating activities relate to providing services to customers, rather than selling goods.

FOCUS COMPANY: Walmart

Seventeen years after the company was founded, Walmart rang up yearly sales of $1 billion. Fourteen years later, it sold that much in a week. Thanks to you and the 200 million other Americans who shop at Walmart, its sales now average over $1 billion a day. And that's not all. Walmart has been able to earn sizable profits, even during difficult economic times. One secret to its success is the state-of-the-art accounting system that controls Walmart's merchandise sales and cash collections. In this chapter, you will learn about this kind of system and the other aspects of merchandising companies that make them unique and interesting. You'll also learn how to analyze a merchandiser's financial statements to figure out the amount of mark-up that it includes in the prices you pay. You might be surprised by how much you're contributing to Walmart's profits.

www.walmart.com

THIS IS NOW

This chapter focuses on companies that sell merchandise to customers, and the way they control and report their operating results.

Understand the business	Study the accounting methods	Evaluate the results	Review the chapter
• Operating cycles • Internal control	• Controlling and reporting cash • Controlling and reporting merchandise sales	• Gross profit analysis	• Demonstration cases • Chapter summary • Key terms • Homework helper • Practice material

Understand the Business

OPERATING CYCLES

For any company to be successful, it must complete its operating cycle efficiently. **The operating cycle is a series of activities that a company undertakes to generate revenues and, ultimately, cash.** Exhibit 6.1 contrasts the operating cycles of service and merchandising companies.

Service companies such as WorldGym follow a simple operating cycle: sell services to customers, collect cash from them, and use that money to pay for operating expenses. **Merchandising companies** differ in that their cycle begins with buying products. These products, which are called Inventory, are sold to customers, which leads to collecting cash that can be used to pay for operating expenses and buy more inventory. Merchandising companies such as Walmart and Costco are called **retailers** when they sell directly to individual consumers and **wholesalers** when they sell their inventory to retail businesses for resale to consumers. This chapter applies equally to both retail and wholesale merchandisers. This chapter does not include **manufacturing companies** such as Mattel and Goodyear because they make rather than buy the products they sell, which introduces complexities that are beyond this introductory course. Accounting for manufacturing companies is explained in managerial and cost accounting courses.

Merchandising companies aim to reduce the time needed to complete their operating cycles. To promote this efficiency, companies establish and follow specific procedures and policies that describe how the business is to be run. These procedures and policies are called **internal controls.** In your personal life, internal controls include basic precautions such as locking your car door and checking the accuracy of your banking records. When internal controls operate effectively, they contribute not only to improving operating efficiency, but also to reducing waste, minimizing unintentional errors, and deterring fraud. It's little wonder, then, that Walmart has established world-class internal controls at each of its 9,000 store locations.

EXHIBIT 6.1 Operating Cycles for Service and Merchandising Companies

INTERNAL CONTROL

Learning Objective 6-2
Explain common principles and limitations of internal control.

Internal control is important to all types and sizes of organizations, especially after the business failures and accounting scandals involving Enron and other companies in the early 2000s. As you may recall from Chapter 5, the Sarbanes-Oxley (SOX) Act requires all public companies to assess the effectiveness of internal controls over financial reporting. **Effective internal controls play an essential role in creating an ethical business environment, improving financial performance, and preventing fraud.** A 2010 report by the Association for Certified Fraud Examiners identifies a lack of internal controls as the *primary* factor in 38 percent of fraud cases.

Common Control Principles

From the perspective of a company's chief executive officer (CEO), chief financial officer (CFO), and board of directors, internal control is a broad concept that includes setting strategic objectives, identifying risks the company faces, hiring good employees, instilling ethical principles in them, motivating them to achieve the company's objectives, and providing the resources and information they need to fulfill those objectives. These broad controls are supported by basic control principles that are used throughout the company. We focus on five key control principles that you are likely to see in your own work. We want you to understand why these controls exist so that when you encounter them on the job, you will appreciate them and ensure that others respect them.

All good systems of internal control are based on these five common principles, which are summarized in Exhibit 6.2. These principles are typically applied to all aspects of a company's

EXHIBIT 6.2 Five Common Principles of Internal Control

	Principle	Explanation	Examples	
1	Establish responsibility	Assign each task to only one employee.	Each Walmart cashier uses a different cash drawer.	
2	Segregate duties	Do not make one employee responsible for all parts of a process.	Walmart's inventory buyers do not also approve payments to suppliers.	
3	Restrict access	Do not provide access to assets or information unless it is needed to fulfill assigned responsibilities.	Walmart secures valuable assets such as cash and restricts access to its computer systems (via passwords, firewalls).	
4	Document procedures	Prepare documents to show activities that have occurred.	Walmart pays suppliers using prenumbered checks and digitally documented electronic fund transfers.	
5	Independently verify	Check others' work.	Walmart compares the cash balances in its accounting records to the cash balances reported by its bank, and accounts for any differences.	

business activities, including human resource management, finance, marketing, and general business operations. Our focus here, however, is on their relationship to accounting.

① **Establish responsibility.** Whenever possible, assign each task to only one employee. Doing so will allow you to determine who caused any errors or thefts that occur. That's the reason Walmart assigns a separate cash register drawer to each employee at the beginning of a shift. If two cashiers were to use the same drawer, it would be impossible to know which cashier caused the drawer to be short on cash. With only one person responsible for adding and removing money from the drawer, there's no doubt about who is responsible for a cash shortage. That leads to more training, supervision, or dismissal.

② **Segregate duties.** **Segregation of duties** involves assigning responsibilities so that one employee can't make a mistake or commit a dishonest act without someone else discovering it. That's why Walmart's inventory buyers do not approve payments to suppliers. Without this control, buyers could create their own fictitious supply company and approve unwarranted payments from Walmart to the supply company. Segregation of duties is most effective when a company assigns responsibilities for related activities to two or more people, and assigns responsibilities for recordkeeping to people who do not handle the assets for which they are accounting. One employee should not initiate, approve, record, and have access to the items involved in the same transaction.

> **YOU SHOULD KNOW**
>
> **Segregation of duties:** An internal control designed into the accounting system to prevent an employee from making a mistake or committing a dishonest act as part of one assigned duty, and then also covering it up through another assigned duty.

③ **Restrict access.** Some controls involve rather obvious steps such as physically locking up valuable assets and electronically securing access to other assets and information. Walmart restricts access to check-signing equipment, requires a password to open cash registers, and protects computer systems with firewalls. The company provides access to important assets and valuable information on an as-needed basis. If employees do not need assets or information to fulfill their assigned responsibilities, they are denied access.

④ **Document procedures.** Digital and paper documents are such common features of business that you may not realize they represent an internal control. By documenting each business activity, a company creates a record of whether goods were shipped, customers were billed, cash was received, and so on. Without these documents, a company wouldn't know what transactions have been or need to be entered into the accounting system. To enhance this control, most companies assign sequential numbers to their documents and then check at the end of every accounting period that each document number corresponds to one and only one accounting entry. Walmart's computer system automatically assigns sequential numbers to cash sales so that the accounting staff can ensure that every sale has been recorded.

⑤ **Independently verify.** A business can perform independent verification in various ways. The most obvious is to hire someone (an auditor) to check that the work done by others within the company is appropriate and supported by documentation. Independent verification also can be made part of a person's job. For example, before Walmart issues a check to pay the bill for a truckload of merchandise, a clerk first verifies that the bill relates to goods actually received and is calculated correctly. A third form of independent verification involves comparing the company's accounting information to information kept by an independent third party. For example, the company may compare internal cash records to a statement of account issued by the bank. The next section of this chapter demonstrates this procedure, called a bank reconciliation.

Control Limitations

Internal controls can never completely prevent and detect errors and fraud for two reasons. First, an organization will implement internal controls only to the extent that their benefits exceed their costs. Walmart could nearly eliminate shoplifting by body searching every customer who leaves the store, but such an irritating policy would soon drive customers away. The cost of the lost sales would far exceed the benefits of reduced shoplifting. For smaller companies, the cost of hiring additional employees to fully segregate duties exceeds the benefits. In these cases, other controls such as independent verification by top management must compensate for the lack of segregation of duties. A second limitation is that internal controls can fail as a result of human error or fraud. People do make simple mistakes in performing control procedures, especially if they are tired, careless, or confused. Criminally minded employees have been known to **override** (disarm) internal controls or **collude** (work together) to get around them.

SPOTLIGHT ON Controls

Is That a Control, Too?

The five principles covered in this section do not represent all possible forms of internal control. Many other policies and procedures exist, some of which contribute in subtle ways to internal control. For example, most businesses establish a **mandatory vacation** policy for employees who handle cash because it is difficult for them to cover prior thefts while they are away from the business. Another simple control is an **anonymous hotline** that allows anyone to tip off independent auditors about suspected fraud. The Association of Certified Fraud Examiners claims that more than 40 percent of workplace fraud cases are identified in this way. A final example of a control that can limit losses from theft is **bonding** employees, which involves obtaining an insurance policy that partially reimburses the organization for losses caused by employee fraud.

Study the Accounting Methods

CONTROLLING AND REPORTING CASH

> **Learning Objective 6-3**
> Apply internal control principles to cash receipts and payments.

Internal control of cash is important to any organization for two main reasons. First, because the volume of cash transactions is enormous, any cash handling errors can quickly add up. By our estimates, Walmart received about $418 billion from customers in 2011 and paid $393 billion for inventory, wages, and other operating expenses. Second, because cash is valuable, portable, and "owned" by the person who possesses it, thieves often target it. The Association of Certified Fraud Examiners reports that 85 percent of all known asset thefts involve cash. The following discussion describes common applications of internal control principles to cash receipts and cash payments.

Cash Receipts

Businesses can receive cash in two different ways. They can receive it in person at the time of a sale, or they can receive it from a remote source as payment on an account. Most businesses, including Walmart, receive cash either physically, in the form of dollars, coins, and checks payable to the business, or through electronic transactions involving credit cards, debit cards, and electronic funds transfers. Regardless of the way or form in which a business receives cash, **the primary internal control goal for cash receipts is to ensure that the business receives the appropriate amount of cash and safely deposits it in the bank.**

Cash Received in Person   To properly segregate duties involving cash receipts, specific responsibilities are established and usually assigned to three different employee groups, as shown in Exhibit 6.3. First, cashiers are responsible for collecting cash and issuing a receipt at the point of sale. Second, a supervisor is responsible for taking custody of the cash at the end of each cashier's shift and depositing it in the bank. Third, members of the accounting staff are responsible for ensuring that the receipts from cash sales are properly recorded in the accounting system. Segregating the duties ensures that those who handle the cash (the cashiers and supervisor) do not have access to those who record it (the accounting staff). If this segregation of duties did not exist, employees could steal the cash and cover up the theft by changing the accounting records.

As Exhibit 6.3 also shows, specific responsibilities are assigned to each employee. For example, boxes 1–3 indicate that the cashier uses the cash register and its accompanying point-of-sale accounting system to perform three important functions: (1) document the amount charged for each item sold, (2) restrict access to cash, and (3) summarize the total cash sales. In documenting each item sold (both on screen and on a paper receipt), the cash register reduces errors by allowing customers to dispute any overcharges. By restricting access, the cash register reduces the risk of cash being lost or stolen. By summarizing the total cash sales, the cash register provides an independent record of the amount of cash the cashier should have collected and passed on for deposit at the bank. The cashier uses this information when completing a cash count sheet at the end of each shift. The cash count sheet documents the amount of cash the cashier received and determines any cash short or over that occurred during the shift.

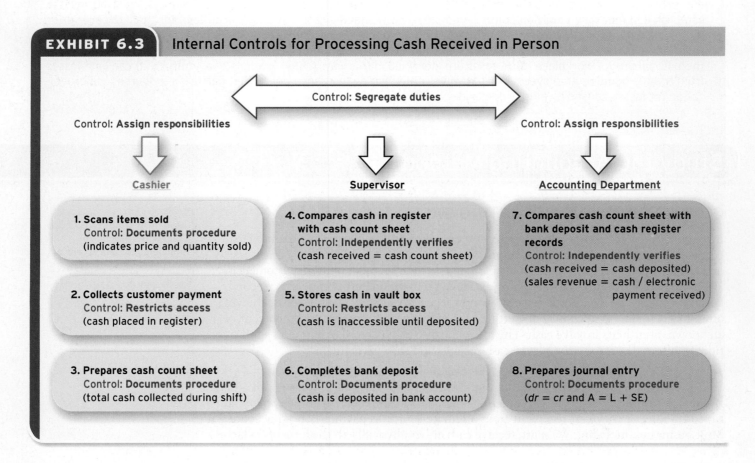

EXHIBIT 6.3   **Internal Controls for Processing Cash Received in Person**

Control: **Segregate duties**

Control: **Assign responsibilities**

Control: **Assign responsibilities**

Cashier   **Supervisor**   **Accounting Department**

1. Scans items sold
Control: **Documents procedure**
(indicates price and quantity sold)

4. Compares cash in register with cash count sheet
Control: **Independently verifies**
(cash received = cash count sheet)

7. Compares cash count sheet with bank deposit and cash register records
Control: **Independently verifies**
(cash received = cash deposited)
(sales revenue = cash / electronic payment received)

2. Collects customer payment
Control: **Restricts access**
(cash placed in register)

5. Stores cash in vault box
Control: **Restricts access**
(cash is inaccessible until deposited)

3. Prepares cash count sheet
Control: **Documents procedure**
(total cash collected during shift)

6. Completes bank deposit
Control: **Documents procedure**
(cash is deposited in bank account)

8. Prepares journal entry
Control: **Documents procedure**
($dr = cr$ and A = L + SE)

Exhibit 6.3 also shows, in boxes 4–6, that the supervisor performs important controls such as independently verifying each cashier's count sheet, a copy of which is sent to the accounting department. The supervisor is also responsible for placing the cash in a locked vault until it is taken to the bank for deposit. At that time, a deposit slip listing the amounts included in the deposit is prepared and presented to the bank for a teller to verify. After verifying and receiving the funds, the bank teller stamps the deposit slip, which is then forwarded to the company's accounting department.

The accounting department compares the record of cash sales maintained by the cash register with the count sheet prepared by the cashier and the stamped bank deposit slip returned by the bank. This comparison provides independent verification that the amount of cash rung up at the time of sale was deposited into the bank account. Based on this information, a journal entry is prepared to record Sales Revenue at the amount rung up by the cash register and Cash at the amount deposited in the bank. Any difference between the two amounts is recorded in a Cash Shortage (or Overage) account, which is reported on the income statement as a miscellaneous expense (or revenue). For example, if cashiers rung up sales totaling $6,100, but had only $6,097 to deposit, the following financial statement effects would be recorded with the journal entry that follows.

① Analyze

	Assets		=	Liabilities	+	Stockholders' Equity	
Cash		+6,097				Sales Revenue (+R)	+6,100
						Cash Shortage (+E)	−3

② Record

dr Cash (+A)	6,097	
dr Cash Shortage (+E, −SE)	3	
cr Sales Revenue (+R, +SE)		6,100

Cash Received from a Remote Source

Cash Received by Mail Businesses receive checks in the mail when customers pay on account. Because this cash is not received in the form of currency and coins, a cashier is not needed to enter these amounts into a cash register. Instead, the clerk who opens the mail performs this function. In fact, to visualize the following description, you need only glance back at Exhibit 6.3 and replace boxes 1–5 with the following duties performed by a mail clerk.

Like a cash register, the mail clerk lists all amounts received on a cash receipt list, which also includes the customers' names and the purpose of each payment. The customer typically explains the purpose of the payment using a **remittance advice,** which the customer includes with the payment. Ideally, someone supervises the clerk who opens the mail to ensure that he or she takes no cash that may have been remitted by a customer. As evidence of this supervision, both the mail clerk and the supervisor sign the completed cash receipts list. To ensure that no one diverts the checks for personal use, the clerk stamps each check "For Deposit Only," which instructs the bank to deposit the check in the company's account rather than exchange it for cash.

After these steps have been completed, the cash received is separated from the record of cash received. Checks and money orders are given to the person who prepares the bank deposit whereas the cash receipts list and remittance advices are sent to the accounting department. As in step 7 of Exhibit 6.3, the accounting department then independently verifies that all cash received by mail was deposited in the bank by ensuring that the total on the cash receipts list equals the stamped deposit slip received from the bank. The accounting department then uses the cash receipts list to record the journal entries that debit Cash and credit Accounts Receivable from each customer.

Cash Received Electronically Businesses also receive payments from customers via **electronic funds transfer (EFT).** An EFT occurs when a customer electronically transfers funds from its bank account to the company's bank account. Most businesses encourage customers to use EFTs because they speed up collections. A company may not receive mailed payments for five to seven days, but it receives EFTs immediately. And because these payments are deposited directly into the company's bank account, EFTs eliminate the need for some internal controls. To process an EFT, the accounting department merely records journal entries to debit Cash and credit each customer's account receivable.

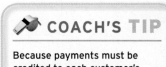

COACH'S TIP

Because payments must be credited to each customer's account, it is important that the cash receipt list include the customer's name and payment purpose.

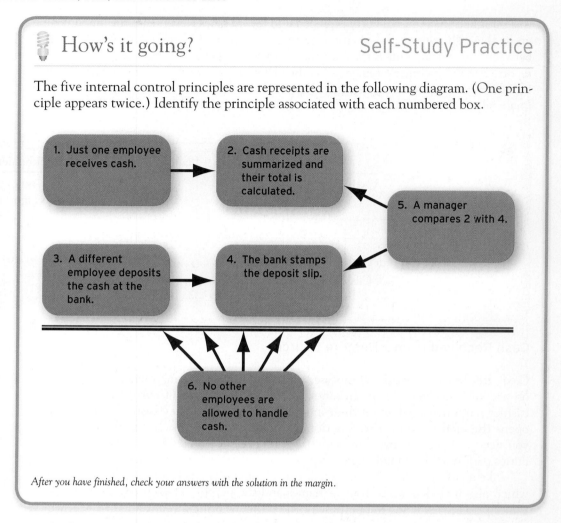

How's it going? Self-Study Practice

The five internal control principles are represented in the following diagram. (One principle appears twice.) Identify the principle associated with each numbered box.

1. Just one employee receives cash.

2. Cash receipts are summarized and their total is calculated.

5. A manager compares 2 with 4.

3. A different employee deposits the cash at the bank.

4. The bank stamps the deposit slip.

6. No other employees are allowed to handle cash.

After you have finished, check your answers with the solution in the margin.

Solution to Self-Study Practice
1. Establish responsibility
2. Document procedures
3. Segregate duties
4. Document procedures
5. Independently verify
6. Restrict access

Cash Payments

Companies rarely use dollar bills and coins to pay for purchases. Instead, most cash payments involve (1) writing a check or completing an electronic funds transfer (EFT) to a supplier, or (2) paying employees via EFT. **The primary goal of internal controls for cash payments is to ensure that the business pays only for properly authorized transactions.**

Cash Paid by Check for Purchases on Account   Businesses usually purchase goods and services on account and pay for them later by check or EFT. Most companies rely on a voucher system to control these transactions. A **voucher system** is a process for approving and documenting all purchases and payments made on account. A voucher is simply a collection of documents prepared at each step in the system. See Exhibit 6.4 for the typical steps involved in obtaining goods or services from a supplier and the documentation prepared at each step. Exhibit 6.4 also gives some examples of the related cash controls and applicable control principles. **Study this exhibit in detail,** noticing how at each step employee responsibilities are limited to specific tasks that occur only after obtaining and documenting proper authorization in the prior step. The purchasing, receiving, and bill payment duties are segregated to ensure that the company obtains and pays only for the goods or services that have been properly authorized.

Cash Paid to Employees via Electronic Funds Transfer   Most companies pay cash to their employees through EFTs, which are known by employees as **direct deposits.** The company initiates the EFT when it instructs its bank to transfer the net pay due each employee directly from the company's bank account to each employee's checking account. This system is convenient and efficient for the employer because it eliminates

EXHIBIT 6.4	Steps, Documentation, and Controls in a Voucher System

Steps	Documentation	Sample Control(s)		Control Principle
1. Request that goods or services be ordered.	Purchase requisition	Ensure that the request is made by someone who is approved to order goods or services of the type and amount requested.	1	Establish responsibility.
2. Order goods or services.	Purchase order	Place the order only with approved suppliers at approved prices.	3	Restrict access.
3. Receive goods or services.	Receiving report	Prepare a list of goods received.	4	Document procedures.
		Notify the accounting department so that the purchase and liability can be recorded.	2	Segregate duties.
4. Obtain bill for goods or services.	Supplier invoice	Ensure that the supplier charges only for items received at approved prices.	5	Independently verify.
5. Write check or initiate an EFT to pay the bill.	Company check or EFT transaction number	Use prenumbered checks and account for their sequence. Missing checks may signal theft.	4	Document procedures.
		Make payments only when a purchase is supported by complete voucher documentation.	5	Independently verify.
		Mark the voucher "paid" after it is paid to avoid duplicating the payment.	4	Document procedures.
		Notify the accounting department of the payment so that it can be recorded.	2	Segregate duties.

the tasks of physically writing and distributing the checks and for the employee who has access to the funds without having to deposit a check. One risk, however, is that the bank might accidentally overpay or underpay an employee by transferring the wrong amount of money out of the company's bank account.

To avoid this risk, many companies use an imprest system for paying employees. An **imprest system** restricts the total amount paid to others by limiting the amount of money available to be transferred. Using an imprest payroll system, the company instructs the bank to transfer the total net pay of all employees for the pay period out of the company's general bank account and into a special payroll account established for that purpose. Then the bank transfers the individual amounts from the payroll account to the employees' checking accounts. If the transfers occur without error, the special payroll account equals zero after all employees have been paid. If the account is overdrawn or a balance remains, the company knows that an error has occurred.

An imprest payroll system is one example of how banking procedures can help a company control its cash. Other basic banking procedures contribute to a company's internal control, as discussed in the next section.

Bank Procedures and Reconciliation

Banks provide important services to individuals and businesses. They accept deposits, process payments to others, and provide statements that account for these and other transactions. Their services help businesses to control cash in several ways:

1. **Restricting access.** Because banks provide a secure place to deposit cash, businesses need to keep only a limited amount of cash on hand, which reduces the risk that it will be stolen or misplaced.

2. **Documenting procedures.** By processing payments made by check or EFT, banks facilitate and document business transactions.

> **YOU SHOULD KNOW**
> **Imprest system:** A process that controls the amount paid to others by limiting the total amount of money available for making payments to others.

> **Learning Objective 6-4**
> Perform the key control of reconciling cash to bank statements.

3. **Independently verifying.** Company accountants can use the statement of account prepared by the bank to double-check the accuracy of the cash records. By comparing these two sets of records and investigating any differences, they can verify that the company's records are accurate or identify necessary adjustments.

The process of comparing two sets of records is called reconciling. Thus, the internal accounting report that compares the company's cash records with the bank's is a **bank reconciliation.** A bank reconciliation is a key internal control because it provides independent verification of all cash transactions that the bank has processed for the company. This procedure is done monthly, ideally by a company employee whose duties are segregated from recording and handling cash. You should prepare a bank reconciliation in your own life too, every month. To prepare a bank reconciliation, you must first understand the items on a bank statement.

YOU SHOULD KNOW

Bank reconciliation: An internal report prepared to verify the accuracy of both the bank statement and the cash accounts of a business or individual.

Bank Statement   Large businesses such as Walmart can have many bank accounts. For each account a business opens, the bank generates a statement that it makes available online. The format varies from bank to bank, but the statement in Exhibit 6.5 is typical. This statement, prepared by Texas Commerce Bank for one of the accounts opened by Wonderful Merchandise and Things (WMT), provides an overall summary of the activity in the account (labeled ① in Exhibit 6.5). The summary is followed by a list of specific transactions posted to the account (labeled ② through ④) and a running balance in the account (labeled ⑤). In the following section, we explain the transactions that caused changes in the account's balance.

Checks Cleared   After a check is written, the payee (to whom the check is written) usually presents the check to a financial institution for deposit or cash. That financial institution contacts the check writer's bank, which in turn withdraws the amount of the

---

EXHIBIT 6.5   Sample Bank Statement

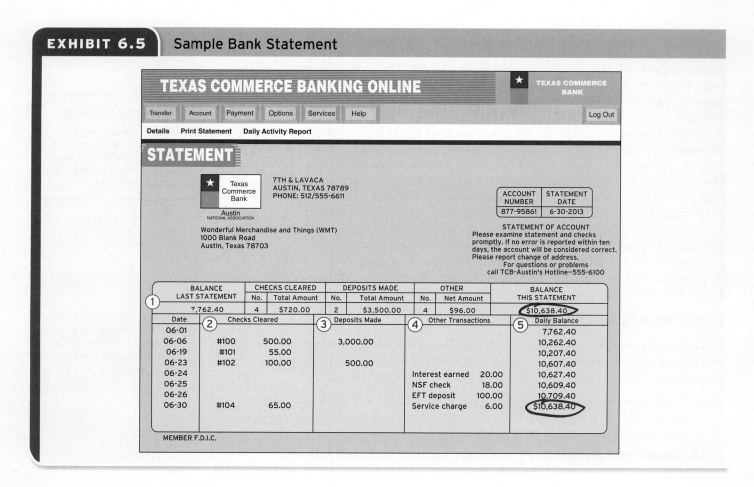

check from the check writer's account and reports it as a deduction on the bank statement. The check is then said to have **cleared the bank.**

Checks are listed on the bank statement in the order in which they clear the bank. Look closely at column ② in Exhibit 6.5 and you will see that four checks cleared the bank in June. Because WMT's checks are used in their prenumbered order, the bank statement provides a hint that check 103 did not clear the bank this month. (This fact will be important later when we prepare the bank reconciliation.)

Deposits Made   Deposits are listed on the bank statement in the order in which the bank processes them. If you make a deposit after the bank closes (using an ATM or a night deposit chute), it will not appear on the bank statement until the bank processes it the following business day. Knowing this detail will help you to prepare the bank reconciliation.

Other Transactions   The balance in a bank account can change for a variety of reasons other than checks and deposits. For example, the account balance increases when the account earns interest and when funds are transferred into the account electronically. The account balance decreases when the bank charges a service fee or transfers funds out of the account electronically.

To understand how these items are reported on a bank statement, it is important to realize that **the bank statement is presented from the bank's point of view.** The amounts in a company's bank account are liabilities to the bank because they will eventually be used by or returned to the account holder. As with all liabilities, increases are reported as credits on the bank statement. Amounts that are removed from a bank account reduce the bank's liability, so they are reported as debits on the bank statement. Banks typically explain the reasons for these increases (credits) and decreases (debits) with symbols or in a short memo, appropriately called a credit memo or debit memo.

COACH'S TIP

Bank statements often refer to checks as debits and deposits as credits. This apparent reversal of debit and credit rules occurs because the bank reports from its perspective, not yours. To the bank, your account is a liability that decreases when you take money out (debit the liability) and increases when you deposit money (credit the liability).

Need for Reconciliation   A bank reconciliation involves comparing the company's records to the bank's statement of account to determine whether they agree. The company's records can differ from the bank's records for two basic reasons: (1) the company has recorded some items that the bank doesn't know about at the time it prepares the statement of account or (2) the bank has recorded some items that the company doesn't know about until the bank statement is examined. Exhibit 6.6 lists specific causes of these differences, which we discuss below.

EXHIBIT 6.6	**Reconciling Differences**

Your Bank May Not Know About	You May Not Know About

1. Errors made by the bank
2. Time lags
  a. Deposits that you made recently
  b. Checks that you wrote recently
	3. Interest the bank has put into your account
	4. Electronic funds transfers (EFTs)
	5. Service charges taken out of your account
	6. Customer checks you deposited but that bounced
	7. Errors made by you

COACH'S TIP

You'll need to adjust your cash records only for items that appear on the right-hand side of this table.

1. **Bank errors.** Bank errors happen in real life, just as they do in Monopoly. If you discover a bank error, you should ask the bank to correct its records, but you should not change yours.

2. **Time lags.** Time lags are common. A time lag occurs, for example, when you make a deposit after the bank's normal business hours. You know you made the deposit, but your bank does not know until it processes the deposit the next day. Time lags involving deposits are called **deposits in transit.** Another common time lag is an **outstanding check.** This lag occurs when you write and mail a

check to a company, but your bank doesn't find out about it until that company deposits the check in its own bank, which then notifies your bank. As you will see later, although deposits in transit and outstanding checks may be a significant part of a bank reconciliation, they do not require any further action on your part because you have already recorded them.

3. **Interest deposited.** You may know that your bank pays interest, but you probably do not know exactly how much interest you'll get because it varies depending on the average balance in your account. When you read your bank statement, you'll learn how much interest to add to your records.

4. **Electronic funds transfer (EFT).** It doesn't happen every day, but occasionally funds may be transferred into or out of your account without your knowing about it. If you discover these electronic transfers on your bank statement, you will need to adjust your records.

5. **Service charges.** These are the amounts the bank charges for processing your transactions. Rather than send you a bill and wait for you to pay it, the bank just takes the amount directly out of your account. You will need to reduce the Cash balance in your accounting records for these charges.

6. **NSF checks.** Checks that were deposited in the bank but were later rejected ("bounced") because of insufficient funds in the check writer's account are referred to as **NSF (not sufficient funds) checks.** Because the bank increased your account when the check was deposited, the bank decreases your account when it discovers that the deposit was not valid. You will need to reduce your Cash balance by the amount of these bounced checks (and any additional bank charges), and you will have to try to collect these amounts from the check writer.

7. **Your errors.** You may have made mistakes or forgotten to record some amounts in your checkbook. If so, you will need to adjust your records for these items.

Bank Reconciliation The ending cash balance as shown on the bank statement does not usually agree with the ending cash balance shown by the related Cash account on the books of the company. For example, the Cash account of WMT at the end of June might contain the information shown in the following T-account.

dr +		Cash (A)		cr −
June 1 balance	7,762.40			
June 6 deposit	3,000.00	500.00	Check # 100 written June 4	
June 23 deposit	500.00	55.00	Check # 101 written June 17	
June 30 deposit	1,800.00	100.00	Check # 102 written June 20	
		145.00	Check # 103 written June 24	
		56.00	Check # 104 written June 30	
		815.00	Check # 105 written June 30	
Ending balance	11,391.40			

Notice that WMT's ending cash balance of $11,391.40 differs from the $10,638.40 ending cash balance shown on the bank statement in Exhibit 6.5 (page 258). To determine the appropriate cash balance, these balances need to be reconciled.

Exhibit 6.7 shows the bank reconciliation prepared by WMT for the month of June. The completed reconciliation finds that the up-to-date cash balance is $11,478.40, an amount that differs from both the bank's statement and WMT's accounting records. This balance is the amount that WMT will report as Cash on its balance sheet after adjusting its records with the journal entries that we present later.

| EXHIBIT 6.7 | Sample Bank Reconciliation |

WMT BANK RECONCILIATION
At June 30, 2013

UPDATES TO BANK STATEMENT			UPDATES TO COMPANY'S BOOKS	
Ending cash balance per bank statement		$10,638.40	Ending cash balance per books	$11,391.40
Additions			Additions	
(1) Deposit in transit		1,800.00	(3a) Interest received from the bank	20.00
		12,438.40	(3b) EFT received from customer	100.00
				11,511.40
Deductions				
(2) Outstanding checks:			Deductions	
# 103	145.00		(3c) NSF check of R. Smith	18.00
# 105	815.00	960.00	(3d) Bank service charges	6.00
Up-to-date ending cash balance		$11,478.40	(3e) Error in recording check no. 104	9.00
			Up-to-date ending cash balance	$11,478.40

To prepare the bank reconciliation in Exhibit 6.7, WMT compared the entries in its Cash account to the bank statement (Exhibit 6.5) with the following goals:

1. **Identify the deposits in transit.** A comparison of WMT's recorded deposits with those listed on the bank statement revealed that WMT made a deposit of $1,800 on June 30 that was not listed on the bank statement. More than likely, the bank will process this deposit the next business day (July 1). WMT doesn't have to change its records for this item because it already was recorded in WMT's books on June 30. It is simply a timing difference so WMT entered the amount on the bank reconciliation as an addition to update the bank's records.

2. **Identify the outstanding checks.** A comparison of the checks listed on the bank statement with the company's record of written checks showed checks numbered 103 and 105 were still outstanding at the end of June (that is, they had not cleared the bank). They were entered on the reconciliation (in Exhibit 6.7) as a deduction from the bank account because the bank will eventually reduce the account balance when these checks clear the bank. (WMT had already deducted Checks 103 and 105 from its cash records.)

3. **Record other transactions on the bank statement and correct your errors.**
   a. **Interest received** from the bank, $20—entered on the bank reconciliation in Exhibit 6.7 as an addition to the book balance because it's included in the bank balance but not yet in the company's books.
   b. **Electronic funds transfer** received from customer, $100—entered on the bank reconciliation as an addition to the book balance because it's included in the bank balance but not yet in the company's books.
   c. **NSF check** rejected, $18—entered on the bank reconciliation as a deduction from the book balance because it was deducted from the bank statement balance but has not yet been deducted from the company's cash records.
   d. **Service charges,** $6—entered on the bank reconciliation as a deduction from the book balance because it has been deducted from the bank balance but not yet removed from the Cash account in the company's books.
   e. **Your company errors,** $9—after accounting for the items listed above, WMT found that the reconciliation was out of balance by $9. Upon checking the journal entries made during the month, WMT found that Check 104 was recorded in the company's accounts as $56 when, in fact, the check had been

COACH'S TIP

This example involves the company's error in recording the amount of the check. In other cases, the bank errs if it processes the check at the wrong amount. In all instances, the amount written on the check is the correct amount at which the transaction should be recorded.

filled out for $65 (in payment of Accounts Payable). As Exhibit 6.5 shows (on page 258), the bank correctly processed the check (on June 30) as $65. To correct its own error, WMT must deduct $9 ($65 − $56) from the Company's Books side of the bank reconciliation.

Now that we know the up-to-date cash balance is $11,478.40, we need to prepare and record journal entries that will bring the Cash account to that balance. Remember that the entries on the Bank Statement side of the bank reconciliation do not need to be adjusted by WMT because they will work out automatically when the bank processes them next month. **Only the items on the Company's Books side of the bank reconciliation need to be recorded in the company's records,** using the following journal entries:

Interest Received:

(a)	dr Cash (+A)	....	20	
	cr Interest Revenue (+R, +SE)	....		20

To record interest received from the bank.

EFT Received from Customer:

(b)	dr Cash (+A)	....	100	
	cr Accounts Receivable (−A)	....		100

To record electronic funds transfer received from customer.

Customer's Check Rejected as NSF:

(c)	dr Accounts Receivable (+A)	....	18	
	cr Cash (−A)	....		18

To record amount rejected by bank and still owed by customer.

Service Charges:

(d)	dr Office Expenses (+E, −SE)	....	6	
	cr Cash (−A)	....		6

To record service charge deducted by bank.

Company Error (Understated Payment to Supplier):

(e)	dr Accounts Payable (−L)	....	9	
	cr Cash (−A)	....		9

To correct error made in recording a check paid to a creditor.

 How's it going?   Self-Study Practice

Indicate which of the following items discovered when preparing a bank reconciliation for Target will need to be recorded in the Cash account on the company's books.

1. Outstanding checks.

2. Deposits in transit.

3. Bank service charges.

4. NSF checks that were deposited.

After you have finished, check your answers with the solution in the margin.

Reporting Cash and Cash Equivalents The account called Cash on the balance sheet includes **cash** deposited with banks as well as cash on hand (also called petty cash) and cash equivalents. **Cash equivalents** are short-term, highly liquid investments purchased within three months of maturity. They are considered equivalent to cash because they are both readily convertible to known amounts of cash and so near to maturity that there is little risk their value will change. In your personal life, cash equivalents could include certificates of deposit (CDs) you've purchased within three months of maturity.

> **YOU SHOULD KNOW**
>
> **Cash:** Money or any instrument that banks will accept for deposit and immediate credit to a company's account. **Cash equivalents:** Short-term, highly liquid investments purchased within three months of maturity.

SPOTLIGHT ON Controls

www.mhhe.com/phillips4e

Granny Does Time

Grandmothers seem so trustworthy. But in one well-known case, a granny stole nearly half a million dollars from the small company where she worked as a bookkeeper. How did she do it? It was easy because the owner knew little accounting, so he gave her responsibility for all of the company's accounting work but never independently verified her work. Granny realized this lack of internal control gave her unlimited opportunity, so she wrote checks to herself and recorded them as inventory purchases. Then, when she did the bank reconciliation, she destroyed the checks to cover her tracks. Granny kept this fraud going for eight years, but then confessed after becoming overwhelmed with guilt. If you're wondering why no one ever became suspicious about the recorded inventory purchases that didn't actually occur, keep reading. The next section will tell you why.

CONTROLLING AND REPORTING MERCHANDISE SALES

The success of all merchandisers depends on their ability to sell large quantities of merchandise at prices that exceed their cost. Knowing this, merchandisers carefully track their inventory transactions and provide information on:

> **Learning Objective 6-5**
> Explain the use of a perpetual inventory system as a control.

1. Inventory quantities, so that managers can control inventory levels.
2. Inventory costs, so that managers can set appropriate selling prices.
3. Sales and related costs, so that financial statements can be prepared and used to evaluate the amount of profit generated from merchandise sales in the current period. Until inventory is sold, it is an asset reported at its cost on the balance sheet. After inventory is sold, its cost is removed from the balance sheet and reported on the income statement as an expense, called Cost of Goods Sold. The difference between the selling price (reported as Sales Revenue) and the Cost of Goods Sold is the gross profit earned by the merchandiser.

To perform these functions, companies can use either of two types of inventory accounting systems: perpetual or periodic.

Perpetual Inventory System

A **perpetual inventory system** updates inventory records every time an item is bought, sold, or returned. You may not realize it, but the bar-code readers at Walmart's checkouts serve two purposes: (1) they calculate and record the sales revenue for each product you're buying, and (2) they remove the product and its cost from Walmart's inventory records. Similar scanners are used back in the "employees only" part of the store, where products are unloaded from the trucks or returned to suppliers. As a result of this continuous, or "perpetual," updating, the balances in Walmart's Inventory and Cost of Goods Sold accounts are always up to date.

> **YOU SHOULD KNOW**
>
> **Perpetual inventory system:** Inventory records are updated "perpetually," every time inventory is bought, sold, or returned.

Periodic Inventory System

Unlike a perpetual system, which updates the inventory records immediately after each purchase, sale, and return of merchandise, a **periodic inventory system** updates the inventory records only at the end of the accounting period. Although simple to maintain, a major drawback of a periodic system is that accurate records of the inventory on hand and the inventory that has been sold are unavailable. To determine these amounts, employees must physically count the inventory, which they do at the end of the period, when the store is "closed for inventory." This inventory count is then used to adjust the balances for Inventory and Cost of Goods Sold.

Inventory Control

A perpetual inventory system provides the best inventory control because its continuous tracking of transactions allows companies to instantly determine the quantity of products on the shelves and to evaluate the amount of time they have spent there. Using this information, companies can better manage their inventory and save a great deal of money in financing and storage charges. Another benefit of a perpetual inventory system is that it allows managers to estimate **shrinkage,** the term for loss of inventory from theft, fraud, and error. You might wonder how companies can estimate how much of their inventory is missing, because isn't it, by definition, *missing?* They use the information in the perpetual inventory system and their understanding of the following inventory equation. Assume Walmart reports the following for one of its lines of cell phones.

Equation	Information in the company's perpetual records						Physical inventory count
	Quantity		Cost per Unit		Total Cost		
Beginning Inventory	3	×	$100	=	$300		
+ Purchases	3	×	$100	=	300		
− Goods Sold	(2)	×	$100	=	(200)	vs.	
= Ending Inventory	4	×	$100	=	$400		

Because a perpetual inventory system records all goods purchased and sold, the ending inventory in the company's perpetual records indicates how many units should be on hand. In our example, four units should be on hand at a unit cost of $100, for a total cost of $400. By physically counting the inventory that is actually on hand, the company can determine whether items have been physically removed without being recorded as an approved transaction. Calculate shrinkage by subtracting the cost of inventory counted from that recorded in the perpetual inventory system. In our example, just three units were on hand, so the shrinkage was one unit, with a cost of $100.

You can't do this kind of detective work with a periodic inventory system because it doesn't provide an up-to-date record of the inventory that should be on hand when you count it. Also, even if you're using a perpetual inventory system, you still need to count the inventory occasionally (at least yearly) to ensure the accounting records are accurate and any shrinkage is detected. If you don't do this physical count, you could end up like the company in the Spotlight on Controls on page 263. The grandmother was able to falsely record payments to herself as if they were inventory purchases because no one checked to see whether the recorded inventory actually existed.

Until recently, perpetual inventory systems were too costly for most merchandisers to implement. Today, however, computerized inventory systems have become so cheap that most merchandisers use a perpetual system. Accordingly, this chapter focuses on the accounting process that perpetual systems use. Because you may still encounter a periodic system, particularly in small companies, we discuss the accounting process for periodic systems in Chapter 7.

Sources of Inventory Shrinkage

Independent verification of inventory quantities is important. A recent study suggests that more than $37 billion of inventory goes missing from U.S. retailers each year.* Although shoplifting is a major cause of shrinkage (accounting for 33 percent of lost units), an even larger portion (44 percent) results from employee theft. To avoid hiring dishonest employees, companies screen job applicants using employment and criminal background checks. To deter and detect employee theft, they use security tags, surveillance cameras, and complex computer programs that monitor cash registers.

*Richard Hollinger, "2010 National Retail Security Survey," University of Florida, 2011.

Sales of Merchandise Inventory

As required by the revenue recognition principle, merchandisers record revenue when it is earned. Merchandisers earn revenues by making a "sale," which means transferring ownership of merchandise to a customer, either for cash or on credit. For a retail merchandiser like Walmart, this transfer of ownership occurs when a customer buys and takes possession of the goods at checkout. For a wholesale merchandiser that ships goods to a customer, the transfer of ownership occurs at a time stated in the written sales agreement. The sales agreement will specify one of two possible times:

1. **FOB shipping point**—the sale is recorded when the goods leave the seller's shipping department.
2. **FOB destination**—the sale is recorded when the goods reach their destination (the customer).

Unless otherwise indicated, the examples in this book assume that ownership transfers when goods are shipped (FOB shipping point), which usually means the buyer pays for all transportation costs.[1]

Every merchandise sale has two components, each of which requires an entry in a perpetual inventory system:

1. **Selling price.** Walmart's *sales price* is recorded as an increase in Sales Revenue and a corresponding increase in either Cash (for a cash sale) or Accounts Receivable (for a credit sale).
2. **Cost.** The *cost* that Walmart incurred to initially buy the merchandise is removed from Inventory and reported as an expense called Cost of Goods Sold (CGS).

For example, assume Walmart sells two Schwinn mountain bikes at a selling price of $200 per bike, for a total of $400 cash. The bikes had previously been recorded in Walmart's Inventory at a total cost of $350. This transaction is illustrated, analyzed, and recorded in Exhibit 6.8.

Notice in Exhibit 6.8 that the first part of Walmart's journal entry involving Cash and Sales Revenue is recorded at the total selling price ($400). The second part involving Cost of Goods Sold and Inventory uses Walmart's total cost ($350). The $50 difference between selling price and cost ($400 − $350) is called the *gross profit*. **Gross profit is not directly recorded in an account by itself,** but instead is

Learning Objective 6-6
Analyze sales transactions under a perpetual inventory system.

YOU SHOULD KNOW

FOB shipping point: A term of sale indicating that goods are owned by the customer the moment they leave the seller's premises. **FOB destination:** A term of sale indicating that goods are owned by the seller until they are delivered to the customer.

---

[1]Any transportation costs paid by the seller (called freight-out) are reported as Delivery Expenses on the seller's income statement. Chapter 7 discusses buyers' accounting for transportation costs.

EXHIBIT 6.8   Sale of Merchandise in a Perpetual System

a subtotal produced by subtracting Cost of Goods Sold from Sales Revenue on the income statement.

To keep things simple, we use only one Sales Revenue account and one Cost of Goods Sold account for our examples. In the workplace, however, merchandising companies use different Sales and Cost of Goods Sold accounts for different product lines. This allows managers at Walmart to separately evaluate sales of different products. When reporting to external financial statement users, Walmart combines these individual accounts into a single number for Sales and a single number for Cost of Goods Sold, which avoids cluttering its income statement with numerous accounts and also prevents its competitors from discovering details about its sales of specific products.

Sales Returns and Allowances

When goods sold to a customer arrive in damaged condition or are otherwise unsatisfactory, the customer can (1) return them for a full refund or (2) keep them and ask for a reduction in the selling price, called an *allowance*. These **sales returns and allowances** require Walmart to revise the previously recorded sale and, in the case of returns, to revise the previously recorded inventory reduction and cost of goods sold. To illustrate this, suppose that after Walmart sold the two Schwinn mountain bikes, the customer returned one to Walmart. Assuming that the bike is still like new, Walmart would refund the $200 selling price to the customer and take the bike back into inventory.

To account for this transaction, Walmart would make two entries to basically reverse the entries recorded when the bike was sold. We say "basically" because there is one catch: Walmart does not directly reduce its Sales Revenue account. Instead, Walmart tracks sales returns and allowances in a contra-revenue account that is deducted from total sales revenue.

COACH'S TIP

To indicate that an increase in a contra-revenue account reduces revenues, which reduces stockholders' equity, use (+xR, −SE).

Just as a contra-asset account such as Accumulated Depreciation reduces the total in an asset account such as Equipment, a contra-revenue account such as Sales Returns and Allowances reduces the total in a revenue account such as Sales Revenues. **Using a contra-revenue account instead of directly reducing the Sales account allows Walmart to track the value of goods returned,** providing clues about whether customers are happy with the quality and price of Walmart's products.[2] Sales returns are recorded as follows:

① Analyze

	Assets		=	Liabilities	+	Stockholders' Equity	
Cash	−200	=				Sales Returns & Allowances (+xR)	−200
Inventory	+175	=				Cost of Goods Sold (−E)	+175

② Record

dr Sales Returns & Allowances (+xR, −SE)	200	
cr Cash (−A)..		200
dr Inventory (+A)	175	
cr Cost of Goods Sold (−E +SE)........................		175

Sales on Account and Sales Discounts

To encourage customers to promptly pay for sales made on credit, a merchandiser often specifies payment terms such as "2/10, n/30." The "2/10" means that if the customer pays by the 10th day after the sale date, a 2 percent **sales discount** will be deducted from the selling price. The "n/30" part implies that if payment is not made within the 10-day discount period, the full amount will be due 30 days after the date of sale. See Exhibit 6.9 for an illustration of a 2/10, n/30 sale that occurred on November 1.

When a sales discount is offered to and later taken by the customer, the seller accounts for two transactions: (1) the initial sale, and (2) the sales discount taken by the customer. Suppose Walmart's warehouse store (Sam's Club) sells printer paper on

> **YOU SHOULD KNOW**
>
> **Sales discount:** A sales price reduction given to customers for prompt payment of their account balance.

EXHIBIT 6.9 Interpreting Credit Terms

Discount percentage offered

Number of days in discount period

"Net" sale (after returns and allowances)

Maximum credit period

2/10, n/30

2% discount period

November 1	November 11	November 30
Date of sale	End of discount period	End of credit period

---

[2]We have assumed that the return occurs in the same period as the sale. When significant returns are likely to occur after the period of sale, the seller records an estimate of those expected returns, using methods described in Chapter 8. We also have assumed the returned bike was as good as new. Chapter 7 describes how to account for damaged inventory.

account to a local business for $1,000 with payment terms of 2/10, n/30. The paper had cost Sam's Club $700. Walmart accounts for this initial sale as follows:

1 Analyze

Assets	=	Liabilities	+	Stockholders' Equity	
Accounts Receivable +1,000				Sales Revenue (+R)	+1,000
Inventory −700				Cost of Goods Sold (+E)	−700

2 Record

dr Accounts Receivable (+A)...	1,000	
cr Sales Revenue (+R, +SE)...		1,000
dr Cost of Goods Sold (+E, −SE)..	700	
cr Inventory (−A)		700

To take advantage of the 2 percent discount, the customer must pay Walmart within 10 days. If the customer does so, it will deduct the $20 discount (2% × $1,000) from the total owed ($1,000), and then pay $980 to Walmart. Walmart accounts for the $20 sales discount using a contra-revenue account, as follows:

1 Analyze

Assets	=	Liabilities	+	Stockholders' Equity	
Cash + 980				Sales Discounts (+xR)	−20
Accounts Receivable −1,000					

2 Record

dr Cash (+A)	980	
dr Sales Discounts (+xR, −SE)	20	
cr Accounts Receivable (−A)...		1,000

COACH'S TIP

Sales discounts are calculated after taking into account any sales returns and allowances. Customers that pay a portion of what they owe are entitled to a discount on that portion if they pay within the discount period.

If the customer doesn't pay by the end of the discount period, Walmart would not allow the customer to take a discount for early payment. Instead, the customer would have to pay the full $1,000, which Walmart would record as an increase in Cash (debit) and a decrease in Accounts Receivable (credit). What if a customer doesn't pay at all? We discuss that important issue in detail in Chapter 8.

Before leaving the topic of sales discounts, we should clear up a common misconception. Sales discounts differ from the "discount" that you get as a consumer buying clearance items at a reduced selling price. Reductions in the selling price of merchandise that occur before a sale is made—what Walmart calls "rolling back" prices—are not captured in the accounting system because they are not transactions. To be considered a transaction, a sales discount must occur after the initial sale has been made. These types of sales discounts are given in business-to-business (B2B) transactions for prompt payment on account. We're sorry to say that, as a consumer, you're not likely to be offered this kind of discount.

Summary of Sales-Related Transactions

The sales returns and allowances and sales discounts introduced in this section were recorded using contra-revenue accounts. Exhibit 6.10 summarizes how they are reported on the income statement. See the Homework Helper on page 276 for further illustration.

EXHIBIT 6.10	Reporting Effects of Sales-Related Transactions

Sales Revenue	$1,400	**Selling price** of 2 bikes ($400) + paper ($1,000)
Less: Sales Returns and Allowances	(200)	**Selling price** of returned bike ($200)
Sales Discounts	(20)	**Selling price** of paper ($1,000) × 2% (discount)
Net Sales	1,180	$1,400 − 200 − 20 = 1,180
Cost of Goods Sold	875	**Cost** of 2 bikes ($350) − returned bike ($175) + paper ($700)
Gross Profit	305	$1,180 − 875 = 305

SPOTLIGHT ON Financial Reporting

The Makeup of Net Sales

The internal control of **documenting** sales discounts, returns, and allowances in contra-revenue accounts allows managers to monitor and control how these items affect the company's revenues. For example, frequent returns of defective products would show up as an increase in the Sales Returns and Allowances account. In response to an increase in this account, Walmart's managers might decide to discontinue the product or find a new supplier.

Details relating to sales discounts and returns are key to a merchandiser's business operations. To avoid revealing these secrets to competitors, most companies report these contra-accounts only in financial statements prepared for internal use, as in Exhibit 6.10. Externally reported income statements usually begin with **Net Sales,** as in Exhibit 6.11.

Evaluate the Results

GROSS PROFIT ANALYSIS

To survive, a merchandiser must sell goods for more than their cost. Sure, cash has to be controlled, but there won't be much cash to control unless goods are sold at a profit. That's the only way companies like Walmart can generate enough money to cover operating expenses. To show how much profit is earned from product sales, without being clouded by other operating costs, merchandise companies often present their income statement using a multistep format.

A **multistep income statement** is similar to what you saw in the first few chapters, with expenses being subtracted from revenues to arrive at net income. The difference is that a multistep format separates the revenues and expenses that relate to core operations from all the other (peripheral) items that affect net income. For merchandisers, a key measure is the amount of profit earned over the cost of goods sold, so their multistep income statements separate Cost of Goods Sold from other expenses. As shown in Exhibits 6.10 and 6.11, this extra step produces a subtotal called **gross profit,** which is the profit the company earned from selling goods, over and above the cost of the goods. If you buy something for $70 and sell it for $100, you'll have a gross profit of $30.

Notice in Exhibit 6.11 that after the gross profit line, the multistep income statement presents other items in a format similar to what you saw for a service company in Chapter 3 (Exhibit 3.2). The category called *Selling, General, and Administrative Expenses* includes a variety of operating expenses such as wages, utilities, advertising, rent, and the costs of delivering merchandise to customers. These expenses are subtracted from gross profit to yield Income from Operations, which is a measure of the company's income from regular operating activities, before considering the effects of interest, income taxes, and any nonrecurring items.

> **Learning Objective 6-7**
> Analyze a merchandiser's multistep income statement.

> **YOU SHOULD KNOW**
>
> **Multistep income statement:** Presents important subtotals, such as gross profit, to help distinguish core operating results from other, less significant items that affect net income.
>
> **Gross profit** (also called *gross margin* or simply *margin*): Net sales minus cost of goods sold. It is a subtotal, not an account.

| EXHIBIT 6.11 | Sample Multistep Income Statement | Walmart |

WALMART STORES, INC.
Income Statements
For the Years Ended January 31
(amounts in millions)

	2009	2010	2011
Net Sales	$401,087	$405,132	$418,952
Cost of Goods Sold	303,941	304,444	315,287
Gross Profit	97,146	100,688	103,665
Selling, General, and Administrative Expense	77,546	79,639	81,020
Income from Operations	19,600	21,049	22,645
Other Revenues	914	477	1,323
Income before Income Tax Expense	20,514	21,526	23,968
Income Tax Expense	7,133	7,156	7,579
Net Income	$ 13,381	$ 14,370	$ 16,389

Gross Profit Percentage

Let's focus again on the gross profit line on the income statement in Exhibit 6.11. Although the dollar amount of gross profit can be impressive—yes, Walmart really did generate over $103 billion of gross profit in the year ended January 31, 2011—this number is difficult to interpret by itself. In Exhibit 6.11, we see that Walmart's gross profit increased throughout the three years. The difficulty in interpreting this is that Walmart also increased its net sales over these three years, so we don't know whether the increase in gross profit dollars arises solely because Walmart increased its sales volume or whether it also is generating more profit per sale. To determine the amount of gross profit included in each dollar of sales, analysts typically evaluate the gross profit percentage.

Accounting Decision Tools		
Name of Measure	**Formula**	**What It Tells You**
Gross profit percentage	$\dfrac{\text{Net Sales} - \text{CGS}}{\text{Net Sales}} \times 100$	• The percentage of profit earned on each dollar of sales, after considering the cost of products sold • A higher ratio means that greater profit is available to cover operating and other expenses

YOU SHOULD KNOW

Gross profit percentage: A ratio indicating the percentage of profit earned on each dollar of sales, after considering the cost of products sold.

The **gross profit percentage** measures the percentage of profit earned on each dollar of sales. A higher gross profit percentage means that the company is selling products for a greater markup over its cost. This ratio can be used to (1) analyze changes in the company's operations over time, (2) compare one company to another, and (3) determine whether a company is earning enough on each sale to cover its operating expenses.

The graphic in the margin shows that Walmart's gross profit percentage decreased from 24.8 percent to 24.7 percent across the years ended January 31, 2010 and 2011. Thus, the increase in total dollars of gross profit reported in those years (from $100,688 to $103,665) could only be caused by an increase in sales volume, not an increase in gross profit per sale.

You might wonder whether it's worth talking about a mere 0.1% change in the gross profit percentage, but a small change in this ratio can lead to a big change in net income. In Walmart's case, because the company has such a huge sales volume (more than $400 billion), even just one-tenth of a percentage point decrease in gross profit translates into almost half a billion dollars of lost profit. Yes, that's billion with a b ($400 billion × 0.001 = $0.4 billion).

Comparing Operating Results across Companies, Industries, and Time

Be aware that gross profit percentages can vary greatly between companies. Walmart's gross profit percentage of 24.7 percent is characteristic of its slogan of "Saving people money so they can live better." Walmart's strategy is to earn a relatively small amount of profit on each dollar of sales, but to compensate by generating a huge volume of sales. In contrast, high-end department stores carry brand-name fashions with high-end prices, resulting in fewer sales, but more profit on each sale. In 2011, Saks reported a 40.1 percent gross profit percentage.

Gross profit percentages can vary across industries too. Oil and gas exploration companies recently reported an average gross profit percentage of 63.5 percent, which they need to cover their research and exploration expenses.[3]

As the following spotlight indicates, gross profit percentages also reveal changes in the economy over time.

WALMART'S GROSS PROFIT PERCENTAGE

Year-ended January 31,	2009	2010	2011
$\dfrac{\text{Gross Profit}}{\text{Net Sales}}$ =	$\dfrac{\$\ 97,146}{\$401,087}$	$\dfrac{\$100,688}{\$405,132}$	$\dfrac{\$103,665}{\$418,952}$
=	0.242	0.248	0.247
	× 100	× 100	× 100
=	24.2%	24.8%	24.7%

Gross Profit Percentage by Industry

Source: eStatement Studies, 2011–12.

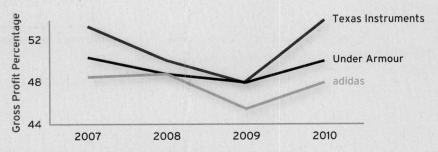

[3] Industry statistics were retrieved on December 19, 2011, from ycharts.com/sectors.

REVIEW THE CHAPTER

DEMONSTRATION CASE A: BANK RECONCILIATION

Bardash Corporation has just received its checking account statement for the month ended September 30. The bank's statement of account showed the following:

Bank balance, September 1	$1,150
Deposits during September	650
Checks cleared during September	900
Bank service charge	25
Interest earned	5
EFT received from Bardash customer	20
NSF check written by Bardash customer	(15)
Bank balance, September 30	885

The bank had not yet reported a deposit of $50 made on September 29 and a Bardash check for $200 had not cleared its account. Bardash's September 30 Cash balance was $759. The company's accountant discovered that one of Bardash's checks for $19 paid on account to a supplier had been recorded as $10.

Required:

1. Complete the September bank reconciliation. What adjustments, if any, does Bardash need to make?
2. Why is it important for individuals and businesses to prepare a bank reconciliation each month?

Suggested Solution

1. Bardash's bank reconciliation:

Updates to Bank Statement		Updates to Company's Books	
September 30 cash balance	$ 885	September 30 cash balance	$759
Additions		Additions	
Deposit in transit	50	(a) Interest earned	5
Deductions		(b) EFT from customer	20
Outstanding check	(200)	Deductions	
Up-to-date cash balance	$ 735	(c) Bank service charge	(25)
		(d) NSF check	(15)
		(e) Recording error	(9)
		Up-to-date cash balance	$735

Bardash needs to record the following reconciling entries:

(a)	dr Cash (+A)	5	
	cr Interest Revenue (+R, +SE)		5
(b)	dr Cash (+A)	20	
	cr Accounts Receivable (−A)		20
(c)	dr Office Expenses (+E, −SE)	25	
	cr Cash (−A)		25
(d)	dr Accounts Receivable (+A)	15	
	cr Cash (−A)		15
(e)	dr Accounts Payable (−L)	9	
	cr Cash (−A)		9

2. Bank statements, whether personal or business, should be reconciled each month to help ensure that a correct balance is reflected in the depositor's books. Failure to reconcile a bank statement increases the chance that an error will not be discovered and may result in NSF checks being written. Businesses reconcile their bank statements for an additional reason: The up-to-date balance that is calculated during reconciliation is reported on the balance sheet.

DEMONSTRATION CASE B: MERCHANDISE SALES

Assume Oakley, Inc.—the maker of sunglasses, goggles, and other products—made merchandise costing $137,200 and sold it on credit to Sunglass Hut for $405,000 with terms 2/10, n/30. Some of the merchandise differed from what Sunglass Hut had ordered, so Oakley agreed to give an allowance of $5,000. Sunglass Hut satisfied the remaining balance (of $400,000) by paying within the discount period.

Sunglass Hut

Required:

1. Assuming that Oakley uses a perpetual inventory system, analyze the accounting equation effects and record the journal entries that Oakley would use for the following transactions:

   a. Sale from Oakley to Sunglass Hut.
   b. Allowance granted by Oakley.
   c. Payment made by Sunglass Hut to Oakley.

2. Compute Oakley's net sales, assuming that sales returns and allowances and sales discounts are treated as contra-revenues.

3. Compute Oakley's gross profit and gross profit percentage on the sale. Compare this ratio to the 65.7 percent gross profit percentage earned in 2010 by the Luxottica Group—the Italian company that makes Killer Loop® and Ray-Ban® sunglasses, which are sold through its Sunglass Hut stores. What does it imply about the two companies?

> **COACH'S TIP**
>
> Note that transaction b depicts an allowance but no return of goods. Because no goods are returned, Oakley does not increase its Inventory and decrease its Cost of Goods Sold, but it does account for the allowance's effect on the selling price.

Suggested Solution

1. a. Sale from Oakley to Sunglass Hut

1 Analyze

Assets		= Liabilities +	Stockholders' Equity	
Accounts Receivable	+405,000		Sales Revenue (+R)	+405,000
Inventory	−137,200		Cost of Goods Sold (+E)	−137,200

2 Record

dr Accounts Receivable (+A)... 405,000
   cr Sales Revenue (+R, +SE)... 405,000
dr Cost of Goods Sold (+E, −SE)... 137,200
   cr Inventory (−A) 137,200

b. Allowance granted by Oakley

1 Analyze

Assets		= Liabilities +	Stockholders' Equity	
Accounts Receivable	−5,000		Sales Returns and Allowances (+xR)	−5,000

2 Record

dr Sales Returns and Allowances (+xR, −SE)...................... 5,000
   cr Accounts Receivable (−A)... 5,000

c. Payment made by Sunglass Hut to Oakley

1 Analyze

Assets		= Liabilities +	Stockholders' Equity	
Cash	+392,000		Sales Discounts (+xR)	−8,000
Accounts Receivable	−400,000			

2 Record

dr **Cash** (+A)	392,000	
dr **Sales Discounts** (+xR, −SE).....................................	8,000	
cr **Accounts Receivable** (−A)...		400,000

2. Sales returns and allowances and sales discounts should be subtracted from sales revenue to compute net sales:

Sales Revenue		$405,000
Less: Sales Returns and Allowances		5,000
Sales Discounts		8,000*
Net Sales		392,000
*$8,000 = 2% × ($405,000 − $5,000)		

3. Gross profit and gross profit percentage are calculated as follows:

	In Dollars	Percent of Net Sales
Net Sales (calculated in 2.)	$392,000	100.0%
Less: Cost of Goods Sold	137,200	35.0
Gross Profit	$254,800	65.0%

The 65% gross profit percentage indicates that Oakley generates 65 cents of gross profit on each dollar of sales. This is 0.7 cents less gross profit on each dollar of sales than Luxottica (0.7 = 65.7 − 65.0). This difference implies that Luxottica is including a slightly higher markup in its selling prices than Oakley.

CHAPTER SUMMARY

LO 6-1   **Distinguish among service, merchandising, and manufacturing operations. p. 250**

- Service companies sell services rather than physical goods; consequently, their income statements show costs of services rather than cost of goods sold.

- Merchandise companies sell goods that have been obtained from a supplier. Retail merchandise companies sell directly to consumers whereas wholesale merchandise companies sell to retail companies.

- Manufacturing companies sell goods that they have made themselves.

LO 6-2   **Explain common principles and limitations of internal control. p. 251**

- The concept of internal control is broad. Most employees working within a company will encounter five basic principles: (1) establish responsibility for each task; (2) segregate duties so that one employee cannot initiate, record, approve, and handle a single transaction; (3) restrict access to those employees who have been assigned responsibility; (4) document procedures performed; and (5) independently verify work done by others inside and outside the business.

- Internal controls may be limited by cost, human error, and fraud.

Apply internal control principles to cash receipts and payments. p. 253 **LO 6-3**

- When applied to cash receipts, internal control principles require that (1) cashiers be held individually responsible for the cash they receive, (2) different individuals be assigned to receive, maintain custody of, and record cash, (3) cash be stored in a locked safe until it has been securely deposited in a bank, (4) cash register receipts, cash count sheets, daily cash summary reports, and bank deposit slips be prepared to document the cash received and deposited, and (5) cash register receipts be matched to cash counts and deposit slips, to independently verify that all cash was received and deposited.

- When applied to cash payments, internal control principles require that (1) only certain individuals or departments initiate purchase requests, (2) different individuals be assigned to order, receive, and pay for purchases, (3) access to checks and valuable property be restricted, (4) purchase requisitions, purchase orders, receiving reports, and pre-numbered checks be used to document the work done, and (5) each step in the payment process occurs only after the preceding step has been independently verified using the documents listed in (4).

Perform the key control of reconciling cash to bank statements. p. 257 **LO 6-4**

- The bank reconciliation requires determining two categories of items: (1) those that have been recorded in the company's books but not in the bank's statement of account, and (2) those that have been reported in the bank's statement of account but not in the company's books. The second category of items provides the data needed to adjust the Cash account to the balance that will be reported on the balance sheet.

Explain the use of a perpetual inventory system as a control. p. 263 **LO 6-5**

- Perpetual inventory systems protect against undetected theft because they provide an up-to-date record of inventory that should be on hand at any given time, which can be compared to a count of the physical quantity that actually is on hand.

- Perpetual inventory systems serve to promote efficient and effective operations because they are updated every time inventory is purchased, sold, or returned.

Analyze sales transactions under a perpetual inventory system. p. 265 **LO 6-6**

- In a perpetual inventory system, two entries are made every time inventory is sold: one entry records the sale (and corresponding debit to Cash or Accounts Receivable) and the other entry records the Cost of Goods Sold (and corresponding credit to Inventory).

- Sales discounts and sales returns and allowances are reported as contra-revenues, reducing net sales.

Analyze a merchandiser's multistep income statement. p. 269 **LO 6-7**

- One of the key items in a merchandiser's multistep income statement is gross profit, which is a subtotal calculated by subtracting cost of goods sold from net sales. The gross profit percentage is calculated and interpreted as follows.

Accounting Decision Tools

Name of Measure	Formula	What It Tells You
Gross profit percentage	$\dfrac{\text{Net Sales} - \text{CGS}}{\text{Net Sales}} \times 100$	• The percentage of profit earned on each dollar of sales, after considering the cost of products sold • A higher ratio means that greater profit is available to cover operating and other expenses

KEY TERMS

Bank Reconciliation p. 258

Cash p. 263

Cash Equivalents p. 263

FOB Destination p. 265

FOB Shipping Point p. 265

Gross Profit (or Gross Margin) p. 269

Gross Profit Percentage p. 270

Imprest System p. 257

Internal Controls p. 250

Manufacturing Company p. 250

Merchandising Company p. 250

Multistep Income Statement p. 269

NSF (Not Sufficient Funds) Check p. 260

Periodic Inventory System p. 264

Perpetual Inventory System p. 263

Sales Discount p. 267

Sales Returns and Allowances p. 266

Segregation of Duties p. 252

Service Company p. 250

Shrinkage p. 264

Voucher System p. 256

See complete definitions in the glossary in the back of this text.

HOMEWORK HELPER

Multistep Income Statement Format (heading omitted)

Sales Revenue	$100,000
Less: Sales Returns and Allowances	(2,500)
Sales Discounts	(1,500)
Net Sales	96,000
Cost of Goods Sold	55,000
Gross Profit	41,000
Selling, General, and Administrative Expenses	21,000
Income from Operations	20,000
Other Revenue (Expenses)	5,000
Income before Income Tax Expense	25,000
Income Tax Expense	10,000
Net Income	$ 15,000

Reported Internally / Reported Externally

Alternative terms

- Gross profit is also called gross margin or margin.

Helpful reminders

- When preparing a bank reconciliation, your goals are to determine which transactions the bank has not yet processed and which transactions your company has not yet processed. You will record transactions correctly processed by the bank but not yet processed by your company.
- Sales Returns have two components: (1) an adjustment to the selling price (record a contra-revenue and a decrease in Cash or Accounts Receivable) and (2) return of goods previously recorded as sold (record an increase in Inventory and a decrease in Cost of Goods Sold). Sales Allowances involve only the first component, because no goods are returned to the seller.

Frequent mistakes

- Discounts (or "markdowns") in the selling price of merchandise occur prior to making a sale, so they are not recorded. Sales Discounts, given to customers after making a sale, are recorded in a contra-revenue account, to offset the Sales Revenue recorded on the initial sales transaction.
- Gross profit percentage is calculated as a percentage of Net Sales, not as a percentage of Total Revenue or Cost of Goods Sold.

PRACTICE MATERIAL

QUESTIONS (⊖ Symbol indicates questions that require analysis from more than one perspective.)

1. What is the distinction between service and merchandising companies? What is the distinction between merchandising and manufacturing companies? What is the distinction between retail and wholesale merchandising companies?

2. From the perspective of a CEO or CFO, what does internal control mean?

3. What are five common internal control principles?

4. Why is it a good idea to assign each task to only one employee?

5. Why should responsibilities for certain duties, like cash handling and cash recording, be separated? What types of responsibilities should be separated?

6. What are some of the methods for restricting access?

7. In what ways does documentation act as a control?

8. In what ways can independent verification occur?

9. In what way does a mandatory vacation policy act as a control?

10. What are two limitations of internal control?

11. What is the primary internal control goal for cash receipts?

12. What internal control functions are performed by a cash register and point-of-sale system? How are these functions performed when cash is received by mail? ⊖

13. How is cash received in person independently verified?

14. What is the primary internal control goal for cash payments?

15. What are the purposes of a bank reconciliation? What balances are reconciled?

16. Define Cash and Cash Equivalents, and indicate the types of items that should be reported as cash and cash equivalents.

17. What is the main distinction between perpetual and periodic inventory systems? Which type of system provides better internal control over inventory? Explain why.

18. Why is a physical count of inventory necessary in a periodic inventory system? Why is it still necessary in a perpetual inventory system?

19. What is the difference between FOB shipping point and FOB destination? How do these terms relate to the revenue principle?

20. Describe in words the journal entries that are made in a perpetual inventory system when inventory is sold on credit.

21. What is the distinction between *Sales Returns and Sales Allowances?*

22. What is a Sales Discount? Use 1/10, n/30 in your explanation.

23. In response to the weak economy, your company's sales force is urging you, the sales manager, to change sales terms from 1/10, n/30 to 2/10, n/45. Explain what these terms mean and how this switch could increase or decrease your company's profits. ⊖

24. Explain the difference between Sales Revenue and Net Sales.

25. Why are contra-revenue accounts used rather than directly deducting from the Sales Revenue account?

26. What is gross profit? How is the gross profit percentage computed? Illustrate its calculation and interpretation assuming Net Sales is $100,000 and Cost of Goods Sold is $60,000.

MULTIPLE CHOICE

1. Mountain Gear, Inc., buys bikes, tents, and climbing supplies from Rugged Rock Corporation for sale to consumers. What type of company is Mountain Gear, Inc.?

   a. Service
   b. Retail merchandiser
   c. Wholesale merchandiser
   d. Manufacturer

2. Which of the following does not enhance internal control?

   a. Assigning different duties to different employees.
   b. Ensuring adequate documentation is maintained.
   c. Allowing access only when required to complete assigned duties.
   d. None of the above—all enhance internal control.

3. Which of the following internal control principles underlies the requirement that all customers be given a sales receipt?

   a. Segregate duties
   b. Establish responsibility
   c. Restrict access
   d. Document procedures

4. Upon review of your company's bank statement, you discover that you recently deposited a check from a customer that was rejected by your bank as NSF. Which of the following describes the actions to be taken when preparing your company's bank reconciliation?

Balance per Bank	Balance per Book
a. Decrease	No change
b. Increase	Decrease
c. No change	Decrease
d. Decrease	Increase

5. Upon review of the most recent bank statement, you discover that a check was made out to your supplier for $76 but was recorded in your Cash and Accounts Payable accounts as $67. Which of the following describes the actions to be taken when preparing your bank reconciliation?

Balance per Bank	Balance per Book
a. Decrease	No change
b. Increase	Decrease
c. No change	Decrease
d. Decrease	Increase

6. Which of the following is false regarding a perpetual inventory system?

    a. Physical counts are never needed because records are maintained on a transaction-by-transaction basis.

    b. The Inventory records are updated with each inventory purchase, sale, or return transaction.

    c. Cost of Goods Sold is increased as sales are recorded.

    d. A perpetual inventory system can be used to detect shrinkage.

7. Sales discounts with terms 2/10, n/30 mean

    a. 10 percent discount for payment received within 30 days of the date of sale.

    b. 2 percent discount for payment received within 10 days or the full amount (less returns) is due within 30 days.

    c. Two-tenths of a percent discount for payment received within 30 days.

    d. None of the above.

8. Which of the following is not a component of Net Sales?

    a. Sales Returns and Allowances

    b. Sales Discounts

    c. Cost of Goods Sold

    d. Sales Revenue

9. A $1,000 sale is made on May 1 with terms 2/10, n/30. Items with a $100 selling price are returned on May 3. What amount, if received on May 9, will be considered payment in full?

    a. $700

    b. $800

    c. $882

    d. $900

10. This year your company has purchased less expensive merchandise inventory but has not changed its selling prices. What effect will this change have on the company's gross profit percentage this year, in comparison to last year?

    a. The ratio will not change.

    b. The ratio will increase.

    c. The ratio will decrease.

    d. Cannot determine.

> For answers to the Multiple-Choice Questions **see page Q1** located in the last section of the book.

MINI-EXERCISES

McGraw Hill **connect** |ACCOUNTING

LO 6-1

M6-1 Distinguishing among Operating Cycles

Identify the type of business as service (S), retail merchandiser (RM), wholesale merchandiser (WM), or manufacturer (M) for each of the following.

_____ 1. The company reports no inventory on its balance sheet.

_____ 2. The company is a true "middleman," buying from a manufacturer and selling to other companies.

_____ 3. The company's inventory includes raw materials that will be processed into ready-to-use goods.

_____ 4. The company sells goods to consumers.

LO 6-2, 6-3

M6-2 Identifying Internal Controls over Financial Reporting

Fox Erasing has a system of internal control with the following procedures. Match the procedure to the corresponding internal control principle.

Procedure	Internal Control Principle
_____ 1. The treasurer signs checks.	A. Establish responsibility
_____ 2. The treasurer is not allowed to make bank deposits.	B. Segregate duties
_____ 3. The company's checks are prenumbered.	C. Restrict access
_____ 4. Unused checks are stored in the vault.	D. Document procedures
_____ 5. A bank reconciliation is prepared each month.	E. Independently verify

M6-3 Identifying Internal Control Principles Applied by a Merchandiser   LO 6-2

Identify the internal control principle represented by each point in the following diagram.

1. One office employee places all merchandise orders.

4. Merchandise orders are recorded on a purchase order form.

6. Goods billed by suppliers are compared to purchase orders and receiving reports before being paid.

2. Goods are received only by warehouse employees.

5. Receiving reports are completed to indicate goods received.

3. The warehouse is locked and activities electronically monitored.

M6-4 Matching Cash Receipt Processes to Internal Control Principles   LO 6-3

Match each of the following cash receipt activities to the internal control principle to which they best relate. Enter the appropriate letter in the space provided.

_____ 1. A list of checks received in the mail is prepared.

_____ 2. Total cash receipts are compared to the amount on the bank deposit slip.

_____ 3. A password is required to open the cash register.

_____ 4. Price changes at the checkout require a manager's approval.

_____ 5. Cashiers are required to count the cash in their register at the beginning and end of each shift.

A. Establish responsibility

B. Segregate duties

C. Restrict access

D. Document procedures

E. Independently verify

M6-5 Identifying Internal Control Weaknesses in Descriptions of Cash Receipts Process   LO 6-3

Each situation below describes an internal control weakness in the cash receipts process. Identify which of the five internal control principles is violated, explain the weakness, and then suggest a change that would improve internal control.

a. Cashiers prepare a cash count summary, attach tapes from the cash register showing total receipts, and then prepare a bank deposit slip, which they take to the bank for deposit. After the deposit is made, all documents are forwarded to the accounting department for review and recording.

b. The receptionist opens the mail each morning, sorts it into piles, and then gives checks received from customers to the mail clerk for delivery to the accounting department, where a cash receipts list is prepared.

c. The accounting department receives cash register totals each day and promptly files them by cash register number. The accounting department also receives cash count sheets from cashiers each day and files them by employee number. The accounting department receives stamped bank deposit slips the morning after the bank deposit is made, prepares the journal entry, and files the deposit slips by date.

d. To avoid boredom, the employee who works the cash register at the movie theater trades off with either the employee who collects the tickets or an employee who works at the concessions stand.

e. To enhance efficiency, cashiers are assigned the responsibility of authorizing price changes at the cash register.

LO 6-3   **M6-6 Matching Cash Payment Processes to Internal Control Principles**

Match each of the following cash payment activities to the internal control principle to which they best relate. Enter the appropriate letter in the space provided.

_____ 1. The business manager has the only key to the check-signing equipment.

_____ 2. The purchasing manager orders all goods and services for the business.

_____ 3. A bank reconciliation is prepared monthly.

_____ 4. Prenumbered checks are used for all payments.

_____ 5. The company asks suppliers to deliver their merchandise to the warehouse but mail their invoices to the accounting department.

A. Establish responsibility

B. Segregate duties

C. Restrict access

D. Document procedures

E. Independently verify

LO 6-3   **M6-7 Identifying Internal Control Weaknesses in Descriptions of Cash Payment Processes**

Each situation below describes an internal control weakness in the cash payments process. Identify which of the five internal control principles is violated, explain the weakness, and then suggest a change that would improve internal control.

a. The warehouse clerk is responsible for ordering inventory when levels become low and advising the accounting department to issue a payment to the supplier when ordered goods are received.

b. For each purchase, the accountant compares the purchase order (prepared by the purchasing manager) to the receiving report (prepared by warehouse employees), and then attaches these documents to the corresponding supplier invoice and files them by supplier name. The accountant then prepares a check, which the owner merrily signs and sends to the mail clerk for mailing.

c. The check-signing machine is stored with a supply of blank checks in the lunch room closet.

d. Purchase orders can be approved by the purchasing manager, accountant, or warehouse supervisor, depending on who is least busy.

LO 6-4   **M6-8 Organizing Items on the Bank Reconciliation**

Indicate whether the following items would be added (+) or subtracted (−) from the company's books or the bank statement side of a bank reconciliation.

Reconciling Item	Bank Statement	Company's Books
a. Outstanding checks of $12,000		
b. Bank service charge of $15		
c. Deposit in transit of $2,300		
d. Interest earned of $5		

LO 6-4   **M6-9 Preparing Journal Entries after a Bank Reconciliation**

Using the information in M6-8, prepare any journal entries needed to adjust the company's books.

LO 6-5   **M6-10 Calculating Shrinkage in a Perpetual Inventory System**

Corey's Campus Store has $4,000 of inventory on hand at the beginning of the month. During the month, the company buys $41,000 of merchandise and sells merchandise that had cost $30,000.

At the end of the month, $13,000 of inventory is on hand. How much shrinkage occurred during the month?

M6-11 Calculating Shrinkage and Gross Profit in a Perpetual System

LO 6-5, 6-7

Nord Store's perpetual accounting system indicated ending inventory of $20,000, cost of goods sold of $100,000, and net sales of $150,000. A year-end inventory count determined that goods costing $15,000 were actually on hand. Calculate (a) the cost of shrinkage, (b) an adjusted cost of goods sold (assuming shrinkage is charged to cost of goods sold), (c) gross profit percentage before shrinkage, and (d) gross profit percentage after shrinkage.

M6-12 Reporting Net Sales and Gross Profit with Sales Discounts

LO 6-6

Merchandise costing $2,000 is sold for $3,000 on terms 2/10, n/30. If the buyer pays within the discount period, what amount will be reported on the income statement as net sales and as gross profit?

M6-13 Recording Journal Entries for Sales and Sales Discounts

LO 6-6

Using the information in M6-12, prepare the journal entries needed at the time of sale and collection, assuming the company uses a perpetual inventory system.

M6-14 Choosing between FOB Shipping Point and FOB Destination

LO 6-6

In its 2011 annual report, American Eagle Outfitters states that its "e-commerce operation records revenue upon the estimated customer receipt date of the merchandise." Is this FOB shipping point or FOB destination? If American Eagle were to change to the other terms of shipment, would it report its Sales Revenues earlier, or later?

AMERICAN EAGLE OUTFITTERS
ae.com

M6-15 Journal Entries to Record Sales Discounts

LO 6-6

Inventory that cost $500 is sold for $700, with terms of 2/10, n/30. Give the journal entries to record (a) the sale of merchandise and (b) collection of the accounts receivable assuming that it occurs during the discount period.

M6-16 Preparing a Multistep Income Statement

LO 6-7

Sellall Department Stores reported the following amounts in its adjusted trial balance prepared as of its December 31, 2013, year-end: Administrative Expenses, $2,400; Cost of Goods Sold, $22,728; Income Tax Expense, $3,000; Interest Expense, $1,600; Interest Revenue, $200; General Expenses, $2,600; Sales Revenue, $42,000; Sales Discounts, $2,200; Sales Returns and Allowances, $1,920; and Delivery (freight-out) Expense, $300. Prepare a multistep income statement for distribution to external financial statement users, using a format similar to Exhibit 6.11.

M6-17 Computing and Interpreting the Gross Profit Percentage

LO 6-7

Using the information in M6-16, calculate the gross profit percentage for 2013. How has Sellall performed, relative to the gross profit percentages reported for Walmart in the chapter?

M6-18 Computing and Interpreting the Gross Profit Percentage

LO 6-7

Ziehart Pharmaceuticals reported Net Sales of $178,000 and Cost of Goods Sold of $58,000. Candy Electronics Corp. reported Net Sales of $36,000 and Cost of Goods Sold of $26,200. Calculate the gross profit percentage for both companies. From these calculations, can you determine which company is more successful? Explain.

M6-19 Calculating the Impact of the Economic Crisis and Changes in Gross Profit Percentage on Operating Income

LO 6-7

Luxottica Group

Luxottica Group, the Italian company that sells Ray Ban and Killer Loop sunglasses, reported a gross profit percentage of 66.4 percent in 2008 and 65.4 percent in 2009. In each of these two years, the company's net sales was steady at 5 million euro. Luxottica's operating expenses were 2.6 million euro in each year. How much more (or less) income from operations did Luxottica report in 2009 than in 2008?

M6-20 Determining the Cause of Decreasing Gross Profit

LO 6-7

Fortune Brands, Inc., sells a variety of products including Titleist and Pinnacle golf balls, Footjoy golf shoes, and Master Lock padlocks. Like many other companies, Fortune Brands reported a drop in net sales from $7.6 billion in 2008 to $6.7 billion in 2009, and a drop in gross profit from

$3.6 billion in 2008 to $3.5 billion in 2009. Based on these numbers, determine whether the drop in gross profit was caused by a decline in gross profit per sale, a decline in sales volume, or a combination of the two.

EXERCISES

LO 6-2   **E6-1 Identifying Internal Control Principle and Financial Reporting Control Objective**

At most movie theaters, one employee sells tickets and another employee collects them. One night, when you're at the movies, your friend comments that this is a waste of the theater's money.

Required:

1. Identify the name of the control principle to which this situation relates.
2. Explain to your friend what could happen if the same person did both jobs.

LO 6-2   **E6-2 Identifying Financial Reporting Control Objectives**

Your student club recently volunteered to go door-to-door collecting cash donations on behalf of a local charity. The charity's accountant went berserk when you said you wrote receipts only for donors who asked for one.

Required:

Identify the control principle that you violated, and explain why the accountant reacted so strongly. What controls might be appropriate to use in the future?

LO 6-3   **E6-3 Identifying Internal Control Principles in Cash Receipt Processes**

Locker Rentals Corp. (LRC) operates locker rental services at several locations throughout the city including the airport, bus depot, shopping malls, and athletics facilities. Unlike some of the old mechanical lockers that charge a fixed amount per use, LRC's lockers operate electronically and are able to charge based on hours of use. The locker system transmits a daily message to LRC's office indicating the number of hours that lockers have been used, which the office manager uses to determine when cash should be picked up at each location. LRC's cash receipts system is described below.

a. Two employees ("cash collection clerks") are responsible for collecting cash from the lockers. Based on instructions from the office manager, one clerk collects cash from specific locations on the west side of the city and the other collects from specific locations on the east side.
b. When each cash collection clerk returns the cash, a supervisor counts the cash and prepares a cash count sheet.
c. The supervisor summarizes the cash count sheets in a prenumbered daily cash summary, and files the prenumbered cash count sheets by date.
d. The supervisor places the cash in a locked cashbox until it is taken to the bank for deposit.
e. The supervisor, not the cash collection clerks, takes the cash to the bank for deposit.
f. The supervisor prepares a duplicate deposit slip, which the bank stamps after the deposit is made, to indicate the date and amount of the deposit.
g. The supervisor sends the stamped bank deposit slip and daily cash summary to the accountant, who compares them before preparing a journal entry debiting Cash and crediting Locker Rental Revenue.

Required:

1. For each statement (a)–(g), identify the internal control principle being applied.
2. After several months, LRC's supervisor is arrested for stealing nearly $10,000 from the company. Identify the internal control weakness that allowed this theft to occur.

LO 6-3   **E6-4 Identifying Internal Control Principles in Cash Payment Processes**

Home Repair Corp. (HRC) operates a building maintenance and repair business. The business has three office employees—a sales manager, a materials/crew manager, and an accountant. HRC's cash payments system is described below.

a. After a contract is signed with a customer, the sales manager prepares a prenumbered purchase requisition form that indicates the materials needed for the work at the repair site.
b. Based on the purchase requisition form, the materials/crew manager prepares and sends a prenumbered purchase order to suppliers of materials, advising them of the specific materials needed and the repair site to which they should be delivered.
c. The materials/crew manager is the only employee authorized to order goods.
d. Upon receiving a supplier's invoice, the accountant compares it to terms indicated on the purchase order, noting in particular the prices charged and quantity ordered.
e. If these documents are in agreement, the accountant prepares a prenumbered check, stamps the invoice "paid," and prepares a journal entry to record the payment. The journal entry explanation references the sequential number on the purchase order.
f. HRC's owner prepares a monthly bank reconciliation, and review checks returned with the bank statement to ensure they have been issued to valid suppliers.

Required:

1. For each statement (a)–(f), identify the internal control principle being applied.
2. Using the above description, prepare a list of steps and documentation similar to Exhibit 6.4. Which document in Exhibit 6.4 is excluded from the above description?
3. After several months, HRC's materials/crew manager is arrested for having $20,000 of materials delivered to his home, but charged to the company. Identify the internal control weakness that allowed this theft to occur.

E6-5 Preparing a Bank Reconciliation and Journal Entries, and Reporting Cash

LO 6-4

Hills Company's June 30, 2013, bank statement and the June ledger account for cash are summarized here:

BANK STATEMENT				
	Checks	Deposits	Other	Balance
Balance, June 1, 2013				$ 7,200
Deposits during June		$18,000		25,200
Checks cleared during June	$19,100			6,100
Bank service charges			$30	6,070
Balance, June 30, 2013				6,070

Cash (A)						
June 1	Balance	6,800				
June	Deposits	19,000	19,400	Checks written	June	
June 30	Balance	6,400				

Required:

1. Prepare a bank reconciliation. A comparison of the checks written with the checks that have cleared the bank shows outstanding checks of $700. Some of the checks that cleared in June were written prior to June. No deposits in transit were noted in May, but a deposit is in transit at the end of June.
2. Give any journal entries that should be made as a result of the bank reconciliation.
3. What is the balance in the Cash account after the reconciliation entries?
4. In addition to the balance in its bank account, Hills Company also has $300 cash on hand. This amount is recorded in a separate T-account called Cash on Hand. What is the total amount of cash that should be reported on the balance sheet at June 30?

LO 6-4 **E6-6 Preparing a Bank Reconciliation and Journal Entries, and Reporting Cash**

The September 30, 2014, bank statement for Cadieux Company and the September ledger account for cash are summarized here:

BANK STATEMENT				
	Checks	Deposits	Other	Balance
Balance, September 1, 2014				$2,000
September 7			NSF check $100	1,900
September 11		$3,000		4,900
September 12	#101 $ 800			4,100
September 17	#102 1,700			2,400
September 26	#103 2,300			100
September 29			EFT deposit 150	250
September 30			Service charge 20	230

Cash (A)				
Sept 1 Balance	2,000			
Sept 10	3,000	800	Sept 10	#101
Sept 30	2,500	1,700	Sept 15	#102
		2,300	Sept 22	#103
		50	Sept 28	#104
Sept 30 Balance	2,650			

No outstanding checks and no deposits in transit were noted in August. However, there are deposits in transit and checks outstanding at the end of September. The NSF check and electronic funds transfer (EFT) involved transactions with Cadieux Company's customers.

Required:

1. Prepare a bank reconciliation.
2. Give any journal entries that should be made as the result of the bank reconciliation.
3. What should the balance in the Cash account be after recording the journal entries in requirement 2?
4. If the company also has $400 of cash on hand (recorded in a separate account), what total amount of cash should the company report on the September 30 balance sheet?

LO 6-5 **E6-7 Identifying Shrinkage and Other Missing Inventory Information**

Calculate the missing information for each of the following independent cases:

Cases	Beginning Inventory	Purchases	Cost of Goods Sold	Ending Inventory (perpetual system)	Ending Inventory (as counted)	Shrinkage
A	$100	$700	$300	?	$420	$?
B	200	800	?	150	150	?
C	150	500	200	450	?	10
D	260	?	650	210	200	?

LO 6-5 **E6-8 Inferring Shrinkage Using a Perpetual Inventory System**

JCPenney Company, Inc.

JCPenney Company, Inc., is a major retailer with department stores in 49 states and Puerto Rico. The main part of the company's business consists of providing merchandise and services to consumers through department stores. In 2010, JCPenney reported cost of goods sold of $10,799 million, ending inventory for the current year of $3,213 million, and ending inventory for the previous year (2009) of $3,024 million.

Required:

If you knew that the cost of inventory purchases was $11,289 million, could you estimate the cost of shrinkage during the year? If so, prepare the estimate and, if not, explain why.

E6-9 Reporting Net Sales with Credit Sales and Sales Discounts   LO 6-6

During the months of January and February, Solitare Corporation sold goods to three customers. The sequence of events was as follows:

Jan. 6	Sold goods for $100 to Wizard Inc. with terms 2/10, n/30. The goods cost Solitare $70.
6	Sold goods to SpyderCorp. for $80 with terms 2/10, n/30. The goods cost Solitare $60.
14	Collected cash due from Wizard Inc.
Feb. 2	Collected cash due from SpyderCorp.
28	Sold goods for $50 to Bridges with terms 2/10, n/45. The goods cost Solitare $30.

Required:

Assuming that Sales Discounts are reported as contra-revenue, compute Net Sales for the two months ended February 28.

E6-10 Recording Journal Entries for Net Sales with Credit Sales and Sales Discounts   LO 6-6

Using the information in E6-9, prepare journal entries to record the transactions, assuming Solitare uses a perpetual inventory system.

E6-11 Reporting Net Sales with Credit Sales and Sales Discounts   LO 6-6

The following transactions were selected from the records of Evergreen Company:

July 12	Sold merchandise to Wally Butler, who paid the $1,000 purchase with cash. The goods cost Evergreen Company $600.
15	Sold merchandise to Claudio's Chair Company at a selling price of $5,000 on terms 3/10, n/30. The goods cost Evergreen Company $3,500.
20	Sold merchandise to Otto's Ottomans at a selling price of $3,000 on terms 3/10, n/30. The goods cost Evergreen Company $1,900.
23	Collected payment from Claudio's Chair Company from the July 15 sale.
Aug. 25	Collected payment from Otto's Ottomans from the July 20 sale.

Required:

Assuming that Sales Discounts are reported as contra-revenue, compute Net Sales for the two months ended August 31.

E6-12 Recording Journal Entries for Net Sales with Credit Sales and Sales Discounts   LO 6-6

Using the information in E6-11, prepare journal entries to record the transactions, assuming Evergreen Company uses a perpetual inventory system.

E6-13 Reporting Net Sales with Credit Sales, Sales Discounts, and Sales Returns   LO 6-6

The following transactions were selected from among those completed by Bear's Retail Store in 2013:

Nov. 20	Sold two items of merchandise to Cheryl Jahn, who paid the $400 sales price in cash. The goods cost Bear's $300.
25	Sold 20 items of merchandise to Vasko Athletics at a selling price of $4,000 (total); terms 3/10, n/30. The goods cost Bear's $2,500.
28	Sold 10 identical items of merchandise to Nancy's Gym at a selling price of $6,000 (total); terms 3/10, n/30. The goods cost Bear's $4,000.
29	Nancy's Gym returned one of the items purchased on the 28th. The item was in perfect condition, and credit was given to the customer.
Dec. 6	Nancy's Gym paid the account balance in full.
30	Vasko Athletics paid in full for the invoice of November 25, 2013.

Required:

Assuming that Sales Returns and Sales Discounts are reported as contra-revenues, compute Net Sales for the two months ended December 31, 2013.

LO 6-6

E6-14 Recording Journal Entries for Net Sales with Credit Sales, Sales Discounts, and Sales Returns

Using the information in E6-13, prepare journal entries to record the transactions, assuming Bear's Retail Store uses a perpetual inventory system.

LO 6-6, 6-7

E6-15 Determining the Effects of Credit Sales, Sales Discounts, and Sales Returns and Allowances on Income Statement Categories

Rockland Shoe Company records Sales Returns and Allowances and Sales Discounts as contra-revenues. Complete the following table, indicating the amount and direction of effect (+ for increase, − for decrease, and NE for no effect) of each transaction on each item reported in Rockland's income statement prepared for internal use. Be sure to total the effects.

July 12	Rockland sold merchandise to Kristina Zee at its factory store. Kristina paid for the $300 purchase in cash. The goods cost Rockland $160.
15	Sold merchandise to Shoe Express at a selling price of $5,000, with terms 3/10, n/30. Rockland's cost was $3,000.
20	Collected cash due from Shoe Express.
21	Sold merchandise to Fleet Foot Co. at a selling price of $2,000, with terms 2/10, n/30. Rockland's cost was $1,200.
23	Fleet Foot Co. returned $1,000 of shoes and promised to pay for the remaining goods in August. The returned shoes were in perfect condition and had cost Rockland $600.

Transaction Date:	July 12	July 15	July 20	July 21	July 23	Totals
Sales Revenues						
Sales Returns and Allowances						
Sales Discounts						
Net Sales						
Cost of Goods Sold						
Gross Profit						

LO 6-6, 6-7

E6-16 Analyzing and Recording Sales and Gross Profit with and without Sales Discounts

Cycle Wholesaling sells merchandise on credit terms of 2/10, n/30. A sale for $800 (cost of goods sold of $500) was made to Sarah's Cycles on February 1, 2013. Assume Cycle Wholesaling uses a perpetual inventory system.

Required:

1. Give the journal entry Cycle Wholesaling would make to record the sale to Sarah's Cycles.
2. Give the journal entry to record the collection of the account, assuming it was collected in full on February 9, 2013.
3. Give the journal entry, assuming, instead, that the account was collected in full on March 2, 2013.
4. Calculate the gross profit percentage for the sale to Sarah's Cycles, assuming the account was collected in full on February 9, 2013.

LO 6-7

E6-17 Inferring Missing Amounts Based on Income Statement Relationships

Supply the missing dollar amounts for the income statement of Williamson Company for each of the following independent cases:

	Case A	Case B	Case C
Sales Revenues	$8,000	$6,000	$?
Sales Returns and Allowances	150	?	275
Net Sales	?	?	5,920
Cost of Goods Sold	5,750	4,050	5,400
Gross Profit	?	1,450	?

E6-18 Analyzing Gross Profit Percentage on the Basis of a Multistep Income Statement   **LO 6-7**

The following summarized data were provided by the records of Mystery Incorporated for the year ended December 31, 2013:

Administrative Expense	$ 19,000
Cost of Goods Sold	165,000
Income Tax Expense	17,600
Sales Returns and Allowances	7,000
Selling Expense	40,200
Sales of merchandise on cash	240,000
Sales of merchandise for credit	42,000

Required:

1. Based on these data, prepare a multistep income statement for internal reporting purposes (showing all appropriate subtotals and totals).
2. What was the amount of gross profit? What was the gross profit percentage (calculated using the formula shown in this chapter)? Explain what these two amounts mean.
3. Evaluate the 2013 results in light of the company's 38% gross profit percentage in 2012.

E6-19 Analyzing Gross Profit Percentage on the Basis of an Income Statement   **LO 6-7**

Wolverine World Wide Inc. prides itself as being the "world's leading marketer of U.S. branded non-athletic footwear." The following data (in millions) were taken from its annual report for the fiscal year ended January 1, 2011:

Wolverine World Wide Inc.

Sales of Merchandise	$1,249
Income Tax Expense	39
Cash Dividends Paid	21
Selling and Administrative Expense	347
Cost of Products Sold	755
Interest Expense	571
Other Revenues	1,366

Required:

1. Based on these data, prepare a multistep income statement.
2. How much was the gross profit? What was the gross profit percentage? (Round to the nearest tenth of a percent.) Explain what these two amounts mean.
3. Evaluate the results in light of the company's 39.8% gross profit percentage in the prior year.
4. Compare Wolverine's gross profit percentage to Walmart's average gross profit percentage of 24.7%. From this information, can you determine which company is more successful? Why or why not?

E6-20 Evaluating the Effect of Discounts and Returns on Gross Profit   **LO 6-7**

One of the few companies to ever report the extent of sales discounts and returns was sunglass maker Oakley, Inc. In the Management Discussion and Analysis section of its 2005 annual report, Oakley reported the following information about its Sales Discounts and Returns.

	Year Ended December 31,	
(in thousands)	2005	2004
Gross Sales	$693,342	$621,652
Sales Discounts and Returns	(45,211)	(36,184)
Net Sales	648,131	585,468
Cost of Goods Sold	277,230	262,483
Gross Profit	370,901	322,985

Required:

1. For each year, calculate the percentage of sales discounts and returns by dividing Sales Discounts and Returns by Gross Sales and multiplying by 100. Based on these percentages, explain whether Sales Discounts and Returns have a greater impact in 2005 or 2004.

2. For each year, calculate the gross profit percentage using the formula shown in this chapter (i.e., using net sales). Did Oakley's gross profit improve or worsen in 2005, as compared to 2004?

COACHED PROBLEMS

LO 6-3   **CP6-1 Evaluating Internal Control Strengths and Weaknesses in Cash Receipts and Disbursements**

The following procedures are used by Richardson Light Works.

a. When customers pay cash for lighting products, the cash is placed in a cash register and a receipt is issued to the customer.
b. At the end of each day, the cash is counted by the cashier and a cash count sheet is prepared.
c. The manager checks the accuracy of the cash count sheet before taking the cash to the bank for deposit.
d. The journal entry to record cash sales is prepared using the cash count sheets.
e. Checks are written to suppliers immediately after supplier invoices are received.
f. Receiving reports are prepared to indicate the quantity and condition of goods received from suppliers, based on inspections made by warehouse personnel.

Required:

1. Indicate whether each procedure represents a strength or weakness. Explain your reasons.
2. For each weakness, describe a change in procedures that would address the weakness.

LO 6-4   **CP6-2 Preparing a Bank Reconciliation and Journal Entries, and Reporting Cash**

The April 30, 2013, bank statement for KMaxx Company and the April ledger account for cash are summarized here:

BANK STATEMENT					
	Checks		Deposits	Other	Balance
Balance, April 1, 2013					$6,000
April 5	#101	$700			5,300
April 9			$2,500		7,800
April 12	#102	200			7,600
April 19	#103	500			7,100
April 22	#104	1,000			6,100
April 27				EFT payment $200	5,900
April 29				NSF check 100	5,800
April 30				Service charge 25	5,775

Cash (A)				
April 1 Balance	6,000			
April 8	2,500	700	April 2	#101
April 28	500	200	April 10	#102
		500	April 15	#103
		1,100	April 20	#104
		300	April 29	#105
April 30 Balance	6,200			

No outstanding checks and no deposits in transit were noted in March. However, there are deposits in transit and checks outstanding at the end of April. The electronic funds transfer (EFT) involved an automatic monthly payment to one of KMaxx's creditors. Check #104 was written for $1,100. The NSF check had been received from a customer.

Required:

1. Prepare a bank reconciliation for April.
    TIP: Put a check mark beside each item that appears on both the bank statement and what's already been recorded in the accounting records (shown in the T-account). Items left unchecked will be used in the bank reconcil ation.
2. Give any journal entries that should be made as a result of the bank reconciliation.
    TIP: Remember to make entries only for items that affect the company's books, not the bank.
3. What should the balance in the Cash account be after recording the journal entries in requirement 2?
4. If the company also has $1,000 of cash on hand (recorded in a separate account), what total amount should the company report as Cash and Cash Equivalents on the April 30 balance sheet?

CP6-3 Identifying Outstanding Checks and Deposits in Transit and Preparing a Bank Reconciliation and Journal Entries

LO 6-4

The August 2013 bank statement and cash T-account for Martha Company follow:

BANK STATEMENT				
Date	Checks	Deposits	Other	Balance
Aug. 1				$17,470
2	$300			17,170
3		$12,000		29,170
4	400			28,770
5	250			28,520
9	890			27,630
10	310			27,320
15		4,000		31,320
21	400			30,920
24	21,000			9,920
25		7,000		16,920
30	800			16,120
30			Interest earned $20	16,140
31			Service charge 10	16,130

Cash (A)				
Aug. 1 Balance	17,470	Checks written		
Deposits				
Aug. 2	12,000	300	Aug. 1	
12	4,000	400	2	
24	7,000	250	3	
31	5,000	310	4	
		890	5	
		290	15	
		550	17	
		800	18	
		400	19	
		21,000	23	
Aug. 31 Balance	20,280			

No deposits were in transit and no checks were outstanding at the end of July.

Required:

1. Identify and list the deposits in transit at the end of August.

   TIP: Put a check mark beside each item that appears on both the bank statement and what's already been recorded in the accounting records (shown in the T-account).

2. Identify and list the outstanding checks at the end of August.

3. Prepare a bank reconciliation for August.

   TIP: Any item in the accounting records without check marks should appear on the bank statement side of the bank reconciliation. Any items in the bank statement without check marks should appear on the company's books side of the bank reconciliation.

4. Give any journal entries that the company should make as a result of the bank reconciliation. Why are they necessary?

5. After the reconciliation journal entries are posted, what balance will be reflected in the Cash account in the ledger?

6. If the company also has $100 on hand, which is recorded in a different account called Cash on Hand, what total amount of Cash and Cash Equivalents should be reported on the August 31, 2013, balance sheet?

LO 6-7 **CP6-4 Preparing a Multistep Income Statement with Sales Discounts and Sales Returns and Allowances and Computing the Gross Profit Percentage**

Psymon Company, Inc., sells construction equipment. The annual fiscal period ends on December 31. The following adjusted trial balance was created from the general ledger accounts on December 31, 2013:

Account Titles	Debits	Credits
Cash	$ 42,000	
Accounts Receivable	18,000	
Inventory	65,000	
Property and Equipment	50,000	
Accumulated Depreciation		$ 21,000
Liabilities		30,000
Contributed Capital		90,000
Retained Earnings, January 1, 2013		11,600
Sales Revenue		182,000
Sales Returns and Allowances	7,000	
Sales Discounts	8,000	
Cost of Goods Sold	98,000	
Selling Expense	17,000	
Administrative Expense	18,000	
General Expenses	2,000	
Income Tax Expense	9,600	
Totals	$334,600	$334,600

Required:

1. Prepare a multistep income statement that would be used for internal reporting purposes. Treat Sales Discounts and Sales Returns and Allowances as contra-revenue accounts.

   TIP: Some of the accounts listed will appear on the balance sheet rather than the income statement.

2. Prepare a multistep income statement that would be used for external reporting purposes, beginning with the amount for Net Sales.

3. Compute and interpret the gross profit percentage (using the formula shown in this chapter).

LO 6-6, 6-7 **CP6-5 Recording Cash Sales, Credit Sales, Sales Discounts, Sales Returns, and Sales Allowances and Analyzing Gross Profit Percentage**

Campus Stop, Incorporated, is a student co-op. Campus Stop uses a perpetual inventory system. The following transactions (summarized) have been selected from 2013:

a. Sold merchandise for cash (cost of merchandise $152,070). $275,000

b. Received merchandise returned by customers as unsatisfactory (but in perfect condition), for cash refund (original cost of merchandise $800).   1,600

c.	Sold merchandise (costing $9,000) to a customer, on account with terms 2/10, n/30.	20,000
d.	Collected half of the balance owed by the customer in (c) within the discount period.	9,800
e.	Granted an allowance to the customer in (c).	1,800

Required:

1. Compute Sales Revenue, Net Sales, and Gross Profit for Campus Stop.
2. Compute the gross profit percentage (using the formula shown in this chapter).
3. Prepare journal entries to record transactions (a)–(e).
4. Campus Stop is considering a contract to sell merchandise to a campus organization for $15,000. This merchandise will cost Campus Stop $12,000. Would this contract increase (or decrease) Campus Stop's gross profit and gross profit percentage? How should Campus Stop decide whether to accept the contract?

    TIP: The impact on gross profit (a dollar amount) may differ from the impact on gross profit percentage.

CP6-6 Sales Transactions between Wholesale and Retail Merchandisers, with Sales Allowances and Sales Discounts Using a Perpetual Inventory System LO 6-6, 6-7

The transactions listed below are typical of those involving Amalgamated Textiles and American Fashions. Amalgamated is a wholesale merchandiser and American Fashions is a retail merchandiser. Assume all sales of merchandise from Amalgamated to American Fashions are made with terms 2/10, n/30, and that the two companies use perpetual inventory systems. Assume the following transactions between the two companies occurred in the order listed during the year ended December 31, 2013.

a. Amalgamated sold merchandise to American Fashions at a selling price of $230,000. The merchandise had cost Amalgamated $175,000.
b. Two days later, American Fashions complained to Amalgamated that some of the merchandise differed from what American Fashions had ordered. Amalgamated agreed to give an allowance of $5,000 to American Fashions.
c. Just three days later, American Fashions paid Amalgamated, which settled all amounts owed.

Required:

1. For each of the events (a) through (c), indicate the amount and direction of the effect (+ for increase, − for decrease, and NE for no effect) on Amalgamated Textiles in terms of the following items.

Sales Revenues	Sales Returns and Allowances	Sales Discounts	Net Sales	Cost of Goods Sold	Gross Profit

2. Which of the above items are likely to be reported on Amalgamated's external financial statements, and which items will be combined "behind the scenes"?

3. Prepare the journal entries that Amalgamated Textiles would record, and show any computations.

    TIP: When using a perpetual inventory system, the seller always makes two journal entries when goods are sold.

GROUP A PROBLEMS

 |ACCOUNTING LO 6-3

PA6-1 Evaluating Internal Control Strengths and Weaknesses in Cash Receipts and Disbursements

The following procedures are used by The Taco Shop.

a. Customers pay cash for all food orders. Cash is placed in a cash register and a receipt is issued upon request by the customer.
b. At the end of each day, the cashier counts the cash, prepares a cash count sheet, and has the manager review and sign the cash count sheet.

c.   At three times during the day, excess cash is removed from the cash registers and placed in a vault until it is taken for night deposit at the local bank.

d.   Orders for drink cups, straws, condiments, and other supplies are written on prenumbered purchase order forms and are approved by the manager before being sent to an authorized supplier.

e.   When supplies are received, they are stacked just inside the back door to the kitchen, which is left unlocked because part-time employees frequently arrive and leave at various times during the day.

Required:

1.   Indicate whether each procedure represents a strength or weakness. Explain your reasons.

2.   For each weakness, describe a change in procedures that would address the weakness.

LO 6-4   **PA6-2 Preparing a Bank Reconciliation and Journal Entries, and Reporting Cash**

The bookkeeper at Martin Company has asked you to prepare a bank reconciliation as of May 31, 2013. The May 31, 2013, bank statement and the May T-account for cash showed the following (summarized):

Martin Company's bank reconciliation at the end of April 2013 showed a cash balance of $18,800. No deposits were in transit at the end of April, but a deposit was in transit at the end of May.

BANK STATEMENT					
	Checks		Deposits	Other	Balance
Balance, May 1, 2013					$18,800
May 2			$ 8,000		26,800
May 5	#301	$11,000			15,800
May 7	#302	6,000			9,800
May 8			10,000		19,800
May 14	#303	500			19,300
May 17				Interest $120	19,420
May 22				NSF check 280	19,140
May 27	#304	4,600			14,540
May 31				Service charge 60	14,480
Balance, May 31, 2013					14,480

Cash (A)				
May 1	Balance	18,800		
May 1		8,000	11,000	#301 May 2
May 7		10,000	6,000	#302 May 4
May 29		6,000	500	#303 May 11
			4,600	#304 May 23
			1,300	#305 May 29
May 31	Balance	19,400		

Required:

1.   Prepare a bank reconciliation for May.

2.   Prepare any journal entries required as a result of the bank reconciliation. Why are they necessary?

3. After the reconciliation journal entries are posted, what balance will be reflected in the Cash account in the ledger?

4. If the company also has $50 on hand, which is recorded in a different account called Cash on Hand, what total amount of Cash and Cash Equivalents should be reported on the balance sheet at the end of May?

PA6-3 Identifying Outstanding Checks and Deposits in Transit and Preparing a Bank Reconciliation and Journal Entries

LO 6-4

The December 2013 bank statement and cash T-account for Stewart Company follow:

BANK STATEMENT					
Date	Checks	Deposits	Other		Balance
Dec. 1					$48,000
2	$ 500				47,500
4	7,000				40,500
6	120				40,380
11	550	$28,000			67,830
13	1,900				65,930
17	12,000				53,930
23	60	36,000			89,870
26	900				88,970
28	2,200				86,770
30	17,000	19,000	NSF*	$300	88,470
31	1,650		Interest earned	50	86,870
31			Service charge	150	86,720

*NSF check from J. Left, a customer.

Cash (A)				
Dec. 1 Balance	48,000	Checks written during December:		
Deposits				
Dec. 11	28,000	500		60
23	36,000	7,000		900
30	19,000	120		150
31	13,000	550		17,000
		1,900		4,500
		12,000		1,650
		2,200		
Dec. 31 Balance	95,470			

There were no deposits in transit or outstanding checks at November 30.

Required:

1. Identify and list the deposits in transit at the end of December.
2. Identify and list the outstanding checks at the end of December.
3. Prepare a bank reconciliation for December.
4. Give any journal entries that the company should make as a result of the bank reconciliation. Why are they necessary?
5. After the reconciliation journal entries are posted, what balance will be reflected in the Cash account in the ledger?
6. If the company also has $300 on hand, which is recorded in a different account called Cash on Hand, what total amount of Cash and Cash Equivalents should be reported on the December 31, 2013, balance sheet?

LO 6-7 **PA6-4 Preparing a Multistep Income Statement with Sales Discounts and Sales Returns and Allowances and Computing the Gross Profit Percentage**

Big Tommy Corporation is a local grocery store organized seven years ago as a corporation. The store is in an excellent location, and sales have increased each year. At the end of 2013, the bookkeeper prepared the following statement (assume that all amounts are correct, but note the incorrect terminology and format):

	Debit	Credit
BIG TOMMY CORPORATION		
Profit and Loss		
December 31, 2013		
Sales		$420,000
Cost of Goods Sold	$279,000	
Sales Returns and Allowances	10,000	
Sales Discounts	6,000	
Selling Expense	58,000	
Administrative Expense	16,000	
General Expenses	1,000	
Income Tax Expense	15,000	
Net Profit	35,000	
Totals	$420,000	$420,000

Required:

1. Prepare a properly formatted multistep income statement that would be used for internal reporting purposes. Treat Sales Returns and Allowances and Sales Discounts as contra-revenue accounts.

2. Prepare a properly formatted multistep income statement that would be used for external reporting purposes, beginning with the amount for Net Sales.

3. Compute and interpret the gross profit percentage (using the formula shown in this chapter).

LO 6-6, 6-7 **PA6-5 Recording Sales with Discounts and Returns and Analyzing Gross Profit Percentage**

Hair World Inc. is a wholesaler of hair supplies. Hair World uses a perpetual inventory system. The following transactions (summarized) have been selected from 2013:

a.	Sold merchandise for cash (cost of merchandise $28,797).	$51,200
b.	Received merchandise returned by customers as unsatisfactory (but in perfect condition), for cash refund (original cost of merchandise $360).	600
c.	Sold merchandise (costing $4,750) to a customer, on account with terms 2/10, n/30.	10,000
d.	Collected half of the balance owed by the customer in (c) within the discount period.	4,900
e.	Granted an allowance to the customer in (c).	160

Required:

1. Compute Sales Revenue, Net Sales, and Gross Profit for Hair World.
2. Compute the gross profit percentage (using the formula shown in this chapter).
3. Prepare journal entries to record transactions (a)–(e).
4. Hair World is considering a contract to sell merchandise to a hair salon chain for $15,000. This merchandise will cost Hair World $10,000. Would this contract increase (or decrease) Hair World's gross profit and gross profit percentage? How should Hair World decide whether to accept the contract?

PA6-6 Reporting Sales Transactions between Wholesale and Retail LO 6-6, 6-7
       Merchandisers, with Sales Allowances and Sales Discounts Using
       a Perpetual Inventory System

The transactions listed below are typical of those involving New Books Inc. and Readers' Corner. New Books is a wholesale merchandiser and Readers' Corner is a retail merchandiser. Assume all sales of merchandise from New Books to Readers' Corner are made with terms 2/10, n/30, and that the two companies use perpetual inventory systems. Assume the following transactions between the two companies occurred in the order listed during the year ended August 31, 2013.

a. New Books sold merchandise to Readers' Corner at a selling price of $550,000. The merchandise had cost New Books $415,000.

b. Two days later, Readers' Corner complained to New Books that some of the merchandise differed from what Readers' Corner had ordered. New Books agreed to give an allowance of $10,000 to Readers' Corner.

c. Just three days later, Readers' Corner paid New Books, which settled all amounts owed.

Required:

1. For each of the events (a) through (c), indicate the amount and direction of the effect (+ for increase, − for decrease, and NE for no effect) on New Books in terms of the following items.

Sales Revenues	Sales Returns and Allowances	Sales Discounts	Net Sales	Cost of Goods Sold	Gross Profit

2. Which of the above items are likely to be reported on New Books' external financial statements, and which items will be combined "behind the scenes"?

3. Prepare the journal entries that New Books would record, and show any computations.

GROUP B PROBLEMS

connect |ACCOUNTING   LO 6-3

PB6-1 Evaluating Internal Control Strengths and
       Weaknesses in Cash Receipts and Disbursements

The following procedures are used by Complete Wholesale Incorporated.

a. All sales are made on account, with each sale being indicated on a sequentially numbered sales invoice.

b. Customer payments are received in the mail by the office receptionist, who sends the checks to a cashier for deposit and the remittance advices to the accounting department for recording against the customer's account balance.

c. The office receptionist is assigned the job of handling all customer complaints.

d. When a customer has a legitimate complaint about goods sold to the customer on account, the receptionist will phone the accounting department to request that the customer's account be credited for the sales allowance.

e. The company's inventory is stored in a locked warehouse that is monitored by surveillance cameras.

f. Payments to the company's suppliers are made only after the supplier's invoice is received and compared to the receiving report.

Required:

1. Indicate whether each procedure represents a strength or weakness. Explain your reasons.

2. For each weakness, describe a change in procedures that would address the weakness.

LO 6-4   **PB6-2 Preparing a Bank Reconciliation and Journal Entries and Reporting Cash**

The bookkeeper at Tony Company has asked you to prepare a bank reconciliation as of February 28, 2013. The February 28, 2013, bank statement and the February T-account for cash showed the following (summarized):

BANK STATEMENT					
		Checks	Deposits	Other	Balance
Balance, February 1, 2013					$49,400
February 2	#101	$15,000			34,400
February 4			$ 7,000		41,400
February 5				NSF $320	41,080
February 9	#102	11,000			30,080
February 12	#103	7,500			22,580
February 14			9,500		32,080
February 19	#104	9,000			23,080
February 23			14,150		37,230
February 26	#105	6,700			30,530
February 27				Interest earned 150	30,680
February 28				Service charge 40	30,640

Cash (A)				
Feb 1	Balance	49,400		
Feb 2		7,000	15,000	Feb 1 #101
Feb 13		9,500	11,000	Feb 7 #102
Feb 21		14,150	7,500	Feb 11 #103
Feb 28		7,800	9,000	Feb 17 #104
			6,700	Feb 25 #105
			1,200	Feb 29 #106
Feb 28	Balance	37,450		

Tony Company's bank reconciliation at the end of January 2013 showed no outstanding checks. No deposits were in transit at the end of January, but a deposit was in transit at the end of February.

Required:

1. Prepare a bank reconciliation for February.
2. Prepare any journal entries required as a result of the bank reconciliation. Why are they necessary?
3. After the reconciliation journal entries are posted, what balance will be reflected in the Cash account in the ledger?
4. If the company also has $50 on hand, which is recorded in a different account called Cash on Hand, what total amount of Cash and Cash Equivalents should be reported on the balance sheet at the end of February?

PB6-3 Identifying Outstanding Checks and Deposits n Transit and Preparing   LO 6-4
a Bank Reconciliation and Journal Entries

The September 2014 bank statement and cash T-account for Terrick Company follow:

		BANK STATEMENT			
Date	Checks	Deposits	Other		Balance
Sept. 1					$ 75,900
2	$ 620				75,280
4	2,000				73,280
6	1,500				71,780
11	300	14,000			85,480
13	650				84,830
17	1C,000				74,830
23	90	27,000			101,740
26	700				101,040
28	8,000				93,040
29	730	17,000	NSF*	$500	108,810
30	400		Interest earned	60	108,470
30			Service charge	40	108,430

*NSF check from B. Frank, a customer.

		Cash (A)			
Sept. 1	Balance	75,900	Checks written during September:		
Deposits			620	8,000	
Sept. 11		14,000	2,000	730	
23		27,000	1,500	400	
29		17,000	300	500	
30		21,000	650	6,00C	
			10,000	9C	
			700		
Sept. 30	Balance	123,410			

There were no deposits in transit or outstanding checks at August 31.

Required:

1. Identify and list the deposits in transit at the end of September.
2. Identify and list the outstanding checks at the end of September.
3. Prepare a bank reconciliation for September.
4. Give any journal entries that the company should make as a result of the bank reconciliation. Why are they necessary?
5. After the reconciliation journal entries are posted, what balance will be reflected in the Cash account in the ledger?
6. If the company also has $200 on hand, which is recorded in a different account called Cash on Hand, what total amount of Cash and Cash Equivalents should be reported on the September 30, 2014, balance sheet?

PB6-4 Preparing a Multistep Income Statement with Sales Discounts and Sales   LO 6-7
Returns and Allowances and Computing the Gross Profit Percentage

Emily's Greenhouse Corporation is a local greenhouse organized 10 years ago as a corporation. The greenhouse is in an excellent location, and sales have increased each year. At the end of

2014, the bookkeeper prepared the following statement (assume that all amounts are correct, but note the incorrect terminology and format):

EMILY'S GREENHOUSE CORPORATION
Profit and Loss
December 31, 2014

	Debit	Credit
Sales		$504,000
Cost of Goods Sold	$311,000	
Sales Returns and Allowances	11,000	
Sales Discounts	8,000	
Selling Expense	61,000	
Administrative Expense	13,000	
General Expenses	3,000	
Income Tax Expense	18,000	
Net Profit	79,000	
Totals	$504,000	$504,000

Required:

1. Prepare a properly formatted multistep income statement that would be used for internal reporting purposes. Treat Sales Returns and Allowances and Sales Discounts as contra-revenue accounts.

2. Prepare a properly formatted multistep income statement that would be used for external reporting purposes, beginning with the amount for Net Sales.

3. Compute and interpret the gross profit percentage (using the formula shown in this chapter).

LO 6-6, 6-7   PB6-5 Recording Sales and Purchases with Discounts and Returns and Analyzing Gross Profit Percentage

Larry's Building Supplies (LBS) is a locally owned and operated hardware store. LBS uses a perpetual inventory system.

The following transactions (summarized) have been selected from 2013:

a.	Sold merchandise for cash (cost of merchandise $224,350).	$500,000
b.	Received merchandise returned by customers as unsatisfactory (but in perfect condition), for cash refund (original cost of merchandise $1,900).	3,000
c.	Sold merchandise (costing $3,000) to a customer, on account with terms 2/10, n/30.	5,000
d.	Collected half of the balance owed by the customer in (*c*) within the discount period.	2,450
e.	Granted an allowance to the customer in (*c*).	950

Required:

1. Compute Sales Revenue, Net Sales, and Gross Profit for LBS.

2. Compute the gross profit percentage (using the formula shown in this chapter).

3. Prepare journal entries to record transactions (*a*)–(*e*).

4. LBS is considering a contract to sell building supplies to a local home builder for $20,000. These materials will cost LBS $16,000. Would this contract increase (or decrease) LBS's gross profit and gross profit percentage? How should LBS decide whether to accept the contract?

LO 6-5, 6-6, 6-7   PB6-6 Reporting Sales Transactions between Wholesale and Retail Merchandisers, with Sales Allowances and Sales Discounts Using a Perpetual Inventory System

The transactions listed below are typical of those involving Southern Sporting Goods and Sports R Us. Southern Sporting Goods is a wholesale merchandiser and Sports R Us is a retail merchandiser. Assume all sales of merchandise from Southern Sporting Goods to Sports R Us are made with terms 2/10, n/30, and that the two companies use perpetual inventory systems. Assume the following transactions between the two companies occurred in the order listed during the year ended December 31, 2014.

a. Southern Sporting Goods sold merchandise to Sports R Us at a selling price of $125,000. The merchandise had cost Southern Sporting Goods $94,000.

b. Two days later, Sports R Us complained to Southern Sporting Goods that some of the merchandise differed from what Sports R Us had ordered. Southern Sporting Goods agreed to give an allowance of $3,000 to Sports R Us.

c. Just three days later Sports R Us paid Southern Sporting Goods, which settled all amounts owed.

Required:

1. For each of the events (*a*) through (*c*), indicate the amount and direction of the effect (+ for increase, − for decrease, and NE for no effect) on Southern Sporting Goods in terms of the following items.

Sales Revenues	Sales Returns and Allowances	Sales Discounts	Net Sales	Cost of Goods Sold	Gross Profit

2. Which of the above items are likely to be reported on Southern Sporting Goods' external financial statements, and which items will be combined "behind the scenes"?

3. Prepare the journal entries that Southern Sporting Goods would record and show any computations.

SKILLS DEVELOPMENT CASES

S6-1 Finding Financial Information

LO 6-2, 6-7

Refer to the financial statements of The Home Depot in Appendix A at the end of this book, or download the annual report from the *Cases* section of the text's Web site at www.mhhe.com/phillips4e.

Required:

1. What amount of Net Sales does the company report during the year ended January 30, 2011?
   a. $47,298
   b. $66,176
   c. $44,639
   d. $67,997

2. Assuming that Cost of Sales is the company's term for Cost of Goods Sold, compute the company's gross profit percentage for the most recent two years.
   a. 34.3% and 33.9%
   b. 33.9% and 33.7%
   c. 33.7% and 34.3%
   d. 65.7% and 66.1%

3. Assume that The Home Depot experienced no shrinkage in the most current year. Using the balance sheet and income statement, estimate the amount of purchases in the year ended January 30, 2011.
   a. $10,188
   b. $45,130
   c. $44,693
   d. $10,625

S6-2 Comparing Financial Information

LO 6-2, 6-7

Lowe's

Refer to the financial statements of The Home Depot in Appendix A and Lowe's in Appendix B at the end of this book, or download the annual reports from the *Cases* section of the text's Web site at www.mhhe.com/phillips4e.

1. Does Lowe's report higher or lower Net Sales than The Home Depot during the year ending near January 31, 2011?

2. Assuming that Cost of Sales is the same thing as Cost of Goods Sold, compute Lowe's gross profit percentage for the most recent two years. Is it greater or less than The Home Depot's? Based on this, where are consumers likely to find lower mark-ups?

3. Assume that Lowe's and The Home Depot experienced no shrinkage in the most recent year. Using the balance sheet and income statement, estimate the amount of purchases in the 2010–2011 year. How much greater (or less) were Lowe's purchases than The Home Depot's in that year?

4. Refer to the "Report of Independent Registered Public Accounting Firm" in The Home Depot's annual report and Lowe's annual report. Were the two companies' internal controls operating effectively? What are the "inherent limitations" of internal control to which KPMG is referring?

S6-3 Internet-Based Team Research: Examining an Annual Report

LO 6-1, 6-7

As a team, select an industry to analyze. Using your Web browser, each team member should access the annual report or 10-K for one publicly traded company in the industry, with each member selecting a different company. (See S1-3 in Chapter 1 for a description of possible resources for these tasks.)

Required:

1. On an individual basis, each team member should write a short report that incorporates the following:
   a. Describe the company's business in sufficient detail to be able to classify it as a service, merchandising, or manufacturing company. What products or services does the company provide?
   b. Calculate the gross profit percentage at the end of the current and prior year, and explain any change between the two years.

2. Then, as a team, write a short report comparing and contrasting your companies using these attributes. Discuss any patterns across the companies that you as a team observe. Provide potential explanations for any differences discovered.

LO 6-2, 6-5

S6-4 Ethical Decision Making: A Real-Life Example

When some people think about inventory theft, they imagine a shoplifter running out of a store with goods stuffed inside a jacket or bag. But that's not what the managers thought at the Famous Footwear store on Chicago's Madison Street. No, they suspected their own employees were the main cause of their unusually high shrinkage. One scam involved dishonest cashiers who would let their friends take a pair of Skechers without paying for them. To make it look like the shoes had been bought, cashiers would ring up a sale, but instead of charging $50 for shoes, they would charge only $2 for a bottle of shoe polish. That's when the company's managers decided to put its accounting system to work. In just two years, the company cut its Madison Street inventory losses in half. Here's how a newspaper described the store's improvements:

> **Retailers Crack Down on Employee Theft**
> *SouthCoast Today*, September 10, 2000, Chicago
> By Calmetta Coleman, *Wall Street Journal* Staff Writer
>
> . . . Famous Footwear installed a chainwide register-monitoring system to sniff out suspicious transactions, such as unusually large numbers of refunds or voids, or repeated sales of cheap goods.
>
> . . . [B]efore an employee can issue a cash refund, a second worker must be present to see the customer and inspect the merchandise.
>
> . . . [T]he chain has set up a toll-free hotline for employees to use to report suspicions about co-workers.

These improvements in inventory control came as welcome news for investors and creditors of Brown Shoe Company, the company that owns Famous Footwear. Despite these improvements at the Chicago store, Brown Shoe has been forced to shut down operations in other cities.

Required:

1. Explain how the register-monitoring system would allow Famous Footwear to cut down on employee theft.
2. What is the name of the control principle that is addressed by Famous Footwear's new cash refund procedure?
3. If Famous Footwear used a periodic inventory system, rather than a perpetual inventory system, how would the company detect shrinkage?
4. Think of and describe at least four different parties that are harmed by the type of inventory theft described in this case.

LO 6-6, 6-7

S6-5 Ethical Decision Making: A Mini-Case

Assume you work as an accountant in the merchandising division of a large public company that makes and sells athletic clothing. To encourage the merchandising division to earn as much profit on each individual sale as possible, the division manager's pay is based, in part, on the division's gross profit percentage. To encourage control over the division's operating expenses, the manager's pay also is based on the division's net income.

You are currently preparing the division's financial statements. The division had a good year, with sales of $100,000, cost of goods sold of $50,000, sales returns and allowances of $6,000, sales discounts of $4,000, and other selling expenses of $30,000. (Assume the division does not report income taxes.) The division manager stresses that "*it would be in your personal interest*" to classify sales returns and allowances and sales discounts as selling expenses rather than as contra-revenues on the division's income statement. He justifies this "friendly advice" by saying that he's not asking you to fake the numbers—he just believes that those items are more accurately reported as expenses. Plus, he claims, being a division of a larger company, you don't have to follow GAAP.

Required:

1. Prepare an income statement for the division using the classifications shown in this chapter. Using this income statement, calculate the division's gross profit percentage.
2. Prepare an income statement for the division using the classifications advised by the manager. Using this income statement, calculate the division's gross profit percentage.
3. What reason (other than reporting "more accurately") do you think is motivating the manager's advice to you?
4. Do you agree with the manager's statement that "he's not asking you to fake the numbers"?
5. Do you agree with the manager's statement about not having to follow GAAP?
6. How should you respond to the division manager's "friendly advice"?

S6-6 Critical Thinking: Analyzing Internal Control Weaknesses

LO 6-2

Snake Creek Company has a trusted employee who, as the owner said, "handles all of the bookkeeping and paperwork for the company." This employee is responsible for counting, verifying, and recording cash receipts and payments, making the weekly bank deposit, preparing checks for major expenditures (signed by the owner), making small expenditures from the cash register for daily expenses, and collecting accounts receivable. The owner asked the local bank for a $20,000 loan. The bank asked that an audit be performed covering the year just ended. The independent auditor (a local CPA), in a private conference with the owner, presented some evidence of the following activities of the trusted employee during the past year:

a. Cash sales sometimes were not entered in the cash register, and the trusted employee pocketed approximately $50 per month.
b. Cash taken from the cash register (and pocketed by the trusted employee) was replaced with expense memos with fictitious signatures (approximately $12 per day).
c. $300 collected on an account receivable from a valued out-of-town customer was pocketed by the trusted employee and was covered by making a $300 entry as a debit to Sales Returns and a credit to Accounts Receivable.
d. $800 collected on an account receivable from a local customer was pocketed by the trusted employee and was covered by making an $800 entry as a debit to Sales Discounts and a credit to Accounts Receivable.

Required:

1. What was the approximate amount stolen during the past year?
   TIP: Assume employees work 5 days a week, 52 weeks a year.
2. What would be your recommendations to the owner?

S6-7 Preparing Multistep Income Statements and Calculating Gross Profit Percentage

LO 6-6, 6-7

Assume that you have been hired by Big Sky Corporation as a summer intern. The company is in the process of preparing its annual financial statements. To help in the process, you are asked to prepare an income statement for internal reporting purposes and an income statement for external reporting purposes. Your boss has also requested that you determine the company's gross profit percentage based on the statements that you are to prepare. The following adjusted trial balance was created from the general ledger accounts on May 31, 2013.

Account Titles	Debits	Credits
Cash	$ 57,000	
Accounts Receivable	67,000	
Inventory	103,000	
Property and Equipment	252,000	
Accumulated Depreciation		$103,000
Liabilities		75,000
Contributed Capital		120,000
Retained Earnings, June 1, 2012		145,900
Sales Revenue		369,000
Sales Returns and Allowances	9,500	
Sales Discounts	14,000	
Cost of Goods Sold	248,000	
Selling Expense	19,000	
Administrative Expense	23,000	
General Expenses	5,000	
Income Tax Expense	15,400	
Totals	$812,900	$812,900

Your boss wants you to create the spreadsheet in a way that automatically recalculates net sales and any other related amounts whenever changes are made to the contra-revenue accounts. To do this, you know that you'll have to use formulas throughout the worksheets and even import or link cells from one worksheet to another. Your friend Owen, an accountant, is willing to help.

From:	Owentheaccountant@yahoo.com
To:	Helpme@hotmail.com
Cc:	
Subject:	Excel Help

Sounds like you are going to get some great experience this summer. Okay, to import a number from another spreadsheet, you first click on the cell where you want the number to appear. For example, if you want to enter the Net Sales balance in the external income statement, click on the cell in the external income statement where the Net Sales number is supposed to appear. Enter the equals sign (=) and then click on the tab that takes you to the worksheet containing the internal income statement. In that worksheet, click on the cell that contains the amount you want to import into the external income statement and then press enter. This will create a link from the internal income statement cell to the external income statement cell. Here's a screen shot showing the formula that will appear after you import the number.

S6-7 - Microsoft Excel

Home | Insert | Page Layout | Formulas | Data | Review | View | Acrobat

G5 f_x ='Internal Income Statement'!G8

	A	B	C	D	E	F	G	H
1				Big Sky Corporation				
2				Income Statement				
3				For the Year Ended May 31, 2013				
4								
5	Net sales						345,500	
6	Cost of goods sold						248,000	
7	Gross profit							
8								

Internal Income Statement   **External Income Statement**

Ready   100%

Don't forget to save the file using a name that indicates who you are.

Required:

Enter the trial balance information into a spreadsheet and complete the following:

1. Prepare a multistep income statement that would be used for internal reporting purposes. Classify sales returns and allowances and sales discounts as contra-revenue accounts.

2. Prepare a multistep income statement that would be used for external reporting purposes, beginning with the amount for Net Sales.

3. Compute the gross profit percentage.

CONTINUING CASES

LO 6-6, 6-7   **CC6-1 Accounting for Merchandising Operations**

Nicole's Getaway Spa (NGS) has been so successful that Nicole has decided to expand her spa by selling merchandise. She sells things such as nail polish, at-home spa kits, cosmetics, and aromatherapy items. Nicole uses a perpetual inventory system and is starting to realize all of the work that is created when inventory is involved in a business. The following transactions were selected from among those completed by NGS in August.

Aug. 2   Sold 10 items of merchandise to Salon World on account at a selling price of $1,000 (total); terms 2/10, n/30. The goods cost NGS $650.

Aug. 3   Sold 5 identical items of merchandise to Cosmetics R Us on account at a selling price of $500 (total); terms 2/10, n/30. The goods cost NGS $400.

Aug. 6   Cosmetics R Us returned one of the items purchased on August 3. The item could still be sold by NGS in the future, and credit was given to the customer.

Aug. 10   Collected payment from Salon World, fully paying off the account balance.

Aug. 20   Sold two at-home spa kits to Meghan Witzel for $300 cash. The goods cost NGS $96.

Aug. 22   Cosmetics R Us paid its remaining account balance in full.

Required:

1. Prepare journal entries for each transaction.
2. Calculate the amount of Net Sales and Cost of Goods Sold for the transactions listed above. What is Nicole's Getaway Spa's gross profit percentage? Explain to Nicole what this gross profit percentage means.
3. At the end of August, Nicole noticed that the bank account balance did not equal the company's Cash account balance. Explain to her why these balances do not equal and what related internal control she needs to establish.

CC6-2 Wiki Art Gallery (WAG)

LO 6-2, 6-7

Access the Wiki Art Gallery (WAG) instructional case in Connect, and read the case in sufficient depth to answer the following questions.

1. Is the revenue recognition policy used by Wiki Art Gallery (WAG) for artwork sales in accordance with the revenue recognition principle? Why or why not?
   a. Yes, the artwork sales policy is in accordance with the revenue recognition principle because WAG reports sales using FOB shipping point.
   b. Yes, the artwork sales policy is in accordance with the revenue recognition principle because WAG reports sales using FOB destination.
   c. No, the artwork sales policy is not in accordance with the revenue recognition principle because WAG reports revenue as it is earned each month.
   d. No, the artwork sales policy is not in accordance with the revenue recognition principle because WAG reports revenue before it fulfills its obligation to transfer ownership of the artwork to the customer.

2. WAG presents a single-step income statement. Reorganize it into a multistep format to calculate the gross profit from artwork sales in 2011 and 2010 and the gross profit percentage from artwork sales in 2011 and 2010. Which of the following is consistent with the amounts reported by WAG?
   a. Gross profit from artwork sales was $58,225 in 2011 and $10,400 in 2010, and the gross profit percentage was 72.2% in 2011 and 34.2% in 2010.
   b. Gross profit from artwork sales was $58,225 in 2011 and $10,400 in 2010, and the gross profit percentage was 41.6% in 2011 and 14.9% in 2010.
   c. Gross profit from artwork sales was $63,061 in 2011 and $2,417 in 2010, and the gross profit percentage was 45.0% in 2011 and 3.45% in 2010.
   d. Gross profit from artwork sales was $22,375 in 2011 and $20,000 in 2010, and the gross profit percentage was 27.8% in 2011 and 65.8% in 2010.

3. Recalculate WAG's gross profit and gross percentage for 2011 after removing the effects of the sale to TEAC. Which of the following is consistent with these revised amounts?
   a. The revised gross profit would be $30,600, resulting in a gross profit percentage of 38.0%.
   b. The revised gross profit would be $8,225, resulting in a gross profit percentage of 26.9%.
   c. The revised gross profit would be $10,600, resulting in a gross profit percentage of 34.6%.
   d. The revised gross profit would be $10,225, resulting in a gross profit percentage of 33.4%.

Inventories and Cost of Goods Sold

YOUR LEARNING OBJECTIVES

Understand the business

LO 7-1   Describe the issues in managing different types of inventory.

Study the accounting methods

LO 7-2   Explain how to report inventory and cost of goods sold.

LO 7-3   Compute costs using four inventory costing methods.

LO 7-4   Report inventory at the lower of cost or market.

LO 7-5   Analyze and record inventory purchases, transportation, returns and allowances, and discounts.

Evaluate the results

LO 7-6   Evaluate inventory management by computing and interpreting the inventory turnover ratio.

Review the chapter

Supplemental material

LO 7-S1   Compute inventory costs in perpetual systems.

LO 7-S2   Determine the effects of inventory errors.

LO 7-S3   Record inventory transactions in a periodic system.

THAT WAS THEN

In the previous chapter, we focused on selling goods that were purchased at the same cost per unit.

FOCUS COMPANY: American Eagle Outfitters

AMERICAN EAGLE
OUTFITTERS
ae.com

Whether you are shopping for gasoline, groceries, or a new electronic gadget, prices always seem to be changing. The political situation in oil-producing nations can cause a stunning increase in prices at the pump. A late freeze in Florida can hike the price of orange juice. Increasing competition can dramatically lower the cost of that new tablet.

Like you, companies face similar changes when they purchase or produce goods. For some products, unit costs increase over time and, for others, technological innovation causes unit costs to decrease. Either way, inventory is likely to include some items that were acquired at a lower unit cost and others that were acquired at a higher unit cost.

Suppose clothing retailer American Eagle Outfitters buys three batches of its AE Fleece Jackets at a cost of $20 per jacket for the first batch, $30 per jacket for the second batch, and $40 per jacket for the third. When American Eagle sells a jacket, what cost should it use to compute the Cost of Goods Sold? And, what happens at the end of the season when the value of its jackets falls below cost? As you will learn in this chapter, accounting rules allow different methods to be used when accounting for inventory, each of which leads to reporting different dollar amounts for Cost of Goods Sold (and the items remaining in inventory). This flexibility allows managers to choose the method that best fits their business environment. But it also means that you must know which method managers are using and how it works. That's what we'll look at in this chapter.

www.ae.com

THIS IS NOW

This chapter demonstrates how to account for goods purchased at different unit costs.

305

Understand the business	Study the accounting methods	Evaluate the results	Review the chapter
• Inventory management decisions • Types of inventory	• Balance sheet and income statement reporting • Inventory costing methods • Lower of cost or market • Recording inventory transactions	• Inventory turnover analysis	• Demonstration case • Chapter summary • Key terms • Homework helper • Practice material

Understand the Business

Learning Objective 7-1
Describe the issues in managing different types of inventory.

INVENTORY MANAGEMENT DECISIONS

You may not make or sell inventory, but you buy it all the time. The things that concern you as a consumer also concern managers who make inventory decisions. The primary goals of inventory managers are to (1) maintain a sufficient **quantity** of inventory to meet customers' needs and (2) ensure inventory **quality** meets customers' expectations and company standards. At the same time, they try to (3) minimize the **cost** of acquiring and carrying inventory (including costs related to purchasing, production, storage, spoilage, theft, obsolescence, and financing). These factors are tricky to manage because as one of them changes (e.g., quality) so, too, do the others (e.g., cost). Ultimately, inventory management often comes down to purchasing goods that can be sold soon after they are acquired.

TYPES OF INVENTORY

The generic term *inventory* means goods that are held for sale in the normal course of business or are used to produce other goods for sale. Merchandisers hold **merchandise inventory,** which consists of products acquired in a finished condition, ready for sale without further processing. Manufacturers often hold three types of inventory, with each representing a different stage in the manufacturing process. They start with **raw materials inventory** such as plastic, steel, or fabrics. When these raw materials enter the production process, they become part of **work in process inventory,** which includes goods that are in the process of being manufactured. When completed, work in process inventory becomes **finished goods inventory,** which is ready for sale just like merchandise inventory. For purposes of this chapter, we'll focus on merchandise inventory, but be aware that the concepts we cover apply equally to manufacturers' inventory.

Two other accounting terms may be used to describe inventory. **Consignment inventory** refers to goods a company is holding on behalf of the goods' owner. Typically, this arises when a company is willing to sell the goods for the owner (for a fee) but does not want to take ownership of the goods in the event the goods are difficult to sell. Consignment inventory is reported on the balance sheet of the owner, not the company holding the inventory. **Goods in transit** are inventory items being transported. This type of inventory is reported on the balance sheet of the owner, not the company transporting it. As you may remember from Chapter 6, ownership of inventory is determined by the terms of the inventory sales agreement. If a sale is made FOB destination, the goods belong to the seller until they reach their destination (the customer). If a sale is made FOB shipping point, inventory belongs to the customer at the point of shipping (from the seller's premises).

Study the Accounting Methods

BALANCE SHEET AND INCOME STATEMENT REPORTING

Because inventory will be used or converted into cash within one year, it is reported on the balance sheet as a current asset. Goods placed in inventory are initially recorded at cost, which is the amount paid to acquire the asset and prepare it for sale. See Exhibit 7.1 for the way American Eagle reports inventory.

> **Learning Objective 7-2**
> Explain how to report inventory and cost of goods sold.

AMERICAN EAGLE
OUTFITTERS
ae.com

EXHIBIT 7.1	Reporting Inventory on the Balance Sheet (Partial)

AMERICAN EAGLE OUTFITTERS, INC.
Balance Sheets (Partial)

(in millions)	January 29, 2011	January 30, 2010
Assets		
Current Assets		
Cash and Cash Equivalents	$668	$694
Short-term Investments	67	5
Inventory	301	326
Accounts and Note Receivable	37	35
Prepaid Expenses and Other	102	107

When a company sells goods, it removes their cost from the Inventory account and reports the cost on the income statement as the expense Cost of Goods Sold. See Exhibit 7.2 for how American Eagle reports the Cost of Goods Sold (CGS) on its partial income statement. Notice that it follows directly after Net Sales. The difference between these two line items is a subtotal called Gross Profit.

AMERICAN EAGLE
OUTFITTERS
ae.com

EXHIBIT 7.2	Reporting Cost of Goods Sold on the Income Statement (Partial)

AMERICAN EAGLE OUTFITTERS, INC.
Income Statements (Partial)
For the Years Ended

(in millions)	January 29, 2011	January 30, 2010	January 31, 2009
Net Sales	$2,968	$2,940	$2,949
Cost of Goods Sold	1,797	1,767	1,752
Gross Profit	1,171	1,173	1,197

Cost of Goods Sold Equation

Although the cost of inventory and the cost of goods sold are reported on different financial statements, they are related. A company starts each accounting period with a stock of inventory called **beginning inventory (BI).** During the accounting period, new **purchases (P)** are added to the beginning inventory. As in Exhibit 7.3, the sum of these two amounts (BI + P) becomes the cost of **goods available for sale** during the period.

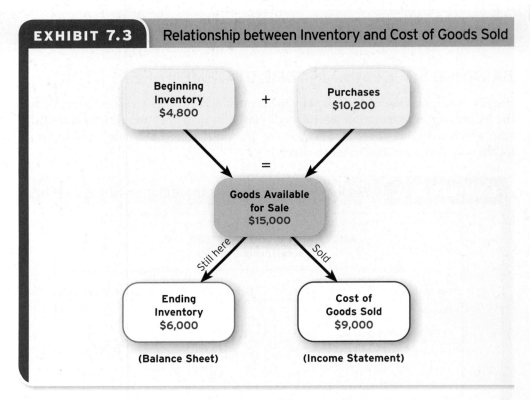

EXHIBIT 7.3   Relationship between Inventory and Cost of Goods Sold

Goods available for sale either will be sold during the period (reported as the cost of goods sold on the income statement) or not (reported as **ending inventory (EI)** on the balance sheet). The ending inventory for one accounting period then becomes the beginning inventory for the next period. The **cost of goods sold (CGS) equation** summarizes the relationships between these inventory amounts:

$$\text{BI} + \text{P} - \text{CGS} = \text{EI}$$

To illustrate the CGS equation, assume that, as in Exhibit 7.3, American Eagle Outfitters began the period with $4,800 of Vintage Jeans in beginning inventory. During the period, the company purchased more of these jeans for $10,200. This meant that American Eagle had goods costing $15,000 that were available for sale. If the cost of goods sold for the period was $9,000, $6,000 of jeans was left in inventory at the end of the period. These amounts can be represented in the following cost of goods sold equation or Inventory T-account:

Cost of Goods Sold Calculation	
Beginning Inventory	$ 4,800
+ Purchases	+10,200
Goods Available for Sale	15,000
− Cost of Goods Sold	− 9,000
Ending Inventory	$ 6,000

+	Inventory (A)		−
Beginning Inventory	4,800		
Purchases of Inventory	10,200	9,000	Cost of Goods Sold
Ending Inventory	6,000		

If one of the values in the cost of goods sold equation is unknown, you can use either the cost of goods sold equation or the inventory T-account to solve for the missing value. See for yourself in the following Self-Study Practice.

 How's it going?   Self-Study Practice

Use the cost of goods sold equation to solve for the missing information for cases 1 and 2. Then enter the information for either case 1 or case 2 into the T-account on the right.

		Case 1	Case 2
Beginning Inventory	5 units × $10	$ 50	$ 50
+ Purchases	20 units × $10	200	200
Goods Available for Sale			250
− Ending Inventory		100	
Cost of Goods Sold			$150

dr −	Inventory		cr −
Beginning	50		
Purchases	200		
Goods Available			
		Goods Sold	
Ending Inventory			

After you have finished, check your answers with the solution in the margin.

Solution to Self-Study Practice
Case 1: Goods available = $250, CGS = $150
Case 2: Ending inventory = $100

dr +	Inventory		cr −
Beginning Inventory	50		
Purchases	200		
Goods Available	250	150	Goods Sold
Ending Inventory	100		

INVENTORY COSTING METHODS

Learning Objective 7-3
Compute costs using four inventory costing methods.

In the example presented in the Self-Study Practice, the cost of all units of the item was the same—$10. If inventory costs normally remained constant, we'd be done right now. But just as you notice every time you fill up your car with gas, the cost of goods does not always stay the same. In recent years, the costs of many items have risen moderately. In other cases, such as electronic products, costs have dropped dramatically.

When the costs of inventory change over time, it is not obvious how to determine the cost of goods sold (and the cost of ending inventory). To see why, think about the following simple example:

May 3	Purchased 1 unit for **$70**.
May 5	Purchased 1 more unit for **$75**.
May 6	Purchased 1 more unit for **$95**.
May 8	Sold 2 units for **$125** each.

The sale on May 8 of two units, at a selling price of $125 each, would generate sales revenue of $250 ($125 × 2), but what amount would be considered the cost of goods sold? The answer depends on which goods are reported as sold.

Four generally accepted inventory costing methods are available for determining the cost of goods sold and the cost of goods remaining in ending inventory. The method chosen does not have to correspond to the physical flow of goods, so any one of these four methods is acceptable under GAAP in the United States.

The **specific identification** method individually identifies and records the cost of each item sold as Cost of Goods Sold. This method requires accountants to keep track of the purchase cost of each item. In the example just given, if the items sold were identified as the ones received on May 3 and May 6, which cost $70 and $95, the total cost of those items ($70 + $95 = $165) would be reported as Cost of Goods Sold. The cost of the remaining item ($75) would be reported as Inventory on the balance sheet at the end of the period. Companies tend to use the specific identification method when accounting for individually expensive and unique items. Toll Brothers, the country's leading builder of luxury homes, reports the costs of home construction using the specific identification method. Car Max, a national auto dealership, uses specific identification too.

The units within each American Eagle product line are identical, so the company does not use the specific identification method. Like most companies, American Eagle

YOU SHOULD KNOW

Specific identification:
The inventory costing method that identifies the cost of the specific item that was sold.

uses one of the three other cost flow methods to account for inventory items. These three other inventory costing methods are **not based on the physical flow** of goods on and off the shelves. Instead, these methods are based on **assumptions** that accountants make about the flow of inventory costs. These three cost flow assumptions are applied to our simple three-unit example in Exhibit 7.4.

1. **First-in, first-out (FIFO)** assumes that the inventory costs flow out in the order the goods are received. As in Exhibit 7.4, the earliest items received, the $70 and $75 units received on May 3 and 5, become the $145 Cost of Goods Sold on the income statement and the remaining $95 unit received on May 6 becomes ending Inventory on the balance sheet.

2. **Last-in, first-out (LIFO)** assumes that the inventory costs flow out in the opposite of the order the goods are received. As in Exhibit 7.4, the latest items received, the $95 and $75 units received on May 6 and 5, become the $170 Cost of Goods Sold on the income statement, and the remaining $70 unit received on May 3 becomes ending Inventory on the balance sheet.

3. **Weighted average cost** uses the weighted average of the costs of goods available for sale for both the cost of each item sold and those remaining in inventory. As in Exhibit 7.4, the average of the costs [($70 + $75 + $95) ÷ 3 = $80] is assigned to the two items sold, resulting in $160 as Cost of Goods Sold on the income statement. The same $80 average cost is assigned to the one item in ending Inventory reported on the balance sheet.

As Exhibit 7.4 illustrates, the choice of cost flow assumption can have a major effect on Gross Profit on the income statement and Inventory on the balance sheet. Walgreens, for example, would report $1.5 billion more gross profit if it used FIFO rather than LIFO. But doing so would also increase the company's income taxes, so it stays with LIFO.

Notice that **although they're called "inventory" costing methods, their names actually describe how to calculate the cost of goods sold.** That is, the "first-out" part of FIFO and LIFO refers to the goods that are sold (i.e., first out) not the goods that are still in ending inventory. Also notice that the cost flows assumed for LIFO are the opposite of FIFO, and weighted average is a middle-of-the-road method.

EXHIBIT 7.4 | Cost Flow Assumptions and Financial Statement Effects

Inventory Cost Flow Computations

Now that you've seen how these cost flow assumptions work and that they actually make a difference in a company's balance sheet and income statement, you're ready for a more realistic example. So, let's assume that during the first week of October American Eagle entered into the following transactions for its Henley T-shirt product line. All sales were made at a selling price of $15 per unit. These sales occurred after American Eagle made two batches of T-shirt purchases, which were added to inventory purchased the previous month.

Date	Description	# of Units	Cost per Unit	Total Cost
Oct. 1	Beginning Inventory	10	$ 7	$ 70
Oct. 3	Purchase	30	8	240
Oct. 5	Purchase	10	10	100
	Goods Available for Sale	50		410
Oct. 6	Sales	(35)	To calculate	To calculate
	Ending Inventory	15	To calculate	To calculate

FIFO (First-in, first-out) The first-in, first-out (FIFO) method assumes that the oldest goods (the first in to inventory) are the first ones sold (the first out of inventory). So **to calculate the cost of the 35 units sold, use the costs of the first-in (oldest) goods** (10 units at $7 plus 25 of the 30 units at $8 = a total of $270). The **costs of the newer goods are included in the cost of the ending inventory** (10 units at $10 plus 5 units remaining from the 30 units at $8 = a total of $140). These calculations are summarized in the table below.

FIFO		
Beginning Inventory	10 units × $7	$ 70
+ Purchases	30 units × $8	240
	10 units × $10	100
Goods Available for Sale		410
− Ending Inventory (10 × $10) + (5 × $8)		**140**
Cost of Goods Sold (10 × $7) + (25 × $8)		$270

Notice in the table that the Cost of Goods Sold can be calculated directly (10 times $7 plus 25 times $8 = a total of $270) or it can be "backed into" by subtracting the cost of ending inventory from the cost of goods available for sale ($410 − $140 = $270). This latter approach is helpful if the number of units sold is not known, which can occur when a company uses a periodic inventory system.[1]

LIFO (Last-in, first-out) The last-in, first-out (LIFO) method assumes that the newest goods (the last in to inventory) are the first ones sold (the first out of inventory). So **to calculate the cost of the 35 units sold, use the costs of the last-in (newest) goods** (10 units at $10 plus 25 of the 30 units at $8 = total of $300). The **costs of the older goods, including those in beginning inventory, are included in the cost of the**

---

[1]By showing all purchases taking place before any Sales and Cost of Goods Sold are computed, we are demonstrating a periodic inventory system. You might think it's odd that we use a periodic system when we said in Chapter 6 that most modern companies use perpetual inventory systems. We actually have several good reasons for doing this, which we explain in Supplement 7A at the end of this chapter. To learn how cost flow assumptions are applied in more complex situations involving perpetual inventory systems, see Supplement 7A. For purposes of examples shown in the chapter and for problem materials at the end of this chapter, we assume no shrinkage (a topic discussed in Chapter 6).

ending inventory (10 units at $7 plus 5 units remaining from the 30 units at $8 = a total of $110). These calculations are summarized in the table below.

LIFO		
Beginning Inventory	10 units × $7	$ 70
+ Purchases	30 units × $8	240
	10 units × $10	100
Goods Available for Sale		410
− Ending Inventory (10 × $7) + (5 × $8)		**110**
Cost of Goods Sold (10 × $10) + (25 × $8)		$300

As in the table, Cost of Goods Sold can be calculated directly (10 times $10 plus 25 times $8 = a total of $300) or it can be "backed into" by subtracting the cost of ending inventory from the cost of goods available for sale ($410 − $110 = $300). We actually recommend that you do both, as a way to double-check your calculations.

Weighted Average Cost   The weighted average cost method is calculated in two steps. The first step is to calculate the total cost of the goods available for sale. You multiply the number of units at each cost by the cost per unit and then add to get the total cost:

Beginning Inventory	10 units × $7	$ 70
+ Purchases	30 units × $8	240
	10 units × $10	100
Goods Available for Sale	**50 units**	**$410**

Then you calculate the weighted average cost per unit using the following formula:

$$\text{Weighted Average Cost} = \frac{\text{Cost of Goods Available for Sale}}{\text{Number of Units Available for Sale}} = \frac{\$410}{50 \text{ units}} = \frac{\$8.20}{\text{per unit}}$$

Cost of goods sold and ending inventory are both calculated using the same weighted average cost per unit, as in the following table.

Weighted Average		
Beginning Inventory	10 units × $7	$ 70
+ Purchases	30 units × $8	240
	10 units × $10	100
Goods Available for Sale	**50 units**	410
− Ending Inventory (15 × $8.20)		123
Cost of Goods Sold (35 × $8.20)		$287

Financial Statement Effects   Exhibit 7.5 summarizes the financial statement effects of the FIFO, LIFO, and weighted average cost methods. Remember that these methods differ only in the way they split the cost of goods available for sale between ending inventory and cost of goods sold. If a cost goes into Inventory, it doesn't go into Cost of Goods Sold. Thus, the method that assigns the highest cost to ending inventory will assign the lowest cost to cost of goods sold (and vice versa). As you can see in Exhibit 7.5, the effect on Cost of Goods Sold affects many other items on the income statement including Gross Profit, Income from Operations, Income before Income Tax Expense, Income Tax Expense, and Net Income.

EXHIBIT 7.5	Financial Statement Effects of Inventory Costing Methods

Effects on the Income Statement	FIFO	LIFO	Weighted Average
Sales	$525	$525	$525
Cost of Goods Sold	270	300	287
Gross Profit	255	225	238
Operating Expenses	125	125	125
Income from Operations	130	100	113
Other Revenue (Expenses)	20	20	20
Income before Income Tax Expense	150	120	133
Income Tax Expense (assume 30%)	45	36	40
Net Income	$105	$ 84	S 93
Effects on the Balance Sheet			
Inventory	$140	$110	S123

Depending on whether costs are rising or falling, different methods have different effects on the financial statements. **When costs are rising,** as they are in our example, FIFO produces a higher inventory value (making the balance sheet **appear** to be stronger) and a lower cost of goods sold (resulting in a higher gross profit, which makes the company look more profitable). **When costs are falling,** these effects are reversed; FIFO produces a lower ending inventory value and a higher cost of goods sold—a double whammy. These are not "real" economic effects, however, because the same number of units is sold or held in ending inventory under either method. The following graphic summarizes the effects:

Tax Implications and Cash Flow Effects Given the financial statement effects, you might wonder why a company would ever use a method that produces a lower inventory amount and a higher cost of goods sold. The answer is suggested in Exhibit 7.5, in the line called Income Tax Expense. When faced with increasing costs per unit, as in our example, **a company that uses FIFO will have a higher income tax expense.** This income tax effect is a real cost, in the sense that the company will actually have to pay more income taxes in the current year, thereby reducing the company's cash.

 How's it going?   Self-Study Practice

Ultimo Euromoda, Inc., purchased one designer suit at a cost of $200 and then purchased three more for $400 each. Three of the suits are then sold at a price of $1,000 each. Compute the Sales Revenue, Cost of Goods Sold, Gross Profit, and the cost of ending Inventory using (a) FIFO, (b) weighted average, and (c) LIFO. Which inventory costing method will minimize Ultimo's income taxes?

After you have finished, check your answers with the solution in the margin.

Solution to Self-Study Practice

	(a) FIFO	(b) Weighted Average	(c) LIFO
Sales Revenue (3 × $1,000)	$3,000	$3,000	$3,000
Cost of Goods Sold*	1,000	1,050	1,200
Gross Profit	2,000	1,950	1,800
Ending Inventory	$ 400	$ 350	$ 200

*(a) $1,000 = (1 × $200) + (2 × $400); (b) $1,050 = 3 × [(1 × $200) + (3 × $400)]/4; (c) $1,200 = 3 × $400

LIFO minimizes Ultimo's gross profit and, therefore, minimizes its income taxes.

Consistency in Reporting A common question is whether managers are free to choose LIFO one period, FIFO the next, and then go back to LIFO, depending on whether unit costs are rising or declining during the period. Because this switching would make it difficult to compare financial results across periods, accounting rules discourage it. A change in method is allowed only if it improves the accuracy of the company's financial results. A company can, however, use different methods for inventories that differ in nature or use, provided that the methods are used consistently over time. Tax rules also limit the methods that can be used. In the United States, the LIFO Conformity Rule requires that if LIFO is used on the income tax return, it also must be used in financial statement reporting.

SPOTLIGHT ON The World

No LIFO

Approximately 35 percent of companies in the United States use LIFO,* but **International Financial Reporting Standards (IFRS) do not allow LIFO** so a switch from U.S. GAAP to IFRS would require many U.S. companies to stop using LIFO in their financial statements. And if these companies stop using LIFO in their financial statements, the LIFO Conformity Rule will require that they stop using LIFO in their tax returns. Without LIFO, these companies would have higher tax bills (as illustrated in Exhibit 7.5), the total cost of which is estimated to be more than $100 billion.[‡] In his 2013 budget proposal to Congress, President Obama proposed to disallow LIFO. At the time of writing this textbook, the matter had not been resolved.

*American Institute of Certified Public Accountants, *Accounting Trends and Techniques,* 63rd ed. 2010.

[‡]House Ways and Means Committee, H.R. 3970, Tax Reduction and Reform Act of 2007 (October 29, 2007).

LOWER OF COST OR MARKET

The value of inventory can fall below its recorded cost for two reasons: (1) it's easily replaced by identical goods at a lower cost, or (2) it's become outdated or damaged. The first case is common for high-tech electronics. As companies become more efficient at making these cutting-edge products, they become cheaper to make. The second case commonly occurs with fad items or seasonal goods such as American Eagle's winter coats, which tend to drop in value at the end of the season.

In either instance, when the value of inventory falls below its recorded cost, GAAP require that the inventory be written down to its lower market value. This rule is known as reporting inventories at the **lower of cost or market (LCM)**. It results in reporting inventory conservatively, at an amount that does not exceed its actual value. Also, by recording the write-down in the period in which a loss in value occurs, companies better match their revenues and expenses of that period.

YOU SHOULD KNOW

Lower of cost or market (LCM): A valuation rule that requires inventory to be written down when its market value falls below its cost.

Let's look at how the inventory write-down is determined and recorded. Assume that American Eagle's ending inventory includes two items whose replacement costs have recently changed: leather coats and vintage jeans.[2] The replacement costs of these items can be used as estimates of market value and compared to the original recorded cost per unit. You then take the lower of those two amounts (the lower of cost or market) and multiply it by the number of units on hand. The result is the amount at which the inventory should be reported after all adjustments have been made:

Item	Cost per Item	Market Value per Item	LCM per Item	Quantity	Total Lower of Cost or Market	Recorded Total Cost
Leather coats	$165	**$150**	$150	1,000	**$150** × 1,000 = $150,000	$165,000
Vintage jeans	**20**	25	20	400	**$ 20** × 400 = 8,000	8,000

[2]We apply lower of cost or market on an item basis. It also may be applied on a product category basis.

Because the market value of the 1,000 leather coats ($150 × 1,000) is **lower** than the recorded cost ($165 × 1,000), the recorded amount for ending inventory should be written down by $15 per unit ($165 − $150). Thus, the total write-down should be $15,000 ($15 × 1,000). The effect of this write-down on the accounting equation and the journal entry to record it would be:

1 Analyze

Assets	=	Liabilities	+	Stockholders' Equity	
Inventory −15,000	=			Cost of Goods Sold (+E)	−15,000

2 Record

(a)	dr Cost of Goods Sold (+E −SE)	15,000	
	cr Inventory (−A)		15,000

Because the market value of the vintage jeans ($25) is higher than the original cost ($20), no write-down is necessary. The vintage jeans remain on the books at their cost of $20 per unit ($8,000 in total). Their value should not be increased based on the higher replacement cost because GAAP require that they be reported at the **lower** of cost or market.

Most companies report their inventory write-down expense as Cost of Goods Sold, even though the written-down goods may not have been sold. This reporting is appropriate because writing down goods that haven't yet sold is a necessary cost of carrying the goods that did sell. By recording the write-down in the period in which a loss in value occurs, companies better match their revenues and expenses of that period.

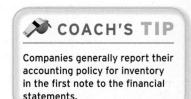

COACH'S TIP

Companies generally report their accounting policy for inventory in the first note to the financial statements.

SPOTLIGHT ON **Financial Reporting**

Blackberry PlayBook Leaves Sour Taste

When the maker of Blackberry devices, Research in Motion (RIM), recently announced a $485 million LCM write-down on its inventory of first generation PlayBooks, investors reacted by selling their shares in the company. Within just one day of the announcement, the company's stock price fell by 9.2%, to only $17 per share. Investors knew the write-down signaled bad news for the tablet.

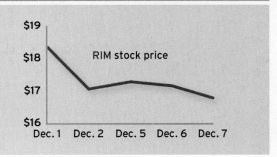

Because investors and analysts view an inventory LCM write-down as a sign of inventory management problems, some executives go out of their way to avoid them, as the Spotlight on Ethics on the following page explains. The failure to follow inventory LCM rules is one of the most common types of financial statement misstatements. To learn more about how this misstatement and other inventory errors can affect the financial statements, see Supplement 7B at the end of this chapter.

RECORDING INVENTORY TRANSACTIONS

To this point in the chapter, we have described the requirement that inventory be reported at the lower of cost or market, and we have shown how those values are determined. But we haven't discussed the details about how to record inventory transactions. Until now, we have considered only inventory purchases but not other related

Learning Objective 7-5
Analyze and record inventory purchases, transportation, returns and allowances, and discounts.

transactions including transportation, purchase returns and allowances, and purchase discounts. In this section, we demonstrate the accounting for these other transactions. For purposes of this demonstration, we record all inventory-related transactions in the Inventory account. This approach is generally associated with a **perpetual inventory system** because it maintains an up-to-date balance in the Inventory account at all times. An alternative approach, which maintains separate accounts for purchases, transportation, and so on, is generally used in a **periodic inventory system** and is demonstrated in Supplement 7C at the end of this chapter.

Inventory Purchases

To enhance efficiency and internal control, most companies buy inventory on credit rather than with cash. If American Eagle Outfitters purchases $10,500 of vintage jeans on credit, the transaction would affect the accounting equation and would be recorded as follows.

① Analyze

Assets		=	Liabilities		+	Stockholders' Equity
Inventory	+10,500		Accounts Payable	+10,500		

② Record

dr Inventory (+A) 10,500
    cr Accounts Payable (+L) 10,500

The $10,500 owed to the supplier remains in Accounts Payable until it is paid, at which time Accounts Payable is decreased (with a debit) and Cash is decreased (with a credit). The Inventory account remains at $10,500, unless the inventory is sold or any of the following transactions occur.

Transportation Cost

The inventory that American Eagle purchases does not magically appear in its stores. It must be shipped from the supplier to American Eagle. If the terms are **FOB shipping point,** the purchaser pays for the shipping. If the terms are **FOB destination,** the seller pays for the shipping. When the purchaser pays for the shipping, the additional cost of transporting the goods (called freight-in) is added to the Inventory account.

Assume that American Eagle pays $400 cash to a trucker who delivers the $10,500 of vintage jeans to one of its stores. American Eagle would account for this transportation cost as follows:

1 Analyze

	Assets		=	Liabilities	+ Stockholders' Equity
Cash		−400			
Inventory		+400			

2 Record

dr Inventory (+A) 400
    cr Cash (−A)   400

In general, a purchaser should **include in the Inventory account any costs needed to get the inventory into a condition and location ready for sale.** Costs that are incurred after the inventory has been made ready for sale, such as freight-out to deliver goods to customers, should be treated as selling expenses.

Purchase Returns and Allowances

When goods purchased from a supplier arrive in damaged condition or fail to meet specifications, the buyer can (1) return them for a full refund or (2) keep them and ask for a cost reduction, called an allowance. Either way, these **purchase returns and allowances** are accounted for by reducing the cost of the inventory and either recording a cash refund or by reducing the liability owed to the supplier.

Assume, for example, that American Eagle returned some of the vintage jeans to the supplier and received a $500 reduction in the balance owed. This purchase return would be analyzed and recorded as follows:

> **YOU SHOULD KNOW**
>
> **Purchase returns and allowances:** A reduction in the cost of inventory purchases associated with unsatisfactory goods.

1 Analyze

	Assets		=	Liabilities		+ Stockholders' Equity
Inventory		−500	Accounts Payable		−500	

2 Record

dr Accounts Payable (−L)... 500
    cr Inventory (−A)   500

Purchase Discounts

When inventory is bought on credit, terms such as "2/10, n/30" may be specified. Chapter 6 provided a lengthy description of how to interpret these terms from the seller's perspective. From the purchaser's perspective, these terms mean that the purchaser is allowed to deduct a 2 percent **purchase discount** if payment is made within 10 days of the date of purchase, otherwise the purchase cost (net of any returns or allowances) is due within 30 days of the purchase date.

When offered a purchase discount at the time of purchase, the purchaser accounts for it in two stages. Initially, the purchase is accounted for at full cost. Later, if payment is made within the discount period, the purchaser reduces the Inventory account by the amount of the discount because it effectively reduces the cost of the inventory. The purchase discount is calculated using the net amount owing to the supplier, after considering purchase returns and allowances.

Assume, for example, that American Eagle's purchase of vintage jeans for $10,500 occurred with terms 2/10, n/30. The initial purchase would be accounted for as shown earlier, by recording a $10,500 increase in Inventory (with a debit) and a $10,500

> **YOU SHOULD KNOW**
>
> **Purchase discount:** A cash discount received for prompt payment of a purchase on account.

> **COACH'S TIP**
>
> The discount would not be applied to the freight-in unless the trucking company offered a discount.

increase in Accounts Payable (with a credit). In our example, American Eagle returned inventory costing $500 and received a $500 reduction in its Accounts Payable. Consequently, American Eagle owed the supplier $10,000 for the purchase. Multiplying this balance by the 2 percent discount, we find that American Eagle's purchase discount is $200 (2% × $10,000 = $200). This discount means that American Eagle has to pay only $9,800 ($10,000 − $200 = $9,800) to fully satisfy its $10,000 of Accounts Payable. The $200 discount also reduces the cost of inventory as follows:

① Analyze

	Assets	=	Liabilities	+ Stockholders' Equity
Cash	−9,800	Accounts Payable	−10,000	
Inventory	−200			

② Record

dr Accounts Payable (−L)	10,000	
cr Cash (−A)		9,800
cr Inventory (−A)		200

COACH'S TIP

To review how to account for sales of inventory, see page 265 in Chapter 6.

Summary of Inventory Transactions

You have now seen how several types of inventory transactions affect the Inventory account on the balance sheet. Exhibit 7.6 summarizes, in table and T-account forms, how these transactions affect inventory, assuming beginning inventory was $4,800. Take a moment to flip back to Exhibit 7.3 on page 308 so that you can see that these are the values that will either become assigned to Cost of Goods Sold (when the goods are sold) or remain in Inventory.

EXHIBIT 7.6	Effects of Inventory Transactions Related to Purchases

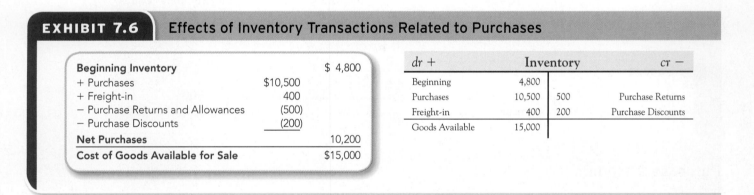

Beginning Inventory		$ 4,800
+ Purchases	$10,500	
+ Freight-in	400	
− Purchase Returns and Allowances	(500)	
− Purchase Discounts	(200)	
Net Purchases		10,200
Cost of Goods Available for Sale		$15,000

dr +	Inventory		cr −
Beginning	4,800		
Purchases	10,500	500	Purchase Returns
Freight-in	400	200	Purchase Discounts
Goods Available	15,000		

Evaluate the Results

INVENTORY TURNOVER ANALYSIS

Learning Objective 7-6
Evaluate inventory management by computing and interpreting the inventory turnover ratio.

If a company's inventory balance increases from $100,000 in one period to $130,000 in the next, is that good news or bad news? If the increase occurs because management is building up stock in anticipation of higher sales, it could be good news. But if it results from an accumulation of old inventory items that nobody wants, it is probably bad news. Those who work inside the company can easily determine whether the change is good or bad news by talking with the sales managers. But if you are looking at the company's financial statements from the outside, how can you tell?

EXHIBIT 7.7	Inventory Turnover Analysis

The method most analysts use to evaluate such changes is called inventory turnover analysis. Exhibit 7.7 illustrates the idea behind inventory turnover analysis. As a company buys goods, its inventory balance goes up; as it sells goods, its inventory balance goes down. This process of buying and selling, which is called **inventory turnover**, is repeated over and over during each accounting period for each line of products.

Analysts can assess how many times, on average, inventory has been bought and sold during the period by calculating the inventory turnover ratio. A higher ratio indicates that inventory moves more quickly from purchase to sale, reducing storage and obsolescence costs. Because less money is tied up in inventory, the excess can be invested to earn interest or reduce borrowing, which reduces interest expense. More efficient purchasing and production techniques as well as high product demand will boost this ratio. A sudden decline in the inventory turnover ratio may signal an unexpected drop in demand for the company's products or sloppy inventory management.

Rather than evaluate the **number of times** inventory turns over during the year, some analysts prefer to think in terms of the **length of time** (in days) required to sell inventory. Converting the inventory turnover ratio to the number of days needed to sell the inventory is easy. You simply divide 365 days by the year's inventory turnover ratio to get the **days to sell**. This measure provides the same basic information, but it is a little easier to interpret than the inventory turnover ratio. In terms of Exhibit 7.7, the inventory turnover ratio indicates the number of loops in a given period; days to sell indicates the average number of days between loops.

> **YOU SHOULD KNOW**
>
> **Inventory turnover:** The process of buying and selling inventory.

> **YOU SHOULD KNOW**
>
> **Days to sell:** A measure of the average number of days from the time inventory is bought to the time it is sold.

Accounting Decision Tools		
Name of Measure	**Formula**	**What It Tells You**
Inventory turnover ratio	$\dfrac{\text{Cost of Goods Sold}}{\text{Average Inventory}}$	• The number of times inventory turns over during the period • A higher ratio means faster turnover
Days to sell	$\dfrac{365}{\text{Inventory Turnover Ratio}}$	• Average number of days from purchase to sale • A higher number means a longer time to sell

Comparison to Benchmarks

Inventory turnover ratios and the number of days to sell can be helpful in comparing different companies' inventory management practices. But use them cautiously because these measures can vary significantly between industries. For merchandisers, inventory turnover refers to buying and selling goods, whereas for manufacturers, it refers to producing inventory and delivering it to customers. These differences are reflected in Exhibit 7.8, which shows that McDonald's has a turnover ratio of 49.1, which means it takes about 7–8 days to sell its entire food inventory (including the stuff in its freezers). The motorcycles at Harley-Davidson hog more time, as indicated by its inventory turnover ratio of 8.5, which equates to nearly 43 days to produce and sell. American Eagle's inventory turned over only 5.7 times during the year, which is just once every 64 days.

EXHIBIT 7.8	Summary of Inventory Turnover Ratio Analyses

Company	Relevant Information (in millions)			Fiscal 2010 Inventory Turnover Calculation	Fiscal 2010 Days to Sell Calculation
HARLEY-DAVIDSON MOTORCYCLES		**Fiscal 2010**	**Fiscal 2009**	$\dfrac{\$2{,}749}{(\$326 + \$323)/2} = 8.5 \text{ times}$	$\dfrac{365 \text{ days}}{8.5 \text{ times}} = 42.9 \text{ days}$
	CGS	$2,749	$2,901		
	Inventory	326	323		
M **i'm lovin' it**		**Fiscal 2010**	**Fiscal 2009**	$\dfrac{\$5{,}300}{(\$110 + \$106)/2} = 49.1 \text{ times}$	$\dfrac{365 \text{ days}}{49.1 \text{ times}} = 7.4 \text{ days}$
	CGS	$5,300	$5,178		
	Inventory	110	106		
AMERICAN EAGLE OUTFITTERS ae.com		**Fiscal 2010**	**Fiscal 2009**	$\dfrac{\$1{,}797}{(\$301 + \$326)/2} = 5.7 \text{ times}$	$\dfrac{365 \text{ days}}{5.7 \text{ times}} = 64.0 \text{ days}$
	CGS	$1,797	$1,767		
	Inventory	301	326		

Inventory turnover also can vary significantly between companies within the same industry, particularly if they take different approaches to pricing their inventories. In Chapter 6, we saw that Walmart follows a low-cost pricing policy, which means setting its sales prices only slightly above cost. This policy led Walmart to earn about 24.7 cents of gross profit on each dollar of sales whereas Saks earned 40.1 cents of gross profit. But when you consider the inventory turnover measures, you can see the full implications of this pricing policy. Walmart turns its inventory over about 9.1 times a year (40 days), whereas Saks turns inventory over 2.5 times a year (146 days). **Often, the company with a lower gross profit percentage has a faster inventory turnover.**

With inventory turnover ratios varying between industries and companies, it's most useful to compare a company's turnover with its own results from prior periods. For practice at computing and comparing to prior periods, try the Self-Study Practice below. Following that, in the Spotlight on Financial Reporting, see how the recent financial crisis affected inventory turnovers.

💡 How's it going?   Self-Study Practice

American Eagle's balance sheet and income statement information for prior years are presented in Exhibits 7.1 and 7.2 (page 307).

(a) Calculate American Eagle's inventory turnover and days to sell for the year ended January 31, 2010 (Fiscal 2009). The inventory balance on January 31, 2009, was $295 (million).

Fiscal 2009 Inventory Turnover: Fiscal 2009 Days to Sell:

$$\frac{\boxed{}}{(\boxed{} + \boxed{})/2} = \boxed{} \text{ times} \qquad \frac{365 \text{ days}}{\boxed{} \text{ times}} = \boxed{} \text{ days}$$

(b) Did American Eagle's inventory turnover improve, decline, or remain unchanged between Fiscal 2009 (calculated in a) and Fiscal 2010 (shown in Exhibit 7.8)?

After you have finished, check your answers with the solution in the margin.

Solution to Self-Study Practice

a. $\dfrac{\$1{,}767}{(\$326 + \$295)/2} = 5.7 \text{ times}$

$365 \div 5.7 = 64.0 \text{ days}$

b. American Eagle's inventory turnover (and days to sell) remained unchanged.

Days to Sell Before and After the Financial Crisis

The graph below shows a big spike in the number of days that (John) Deere & Company, Texas Instruments, and Caterpillar took to sell their inventories during the financial crisis that began in late 2008 and extended into 2009. These manufacturers found that their customers had to reduce spending during the crisis, which in turn caused the manufacturers' inventory levels to rise quickly. Increasing inventory levels, coupled with declining sales and cost of goods sold, led to slower inventory turnover and a big jump in the number of days to sell.

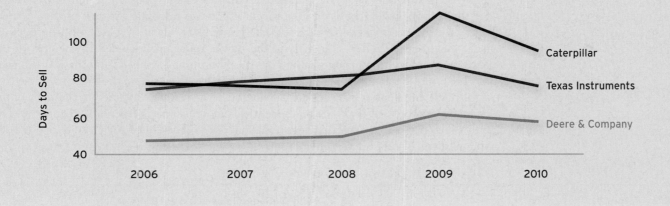

SUPPLEMENT 7A   FIFO, LIFO, AND WEIGHTED AVERAGE IN A PERPETUAL INVENTORY SYSTEM

> **Learning Objective 7-S1**
> Compute inventory costs in perpetual systems.

There were several good reasons for showing, in the previous sections of this chapter, how cost flow assumptions are applied in a periodic inventory system, even though most modern companies use perpetual inventory systems. First, only the LIFO and weighted average calculations differ between periodic and perpetual inventory systems. As we show in the following example, FIFO calculations don't differ between periodic and perpetual systems. Nearly half of all U.S. companies use FIFO, so even if they calculate costs under a perpetual system, it is identical to calculating costs under a periodic system. Second, most LIFO companies actually use FIFO during the period and then adjust to LIFO at the end of the period. By waiting to the end of the period to calculate this LIFO adjustment, it's *as if* all purchases during the period were recorded before the Cost of Goods Sold is calculated and recorded. In other words, it's as if these companies use a periodic inventory system to determine their LIFO inventory numbers, even though they actually track the number of units bought and sold on a perpetual basis. Third, companies typically adjust their records at year-end to match a physical count of the inventory on hand, so as a practical matter, these companies are in substance on a periodic costing system. Fourth, the periodic inventory system is easier to visualize, so it's easier for you to learn.

Despite these reasons, it can be useful to know how to apply cost flow assumptions in a perpetual inventory system. In this supplement, we show how to calculate the Cost of Goods Sold and cost of ending Inventory on a perpetual basis using the same basic cost flow information used in the body of the chapter (on pages 311–312). The only difference in the following table is that we have assumed the sales occurred on October 4, prior to the final inventory purchase.

Date	Description	# of Units	Cost per Unit	Total Cost
Oct. 1	Beginning Inventory	10	$ 7	$ 70
Oct. 3	Purchase	30	$ 8	240
Oct. 4	Sales	(35)	To calculate	To calculate
Oct. 5	Purchase	10	$10	100
	Ending Inventory	**15**	**To calculate**	**To calculate**

FIFO (First-in, First-out)

The first-in, first-out (FIFO) method assumes that the oldest goods (the first in to inventory) are the first ones sold (the first out of inventory). So **to calculate the cost of the 35 units sold, use the costs of the first-in (oldest) goods** (10 units at $7 plus 25 of the 30 units at $8 = a total of $270). The **costs of the newer goods are included in the cost of the ending inventory** (5 units remaining from the 30 units at $8 plus 10 units at $10 = a total of $140). These calculations are summarized in the left-hand side of the following table (the right-hand side summarizes periodic calculations, which were explained in the body of the chapter). As you can see, FIFO yields identical amounts under perpetual and periodic. The only difference is that perpetual does not allow you to "back into" the Cost of Goods Sold; you must calculate it directly.

FIFO – Perpetual

Beginning Inventory	10 units × $7	$ 70
+ Purchases	30 units × $8	240
	10 units × $10	100
Goods Available for Sale		410
− **Cost of Goods Sold** (10 × $7) + (25 × $8)		**270**
Ending Inventory (10 × $10) + (5 × $8)		**$140**

FIFO – Periodic (Shown on page 311)

Beginning Inventory	10 units × $7	$ 70
+ Purchases	30 units × $8	240
	10 units × $10	100
Goods Available for Sale		410
− **Ending Inventory** (10 × $10) + (5 × $8)		**140**
Cost of Goods Sold (10 × $7) + (25 × $8)		**$270**

LIFO (Last-in, First-out)

The last-in, first-out (LIFO) method assumes that the newest goods (the last in to inventory) as of the date of the sale are the first ones sold (the first out of inventory). So **to calculate the cost of the 35 units sold, use the costs of the last-in (newest) goods as of the date of the sale** (30 units at $8 plus 5 of the 10 units at $7 = a total of $275). **The costs of the older goods** (5 units remaining from the 10 units at $7 = $35) **plus any later purchases** (10 units at $10 = $100) **are included in the cost of the ending inventory** ($35 + $100 = $135). These calculations appear in the following table on the left.

LIFO – Perpetual

Beginning Inventory	10 units × $7	$ 70
+ Purchase	30 units × $8	240
Goods Available for Sale		310
− **Cost of Goods Sold** (30 × $8) + (5 × $7)		275
Goods Available for Sale	5 units × $7	35
+ Purchase	10 units × $10	100
Ending Inventory (5 × $7) + (10 × $10)		**$135**

LIFO – Periodic (shown on page 312)

Beginning Inventory	10 units × $7	$ 70
+ Purchases	30 units × $8	240
	10 units × $10	100
Goods Available for Sale		410
− **Ending Inventory** (10 × $7) + (5 × $8)		**110**
Cost of Goods Sold (10 × $10) + (25 × $8)		**$300**

Notice that LIFO–Perpetual calculates Cost of Goods Sold using the cost of goods last-in at the time of the sale, whereas LIFO–Periodic uses the cost of goods last-in at the end of the period.

Weighted Average Cost

In a perpetual inventory system, the weighted average cost must be calculated each time a sale is recorded. Use the same two steps shown in the body of the chapter: (1) calculate the total cost of the goods available for sale, and (2) divide by the number of units available for sale. For example, in the following table on the left, the weighted average cost at the time of sale is calculated by dividing $310 by the 40 units available for sale ($310 ÷ 40 = $7.75 per unit). This cost is then multiplied by the number of units sold to calculate Cost of Goods Sold (35 × $7.75 = $271.25). The remaining 5 units are also valued at the same weighted average cost (5 × $7.75 = $38.75). Additional inventory purchases ($100) are added to these inventory costs to calculate the cost of ending inventory ($38.75 + $100 = $138.75).[3]

Weighted Average – Perpetual

Beginning Inventory	10 units × $7	$ 70.00
+ Purchase	30 units × $8	240.00
Goods Available for Sale	40 units	310.00
− **Cost of Goods Sold** (35 × $7.75)		**271.25**
Goods Available for Sale	5 units	38.75
+ Purchase	10 units × $10	100.00
Ending Inventory	15 units	**$138.75**

Weighted Average – Periodic (shown on page 312)

Beginning Inventory	10 units × $7	$ 70
+ Purchases	30 units × $8	240
	10 units × $10	100
Goods Available for Sale	50 units	410
− **Ending Inventory** (15 × $8.20)		**123**
Cost of Goods Sold (35 × $8.20)		**$287**

Financial Statement Effects

Exhibit 7A.1 summarizes the financial statement effects of using a perpetual inventory system with FIFO, LIFO, or weighted average cost methods. These methods differ only in the way they split the cost of goods available for sale between ending inventory and cost of goods sold. If a cost goes into Cost of Goods Sold, it must be taken out of Inventory.

EXHIBIT 7A.1	Financial Statement Effects of Inventory Costing Methods (Perpetual)

Effects on the Income Statement	FIFO	LIFO	Weighted Average
Sales	$525	$525	$ 525.00
Cost of Goods Sold	270	275	271.25
Gross Profit	255	250	253.75
Effects on the Balance Sheet			
Inventory	$140	$135	$138.75

[3]If inventory is sold immediately after the $100 purchase, the weighted average cost will need to be calculated again ($138.75 ÷ 15 = $9.25 per unit). Notice the change in weighted average cost from $7.75 to $9.25 per unit. Because the weighted average unit cost changes, weighted average perpetual is also called the moving average method.

Thus, the method that assigns the highest cost to cost of goods sold assigns the lowest cost to ending inventory (and vice versa).

SUPPLEMENT 7B   THE EFFECTS OF ERRORS IN ENDING INVENTORY

> **Learning Objective 7-S2**
> Determine the effects of inventory errors.

As mentioned earlier in the chapter, the failure to correctly apply the LCM rule to ending inventory is considered an error. Other errors can occur when inappropriate quantities or unit costs are used in calculating inventory cost. Regardless of the reason, errors in inventory can significantly affect both the balance sheet and the income statement. As the cost of goods sold equation indicates, a direct relationship exists between ending inventory and cost of goods sold because items not in the ending inventory are assumed to have been sold. Thus, any errors in ending inventory will affect the balance sheet (current assets) and the income statement (Cost of Goods Sold, Gross Profit, and Net Income). The effects of inventory errors are felt in more than one year because the ending inventory for one year becomes the beginning inventory for the next year.

To determine the effects of inventory errors on the financial statements in both the current year and the following year, use the cost of goods sold equation. For example, let's assume that ending inventory was overstated in 2012 by $10,000 due to an error that was not discovered until 2013. This would have the following effects in 2012:

2012	
Beginning Inventory	Accurate
+ Purchases	Accurate
− Ending Inventory	Overstated $10,000
= Cost of Goods Sold	Understated $10,000

Because Cost of Goods Sold was understated, Gross Profit and Income before Income Tax Expense would be overstated by $10,000 in 2012, as shown in Exhibit 7B.1. (Net Income would be overstated as well, although the effects would be offset somewhat by overstated Income Tax Expense.)

The 2012 ending inventory becomes the 2013 beginning inventory, so even if 2013 ending inventory is calculated correctly, the error in 2012 creates an error in 2013, as shown in the following table:

2013	
Beginning Inventory	Overstated $10,000
+ Purchases	Accurate
− Ending Inventory	Accurate
= Cost of Goods Sold	Overstated $10,000

Because Cost of Goods Sold is overstated in 2013, that year's Gross Profit and Income before Income Tax Expense would be understated by the same amount in 2013. (Net Income would be understated as well, although the effects would be offset somewhat by understated Income Tax Expense.)

EXHIBIT 7B.1	**Two-Year Income Effects of Inventory Error**

	2012		2013	
	With an Error	**Without an Error**	**With an Error**	**Without an Error**
Sales	$120,000	$120,000	$110,000	$110,000
Beginning Inventory	$ 50,000	$ 50,000	**$45,000**	**$35,000**
Purchases	75,000	75,000	70,000	70,000
Cost of Goods Available for Sale	125,000	125,000	115,000	105,000
Ending Inventory	**45,000**	**35,000**	20,000	20,000
Cost of Goods Sold	80,000	90,000	95,000	85,000
Gross Profit	40,000	30,000	15,000	25,000
Operating Expenses	10,000	10,000	10,000	10,000
Net Income (before income tax)	$ 30,000	$ 20,000	$ 5,000	$ 15,000

Net Income overstated by $10,000 ⟶ Cancels out ⟵ Net Income understated by $10,000

Ignoring income taxes, the effects of these errors on Net Income in each of the two years is shown in Exhibit 7B.1. Notice that the Cost of Goods Sold is understated in the first year and overstated in the second year. Over the two years, these errors offset one another. Inventory errors will "self-correct" like this only if ending inventory is accurately calculated at the end of the following year and adjusted to that correct balance. (That these errors are self-correcting does not make them "OK." They are errors.)

SUPPLEMENT 7C RECORDING INVENTORY TRANSACTIONS IN A PERIODIC SYSTEM

> **Learning Objective 7-S3**
> Record inventory transactions in a periodic system.

As you have learned, businesses using a periodic inventory system update inventory records only at the end of the accounting period. Unlike a perpetual inventory system, a periodic system does not track the cost of goods sold during the accounting period.

This supplement illustrates typical journal entries made when using a periodic inventory system. The table that follows contrasts those entries with the entries that would be recorded using a perpetual inventory system. A summary of the effects of the journal entries on the accounting equation follows them. Note that the total effects and the resulting financial statements are identical. Only the timing and nature of the entries differ.

Assume for the purposes of this illustration that an electronics retailer stocks and sells just one item and that only the following events occurred in 2013:

Jan. 1	Beginning inventory: 80 units at a unit cost of $60.
Apr. 14	Purchased 170 additional units on account at a unit cost of $60.
Nov. 30	Sold 150 units on account at a unit sales price of $80.
Dec. 31	Counted 100 units at a unit cost of $60.

PERIODIC RECORDS	PERPETUAL RECORDS

A. Record purchases:

April 14, 2013:

Purchases (+A) (170 units at $60)	10,200	
Accounts Payable (+L)		10,200

B. Record sales (but not cost of goods sold):

November 30, 2013:

Accounts Receivable (+A)	12,000	
Sales Revenue (+R, +SE) (150 units at $80)		12,000

No cost of goods sold entry

C. Record end-of-period adjustments:

　a. Count the number of units on hand.
　b. Compute the dollar valuation of the ending inventory.
　c. Compute and record the cost of goods sold.

Beginning Inventory (last period's ending) (80 units at $60)	$ 4,800
Add: Net Purchases	10,200
Cost of Goods Available for Sale	15,000
Deduct: Ending Inventory (physical count—100 units at $60)	6,000
Cost of Goods Sold	$ 9,000

December 31, 2013:

Transfer beginning inventory and net purchases to cost of goods sold (act as if all goods were sold):

Cost of Goods Sold (+E, −SE)	15,000	
Inventory (−A) (beginning)		4,800
Purchases (−A)		10,200

Adjust the cost of goods sold by subtracting the amount of ending inventory still on hand (recognize that not all goods were sold):

Inventory (+A) (ending)	6,000	
Cost of Goods Sold (−E, +SE)		6,000

A. Record purchases:

April 14, 2013:

Inventory (+A) (170 units at $60)	10,200	
Accounts Payable (+L)		10,200

B. Record sales and cost of goods sold:

November 30, 2013:

Accounts Receivable (+A)	12,000	
Sales Revenue (+R, +SE) (150 units at $80)		12,000

Cost of Goods Sold (+E, −SE)	9,000	
Inventory (−A) (150 units at $60)		9,000

C. Record end-of-period adjustments:

At the end of the accounting period, the balance in the Cost of Goods Sold account is reported on the income statement. Computing the cost of goods sold is not necessary because the **Cost of Goods Sold** account is up to date. Also, the **Inventory** account shows the ending inventory amount reported on the balance sheet. A physical inventory count is still necessary to assess the accuracy of the perpetual records and identify theft and other forms of shrinkage. Any shrinkage would be recorded by reducing the **Inventory** account and increasing an expense account (such as **Inventory Shrinkage** or **Cost of Goods Sold**). This illustration assumes that no shrinkage has been detected.

No entries

PERIODIC	PERPETUAL

PERIODIC

Assets	=	Liabilities	+	Stockholders' Equity
Purchases +10,200		Accounts Payable +10,200		
Accts. Rec. +12,000				Sales Revenue (+R) +12,000
Inventory −4,800				Cost of Goods Sold (+E) −15,000
Purchases −10,200				
Inventory +6,000				Cost of Goods Sold (−E) +6,000
Totals **+13,200**	**=**	**+10,200**		**+3,000**

PERPETUAL

Assets	=	Liabilities	+	Stockholders' Equity
Inventory +10,200		Accounts Payable +10,200		
Accts. Rec. +12,000				Sales Revenue (+R) +12,000
Inventory −9,000				Cost of Goods Sold (+E) −9,000
Totals **+13,200**	**=**	**+10,200**		**+3,000**

REVIEW THE CHAPTER

DEMONSTRATION CASE

Ebert Electronics sells one line of consumer electronics. Assume that the following summarized transactions were completed during the month ended January 31, 2013, in the order given.

	Units	Unit Cost
Beginning inventory (January 1)	11	$200
New inventory purchases (January 3)	5	209
New inventory purchases (January 4)	9	220
Sale (January 5 at a price of $420 per item)	(12)	
Ending inventory (January 31)	13	

Required:

1. Using the formats shown in the chapter, compute the Cost of Goods Available for Sale, Ending Inventory, and Cost of Goods Sold under (a) FIFO, (b) LIFO, and (c) weighted average.
2. Which method would minimize income taxes? Explain your answer.
3. Assuming that operating expenses were $500 and the income tax rate is 25 percent, prepare the income statement for the month using the method selected in requirement 2.
4. If the replacement cost fell to $205 in February, compute the adjustment that would be made to the Inventory account assuming the company uses (a) FIFO, (b) LIFO, and (c) weighted average.
5. Describe the impact of an adjustment in requirement 4 on the inventory turnover ratio. Computations are not required.

Suggested Solution

1.

(a) FIFO

Beginning Inventory	11 units × $200	$ 2,200
+ Purchases	5 units × $209	1,045
	9 units × $220	1,980
Goods Available for Sale		5,225
− Ending Inventory (9 × $220) + (4 × $209)		**2,816**
Cost of Goods Sold (11 × $200) + (1 × $209)		**$2,409**

(b) LIFO

Beginning Inventory	11 units × $200	$ 2,200
+ Purchases	5 units × $209	1,045
	9 units × $220	1,980
Goods Available for Sale		5,225
− Ending Inventory (11 × $200) + (2 × $209)		**2,618**
Cost of Goods Sold (9 × $220) + (3 × $209)		**$2,607**

(c) Weighted Average

Beginning Inventory	11 units × $200	$ 2,200
+ Purchases	5 units × $209	1,045
	9 units × $220	1,980
Goods Available for Sale	25 units	5,225

$$\text{Weighted Average Cost} = \frac{\text{Cost of Goods Available for Sale}}{\text{Number of Units Available for Sale}} = \frac{\$5,225}{25 \text{ units}} = \$209 \text{ per unit}$$

(c) Weighted Average

Beginning Inventory	11 units × $200	$ 2,200
+ Purchases	5 units × $209	1,045
	9 units × $220	1,980
Goods Available for Sale		5,225
− **Ending Inventory** (13 × $209)		**2,717**
Cost of Goods Sold (12 × $209)		**$2,508**

2. LIFO would minimize income taxes. Because costs are rising, LIFO produces higher Cost of Goods Sold, lower Income before Income Tax Expense, and lower Income Tax Expense.

3.

EBERT ELECTRONICS
Income Statement
For the Month Ended January 31, 2013

Sales (12 × $420)	$5,040
Cost of Goods Sold	2,607
Gross Profit	2,433
Operating Expenses	500
Income before Income Tax Expense	1,933
Income Tax Expense (25%)	483
Net Income	$1,450

4. The total market value of the 13 units in ending inventory, with a per unit replacement cost of $205, is $2,665 (13 × $205 = $2,665). The LCM analysis follows:

	Cost	Market	LCM	Adjustment Needed
(a) FIFO	$2,816	$2,665	$2,665	$(151) = $2,816 − $2,665
(b) LIFO	$2,618	$2,665	$2,618	0
(c) Weighted Average	$2,717	$2,665	$2,665	(52) = $2,717 − $2,665

5. An adjustment for LCM decreases the Inventory balance and increases the Cost of Goods Sold. Both of these changes (individually or together) increase the inventory turnover ratio.

CHAPTER SUMMARY

LO 7-1   **Describe the issues in managing different types of inventory. p. 306**

- Make or buy a sufficient *quantity* of *quality* products, at the lowest possible *cost*, so that they can be sold as quickly as possible to earn the desired amount of gross profit.
- *Merchandise inventory* is bought by merchandisers in a ready to sell format. When *raw materials* enter a manufacturer's production process, they become *work in process* inventory, which is further transformed into *finished goods* that are ultimately sold to customers.

LO 7-2   **Explain how to report inventory and cost of goods sold. p. 307**

- The costs of goods purchased are added to Inventory (on the balance sheet).
- The costs of goods sold are removed from Inventory and reported as an expense called Cost of Goods Sold (on the income statement).
- The costs remaining in Inventory at the end of a period become the cost of Inventory at the beginning of the next period.
- The relationships among beginning inventory (BI), purchases (P), ending inventory (EI), and cost of goods sold (CGS) are: BI + P − EI = CGS or BI + P − CGS = EI.

Compute costs using four inventory costing methods. p. 309 LO 7-3

- Under GAAP, any of four generally accepted methods can be used to allocate the cost of inventory available for sale between goods that are sold and goods that remain on hand at the end of the accounting period.

- Specific identification assigns costs to ending inventory and cost of goods sold by tracking and identifying each specific item of inventory.

- Under FIFO, the costs first in are assigned to cost of goods sold, and the costs last in (most recent) are assigned to the inventory that is still on hand in ending inventory.

- Under LIFO, the costs last in are assigned to cost of goods sold, and the costs first in (oldest) are assigned to the inventory that is still on hand in ending inventory.

- Under weighted average cost, the weighted average cost per unit of inventory is assigned equally to goods sold and those still on hand in ending inventory.

Report inventory at the lower of cost or market. p. 314 LO 7-4

- The LCM rule ensures inventory assets are not reported at more than they are worth.

Analyze and record inventory purchases, transportation, returns and allowances, and discounts. p. 315 LO 7-5

- The Inventory account should include costs incurred to get inventory into a condition and location ready for sale.

- The cost of inventory includes its purchase price and transportation (freight-in) minus cost reductions for purchase returns and allowances and purchase discounts. Costs to deliver inventory to customers (freight-out) are a selling expense and are not included in inventory.

Evaluate inventory management by computing and interpreting the inventory turnover ratio. p. 318 LO 7-6

- The inventory turnover ratio measures the efficiency of inventory management. It reflects how many times average inventory was acquired and sold during the period. The inventory turnover ratio is calculated by dividing Cost of Goods Sold by Average Inventory.

Accounting Decision Tools

Name of Measure	Formula	What It Tells You
Inventory turnover ratio	$\dfrac{\text{Cost of Goods Sold}}{\text{Average Inventory}}$	• The number of times inventory turns over during the period • A higher ratio means faster turnover
Days to sell	$\dfrac{365}{\text{Inventory Turnover Ratio}}$	• Average number of days from purchase to sale • A higher number means a longer time to sell

KEY TERMS

Cost of Goods Sold (CGS)
  Equation p. 308
Days to Sell p. 319
First-In, First-Out (FIFO) p. 310
Goods Available for Sale p. 308

Inventory Turnover p. 319
Last-In, First-Out (LIFO) p. 310
Lower of Cost or Market
  (LCM) p. 314

Purchase Discounts p. 317
Purchase Returns and Allowances p. 317
Specific Identification p. 309
Weighted Average Cost p. 310

See complete definitions in the glossary in the back of this text.

HOMEWORK HELPER

Alternative terms

- Cost of Goods Sold is also called Cost of Sales.
- Days to Sell is also called "days in inventory" and "days' sales in inventory."

Helpful reminders

- The "first-out" part of FIFO and LIFO describes the costs going out of inventory into Cost of Goods Sold. To calculate ending inventory cost using LIFO, think FIST (first-in, still there). For FIFO inventory, think LIST (last-in, still there).
- Purchase discounts are calculated after taking into account any purchase returns and allowances. A partial payment within the discount period (such as one-half of the total cost) usually entitles the purchaser to a partial discount (apply the discount to one-half of the total cost).

Frequent mistakes

- Purchase discounts should not be calculated on transportation costs unless the shipping company offers a purchase discount for early payment. Purchase discounts should not be calculated on merchandise returned to the supplier.
- When calculating weighted average cost, do not simply average the costs per unit. Instead, divide the total cost of goods available for sale by the number of goods available for sale.
- Do not use Sales Revenue when calculating inventory turnover (use Cost of Goods Sold). Also, use the average inventory, not the ending Inventory balance.

PRACTICE MATERIAL

QUESTIONS (⊜ Symbol indicates questions that require analysis from more than one perspective.)

1. What are three goals of inventory management?

2. Describe the specific types of inventory reported by merchandisers and manufacturers.

3. If a Chicago-based company ships goods on September 30 to a customer in Hawaii with sales terms FOB destination, does the Chicago-based company include the inventory or the sale in its September financial statements?

4. Define *goods available for sale*. How does it differ from cost of goods sold?

5. Define *beginning inventory* and *ending inventory*.

6. The chapter discussed four inventory costing methods. List the four methods and briefly explain each.

7. Which inventory cost flow method is most similar to the flow of products involving (a) a gumball machine, (b) bricks off a stack, and (c) gasoline out of a tank?

8. "Where possible, the inventory costing method should mimic actual product flows." Do you agree? Explain.

9. Contrast the effects of LIFO versus FIFO on ending inventory when (a) costs are rising and (b) costs are falling.

10. Contrast the income statement effect of LIFO versus FIFO (on Cost of Goods Sold and Gross Profit) when (a) costs are rising and (b) costs are falling.

11. Several managers in your company are experiencing personal financial problems and have asked that your company switch from LIFO to FIFO so that they can receive bigger bonuses, which are tied to the company's net income. How would you respond to this request if you were the company's chief financial officer (CFO)? Would such a switch help the managers? Who could it hurt? ⊜

12. Explain briefly the application of the LCM rule to ending inventory. Describe its effect on the balance sheet and income statement when market is lower than cost.

13. Describe how transportation costs to obtain inventory (freight-in) are accounted for by a merchandising company using a perpetual inventory system. Explain the reasoning behind this accounting treatment.

14. As a sales representative for a publicly traded pharmaceutical company, you become aware of new evidence that one of your company's main drugs has significant life-threatening side effects that were not previously reported. Your company has a significant inventory of this drug. What income statement accounts other than Net Sales will be affected by the news? A friend asks you whether he should invest in your company. What should you say? ⊜

15. You work for a made-to-order clothing company, whose reputation is based on its fast turnaround from order to delivery. The owner of your company is considering outsourcing much of the clothing production because she thinks this will improve inventory turnover and customer satisfaction. In what way is she correct? In what way might she be wrong? ⊜

16. (Supplement 7A) Distinguish perpetual inventory systems from periodic inventory systems by describing when and how cost of goods sold is calculated when using LIFO.

17. (Supplement 7B) Explain why an error in ending inventory in one period affects the following period.

18. (Supplement 7C) The summary in Supplement 7C shows two entries recorded in a periodic system that are not recorded in a perpetual system and only one entry in the perpetual system that is not recorded in a periodic system. Why then is a periodic system considered less onerous than a perpetual system?

MULTIPLE CHOICE

1. Which of the following statements are true regarding Cost of Goods Sold?

   (i) Cost of Goods Sold represents the costs that a company incurred to purchase or produce inventory in the current period.

   (ii) Cost of Goods Sold is an expense on the income statement.

   (iii) Cost of Goods Sold is affected by the inventory method selected by a company (FIFO, LIFO, etc.).

   a. (i) only   c. (ii) and (iii)
   b. (ii) only   d. All of the above.

2. The inventory costing method selected by a company can affect

   a. The balance sheet.
   b. The income statement.
   c. The statement of retained earnings.
   d. All of the above.

3. Which of the following is not a name for a specific type of inventory?

   a. Finished goods.   c. Raw materials.
   b. Merchandise inventory.   d. Goods available for sale.

4. Each period, the Cost of Goods Available for Sale is allocated between

   a. Assets and Liabilities.   c. Assets and Revenues.
   b. Assets and Expenses.   d. Expenses and Liabilities.

5. A New York bridal dress designer that makes high-end custom wedding dresses and needs to know the exact cost of each dress most likely uses which inventory costing method?

   a. FIFO   c. Weighted Average
   b. LIFO   d. Specific Identification

6. If costs are rising, which of the following will be true?

   a. The cost of goods sold will be greater if LIFO is used rather than weighted average.
   b. The cost of ending inventory will be greater if FIFO is used rather than LIFO.
   c. The gross profit will be greater if FIFO is used rather than LIFO.
   d. All of the above are true.

7. Which inventory method provides a better matching of current costs with sales revenue on the income statement but also results in older values being reported for inventory on the balance sheet?

   a. FIFO   c. LIFO
   b. Weighted Average   d. Specific Identification

8. Which of the following regarding the *lower of cost or market* rule for inventory are true?

   (i) The lower of cost or market rule is an example of the historical cost principle.

   (ii) When the replacement cost of inventory drops below the original cost of inventory shown in the financial records, net income is reduced.

   (iii) When the replacement cost of inventory drops below the original cost of inventory shown in the financial records, total assets are reduced.

   a. (i) only   c. (ii) and (iii)
   b. (ii) only   d. All of the above.

9. An increasing inventory turnover ratio

   a. Indicates a longer time span between the ordering and receiving of inventory.
   b. Indicates a shorter time span between the ordering and receiving of inventory.
   c. Indicates a shorter time span between the purchase and sale of inventory.
   d. Indicates a longer time span between the purchase and sale of inventory.

10. A company that purchases inventory costing $10,000 on terms 2/10, n/30, but first returns one-half of those goods, will receive a discount of what amount if it pays on the last day of the discount period?

   a. $0   c. $200
   b. $100   d. $5,000

> For answers to the Multiple-Choice Questions **see page Q1** located in the last section of the book.

MINI-EXERCISES

Mc Graw Hill **connect** |ACCOUNTING

M7-1 Items Included in Inventory

LO 7-1

Explain whether the following items should be included in the inventory of The Knot, Inc., a company that arranges and supplies wedding services for couples and other wedding consultants.

The Knot, Inc.

a. Goods are being held by The Knot on consignment from Emerald Bridal.
b. Goods in transit to Winston Wedding Consultants, sold by The Knot FOB shipping point.
c. Goods in transit to The Knot, purchased by The Knot FOB shipping point.

LO 7-1

M7-2 Matching Inventory Items to Type of Business

Match the type of inventory with the type of business by placing checkmarks in the applicable columns:

	Type of Business	
Type of Inventory	Merchandising	Manufacturing
Merchandise		
Finished goods		
Work in process		
Raw materials		

LO 7-2

Dillard's, Inc.

M7-3 Inferring Purchases Using the Cost of Goods Sold Equation

Dillard's, Inc., operates 308 department stores located in 29 states primarily in the Southwest, Southeast, and Midwest. In its annual report for the year ended January 29, 2011, the company reported Cost of Goods Sold of $3,976 million, ending inventory for the current year of $1,290 million, and ending inventory for the previous year of $1,301 million. Is it possible to develop a reasonable estimate of the merchandise purchases for the year? If so, prepare the estimate. If not, explain why.

LO 7-3

M7-4 Matching Financial Statement Effects to Inventory Costing Methods

Complete the following table by indicating which inventory costing method (FIFO or LIFO) would lead to the effects noted in the rows, for each of the circumstances described in the columns.

	1. Declining Costs	2. Rising Costs
a. Lowest net income		
b. Lowest ending inventory		

LO 7-3

M7-5 Matching Inventory Costing Method Choices to Company Circumstances

Indicate whether a company interested in minimizing its income taxes should choose the FIFO or LIFO inventory costing method under each of the following circumstances.

a. Declining costs _____
b. Rising costs _____

LO 7-3

M7-6 Calculating Cost of Goods Available for Sale, Ending Inventory, Sales, Cost of Goods Sold, and Gross Profit under Periodic FIFO, LIFO, and Weighted Average Cost

Given the following information, calculate cost of goods available for sale and ending inventory, then sales, cost of goods sold, and gross profit, under (a) FIFO, (b) LIFO, and (c) weighted average. Assume a periodic inventory system is used.

		Units	Unit Cost	Unit Selling Price
July 1	Beginning Inventory	50	$10	
July 13	Purchase	250	13	
July 25	Sold	(100)		$15
July 31	Ending Inventory	200		

LO 7-3

M7-7 Calculating Cost of Goods Available for Sale, Cost of Goods Sold, and Ending Inventory under FIFO, LIFO, and Weighted Average Cost (Periodic Inventory)

Aircard Corporation tracks the number of units purchased and sold throughout each accounting period, but applies its inventory costing method at the end of each period as if it uses a periodic inventory system. Given the following information, calculate the cost of goods available for sale, ending inventory, and cost of goods sold, if Aircard uses (a) FIFO, (b) LIFO, or (c) weighted average cost.

		Units	Unit Cost
July 1	Beginning Inventory	2,000	$40
July 5	Sold	1,000	
July 13	Purchased	6,000	44
July 17	Sold	3,000	
July 25	Purchased	8,000	50
July 27	Sold	5,000	

M7-8 Calculating Cost of Goods Available for Sale, Cost of Goods Sold, and Ending Inventory under Periodic FIFO, LIFO, and Weighted Average Cost   LO 7-3

In its first month of operations, Literacy for the Illiterate opened a new bookstore and bought merchandise in the following order: (1) 300 units at $7 on January 1, (2) 450 units at $8 on January 8, and (3) 750 units at $9 on January 29. Assuming 900 units are on hand at the end of the month, calculate the cost of goods available for sale, ending inventory, and cost of goods sold under the (a) FIFO, (b) LIFO, and (c) weighted average cost flow assumptions. Assume a periodic inventory system is used.

M7-9 Reporting Inventory under Lower of Cost or Market   LO 7-4

The Jewel Fool had the following inventory items on hand at the end of the year.

	Quantity	Cost per Item	Replacement Cost per Item
Necklaces	10	$75	$70
Bracelets	50	40	60

Determine the lower of cost or market per unit and the total amount that should be reported on the balance sheet for each item of inventory.

M7-10 Preparing the Journal Entry to Record Lower of Cost or Market (LCM) Adjustments   LO 7-4

In its 2012 annual report Research in Motion reported that it wrote down its PlayBook inventory by $485,000,000 because its cost exceeded its market value. Show the effects of this adjustment on the accounting equation and show the journal entry that the company would have made to record it.

Research in Motion

M7-11 Evaluating Inventory Cost Components   LO 7-5

Assume Anderson's General Store bought, on credit, a truckload of merchandise from American Wholesaling costing $23,000. If the company was charged $650 in transportation cost by National Trucking, immediately returned goods to American Wholesaling costing $1,200, and then took advantage of American Wholesaling's 2/10, n/30 purchase discount, how much did this inventory cost Anderson's?

M7-12 Preparing Journal Entries for Purchases, Purchase Discounts, and Purchase Returns Using a Perpetual System   LO 7-5

Using the information in M7-11, prepare journal entries to record the inventory transactions, assuming Anderson's uses a perpetual inventory system.

M7-13 Recording Journal Entries for Purchases and Sales Using a Perpetual Inventory System   LO 7-2, 7-5

Inventory at the beginning of the year cost $13,400. During the year, the company purchased (on account) inventory costing $84,000. Inventory that had cost $80,000 was sold on account for $95,000. At the end of the year, inventory was counted and its cost was determined to be $17,400. (a) Show the cost of goods sold equation using these numbers (b) What was the dollar amount of Gross Profit? (c) Prepare journal entries to record these transactions, assuming a perpetual inventory system is used.

LO 7-6

M7-14 Determining the Effects of Inventory Management Changes on the Inventory Turnover Ratio

Indicate the most likely effect of the following changes in inventory management on the inventory turnover ratio (+ for increase, − for decrease, and NE for no effect).

_____ a. Inventory delivered by suppliers daily (small amounts) instead of weekly (larger amounts).

_____ b. Shorten production process from 10 days to 8 days.

_____ c. Extend payments for inventory purchases from 15 days to 30 days.

LO 7-6

Dillard's

★macy's

M7-15 Calculating the Inventory Turnover Ratio and Days to Sell

Using the data in M7-3, calculate to one decimal place the inventory turnover ratio and days to sell for Dillard's. In a recent year, Macy's reported an inventory turnover ratio of 3.2. Which company's inventory turnover is faster?

LO 7-S1

M7-16 (Supplement 7A) Calculating Cost of Goods Sold and Ending Inventory under FIFO and LIFO (Perpetual Inventory)

Refer to M7-7. Calculate the cost of ending inventory and cost of goods sold assuming a perpetual inventory system is used in combination with (a) FIFO and (b) LIFO.

LO 7-S1

M7-17 (Supplement 7A) Calculating Cost of Goods Sold and Ending Inventory under Perpetual FIFO, LIFO, and Weighted Average Cost

Repeat M7-8, except assume Literacy for the Illiterate uses a perpetual inventory system and it sold 600 units between January 9 and January 28.

LO 7-S2

M7-18 (Supplement 7B) Determining the Financial Statement Effects of Inventory Errors

Assume the 2012 ending inventory of Shea's Shrimp Shack was understated by $10,000. Explain how this error would affect the amounts reported for cost of goods sold and gross profit for 2012 and 2013.

LO 7-S2

M7-19 (Supplement 7B) Determining the Financial Statement Effects of Inventory Errors

Repeat M7-18, except assume the 2012 ending inventory was _over_stated by $100,000.

EXERCISES

LO 7-1, 7-2

PC Mall, Inc.

E7-1 Items Included in Inventory

PC Mall, Inc., is a direct marketer of computer hardware, software, peripherals, and electronics. In a recent annual report, the company reported that its revenue is "recognized upon receipt of the product by the customer" and that its "inventories include goods-in-transit to customers."

Required:

1. Indicate whether PC Mall's sales terms are FOB shipping point or FOB destination.
2. Assume PC Mall sold inventory on account to eCOST.com on December 28, 2012, which was to be delivered January 3, 2013. The inventory cost PC Mall $25,000 and the selling price was $30,000. What amounts, if any, related to this transaction would be reported on PC Mall's balance sheet and income statement in 2012? In 2013?
3. PC Mall placed inventory on consignment with one of its customers. Would this inventory have been reported on the balance sheet of PC Mall or its customer?
4. Assume PC Mall purchased electronics on December 29, 2012, which were received on January 2, 2013. For these goods to be included in PC Mall's inventory on December 31, 2012, would the terms have been under FOB destination or FOB shipping point?

LO 7-2

E7-2 Inferring Missing Amounts Based on Income Statement Relationships

Supply the missing dollar amounts for the income statement of Lewis Retailers for each of the following independent cases:

Cases	Sales Revenue	Beginning Inventory	Purchases	Cost of Goods Available for Sale	Cost of Goods Sold	Cost of Ending Inventory	Gross Profit
A	$ 700	$100	$800	?	$300	$?	$?
B	900	200	800	?	?	150	?
C	?	100	?	?	200	300	400
D	800	?	600	?	650	250	?
E	1,000	50	900	?	?	?	500

E7-3 Inferring Missing Amounts Based on Income Statement Relationships

LO 7-2

Supply the missing dollar amounts for the income statement of Clark Retailers for each of the following independent cases:

Cases	Sales Revenue	Beginning Inventory	Purchases	Total Available	Ending Inventory	Cost of Goods Sold	Gross Profit	Selling and General Expenses	Income from Operations
A	$800	$100	$700	$?	$500	$?	$?	$200	$?
B	900	200	700	?	?	?	?	150	0
C	?	100	?	?	200	200	400	150	?
D	800	?	600	?	300	?	?	250	100

E7-4 Inferring Merchandise Purchases

LO 7-2

The Gap, Inc.

The Gap, Inc., is a specialty retailer that operates stores selling clothes under the trade names Gap, Banana Republic, and Old Navy. Assume that you are employed as a stock analyst and your boss has just completed a review of the annual report of The Gap, Inc., for the year ended January 31, 2011. She provided you with her notes, but they are missing some information that you need. Her notes show that the ending inventory for Gap in the current year was $1,602 million and in the previous year it was $1,477 million. Net Sales for the current year were $14,664 million. Gross Profit was $5,889 million and Net Income was $1,204 million. For your analysis, you determine that you need to know the amount of Cost of Goods Sold and Purchases for the year.

Required:

Do you need to ask your boss for her copy of the annual report, or can you develop the information from her notes? Explain and show calculations.

E7-5 Calculating Cost of Ending Inventory and Cost of Goods Sold under Periodic FIFO, LIFO, and Weighted Average Cost

LO 7-3

Oahu Kiki tracks the number of units purchased and sold throughout each accounting period but applies its inventory costing method at the end of each month, as if it uses a periodic inventory system. Assume Oahu Kiki's records show the following for the month of January. Sales totaled 240 units.

	Date	Units	Unit Cost	Total Cost
Beginning Inventory	January 1	120	$ 80	$ 9,600
Purchase	January 15	380	90	34,200
Purchase	January 24	200	110	22,000

Required:

1. Calculate the number and cost of goods available for sale
2. Calculate the number of units in ending inventory.
3. Calculate the cost of ending inventory and cost of goods sold using the (a) FIFO, (b) LIFO, and (c) weighted average cost methods.

LO 7-3   **E7-6 Analyzing and Interpreting the Financial Statement Effects of Periodic FIFO, LIFO, and Weighted Average Cost**

Orion Iron Corp. tracks the number of units purchased and sold throughout each year but applies its inventory costing method at the end of the year, as if it uses a periodic inventory system. Assume its accounting records provided the following information at the end of the annual accounting period, December 31, 2012.

Transactions	Units	Unit Cost
a. Inventory, December 31, 2011	300	$12
For the year 2012:		
b. Purchase, April 11	900	10
c. Purchase, June 1	800	13
d. Sale, May 1 (sold for $40 per unit)	300	
e. Sale, July 3 (sold for $40 per unit)	600	
f. Operating expenses (excluding income tax expense), $19,500		

Required:

1. Calculate the number and cost of goods available for sale.
2. Calculate the number of units in ending inventory.
3. Compute the cost of ending inventory and cost of goods sold under (a) FIFO, (b) LIFO, and (c) weighted average cost.
4. Prepare an Income Statement that shows 2012 amounts for the FIFO method in one column, the LIFO method in another column, and the weighted average method in a final column. Include the following line items in the income statement: Sales, Cost of Goods Sold, Gross Profit, Operating Expenses, and Income from Operations.
5. Compare the Income from Operations and the ending inventory amounts that would be reported under the three methods. Explain the similarities and differences.
6. Which inventory costing method may be preferred by Orion Iron Corp. for income tax purposes? Explain.

LO 7-3   **E7-7 Analyzing and Interpreting the Financial Statement Effects of FIFO, LIFO, and Weighted Average Cost**

Scoresby Inc. tracks the number of units purchased and sold throughout each year but applies its inventory costing method at the end of the year, as if it uses a periodic inventory system. Assume its accounting records provided the following information at the end of the annual accounting period, December 31, 2013.

Transactions	Units	Unit Cost
a. Inventory, December 31, 2012	3,000	$ 8
For the year 2013:		
b. Purchase, March 5	9,500	9
c. Purchase, September 19	5,000	11
d. Sale, April 15 (sold for $29 per unit)	4,000	
e. Sale, October 31 (sold for $31 per unit)	8,000	
f. Operating expenses (excluding income tax expense), $250,000		

Required:

1. Calculate the number and cost of goods available for sale.
2. Calculate the number of units in ending inventory.
3. Compute the cost of ending inventory and cost of goods sold under (a) FIFO, (b) LIFO, and (c) weighted average cost.
4. Prepare an income statement that shows 2013 amounts for the FIFO method in one column, the LIFO method in another column, and the weighted average method in a final column. Include the following line items in the income statement: Sales, Cost of Goods Sold, Gross Profit, Operating Expenses, and Income from Operations.
5. Compare the Income from Operations and the ending inventory amounts that would be reported under the three methods. Explain the similarities and differences.
6. Which inventory costing method may be preferred by Scoresby for income tax purposes? Explain.

E7-8 Evaluating the Effects of Inventory Methods on Income from Operations, Income Taxes, and Net Income (Periodic)   LO 7-3

Courtney Company uses a periodic inventory system. Data for 2012: beginning merchandise inventory (December 31, 2011), 1,000 units at $35; purchases, 4,000 units at $38; operating expenses (excluding income taxes), $91,500; ending inventory per physical count at December 31, 2012, 900 units; sales price per unit, $75; and average income tax rate, 30%.

Required:

1. Prepare income statements under the FIFO, LIFO, and weighted average costing methods. Use a format similar to the following:

Income Statement	Units	Inventory Costing Method		
		FIFO	LIFO	Weighted Average
Sales Revenue	_____	$_____	$_____	$_____
Cost of Goods Sold*	_____	_____	_____	_____
Gross Profit		_____	_____	_____
Operating Expenses		_____	_____	_____
Income from Operations		_____	_____	_____
Income Tax Expense		_____	_____	_____
Net Income		_____	_____	_____

*Cost of goods sold equation:

Beginning Inventory	_____	$_____	$_____	$_____
Purchases	_____	_____	_____	_____
Goods Available for Sale	_____	_____	_____	_____
Ending Inventory	_____	_____	_____	_____
Cost of Goods Sold	_____	_____	_____	_____

2. Between FIFO and LIFO, which method is preferable in terms of (a) maximizing income from operations or (b) minimizing income taxes? Explain.
3. What would be your answer to requirement 2 if costs were falling? Explain.

E7-9 Choosing LIFO versus FIFO When Costs Are Rising and Falling   LO 7-3

Use the following information to complete this exercise: sales, 550 units for $12,500; beginning inventory, 300 units; purchases, 400 units; ending inventory, 150 units; and operating expenses, $4,000. Begin by setting up the following table and then complete the requirements that follow.

	Costs Rising		Costs Falling	
	Situation A	Situation B	Situation C	Situation D
	FIFO	LIFO	FIFO	LIFO
Sales Revenue	$12,500	$12,500	$12,500	$12,500
Beginning Inventory	$3,600			
Purchases	5,200	_____	_____	_____
Goods Available for Sale	8,800			
Ending Inventory	1,950	_____	_____	_____
Cost of Goods Sold	6,850	_____	_____	_____
Gross Profit	5,650			
Operating Expenses	4,000	4,000	4,000	4,000
Income from Operations	1,650			
Income Tax Expense (30%)	495	_____	_____	_____
Net Income	$ 1,155	_____	_____	_____

Required:

1. Complete the table for each situation. In Situations A and B (costs rising), assume the following: beginning inventory, 300 units at $12 = $3,600; purchases, 400 units at $13 = $5,200. In Situations C and D (costs falling), assume the opposite; that is, beginning inventory, 300 units at $13 = $3,900; purchases, 400 units at $12 = $4,800. Use periodic inventory procedures.

2. Describe the relative effects on Income from Operations as demonstrated by requirement 1 when costs are rising and when costs are falling.

3. Describe the relative effects on Income Tax Expense for each situation.

LO 7-4   **E7-10 Reporting Inventory at Lower of Cost or Market**

Peterson Furniture Designs is preparing the annual financial statements dated December 31, 2012. Ending inventory information about the five major items stocked for regular sale follows:

		Ending Inventory, 2012			
Item	Quantity on Hand	Unit Cost When Acquired (FIFO)	Market Value at Year-End	LCM per Item	Total LCM
Alligator Armoires	50	$30	$24		
Bear Bureaus	75	40	40		
Cougar Beds	10	50	52		
Dingo Cribs	30	30	30		
Elephant Dressers	400	15	12		

Required:

1. Complete the final two columns of the table and then compute the amount that should be reported for the 2012 ending inventory using the LCM rule applied to each item.

2. Prepare the journal entry that Peterson Furniture Designs would record on December 31, 2012.

LO 7-4   **E7-11 Reporting Inventory at Lower of Cost or Market**

Sandals Company was formed on January 1, 2013, and is preparing the annual financial statements dated December 31, 2013. Ending inventory information about the four major items stocked for regular sale follows:

	Ending Inventory, 2013		
Product Line	Quantity on Hand	Unit Cost When Acquired (FIFO)	Market Value at Year-End
Air Flow	20	$12	$14
Blister Buster	75	40	38
Coolonite	35	55	50
Dudesly	10	30	35

Required:

1. Compute the amount that should be reported for the 2013 ending inventory using the LCM rule applied to each item.

2. How will the write-down of inventory to lower of cost or market affect the company's expenses reported for the year ended December 31, 2013?

3. How would the inventory costing method used by Sandals Company to account for its inventory be affected by a switch from GAAP to IFRS?

LO 7-4   **E7-12 Failing to Report Inventory at the Lower of Cost or Market**

DHB Industries   David H. Brooks, a university graduate with an accounting degree and the former CEO of DHB Industries, Inc., was charged in October 2007 with accounting and securities fraud for failing to report the company's inventory at the lower of cost or market. From 2001 to 2005, DHB purchased large quantities of a material called Zylon and used it in making bulletproof vests that were sold to the U.S. military and local law enforcement agencies. During this same period, DHB learned that Zylon deteriorated rapidly when exposed to light, heat, and body perspiration. DHB knew that one of its competitors, Second Chance Body Armor, had stopped using Zylon in its vests and, eventually, discontinued its business because customer demand for its Zylon-based vests had evaporated. DHB did not write down its own inventory of Zylon and Zylon-based vests because it had a large contract to supply the U.S. military with bulletproof vests. In its financial statements for the year ended December 31, 2004, DHB reported inventories of $86 million, sales of $90 million, net income of $8.3 million, but no inventory write-down. Yet, only eight months later, DHB admitted it should have written down its inventory by $18 million.

Required:

1. Show the impact of the inventory write-down on the accounting equation, and also show the journal entry that should have been recorded on December 31, 2004.
2. Calculate (a) the Inventory balance that should have been reported on December 31, 2004, and (b) the amount of Net Income that should have been reported for the year ended December 31, 2004. (Assume the inventory write-down does not affect income tax.)
3. DHB's share price reached an all-time high ($20–$22 per share) in November and December 2004, but then the company's CEO, CFO, and other executives began selling their shares in the company. Within a few weeks, they had cashed in over $200 million of stock. In August 2005, after DHB announced its inventory would have to be written down, the stock price fell to less than $5 per share. If you were an attorney representing DHB's investors, what evidence would you present to assert that a fraud had occurred? If you were an attorney defending DHB, what counterarguments would you make?

E7-13 **Reporting Purchases and Purchase Discounts Using**   LO 7-5
       a Perpetual Inventory System

During the months of January and February, Axe Corporation purchased goods from three suppliers. The sequence of events was as follows:

Jan. 6	Purchased goods for $1,200 from Green with terms 2/10, n/30.
6	Purchased goods from Munoz for $900 with terms 2/10, n/30.
14	Paid Green in full.
Feb. 2	Paid Munoz in full.
28	Purchased goods for $350 from Reynolds with terms 2/10, n/45.

Required:

Assume that Axe uses a perpetual inventory system, the company had no inventory on hand at the beginning of January, and no sales were made during January and February. Calculate the cost of inventory as of February 28.

E7-14 **Recording Journal Entries for Purchases and Purchase Discounts**   LO 7-5
       Using a Perpetual Inventory System

Using the information in E7-13, prepare journal entries to record the transactions, assuming Axe uses a perpetual inventory system.

E7-15 **Reporting Purchases, Purchase Discounts, and Purchase Returns**   LO 7-5
       Using a Perpetual Inventory System

During the month of June, Ace Incorporated purchased goods from two suppliers. The sequence of events was as follows:

June 3	Purchased goods for $4,100 from Diamond Inc. with terms 2/10, n/30.
5	Returned goods costing $1,100 to Diamond Inc. for full credit.
6	Purchased goods from Club Corp. for $1,000 with terms 2/10, n/30.
11	Paid the balance owed to Diamond Inc.
22	Paid Club Corp. in full.

Required:

Assume that Ace uses a perpetual inventory system and that the company had no inventory on hand at the beginning of the month. Calculate the cost of inventory as of June 30.

LO 7-5   **E7-16 Recording Journal Entries for Purchases, Purchase Discounts, and Purchase Returns Using a Perpetual Inventory System**

Using the information in E7-15, prepare journal entries to record the transactions, assuming Ace uses a perpetual inventory system.

LO 7-6

Polaris Industries Inc.
Arctic Cat

E7-17 Analyzing and Interpreting the Inventory Turnover Ratio

Polaris Industries Inc. is the biggest snowmobile manufacturer in the world. It reported the following amounts in its financial statements (in millions):

	2010	2009	2008	2007
Net Sales Revenue	$1,991	$1,566	$1,948	$1,780
Cost of Goods Sold	1,461	1,173	1,502	1,387
Average Inventory	208	201	220	224

Required:

1. Calculate to one decimal place the inventory turnover ratio and average days to sell inventory for 2010, 2009, and 2008.

2. Comment on any trends, and compare the effectiveness of inventory managers at Polaris to inventory managers at its main competitor, Arctic Cat, where inventory turns over 3.6 times per year (101.4 days to sell). Both companies use the same inventory costing method (FIFO).

LO 7-2, 7-3, 7-6   **E7-18 Analyzing and Interpreting the Effects of the LIFO/FIFO Choice on Inventory Turnover Ratio**

Simple Plan Enterprises uses a periodic inventory system. Its records showed the following:

Inventory, December 31, 2012, using FIFO → 38 Units @ $14 = $532
Inventory, December 31, 2012, using LIFO → 38 Units @ $10 = $380

Transactions	Units	Unit Cost	Total Cost
Purchase, January 9, 2013	50	15	$ 750
Purchase, January 20, 2013	100	16	1,600
Sale, January 11, 2013 (at $38 per unit)	80		
Sale, January 27, 2013 (at $39 per unit)	56		

Required:

1. Compute the number and cost of goods available for sale, the cost of ending inventory, and the cost of goods sold under FIFO and LIFO.

2. Compute the inventory turnover ratio under the FIFO and LIFO inventory costing methods (show computations).

3. Based on your answer to 2, explain whether analysts should consider the inventory costing method when comparing companies' inventory turnover ratios.

LO 7-S1   **E7-19 (Supplement 7A) Calculating Cost of Ending Inventory and Cost of Goods Sold under Perpetual FIFO and LIFO**

Refer to the information in E7-5. Assume Oahu Kiki applies its inventory costing method perpetually at the time of each sale. The company sold 240 units between January 16 and 23. Calculate the cost of ending inventory and the cost of goods sold using the FIFO and LIFO methods.

E7-20 **(Supplement 7A) Calculating Cost of Ending Inventory and Cost of Goods   LO 7-S1
Sold under Perpetual FIFO and LIFO**

Refer to the information in E7-6. Assume Orion Iron applies its inventory costing method perpetually at the time of each sale. Calculate the cost of ending inventory and the cost of goods sold using the FIFO and LIFO methods.

E7-21 **(Supplement 7B) Analyzing and Interpreting the Impact of an   LO 7-S2
Inventory Error**

Dallas Corporation prepared the following two income statements:

	First Quarter 2012		Second Quarter 2012	
Sales Revenue		$15,000		$18,000
Cost of Goods Sold				
Beginning Inventory	$ 3,000		$ 4,000	
Purchases	7,000		12,000	
Goods Available for Sale	10,000		16,000	
Ending Inventory	4,000		9,000	
Cost of Goods Sold		6,000		7,000
Gross Profit		9,000		11,000
Operating Expenses		5,000		6,000
Income from Operations		$ 4,000		$ 5,000

During the third quarter, the company's internal auditors discovered that the ending inventory for the first quarter should have been $4,400. The ending inventory for the second quarter was correct.

Required:

1. What effect would the error have on total Income from Operations for the two quarters combined? Explain.
2. What effect would the error have on Income from Operations for each of the two quarters? Explain.
3. Prepare corrected income statements for each quarter. Ignore income taxes.

E7-22 **(Supplement 7C) Recording Purchases and Sales Using Perpetual   LO 7-S3
and Periodic Inventory Systems**

Kangaroo Jim Company reported beginning inventory of 100 units at a per unit cost of $25. It had the following purchase and sales transactions during 2012:

Jan. 14	Sold 25 units at unit sales price of $45 on account.
Apr. 9	Purchased 15 additional units at a per unit cost of $25 on account.
Sep. 2	Sold 50 units at a sales price of $50 on account.
Dec. 31	Counted inventory and determined 40 units were still on hand.

Required:

Record each transaction, assuming that Kangaroo Jim Company uses (a) a perpetual inventory system and (b) a periodic inventory system.

COACHED PROBLEMS

|ACCOUNTING   **LO 7-3**

CP7-1 **Analyzing the Effects of Four Alternative
Inventory Costing Methods**

Scrappers Supplies tracks the number of units purchased and sold throughout each accounting period but applies its inventory costing method at the end of each period, as if it uses a periodic inventory system. Assume its accounting records provided the following information at the end of the annual accounting period, December 31, 2013.

Transactions	Units	Unit Cost
Beginning inventory, January 1, 2013	200	$30
Transactions during 2013:		
a. Purchase on account, March 2	300	32
b. Cash sale, April 1 ($46 each)	(350)	
c. Purchase on account, June 30	250	36
d. Cash sale, August 1 ($46 each)	(50)	

TIP: Although the purchases and sales are listed in chronological order, Scrappers determines the cost of goods sold *after* all of the purchases have occurred.

Required:

1. Compute the cost of goods available for sale, cost of ending inventory, and cost of goods sold at December 31, 2013, under each of the following inventory costing methods:

   a. Last-in, first-out.
   b. Weighted average cost.
   c. First-in, first-out.
   d. Specific identification, assuming that the April 1, 2013, sale was selected one-fifth from the beginning inventory and four-fifths from the purchase of March 2, 2013. Assume that the sale of August 1, 2013, was selected from the purchase of June 30, 2013.

2. Of the four methods, which will result in the highest gross profit? Which will result in the lowest income taxes?

LO 7-4   **CP7-2 Evaluating the Income Statement and Income Tax Effects of Lower of Cost or Market**

Smart Company prepared its annual financial statements dated December 31, 2013. The company used the FIFO inventory costing method, but it failed to apply LCM to the ending inventory. The preliminary 2013 income statement follows:

Sales Revenue		$280,000
Cost of Goods Sold		
Beginning Inventory	$ 30,000	
Purchases	182,000	
Goods Available for Sale	212,000	
Ending Inventory (FIFO cost)	44,000	
Cost of Goods Sold		168,000
Gross Profit		112,000
Operating Expenses		61,000
Income from Operations		51,000
Income Tax Expense (30%)		15,300
Net Income		$ 35,700

TIP: Inventory write-downs do not affect the cost of goods available for sale. Instead, the effect of the write-down is to reduce ending inventory, which increases Cost of Goods Sold and then affects other amounts reported lower in the income statement.

Assume that you have been asked to restate the 2013 financial statements to incorporate LCM. You have developed the following data relating to the 2013 ending inventory:

		Purchase Cost		Current Replacement
Item	Quantity	Per Unit	Total	Cost per Unit (Market)
A	3,000	$3	$ 9,000	$4
B	1,500	4	6,000	2
C	7,000	2	14,000	4
D	3,000	5	15,000	2
			$44,000	

Required:

1. Restate the income statement to reflect LCM valuation of the 2013 ending inventory. Apply LCM on an item-by-item basis and show computations.
2. Compare and explain the LCM effect on each amount that was changed in requirement 1.
3. What is the conceptual basis for applying LCM to merchandise inventories?

CP7-3 Accounting for Inventory Purchase Transactions including Allowances and Discounts Using a Perpetual Inventory System

Use the information in CP6-6 (page 291 in Chapter 6) to complete the following requirements.

Required:

1. Indicate the effect (direction and amount) of each transaction on the Inventory balance of American Fashions.
2. Prepare the journal entries that American Fashions would record and show any computations.
   TIP: The selling price charged by the seller is the purchaser's cost.

CP7-4 Calculating and Interpreting the Inventory Turnover Ratio and Days to Sell

Best Buy is a leading national retailer of brand-name consumer electronics, personal computers, and entertainment software. The company reported the following amounts in its financial statements (in millions).

	2011	2010
Net Sales Revenue	$50,272	$49,694
Cost of Goods Sold	37,611	37,534
Beginning Inventory	5,486	4,753
Ending Inventory	5,896	5,486

LO 7-6

Best Buy
GameStop

Required:

1. Determine the inventory turnover ratio and average days to sell inventory for 2011 and 2010. Round your answers to one decimal place.
   TIP: Remember to use costs in both the numerator (CGS) and denominator (average inventory).
2. Comment on any changes in these measures, and compare the effectiveness of inventory managers at Best Buy with GameStop, where inventory turns over 6.0 times per year (61 days to sell).

CP7-5 (Supplement 7A) Analyzing the Effects of the LIFO Inventory Method in a Perpetual Inventory System

Using the information in CP7-1, calculate the Cost of Goods Sold and Ending Inventory for Scrappers Supplies assuming it applies the LIFO cost method perpetually at the time of each sale. Compare these amounts to the periodic LIFO calculations in requirement 1a of CP7-1. Does the use of a perpetual inventory system result in a higher or lower Cost of Goods Sold when costs are rising?
   TIP: In CP7-5, the sale of 350 units on April 1 is assumed, under LIFO, to consist of the 300 units purchased March 2 and 50 units from beginning inventory.

LO 7-S1

CP7-6 (Supplement 7B) Analyzing and Interpreting the Effects of Inventory Errors

Partial income statements for Murphy & Murphy (M & M) reported the following summarized amounts:

LO 7-S2

	2010	2011	2012	2013
Net Sales	$50,000	$49,000	$71,000	$58,000
Cost of Goods Sold	32,500	35,000	43,000	37,000
Gross Profit	17,500	14,000	28,000	21,000

After these amounts were reported, M & M's accountant determined that the inventory on December 31, 2011, was understated by $3,000. The inventory balance on December 31, 2012, was accurately stated.

Required:

1. Restate the partial income statements to reflect the correct amounts, after fixing the inventory error.
2. Compute the gross profit percentage for all four years both (*a*) before the correction and (*b*) after the correction. Does the pattern of gross profit percentages lend confidence to your corrected amounts? Explain. Round your answer to the nearest percentage.
   TIP: Gross profit percentage is calculated as (Gross Profit ÷ Net Sales) × 100.

LO 7-S3 **CP7-7 (Supplement 7C) Journalizing Inventory Transactions Using a Periodic Inventory System**

Prepare journal entries to record the transactions in CP7-1 assuming that a periodic inventory system is used, with inventory costs being determined on a FIFO basis.

GROUP A PROBLEMS

LO 7-3 **PA7-1 Analyzing the Effects of Four Alternative Inventory Methods in a Periodic Inventory System**

Gladstone Company tracks the number of units purchased and sold throughout each accounting period but applies its inventory costing method at the end of each period, as if it uses a periodic inventory system. Assume its accounting records provided the following information at the end of the annual accounting period, December 31, 2012.

Transactions	Units	Unit Cost
Beginning inventory, January 1, 2012	1,800	$50
Transactions during 2012:		
a. Purchase, January 30	2,500	62
b. Sale, March 14 ($100 each)	(1,450)	
c. Purchase, May 1	1,200	80
d. Sale, August 31 ($100 each)	(1,900)	

Required:

1. Compute the amount of goods available for sale, ending inventory, and cost of goods sold at December 31, 2012, under each of the following inventory costing methods:
   a. Last-in, first-out.
   b. Weighted average cost.
   c. First-in, first-out.
   d. Specific identification, assuming that the March 14, 2012, sale was selected two-fifths from the beginning inventory and three-fifths from the purchase of January 30, 2012. Assume that the sale of August 31, 2012, was selected from the remainder of the beginning inventory, with the balance from the purchase of May 1, 2012.
2. Of the four methods, which will result in the highest gross profit? Which will result in the lowest income taxes?

LO 7-4 **PA7-2 Evaluating the Income Statement and Income Tax Effects of Lower of Cost or Market**

Springer Anderson Gymnastics prepared its annual financial statements dated December 31, 2012. The company used the FIFO inventory costing method, but it failed to apply LCM to the ending inventory. The preliminary 2012 income statement follows:

Sales Revenue		$140,000
Cost of Goods Sold		
Beginning Inventory	$ 15,000	
Purchases	91,000	
Goods Available for Sale	106,000	
Ending Inventory (FIFO cost)	22,000	
Cost of Goods Sold		84,000
Gross Profit		56,000
Operating Expenses		31,000
Income from Operations		25,000
Income Tax Expense (30%)		7,500
Net Income		$ 17,500

Assume that you have been asked to restate the 2012 financial statements to incorporate LCM. You have developed the following data relating to the 2012 ending inventory:

		Purchase Cost		Current Replacement
Item	Quantity	Per Unit	Total	Cost per Unit (Market)
A	1,500	$3	$ 4,500	$4
B	750	4	3,000	2
C	3,500	2	7,000	1
D	1,500	5	7,500	3
			$22,000	

Required:

1. Restate the income statement to reflect LCM valuation of the 2012 ending inventory. Apply LCM on an item-by-item basis and show computations.
2. Compare and explain the LCM effect on each amount that was changed in requirement 1.
3. What is the conceptual basis for applying LCM to merchandise inventories?

PA7-3 Accounting for Inventory Purchase Transactions Including Allowances and Discounts Using a Perpetual Inventory System

LO 7-5

Use the information in PA6-6 (page 295 in Chapter 6) to complete the following requirements.

Required:

1. Indicate the effect (direction and amount) of each transaction on the Inventory balance of Readers' Corner.
2. Prepare the journal entries that Readers' Corner would record and show any computations.

PA7-4 Calculating and Interpreting the Inventory Turnover Ratio and Days to Sell

LO 7-6

Harman International Industries is a world leading producer of loudspeakers and other electronics products, which are sold under brand names like JBL, Infinity, and Harman/Kardon. The company reported the following amounts in its financial statements (in millions):

Harman International Industries
Pioneer Corporation

	2010	2009
Net Sales	$3,364	$2,855
Cost of Goods Sold	2,479	2,210
Beginning Inventory	334	391
Ending Inventory	353	334

Required:

1. Determine the inventory turnover ratio and average days to sell inventory for 2010 and 2009. Round to one decimal place.
2. Comment on any changes in these measures, and compare the effectiveness of inventory managers at Harman to inventory managers at Pioneer Corporation, where inventory turns over 5.2 times per year (70 days to sell). Both companies use the same inventory costing method (FIFO).

LO 7-S1   **PA7-5 (Supplement 7A) Analyzing the Effects of the LIFO Inventory Method in a Perpetual Inventory System**

Using the information in PA7-1, calculate the cost of goods sold and ending inventory for Gladstone Company assuming it applies the LIFO cost method perpetually at the time of each sale. Compare these amounts to the periodic LIFO calculations in requirement 1a of PA7-1. Does the use of a perpetual inventory system result in a higher or lower cost of goods sold when costs are rising?

LO 7-S2   **PA7-6 (Supplement 7B) Analyzing and Interpreting the Effects of Inventory Errors**

Partial income statements for Sherwood Company summarized for a four-year period show the following:

	2010	2011	2012	2013
Net Sales	$2,000,000	$2,400,000	$2,500,000	$3,000,000
Cost of Goods Sold	1,400,000	1,660,000	1,770,000	2,100,000
Gross Profit	600,000	740,000	730,000	900,000

An audit revealed that in determining these amounts, the ending inventory for 2011 was overstated by $20,000. The inventory balance on December 31, 2012, was accurately stated. The company uses a periodic inventory system.

Required:

1. Restate the partial income statements to reflect the correct amounts, after fixing the inventory error.
2. Compute the gross profit percentage for each year (a) before the correction and (b) after the correction, rounding to the nearest percentage. Do the results lend confidence to your corrected amounts? Explain.

LO 7-S3   **PA7-7 (Supplement 7C) Journalizing Inventory Transactions Using a Periodic Inventory System**

Prepare journal entries to record the transactions in PA7-1 assuming that a periodic inventory system is used, with inventory costs being determined on a FIFO basis.

GROUP B PROBLEMS

LO 7-3   **PB7-1 Analyzing the Effects of Four Alternative Inventory Methods in a Periodic Inventory System**

Mojo Industries tracks the number of units purchased and sold throughout each accounting period but applies its inventory costing method at the end of each period, as if it uses a periodic inventory system. Assume its accounting records provided the following information at the end of the accounting period, January 31, 2012. The inventory's selling price is $9 per unit.

Transactions	Unit Cost	Units	Total Cost
Inventory, January 1, 2012	$2.50	250	$625
Sale, January 10		(200)	
Purchase, January 12	3.00	300	900
Sale, January 17		(150)	
Purchase, January 26	4.00	80	320

Required:

1. Compute the amount of goods available for sale, ending inventory, and cost of goods sold at January 31, 2012, under each of the following inventory costing methods:
   a. Weighted average cost.
   b. First-in, first-out.
   c. Last-in, first-out.
   d. Specific identification, assuming that the January 10 sale was from the beginning inventory and the January 17 sale was from the January 12 purchase.

2. Of the four methods, which will result in the highest gross profit? Which will result in the lowest income taxes?

PB7-2 Evaluating the Income Statement and Income Tax Effects of Lower of Cost or Market

LO 7-4

Mondetta Clothing prepared its annual financial statements dated December 31, 2013. The company used the FIFO inventory costing method, but it failed to apply LCM to the ending inventory. The preliminary 2013 income statement follows:

Net Sales		$420,000
Cost of Goods Sold		
Beginning Inventory	$ 45,000	
Purchases	273,000	
Goods Available for Sale	318,000	
Ending Inventory (FIFO cost)	66,000	
Cost of Goods Sold		252,000
Gross Profit		168,000
Operating Expenses		93,000
Income from Operations		75,000
Income Tax Expense (30%)		22,500
Net Income		$ 52,500

Assume that you have been asked to restate the 2013 financial statements to incorporate LCM. You have developed the following data relating to the 2013 ending inventory:

Item	Quantity	Acquisition Cost Per Unit	Total	Current Replacement Cost per Unit (Market)
A	3,000	$4.50	$13,500	$6.00
B	1,500	6.00	9,000	3.00
C	7,000	3.00	21,000	6.00
D	3,000	7.50	22,500	4.50
			$66,000	

Required

1. Restate the income statement to reflect LCM valuation of the 2013 ending inventory. Apply LCM on an item-by-item basis and show computations.
2. Compare and explain the LCM effect on each amount that was changed in requirement 1.
3. What is the conceptual basis for applying LCM to merchandise inventories?

PB7-3 Accounting for Inventory Purchase Transactions Including Allowances and Discounts Using a Perpetual Inventory System

LO 7-5

Use the information in PB6-6 (page 298 in Chapter 6) to complete the following requirements.

Required:

1. Indicate the effect (direction and amount) of each transaction on the Inventory balance of Sports R Us.

2. Prepare the journal entries that Sports R Us would record and show any computations.

LO 7-6

Amazon.com
Barnes & Noble, Inc.

PB7-4 Calculating and Interpreting the Inventory Turnover Ratio and Days to Sell

Amazon.com reported the following amounts in its financial statements (in millions):

	2010	2009
Net Sales	$34,204	$24,509
Cost of Goods Sold	26,561	18,978
Beginning Inventory	2,171	1,399
Ending Inventory	3,202	2,171

Required:

1. Determine the inventory turnover ratio and average days to sell inventory for 2010 and 2009. Round to one decimal place.

2. Comment on any changes in these measures and compare the inventory turnover at Amazon.com to inventory turnover at Barnes & Noble, Inc., where inventory turned over 3.2 times during 2010 (114.1 days to sell). Based on your own experience, what's the key difference between Amazon.com and Barnes & Noble that leads one company's results to be the picture of efficiency and the other to seem like a library?

LO 7-S1

PB7-5 (Supplement 7A) Analyzing the Effects of the LIFO Inventory Method in a Perpetual Inventory System

Using the information in PB7-1, calculate the cost of goods sold and ending inventory for Mojo Industries assuming it applies the LIFO cost method perpetually at the time of each sale. Compare these amounts to the periodic LIFO calculations in requirement 1(c) of PB7-1. Does the use of a perpetual inventory system result in a higher or lower cost of goods sold when costs are rising?

LO 7-S2

PB7-6 (Supplement 7B) Analyzing and Interpreting the Effects of Inventory Errors

Spears & Cantrell announced inventory had been overstated by $30 at the end of its 2012 second quarter. The error wasn't discovered and corrected in the company's periodic inventory system until after the end of the third quarter. The following table shows the amounts that were originally reported by the company.

	Q1	Q2	Q3
Net Sales	$3,000	$3,600	$3,750
Cost of Goods Sold	2,100	2,490	2,655
Gross Profit	900	1,110	1,095

Required:

1. Restate the income statements to reflect the correct amounts, after fixing the inventory error.

2. Compute the gross profit percentage for each quarter (a) before the correction and (b) after the correction, rounding to the nearest percentage. Do the results lend confidence to your corrected amounts? Explain.

LO 7-S3

PB7-7 (Supplement 7C) Journalizing Inventory Transactions Using a Periodic Inventory System

Prepare journal entries to record the transactions in PB7-1 assuming that a periodic inventory system is used, with inventory costs being determined on a FIFO basis.

COMPREHENSIVE PROBLEMS

C7-1 Accounting for Inventory Orders, Purchases, Sales, Returns, and Discounts (Chapters 6 and 7)

LO 6-6, 6-7, 7-5

On October 1, the Business Students' Society (BSS) placed an order for 100 golf shirts at a unit cost of $20, under terms 2/10, n/30. The order was received on October 10, but 20 golf shirts had been damaged in shipment. On October 11, the damaged golf shirts were returned. On October 12, the BSS complained that the remaining golf shirts were slightly defective so the supplier granted a $100 allowance. The BSS paid for the golf shirts on October 13. During the first week of October, the BSS received student and faculty orders for 80 golf shirts, at a unit price of $37.50, on terms 2/10, n/30. The golf shirts were delivered to these customers on October 18. Unfortunately, customers were unhappy with the golf shirts, so BSS permitted them to be returned or given an allowance of $12.50 per shirt. Half of the golf shirts were returned on October 21, and the remaining 40 customers were granted the allowance on account on October 22. The customers paid their remaining balances during the week of October 25.

Required:

1. Prepare journal entries for the transactions described above, using the date of each transaction as its reference. Assume BSS uses perpetual inventory accounts.
2. Report the financial effects of the above transactions in a multistep income statement for the month ended October 31. Assume operating expenses, other than cost of goods sold, are $100 and income tax expense is $45.
3. Determine the percentage of net sales that is available to cover operating expenses other than cost of goods sold. By what name is this percentage commonly known?

C7-2 Computing and Evaluating Financial Statement Effects of Alternative Inventory Costing Methods (Chapters 2 and 7)

LO 2-5, 7-3

You have been given responsibility for overseeing a bank's small business loans division. The bank has included loan covenants requiring a minimum current ratio of 1.8 in all small business loans. When you ask which inventory costing method the covenant assumes, the previous loans manager gives you a blank look. To explain to him that a company's inventory costing method is important, you present the following balance sheet information.

Current assets other than inventory	$ 10
Inventory	(a)
Other (noncurrent) assets	107
Total assets	$ (b)
Current liabilities	$ 36
Other (noncurrent) liabilities	44
Stockholders' equity	(d)
Total liabilities and stockholders' equity	$ (c)

You ask the former loans manager to find amounts for (a), (b), (c), and (d) assuming the company began the year with 5 units of inventory at a unit cost of $11, then purchased 8 units at a cost of $12 each, and finally purchased 6 units at a cost of $16 each. A year-end inventory count determined that 4 units are on hand.

Required:

1. Determine the amount for (a) using FIFO, and then calculate (b) through (d).
2. Determine the amount for (a) using Weighted Average, and then calculate (b) through (d).
3. Determine the amount for (a) using LIFO, and then calculate (b) through (d).
4. Determine the current ratios using (i) FIFO, (ii) Weighted Average, and (iii) LIFO, and explain why these ratios differ.
5. Determine whether the company would be in violation or compliance with the loan covenant if the company were to use (i) FIFO, (ii) Weighted Average, and (iii) LIFO.

LO 4-2, 6-6, 7-3, 7-5, 7-6   **C7-3** **Recording Inventory Transactions, Making Accrual and Deferral Adjustments, and Preparing and Evaluating Financial Statements (Chapters 4, 6, and 7)**

College Coasters is a San Antonio–based merchandiser specializing in logo-adorned drink coasters. The company reported the following balances in its unadjusted trial balance at December 1, 2012.

Cash	$10,005	Accounts Payable	$ 1,500	Cost of Goods Sold	$8,900
Accounts Receivable	2,000	Wages Payable	300	Rent Expense	1,100
Inventory	500	Taxes Payable	0	Wages Expense	2,000
Prepaid Rent	600	Contributed Capital	6,500	Depreciation Expense	110
Equipment	810	Retained Earnings	3,030	Income Tax Expense	0
Accumulated Depreciation	110	Sales Revenue	15,985	Selling Expenses	1,400

The company buys coasters from one supplier. All amounts in Accounts Payable on December 1 are owed to that supplier. The inventory on December 1, 2012, consisted of 1,000 coasters, all of which were purchased in a batch on July 10 at a unit cost of $0.50. College Coasters records its inventory using perpetual inventory accounts and the FIFO cost flow method.

During December 2012, the company entered into the following transactions. Some of these transactions are explained in greater detail below.

Dec. 1   Purchased 500 coasters on account from the regular supplier at a unit cost of $0.52, with terms of 2/10, n/30.

Dec. 2   Purchased 1,000 coasters on account from the regular supplier at a unit cost of $0.55, with terms of 2/10, n/30.

Dec. 15   Paid the supplier $1,600 cash on account.

Dec. 17   Sold 2,000 coasters on account at a unit price of $0.90.

Dec. 23   Paid employees $500, $300 of which related to work done in November and $200 for wages up to December 22.

Dec. 24   Collected $1,000 from customers on account.

Dec. 31   Loaded 1,000 coasters on a cargo ship to be delivered to a customer in Hawaii. The sale was made FOB destination with terms of 2/10, n/30.

Other relevant information includes the following:

a. College Coasters has not yet recorded $200 of selling expenses incurred in December on account.

b. The company estimates that the equipment depreciates at a rate of $10 per month. One month of depreciation needs to be recorded.

c. Wages for the period from December 23–31 are $100 and will be paid on January 15, 2013.

d. The $600 of Prepaid Rent relates to a six-month period ending on May 31, 2013.

e. No shrinkage or damage was discovered when the inventory was counted on December 31, 2012.

f. The company did not declare dividends and there were no transactions involving contributed capital.

g. The company has a 30 percent tax rate and has made no tax payments this year.

Required:

1. Analyze the accounting equation effects of each transaction and any adjustments required at month-end.

2. Prepare journal entries to record each transaction and any adjustments required at month-end.

3. Summarize the journal entries in T-accounts. Be sure to include the balances on December 1, 2012, as beginning account balances.

4. Prepare the year-end Income Statement, Statement of Stockholders' Equity, and classified Balance Sheet, using the formats presented in Exhibits 6.11, 5.8, and 5.6.

5. Calculate to one decimal place the inventory turnover ratio and days to sell in 2012, assuming that inventory was $500 on January 1, 2012. Evaluate these measures in comparison to an inventory turnover ratio of 12.0 during the year ended December 31, 2011.

SKILLS DEVELOPMENT CASES

S7-1 Finding Financial Information

|ACCOUNTING   LO 7-2, 7-4, 7-6

Refer to the financial statements of The Home Depot in Appendix A at the end of this book, or download the annual report from the *Cases* section of the text's Web site at www.mhhe.com/phillips4e.

1. How much inventory does the company hold on January 30, 2011? Does this represent an increase or decrease in comparison to the prior year?
   a. $10,188 (Decrease)
   b. $10,188 (Increase)
   c. $10,625 (Decrease)
   d. $10,625 (Increase)

2. What method(s) does the company use to determine the cost of its inventory? Describe where you found this information.
   a. LIFO; Note 1
   b. FIFO; Note 1
   c. Weighted average cost; the Balance Sheet
   d. Specific Identification; Management's Discussion and Analysis

3. Compute to one decimal place the company's inventory turnover ratio and days to sell for the most recent year.
   a. 4.3 and 84.9
   b. 4.2 and 86.9
   c. 6.5 and 56.2
   d. 4.6 and 79.3

4. Does the company believe FIFO, or weighted average cost, is a better method?
   TIP: See financial statement Note 3.
   a. FIFO
   b. Weighted average cost

S7-2 Comparing Financial Information

LO 7-2, 7-4, 7-6

Lowe's

Refer to the financial statements of The Home Depot in Appendix A and Lowe's in Appendix B at the end of this book, or download the annual reports from the *Cases* section of the text's Web site at www.mhhe.com/phillips4e.

1. Does Lowe's hold more or less inventory than The Home Depot at the end of January 2011?

2. Does Lowe's follow the lower of cost or market rule? What method does Lowe's use to determine the cost of its inventory? Comment on how this affects comparisons you might make between Lowe's and The Home Depot's inventory turnover ratios.

3. Compute to one decimal place Lowe's inventory turnover ratio and days to sell for the 2010–11 fiscal year and compare to The Home Depot's. What does this analysis suggest to you?

S7-3 Internet-Based Team Research: Examining an Annual Report

LO 7-1, 7-2, 7-3, 7-4, 7-6

As a team, select an industry to analyze. Using your Web browser, each team member should access the annual report or 10-K for one publicly traded company in the industry, with each member selecting a different company. (See S1-3 in Chapter 1 for a description of possible resources for these tasks.)

Required:

1. On an individual basis, each team member should write a short report that incorporates the following:
   a. Describe the types of inventory held by the company. Does the company indicate its inventory management goals anywhere in its annual report?
   b. Describe the inventory costing method that is used. Why do you think the company chose this method rather than the other acceptable methods? Do you think its inventory costs are rising or falling?

    c. Calculate the inventory turnover ratio for the current and prior year, and explain any change between the two years. (To obtain the beginning inventory number for the prior year, you will need the prior year's annual report.)

    d. Search the 10-K for information about the company's approach for applying the LCM rule to inventory. Did the company report the amount of inventory written down during the year?

2. Then, as a team, write a short report comparing and contrasting your companies using these attributes. Discuss any patterns across the companies that you as a team observe. Provide potential explanations for any differences discovered.

LO 7-2, 7-4

S7-4 Ethical Decision Making: A Real-Life Example

Phar-Mor

This case is based on an inventory fraud at Phar-Mor, and is available online at www.mhhe.com/phillips4e. By completing this case, you will learn to identify clues of inventory misreporting.

LO 7-3

S7-5 Ethical Decision Making: A Mini-Case

This case is available online at www.mhhe.com/phillips4e. By completing this case, you will learn how the choice of inventory method can influence a manager's ability to meet profit expectations.

LO 7-3

S7-6 Critical Thinking: Income Manipulation under the LIFO Inventory Method

Mandalay Industries is a private company that sells electronic test equipment. During the year 2013, the inventory records reflected the following:

	Units	Unit Cost	Total Cost
Beginning Inventory	15	$12,000	$180,000
Purchases	40	10,000	400,000
Sales (45 units at $25,000 each)			

To minimize income taxes, inventory is valued at cost using the LIFO inventory method. On December 28, 2013, Mandalay's supplier increased the unit cost of new test equipment to $15,000.

Required:

1. Determine the company's Income from Operations and the cost of ending inventory. The company's operating expenses (excluding Cost of Goods Sold) were $300,000 and the company applies LIFO with a periodic inventory system.

2. Mandalay's management is considering buying 20 additional units on December 31, 2013, at $15,000 each. Redo the income statement and ending inventory calculations, assuming that this purchase is made on December 31, 2013.

3. How much did Income from Operations change because of the decision to purchase additional units on December 31, 2013? Is there any evidence of deliberate income manipulation? Is this tax fraud? Explain.

LO 7-4

S7-7 Calculating and Recording the Effects of Lower of Cost or Market (LCM) on Ending Inventory

This case is available online at www.mhhe.com/phillips4e. By completing this case, you will learn to use a spreadsheet to compute the amount of write-down to record after applying LCM to inventory.

CONTINUING CASES

LO 7-3, 7-5, 7-6

CC7-1 Accounting for Changing Inventory Costs

In October 2013, Nicole eliminated all existing inventory of cosmetic items. The trouble of ordering and tracking each product line had exceeded the profits earned. In December, a supplier asked her to sell a prepackaged spa kit. Feeling she could manage a single product line, Nicole agreed. Nicole's Getaway Spa would make monthly purchases from the supplier at a cost that included production costs and a transportation charge. Nicole's Getaway Spa would keep track of its new inventory using a perpetual inventory system.

On December 30, 2013, Nicole's Getaway Spa purchased 10 units at a total cost of $6 per unit. Nicole purchased 40 more units at $8 in February 2014, but returned 15 defective units to her supplier. In March, Nicole purchased 15 units at $10 per unit. In May, 50 units were purchased at $10 per unit; however, Nicole took advantage of a 2/10, n/30 discount from her supplier. In June, NGS sold 50 units at a selling price of $12 per unit and 35 units at $10 per unit.

Required:

1. Explain whether the transportation cost included in each purchase should be recorded as a cost of the inventory or immediately expensed.

2. Compute the Cost of Goods Available for Sale, Cost of Goods Sold, and Cost of Ending Inventory using the first-in, first-out (FIFO) method.

3. Calculate the inventory turnover ratio (round to one decimal place), using the inventory on hand at December 31, 2013, as the beginning inventory. The supplier reported that the typical inventory turnover ratio was 6.0. How does NGS's ratio compare?

4. Would a different inventory cost flow assumption allow Nicole's Getaway Spa to better minimize its income tax?

CC7-2 Wiki Art Gallery (WAG)

LO 7-3, 7-4

Access the Wiki Art Gallery (WAG) instructional case in Connect, and read the case in sufficient depth to answer the following questions.

1. What inventory costing method(s) does Wiki Art Gallery (WAG) use for determining the cost of artwork purchased as individual pieces?

    a. WAG uses FIFO.
    b. WAG uses Specific Identification.
    c. WAG uses a combination of FIFO and Specific Identification.
    d. WAG uses a combination of Average Cost and Specific Identification.

2. What assumption is WAG making when accounting for the cost of artwork purchased in lots?

    a. WAG is assuming the first artwork purchased is the first artwork sold.
    b. WAG is assuming the last artwork purchased is the first artwork sold.
    c. WAG is assuming the pieces of artwork are interchangeable and do not vary in value.
    d. WAG is assuming the pieces of artwork are uniquely identifiable.

3. For the 20 original oil paintings purchased on August 20, determine the amounts that WAG included in the cost of artwork sold and cost of artwork remaining in ending inventory after the sale of two pieces to TEAC.

    a. Cost of artwork sold includes $20,000 and ending inventory includes $20,000.
    b. Cost of artwork sold includes $10,000 and ending inventory includes $10,000.
    c. Cost of artwork sold includes $18,000 and ending inventory includes $2,000.
    d. Cost of artwork sold includes $2,000 and ending inventory includes $18,000.

4. Assume that the two paintings sold to TEAC represented 40 percent of the total value of the 20 original oil paintings purchased on August 20. Determine the amounts that WAG would include in the cost of artwork sold and cost of artwork remaining in ending inventory after the sale of two pieces to TEAC.

    a. Cost of artwork sold would include $8,000 and ending inventory would include $12,000.
    b. Cost of artwork sold would include $12,000 and ending inventory would include $8,000.
    c. Cost of artwork sold would include $8,000 and ending inventory would include $20,000.
    d. Cost of artwork sold would include $20,000 and ending inventory would include $8,000.

5. WAG's notes to the financial statements indicate the company reports its inventory at the lower of cost or market. What facts suggest a write-down may be required but has not been recorded by WAG?

    a. The market value of inventory is estimated by WAG's management, and Rob may be biased in thinking that WAG's inventory can be sold to TEAC.
    b. WAG's inventory contains aging, less attractive items.
    c. The 2011 income statement does not include an inventory write-down expense.
    d. All of the above.

Receivables, Bad Debt Expense, and Interest Revenue

YOUR LEARNING OBJECTIVES

Understand the business

LO 8-1   Describe the trade-offs of extending credit.

Study the accounting methods

LO 8-2   Estimate and report the effects of uncollectible accounts.

LO 8-3   Compute and report interest on notes receivable.

Evaluate the results

LO 8-4   Compute and interpret the receivables turnover ratio.

Review the chapter

Supplemental material

LO 8-S1   Record bad debts using the direct write-off method.

THAT WAS THEN

In previous chapters, we quietly assumed that all sales on account ultimately are collected as cash.

FOCUS COMPANY: VF Corporation (VFC)

vfc.com

One company is responsible for making North Face jackets, JanSport backpacks, Wrangler jeans, and Vans shoes. That company, VF Corporation, or simply "VFC," sells its products on account to major customers including Walmart, Macy's, and Target, as well as to many smaller retailers that you likely haven't heard of including Adventure 16, Paragon Sporting Goods, and Tactics. After making a sale to its customers, VFC faces the challenge of trying to collect the amount owed. Inevitably, some of VFC's customers will not pay the full amount owed, either because they dispute the price or quality of VFC's products or the customers have run into financial difficulties. This risk of failing to collect the full amount of its Accounts Receivable is a major concern for VFC's managers and investors, and it presents interesting challenges for the company's accountants, as you will read in this chapter.

THIS IS NOW

In this chapter, you'll learn how companies handle the situation where customers don't pay all that they owe.

Understand the business	Study the accounting methods	Evaluate the results	Review the chapter
• Pros and cons of extending credit	• Accounts receivable and bad debts • Methods for estimating bad debts • Notes receivable and interest revenue • Recording notes receivable and interest revenue	• Receivables turnover analysis	• Demonstration cases • Chapter summary • Key terms • Homework helper • Practice material

Understand the Business

What factors do managers consider when extending credit on account (accounts receivable) or lending to others under contract (notes receivable)?

PROS AND CONS OF EXTENDING CREDIT

Learning Objective 8-1
Describe the trade-offs of extending credit.

VFC allows business customers (like Walmart and Macy's) to open an account and buy items on credit, yet its outlet stores do not extend this option to you—the individual consumer. The reason VFC is willing to create an account receivable from business customers but not individual consumers is that doing so involves different advantages and disadvantages. The advantage of extending credit is that it helps customers buy products and services, thereby increasing the seller's revenues. The disadvantages of extending credit are the following additional costs introduced:

1. **Increased wage costs.** If credit is extended, VFC will have to hire people to (a) evaluate whether each customer is creditworthy, (b) track how much each customer owes, and (c) follow up to collect the receivable from each customer.

2. **Bad debt costs.** Inevitably, some customers dispute what they owe, or they run into financial difficulties and pay only a fraction of their account balances. These "bad debts," as they are called, can be a significant additional cost of extending credit. At September 30, 2011, VFC estimated that over 3.5 percent of its receivables would not be collected.

3. **Delayed receipt of cash.** Even if VFC were to collect in full from customers, it would likely have to wait 30–60 days before receiving the cash. During this period, VFC may have to take out a short-term bank loan to pay for other business activities. The interest on such a loan would be another cost of extending credit to customers.

SPOTLIGHT ON Business Decisions

Deciding Whether to Grant Credit

Many companies, including VFC, do not grant credit to individual consumers because the expected costs outweigh the benefits. However, some companies such as Target Corporation are able to profit by extending credit to individuals. Through its Target credit card program, Target allows consumers to purchase merchandise on credit. For Target, extending credit has allowed the company to generate more profit,* even in 2008 and 2009, when the economy struggled and Target's bad debts soared:

Credit program results (in millions):	2007	2008	2009	2010
Gross profit	$ 1,896	$ 2,064	$ 1,922	$ 1,604
Wages and administration expense	485	491	439	452
Bad debt expense	**481**	**1,251**	**1,185**	**528**
Interest expense	133	167	97	83
Additional net profit	$ 797	$ 155	$ 201	$ 541

*Target Corporation Form 10-K, Item 7, Management's Discussion and Analysis.

Most managers find that the additional revenue (or, more accurately, the gross profit) to be gained from selling on account to business customers is greater than the additional costs mentioned above.

Similar advantages and disadvantages are considered when deciding whether to create notes receivable. A **note receivable** is created when a formal written contract ("note") is established outlining the terms by which a company will receive amounts it is owed. Notes receivable differ from accounts receivable in that notes generally charge interest from the day they are signed to the day they are collected. Notes receivable are viewed as a stronger legal claim than accounts receivable, but a new note needs to be created for every transaction, so they are used less frequently—typically when a company sells large dollar-value items (e.g., cars), offers extended payment periods, or lends money to individuals or businesses.

> **YOU SHOULD KNOW**
>
> **Note receivable:** A promise that requires another party to pay the business according to a written agreement.

Study the Accounting Methods

ACCOUNTS RECEIVABLE AND BAD DEBTS

You already know from earlier chapters that **accounts receivable** arise from the sale of goods or services on credit. What you may not know is that some accounts receivable are never collected. Like that "friend" of yours who *says* he'll pay you later but for one reason or another never gets around to it, some customers just do not pay their bills.

Two objectives when accounting for accounts receivable and bad debts are: (1) report Accounts Receivable at the amount the company expects to collect ("net realizable value"), and (2) match the cost of bad debts to the accounting period in which the related credit sales are made. These two objectives point to the same solution: reduce both Accounts Receivable and Net Income by the amount of credit sales that are unlikely to be collected as cash.

The only problem with this solution is that time will pass before VFC discovers which particular credit sales and customer balances aren't going to be collected. These bad debts will likely be discovered in an accounting period following the sale,

> **Learning Objective 8-2**
> Estimate and report the effects of uncollectible accounts.

> **YOU SHOULD KNOW**
>
> **Accounts receivable:** Amounts owed to a business by its customers.

rather than in the same period as the sale. As Exhibit 8.1 shows, if you record sales in one period when they occur and bad debts in a different period when they are discovered, you will violate the **expense recognition ("matching") principle.** This failure to match Bad Debt Expense with Sales Revenue in the same period will lead to distorted views of Net Income in the period of the sale as well as in the period the bad debt is discovered.

EXHIBIT 8.1	Distortion Occurs If Bad Debts Are Not Matched to Sales

PERIOD 1 (Credit Sale Occurs)		PERIOD 2 (Bad Debt Discovered)	
Sales Revenues	$10,000	Sales Revenues	$ 0
Cost of Goods Sold	8,000	Cost of Goods Sold	0
Bad Debt Expense	0	Bad Debt Expense	1,000
Net Income	$ 2,000	Net Income (Loss)	$ (1,000)

Clearly, we need to **record bad debts in the same period as the sale.** The only way to do this is to record an estimate of the amount of bad debts that are likely to arise. Later, the accounting records can be adjusted when uncollectible amounts become known with certainty. This approach is called the **allowance method** and it follows a two-step process, which we'll walk you through below:

1. Make an end-of-period adjustment to **record the estimated bad debts in the period credit sales occur.**

2. Remove ("write off") specific customer balances when they are known to be uncollectible.

1. Adjust for Estimated Bad Debts

Credit sales, when first recorded, affect both the balance sheet (an increase in Accounts Receivable) and the income statement (an increase in Sales Revenue). Thus, to account for any bad credit sales that have been included in Sales Revenue and Accounts Receivable, we record offsetting amounts in both the balance sheet and income statement. This adjustment is made at the end of each accounting period to reduce Accounts Receivable (using a contra-asset account called Allowance for Doubtful Accounts) and reduce Net Income (using an expense account called **Bad Debt Expense**). If VFC were to estimate $900 of bad debts this period, the effects on the accounting equation and adjusting journal entry to record them would be:

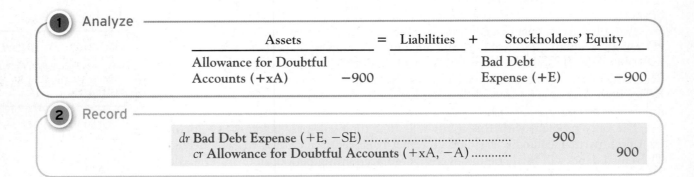

① Analyze

	Assets	=	Liabilities	+	Stockholders' Equity	
Allowance for Doubtful Accounts (+xA)	−900				Bad Debt Expense (+E)	−900

② Record

dr Bad Debt Expense (+E, −SE) 900
   cr Allowance for Doubtful Accounts (+xA, −A) 900

Exhibit 8.2 uses blue and red text to show how the accounts in the end-of-period adjusting entry partially offset the original sales on account. The exhibit also shows where the accounts appear in the balance sheet and income statement.[1]

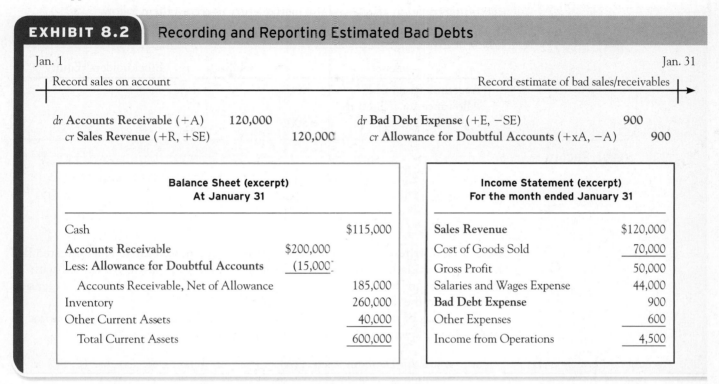

EXHIBIT 8.2   Recording and Reporting Estimated Bad Debts

Jan. 1   Jan. 31

Record sales on account   Record estimate of bad sales/receivables

dr Accounts Receivable (+A)   120,000   dr **Bad Debt Expense** (+E, −SE)   900
    cr Sales Revenue (+R, +SE)   120,000   cr **Allowance for Doubtful Accounts** (+xA, −A)   900

| **Balance Sheet (excerpt)** | | |
At January 31		
Cash		$115,000
Accounts Receivable	$200,000	
Less: **Allowance for Doubtful Accounts**	(15,000)	
Accounts Receivable, Net of Allowance		185,000
Inventory		260,000
Other Current Assets		40,000
Total Current Assets		600,000

| **Income Statement (excerpt)** | |
For the month ended January 31	
Sales Revenue	$120,000
Cost of Goods Sold	70,000
Gross Profit	50,000
Salaries and Wages Expense	44,000
Bad Debt Expense	900
Other Expenses	600
Income from Operations	4,500

Like all contra-asset accounts, such as Accumulated Depreciation, the Allowance for Doubtful Accounts is a permanent account, so its balance carries forward from one accounting period to the next. Bad Debt Expense, which is a temporary account, will have its balance closed (zeroed out) at the end of each accounting period. Consequently, the balance in the Allowance for Doubtful Accounts will differ from the balance in Bad Debt Expense, except during the first year that the Allowance for Doubtful Accounts is used. This explains why the Allowance for Doubtful Accounts in the balance sheet in Exhibit 8.2 does not equal the Bad Debt Expense in the January income statement.

For billing and collection purposes, VFC internally keeps a separate accounts receivable account (called a **subsidiary account**) for each customer. The total of these accounts is reported as Accounts Receivable on the balance sheet. Given this, you might wonder why the estimated uncollectible accounts aren't taken directly out of these individual accounts. The reason is that, at the time the Allowance for Doubtful Accounts is estimated, no one knows which particular customers' accounts receivable are uncollectible. If VFC were to remove the specific customer accounts believed to be uncollectible, it would lose track of which customers still owed money. If this were to happen, VFC would no longer know which customers it should continue pursuing for payment.

> **COACH'S TIP**
>
> Accounts Receivable, Net of Allowance (shown in Exhibit 8.2) is not a separate account. It is a subtotal that is computed by subtracting the contra-asset account *Allowance for Doubtful Accounts* from the asset account *Accounts Receivable*.

2. Remove (Write Off) Specific Customer Balances

Throughout the year, when it becomes clear that a particular customer will never pay, VFC removes the customer's account from the accounts receivable records. By removing the receivable, VFC no longer needs to make an allowance for it, so the company removes the corresponding amount from the Allowance for Doubtful Accounts. Removing the uncollectible account and a corresponding amount from the allowance is called a **write-off**. The purpose of writing off some or all of a customer's account balance is to remove amounts that are known with near certainty to have no chance of collection.

> **YOU SHOULD KNOW**
>
> **Write-off:** The act of removing an uncollectible account and its corresponding allowance from the accounting records.

---

[1]At the time of writing this text, the FASB and IASB had issued a proposal that would require bad debts to be reported on the income statement as a contra-revenue account rather than an expense account. This proposal is not expected to be implemented until 2015, so we show bad debts as an expense.

To illustrate, assume VFC decides to write off an $800 receivable from Fast Fashions. VFC would record an $800 decrease in Accounts Receivable, which would be offset by an $800 decrease in the contra-account Allowance for Doubtful Accounts. These accounting equation effects and the journal entry to record them follow.

① Analyze

	Assets		=	Liabilities	+	Stockholders' Equity
Accounts Receivable		−800				
Allowance for Doubtful Accounts (−xA)		+800				

② Record

dr Allowance for Doubtful Accounts (−xA, +A) 800
   cr Accounts Receivable (−A)... 800

Notice that **a write-off does not affect income statement accounts.** The estimated Bad Debt Expense relating to these uncollectible accounts was already recorded with an adjusting entry in the period the sale was recorded. Therefore, no additional expense is incurred when the account is finally written off.

The effects of these two steps on VFC's accounting records can be summarized in terms of the following changes in the related T-accounts:

dr + Accounts Receivable (A) cr −		dr − Allow. for Doubtful Accts. (xA) cr +		dr + Bad Debt Expense (E, SE) cr −	
1/1 Bal. 200,000			14,100 1/1 Bal. 900 **(1) Estimate**	1/1 Bal. 0 **(1) Estimate** 900	
1/31 Bal. 200,000			15,000 1/31 Bal.	1/31 Bal. 900	
	800 (2) Write-off	(2) Write-off 800			
2/28 Bal. 199,200			14,200 2/28 Bal.		

Notice that the write-off decreased both the total Accounts Receivable and Allowance for Doubtful Accounts by the same amount ($800). Consequently, the **net** receivable balance on February 28 ($185,000 = $199,200 − $14,200) is unchanged from the net receivable balance on January 31 ($185,000 = $200,000 − $15,000). Write-offs merely remove receivable balances that were previously accounted for as uncollectible.

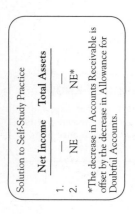

Solution to Self-Study Practice

	Net Income	Total Assets
1.	−	−
2.	NE	NE*

*The decrease in Accounts Receivable is offset by the decrease in Allowance for Doubtful Accounts.

💡 How's it going?   Self-Study Practice

Indicate the effect (+ / − / No Effect) of the following on net income and total assets.

	Net Income	Total Assets
1. Polaris Industries recorded an increase in estimated bad debts on December 31, 2013.		
2. Kellogg's wrote off twelve customer account balances during 2013.		

After you have finished, check your answers with the solution in the margin.

METHODS FOR ESTIMATING BAD DEBTS

In the examples given so far, we simply stated the estimated amount of uncollectibles to record. In the workplace, these bad debts must be estimated. Such estimates may be based on either (1) a **percentage of credit sales** for the period or (2) an **aging of accounts receivable**. Both methods are acceptable under GAAP and IFRS. The percentage of credit sales method is simpler to apply, but the aging method uses more detailed data and therefore is generally more accurate. Some companies use the simpler method on a monthly basis and the more accurate method on a quarterly or annual basis.

Percentage of Credit Sales Method

The percentage of credit sales method estimates bad debt expense by multiplying the historical percentage of bad debt losses by the current period's credit sales. Assume, for example, that VFC has experienced bad debt losses of ¾ of 1 percent of credit sales in prior periods. If credit sales in January total $120,000, VFC could estimate the month's bad debt expense as:

Credit sales this month	$120,000
× Bad debt loss rate (0.75%)	× 0.0075
Bad debt expense this month	$ 900

This estimate would be recorded using the journal entry previously shown on page 358.

Aging of Accounts Receivable Method

Whereas the percentage of credit sales method focuses on estimating Bad Debt Expense for the period, the aging of accounts receivable method focuses on estimating the ending balance in the Allowance for Doubtful Accounts. The aging method gets its name because it is based on the "age" of each amount in Accounts Receivable. The older and more overdue an account receivable becomes, the less likely it is to be collectible. Based on this idea, credit managers and accountants use their experience to estimate what portion of receivables of a specific age will not be paid.

To illustrate the aging of accounts receivable method, we assume VFC applies this method to its accounts receivable balances when its quarter ends on March 31. The method includes three steps as shown in Exhibit 8.3:

 Prepare an aged listing of accounts receivable with totals for each age category. Most accounting software will produce this report automatically by counting back the number of days to when each receivable was first recorded.

> **YOU SHOULD KNOW**
>
> **Percentage of credit sales method** (also called the income statement approach): Estimates bad debts based on the historical percentage of sales that lead to bad debt losses. **Aging of accounts receivable method** (also called the balance sheet approach): Estimates uncollectible accounts based on the age of each account receivable.

EXHIBIT 8.3 Estimating Uncollectible Amounts with an Aging of Accounts Receivable

Customer	Total	Number of Days Unpaid			
		0–30	31–60	61–90	Over 90
Adam's Sports	$ 700	$ 400	$ 200	$ 100	
Momentum Clothes	2,300				$ 2,300
Others (not shown to save space)	189,000	97,600	49,800	37,900	3,700
Zoom Athletics	6,000	4,000	2,000		
Total Accounts Receivable	**$198,000**	**$102,000**	**$52,000**	**$38,000**	**$6,000**
Estimated Uncollectible (%)		× 2%	× 10%	× 20%	× 40%
Estimated Uncollectible ($)	**$ 17,240**	**$ 2,040**	**$ 5,200**	**$ 7,600**	**$2,400**

←Step ❶ —Age
←Step ❷ —Estimate
←Step ❸ —Compute

② **Estimate bad debt loss percentages for each category.** The percentage each company uses varies according to its circumstances and past experience. Generally, higher percentages are applied to increasingly older receivables.

③ **Compute the total estimate by multiplying the totals in Step 1 by the percentages in Step 2 and then summing across all categories.** The total across all aging categories ($2,040 + $5,200 + $7,600 + $2,400 = **$17,240**) equals the balance to which the Allowance for Doubtful Accounts will need to be adjusted at the end of the period.

Allowance for		
dr − Doubtful Accounts cr +		
	14,200	Unadj. bal.
	?	AJE
	17,240	Desired bal.

The amount computed in Step 3 is the desired balance in the Allowance for Doubtful Accounts, not the amount of the adjustment. To compute the amount of the adjustment, you must determine how much to increase (credit) the Allowance for Doubtful Accounts to reach the desired adjusted balance computed in Step 3. For example, assume VFC had an unadjusted credit balance in the Allowance for Doubtful Accounts of $14,200 on March 31 and computed a desired credit balance of $17,240 as shown in Exhibit 8.3. An adjustment of **$3,040** ($17,240 − $14,200) needs to be recorded as a credit to the account. A corresponding amount is debited to Bad Debt Expense, as follows.

① Analyze

	Assets	=	Liabilities	+	Stockholders' Equity	
Allowance for Doubtful Accounts (+xA)	−3,040				Bad Debt Expense (+E)	−3,040

② Record

dr Bad Debt Expense (+E, −SE)	3,040	
cr Allowance for Doubtful Accounts (+xA, −A)............		3,040

③ Summarize

dr − Allow. for Doubtful Accts. (xA) cr +				dr + Bad Debt Expense (E, SE) cr −		
	14,200	Unadj. bal.		Beg. bal.	900	
	3,040	AJE		AJE	3,040	
	17,240	Adj. bal.		End. bal.	3,940	

Although the Allowance for Doubtful Accounts normally has a credit balance, it may have a **debit balance** before it is adjusted. This happens when a company has recorded write-offs that exceed previous estimates of uncollectible accounts. If this happens, you can still calculate the amount of the adjustment needed to reach the desired balance under the aging of accounts receivable method. The only difference is that to reach the desired balance, you need to record an amount equal to the desired balance **plus** the existing debit balance. After the adjustment is recorded, the Allowance for Doubtful Accounts will once again return to a credit balance.

SPOTLIGHT ON Business Decisions

Focus Collection Efforts with the Aged Listing of Accounts Receivable

The aged listing of accounts receivable, shown in Exhibit 8.3, is useful when estimating uncollectible accounts. It also is useful when credit managers identify customers at risk of failing to pay their accounts. Some sources report that this risk doubles every month that an account ages beyond 90 days. Knowing this, employees in VFC's credit department would be especially concerned with the $2,300 shown in Exhibit 8.3 as receivable from Momentum Clothes. If a follow-up phone call does not prompt the customer to pay, VFC could turn the account over to a collection agency.

💡 How's it going?   Self-Study Practice

For the years ended March 31, 2011 and 2010, Mad Catz reported credit balances in the Allowance for Doubtful Accounts of approximately $6,300 and $4,800 respectively. Assume it also reported that write-offs during the year ended March 31, 2011, amounted to $7,500. Assuming no other changes in the account, what amount did Mad Catz record as Bad Debt Expense for the period? Use the following T-accounts to solve for the missing value.

dr –	Allow. for Doubtful Accts. (xA)	cr +		dr +	Bad Debt Expense (E, SE)	cr –
	4,800	March 31, 2010		Beg. bal.	0	
[ ]	[ ]	Estimate		Estimate	[ ]	
		March 31, 2011		March 31, 2011		

After you have finished, check your answers with the solution in the margin.

Other Issues

Revising Estimates Bad debt estimates always differ from the amounts that are later written off. If these differences are material, companies are required to revise their bad debt estimates for the current period. That is, they correct overestimates of prior periods by lowering estimates in the current period, or they raise estimates in the current period to correct underestimates of prior periods.

Account Recoveries In the same way that someone you've written off as a friend might do something to win you back, a customer might pay an account balance that was previously written off. Collection of a previously written off account is called a **recovery** and it is accounted for in two parts. First, put the receivable back on the books by recording the opposite of the write-off. Second, record the collection of the account. To illustrate, let's assume that VFC collects the $800 from Fast Fashions that was previously written off. This recovery would be recorded with the following journal entries:

(1)	dr Accounts Receivable (+A)...	800	
	cr Allowance for Doubtful Accounts (+xA, −A)....		800
(2)	dr Cash (+A)	800	
	cr Accounts Receivable (−A).....................................		800

Reverse the write-off

Record the collection

Look closely at the journal entries for recording a recovery and you'll see that Accounts Receivable is debited and then credited for $800. It's tempting to cancel these two out, but don't do it because it would create an inaccurate credit history for the customer. After all is said and done, the customer's balance was removed because it was actually collected, not written off, so the accounting records should reflect that.

Alternative Methods You should be aware that some small companies don't use the allowance method. Instead, they use an alternative approach called the **direct write-off method,** which we demonstrate in Supplement 8A at the end of this chapter. This

Solution to Self-Study Practice

dr –	Allow. for Doubtful Accts.	cr +
Write-offs 7,500	4,800	March 31, 2010
	9,000	Estimate
	6,300	March 31, 2011

dr +	Bad Debt Expense	cr –
	Beg. bal.	0
	Estimate	9,000
	Adj. bal.	9,000

Beginning + Bad debt estimate − Write-offs = Ending
4,800 + X − 7,500 = 6,300; which implies X = 9,000

COACH'S TIP

Like the initial write-off, a recovery does not affect Net Income.

alternative method records Bad Debt Expense only when a company writes off specific accounts. Although this alternative method is easier to use, it overstates the value of Accounts Receivable and it violates the expense recognition principle as explained in Supplement 8A. Thus, it is not considered a generally accepted accounting method. However, the Internal Revenue Service (IRS), which discourages the use of accounting estimates, requires this method for tax purposes.

NOTES RECEIVABLE AND INTEREST REVENUE

> **Learning Objective 8-3**
> Compute and report interest on notes receivable.

A company reports Notes Receivable if it uses a promissory note to document its right to collect money from another party. This usually happens in the following three situations: (1) the company loans money to employees or businesses, (2) the company sells expensive items for which customers require an extended payment period, or (3) the company converts an existing account receivable to a note receivable to allow an extended payment period.

The accounting issues for notes receivable are similar to those for accounts receivable, with one exception. Unlike accounts receivable, which are interest-free until they become overdue, notes receivable charge interest from the day they are created to the day they are due (their **maturity date**). Although interest on a note receivable is earned each day, interest payments typically are received only once or twice a year. This means that a company with a note receivable needs to accrue Interest Revenue and Interest Receivable. Let's look at how to calculate interest.

Calculating Interest

> **YOU SHOULD KNOW**
>
> **Interest formula:** $I = P \times R \times T$ where I = interest calculated, P = principal, R = annual interest rate, and T = time period covered in the interest calculation (number of months out of 12).

To calculate interest, you need to consider three variables: (1) the **principal**, which is the amount of the note receivable, (2) the annual **interest rate** charged on the note, and (3) the **time** period covered in the interest calculation. Because **interest rates are always stated as an annual percentage even if the note is for less than a year,** the time period is the portion of a year for which interest is calculated. Ask yourself how many months out of 12 or how many days out of 365 the interest period covers. Then use the following **interest formula** to calculate the interest:

> ### COACH'S TIP
>
> The "time" variable refers to the portion of a year for which interest is calculated, not the portion of the note's entire life. A 2-month interest calculation on a 3-year note has a time variable of 2/12 not 2/36.

$$\text{Interest (I)} = \text{Principal (P)} \times \text{Interest Rate (R)} \times \text{Time (T)}$$

Many financial institutions use the number of days out of 365 to compute interest. In doing homework assignments, assume that the time is measured in terms of number of months out of 12. See Exhibit 8.4 for the computation of interest for three notes with different terms and different lengths of interest periods. Notice how the time variable in the calculation depends on the interest period, not the due date for the note.

EXHIBIT 8.4	Sample Interest Computations

GIVEN INFORMATION		INTEREST CALCULATION				
Terms of note	Interest period	Principal	Rate	Time		Interest
$100,000, 6%, due in two years	January 1–December 31	$100,000 ×	6% ×	12/12	=	$6,000
$100,000, 6%, due in one year	January 1–October 31	100,000 ×	6 ×	10/12	=	5,000
$100,000, 6%, due in 100 days	November 1–December 31	100,000 ×	6 ×	2/12	=	1,000

RECORDING NOTES RECEIVABLE AND INTEREST REVENUE

The four key events that occur with any note receivable are (1) establishing the note, (2) accruing interest earned but not received, (3) recording interest payments received, and (4) recording principal payments received. Assume that on November 1, 2012, VFC lent $100,000 to a company by creating a note that required the company to pay VFC 6 percent interest and the $100,000 principal on October 31, 2013. VFC prepared year-end financial statements as of December 31, 2012, but made no other adjustments for interest during the year.

Establishing a Note Receivable

The $100,000 loan that created the note receivable has the following accounting equation effects, which VFC would record using the following journal entry:

1 Analyze

	Assets	=	Liabilities	+	Stockholders' Equity
Note Receivable	+100,000				
Cash	−100,000				

2 Record

dr Note Receivable (+A) 100,000
  cr Cash (−A) 100,000

No interest is recorded on the day the note is established. Interest is earned over time.

Accruing Interest Earned

Under accrual basis accounting, interest revenue is recorded when it is earned. Rather than record the interest earned as each day passes, VFC waits until it either receives an interest payment or reaches the end of its accounting period.

The timeline in Exhibit 8.5 shows how VFC should account for interest on the note over its one-year term. Between the date of the note's creation (November 1, 2012) and the year-end (December 31, 2012), VFC earned two months of interest revenue (the red portion of the time line). As you learned in Chapter 4, when a company has earned interest in the current period but has not yet recorded the interest, the company must make an adjusting entry at the end of the current period to accrue the interest earned. The amount of interest for the two months of 2012 is computed as:

> **COACH'S TIP**
>
> Except for banks, interest is considered a peripheral source of revenue, so it is reported on the income statement immediately following the Income from Operations subtotal.

Interest (I) = Principal (P) × Interest Rate (R) × Time (T)
$1,000 = $100,000 ×   6%   × **2**/12

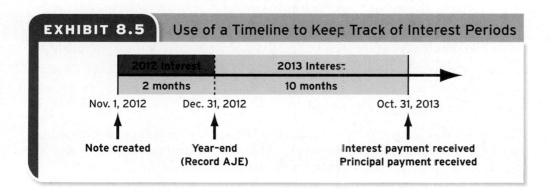

EXHIBIT 8.5 Use of a Timeline to Keep Track of Interest Periods

2012 Interest	2013 Interest
2 months	10 months

Nov. 1, 2012   Dec. 31, 2012   Oct. 31, 2013

Note created   Year-end   Interest payment received
            (Record AJE)   Principal payment received

The effect of this adjustment, along with the adjusting journal entry to record the $1,000 of interest revenue that is receivable on December 31, 2012, follows.

① Analyze

	Assets	= Liabilities +	Stockholders' Equity
Interest Receivable	+1,000		Interest Revenue (+R) +1,000

② Record

dr Interest Receivable (+A)	1,000	
cr Interest Revenue (+R, +SE)		1,000

Recording Interest Received

On October 31, 2013, VFC receives a cash interest payment of $6,000 (= $100,000 × 6% × 12/12). As shown on the following timeline, this $6,000 of interest includes the $1,000 that was accrued as Interest Receivable at December 31, 2012, plus $5,000 of interest revenue earned during the 10-month period from January 1 to October 31, 2013, which had yet to be recorded.

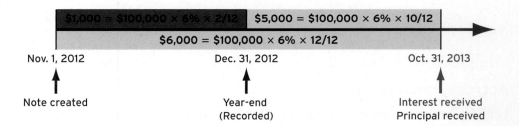

$1,000 = $100,000 × 6% × 2/12	$5,000 = $100,000 × 6% × 10/12	
$6,000 = $100,000 × 6% × 12/12		

Nov. 1, 2012	Dec. 31, 2012	Oct. 31, 2013
↑	↑	↑
Note created	Year-end (Recorded)	Interest received Principal received

When VFC receives the interest payment, it will record the $6,000 Cash, and it will reduce the $1,000 Interest Receivable that was previously recorded and record the remaining $5,000 as Interest Revenue in 2013. These effects and the journal entry to record them follow:

① Analyze

	Assets	= Liabilities +	Stockholders' Equity
Cash	+6,000		Interest Revenue (+R) +5,000
Interest Receivable	−1,000		

② Record

dr Cash (+A)	6,000	
cr Interest Receivable (−A)		1,000
cr Interest Revenue (+R, +SE)		5,000

Recording Principal Received

The collection of a note receivable is accounted for just like the collection of an account receivable. Assuming that VFC receives the $100,000 principal that is due, the accounting equation effects and journal entry for this transaction would be:

1 Analyze

	Assets	= Liabilities +	Stockholders' Equity
Cash	+100,000		
Note Receivable	−100,000		

2 Record

dr Cash (+A) 100,000
  cr Note Receivable (−A) 100,000

Accounting for Uncollectible Notes

Just as companies may not collect their accounts receivable in full, they also might not collect the full principal (and interest) that they are owed on a note receivable. When the collection of notes receivable is in doubt, a company should record an Allowance for Doubtful Accounts against the Notes Receivable, just as it records an Allowance for Doubtful Accounts against Accounts Receivable.

 How's it going? — Self-Study Practice

Assume that Mad Catz loaned $12,000 to an employee on October 1, 2012, by creating a note that required that the employee pay the principal and 8 percent interest on September 30, 2013. Assume that the company makes adjusting entries only at year-end on December 31.

1. Record the creation of the note.
2. Record any necessary end-of-period adjusting entry to be made at the end of 2012.
3. Record the receipt of interest and principal on September 30, 2013.

After you have finished, check your answers with the solution in the margin.

Solution to Self-Study Practice
1. dr Note Receivable (+A) 12,000
   cr Cash (−A).......... 12,000
2. dr Interest Receivable (+A) ($12,000 × 8% × 3/12) 240
   cr Interest Revenue (+R, +SE) 240
3. dr Cash (+A) ($12,000 × 8% × 12/12) 960
   cr Interest Receivable (−A) ($12,000 × 8% × 3/12) 240
   cr Interest Revenue (+R, +SE) ($12,000 × 8% × 9/12) 720
   dr Cash (+A) 12,000
   cr Note Receivable (−A) 12,000

SPOTLIGHT ON Ethics

www.mhhe.com/phillips4e

Resetting the Clock

Earlier in this chapter, you saw that as customer balances get older, the Allowance for Doubtful Accounts should be increased. Because increases in the Allowance for Doubtful Accounts require increases in Bad Debt Expense, the result of older customer accounts should be a decrease in net income.

  A credit manager at MCI knew about these accounting effects. To avoid reducing net income, he "reset the clock" on amounts owed by customers. He did so by making loans to customers, who then used the money to pay off their account balances. By replacing old accounts receivable with new notes receivable, he avoided recording approximately $70 million in bad debts. His scheme didn't last long, though. After the fraud was revealed, the credit manager spent several years in prison and he has been working to pay off over $10 million in fines. To learn more about this fraud, see S8-4 at the end of this chapter.

Learning Objective 8-4
Compute and interpret the receivables turnover ratio.

Evaluate the Results

RECEIVABLES TURNOVER ANALYSIS

YOU SHOULD KNOW

Receivables turnover: The process of selling and collecting on account. The receivables turnover ratio determines the average number of times this process occurs during the period.

Managers, directors, investors, and creditors can evaluate the effectiveness of a company's credit-granting and collection activities by conducting a receivables turnover analysis. The idea behind a receivables turnover analysis is shown in Exhibit 8.6. When a company sells goods or services on credit, its receivables balance goes up, and when it collects from customers, the receivables balance goes down. This process of selling and collecting is called **receivables turnover** and it is repeated over and over during each accounting period, for each customer.

EXHIBIT 8.6 Receivables Turnover Analysis

COACH'S TIP

The bottom of the receivables turnover ratio uses the average beginning and ending Net Receivables, so that it spans the same period as the numerator. Ideally, the ratio would use only credit sales, but this is not reported separately, so use Net Sales Revenue instead.

The receivables turnover ratio indicates how many times, on average, this process of selling and collecting is repeated during the period. The higher the ratio, the faster the collection of receivables. And the faster the collection of receivables, the shorter your company's operating cycle, which means more cash available for running the business. A low turnover ratio can be a warning sign, suggesting that the company is allowing too much time for customers to pay. As you learned earlier in this chapter (on page 361), the longer an account goes without being collected, the bigger the risk that it will never be collected. Analysts watch for changes in the receivables turnover ratio because a sudden decline may mean that a company is recording sales of merchandise that customers are likely to return later. It also may mean that the company is selling to less financially secure customers or is allowing customers more time to pay their accounts to entice them to buy as much as possible—a practice known as **channel stuffing.**

YOU SHOULD KNOW

Days to collect: A measure of the average number of days from the time a sale is made on account to the time it is collected.

Rather than evaluate the **number of times** accounts receivable turn over during a year, some people find it easier to think in terms of the **length of time** (in days) it takes to collect accounts receivable (called **days to collect**). Converting the year's receivables turnover ratio into the average days to collect is easy. Simply divide 365 by the year's receivables turnover ratio. This alternative measure provides the same basic information about the company's ability to collect receivables, but it's a little easier to interpret. In terms of Exhibit 8.6, the receivables turnover ratio counts the number of loops in a given period of time, whereas days to collect tells you the average number of days between loops.

Accounting Decision Tools		
Name of Measure	Formula	What It Tells You
Receivables turnover ratio	$\dfrac{\text{Net Sales Revenue}}{\text{Average Net Receivables}}$	• The number of times receivables turn over during the period • A higher ratio means faster (better) turnover
Days to collect	$\dfrac{365}{\text{Receivables Turnover Ratio}}$	• Average number of days from sale on account to collection • A higher number means a longer (worse) time to collect

Comparison to Benchmarks

Credit Terms By calculating days to collect you can compare a company's collection performance to its stated collections policy. You might remember from Chapter 6 that when companies sell on account, they specify the length of credit period (as well as any discounts for prompt payment). By comparing the number of days to collect to the length of credit period, you can gain a sense of whether customers are complying with the stated policy. Managers inside a company watch this closely, and so do investors and creditors on the outside. Why? If customers appear to be disregarding the stated credit period, that may be a sign they are dissatisfied with the product or service they bought.

SPOTLIGHT ON Financial Reporting

www.mhhe.com/phillips4e

Days to Collect before and after the Financial Crisis

Kellogg Company—the cereal maker—provides information about its normal credit policies in its annual report. Kellogg indicates that its stated policy is to require payment from customers within 16 days of making a sale (**1/15, n/16**). During the financial crisis of 2008 and 2009, the company experienced an increase in its days to collect from about 19 to 27 days, suggesting that customers were finding it difficult to meet the stated credit terms. Other companies also experienced a jump in days to collect between 2007 and 2009, including Caterpillar (68 to 85 days), Hewlett-Packard (43 to 53 days), and K·Swiss (35 to 47 days).

Other Companies Receivables turnover ratios and the number of days to collect often vary across industries. To illustrate, we have calculated these measures in Exhibit 8.7 for VFC, Kellogg (the cereal maker), and Skechers (a footwear company). As Exhibit 8.7 shows, VFC turned over its receivables 9.8 times, which is once every 37.2 days. Kellogg had a turnover ratio of 13.6 times, which means a collection period of about 27 days. Skechers shuffled along behind, with a receivables turnover ratio of 8.3, which is about 44 days to collect. Because these measures typically vary between industries, you should compare a company's turnover only with other companies in the same

---

EXHIBIT 8.7 Summary of Receivables Turnover Ratio Analyses

Company	Relevant Information (in millions)			Fiscal 2010 Receivables Turnover Calculation	Fiscal 2010 Days to Collect Calculation
		Fiscal 2010	Fiscal 2009		
	Net Sales	$7,625	$7,143	$\dfrac{\$7,625}{(\$773 + \$776)/2} = 9.8 \text{ times}$	$\dfrac{365 \text{ days}}{9.8 \text{ times}} = 37.2 \text{ days}$
	Net Accounts Receivable	773	776		
		Fiscal 2010	Fiscal 2009		
KELLOGG'S	Net Sales	$12,397	$12,575	$\dfrac{\$12,397}{(\$883 + \$942)/2} = 13.6 \text{ times}$	$\dfrac{365 \text{ days}}{13.6 \text{ times}} = 26.8 \text{ days}$
	Net Accounts Receivable	883	942		
		Fiscal 2010	Fiscal 2009		
SKECHERS	Net Sales	$2,007	$1,436	$\dfrac{\$2,007}{(\$266 + \$220)/2} = 8.3 \text{ times}$	$\dfrac{365 \text{ days}}{8.3 \text{ times}} = 44.0 \text{ days}$
	Net Accounts Receivable	266	220		

industry or with its figures from prior periods. For practice at computing and comparing to prior periods, try the Self-Study Practice that follows.

 How's it going?   Self-Study Practice

VFC reported net accounts receivable of $851 (million) at the end of Fiscal 2008.

(*a*) Use this information, along with that in Exhibit 8.7, to calculate VFC's receivables turnover and days to collect in Fiscal 2009.

Fiscal 2009 Receivables Turnover:

$$\frac{[\qquad]}{([\qquad]+[\qquad])/2} = [\qquad] \text{ times}$$

Fiscal 2009 Days to Collect:

$$\frac{365 \text{ days}}{[\qquad] \text{ times}} = [\qquad] \text{ days}$$

(*b*) Did VFC's receivables turnover improve or decline from Fiscal 2009 (calculated in *a*) to 2010 (shown in Exhibit 8.7)?

After you have finished, check your answers with the solution in the margin.

Solution to Self-Study Practice

a. $\dfrac{\$7,143}{(\$776 + \$851)/2} = 8.8$ times

$365 \div 8.8 = 41.5$ days

b. VFC's receivables turnover improved in 2010 (4.3 days faster).

Speeding Up Collections

Factoring Receivables   To generate the cash needed to pay for a company's business activities, managers must ensure that receivables are collected on a timely basis. One way to speed up collections of sluggish receivables is to start hounding customers for payment. But this forceful approach is time-consuming, costly, and can annoy customers and cause them to take their business elsewhere. An alternative approach is to sell outstanding accounts receivable to another company (called a **factor**). The way this **factoring** arrangement works is that your company receives cash for the receivables it sells to the factor (minus a factoring fee) and the factor then has the right to collect the outstanding amounts owed by your customers. Factoring is a fast and easy way for your company to get cash for its receivables, but with costs. First, factoring could send a potentially negative message because it might be seen as a last resort for collecting accounts. Second, the factoring fee can be as much as 3 percent of the receivables sold. In its 2009 annual report, VFC reported that it sold $240 million of receivables to a factor, and was charged a fee of $400,000, which VFC reported as a Miscellaneous Expense. Other companies that regularly sell receivables report the cost of factoring on the income statement as a selling expense.

Credit Card Sales   Another way to avoid lengthy collection periods is to allow customers to pay for goods using PayPal or national credit cards like Visa, MasterCard, American Express, and Discover Card. Unlike private credit card programs that require the seller to pursue collection from customers, PayPal sends the money immediately and national credit card companies pay the seller within one to three days of the sale. Some banks accept credit card receipts as overnight deposits into the company's bank account as if they're cash. This not only speeds up the seller's cash collection, but also reduces losses from customers writing bad checks. But, just like factoring, these benefits come at a cost. PayPal and credit card companies charge a fee for their services, often around 3 percent of the total sales price. If sales amounted to $100,000, a fee of $3,000 would be deducted, leaving the equivalent of $97,000 cash. These transaction fees are included with selling expenses on the income statement.

SPOTLIGHT ON Controls

Segregating Collections and Write-Offs

One way to control accounts receivable is to ensure that the same person does not both receive collections from customers and write off account balances. This segregation of duties helps to prevent errors and fraud. Without adequate segregation between these duties, a single dishonest employee could divert customer payments to his or her own bank account and then cover up the theft by writing off the customer's balance.

SUPPLEMENT 8A DIRECT WRITE-OFF METHOD

As described earlier in this chapter, an alternative method exists to account for uncollectible accounts. This alternative approach, called the **direct write-off method**, does not estimate bad debts and does not use an Allowance for Doubtful Accounts. Instead, it reports Sales when they occur and Bad Debt Expense when it is discovered. This is required for tax purposes but it is not acceptable under generally accepted accounting principles or IFRS. Consequently, it isn't used very often for external financial reporting.

> **Learning Objective 8-S1**
> Record bad debts using the direct write-off method.

The reason the direct write-off method isn't considered a GAAP method is that it reports Accounts Receivable at the total amount owed by customers (an overly optimistic point of view) rather than what is estimated to be collectible (a more realistic viewpoint). The direct write-off method also breaks the expense recognition ("matching") principle by recording Bad Debt Expense in the period customer accounts are determined to be bad rather than the period when the credit sales are actually made. As illustrated in Exhibit 8.1 on page 358, the failure to match Bad Debt Expense to Sales has a distorting effect on Net Income in the period of the sale as well as in later periods when bad debts are discovered. The only advantage of this method is that it doesn't require estimating uncollectible amounts.

> **YOU SHOULD KNOW**
> **Direct write-off method:** A non-GAAP alternative to the allowance method of accounting for uncollectible accounts.

Under the direct write-off method, no journal entries are made until a bad debt is discovered. The journal entry used by the direct write-off method to record $1,000 of Bad Debt Expense when a customer account is determined to be uncollectible is:

> *dr* **Bad Debt Expense** (+E, −SE) 1,000
>   *cr* **Accounts Receivable** (−A) 1,000

REVIEW THE CHAPTER

DEMONSTRATION CASE A: BAD DEBTS

Shooby Dooby Shoe (SDS) reported credit sales of $95,000 during January 2013. Later in 2013, SDS determined that it would not be able to collect a $500 account balance that was owed by a deceased customer (Captain Cutler). SDS uses the percentage of credit sales method for estimating monthly Bad Debt Expense, and the aging of accounts receivable method at its December 31 year-end.

Required:

1. If SDS estimates that 1 percent of credit sales will result in bad debts, what will be the effects on the accounting equation of recording the January 2013 estimate? Prepare the journal entry to record these effects.

2. Show how the write-off of the account receivable from Captain Cutler would affect the accounting equation, and prepare the journal entry to record these effects.

3. Assume that SDS estimates that $11,000 of its year-end Accounts Receivable is uncollectible as shown below. As of December 31, 2013, the Allowance for Doubtful Accounts had an unadjusted credit balance of $3,000. Show the accounting equation effects of recording the bad debt estimate, and prepare a journal entry to record these effects.

		Number of Days Unpaid			
	Total	0–30	31–60	61–90	>90
Total Accounts Receivable	$171,000	$50,000	$80,000	$40,000	$1,000
Estimated uncollectible (%)		× 1%	× 5%	× 15%	× 50%
Estimated uncollectible ($)	$ 11,000	$ 500	$ 4,000	$ 6,000	$ 500

4. Assume that SDS reported Net Sales of $950,000 in 2013, Net Accounts Receivable of $160,000 at December 31, 2013, and $167,586 at December 31, 2012. Calculate the receivables turnover ratio for 2013.

5. If the receivables turnover ratio was 6.4 in 2012, what was the number of days to collect in 2012? Given your calculations in 4, conclude whether SDS collections are faster or slower in 2013 than in 2012.

Suggested Solution

1. The percentage of credit sales method multiplies historical bad debt losses (1%) by this period's credit sales ($95,000) to directly estimate the amount of Bad Debt Expense to record ($950 = 1% × $95,000).

Assets		=	Liabilities	+	Stockholders' Equity	
Allowance for Doubtful					Bad Debt Expense (+E)	−950
Accounts (+xA)	−950					

dr Bad Debt Expense (+E, −SE)(0.01 × $95,000) 950
    cr Allowance for Doubtful Accounts (+xA, −A)................. 950

2.

Assets		= Liabilities + Stockholders' Equity
Accounts Receivable	−500	
Allowance for Doubtful Accounts (−xA)	+500	

dr Allowance for Doubtful Accounts (−xA, +A)...................... 500
    cr Accounts Receivable (−A) 500

3. Under the aging of accounts receivable method, we determine the estimated balance for the Allowance for Doubtful Accounts ($11,000) and then subtract its unadjusted balance ($3,000) to determine the amount of the adjustment ($8,000 = $11,000 − $3,000).

Assets		=	Liabilities	+	Stockholders' Equity	
Allowance for Doubtful					Bad Debt Expense (+E)	−8,000
Accounts (+xA)	−8,000					

dr Bad Debt Expense (+E, −SE)... 8,000
    cr Allowance for Doubtful Accounts (+xA, −A)................. 8,000

4. Receivables turnover ratio is calculated as Net Sales ÷ Average Net Accounts Receivable. The average net accounts receivable in 2013 was $163,793 (= ($160,000 + $167,586)/2), so the receivables turnover ratio for 2013 was 5.8 (= $950,000 ÷ $163,793).

5. Days to collect is calculated as 365 ÷ receivables turnover ratio. The 6.4 turnover in 2012 equates to 57 days (and the 5.8 turnover in 2013 equates to 63 days). Collections are slower in 2013 than in 2012.

DEMONSTRATION CASE B: NOTES RECEIVABLE

As of February 28, 2010, Rocky Mountain Chocolate Factory, Inc. (RMCF), reported it had approximately $360,000 of Notes Receivable, with an annual interest rate of 8 percent. As a public company, RMCF prepares financial statements for external reporting every quarter, ending on May 31, August 31, November 30, and February 28. Assume that the notes were created on March 1, 2009, when money was loaned to another company and that RMCF receives interest payments semi-annually, on July 31 and January 31.

Required:

1. Using the interest formula, calculate the amount of interest that RMCF earns each month on the notes.

2. Using the interest formula, calculate the amount of interest payment that RMCF received on July 31, 2010, and on January 31, 2011.

3. Prepare a timeline showing the amount of interest earned each quarter and received on each payment date.

4. Prepare journal entries to record the note's issuance, interest earned, and interest payments received for each quarter and on each payment date.

Suggested Solution

1. Interest earned = Principal × Interest Rate × Time
   $$= \$360{,}000 \times 8\% \times 1/12 = \$2{,}400 \text{ per month.}$$

2. The period from March 1 to July 31 is five months whereas the period from August 1 to January 31 is six months.

   Interest payment = Principal × Interest Rate × Time
   $$= \$360{,}000 \times 8\% \times 5/12 = \$12{,}000 \text{ on July 31.}$$

   Interest payment = Principal × Interest Rate × Time
   $$= \$360{,}000 \times 8\% \times 6/12 = \$14{,}400 \text{ on January 31.}$$

3. Timeline

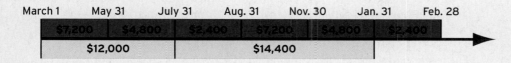

4. Journal Entries

   March 1, 2009 (Notes Issued)

dr Notes Receivable (+A)	360,000	
cr Cash (−A)		360,000

   May 31, 2009 (Interest Accrued)

dr Interest Receivable (+A)	7,200	
cr Interest Revenue (+R, +SE)		7,200

   July 31, 2009 (Interest Payment Received)

dr Cash (+A)	12,000	
cr Interest Receivable (−A)		7,200
cr Interest Revenue (+R, +SE)		4,800

   August 31, 2009 (Interest Accrued)

dr Interest Receivable (+A)	2,400	
cr Interest Revenue (+R, +SE)		2,400

   November 30, 2009 (Interest Accrued)

dr Interest Receivable (+A)	7,200	
cr Interest Revenue (+R, +SE)		7,200

January 31, 2010 (Interest Payment Received)

dr Cash (+A)	14,400	
cr Interest Receivable (−A)		9,600
cr Interest Revenue (+R, +SE)		4,800

February 28, 2010 (Interest Accrued)

dr Interest Receivable (+A)	2,400	
cr Interest Revenue (+R, +SE)		2,400

CHAPTER SUMMARY

LO 8-1   Describe the trade-offs of extending credit. p. 356

- By extending credit to customers, a company is likely to attract a greater number of customers willing to buy from it.

- The additional costs of extending credit include increased wage costs, bad debt costs, and delayed receipt of cash.

LO 8-2   Estimate and report the effects of uncollectible accounts. p. 357

- Under generally accepted accounting principles, companies must use the allowance method to account for uncollectibles. This method involves the following steps:
    1. Estimate and record uncollectibles with an end-of-period adjusting journal entry that increases Bad Debt Expense (debit) and increases the Allowance for Doubtful Accounts (credit).
    2. Identify and write off specific customer balances in the period that they are determined to be uncollectible.

- The adjusting entry (in 1) reduces Net Income as well as Net Accounts Receivable. The write-off (in 2) has offsetting effects on Accounts Receivable and the Allowance for Doubtful Accounts, ultimately yielding no net effect on Net Accounts Receivable or on Net Income.

LO 8-3   Compute and report interest on notes receivable. p. 364

- Interest is calculated by multiplying the principal, interest rate, and time period (number of months out of 12). As time passes and interest is earned on the note, accountants must record an adjusting journal entry that accrues the interest revenue that is receivable on the note.

LO 8-4   Compute and interpret the receivables turnover ratio. p. 368

- The receivables turnover ratio measures the effectiveness of credit-granting and collection activities. It reflects how many times average trade receivables were recorded and collected during the period.

- Analysts and creditors watch this ratio because a sudden decline may mean that a company is extending payment deadlines in an attempt to prop up lagging sales. Or it may mean that a company is recording sales of merchandise that customers are likely to return later.

Accounting Decision Tools

Name of Measure	Formula	What It Tells You
Receivables turnover ratio	$\dfrac{\text{Net Sales Revenue}}{\text{Average Net Receivables}}$	• The number of times receivables turn over during the period • A higher ratio means faster (better) turnover
Days to collect	$\dfrac{365}{\text{Receivables Turnover Ratio}}$	• Average number of days from sale on account to collection • A higher number means a longer (worse) time to collect

KEY TERMS

Accounts Receivable p. 357

Aging of Accounts Receivable
Method p. 361

Allowance Method p. 358

Bad Debt Expense p. 358

Days to Collect p. 368

Direct Write-Off Method p. 371

Factoring p. 370

Interest Formula p. 364

Notes Receivable p. 357

Percentage of Credit Sales
Method p. 361

Receivables Turnover p. 368

Write-Off p. 359

See complete definitions in the glossary in the back of this text.

HOMEWORK HELPER

Alternative terms

- Days to Collect is also called "days' sales outstanding."

Helpful reminders

- The percentage of credit sales method calculates the amount to record as Bad Debt Expense. The aging of accounts receivable method calculates the desired balance in the Allowance for Doubtful Accounts. This desired balance is compared to the existing balance to determine the amount to record as Bad Debt Expense.
- Interest rates always are for a full year. To calculate interest for a shorter period, multiply the interest rate by the fraction of the year for which you are calculating interest.

Frequent mistakes

- Some students mistakenly think a write-off is an expense. It isn't. It is merely a way to clean up the accounts receivable records. Under the allowance method, no Bad Debt Expense is recorded when removing (writing off) specific customer accounts.

PRACTICE MATERIAL

QUESTIONS (☻ Symbol indicates questions that require analysis from more than one perspective.)

1. What are the advantages and disadvantages of extending credit to customers?

2. In April 2006, Kohl's Corporation decided to discontinue its Kohl's credit card operations. What factors would this department store company have considered prior to making this decision? ☻

3. Which basic accounting principles does the allowance method of accounting for bad debts satisfy?

4. Using the allowance method, is Bad Debt Expense recognized in the period in which (a) sales related to the uncollectible account were made or (b) the seller learns that the customer is unable to pay?

5. What is the effect of the write-off of uncollectible accounts (using the allowance method) on (a) net income and (b) net accounts receivable?

6. How does the use of calculated estimates differ between the aging of accounts receivable method and the percentage of credit sales method?

7. A local phone company had a customer who rang up $300 in charges during September 2012, but did not pay. Despite reminding the customer of this balance, the company was unable to collect in October, November, or December. In March 2013, the company finally gave up and wrote off the account balance. What amount of Sales, Bad Debt Expense, and Net Income would the phone company report from these events in 2012 and 2013 if it used the allowance method of accounting for uncollectible accounts? Assume the company estimates 5 percent of credit sales will go bad.

8. What is the primary difference between accounts receivable and notes receivable?

9. What are the three components of the interest formula? Explain how this formula adjusts for interest periods that are less than a full year.

10. As of July 31, 2011, Krispy Kreme Doughnuts had $230,000 of Notes Receivable due before July 31, 2012, $21,646,000 of Accounts Receivable, and $1,307,000 in its Allowance for Doubtful Accounts (all related to accounts receivable). How should these accounts be reported on a balance sheet prepared following GAAP? What if the balance sheet follows IFRS, as described in Chapter 5?

11. Does an increase in the receivables turnover ratio generally indicate faster or slower collection of receivables? Explain.

12. What two approaches can managers take to speed up sluggish collections of receivables? List one advantage and disadvantage for each approach.

13. When customers experience economic difficulties, companies consider extending longer credit periods. What are the possible consequences of longer credit periods on Sales, Accounts Receivable, Allowance for Doubtful Accounts, Net Income, and the receivables turnover ratio? ●

14. (Supplement 8A) Describe how (and when) the direct write-off method accounts for uncollectible accounts. What are the disadvantages of this method?

15. (Supplement 8A) Refer to question 7. What amounts would be reported if the direct write-off method were used? Which method (allowance or direct write-off) more accurately reports the financial results?

MULTIPLE CHOICE

1. When a company using the allowance method writes off a specific customer's account receivable from the accounting system, how many of the following are true?

   - Total stockholders' equity remains the same.
   - Total assets remain the same.
   - Total expenses remain the same.

   a. None   c. Two
   b. One   d. Three

2. When using the allowance method, as Bad Debt Expense is recorded,

   a. Total assets remain the same and stockholders' equity remains the same.
   b. Total assets decrease and stockholders' equity decreases.
   c. Total assets increase and stockholders' equity decreases.
   d. Total liabilities increase and stockholders' equity decreases.

3. For many years, Carefree Company has estimated Bad Debt Expense using the aging of accounts receivable method. Assuming Carefree has no write-offs or recoveries, its estimate of uncollectible receivables resulting from the aging analysis equals

   a. Bad Debt Expense for the current period.
   b. The ending balance in the Allowance for Doubtful Accounts for the period.
   c. The change in the Allowance for Doubtful Accounts for the period.
   d. Both (a) and (c).

4. Which of the following best describes the proper presentation of accounts receivable in the financial statements?

   a. Accounts Receivable plus the Allowance for Doubtful Accounts in the asset section of the balance sheet.
   b. Accounts Receivable in the asset section of the balance sheet and the Allowance for Doubtful Accounts in the expense section of the income statement.
   c. Accounts Receivable less Bad Debt Expense in the asset section of the balance sheet.
   d. Accounts Receivable less the Allowance for Doubtful Accounts in the asset section of the balance sheet.

5. If the Allowance for Doubtful Accounts opened with a $10,000 credit balance, had write-offs of $5,000 (with no recoveries) during the period, and had a desired ending balance of $20,000 based on an aging analysis, what was the amount of Bad Debt Expense?

   a. $5,000   c. $15,000
   b. $10,000   d. $20,000

6. When an account receivable is "recovered"

   a. Total assets increase.
   b. Total assets decrease.
   c. Stockholders' equity increases.
   d. None of the above.

7. If a 10 percent note receivable for $10,000 is created on January 1, 2012, and it has a maturity date of December 31, 2016,

   a. No interest revenue will be recorded in 2012.
   b. The note receivable will be classified as a current asset.
   c. Interest Revenue of $1,000 will be recorded in 2012.
   d. None of the above.

8. If the receivables turnover ratio decreased during the year,

   a. The days to collect also decreased.
   b. Receivables collections slowed down.
   c. Sales Revenues increased at a faster rate than Accounts Receivable increased.
   d. None of the above.

9. In 2010, Coca-Cola Enterprises had a receivables turnover ratio of 7.9. Which of the following actions could Coca-Cola take to cause the ratio to increase?

   a. Pursue collections more aggressively.
   b. Increase the percentages used to estimate bad debts.
   c. Factor its receivables.
   d. All of the above.

10. All else equal, if VFC incurs a 3 percent fee to factor $10,000 of its Accounts Receivable, its Net Income will

   a. Increase by $10,000.   c. Increase by $300.
   b. Increase by $9,700.   d. Decrease by $300.

For answers to the Multiple-Choice Questions **see page Q1** located in the last section of the book.

MINI-EXERCISES

Mc Graw Hill connect | ACCOUNTING

LO 8-1   **M8-1 Evaluating the Decision to Extend Credit**

Nutware Productions Inc. generated sales of $30,000 and gross profit of $10,000 last year. The company estimates that it would have generated sales of $60,000 had it extended credit, but there would be additional costs for associated wages and bad debts totaling $25,000. Should the company extend credit?

M8-2 Evaluating the Decision to Extend Credit   LO 8-1

Last year, Pastis Productions reported $100,000 in sales and $40,000 in cost of goods sold. The company estimates it would have doubled its sales had it allowed customers to buy on credit, but it also would have incurred $50,000 in additional expenses relating to wages, bad debts, and interest. Should Pastis Productions extend credit?

M8-3 Reporting Accounts Receivable and Recording Write-Offs Using   LO 8-2
the Allowance Method

At the end of 2012, Extreme Fitness has adjusted balances of $800,000 in Accounts Receivable and $55,000 in Allowance for Doubtful Accounts. On January 2, 2013, the company learns that certain customer accounts are not collectible, so management authorizes a write-off of these accounts totaling $10,000.

a. Show how the company would have reported its receivable accounts on December 31, 2012. As of that date, what amount did Extreme Fitness expect to collect?
b. Prepare the journal entry to write off the accounts on January 2, 2013.
c. Assuming no other transactions occurred between December 31, 2012, and January 3, 2013, show how Extreme Fitness would have reported its receivable accounts on January 3, 2013. As of that date, what amount did Extreme Fitness expect to collect? Has this changed from December 31, 2012? Explain why or why not.

M8-4 Recording Recoveries Using the Allowance Method   LO 8-2

Let's go a bit further with the example from M8-3. Assume that on February 2, 2013, Extreme Fitness received a payment of $500 from one of the customers whose balance had been written off. Prepare the journal entries to record this transaction.

M8-5 Recording Write-Offs and Bad Debt Expense Using the Allowance Method   LO 8-2

Prepare journal entries for each transaction listed.

a. At the end of June, bad debt expense is estimated to be $14,000.
b. In July, customer balances are written off in the amount of $7,000.

M8-6 Determining Financial Statement Effects of Write-Offs and Bad Debt   LO 8-2
Expense Using the Allowance Method

Using the following categories, indicate the effects of the following transactions. Use + for increase and − for decrease and indicate the accounts affected and the amounts.

Assets	=	Liabilities	−	Stockholders' Equity

a. During the period, customer balances are written off in the amount of $10,000.
b. At the end of the period, bad debt expense is estimated to be $8,000.

M8-7 Estimating Bad Debts Using the Percentage of Credit Sales Method   LO 8-2

Assume Simple Co. had credit sales of $250,000 and cost of goods sold of $150,000 for the period. Simple uses the percentage of credit sales method and estimates that 1 percent of credit sales would result in uncollectible accounts. Before the end-of-period adjustment is made, the Allowance for Doubtful Accounts has a credit balance of $250. What amount of Bad Debt Expense would the company record as an end-of-period adjustment?

M8-8 Estimating Bad Debts Using the Aging Method   LO 8-2

Assume that Simple Co. had credit sales of $250,000 and cost of goods sold of $150,000 for the period. Simple uses the aging method and estimates that the appropriate ending balance in the Allowance for Doubtful Accounts is $3,000. Before the end-of-period adjustment is made, the Allowance for Doubtful Accounts has a credit balance of $250. What amount of Bad Debt Expense would the company record as an end-of-period adjustment?

M8-9 Recording Bad Debt Estimates Using the Two Estimation Methods   LO 8-2

Using the information in M8-7 and M8-8, prepare the journal entry to record the end-of-period adjustment for bad debts under the (a) percentage of credit sales method, and (b) aging of accounts receivable method. Which of these methods is required by GAAP?

LO 8-3 **M8-10 Using the Interest Formula to Compute Interest**

Complete the following table by computing the missing amounts (?) for the following independent cases.

Principal Amount on Note Receivable	Annual Interest Rate	Time Period	Interest Earned
a. $100,000	10%	6 months	?
b. $50,000	?	9 months	$3,000
c. ?	10%	12 months	$4,000

LO 8-3 **M8-11 Recording Note Receivable Transactions**

Nova Corporation hired a new product manager and agreed to provide her a $20,000 relocation loan on a six-month, 7 percent note. Prepare journal entries to record the following transactions for Nova Corporation. Rather than use letters to reference each transaction, use the date of the transaction.

a.   The company loans the money on January 1, 2013.
b.   The new employee pays Nova the full principal and interest on its maturity date.

LO 8-3 **M8-12 Recording Note Receivable Transactions**

RecRoom Equipment Company received an $8,000, six-month, 6 percent note to settle an $8,000 unpaid balance owed by a customer. Prepare journal entries to record the following transactions for RecRoom. Rather than use letters to reference each transaction, use the date of the transaction.

a.   The note is accepted by RecRoom on November 1, 2012, causing the company to increase its Notes Receivable and decrease its Accounts Receivable.
b.   RecRoom adjusts its records for interest earned to December 31, 2012.
c.   RecRoom receives the principal and interest on the note's maturity date.

LO 8-2, 8-3 **M8-13 Reporting Accounts and Notes Receivable in a Classified Balance Sheet**

Caterpillar, Inc.

Caterpillar, Inc., reported the following accounts and amounts (in millions) in its December 31, 2010, year-end financial statements. Prepare the current assets section of a classified balance sheet. Assume that the Allowance for Doubtful Accounts relates to Accounts Receivable rather than Notes Receivable.

Accounts Payable	$ 5,856	Long-Term Debt	$30,675
Accounts Receivable	17,149	Long-Term Notes Receivable	12,057
Accumulated Depreciation	12,367	Notes Receivable—Current	931
Allowance for Doubtful Accounts	357	Other Current Assets	908
Cash and Cash Equivalents	3,592	Other Current Liabilities	12,239
Inventories	9,587	Other Noncurrent Assets	7,614
Loans Payable—Current	3,925	Property, Plant, and Equipment	24,906

LO 8-4 **M8-14 Determining the Effects of Credit Policy Changes on Receivables Turnover Ratio and Days to Collect**

Indicate the most likely effect of the following changes in credit policy on the receivables turnover ratio and days to collect (+ for increase, − for decrease, and NE for no effect).

a.   Granted credit with shorter payment deadlines.
b.   Granted credit to less creditworthy customers.
c.   Increased effectiveness of collection methods.

LO 8-4 **M8-15 Evaluating the Effect of Factoring on the Receivables Turnover Ratio and Computing the Cost of Factoring**

After noting that its receivables turnover ratio had declined, Imperative Company decided for the first time in the company's history to sell $500,000 of receivables to a factoring company. The factor charges a factoring fee of 3 percent of the receivables sold. How much cash does Imperative receive on the sale? Calculate the factoring fee and describe how it is reported by Imperative Company. All else equal, how will this affect Imperative's receivables turnover ratio in the future?

M8-16 (Supplement 8A) Recording Write-Offs and Reporting Accounts Receivable Using the Direct Write-Off Method   LO 8-S1

Complete all the requirements of M8-3, except assume that Extreme Fitness uses the direct write-off method. Note that this means Extreme does not have an Allowance for Doubtful Accounts balance.

EXERCISES

E8-1 Recording Bad Debt Expense Estimates and Write-Offs Using the Aging of Receivables Method   LO 8-2

At the end of 2013, Blackhorse Productions, Inc., used the aging of accounts receivable method to estimate that its Allowance for Doubtful Accounts should be $19,750. The account had an unadjusted credit balance of $10,000 at December 31, 2013.

Required:

Prepare journal entries for each transaction.

a. The appropriate bad debt adjustment was recorded for the year 2013.
b. On January 31, 2014, an account receivable for $1,000 from March 2013 was determined to be uncollectible and was written off.

E8-2 Determining Financial Statement Effects of Bad Debt Expense Estimates and Write-Offs   LO 8-2

For each transaction listed in E8-1, indicate the amount and direction (+ or −) of effects on the financial statement accounts and on the overall accounting equation.

Assets	=	Liabilities	+	Stockholders' Equity

E8-3 Recording, Reporting, and Evaluating a Bad Debt Estimate Using the Percentage of Credit Sales Method   LO 8-2

During the year ended December 31, 2012, Kelly's Camera Shop had sales revenue of $170,000, of which $85,000 was on credit. At the start of 2012, Accounts Receivable showed a $10,000 debit balance, and the Allowance for Doubtful Accounts showed a $600 credit balance. Collections of accounts receivable during 2012 amounted to $68,000.

Data during 2012 follow:

a. On December 10, 2012, a customer balance of $1,500 from a prior year was determined to be uncollectible, so it was written off.
b. On December 31, 2012, a decision was made to continue the accounting policy of basing estimated bad debt losses on 2 percent of credit sales for the year.

Required:

1. Give the required journal entries for the two events in December 2012.
2. Show how the amounts related to Accounts Receivable and Bad Debt Expense would be reported on the balance sheet and income statement for 2012.
3. On the basis of the data available, does the 2 percent rate appear to be reasonable? Explain.

E8-4 Recording Write-Offs and Recoveries   LO 8-2

Prior to recording the following, Elite Electronics, Incorporated, had a credit balance of $2,000 in its Allowance for Doubtful Accounts.

Required:

Prepare journal entries for each transaction.

a. On August 31, 2013, a customer balance for $300 from a prior year was determined to be uncollectible and was written off.
b. On December 15, 2013, the customer balance for $300 written off on August 31, 2013, was collected in full.

LO 8-2   **E8-5 Determining Financial Statement Effects of Write-Offs and Recoveries**

For each transaction listed in E8-4, indicate the amount and direction (+ or −) of effects on the financial statement accounts and on the overall accounting equation.

Assets	=	Liabilities	+	Stockholders' Equity

LO 8-2   **E8-6 Computing Bad Debt Expense Using Aging of Accounts Receivable Method**

Young and Old Corporation (YOC) uses two aging categories to estimate uncollectible accounts. Accounts less than 60 days are considered young and have a 5% uncollectible rate. Accounts more than 60 days are considered old and have a 40% uncollectible rate.

Required:

1. If YOC has $100,000 of young accounts and $400,000 of old accounts, how much should be reported in the Allowance for Doubtful Accounts?
2. If YOC's Allowance for Doubtful Accounts currently has an unadjusted credit balance of $40,000, how much should be credited to the account?
3. If YOC's Allowance for Doubtful Accounts has an unadjusted debit balance of $5,000, how much should be credited to the account?
4. Explain how YOC's Allowance for Doubtful Accounts could have a debit balance.

LO 8-2   **E8-7 Computing Bad Debt Expense Using Aging of Accounts Receivable Method**

Brown Cow Dairy uses the aging approach to estimate Bad Debt Expense. The balance of each account receivable is aged on the basis of three time periods as follows: (1) 1–30 days old, $12,000; (2) 31–90 days old, $5,000; and (3) more than 90 days old, $3,000. Experience has shown that for each age group, the average loss rate on the amount of the receivable due to uncollectibility is (1) 5 percent, (2) 10 percent, and (3) 20 percent, respectively. At December 31, 2013 (end of the current year), the Allowance for Doubtful Accounts balance was $800 (credit) before the end-of-period adjusting entry is made.

Required:

1. Prepare a schedule to estimate an appropriate year-end balance for the Allowance for Doubtful Accounts.
2. What amount should be recorded as Bad Debt Expense for the current year?
3. If the unadjusted balance in the Allowance for Doubtful Accounts was a $600 debit balance, what would be the amount of Bad Debt Expense in 2013?

LO 8-2   **E8-8 Recording and Reporting Allowance for Doubtful Accounts Using the Percentage of Credit Sales and Aging of Accounts Receivable Methods**

Innovative Tech Inc. (ITI) uses the percentage of credit sales method to estimate bad debts each month and then uses the aging method at year-end. During November 2013, ITI sold services on account for $100,000 and estimated that ½ of one percent of those sales would be uncollectible. At its December 31 year-end, total Accounts Receivable is $89,000, aged as follows: (1) 1–30 days old, $75,000; (2) 31–90 days old, $10,000; and (3) more than 90 days old, $4,000. Experience has shown that for each age group, the average rate of uncollectibility is (1) 10 percent, (2) 20 percent, and (3) 40 percent, respectively. Before the end-of-year adjusting entry is made, the Allowance for Doubtful Accounts has a $1,600 credit balance at December 31, 2013.

Required:

1. Prepare the November 2013 adjusting entry for bad debts.
2. Prepare a schedule to estimate an appropriate year-end balance for the Allowance for Doubtful Accounts.
3. Prepare the December 31, 2013, adjusting entry.
4. Show how the various accounts related to accounts receivable should be shown on the December 31, 2013, balance sheet.

LO 8-2   **E8-9 Recording and Determining the Effects of Write-Offs, Recoveries, and Bad Debt Expense Estimates on the Balance Sheet and Income Statement**

Fraud Investigators Inc. operates a fraud detection service.

Required:

1. Prepare journal entries for each transaction below.

   a. On March 31, 10 customers were billed for detection services totaling $25,000.

   b. On October 31, a customer balance of $1,500 from a prior year was determined to be uncollectible and was written off.

   c. On December 15, a customer paid an old balance of $900, which had been written off in a prior year.

   d. On December 31, $500 of bad debts were estimated and recorded for the year.

2. Complete the following table, indicating the amount and effect (+ for increase, − for decrease, and NE for no effect) of each transaction. Ignore income taxes.

Transaction	Net Receivables	Net Sales	Income from Operations
a			
b			
c			
d			

E8-10 Recording Note Receivable Transactions, Including Accrual Adjustment for Interest   LO 8-3

The following transactions took place for Smart Solutions Inc.

2012

July   1   Loaned $70,000 to an employee of the company and received back a one-year, 10 percent note.

Dec. 31   Accrued interest on the note.

2013

July   1   Received interest and principal on the note. (No interest has been recorded since December 31.)

Required:

Prepare the journal entries that Smart Solutions Inc. would record for the above transactions.

E8-11 Recording Note Receivable Transactions, Including Accrual Adjustment for Interest   LO 8-3

The following transactions took place for Parker's Grocery.

Jan.   1   Loaned $50,000 to a cashier of the company and received back a one-year, 8 percent note.

June 30   Accrued interest on the note.

Dec. 31   Received interest and principal on the note. (No interest has been recorded since June 30.)

Required:

Prepare the journal entries that Parker's Grocery would record for the above transactions.

E8-12 Recording Note Receivable Transactions, Including Accrual Adjustment for Interest   LO 8-3

To attract retailers to its shopping center, the Marketplace Mall will lend money to tenants under formal contracts, provided that they use it to renovate their store space. On November 1, 2013, the company loaned $100,000 to a new tenant on a one-year note with a stated annual interest rate of 9 percent. Interest is to be received by Marketplace Mall on April 30, 2014, and at maturity on October 31, 2014.

Required:

Prepare journal entries that Marketplace Mall would record related to this note on the following dates: (a) November 1, 2013; (b) December 31, 2013 (Marketplace Mall's fiscal year-end); (c) April 30, 2014; and (d) October 31, 2014.

LO 8-2, 8-4

E8-13 Using Financial Statement Disclosures to Infer Write-Offs and Bad Debt Expense and to Calculate the Receivables Turnover Ratio

Microsoft Corporation

Microsoft Corporation develops, produces, and markets a wide range of computer software including the Windows operating system. Microsoft reported the following information about Net Sales Revenue and Accounts Receivable (all amounts in millions).

	June 30, 2010	June 30, 2009
Accounts Receivable, Net of Allowances of $375 and $451	$13,014	$11,192
Net Revenues	62,484	58,437

According to its Form 10-K, Microsoft recorded Bad Debt Expense of $45 and did not recover any previously written off accounts during the year ended June 30, 2010.

Required:

1. What amount of accounts receivable was written off during the year ended June 30, 2010?
2. What was Microsoft's receivables turnover ratio (to one decimal place) in the current year?

LO 8-2

E8-14 Using Financial Statement Disclosures to Infer Bad Debt Expense

SEARS

The 2011 annual report for Sears Holding Corporation contained the following information:

(in millions)	2011	2010
Accounts Receivable	$719	$691
Allowance for Doubtful Accounts	36	39
Accounts Receivable, Net	$683	$652

Assume that accounts receivable write-offs amounted to $13 during 2011 and $3 during 2010, and that Sears did not record any recoveries.

Required:

Determine the Bad Debt Expense for 2011 based on the above facts.

LO 8-2, 8-4

E8-15 Determining the Effects of Uncollectible Accounts on the Receivables Turnover Ratio

Refer to the information about Sears given in E8-14.

Required:

Complete the following table indicating the direction of the effect (+ for increase, − for decrease, and NE for no effect) of each transaction during 2011:

Transaction	Net Credit Sales	Average Net Accounts Receivable	Receivables Turnover Ratio
a. Writing off uncollectible accounts.			
b. Recording bad debt expense.			

LO 8-4

E8-16 Analyzing and Interpreting Receivables Turnover Ratio and Days to Collect

FedEx Corporation

A recent annual report for FedEx Corporation contained the following data (in millions):

May 31	2010	2009
Accounts Receivable	$ 4,329	$ 3,587
Less: Allowance for Doubtful Accounts	66	196
Accounts Receivable, Net of Allowance	$ 4,163	$ 3,391
Net Sales (assume all on credit)	$34,734	$35,497

Required:

1. Determine the receivables turnover ratio and days to collect for 2010. Round your answers to one decimal place.
2. Explain the meaning of each number.

E8-17 (Supplement 8A) Recording Write-Offs and Reporting Accounts Receivable Using the Direct Write-Off Method

LO 8-S1

Trevorson Electronics is a small company privately owned by Jon Trevorson, an electrician who installs wiring in new homes. Because the company's financial statements are prepared only for tax purposes, Jon uses the direct write-off method. During 2012, its first year of operations, Trevorson Electronics sold $30,000 of services on account. The company collected $26,000 of these receivables during the year, and Jon believed that the remaining $4,000 was fully collectible. In 2013, Jon discovered that none of the $4,000 would be collected, so he wrote off the entire amount. To make matters worse, Jon sold only $5,000 of services during the year.

Required:

1. Prepare journal entries to record the transactions in 2012 and 2013.
2. Using only the information provided (ignore other operating expenses), prepare comparative income statements for 2012 and 2013. Was 2012 really as profitable as indicated by its income statement? Was 2013 quite as bad as indicated by its income statement? What should Jon do if he wants better information for assessing his company's ability to generate profit?

COACHED PROBLEMS

 |ACCOUNTING

CP8-1 Recording Accounts Receivable Transactions Using Two Estimation Methods

LO 8-2

The A.T. Cross Company is well known for its Cross pens. The company recently reported the following amounts in its unadjusted trial balance as of December 31, 2010.

A.T. Cross Company

	Debits	Credits
Accounts Receivable	$30,691,000	
Allowance for Doubtful Accounts		$ 952,000
Sales Revenue		158,312,000

Required:

1. Assume Cross uses ¼ of 1 percent of sales to estimate its bad debt expense for the year. Prepare the adjusting journal entry required at December 31, 2010, for recording Bad Debt Expense.
   TIP: The percentage of credit sales method directly calculates Bad Debt Expense.
2. Assume instead that Cross uses the aging of accounts receivable method and estimates that $1,007,000 of Accounts Receivable will be uncollectible. Prepare the adjusting journal entry required at December 31, 2010, for recording bad debt expense.
   TIP: The aging of accounts receivable method focuses on calculating what the adjusted Allowance for Doubtful Accounts balance should be. You need to consider the existing balance when determining the adjustment.

3. Repeat requirement 2, except this time assume the unadjusted balance in Cross's Allowance for Doubtful Accounts at December 31, 2010, was a debit balance of $10,050.

4. If one of Cross's main customers declared bankruptcy in 2012, what journal entry would be used to write off its $10,000 balance?

LO 8-2, 8-3

Sonic Corp.

CP8-2 Interpreting Disclosure of Allowance for Doubtful Accounts

Sonic Corp. runs the largest chain of drive-in restaurants in the United States. In its 2010 10-K, Sonic reported the following changes in the Allowance for Doubtful Accounts (in thousands):

Balance at Beginning of Period	Charged to Bad Debt Expense	Amounts Written Off	Balance at End of Period
$879	$2,470	$139	$3,210

Required:

1. Create a T-account for the Allowance for Doubtful Accounts and enter into it the amounts from the above schedule. Then write the T-account in equation format to prove that the above items account for the changes in the account.
   TIP: The allowance increases when estimates are charged to Bad Debt Expense and when recoveries are reported. The allowance decreases when accounts are written off.

2. Record summary journal entries related to (a) estimating bad debt expense, and (b) write-offs of specific balances during the year.
   TIP: Use the generic account name "Receivables" to refer to the combined accounts receivable and notes receivable.

3. If Sonic had written off an additional $20,000 of accounts receivable during the period, how would Net Receivables have been affected? How would Net Income have been affected?

LO 8-3

CP8-3 Recording Notes Receivable Transactions

Jung & Newbicalm Advertising (JNA) recently hired a new creative director, Howard Rachell, for its Madison Avenue office in New York. To persuade Howard to move from San Francisco, JNA agreed to advance him $100,000 on April 30, 2012, on a one-year, 10 percent note, with interest payments required on October 31, 2012, and April 30, 2013. JNA issues quarterly financial statements on March 31, June 30, September 30, and December 31.

Required:

1. Prepare the journal entry that JNA will make to record the promissory note created on April 30, 2012.
   TIP: See Demonstration Case B for a similar problem.

2. Prepare the journal entries that JNA will make to record the interest accruals at each quarter end and interest payments at each payment date.
   TIP: Interest receivable will be accrued at the end of each quarter, and then will be reduced when the interest payment is received.

3. Prepare the journal entry that JNA will make to record the principal payment at the maturity date.

LO 8-2, 8-3

CP8-4 Accounting for Accounts and Notes Receivable Transactions

Execusmart Consultants has provided business consulting services for several years. The company uses the percentage of credit sales method to estimate bad debts for internal monthly reporting purposes. At the end of each quarter, the company adjusts its records using the aging of accounts receivable method. The company entered into the following partial list of transactions during the first quarter of 2013.

a. During January, the company provided services for $200,000 on credit.
b. On January 31, the company estimated bad debts using 1 percent of credit sales.
c. On February 4, the company collected $100,000 of accounts receivable.
d. On February 15, the company wrote off a $500 account receivable.
e. During February, the company provided services for $150,000 on credit.
f. On February 28, the company estimated bad debts using 1 percent of credit sales.
g. On March 1, the company loaned $12,000 to an employee who signed a 10% note, due in 3 months.
h. On March 15, the company collected $500 on the account written off one month earlier.

i. On March 31, the company accrued interest earned on the note.
j. On March 31, the company adjusted for uncollectible accounts, based on the following aging analysis. Allowance for Doubtful Accounts has an unadjusted credit balance of $6,000.

Customer	Total	Number of Days Unpaid			
		0–30	31–60	61–90	Over 90
Arrow Ergonomics	$ 1,000	$ 500	$ 400	$ 100	
Asymmetry Architecture	2,000				$ 2,000
Others (not shown to save space)	85,000	34,000	42,000	5,000	4,000
Weight Whittlers	2,000	2,000			
Total Accounts Receivable	**$90,000**	**$36,500**	**$42,400**	**$5,100**	**$6,000**
Estimated Uncollectible (%)		**2%**	**10%**	**20%**	**40%**

Required:

1. For items a–j, analyze the amount and direction (+ or −) of effects on specific financial statement accounts and the overall accounting equation and prepare journal entries.
    TIP: In item j, you must first calculate the desired ending balance before adjusting the Allowance for Doubtful Accounts.
2. Show how Accounts Receivable and related accounts would be reported in the current assets section of a classified balance sheet.
3. Name the accounts related to Accounts Receivable and Note Receivable that would be reported on the income statement and indicate whether they would appear before, or after, Income from Operations.

CP8-5 Analyzing Allowance for Doubtful Accounts, Receivables Turnover Ratio, and Days to Collect

LO 8-4

Mattel and Hasbro are two of the largest and most successful toymakers in the world, in terms of the products they sell and their receivables management practices. To evaluate their ability to collect on credit sales, consider the following information reported in their annual reports (amounts in millions).

Mattel, Inc.

Fiscal Year Ended:	Mattel			Hasbro		
	2010	2009	2008	2010	2009	2008
Net Sales	$5,856	$5,431	$5,918	$4,002	$4,068	$4,022
Accounts Receivable	1,168	774	900	992	1,072	644
Allowance for Doubtful Accounts	22	25	26	31	33	32
Accounts Receivable, Net of Allowance	1,146	749	874	961	1,039	612

Required:

1. Calculate the receivables turnover ratios and days to collect for Mattel and Hasbro for 2010 and 2009. (Round your final answers to one decimal place.)
    TIP: In your calculations, use average Accounts Receivable, Net of Allowance.
2. Which of the companies was quicker to convert its receivables into cash in 2010? in 2009?

GROUP A PROBLEMS

|ACCOUNTING

PA8-1 Recording Accounts Receivable Transactions Using the Aging Method

LO 8-2

Kraft Foods Inc. is the second-largest food and beverage company in the world. Assume the company recently reported the following amounts in its unadjusted trial balance as of December 31, 2010 (all amounts in millions):

Kraft Foods Inc.

	Debits	Credits
Accounts Receivable	$6,785	
Allowance for Doubtful Accounts		$ 121
Sales (assume all on credit)		49,207

Required:

1. Assume Kraft uses ½ of 1 percent of sales to estimate its Bad Debt Expense for the year. Prepare the adjusting journal entry required for the year, assuming no Bad Debt Expense has been recorded yet.

2. Assume instead that Kraft uses the aging of accounts receivable method and estimates that $233 of its Accounts Receivable will be uncollectible. Prepare the adjusting journal entry required at December 31, 2010, for recording Bad Debt Expense.

3. Repeat requirement 3, except this time assume the unadjusted balance in Kraft's Allowance for Doubtful Accounts at December 31, 2010, was a debit balance of $20.

4. If one of Kraft's main customers declared bankruptcy in 2011, what journal entry would be used to write off its $15 balance?

LO 8-2

Heelys, Inc.

PA8-2 Interpreting Disclosure of Allowance for Doubtful Accounts

Heelys, Inc., designs and sells footwear with the wheel in the heel, worn by annoying kids at shopping malls. It recently disclosed the following information concerning the Allowance for Doubtful Accounts on its Form 10-K annual report.

SCHEDULE II
Valuation and Qualifying Accounts
(dollars in thousands)

Allowance for Doubtful Accounts	Balance at Beginning of Year	Additions Charged to Bad Debt Expense	Write-Offs	Balance at End of Year
2008	$189	$ 0	$ 69	$120
2009	120	356	62	414
2010	414	131	?	237

Required:

1. Create a T-account for the Allowance for Doubtful Accounts and enter into it the 2008 amounts from the above schedule. Then write the T-account in equation format to prove that the above items account for the changes in the account.

2. Heelys reported sales of $70 million in 2008. Why might its Bad Debt Expense equal zero that year?

3. Record summary journal entries for 2009 related to (a) estimating Bad Debt Expense and (b) writing off specific balances.

4. Supply the missing dollar amount noted by ? for 2010.

5. If Heelys had written off an additional $20 of Accounts Receivable during 2010, how would Net Receivables have been affected? How would Net Income have been affected?

LO 8-3

PA8-3 Recording Notes Receivable Transactions

C&S Marketing (CSM) recently hired a new marketing director, Jeff Otos, for its downtown Minneapolis office. As part of the arrangement, CSM agreed on February 28, 2012, to advance Jeff $50,000 on a one-year, 8 percent note, with interest to be paid at maturity on February 28, 2013. CSM prepares financial statements on June 30 and December 31.

Required:

1. Prepare the journal entry that CSM will make when the note is established.

2. Prepare the journal entries that CSM will make to accrue interest on June 30 and December 31.

3. Prepare the journal entry that CSM will make to record the interest and principal payments on February 28, 2013.

LO 8-2, 8-3

PA8-4 Accounting for Accounts and Notes Receivable Transactions

Web Wizard, Inc., has provided information technology services for several years. The company uses the percentage of credit sales method to estimate bad debts for internal monthly reporting purposes. At the end of each quarter, the company adjusts its records using the aging of accounts receivable method. The company entered into the following partial list of transactions during the first quarter of 2013.

a. During January, the company provided services for $40,000 on credit.
b. On January 31, the company estimated bad debts using 1 percent of credit sales.
c. On February 4, the company collected $20,000 of accounts receivable.
d. On February 15, the company wrote off a $100 account receivable.
e. During February, the company provided services for $30,000 on credit.
f. On February 28, the company estimated bad debts using 1 percent of credit sales.
g. On March 1, the company loaned $2,400 to an employee who signed a 6% note, due in 6 months.
h. On March 15, the company collected $100 on the account written off one month earlier.
i. On March 31, the company accrued interest earned on the note.
j. On March 31, the company adjusted for uncollectible accounts, based on an aging analysis (below). Allowance for Doubtful Accounts has an unadjusted credit balance of $1,200.

Customer	Total	Number of Days Unpaid			
		0–30	31–60	61–90	Over 90
Alabama Tourism	$ 200	$ 100	$ 80	$ 20	
Bayside Bungalows	400				$ 400
Others (not shown to save space)	17,000	6,800	8,400	1,000	800
Xciting Xcursions	400	400			
Total Accounts Receivable	**$18,000**	**$7,300**	**$8,480**	**$1,020**	**$1,200**
Estimated uncollectible (%)		**2%**	**10%**	**20%**	**40%**

Required:

1. For items *a–j*, analyze the amount and direction (+ or −) of effects on specific financial statement accounts and the overall accounting equation and prepare journal entries.
2. Show how Accounts Receivable and related accounts would be reported in the current assets section of a classified balance sheet.
3. Name the accounts related to Accounts Receivable and Note Receivable that would be reported on the income statement and indicate whether they would appear before, or after, Income from Operations.

PA8-5 Analyzing Allowance for Doubtful Accounts, Receivables Turnover Ratio, and Days to Collect

LO 8-4

Coca-Cola
PepsiCo

Coca-Cola and PepsiCo are two of the largest and most successful beverage companies in the world in terms of the products that they sell and their receivables management practices. To evaluate their ability to collect on credit sales, consider the following information reported in their 2010, 2009, and 2008 annual reports (amounts in millions).

Fiscal Year Ended:	Coca-Cola			PepsiCo		
	2010	2009	2008	2010	2009	2008
Net Sales	$35,119	$30,990	$31,944	$57,838	$43,232	$43,251
Accounts Receivable	4,478	3,813	3,141	6,467	4,714	3,784
Allowance for Doubtful Accounts	48	55	51	144	90	70
Accounts Receivable, Net of Allowance	4,430	3,758	3,090	6,323	4,624	3,714

Required:

1. Calculate the receivables turnover ratios and days to collect for Coca-Cola and PepsiCo for 2010 and 2009. (Round to one decimal place.)
2. Which of the companies is quicker to convert its receivables into cash?

GROUP B PROBLEMS

LO 8-2   **PB8-1** **Recording Accounts Receivable Transactions Using the Allowance Method**

Intel Corporation

Intel Corporation is a well-known supplier of computer chips, boards, systems, and software building blocks. Assume the company recently reported the following amounts in its unadjusted trial balance at its year-end of December 25, 2010 (all amounts in millions):

	Debits	Credits
Accounts Receivable	$2,895	
Allowance for Doubtful Accounts		$ 19
Sales (assume all on credit)		43,623

Required:

1. Assume Intel uses ¼ of 1 percent of sales to estimate its Bad Debt Expense for the year. Prepare the adjusting journal entry required for the year, assuming no Bad Debt Expense has been recorded yet.

2. Assume instead that Intel uses the aging of accounts receivable method and estimates that $40 of its Accounts Receivable will be uncollectible. Prepare the adjusting journal entry required at December 25, 2010, for recording Bad Debt Expense.

3. Repeat requirement 2, except this time assume the unadjusted balance in Intel's Allowance for Doubtful Accounts at December 25, 2010, was a debit balance of $20.

4. If one of Intel's main customers declared bankruptcy in 2011, what journal entry would be used to write off its $15 balance?

LO 8-2   **PB8-2** **Interpreting Disclosure of Allowance for Doubtful Accounts**

Xerox Corporation

Xerox Corporation is the company that made the photocopier popular, although it now describes itself as a technology and services enterprise that helps businesses deploy document management strategies and improve productivity. It recently disclosed the following information concerning the allowance for doubtful accounts on its Form 10-K annual report.

SCHEDULE II				
Valuation and Qualifying Accounts				
(dollars in millions)				
Allowance for Doubtful Accounts	Balance at Beginning of Year	Additions Charged to Bad Debt Expense	Write- Offs	Balance at End of Year
2008	$128	$ 72	$69	$131
2009	131	109	a	148
2010	148	b	82	112

Required:

1. Create a T-account for the Allowance for Doubtful Accounts and enter into it the 2008 amounts from the above schedule. Then, write the T-account in equation format to prove that the above items account for the changes in the account.

2. Record summary journal entries for 2008 related to (*i*) estimating bad debt expense and (*ii*) writing off specific balances.

3. Supply the missing dollar amounts for *a* and *b*.

4. If Xerox had written off an additional $20 of accounts receivable during 2010, how would it have affected Net Accounts Receivable? How would the write-off have affected Net Income? Explain.

LO 8-3   **PB8-3** **Recording Notes Receivable Transactions**

Stinson Company recently agreed to loan an employee $100,000 for the purchase of a new house. The loan was executed on May 31, 2013, and is a one-year, 6 percent note, with interest payments required on November 30, 2013, and May 31, 2014. Stinson issues quarterly financial statements on March 31, June 30, September 30, and December 31.

Required:

1. Prepare the journal entry that Stinson will make when the note is established.
2. Prepare the journal entries that Stinson will make to record the interest accruals at each quarter end and interest payments at each payment date.
3. Prepare the journal entry that Stinson will make to record the principal payment at the maturity date.

PB8-4 Accounting for Accounts and Notes Receivable Transactions

LO 8-2, 8-3

Elite Events Corporation has provided event planning services for several years. The company uses the percentage of credit sales method to estimate bad debts for internal monthly reporting purposes. At the end of each quarter, the company adjusts its records using the aging of accounts receivable method. The company entered into the following partial list of transactions during the first quarter of 2013.

a. During January, the company provided services for $300,000 on credit.
b. On January 31, the company estimated bad debts using 1 percent of credit sales.
c. On February 4, the company collected $250,000 of accounts receivable.
d. On February 15, the company wrote off a $3,000 account receivable.
e. During February, the company provided services for $250,000 on credit.
f. On February 28, the company estimated bad debts using 1 percent of credit sales.
g. On March 1, the company loaned $15,000 to an employee who signed a 4% note, due in 9 months.
h. On March 15, the company collected $3,000 on the account written off one month earlier.
i. On March 31, the company accrued interest earned on the note.
j. On March 31, the company adjusted for uncollectible accounts, based on the following aging analysis. Allowance for Doubtful Accounts has an unadjusted credit balance of $9,000.

| Customer | Total | Number of Days Unpaid | | | |
		0–30	31–60	61–90	Over 90
Aerosmith	$ 2,000	$ 1,000	$ 1,000		
Biggie Small	2,000			$ 1,000	$ 1,000
Others (not shown to save space)	99,000	39,000	42,000	9,000	9,000
ZZ Top	7,000	7,000			
Total Accounts Receivable	**$110,000**	**$47,000**	**$43,000**	**$10,000**	**$10,000**
Estimated uncollectible (%)		**5%**	**10%**	**20%**	**40%**

Required:

1. For items a–j, analyze the amount and direction (+ or −) of effects on specific financial statement accounts and the overall accounting equation and prepare journal entries.
2. Show how Accounts Receivable and related accounts would be reported in the current assets section of a classified balance sheet.
3. Name the accounts related to Accounts Receivable and Note Receivable that would be reported on the income statement and indicate whether they would appear before, or after, Income from Operations.

PB8-5 Analyzing Allowance for Doubtful Accounts, Receivables Turnover Ratio, and Days to Collect

LO 8-4

Target

Walmart and Target are two of the largest and most successful retail chains in the world. To evaluate their ability to collect on credit sales, consider the following information reported in their annual reports (amounts in millions).

| | Walmart | | | Target | | |
Fiscal Year Ended January 31:	2011	2010	2009	2011	2010	2009
Net Sales	$418,952	$405,132	$401,244	$65,786	$63,435	$62,894
Accounts Receivable, Net of Allowance	5,089	4,144	3,905	6,153	6,966	8,084

Required:

1. Calculate the receivables turnover ratios and days to collect for Walmart and Target for the years ended January 31, 2011 and 2010. (Round to one decimal place.)

2. Which of the companies is quicker to convert its receivables into cash?

COMPREHENSIVE PROBLEM

LO 6-6, 8-2   **C8-1 Recording and Reporting Credit Sales and Bad Debts Using the Aging of Accounts Receivable Method (Chapters 6 and 8)**

Walgreens

Okay Optical, Inc., (OOI) began operations in January 2013, selling inexpensive sunglasses to large retailers like Walgreens and other smaller stores. Assume the following transactions occurred during its first six months of operations.

January 1   Sold merchandise to Walgreens for $20,000; the cost of these goods to OOI was $12,000.

February 12   Received payment in full from Walgreens.

March 1   Sold merchandise to Bravis Pharmaco on account for $3,000; the cost of these goods to OOI was $1,400.

April 1   Sold merchandise to Tony's Pharmacy on account for $8,000. The cost to OOI was $4,400.

May 1   Sold merchandise to Anjuli Stores on account for $2,000; the cost to OOI was $1,200.

June 17   Received $6,500 on account from Tony's Pharmacy.

Required:

1. Complete the following aged listing of customer accounts at June 30.

| | | Unpaid Since | | | |
| | | June (one month) | May (two months) | April (three months) | March (greater than three months) |
Customer	Total Balance				
Anjuli Stores	$2,000		$2,000		
Bravis Pharmaco	3,000				$3,000
Tony's Pharmacy					
Walgreens					

2. Estimate the Allowance for Doubtful Accounts required at June 30, 2013, assuming the following uncollectible rates: one month, 1 percent; two months, 5 percent; three months, 20 percent; more than three months, 40 percent.

3. Show how OOI would report its accounts receivable on its June 30 balance sheet. What amounts would be reported on an income statement prepared for the six-month period ended June 30, 2013?

4. Bonus Question: In July 2013, OOI collected the balance due from Bravis Pharmaco but discovered that the balance due from Tony's Pharmacy needed to be written off. Using this information, determine how accurate OOI was in estimating the Allowance for Doubtful Accounts needed for each of these two customers and in total.

SKILLS DEVELOPMENT CASES

S8-1 Finding Financial Information

LO 8-2, 8-4

Refer to the financial statements of The Home Depot in Appendix A at the end of this book, or download the 2011 annual report from the *Cases* section of the text's Web site at www.mhhe.com/phillips4e.

1. Where does the company report the amount of its Allowance for Doubtful Accounts? (*Hint:* The company refers to its Allowance for Doubtful Accounts as a "Valuation Reserve" related to Accounts Receivable.)
    a. On the balance sheet.
    b. In the notes.
    c. In both the balance sheet and notes.
    d. Not at all.
2. Compute the company's receivables turnover ratio and days to collect for the year ended January 31, 2011.
    a. 62.7 times and 5.8 days
    b. 74.0 times and 4.9 days
    c. 68.6 times and 5.3 days
    d. 66.4 times and 5.5 days

S8-2 Comparing Financial Information

LO 8-2, 8-4

Lowe's

Refer to the financial statements of Lowe's in Appendix B at the end of this book, or download the annual report from the *Cases* section of the text's Web site at www.mhhe.com/phillips4e.

1. Does the company report Accounts Receivable or an Allowance for Doubtful Accounts in its financial statements? Explain why it does or does not.
2. Based on your observations for requirement 1, describe the usefulness of the receivables turnover ratio and days to collect analyses for companies that are involved in home improvement retail sales.

S8-3 Internet-Based Team Research: Examining an Annual Report

LO 8-2, 8-4

As a team, select an industry to analyze. Using your Web browser, each team member should access the annual report or 10-K for one publicly traded company in the industry, with each member selecting a different company. (See S1-3 in Chapter 1 for a description of possible resources for these tasks.)

Required:

1. On an individual basis, each team member should write a short report that incorporates the following:
    a. Calculate the receivables turnover ratio for the current and prior year, and explain any change between the two years. (To obtain the beginning accounts receivable number for the prior year, you will need the prior year's annual report.)
    b. Look in the 10-K for the Schedule II analysis of "Valuation and Qualifying Accounts," which provides additional disclosures concerning the Allowance for Doubtful Accounts. From this schedule, determine the level of Bad Debt Expense, as a percentage of sales, for the current and prior year.
2. Then, as a team, write a short report comparing and contrasting your companies using these attributes. Discuss any patterns across the companies that you as a team observe. Provide potential explanations for any differences discovered.

S8-4 Ethical Decision Making: A Real-Life Example

LO 8-2, 8-3

MCI

You work for a company named MCI and you have been assigned the job of adjusting the company's Allowance for Doubtful Accounts balance. You obtained the following aged listing of customer account balances for December.

Accounts Receivable Aged Listing—December 31						
Customer	Total	0–30 days	31–60 days	61–90 days	91–120 days	>120 days
AfriTel	40,000	20,000	10,000	5,000	5,000	0
CT&T	0	0	0	0	0	0
GlobeCom	28,000	0	18,000	8,000	1,000	1,000
Hi-Rim	35,000	0	0	0	0	35,000
Level 8	162,000	63,000	44,000	29,000	13,000	13,000
NewTel	0	0	0	0	0	0
Telemedia	0	0	0	0	0	0
Others	485,000	257,000	188,000	28,000	11,000	1,000
TOTAL	**750,000**	**340,000**	**260,000**	**70,000**	**30,000**	**50,000**

Historically, bad debt loss rates for each aging category have been 1% (0–30 days), 5% (31–60 days), 8% (61–90 days), 10% (91–120 days), and 50% (> 120 days). Using these rates, you calculate a desired balance for the allowance. No entries have been made to the account since the end of November when the account had a credit balance of $46,820.

To check the reasonableness of the calculated balance, you obtain the aged listings for prior months (shown below). As you scan the listings, you notice an interesting pattern. Several account balances, which had grown quite large by the end of November, had disappeared in the final month of the year. You ask the accounts receivable manager, Walter Pavlo, what happened. He said the customers "obtained some financing . . . I guess out of nowhere" and they must have used it to pay off their account balances.

Total Accounts Receivable as of . . .						
	Q1	Q2	Q3		Q4	
Customer	(March 31)	(June 30)	(September 30)	(October 31)	(November 30)	(December 31)
AfriTel	19,000	19,000	21,000	16,000	20,000	40,000
CT&T	0	30,000	100,000	100,000	100,000	0
GlobeCom	29,000	28,000	31,000	27,000	28,000	28,000
Hi-Rim	0	0	25,000	35,000	35,000	35,000
Level 8	229,000	229,000	198,000	174,000	190,000	162,000
NewTel	0	0	25,000	25,000	25,000	0
Telemedia	0	0	2,000	2,000	2,000	0
Others	524,000	489,000	375,000	503,000	463,000	485,000
TOTAL	**801,000**	**795,000**	**777,000**	**882,000**	**863,000**	**750,000**

Required:

1. Calculate the balance that should be reported in Allowance for Doubtful Accounts as of December 31.
2. Prepare the adjusting journal entry that is required on December 31.
3. Show how Accounts Receivable would be reported on the balance sheet at December 31.
4. If the balances for CT&T, NewTel, and Telemedia at the end of November continued to exist at the end of December (in the over 120 days category), what balance would you have estimated for the Allowance for Doubtful Accounts on December 31? Would this have changed MCI's net income in the current year? Explain.
5. A few days later, you overhear Mr. Pavlo talking about the account receivable from Hi-Rim. Apparently, MCI will soon loan Hi-Rim some money, creating a note receivable. Hi-Rim will use the money to pay off the Accounts Receivable balance it owes to MCI. You are aware that Mr. Pavlo receives a bonus based on MCI's net income. Should you investigate this matter further? Explain why or why not.

Epilogue: The events described above are based on an article in the June 10, 2002, issue of *Forbes* magazine that describes how, in the mid-1990s, Walter Pavlo was pressured to commit accounting fraud at MCI. Ironically, MCI was later taken over by WorldCom—the company that went on to commit the world's largest accounting fraud at the time.

S8-5 Ethical Decision Making: A Mini-Case

LO 8-2

This case is available online at www.mhhe.com/phillips4e. By completing this case, you will learn what "earnings management" and "smoothing earnings" mean, and you will see how it occurs when estimates of uncollectible accounts are unethically biased.

S8-6 Critical Thinking: Analyzing

LO 8-1, 8-4

Problem Solved Company has been operating for five years as a software consulting firm. During this period, it has experienced rapid growth in Sales Revenue and in Accounts Receivable. To solve its growing receivables problem, the company hired you as its first corporate controller. You have put into place more stringent credit-granting and collection procedures that you expect will reduce receivables by approximately one-third by year-end. You have gathered the following data related to the changes (in thousands):

	(in thousands)	
	Beginning of Year	End of Year (projected)
Accounts Receivable	$1,000,608	$660,495
Less: Allowance for Doubtful Accounts	36,800	10,225
Accounts Receivable, Net	$ 963,808	$650,270
	Prior Year	Current Year (projected)
Net Sales (assume all on credit)	$7,515,444	$7,015,069

Required:

1. Compute, to one decimal place, the accounts receivable turnover ratio based on three different assumptions:
   a. The stringent credit policies reduce Accounts Receivable, Net and decrease Net Sales as projected in the table.
   b. The stringent credit policies reduce Accounts Receivable, Net as projected in the table but do not decrease Net Sales from the prior year.
   c. The stringent credit policies are not implemented, resulting in no change from the beginning of the year Accounts Receivable balance and no change in Net Sales from the prior year.

2. On the basis of your findings in requirement 1, write a brief memo to the chief financial officer explaining the potential benefits and drawbacks of more stringent credit policies and how they are likely to affect the accounts receivable turnover ratio.

S8-7 Using an Aging Schedule to Estimate Bad Debts and Improve Collections from Customers

LO 8-2

Assume you were recently hired by Caffe D'Amore, the company that formulated the world's first flavored instant cappuccino and now manufactures several lines of coffee flavored cappuccino mixes. Given the company's tremendous sales growth, Caffe D'Amore's receivables also have grown. Your job is to evaluate and improve collections of the company's receivables.

By analyzing collections of accounts receivable over the past five years, you were able to estimate bad debt loss rates for balances of varying ages. To estimate this year's uncollectible accounts, you jotted down the historical loss rates on the last page of a recent aged listing of outstanding customer balances (see below).

		Number of Days Unpaid				
Customer	Total	1–30	31–60	61–90	91–120	Over 120
Subtotal from previous page	$280,000	$150,000	$60,000	$40,000	$20,000	$10,000
Jumpy Jim's Coffee	1,000					1,000
Pasadena Coffee Company	24,500	14,500	8,000	2,000		
Phillips Blender House	17,000	12,000	4,000		1,000	
Pugsly's Trading Post	26,600	19,600	7,000			
Q-Coffee	12,400	8,400	3,000	1,000		
Special Sips	10,000	6,000	4,000			
Uneasy Isaac's	3,500	500				3,000
Total accounts receivable	**375,000**	**211,000**	**86,000**	**43,000**	**21,000**	**14,000**
Bad debt loss rates		**1%**	**5%**	**10%**	**15%**	**30%**

Required:

1. Enter the above totals in a spreadsheet and then insert formulas to calculate the total estimated uncollectible balance.

2. Prepare the year-end adjusting journal entry to adjust the Allowance for Doubtful Accounts to the balance you calculated above. Assume the allowance account has an unadjusted credit balance of $8,000.

3. Of the customer account balances shown above on the last page of the aged listing, which should be your highest priority for contacting and pursuing collection?

4. Assume Jumpy Jim's Coffee account is determined to be uncollectible. Prepare the journal entry to write off the entire account balance.

CONTINUING CASES

LO 8-2, 8-4 **CC8-1 Accounting for Receivables and Uncollectible Accounts**

The following transactions occurred over the months of September to December 2014 at Nicole's Getaway Spa (NGS).

September	Sold spa merchandise to Ashley Welch Beauty for $1,800 on account; the cost of these goods to NGS was $900.
October	Sold merchandise to Kelly Fast Nail Gallery for $450 on account; the cost of these goods to NGS was $200.
November	Sold merchandise to Raea Gooding Wellness for $300 on account; the cost of these goods to NGS was $190.
December	Received $1,200 from Ashley Welch Beauty for payment on its account.

Required:

1. Prepare journal entries for each of the transactions. Assume a perpetual inventory system.

2. Estimate the Allowance for Doubtful Accounts required at December 31, 2014, assuming the only receivables outstanding at December 31, 2014, arise from the transactions listed above. NGS uses the aging of accounts receivable method with the following uncollectible rates: one month, 2%; two months, 5%; three months, 20%; more than three months, 35%.

3. The Allowance for Doubtful Accounts balance was $47 (credit) before the end-of-period adjusting entry is made. Prepare the journal entry to account for the Bad Debt Expense.

4. Assume the end of the previous year showed net accounts receivable of $800, and net sales for the current year is $9,000. Calculate the accounts receivable turnover ratio (round to one decimal place).

5. Audrey's Mineral Spa has an accounts receivable turnover ratio of 12.0 times. How does NGS compare to this competitor?

LO 8-3, 8-4 **CC8-2 Wiki Art Gallery (WAG)**

Access the Wiki Art Gallery (WAG) instructional case in Connect, and read the case in sufficient depth to answer the following questions.

1. What method for recording bad debts does Wiki Art Gallery (WAG) use and does this method conform to generally acceptable accounting principles?
    a. WAG uses the direct write-off method, which is not in accordance with GAAP.
    b. WAG uses the allowance method with estimates based on aging of receivables, which is in accordance with GAAP.
    c. WAG uses the allowance method with estimates based on percentage of sales, which is in accordance with GAAP.
    d. WAG uses the allowance method with estimates based on percentage of sales, which is not in accordance with GAAP.

2. Which of the following suggests WAG has not adequately allowed for bad debts in 2011?

   a. WAG has changed its bad debt estimation percentage between 2010 and 2011.

   b. WAG has changed its bad debt estimation method between 2010 and 2011.

   c. WAG has calculated bad debts on artwork sales but not artist fees.

   d. WAG has calculated bad debts on artist fees but not artwork sales.

3. WAG wrote off uncollectible customer accounts in 2011. Using information in Note 2 of the financial statements, determine the total amount of the 2011 write-off, and indicate whether this amount was greater than, equal to, or less than the amount of estimated bad debts recorded in 2011.

   a. WAG wrote off $300 in 2011, which is equal to the amount of bad debts estimated in 2011.

   b. WAG wrote off $250 in 2011, which is less than the amount of bad debts estimated in 2011.

   c. WAG wrote off $50 in 2011, which is less than the amount of bad debts estimated in 2011.

   d. WAG wrote off $347 in 2011, which is greater than the amount of bad debts estimated in 2011.

4. Calculate the number of days to collect in 2011 and explain what it suggests about the collectibility of the amount reported as net accounts receivable.

   a. The number of days to collect was 3.7, which suggests WAG is unlikely to collect the amount reported as net accounts receivable.

   b. The number of days to collect was 98.1, which suggests WAG is unlikely to collect the amount reported as net accounts receivable.

   c. The number of days to collect was 3.7, which suggests WAG is likely to collect the amount reported as net accounts receivable.

   d. The number of days to collect was 98.1, which suggests WAG is likely to collect the amount reported as net accounts receivable.

5. What would be the financial impact if WAG were to increase its estimate of bad debts in 2011?

   a. WAG's bad debt expense would increase.

   b. WAG's net income would decrease.

   c. WAG's selling price would decrease.

   d. All of the above.

Long-Lived Tangible and Intangible Assets

YOUR LEARNING OBJECTIVES

Understand the business

LO 9-1 Define, classify, and explain the nature of long-lived assets.

Study the accounting methods

LO 9-2 Apply the cost principle to the acquisition of long-lived assets.

LO 9-3 Apply various depreciation methods as economic benefits are used up over time.

LO 9-4 Explain the effect of asset impairment on the financial statements.

LO 9-5 Analyze the disposal of long-lived tangible assets.

LO 9-6 Analyze the acquisition, use, and disposal of long-lived intangible assets.

Evaluate the results

LO 9-7 Interpret the fixed asset turnover ratio.

LO 9-8 Describe factors to consider when comparing companies' long-lived assets.

Review the chapter

Supplemental material

LO 9-S1 Analyze and report depletion of natural resources.

LO 9-S2 Calculate changes in depreciation arising from changes in estimates of capitalized cost.

THAT WAS THEN

In the past few chapters, you learned about the sale of goods and services to customers.

FOCUS COMPANY: Cedar Fair

Cedar Fair. L.P.

Most people agonize over how much money to spend on a house or which car to buy. After all, they will own these expensive items for many years to come. The same concerns exist when companies acquire long-lived assets. One of the major challenges business managers face is determining the right amount to invest in long-lived assets.

The task is especially challenging for companies such as Disney, Six Flags, and Cedar Fair, which operate amusement parks. Unlike merchandising companies, an amusement park cannot build up an inventory of unused roller-coaster seats to be sold sometime in the future. If managers build more rides than needed to satisfy park-goers, some rides will run with empty seats. Although the company will still incur all the costs of running the rides, it will generate only a fraction of the potential revenue. On the other hand, amusement parks can also run into trouble if they have too few rides to satisfy patrons. Fortunately for managers, accounting reports provide information to evaluate a company's investment in long-lived assets.

In this chapter, you will study specific long-lived asset decisions at Cedar Fair, which is headquartered in Sandusky, Ohio, and owns and operates 11 amusement parks, seven water parks, and five hotels throughout North America. You will see the significant effect that long-lived assets can have on a company's financial statements. Although manufacturing companies, retailers, and even airlines must deal with the same issues as Cedar Fair, the impact on this amusement park company is particularly significant because it relies almost exclusively on long-lived assets. As of December 31, 2010, in fact, Cedar Fair's rides, hotels, and other long-lived assets accounted for more than 94 percent of its total assets.

www.cedarfair.com

THIS IS NOW

This chapter focuses on the assets that enable companies to produce and sell goods and services.

Understand the business	Study the accounting methods	Evaluate the results	Review the chapter
• Definition and classification	• Tangible assets • Intangible assets	• Turnover analysis • Impact of depreciation differences	• Demonstration case • Chapter summary • Key terms • Homework helper • Practice material

Understand the Business

DEFINITION AND CLASSIFICATION

Long-lived assets are business assets acquired for use over one or more years. These assets are not intended for resale. Instead, they are considered "productive" assets in the sense that they enable the business to produce the goods or services that the business then sells to customers. Examples include the ovens in which Pizza Aroma bakes pizza, the stores where Walmart sells merchandise, and the legal rights that restrict use of the Activision logo. So when you hear the term "long-lived assets," think more broadly than just rusty old equipment. This class of assets includes two major types: tangible and intangible.

1. **Tangible assets.** These are long-lived assets that have physical substance, which simply means that you can see, touch, or kick them. The most prominent examples of tangible assets are land, buildings, machinery, vehicles, office equipment, and furniture and fixtures. These assets are typically grouped into a single line item on the balance sheet called Property, Plant, and Equipment. Because many long-lived tangible assets are fixed in place, they are also known as **fixed assets.** Cedar Fair's tangible assets include roller coasters, hotels, and land in the western, midwestern, and northeastern United States.

2. **Intangible assets.** These long-lived assets have special rights but no physical substance. The existence of most intangible assets is indicated only by legal documents that describe their rights. Compared to the tangible assets that you see in daily life, such as store buildings and cash registers, intangible assets are probably less familiar to you. For this reason, we'll describe the various types of intangibles in detail later in this chapter. For now you can think of this category as including brand names, trademarks, and licensing rights such as the ones that allow Cedar Fair to use PEANUTS® characters throughout its amusement parks.

A third category of long-lived assets that are depleted over time, like an oil well or gold mine, is common in natural resource industries. Chapter Supplement 9A describes how to account for these natural resource assets.

EXHIBIT 9.1	Cedar Fair's Assets		

		AT DECEMBER 31	
(in millions)		**2010**	**2009**
Assets			
Current Assets		$ 70	$ 60
(details omitted to save space)			
Property and Equipment			
Land		310	310
Land Improvements		320	330
Buildings		580	590
Rides and Equipment		1,400	1,350
Construction in Progress		20	40
Property and Equipment, at cost		2,630	2,620
Less: Accumulated Depreciation		(950)	(830)
Property and Equipment, net		1,680	1,790
Goodwill and Other Intangible Assets		290	280
Other Assets		50	20
Total Assets		$2,090	$2,150

> **COACH'S TIP**
>
> Accumulated Depreciation is reported here as a total for the entire tangible assets category. Alternatively, it can be reported separately for each type of tangible asset.

Exhibit 9.1 shows how Cedar Fair reported long-lived assets on its 2010 balance sheet. From this exhibit, you can see how important tangible and intangible assets are to Cedar Fair. Of the nearly $2.1 billion in total assets at December 31, 2010, Cedar Fair owned long-lived assets totaling $1.97 billion ($1,680 + $290 = $1,970, in millions).

Study the Accounting Methods

In this section, you will study the accounting decisions that relate to long-lived assets. We'll start with tangible long-lived assets and consider key accounting decisions related to their (1) acquisition, (2) use, and (3) disposal. Accounting for intangible assets will be the focus of the last part of this section.

TANGIBLE ASSETS

> **Learning Objective 9-2**
> Apply the cost principle to the acquisition of long-lived assets.

Most companies own a variety of tangible assets. Earlier chapters introduced you to the most common examples: land, buildings, equipment, and automobiles. Other, less common examples include land improvements and construction in progress—both of which Cedar Fair reported on its balance sheet in Exhibit 9.1. **Land improvements** include the sidewalks, pavement, landscaping, fencing, lighting, and sprinkler systems that are added to improve the usefulness of land. Land improvements differ from land in that they deteriorate over time, whereas land is assumed to last forever. **Construction in progress** includes the costs of constructing new buildings and equipment. When construction is finished, these costs are moved from this account into the building or equipment account to which they relate.

Acquisition of Tangible Assets

The general rule for tangible assets under the cost principle is that **all reasonable and necessary costs to acquire and prepare an asset for use should be recorded as a cost of the asset.** Accountants say costs have been **capitalized** when they are recorded as assets (rather than as expenses).

Deciding whether a cost is a reasonable and necessary cost to acquire or prepare tangible assets for use can involve a great deal of judgment. Because capitalizing costs has a significant impact on both the balance sheet (it increases assets) and the income statement (it decreases expenses), some dishonest accountants and managers have exploited the judgment involved in this decision by capitalizing costs that should have been expensed. A well-known example of this tactic is described in the following Spotlight on Ethics feature. As you read the feature and the next couple of pages, focus on distinguishing between what types of costs should be capitalized and what types should be expensed.

SPOTLIGHT ON Ethics

www.mhhe.com/phillips4e

Simple Violations, Serious Consequences

In the early 2000s, executives at WorldCom (now part of Verizon) committed an $11 billion fraud by capitalizing costs that should have been expensed. Their decision caused WorldCom to report huge increases in assets (rather than expenses) when the costs were incurred. The result was a balance sheet that appeared stronger (more total assets) and an income statement that appeared more profitable (lower expenses) than would have been the case had the costs been expensed. Learn more about this fraud in Case S9-4 at the end of this chapter.

The illustration that follows shows the types of costs that should be capitalized when a tangible asset is acquired. All are necessary for acquiring and preparing tangible assets for use. Notice that they are not limited to the amounts paid to purchase or construct the assets. For example, the Land account at Cedar Fair would include legal fees for title searches, fees for land surveys, and commissions paid to brokers when purchasing the land on Ohio's Sandusky Bay shown in the photograph on the left. Take a moment right now to read the lists of costs that should be capitalized when buildings (middle) and equipment (right) are acquired.

Land

Purchase cost
Legal fees
Survey fees
Title search fees

Equipment

Purchase/construction cost
Sales taxes
Transportation costs
Installation costs

Buildings

Purchase/construction cost
Legal fees
Appraisal fees
Architect fees

If a company buys land, a building, or a piece of used equipment and incurs demolition, renovation, or repair costs before it can be used, these additional costs would be capitalized as a cost of the land, building, or equipment. These costs are capitalized because they are needed to prepare the asset for use.

In some cases, land, buildings, and equipment are purchased together. On June 30, 2006, Cedar Fair bought all five amusement parks from Paramount Parks for $1.2 billion. When this type of "basket purchase" occurs, the total cost is split among the assets in proportion to the market value of the assets as a whole. For example, if Cedar Fair were to pay $10 million for a hotel and the land surrounding it, based on an appraisal that estimates that the land contributes 40 percent of the property's value and the building contributes 60 percent, Cedar Fair would record 40 percent of the total cost as land ($4 million) and the other 60 percent as buildings ($6 million). Splitting the total purchase price among individual assets is necessary because they may be used over different periods. For example, the hotel may be used over 50 years. However, **land is never used up,** so any costs assigned to Land will remain in that account until Cedar Fair sells the land.

SPOTLIGHT ON The World

Component Allocation

IFRS takes the idea of a basket purchase one step further. The cost of an individual asset's components is allocated among each significant component and then depreciated separately over that component's useful life. For example, British Airways (now merged into International Airlines Group) separates the cost of an aircraft between its body and engines and interior cabin space, and then depreciates the body and engines over 18 to 25 years, and the cabin interior over 5 years.

5 Years

18 to 25 Years

To illustrate how the costs of tangible assets are recorded, let's consider the Top Thrill Dragster that Cedar Fair purchased from Intamin, a Swiss roller-coaster manufacturer. When it was purchased, the Top Thrill Dragster was the biggest, fastest roller coaster in the world. Some of its specs are shown in the following graphic.

Top Thrill Dragster

Ride Height:	42 stories
Vertical Drop:	400 ft.
Track Length:	2,800 ft.
Ride Time:	17 seconds
Angle of Descent:	90 degrees
Angle of Twist:	270 degrees
Launch Speed:	120 mph in 4 seconds
Ride Capacity:	1,500 riders per hour

Assume the list price for the roller coaster (including sales tax) was $26 million but that Cedar Fair received a $1 million discount. In other words, the roller coaster's net purchase price to Cedar Fair was $25 million. Assume too that Cedar Fair paid $125,000 to have the roller coaster delivered and another $625,000 to have it assembled and prepared for use. Since these expenditures are necessary to acquire and prepare the asset for use, Cedar Fair would capitalize the expenditures as part of the cost of the asset as follows:

List price	$26,000,000
Less: Discount	1,000,000
Net invoice price	25,000,000
Add: Transportation costs paid by Cedar Fair	125,000
Installation costs paid by Cedar Fair	625,000
Total cost of the roller coaster	$25,750,000

The total $25,750,000 cost would be the amount Cedar Fair recorded in the Rides and Equipment account regardless of how the company paid for or financed the roller coaster. As you will see next, the method of payment or financing affects only whether the purchase reduces cash, increases liabilities, or both.

Cash Purchase   If Cedar Fair paid cash for the roller coaster and related transportation and installation costs, the effects of the transaction and the journal entry to record these effects would be:

1 Analyze

	Assets	=	Liabilities	+	Stockholders' Equity
Cash	−25,750,000				
Rides and Equipment	+25,750,000				

2 Record

dr Rides and Equipment (+A)	25,750,000	
cr Cash (−A)		25,750,000

You might find it hard to believe that Cedar Fair would pay cash for assets that cost more than $25 million, but this isn't unusual. Companies often pay with cash generated from operations or with cash that has been borrowed. In addition, it's possible the seller may extend credit to the buyer, a situation we examine next.

Credit Purchase   If we assume Cedar Fair signed a note payable for the new roller coaster and paid cash for the transportation and installation costs, the accounting equation effects and journal entry would be:

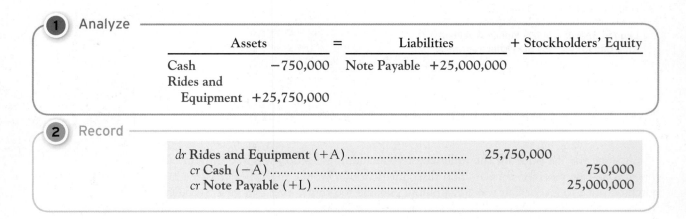

1 Analyze

	Assets	=	Liabilities	+	Stockholders' Equity
Cash	−750,000	Note Payable	+25,000,000		
Rides and Equipment	+25,750,000				

2 Record

dr Rides and Equipment (+A)	25,750,000	
cr Cash (−A)		750,000
cr Note Payable (+L)		25,000,000

How's it going?   Self-Study Practice

In a recent year, the New Bakery Company of Zanesville, Ohio, opened a new baking plant that can make 200,000 buns per hour. The equipment cost $21 million. Assume New Bakery financed the equipment purchase using a promissory note and paid in cash $900,000 of sales tax, $60,000 of transportation costs, and $40,000 of installation costs before the equipment could be used. Indicate the effects of the purchase on the accounting equation and give the journal entry to record the purchase.

1 Analyze

Assets	=	Liabilities	+	Stockholders' Equity

2 Record

After you have finished, check your answers with the solutions in the margin.

Solution to Self-Study Practice

1.

Assets	=	Liabilities	+	Stockholders' Equity
Equipment +22,000,000		Note Payable +21,000,000		
Cash −1,000,000				

2. dr Equipment (+A) 22,000,000
   cr Cash (−A) 1,000,000
   cr Note Payable (+L) 21,000,000

Before we leave this section, we should mention that not all fixed asset costs are capitalized. The cost of some fixed assets, like staplers or hole punches, is such a small dollar amount that it's not worth the trouble of recording them as fixed assets. Ford Motor Company, with over $23 billion in property and equipment, reports in its financial statement notes that it expenses all expenditures less than $2,500. Such policies are acceptable because immaterial amounts (small in relation to the company) will not affect users' analysis of financial statements. **Other costs that are expensed when incurred include insurance for fixed assets in use, interest on loans to purchase fixed assets, and ordinary repairs and maintenance,** as discussed in the next section.

Use of Tangible Assets

Maintenance Costs Incurred during Use   Most tangible assets require substantial expenditures over the course of their lives to maintain or enhance their operation. Maintenance is a big deal in the roller-coaster industry where safety is vital. Companies in this industry spend a lot of money on two types of maintenance: (1) ordinary repairs and maintenance and (2) extraordinary repairs and maintenance.

1. **Ordinary repairs and maintenance. Ordinary repairs and maintenance** are expenditures for the routine maintenance and upkeep of long-lived assets. Just like an oil change for your car, these are recurring, relatively small expenditures that do not directly increase an asset's usefulness. Because these costs occur frequently to maintain the asset's productive capacity for a short time, they are recorded as expenses in the current period. Because these expenses are matched to revenues, ordinary repairs and maintenance are sometimes called **revenue expenditures.**

   In the case of Cedar Fair, ordinary repairs and maintenance would include greasing the tracks on the Steel Venom roller coaster at Valleyfair in Minnesota. It would also include replacing the lights on the eight-story Giant Gondola wheel at Michigan's Adventure and tightening the seams on a water slide at Knott's Soak City in California.

YOU SHOULD KNOW

Ordinary repairs and maintenance: Expenditures for routine operating upkeep of long-lived assets; they are recorded as expenses.

2. Extraordinary repairs, replacements, and additions. In contrast to ordinary repairs and maintenance, **extraordinary repairs** occur infrequently, involve large expenditures, and increase an asset's usefulness through enhanced efficiency, capacity, or lifespan. Examples include additions, major overhauls, complete reconditioning, and major replacements and improvements, such as the replacement of the passenger train on a roller coaster. Because these costs increase the usefulness of tangible assets beyond their original condition, they are added to the appropriate long-lived asset accounts. Because doing so means capitalizing costs, these extraordinary repairs, replacements, and additions are called **capital expenditures.**

 How's it going?   Self-Study Practice

As you know from living in a house, apartment, or residence hall, buildings often require maintenance and repair. For each of the following expenditures, indicate whether it should be expensed in the current period or capitalized.

Expense or Capitalize?

1. Replacing electrical wiring throughout the building.
2. Repairing the hinge on the front door of the building.
3. Yearly cleaning of the building's air conditioning filters.
4. Making major structural improvements to a clubhouse.

After you have finished, check your answers with the solution in the margin.

Depreciation Expense   In addition to repairs and maintenance expense, a company reports depreciation expense every period that buildings and equipment are used to generate revenue. Depreciation doesn't involve new payments for using the asset. Rather, **depreciation** is the allocation of existing costs that were already recorded as a long-lived asset. Think of the cost of a long-lived asset as a big prepayment for future benefits. As that asset is used, those prepaid benefits are used up, so the asset needs to be decreased each period. This decrease in the asset creates an expense, which is reported on the income statement and matched against the revenue generated by the asset, as required by accrual accounting.

As you learned in Chapter 4, depreciation affects one income statement account and one balance sheet account. The income statement account, Depreciation Expense, reports the depreciation of the current period. The balance sheet account, Accumulated Depreciation, contains the current period's depreciation as well as that of prior periods. It is an **accumulation** over several periods. The effects of $130 of depreciation on the accounting equation and the journal entry to record them follow:

1 Analyze

Assets	= Liabilities +	Stockholders' Equity
Accumulated Depreciation (+xA) −130		Depreciation Expense (+E) −130

2 Record

dr Depreciation Expense (+E, −SE)	130	
cr Accumulated Depreciation (+xA, −A)		130

Exhibit 9.2 shows how Cedar Fair reported its depreciation in 2010. The income statement on the right shows the $127 million of Depreciation Expense in 2010. The balance sheet on the left shows that this $127 million, when combined with depreciation of prior years, brought the total Accumulated Depreciation to $950 million at December 31, 2010. The $1,680 difference between the Property and Equipment's $2,630 cost and $950 of Accumulated Depreciation is called the **book (or carrying) value**. Most companies report a breakdown of these totals by class of asset (e.g., buildings, equipment) in their financial statement notes.

> **YOU SHOULD KNOW**
>
> **Book (or carrying) value:** The acquisition cost of an asset less accumulated depreciation.

EXHIBIT 9.2	Reporting Depreciation on the Balance Sheet and Income Statement	Cedar Fair. L.P.

(in millions) **Balance Sheet**	Dec. 31, 2010
Assets	
Property and Equipment, at cost	$2,630
Less: **Accumulated Depreciation**	(950)
Property and Equipment, net	1,680

(in millions) **Income Statement**	2010
Net Revenues	$978
Operating Expenses:	
Food and Operating Expenses	498
Selling, General, and Other	134
Depreciation Expense	127
Loss on Disposals and Impairments	65
Total Operating Expenses	824
Income from Operations	154

One way to interpret the information in Exhibit 9.2 is that the Property and Equipment's $2,630 million cost represents the assets' total economic benefits. Thus, $127 million of Depreciation Expense means Cedar Fair used up about 5 percent ($127/$2,630 = 0.048) of the assets' benefits in 2010. As of December 31, 2010, over 36 percent ($950/$2,630 = 0.361) of their total benefits had been used up.

To fully understand the depreciation numbers in Exhibit 9.2, you need to know how they are calculated. Depreciation calculations are based on the following three items:

1. **Asset cost.** This includes all the asset's capitalized costs, including the purchase cost, sales tax, legal fees, and other costs needed to acquire and prepare the asset for use.

2. **Useful life. Useful life** is an estimate of the asset's useful economic life to the company (not its economic life to all potential users). It may be expressed in terms of years or units of capacity, such as the number of units it can produce or the number of miles it will travel. **Land is the only tangible asset that's assumed to have an unlimited (indefinite) useful life. Because of this, land is not depreciated.**

3. **Residual value. Residual (or salvage) value** is an estimate of the amount the company will receive when it disposes of the asset. Cedar Fair will recover some of the initial cost of its roller coasters when it disposes of them by either selling them "as is" to local amusement companies or by dismantling them and selling their parts to other roller coaster or scrap metal companies.

> **YOU SHOULD KNOW**
>
> **Useful life:** The expected service life of an asset to the present owner.
> **Residual (or salvage) value:** The estimated amount to be recovered at the end of the company's estimated useful life of an asset.

The basic idea of depreciation is to match the economic benefit that will be used up (asset cost minus residual value) to the periods the asset will be used to generate revenue (useful life). Residual value is considered when calculating depreciation because we want to leave a little of the asset's cost in the accounts after we have finished depreciating it. We do this because, when we dispose of the asset, we're likely to get back some of the money we initially paid for the asset. So the amount to be depreciated over the asset's life is the difference between its cost and residual value, an amount called the **depreciable cost.** A company should record depreciation each year of an asset's useful life until its total accumulated depreciation equals its depreciable cost. After that, the company should report no additional depreciation expense, even if the company continues to use the asset.

> **YOU SHOULD KNOW**
>
> **Depreciable cost:** The portion of the asset's cost that will be used in generating revenue; calculated as asset cost minus residual value.

If every company used the same techniques for calculating depreciation, we'd stop right here. But they don't. Companies own different assets and use them differently, so they are allowed to choose from several alternative depreciation methods. These alternative depreciation methods produce different patterns of depreciation as represented by the depreciation amounts recorded each year.

Depreciation Methods   **The depreciation method chosen for each type of property, plant, and equipment should reflect the pattern in which those assets' economic benefits are used up.** We discuss the three most common depreciation methods:

1. **Straight-line**—when usage is the same each period.

2. **Units-of-production**—when usage varies each period.

3. **Declining-balance**—when the asset is more efficient (generates more revenues) in early years but less so over time.

To show how each method works, let's assume that Cedar Fair acquired a new go-kart ride on January 1, 2012. The relevant information is shown in Exhibit 9.3.

EXHIBIT 9.3 | **Information for Depreciation Computations**

CEDAR FAIR—Acquisition of a New Go-Kart Ride

Cost, purchased on January 1, 2012	$62,500
Estimated residual value	$2,500
Estimated useful life	3 years; 100,000 miles

Straight-Line Method   Managers choose the **straight-line depreciation method** when an asset is expected to be used up in equal amounts each period of the asset's estimated useful life. The straight-line formula for estimating annual depreciation expense is:

Straight-Line Formula

$$\underbrace{(\text{Cost}-\text{Residual Value})}_{\text{Depreciable cost}} \times \underbrace{\frac{1}{\text{Useful life}}}_{\text{Depreciation rate}} = \text{Depreciation Expense}$$

In the straight-line formula, Cost − Residual Value is the total amount to be depreciated (the depreciable cost). The depreciation rate is 1/Useful Life. Using the information in Exhibit 9.3, the depreciation expense for Cedar Fair's new ride is $20,000 per year, calculated in the following depreciation schedule:

Straight-line (Cost − Residual Value) × (1/Useful Life)		INCOME STATEMENT	BALANCE SHEET		
Year	Yearly Computation	Depreciation Expense	Cost −	Accumulated Depreciation =	Book Value
At acquisition			$ 62,500	$ 0	$ 62,500
2012	($62,500 − $2,500) × (1/3) amounts for	$20,000	62,500	20,000	42,500
2013	($62,500 − $2,500) × (1/3) adjusting entry	20,000	62,500	40,000	22,500
2014	($62,500 − $2,500) × (1/3) each period	20,000	62,500	60,000	2,500
	Total	$60,000		↑	↑
				used cost to-date	unused cost to-date

Take a moment to study the straight-line depreciation schedule. Notice that as the name straight line suggests,

1. Depreciation Expense is a constant amount each year.
2. Accumulated Depreciation increases by an equal amount each year.
3. Book Value decreases by the same equal amount each year.

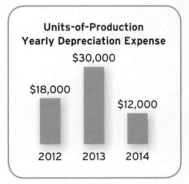

**Straight-Line
Yearly Depreciation Expense**
$20,000 $20,000 $20,000
2012   2013   2014

Notice too that at the end of the asset's life, accumulated depreciation ($60,000) equals the asset's depreciable cost ($62,500 − $2,500), and book value ($2,500) equals residual value.

As you will see with other depreciation methods the amount of depreciation depends on estimates of an asset's useful life and residual value at the end of that life. A question people often ask is: **How do accountants estimate useful lives and residual values?** While some of this information can be obtained from the asset's supplier or from other sources such as reseller databases or insurance companies, the simple answer is that professional judgment is required. Because useful lives and residual values are difficult to estimate with precision, accountants are encouraged to update their calculations regularly (see Supplement 9B at the end of this chapter).

Units-of-Production Yearly Depreciation Expense
$30,000
$18,000
$12,000
2012   2013   2014

Units-of-Production Method

Choose the **units-of-production depreciation method** if the amount of asset production varies significantly from period to period. An asset's production can be defined in terms of miles, products, or machine-hours. The units-of-production formula for estimating depreciation expense is:

Units-of-Production Formula

$$(\text{Cost} - \text{Residual Value}) \times \frac{\text{Actual Production this Period}}{\text{Estimated Total Production}} = \text{Depreciation Expense}$$

> **YOU SHOULD KNOW**
>
> **Units-of-production depreciation method:** Allocates the depreciable cost of an asset over its useful life based on the relationship of its periodic output to its total estimated output.

If the go-kart ride in Exhibit 9.3 was driven 30,000 miles in 2012, 50,000 miles in 2013, and 20,000 miles in 2014, the units-of-production method would calculate depreciation in each year of the asset's life as follows:

Units-of-production (Cost − Residual Value) × (Actual/Estimated Total Production)		INCOME STATEMENT	BALANCE SHEET		
Year	Yearly Computation	Depreciation Expense	Cost −	Accumulated Depreciation =	Book Value
At acquisition			$62,500	$ 0	$62,500
2012	($62,500 − $2,500) × (30,000/100,000 miles)	$18,000	62,500	18,000	44,500
2013	($62,500 − $2,500) × (50,000/100,000 miles)	30,000	62,500	48,000	14,500
2014	($62,500 − $2,500) × (20,000/100,000 miles)	12,000	62,500	60,000	2,500
	Total	$60,000			

Under the units-of-production method, the depreciation expense, accumulated depreciation, and book value vary from period to period, depending on the number of units produced.

Declining-Balance Method

The **declining-balance depreciation method** is used to report more depreciation expense in the early years of an asset's life when the asset is more efficient and less in later years as the asset becomes less efficient. Because this method speeds up depreciation reporting, it is sometimes called an accelerated method. Although accelerated methods are used infrequently for financial reporting purposes in the United States, they are used commonly in financial reporting in other countries, such as Japan and Canada, as well as in tax reporting in the United States (a point we discuss in greater detail later).

> **YOU SHOULD KNOW**
>
> **Declining-balance depreciation method:** Assigns more depreciation to early years of an asset's life and less depreciation to later years.

Double-Declining Yearly Depreciation Expense

The declining-balance method applies a depreciation rate to the book value of the asset at the beginning of each accounting period. **Notice that the following formula uses book value (Cost − Accumulated Depreciation) rather than depreciable cost (Cost − Residual Value).** This slight difference in the formula produces declining amounts of depreciation as the asset ages. Because the 2/Useful Life rate used in the formula is double the straight-line rate, this particular version of the declining-balance method is called the **double-declining-balance depreciation method.**

Double-Declining-Balance Formula

$$(\text{Cost} - \underbrace{\text{Accumulated Depreciation}) \times \frac{2}{\text{Useful life}}}_{\text{Book value at beginning of period}} = \text{Depreciation Expense}$$

This formula uses the accumulated depreciation balance at the beginning of each year. In the first year of an asset's life, the beginning balance in Accumulated Depreciation is zero. However, with each passing year as additional depreciation is recorded, the Accumulated Depreciation balance increases, causing the amount of double-declining depreciation expense to decline over time.

Because **residual value is not included in the formula for the declining-balance method of computing depreciation expense,** you must take extra care to ensure that an asset's book value is not depreciated beyond its residual value. If the calculated amount of depreciation for the year would reduce the book value below the asset's residual value, you must record a lower amount of depreciation so that the book value will equal the residual value. If this happens in a year prior to the last year of the asset's useful life, no additional depreciation is calculated, to keep book value equal to residual value. The following depreciation schedule illustrates this point.

Double-declining-balance
(Cost − Accumulated Depreciation) × (2/Useful Life)

| | | INCOME STATEMENT | BALANCE SHEET | | |
| | | Depreciation | | Accumulated | Book |
Year	Yearly Computation	Expense	Cost −	Depreciation =	Value
At acquisition			$62,500	$ 0	$62,500
2012	($62,500 − $0) × (2/3)	$41,667	62,500	41,667	20,833
2013	($62,500 − $41,667) × (2/3)	13,889	62,500	55,556	6,944
2014	($62,500 − $55,556) × (2/3)	~~4,629~~	62,500	~~60,185~~	~~2,315~~
		4,444	62,500	60,000	**2,500**
	Total	$60,000			

Notice that the calculated depreciation expense for 2014 ($4,629) would not be recorded because it would cause the asset's book value to fall below its residual value. Instead, in the final year of the asset's life, just enough depreciation ($4,444) is recorded to make the book value of the asset equal its residual value of **$2,500.**

Summary of Depreciation Methods   See Exhibit 9.4 for a summary of the depreciation expense that would be reported in each year of our example under the three alternative depreciation methods. Notice that **the amount of depreciation expense recorded in each year of an asset's life depends on the method that is used. That means that the amount of net income that is reported can vary, depending on the depreciation method used.** At the end of an asset's life, after it has been fully depreciated, the total amount of depreciation will equal the asset's depreciable cost regardless of the depreciation method used.

| EXHIBIT 9.4 | Differences in Depreciation Expense by Method |

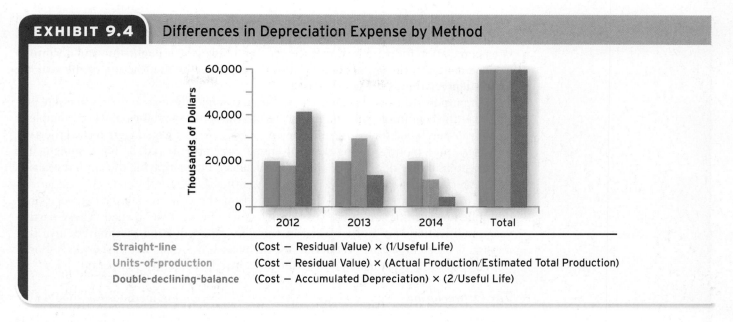

Straight-line	(Cost − Residual Value) × (1/Useful Life)
Units-of-production	(Cost − Residual Value) × (Actual Production/Estimated Total Production)
Double-declining-balance	(Cost − Accumulated Depreciation) × (2/Useful Life)

Different depreciation methods can be used for different classes of assets provided they are used consistently over time so that financial statement users can compare results across periods. The methods that companies use most frequently are shown in the margin. The straight-line method is the preferred choice because it is the easiest to use and understand, and it does a good job of matching depreciation expense to revenues when assets are used evenly over their useful lives. The units-of-production method is the typical choice when asset use fluctuates significantly from period to period. Declining-balance methods apply best to assets that are most productive when they are new but quickly lose their usefulness as they get older.

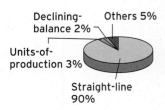

How's it going? Self-Study Practice

Assume that Cedar Fair has acquired new equipment at a cost of $24,000. The equipment has an estimated life of six years, an estimated operating life to the company of 5,000 hours, and an estimated residual value of $3,000. Determine depreciation expense for the **second year** under each of the following methods:

1. Straight-line method.

   $(24,000 −   ) ×   /6 = $

2. Double-declining-balance method.

   Year 1 : $(24,000 −   ) ×   /   = $
   Year 2 : $(24,000 −   ) ×   /   = $

3. Units-of-production method (assume the equipment ran for 800 hours in Year 2).

   $(−   ) ×   /5,000 = $

After you have finished, check your answers with the solutions in the margin.

Partial-Year Depreciation Calculations   Purchases of long-lived assets seldom occur on the first day of the accounting period. Consequently, the need arises to calculate depreciation for periods shorter than a year. **Under the straight-line and declining-balance methods, the annual depreciation is multiplied by the fraction of the year for which depreciation is being calculated.**

For purposes of these calculations, accountants typically assume that assets were purchased at the beginning of the month nearest to the actual purchase date. For example, if Cedar Fair purchased the go-kart ride on October 7, 2012, it would have owned the asset for about three months during the year ended December 31, 2012. Thus, straight-line depreciation for the ride in 2012 would be calculated by multiplying the annual straight-line depreciation of $20,000 by 3 ÷ 12, representing the 3 months of 12 that Cedar Fair owned it. Similarly, if an asset is disposed of during the year, the annual depreciation is multiplied by the fraction of the year during which the asset was owned. **These partial-year modifications are not required in the units-of-production method because that method is based on actual production for the period.** If the accounting period is shorter than a year, the level of actual production already reflects that shorter period.

Tax Depreciation   Before we leave the topic of depreciation methods, we should note that most companies use one method of depreciation for reporting to stockholders and a different method for determining income taxes. Keeping two sets of accounting records like this is both ethical and legal because the primary objective of financial reporting differs from that of income tax reporting.

Financial Reporting	Income Tax Reporting
Objective: Provide economic information about a business that is useful in projecting its future cash flows.	Objective: Raise sufficient tax revenues to pay for the expenditures of the federal government and to encourage certain social and economic behaviors.

One of the behaviors the government wants to encourage is economic renewal and growth. Thus, the IRS allows companies to deduct larger amounts of tax depreciation in the early years of an asset's life than what GAAP allows.[1] The larger tax deduction reduces the company's income taxes significantly in the years immediately following the purchase of a long-lived asset.

Although the IRS allows super-sized deductions in the early years of an asset's life, it doesn't allow a company to depreciate more than an asset's depreciable cost over its life. So the tax savings enjoyed in the early years of an asset's life will eventually be returned to the government in later years of that asset's life. The tax payment that is put off (deferred) as a result of taking large tax deductions for depreciation is reported as a long-term liability called Deferred Income Tax. Although the deferral delays the payment of taxes only temporarily, it can be worth the effort of keeping two sets of records. The following companies report that they deferred significant tax obligations in recent years by choosing different depreciation methods for tax and financial reporting purposes.

Company	Deferred Income Tax Liabilities	Percentage Due to Applying Different Depreciation Methods
AT&T Corp.	$34,172 million	95%
ExxonMobil Corp.	42,657 million	91
Cedar Fair	180 million	95

[1]Most corporations use the IRS-approved Modified Accelerated Cost Recovery System (MACRS) to calculate depreciation expense for their tax returns. MACRS is similar to the declining-balance method and is applied over relatively short asset lives set by the IRS to yield high tax deductions for depreciation expense in the early years.

The preceding table shows that, like most individuals, companies follow an economic rule called the **least and latest rule.** All taxpayers want to pay the least tax that is legally permitted, and at the latest possible date. If you had the choice of paying $1,000 to the federal government at the end of this year or at the end of next year, you would choose the end of next year. Doing so would allow you to invest the money for an extra year and earn a return on your investment.

Asset Impairment Losses

As a result of recording depreciation, an asset's book value declines as it ages. However, because **depreciation is not intended to report an asset at its current value,** an asset's book value could exceed its current value, particularly if the asset becomes impaired. **Impairment** occurs when events or changed circumstances cause the estimated future cash flows from a long-lived asset to fall below its book value. If an asset's estimated future cash flows are less than its book value, the book value should be written down to what the asset is worth (called fair value) with the amount of the write-down reported as an impairment loss. Impairment losses are classified as an operating expense on the income statement and reported above the Income from Operations subtotal, as shown in Exhibit 9.2 on page 405.[2]

Cedar Fair recorded a $3 million write-down about 10 years ago after a rare engineering phenomenon called "vortex shedding" caused a steel support tower in one of its VertiGo slingshot rides to snap during the off-season. More recently, in 2010, the company recorded a $63 million write-down of its Great America theme park in California. To see how this event would be accounted for, assume that the book value of Great America's rides was $663 million. If the fair value of the rides was estimated to be $600 million—an amount that represents what other amusement park companies and scrap dealers might pay for the rides—then the impairment loss would be calculated as $663 million minus $600 million. The effects of the resulting $63 million loss on impairment and the journal entry to record it would be:

> **Learning Objective 9-4**
> Explain the effect of asset impairment on the financial statements.

> **YOU SHOULD KNOW**
> **Impairment:** Occurs when the cash to be generated by an asset is estimated to be less than the carrying value of that asset.

1 Analyze

Assets	=	Liabilities	+	Stockholders' Equity
Rides and Equipment −63,000,000				Loss on Impairment (+E) −63,000,000

2 Record

dr Loss on Impairment (+E, −SE) 63,000,000	
cr Rides and Equipment (−A)...................................	63,000,000

Disposal of Tangible Assets

A business may voluntarily decide not to hold a long-term asset for its entire life. For example, your local gym might decide to replace its treadmills with elliptical trainers. Or, if a company discontinues a product, it may sell the equipment that was used to make the product. To get rid of used assets, companies do just what you do. They trade them in on a new asset, sell them on eBay, or "retire" them to a junkyard.

> **Learning Objective 9-5**
> Analyze the disposal of long lived tangible assets.

---

[2]Accounting standards do not clearly indicate where all items should be reported in the income statement. Consequently, the Securities and Exchange Commission (SEC) sometimes provides this guidance by commenting on company practices. In its fifth edition of *SEC Comment Letters*, the SEC indicates its Rule 5-03 implies that gains and losses relating to fixed and intangible assets should be included in operating income.

The disposal of a depreciable asset usually requires two accounting adjustments:

1. **Update the Depreciation Expense and Accumulated Depreciation accounts.** If a long-lived asset is disposed of during the year, it should be depreciated to the date of disposal using the partial-year calculations explained on page 410.

2. **Record the disposal.** All disposals of long-lived assets require that you account for (1) the book value of the items given up, (2) the value of the items received on disposal, and (3) any difference between the two amounts, which reflects a gain or loss on the disposal. Any gain or loss on the disposal is included on the income statement when calculating Income from Operations, as Cedar Fair did in 2010 (see Exhibit 9.2) on page 405.

Earlier in this chapter, you saw how to compute and record depreciation expense on a long-lived asset (step 1 above), so let's look instead at an example where we only have to record the disposal (step 2). Assume that, at the end of year 16, Cedar Fair sold one of its hotels for $3 million cash. The original $20 million cost of the hotel was depreciated using the straight-line method over 20 years with no residual value ($1 million depreciation expense per year). Based on the numbers for this example, the book value is

COACH'S TIP

Be sure to reduce both the asset and accumulated depreciation accounts for their full cost and accumulated depreciation (updated to the time of disposal).

Original cost	$20,000,000
Less: Accumulated Depreciation ($1,000,000 × 16 years)	16,000,000
Book value (BV) at date of sale	$ 4,000,000

The gain or loss on disposal is calculated as the difference between the asset's selling price and its book value (BV). The selling price ($3,000,000) is less than the book value ($4,000,000), so the difference ($1,000,000) is reported as a loss on disposal.

Selling price	$3,000,000
Less: Book value (BV) at disposal	4,000,000
Loss on disposal	($1,000,000)

The effects of the loss and hotel disposal on Cedar Fair are shown below, along with the journal entry to record them.

1 Analyze

Assets		= Liabilities +	Stockholders' Equity	
Buildings	−20,000,000		Loss on	
Accumulated			Disposal (+E)	−1,000,000
Depreciation (−xA)	+16,000,000			
Cash	+3,000,000			

2 Record

dr Cash (+A)	3,000,000	
dr Accumulated Depreciation (−xA, +A)	16,000,000	
dr Loss on Disposal (+E, −SE)	1,000,000	
cr Buildings (−A)		20,000,000

Loss on Disposal is recorded just like any other expense (with a debit). Had the selling price exceeded the book value, Cedar Fair would have recorded a gain on disposal (with a credit) as shown in the following Self-Study Practice.

How's it going? Self-Study Practice

Assume that Cedar Fair sold the hotel described above at the end of year 16 for $5,000,000 cash. Also assume that depreciation had been updated to that point in time, resulting in Accumulated Depreciation of $16,000,000 at the time of sale. Complete the accounting equation effects and the journal entry for this disposal below.

1 Analyze

Assets		= Liabilities + Stockholders' Equity
Buildings	−20,000,000	
Accumulated		
Depreciation (−xA)		
Cash	+5,000,000	

2 Record

After you have finished, check your answers with the solution in the margin.

Solution to Self-Study Practice

1.	Assets	=	Liabilities	+	Stockholders' Equity
Buildings −20,000,000					
Acc. Depn. +16,000,000					
Cash +5,000,000					Gain on Disposal (+R) + 1,000,000

2. dr Cash (+A) 5,000,000
   dr Accumulated Depreciation (−xA, +A) ... 16,000,000
   cr Buildings (−A) 20,000,000
   cr Gain on Disposal (+R, +SE) 1,000,000

INTANGIBLE ASSETS

Intangible assets are long-lived assets that lack physical substance. Their existence is indicated by legal documents of the types described below.

- **Trademarks.** A trademark is a special name, image, or slogan identified with a product or company, like the name Kleenex or the image of McDonald's golden arches. The symbol® signifies a trademark registered with the U.S. Patent and Trademark Office and ™ indicates unregistered trademarks. Both are intangible assets.

- **Copyrights.** A copyright gives the owner the exclusive right to publish, use, and sell a literary, musical, artistic, or dramatic work for a period not exceeding 70 years after the author's death. The book you are reading is copyrighted. It is illegal, therefore, for an instructor to copy several chapters from this book and hand them out in class without first obtaining permission from the copyright owner.

- **Patents.** A patent is an exclusive right granted by the federal government to the patent owner that prevents others from using, manufacturing, or selling the patented item for 20 years. One of the first roller-coaster patents was granted in 1884 for what was then called a "gravity pleasure road."

- **Technology.** Technology assets include software and Web development work. Google, Inc., reported $915 million of these assets at the end of 2010. Most companies use up intangible technology assets over a relatively short time (three to seven years).

- **Licensing rights.** Licensing rights are limited permissions to use something according to specific terms and conditions. Your university or college likely has obtained the licensing right to make computer programs available for use on your campus network. A licensing right also allows Cedar Fair to showcase Snoopy at its parks.

- **Franchises.** A franchise is a contractual right to sell certain products or services, use certain trademarks, or perform activities in a geographical region. For

Learning Objective 9-6
Analyze the acquisition, use, and disposal of long lived intangible assets.

YOU SHOULD KNOW

Trademark: A special name, image, or slogan identified with a product or company.
Copyright: A form of protection provided to the original authors of literary, musical, artistic, dramatic, and other works of authorship.
Patent: A right to exclude others from making, using, selling, or importing an invention.
Technology assets: Acquired computer software and development costs.
Licensing rights: The limited permission to use property according to specific terms and conditions set out in a contract.

YOU SHOULD KNOW

Franchise: A contractual right to sell certain products or services, use certain trademarks, or perform activities in a certain geographical region.
Goodwill: The premium a company pays to obtain the favorable features associated with another company.

example, a business can buy franchise rights that allow it to use the Krispy Kreme name, store format, recipes, and ingredients by paying an up-front fee ranging from $10,000 to $50,000 per store plus ongoing fees of 6 percent of store sales.[3]

- **Goodwill.** **Goodwill** tops the charts as the most frequently reported intangible asset. It encompasses lots of good stuff like a favorable location, an established customer base, a great reputation, and successful business operations. Although many companies have probably built up their own goodwill, GAAP do not allow it to be reported as an intangible asset on the balance sheet unless it has been purchased from another company. To understand the reasons behind this, keep reading. We explain them in the next section.

Acquisition, Use, and Disposal

Acquisition   The costs of intangible assets are recorded as assets only if they have been purchased. If an intangible asset is being self-constructed or internally developed, its costs generally are reported as **research and development** expenses. The primary reason that the cost of self-developed intangibles is reported as an expense rather than an asset is that it's easy for people to claim that they've developed a valuable (but invisible) intangible asset. But to believe what they are saying, you really need to see some evidence that it's actually worth what they say it's worth. And that only happens when someone gives up their hard-earned cash to buy it. At that time, the purchaser records the intangible asset at its acquisition cost. This general rule applies to trademarks, copyrights, patents, licensing rights, franchises, and goodwill.

YOU SHOULD KNOW

Research and development: Expenditures that may someday lead to patents, copyrights, or other intangible assets; the uncertainty about their future benefits requires that they be expensed.

Goodwill is a peculiar intangible asset because it represents the value paid for the unidentifiable assets of another business. You might wonder how you can value something you can't identify, but it is possible. When one company buys another business, the purchase price often is greater than the appraised value of all of the **net assets** of the business. Why would a company pay more for a business as a whole than if it bought the assets individually? The answer is to obtain its goodwill, which encompasses intangible benefits such as its good location or strong management team.

YOU SHOULD KNOW

Net assets: The shorthand term used to refer to assets minus liabilities.

SPOTLIGHT ON Business Decisions

Valuing Goodwill in a Business Acquisition

Most business acquisitions involve goodwill. For example, in 2006 Cedar Fair bought five theme parks from Paramount Parks. The total purchase price that Cedar Fair agreed to pay ($1.2 billion) exceeded the fair value of Paramount's net assets ($890 million). As shown below, Cedar Fair paid this extra $310 million to acquire the goodwill associated with the theme parks' businesses.

Cedar Fair Purchases Paramount Parks		
(in millions)		
Purchase price		**$1,200**
Assets purchased and liabilities assumed		
Current assets	$ 70	
Property and equipment	1,000	
Intangible assets	80	
Debt and other liabilities	(260)	
Net assets, at fair value		890
Goodwill		$ 310

---

[3]Krispy Kreme Form 10-K annual report for the year ended January 30, 2011.

Use   The accounting rules that apply to the use of intangible assets, after they have been purchased, depend on whether the intangible asset has a limited or unlimited life.

- **Limited life.** The cost of intangible assets with a limited life (copyrights, patents, licensing rights, and franchises) is spread on a **straight-line** basis over each period of useful life in a process called **amortization**, which is similar to depreciation. Most companies do not estimate a residual value for their intangible assets because, unlike tangible assets that can be sold as scrap, intangibles usually have no value at the end of their useful lives. Amortization is reported as an expense each period on the income statement and also is subtracted directly from the applicable intangible asset accounts on the balance sheet.[4]

> **YOU SHOULD KNOW**
>
> **Amortization:** The process of allocating the cost of intangible assets over their limited useful lives.

To illustrate, assume Cedar Fair purchased a patent for an uphill water-coaster for $800,000 and intends to use it for 20 years. Each year, the company would record $40,000 in Amortization Expense ($800,000 ÷ 20 years). The effect of this amortization and the journal entry to record it follow:

1 Analyze

	Assets	= Liabilities +	Stockholders' Equity	
Patents	−40,000		Amortization Expense (+E)	−40,000

2 Record

dr Amortization Expense (+E, −SE)	40,000	
cr Patents (−A)		40,000

- **Unlimited life.** Intangibles with unlimited or indefinite lives (trademarks and goodwill) are not amortized.

All intangible assets are tested at least annually for possible impairment, just like long-lived tangible assets. If an intangible asset is impaired, its book value is written down (reduced) to its fair value and the amount of the reduction is reported as an expense. For example, in 2010, Cedar Fair determined that declining economic conditions had impaired its Goodwill and Other Intangible Assets by approximately $2 million. These assets were written down on the balance sheet to their remaining fair value of $290 million (shown in Exhibit 9.1), with the $2 million reduction included in the $65 million Loss on Impairment on the income statement (shown in Exhibit 9.2 on page 405).

Disposal   Just like long-lived tangible assets, disposals of intangible assets result in gains (or losses) if the amounts received on disposal are greater than (less than) their book values.

The accounting rules for long-lived tangible and intangible assets are summarized and compared in the Homework Helper section on page 426.

---

[4]Consistent with the procedure for recording accumulated depreciation, an Accumulated Amortization account may be used. In practice, however, most companies directly reduce the intangible asset account.

SPOTLIGHT ON The World

Differences between GAAP and IFRS

IFRS differ from GAAP somewhat in accounting for tangible and intangible assets. Two of the most significant differences are summarized below. GAAP requires tangible and intangible assets to be recorded at cost and not revalued for later increases in asset values. In contrast, IFRS allows companies the option of reporting these assets at fair values (e.g., appraisals), provided they use the fair value method consistently each year. IFRS also requires companies to capitalize costs of developing intangible assets, such as prototypes for making new products or tools. GAAP generally expenses such development costs because of the uncertainty of their value.

GAAP	IFRS
Cost versus Fair Value	**Cost versus Fair Value**
• Must record at cost	• Choose between either cost **or fair value**
• Adjust for depreciation and impairment	• Adjust for depreciation and impairment
• Do not record increases in value	• **If using fair value, record increases in value**
Research and Development	**Research and Development**
• Expense all costs of researching and developing intangible assets	• Expense research costs but **capitalize measurable costs of developing intangible assets**

Until the United States switches to IFRS, you should carefully read the financial statement notes of any non-U.S. company you analyze. Euro Disney and LEGO reported in 2010 that they chose to use historical costs just like Cedar Fair, but they could have chosen instead to use fair value.

Evaluate the Results

TURNOVER ANALYSIS

Learning Objective 9-7
Interpret the fixed asset turnover ratio.

A primary goal of financial analysts is to evaluate how well management uses long-lived tangible assets to generate revenues. The fixed asset turnover ratio provides a good measure of this aspect of managerial performance. It is calculated as shown in the table that follows. The denominator uses the value of **average** net fixed assets (property and equipment) over the same period as the revenue in the numerator. You can calculate the average net fixed assets by summing the beginning and ending balances in fixed assets (net of accumulated depreciation) and dividing by 2.

Accounting Decision Tools

Name of Measure	Formula	What It Tells You
Fixed asset turnover ratio	$\dfrac{\text{Net Revenue}}{\text{Average Net Fixed Assets}}$	• Indicates dollars of revenue generated for each dollar invested in fixed assets (long-lived tangible assets) • A higher ratio implies greater efficiency

EXHIBIT 9.5	Summary of Fixed Asset Turnover Ratio Analyses

Company	Relevant Information (in millions)		2010 Fixed Asset Turnover Calculation
	2010	**2009**	
Cedar Fair, L.P. Net revenue	$ 978	$ 916	$\dfrac{\$978}{(\$1,680 + \$1,780)/2} = 0.57$
Net fixed assets	1,680	1,780	
Six Flags Net revenue	$ 976	$ 899	$\dfrac{\$976}{(\$1,370 + \$1,480)/2} = 0.68$
Net fixed assets	1,370	1,480	
YAHOO! Net revenue	$6,320	$6,460	$\dfrac{\$6,320}{(\$1,650 + \$1,430)/2} = 4.10$
Net fixed assets	1,650	1,430	

The fixed asset turnover ratio measures the dollars of revenue generated by each dollar invested in (tangible) fixed assets. Just as the number of miles per gallon provides a measure of a car's fuel efficiency, the fixed asset turnover ratio provides a measure of fixed asset operating efficiency. Generally speaking, a high or increasing turnover ratio relative to others in the industry suggests better than average use of fixed assets in the sense that each dollar of fixed assets is generating higher than average revenue.

Be aware that fixed asset turnover ratios can vary across industries because capital intensity—the need for tangible assets—varies widely. Compared to **Cedar Fair** and **Six Flags**, a company such as **Yahoo!** needs fewer fixed assets to generate revenue, so it has a higher turnover ratio. Exhibit 9.5 shows the fixed asset turnover ratios for the three companies in 2010. Practice computing this ratio and comparing it to prior periods by trying the Self-Study Practice that follows.

 How's it going?   Self-Study Practice

Cedar Fair reported net fixed assets of $1,800 (million) at December 31, 2008.

a. Use this information, along with that in Exhibit 9.5, to calculate Cedar Fair's fixed asset turnover ratio in 2009.

$$\frac{}{(+)/2} =$$

b. Did Cedar Fair's fixed asset turnover improve or decline from 2009 (calculated in *a*) to 2010 (shown in Exhibit 9.5)?

After you have finished, check your answers with the solutions in the margin.

Fixed Asset Turnover before and after the Financial Crisis

Revenue at amusement parks declined in 2009 as people became increasingly concerned about their jobs and the economy. They didn't go to the parks as often and when they did go, they spent less on food, merchandise, and games. This decline in revenue led to a significant drop in the fixed asset turnover ratios of the three leading amusement parks in the United States, as shown in the accompanying graph. Fortunately this decline was short-lived. When the economy began to recover in 2010, the companies reported significant increases in their fixed asset turnover ratios, driven by increases in admissions and concessions revenue.

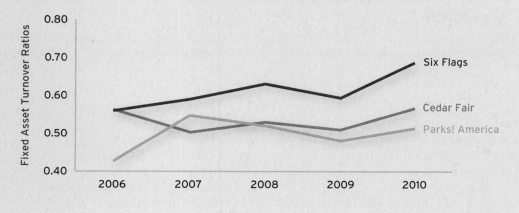

IMPACT OF DEPRECIATION DIFFERENCES

Learning Objective 9-8
Describe factors to consider when comparing companies' long-lived assets.

 COACH'S TIP

For tips and practice involving the calculations in Exhibit 9.6, try S9-7 at the end of this chapter.

Just as differences in the nature of business operations affect financial analyses and the conclusions you draw from them, so too do differences in depreciation. Depreciation varies from one company to the next as a result of differences in depreciation methods, estimated useful lives, and estimated residual values. In this section, we present a simple example to show how different depreciation methods can affect financial analysis throughout the life of a long-lived asset. Do not be fooled by the simplicity of the example. Differences in depreciation can have a significant impact in the real world.

Assume that Cedar Fair and Six Flags each acquired a new roller coaster at the beginning of the year for $15.5 million. The two companies estimate that the roller coasters will have residual values of $1.5 million at the end of their seven-year useful lives. Assume too that everything about the roller coasters is identical. However, Cedar Fair uses the straight-line depreciation method and Six Flags uses the double-declining-balance method. Exhibit 9.6 shows the yearly depreciation reported by the two companies (rounded to the nearest thousand dollars). Notice that early in the asset's life, before year 4, the straight-line depreciation expense reported by Cedar Fair is less than the declining-balance depreciation expense reported by Six Flags. Thus, even if the two companies attract exactly the same number of customers and earn exactly the same total revenues, their reported net incomes will differ each year simply because they use two different (but equally acceptable) methods of depreciation. This example shows why a user of financial statements needs to understand the accounting methods companies use.

These differences in depreciation affect more than just depreciation expense, however. Taking this example one step further, assume that the two companies sell

CHAPTER 9 Long-Lived Tangible and Intangible Assets **419**

EXHIBIT 9.6 — Straight-Line versus Double-Declining-Balance Depreciation Schedules

| | CEDAR FAIR (STRAIGHT LINE) | | | SIX FLAGS (DOUBLE-DECLINING BALANCE) | | |
Depreciation Expense	Accumulated Depreciation	Book Value	Year	Depreciation Expense	Accumulated Depreciation	Book Value
$2,000,000	$ 2,000,000	$13,500,000	1	$4,429,000	$ 4,429,000	$11,071,000
2,000,000	4,000,000	11,500,000	2	3,163,000	7,592,000	7,908,000
2,000,000	6,000,000	9,500,000	3	2,259,000	9,851,000	5,649,000
2,000,000	8,000,000	7,500,000	4	1,614,000	11,465,000	4,035,000
2,000,000	10,000,000	5,500,000	5	1,153,000	12,618,000	2,882,000
2,000,000	12,000,000	3,500,000	6	823,000	13,441,000	2,059,000
2,000,000	14,000,000	1,500,000	7	559,000	14,000,000	1,500,000

the roller coasters at the end of year 4 for $6,000,000. Because the disposal occurs on the last day of the year, the companies will record a full year of depreciation prior to the disposal. Thus, at the time of disposal, Cedar Fair's roller coaster will have a book value of $7,500,000, but Six Flags' roller coaster will have a book value of $4,035,000 (see the highlighted line in Exhibit 9.6). To account for the disposal at the end of year 4, the companies record what they received, remove what they gave up (the book value of the asset), and recognize a gain or loss for the difference between what was received and what was given up. Exhibit 9.7 shows the calculations for the two companies.

Based on the information in Exhibit 9.7, which company appears to be better managed? Someone who does not understand accounting is likely to say that Six Flags is better managed because it reported a gain on disposal whereas Cedar Fair reported a loss. You know that cannot be right, however, because both companies experienced exactly the same events. They bought the same asset at the same cost ($15.5 million) and sold it for the same amount of money ($6 million). The only difference between them is that Cedar Fair reported less depreciation over the years leading up to the disposal, so its roller coaster had a larger book value at the time of disposal. Six Flags reported more depreciation, so its roller coaster had a smaller book value at the time of disposal. As a financial statement user, you should realize that **any gain or loss on disposal on the income statement tells you as much about the method used to depreciate assets as about management's apparent ability to successfully negotiate the sale of long-lived assets.**

EXHIBIT 9.7 — Calculation of Gain/Loss on Disposal

	Cedar Fair	Six Flags
Selling price	$ 6,000,000	$6,000,000
Book value (see Exhibit 9.6)	(7,500,000)	(4,035,000)
Gain (loss) on disposal	$(1,500,000)	$1,965,000

Although the previous example concerned different depreciation methods, the same effects can occur for two companies that use the same depreciation method but different estimated useful lives or residual values. Useful lives can vary for several reasons including differences in (1) the type of equipment used, (2) the frequency of repairs, (3) the frequency and duration of use, and (4) the accuracy of management's estimates. How large can these differences be? Even within the same industry, sizable differences can occur. The notes to the financial statements of various companies in the airline industry, for example, reveal the following differences in the estimated useful lives of airplanes and other flight equipment:

Company	Estimated Life (in years)
US Airways	Up to 30
Southwest Airlines	Up to 25
Alaska Airlines	Up to 20
Singapore Airlines	Up to 15

YOU SHOULD KNOW

EBITDA: An abbreviation for "earnings before interest, taxes, depreciation, and amortization," which is a measure of operating performance that some managers and analysts use in place of net income.

Some analysts try to sidestep such differences in depreciation calculations by focusing on financial measures that exclude the effects of depreciation. One popular measure is called **EBITDA** (pronounced something like *'e bit, duh*), which stands for "earnings before interest, taxes, depreciation, and amortization." Analysts calculate EBITDA by starting with net income and then adding back depreciation and amortization expense (as well as nonoperating expenses such as interest and taxes). The idea is that this measure allows analysts to conduct financial analyses without having to deal with possible differences in depreciation and amortization.

Learning Objective 9-S1
Analyze and report depletion of natural resources.

SUPPLEMENT 9A   NATURAL RESOURCES

Industries such as oil and gas, mining, and timber harvesting rely significantly on a third category of long-lived assets called *natural resources*. These natural resources, whether in the form of oil wells, mineral deposits, or timber tracts, provide the raw materials for products that are sold by companies like ExxonMobil and International Paper. When a company first acquires or develops a natural resource, the cost of the natural resource is recorded in conformity with the **cost principle.** As the natural resource is used up, its acquisition cost must be split among the periods in which revenues are earned in conformity with the **expense recognition ("matching") principle.** The term **depletion** describes the process of allocating a natural resource's cost over the period of its extraction or harvesting. The units-of-production method is often used to compute depletion.

YOU SHOULD KNOW

Depletion: The process of allocating a natural resource's cost over the period of its extraction or harvesting.

Depletion is similar to the concepts of depreciation and amortization discussed earlier in the chapter for tangible and intangible assets, with one important exception. When a natural resource such as timberland is depleted, the company obtains inventory (logs). Because depletion of the natural resource is necessary to obtain the inventory, the depletion computed during a period is added to the cost of the inventory, not expensed in the period. For example, if a timber tract costing $530,000 is depleted over its estimated cutting period based on a "cutting" rate of approximately 20 percent per year, it would be depleted by $106,000 each year. Recording this depletion would have the following effects on the company's accounting equation, which would be recorded with the journal entry shown below.

1 Analyze

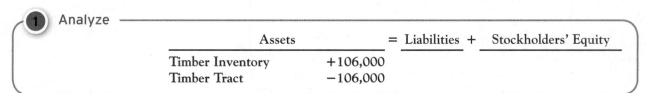

	Assets		= Liabilities +	Stockholders' Equity
Timber Inventory	+106,000			
Timber Tract	−106,000			

② Record

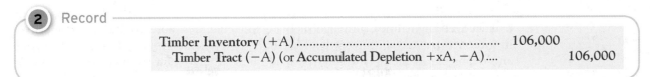

Timber Inventory (+A)	106,000	
Timber Tract (−A) (or **Accumulated Depletion** +xA, −A)		106,000

Timber Inventory remains as an asset on the balance sheet until it is sold, at which time its cost is removed from the balance sheet and reported on the income statement as an expense called Cost of Goods Sold.

SUPPLEMENT 9B   CHANGES IN DEPRECIATION

Learning Objective 9-S2
Calculate changes in depreciation arising from changes in estimates or capitalized cost.

The amount of depreciation and amortization depends on three items: an asset's recorded cost, its estimated useful life, and its estimated residual value. When any one of these items changes, the amount of depreciation and amortization needs to change. For example, in 2009, Cedar Fair changed its amortization calculations because it shortened the estimated useful life of certain intangible assets after deciding to discontinue its licensing agreement with Nickelodeon. In other instances, when the company made extraordinary repairs that increased a roller coaster's recorded cost, it needed to revise depreciation for the remaining years of that asset's estimated life.

To compute the new depreciation expense due to the changes described above, substitute the book value for the original acquisition cost, the new residual value for the original residual value, and the estimated remaining life for the original useful life. As an illustration, the formula using the straight-line method follows:

$$\text{(Cost} - \text{Residual Value)} \times \frac{1}{\text{Useful Life}} = \text{Depreciation Expense}$$

$$\text{(Book Value} - \text{New Residual Value)} \times \frac{1}{\text{Remaining Life}} = \text{Depreciation Expense}$$

Assume Cedar Fair purchased the largest and fastest roller coaster in the universe for $60,000,000 with an estimated useful life of 20 years and estimated residual value of $3,000,000. Shortly after the start of year 5, Cedar Fair changed the initial estimated life to 25 years and lowered the estimated residual value to $2,400,000. At the end of year 5, the computation of the new amount for depreciation expense is as follows:

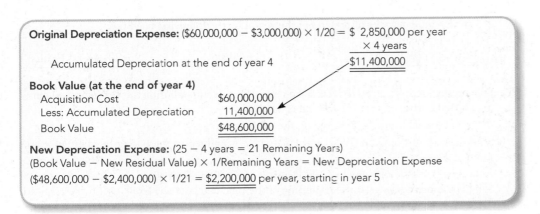

Original Depreciation Expense: ($60,000,000 − $3,000,000) × 1/20 = $ 2,850,000 per year
$\qquad\qquad\qquad\qquad\qquad\qquad\qquad\qquad\qquad\qquad\qquad\qquad$ × 4 years

Accumulated Depreciation at the end of year 4 $\qquad$ $11,400,000

Book Value (at the end of year 4)

Acquisition Cost	$60,000,000
Less: Accumulated Depreciation	11,400,000
Book Value	$48,600,000

New Depreciation Expense: (25 − 4 years = 21 Remaining Years)
(Book Value − New Residual Value) × 1/Remaining Years = New Depreciation Expense
($48,600,000 − $2,400,000) × 1/21 = $2,200,000 per year, starting in year 5

Companies may also change depreciation *methods* (for example, from declining-balance to straight-line), although such a change requires more disclosure, as described in intermediate accounting textbooks. Under GAAP, changes in accounting estimates and depreciation methods should be made only when a new estimate or accounting method "better measures" the periodic income of the business.

REVIEW THE CHAPTER

DEMONSTRATION CASE

Diversified Industries (DI) started as a house construction company. In recent years, it has expanded into heavy construction, ready-mix concrete, sand and gravel, construction supplies, and earth-moving services. The company completed the following transactions during 2013. Amounts have been simplified.

Jan. 1	The management decided to buy a 10-year-old building for $175,000 and the land on which it was situated for $130,000. DI paid $100,000 in cash and signed a note payable for the rest.
Jan. 3	DI paid $38,000 in cash for renovations to the building prior to its use.
July 10	DI paid $1,200 cash for ordinary repairs on the building.
Dec. 31	DI considered the following information to determine year-end adjustments:

a. The building will be depreciated on a straight-line basis over an estimated useful life of 30 years. The estimated residual value is $33,000.
b. DI purchased another company two years ago at $100,000 more than the fair values of the net assets acquired. The goodwill has an unlimited life.
c. At the beginning of the year, DI owned equipment with a cost of $650,000 and accumulated depreciation of $150,000. The equipment is being depreciated using the double-declining-balance method, with a useful life of 20 years and no residual value.
d. At year-end, DI tested its long-lived assets for possible impairment of their value. Included in its equipment was a piece of old excavation equipment with a cost of $156,000 and book value of $120,000 after making the adjustment for (c). Due to its smaller size and lack of safety features, the old equipment has limited use. The future cash flows and fair value are expected to be $35,000. Goodwill was found to be not impaired.

December 31, 2013, is the end of the annual accounting period.

Required:

1. Indicate the accounts affected and the amount and direction (+ for increase and − for decrease) of the effect of each of the preceding events and required adjustments on the financial statement categories at the end of the year. Use the following headings:

Date	Assets	=	Liabilities	+	Stockholders' Equity

2. Prepare the journal entries to record each event that occurred during the year and the adjusting journal entries required at December 31.
3. Which accounts would be reported on the income statement? Where?
4. Show how the December 31, 2013, balance sheet would report these long-lived tangible and intangible assets.
5. Assuming that the company had Net Revenue of $1,000,000 for the year and a book value of $500,000 for fixed assets at the beginning of the year, compute the fixed asset turnover ratio. Explain its meaning and evaluate it relative to the prior year's ratio of 1.5.

Suggested Solution

1. Effects of events (with computations in notes below the table):

Date	Assets		=	Liabilities	+	Stockholders' Equity	
Jan. 1	Cash	−100,000		Note Payable	+205,000		
	Land	+130,000					
	Building	+175,000					
Jan. 3 (Note 1)	Cash	−38,000					
	Building	+38,000					
July 10 (Note 2)	Cash	−1,200				Repairs and Maintenance Expense (+E)	−1,200
Dec. 31 (a) (Note 3)	Accumulated Depreciation (+xA)	−6,000				Depreciation Expense (+E)	−6,000
Dec. 31 (b) (Note 4)	No entry						
Dec. 31 (c) (Note 5)	Accumulated Depreciation (+xA)	−50,000				Depreciation Expense (+E)	−50,000
Dec. 31 (d) (Note 6)	Equipment	−85,000				Impairment Loss (+E)	−85,000

Notes

(1) Capitalize the $38,000 expenditure because it is necessary to prepare the asset for use.

(2) This is an ordinary repair and should be expensed.

(3)

Cost of building		**Straight-line depreciation (building)**
Initial payment	$175,000	($213,000 cost − $33,000 residual value) ×
Renovations prior to use	38,000	1/30 years = $6,000 annual depreciation
Acquisition cost	$213,000	

(4) Goodwill has an indefinite life and is therefore not amortized. Goodwill is tested for impairment but as described later in the case, was found to be not impaired.

(5) **Double-declining-balance depreciation (equipment)**

($650,000 cost − $150,000 accumulated depreciation) × 2/20 years = $50,000 depreciation for the year.

(6) **Asset impairment test**

The book value of the old equipment ($120,000) exceeds expected future cash flows ($35,000). The asset has become impaired, so it needs to be written down to its fair value.

Impairment loss:	
Book Value	$120,000
Fair Value	(35,000)
Impairment Loss	$ 85,000

2. Journal entries for events during the year:

Jan. 1, 2013	dr Land (+A)..	130,000	
	dr Building (+A)...................................	175,000	
	cr Cash (−A)		100,000
	cr Note Payable (+L).........................		205,000
Jan. 3, 2013	dr Building (+A)...................................	38,000	
	cr Cash (−A)		38,000
July 10, 2013	dr Repairs and Maintenance Expense (+E, −SE)......	1,200	
	cr Cash (−A)		1,200

Adjusting journal entries at December 31, 2013:

   a. *dr* **Depreciation Expense** (+E, −SE).. 6,000

         cr **Accumulated Depreciation—Building** (+xA, −A)   6,000

   b. No adjusting journal entry required because goodwill is assumed to have an unlimited (or indefinite) life.

   c. *dr* **Depreciation Expense** (+E, −SE).. 50,000

         cr **Accumulated Depreciation—Equipment** (+xA, −A)   50,000

   d. *dr* **Impairment Loss** (+E, −SE) 85,000

         cr **Equipment** (−A)...   85,000

3. The income statement would report Depreciation Expense, Repairs and Maintenance Expense, and Impairment Loss as operating expenses included in the computation of Income from Operations.

4. Partial balance sheet, December 31, 2013:

Assets	
Property, Plant, and Equipment	
Land	$130,000
Building	213,000
Equipment	565,000*
Property, Plant, and Equipment, at cost	908,000
Less: Accumulated Depreciation	(206,000)†
Property, Plant, and Equipment, net	702,000
Goodwill	100,000

* $565,000 = $650,000 − $85,000
† $206,000 = $6,000 + $150,000 + $50,000

5. Fixed asset turnover ratio:

$$\frac{\text{Net Revenue}}{(\text{Beginning Net Fixed Asset Balance} + \text{Ending Net Fixed Asset Balance})/2} = \frac{\$1,000,000}{(\$500,000 + \$702,000)/2} = 1.66$$

The fixed asset turnover ratio measures the company's efficiency at using its investment in property, plant, and equipment to generate revenue. Approximately $1.66 of revenue was generated for each dollar of fixed assets, which is an improvement over last year's 1.5.

CHAPTER SUMMARY

LO 9-1   **Define, classify, and explain the nature of long-lived assets. p. 398**

- Long-lived assets are those that a business retains for long periods of time for use in the course of normal operations rather than for sale. They may be divided into tangible assets (land, buildings, equipment) and intangible assets (including goodwill, patents, and franchises).

LO 9-2   **Apply the cost principle to the acquisition of long-lived assets. p. 399**

- The acquisition cost of property, plant, and equipment is the cash-equivalent purchase price plus all reasonable and necessary expenditures made to acquire and prepare the asset for its intended use. Expenditures made after the asset is in use are either expensed or capitalized as a cost of the asset:
  - **a.** Expenditures are expensed if they recur frequently, involve relatively small amounts, and do not directly lengthen the asset's useful life. These are considered ordinary repairs and maintenance expense.
  - **b.** Expenditures are capitalized as a cost of the asset if they provide benefits for one or more accounting periods beyond the current period. This category includes extraordinary repairs, replacements, and additions.

Apply various depreciation methods as economic benefits are used up over time. p. 406

LO 9-3

- In conformity with the matching principle, the cost of long-lived tangible assets (less any estimated residual value) is allocated to depreciation expense over each period benefited by the assets.

- Because of depreciation, the book value of an asset declines over time and net income is reduced by the amount of the expense.

- Common depreciation methods include straight-line (a constant amount over time), units-of-production (a variable amount over time), and double-declining-balance (a decreasing amount over time).

Explain the effect of asset impairment on the financial statements. p. 411

LO 9-4

- When events or changes in circumstances reduce the estimated future cash flows of a long-lived asset below its book value, the book value of the asset should be written down, with the amount of the write-down reported as an impairment loss.

Analyze the disposal of long-lived tangible assets. p. 411

LO 9-5

When assets are disposed of through sale or abandonment,

- Record additional depreciation arising since the last adjustment was made.

- Remove the cost of the old asset and its related accumulated depreciation.

- Recognize the cash proceeds (if any).

- Recognize any gains or losses when the asset's book value is not equal to the cash received.

Analyze the acquisition, use, and disposal of long-lived intangible assets. p. 413

LO 9-6

- Intangible assets are recorded at cost, but only when purchased. The costs of most internally developed intangible assets are expensed as research and development when incurred.

- Intangibles are reported at book value on the balance sheet.

- Amortization is calculated for intangibles with limited useful lives, using the straight-line method.

- Intangibles with unlimited useful lives, including goodwill, are not amortized, but are reviewed for impairment.

Interpret the fixed asset turnover ratio. p. 416

LO 9-7

- The fixed asset turnover ratio measures the company's efficiency at using its investment in property, plant, and equipment to generate sales. Higher turnover ratios imply greater efficiency.

Describe factors to consider when comparing companies' long-lived assets. p. 418

LO 9-8

- Companies in different industries require different levels of investment in long-lived assets. Beyond that, you should consider whether differences exist in depreciation methods, estimated useful lives, and estimated residual values, which can affect the book value of long-lived assets as well as ratios calculated using these book values and any gains or losses reported at the time of asset disposal.

Accounting Decision Tools

Name of Measure	Formula	What It Tells You
Fixed asset turnover ratio	$\dfrac{\text{Net Revenue}}{\text{Average Net Fixed Assets}}$	• Dollars of revenue generated for each dollar invested in (tangible) fixed assets • A higher ratio implies greater efficiency

KEY TERMS

Amortization p. 415

Book (or Carrying) Value p. 405

Capitalize p. 400

Copyright p. 413

Declining-Balance Depreciation
   Method p. 407

Depletion p. 420

Depreciable Cost p. 405

Depreciation p. 404

EBITDA p. 420

Extraordinary Repairs p. 404

Franchise p. 414

Goodwill p. 414

Impairment p. 411

Licensing Right p. 413

Long-Lived Assets p. 398

Net Assets p. 414

Ordinary Repairs and Maintenance p. 403

Patent p. 413

Research and Development p. 414

Residual (or Salvage) Value p. 405

Straight-Line Depreciation Method p. 406

Technology Assets p. 413

Trademark p. 413

Units-of-Production Depreciation
   Method p. 407

Useful Life p. 405

See complete definitions in the glossary in the back of this text.

HOMEWORK HELPER

Stage	Subject	Tangible Assets	Intangible Assets
Acquire	**Purchased asset**	Capitalize all related costs	Capitalize all related costs
Use	***Repairs and maintenance***		
	Ordinary	Expense related costs	Not applicable
	Extraordinary	Capitalize related costs	Not applicable
	Depreciation/amortization		
	Limited life	One of several methods: • Straight-line • Units-of-production • Declining-balance	Straight-line method
	Unlimited life	Do not depreciate (e.g., land)	Do not amortize (e.g., goodwill)
	Impairment test	Write down if necessary	Write down if necessary
Dispose	***Report gain (loss) when . . .***	Receive more (less) on disposal than book value	Receive more (less) on disposal than book value

Alternative terms

- Declining-balance depreciation methods are also called accelerated methods.

Helpful reminders

- Costs that benefit future periods are capitalized as assets. Costs that benefit only the current period are recorded as expenses.
- See Exhibit 9.2 for an income statement showing where to report Depreciation Expense and Losses from Disposals and Impairments.
- Declining-balance depreciation methods subtract Accumulated Depreciation, not residual value, from the asset's cost. For this reason, take extra care to ensure that you stop depreciating the asset when its book value equals its residual value.

Frequent mistakes

- Depreciation does not represent a decline in the current value of an asset; declines in asset values are recorded as impairment losses, not depreciation. The purpose of depreciation is to allocate the cost of a long-lived asset to each period in which the asset is used to generate revenue.
- To record an asset disposal, remove its cost and accumulated depreciation separately, rather than remove just its book value from the asset's account.

PRACTICE MATERIAL

QUESTIONS (Symbol indicates questions that require analysis from more than one perspective.)

1. Define long-lived assets. What are the two common categories of long-lived assets? Describe each.

2. Under the cost principle, what amounts should be recorded as a cost of a long-lived asset?

3. What is the term for recording costs as assets rather than as expenses? Describe how the decision to record costs as assets, rather than expenses, affects the balance sheet and income statement.

4. Waste Management, Inc., regularly incurs costs (e.g., salaries, legal fees, travel) to find new locations for landfill sites. What reasons support capitalizing these costs? What reasons support expensing these costs?

5. Distinguish between ordinary repairs and extraordinary repairs. How is each accounted for?

6. Describe the relationship between the matching principle and accounting for long-lived assets.

7. Why are different depreciation methods allowed?

8. In computing depreciation, three values must be known or estimated. Identify and describe each.

9. What type of depreciation expense pattern is used under each of the following methods and when is its use appropriate?
   a. The straight-line method.
   b. The units-of-production method.
   c. The double-declining-balance method.

10. After merging with Northwest Airlines, Delta Airlines increased the estimated useful life and increased the estimated residual value of its flight equipment. All else equal, how will each of these changes affect Delta's Depreciation Expense and Net Income?

11. A local politician claimed, "to reduce the government's deficit, it's time we require companies to start paying their deferred income tax liabilities." Explain to the politician what deferred income taxes represent and why they should not be viewed as accounts payable to the government.

12. What is an *asset impairment*? How is it accounted for?

13. What is book value? When equipment is sold for more than book value, how is the transaction recorded? How is it recorded when the selling price is less than book value?

14. Distinguish between depreciation and amortization.

15. Define *goodwill*. When is it appropriate to record goodwill as an intangible asset? When is its value decreased?

16. FedEx Corporation reports the cost of its aircraft in a single category called Flight Equipment. What impact will IFRS have on this aspect of FedEx's accounting?

17. How is the fixed asset turnover ratio computed? Explain its meaning.

18. Johnson & Johnson, the maker of Tylenol, uses GAAP. Bayer, the maker of aspirin, uses IFRS. Explain what complications might arise when comparing the Property, Plant, and Equipment of these two companies.

19. (Supplement 9A) How does depletion affect the balance sheet and income statement? Why is depletion accounted for in a manner that differs from depreciation and amortization?

20. (Supplement 9B) Over what period should an addition to an existing long-lived asset be depreciated? Explain.

MULTIPLE CHOICE

1. Which of the following should be capitalized when a piece of production equipment is acquired for a factory?
   a. Sales tax.   c. Installation costs.
   b. Transportation costs.   d. All of the above.

2. When recording depreciation, which of the following statements is true?
   a. Total assets increase and stockholders' equity increases.
   b. Total assets decrease and total liabilities increase.
   c. Total assets decrease and stockholders' equity increases.
   d. None of the above are true.

3. Under what depreciation method(s) is an asset's book value used to calculate depreciation each year?
   a. Straight-line method.
   b. Units-of-production method.
   c. Declining-balance method.
   d. All of the above.

4. A company wishes to report the highest earnings possible according to GAAP. Therefore, when calculating depreciation for financial reporting purposes,

   a. It will follow the MACRS depreciation rates prescribed by the IRS.
   b. It will estimate the shortest lives possible for its assets.
   c. It will estimate the longest lives possible for its assets.
   d. It will estimate lower residual values for its assets.

5. Barber, Inc., depreciates its building on a straight-line basis. A building was purchased on January 1, 2013, and it had an estimated useful life of 20 years and a residual value of $20,000. The company's Depreciation Expense for 2013 was $20,000 on the building. What was the original cost of the building?
   a. $360,000   c. $400,000
   b. $380,000   d. $420,000

6. Thornton Industries purchased a machine on July 1, 2013, for $45,000 and is depreciating it with the straight-line method over a life of 10 years, using a residual value of $3,000. Depreciation Expense for the machine for the year ended December 31, 2013, is
   a. $2,100   c. $4,200
   b. $2,250   d. $4,500

7. ACME, Inc., uses straight-line depreciation for all of its depreciable assets. ACME sold a used piece of machinery on December 31, 2013, that it purchased on January 1, 2012, for $10,000. The asset had a five-year life, zero residual value, and Accumulated Depreciation as of December 31, 2013, of $4,000. If the sales price of the used machine was $7,500, the resulting gain or loss on disposal was which of the following amounts?

   a. Loss of $2,500
   b. Gain of $3,500
   c. Loss of $1,500
   d. Gain of $1,500

8. What assets should be amortized using the straight-line method?

   a. Land.
   b. Intangible assets with limited lives.
   c. Intangible assets with unlimited lives.
   d. All of the above.

9. How many of the following statements regarding goodwill are true?

   • Goodwill is not reported unless purchased in an exchange.
   • Goodwill must be reviewed annually for possible impairment.
   • Impairment of goodwill results in a decrease in net income.

   a. None
   b. One
   c. Two
   d. Three

10. The Simon Company and the Allen Company each bought a new delivery truck on January 1, 2012. Both companies paid exactly the same cost, $30,000, for their respective vehicles. As of December 31, 2013, the book value of Simon's truck was less than the Allen Company's book value for the same vehicle. Which of the following are acceptable explanations for the difference in book value?

    a. Both companies elected straight-line depreciation, but the Simon Company used a longer estimated life.
    b. The Simon Company estimated a lower residual value, but both estimated the same useful life and both elected straight-line depreciation.
    c. Because GAAP specifies rigid guidelines regarding the calculation of depreciation, this situation is not possible.
    d. None of the above explain the difference in book value.

For answers to the Multiple-Choice Questions **see page Q1** located in the last section of the book.

MINI-EXERCISES

McGraw Hill **connect** |ACCOUNTING

LO 9-1, 9-3, 9-6   **M9-1 Classifying Long-Lived Assets and Related Cost Allocation Concepts**

For each of the following long-lived assets, indicate its nature and related cost allocation concept. Use the abbreviations shown on the right:

Asset	Nature	Cost Allocation		Nature
1. Property	_____	_____	B	Building
2. Delivery vans	_____	_____	E	Equipment
3. Warehouse	_____	_____	I	Intangible
4. Trademark	_____	_____	L	Land
5. New engine	_____	_____		
6. Franchise	_____	_____		Cost Allocation
7. Software license	_____	_____	A	Amortization
8. Computers	_____	_____	D	Depreciation
9. Production plant	_____	_____	NO	No cost allocation

LO 9-2, 9-6   **M9-2 Deciding Whether to Capitalize or Expense**

American Golf Corporation

American Golf Corporation operates over 110 golf courses throughout the country. For each of the following items, enter the correct letter to show whether the cost should be capitalized (C) or expensed (E).

Transactions

_____ 1. Purchased a golf course in Orange County, California.

_____ 2. Paid a landscaping company to clear one hundred acres of land on which to build a new course.

____ 3. Paid a landscaping company to apply fertilizer to the fairways on its Coyote Hills Golf Course.

____ 4. Hired a building maintenance company to build a 2,000 square foot addition on a clubhouse.

____ 5. Hired a building maintenance company to replace the locks on a clubhouse and equipment shed.

____ 6. Paid an advertising company to create a campaign to build goodwill.

M9-3 Deciding Whether to Capitalize an Expense

LO 9-2, 9-6

For each of the following items, enter the correct letter to show whether the expenditure should be capitalized (C) or expensed (E).

Transactions
_____

____ 1. Purchased a machine, $70,000; gave long-term note.

____ 2. Paid $600 for ordinary repairs.

____ 3. Purchased a patent, $45,300 cash.

____ 4. Paid cash, $200,000, for addition to old building.

____ 5. Paid $20,000 for monthly salaries.

____ 6. Paid $250 for routine maintenance.

____ 7. Paid $16,000 for extraordinary repairs.

M9-4 Computing Book Value (Straight-Line Depreciation)

LO 9-3

Calculate the book value of a three-year-old machine that cost $400,000, has an estimated residual value of $40,000, and has an estimated useful life of four years. The company uses straight-line depreciation.

M9-5 Computing Book Value (Units-of-Production Depreciation)

LO 9-3

Calculate the book value of a three-year-old machine that cost $400,000, has an estimated residual value of $40,000, and has an estimated useful life of 20,000 machine hours. The company uses units-of-production depreciation and ran the machine 3,000 hours in year 1, 8,000 hours in year 2, and 6,000 hours in year 3.

M9-6 Computing Book Value (Double-Declining-Balance Depreciation)

LO 9-3

Calculate the book value of a three-year-old machine that cost $400,000, has an estimated residual value of $40,000, and has an estimated useful life of four years. The company uses double-declining-balance depreciation. Round to the nearest dollar.

M9-7 Calculating Partial-Year Depreciation

LO 9-3

Calculate the amount of depreciation to report during the year ended December 31, 2013, for equipment that was purchased at a cost of $43,000 on October 1, 2013. The equipment has an estimated residual value of $3,000 and an estimated useful life of five years or 20,000 hours. Assume the equipment was used for 1,000 hours from October 1 to December 31 and the company uses: (a) straight-line, (b) double-declining-balance, or (c) units-of-production depreciation.

M9-8 Understanding the Significance of Asset Impairment Losses

LO 9-4

General Motors Corporation

For the year ended December 31, 2008, General Motors Corporation reported a Loss from Operations of $20 billion. The following asset impairment losses were included among its operating expenses.

Goodwill impairment	$ 610 million
HUMMER equipment impairment	290 million
Saab equipment impairment	500 million
Other impairment losses	1,100 million
Total impairment losses	$2,500 million

Do GM's asset impairment losses seem significant in terms of total dollar value? What percentage of the company's 2008 operating loss was explained by asset impairments? Why might GM write down its HUMMER and Saab production equipment, but not its Chevrolet production equipment?

LO 9-5

M9-9 Recording the Disposal of a Long-Lived Asset

Prepare journal entries to record these transactions: (*a*) Morrell Corporation disposed of two computers at the end of their useful lives. The computers had cost $4,800 and their Accumulated Depreciation was $4,800. No residual value was received. (*b*) Assume the same information as (*a*), except that Accumulated Depreciation, updated to the date of disposal, was $3,600.

LO 9-5

M9-10 Reporting and Recording the Disposal of a Long-Lived Asset (Straight-Line Depreciation)

As part of a major renovation at the beginning of the year, Atiase Pharmaceuticals, Inc., sold shelving units (recorded as Equipment) that were 10 years old for $800 cash. The shelves originally cost $6,400 and had been depreciated on a straight-line basis over an estimated useful life of 10 years with an estimated residual value of $400. Assuming that depreciation has been recorded to the date of sale, show the effect of the disposal on the accounting equation. Prepare the journal entry to record the sale of the shelving units.

LO 9-6

M9-11 Capitalizing versus Expensing Intangible Asset Costs

Most highly visible companies spend significant amounts of money to protect their intellectual property, ensuring that no one uses this property without direct permission. For example, to include logos throughout this book, we had to obtain written permission from each company—a process that stretched over nearly a year and often resulted in requests being denied. Discuss whether companies should capitalize or expense the money paid to employees who evaluate requests for use of their logos and who search for instances where the companies' intellectual property has been used without permission. Draw an analogy to similar costs incurred for employees responsible for the use and upkeep of tangible assets.

LO 9-6

M9-12 Computing Goodwill and Patents

Taste-T Company has been in business for 30 years and has developed a large group of loyal restaurant customers. Down Home Foods made an offer to buy Taste-T Company for $6,000,000. The market value of Taste-T's recorded assets, net of liabilities, on the date of the offer is $5,600,000. Taste-T also holds a patent for a fluting machine that the company invented (the patent with a market value of $200,000 was never recorded by Taste-T because it was developed internally). How much has Down Home Foods included for intangibles in its offer of $6,000,000? Assuming Taste-T accepts this offer, which company will report Goodwill on its balance sheet?

LO 9-7

M9-13 Computing and Evaluating the Fixed Asset Turnover Ratio

The following information was reported by Amuse Yourself Parks (AYP) for 2010:

Net fixed assets (beginning of year)	$8,450,000
Net fixed assets (end of year)	8,250,000
Net sales for the year	4,175,000
Net income for the year	1,700,000

Compute the company's fixed asset turnover ratio for the year. What can you say about AYP's fixed asset turnover ratio when compared to Cedar Fair's 2010 ratio in Exhibit 9.5?

M9-14 (Supplement 9A) Recording Depletion for a Natural Resource

Saskatchewan Forestry Company purchased a timber tract for $600,000 and estimates that it will be depleted evenly over its 10-year useful life with no residual value. Show the journal entry that would be recorded if 10 percent of the total timber is cut and placed into inventory during the current year.

M9-15 (Supplement 9B) Computing Revised Depreciation after Change in Cost and Estimated Life

Plummer Industries purchased a machine for $43,800 and is depreciating it with the straight-line method over a life of 8 years, using a residual value of $3,000. At the beginning of the sixth year, an extraordinary repair was made costing $7,500, the estimated useful life was extended to 13 years, and no change was made to the estimated residual value. Calculate depreciation expense for year 6, rounded to the nearest dollar.

EXERCISES

E9-1 Preparing a Classified Balance Sheet

|ACCOUNTING   LO 9-1, 9-7

The following is a list of account titles and amounts (in millions) reported at December 26, 2010, by Hasbro, Inc., a leading manufacturer of games, toys, and interactive entertainment software for children and families:

Buildings	$197	Goodwill	$475
Prepaids and Other Current Assets	168	Equipment	460
Allowance for Doubtful Accounts	31	Accumulated Depreciation	430
Other Noncurrent Assets	663	Inventories	364
Cash and Cash Equivalents	728	Other Intangibles	501
Accounts Receivable	992	Land	7

Required:

1. Prepare the asset section of a classified balance sheet for Hasbro, Inc.
2. Using Hasbro's 2010 Net Sales Revenue of $4,002 (million) and its Net Fixed Assets of $221 (million) at December 30, 2009, calculate the fixed asset turnover ratio for 2010. Has the company generated more or less revenue from each dollar of fixed assets than in 2009, when the ratio was 20.76?

E9-2 Computing and Recording a Basket Purchase and Straight-Line Depreciation

LO 9-2, 9-3

Bridge City Consulting bought a building and the land on which it is located for $182,000 cash. The land is estimated to represent 70 percent of the purchase price. The company paid $22,000 for building renovations before it was ready for use.

Required:

1. Explain how the renovation costs should be accounted for.
2. Give the journal entry to record all expenditures. Assume that all transactions were for cash and they occurred at the start of the year.
3. Compute straight-line depreciation on the building at the end of one year, assuming an estimated 12-year useful life and a $4,600 estimated residual value.
4. What should be the book value of the land and building at the end of year 2?

E9-3 Determining Financial Statement Effects of an Asset Acquisition and Straight-Line Depreciation

LO 9-2, 9-3

O'Connor Company ordered a machine on January 1, 2012, at a purchase price of $40,000. On the date of delivery, January 2, 2012, the company paid $10,000 on the machine and signed a long-term note payable for the balance. On January 3, 2012, it paid $350 for freight on the machine. On January 5, O'Connor paid installation costs relating to the machine amounting to $2,400. On December 31, 2012 (the end of the accounting period), O'Connor recorded depreciation on the machine using the straight-line method with an estimated useful life of 10 years and an estimated residual value of $4,750.

Required:

1. Indicate the effects (accounts, amounts, and + or −) of each transaction (on January 1, 2, 3, and 5) on the accounting equation. Use the following schedule:

Date	Assets	=	Liabilities	+	Stockholders' Equity

2. Compute the acquisition cost of the machine.
3. Compute the depreciation expense to be reported for 2012.
4. What should be the book value of the machine at the end of 2013?

LO 9-2, 9-3   **E9-4 Recording Straight-Line Depreciation and Repairs**

Wiater Company operates a small manufacturing facility. On January 1, 2013, an asset account for the company showed the following balances:

Manufacturing equipment	$160,000
Accumulated depreciation through 2012	100,000

During the first week of January 2013, the following expenditures were incurred for repairs and maintenance:

Routine maintenance and repairs on the equipment	$ 1,850
Major overhaul of the equipment that improved efficiency	24,000

The equipment is being depreciated on a straight-line basis over an estimated life of 15 years with a $10,000 estimated residual value. The annual accounting period ends on December 31.

Required:

Indicate the effects (accounts, amounts, and + or −) of the following two items on the accounting equation, using the headings shown below.

1. The adjustment for depreciation made at the end of 2012.
2. The two expenditures for repairs and maintenance during January 2013.

Item	Assets	=	Liabilities	+	Stockholders' Equity

LO 9-2, 9-3   **E9-5 Determining Financial Statement Effects of Straight-Line Depreciation and Repairs**

Refer to the information in E9-4.

Required:

1. Give the adjusting journal entry that would have been made at the end of 2012 for depreciation on the manufacturing equipment.
2. Starting at the beginning of 2013, what is the remaining estimated life?
3. Give the journal entries to record the two expenditures for repairs and maintenance during 2013.

LO 9-3   **E9-6 Computing Depreciation under Alternative Methods**

Solar Innovations Corporation bought a machine at the beginning of the year at a cost of $22,000. The estimated useful life was five years, and the residual value was $2,000. Assume that the estimated productive life of the machine is 10,000 units. Expected annual production was: year 1, 2,000 units; year 2, 3,000 units; year 3, 2,000 units; year 4, 2,000 units; and year 5, 1,000 units.

Required:

1. Complete a depreciation schedule for each of the alternative methods. Round answers to the nearest dollar.
   a. Straight-line.
   b. Units-of-production.
   c. Double-declining-balance.

		Income Statement	Balance Sheet		
Year	Computation	Depreciation Expense	Cost	Accumulated Depreciation	Book Value
At acquisition					
1					

2. Which method will result in the highest net income in year 2? Does this higher net income mean the machine was used more efficiently under this depreciation method?

E9-7 Computing Depreciation under Alternative Methods

Sonic Corporation purchased and installed electronic payment equipment at its drive-in restaurants in San Marcos, TX, at a cost of $27,000. The equipment has an estimated residual value of $1,500. The equipment is expected to process 255,000 payments over its three-year useful life. Per year, expected payment transactions are 61,200, year 1; 140,250, year 2; and 53,550, year 3.

LO 9-3

Sonic Corporation

Required:

Complete a depreciation schedule for each of the alternative methods.

1. Straight-line.
2. Units-of-production.
3. Double-declining-balance.

| | | Income Statement | Balance Sheet | | |
| | | Depreciation | | Accumulated | |
Year	Computation	Expense	Cost	Depreciation	Book Value
At acquisition					
1					

E9-8 Interpreting Management's Choice of Different Depreciation Methods for Tax and Financial Reporting

The annual report for FedEx Corporation includes the following information:

LO 9-3

FedEx Corporation

> For financial reporting purposes, we record depreciation and amortization of property and equipment on a straight-line basis over the asset's service life. For income tax purposes, depreciation is computed using accelerated methods.

Required:

Explain why FedEx uses different methods of depreciation for financial reporting and tax purposes.

E9-9 Inferring Asset Age from Straight-Line Depreciation

On January 1, 2013, the records of Tasty Treats Corporation (TTC) showed the following regarding production equipment:

LO 9-3

Equipment (estimated residual value, $4,000)	$16,000
Accumulated Depreciation (straight-line, one year)	2,000

Required:

Based on the data given, compute the estimated useful life of the equipment.

E9-10 Exploring Financial Statement Effects of Asset Impairment

Refer to E9-9.

LO 9-4

Required:

If TTC's management estimated that the equipment had future cash flows and a fair value of only $6,800 at December 31, 2013, how would this affect TTC's balance sheet and income statement? Explain.

E9-11 Demonstrating the Effect of Book Value on Reporting an Asset Disposal

FedEx Corporation is the world's leading express-distribution company. In addition to the world's largest fleet of all-cargo aircraft, the company has more than 56,700 ground vehicles that pick up and deliver packages. Assume that FedEx sold a delivery truck for $16,000. FedEx had originally purchased the truck for $28,000, and had recorded depreciation for three years.

LO 9-5

FedEx Corporation

Required:

1. Calculate the amount of gain or loss on disposal, assuming that Accumulated Depreciation was: (*a*) $12,000, (*b*) $10,000, and (*c*) $15,000.

2. Using the following structure, indicate the effects (accounts, amounts, and + or −) for the disposal of the truck, assuming that Accumulated Depreciation was: (a) $12,000, (b) $10,000, and (c) $15,000.

Assets	=	Liabilities	+	Stockholders' Equity

3. Based on the three preceding situations, explain how the amount of depreciation recorded up to the time of disposal affects the amount of gain or loss on disposal.

4. Prepare the journal entry to record the disposal of the truck, assuming that Accumulated Depreciation was: (a) $12,000, (b) $10,000, and (c) $15,000.

LO 9-6   **E9-12 Computing and Reporting the Acquisition and Amortization of Three Different Intangible Assets**

Bluestone Company had three intangible assets at the end of 2014 (end of the accounting year):

a. A patent purchased from Miller Co. on January 1, 2014, for a cash cost of $9,300. When purchased, the patent had an estimated life of fifteen years.

b. A trademark was registered with the federal government for $10,000. Management estimated that the trademark could be worth as much as $200,000 because it has an indefinite life.

c. Computer licensing rights were purchased on January 1, 2014, for $60,000. The rights are expected to have a five-year useful life to the company.

Required:

1. Compute the acquisition cost of each intangible asset.
2. Compute the amortization of each intangible for the year ended December 31, 2014.
3. Show how these assets and any related expenses should be reported on the balance sheet and income statement for 2014.

LO 9-4, 9-6   **E9-13 Recording the Purchase, Amortization, and Impairment of a Patent**

Nutek, Inc.   Nutek, Inc., holds a patent for the Full Service™ handi-plate, which the company described as "a patented plastic buffet plate that allows the user to hold both a plate and cup in one hand" and that "has a multitude of uses including social gatherings such as backyard barbecues, buffets, picnics, and parties of any kind." (No, we're not making this up.) Nutek also purchased a patent for $1,000,000 for "a specialty line of patented switch plate covers and outlet plate covers specifically designed to light up automatically when the power fails." Assume the switch plate patent was purchased January 1, 2013, and it is being amortized over a period of 10 years. Assume Nutek does not use an accumulated amortization account but instead charges amortization directly against the intangible asset account.

Required:

1. Describe the effects of the purchase and amortization of the switch plate patent on the 2013 balance sheet and income statement.
2. Give the journal entries to record the purchase and amortization of the switch plate patent in 2013.
3. After many months of unsuccessful attempts to manufacture the switch plate covers, Nutek determined the patent was significantly impaired and its book value on January 1, 2014, was written off. Describe the financial statement effects of accounting for the asset impairment and give the journal entry to record the impairment.

LO 9-7   **E9-14 Computing and Interpreting the Fixed Asset Turnover Ratio from a Financial Analyst's Perspective**

Apple Inc.   The following data were included in a recent Apple Inc. annual report (in millions):

	2007	2008	2009	2010	2011
Net revenue	$24,006	$32,479	$42,905	$65,225	$108,249
Net property, plant, and equipment	1,832	2,455	2,954	4,768	7,777

Required:

1. Compute Apple's fixed asset turnover ratio for 2008, 2009, 2010, and 2011. Round your answer to one decimal place.

2. Was Apple able to maintain its strong financial performance in recent years when the economy was faltering?

E9-15   Computing Depreciation and Book Value for Two Years Using Alternative Depreciation Methods and Interpreting the Impact on the Fixed Asset Turnover Ratio   LO 9-3, 9-7

Torge Company bought a machine for $65,000 cash. The estimated useful life was five years, and the estimated residual value was $5,000. Assume that the estimated useful life in productive units is 150,000. Units actually produced were 40,000 in year 1 and 45,000 in year 2.

Required:

1. Determine the appropriate amounts to complete the following schedule. Show computations.

	Depreciation Expense for		Book Value at the End of	
Method of Depreciation	Year 1	Year 2	Year 1	Year 2
Straight-line				
Units-of-production				
Double-declining-balance				

2. Which method would result in the lowest net income for year 1? For year 2?
3. Which method would result in the lowest fixed asset turnover ratio for year 1? Why?

E9-16   (Supplement 9A) Calculating and Reporting Depletion   LO 9-S1

Texas Oil Company (TOC) paid $3,000,000 for an oil reserve estimated to hold 50,000 barrels of oil. Oil production is expected to be 10,000 barrels in year 1, 30,000 barrels in year 2, and 10,000 barrels in year 3. TOC expects to begin selling barrels from its oil inventory in year 2.

Required:

Assuming these estimates are accurate, describe the amounts, financial statements, and classifications that would be used for the oil reserves and oil inventory at the end of year 1.

E9-17   (Supplement 9B) Determining Financial Statement Effects of a Change in Estimate   LO 9-S2

Refer to E9-4.

Required:

1. Indicate the effects (accounts, amounts, and + or −) of the 2013 adjustment for depreciation of the manufacturing equipment, assuming no change in the estimated life or residual value. Show computations.

Date	Assets	=	Liabilities	+	Stockholders' Equity

2. Give the adjusting entry that should be made at the end of 2013 for depreciation.

COACHED PROBLEMS

CP9-1   Computing Acquisition Cost and Recording Depreciation under Three Alternative Methods

Mc Graw Hill **connect** |ACCOUNTING   LO 9-2, 9-3

At the beginning of the year, Young Company bought three used machines from Vince, Inc. The machines immediately were overhauled, installed, and started operating. Because the machines were different, each was recorded separately in the accounts.

	Machine A	Machine B	Machine C
Amount paid for asset	$7,600	$25,600	$9,300
Installation costs	200	600	500
Renovation costs prior to use	1,500	1,200	1,000
Repairs after production began	400	350	325

By the end of the first year, each machine had been operating 7,000 hours.

Required:

1. Compute the cost of each machine. Explain the rationale for capitalizing or expensing the various costs.
2. Give the journal entry to record depreciation expense at the end of year 1, assuming the following:

	Estimates		
Machine	Life	Residual Value	Depreciation Method
A	5 years	$ 600	Straight-line
B	40,000 hours	1,000	Units-of-production
C	6 years	2,000	Double-declining-balance

TIP: Remember that the formula for double-declining-balance uses cost minus accumulated depreciation (not residual value).

LO 9-5 **CP9-2 Recording and Interpreting the Disposal of Long-Lived Assets**

During 2014, Martinez Company disposed of two different assets. On January 1, 2014, prior to their disposal, the accounts reflected the following:

Asset	Original Cost	Residual Value	Estimated Life	Accumulated Depreciation (straight line)
Machine A	$76,200	$4,200	15 years	$62,400 (13 years)
Machine B	20,000	2,000	8 years	13,500 (6 years)

The machines were disposed of in the following ways:

a. Machine A: Sold on January 2, 2014, for $20,000 cash.
b. Machine B: On January 2, 2014, this machine suffered irreparable damage from an accident and was removed immediately by a salvage company at no cost.

Required:

1. Give the journal entries related to the disposal of each machine at the beginning of 2014.
   TIP: When no cash is received on disposal, the loss on disposal will equal the book value of the asset at the time of disposal.
2. Explain the accounting rationale for the way that you recorded each disposal.

LO 9-2, 9-3, 9-6 **CP9-3 Analyzing and Recording Long-Lived Asset Transactions with Partial-Year Depreciation**

Palmer Cook Productions manages and operates two rock bands. The company entered into the following transactions during a recent year.

January 2	Purchased a tour bus for $80,000 by paying $20,000 cash and signing a $60,000 note due in two years.
January 8	The bus was painted with the logos of the two bands at a cost of $350, on account.
January 30	Wrote a check for the amount owed on account for the work completed on January 8.

February 1   Purchased new speakers and amplifiers and wrote a check for the full $12,000 cost.

February 8   Paid $250 cash to tune up the tour bus.

March   1   Paid $20,000 cash and signed a $190,000 five-year note to purchase a small office building and land. An appraisal indicated that the building and land contributed equally to the total price.

March   31   Paid $90,000 cash to acquire the goodwill and certain tangible assets of Kris' Myth, Inc. The fair values of the tangible assets acquired were: $20,000 for band equipment and $60,000 for recording equipment.

Required:

1. Analyze the accounting equation effects and record journal entries for each of the transactions.
    TIP: Goodwill is recorded as the excess of the purchase price over the fair value of individual assets.

2. For the tangible and intangible assets acquired in the preceding transactions, determine the amount of depreciation and amortization that Palmer Cook Productions should report for the quarter ended March 31. For convenience, the equipment and vehicle are depreciated the same way, using the straight-line method with a useful life of five years and no residual value. The building is depreciated using the double-declining-balance method, with a 10-year useful life and residual value of $20,000.
    TIP: Calculate depreciation from the acquisition date to the end of the quarter.

3. Prepare a journal entry to record the depreciation calculated in requirement 3.

4. What advice would you offer the company in anticipation of switching to IFRS in the future?
    TIP: Consider whether the vehicle and different types of equipment should be grouped together.

GROUP A PROBLEMS

PA9-1 Computing Acquisition Cost and Recording Depreciation under Three Alternative Methods |ACCOUNTING   LO 9-2, 9-3

At the beginning of the year, Grillo Industries bought three used machines from Freeman Incorporated. The machines immediately were overhauled, installed, and started operating. Because the machines were different, each was recorded separately in the accounts.

	Machine A	Machine B	Machine C
Cost of the asset	$9,000	$38,200	$22,000
Installation costs	800	2,100	1,200
Renovation costs prior to use	600	1,700	2,200
Repairs after production began	500	600	700

By the end of the first year, each machine had been operating 8,000 hours.

Required:

1. Compute the cost of each machine. Explain the rationale for capitalizing or expensing the various costs.

2. Give the journal entry to record depreciation expense at the end of year 1, assuming the following:

	Estimates		
Machine	Life	Residual Value	Depreciation Method
A	4 years	$1,000	Straight-line
B	30,000 hours	4,500	Units-of-production
C	10 years	1,400	Double-declining-balance

LO 9-5   **PA9-2 Recording and Interpreting the Disposal of Long-Lived Assets**

During 2013, Ly Company disposed of two different assets. On January 1, 2013, prior to their disposal, the accounts reflected the following:

Asset	Original Cost	Residual Value	Estimated Life	Accumulated Depreciation (straight line)
Machine A	$30,000	$3,000	5 years	$ 21,600 (4 years)
Machine B	59,200	3,200	14 years	$44,000 (11 years)

The machines were disposed of in the following ways:

a.   Machine A: Sold on January 1, 2013, for $9,000 cash.

b.   Machine B: On January 1, 2013, this machine suffered irreparable damage from an accident and was removed immediately by a salvage company at no cost.

Required:

1.   Give the journal entries related to the disposal of each machine at the beginning of 2013.

2.   Explain the accounting rationale for the way that you recorded each disposal.

LO 9-2, 9-3, 9-6   **PA9-3 Analyzing and Recording Long-Lived Asset Transactions with Partial-Year Depreciation**

Precision Construction entered into the following transactions during a recent year.

January 2	Purchased a bulldozer for $250,000 by paying $20,000 cash and signing a $230,000 note due in five years.
January 3	Replaced the steel tracks on the bulldozer at a cost of $20,000, purchased on account.
January 30	Wrote a check for the amount owed on account for the work completed on January 3.
February 1	Replaced the seat on the bulldozer and wrote a check for the full $800 cost.
March 1	Paid $3,600 cash for the rights to use computer software for a two-year period.

Required:

1.   Analyze the accounting equation effects and record journal entries for each of the transactions.

2.   For the tangible and intangible assets acquired in the preceding transactions, determine the amount of depreciation and amortization that Precision Construction should report for the quarter ended March 31. The equipment is depreciated using the double-declining-balance method with a useful life of five years and $40,000 residual value.

3.   Prepare a journal entry to record the depreciation calculated in requirement 2.

4.   What advice would you offer the company in anticipation of switching to IFRS in the future?

LO 9-1, 9-2, 9-3, 9-4, 9-5, 9-6

PA9-4 Recording Transactions and Adjustments for Tangible and Intangible Assets

The following transactions and adjusting entries were completed by a paper-packaging company called Gravure Graphics International. The company uses straight-line depreciation for trucks and other vehicles, double-declining-balance depreciation for buildings, and straight-line amortization for patents.

January 2, 2013	Paid $95,000 cash to purchase storage shed components.
January 3, 2013	Paid $5,000 cash to have the storage shed erected. The storage shed has an estimated life of 10 years, and a residual value of $10,000.
April 1, 2013	Paid $38,000 cash to purchase a pickup truck for use in the business. The truck has an estimated useful life of five years, and a residual value of $8,000.
May 13, 2013	Paid $250 cash for repairs to the pickup truck.
July 1, 2013	Paid $20,000 cash to purchase patent rights on a new paper bag manufacturing process. The patent is estimated to have a remaining useful life of five years.

December 31, 2013	Recorded depreciation and amortization on the pickup truck, storage shed, and patent.
June 30, 2014	Sold the pickup truck for $33,000 cash. (Record the depreciation on the truck prior to recording its disposal.)
December 31, 2014	Recorded depreciation on the storage shed. Determined that the patent was impaired and wrote off its remaining book value (i.e., wrote down the book value to zero).

Required:

Give the journal entries required on each of the above dates.

GROUP B PROBLEMS

PB9-1 Computing Acquisition Cost and Recording Depreciation under Three Alternative Methods | ACCOUNTING   LO 9-2, 9-3

At the beginning of the year, Oakmont Company bought three used machines from American Manufacturing, Inc. The machines immediately were overhauled, installed, and started operating. Because the machines were different, each was recorded separately in the accounts.

	Machine A	Machine B	Machine C
Amount paid for asset	$19,600	$10,100	$9,800
Installation costs	300	500	200
Renovation costs prior to use	100	300	600
Repairs after production began	220	900	480

By the end of the first year, each machine had been operating 4,000 hours.

Required:

1. Compute the cost of each machine. Explain the rationale for capitalizing or expensing the various costs.
2. Give the journal entry to record depreciation expense at the end of year 1, assuming the following:

Machine	Estimates — Life	Residual Value	Depreciation Method
A	7 years	$1,100	Straight-line
B	40,000 hours	900	Units-of-production
C	4 years	2,000	Double-declining-balance

PB9-2 Recording and Interpreting the Disposal of Long-Lived Assets   LO 9-5

During 2013, Rayon Corporation disposed of two different assets. On January 1, 2013, prior to their disposal, the accounts reflected the following:

Asset	Original Cost	Residual Value	Estimated Life	Accumulated Depreciation (straight line)
Machine A	$60,000	$11,000	7 years	$28,000 (4 years)
Machine B	14,200	1,925	5 years	7,365 (3 years)

The machines were disposed of in the following ways:

a. Machine A: Sold on January 2, 2013, for $33,500 cash.
b. Machine B: On January 2, 2013, this machine suffered irreparable damage from an accident and was removed immediately by a salvage company at no cost.

Required:

1. Give the journal entries related to the disposal of each machine at the beginning of 2013.
2. Explain the accounting rationale for the way that you recorded each disposal.

LO 9-2, 9-3, 9-6   **PB9-3**   **Analyzing and Recording Long-Lived Asset Transactions with Partial-Year Depreciation**

Randy's Restaurant Company (RRC) entered into the following transactions during a recent year.

April 1	Purchased a new food locker for $5,000 by paying $1,000 cash and signing a $4,000 note due in six months.
April 2	Installed an air conditioning system in the food locker at a cost of $3,000, purchased on account.
April 30	Wrote a check for the amount owed on account for the work completed on April 2.
May 1	A local carpentry company repaired the restaurant's front door, for which RRC wrote a check for the full $120 cost.
June 1	Paid $9,120 cash for the rights to use the name and store concept created by a different restaurant that has been successful in the region. For the next four years, RRC will operate under the Mullet Restaurant name, with the slogan "business customers in the front, and partiers in the back."

Required:

1. Analyze the accounting equation effects and record journal entries for each of the transactions.
2. For the tangible and intangible assets acquired in the preceding transactions, determine the amount of depreciation and amortization that Randy's Restaurant Company should report for the quarter ended June 30. For convenience, the food locker and air-conditioning system are depreciated as a group using the straight-line method with a useful life of five years and no residual value.
3. Prepare a journal entry to record the depreciation calculated in requirement 2.
4. What advice would you offer the company in anticipation of switching to IFRS in the future?

LO 9-1, 9-2, 9-3, 9-4, 9-5, 9-6   **PB9-4**   **Recording Transactions and Adjustments for Tangible and Intangible Assets**

The following transactions and adjusting entries were completed by a local delivery company called Fast Delivery. The company uses straight-line depreciation for delivery vehicles, double-declining-balance depreciation for buildings, and straight-line amortization for franchise rights.

January 2, 2014	Paid $175,000 cash to purchase a small warehouse building near the airport. The building has an estimated life of 20 years, and a residual value of $15,000.
July 1, 2014	Paid $40,000 cash to purchase a delivery van. The van has an estimated useful life of five years, and a residual value of $8,000.
October 2, 2014	Paid $500 cash to paint a small office in the warehouse building.
October 13, 2014	Paid $150 cash to get the oil changed in the delivery van.
December 1, 2014	Paid $90,000 cash to UPS to begin operating Fast Delivery business as a franchise using the name The UPS Store. This franchise right expires in five years.
December 31, 2014	Recorded depreciation and amortization on the delivery van, warehouse building, and franchise right.
June 30, 2015	Sold the warehouse building for $140,000 cash. (Record the depreciation on the building prior to recording its disposal.)
December 31, 2015	Recorded depreciation on the delivery van and amortization on the franchise right. Determined that the franchise right was not impaired in value.

Required:

Give the journal entries required on each of the above dates.

COMPREHENSIVE PROBLEM

C9-1 Accounting for Operating Activities (Including Depreciation) and Preparing Financial Statements (Chapters 3, 4, 8, and 9)

|ACCOUNTING   LO 3-3, 4-2, 8-2, 9-2, 9-3

Grid Iron Prep Inc. (GIPI) is a service business incorporated in January 2013 to provide personal training for athletes aspiring to play college football. The following transactions occurred during the year ended December 31, 2013.

a. GIPI issued stock in exchange for $100,000 cash.
b. GIPI purchased a gymnasium building and gym equipment at the beginning of the year for $50,000, 80% of which related to the gymnasium and 20% to the equipment.
c. GIPI paid $260 cash to have the gym equipment refurbished before it could be used.
d. GIPI collected $36,000 cash in training fees during the year, of which $2,000 were customer deposits to be earned in 2014.
e. GIPI paid $23,000 of wages and $7,000 in utilities.
f. GIPI provided $4,000 in training during the final month of the year and expected collection in 2014.
g. GIPI will depreciate the gymnasium building using the straight-line method over 20 years with a residual value of $2,000. Gym equipment will be depreciated using the double-declining method, with an estimated residual value of $2,250 at the end of its four-year useful life.
h. GIPI received a bill for $350 of advertising done during December. The bill has not been paid or recorded.
i. GIPI will record an estimated 3 percent of its Accounts Receivable as not collectible.
j. GIPI's income tax rate is 30%. Assume depreciation for tax is the same amount as depreciation for financial reporting purposes.

Required:

1. Prepare journal entries to record the transactions and adjustments listed in (a)–(j).

2. Prepare GIPI's annual income statement, statement of retained earnings, and classified balance sheet.

SKILLS DEVELOPMENT CASES

S9-1 Finding Financial Information

|ACCOUNTING   LO 9-2, 9-3, 9-6, 9-7

Refer to the financial statements of The Home Depot in Appendix A at the end of this book, or download the annual report from the *Cases* section of the text's Web site at www.mhhe.com/phillips4e.

Required:

1. What is the amount of Accumulated Depreciation and Amortization at January 30, 2011? What percentage is this of the total cost of property and equipment?
    a. $13,325; 34.7%   c. $1,616; 4.0%
    b. $13,325; 33.2%   d. $1,616; 4.2%

2. What amount of Depreciation and Amortization Expense was reported for the year ended January 30, 2011? What percentage of net sales is it?
    a. $13,325; 19.6%   c. $1,616; 2.4%
    b. $13,325; 20.1%   d. $1,616; 10.2%

3. What is the fixed asset turnover ratio for the year ended January 30, 2011?
    a. 2.71   c. 2.59
    b. 1.77   d. 2.69

S9-2 Comparing Financial Information

LO 9-2, 9-3, 9-6, 9-7, 9-8

Refer to the financial statements of The Home Depot in Appendix A and Lowe's in Appendix B at the end of this book, or download the annual reports from the *Cases* section of the text's Web site at www.mhhe.com/phillips4e.

Required:

1. What method of depreciation does Lowe's use?

Lowe's

2. Refer to Note 4 in Lowe's annual report. What amount of Accumulated Depreciation did Lowe's report at January 28, 2011? What percentage is this of the total cost of property and equipment? Is this a larger (or smaller) percentage of the total cost of property and equipment than for The Home Depot (in S9-1)? What does it suggest to you about the length of time the assets have been depreciated?

3. Lowe's estimated useful life of buildings is shorter than that estimated by The Home Depot. How will this affect the fixed asset turnover ratios of the two companies?

4. What amount of Depreciation Expense was reported on Lowe's income statement for the year ended January 28, 2011? What percentage of net sales is it? Compare this percentage to that of The Home Depot and describe what this implies about the two companies' operations.

5. What is Lowe's fixed asset turnover ratio for the current year? Compare this ratio to that of The Home Depot and describe what it implies about the operations of the two companies.

LO 9-1, 9-3, 9-6, 9-7   **S9-3 Internet-Based Team Research: Examining an Annual Report**

As a team, select an industry to analyze. Using your Web browser, each team member should access the annual report or 10-K for one publicly traded company in the industry, with each member selecting a different company. (See S1-3 in Chapter 1 for a description of possible resources for these tasks.)

Required:

1. On an individual basis, each team member should write a short report that incorporates the following:
   a. Describe the depreciation methods used.
   b. Compute the percentage of fixed asset cost that has been depreciated. What does this imply about the length of time the assets have been depreciated?
   c. Compute the fixed asset turnover ratios for the current and prior years. What does this tell you about the efficiency of the company's asset use?
   d. Describe the kinds of intangible assets, if any, that the company reports on the balance sheet.
2. Then, as a team, write a short report comparing and contrasting your companies using these attributes. Discuss any patterns across the companies that you as a team observe. Provide potential explanations for any differences discovered.

LO 9-2, 9-7   **S9-4 Ethical Decision Making: A Real-Life Example**

WorldCom
Verizon

This case is based on a cost capitalization fraud at WorldCom (now part of Verizon). The case is available online at www.mhhe.com/phillips4e. To complete this case, you will calculate and interpret the three ratios introduced in this chapter.

LO 9-3   **S9-5 Ethical Decision Making: A Mini-Case**

Assume you are one of three members of the accounting staff working for a small, private company. At the beginning of this year, the company expanded into a new industry by acquiring equipment that will be used to make several new lines of products. The owner and general manager of the company has indicated that, as one of the conditions for providing financing for the new equipment, the company's bank will receive a copy of the company's annual financial statements. Another condition of the loan is that the company's total assets cannot fall below $250,000. Violation of this condition gives the bank the option to demand immediate repayment of the loan. Before making the adjustment for this year's depreciation, the company's total assets are reported at $255,000. The owner has asked you to take a look at the facts regarding the new equipment and "work with the numbers to make sure everything stays onside with the bank."

A depreciation method has not yet been adopted for the new equipment. Equipment used in other parts of the company is depreciated using the double-declining-balance method. The cost of the new equipment was $35,000 and the manager estimates it will be worth "at least $7,000" at the end of its four-year useful life. Because the products made with the new equipment are only beginning to catch on with consumers, the company used the equipment to produce just 4,000 units this year. It is expected that, over all four years of its useful life, the new equipment will make a total of 28,000 units.

Required:

1. Calculate the depreciation that would be reported this year under each of the three methods shown in this chapter. Which of the methods would meet the owner's objective?

2. Evaluate whether it is ethical to recommend that the company use the method identified in requirement 1. What two parties are most directly affected by this recommendation? How would each party benefit from or be harmed by the recommendation? Does the recommendation violate any laws or applicable rules? Are there any other factors that you would consider before making a recommendation?

S9-6 Critical Thinking: Analyzing the Effects of Depreciation Policies on Income

LO 9-3, 9-5, 9-8

As an aspiring financial analyst, you have applied to a major Wall Street firm for a summer job. To screen potential applicants, the firm provides you a short case study and asks you to evaluate the financial success of two hypothetical companies that started operations on January 1, 2012. Both companies operate in the same industry, use very similar assets, and have very similar customer bases. Among the additional information provided about the companies are the following comparative income statements.

	Fast Corporation		Slow Corporation	
	2012	2013	2012	2013
Net Sales	$60,000	$60,000	$60,000	$60,000
Cost of Goods Sold	20,000	20,000	20,000	20,000
Gross Profit	40,000	40,000	40,000	40,000
Selling, General, and Administrative Expenses	19,000	19,000	19,000	19,000
Depreciation Expense	10,667	3,555	5,000	5,000
Loss (Gain) on Disposal	—	(2,222)	—	2,000
Income from Operations	$10,333	$19,667	$16,000	$14,000

Required:

Prepare an analysis of the two companies with the goal of determining which company is better managed. If you could request two additional pieces of information from these companies' financial statements, describe specifically what they would be and explain how they would help you to make a decision.

S9-7 Preparing Depreciation Schedules for Straight-Line and Double-Declining-Balance

LO 9-3

To make some extra money, you've started preparing templates of business forms and schedules for others to download from the Internet (for a small fee). After relevant information is entered into each template, it automatically performs calculations using formulas you have entered into the template. For the depreciation template, you decide to produce two worksheets—one that calculates depreciation and book value under the straight-line method and another that calculates these amounts using the double-declining-balance method. The templates perform straightforward calculations of depreciation and book value, when given the cost of an asset, its estimated useful life, and its estimated residual value. These particular templates won't handle disposals or changes in estimates—you plan to create a deluxe version for those functions. To illustrate that your templates actually work, you enter the information used to produce the depreciation schedules shown in Exhibit 9.6, with Cedar Fair and Six Flags as examples.

Although you're confident you can use appropriate formulas in the spreadsheet to create a template for the straight-line method, you're a little uncertain about how to make the double-declining-balance method work. As usual, you e-mail your friend Owen for advice. Here's what he said:

From:	Owentheaccountant@yahoo.com
To:	Helpme@hotmail.com
Cc:	
Subject:	Excel Help

I wish I'd thought of charging money for showing how to do ordinary accounting activities. You'd have made me rich by now. Here's how to set up your worksheets. Begin by creating an "input values" section. This section will allow someone to enter the asset cost, residual value, and estimated life in an area removed from the actual depreciation schedule. You don't want someone accidentally entering amounts over formulas that you've entered into the schedule.

The cells from the input values section will be referenced by other cells in the depreciation schedule. You will want to enter formulas in the cells for the first year row, and then copy and paste them to rows for the other years. When doing this, you will need to use what is called an "absolute reference," which means that the cell reference does not change when one row is copied and pasted to a different row. Unlike an ordinary cell reference that has a format of A1, an absolute reference has the format of A1, which prevents the spreadsheet from changing either the column (A) or row (1) when copying the cell to other cells. You may find this useful when preparing both the straight-line and double-declining-balance schedules.

To create the depreciation schedules, use five columns labeled: (1) year, (2) beginning of year accumulated depreciation, (3) depreciation, (4) end of year accumulated depreciation, and (5) end of year book value.

The double-declining-balance template will be the trickiest to create because you need to be concerned that the book value is not depreciated below the residual value in the last year of the asset's life. To force the template to automatically watch for this, you will need to use the IF function. I have included a screenshot of a template I created, using the IF function to properly calculate depreciation for all years of the asset's life. Notice the formula shown in the formula bar at the top.

Required:

Create the spreadsheet templates to calculate depreciation and book value using the straight-line and double-declining-balance methods. Demonstrate that the template works by reproducing the schedules in Exhibit 9.6.

TIP: To switch between displaying cell formulas and their values, press CTRL and ~ (tilde) at the same time. Also, use Excel's help feature to obtain further information about the IF function.

CONTINUING CASES

LO 9-3, 9-5   **CC9-1 Accounting for the Use and Disposal of Long-Lived Assets**

Nicole's Getaway Spa (NGS) purchased a hydrotherapy tub system to add to the wellness programs at NGS. The machine was purchased at the beginning of 2014 at a cost of $7,000.

The estimated useful life was five years, and the residual value was $500. Assume that the estimated productive life of the machine is 13,000 hours. Expected annual production was: year 1, 3,100 hours; year 2, 2,500 hours; year 3, 3,400 hours; year 4, 2,200 hours and year 5, 1,800 hours.

Required:

1. Complete a depreciation schedule for each of the alternative methods.
   a. Straight-line.
   b. Units-of-production.
   c. Double-declining-balance.

2. Assume NGS sold the hydrotherapy tub system for $2,100 at the end of 2016. Prepare the journal entry to account for the disposal of this asset under the three different methods.

3. The following amounts were forecast for the year ended December 31, 2016: Sales Revenues $42,000; Cost of Goods Sold $33,000; Other Operating Expenses $4,000; and Interest Expense $800. Create an income statement for the year ended December 31, 2016 for each of the different depreciation methods, ending at Income before Income Tax Expense. (Don't forget to include a loss or gain on disposal for each method.)

CC9-2 Wiki Art Gallery (WAG)

LO 9-3, 9-4

Access the Wiki Art Gallery (WAG) instructional case in Connect, and read the case in sufficient depth to answer the following questions.

1. What method for depreciation does Wiki Art Gallery (WAG) use and is this method generally accepted?
   a. WAG uses the capitalization method, which is in accordance with GAAP.
   b. WAG uses the straight-line method, which is in accordance with GAAP.
   c. WAG uses the declining-balance method, which is in accordance with GAAP.
   d. WAG uses the units-of-production method, which is in accordance with GAAP.

2. Calculate the amount of 2011 depreciation expense that WAG recorded on the old computer equipment and on the new computer equipment.
   a. WAG recorded $206 on the old equipment and $180 on the new equipment.
   b. WAG recorded $825 on the old equipment and $180 on the new equipment.
   c. WAG recorded $825 on the old equipment and $386 on the new equipment.
   d. Cannot be determined with the information provided.

3. Which aspect(s) of WAG's accounting for Web site development costs in 2011 may be inappropriate?
   a. WAG capitalized $9,000 despite $7,000 being a regularly recurring cost.
   b. WAG began amortizing only after the Web site development costs were paid.
   c. The six-year useful life overstates the likely period of benefit.
   d. All of the above.

4. By what amount would WAG's net income change if WAG were to adopt a two-year useful life for the new computer equipment, appropriately capitalize the Web development cost, and amortize the capitalized Web costs over a three-year life?
   a. WAG's net income would decrease by $928.
   b. WAG's net income would decrease by $1,233.
   c. WAG's net income would decrease by $1,867.
   d. WAG's net income would decrease by $7,928.

10 Liabilities

YOUR LEARNING OBJECTIVES

Understand the business

LO 10-1 Explain the role of liabilities in financing a business.

Study the accounting methods

LO 10-2 Explain how to account for common types of current liabilities.

LO 10-3 Analyze and record bond liability transactions.

LO 10-4 Describe how to account for contingent liabilities.

Evaluate the results

LO 10-5 Calculate and interpret the quick ratio and the times interest earned ratio.

Review the chapter

Supplemental material

LO 10-S1 Use straight-line bond amortization.

LO 10-S2 Use effective-interest bond amortization.

LO 10-S3 Use simplified effective-interest bond amortization.

THAT WAS THEN

Previous chapters focused on items related to the assets section of the balance sheet.

FOCUS COMPANY: General Mills

GENERAL MILLS

They've turned in the reports, and they're just waiting to hear their letter grade. They're expecting an A and would be devastated if it's a B. Sounds like some high-achieving students, right? It could be. But it's actually the Jolly Green Giant, Lucky the Leprechaun, the Pillsbury Doughboy, and their corporate bosses at General Mills. That's right. This magically delicious company and all its characters receive a letter grade just like you and your friends. Their grading process differs a bit from yours, because their grade is assigned by credit rating agencies like Standard & Poor's, Fitch, and Moody's, indicating the company's ability to pay its liabilities on a timely basis. Another difference is that their grades can range from AAA to D. The AAA rating is given to companies in rock-solid financial condition, and the D goes to those likely to pay less than half of what they owe. In general, anything above BB is considered a good to high-quality credit rating, which is what General Mills typically earns. Anything below BB is called "junk."

In this chapter, you will learn about the accounting procedures and financial ratios used to report and interpret liabilities, and how they influence credit ratings. Although we focus on corporate reporting and analyses, this chapter also can help you to understand the kind of information others use to evaluate your own personal credit rating.

www.generalmills.com

THIS IS NOW

This chapter focuses on items related to the liabilities section of the balance sheet.

Understand the business	Study the accounting methods	Evaluate the results	Review the chapter
• The role of liabilities	• Measuring liabilities • Current liabilities • Long-term liabilities • Contingent liabilities	• Quick ratio • Times interest earned ratio	• Demonstration cases • Chapter summary • Key terms • Homework helper • Practice material

Understand the Business

Learning Objective 10-1
Explain the role of liabilities in financing a business.

THE ROLE OF LIABILITIES

Liabilities play a significant role in financing most business activities. Liabilities are created when a company buys goods and services on credit, obtains short-term loans to cover gaps in cash flows, and issues long-term debt to obtain money for expanding into new regions and markets. The importance of liabilities became most apparent during the financial crisis of 2008–2009. Soon after banks restricted their lending activities and suppliers tightened their credit terms, companies began to fail. Circuit City, for example, filed for bankruptcy protection just one week after its suppliers required the company to pay cash on delivery (C.O.D.).

General Mills survived the financial crisis because it was able to pay suppliers on time and its BBB+ credit rating helped it obtain short-term financing as needed. To provide long-term financial stability, the company also arranged debt financing that will not come due until the year 2040. With these critical sources of financing in place, the company has been able to ride out the rough economic times.

To help financial statement users know when liabilities must be repaid, companies prepare a classified balance sheet, as shown in Exhibit 10.1. In Chapter 2, you learned that a classified balance sheet reports current liabilities separate from other liabilities. Technically, **current liabilities** are defined as short-term obligations that will be paid with current assets within the company's current operating cycle or within one year of the balance sheet date, whichever is longer. Practically, this definition can be simplified as liabilities that are due within one year (because most companies have operating cycles that are shorter than a year). This means that, as shown in Exhibit 10.1, General Mills will have to pay over $3.6 billion in the year following its 2011 fiscal year. An additional $8.4 billion will need to be paid in the longer term. Although these long-term obligations rarely get a separate subheading of their own, people often refer to them as noncurrent or long-term liabilities.

YOU SHOULD KNOW

Current liabilities: Short-term obligations that will be paid with current assets within the current operating cycle or one year, whichever is longer.

EXHIBIT 10.1	Excerpt from General Mills's Balance Sheet

(in millions)	2011	2010
Liabilities		
Current Liabilities		
Accounts Payable	$ 995	$ 850
Accrued Liabilities (see Exhibit 10.2)	1,322	1,762
Notes Payable	311	1,050
Current Portion of Long-term Debt	1,031	107
Total Current Liabilities	3,659	3,769
Long-term Debt	5,543	5,268
Deferred Income Taxes	1,127	875
Other Liabilities	1,733	2,119
Total Liabilities	12,062	12,031

Study the Accounting Methods

MEASURING LIABILITIES

As Exhibit 10.1 illustrates, General Mills owed various types of liabilities at the end of its 2011 fiscal year. In this section, we will describe each of these liabilities and the methods used to account for them. In general, the amount reported for each liability is the result of three factors:

> **Learning Objective 10-2**
> Explain how to account for common types of current liabilities.

1. **The initial amount of the liability.** Initially, the company records each liability at its cash equivalent, which is the amount of cash a creditor would accept to settle the liability immediately after a transaction or event creates the liability.

2. **Additional amounts owed to the creditor.** The company increases liabilities whenever additional obligations arise, by purchasing goods and services or incurring interest charges over time.

3. **Payments or services provided to the creditor.** The company decreases liabilities whenever the company makes a payment or provides services to the creditor.

Notice that a liability is first recorded at a cash-equivalent amount, which excludes interest charges. **Interest arises only when time passes, so no interest is recorded on the day the company purchases an item on account or the day the company receives a loan.** This practice makes sense because if you borrowed $10 from a friend and paid it back a split-second later, you wouldn't have to pay interest.

CURRENT LIABILITIES

Let's look more closely at each current liability listed in Exhibit 10.1.

Accounts Payable

You've used this account in previous chapters, so we'll keep this discussion short. Accounts Payable is increased (credited) when a company receives goods or services on credit, and it is decreased (debited) when the company pays on its account. Accounts Payable is interest free unless it becomes overdue.

Accrued Liabilities

Chapter 4 showed how to use an adjusting journal entry at the end of the accounting period to record increases in both Wages Expense (debit) and Wages Payable (credit) when a company had incurred but not yet paid that period's wages. Similar adjustments

EXHIBIT 10.2 | Accrued Liabilities Note (Excerpt)

GENERAL MILLS

(in millions)	2011
Accrued Advertising	$ 463
Accrued Payroll	303
Accrued Taxes	80
Accrued Interest	114
Other	362
Total Accrued Liabilities	$1,322

YOU SHOULD KNOW

Accrued liabilities: Liabilities for expenses that have been incurred but not paid at the end of the accounting period.

were made for interest incurred but not paid, and income taxes incurred but not paid. Because these adjustments are called *accruals*, the liabilities (Wages Payable, Interest Payable, etc.) are generally referred to as *accrued liabilities*. **Accrued liabilities** relate to various unpaid expenses, including advertising, electricity, corporate income tax, interest, payroll tax, and warranties. General Mills itemizes its $1.3 billion of Accrued Liabilities in a note to its financial statements, similar to Exhibit 10.2.

Accrued Payroll In addition to Wages Payable, companies record liabilities for other aspects of payroll. Two significant payroll liabilities relate to payroll deductions and employer payroll taxes.

Payroll Deductions Payroll deductions are amounts subtracted from employees' gross earnings to determine their net pay. **Gross earnings** are computed by multiplying the time worked by the pay rate promised by the employer (40 hours × $15 per hour = $600 gross earnings). From these gross earnings, certain **payroll deductions** are subtracted, for items such as income tax, FICA tax, and charitable donations. The tear-away portion of the paycheck shown in Exhibit 10.3 illustrates payroll deductions totaling $116.80. **Net pay** equals gross earnings less payroll deductions ($483.20 = $600.00 − $116.80).

You might think your employer keeps the deductions from your gross earnings, but that's not true. Your employer is obligated to remit those deductions to another organization or government agency on your behalf. As Exhibit 10.3 shows, **payroll deductions create current liabilities for your employer.**

Payroll deductions are either required by law or voluntarily requested by employees. The law requires that employers deduct federal income tax (and possibly state, county, and city income tax) from each employee's gross earnings. The law also requires, through the Federal Insurance Contributions Act, that each employee support Medicare and Social Security

EXHIBIT 10.3 | Accounting for Gross Earnings, Payroll Deductions, and Net Pay

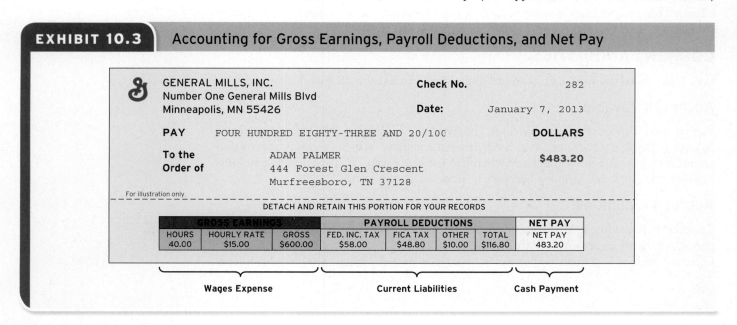

through employee payroll deductions called **FICA taxes.** In 2012, employers were required to deduct 1.45 percent from each employee's earnings for Medicare and 6.2 percent (on earnings up to $110,100) for Social Security. Employers use these same methods to account for any other payroll deductions (including voluntary deductions for charitable donations, parking, union dues, retirement savings, etc.). The employer classifies payroll deductions as *current* liabilities because they must be paid no more than one month after the payroll date.

To illustrate how to record these items, let's assume (for simplicity) that General Mills has 1,000 workers just like the employee in Exhibit 10.3. The accounting equation effects and journal entry for these 1,000 workers would be as follows:

1 Analyze

Assets	=	Liabilities		+	Stockholders' Equity	
Cash −483,200		Withheld Income Tax Payable	+58,000		Wages Expense (+E)	−600,000
		FICA Payable	+48,800			
		United Way Payable	+10,000			

2 Record

dr Wages Expense (+E, −SE)	600,000	
cr Withheld Income Tax Payable (+L)		58,000
cr FICA Payable (+L)		48,800
cr United Way Payable (+L)		10,000
cr Cash (−A)		483,200

Employer Payroll Taxes   Beyond paying employees and remitting payroll deductions, employers have other responsibilities that lead to substantial additional labor costs. According to the U.S. Department of Labor, **in 2011, nearly 30 percent of labor costs were for costs other than salaries and wages.** In the remainder of this section, we consider two employer payroll taxes: FICA and unemployment taxes.

Like their employees, all employers are required to pay FICA taxes. The required contribution is 100% of total employee contributions (called a "matching" contribution). In addition, employers are required by the Federal Unemployment Tax Act (FUTA) and State Unemployment Tax Act (SUTA) to pay unemployment taxes. The rates for these taxes vary by industry, state, and employer history but can be substantial, as shown in the pie chart.

To illustrate how these payroll expenses affect the accounting records, let's assume General Mills was required to contribute $48,800 for FICA, $750 for federal unemployment tax, and $4,000 for state unemployment tax. These payroll taxes are extra costs the employer incurs beyond the costs of salaries and wages, so they are reported as an additional operating expense on the income statement. Until they have been paid, the liabilities for these taxes are recorded in current liability accounts, as follows:

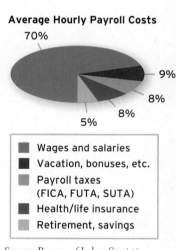

Average Hourly Payroll Costs

70%
9%
8%
8%
5%

- ■ Wages and salaries
- ■ Vacation, bonuses, etc.
- ■ Payroll taxes (FICA, FUTA, SUTA)
- ■ Health/life insurance
- ■ Retirement, savings

Source: Bureau of Labor Statistics.

1 Analyze

Assets	=	Liabilities		+	Stockholders' Equity	
		FICA Payable	+48,800		Payroll Tax	
		Federal Unemployment Tax Payable	+750		Expense (+E)	−53,550
		State Unemployment Tax Payable	+4,000			

2 Record

dr Payroll Tax Expense (+E, −SE)...	53,550	
cr FICA Payable (+L)...		48,800
cr Federal Unemployment Tax Payable (+L)...................		750
cr State Unemployment Tax Payable (+L).......................		4,000

When the employer pays these taxes (and the payroll deductions shown at the top of this page), it decreases the liability accounts (with debits) and decreases its Cash account (with a credit).

COACH'S TIP

The adjusting journal entry to accrue income taxes was presented in Chapter 4 on pages 156-157.

Accrued Income Taxes   Corporations pay taxes not only on payroll but also on income they earn, just like you. The corporate tax return, which the IRS calls a Form 1120, is similar to the company's income statement, except that it calculates *taxable* income by subtracting tax-allowed expenses from revenues. This taxable income is then multiplied by a tax rate, which for most large corporations is about 35 percent. Corporate income taxes are due two and a half months after year-end, although most corporations are required to pay advance installments during the year.

Notes Payable

The next liability reported by General Mills in Exhibit 10.1 is Notes Payable. This liability represents the amount the company owes to others as a result of issuing promissory notes. It is the flipside of the notes receivable transactions that were explained in Chapter 8.

Four key events occur with any note payable: (1) establishing the note, (2) accruing interest incurred but not paid, (3) recording interest paid, and (4) recording principal paid. Financial effects are recorded for each of these four events. As an example, assume that on November 1, 2012, General Mills borrowed $100,000 cash on a one-year note that required General Mills to pay 6 percent interest and $100,000 principal, both on October 31, 2013.

1. **Establish the note payable.** The $100,000 loan that created the note payable has the following accounting equation effects, which General Mills would record using the following journal entry:

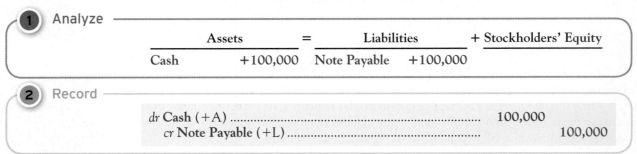

1 Analyze

	Assets	=	Liabilities	+ Stockholders' Equity
Cash	+100,000		Note Payable +100,000	

2 Record

dr **Cash** (+A)	100,000	
cr **Note Payable** (+L)		100,000

2. **Accrue interest incurred but not paid.** Interest occurs as time passes. It is not owed the day the note is established, but rather it accumulates as each day passes. Under accrual accounting, interest must be recorded as it is incurred over time. The timeline in Exhibit 10.4 shows how General Mills should account for the interest incurred on the note over its one-year term. In reality, General Mills would record an adjustment each month or quarter for interest incurred in that period, but for simplicity, we have assumed it occurs only once, at the end of the year. From the date the note was established (November 1, 2012) to the end of the year (December 31, 2012), General Mills incurred two months of interest expense.

The amount of interest to record for **two** months is computed using the interest formula, as follows:

$$\text{Interest (I)} = \text{Principal (P)} \times \text{Interest Rate (R)} \times \text{Time (T)}$$
$$\$1,000 = \$100,000 \times 6\% \times 2/12$$

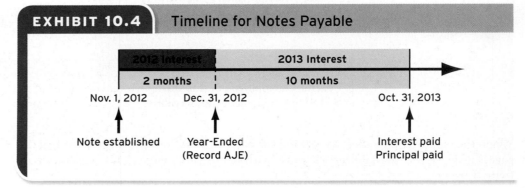

EXHIBIT 10.4   Timeline for Notes Payable

2012 Interest	2013 Interest	
2 months	10 months	
Nov. 1, 2012	Dec. 31, 2012	Oct. 31, 2013
↑	↑	↑
Note established	Year-Ended (Record AJE)	Interest paid Principal paid

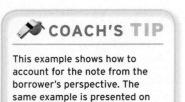
COACH'S TIP

This example shows how to account for the note from the borrower's perspective. The same example is presented on pages 365-367 from the lender's perspective.

The effect of this adjustment, along with the adjusting journal entry to record the $1,000 of interest expense that is payable on December 31, 2012. is as follows:

1 Analyze

Assets	=	Liabilities	+	Stockholders' Equity
		Interest Payable +1,000	Interest Expense (+E)	−1,000

2 Record

dr Interest Expense (+E, −SE)	1,000
cr Interest Payable (+L)	1,000

3. **Record interest paid.** The timeline in Exhibit 10.4 shows that on October 31, 2013, General Mills pays both the principal and the interest. Although the company is likely to pay both amounts with a single check, it is instructive to consider these payments separately. In this step, we analyze and record the interest payment. The interest payment is $6,000 (= $100,000 × 6% × 12/12). As shown in the following timeline, this $6,000 interest payment includes the $1,000 that was accrued as Interest Payable at December 31, 2012, plus $5,000 interest expense incurred during the 10 months between January 1 and October 31, 2013.

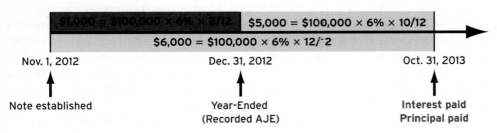

$1,000 = $100,000 × 6% × 2/12	$5,000 = $100,000 × 6% × 10/12
$6,000 = $100,000 × 6% × 12/12	

Nov. 1, 2012	Dec. 31, 2012	Oct. 31, 2013
Note established	Year-Ended (Recorded AJE)	Interest paid Principal paid

The $6,000 interest payment is analyzed and recorded as follows:

1 Analyze

Assets	=	Liabilities	+	Stockholders' Equity
Cash −6,000		Interest Payable −1,000		Interest Expense (+E) −5,000

2 Record

dr Interest Payable (−L)..........................	1,000	
dr Interest Expense (+E, −SE)	5,000	
cr Cash (−A)		6,000

4. **Record principal paid.** The accounting equation effects and journal entry to record the $100,000 principal payment on October 31, 2013, are as follows:

1 Analyze

Assets	=	Liabilities	+ Stockholders' Equity
Cash −100,000		Note Payable −100,000	

2 Record

dr Note Payable (−L) ...._...........................	100,000	
cr Cash (−A) ...._.....................		100,000

Solution to Self-Study Practice

Assets	=	Liabilities	+	Stockholders' Equity
Dec. 1 Cash +12,000	=	Note Payable +12,000		
Dec. 31		Interest Payable +50		Interest Expense (+E) −50

($50 = $12,000 × 5% × 1/12)

How's it going?   Self-Study Practice

Assume Starbucks issues a 5 percent, $12,000 note on December 1. How would this transaction and the month-end interest adjustment affect the accounting equation?

1 Analyze

	Assets	=	Liabilities	+	Stockholders' Equity
December 1					
December 31					

After you have finished, check your answers with the solution in the margin.

Current Portion of Long-term Debt

Remember when you were in grade 9 and it seemed as if it would be forever before you'd graduate from high school? At that time, graduation was something that would happen in the long term. Later, when you became a senior, graduation became a current event—one that was less than a year away. A similar progression occurs with long-term debt.

If a company borrows money with the promise to repay it in two years, the loan is classified as a long-term debt. The company reports only the accrued interest on the loan as a current liability in that year's balance sheet. After a year has passed, however, the loan becomes a current liability (just as your graduation became a current event when you reached your senior year). When that happens, the borrower must report the loan in the Current Liabilities section of the balance sheet. Rather than create a different account for this, accountants simply remove the amount of principal to be repaid in the upcoming year from the total long-term debt and report it as a current liability, Current Portion of Long-term Debt.

The final line item in the Current Liabilities section of the General Mills balance sheet provides an example (see Exhibit 10.1, page 449). Notice that in 2011, General Mills reported a current liability for the $1,031 (million) of long-term debt that was expected to be paid in 2012. This reclassification of long-term debt into current liabilities is needed so that the balance sheet accurately reports the dollar amount of existing liabilities that will be paid in the upcoming year.

Solution to Self-Study Practice

	At December 31	
	2013	2012
Current Liabilities		
Current Portion of Long-term Debt	$2,000	$ 1,000
Long-term Debt	7,000	9,000
Total Liabilities	$9,000	$10,000

How's it going?   Self-Study Practice

Assume that on December 31, 2012, DIRECTV borrowed $10,000, a portion of which is to be repaid each year on November 30. Specifically, DIRECTV will make the following principal payments: $1,000 in 2013, $2,000 in 2014, $3,000 in 2015, and $4,000 in 2016. Show how this loan will be reported on the balance sheets on December 31, 2013 and 2012, assuming that principal payments will be made when required.

	At December 31	
	2013	2012
Current Liabilities:		
Current Portion of Long-term Debt	$	$
Long-term Debt		
Total Liabilities	$9,000	$10,000

After you have finished, check your answers with the solution in the margin.

SPOTLIGHT ON The World

Violated Loan Covenants

Most lending agreements allow the lender to revise loan terms (e.g., interest rates, due dates) if a borrower's financial condition deteriorates significantly. These escape hatches, called **loan covenants,** are often based on financial statement ratios such as those in earlier chapters. Under GAAP, if a company violates loan covenants on long-term debt but renegotiates the loan prior to releasing its financial statements, the debt remains classified as long-term. Under IFRS, the company must reclassify that long-term debt as a current liability even if renegotiated.

Additional Current Liabilities

Because of the nature of General Mills's business, the company does not have some current liabilities that are common to other companies. This section covers two such liabilities.

Sales Tax Payable   Retail companies are required to charge a sales tax in all but five states (Alaska, Delaware, Montana, New Hampshire, and Oregon). Retailers collect sales tax from consumers at the time of sale and forward it to the state government. Just like payroll taxes, the tax collected by the company is reported as a current liability until it is forwarded to the government. Sales tax is not an expense to the retailer because it is simply collected and passed on to the government. So if Best Buy sold a television for $1,000 cash plus 5 percent sales tax, Best Buy would collect $1,050 cash, earn $1,000 in sales revenue, and recognize a $50 liability (= 5% × $1,000) for the sales tax collected. The financial effects of this sale are analyzed below and would be recorded with the journal entry that follows:

COACH'S TIP

The sale shown below would be accompanied (in a perpetual inventory system) by an increase in Cost of Goods Sold (recorded with a debit) and a decrease in Inventory (recorded with a credit).

1 Analyze

	Assets	=	Liabilities		+	Stockholders' Equity	
Cash	+1,050		Sales Tax Payable	+50		Sales Revenue (+R)	+1,000

2 Record

dr **Cash** (+A)	1,050	
cr **Sales Tax Payable** (+L) ($1,000 × 5%)		50
cr **Sales Revenue** (+R, +SE)		1,000

When Best Buy pays the sales tax to the state government, its accountants will reduce Sales Tax Payable (with a debit) and reduce Cash (with a credit).

Unearned Revenue   In Chapter 4, you learned that some companies receive cash before they provide goods or services to customers. Airlines are paid in advance of providing flights, retailers receive cash for gift cards that can be used for future purchases of goods and services, and other companies receive money for subscriptions and events before they begin. Live Nation Entertainment (LYV), the owner of Ticketmaster, provides a great example of this type of liability. Consider what happened when LYV received $8 million cash on May 14, 2010, when tickets went on sale for two Lady Gaga concerts on February 21 and 22, 2011, at Madison Square Garden. Because LYV received cash before providing concert services, accountants initially recorded a liability in the account Unearned Revenue. As the concert services were provided, LYV reduced this liability and reported the earned concert fees as revenue.

That is, LYV recorded the following financial effects and related journal entries on May 14, 2010, when it received $8 million for advance ticket sales for the February 2011 concerts:

1. Receive cash and create a liability (on May 14):

① Analyze

Assets		=	Liabilities		+	Stockholders' Equity
Cash	+8		Unearned Revenue	+8		

② Record

dr Cash (+A)	8
cr Unearned Revenue (+L)	8

2. Fulfill part of the liability and earn revenue (on February 21):

① Analyze

Assets	=	Liabilities		+	Stockholders' Equity	
		Unearned Revenue	−4		Concert Revenue (+R)	+4

② Record

dr Unearned Revenue (−L)	4
cr Concert Revenue (+R, +SE)	4

When the February 22 concert was held, LYV made another adjustment like the one in step 2 to show that it fulfilled its remaining obligation and earned $4 million more in concert revenue.

LONG-TERM LIABILITIES

Like most companies, General Mills reports several long-term liabilities on its balance sheet (see Exhibit 10.1). Common long-term liabilities include long-term notes payable, deferred income taxes, and bonds payable. Long-term notes payable are accounted for in the same way as the short-term notes payable discussed in the previous section (except, of course, long-term notes are on the books for more than one year). Liabilities for deferred income taxes were explained in Chapter 9; they represent the amount of tax put off (deferred) by taking tax deductions on the corporation's income tax return that are greater than the expenses subtracted on the income statement. This section focuses on accounting for bonds that a company issues to obtain a significant amount of financing. Later, in Chapter 11, after you become more familiar with this form of long-term debt financing, we will compare it to alternative forms of long-term (equity) financing.

Bonds

Occasionally, governments and very large companies such as General Mills need to borrow more money than any single lender can provide. In May 2011, for example, General Mills needed to borrow $700 million. Because issuing a promissory note for such a large amount of money was impractical, the company instead issued bonds. A sample bond certificate is shown here.

Bonds are financial instruments that outline the future payments a company promises to make in exchange for receiving a sum of money now. From the company's perspective, the bond is a long-term liability. From the bondholder's perspective, the bond is an investment. After a company issues the bonds, they can be traded on established exchanges such as the New York Bond Exchange. The ability to sell a bond on the bond exchange is attractive to bondholders because it provides them liquidity, or the ability to receive cash for the bond whenever they wish to sell it. In return for this liquidity, bondholders will accept a lower interest rate, which benefits the company by lowering the cost of long-term borrowing.

As you can see from the sample bond certificate, three key elements of a bond are (1) the **maturity date**, (2) the amount payable on the maturity date (often called the **face value**), and (3) the **stated interest rate**. In most cases, the face value of each bond is $1,000. The stated interest rate is always expressed as an annual rate although many bonds require interest payments every six months (that is, semiannually). Each interest payment is computed by multiplying the face value times the stated interest rate (times the fraction of the year if payments are made semiannually). As you will see later, for good economic reasons, bonds may be priced at amounts above or below their face value. A bond's price does not affect the amount of each interest payment, however. For example, a 6 percent bond with a face value of $1,000 will always pay interest of $60 cash each year (= $1,000 × 6% × 12/12).

Bond Pricing

Neither the company nor its financial advisers determine the price at which bonds issue. Instead, investors in the market establish the issue price. The bond **issue price** represents the amount that investors are willing to pay on the issue date in exchange for the cash payments that the company promises to make over the life of the bond. Theoretically, this amount is based on a mathematical calculation called a **present value**, which is described in Appendix C at the end of this book. (Case C on page C10 shows the calculations for the $1,000, 6 percent General Mills bond.)

SPOTLIGHT ON Financial Reporting

Bond Prices in the Financial Press

The financial press (and Yahoo! Finance bond center) reports bond prices each day based on transactions that occurred on the bond exchange. The following is typical of the information you will find:

GENERAL MILLS

Company Name	Maturity	INTEREST RATE Stated	INTEREST RATE Market	Bond Price
Best Buy	2021	5.50	6.15	95.50
General Mills	2016	6.00	4.00	107.26
Home Depot	2040	5.40	4.28	118.30

This listing reports that the General Mills bond will mature in the year 2016. It has a stated interest rate of 6.00 percent. At the present time, 4.00 is the typical interest rate earned by investors in the market when buying similar bonds. Because the 6.00 percent stated interest rate is better than the 4.00 percent market interest rate, investors are attracted to the General Mills bond. Consequently, they are willing to pay a higher bond price. The bond price is quoted as a percentage of face value. In this case, investors were willing to pay 107.26 percent of face value, or $1,072.60 for each $1,000 bond (107.26% × $1,000).

When companies issue bonds, they try to offer competitive interest rates. However, changing economic events can cause the bond's stated interest rate to differ from the market's desired rate, which affects the bond's attractiveness and its price. After a bond has issued, the market's desired rate fluctuates frequently, which affects the bond price in the market. **Daily fluctuations in the market do not directly involve the company, so they are not considered transactions of the company.** Except in rare situations, a company accounts for its bond liability using the bond price and interest rates that existed when the bonds were first issued to the market.

Accounting for a Bond Issue

Although it is useful to know how to determine bond prices, it is not a necessary step in accounting for a bond issue. Instead, what we need to know is the amount of cash the company receives from investors when the bonds are first issued. This amount may be equal to the face value, above the face value, or below the face value. A bond issued for more than its face value is said to have been issued at a **premium**, which is the excess of the bond's issue price over its face value. A bond issued for less than its face value is said to have been issued at a **discount**, which is the amount by which the issue price falls short of the bond's face value. The following sections show how to account for bonds issued at face value, at a premium, and at a discount.

Bonds Issued at Face Value If General Mills receives $100,000 cash in exchange for issuing 100 bonds at their $1,000 face value, the transaction will be analyzed and recorded as follows:

① Analyze

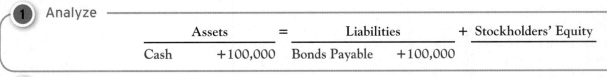

	Assets	=	Liabilities	+ Stockholders' Equity
Cash	+100,000	Bonds Payable	+100,000	

② Record

dr Cash (+A) 100,000
   cr Bonds Payable (+L) 100,000

Bonds Issued at a Premium If General Mills issues 100 of its $1,000 bonds at a price of 107.26, the company will receive $107,260 (= 100 × $1,000 × 1.0726). Thus, the cash-equivalent amount is $107,260, which represents the total liability on that date. The company's accountants will distinguish the $100,000 total face value from the $7,260 premium by recording them in separate liability accounts as follows:

① Analyze

	Assets	=	Liabilities	+ Stockholders' Equity
Cash	+107,260	Bonds Payable	+100,000	
		Premium on		
		Bonds Payable	+7,260	

② Record

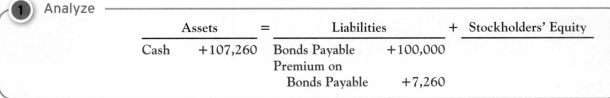

dr Cash (+A) 107,260
   cr Bonds Payable (+L) 100,000
   cr Premium on Bonds Payable (+L) 7,260

Why would bondholders be willing to pay a premium? For the same reason that you might pay a premium to acquire tickets to a great concert or a big game. If a bond offers something attractive, such as a high interest rate, bondholders may be willing to pay a premium to acquire it.

COACH'S TIP

Although Discount on Bonds Payable is recorded with a debit, it is not an asset—it is a contra-liability.

Bonds Issued at a Discount If General Mills receives $93,376 for bonds with a total face value of $100,000, the cash-equivalent amount is $93,376, which represents the liability on that date. As shown in the analyze step below, the discount of $6,624 (= $100,000 − $93,376) offsets the face value, so accountants will record it in a contra-liability account, which we identify using "xL." A contra-liability account is recorded as a debit as in the journal entry that follows:

① Analyze

	Assets	=	Liabilities	+ Stockholders' Equity
Cash	+93,376	Bonds Payable	+100,000	
		Discount on Bonds		
		Payable (+xL)	−6,624	

② Record

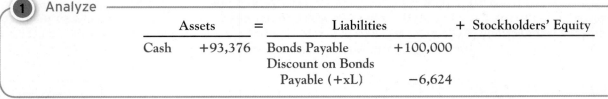

dr Cash (+A) 93,376
dr Discount on Bonds Payable (+xL, −L) 6,624
   cr Bonds Payable (+L) 100,000

Why would companies be willing to discount a bond? The answer is that they must if they want to issue it. If a bond promises to pay interest at a stated rate of 6 percent when other financial instruments offer 8 percent, no one will be willing to buy the bond unless the company discounts it. The discount reduces the initial bond price for investors without changing the stated interest payments and the face value paid to them at maturity. In effect, a discount increases the return that bondholders earn on their initial investment.

To illustrate, suppose you could buy a $1,000 bond that pays a stated interest rate of 6 percent and matures in one year. After one year, you would receive the stated interest of $60 ($1,000 × 6% × 12/12) plus the face value of $1,000. If you had paid $1,000 for the bond, you would receive 1.06 times as much as your initial investment [($60 + $1,000) ÷ $1,000]—a return of 6 percent. If instead the bond price were discounted $19, so that you paid only $981 for it, you would receive 1.08 times as much as your initial investment [($60 + $1,000) ÷ $981 = 1.08]—a return of 8 percent. This percentage represents both the bondholder's rate of return and the company's cost of borrowing. It is commonly referred to as the **market interest rate**.

Reporting Bond Liabilities The total face value of a bond plus any related premium or minus any related discount is reported in the liabilities section of the balance sheet as in Exhibit 10.5 for our three examples The amount of the bond liability, after taking into account any premium or discount, is referred to as the bond's **carrying value.**

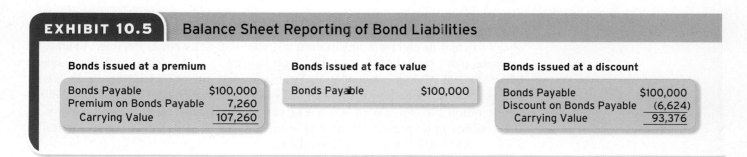

EXHIBIT 10.5 | **Balance Sheet Reporting of Bond Liabilities**

Bonds issued at a premium

Bonds Payable	$100,000
Premium on Bonds Payable	7,260
Carrying Value	107,260

Bonds issued at face value

Bonds Payable	$100,000

Bonds issued at a discount

Bonds Payable	$100,000
Discount on Bonds Payable	(6,624)
Carrying Value	93,376

To determine whether a bond will be issued at a premium, at face value, or at a discount, you need consider only the relationship between the stated interest rate on the bond (what the bond pays in cash) and the market interest rate (the return that bondholders require). Exhibit 10.6 illustrates this relationship.

EXHIBIT 10.6 | **Relationships between Interest Rates and Bond Pricing**

What the bonds say	What if bondholders desire...	What bondholders think	The bonds issue at
	4% Market interest rate	I'll pay more than face value.	Premium
6% Stated interest rate	6% Market interest rate	It's just enough.	Face value
	8% Market interest rate	I'm not attracted (yet).	Discount

Before you continue, try the following Self-Study Practice.

 How's it going?   Self-Study Practice

For each of the following independent situations, indicate whether the bonds were issued at a premium, at a discount, or at face value.

1. Stated interest rate = 7% and market interest rate = 7%.
2. Stated interest rate = 5% and market interest rate = 6%.
3. Bond issue price = $10,100 and bond face value = $10,000.

After you have finished, check your answers with the solution in the margin.

Interest Expense

As time passes, a bond liability creates interest expense, which is matched to each period in which the liability is owed. Because interest expense arises from a financing decision (not an operating decision), it is reported below the Income from Operations line on the company's income statement.

Interest on Bonds Issued at Face Value   For bonds issued at face value, the process of calculating and recording interest is similar to that for Notes Payable. Assume, for example, that General Mills issues bonds on January 1, 2013, at their total face value of $100,000. If the bonds carry an annual stated interest rate of 6 percent payable in cash on December 31 of each year, General Mills will need to accrue an expense and liability for interest at the end of each accounting period. For the first month ended January 31, 2013, assuming no previous accrual of interest, General Mills would record interest of $500 (= $100,000 × 6% × 1/12) as follows:

1 Analyze

Assets	=	Liabilities	+	Stockholders' Equity	
		Interest Payable +500		Interest Expense (+E)	−500

2 Record

dr Interest Expense (+E, −SE)	500	
cr Interest Payable (+L)		500

General Mills would continue to calculate and record interest this way each month until the interest is paid. When interest is paid, Interest Payable will be decreased (with a debit) and Cash will be decreased (with a credit) for the amount paid.

Interest on Bonds Issued at a Premium   When bonds issue at a premium, the bond issuer receives more cash on the issue date than it repays on the maturity date. For example, in our earlier illustration of bonds issued at a premium, General Mills received $107,260 but repays only $100,000 at maturity. The $7,260 difference isn't exactly "free money" for General Mills but rather is a reduction in the company's cost of borrowing. For accounting purposes, we match the reduced borrowing cost to the periods in which interest expense is recorded. This process, called **bond amortization,** makes the Interest Expense smaller than the actual interest payment and, at the same time, causes the balance in Premium on Bonds Payable to decline each period, as shown in Exhibit 10.7.

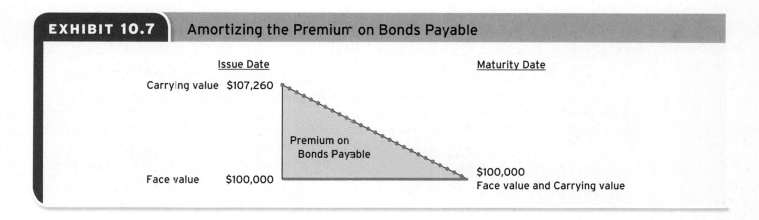

EXHIBIT 10.7 | Amortizing the Premium on Bonds Payable

Issue Date   Maturity Date

Carrying value $107,260

Premium on Bonds Payable

Face value $100,000 $100,000 Face value and Carrying value

Procedures for amortizing bond premiums are explained in Chapter Supplements 10A, 10B, and 10C. If you have been assigned any of these supplements, don't jump to them yet. We'll tell you later when it's best to read them.

Interest on Bonds Issued at a Discount   When bonds issue at a discount, the bond issuer receives less cash on the issue date than it repays on the maturity date. For example, in our earlier illustration of bonds issued at a discount, General Mills receives $93,376 on the issue date but repays $100,000 at maturity. For General Mills, the $6,624 discount represents an extra cost of borrowing, over and above each interest payment. For accounting purposes, we match the extra borrowing cost to the periods in which interest is recorded. This amortization causes the Interest Expense to be more than the interest payment and, at the same time, causes Discount on Bonds Payable to decrease each period. As the Discount on Bonds Payable decreases, the carrying value of the liability increases until it reaches $100,000 on the maturity date, as illustrated in Exhibit 10.8.

EXHIBIT 10.8 | Amortizing the Discount on Bonds Payable

Issue Date   Maturity Date

Face value $100,000 $100,000 Face value

Discount on Bonds Payable   (0) Discount

$100,000 Carrying value

Discount (6,624)

Carrying value $ 93,376

At this point, you should read any of the assigned chapter supplements, then come back here and continue with the remainder of this section. The chapter supplements begin on page 466.

Bond Retirements

Retirement at Maturity   Most bonds are retired (paid off) at maturity. If interest has been fully paid at the time of maturity, the only remaining account to settle will be Bonds Payable. Assuming the General Mills bonds in our example were retired with a payment equal to their $100,000 face value, the transaction would be analyzed and recorded as follows:

1 Analyze

	Assets	=	Liabilities	+ Stockholders' Equity
Cash	−100,000	Bonds Payable	−100,000	

2 Record

dr Bonds Payable (−L) 100,000
   cr Cash (−A)   100,000

Early Retirement   Rather than wait until the maturity date to retire bonds, a company may retire them early. Companies with a lot of cash often retire their bonds early to avoid the related interest expense. Even companies that do not have extra cash may decide to retire their bonds early if interest rates have fallen since issuing the original bonds. In this case, the companies would issue new bonds at the lower interest rate and use the money they receive from the new bonds to retire the old ones before maturity. Again, this decision reduces interest expense, which increases future earnings.

The early retirement of bonds has three financial effects. The company (1) pays cash, (2) eliminates the bond liability, and (3) reports either a gain or a loss. A gain arises if the cash paid to retire the bonds is less than the carrying value of the bond liability. A loss is incurred if the company pays more than the carrying value at the time of retirement.

To illustrate these effects, assume that in 2003, General Mills issued $100,000 of bonds at face value. Ten years later, in 2013, the company retired the bonds early. At the time, the bond price was 102, so General Mills made a payment of $102,000 (= $100,000 × 1.02) to retire the bonds. This transaction would be analyzed and recorded as follows:

1 Analyze

	Assets	=	Liabilities	+	Stockholders' Equity	
Cash	−102,000	Bonds Payable	−100,000		Loss on Bond	
					Retirement (+E)	−2,000

2 Record

dr Bonds Payable (−L) 100,000
dr Loss on Bond Retirement (+E, −SE) 2,000
   cr Cash (−A)   102,000

Notice two features of this example. First, because the bond retirement is a financing decision, the loss would be reported after the Income from Operations line on the income statement. Second, this retirement example does not involve the removal of a bond discount or bond premium account because the bonds were issued at face value. If the bonds had been issued below or above face value, any premium or discount balance that existed at the time of retirement would need to be removed as well.

Types of Bonds

When you first start learning about bonds, it may seem the number of new terms that describe the bonds are limitless. These terms can generally be grouped into two categories: (1) those that describe the type of organization that issued the bonds and (2) those that describe specific features of the bond. In the first category are bonds issued by the U.S. Treasury Department ("treasuries"); municipal organizations such as states, cities, counties, and towns ("munis"); and corporations ("corporates"). In the second category are bonds that are backed by collateral ("secured") or not ("debentures"), that the issuing corporation can call in and exchange for cash ("callable") or convert into shares of its stock ("convertible"), and that mature in a series of installments ("serial bonds") or include no periodic interest payments ("zero-coupon bonds" and "strips"). The basic procedures shown in the previous sections for recording bond liabilities and interest expense apply equally to these various types of bonds.

CONTINGENT LIABILITIES

Learning Objective 10-4
Describe how to account for contingent liabilities.

Contingent liabilities are potential liabilities that arise as a result of past transactions or events, but their ultimate resolution depends (is contingent) on a future event. Contingent liabilities differ from other liabilities discussed in this chapter because their dependence on a future event introduces a great deal of uncertainty. For example, consider the product warranties on watches and computers. These warranties obligate the company to repair defective products for a limited time, but the ultimate cost of those repairs depends on future events including the number of warranty claims, labor rates, and supply costs. Even more uncertainty is introduced when accounting for lawsuits against the company. Some suits may be defended successfully but others may result in huge penalties, such as the $158 million Johnson & Johnson agreed to in 2011 for illegally marketing its Risperdal drug in Texas. Given the uncertainties of contingent events, accounting rules require the company to evaluate whether it is likely to be found liable and, if so, whether the amount of the liability is estimable (yes, that's a word). If the liability is probable, an expense and liability are accrued as shown in Exhibit 10.9. If a contingent liability is possible but not probable or its amount cannot be estimated, a liability is not recorded in the accounting records. Instead, any potential liability and related loss is described in a note to the financial statements, as shown below in a General Mills excerpt.

YOU SHOULD KNOW

Contingent liabilities: Potential liabilities that have arisen as a result of a past transaction or event; their ultimate outcome will not be known until a future event occurs or fails to occur.

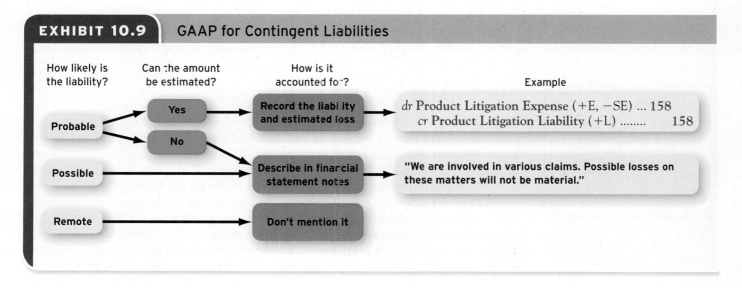

EXHIBIT 10.9   GAAP for Contingent Liabilities

How likely is the liability?	Can the amount be estimated?	How is it accounted for?	Example
Probable	Yes	Record the liability and estimated loss	*dr* Product Litigation Expense (+E, −SE) ... 158 *cr* Product Litigation Liability (+L) 158
	No		
Possible		Describe in financial statement notes	"We are involved in various claims. Possible losses on these matters will not be material."
Remote		Don't mention it	

SPOTLIGHT ON The World

Just How Certain Are You?

Under GAAP, contingent liabilities (and corresponding losses) are recorded if the estimated loss is probable. Under IFRS, contingent liabilities (and corresponding losses) are recorded if the estimated loss is "more likely than not" to occur. The threshold under IFRS is lower than that under GAAP, which should cause more contingent liabilities to be reported under IFRS than under GAAP.

Now that you have seen how liabilities are accounted for inside a company, let's consider them again from the outside. How do users judge whether liabilities are likely to be repaid in full?

Evaluate the Results

Learning Objective 10-5
Calculate and interpret the quick ratio and the times interest earned ratio.

In evaluating a company's ability to pay its liabilities, you want to assess whether the company has the assets available to pay what it currently owes, and whether the company is likely to generate the resources needed to pay future amounts that will be owed. Two financial ratios are commonly used to make these assessments: the quick ratio and the times interest earned ratio.

Accounting Decision Tools

Name of Measure	Formula	What It Tells You
Quick ratio	$\dfrac{\text{(Cash + Short-term Investments + Accounts Receivable, Net)}}{\text{Current Liabilities}}$	• Whether liquid assets are sufficient to pay current liabilities • The higher the number the better able to quickly pay
Times interest earned ratio	$\dfrac{\text{(Net Income + Interest Expense + Income Tax Expense)}}{\text{Interest Expense}}$	• Whether sufficient resources are generated to cover interest costs • The higher the number the better the coverage

QUICK RATIO

> **YOU SHOULD KNOW**
>
> **Quick ratio:** The ratio of liquid assets to current liabilities; liquid assets include cash and cash equivalents, short-term investments, and accounts receivable (net of doubtful accounts).

The **quick ratio** is similar to the current ratio introduced in Chapter 2. Both ratios compare a company's current assets to its current liabilities. Rather than consider all current assets, however, the quick ratio focuses on just the assets that can be quickly converted into cash. These liquid assets, as they are called, typically include cash and cash equivalents, short-term investments, and accounts receivable (net of doubtful accounts).

As with all ratios, judgment is required to interpret the quick ratio. Generally speaking, a high quick ratio suggests a high ability to pay current liabilities. For example, a quick ratio greater than 1.0 implies a company could pay all its current liabilities immediately if it were required to. However, lower ratios do not necessarily imply a company will be unable to pay its current liabilities. For example, at the end of its 2011 fiscal year, General Mills reported $620 million of cash and cash equivalents, no short-term investments, and $1,162 million of net accounts receivable. Using these numbers and the $3,659 million in total current liabilities shown in Exhibit 10.1, we can calculate the quick ratio for General Mills as follows:

$$\frac{\textbf{Cash + Short-term Investments + Accounts Receivable, Net}}{\textbf{Current Liabilities}} = \frac{\$620 + \$0 + \$1,162}{\$3,659} = 0.487$$

A quick ratio of 0.487 implies that General Mills would be able to pay only 48.7 percent of its current liabilities, if forced to pay them immediately. However, this interpretation overlooks a few important facts. First, not all current liabilities are to be paid immediately. The $1.3 billion of Notes Payable and Current portion of long-term debt in Exhibit 10.1 may not be payable until late in the following year and, at that time, could be refinanced over even longer periods. Second, General Mills generates over $4 million in cash from its operations each day. These huge future cash inflows aren't included in the existing cash balance. Third, the company has arranged a **line of credit**, as discussed in the following spotlight feature.

SPOTLIGHT ON Financial Reporting

Surviving a Financial Crunch

In difficult economic times, it is imperative for companies to have adequate financing in place. Prior to the economic downturn in 2008, General Mills had established a line of credit that provides up to $3 billion cash on an as-needed basis. Rather than hold extra cash, General Mills uses its line of credit to borrow only when money is needed. Not all companies are able to establish lines of credit, but those that do are able to survive with a quick ratio less than 1.0. To determine whether a company has a line of credit available, be sure to read the company's notes to the financial statements. General Mills reports its $2.9 billion line of credit in its long-term debt note.

TIMES INTEREST EARNED RATIO

One way to judge a company's ability to pay interest is to ask whether it has generated enough income to cover its interest expense. The measure that most analysts use for this purpose is the **times interest earned ratio** (also called a fixed charge coverage ratio).

The accounting decision tools feature (on page 464) showed the formula for the times interest earned ratio. Notice that in this ratio, interest and income tax expenses are added back into net income. The reason for this is simple: Analysts want to know whether a company generates enough income to cover its interest expense **before the costs of financing and taxes.** In general, a high times interest earned ratio is viewed more favorably than a low one. A high ratio indicates an extra margin of protection should the company's profitability decline in the future.

Using information from General Mills's 2011 income statement (online at sec.gov), we can compute the times interest earned ratio as follows:

$$\frac{\textbf{Net Income + Interest Expense + Income Tax Expense}}{\textbf{Interest Expense}} = \frac{\$1,798 + \$346 + \$721}{\$346} = 8.28$$

This ratio means that General Mills generates $8.28 of income (before the costs of financing and taxes) for each dollar of interest expense. Reaching this level of interest coverage was important to General Mills because its long-term debt note reported that loan covenants required a minimum ratio of 2.5.

Every now and then you will see a times interest earned ratio that is less than 1.0 or even negative. **When the times interest earned ratio is less than 1.0, a company is not generating enough income to cover its interest expense.** Companies with recurring negative times interest earned ratios survive only a few years before declaring bankruptcy.

SUPPLEMENT 10A STRAIGHT-LINE METHOD OF AMORTIZATION

Exhibits 10.7 and 10.8 illustrated how a bond premium or discount decreases each year, until it is completely eliminated on the bond's maturity date. This process is called amortizing the bond premium or discount. The **straight-line method of amortization** reduces the premium or discount by an equal amount each period. Because this method results in an equal amount each period, it is easy to apply. However, it distorts the financial results somewhat because it produces an equal Interest Expense each period, even though the bond's carrying value changes each period. For this reason, the straight-line method may be used only when it does not materially differ from the effective-interest method of amortization (presented in Supplement 10B).

Bond Premiums

In our earlier example of bonds issued at a premium, General Mills received $107,260 on the issue date (January 1, 2013) but repays only $100,000 at maturity (December 31, 2016). The $7,260 difference is considered a reduction in the company's borrowing cost over the four-year period the bond is owed. Under the straight-line method, this $7,260 is spread evenly as a reduction in interest expense over the four years ($7,260 ÷ 4 = $1,815 per year). So when General Mills makes its yearly $6,000 cash payment for interest, it will report Interest Expense of only $4,185 ($6,000 − $1,815). The remainder of the $6,000 cash payment is reported as a reduction in the bond liability, as follows:

1 Analyze

Assets	=	Liabilities	+	Stockholders' Equity
Cash −6,000		Premium on Bonds Payable −1,815		Interest Expense (+E) −4,185

2 Record

dr Interest Expense (+E, −SE)...	4,185	
dr Premium on Bonds Payable (−L).......................................	1,815	
cr Cash (−A)		6,000

In effect, the $6,000 payment includes both an interest component ($4,185) and a repayment of the bond liability ($1,815). The accounting equation effects and journal entry shown above will be recorded each year on December 31 until the bonds mature. The following bond amortization schedule summarizes the journal entry effects each period (on the left) and the updated balance sheet account balances (on the right):

Bond Premium Amortization Schedule: Straight-Line Method

	Journal Entry Components			Balance Sheet Accounts		
	(A)	(B) Amortized	(C) (= A − B) Interest	(D) Bonds	(E) Premium on	(F) (= D + E) Carrying
Period Ended	Cash Paid	Premium	Expense	Payable	Bonds Payable	Value
01/01/2013				$100,000	$7,260	$107,260
12/31/2013	$6,000	$1,815	$4,185	100,000	5,445	105,445
12/31/2014	6,000	1,815	4,185	100,000	3,630	103,630
12/31/2015	6,000	1,815	4,185	100,000	1,815	101,815
12/31/2016	6,000	1,815	4,185	100,000	0	100,000

Bond Discounts

A discount arises when the bond issuer receives less cash than the issuer repays at maturity. In effect, a discount increases the company's cost of borrowing, so amortization of the discount causes interest expense to be higher than the interest payment each period. To report this effect, accountants record a decrease in Discount on Bonds Payable and an increase in Interest Expense.

In our earlier example, General Mills received $93,376 for four-year bonds with a total face value of $100,000, implying a discount of $6,624. Using the straight-line method, amortization of the discount in each of the four years that the bonds remain unpaid would be $1,656 (= $6,624 ÷ 4). This amount would be added to the interest to be paid ($6,000) to calculate the amount of Interest Expense ($7,656). The effects would be recorded as follows:

1 Analyze

Assets	=	Liabilities	+	Stockholders' Equity
Cash −6,000		Discount on Bonds Payable (−xL) +1,656		Interest Expense (+E) −7,656

2 Record

dr Interest Expense (+E, −SE) 7,656
    cr Discount on Bonds Payable (−xL, +L)   1,656
    cr Cash (−A)   6,000

The accounting equation effects and journal entry shown above would be recorded each year on December 31 until the bonds mature. The following bond amortization schedule summarizes the effects that must be recorded each period (on the left), producing the end-of-year balance sheet account balances (on the right):

Bond Discount Amortization Schedule: Straight-Line Method

	Journal Entry Components				Balance Sheet Accounts		
Period Ended	**(A)** Cash Paid	**(B)** Amortized Discount	**(C) (= A + B)** Interest Expense		**(D)** Bonds Payable	**(E)** Discount on Bonds Payable	**(F) (= D − E)** Carrying Value
01/01/2013					$100,000	$6,624	$ 93,376
12/31/2013	$6,000	$1,656	$7,656		100,000	4,968	95,032
12/31/2014	6,000	1,656	7,656		100,000	3,312	96,688
12/31/2015	6,000	1,656	7,656		100,000	1,656	98,344
12/31/2016	6,000	1,656	7,656		100,000	0	100,000

SUPPLEMENT 10B   EFFECTIVE-INTEREST METHOD OF AMORTIZATION

The **effective-interest method of amortization** is considered a conceptually superior method of accounting for bonds because it correctly calculates interest expense by multiplying the true cost of borrowing times the amount of money actually owed to investors. The true cost of borrowing is the market interest rate that investors used to determine the bond issue price. The actual amount owed to investors is the carrying value of the bond, which equals the cash received when the bond was issued plus any interest that has been incurred but not yet paid.

To clearly understand the effective-interest method, it helps to see how a bond's issue price depends on the market interest rate. As we mentioned in the chapter, investors in the market decide how much to pay for a bond by using a mathematical calculation called a **present value.** You can read instructions about how to calculate present values in Appendix C at the end of this book, but for now just focus on understanding what a present value is. Present value is the idea that something is worth more if you get it today than

Learning Objective 10-S2
Use effective-interest bond amortization.

YOU SHOULD KNOW

Effective-interest method of amortization: Allocates the amount of bond premium or discount over each period of a bond's life in amounts corresponding to the bond's carrying value.

if you get it sometime in the future. For example, if someone offered to pay you $100,000 today or $100,000 five years from now, you'd be better off taking it today. You could invest the money and earn interest for five years, making it worth more than $100,000. The same idea explains why you could be equally happy with receiving $100,000 in five years or some smaller amount today. To figure out how much this smaller amount is, you just calculate the present value of $100,000. The only pieces of information you need for this calculation are (1) the amounts to be received in the future, (2) the number of months between now and then, and (3) the interest rate you expect to earn during that time.

In the bond context, investors calculate the present value of the amounts received periodically (at the stated interest rate) and at maturity (the face value), using the interest rate that they want to earn. We have summarized this calculation in Exhibit 10B.1 for General Mills's 6 percent, four-year bond. We show three different scenarios, with each one involving different market interest rates but the same 6 percent stated interest rate. The first column calculates the amount of money that investors would be willing to give up if they needed to earn 4 percent on the amount they pay for the bond. The second column calculates the amount investors would pay if they wanted to earn an interest rate of 6 percent. The third column calculates the amount that investors would be willing to pay if they wanted to earn 8 percent on the amount they pay for the bond. (For detailed calculations underlying the amounts in Exhibit 10B.1, see Appendix C at the end of the book.)

EXHIBIT 10B.1   Computing the Present Value of Bond Payments

	MARKET INTEREST RATES		
	4%	6%	8%
Present value of $100,000 face value (principal) paid four years from now	$ 85,480	$ 79,210	$ 73,503
Present value of $6,000 (6% stated interest rate) paid once a year for four years	21,780	20,790	19,873
Bond price	**$107,260**	**$100,000**	**$93,376**

Notice that when the bond pays interest at a rate that exactly matches the rate required by investors in the market (6 percent), they are willing to pay face value ($100,000) for it. If the 6 percent interest rate stated on the bond is more than investors require (4 percent), they will pay a premium for the bond (as shown in the first column). If the 6 percent interest promised is less than the market interest rate (8 percent), investors pay less than face value for the bond, resulting in a discounted bond price as indicated in the third column. Let's now look at what happens to a bond premium and discount under the effective-interest amortization method.

Bond Premiums

In our earlier example of a bond premium, General Mills promised to make cash interest payments each year at a stated rate of 6 percent. Investors found this stated interest rate attractive, so the bond issued at a $7,260 premium. When General Mills adds this $7,260 premium to the $100,000 face value, it reports a carrying value of $107,260 (= $100,000 + $7,260) on January 1, 2013. Exhibit 10B.1 indicates that the $107,260 total implies the market interest rate was 4 percent. General Mills uses this market interest rate to calculate its **Interest Expense** on the bond, using a variation of the interest formula. For example, General Mills calculates Interest Expense in the first year ended December 31, 2013, as follows:

2013:	**Interest (I)**	=	**Principal (P)**	×	**Interest Rate (R)**	×	**Time (T)**
	Interest Expense	=	Carrying Value	×	Market Interest Rate	×	n/12
	$4,290	=	$107,260	×	4%	×	12/12

Use the information *stated* on the *face* of the bond to calculate the **cash interest payment**:

> **Interest (I) = Principal (P) × Interest Rate (R) × Time (T)**
> **Cash Payment = Face Value × Stated Interest Rate × n/12**
> $6,000 = $100,000 × 6% × 12/12

Because the $6,000 cash interest payment exceeds the $4,290 Interest Expense by $1,710 ($6,000 − $4,290 = $1,710), General Mills records a $1,710 reduction in its bond liability. In effect, the $6,000 cash payment includes both an interest component ($4,290) and a partial repayment of the bond liability ($1,710), as analyzed and recorded below:

① Analyze

Assets	=	Liabilities	+	Stockholders' Equity
Cash −6,000		Premium on Bonds Payable −1,710		Interest Expense (+E) −4,290

② Record

dr Interest Expense (+E, −SE)	4,290	
dr Premium on Bonds Payable (−L)	1,710	
cr Cash (−A)		6,000

Similar calculations and accounting effects occur each period until the bonds mature. The only thing to watch out for is that the carrying value of the bond liability decreases each year because the cash payment includes a partial repayment of the bond liability. For example, after the above entry is recorded on December 31, 2013, the Premium on Bonds Payable decreases by $1,710, from $7,260 to $5,550. Thus, the Interest Expense for the second year of the bond (for the year ended December 31, 2014) is:

Premium on Bonds Payable (L)	
	7,260 1/1/2013
12/31/2013 1,710	
	5,550 12/31/2013

> **2014:**   **Interest (I) = Principal (P) × Interest Rate (R) × Time (T)**
> **Interest Expense = Carrying Value × Market Interest Rate × n/12**
> $4,222 = $105,550 × 4% × 12/12

The following bond amortization schedule summarizes the effects that must be recorded each period (on the left), producing the end-of-year balance sheet account balances (on the right):

Bond Premium Amortization Schedule: Effective-Interest Method

	Journal Entry Components				Balance Sheet Accounts		
	(A)	(B) Interest	(C) (= A − B) Amortized		(D) Bonds	(E) Premium on	(F) (= D + E) Carrying
Period Ended	Cash Paid	Expense	Premium		Payable	Bonds Payable	Value
01/01/2013					$100,000	$7,260	$107,260
12/31/2013	$6,000	$4,290	$1,710		100,000	5,550	105,550
12/31/2014	6,000	4,222	1,778		100,000	3,772	103,772
12/31/2015	6,000	4,151	1,849		100,000	1,923	101,923
12/31/2016	6,000	4,077	1,923		100,000	0	100,000

Bond Discounts

In our earlier example of a bond discount, General Mills promised to make cash interest payments each year at a stated rate of 6 percent. Investors did not find this stated interest rate attractive, so the bond issued at a $6,624 discount. When General Mills subtracts this $6,624 discount from the $100,000 face value, it reports a carrying value of $93,376 (= $100,000 − $6,624) on January 1, 2013. Exhibit 10B.1 indicates that the $93,376 implies the market interest rate was 8 percent. General Mills uses this market interest rate to calculate its **Interest Expense** on the bond, as we did in the case of a bond premium. The Interest Expense for the first year ended December 31, 2013, is calculated as:

2013:	**Interest (I)**	=	**Principal (P)**	×	**Interest Rate (R)**	×	**Time (T)**
	Interest Expense	=	**Carrying Value**	×	**Market Interest Rate**	×	**n/12**
	$7,470	=	$93,376	×	8%		× 12/12

Use the information *stated* on the *face* of the bond to calculate the **cash** interest payment:

	Interest (I)	=	**Principal (P)**	×	**Interest Rate (R)**	×	**Time (T)**
	Cash Payment	=	**Face Value**	×	**Stated Interest Rate**	×	**n/12**
	$6,000	=	$100,000	×	6%		× 12/12

Because the $7,470 Interest Expense is more than the $6,000 cash paid, General Mills records the $1,470 difference ($7,470 − $6,000 = $1,470) as an increase in its bond liability. As illustrated in Exhibit 10.8 (on page 461), the increase in the bond liability is achieved by decreasing the contra-liability Discount on Bonds Payable. These effects are analyzed and recorded as follows:

① Analyze

Assets	=	Liabilities	+	Stockholders' Equity
Cash −6,000		Discount on Bonds Payable (−xL) +1,470		Interest Expense (+E) −7,470

② Record

dr Interest Expense (+E, −SE)	7,470	
cr Discount on Bonds Payable (−xL, +L)........................		1,470
cr Cash (−A)		6,000

Discount on Bonds Payable (xL)	
1/1/2013 6,624	
	1,470 12/31/2013
12/31/2013 5,154	

The T-account presented in the margin shows how the above journal entry reduces Discount on Bonds Payable. A reduction of this contra-liability account increases the carrying value of the long-term liability, as you can see by moving from left to right in Exhibit 10B.2.

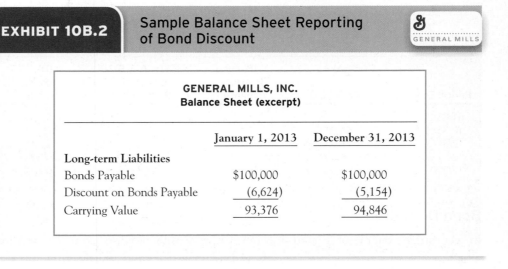

EXHIBIT 10B.2   Sample Balance Sheet Reporting of Bond Discount

GENERAL MILLS

GENERAL MILLS, INC.
Balance Sheet (excerpt)

	January 1, 2013	December 31, 2013
Long-term Liabilities		
Bonds Payable	$100,000	$100,000
Discount on Bonds Payable	(6,624)	(5,154)
Carrying Value	93,376	94,846

Let's now consider the interest expense for 2014. As in 2013, the 2014 interest expense is calculated using the market interest rate. However, the carrying value of bonds owed at the end of 2013 increased, as shown in Exhibit 10B.2. Thus, interest expense also will increase in 2014, calculated as follows:

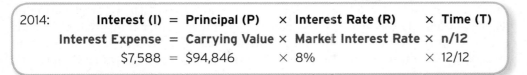

2014:	**Interest (I)** =	**Principal (P)**	× **Interest Rate (R)**	× **Time (T)**
	Interest Expense =	Carrying Value ×	Market Interest Rate ×	n/12
	$7,588 =	$94,846 ×	8% ×	12/12

Because the Interest Expense ($7,588) is greater than the cash payment ($6,000), the bond liability is increased (by reducing the contra-liability). This is reflected in the accounting equation and recorded with the journal entry on December 31, 2014, as follows:

1 Analyze

Assets	=	Liabilities	+	Stockholders' Equity
Cash −6,000		Discount on		Interest
		Bonds Payable (−xL) +1,588		Expense (+E) −7,588

2 Record

dr Interest Expense (+E, −SE)	7,588	
cr Discount on Bonds Payable (−xL, +L)		1,588
cr Cash (−A)		6,000

The following bond amortization schedule summarizes the effects that must be recorded each period (on the left), producing the end-of-year balance sheet account balances (on the right):

Bond Discount Amortization Schedule: Effective-Interest Method						
Journal Entry Components				**Balance Sheet Accounts**		
	(A)	**(B)** Interest Expense	**(C) (= B − A)** Amortized Discount	**(D)** Bonds Payable	**(E)** Discount on Bonds Payable	**(F) (= D − E)** Carrying Value
Period Ended	**Cash Paid**					
01/01/2013				$100,000	$6,624	$ 93,376
12/31/2013	$6,000	$7,470	$1,470	100,000	5,154	94,846
12/31/2014	6,000	7,588	1,588	100,000	3,566	96,434
12/31/2015	6,000	7,715	1,715	100,000	1,851	98,149
12/31/2016	6,000	7,851	1,851	100,000	0	100,000

SUPPLEMENT 10C SIMPLIFIED EFFECTIVE-INTEREST AMORTIZATION

The approach shown in this supplement presents a simplified explanation of how to account for bond liabilities and interest expense. You should be aware that this approach involves taking a shortcut. While the shortcut will help you to focus on the line items that ultimately are reported on the financial statements, it requires that we ignore a few accounts that are typically used behind the scenes in real-world accounting systems. Be sure to check your course syllabus to see whether you are expected to read this supplement.

If you're like most people, you probably have to concentrate really hard when you are told the carrying value of a bond is increased by decreasing a contra-liability account. You may even whisper this thought quietly to yourself a few times before it starts making sense. In this section, we present a shortcut when accounting for bonds that will allow you to avoid thinking in "double-negatives" like this. Hopefully it will also help you to stop whispering to yourself when you read.

Accounting for the Bond Issue

The shortcut involves simplifying only one aspect of what you studied earlier in this chapter. Rather than record a discount or premium in a separate account, we combine the discount or premium with the bond's face value in a single account that we will call Bonds Payable, Net. This name is used to remind you that we are focusing on what is ultimately reported in the financial statements rather than what is actually used behind the scenes. The following journal entries demonstrate how the shortcut is applied to the three earlier bond examples (issued at a premium, at face value, and at a discount).

	Premium	Face Value	Discount
dr Cash (+A)	107,260	100,000	93,376
cr Bonds Payable, Net (+L)	107,260	100,000	93,376

Interest Expense

As time passes, the company incurs Interest Expense on its bond liability. Because the bond liability was recorded in a single account, the interest calculation is the same whether the bond has been issued at a premium or discount. The following version of the interest formula is used to compute Interest Expense.

> **Interest (I) = Principal (P)   × Interest Rate (R)   × Time (T)**
> **Interest Expense = Bonds Payable, Net × Market Interest Rate × n/12**

The market interest rate is determined by using present value techniques (discussed in Appendix C) that relate the bond's issue price to the payments promised over the life of the bond. The market interest rate also can be determined using the XIRR and RATE functions in Excel.

Bond Premiums

Our bond premium example indicated that General Mills received $107,260 on the issue date, which we would record in Bonds Payable, Net, using the journal entry shown above. The $107,260 issue price implies a 4 percent market interest rate. The bonds promise to pay the 6 percent stated interest rate on their total face value of $100,000. This information is used to compute Interest Expense and the annual cash payment as follows:

> 2013:   **Interest (I) = Principal (P)   × Interest Rate (R)   × Time (T)**
> **Interest Expense = Bonds Payable, Net × Market Interest Rate × n/12**
> $4,290 = $107,260   × 4%   × 12/12

> **Interest (I) = Principal (P) × Interest Rate (R)   × Time (T)**
> **Cash Payment = Face Value   × Stated Interest Rate × n/12**
> $6,000 = $100,000   × 6%   × 12/12

Because the $6,000 cash interest payment exceeds the $4,290 Interest Expense by $1,710 ($6,000 − $4,290 = $1,710), General Mills records a $1,710 reduction in Bonds

Payable, Net. In effect, the $6,000 cash payment includes both an interest compo-
nent ($4,290) and a partial repayment of the bond liability ($1,710), as analyzed and
recorded below:

1 Analyze

Assets	=	Liabilities	+	Stockholders' Equity
Cash −6,000		Bonds Payable, Net −1,710		Interest Expense (+E) −4,290

2 Record

dr Interest Expense (+E, −SE) 4,290
dr Bonds Payable, Net (−L)...... 1,710
   cr Cash (−A) 6,000

Similar calculations and accounting effects occur each period until the bonds
mature. The only thing to watch out for is that Bonds Payable, Net decreases each
year because the cash payment includes a partial repayment of the bond liability.
For example, after the above entry is recorded on December 31, 2013, Bonds Payable, Net decreases by $1,710, from $107,260 to $105,550. This new balance is used
to compute Interest Expense for the second year of the bond (for the year ended
December 31, 2014):

Bonds Payable, Net (L)	
	107,260 1/1/2013
12/31/2013 1,710	
	105,550 12/31/2013

2014:	Interest (I) =	Principal (P)	× Interest Rate (R)	× Time (T)
Interest Expense =		Bonds Payable, Net ×	Market Interest Rate ×	n/12
$4,222 =		$105,550	× 4%	× 12/12

Because the $6,000 annual cash payment exceeds the $4,222 Interest Expense by
$1,778 ($6,000 − $4,222 = $1,778), General Mills records a $1,778 reduction in Bonds
Payable, Net in 2014. In effect, the $6,000 cash payment includes both an interest com-
ponent ($4,222) and a partial repayment of the bond liability ($1,778). As the following
amortization schedule shows, the bond liability continues to decrease until, at maturity,
it reaches the bonds' face value ($100,000).

	Bond Premium Amortization Schedule: Simplified Method				
	Beginning of Year	Changes During the Year			End of Year
Period	(A) Bonds Payable, Net	(B) Interest Expense	(C) Cash Paid	(D) = (C − B) Reduction in Bonds Payable, Net	(E) = (A − D) Bonds Payable, Net
1/1/13–12/31/13	$107,260	$4,290	$6,000	$1,710	$105,550
1/1/14–12/31/14	105,550	4,222	6,000	1,778	103,772
1/1/15–12/31/15	103,772	4,151	6,000	1,849	101,923
1/1/16–12/31/16	101,923	4,077	6,000	1,923	100,000

Bond Discounts

Our bond discount example indicated that General Mills received $93,376 on the
issue date, which we would record in Bonds Payable, Net, using the journal entry
shown on page 472. This issue price implies an 8 percent market interest rate. The
bonds promise to pay the 6 percent stated interest rate on their total face value of

$100,000. This information is used to compute Interest Expense and the annual cash payment as follows:

2013:	Interest (I)	=	Principal (P)	× Interest Rate (R)	× Time (T)
	Interest Expense	=	Bonds Payable, Net	× Market Interest Rate	× n/12
	$7,470	=	$93,376	× 8%	× 12/12

	Interest (I)	=	Principal (P)	× Interest Rate (R)	× Time (T)
	Cash Payment	=	Face Value	× Stated Interest Rate	× n/12
	$6,000	=	$100,000	× 6%	× 12/12

Because the $7,470 Interest Expense is more than the $6,000 cash paid, General Mills records the $1,470 difference ($7,470 − $6,000 = $1,470) as an increase in its liability Bonds Payable, Net, as follows:

1 Analyze

Assets	=	Liabilities	+	Stockholders' Equity
Cash −6,000		Bonds Payable, Net +1,470		Interest Expense (+E) −7,470

2 Record

dr Interest Expense (+E, −SE)	7,470	
cr Bonds Payable, Net (+L)		1,470
cr Cash (−A)		6,000

Recording the $1,470 as the liability Bonds Payable, Net is appropriate because General Mills will pay this amount at maturity, as part of the face value of the bond.

Similar calculations and accounting effects occur each period until the bonds mature. The only thing to watch out for is that Bonds Payable, Net increases each year because the cash payment is less than the interest expense. For example, after the above entry is recorded on December 31, 2013, Bonds Payable, Net increases by $1,470, from $93,376 to $94,846. This new balance is used to compute Interest Expense for the second year of the bond (for the year ended December 31, 2014):

Bonds Payable, Net (L)	
	93,376 1/1/2013
	1,470 12/31/2013
	94,846 12/31/2013

2014:	Interest (I)	=	Principal (P)	× Interest Rate (R)	× Time (T)
	Interest Expense	=	Bonds Payable, Net	× Market Interest Rate	× n/12
	$7,588	=	$94,846	× 8%	× 12/12

Because the $7,588 Interest Expense exceeds the $6,000 annual cash payment by $1,588 ($7,588 − $6,000 = $1,588), General Mills records a $1,588 increase in Bonds Payable, Net in 2014. In effect, the $1,588 in unpaid interest will be paid at maturity. As the following amortization schedule shows, the bond liability continues to increase until, at maturity, it reaches the bonds' face value ($100,000).

Bond Discount Amortization Schedule: Simplified Method

	Beginning of Year	Changes During the Year			End of Year
Period	(A) Bonds Payable, Net	(B) Interest Expense	(C) Cash Paid	(D) = (B − C) Reduction in Bonds Payable, Net	(E) = (A + D) Bonds Payable, Net
1/1/13–12/31/13	$93,376	$7,470	$6,000	$1,470	$ 94,846
1/1/14–12/31/14	94,846	7,588	6,000	1,588	96,434
1/1/15–12/31/15	96,434	7,715	6,000	1,715	98,149
1/1/16–12/31/16	98,149	7,851	6,000	1,851	100,000

REVIEW THE CHAPTER

DEMONSTRATION CASE A: ACCRUED LIABILITIES AND UNEARNED REVENUE

Online Games, Inc., reported the following information in its accounting records on December 31, 2013.

Annual subscription payments received in December 2013 for 2014 services	$12,000
Gross salaries earned by employees (December 26–31, 2013)	3,600
Income taxes withheld from employees (December 26–31, 2013)	550
FICA taxes withheld from employees (December 26–31, 2013)	210
Net payment to employees (made on December 31, 2013)	2,840

The 2014 subscription payments will be earned equally throughout each month of 2014. The employees were paid $2,840 on December 31, 2013, but the withholdings have not yet been remitted nor have the matching employer FICA contributions.

Required:

1. Describe how the 2014 subscription payments should be reported in the balance sheet and income statement on (a) December 31, 2013, and (b) January 31, 2014.
2. Show the accounting equation effects and give the journal entries for (a) the receipt of annual subscription payments in December 2013, and (b) any required adjustments for the subscription payments on January 31, 2014.
3. Compute the total payroll costs relating to the period from December 26–31, 2013. (Assume $280 in total unemployment taxes.)
4. Show the accounting equation effects and give the journal entries on December 31, 2013, to adjust for (a) salaries and wages, and (b) payroll taxes relating to December 26–31, 2013.

Suggested Solution

1. **a.** On December 31, 2013, the $12,000 of advance subscription payments would be reported on the balance sheet as a current liability called Unearned Revenue. No amounts relating to 2014 subscription services would be reported in the 2013 income statement.
   b. On January 31, 2014, one month of subscription services would be earned, so Unearned Revenue on the balance sheet would be reduced by $1,000 (= $12,000 × 1/12) and Subscription Revenue on the income statement would be increased by $1,000.

2. **a.** <u>December 2013 (receipt of 2014 subscription payments):</u>

Assets	=	Liabilities	+	Stockholders' Equity
Cash +12,000		Unearned Revenue +12,000		

   dr Cash (+A) 12,000
      cr Unearned Revenue (+L)   12,000

   b. <u>January 31, 2014 (earned one month of 2014 subscriptions):</u>

Assets	=	Liabilities	+	Stockholders' Equity
		Unearned Revenue −1,000		Subscription Revenue (+R) +1,000

   dr Unearned Revenue (−L) 1,000
      cr Subscription Revenue (+R, +SE).........   1,000

3. <u>Computation of total payroll costs:</u>

Salaries and wages:	Net pay to employees	$2,840
	Income taxes withheld from employees	550
	FICA taxes withheld from employees	210
	Total cost of salaries and wages	3,600
Employer payroll taxes:	FICA taxes (matching contribution)	210
	Unemployment taxes	280
Total payroll costs:		$4,090

4a. <u>Salaries and wage costs:</u>

Assets	=	Liabilities	+	Stockholders' Equity	
Cash −2,840		Withheld Income		Salaries and Wages Expense (+E)	−3,600
		Taxes Payable +550			
		FICA Payable +210			

dr Salaries and Wages Expense (+E, −SE) 3,600
    cr Withheld Income Taxes Payable (+L)... 550
    cr FICA Payable (+L)... 210
    cr Cash (−A) 2,840

4b. <u>Employer-related payroll costs:</u>

Assets	=	Liabilities	+	Stockholders' Equity	
		FICA Payable +210		Payroll Tax Expense (+E)	−490
		Unemployment			
		Tax Payable +280			

dr Payroll Tax Expense (+E, −SE) 490
    cr FICA Payable (+L)... 210
    cr Unemployment Tax Payable (+L)... 280

DEMONSTRATION CASE B: NOTES PAYABLE AND ACCRUED INTEREST

Caterpillar, Inc.

Assume that on December 3, 2010, Caterpillar, Inc., had received $350 million when it issued promissory notes that will mature in 2015. The notes pay interest at the annual rate of 7.00 percent, which was comparable to other interest rates available in the market. Caterpillar's fiscal year ends on December 31. On December 31, 2010, Caterpillar had $20.4 billion in Cash, Short-term Investments, and Accounts Receivable, Net and $22.0 billion in current liabilities.

Required:

1. Describe which sections of Caterpillar's classified balance sheet are affected by its issuance of promissory notes.
2. Give the journal entry on December 3, 2010, to record the issuance of the notes.
3. Give the journal entry on December 31, 2010, to record one month of interest expense, assuming none had been accrued prior to that date.
4. Compute Caterpillar's quick ratio at December 31, 2010. What proportion of its current liabilities could Caterpillar pay quickly if it were required to? What was the likely effect (increase or decrease) of the note issuance on the company's quick ratio?

Suggested Solution

1. The issuance of notes increases Caterpillar's Cash (a current asset) and its Notes Payable (a long-term liability) by $350 million.
2. December 3, 2010 (issuance date):

    dr Cash (+A)... 350,000,000
        cr Notes Payable (+L) 350,000,000

3. December 31, 2010 (accrual of interest expense for one month):

    dr Interest Expense (+E, −SE) ($350,000,000 × 7.00% × 1/12)...... 2,041,667
        cr Interest Payable (+L)... 2,041,667

4. December 31, 2010, quick ratio = (Cash + Short-term Investments + Accounts Receivable, Net) ÷ Current Liabilities
= $20.4 ÷ $22.0 = 0.93

The quick ratio of 0.93 implies that Caterpillar could quickly pay 93 percent of its current liabilities if it were required to.

The issuance of the notes increases the quick ratio, because Cash increased by $350 million, but the only increase in current liabilities was a relatively small amount of Interest Payable. The $350 million in Notes Payable increased long-term liabilities.

DEMONSTRATION CASE C: BONDS PAYABLE

To raise funds to build a new plant, Reed Company issued bonds with the following terms:

> Face value of the bonds: $100,000.
> Dates: Issued January 1, 2013; due in 5 years on January 1, 2018.
> Interest rate: 6 percent per year, payable on December 31 each year.

The bonds were issued on January 1, 2013, at 104.3, implying a 5 percent market rate of interest. The annual accounting period for Reed Company ends on December 31.

Required:

1. How much cash did Reed Company receive from the issuance of the bonds? Show computations.
2. What was the amount of premium on the bonds payable? Over how many months should it be amortized?
3. Show the accounting equation effects and give the journal entry on January 1, 2013, for recording the issuance of the bonds.
4. (Supplement 10A) Show the accounting equation effects and give the journal entry required on December 31, 2013, relating to interest on the bond. Use the straight-line amortization method.
5. (Supplement 10B) Show the accounting equation effects and give the journal entry required on December 31, 2013, relating to interest on the bond. Use the effective-interest amortization method.
6. (Supplement 10C) Show the accounting equation effects and give the journal entries required on January 1, 2013, relating to the bond issuance and on December 31, 2013, relating to interest on the bond. Use the simplified effective-interest amortization method.

Suggested Solution

1. Issue price of the bonds: $100,000 × 104.3% = $104,300.
2. Premium on the bonds payable: $104,300 − $100,000 = $4,300.
   Months amortized: From date of issue, January 1, 2013, to maturity date, January 1, 2018
   = 5 years × 12 months per year = 60 months.
3. January 1, 2013 (issuance date):

Assets		=	Liabilities		+	Stockholders' Equity
Cash	+104,300		Bonds Payable	+100,000		
			Premium on			
			Bonds Payable	+4,300		

dr Cash (+A) 104,300
  cr Premium on Bonds Payable (+L)................................. 4,300
  cr Bonds Payable (+L) 100,000

4. December 31, 2013:

Assets		=	Liabilities		+	Stockholders' Equity	
Cash	−6,000		Premium on			Interest Expense (+E)	−5,140
			Bonds Payable	−860			

dr Premium on Bonds Payable (−L) ($4,300 × 12/60 months)........ 860
dr Interest Expense (+E, −SE) ($6,000 − $860)............................ 5,140
  cr Cash (−A) ($100,000 × 6% × 12/12) 6,000

5. December 31, 2013:

Assets		=	Liabilities		+	Stockholders' Equity	
Cash	−6,000		Premium on Bonds Payable	−785		Interest Expense (+E)	−5,215

dr Interest Expense (+E, −SE) ($104,300 × 5% × 12/12)................... 5,215
dr Premium on Bonds Payable (−L) ($6,000 − $5,215)...................... 785
   cr Cash (−A) ($100,000 × 6% × 12/12)   6,000

6. January 1, 2013 (issuance date):

Assets		=	Liabilities		+	Stockholders' Equity
Cash	+104,300		Bonds Payable, Net	+104,300		

dr Cash (+A).. 104,300
   cr Bonds Payable, Net (+L)   104,300

December 31, 2013 (interest accrual):

Assets		=	Liabilities		+	Stockholders' Equity	
Cash	−6,000		Bonds Payable, Net	−785		Interest Expense (+E)	−5,215

dr Interest Expense (+E, −SE) ($104,300 × 5% × 12/12)................... 5,215
dr Bonds Payable, Net (−L) ($6,000 − $5,215)................................... 785
   cr Cash (−A) ($100,000 × 6% × 12/12)   6,000

CHAPTER SUMMARY

LO 10-1   **Explain the role of liabilities in financing a business. p. 448**

- Liabilities play a vital role in allowing a business to buy goods and services on credit, cover gaps in cash flows, and expand into new regions and markets.

- Liabilities are classified as current if due to be paid with current assets within the current operating cycle of the business or within one year of the balance sheet date (whichever is longer). All other liabilities are considered long-term.

LO 10-2   **Explain how to account for common types of current liabilities. p. 449**

- Liabilities are initially reported at their cash equivalent value, which is the amount of cash that a creditor would accept to settle the liability immediately after the transaction or event occurred.

- Liabilities are increased whenever additional obligations arise (including interest) and are reduced whenever the company makes payments or provides services to the creditor.

LO 10-3   **Analyze and record bond liability transactions. p. 456**

- For most public issuances of debt (bonds), the amount borrowed by the company does not equal the amount repaid at maturity. The effect of a bond discount is to provide the borrower less money than the value stated on the face of the bond, which increases the cost of borrowing above the interest rate stated on the bond. The effect of a bond premium is to provide the borrower more money than the face value repaid at maturity, which decreases the cost of borrowing below the stated interest rate.

- Interest Expense reports the cost of borrowing, which equals the periodic interest payments plus (or minus) the amount of the bond discount (or premium) amortized in that interest period.

LO 10-4   **Describe how to account for contingent liabilities. p. 463**

- A contingent liability is a potential liability (and loss) that has arisen as a result of a past transaction or event. Its ultimate outcome will not be known until a future event occurs or fails to occur. Under GAAP, it is recorded when probable and estimable.

Calculate and interpret the quick ratio and the times interest earned ratio. p. 464   LO 10-5

- The quick ratio measures the company's ability to pay its current liabilities using current assets that are quickly converted into cash.
- The times interest earned ratio measures a company's ability to meet its interest obligations with resources generated from its profit-making activities.

Accounting Decision Tools		
Name of Measure	Formula	What It Tells You
Quick ratio	$\dfrac{\text{(Cash + Short-term Investments + Accounts Receivable, Net)}}{\text{Current Liabilities}}$	• Whether liquid assets are sufficient to pay current liabilities • The higher the number the better able to quickly pay
Times interest earned ratio	$\dfrac{\text{(Net Income + Interest Expense + Income Tax Expense)}}{\text{Interest Expense}}$	• Whether sufficient resources are generated to cover interest costs • The higher the number the better the coverage

KEY TERMS

Accrued Liabilities p. 450
Contingent Liability p. 463
Current Liabilities p. 448
Discount p. 457
Effective-Interest Method of Amortization (Supplement 10B) p. 467

Face Value p. 457
Issue Price p. 457
Line of Credit p. 465
Market Interest Rate p. 459
Maturity Date p. 457
Premium p. 457

Present Value p. 457
Quick Ratio p. 464
Stated Interest Rate p. 457
Straight-Line Method of Amortization (Supplement 10A) p. 466
Times Interest Earned Ratio p. 465

See complete definitions in the glossary in the back of this text.

HOMEWORK HELPER

Alternative terms

- The stated interest rate on a bond is also called the coupon rate or contract rate. The market interest rate is also called the effective interest rate or yield rate.
- The word amortize comes from the root word "mort," which means to kill or eliminate; as bond discounts and premiums are amortized, they are gradually eliminated.
- The quick ratio is also called the acid test ratio.

Helpful reminders

- From the employer's perspective, payroll deductions create liabilities, not expenses. They are not expenses because they do not increase the employer's wages and salaries cost; they simply redirect part of the wages and salaries payments to a government agency or other organization, rather than to employees.
- Bonds issue above face value (at a premium) if their stated interest rate is attractive (more than the market interest rate). If bonds have issued at a premium, their periodic cash payments will be greater than the interest expense, causing a reduction in the bond liability's carrying value.
- Bonds issue below face value (at a discount) if their stated interest is unattractive (less than the market interest rate). If bonds have issued at a discount, their periodic cash payments will be less than the interest expense, causing an increase in the bond liability's carrying value.

Frequent mistakes

- Use the stated interest rate, not the market interest rate, to calculate the cash paid periodically on a bond. (The market interest rate is used to calculate Interest Expense when using the effective-interest method.)

PRACTICE MATERIAL

QUESTIONS (⊖Symbol indicates questions that require analysis from more than one perspective.)

1. Describe three ways in which liabilities are used to finance business activities.
2. Define *liability*. What's the difference between a current liability and a long-term liability?
3. What three factors influence the dollar amount reported for liabilities?
4. Define *accrued liability*. Give an example of a typical accrued liability.
5. Why is Unearned Revenue considered a liability?
6. Why are payroll taxes and sales taxes considered liabilities?
7. Your company plans to hire an employee at a yearly salary of $70,000. Someone in your company says the actual cost will be lower because of payroll deductions. Someone else says it will be higher. Who is right? What is likely to be the total cost to the company? Explain. ⊖
8. If a company has a long-term loan that has only two years remaining until it matures, how is it reported on the balance sheet (*a*) this year, and (*b*) next year?
9. What are the reasons that some bonds are issued at a discount and others are issued at a premium?
10. What is the difference between the stated interest rate and the market interest rate on a bond?
11. Will the stated interest rate be higher than the market interest rate or will the market interest rate be higher than the stated interest rate when a bond is issued at (*a*) face value, (*b*) a discount, and (*c*) a premium?
12. What is the carrying value of a bond payable?
13. What is the quick ratio? How is it related to the classification of liabilities?
14. What is the difference between a secured bond and a debenture? Which type carries more risk for the lender?
15. What is a contingent liability? How is a contingent liability reported under GAAP? How does this differ under IFRS?
16. (Supplement 10A) How is interest expense calculated using the straight-line method of amortization for a bond issued at (*a*) a discount and (*b*) a premium?
17. (Supplement 10B) How is interest expense calculated using the effective-interest method of amortization for a bond issued at (*a*) a discount and (*b*) a premium?
18. (Supplement 10C) How is interest expense calculated using the simplified approach to the effective-interest method for a bond issued at (*a*) a discount and (*b*) a premium?

MULTIPLE CHOICE

1. Which of the following best describes Accrued Liabilities?
   a. Long-term liabilities.
   b. Current amounts owed to suppliers of inventory.
   c. Expenses incurred, but not paid at the end of the accounting period.
   d. Revenues that have been collected, but not earned.
2. As of February 28, 2012, American Greetings Corporation had 7,400 full-time and 17,400 part-time employees. Assume that in the last pay period of the year, the company paid $8,000,000 to employees after deducting $2,000,000 for employee income taxes, $612,000 for FICA taxes, and $700,000 for other purposes. No payments have been made to the government relating to these taxes. Which of the following statements is true regarding this pay period?
   a. FICA Taxes Payable should be $612,000.
   b. FICA Taxes Payable should be $1,224,000.
   c. Salaries and Wages Expense should be $8,000,000.
   d. None of the above is true.
3. Assume that Warnaco Group Inc., the makers of Calvin Klein underwear, borrowed $100,000 from the bank to be repaid over the next five years, with principal payments beginning next month. Which of the following

best describes the presentation of this debt in the balance sheet as of today (the date of borrowing)?
   a. $100,000 in the long-term liability section.
   b. $100,000 *plus* the interest to be paid over the five-year period in the long-term liability section.
   c. A portion of the $100,000 in the current liability section, and the remainder of the principal in the long-term liability section.
   d. A portion of the $100,000 plus interest in the current liability section, and the remainder of the principal plus interest in the long-term liability section.
4. Assume that Speedo International received $400,000 for long-term promissory notes that were issued on November 1. The notes pay interest on April 30 and October 31 at the annual rate of 6 percent, which was comparable to other interest rates in the market at that time. Which of the following journal entries would be required at December 31?

   a. *dr* Interest Expense........................... 4,000
          cr Interest Payable......................   4,000

   b. *dr* Interest Expense........................... 4,000
          cr Cash...   4,000

c. *dr* Interest Expense.......................... 4,000
   dr Interest Payable.......................... 8,000
     cr Cash..   12,000

d. *dr* Interest Expense.......................... 8,000
   dr Interest Payable.......................... 4,000
     cr Cash..   12,000

5. Which of the following does not impact the calculation of the cash interest payments to be made to bondholders?

  a. Face value of the bond.

  b. Stated interest rate.

  c. Market interest rate.

  d. The length of time between payments.

6. Which of the following is false when a bond is issued at a premium?

  a. The bond will issue for an amount above its face value.

  b. Interest expense will exceed the cash interest payments.

  c. The market interest rate is lower than the stated interest rate.

  d. The issue price will be quoted at a number greater than 100.

7. To determine if a bond will be issued at a premium, discount, or at face value, one must know which of the following pairs of information?

  a. The face value and the stated interest rate on the date the bonds were issued.

  b. The face value and the market interest rate on the date the bonds were issued.

  c. The stated interest rate and the market interest rate on the date the bonds were issued.

  d. You can't tell without having more information.

8. A bond is issued at a price of 103 and retired early at a price of 97. Which of the following is true?

  a. A gain will be reported on the income statement when the bond is issued.

  b. A loss will be reported on the income statement when the bond is issued.

  c. A gain will be reported on the income statement when the bond is retired.

  d. A loss will be reported on the income statement when the bond is retired.

9. In a recent year, Land O' Lakes, Inc., reported (in millions) Income from Operations of $206, Net Income of $160, Interest Expense of $63, and Income Tax Expense of $15. What was this dairy company's times interest earned ratio (rounded) for the year?

  a. 1.49   c. 3.27

  b. 2.53   d. 3.78

10. Big Hitter Corp. is facing a class-action lawsuit in the upcoming year. It is possible, but not probable, that the company will have to pay a settlement of approximately $2,000,000 in the upcoming year. How would this fact be reported, if at all, in the financial statements prepared at the end of the current month using GAAP?

  a. Report $2,000,000 as a current liability.

  b. Report $2,000,000 as a long-term liability.

  c. Describe the potential liability in the notes to the financial statements.

  d. Reporting is not required in this case.

> For answers to the Multiple-Choice Questions **see page Q1** located in the last section of the book.

MINI-EXERCISES

McGraw Hill connect | ACCOUNTING

M10-1 Recording Unearned Revenues

LO 10-2

A local theater company sells 1,500 season ticket packages at a price of $250 per package. The first show in the ten-show season starts this week. Show the accounting equation effects and prepare the journal entries related to (*a*) the sale of the season tickets before the first show and (*b*) the revenue earned after putting on the first show.

M10-2 Recording Sales and State Tax

LO 10-2

Ahlers Clocks

Ahlers Clocks is a retailer of wall, mantle, and grandfather clocks and is located in the Empire Mall in Sioux Falls, South Dakota. Assume that a grandfather clock was sold for $10,000 cash plus 4 percent sales tax. The clock had originally cost Ahlers $6,000. Show the accounting equation effects and prepare the journal entries related to this transaction. Assume Ahlers uses a perpetual inventory system, as explained in Chapter 6.

M10-3 Calculating Payroll Tax Liabilities

LO 10-2

Lightning Electronics is a midsize manufacturer of lithium batteries. The company's payroll records for the November 1–14 pay period show that employees earned wages totaling $50,000 but that employee income taxes totaling $7,000 and FICA taxes totaling $2,625 were withheld from this amount. The net pay was directly deposited into the employees' bank accounts. What was the amount of net pay? Assuming Lighting Electronics must also pay $250 of unemployment taxes for this pay period, what amount would be reported as the total payroll costs?

M10-4 Reporting Payroll Tax Liabilities

LO 10-2

Refer to M10-3. Prepare the journal entry or entries that Lightning would use to record the payroll. Include both employee and employer taxes.

LO 10-2   **M10-5 Reporting Current and Noncurrent Portions of Long-term Debt**

Assume that on December 1, 2013, your company borrowed $15,000, a portion of which is to be repaid each year on November 30. Specifically, your company will make the following principal payments: 2014, $2,000; 2015, $3,000; 2016, $4,000; and 2017, $6,000. Show how this loan will be reported in the December 31, 2014 and 2013 balance sheets, assuming that principal payments will be made when required.

LO 10-2   **M10-6 Recording a Note Payable**

Greener Pastures Corporation borrowed $1,000,000 on November 1, 2012. The note carried a 9 percent interest rate with the principal and interest payable on June 1, 2013. Show the accounting equation effects and prepare the journal entries for (a) the note issued on November 1 and (b) the interest accrual on December 31.

LO 10-2   **M10-7 Reporting Interest and Long-term Debt, Including Current Portion**

Barton Chocolates used a promissory note to borrow $1,000,000 on July 1, 2012, at an annual interest rate of 6 percent. The note is to be repaid in yearly installments of $200,000, plus accrued interest, on June 30 of every year until the note is paid in full (on June 30, 2017). Show how the results of this transaction would be reported in a classified balance sheet prepared as of December 31, 2012.

LO 10-3   **M10-8 Determining Bond Discount or Premium from Quoted Price**

Ford Motor Company

On May 9, 2011, finance.yahoo.com/bonds quoted a bond price of 129.7 for Ford Motor Company's 9.3 percent bonds maturing on March 1, 2030. Were the bonds selling at a discount or premium? Does this mean the market interest rate for comparable bonds was higher or lower than 9.3 percent?

LO 10-3   **M10-9 Computing and Reporting a Bond Liability at an Issuance Price of 97**

E-Tech Initiatives Limited plans to issue $500,000, 10-year, 4 percent bonds. Interest is payable annually on December 31. All of the bonds will be issued on January 1, 2013. Show how the bonds would be reported on the January 2, 2013, balance sheet if they are issued at 97.

LO 10-3   **M10-10 Computing and Reporting a Bond Liability at an Issuance Price of 102**

Repeat M10-9 assuming the bonds are issued at 102.

LO 10-3   **M10-11 Recording Bonds Issued at Face Value**

Schlitterbahn Waterslide Company issued 25,000, 10-year, 5 percent, $100 bonds on January 1, 2013, at face value. Interest is payable each December 31. Show the accounting equation effects and prepare journal entries for (a) the issuance of these bonds on January 1, 2013, and (b) the interest payment on December 31, 2013.

LO 10-4   **M10-12 Reporting a Contingent Liability**

Buzz Coffee Shops is famous for its large servings of hot coffee. After a famous case involving McDonald's, the lawyer for Buzz warned management (during 2011) that it could be sued if someone were to spill hot coffee and be burned. "With the temperature of your coffee, I can guarantee it's just a matter of time before you're sued for $1,000,000." Buzz felt the likelihood was remote. Unfortunately, in 2013, the lawyer's prediction came true when a customer filed suit. After consulting with his attorney, Buzz felt the loss was possible but not likely or probable. The case went to trial in 2014, and the jury awarded the customer $400,000 in damages, which the company immediately appealed. Buzz felt a loss was probable but believed a lower amount could be negotiated. During 2015, the customer and the company settled their dispute for $150,000. What is the proper reporting of this liability each year from 2013 through 2015 under GAAP? Would the reporting differ under IFRS?

LO 10-5   **M10-13 Computing the Quick Ratio and the Times Interest Earned Ratio**

The balance sheet for Shaver Corporation reported the following: cash $5,000; short-term investments $10,000; net accounts receivable $35,000; inventory $40,000; prepaids $10,000; current liabilities, $40,000; total stockholders' equity, $90,000; net income, $3,320; interest expense, $4,400; income before income taxes, $5,280. Compute Shaver's quick ratio and times interest earned ratio. Based on these ratios, does it appear Shaver will be able to meet its obligations to pay current liabilities and future interest obligations as they become payable?

M10-14 Analyzing the Impact of Transactions on the Quick Ratio   LO 10-5

BSO, Inc., has liquid assets of $600,000 and current liabilities of $500,000, resulting in a quick ratio of 1.2. For each of the following transactions, determine whether the quick ratio will increase, decrease, or remain the same. Each item is independent.

a. Purchased $20,000 of new inventory on credit.
b. Paid accounts payable in the amount of $50,000.
c. Recorded accrued salaries in the amount of $100,000.
d. Borrowed $250,000 from a local bank, to be repaid in 90 days.

M10-15 (Supplement 10A) Recording Bond Issuance and Interest Payment   LO 10-S1
(Straight-Line Amortization)

Simko Company issued $600,000, 10-year, 5 percent bonds on January 1, 2012. The bonds were issued for $580,000. Interest is payable annually on December 31. Using straight-line amortization, prepare journal entries to record (a) the bond issuance on January 1, 2012, and (b) the payment of interest on December 31, 2012.

M10-16 (Supplement 10B) Recording Bond Issuance and Interest Payment   LO 10-S2
(Effective-Interest Amortization)

Clem Company issued $800,000, 10-year, 5 percent bonds on January 1, 2012. The bonds sold for $741,000. Interest is payable annually on December 31. Using effective-interest amortization, prepare journal entries to record (a) the bond issuance on January 1, 2012, and (b) the payment of interest on December 31, 2012. The market interest rate on the bonds is 6 percent.

M10-17 (Supplement 10C) Recording Interest Accrual and Interest Payment   LO 10-S3
(Simplified Approach to Effective-Interest Amortization)

On January 1, 2012, Buchheit Enterprises reported $95,000 in a liability called "Bonds Payable, Net." This liability related to a $100,000 bond with a stated interest rate of 5 percent that was issued when the market interest rate was 6 percent. Assuming that interest is paid December 31 each year, prepare the journal entry to record interest paid on December 31, 2012, using the simplified effective-interest method shown in chapter supplement 10C.

EXERCISES

E10-1 Determining Financial Statement Effects   LO 10-2
of Transactions Involving Notes Payable

Many businesses borrow money during periods of increased business activity to finance inventory and accounts receivable. Target Corporation is one of America's largest general merchandise retailers. Each Christmas, Target builds up its inventory to meet the needs of Christmas shoppers. A large portion of Christmas sales are on credit. As a result, Target often collects cash from the sales several months after Christmas. Assume that on November 1, 2013, Target borrowed $6 million cash from Metropolitan Bank and signed a promissory note that matures in six months. The interest rate was 8.0 percent payable at maturity. The accounting period ends December 31.

Target Corporation

Required:

1. Indicate the accounts, amounts, and effects (+ for increase, − for decrease, and NE for no effect) of the (a) issuance of the note on November 1, (b) impact of the adjusting entry on December 31, 2013, and (c) the payment of the note and interest on April 30, 2014, on the accounting equation. Use the following structure for your answer:

Date	Assets	=	Liabilities	+	Stockholders' Equity

2. If Target needs extra cash every Christmas season, should management borrow money on a long-term basis to avoid negotiating a new short-term loan each year? Explain your answer.

LO 10-2   **E10-2 Recording a Note Payable through Its Time to Maturity**

Use the information in E10-1 to complete the following requirements.

Required:

1. Give the journal entry to record the note on November 1, 2013.
2. Give any adjusting entry required on December 31, 2013.
3. Give the journal entry to record payment of the note and interest on the maturity date, April 30, 2014, assuming that interest has not been recorded since December 31, 2013.

LO 10-2   **E10-3 Recording Payroll Costs**

McLoyd Company completed the salary and wage payroll for March 2013. The payroll provided the following details:

Salaries and wages earned	$400,000
Employee income taxes withheld	37,000
FICA taxes withheld	28,600
Unemployment taxes	2,780

Required:

1. Considering both employee and employer payroll taxes, use the preceding information to calculate the total labor cost for the company.
2. Prepare the journal entry to record the payroll for March, including employee deductions (but excluding employer payroll taxes). Employees were paid in March but amounts withheld were not yet remitted.
3. Prepare the journal entry to record the employer's FICA taxes and unemployment taxes.

LO 10-2   **E10-4 Recording Payroll Costs with and without Withholdings**

Assume an employee of Rocco Rock Company earns $1,000 of gross wages during the current pay period, and is required to remit to the government $100 for income tax and $50 for FICA. Consider the following two procedures for paying the employee:

Procedure 1 (Withholdings)	Procedure 2 (No Withholdings)
Rocco Rock Company pays the employee net wages of $850 and will remit income taxes and FICA on behalf of the employee.	Rocco Rock Company pays the employee gross wages of $1,000 and the employee is responsible for remitting income taxes and FICA himself.

Required:

1. Ignoring employer payroll taxes, under each procedure calculate (a) the total labor cost for the company, and (b) the amount of cash the employee will have after satisfying all responsibilities to the government. Do your answers for procedures 1 and 2 differ for (a)? For (b)?
2. Explain why procedure 1 (withholdings) is the approach required by the government.
3. Considering that employers are responsible for matching employees' FICA contributions, explain why employers might also prefer procedure 1 over procedure 2.
4. Prepare the journal entries required by the employer under procedure 1, assuming that the employee is paid in cash, but the withholdings and matching employer FICA contribution have not yet been paid. (Assume no unemployment taxes.)

LO 10-2, 10-5   **E10-5 Determining the Impact of Current Liability Transactions, Including Analysis of the Quick Ratio**

Bryant Company sells a wide range of inventories, which are initially purchased on account. Occasionally, a short-term note payable is used to obtain cash for current use. The following transactions were selected from those occurring during 2013:

a. On January 10, 2013, purchased merchandise on credit for $18,000. The company uses a perpetual inventory system.
b. On March 1, 2013, borrowed $40,000 cash from City Bank and signed a promissory note with a face amount of $40,000, due at the end of six months, accruing interest at an annual rate of 8 percent, payable at maturity.

Required:

1. For each of the transactions, indicate the accounts, amounts, and effects (+ for increase, − for decrease, and NE for no effect) on the accounting equation. Use the following structure:

Date	Assets	=	Liabilities	+	Stockholders' Equity

2. What amount of cash is paid on the maturity date of the note?
3. Discuss the impact of each transaction on the quick ratio. (Assume Bryant Company's quick ratio was 1.10 prior to each transaction.)

E10-6 Determining and Recording the Financial Statement Effects of Unearned Subscription Revenue

LO 10-2

Reader's Digest Association is a publisher of magazines, books, and music collections. The following note is from a recent annual report:

Revenues

Sales of our magazine subscriptions are deferred (as unearned revenue) and recognized as revenues proportionately over the subscription period.

Assume that Reader's Digest (*a*) collected $420 million in 2012 for magazines that will be delivered later in 2012 and 2013, and (*b*) delivered $204 million worth of magazines on these subscriptions in 2012.

Required:

1. Using the information given, indicate the accounts, amounts, and accounting equation effects (+ for increase, − for decrease, and NE for no effect) of transactions (a) and (b).
2. Using the information given, prepare the journal entries that would be recorded in 2012 and 2013.

E10-7 Preparing Journal Entries to Record Issuance of Bonds and Payment of Interest

LO 10-3

On January 1, 2013, Applied Technologies Corporation (ATC) issued $500,000 in bonds that mature in 10 years. The bonds have a stated interest rate of 10 percent. When the bonds were issued, the market interest rate was 10 percent. The bonds pay interest once per year on December 31.

Required:

1. Determine the price at which the bonds were issued and the amount that ATC received at issuance.
2. Prepare the journal entry to record the bond issuance.
3. Prepare the journal entry to record the interest payment on December 31, 2013, assuming no interest has been accrued earlier in the year.

E10-8 Preparing Journal Entries to Record Issuance of Bonds at Face Value, Payment of Interest, and Early Retirement

LO 10-3

On January 1, 2013, Innovative Solutions, Inc., issued $200,000 in bonds at face value. The bonds have a stated interest rate of 6 percent. The bonds mature in 10 years and pay interest once per year on December 31.

Required:

1. Prepare the journal entry to record the bond issuance.
2. Prepare the journal entry to record the interest payment on December 31, 2013. Assume no interest has been accrued earlier in the year.
3. Assume the bonds were retired immediately after the first interest payment at a quoted price of 101. Prepare the journal entry to record the early retirement of the bonds.

LO 10-3, 10-5   **E10-9 Describing the Effects of a Premium Bond Issue and Interest Payment on the Financial Statements, Quick Ratio, and Times Interest Earned Ratio**

Grocery Corporation received $300,328 for $250,000, 11 percent bonds issued on January 1, 2012, at a market interest rate of 8 percent. The bonds stated that interest would be paid each December 31 and that they mature on December 31, 2021.

Required:

1. Describe how the bond issuance affects the 2012 balance sheet and income statement, specifically identifying the account names and direction of effects (ignore amounts). Also, describe its impact, if any, on the quick ratio and times interest earned ratio.

2. Without doing calculations, describe how the balance sheet and income statement are affected by the recording of interest on December 31, 2012. Also, describe the impact, if any, of the December 31 interest payment on the quick ratio and times interest earned ratio.

LO 10-5   **E10-10 Calculating and Interpreting the Quick Ratio and Times Interest Earned Ratio**

Kraft Foods Inc.   At December 31, 2010, Kraft Foods Inc. reported no short-term investments but did report the following amounts (in millions) in its financial statements:

	2010	2009
Cash and Cash Equivalents	$ 2,481	$ 2,101
Accounts Receivable, Net	6,539	5,197
Total Current Liabilities	15,660	11,491
Interest Expense	2,024	1,237
Income Tax Expense	1,147	1,136
Net Income	4,114	3,021

Required:

1. Compute the quick ratio and times interest earned ratio (to two decimal places) for 2010 and 2009.

2. Did Kraft appear to have increased or decreased its ability to pay current liabilities and future interest obligations as they become due?

LO 10-S1   **E10-11 (Supplement 10A) Recording the Effects of a Premium Bond Issue and First Interest Period (Straight-Line Amortization)**

Refer to the information in E10-9 and assume Grocery Corporation uses the straight-line method to amortize the bond premium.

Required:

1. Prepare the journal entry to record the bond issuance.
2. Prepare the journal entry to record the interest payment on December 31, 2012.

LO 10-S2   **E10-12 (Supplement 10B) Recording the Effects of a Premium Bond Issue and First Interest Period (Effective-Interest Amortization)**

Refer to the information in E10-9 and assume Grocery Corporation uses the effective-interest method to amortize the bond premium.

Required:

1. Prepare the journal entry to record the bond issuance.
2. Prepare the journal entry to record the interest payment on December 31, 2012.

LO 10-S3   **E10-13 (Supplement 10C) Recording the Effects of a Premium Bond Issue and First Interest Period (Simplified Effective-Interest Amortization)**

Refer to the information in E10-9 and assume Grocery Corporation accounts for the bond using the shortcut approach shown in Chapter Supplement 10C.

Required:

1. Prepare the journal entry to record the bond issuance.
2. Prepare the journal entry to record the interest payment on December 31, 2012.

E10-14 (Supplement 10A) Recording the Effects of a Discount Bond Issue and First Interest Payment and Preparing a Discount Amortization Schedule (Straight-Line Amortization)

LO 10-S1

On January 1, 2013, when the market interest rate was 9 percent, Seton Corporation completed a $200,000, 8 percent bond issue for $187,163. The bonds were dated January 1, 2013, pay interest each December 31, and mature in 10 years on December 31, 2022. Seton amortizes the bond discount using the straight-line method.

Required:

1. Prepare the journal entry to record the bond issuance.
2. Prepare the journal entry to record the interest payment on December 31, 2013.
3. Prepare a bond discount amortization schedule for these bonds. Round calculations to the nearest dollar.

E10-15 (Supplement 10B) Recording the Effects of a Discount Bond Issue and First Interest Payment and Preparing a Discount Amortization Schedule (Effective-Interest Amortization)

LO 10-S2

Refer to the information in E10-14 and assume Seton Corporation uses the effective-interest method to amortize the bond discount.

Required:

1. Prepare the journal entry to record the bond issuance.
2. Prepare the journal entry to record the interest payment on December 31, 2013.
3. Prepare a bond discount amortization schedule for these bonds. Round calculations to the nearest dollar.

E10-16 (Supplement 10C) Recording the Effects of a Discount Bond Issue and First Interest Payment and Preparing a Discount Amortization Schedule (Simplified Effective-Interest Amortization)

LO 10-S3

Refer to the information in E10-14 and assume Seton Corporation accounts for the bond using the simplified effective-interest method shown in chapter supplement 10C.

Required:

1. Prepare the journal entry to record the bond issuance.
2. Prepare the journal entry to record the interest payment on December 31, 2013.
3. Prepare a bond discount amortization schedule for these bonds. Round calculations to the nearest dollar.

COACHED PROBLEMS

|ACCOUNTING

CP10-1 Determining Financial Effects of Transactions Affecting Current Liabilities with Evaluation of Effects on the Quick Ratio

LO 10-2, 10-5

EZ Curb Company completed the following transactions during 2013. The annual accounting period ends December 31, 2013.

Jan.	8	Purchased merchandise on account at a cost of $14,000. (Assume a perpetual inventory system.)
	17	Paid for the January 8 purchase.
Apr.	1	Received $40,000 from National Bank after signing a 12-month, 6 percent, promissory note.
June	3	Purchased merchandise on account at a cost of $18,000.
July	5	Paid for the June 3 purchase.

Aug. 1	Rented out a small office in a building owned by EZ Curb Company and collected six months' rent in advance amounting to $6,000. (Use an account called Unearned Rent Revenue.)
Dec. 20	Received a $100 deposit from a customer as a guarantee to return a large trailer "borrowed" for 30 days. **TIP:** Consider whether EZ Curb Company has an obligation to return the money when the trailer is returned.
Dec. 31	Determined that wages of $6,500 were earned but not yet paid on December 31 (ignore payroll taxes).
Dec. 31	Adjusted the accounts at year-end, relating to interest.
Dec. 31	Adjusted the accounts at year-end, relating to rent.

Required:

1. For each listed transaction and related adjusting entry, indicate the accounts, amounts, and effects (+ for increase, − for decrease, and NE for no effect) on the accounting equation, using the following format:

Date	Assets	=	Liabilities	+	Stockholders' Equity

2. For each transaction and related adjusting entry, state whether the quick ratio is increased, decreased, or there is no change. (Assume EZ Curb Company's quick ratio has always been greater than 1.0.)

LO 10-2, 10-5

CP10-2 Recording and Reporting Current Liabilities with Evaluation of Effects on the Quick Ratio

Using data from CP10-1, complete the following requirements.

Required:

1. Prepare journal entries for each of the transactions.
2. Prepare any adjusting entries required on December 31, 2013.
3. Show how all of the liabilities arising from these items are reported on the balance sheet at December 31, 2013.
4. Complete requirement 2 of CP10-1, if you have not already done so.

LO 10-2

CP10-3 Recording and Reporting Current Liabilities

During 2013, Riverside Company completed the following two transactions. The annual accounting period ends December 31.

a. On December 31, 2013, calculated the payroll, which indicates gross earnings for wages ($130,000), payroll deductions for income tax ($13,000), payroll deductions for FICA ($10,000), payroll deductions for United Way ($2,000), employer contributions for FICA (matching), state unemployment taxes ($1,100), and federal unemployment taxes ($200). Employees were paid in cash, but these payments and the corresponding payroll deductions and employer taxes have not yet been recorded.

b. Collected rent revenue of $3,600 on December 10, 2013, for office space that Riverside rented to another business. The rent collected was for 30 days from December 11, 2013, to January 10, 2014, and was credited in full to Unearned Rent Revenue.

Required:

1. Give the journal entries to record payroll on December 31, 2013.
2. Give (a) the journal entry for the collection of rent on December 10, 2013, and (b) the adjusting journal entry on December 31, 2013.
   TIP: Notice that the revenue recorded on December 10 includes revenue for 10 days (out of 30) that isn't earned until after December 31.
3. Show how any liabilities related to these items should be reported on the company's balance sheet at December 31, 2013.
4. Explain why the accrual basis of accounting provides more relevant information to financial analysts than the cash basis.

CP10-4 Comparing Bonds Issued at Par, Discount, and Premium

Sikes Corporation, whose annual accounting period ends on December 31, issued the following bonds:

> Date of bonds: January 1, 2012
> Maturity amount and date: $200,000 due in 10 years (December 31, 2021)
> Interest: 10 percent per year payable each December 31
> Date issued: January 1, 2012

Required:

1. Provide the following amounts to be reported on the January 1, 2012, financial statements immediately after the bonds are issued:

	Case A (issued at 100)	Case B (at 96)	Case C (at 102)
a. Bonds payable	$	$	$
b. Unamortized premium (or discount)			
c. Carrying value			

TIP: See Exhibit 10.5 for an illustration distinguishing Bonds Payable from their carrying value.

2. Assume that a retired person has written to you (an investment adviser) asking, "Why should I buy a bond at a premium when I can find one at a discount? Isn't that stupid? It's like paying list price for a car instead of negotiating a discount." Write a brief message in response to the question.

CP10-5 Determining Financial Statement Reporting of Contingent Liabilities

Brunswick Corporation is a multinational company that manufactures and sells marine and recreational products. A prior annual report contained the following information:

> **Litigation**
>
> A jury awarded $44.4 million in damages in a suit brought by ndependent Boat Builders, Inc., a buying group of boat manufacturers and its 22 members. Under the antitrust laws, the damage award has been tripled, and the plaintiffs will be entitled to their attorney's fees and interest. The Company has filed an appeal contending the verdict was erroneous as a matter of law, both as to liability and damages.

Required:

What are the alternative ways in which Brunswick could account for this litigation?
    TIP: Consider the different possible outcomes that could arise from the appeal.

CP10-6 (Supplement 10A) Recording Bond Issuance and Interest Payments (Straight-Line Amortization)

Southwest Corporation issued bonds with the following details:

> Face value: $600,000
> Interest: 9 percent per year payable each December 31
> Terms: Bonds dated January 1, 2012, due five years from that date

The annual accounting period ends December 31. The bonds were issued at 104 on January 1, 2012, when the market interest rate was 8 percent. Assume the company uses straight-line amortization and adjusts for any rounding errors when recording interest expense in the final year.

Required:

1. Compute the issue price of the bonds in dollars (show computations).
   TIP: The issue price typically is quoted at a percentage of face value.
2. Give the journal entry to record the issuance of the bonds.
3. Give the journal entries to record the payment of interest on December 31, 2012 and 2013.
4. How much interest expense would be reported on the income statements for 2012 and 2013? Show how the liability related to the bonds should be reported on the balance sheets at December 31, 2012 and 2013.

LO 10-S2   **CP10-7 (Supplement 10B) Recording Bond Issuance and Interest Payments (Effective-Interest Amortization)**

Complete the requirements of CP10-6, assuming Southwest Corporation uses effective-interest amortization.

LO 10-S3   **CP10-8 (Supplement 10C) Recording Bond Issuance and Interest Payments (Simplified Approach to Effective-Interest Amortization)**

Complete the requirements of CP10-6, assuming Southwest Corporation uses simplified effective-interest amortization shown in Chapter Supplement 10C.

LO 10-S1   **CP10-9 (Supplement 10A) Completing an Amortization Schedule (Straight-Line Amortization)**

The Peg Corporation (TPC) issued bonds and received cash in full for the issue price. The bonds were dated and issued on January 1, 2012. The stated interest rate was payable at the end of each year. The bonds mature at the end of four years. The following schedule has been prepared (amounts in thousands):

Date	Cash	Interest	Amortization	Balance
January 1, 2012				$6,101
End of year 2012	$450	$425	$25	?
End of year 2013	450	?	25	6,051
End of year 2014	450	?	25	6,026
End of year 2015	450	424	26	6,000

Required:

1. Complete the amortization schedule.
   TIP: The switch in amortization from $25 to $26 in 2015 is caused by rounding.
2. What was the maturity amount (face value) of the bonds?
3. How much cash was received at date of issuance of the bonds?
4. Was there a premium or a discount? If so, which and how much was it?
5. How much cash is paid for interest each period and will be paid in total for the full life of the bond issue?
6. What is the stated interest rate?
7. What is the market interest rate?
8. What amount of interest expense should be reported on the income statement each year?
9. Show how the bonds should be reported on the balance sheet at the end of 2013 and 2014.

LO 10-S2, 10-S3   **CP10-10 (Supplements 10B or 10C) Completing an Amortization Schedule (Effective-Interest Amortization or Simplified Effective-Interest)**

Hondor Corporation issued bonds and received cash in full for the issue price. The bonds were dated and issued on January 1, 2012. The stated interest rate was payable at the end of each year. The bonds mature at the end of four years. The following schedule has been completed (amounts in thousands):

Date	Cash	Interest	Amortization	Balance
January 1, 2012				$6,101
End of year 2012	$450	$427	$23	6,078
End of year 2013	450	426	24	6,054
End of year 2014	450	?	?	?
End of year 2015	450	?	28	6,000

Required:

1. Complete the amortization schedule.
2. What was the maturity amount (face value) of the bonds?
3. How much cash was received at date of issuance (sale) of the bonds?
4. Was there a premium or a discount? If so, which and how much was it?
5. How much cash is paid for interest each period and will be paid in total for the full life of the bond issue?
6. What is the stated interest rate?

   TIP: The stated interest rate can be calculated by comparing the cash payment to the face value of the bond.

7. What is the market interest rate?
8. What amount of interest expense should be reported on the income statement each year?
9. Show how the bonds should be reported on the balance sheet at the end of 2012 and 2013.

GROUP A PROBLEMS

|ACCOUNTING   LO 10-2, 10-5

PA10-1 Determining Financial Effects of Transactions Affecting Current Liabilities with Evaluation of Effects on the Quick Ratio

Jack Hammer Company completed the following transactions during 2013. The annual accounting period ends December 31, 2013.

Apr. 30	Received $600,000 from Commerce Bank after signing a 12-month, 6 percent, promissory note.
June 6	Purchased merchandise on account at a cost of $75,000. (Assume a perpetual inventory system.)
July 15	Paid for the June 6 purchase.
Aug. 31	Signed a contract to provide security service to a small apartment complex and collected six months' fees in advance amounting to $24,000. (Use an account called Unearned Service Revenue.)
Dec. 31	Determined salary and wages of $40,000 were earned but not yet paid as of December 31 (ignore payroll taxes).
Dec. 31	Adjusted the accounts at year-end, relating to interest.
Dec. 31	Adjusted the accounts at year-end, relating to security service.

Required:

1. For each listed transaction and related adjusting entry, indicate the accounts, amounts, and effects (+ for increase, − for decrease, and NE for no effect) on the accounting equation, using the following format:

Date	Assets	=	Liabilities	+	Stockholders' Equity

2. For each item, state whether the quick ratio is increased, decreased, or there is no change. (Assume Jack Hammer's quick ratio is greater than 1.0.)

PA10-2 Recording and Reporting Current Liabilities with Evaluation of Effects on the Quick Ratio   LO 10-2, 10-5

Using data from PA10-1, complete the following requirements.

Required:

1. Prepare journal entries for each of the transactions.
2. Prepare all adjusting entries required on December 31, 2013.
3. Show how all of the liabilities arising from these items are reported on the balance sheet at December 31, 2013.
4. Complete requirement 2 of PA10-1, if you have not already done so.

LO 10-2   **PA10-3 Recording and Reporting Current Liabilities**

During 2013, Lakeview Company completed the following two transactions. The annual accounting period ends December 31.

a. On December 31, 2013, calculated the payroll, which indicates gross earnings for wages ($80,000), payroll deductions for income tax ($8,000), payroll deductions for FICA ($6,000), payroll deductions for American Cancer Society ($3,000), employer contributions for FICA (matching), state unemployment taxes ($500), and federal unemployment taxes ($100). Employees were paid in cash, but payments for the corresponding payroll deductions have not yet been made and employer taxes have not yet been recorded.

b. Collected rent revenue of $6,000 on December 10, 2013, for office space that Lakeview rented to another business. The rent collected was for 30 days from December 11, 2013, to January 10, 2014, and was credited in full to Unearned Rent Revenue.

Required:

1. Give the journal entries to record payroll on December 31, 2013.
2. Give (a) the journal entry for the collection of rent on December 10, 2013, and (b) the adjusting journal entry on December 31, 2013.
3. Show how any liabilities related to these items should be reported on the company's balance sheet at December 31, 2013.

LO 10-3   **PA10-4 Comparing Bonds Issued at Par, Discount, and Premium**

Net Work Corporation, whose annual accounting period ends on December 31, issued the following bonds:

> Date of bonds: January 1, 2012
> Maturity amount and date: $200,000 due in 10 years (December 31, 2021)
> Interest: 10 percent per year payable each December 31
> Date issued: January 1, 2012

Required:

1. Provide the following amounts to be reported on the January 1, 2012, financial statements immediately after the bonds were issued:

	Case A (issued at 100)	Case B (at 98)	Case C (at 102)
a. Bonds payable	$	$	$
b. Unamortized premium (or discount)			
c. Carrying value			

2. Assume that you are an investment adviser and a retired person has written to you asking, "Why should I buy a bond at a premium when I can find one at a discount? Isn't that stupid? It's like paying list price for a car instead of negotiating a discount." Write a brief message in response to the question.

LO 10-4   **PA10-5 Determining Financial Statement Reporting of Contingent Liabilities**

Macromedia, Inc.   Macromedia, Inc., is the original maker of shockwave and flash technologies. One of its annual reports indicated that a lawsuit had been filed against the company and five of its former officers for securities fraud in connection with allegedly making false or misleading statements about its financial results. The lawsuit was settled out of court, as described in the following note:

> **Legal**
>
> The settlement amount was $48.0 million, of which approximately $19.5 million was paid by insurance. As a result, the Company recorded a $28.5 million charge as a component of other income (expense) in its consolidated statements of operations.

Required:

Explain why Macromedia didn't record a contingent liability under GAAP when the lawsuit was first filed.

PA10-6 (Supplement 10A) Recording Bond Issue, Interest Payments (Straight-Line Amortization), and Early Bond Retirement

LO 10-S1

On January 1, 2012, Loop Raceway issued 600 bonds, each with a face value of $1,000, a stated interest rate of 5% paid annually on December 31, and a maturity date of December 31, 2014. On the issue date, the market interest rate was 6 percent, so the total proceeds from the bond issue were $583,950. Loop uses the straight-line bond amortization method and adjusts for any rounding errors when recording interest in the final year.

Required:

1. Prepare a bond amortization schedule.
2. Give the journal entry to record the bond issue.
3. Give the journal entries to record the interest payments on December 31, 2012 and 2013.
4. Give the journal entry to record the interest and face value payment on December 31, 2014.
5. Assume the bonds are retired on January 1, 2014, at a price of 98. Give the journal entries to record the bond retirement.

PA10-7 (Supplement 10B) Recording Bond Issue, Interest Payments (Effective-Interest Amortization), and Early Bond Retirement

LO 10-S2

On January 1, 2012, Surreal Manufacturing issued 600 bonds, each with a face value of $1,000, a stated interest rate of 3 percent paid annually on December 31, and a maturity date of December 31, 2014. On the issue date, the market interest rate was 4 percent, so the total proceeds from the bond issue were $583,352. Surreal uses the effective-interest bond amortization method and adjusts for any rounding errors when recording interest in the final year.

Required:

1. Prepare a bond amortization schedule.
2. Give the journal entry to record the bond issue.
3. Give the journal entries to record the interest payments on December 31, 2012 and 2013.
4. Give the journal entry to record the interest and face value payment on December 31, 2014.
5. Assume the bonds are retired on January 1, 2014, at a price of 101. Give the journal entry to record the bond retirement.

PA10-8 (Supplement 10C) Recording Bond Issue, Interest Payments (Simplified Effective-Interest Amortization), and Early Bond Retirement

LO 10-S3

Assume the same facts as PA10-7, except that Surreal uses the simplified effective-interest bond amortization method, as shown in supplement 10C.

Required:

1. Prepare a bond amortization schedule.
2. Give the journal entry to record the bond issue.
3. Give the journal entries to record the interest payments on December 31, 2012 and 2013.
4. Give the journal entry to record the interest and face value payment on December 31, 2014.
5. Assume the bonds are retired on January 1, 2014, at a price of 101. Give the journal entry to record the bond retirement.

GROUP B PROBLEMS

Mc Graw Hill **connect** |ACCOUNTING

PB10-1 Determining Financial Effects of Transactions Affecting Current Liabilities with Evaluation of Effects on the Quick Ratio

LO 10-2, 10-5

Tiger Company completed the following transactions during 2013. The annual accounting period ends December 31, 2013.

Jan. 3	Purchased merchandise on account at a cost of $24,000. (Assume a perpetual inventory system.)
27	Paid for the January 3 purchase.
Apr. 1	Received $80,000 from Atlantic Bank after signing a 12-month, 5 percent, promissory note.
June 13	Purchased merchandise on account at a cost of $8,000.
July 25	Paid for the June 13 purchase.
Aug. 1	Rented out a small office in a building owned by Tiger Company and collected eight months' rent in advance amounting to $8,000. (Use an account called Unearned Rent Revenue.)
Dec. 31	Determined wages of $12,000 were earned but not yet paid on December 31 (ignore payroll taxes).
Dec. 31	Adjusted the accounts at year-end, relating to interest.
Dec. 31	Adjusted the accounts at year-end, relating to rent.

Required:

1. For each listed transaction and related adjusting entry, indicate the accounts, amounts, and effects (+ for increase, − for decrease, and NE for no effect) on the accounting equation, using the following format:

Date	Assets	=	Liabilities	+	Stockholders' Equity

2. For each item, state whether the quick ratio is increased, decreased, or there is no change. (Assume Tiger Company's quick ratio is greater than 1.0.)

LO 10-2, 10-5   **PB10-2 Recording and Reporting Current Liabilities with Evaluation of Effects on the Quick Ratio**

Using data from PB10-1, complete the following requirements.

Required:

1. Prepare journal entries for each of the transactions.
2. Prepare any adjusting entries required on December 31, 2013.
3. Show how all of the liabilities arising from these items are reported on the balance sheet at December 31, 2013.
4. Complete requirement 2 of PB10-1, if you have not already done so.

LO 10-2   **PB10-3 Recording and Reporting Current Liabilities**

During 2013, Sandler Company completed the following two transactions. The annual accounting period ends December 31.

a. On December 31, 2013, calculated the payroll, which indicates gross earnings for wages ($260,000), payroll deductions for income tax ($28,000), payroll deductions for FICA ($20,000), payroll deductions for United Way ($4,000), employer contributions for FICA (matching), state unemployment taxes ($1,700), and federal unemployment taxes ($300). Employees were paid in cash, but payments for the corresponding payroll deductions have not been made and employer taxes have not yet been recorded.
b. Collected rent revenue of $1,500 on December 10, 2013, for office space that Sandler rented to another business. The rent collected was for 30 days from December 11, 2013, to January 10, 2014, and was credited in full to Unearned Revenue.

Required:

1. Give the entries required on December 31, 2013, to record payroll.
2. Give (a) the journal entry for the collection of rent on December 10, 2013, and (b) the adjusting journal entry on December 31, 2013.
3. Show how any liabilities related to these items should be reported on the company's balance sheet at December 31, 2013.

PB10-4 Comparing Bonds Issued at Par, Discount, and Premium

LO 10-3

Marshalls Corporation completed a $500,000, 7 percent bond issue on January 1, 2013. The bonds pay interest each December 31 and mature 10 years from January 1, 2013.

Required:

1. Provide the following amounts to be reported on the January 1, 2013, financial statements immediately after the bonds were issued:

	Case A (issued at 100)	Case B (at 98)	Case C (at 102)
a. Bonds payable	$	$	$
b. Unamortized premium (or discount)			
c. Carrying value			

2. Assume that you are an investment adviser and a retired person has written to you asking, "Why should I buy a bond at a premium when I can find one at a discount? Isn't that stupid? It's like paying list price for a car instead of negotiating a discount." Write a brief message in response to the question.

PB10-5 Recording and Explaining the Early Retirement of Debt

LO 10-3

AMC Entertainment, Inc.

AMC Entertainment, Inc., owns and operates 361 movie theaters worldwide, with 5,203 screens in 31 states. Assume the company issued 11 percent bonds in the amount of $53,000,000 and then used all of these cash proceeds to retire bonds with a coupon rate of 13.6 percent. At that time, the 13.6 percent bonds had a carrying value of $50,000,000.

Required:

1. Prepare the journal entries to record the issuance of the 11 percent bonds and the early retirement of the 13.6 percent bonds. Assume both sets of bonds were issued at face value.
2. How should AMC report any gain or loss on this transaction?
3. What dollar amount of interest expense is AMC saving each year by replacing the 13.6 percent bonds with the 11 percent bonds?

PB10-6 (Supplement 10A) Recording Bond Issue, Interest Payments (Straight-Line Amortization), and Early Bond Retirement

LO 10-S1

On January 1, 2012, Methodical Manufacturing issued 100 bonds, each with a face value of $1,000, a stated interest rate of 5 percent paid annually on December 31, and a maturity date of December 31, 2014. On the issue date, the market interest rate was 4.25 percent, so the total proceeds from the bond issue was $102,070. Methodical uses the straight-line bond amortization method and adjusts for any rounding errors when recording interest in the final year.

Required:

1. Prepare a bond amortization schedule.
2. Give the journal entry to record the bond issue.
3. Give the journal entries to record the interest payments on December 31, 2012 and 2013.
4. Give the journal entry to record the interest and face value payment on December 31, 2014.
5. Assume the bonds are retired on January 1, 2014, at a price of 102. Give the journal entries to record the bond retirement.

PB10-7 (Supplement 10B) Recording Bond Issue, Interest Payments (Effective-Interest Amortization), and Early Bond Retirement

LO 10-S2

Refer to PB10-6. Assume Methodical uses the effective-interest bond amortization method.

Required:

1. Prepare a bond amortization schedule.
2. Give the journal entry to record the bond issue.

3. Give the journal entries to record the interest payments on December 31, 2012 and 2013.

4. Give the journal entry to record the interest and face value payment on December 31, 2014.

5. Assume the bonds are retired on January 1, 2014, at a price of 101. Give the journal entry to record the bond retirement.

LO 10-S3   **PB10-8 (Supplement 10C) Recording Bond Issue, Interest Payments (Simplified Effective-Interest Amortization), and Early Bond Retirement**

Assume the same facts as PB10-6, but now assume that Methodical uses the simplified effective-interest bond amortization method, as shown in supplement 10C.

Required:

1. Prepare a bond amortization schedule.
2. Give the journal entry to record the bond issue.
3. Give the journal entries to record the interest payments on December 31, 2012 and 2013.
4. Give the journal entry to record the interest and face value payment on December 31, 2014.
5. Assume the bonds are retired on January 1, 2014, at a price of 101. Give the journal entry to record the bond retirement.

COMPREHENSIVE PROBLEM

LO 9-3, 9-7, 10-2, 10-5   **C10-1 Calculating Interest and Depreciation Expenses and Effects on Loan Covenant Ratios (Chapters 9 and 10)**

Zoom Car Corporation (ZCC) plans to purchase approximately 100 vehicles on December 31, 2012, for $2 million, plus 11 percent total sales tax. ZCC expects to use the vehicles for 5 years, and then sell them for approximately $420,000. ZCC anticipates the following average vehicle use over each year ended December 31:

	2013	2014	2015	2016	2017
Miles per year	15,000	20,000	10,000	10,000	5,000

To finance the purchase, ZCC signed a 5-year promissory note on December 31, 2012, for $1.8 million, with interest paid annually at the market interest rate of 6 percent. The note carries loan covenants that require ZCC to maintain a minimum times interest earned ratio of 3.0 and a minimum fixed asset turnover ratio of 1.0. ZCC forecasts that the company will generate the following sales and preliminary earnings (prior to recording depreciation on the vehicles and interest on the note). (For purposes of this question, ignore income tax.)

(in 000s)	2013	2014	2015	2016	2017
Sales Revenue	$2,000	$2,500	$2,800	$2,900	$3,000
Income before depreciation and interest expense	1,000	1,200	1,400	1,500	1,600

Required:

1. Calculate the amount of interest expense that would be recorded each year.
2. Calculate the depreciation expense that would be recorded each year, using the following depreciation methods: (a) straight-line, (b) double declining-balance, (c) units-of-production.
3. Using your answers to requirements 1 and 2, determine net income and the two loan covenant ratios in each year, assuming the company chooses the following depreciation methods: (a) straight-line, (b) double declining-balance, (c) units-of-production.
4. Using your answers to requirement 3, indicate whether the loan covenants would be violated under the following depreciation methods: (a) straight-line, (b) double declining-balance, (c) units-of-production.

SKILLS DEVELOPMENT CASES

|ACCOUNTING

S10-1 Finding Financial Information

LO 10-5

Refer to the financial statements of The Home Depot in Appendix A at the end of this book, or download the annual report from the *Cases* section of the text's Web site at www.mhhe.com/phillips4e.

Required:

1. Calculate, to two decimal places, the company's quick ratio using amounts reported in its financial statements for the years ended January 30, 2011, and January 31, 2010.

   a. 1.33 and 1.34
   b. 0.16 and 0.23
   c. 0.28 and 0.36
   d. 1.30 and 1.34

2. Calculate, to two decimal places, the company's times interest earned ratio for the year ended January 30, 2011.

   a. 6.30   c. 10.95
   b. 1.74   d. 3.00

S10-2 Comparing Financial Information

LO 10-5

Refer to the financial statements of The Home Depot in Appendix A and Lowe's in Appendix B at the end of this book, or download the annual reports from the *Cases* section of the text's Web site at www.mhhe.com/phillips4e.

Lowe's

Required:

1. Calculate, to two decimal places, the companies' quick ratios using amounts reported in the financial statements for the years ending in early 2011 and 2010. What do the changes in this ratio suggest about the companies' ability to quickly pay their liabilities? Does it appear that Lowe's or The Home Depot is in a less secure position?

2. Calculate, to two decimal places, the companies' times interest earned ratios for the years ending in early 2012. Does it appear that Lowe's or The Home Depot will be better able to meet future interest obligations as they become payable?

S10-3 Internet-Based Team Research: Examining an Annual Report

LO 10-1, 10-2, 10-3, 10-4, 10-5

As a team, select an industry to analyze. Using your Web browser, each team member should access the annual report or 10-K for one publicly traded company in the industry, with each member selecting a different company. (See S1-3 in Chapter 1 for a description of possible resources for these tasks.)

Required:

1. On an individual basis, each team member should write a short report that incorporates the following:

   a. What are the most significant types of current liabilities owed by the company?
   b. Read the company's financial statement note regarding long-term debt and commitments and contingencies. Does the company have any significant amounts coming due in the next five years?
   c. Compute and analyze the quick ratio and times interest earned ratio.

2. Then, as a team, write a short report comparing and contrasting your companies using these attributes. Discuss any patterns across the companies that you as a team observe. Provide potential explanations for any differences discovered.

S10-4 Ethical Decision Making: A Real-Life Example

LO 10-3

Many retired people invest a significant portion of their money in bonds of corporations because of their relatively low level of risk. During the 1980s, significant inflation caused some interest rates to rise to as high as 15 percent. Retired people who bought bonds that paid only 6 percent continued to earn at the lower rate. During the 1990s, inflation subsided and interest rates declined. Many corporations took advantage of the callability feature of these bonds and retired the bonds early. Many of these early retirements of high interest rate bonds were replaced with low interest rate bonds.

Required:

In your judgment, is it ethical for corporations to continue paying low interest rates when rates increase but to call bonds when rates decrease? Why or why not?

LO 10-3   **S10-5 Ethical Decision Making: A Mini-Case**

Assume that you are a portfolio manager for a large insurance company. The majority of the money you manage is from retired school teachers who depend on the income you earn on their investments. You have invested a significant amount of money in the bonds of a large corporation and have just received news released by the company's president explaining that it is unable to meet its current interest obligations because of deteriorating business operations related to increased international competition. The president has a recovery plan that will take at least two years. During that time, the company will not be able to pay interest on the bonds and, she admits, if the plan does not work, bondholders will probably lose more than half of their money. As a creditor, you can force the company into immediate bankruptcy and probably get back at least 90 percent of the bondholders' money. You also know that your decision will cause at least 10,000 people to lose their jobs if the company ceases operations.

Required:

Given only these two options, what should you do? Consider who would be helped or harmed by the two options.

LO 10-5   **S10-6 Critical Thinking: Evaluating Effects on the Quick Ratio**

Assume you work as an assistant to the chief financial officer (CFO) of Fashions First, Inc. The CFO reminds you that the fiscal year-end is only two weeks away and that he is looking to you to ensure the company stays in compliance with its loan covenant to maintain a quick ratio of 1.25 or higher. A review of the general ledger indicates that cash and other liquid assets total $690,000 and current liabilities are $570,000. Your company has an excess of Cash ($300,000) and an equally large balance in Accounts Payable ($270,000), although none of its Accounts Payable are due until next month.

Required:

1. Determine whether the company is currently in compliance with its loan covenant.
2. Assuming the level of assets and liabilities remains unchanged until the last day of the fiscal year, evaluate whether Fashions First should pay down $90,000 of its Accounts Payable on the last day of the year, before the Accounts Payable become due.

LO 10-S1   **S10-7 (Supplement 10A) Preparing a Bond Amortization Schedule (Straight-Line Amortization)**

Assume the authors of a popular introductory accounting text have hired you to create spreadsheets that will calculate bond discount amortization schedules like those shown in this chapter. As usual, you e-mail your friend Owen for some guidance. Much to your disappointment, you receive an auto-reply message from Owen indicating that he's gone skiing in New Zealand. After a bit of panicking, you realize you can refer to Owen's previous e-mail messages for spreadsheet advice that will help you complete this task. From his advice for Chapter 9, you decide to create a data input section for the stated interest rate, market interest rate, face value, issue price, and years to maturity. The spreadsheet file also will have a separate amortization schedule worksheet that contains only formulas, references to the cells in the data input section, and references to other cells in the amortization schedule. All amounts will be rounded to the nearest dollar (using the Round function in Excel), which means the discount amortization in the final year might be off a few dollars (unless you use the IF function in Excel to eliminate any remaining discount in the final year of the bond's life, in the same way that Owen showed in Chapter 9 for declining-balance depreciation).

Required:

Prepare a worksheet that uses formulas to reproduce the straight-line bond discount amortization schedule shown in Chapter Supplement 10A. Display both the completed spreadsheet and a "formulas revealed" (Ctrl ~) version of it.

S10-8 (Supplement 1OB) Preparing a Bond Amortization Schedule (Effective-Interest Amortization)

LO 10-S2

Refer to the information in S10-7 and prepare a worksheet that uses formulas to reproduce the effective-interest bond discount amortization schedule shown in Chapter Supplement 10B. Display both the completed spreadsheet and a "formulas revealed" (Ctrl ~) version of it.

S10-9 (Supplement 1OC) Preparing a Bond Amortization Schedule (Simplified Effective-Interest Amortization)

LO 10-S3

Refer to the information in S10-7 and prepare a worksheet that uses formulas to reproduce the bond discount amortization schedule shown for simplified effective-interest amortization in Chapter Supplement 10C. Display both the completed spreadsheet and a "formulas revealed" (Ctrl ~) version of it.

CONTINUING CASES

CC10-1 Accounting for Debt Financing

LO 10-2

Nicole thinks that her business, Nicole's Getaway Spa (NGS), is doing really well and she is planning a large expansion. With such a large expansion, Nicole will need to finance some of it using debt. She signed a one-year note payable with the bank for $50,000 with a 6 percent interest rate. The note was issued October 1, 2014, interest is payable semiannually, and the end of Nicole's accounting period is December 31.

Required:

1. Prepare the journal entries required from the issuance of the note until its maturity on September 30, 2015, assuming that no entries are made other than at the end of the accounting period, when interest is payable and when the note reaches its maturity.
2. Is there any similarity between the way Notes Payable and Notes Receivable are accounted for? Explain.

CC10-2 Wiki Art Gallery (WAG)

LO 10-2

Access the Wiki Art Gallery (WAG) instructional case in Connect, and read the case in sufficient depth to answer the following questions.

1. Note 4 to WAG's financial statements indicates that the note payable increased from $20,000 to $25,000. Assume this change in loan balance occurred when the terms of the loan were adjusted on May 31, 2011. Use the interest formula to calculate the amount of interest expense for the periods from October 1, 2010 to May 31, 2011, and from May 31, 2011 to September 30, 2011. What do your calculations suggest about the interest reported by WAG during the 2011 fiscal year?
    a. Interest from October 1, 2010 to May 31, 2011 should be $1,000, and interest from May 31, 2011 to September 30, 2011 should be $1,500. These calculations suggest WAG understated its 2011 interest expense by $1,780.
    b. Interest from October 1, 2010 to May 31, 2011 should be $667, and interest from May 31, 2011 to September 30, 2011 should be $500. These calculations suggest WAG understated its 2011 interest expense by $447.
    c. Interest from October 1, 2010 to May 31, 2011 should be $1,000, and interest from May 31, 2011 to September 30, 2011 should be $500. These calculations suggest WAG understated its 2011 interest expense by $780.
    d. Interest from October 1, 2010 to May 31, 2011 should be $800, and interest from May 31, 2011 to September 30, 2011 should be $400. These calculations suggest WAG understated its 2011 interest expense by $480.
2. What was the effect of Rob cutting his salary by $2,000?
    a. It decreased WAG's selling price by $2,000.
    b. It increased WAG's selling price by $2,000.
    c. It increased WAG's selling price by $10,000.
    d. This was a kind gesture that better aligned Rob's take-home pay with Stephen's cut in dividends. It had no effect on WAG's selling price.

Stockholders' Equity

YOUR LEARNING OBJECTIVES

Understand the business

LO 11-1   Explain the role of stock in financing a corporation.

Study the accounting methods

LO 11-2   Explain and analyze common stock transactions.

LO 11-3   Explain and analyze cash dividends, stock dividends, and stock split transactions.

LO 11-4   Describe the characteristics of preferred stock and analyze transactions affecting preferred stock.

Evaluate the results

LO 11-5   Analyze the earnings per share (EPS), return on equity (ROE), and price/earnings (P/E) ratios.

Review the chapter

Supplemental materials

LO 11-S1   Account for owners' equity in other forms of business.

THAT WAS THEN

The last chapter focused on debt financing, as reported in the liabilities section of the balance sheet.

www.nationalbeverage.com

News about shares of stock is everywhere. You've probably read it in *The Wall Street Journal*, listened to it on MSNBC, or searched for it at Yahoo! Finance. Behind this fascination with stock is a dream that many people share: taking a small amount of money and turning it into a fortune. That's what National Beverage Corp. has managed to do.

National Beverage started out as a small regional drink maker, but has expanded into a successful niche soft-drink company. This success has arisen through National Beverage's acquisition and development of brands such as Shasta, Faygo, Everfresh, and LaCroix. To obtain financing for growing these brands, National Beverage issued its shares to investors through the NASDAQ stock exchange, under the stock ticker symbol "FIZZ." Investors who were lucky enough to buy $1,000 of National Beverage's shares when it first became a public company in September 1991 have seen their investment grow to over $12,735. In comparison, a $1,000 investment in Coca-Cola or PepsiCo in 1991 would now be worth less than $7,000. As the line graph to the right shows, much of National Beverage's stock price improvement relative to Coca-Cola and PepsiCo has occurred in recent years.

In this chapter, you will see how companies like National Beverage account for a variety of stock transactions, including issuances, splits, and dividends. By the end of the chapter, you should understand how each individual National Beverage share that existed in September 1991 has now multiplied into 33 shares.

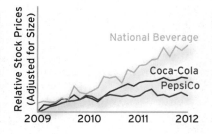

THIS IS NOW

This chapter focuses on equity financing, as reported in the stockholders' equity section of the balance sheet.

ORGANIZATION OF THE CHAPTER

Understand the business	**Study the accounting methods**	**Evaluate the results**	**Review the chapter**
• Corporate ownership • Equity versus debt financing	• Common stock transactions • Stock dividends and stock splits • Preferred stock • Retained earnings	• Earnings per share (EPS) • Return on equity (ROE) • Price/earnings (P/E) ratio	• Demonstration cases • Chapter summary • Key terms • Homework helper • Practice material

Understand the Business

Learning Objective 11-1
Explain the role of stock in financing a corporation.

CORPORATE OWNERSHIP

According to the U.S. Census Bureau, corporations account for about 90 percent of the total sales reported by U.S. businesses.[1] Many Americans own shares in corporations, either directly or indirectly through a mutual fund or pension program.

You probably recall from Chapter 1 that the act of creating a corporation is costly, so why is the corporate form so popular? One reason is that it limits the legal liability of its owners. Another reason is that corporations can raise large amounts of money because investors can easily participate in a corporation's ownership. This ease of participation is related to several factors.

- **Shares of stock can be purchased in small amounts.** You could have become one of National Beverage's owners in 2012 by buying a share of the company's stock for under $17.

- **Ownership interests are transferable.** The shares of public companies are regularly bought and sold on established markets such as the New York Stock Exchange. National Beverage's shares are traded on the NASDAQ under the ticker symbol FIZZ.

- **Stockholders are not liable for the corporation's debts.** Creditors have no legal claim on the personal assets of stockholders like they do on the personal assets belonging to owners of sole proprietorships and partnerships. So if you owned stock in Circuit City, which went bankrupt and was liquidated in 2009, you would lose what you paid to buy the stock but, unless you personally guaranteed the company's debt, you wouldn't have to pay the hundreds of millions the company owed.

The law recognizes a corporation as a separate legal entity. It may own assets, incur liabilities, expand and contract in size, sue others, be sued, and enter into contracts independently of its owners. A corporation exists separate and apart from its owners, which

---

[1]Chapter Supplement 11A discusses accounting for owners' equity in proprietorships, partnerships, and other business forms.

means it doesn't die when its owners die. Thomas Edison died in 1931, but the company he founded (General Electric) continues in existence today.

To protect everyone's rights, the creation and oversight of corporations are tightly regulated by law. Corporations are created by submitting an application to a state government (not the federal government). Because laws vary from state to state, you might decide to create a corporation in a state other than the one in which it operates. Although National Beverage has its headquarters in Fort Lauderdale, it was actually incorporated in Delaware. More than half of the largest corporations in America are incorporated in Delaware because it has some of the most favorable laws for establishing corporations. If the application to create a corporation is approved, the state issues a charter, also called the articles of incorporation, which spells out information about the corporation such as its name, address, nature of business, and ownership structure.

The ownership structure of a corporation can vary from one company to the next. In the most basic form, a corporation must have one type of stock, appropriately called **common stock**. Owners of common stock usually enjoy a number of benefits:

1. **Voting rights.** For each share you own, you get a set number of votes on major issues. Some classes of common stock can carry more votes than others, so watch for this if you care about voting on which accounting firm will be appointed as external auditors and who will serve on the board of directors. (In case you don't remember from Chapter 5, the board of directors is the group that appoints the corporation's officers and governs top management, as shown in Exhibit 11.1.)

2. **Dividends.** Stockholders receive a share of the corporation's profits when distributed as dividends.

3. **Residual claim.** If the company ceases operations, stockholders share in any assets remaining after creditors have been paid.

4. **Preemptive rights.** To retain their ownership percentages, existing stockholders may be given the first chance to buy newly issued stock before it is offered to others.

EQUITY VERSUS DEBT FINANCING

Whenever a company needs a large amount of long-term financing, its executives will have to decide whether to obtain it by issuing new stock to investors (called **equity financing**) or borrowing money from lenders (**debt financing**). Each form of financing

EXHIBIT 11.1 | **Typical Organizational Structure of a Corporation**

Stockholders

↓ Elect

Board of Directors

↓ Appoints

Officers (e.g., CEO, CFO)

↓ Select

- Vice President (Production and Technology)
- Vice President (Sales and Marketing)
- Vice President (Finance and Accounting)
- Vice President (Human Resources)

EXHIBIT 11.2	Advantages of Equity and Debt Financing

Advantages of Equity Financing	Advantages of Debt Financing
1. **Equity does not have to be repaid.** Debt must be repaid or refinanced.	1. **Interest on debt is tax deductible.** Dividends on stock are not tax deductible.
2. **Dividends are optional.** Interest must be paid on debt.	2. **Debt does not change stockholder control.** In contrast, a stock issue gives new stockholders the right to vote and share in the earnings, diluting existing stockholders' control.

has certain advantages over the other, as listed in Exhibit 11.2. These factors play a big role in determining whether equity or debt financing is most appropriate for each particular corporation. One company, for example, might be primarily concerned about the impact of financing on income taxes and decide to rely on debt financing because its interest payments are tax deductible. A different company might be so concerned about being able to pay its existing liabilities that it can't afford to take on additional debt. By using equity financing, which doesn't have to be repaid, the company could obtain the financing it needs. Ultimately, the decision to pursue additional equity or debt financing depends on the circumstances.

Study the Accounting Methods

The first point to note is that **all transactions between a company and its stockholders affect the company's balance sheet accounts only.** They do not affect the company's income statement.

COMMON STOCK TRANSACTIONS

> **Learning Objective 11-2**
> Explain and analyze common stock transactions.

Exhibit 11.3 shows the balance sheet accounts that National Beverage reported in the stockholders' equity section of its balance sheet at the end of its 2011 fiscal year. It includes two familiar line items and two new line items:

1. **Contributed Capital** reports the amount of capital the company received from investors' contributions, in exchange for the company's stock. For this reason, contributed capital represents paid-in capital. As Exhibit 11.3 suggests, contributed capital can include several components, which we'll explain later in this section.

2. **Retained Earnings** reports the cumulative amount of net income earned by the company less the cumulative amount of dividends declared since the corporation was first organized. Retained Earnings represents earned capital.

3. **Treasury Stock** reports shares that were previously owned by stockholders but have been reacquired and are now held by the corporation. To fully understand treasury stock, it's helpful to follow stock transactions through from authorization to issuance and repurchase, as we do in the following section.

4. **Accumulated Other Comprehensive Income** reports unrealized gains and losses, which are temporary changes in the value of certain assets and liabilities the company holds. They can relate to pensions, foreign currencies, and financial investments, such as National Beverage's contracts to stabilize the cost of its aluminum cans. The accounting rules relating to Accumulated Other Comprehensive Income are introduced in Appendix D.

EXHIBIT 11.3   Explanation of National Beverage's Stockholders' Equity

NATIONAL BEVERAGE CORP.
Partial Balance Sheets

(in thousands, except share amounts)	2011	2010	Explanation
STOCKHOLDERS' EQUITY			
Contributed Capital			
Preferred Stock, 7% cumulative, $1 par value	$ 150	$ 150	Stock with special rights
Common Stock, $0.01 par value	503	502	Basic voting stock
Authorized: 75 million shares			Maximum number of shares
Issued: 50.3 and 50.2 million shares			Number of shares distributed
Additional Paid-in Capital (on Common Stock)	29,725	28,150	Amount in excess of par value
Total Contributed Capital	30,378	28,802	Total equity paid-in by investors
Retained Earnings	65,207	130,767	Total equity earned by the company
Treasury Stock (4.1 million shares, at cost)	(18,000)	(18,000)	Stock reacquired by the company
Accumulated Other Comprehensive Income	2,751	3	Unrealized gains and losses
Total Stockholders' Equity	80,336	141,572	

Authorization, Issuance, and Repurchase of Stock

A corporation's charter indicates the maximum number of shares of stock that the corporation is allowed to issue. Look closely at the Contributed Capital section of Exhibit 11.3 and you will see that National Beverage is **authorized** to issue 75 million common shares. The next line in Exhibit 11.3 tells us how many shares have actually been issued. At the end of 2011, 50.3 million common shares have been issued. **Issued shares** will be owned forever by one stockholder or another, unless the company has repurchased them. Shares that have been repurchased by the corporation are called **treasury stock**. National Beverage's treasury stock is shown in Exhibit 11.3 as a negative amount because it represents shares that are no longer outstanding with investors. During the time treasury stock is held by the corporation, the shares do not carry voting, dividend, or other stockholder rights. Shares that are owned by stockholders (not the corporation itself) are called **outstanding shares**.

The relationships among authorized, issued, outstanding, and treasury stock are shown in Exhibit 11.4. Be aware that the number of outstanding shares (46.2) is not reported on the face of the balance sheet but instead has to be computed as the difference between issued shares (50.3) and treasury stock (4.1). Knowing this will help you compute earnings per share, which is a key financial ratio discussed later in this chapter and expressed in terms of the number of outstanding shares.

> **YOU SHOULD KNOW**
>
> **Authorized shares:** The maximum number of shares of capital stock of a corporation that can be issued, as specified in the charter.
> **Issued shares:** Shares of stock that have been distributed by the corporation.
> **Treasury stock:** Issued shares that have been reacquired by the company.
> **Outstanding shares:** Shares that are currently held by stockholders (not the corporation itself).

EXHIBIT 11.4   Authorized, Issued, Outstanding, and Treasury Stock

Authorized	75 million shares

Issued	50.3 million shares

Outstanding	Treasury Stock
46.2 million shares	4.1 million shares

Stock Authorization   Before stock can be issued, its specific rights and characteristics must be authorized and defined in the corporate charter. This authorization does not affect the accounting records, but it does establish certain characteristics that, later, will affect how stock transactions are recorded. One characteristic of importance is the stock's **par value**. Oddly enough, par value has little meaning today. It is an old concept from long ago, originally introduced to prevent stockholders from removing contributed capital of businesses that were about to go bankrupt. Stronger laws and regulations exist today to prevent this from happening, so par value no longer has a business use. Yet, many states still require that corporations specify a par value for stock. Typically, par value is set at a token amount, such as $0.01 per share, as is the case with National Beverage's common stock in Exhibit 11.3. Some states have dropped the requirement to specify a par value and instead allow the issuance of no-par value stock. **No-par value stock** is similar to stock with par value, except it does not have a specified legal value per share. In any event, par value is a legal concept and is not related in any way to the market value of the company's stock.

Stock Issuance   A stock issuance occurs when a corporation distributes its shares to existing or new stockholders, usually in exchange for cash. The very first issuance of a company's stock to the public is called an **initial public offering,** or IPO. This is what most people are referring to when they say a private company is going public. If a company has issued stock previously, additional issuances of new stock by the company are called **seasoned new issues.** Whether stock is issued as part of an IPO or as a seasoned new issue, a company accounts for it in the same way.

Most stock issuances are cash transactions. To illustrate the accounting for a stock issuance, assume that during the next fiscal year, National Beverage issues 100,000 shares of its $0.01 par value stock at the market price existing at the time of issuance of $10 per share. The accounting equation effects of this stock issuance and the journal entry to record them would be:

1 Analyze

	Assets	= Liabilities +	Stockholders' Equity	
Cash	+1,000,000		Common Stock	+1,000
			Additional Paid-In Capital	+999,000

2 Record

dr **Cash** (+A) (100,000 × $10) 1,000,000
  cr **Common Stock** (+SE) (100,000 × $0.01) 1,000
  cr **Additional Paid-In Capital**
    (+SE) ($1,000,000 − $1,000) 999,000

Notice that the increase in Common Stock is the number of shares sold times the par value per share (100,000 × 0.01), and the increase in Additional Paid-in Capital is the amount of cash received in excess of this amount. If the corporate charter does not specify a par value for the stock, the total proceeds from the stock issuance will be entered in the Common Stock account.

Stock Exchanged between Investors   When a company issues stock to the public, the transaction is between the issuing corporation and an investor. After this initial stock issuance, an investor can exchange shares for cash provided by other investors without directly affecting the corporation. For example, if investor Dr. Anne Clem disposed of 1,000 shares of National Beverage stock to Darla Karnes, the company would not record a journal entry on its books. Dr. Clem received cash for the shares, and Mrs. Karnes received stock for the cash she paid. National Beverage did not receive or pay anything. These transactions involve only the owners of the company and not the corporation itself. It's like an auto dealer who records the initial sale of a car to a customer but doesn't later record another sale when the customer sells the car to someone else.

Stock Used to Compensate Employees To encourage employees to work hard for a corporation, employee pay packages often include a combination of base pay, cash bonuses, and stock options. Stock options give employees the option of acquiring the company's stock at a predetermined price, often equal to the then-current market price. If employees work hard and meet the corporation's goals, the company's stock price will increase. Employees can then exercise their option to acquire the company's stock at the lower predetermined price and sell it at the higher price for a profit. If the stock price declines, employees haven't lost anything. Accounting rules require that, at the time the company grants stock options, an expense must be reported for the estimated cost associated with stock options, even if the option price equals the current stock price. The specific accounting procedures for this will be discussed in an intermediate accounting course.

SPOTLIGHT ON Ethics

At Whose Expense?

Some critics claim that stock options, which are intended to give the senior executives of a company the same goals as stockholders, often come at the expense of existing stockholders. When senior executives exercise their stock options to acquire new stock, existing stockholders lose voting power because their percentage of ownership in the company is diluted. Furthermore, critics contend that stock options create an incentive for senior executives to overstate financial results in an attempt to falsely increase the company's stock price so they can exercise their options for huge personal gains.

Repurchase of Stock A corporation may want to repurchase its stock from existing stockholders to: (1) distribute excess cash to stockholders, (2) send a signal to investors that the company itself believes its own stock is worth acquiring, (3) obtain shares that can be reissued as payment for purchases of other companies, and (4) obtain shares to reissue to employees as part of employee stock option plans. Because of Securities and Exchange Commission regulations concerning newly issued shares, it is generally less costly for companies to give employees repurchased shares than to issue new ones.

Most companies record the purchase of treasury stock based on the cost of the shares when they are purchased by the company. This approach is called the cost method. Assume that during the next fiscal year, National Beverage repurchased 50,000 shares of its stock for $25 per share (50,000 shares × $25 = $1,250,000). Using the cost method, the effects of this repurchase on the accounting equation and the journal entry for it would be:

1 Analyze

	Assets	= Liabilities +	Stockholders' Equity	
Cash	−1,250,000		Treasury Stock (+xSE)	−1,250,000

2 Record

dr Treasury Stock (+xSE, −SE)	1,250,000	
cr Cash (−A)		1,250,000

Note that **Treasury Stock is not an asset.** It is a permanent account that is reported as contra-equity, subtracted from total stockholders' equity. This reporting practice makes sense because treasury stock is stock that is not outstanding and therefore should be removed from total stockholders' equity. Look at the third line from the bottom of Exhibit 11.3 on page 505 to see how National Beverage reported its treasury stock.

Solution to Self-Study Practice

1.

Assets	=	Liabilities	+	Stockholders' Equity	
				Common Stock	+10
Cash +21,900				APIC	+21,890

dr Cash (+A) 21,900
  cr Common Stock (+SE) (1,000 × $0.01) 10
  cr Additional Paid-in Capital (+SE) 21,890

2. *dr* Treasury Stock (+xSE, −SE) 10,000
  cr Cash (−A) ($20 × 500) 10,000

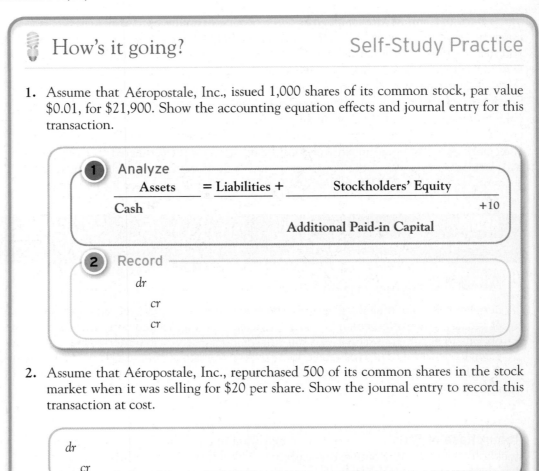

How's it going?   Self-Study Practice

1. Assume that Aéropostale, Inc., issued 1,000 shares of its common stock, par value $0.01, for $21,900. Show the accounting equation effects and journal entry for this transaction.

1 Analyze

Assets	= Liabilities +	Stockholders' Equity	
Cash			+10
		Additional Paid-in Capital	

2 Record

dr
  cr
  cr

2. Assume that Aéropostale, Inc., repurchased 500 of its common shares in the stock market when it was selling for $20 per share. Show the journal entry to record this transaction at cost.

dr
  cr

After you have finished, check your answers with the solution in the margin.

 COACH'S TIP

Notice that the contra-account Treasury Stock is reduced only for the cost of each treasury share. Any amount received for treasury stock in excess of its cost is recorded as an increase in Additional Paid-in Capital, as shown below.

Reissuance of Treasury Stock   When a company reissues shares of its treasury stock, it does not report a gain or loss on sale, even if it issues the shares for more or less than they cost when the company reacquired them. GAAP does not permit a corporation to report income or losses from investments in its own stock because transactions with the owners are not considered profit-making activities. Instead, this type of transaction affects only the balance sheet, just like other stock issuances. To illustrate, let's extend our previous example where National Beverage had repurchased its stock at a cost of $25 per share. If National Beverage reissues 5,000 shares of this treasury stock for $28 per share (5,000 × $28 = $140,000), the accounting equation effects and journal entry would be:

1 Analyze

	Assets	= Liabilities +	Stockholders' Equity	
Cash	+140,000		Treasury Stock (−xSE)	+125,000
			Additional Paid-In Capital	+15,000

2 Record

dr **Cash** (+A) (5,000 × $28) 140,000
  cr **Treasury Stock** (−xSE, +SE) (5,000 × $25) 125,000
  cr **Additional Paid-In Capital** (+SE) [5,000 × ($28 − $25)] 15,000

If treasury stock were reissued at a price below its repurchase price, the difference between the repurchase price ($25 per share) and the reissue price (say, $23 per share) is recorded as a reduction in Additional Paid-in Capital. The accounting equation effects and journal entry for reissuing at an amount less than its cost are:

1 Analyze

	Assets		= Liabilities +	Stockholders' Equity	
Cash	+115,000			Treasury Stock (−xSE)	+125,000
				Additional Paid-In Capital	−10,000

2 Record

dr Cash (+A) (5,000 × $23) 115,000
dr Additional Paid-In Capital (−SE) [5,000 × ($25 − $23)] 10,000
   cr Treasury Stock (−xSE, +SE) (5,000 × $25)   125,000

Dividends on Common Stock

> **Learning Objective 11-3**
> Explain and analyze cash dividends, stock dividends, and stock split transactions.

Investors acquire common stock because they expect a return on their investment. This return can come in two forms: dividends and increases in stock price. Some investors prefer to buy stocks that pay little or no dividends (called a **growth investment**), because companies that reinvest the majority of their earnings tend to increase their future earnings potential, along with their stock price. Dell Corporation, for example, has never paid a dividend, yet if your parents had bought 100 Dell shares when they were first issued on June 22, 1988, for $850, the investment would be worth about $150,000 at the time this chapter was being written. Rather than wait for growth in stock value, other investors, such as retired people who need a steady income, prefer to receive their return in the form of dividends. These people often seek stocks that consistently pay dividends (called an **income investment**), such as Coca-Cola, which has paid cash dividends each year since 1920.

SPOTLIGHT ON Business Decisions

Dividend Policy Affected by Tax Rules

The government introduced a law in 2003 that cut taxes on dividends to 15 percent, but it was set to expire December 31, 2010. Even by mid-December 2010, politicians could not agree whether to extend the tax cut past 2010. National Beverage's board of directors was concerned that if the cut was not extended, its stockholders would pay higher taxes on dividends after December 31, 2010. So, on December 6, 2010, National Beverage declared a $106 million cash dividend and issued a press release to scold "federal lawmakers' lack of fiscal judgment." The government did end up extending the tax cut, on December 17, 2010.

A corporation does not have a legal obligation to pay dividends. It is a decision made by the board of directors, and it is made each time a dividend is to be paid. Once the board of directors formally declares a dividend, a liability is created. When National Beverage declared a dividend, its press release contained the following information:

FORT LAUDERDALE, Fla.—National Beverage Corp. (NASDAQ FIZZ)—"Today, December 6, 2010, being the latest effective date to secure preferential tax treatment for their shareholders, the Board of Directors has . . . [declared] a cash dividend of $2.30 per share. This dividend shall be payable to shareholders of record as of the close of business on December 16, 2010. Payment of dividends shall be made on or before February 14, 2011."

Notice that this announcement contains three important dates: (1) the declaration date (December 6), (2) the date of record (December 16), and (3) the date of payment (February 14).

1. **Declaration Date.** The **declaration date** is the date on which the board of directors officially approves the dividend. As soon as the board makes the declaration, the company records an increase in its liabilities and a corresponding increase in the Dividends Declared account. Dividends Declared is a temporary account that summarizes dividends declared during the year and later is closed to Retained Earnings at year-end, causing a decrease in Retained Earnings. Remember, **dividends are distributions of a company's accumulated prior earnings,** so they are reported on the statement of retained earnings (or the more general statement of stockholders' equity shown in Chapter 5). Dividends declared by a company are not reported on its income statement because they are not expenses. With 46.2 million common shares outstanding (see Exhibit 11.4), National Beverage's $2.30 dividend per share equals $106.26 million (46.2 million × $2.30 = $106.26 million). The accounting equation effects and journal entry to record them would be:

① Analyze

Assets	=	Liabilities	+	Stockholders' Equity
		Dividends Payable 106,260,000		Dividends Declared (+D) −106,260,000

② Record

dr Dividends Declared (+D, −SE) 106,260,000
   cr Dividends Payable (+L) 106,260,000

2. **Date of Record.** After a dividend is declared, the corporation identifies the specific stockholders who will receive the dividend. The **record date** is the date on which this list of current stockholders is finalized. The dividend is payable only to those names listed on the record date. No journal entry is made on this date.

3. **Date of Payment.** The **payment date** is the date on which the cash is disbursed to pay the dividend liability. It follows the date of record, as described in the dividend announcement. Continuing our example above, when the dividend is paid and the liability satisfied on February 14, the accounting equation effects and journal entry are:

① Analyze

Assets	=	Liabilities	+	Stockholders' Equity
Cash −106,260,000		Dividends Payable −106,260,000		

② Record

dr Dividends Payable (−L) 106,260,000
   cr Cash (−A) 106,260,000

These three dates and the corresponding balance sheet effects are summarized in the timeline in Exhibit 11.5.

The declaration of a cash dividend reduces stockholders' equity because Dividends Declared is closed into Retained Earnings at the end of each fiscal year. The payment of a cash dividend similarly reduces Cash (by the same amount). These two observations

EXHIBIT 11.5 | Dividend Dates and Balance Sheet Effects

explain two key financial requirements that the board of directors must consider when declaring a cash dividend:

1. **Sufficient retained earnings.** The corporation must have accumulated a sufficient amount of Retained Earnings to cover the amount of the dividend. State laws often restrict dividends to the balance in Retained Earnings. A company may be further restricted by clauses in its loan agreements that require an even larger minimum balance in Retained Earnings. If the company were to violate such a loan covenant, a lender could require renegotiation of the loan and possibly demand its immediate repayment. **Because restrictions on Retained Earnings can severely limit the ability to pay dividends, accounting rules require that companies disclose any restrictions in their financial statement notes.** National Beverage reported in its 2011 financial statements that "$1,320,000 of retained earnings were restricted from distribution."

2. **Sufficient cash.** The corporation must have sufficient cash to pay the dividend. Cash can be used in many ways, so the mere fact that Retained Earnings has a large credit balance does not mean that the company has sufficient cash to pay a dividend. Remember, retained earnings is not cash.

> **COACH'S TIP**
>
> A lender imposes dividend restrictions because it doesn't want to lend money to a corporation and then have the corporation pay it out in dividends to stockholders.

 How's it going?   Self-Study Practice

Answer the following questions concerning dividends:

1. On which dividend date is a liability created?
2. A cash outflow occurs on which dividend date?
3. What are the two fundamental requirements for the payment of a dividend?

After you have finished, check your answers with the solution in the margin.

Solution to Self-Study Practice
1. Declaration date.
2. Date of payment.
3. Dividends can be paid only if sufficient retained earnings and sufficient cash are both available.

STOCK DIVIDENDS AND STOCK SPLITS

Stock Dividends

The term *dividend*, when used alone with no adjectives, implies a cash dividend. However, some dividends are not paid in cash but in additional shares of stock. These dividends, called **stock dividends,** are distributed to a corporation's stockholders on a pro rata basis at no cost to the stockholder. The phrase *pro rata basis* means that each stockholder receives additional shares equal to the percentage of shares held. A stockholder who owns 10 percent of the outstanding shares would receive 10 percent of any additional shares issued as a stock dividend.

> **YOU SHOULD KNOW**
>
> **Stock dividend:** A dividend that distributes additional shares of a corporation's own stock.

The value assigned to a stock dividend is the subject of much debate. In reality, a stock dividend by itself provides no economic value. All stockholders receive a pro rata distribution of shares, which means that each stockholder owns exactly the same proportion of the company after a stock dividend as he or she did before the dividend. If you get change for a dollar, you do not have more wealth because you hold ten dimes instead of one dollar. Similarly, you are not wealthier when the company declares a stock dividend and gives you (and all other stockholders) more shares of stock.

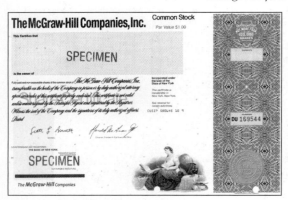

When a stock dividend is issued, the stock market reacts immediately with a proportional decline in the stock price. Theoretically, if the stock price was $60 before a stock dividend that doubles the number of shares outstanding, the price per share would fall to $30. Thus, an investor who owns 100 shares before the stock dividend would own 200 shares after the stock dividend, but the total stock value before (100 × $60 = $6,000) would equal the value after (200 × $30 = $6,000). In reality, the fall in price is not exactly proportional to the number of new shares issued because the stock dividend makes the stock more attractive to investors who acquire stock in round lots (multiples of 100 shares). An investor with $5,000 might not buy a stock selling for $60, for instance, because she cannot afford to buy 100 shares. However, she might buy the stock if the price were less than $60 as the result of a stock dividend. Thus, **one of the main reasons for issuing a stock dividend is that it reduces the market price per share of stock.**

When a stock dividend occurs, the company must decrease Retained Earnings (to show that a dividend was declared) and increase Common Stock (to show that additional shares were issued). The amount recorded depends on whether the stock dividend is classified as large or small. Most stock dividends are classified as large. A large stock dividend involves the distribution of additional shares that amount to more than 20–25 percent of currently outstanding shares. A small stock dividend involves the distribution of shares that amount to less than 20–25 percent of the outstanding shares. Large stock dividends are recorded at the par value of the additional shares issued. Small stock dividends are recorded at the total market value of the shares issued, with the par value recorded in Common Stock and the excess in Additional Paid-in Capital.

On May 25, 2007, National Beverage declared a 20 percent stock dividend on its $0.01 par value common stock, of which 38 million shares were outstanding at the time. The company accounted for it as a large stock dividend by moving $76,000 (=38 million × 20% × $0.01 par value) from Retained Earnings to Common Stock as follows:

1 Analyze

Assets	=	Liabilities	+	Stockholders' Equity	
				Retained Earnings	−76,000
				Common Stock	+76,000

2 Record

dr Retained Earnings (−SE)	76,000	
cr Common Stock (+SE)		76,000

Notice that the stock dividend does not change total stockholders' equity. It changes only the balances of some accounts within stockholders' equity.

Before we leave this section, we must caution you on a potential point of confusion. Some companies refer to 100 percent stock dividends as a "stock split effected as a stock dividend." Although they *say* stock split, they actually mean a stock dividend as described above. A true stock split is different, both in terms of how it is done and how it is accounted for, as we discuss in the following section.

Stock Splits

Stock splits are not dividends. While they are similar to a stock dividend, they are quite different in terms of how they occur and how they affect the stockholders' equity accounts. In a **stock split**, the total number of authorized shares is increased by a specified amount, such as 2-for-1. In this instance, each issued share is called in and two new shares are issued in its place. Cash is not affected when the company splits its stock, so the total resources of the company do not change. It's just like taking a four-piece pizza and cutting each piece into two smaller pieces.

Typically, a stock split involves revising the corporate charter to reduce the per-share par value of all authorized shares, so that the total par value across all shares is unchanged. For instance, if a company with 1 million shares outstanding executes a 2-for-1 stock split, it reduces the per-share par value of its stock from $0.01 to $0.005 and doubles the number of shares outstanding. The decrease in par value per share offsets the increase in the number of shares, so the financial position of the company is not affected and no journal entry is needed. By reading the following illustration from left to right, you can see these offsetting effects on the number of shares and par value per share.

Stockholders' Equity	Before a 2-for-1 Stock Split		After a 2-for-1 Stock Split	
Number of shares outstanding	1,000,000		2,000,000	
Par value per share	$ 0.01		$ 0.005	
Total par value outstanding	$ 10,000		$ 10,000	
Retained earnings	650,000		650,000	
Total stockholders' equity	$ 660,000		$ 660,000	

SPOTLIGHT ON Business Decisions

Choosing Between Stock Dividends and Stock Splits

Both stock dividends and stock splits increase the number of shares outstanding and decrease the per-share market price. A key difference between them is that a stock dividend causes a reduction in Retained Earnings, whereas a "true" stock split doesn't. By itself, this accounting difference might not mean much. Remember, though, that to declare a cash dividend, a company must maintain an adequate balance in Retained Earnings. If you're managing a company that you expect will struggle financially in the future, you'll prefer a stock split because it doesn't reduce Retained Earnings, so it doesn't reduce your ability to declare cash dividends in the future. On the other hand, if you expect your company will be financially successful in the near future, you won't care that a stock dividend reduces Retained Earnings because future earnings will replenish that account to allow cash dividends to be declared. In fact, you'll *want* to declare a stock dividend to show how confident you are of your company's financial outlook. This reasoning suggests that **a company's board of directors may declare a stock dividend rather than a stock split to signal to financial statement users that the company expects significant future earnings** (which will replenish the reduction in Retained Earnings caused by the stock dividend).

Exhibit 11.6 shows the typical components of the stockholders' equity section of the balance sheet and highlights amounts (in blue) that are changed by a 2-for-1 stock split, a 100% stock dividend, and an equivalent ($10,000) cash dividend. Notice that the cash dividend is the only distribution that affects total stockholders' equity because it is the only one that distributes the company's resources to stockholders.

EXHIBIT 11.6 | Comparison of Distributions to Stockholders

Stockholders' Equity	BEFORE	AFTER		
		2-for-1 Stock Split	100% Stock Dividend	$10,000 Cash Dividend
Contributed Capital				
Number of common shares outstanding	1,000,000	2,000,000	2,000,000	1,000,000
Par value per common share	$ 0.01	$ 0.005	$ 0.01	$ 0.01
Common stock, at par	$ 10,000	$ 10,000	$ 20,000	$ 10,000
Additional paid-in capital	30,000	30,000	30,000	30,000
Retained Earnings	650,000	650,000	640,000	640,000
Total stockholders' equity	$ 690,000	$ 690,000	$ 690,000	$ 680,000

Solution to Self-Study Practice
1. *dr* **Retained Earnings** (−SE) 1,000,000
    cr **Common Stock** (+SE)   1,000,000
2. No journal entry is required in the case of a stock split. Theoretically, the new price would be one-half of what it was before the 2-for-1 split ($30 × ½ = $15).

How's it going? Self-Study Practice

Vandalay Industries wanted to reduce the market price of its stock, so it issued 100,000 new shares of common stock (par value $10) in a 100 percent stock dividend when the market value was $30 per share.

1. Prepare the journal entry that Vandalay would use to record this transaction.
2. What journal entry would be required if the transaction instead involved a 2-for-1 stock split? Theoretically, what would be the new stock price after the split?

After you have finished, check your answers with the solution in the margin.

PREFERRED STOCK

Learning Objective 11-4
Describe the characteristics of preferred stock and analyze transactions affecting preferred stock.

YOU SHOULD KNOW

Preferred stock: Stock that has specified rights over common stock.

In addition to common stock, some corporations issue **preferred stock** to a select group of investors. This special form of stock differs from common stock, typically in the following ways:

1. **Preferred stock allows different voting rights.** Preferred stock can carry anywhere from no voting rights to super-voting rights. This flexibility allows a corporation to separate stock ownership from voting control. No voting rights are useful if you want to raise financing from a key stockholder who already owns a lot of common stock and you don't want him to take control. Super-voting rights are useful if you want to issue shares to the public but not give up voting control. Recently, Facebook and Google have adopted such a dual-stock structure.

2. **Dividends on preferred stock, if any, may be paid at a fixed rate,** specified as either a dollar amount or a percentage per share. For example, if dividends are declared on National Beverage's "7%, $1 par value" preferred stock, the dividend will equal 7 cents per share ($0.07 = 7% × $1.00). A fixed dividend can be attractive to certain investors, such as company founders or retirees, who seek a stable income from their investments.

3. **Preferred stock carries priority over common stock.** Preferred stockholders have higher priority than common stockholders if a corporation distributes assets to its owners through dividends or at liquidation. That is, any dividends the corporation declares must be paid to preferred stockholders before they can be paid to common stockholders. Also, if the corporation goes out of business, its assets will be sold and used to pay creditors and then preferred stockholders. Common stockholders are paid last from whatever assets remain after paying preferred stockholders.

SPOTLIGHT ON The World

Under IFRS, preferred stock is typically classified as stockholders' equity. However, if the issuing company is contractually obligated to pay dividends or redeem the stock at a future date, then preferred stock is classified as a liability. This classification can dramatically affect financial ratios that use total stockholders' equity (e.g., return on equity, discussed later in this chapter) or total liabilities (e.g., debt-to-assets ratio in Chapter 5).

Preferred Stock Issuance

Just like a common stock issuance, a preferred stock issuance increases a company's cash and its stockholders' equity. To illustrate, assume that during the upcoming fiscal year, National Beverage issued 10,000 shares of its $1 par value preferred stock for $5 per share ($5 × 10,000 shares = $50,000 cash received). As shown below, the Preferred Stock account increases by its par value for each share issued ($1 × 10,000 = $10,000) and the amount of cash received in excess of par value is recorded as Additional Paid-In Capital—Preferred:

1 Analyze

Assets	=	Liabilities	+	Stockholders' Equity	
Cash +50,000				Preferred Stock	+10,000
				Additional Paid-In Capital—Preferred	+40,000

2 Record

dr Cash (+A) (10,000 × $5)	50,000	
cr Preferred Stock (+SE) (10,000 × $1)		10,000
cr Additional Paid-In Capital—Preferred (+SE)		40,000

Preferred Stock Dividends

Preferred stock offers dividend preferences. The two most common dividend preferences are called current and cumulative.

Current Dividend Preference A **current dividend preference** requires that preferred dividends be paid before paying any dividends to holders of common stock. This preference is a feature of all preferred stock. After the current dividend preference has been met, and if no other preference exists, dividends may be paid to the common stockholders. To illustrate, consider the following example:

> **YOU SHOULD KNOW**
>
> **Current dividend preference:** The feature of preferred stock that grants priority on preferred dividends over common dividends.

> **Flavoria Company**
>
> Preferred stock outstanding, 6%, par $20; 2,000 shares
> Common stock outstanding, par $10; 5,000 shares

Assume the preferred stock carries only a current dividend preference and that the company declares dividends totaling $8,000 in 2012 and $10,000 in 2013. In each year, a fixed amount of the total dividends would first go to the preferred stockholders, and only the excess would go to the common stockholders.

Year	Total Dividends Declared	Dividends on 6% Preferred Stock*	Dividends on Common Stock†
2012	$ 8,000	$2,400	$5,600
2013	10,000	2,400	7,600

* Dividends on preferred stock = $2,000 shares × $20 par value × $6% dividend = $2,400
† Dividends on common stock = Total dividends declared − Dividends on preferred stock

Had Flavoria Company not declared dividends in 2012, preferred stockholders would have had preference to $2,400 of dividends only in 2013. The current dividend preference does not carry over to later years unless the preferred stock is designated as cumulative, as discussed next.

Cumulative Dividend Preference A **cumulative dividend preference** states that if all or a part of the current dividend is not paid in full, the cumulative unpaid amount, known as **dividends in arrears**, must be paid before any future common dividends can be paid. Of course, if the preferred stock is noncumulative, dividends can never be in arrears; any preferred dividends that are not declared are permanently lost. Because preferred stockholders are unwilling to accept this unfavorable feature, preferred stock is usually cumulative.

To illustrate the cumulative preference, assume that Flavoria Company has the same amount of stock outstanding as in the last example. In this case, however, assume that dividends are in arrears for 2010 and 2011. The following table shows that, in 2012, dividends in arrears are satisfied first, followed by the current dividend preference, and the excess goes to common stockholders. In 2013, preferred dividends include only the current preference of that year because dividends in arrears were fulfilled in 2012.

| Year | Total Dividends Declared | DIVIDENDS ON 6% PREFERRED STOCK | | Dividends on Common Stock‡ |
		In Arrears*	Current†	
2012	$ 8,000	$4,800	$2,400	$ 800
2013	10,000	—	2,400	7,600

* Dividends in arrears preference = $2,000 shares × $20 par value × 6% dividend × 2 years = $4,800

† Current dividend preference = 2,000 shares × $20 par value × 6% dividend = $2,400

‡ Dividends on common stock = Total dividends declared − Total dividends on preferred stock

Because dividends are not an actual liability until the board of directors declares them, dividends in arrears are not reported on the balance sheet. Instead, they are disclosed in the notes to the financial statements.

RETAINED EARNINGS

As its name suggests, Retained Earnings represents the company's total earnings that have been retained in the business (rather than being distributed to stockholders). The balance in this account increases when the company reports net income, and it decreases when the company reports a net loss (expenses greater than revenues) or declares cash or stock dividends to stockholders. **Think of retained earnings as the amount of equity that the company itself has generated for stockholders (through profitable operations) but not yet distributed to them.**

Should a company ever accumulate more net losses than net income over its life, it will report a negative (debit) balance in the Retained Earnings account. This amount is (a) shown in parentheses in the stockholders' equity section of the balance sheet, (b) deducted when computing total stockholders' equity, and (c) typically called an **Accumulated Deficit** rather than Retained Earnings.

Evaluate the Results

Now that you know how dividends and other stockholders' equity transactions are accounted for inside a company, it's time to evaluate things from the outside. In this section, you will learn to use three ratios to evaluate how well a company appears to be using its capital to generate returns for the company and, ultimately, for its stockholders.

EARNINGS PER SHARE (EPS)

Learning Objective 11-5
Analyze the earnings per share (EPS), return on equity (ROE), and price/earnings (P/E) ratios.

The most famous of all ratios, earnings per share (EPS), reports how much profit is earned for each share of common stock outstanding. The calculation of EPS can involve many details and intricacies,[2] but in its basic form, it is computed by dividing "bottom line" net income by the average number of common shares outstanding. Most companies report EPS on the income statement immediately below Net Income or in the notes to the financial statements.

You might be wondering why *earnings* per share is so popular when dividends and stock prices ultimately determine the return to stockholders. The reason is that current earnings can predict future dividends and stock prices. If a company generates increased earnings in the current year, it will be able to pay higher dividends in future years. In other words, current EPS influences expectations about future dividends, which investors factor into the current stock price.

Another reason that EPS is so popular is that it allows you to easily compare results over time. For example, in the third quarter of 2011, National Beverage earned net income of $7.4 million, compared to $5.5 million for the same quarter in the previous year. It's hard to know whether the increase is good for stockholders, because it's possible that the increase in net income was accompanied by an increase in the number of shares outstanding. By considering earnings on a per-share basis, we adjust for the effect of additional stock issued, resulting in a clearer picture of what increases mean for each investor. The increase in net income from $5.5 million to $7.4 million actually did translate into EPS growth for the quarter from $0.12 to $0.16.

 COACH'S TIP

Outstanding shares are issued shares minus treasury shares.

Accounting Decision Tools		
Name of Measure	**Formula**	**What It Tells You**
Earnings per share (EPS)	$\dfrac{\text{Net Income}}{\substack{\text{Average Number of} \\ \text{Common Shares Outstanding}}}$	• The amount of income generated for each share of common stock owned by stockholders • A higher ratio means greater profitability
Return on equity (ROE)	$\dfrac{\text{Net Income}}{\text{Average Stockholders' Equity}}$	• The amount of income earned for each dollar of stockholders' equity • A higher ratio means stockholders are likely to enjoy greater returns
Price/Earnings (P/E) ratio	$\dfrac{\text{Current Stock Price (per share)}}{\text{Earnings per Share (annual)}}$	• How many times more than the current year's earnings investors are willing to pay for a company's common stock • A higher number means investors anticipate an improvement in the company's future results

Exhibit 11.7 shows how to calculate EPS for National Beverage and its rival PepsiCo. We should caution you against comparing EPS across companies. The number of shares outstanding for one company can differ dramatically from the number outstanding for a different company, simply because one chooses to issue more shares of stock than the other. Also, as you have seen in earlier chapters, net income can be affected by differences in how two companies cost inventory (Chapter 7), estimate bad debts (Chapter 8), depreciate long-lived tangible assets (Chapter 9), and estimate losses from contingent liabilities (Chapter 10). So, **while EPS is an effective and widely used measure for comparing a company with itself over time, it is not appropriate for comparing across companies.**

---

[2]As explained in intermediate accounting courses, these details include subtracting preferred dividends in the numerator and "weighting" the number of shares by their time outstanding.

EXHIBIT 11.7	Summary of EPS, ROE, and P/E Ratio Analyses

PepsiCo

(in millions, except price)	2011	2010	2009		(in billions, except price)	2011	2010	2009
Net Income	$ 40.8	$ 32.9	$ 24.7		Net Income	$ 6.4	$ 6.3	$ 5.6
Average # shares	46.2	46.1	46.0		Average # shares	1.59	1.61	1.61
Stockholders' equity	$ 80.3	$141.6	$170.0		Stockholders' equity	$ 20.9	$ 21.5	$ 17.4
Stock price	$15.10	$14.01	$10.64		Stock price	$64.27	$63.41	$62.41

		2011	2010				2011	2010
$EPS = \dfrac{\text{Net income}}{\text{Avg. \# shares}}$		$\dfrac{\$40.8}{46.2}$	$\dfrac{\$32.9}{46.1}$		$EPS = \dfrac{\text{Net income}}{\text{Avg. \# shares}}$		$\dfrac{\$6.4}{1.59}$	$\dfrac{\$6.3}{1.61}$
		= $0.88	= $0.71				= $4.03	$3.91

		2011	2010				2011	2010
$ROE = \dfrac{\text{Net income}}{\text{Average SE}}$		$\dfrac{\$40.8}{(\$80.3 + \$141.6)/2}$	$\dfrac{\$32.9}{(\$141.6 + \$170.0)/2}$		$ROE = \dfrac{\text{Net income}}{\text{Average SE}}$		$\dfrac{\$6.4}{(\$20.9 + \$21.5)/2}$	$\dfrac{\$5.7}{(\$21.5 + \$17.4)/2}$
		= 0.368 or 36.8%	= 0.211 or 21.1%				0.302 or 30.2%	0.293 or 29.3%

		2011	2010				2011	2010
$P/E = \dfrac{\text{Stock price}}{\text{EPS}}$		$\dfrac{\$15.10}{\$0.88}$	$\dfrac{\$14.01}{\$0.71}$		$P/E = \dfrac{\text{Stock price}}{\text{EPS}}$		$\dfrac{\$64.27}{\$4.03}$	$\dfrac{\$63.41}{\$3.91}$
		= 17.2	= 19.7				= 15.9	= 16.2

RETURN ON EQUITY (ROE)

Like EPS, return on equity (ROE) reports a company's return to investors. However, rather than relate net income to the average *number* of shares outstanding, the return on equity (ROE) ratio relates net income to the average *dollars* of stockholder investment and earnings reinvested in the company.[3] Because ROE uses dollars contributed to and reinvested in the company, this ratio can be appropriately compared across companies.

According to Yahoo! Finance, the average return on equity for the entire beverage industry in 2011 was 27.0 percent. As Exhibit 11.7 reports, National Beverage's ROE in 2011 was 36.8 percent, up significantly from 21.1 in the prior year. Two factors were responsible for this large jump in National Beverage's ROE. Look closely at the ROE calculation and you will find them both. First, National Beverage's net income was up from $32.9 to $40.8 million. Second, its total stockholders' equity was down—the result of its $106 million dividend discussed earlier in this chapter—causing the denominator to be smaller in 2011 than in 2010. A similar improvement in PepsiCo's ROE in 2011 is reported in 2011, but for different reasons. In PepsiCo's case, the company was able to increase its return by using a strategy called **financial leverage.** Rather than rely on equity financing, PepsiCo relies heavily on debt. PepsiCo has been able to generate more profit from using these borrowed funds than it incurred for interest on that debt. As a result, PepsiCo was able to generate a superior return on equity for stockholders. Financial leverage isn't always the best strategy, though, as another industry competitor (Dr Pepper) discovered in the financial crisis of 2008 when its Interest Expense on debt financing was greater than its Income from Operations.

---

[3]If a company has preferred stock outstanding, the ROE ratio can be adjusted to focus on the common stockholders' perspective. Simply deduct any preferred dividends from net income and exclude any preferred stock accounts from the calculation of average stockholders' equity. This adjustment is not required in National Beverage's case because all its issued preferred stock is held as treasury stock, so it has already been excluded from average stockholders' equity.

PRICE/EARNINGS (P/E) RATIO

While EPS and ROE are useful for evaluating a company's return to stockholders, they don't help you determine what a reasonable price would be for the company's stock. Sophisticated techniques to value a company are taught in advanced courses in finance, but for this course, let's focus on a simple tool. The price/earnings ratio is the most basic way to determine the value investors place on a company's common stock. The P/E ratio, as most people call it, measures how many times more than current year's earnings investors are willing to pay for a company's stock. It is calculated as shown in Exhibit 11.7 by dividing a company's EPS for the year into the stock price at the time its EPS is reported.

Generally, a relatively high P/E ratio means investors expect the company to improve in the future and increase its profits, so they have factored in the future earnings when determining the current stock price. A relatively low P/E ratio typically means that they don't expect strong future performance. P/E ratios can vary significantly across industries, so you'll find them most meaningful when comparing a company over time with itself or with competitors in the same industry. Both National Beverage and PepsiCo showed P/E ratios in 2011 (17.2 and 15.9) that exceeded the industry average (15.1). This suggests that investors were anticipating good things to come from these companies.

 How's it going? Self-Study Practice

National Beverage reported stockholders' equity of $144.6 (million) at its 2008 fiscal year-end.

(a) Use this information, along with that in Exhibit 11.7, to calculate National Beverage's earnings per share (EPS), return on equity (ROE), and price/earnings (P/E) ratios for 2009.

2009 EPS:	2009 ROE:	2009 P/E:
_____ =	_____ =	_____ =
	(+)/2	

(b) Did National Beverage's EPS and ROE improve or decline from 2009 (calculated in a) to 2010 (shown in Exhibit 11.7)? Does the 2009 P/E ratio suggest investors anticipated the changes that occurred in 2010? (Assume the industry average was 8.0.)

After you have finished, check your answers with the solution in the margin.

Solution to Self-Study Practice
a. EPS: $24.7 ÷ 46.0 = 0.54
   ROE: $24.7 ÷ [($170.0 + $144.6)/2] = 0.157
   P/E: $10.64 ÷ 0.54 = 19.7
b. National Beverage's EPS and ROE improved in 2010. Investors appeared to anticipate the improved performance because they were willing to pay 19.7 times earnings to buy a share, when the industry average was only 8.0 times earnings.

SUPPLEMENT 11A OWNERS' EQUITY FOR OTHER FORMS OF BUSINESS

 Learning Objective 11-S1
Account for owners' equity in other forms of business.

Owner's Equity for a Sole Proprietorship

A sole proprietorship is an unincorporated business owned by one person. Only two owner's equity accounts are needed: (1) a capital account for the proprietor (H. Simpson, Capital) and (2) a drawing (or withdrawal) account for the proprietor (H. Simpson, Drawings).

The capital account of a sole proprietorship serves two purposes: to record investments by the owner and to accumulate periodic income or loss. The drawing account is used to record the owner's withdrawals of cash or other assets from the business, similar to recording dividends declared by corporations. The drawing account is closed to the capital account at the end of each accounting period. Thus, after the drawing account is closed, the capital account reflects the cumulative total of all investments by the owner and all earnings of the business less all withdrawals from the entity by the owner.

COACH'S TIP

The capital account is like all the permanent stockholders' equity accounts for a corporation combined into a single account. The drawing account is like the temporary dividends declared account for a corporation.

In most respects, the accounting for a sole proprietorship is the same as for a corporation. Exhibit 11A.1 presents the recording of selected transactions of Homer's Dough Store and a statement of owner's equity, which replaces the statement of retained earnings.

COACH'S TIP

Because a sole proprietorship does not issue stock, its equity is called owner's equity rather than stockholders' equity. We use OE to designate an owner's equity account.

EXHIBIT 11A.1	Accounting for Owner's Equity for a Sole Proprietorship

Selected Entries during 2013

January 1, 2013

H. Simpson started a sole proprietorship by placing $150,000 cash in a bank account opened for the business. The accounting equation effects and journal entry follow:

Assets		=	Liabilities	+	Owner's Equity	
Cash	+150,000				H. Simpson, Capital	+150,000

dr Cash (+A) 150,000
    cr H. Simpson, Capital (+OE) 150,000

During 2013

Each month during the year, Simpson withdrew $1,000 cash from the business for personal living costs. Accordingly, each month the financial effects and required journal entry are:

Assets		=	Liabilities	+	Owner's Equity	
Cash	−1,000				H. Simpson, Drawings (+D)	−1,000

dr H. Simpson, Drawings (+D, −OE) 1,000
    cr Cash (−A) 1,000

Note: At December 31, 2013, after the last withdrawal, the drawings account reflected a debit balance of $12,000.

December 31, 2013

The usual journal entries for the year, including adjusting and closing entries for the revenue and expense accounts, resulted in revenue of $48,000 and expenses of $30,000. The net income of $18,000 was closed to the capital account as follows:

Assets	=	Liabilities	+	Owner's Equity	
				Revenues (−R)	−48,000
				Expenses (−E)	+30,000
				H. Simpson, Capital	+18,000

dr Individual Revenue Accounts (−R, −OE) 48,000
    cr Individual Expense Accounts (−E, +OE) 30,000
    cr H. Simpson, Capital (+OE) 18,000

December 31, 2013

The drawings account was closed as follows:

Assets	=	Liabilities	+	Owner's Equity	
				H. Simpson, Capital	−12,000
				H. Simpson, Drawings (−D)	+12,000

dr H. Simpson, Capital (−OE) 12,000
    cr H. Simpson, Drawings (−D, +OE) 12,000

HOMER'S DOUGH STORE
Statement of Owner's Equity
For the Year Ended December 31, 2013

H. Simpson, Capital, January 1, 2013	$ 0
Add: Capital contribution	150,000
Add: Net income for 2013	18,000
Total	168,000
Less: Withdrawals for 2013	(12,000)
H. Simpson, Capital, December 31, 2013	$156,000

Because a sole proprietorship does not pay income taxes, its financial statements do not report Income Tax Expense or Income Tax Payable. Instead, the net income of a sole proprietorship is taxed when it is included on the owner's personal income tax return. Likewise, the owner's salary is not recognized as an expense in a sole proprietorship because an employer/employee contractual relationship cannot exist with only one party involved. The owner's salary is therefore accounted for as a distribution of profits—a withdrawal—instead of salary expense, as it would be in a corporation.

Owner's Equity for a Partnership

The Uniform Partnership Act, which most states have adopted, defines a partnership as "an association of two or more persons to carry on as co-owners of a business for profit." Small businesses and professionals such as accountants, doctors, and lawyers often use the partnership form of business.

A partnership is formed by two or more persons reaching mutual agreement about the terms of the relationship. The law does not require an application for a charter as in the case of a corporation. Instead, the agreement between the partners constitutes a partnership contract. This agreement should specify matters such as division of income, management responsibilities, transfer or sale of partnership interests, disposition of assets upon liquidation, and procedures to be followed in case of the death of a partner. If the partnership agreement does not specify these matters, the laws of the resident state are binding.

In comparison to a corporation, the primary advantages of a partnership are (1) ease of formation, (2) complete control by the partners, and (3) lack of income taxes on the business itself. The primary disadvantage is the unlimited liability of each partner for the partnership's debts. If the partnership does not have sufficient assets to satisfy outstanding debt, creditors of the partnership can seize each partner's personal assets. In some cases, this can even result in one partner being held responsible for another partner's share of the partnership's debt.

As with a sole proprietorship, accounting for a partnership follows the same underlying principles as any other form of business organization, except for those entries that directly affect owners' equity. Accounting for partners' equity follows the same pattern as for a sole proprietorship, except that separate capital and drawings accounts must be established for each partner. Investments by each partner are credited to that partner's Capital account and withdrawals are debited to the respective Drawings account. The net income of a partnership is divided among the partners in accordance with the partnership agreement and credited to each account. The respective Drawings accounts are closed to the partner Capital accounts. After the closing process, each partner's Capital account reflects the cumulative total of all that partner's investments plus that partner's share of the partnership earnings less all that partner's withdrawals.

Exhibit 11A.2 presents selected journal entries and partial financial statements for AB Partnership to illustrate the accounting for the distribution of income and partners' equity.

Other Business Forms

In addition to sole proprietorships, partnerships, and corporations, other forms of business exist. These forms blend features of the "pure" organizational forms described earlier in this chapter to create hybrid business forms such as S corporations, limited liability partnerships (LLPs), and limited liability companies (LLCs). The LLC in particular is an increasingly common form of business that combines legal characteristics of corporations (such as a separate legal identity and limited liability) with the tax treatment of partnerships (where tax is paid by the individual owners rather than by the business entity itself). Accounting for these hybrid entities generally follows the methods shown earlier in this chapter.

The financial statements of an LLC follow the same format as those for a partnership, which differs from a corporation in the following ways: (1) the financial statements include an additional section entitled Distribution of Net Income; (2) the owners' equity section of the balance sheet is detailed for each owner; (3) the income statement does not report income tax expense because these forms of business do not pay income tax (owners must report their share of the entity's profits on their individual tax returns); and (4) unless other contractual arrangements exist, amounts paid to the owners are not recorded as expenses but instead are accounted for as withdrawals of capital.

EXHIBIT 11A.2   Accounting for Partners' Equity

Selected Entries during 2013

January 1, 2013

A. Able and B. Baker organized AB Partnership on this date. Able contributed $60,000 cash and Baker contributed $40,000 cash to the partnership and they agreed to divide net income (and net loss) 60 percent and 40 percent, respectively. The financial effects of this investment on the business and the journal entry to record them are:

Assets		=	Liabilities	+	Partners' Equity	
Cash	+100,000				A. Able, Capital	+60,000
					B. Baker, Capital	+40,000

dr Cash (+A)	100,000	
cr A. Able, Capital (+OE)		60,000
cr B. Baker, Capital (+OE)		40,000

During 2013

The partners agreed that Able would withdraw $1,000 and Baker $650 per month in cash. Accordingly, each month the following financial effects were recorded with the journal entry that appears below:

Assets		=	Liabilities	+	Partners' Equity	
Cash	−1,650				A. Able, Drawings (+D)	−1,000
					B. Baker, Drawings (+D)	−650

dr A. Able, Drawings (+D, −OE)	1,000	
dr B. Baker, Drawings (+D, −OE)	650	
cr Cash (−A)		1,650

Note: At December 31, 2013, after the last withdrawals, the Drawings account for Able had a debit balance of $12,000 and the Drawings account for Baker had a debit balance of $7,800.

December 31, 2013

Assume that the normal closing entries for the revenue and expense accounts resulted in revenue of $78,000, expenses of $48,000, and net income of $30,000. The partnership agreement specified Able would receive 60 percent of net income ($18,000 = 60% × $30,000) and Baker would get 40 percent ($12,000 = 40% × $30,000). The financial effects and related closing entry follow:

Assets	=	Liabilities	+	Partners' Equity	
				Revenues (−R)	−78,000
				Expenses (−E)	+48,000
				A. Able, Capital	+18,000
				B. Baker, Capital	+12,000

dr Individual Revenue Accounts (−R, −OE)	78,000	
cr Individual Expense Accounts (−E, +OE)		48,000
cr A. Able, Capital (+OE) (60% × $30,000)		18,000
cr B. Baker, Capital (+OE) (40% × $30,000)		12,000

December 31, 2013

The financial effects of closing the drawings accounts and the related closing journal entry are:

Assets	=	Liabilities	+	Partners' Equity	
				A. Able, Capital	−12,000
				B. Baker, Capital	−7,800
				A. Able, Drawings (−D)	+12,000
				B. Baker, Drawings (−D)	+7,800

dr A. Able, Capital (−OE)	12,000	
dr B. Baker, Capital (−OE)	7,800	
cr A. Able, Drawings (−D, +OE)		12,000
cr B. Baker, Drawings (−D, +OE)		7,800

A separate statement of partners' capital, similar to a corporation's statement of stockholders' equity, is customarily prepared to supplement the balance sheet, as shown next:

EXHIBIT 11A.2	Accounting for Partners' Equity (Continued)

AB PARTNERSHIP
Statement of Partners' Equity
For the Year Ended December 31 2013

	A. Able	B. Baker	Total
Partners' equity, January 1, 2013	$ 0	$ 0	$ 0
Add: Additional contributions during the year	60,000	40,000	100,000
Add: Net income for the year	18,000	12,000	30,000
Totals	78,000	52,000	130,000
Less: Drawings during the year	(12,000)	(7,800)	(19,800)
Partners' equity, December 31, 2013	$66,000	$44,200	$110,200

REVIEW THE CHAPTER

DEMONSTRATION CASE A: STOCK ISSUANCE AND REPURCHASES

This case focuses on selected transactions from the first year of operations of Zoogle Corporation, which became a public company on January 1, 2013, for the purpose of operating a lost-pet search business. The charter authorized the following stock:

> Common stock, $0.10 par value, 20,000 shares
> Preferred stock, 5 percent noncumulative, $100 par value, 5,000 shares

The following summarized transactions, selected from 2013, were completed on the dates indicated:

a. Jan. 1   Issued a total of 8,000 shares of $0.10 par value common stock for cash at $50 per share.

b. Feb. 1   Sold 2,000 shares of preferred stock at $102 per share; cash collected in full.

c. July 1   Purchased 400 shares of common stock that had been issued earlier. Zoogle Corporation paid the stockholder $54 per share for the stock, which is currently held in treasury.

d. Aug. 1   Sold 30 shares of the common treasury stock at $54 per share.

e. Dec. 31   The board decided not to declare any dividends for the current year.

Required:

1. Give the appropriate journal entries, and show calculations for each transaction.
2. Prepare the stockholders' equity section of the balance sheet for Zoogle Corporation at December 31, 2013. Assume that Retained Earnings is $31,000.

Suggested Solution

1. Journal entries:

a. Jan. 1, 2013   dr **Cash** (+A) ($50 × $8,000 shares) 400,000
      cr **Common Stock** (+SE) ($0.10 × $8,000 shares) 800
      cr **Additional Paid-In Capital: Common** (+SE) 399,200

b. Feb. 1, 2013   dr **Cash** (+A) ($102 × $2,000 shares) 204,000
      cr **Preferred Stock** (+SE) ($100 par × 2,000 shares) 200,000
      cr **Additional Paid-In Capital: Preferred** (+SE) 4,000
        [($102 − $100) × 2,000 shares]

c. July 1, 2013   dr **Treasury Stock** (+xSE, −SE) 21,600
        cr **Cash** (−A) ($54 × 400 shares) 21,600

d. Aug. 1, 2013 dr **Cash** (+A) ($54 × 30 shares) 1,620
        cr **Treasury Stock** (−xSE, +SE) ($54 × 30 shares) 1,620

e. Dec. 31, 2013   No journal entry is required.

2. Stockholders' equity section of the balance sheet:

ZOOGLE CORPORATION
Partial Balance Sheet
At December 31, 2013

Stockholders' Equity

Contributed Capital

Preferred Stock, 5% (par value $100; 5,000 authorized shares, 2,000 issued and outstanding shares)	$200,000	
Additional Paid-in Capital, Preferred Stock	4,000	
Common Stock ($.10 par value; authorized 20,000 shares, issued 8,000 shares of which 370 shares are held as treasury stock)	800	
Additional Paid-in Capital, Common Stock	399,200	
Total Contributed Capital		$604,000
Retained Earnings		31,000
Treasury Stock, at cost, 370 common shares		(19,980)
Total Stockholders' Equity		615,020

DEMONSTRATION CASE B: CASH AND STOCK DIVIDENDS

This case extends Demonstration Case A by focusing on dividend transactions occurring during Zoogle Corporation's second year. The following summarized transactions, selected from 2014, were completed on the dates indicated:

1. Nov. 1   To make the company's stock more affordable, the board declared and issued a 100 percent stock dividend on the outstanding common stock.

2. Dec. 1   The board declared a cash dividend on the preferred stock, payable on December 22, 2014, to stockholders of record as of December 15, 2014.

3. Dec. 31   The temporary Dividends Declared account was closed.

Required:

Give the appropriate journal entries, and show calculations for each transaction.

Suggested Solution

1. Nov. 1, 2014   dr **Retained Earnings** (−SE) 763
        cr **Common Stock** (+SE) 763
        [(8,000 common shares issued − 370 in treasury) × $0.10]

2. Dec. 1, 2014   dr **Dividends Declared** (+D, −SE) 10,000
        cr **Dividends Payable** (+L) 10,000
        (2,000 preferred shares × $100 par × 5% dividend rate)

Dec. 15, 2014	No journal entry is required.		
Dec. 22, 2014	*dr* **Dividends Payable** (−L)	10,000	
	cr **Cash** (−A)		10,000
3. Dec. 31, 2014	*dr* **Retained Earnings** (−SE)	10,000	
	cr **Dividends Declared** (−D, +SE)		10,000

CHAPTER SUMMARY

Explain the role of stock in financing a corporation. p. 502   LO 11-1

- The law recognizes corporations as separate legal entities. Owners invest in a corporation and receive capital stock that can be bought from and sold to other investors. Stock provides a number of rights, including the rights to vote, to receive dividends, and share in residual assets at liquidation.

Explain and analyze common stock transactions. p. 504   LO 11-2

- A number of key transactions involve common stock: (1) initial issuance of stock, (2) repurchase of stock into treasury, and (3) reissuance of treasury stock. Each is illustrated in this chapter. Note that these transactions have only balance sheet effects; corporations do not report income arising from gains or losses on transactions involving their own stock.

Explain and analyze cash dividends, stock dividends, and stock split transactions. p. 509   LO 11-3

- Cash dividends reduce stockholders' equity (Retained Earnings) and create a liability (Dividends Payable) when they are declared by the board of directors (on the date of declaration). The liability is reduced when the dividends are paid (on the date of payment).

- Stock dividends are pro rata distributions of a company's stock to existing owners. The transaction typically is accounted for by transferring an amount out of Retained Earnings and into contributed capital accounts.

- A stock split also involves the distribution of additional shares to owners but no additional amount is transferred into the contributed capital accounts. Instead, the per-share par value of stock is reduced.

Describe the characteristics of preferred stock and analyze transactions affecting preferred stock. p. 514   LO 11-4

- Preferred stock provides investors certain advantages including current dividend preferences and a preference on asset distributions in the event the corporation is liquidated.

- If preferred stock carries cumulative dividend rights, any part of a current dividend that is not paid (called *dividends in arrears*) must be paid in full before any additional dividends can be paid.

Analyze the earnings per share (EPS), return on equity (ROE), and price/earnings (P/E) ratios. p. 517   LO 11-5

- The earnings per share (EPS) ratio is calculated by dividing net income by the average number of shares of common stock outstanding during the year. This ratio makes it easy to compare a company's earnings over time but it does not allow reliable comparisons across companies because it does not adjust for likely differences in the number of shares that each company has outstanding.

- The return on equity (ROE) ratio relates earnings to each dollar contributed to and retained by the company. Because it is calculated using dollar amounts contributed to and retained by a company, it allows comparisons to be made across companies.

- The price/earnings (P/E) ratio relates the company's current stock price to its most recent annual earnings per share, indicating the value investors place on the company's stock.

Accounting Decision Tools

Name of Measure	Formula	What It Tells You
Earnings per share (EPS)	$$\frac{\text{Net Income}}{\text{Average Number of Common Shares Outstanding}}$$	• The amount of income generated for each share of common stock owned by stockholders • A higher ratio means greater profitability
Return on equity (ROE)	$$\frac{\text{Net Income}}{\text{Average Stockholders' Equity}}$$	• The amount earned for each dollar invested by stockholders • A higher ratio means stockholders are likely to enjoy greater returns
Price/Earnings (P/E) ratio	$$\frac{\text{Current Stock Price (per share)}}{\text{Earnings per Share (annual)}}$$	• How many times more than the current year's earnings investors are willing to pay for a company's common stock • A higher number means investors anticipate an improvement in the company's future results

KEY TERMS

Authorized Shares p. 505

Common Stock p. 503

Cumulative Dividend
  Preference p. 516

Current Dividend
  Preference p. 515

Declaration Date p. 510

Dividends in Arrears p. 516

Issued Shares p. 505

No-Par Value Stock p. 506

Outstanding Shares p. 505

Par Value p. 506

Payment Date p. 510

Preferred Stock p. 514

Record Date p. 510

Stock Dividend p. 511

Stock Split p. 513

Treasury Stock p. 505

See complete definitions in the glossary in the back of this text.

HOMEWORK HELPER

Alternative terms

- Stockholders are also called shareholders.
- Additional Paid-In Capital is also called Capital in Excess of Par.

Helpful reminders

- Large stock dividends are recorded at par value; small stock dividends are recorded at the stock market price, with the excess of market over par accounted for as Additional Paid-In Capital.

Frequent mistakes

- Do not record a liability for dividends in arrears at the end of each year. They are recorded as a liability only when dividends are declared on the cumulative preferred stock.

PRACTICE MATERIAL

QUESTIONS (⊖Symbol indicates questions that require analysis from more than one perspective.)

1. Identify the primary advantages of the corporate form of business.

2. What are the relative advantages of equity versus debt financing?

3. Just prior to filing for bankruptcy protection in 2009, General Motors asked its bondholders to exchange their investment in GM's bonds for GM stock. The bondholders rejected this proposal. Why might GM have proposed this exchange? Why might the bondholders have rejected it? ⊖

4. Explain each of the following terms: (a) authorized common stock, (b) issued common stock, and (c) outstanding common stock.

5. What are the differences between common stock and preferred stock?

6. What is the distinction between par value and no-par value capital stock?

7. What are the usual characteristics of preferred stock?

8. What are the two basic sources of stockholders' equity? Explain each.

9. What is treasury stock? Why do corporations acquire treasury stock?

10. How is treasury stock reported on the balance sheet? How is the "gain or loss" on reissued treasury stock reported on the financial statements?

11. What are the two financial requirements to support the declaration of a cash dividend? What are the effects of a cash dividend on assets and stockholders' equity?

12. What is the difference between cumulative and noncumulative preferred stock?

13. What is a stock dividend? How does a stock dividend differ from a cash dividend?

14. What are the primary reasons for issuing a stock dividend?

15. Your company has been very profitable and expects continued financial success. Its stock price has reached a point where the company needs to make it more affordable. Would you recommend a stock dividend or a stock split? Why? ⊖

16. Identify and explain the three important dates with respect to dividends.

17. Why is the EPS number so popular? What are its limitations?

18. How do stock repurchases affect the EPS and ROE ratios?

19. What is one interpretation of a high P/E ratio?

20. You work for a public company that has relied heavily on debt financing in the past and is now considering a preferred stock issuance to reduce its debt-to-assets ratio. Debt-to-assets is one of the key ratios in your company's loan covenants. Should the preferred stock have a fixed annual dividend rate, or a dividend that is determined yearly? In what way might this decision be affected by IFRS? ⊖

MULTIPLE CHOICE

1. Which feature is not applicable to common stock ownership?
   a. Right to receive dividends before preferred stock shareholders.
   b. Right to vote on appointment of external auditor.
   c. Right to receive residual assets of the company should it cease operations.
   d. All of the above are applicable to common stock ownership.

2. Which statement regarding treasury stock is false?
   a. Treasury stock is considered to be issued but not outstanding.
   b. Treasury stock has no voting, dividend, or liquidation rights.
   c. Treasury stock reduces total stockholders' equity on the balance sheet.
   d. None of the above are false.

3. Which of the following statements about stock dividends is true?
   a. Stock dividends are reported on the income statement.
   b. Stock dividends increase total stockholders' equity.
   c. Stock dividends decrease total stockholders' equity.
   d. None of the above.

4. Which of the following is ordered from the largest number of shares to the smallest number of shares?
   a. Shares authorized, shares issued, shares outstanding.
   b. Shares issued, shares outstanding, shares authorized.
   c. Shares outstanding, shares issued, shares authorized.
   d. Shares in treasury, shares outstanding, shares issued.

5. Which of the following statements about the relative advantages of equity and debt financing is false?
   a. An advantage of equity financing is that it does not have to be repaid.
   b. An advantage of equity financing is that dividends are optional.
   c. An advantage of equity financing is that new stockholders get to vote and share in the earnings of the company.
   d. An advantage of debt financing is that interest is tax deductible.

6. A journal entry is not recorded on what date?
   a. Date of declaration.
   b. Date of record.
   c. Date of payment.
   d. A journal entry is recorded on all of the above dates.

7. Which of the following transactions will increase the return on equity?

   a. Declare and issue a stock dividend.
   b. Split the stock 2-for-1.
   c. Repurchase the company's stock.
   d. None of the above.

8. Which statement regarding dividends is false?

   a. Dividends represent a sharing of corporate profits with owners.
   b. Both stock and cash dividends reduce retained earnings.
   c. Cash dividends paid to stockholders reduce net income.
   d. None of the above statements are false.

9. When treasury stock is purchased with cash, what is the impact on the balance sheet equation?

   a. No change—the reduction of the asset Cash is offset with the addition of the asset Treasury Stock.

   b. Assets decrease and stockholders' equity increases.
   c. Assets increase and stockholders' equity decreases.
   d. Assets decrease and stockholders' equity decreases.

10. In what situation does total stockholders' equity decrease?

    a. When a cash dividend is declared.
    b. When a stock dividend is declared.
    c. When a stock split is announced.
    d. None of the above.

> For answers to the Multiple-Choice Questions **see page Q1** located in the last section of the book.

MINI-EXERCISES

LO 11-1   **M11-1 Equity versus Debt Financing**

Indicate whether each of the following relates to equity (E) or debt (D) financing, and whether it makes that form of financing more, or less, favorable.

_____   1. Interest is tax deductible.

_____   2. Dividends are optional.

_____   3. It must be repaid.

_____   4. Additional stock issuances dilute existing stockholders' control.

LO 11-1   **M11-2 Computing the Number of Issued Shares**

Face 2 Face Corporation reports 100 outstanding shares, 500 authorized shares, and 50 shares of treasury stock. How many shares are issued?

LO 11-1   **M11-3 Computing the Number of Unissued Shares**

The balance sheet for Crutcher Corporation reported 200,000 shares outstanding, 300,000 shares authorized, and 20,000 shares in treasury stock. Compute the maximum number of new shares that Crutcher could issue.

LO 11-2   **M11-4 Analyzing and Recording the Issuance of Common Stock**

To expand operations, Aragon Consulting issued 1,000 shares of previously unissued common stock with a par value of $1. The price for the stock was $50 per share. Analyze the accounting equation effects and record the journal entry for the stock issuance. Would your answer be different if the par value were $2 per share? If so, analyze the accounting equation effects and record the journal entry for the stock issuance with a par value of $2.

LO 11-2   **M11-5 Analyzing and Recording the Issuance of No-Par Value Common Stock**

Refer to M11-4. Assume the issued stock has no par value. Analyze the accounting equation effects and record the journal entry for the issuance of the no-par value stock at $50. Do the effects on total assets, total liabilities, and total stockholders' equity differ from those in M11-4?

LO 11-2, 11-4   **M11-6 Comparing Common Stock and Preferred Stock**

Your parents have just retired and have asked you for some financial advice. They have decided to invest $100,000 in a company very similar to National Beverage Corp. The company has issued both common and preferred stock. Which type of stock would you recommend? What factors are relevant to this recommendation?

M11-7 Determining the Effects of Stock Issuance and Treasury Stock Transactions LO 11-2

Trans Union Corporation issued 5,000 shares for $50 per share in the current year, and it issued 10,000 shares for $37 per share in the following year. The year after that, the company reacquired 20,000 shares of its own stock for $45 per share. Determine the impact (increase, decrease, or no change) of each of these transactions on the following classifications:

1. Total assets.
2. Total liabilities.
3. Total stockholders' equity.
4. Net income.

M11-8 Determining the Amount of a Dividend LO 11-3

Netpass Company has 300,000 shares of common stock authorized, 270,000 shares issued, and 100,000 shares of treasury stock. The company's board of directors declares a dividend of $1 per share of common stock. What is the total amount of the dividend that will be paid?

M11-9 Recording Dividends LO 11-3

On May 20, 2013, the board of directors for Auction.com declared a cash dividend of 50 cents per share payable to stockholders of record on June 14. The dividends will be paid on July 14. The company has 500,000 shares of stock outstanding. Prepare any necessary journal entries for each date.

M11-10 Determining the Impact of a Stock Dividend LO 11-3

Sturdy Stone Tools, Inc., announced a 100 percent stock dividend. Determine the impact (increase, decrease, no change) of this dividend on the following:

1. Total assets.
2. Total liabilities.
3. Common stock.
4. Total stockholders' equity.
5. Market value per share of common stock.

M11-11 Determining the Impact of a Stock Split LO 11-3

Complete the requirements of M11-10 assuming that the company announced a 2-for-1 stock split.

M11-12 Recording a Stock Dividend LO 11-3

To reduce its stock price, Shriver Food Systems, Inc., declared and issued a 100 percent stock dividend. The company has 800,000 shares authorized and 200,000 shares outstanding. The par value of the stock is $1 per share and the market value is $100 per share. Prepare the journal entry to record this large stock dividend.

M11-13 Determining the Amount of a Preferred Dividend LO 11-4

Colliers, Inc., has 100,000 shares of cumulative preferred stock outstanding. The preferred stock pays dividends in the amount of $2 per share but because of cash flow problems, the company did not pay any dividends last year. The board of directors plans to pay dividends in the amount of $600,000 this year. What amount will go to preferred stockholders? How much will be available for common stock dividends?

M11-14 Calculating and Interpreting Earnings per Share (EPS) and Return on Equity (ROE) LO 11-5

Academy Driving School reported the following amount in its financial statements:

	2013	2012
Number of common shares	11,500	11,500
Net income	$ 23,000	$ 18,000
Cash dividends paid on common stock	$ 3,000	$ 3,000
Total stockholders' equity	$240,000	$220,000

Calculate 2013 EPS and ROE. Another driving school in the same city reported a higher net income ($45,000) in 2013, yet its EPS and ROE ratios were lower than those for the Academy Driving School. Explain how this apparent inconsistency could occur.

LO 11-5   **M11-15 Inferring Financial Information Using the P/E Ratio**

In 2012, Rec Room Sports reported earnings per share of $8.50 when its stock price was $212.50. In 2013, its earnings increased by 20 percent. If the P/E ratio remains constant, what is likely to be the price of the stock? Explain.

LO 11-S1   **M11-16 (Supplement 11A) Comparing Owner's Equity to Stockholders' Equity**

On January 2, Daniel Harrison contributed $20,000 to start his business. At the end of the year, the business had generated $30,000 in sales revenues, incurred $18,000 in operating expenses, and distributed $5,000 for Daniel to use to pay some personal expenses. Prepare (*a*) a statement of owner's equity, assuming this is a sole proprietorship, (*b*) the owner's equity section of the balance sheet, assuming this is a sole proprietorship, and (*c*) the stockholder's equity section of the balance sheet, assuming this is a corporation with no-par value stock.

EXERCISES

 |ACCOUNTING

LO 11-1

E11-1 Computing Shares Outstanding

The 2010 annual report for Fortune Brands, the seller of Pinnacle golf balls and MasterLock padlocks, disclosed that 750 million shares of common stock have been authorized. At the end of 2009, 150 million shares had been issued and the number of shares in treasury stock was 84 million. During 2010, 2 million common shares were reissued from treasury, and 1 million common shares were purchased for treasury stock.

Required:

Determine the number of common shares (*a*) issued, (*b*) in treasury, and (*c*) outstanding at the end of 2010.

LO 11-2, 11-3   **E11-2 Reporting Stockholders' Equity and Determining Dividend Policy**

Incentive Corporation was organized in 2012 to operate a financial consulting business. The charter authorized the following capital stock: common stock, par value $4 per share, 12,000 shares. During the first year, the following selected transactions were completed:

a.   Issued 6,000 shares of common stock for cash at $20 per share.
b.   Issued 2,000 shares of common stock for cash at $23 per share.

Required:

1.   Show the effects of each transaction on the accounting equation.
2.   Give the journal entry required for each of these transactions.
3.   Prepare the stockholders' equity section as it should be reported on the 2012 year-end balance sheet. At year-end, the accounts reflected a profit of $100.
4.   Incentive Corporation has $30,000 in the company's bank account. Should the company declare cash dividends at this time? Explain.

LO 11-2, 11-4   **E11-3 Preparing the Stockholders' Equity Section of the Balance Sheet**

North Wind Aviation received its charter during January 2013. The charter authorized the following capital stock:

> Preferred stock: 8 percent, par $10, authorized 20,000 shares.
> Common stock: par $1, authorized 50,000 shares.

During 2013, the following transactions occurred in the order given:

a.   Issued a total of 40,000 shares of the common stock for $15 per share.
b.   Issued 10,000 shares of the preferred stock at $16 per share.

c. Issued 3,000 shares of the common stock at $20 per share and 1,000 shares of the preferred stock at $16.

d. Net income for the first year was $48,000.

Required:

Prepare the stockholders' equity section of the balance sheet at December 31, 2013.

E11-4 Reporting the Stockholders' Equity Section of the Balance Sheet

LO 11-2, 11-3, 11-4

Shelby Corporation was organized in January 2013 to operate an air conditioning sales and service business. The charter issued by the state authorized the following capital stock:

> Common stock, $1 par value, 200,000 shares.
> Preferred stock, $10 par value, 6 percent, 50,000 shares.

During January and February 2013, the following stock transactions were completed:

a. Collected $400,000 cash and issued 20,000 shares of common stock.

b. Issued 15,000 shares of preferred stock at $30 per share; collected in cash.

Net income for 2013 was $50,000; cash dividends declared and paid at year-end were $10,000.

Required:

Prepare the stockholders' equity section of the balance sheet at December 31, 2013.

E11-5 Determining the Effects of the Issuance of Common and Preferred Stock

LO 11-2, 11-4

Inside Incorporated was issued a charter on January 15, 2013, that authorized the following capital stock:

> Common stock, $6 par, 100,000 shares, one vote per share.
> Preferred stock. 7 percent, par value $10 per share, 5,000 shares, nonvoting.

During 2013, the following selected transactions were completed in the order given:

a. Issued 20,000 shares of the $6 par common stock at $18 cash per share.

b. Issued 3,000 shares of preferred stock at $22 cash per share.

c. At the end of 2013, the accounts showed net income of $38,000.

Required:

1. Prepare the stockholders' equity section of the balance sheet at December 31, 2013.

2. Assume that you are a common stockholder. If Inside Incorporated needed additional capital, would you prefer to have it issue additional common stock or additional preferred stock? Explain.

E11-6 Recording and Reporting Stockholders' Equity Transactions

LO 11-2, 11-4

Ava School of Learning obtained a charter at the start of 2013 that authorized 50,000 shares of no-par common stock and 20,000 shares of preferred stock, par value $10. During 2013, the following selected transactions occurred:

a. Collected $40 cash per share from four individuals and issued 5,000 shares of common stock to each.

b. Issued 6,000 shares of common stock to an outside investor at $40 cash per share.

c. Issued 8,000 shares of preferred stock at $20 cash per share.

Required:

1. Give the journal entries indicated for each of these transactions.

2. Prepare the stockholders' equity section of the balance sheet at December 31, 2013. At the end of 2013, the accounts reflected net income of $36,000. No dividends were declared.

LO 11-2, 11-4　**E11-7　Finding Amounts Missing from the Stockholders' Equity Section**

The stockholders' equity section on the December 31, 2012, balance sheet of Chemfast Corporation reported the following amounts:

Contributed Capital	
Preferred Stock (par $20; authorized 10,000 shares, ? issued, of which 1,000 shares are held as treasury stock)	$104,000
Additional Paid-in Capital, Preferred	14,300
Common Stock (no-par; authorized 20,000 shares, issued and outstanding 6,000 shares)	600,000
Retained Earnings	30,000
Treasury Stock, 1,000 Preferred shares at cost	9,500

Assume that no shares of treasury stock have been sold in the past.

Required:

Complete the following statements and show your computations.

1. The number of shares of preferred stock issued was _____.
2. The number of shares of preferred stock outstanding was _____.
3. The average issue price of the preferred stock was $_____ per share.
4. The average issue price of the common stock was $_____.
5. The treasury stock transaction increased (decreased) stockholders' equity by _____.
6. The treasury stock cost $_____ per share.
7. Total stockholders' equity is $_____.

LO 11-2, 11-3　**E11-8　Recording Treasury Stock Transactions and Analyzing Their Impact**

During 2013, the following selected transactions affecting stockholders' equity occurred for Corner Corporation:

Feb.	1	Purchased 400 shares of the company's own common stock at $20 cash per share.
Jul.	15	Issued 100 of the shares purchased on February 1 for $30 cash per share.
Sept.	1	Issued 60 more of the shares purchased on February 1 for $15 cash per share.

Required:

1. Show the effects of each transaction on the accounting equation.
2. Give the indicated journal entries for each of the transactions.
3. What impact does the purchase of treasury stock have on dividends paid?
4. What impact does the reissuance of treasury stock for an amount higher than the purchase price have on net income?

LO 11-2, 11-3　**E11-9　Recording Stockholders' Equity Transactions**

The annual report for Malibu Beachwear reported the following transactions affecting stockholders' equity:

a. Purchased $3.5 million in treasury stock.
b. Declared and paid cash dividends in the amount of $254.2 million.
c. Issued 100 percent common stock dividend involving 222.5 million additional shares with a total par value of $556.3 million.

Required:

1. Indicate the effect (increase, decrease, or no effect) of each of these transactions on total assets, liabilities, and stockholders' equity.
2. Prepare journal entries to record each of these transactions.

LO 11-3, 11-4　**E11-10　Computing Dividends on Preferred Stock and Analyzing Differences**

The records of Hoffman Company reflected the following balances in the stockholders' equity accounts at December 31, 2012:

Common stock, par $12 per share, 40,000 shares outstanding.
Preferred stock, 8 percent, par $10 per share, 6,000 shares outstanding.
Retained earnings, $220,000.

On January 1, 2013, the board of directors was considering the distribution of a $62,000 cash dividend. No dividends were paid during 2011 and 2012.

Required:

1. Determine the total and per-share amounts that would be paid to the common stockholders and to the preferred stockholders under two independent assumptions:

   a. The preferred stock is noncumulative.
   b. The preferred stock is cumulative.

2. Briefly explain why the dividends per share of common stock were less for the second assumption.

3. What factors would cause a more favorable dividend for the common stockholders?

E11-11 Recording the Payment of Dividends and Preparing a Statement of Retained Earnings

LO 11-2, 11-3

The 2012 annual report for Sneer Corporation disclosed that the company declared and paid preferred dividends in the amount of $100,000 in 2012. It also declared and paid dividends on common stock in the amount of $2 per share. During 2012, Sneer had 1 million common shares authorized; 300,000 shares had been issued; and 100,000 shares were in treasury stock. The balance in Retained Earnings was $800,000 on December 31, 2011, and 2012 Net Income was $300,000.

Required:

1. Prepare journal entries to record the declaration, and payment, of dividends on (a) preferred and (b) common stock.

2. Using the information given above, prepare a statement of retained earnings for the year ended December 31, 2013.

E11-12 Analyzing Stock Dividends

LO 11-3

On December 31, 2013, the stockholders' equity section of the balance sheet of R & B Corporation reflected the following:

Common stock (par $10; authorized 60,000 shares, outstanding 25,000 shares)	$250,000
Additional paid-in capital	12,000
Retained earnings	75,000

On February 1, 2014, the board of directors declared a 12 percent stock dividend to be issued April 30, 2014. The market value of the stock on February 1, 2014, was $18 per share.

Required:

1. For comparative purposes, prepare the stockholders' equity section of the balance sheet (a) immediately before the stock dividend and (b) immediately after the stock dividend.
   TIP: Use two columns for the amounts in this requirement.

2. Explain the effects of this stock dividend on the assets, liabilities, and stockholders' equity.

3. How would your answers to requirements 1 and 2 change if the stock dividend were 100%?

E11-13 Journalizing Small and Large Stock Dividends

LO 11-3

Refer to E11-12. Prepare the journal entry to record (a) the small 12 percent stock dividend and, alternatively, (b) the large 100 percent stock dividend mentioned in requirement 3 of E11-12.

LO 11-3

E11-14 Accounting for Dividends during the Credit Crisis

Black & Decker is a leading global manufacturer and marketer of power tools, hardware, and home improvement products. A press release on April 30, 2009, contained the following announcement:

> The Black & Decker Corporation (NYSE: BDK) announced that its board of directors declared a quarterly cash dividend of $0.12 per share of the Corporation's outstanding common stock payable June 26, 2009, to stockholders of record at the close of business on June 12, 2009. This represents a reduction from the $0.42 quarterly dividend paid by the Corporation since 2007. Nolan D. Archibald, Chairman and Chief Executive Officer, commented, "In today's uncertain and challenging economic environment, however, we believe it is important to preserve liquidity. By lowering the dividend to $0.12 per quarter, we will reduce cash outflows by $54 million in 2009. This action will strengthen our balance sheet, improve our credit metrics and provide greater financial flexibility."

At the time of the press release, Black & Decker had 150,000,000 shares authorized and 60 million outstanding. The par value for the company's stock is $.50 per share.

Required:

1. Prepare journal entries as appropriate for each of the three dates mentioned above.
2. Explain how a dividend cut from $0.42 to $0.12 will strengthen the company's balance sheet.

LO 11-3

E11-15 Comparing Stock Dividends and Splits

On July 1, 2013, Jones Corporation had the following capital structure:

Common Stock, par $1; 8,000,000 authorized shares, 100,000 issued and outstanding	$100,000
Additional Paid-in Capital	90,000
Retained Earnings	170,000
Treasury Stock	None

Required:

Complete the following table based on three independent cases involving stock transactions:

Case 1: The board of directors declared and issued a 10 percent stock dividend when the stock price was $8 per share.

Case 2: The board of directors declared and issued a 100 percent stock dividend when the stock price was $8 per share.

Case 3: The board of directors voted a 2-for-1 stock split. The stock price prior to the split was $8 per share.

		Case 1	Case 2	Case 3
Items	Before Stock Transactions	After 10% Stock Dividend	After 100% Stock Dividend	After Stock Split
Number of shares outstanding				
Par per share	$ 1	$	$	$
Common stock account	$	$	$	$
Additional paid-in capital	90,000			
Retained earnings	170,000			
Total stockholders' equity	$	$	$	$

LO 11-3, 11-4

E11-16 Determining the Impact of Cash and Stock Dividends

Superior Corporation has the following capital stock outstanding:

> Preferred stock, 6 percent, par $15, outstanding shares, 8,000.
> Common stock, par $8, outstanding shares, 30,000.

On October 1, 2013, the board of directors declared a full preferred stock dividend, payable on December 20, 2013. On December 20, 2013, the market prices were preferred stock, $40, and common stock, $32.

Required:

Indicate the direction and amount of change in total assets, liabilities, and stockholders' equity as a result of: (a) declaration of the cash dividend on October 1, (b) payment of the cash dividend on December 20, and (c) a 100 percent common stock dividend on December 20.

E11-17 Journalizing Cash Dividends and Stock Dividends

LO 11-3, 11-4

Bogscraft Company has outstanding 60,000 shares of $10 par value common stock and 25,000 shares of $20 par value preferred stock (8 percent). On February 1, 2013, the board of directors voted in favor of an 8 percent cash dividend on the preferred stock. The cash dividends are to be paid on March 15, 2013. A 100 percent stock dividend on the common stock occurred on June 30, 2011, when the common stock price was $30 per share.

Required:

Prepare journal entries to record the events on (a) February 1, (b) March 15, and (c) June 30.

E11-18 Preparing a Statement of Retained Earnings and Partial Balance Sheet and Evaluating Dividend Policy

LO 11-3, 11-5

The following account balances were selected from the records of beverage maker Blake Corporation at December 31, 2013, after all adjusting entries were completed:

Common stock (par $15; authorized 100,000 shares, issued 35,000 shares, of which 1,000 shares are held as treasury stock)	$525,000
Additional paid-in capital—common stock	180,000
Dividends declared and paid in 2013	28,000
Retained earnings, January 1, 2013	76,000
Treasury stock at cost (1,000 shares)	20,000

Net income for the year was $48,000.

Required:

1. Prepare the statement of retained earnings for the year ended December 31, 2013, and the stockholders' equity section of the balance sheet at December 31, 2013.
2. Determine the number of shares of stock that received dividends.
3. Compute the ROE ratio for 2013, assuming total stockholders' equity was $629,000 on December 31, 2012. How does it compare to the 2010 and 2011 ratios shown in Exhibit 11.7?

E11-19 Determining the Effect of a Stock Repurchase on EPS and ROE

LO 11-2, 11-5

Swimtech Pools Inc. (SPI) reported the following in its financial statements for the quarter ended March 31, 2013.

	December 31, 2012	March 31, 2013
Common Stock, $1 par, 50,000 shares outstanding	$ 50,000	$ 50,000
Additional Paid-In Capital	30,000	30,000
Retained Earnings	20,000	20,000
Total Stockholders' Equity	$100,000	$100,000

During the quarter ended March 31, 2013, SPI reported Net Income of $5,000 and declared and paid cash dividends totaling $5,000.

Required:

1. Calculate earnings per share (EPS) and return on equity (ROE) for the quarter ended March 31, 2013.

2. Assume SPI repurchases 10,000 of its common stock at a price of $2 per share on April 1, 2013. Also assume that during the quarter ended June 30, 2013, SPI reported Net Income of $5,000, and declared and paid cash dividends totaling $5,000. Calculate earnings per share (EPS) and return on equity (ROE) for the quarter ended June 30, 2013.

3. Based on your calculations in requirements 1 and 2, what can you conclude about the impact of a stock repurchase on EPS and ROE?

LO 11-S1   **E11-20 (Supplement 11A) Comparing Stockholders' Equity Sections for Alternative Forms of Organization**

Assume for each of the following independent cases that the annual accounting period ends on December 31, 2013, and that the total of all revenue accounts was $150,000 and the total of all expense accounts was $130,000.

Case A: Assume that the business is a *sole proprietorship* owned by Proprietor A. Prior to the closing entries, the Capital account reflected a credit balance of $50,000 and the Drawings account showed a balance of $8,000.

Case B: Assume that the business is a *partnership* owned by Partner A and Partner B. Prior to the closing entries, the owners' equity accounts reflected the following balances: A, Capital, $40,000; B, Capital, $38,000; A, Drawings, $5,000; and B, Drawings, $9,000. Profits and losses are divided equally.

Case C: Assume that the business is a *corporation*. Prior to the closing entries, the stockholders' equity accounts showed the following: Capital Stock, par $10, authorized 30,000 shares, outstanding 15,000 shares; Additional Paid-In Capital, $5,000; Retained Earnings, $65,000.

Required:

1. Give all the closing entries required at December 31, 2013, for each of the separate cases.

2. Show how the equity section of the balance sheet would appear at December 31, 2013, for each case. Show computations.

COACHED PROBLEMS

LO 11-2   **CP11-1 Analyzing Accounting Equation Effects, Recording Journal Entries, and Preparing a Partial Balance Sheet Involving Stock Issuance, Purchase, and Reissuance Transactions**

Worldwide Company obtained a charter from the state in January 2013, which authorized 200,000 shares of common stock, $10 par value. During the first year, the company earned $38,200 and the following selected transactions occurred in the order given:

a. Issued 60,000 shares of the common stock at $12 cash per share.

b. Reacquired 2,000 shares at $15 cash per share from stockholders.

c. Reissued 1,000 of the shares of the treasury stock purchased in transaction (b) two months later at $18 cash per share.

Required:

1. Indicate the effects of each transaction on the accounting equation.

2. Prepare journal entries to record each transaction.

3. Prepare the stockholders' equity section of the balance sheet at December 31, 2013.
   TIP: Because this is the first year of operations, Retained Earnings has a zero balance at the beginning of the year.

CP11-2 Recording Stock Dividends

Activision Blizzard, Inc., reported the following in the notes to its financial statements.

> *Stock Split*—In July, the Board of Directors approved a two-for-one split of our outstanding common shares effected in the form of a stock dividend ("the split"). The split was paid September 5 to shareholders of record as of August 25. The par value of our common stock was maintained at the pre-split amount of $.000001 per share.

Required:

1. Describe the effects that this transaction would have had on the company's financial statements. Assume that 600 million shares were outstanding at the time of the transaction, trading at a stock price of $33.

   TIP: Although the financial statements refer to a stock split, the transaction actually involved a 100% stock dividend. Large stock dividends, such as a 100% dividend, are recorded at par value.

2. Why might the board of directors have decided to declare a stock dividend rather than a stock split?

CP11-3 Finding Missing Amounts

At December 31, 2013, the records of Nortech Corporation provided the following selected and incomplete data:

> Common stock (par $1; no changes during 2013).
> Shares authorized, 500,000.
> Shares issued, ___?___; issue price $22 per share.
> Common Stock account $200,000.
> Shares held as treasury stock, 3,000 shares, cost $20 per share.
> Net income for 2013, $147,750.
> Dividends declared and paid during 2013, $49,250.
> Retained Earnings balance, January 1, 2013, $155,000.

Required:

1. Complete the following:

   Shares authorized _____.

   Shares issued _____.

   Shares outstanding _____.

   TIP: To determine the number of shares issued, divide the balance in the Common Stock account by the par value per share.

2. The balance in Additional Paid-in Capital would be $_____.
3. Earnings per share is $_____.
4. Dividends paid per share of common stock is $_____.
5. Treasury stock should be reported in the stockholders' equity section of the balance sheet in the amount of $_____.
6. Assume that the board of directors approved a 2-for-1 stock split. After the stock split, the par value per share will be $_____.
7. Disregard the stock split (assumed above). Assume instead that a 100 percent stock dividend was declared and issued after the treasury stock had been acquired, when the market price of the common stock was $21. Give any journal entry that should be made.

CP11-4 Comparing Stock and Cash Dividends

Tower Corp. had the following stock outstanding and Retained Earnings at December 31, 2012:

Common Stock (par $8; outstanding, 30,000 shares)	$240,000
Preferred Stock, 8% (par $10; outstanding, 6,000 shares)	60,000
Retained Earnings	280,000

On December 31, 2012, the board of directors is considering the distribution of a cash dividend to the common and preferred stockholders. No dividends were declared during 2010 or 2011. Three independent cases are assumed:

Case A: The preferred stock is noncumulative; the total amount of 2012 dividends would be $12,600.

Case B: The preferred stock is cumulative; the total amount of 2012 dividends would be $14,400. Dividends were not in arrears prior to 2010.

Case C: Same as Case B, except the total dividends are $66,000.

Required:

1. Compute the amount of 2012 dividends, in total and per share, that would be payable to each class of stockholders for each case. Show computations.

   TIP: Preferred stockholders with cumulative dividends are to be paid dividends for any prior years (in arrears) *and* for the current year, before common stockholders are paid.

2. Complete the following schedule, which compares case C to a 100 percent common stock dividend issued when the stock price is $24.

	Amount of Dollar Increase (Decrease)	
Item	Case C (Cash Dividend)	Stock Dividend
Assets	$	$
Liabilities	$	$
Stockholders' Equity	$	$

LO 11-5

CP11-5 Computing and Interpreting Return on Equity (ROE) and Price/Earnings (P/E) Ratios

Aaron's, Inc.
Rent-A-Center, Inc.

Aaron's, Inc., and Rent-A-Center, Inc., are two publicly traded rental companies. They reported the following in their 2010 financial statements (in millions of dollars, except per share amounts and stock prices):

	Aaron's, Inc.		Rent-A-Center, Inc.	
	2010	2009	2010	2009
Net income	$ 118	$ 113	$ 172	$ 168
Total stockholders' equity	979	887	1,354	1,248
Earnings per share	1.44	1.38	2.60	2.52
Stock price when annual results reported	23.85	16.02	32.14	22.24

Required:

1. Compute the 2010 ROE for each company. Express ROE as a percentage rounded to one decimal place. Which company appears to generate greater returns on stockholders' equity in 2010?
   TIP: Remember that the bottom of the ROE ratio uses the *average* stockholders' equity.

2. Compute the 2010 P/E ratio for each company (rounded to one decimal place). Do investors appear to value one company more than the other? Explain.

GROUP A PROBLEMS

LO 11-2

PA11-1 Analyzing Accounting Equation Effects, Recording Journal Entries, and Preparing a Partial Balance Sheet Involving Stock Issuance and Purchase Transactions

Global Marine obtained a charter from the state in January 2013, which authorized 1,000,000 shares of common stock, $5 par value. During the first year, the company earned $400,000 of net income and the following selected transactions occurred in the order given:

 a. Issued 100,000 shares of the common stock at $55 cash per share.
 b. Reacquired 25,000 shares at $50 cash per share.
 c. Reissued 10,000 shares from treasury for $51 per share.
 d. Reissued 10,000 shares from treasury for $49 per share.

Required:

1. Indicate the effects of each transaction on the accounting equation.
2. Prepare journal entries to record each transaction.
3. Prepare the stockholders' equity section of the balance sheet at December 31, 2013.

PA11-2 Recording Cash Dividends

LO 11-3

National Chocolate Corp. produces chocolate bars and snacks under the brand names Blast and Soothe. A press release contained the following information:

> March 5, 2012—National Chocolate Corp. today announced that its Board of Directors has declared a special "one-time" cash dividend of $1 per share on its 100,000 outstanding common shares. The dividend will be paid on April 30 to shareholders of record at the close of business on March 26.

Required:

1. Prepare any journal entries that National Chocolate Corp. should make as the result of information in the preceding report.
2. What two requirements would the board of directors have considered before making the dividend decisions?

PA11-3 Finding Missing Amounts

LO 11-2, 11-3, 11-5

At December 31, 2013, the records of Kozmetsky Corporation provided the following selected and incomplete data:

> Common stock (par $2; no changes during 2013).
> Shares authorized, 5,000,000.
> Shares issued, __?__; issue price $8 per share.
> Shares held as treasury stock, 10,000 shares, cost $6 per share.
> Net income for 2013, $481,000.
> Common Stock account $150,000.
> Dividends declared and paid during 2013, $2 per share.
> Retained Earnings balance, January 1, 2013, $800,000.

Required:

1. Complete the following:
   Shares issued _____.
   Shares outstanding _____.
2. The balance in Additional Paid-in Capital would be $_____.
3. Earnings per share is $_____. Round your answer to two decimal places.
4. Total dividends paid on common stock during 2013 is $_____.
5. Treasury stock should be reported in the stockholders' equity section of the balance sheet in the amount of $_____.
6. Assume that the board of directors voted a 2-for-1 stock split. After the stock split, the par value per share will be $_____.
7. Disregard the stock split (assumed above). Assume instead that a 100 percent stock dividend was declared and issued after the treasury stock had been acquired, when the market price of the common stock was $10. Explain how stockholders' equity will change.

PA11-4 Comparing Stock and Cash Dividends

LO 11-2, 11-3, 11-4

Ritz Company had the following stock outstanding and Retained Earnings at December 31, 2013:

Common stock (par $1; outstanding, 500,000 shares)	$500,000
Preferred stock, 8% (par $10; outstanding, 21,000 shares)	210,000
Retained earnings	900,000

On December 31, 2013, the board of directors is considering the distribution of a cash dividend to the common and preferred stockholders. No dividends were declared during 2011 or 2012. Three independent cases are assumed:

Case A: The preferred stock is noncumulative; the total amount of 2013 dividends would be $30,000.

Case B: The preferred stock is cumulative; the total amount of 2013 dividends would be $30,000. Dividends were not in arrears prior to 2011.

Case C: Same as Case B, except the amount is $75,000.

Required:

1. Compute the amount of dividends, in total and per share, payable to each class of stockholders for each case. Show computations. Round per-share amounts to two decimal places.

2. Complete the following schedule, which compares case C to a 100 percent stock dividend on the outstanding common shares when the stock price was $50.

Item	Amount of Dollar Increase (Decrease)	
	Case C (Cash Dividend)	Stock Dividend
Assets	$	$
Liabilities	$	$
Stockholders' Equity	$	$

LO 11-5

PA11-5 Computing and Interpreting Return on Equity (ROE) and Price/Earnings (P/E) Ratios

Two magazine companies reported the following in their 2012 financial statements:

	BusinessWorld		Fun and Games	
	2012	2011	2012	2011
Net income	$110,000	$108,604	$ 91,420	$172,173
Total stockholders' equity	587,186	512,814	447,151	467,049
Earnings per share	3.20	3.19	2.10	3.98
Stock price when annual results reported	54.40	51.04	32.55	59.70

Required:

1. Compute the 2012 ROE for each company (express ROE as a percentage rounded to one decimal place). Which company appears to generate greater returns on stockholders' equity in 2012?

2. Compute the 2012 P/E ratio for each company. Do investors appear to value one company more than the other? Explain.

GROUP B PROBLEMS

LO 11-2

PB11-1 Analyzing Accounting Equation Effects, Recording Journal Entries, and Preparing a Partial Balance Sheet Involving Stock Issuance and Purchase Transactions

Whyville Corporation obtained its charter from the state in January 2013, which authorized 500,000 shares of common stock, $1 par value. During the first year, the company earned $58,000 and the following selected transactions occurred in the order given:

a. Issued 200,000 shares of the common stock at $23 cash per share.

b. Reacquired 5,000 shares at $24 cash per share to use as stock incentives for senior management.

Required:

1. Indicate the effects of each transaction on the accounting equation.
2. Prepare journal entries to record each transaction.
3. Prepare the stockholders' equity section of the balance sheet at December 31, 2013.

PB11-2 Recording Cash and Stock Dividends

LO 11-3

Yougi Corp. is an animation studio operating in South Florida. A recent press release contained the following information:

> April 1, 2012—Yougi Corp. today announced that its Board of Directors has declared a cash dividend of $0.50 per share on 605,000 outstanding preferred shares. The dividend will be paid on or before May 31, 2012, to preferred shareholders of record at the close of business on May 26, 2012. The Board of Directors also announced a 100% common stock dividend will occur on May 31, 2012, on its 1,900,000 outstanding $0.01 par common stock for stockholders of record on May 26, 2012.

Required:

1. Prepare any journal entries that Yougi Corp. should make as the result of information in the preceding report.
2. What two requirements would the board of directors have considered before making the dividend decision?

PB11-3 Finding Missing Amounts

LO 11-2, 11-3, 11-5

At December 31, 2013, the records of Seacrest Enterprises provided the following selected and incomplete data:

> Common stock (par $1; no changes during 2013).
> Shares authorized, 10,000,000.
> Shares issued, __?__; issue price $10 per share.
> Shares held as treasury stock, 50,000 shares. cost $11 per share.
> Net income for 2013, $1,400,000
> Common Stock account $750,000.
> Dividends declared and paid during 2013, $1 per share.
> Retained Earnings balance, January 1, 2013, $36,400,000.

Required:

1. Complete the following:
   Shares issued _____.
   Shares outstanding _____.
2. The balance in Additional Paid-in Capital would be $_____.
3. Earnings per share is $_____. Round your answer to two decimal places.
4. Total dividends paid on common stock during 2013 is $_____.
5. Treasury stock should be reported in the stockholders' equity section of the balance sheet in the amount of $_____.
6. Assume that the board of directors voted a 2-for-1 stock split. After the stock split, the par value per share will be $_____.
7. Disregard the stock split (assumed above). Assume instead that a 100 percent stock dividend was declared and issued after the treasury stock had been acquired, when the stock price of the common stock was $21. Compute the dollar amount at which to record the stock dividend.

LO 11-2, 11-3, 11-4   **PB11-4 Comparing Stock and Cash Dividends**

Carlos Company had the following stock outstanding and Retained Earnings at December 31, 2013:

Common Stock (par $1; outstanding, 490,000 shares)	$490,000
Preferred Stock, 8% (par $10; outstanding, 19,000 shares)	190,000
Retained Earnings	966,000

On December 31, 2013, the board of directors is considering the distribution of a cash dividend to the common and preferred stockholders. No dividends were declared during 2011 or 2012. Three independent cases are assumed:

Case A: The preferred stock is noncumulative; the total amount of 2013 dividends would be $24,000.

Case B: The preferred stock is cumulative; the total amount of 2013 dividends would be $24,000. Dividends were not in arrears prior to 2011.

Case C: Same as Case B, except the amount is $67,000.

Required:

1. Compute the amount of 2013 dividends, in total and per share, payable to each class of stockholders for each case. Show computations. Round per-share amounts to two decimal places.

2. Complete the following schedule, which compares case C to a 100 percent stock dividend on the outstanding common shares when the stock price was $45.

	Amount of Dollar Increase (Decrease)	
Item	Case C (Cash Dividend)	Stock Dividend
Assets	$	$
Liabilities	$	$
Stockholders' Equity	$	$

LO 11-5   **PB11-5 Computing and Interpreting Return on Equity (ROE)**

Two music companies reported the following in their 2012 financial statements:

	Urban Youth		Sound Jonx	
	2012	2011	2012	2011
Net income	$ 27,500	$ 24,302	$ 41,500	$ 36,739
Total stockholders' equity	387,101	300,399	516,302	521,198
Earnings per share	1.10	1.00	0.95	0.85
Stock price when annual results reported	20.35	18.50	16.15	14.45

Required:

1. Compute the 2012 ROE for each company (express ROE as a percentage rounded to one decimal place). Which company appears to generate greater returns on stockholders' equity in 2012?

2. Compute the 2012 P/E ratio for each company. Do investors appear to value one company more than the other? Explain.

3. Sound Jonx had reacquired 5,000 shares of common stock in 2012 at $13 per share. Recalculate the company's ROE for 2012 assuming that this stock repurchase had not occurred. Does this new ROE change your interpretation of the ROE ratios calculated in requirement 1?

COMPREHENSIVE PROBLEM

C11-1 Financial Reporting of Write-off, Depreciation, Bond Issuance and Common Stock Issuance, Purchase, Reissuance, and Cash Dividends (Chapters 8, 9, 10 and 11)

|ACCOUNTING   LO 8-2, 9-3, 10-3, 11-2, 11-3

American Laser, Inc., reported the following account balances on January 1, 2013.

Accounts Receivable	$ 15,000
Accumulated Depreciation	30,000
Additional Paid-in Capital	90,000
Allowance for Doubtful Accounts	2,000
Bonds Payable	0
Buildings	100,000
Common Stock, 10,000 shares of $1 par	10,000
Notes Payable (due 2016)	10,000
Retained Earnings	120,000
Treasury Stock	0

The company entered into the following transactions during 2013.

Jan. 15   Issued 5,000 shares of $1 par common stock for $50,000 cash.

Feb. 15   Reacquired 3,000 shares of $1 par common stock into treasury for $33,000 cash.

Mar. 15   Reissued 2,000 shares of treasury stock for $24,000 cash.

Aug. 15   Reissued 600 shares of treasury stock for $4,600 cash.

Sept. 15   Declared (but did not yet pay) a $1 cash dividend on each outstanding share of common stock.

Oct.   1   Issued 100, 10-year, $1,000 bonds, at a quoted bond price of 101.

Oct.   3   Wrote off a $500 balance due from a customer who went bankrupt.

Dec. 31   Recorded $10,000 depreciation on the building.

Required:

1. Analyze the effects of each transaction on total assets, liabilities, and stockholders' equity.
2. Prepare journal entries to record each transaction.
3. Prepare the noncurrent liabilities and stockholders' equity sections of the balance sheet at December 31, 2013. At the end of 2013, the adjusted net income was $20,000.

SKILLS DEVELOPMENT CASES

S11-1 Finding Financial Information

|ACCOUNTING   LO 11-2, 11-3, 11-5

Refer to the financial statements of The Home Depot in Appendix A at the end of this book, or download the annual report from the *Cases* section of the text's Web site at www.mhhe.com/phillips4e.

Required:

1. As of January 30, 2011, how many shares of common stock were authorized? How many shares were issued? How many shares were held in treasury?

    a. 10,000,000,000; 1,716,000,000; 99,000,000
    b. 10,000,000,000; 1,722,000,000; 18,000,000
    c. Unlimited: 1,623,000,000; 18,000,000
    d. 10,000,000,000; 1,722,000,000; 99,000,000

2. According to the Retained Earnings column in the Statement of Stockholders' Equity, what was the total dollar amount of cash dividends declared during the year ended January 30, 2011?

    a. $1,521,000,000   c. $1,569,000,000
    b. $1,525,000,000   d. $2,608,000,000

3. According to the income statement, how has The Home Depot's net earnings and basic earnings per share changed over the past three years?

   a. Both net earnings and EPS increased.

   b. Net earnings increased and EPS decreased.

   c. Net earnings decreased and EPS increased.

   d. Both net earnings and EPS decreased.

LO 11-2, 11-3, 11-5

Lowe's

S11-2 Comparing Financial Information

Refer to the financial statements of The Home Depot in Appendix A and Lowe's in Appendix B at the end of this book, or download the annual reports from the *Cases* section of the text's Web site at www.mhhe.com/phillips4e.

Required:

1. Did Lowe's have more or fewer authorized shares of common stock than The Home Depot at the beginning of February 2011?

2. From the Retained Earnings column in the statement of stockholders' equity, what total amount of cash dividends did Lowe's declare during the year ended January 28, 2011? Compared to The Home Depot, is Lowe's policy on dividends better, worse, or just different?

3. How have Lowe's net earnings changed over the past three years? How has the company's basic earnings per share changed over the past three years? According to financial statement note 11, were the changes in EPS caused only by changes in Lowe's net earnings?

LO 11-3, 11-5

S11-3 Internet-Based Team Research: Examining an Annual Report

As a team, select an industry to analyze. Using your Web browser, each team member should access the annual report or 10-K for one publicly traded company in the industry, with each member selecting a different company. (See S1-3 in Chapter 1 for a description of possible resources for these tasks.)

Required:

1. On an individual basis, each team member should write a short report that incorporates the following:

   a. Has the company declared cash or stock dividends during the past three years?

   b. What is the trend in the company's EPS over the past three years?

   c. Compute and analyze the return on equity ratio over the past two years.

2. Then, as a team, write a short report comparing and contrasting your companies using these attributes. Discuss any patterns across the companies that you as a team observe. Provide potential explanations for any differences discovered.

LO 11-1, 11-2

S11-4 Ethical Decision Making: A Real-Life Example

Activision became a public company with an initial public offering of stock on June 9, 1983, at $12 per share. In June 2002, Activision issued 7.5 million additional shares to the public at approximately $33 per share in a seasoned new issue. In October 2002, when its stock was trading at about $22 per share, Activision executives announced that the company would spend up to $150 million to reacquire stock from investors. On January 8, 2003, *The Wall Street Journal* reported that several analysts were criticizing Activision's executives because the company had issued the shares to the public at a high price ($33) and then were offering to reacquire them at the going stock market price, which was considerably lower than the issue price in 2002.

Required:

1. Do you think it was inappropriate for Activision to offer to reacquire the stock at a lower stock price in October 2002?

2. Would your answer to question 1 be different if Activision had not issued additional stock in June 2002?

3. The above *Wall Street Journal* article also reported that, in December 2002, Activision executives had purchased, for their own personal investment portfolios, 530,000 shares of stock in the company at the then-current price of $13.32 per share. If you were an investor, how would you feel about executives buying stock in their own company?

4. Would your answer to question 3 be different if you also learned that the executives had disposed of nearly 2.5 million shares of Activision stock earlier in the year, when the price was at least $26.08 per share?

S11-5 Ethical Decision Making: A Mini-Case

LO 11-3

You are the president of a very successful Internet company that has had a remarkably profitable year. You have determined that the company has more than $10 million in cash generated by operating activities not needed in the business. You are thinking about paying it out to stockholders as a special dividend. You discuss the idea with your vice president, who reacts angrily to your suggestion:

> Our stock price has gone up by 200 percent in the last year alone. What more do we have to do for the owners? The people who really earned that money are the employees who have been working 12 hours a day, six or seven days a week to make the company successful. Most of them didn't even take vacations last year. I say we have to pay out bonuses and nothing extra for the stockholders.

As president, you know that you are hired by the board of directors, which is elected by the stockholders.

Required:

What is your responsibility to both groups? To which group would you give the $10 million? Why?

S11-6 Critical Thinking: Making a Decision as an Investor

LO 11-3

You have retired after a long and successful career as a business executive and now spend a good portion of your time managing your retirement portfolio. You are considering three basic investment alternatives. You can invest in (1) corporate bonds paying 7 percent interest, (2) conservative stocks that pay substantial dividends (typically 5 percent of the stock price every year), and (3) growth-oriented technology stocks that pay no dividends.

Required:

Analyze each of these alternatives and select one. Justify your selection.

S11-7 Charting Stock Price Movement around Important Announcement Dates

LO 11-1, 11-3

Using a Web search engine such as Google, find either an earnings or dividend announcement for two different companies. Using a source such as bigcharts.com, determine the closing stock price for each company for each day during the five business days before and after the announcement. Using a separate worksheet for each company, prepare a line chart of its stock price movement.

Required:

Examine the charts for each company. Does the stock price appear to change as a consequence of their announcements? Explain why or why not.

CONTINUING CASES

McGraw Hill connect®

|ACCOUNTING

CC11-1 Accounting for Equity Financing

LO 11-1, 11-2, 11-3, 11-4, 11-5

Nicole has been financing Nicole's Getaway Spa (NGS) using equity financing. Currently NGS has authorized 100,000 no-par preferred shares and 200,000 $2 par common shares. Outstanding shares include 50,000 preferred shares and 40,000 common shares.

Recently the following transactions have taken place.

a. NGS issues 1,000 preferred shares for $12 a share.
b. NGS repurchases 1,000 common shares for $11 a share.
c. On November 12, 2014, the board of directors declared a $0.10 cash dividend on each outstanding preferred share.
d. The dividend is paid December 20, 2014.

Required:

1. Prepare the journal entries needed for each of the transactions.

2. If you were a common shareholder concerned about your voting rights, would you prefer Nicole to issue additional common shares or additional preferred shares? Why?

3. Describe the overall effect of each transaction on the assets, liabilities, and shareholders' equity of the company. (Use + for increase, − for decrease, and NE for no effect.)

4. How would each transaction affect the ROE ratio?

LO 11-3, 11-5   **CC11-2 Wiki Art Gallery (WAG)**

Access the Wiki Art Gallery (WAG) instructional case in Connect, and read the case in sufficient depth to answer the following questions.

1. Is there any evidence that Rob failed to follow generally accepted accounting principles when preparing WAG's 2011 and 2010 financial statements?
   a. Yes, dividends should have increased rather than decreased from 2010 to 2011.
   b. Yes, as a public company, WAG is required to report its price/earnings ratio.
   c. Yes, dividends should not be reported on the income statement.
   d. No, there were no violations of generally accepted accounting principles.

2. Stephen and Rob agreed to base their agreement on an "earnings multiplier." Which of the following is an alternative name for this concept?
   a. Earnings per share (EPS) ratio.
   b. Return on equity (ROE) ratio.
   c. Price/earnings (P/E) ratio.
   d. None of the above.

ACCOUNTING CAREERS

Although this chapter has discussed equity in a business, you probably want to know how to boost your own personal equity. Pursuing a career in accounting is one way. Even during difficult economic times, accounting positions are abundant. According to the U.S. Department of Labor's most recent projections, employment in accounting is expected to grow 16 percent between 2010 and 2020, resulting in about 20,000 new accounting jobs added each year through 2020.

Accountants may pursue a variety of certifications, including the CPA (Certified Public Accountant), CFE (Certified Fraud Examiner), CMA (Certified Management Accountant), CIA (Certified Internal Auditor), CFM (Certified Financial Manager), Cr. FA (Certified Forensic Accountant), and CFA (Chartered Financial Analyst), among others. For additional information on accounting careers, certifications, salaries, and opportunities, visit www.aicpa.org, www.collegegrad.com, and www.imanet.org.

SUPPLEMENT Overview of Career Choices in Accounting

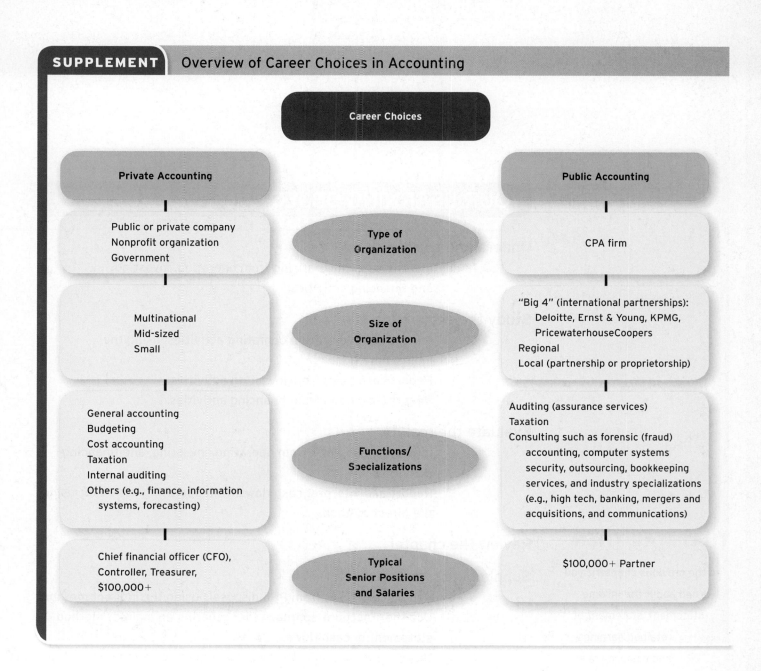

YOUR LEARNING OBJECTIVES

Understand the business

LO 12-1   Identify cash flows arising from operating, investing, and financing activities.

Study the accounting methods

LO 12-2   Report cash flows from operating activities, using the indirect method.

LO 12-3   Report cash flows from investing activities.

LO 12-4   Report cash flows from financing activities.

Evaluate the results

LO 12-5   Interpret cash flows from operating, investing, and financing activities.

LO 12-6   Report and interpret cash flows from operating activities, using the direct method.

Review the chapter

Supplemental material

LO 12-S1   Report cash flows from PPE disposals using the indirect method.

LO 12-S2   Use the T-account approach for preparing an indirect method statement of cash flows.

LO 12-S3   Use the spreadsheet approach for preparing an indirect method statement of cash flows.

THAT WAS THEN

In the previous chapters, you learned about the income statement, statement of retained earnings, and balance sheet.

FOCUS COMPANY: Under Armour, Inc.

www.underarmour.com

Have you ever studied your bank statements to see how much money you bring in and pay out during a typical month? You don't have to be a financial genius to know that if you are spending more than you earn, your savings will quickly disappear, and you will need to get a loan or some other source of financing to see you through.

Most businesses face the same issues you do. In 2007, for example, Under Armour, Inc.–famous for its frictionless sportswear–reported a net cash outflow from day-to-day operating activities. To ensure the company's long-term survival, managers had to stay on top of this change in the cash situation. Fortunately, the company had saved a great deal of cash in prior years. Managers were also able to negotiate some new loans to keep the business from running out of cash. By 2008, the company had turned things around and was again experiencing a positive net cash inflow from its operations, which continued through 2010.

Just like Under Armour's managers, investors and creditors also monitor the company's cash inflows and outflows. Investors want to know whether Under Armour is likely to pay dividends and creditors want to know whether Under Armour is likely to pay them the amounts they are owed. They find information for making such predictions in the statement of cash flows. Similar to your personal bank statement, the statement of cash flows reports changes in a company's cash situation.

THIS IS NOW

This chapter focuses on the fourth main financial statement–the statement of cash flows.

ORGANIZATION OF THE CHAPTER

Understand the business	**Study the accounting methods**	**Evaluate the results**	**Review the chapter**
• Business activities and cash flows • Classifying cash flows	• Relationship to other financial statements • Preparing the statement of cash flows	• Evaluating cash flows • Operating cash flows revisited (direct method)	• Demonstration cases • Chapter summary • Key terms • Homework helper • Practice material

Understand the Business

Learning Objective 12-1
Identify cash flows arising from operating, investing, and financing activities.

BUSINESS ACTIVITIES AND CASH FLOWS

To this point in the course, we've analyzed business activities to identify their financial effects on assets, liabilities, stockholders' equity, revenues, and expenses. We've emphasized that business activities have financial effects even when they don't involve cash. That's why accrual accounting exists. When accurately reported, accrual-based net income is the best measure of a company's profitability during the period.

Despite its importance, net income is not what companies use when they pay wages, dividends, or loans. These activities require cash, so financial statement users need information about the company's cash and changes in its cash. Neither the balance sheet nor the income statement provide this information. The balance sheet shows a company's cash balance at a point in time, but it doesn't explain the activities that caused changes in its cash. Cash may have been generated by the company's day-to-day operations, by the sale of the company's buildings, or by the negotiation of new loans. The income statement doesn't explain changes in cash because it focuses on just the operating results of the business, excluding cash that is received or paid when taking out or paying down loans, issuing or buying the company's own stock, and selling or investing in long-lived assets. Also, the timing of cash receipts and payments may differ from the accrual-based income statement, which reports revenues when they are earned and expenses when they are incurred. Under Armour, for example, reported a hefty amount of net income in each quarter of 2010 yet its related cash flows were negative in three of those four quarters. Such differences between net income and cash flows are the reason that GAAP requires every company to report a statement of cash flows.

The statement of cash flows shows each major type of business activity that caused a company's cash to increase or decrease during the accounting period. For purposes of this statement, cash is defined to include cash and cash equivalents. As explained in Chapter 6, cash equivalents are short-term, highly liquid investments purchased within three months of maturity. They are considered equivalent to cash because they are both (1) readily convertible to known amounts of cash, and (2) so near to maturity that their value is unlikely to change.

SPOTLIGHT ON Ethics

Cash Isn't Estimated

Critics of accrual-based net income claim it can be manipulated because it relies on many estimates (of bad debts, inventory market values, assets' useful lives), but cash flows do not involve estimates so they are not easily manipulated. A cash balance changes only when cash has been received or paid. One particularly dramatic illustration of the subjectivity of net income, but not cash, involved the bankruptcy of a department store chain operated by the W. T. Grant Company. Through biased estimates, the company reported net income for nine consecutive years but then shocked everyone when it declared bankruptcy and shut down the following year. At the time, a statement of cash flows wasn't required. Had it been required, the company would have reported negative operating cash flows in seven of the ten years.

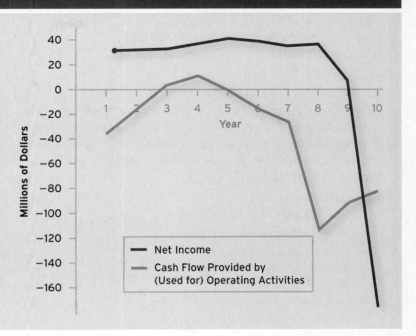

James A. Largay, III, and Clyde P. Stickney, "Cash Flows, Ratio Analysis and the W. T. Grant Company Bankruptcy," *Financial Analysts Journal 36,* no. 4: 51–54, July/August 1980.

CLASSIFYING CASH FLOWS

The statement of cash flows requires that all cash inflows and outflows be classified as relating to the company's operating, investing, or financing activities. This classification of cash flows is useful because most companies experience different cash flow patterns as they develop and mature. Think back to Chapter 2 when Pizza Aroma had just started. The first thing the owner needed to get his idea off the ground was **financing,** which he could then use to **invest** in assets that later would be needed to **operate** his business. At this early stage, financing and investing cash flows were crucial for Pizza Aroma. For an established business, like Activision in Chapter 5, operating activities often are the focus. Financial statement users are interested in a company's ability to generate operating cash flows that will allow it to continue investing in additional assets and repay the financing it originally obtained. Creditors and investors will tolerate poor operating cash flows for only so long before they stop lending to or investing in the company. For any company to survive in the long run, the amount of cash generated through daily operating activities has to exceed the amount spent on them.

A condensed version of Under Armour's statement of cash flows is presented in Exhibit 12.1. Don't worry about the details in the three cash flow categories yet. For now, focus on the categories' totals. Notice that each category can result in net cash inflows (represented by a positive number) or net cash outflows (represented by a negative number by using brackets). The sum of these three categories ($37 − $41 + $7 = $3) represents the overall change in cash on the balance sheet between the beginning and end of the period ($3 + $187 = $190).

Under Armour's 2010 cash flows in Exhibit 12.1 suggest the company is financially healthy. The company generated $37 million cash from its day-to-day operations. This money allowed Under Armour to invest $41 million in additional long-term assets and, combined with $7 million of net cash inflow from financing activities, build its cash balance at the end of the year. To learn the specific causes of these cash flows, you would consider the details of each category, as we will do now.

EXHIBIT 12.1   Under Armour's Condensed Statement of Cash Flows

UNDER ARMOUR, INC. Statement of Cash Flows For the Year Ended December 31, 2010		Explanations
(in millions)		
Cash Flows from Operating Activities		Cash flows related to day-to-day activities
Net income	$ 68	Assume net income (NI) generates cash inflow
Depreciation	17	Depreciation decreased NI but didn't decrease cash
Changes in current assets and current liabilities	(48)	Differences in the timing of net income and cash flows
Net cash provided by operating activities	37	Indicates overall cash impact of operating activities
Cash Flows Used in Investing Activities		Cash flows related to long-term assets
Purchase of equipment	(30)	Cash was used to purchase equipment
Purchase of intangible and other assets	(11)	Cash was used to purchase intangibles
Net cash used in investing activities	(41)	Indicates overall cash impact of investing activities
Cash Flows from Financing Activities		Cash flows from transactions with lenders, investors
Additional borrowings of long-term debt	9	Cash received from borrowing
Payments on long-term debt	(5)	Cash used to repay amounts previously borrowed
Proceeds from stock issuance	3	Cash received from issuing stock
Net cash provided by financing activities	7	Indicates overall cash impact of financing activities
Net Change in Cash and Cash Equivalents	3	$37 + $(41) + $7 = $3
Cash and cash equivalents, beginning of year	187	Cash balance at beginning of the period
Cash and cash equivalents, end of year	$190	Cash balance at end of the period (on balance sheet)

Operating Activities

> **YOU SHOULD KNOW**
>
> **Cash flows from operating activities** (cash flows from operations): Cash inflows and outflows related to components of net income.

Cash flows from operating activities (or **cash flows from operations**) are the cash inflows and outflows related directly to the revenues and expenses reported on the income statement. Operating activities involve day-to-day business activities with customers, suppliers, employees, landlords, and others. Typical cash flows from operating activities include:

Inflows	Outflows
Cash provided by	*Cash used for*
Collecting from customers	Purchasing services (electricity, etc.) and goods for resale
Receiving dividends	Paying salaries and wages
Receiving interest	Paying income taxes
	Paying interest

The difference between these cash inflows and outflows is reported on the statement of cash flows as a subtotal, Net Cash Provided by (Used for) Operating Activities.

Investing Activities

> **YOU SHOULD KNOW**
>
> **Cash flows from investing activities:** Cash inflows and outflows related to the sale or purchase of investments and long-lived assets.

Cash flows from investing activities are the cash inflows and outflows related to the purchase and disposal of investments and long-lived assets. Typical cash flows from investing activities include:

Inflows	Outflows
Cash provided by	*Cash used for*
Sale or disposal of property, plant, and equipment	Purchase of property, plant, and equipment
Sale or maturity of investments in securities	Purchase of investments in securities

The difference between these cash inflows and outflows is reported on the statement of cash flows as a subtotal, Net Cash Provided by (Used in) Investing Activities.

Financing Activities

Cash flows from financing activities include exchanges of cash with stockholders and cash exchanges with lenders (for principal on loans). Common cash flows from financing activities include:

Inflows	Outflows
Cash provided by	*Cash used for*
Borrowing from lenders through formal debt contracts	Repaying principal to lenders
Issuing stock to owners	Repurchasing stock from owners
	Paying cash dividends to owners

The difference between these cash inflows and outflows is reported on the statement of cash flows as a subtotal, Net Cash Provided by (Used in) Financing Activities.

One way to classify cash flows into operating, investing, and financing categories is to think about the balance sheet accounts to which the cash flows relate. **Although exceptions exist, a general rule is that operating cash flows cause changes in current assets and current liabilities, investing cash flows affect noncurrent assets, and financing cash flows affect noncurrent liabilities or stockholders' equity accounts.**[1] Exhibit 12.2 shows how this general rule relates the three sections of the statement of cash flows (SCF) to each of the main sections of a classified balance sheet.

EXHIBIT 12.2 Relationships between Classified Balance Sheet and Statement of Cash Flows (SCF) Categories

SCF Categories	Classified Balance Sheet Categories	
Operating	Current assets	Current liabilities
Investing	Noncurrent assets	Noncurrent liabilities
Financing		Stockholders' equity

How's it going? — Self-Study Practice

Brunswick Corporation produces the Life Fitness line of gym equipment. A listing of some of its cash flows follows. Indicate whether each item is disclosed in the operating activities (O), investing activities (I), or financing activities (F) section of the statement of cash flows.

☐ *a.* Stock issued to stockholders.　　☐ *d.* Purchase of plant and equipment.

☐ *b.* Collections from customers.　　☐ *e.* Purchase of investment securities.

☐ *c.* Interest paid on debt.　　☐ *f.* Cash dividends paid.

After you have finished, check your answers with the solution in the margin.

---

[1]Intermediate accounting courses discuss in detail exceptions to this general rule. Exceptions include investing activities that affect current assets (for example, short-term investments) and financing activities that affect current liabilities (for example, dividends payable and short-term notes payable).

SPOTLIGHT ON The World

Classification Choices under IFRS

To create consistency across companies, GAAP restricts interest and dividend classifications to a single category. IFRS, on the other hand, allows managers to choose between categories, as follows:

	COMPANY PAYS		COMPANY RECEIVES	
	Dividends	Interest	Dividends	Interest
GAAP	F	O	O	O
IFRS	O, F	O, F	O, I	O, I

GAAP classifies dividends paid as financing because they are transactions with stockholders. IFRS allows dividends paid to be classified as operating to assist users in determining the company's ability to pay dividends out of operating cash flows. GAAP requires the other three items to be classified as operating because they enter into the determination of net income. IFRS allows interest paid to be classified as financing because it is a cost of obtaining financial resources. IFRS allows interest and dividends received to be classified as investing because they are returns on investments.

Study the Accounting Methods

RELATIONSHIP TO OTHER FINANCIAL STATEMENTS

The statement of cash flows is intended to provide a cash-based view of a company's business activities during the accounting period. It uses the same transactions that have been reported in the income statement and balance sheet but converts them from the accrual basis to a cash basis. This conversion involves analyzing the income statement and the changes in balance sheet accounts, and relating these changes to the three cash flow categories. To prepare a statement of cash flows, you need the following:

1. **Comparative balance sheets,** showing beginning and ending balances, used in calculating the cash flows from all activities (operating, investing, and financing).
2. **A complete income statement,** used primarily in calculating cash flows from operating activities.
3. **Additional data** concerning selected accounts that increase and decrease as a result of investing and/or financing activities.

The approach to preparing the cash flow statement focuses on changes in the balance sheet accounts. It relies on a simple rearrangement of the balance sheet equation:

$$\text{Assets} = \text{Liabilities} + \text{Stockholders' Equity}$$

First, assets can be split into cash and all other assets, which we'll call **noncash assets:**

$$\text{Cash} + \text{Noncash Assets} = \text{Liabilities} + \text{Stockholders' Equity}$$

If we move the noncash assets to the right side of the equation, we get

$$\text{Cash} = \text{Liabilities} + \text{Stockholders' Equity} - \text{Noncash Assets}$$

Given this relationship, the **changes** in cash between the beginning and end of the period must equal the **changes** in the amounts on the right side of the equation between the beginning and end of the period:

> Change in Cash = Change in (Liabilities + Stockholders' Equity − Noncash Assets)

This equation says that **changes in cash must be accompanied by and can be accounted for by the changes in liabilities, stockholders' equity, and noncash assets.**

PREPARING THE STATEMENT OF CASH FLOWS

Based on the idea that the change in cash equals the sum of the changes in all other balance sheet accounts, we use the following steps to prepare the statement of cash flows:

1 **Determine the change in each balance sheet account.** From this year's ending balance, subtract this year's beginning balance (i.e., last year's ending balance).

2 **Identify the cash flow category or categories to which each account relates.** Use Exhibit 12.2 as a guide, but be aware that some accounts may include two categories of cash flows. Retained Earnings, for example, can include both financing cash flows (paying dividends) and operating cash flows (generating net income). Similarly, Accumulated Depreciation can be affected by operating activities (depreciation for using equipment in daily operations) as well as investing activities (disposing of equipment).

3 **Create schedules that summarize operating, investing, and financing cash flows.**

We will follow these three steps to prepare a statement of cash flows for Under Armour for the year ended December 31, 2010. Step 1 requires that we subtract each account's beginning balance from its ending balance, as we have done in the right side of Exhibit 12.3. Next, for step 2, we have indicated whether each account's cash flows relate to operating (O), investing (I), and/or financing (F) activities. Notice that Cash is not classified as O, I, or F, because Cash is not reported in these three sections but instead appears at the bottom of the statement of cash flows, as shown earlier in Exhibit 12.1. Step 3 in preparing a statement of cash flows is explained in the following sections.

Direct and Indirect Reporting of Operating Cash Flows

Two alternative methods may be used when presenting the operating activities section of the statement of cash flows:

1. The **direct method** reports the total cash inflow or outflow from each main type of transaction (that is, transactions with customers, suppliers, employees, etc.). The difference between these cash inflows and outflows equals the Net Cash Provided by (Used in) Operating Activities.

2. The **indirect method** starts with net income from the income statement and adjusts it by eliminating the effects of items that do not involve cash (for example, depreciation) and including items that do have cash effects. Adjusting net income for these items yields the amount of Net Cash Provided by (Used in) Operating Activities.

Direct Method		Indirect Method	
Cash collected from customers	$1,070	Net income	$68
Cash paid to suppliers of inventory	(585)	Depreciation	17
Cash paid to employees and suppliers of services	(408)		
Cash paid for interest	(1)	Changes in current assets and current liabilities	(48)
Cash paid for income tax	(39)		
Net cash provided by (used in) operating activities	$ 37	Net cash provided by (used in) operating activities	$37

| EXHIBIT 12.3 | Information for Preparing a Statement of Cash Flows |

UNDER ARMOUR, INC.
Balance Sheet*

(in millions)	December 31, 2010	December 31, 2009	Step ① Change	Step ② Related Cash Flow Section
Assets				
Current Assets:			*Change*	*Related Cash Flow Section*
Cash and Cash Equivalents	$190	$187	+3	Cash
Accounts Receivable	102	94	+8	O
Inventories	215	148	+67	O
Prepaid Expenses	35	33	+2	O
Total Current Assets	542	462		
Equipment	163	133	+30	I
Less: Accumulated Depreciation	(87)	(70)	−17	O (note 2 below implies no I)
Intangible and Other Assets	43	32	+11	I
Total Assets	$661	$557		
Liabilities and Stockholders' Equity				
Current Liabilities:				
Accounts Payable	$ 85	$ 69	+16	O
Accrued Liabilities	64	51	+13	O
Total Current Liabilities	149	120		
Long-term Debt	29	25	+4	F
Total Liabilities	178	145		
Stockholders' Equity:				
Contributed Capital	227	224	+3	F
Retained Earnings	256	188	+68	O (note 1 below implies no F)
Total Stockholders' Equity	483	412		
Total Liabilities and Stockholders' Equity	$661	$557		

UNDER ARMOUR, INC.
Income Statement*
For the Year Ended December 31, 2010

(in millions)	
Net Sales	$1,078
Cost of Goods Sold	534
Gross Profit	544
Operating Expenses:	
Selling, General, and Administrative Expenses	419
Depreciation Expense	17
Total Operating Expenses	436
Income from Operations	108
Interest Expense	1
Net Income before Income Tax Expense	107
Income Tax Expense	(39)
Net Income	$ 68

Additional data

1. No dividends were declared or paid.
2. No disposals or impairments of equipment or intangibles occurred.
3. Equipment costing $30 million and Intangibles and Other Assets costing $11 million were purchased with cash.
4. Long-term debt of $5 million was paid and $9 million in new loans was borrowed.
5. Shares of stock were issued for $3 million.

*Certain balances have been adjusted to simplify the presentation.

The point to remember about the direct and indirect methods is that they are simply different ways to arrive at the same number. **Net cash flows provided by (used in) operating activities is always the same under the direct and indirect methods.** Also, the choice between the two methods affects only the operating activities section of the statement of cash flows, not the investing and financing sections.

SPOTLIGHT ON The World

Direct vs. Indirect Method Presentation

GAAP and IFRS currently allow companies to use either the direct or indirect method. The FASB and IASB have recently proposed removing this choice and allowing only the direct method. If adopted, this proposal would significantly change the way companies report their statement of cash flows. Currently, about 99 percent of large U.S. companies, including Under Armour, use the indirect method.

We focus on the indirect method in the following section because it is currently the most commonly used method in the United States. The direct method, which may be required by GAAP and IFRS in the future, is presented in the last section of this chapter.

Learning Objective 12-2
Report cash flows from operating activities, using the indirect method.

Determining Operating Cash Flows Using the Indirect Method

When using the indirect method, the schedule of operating activities has the following format. We explain each of these items below and then, on pages 558–560, we demonstrate how to use Under Armour's information in Exhibit 12.3 to create such a schedule.

> **Net income**
> Items included in net income that do not involve cash
>   + Depreciation
> Changes in current assets and current liabilities
>   + Decreases in current assets
>   − Increases in current assets
>   − Decreases in current liabilities
>   + Increases in current liabilities
> **Net cash flow provided by (used in) operating activities**

Net income. When preparing a schedule to determine operating cash flows using the indirect method, start with net income as reported on the last line of the company's income statement. By starting with net income, it's as if we are assuming all revenues resulted in cash inflows and all expenses resulted in cash outflows. But we know this is not true, however, so we adjust net income to eliminate items that are included in net income but do not involve cash and to include items that were excluded from net income but do involve cash.

+ Depreciation. When initially recording depreciation in the accounting system, we increase Depreciation Expense (with a debit) and increase Accumulated Depreciation (with a credit). Notice that depreciation does not involve cash. To **eliminate** the effect of having deducted Depreciation Expense in the income statement, we add it back in the statement of cash flows.

+ Decreases in current assets. Adding decreases in current assets serves two purposes. First, it **eliminates** the effects of some transactions that decreased net income but did not affect cash in the current period. For example, when Supplies are used, net income decreases but cash is not affected. To eliminate these noncash effects from our cash flow computations, we must add back decreases in Supplies and other current assets. Second, adding decreases in current assets allows us to **include** the cash effects of other transactions that did not affect net income in the current period

COACH'S TIP

Use this table to remember how to adjust for changes in current assets and liabilities. The + and − indicate whether balance sheet changes are added or subtracted in the statement of cash flows.

	Current Assets	Current Liabilities
Increase	−	+
Decrease	+	−

but did increase cash. For example, Cash increases when Accounts Receivable are collected. These cash inflows are captured by adding the amount by which this current asset had decreased.

— Increases in current assets. Subtracting increases in current assets similarly serves two purposes. First, it **eliminates** the effects of transactions that increased net income but did not affect cash in the current period. For example, net income increases when a company provides services on account, but cash is not affected. We eliminate these noncash effects by subtracting increases in current assets. Second, subtracting increases in current assets allows us to **include** the cash effects of other transactions that did not affect net income in the current period but did decrease cash. For example, Cash decreases when a company prepays its insurance or rent, but net income isn't affected until these assets are used up. The cash outflows can be captured by subtracting the increase in these current assets.

— Decreases in current liabilities. Subtracting decreases in current liabilities serves two purposes. First, it **eliminates** the effects of transactions that increased net income but did not affect cash. For example, a company decreases Unearned Revenue and increases net income in the current period when it fulfills its prior obligations to provide services, but cash is not affected. To eliminate these noncash effects, we subtract decreases in current liabilities. Second, subtracting decreases in current liabilities allows us to **include** the cash effects of other transactions that did not affect net income in the current period but did decrease cash. For example, Cash decreases when a company pays wages that were incurred and expensed in a previous period. These cash outflows are captured by subtracting decreases in current liabilities.

+ Increases in current liabilities. Adding increases in current liabilities serves two purposes. First, it **eliminates** the effects of transactions that decreased net income but did not affect cash. For example, when interest is accrued, a company decreases net income but its cash is not affected. To eliminate these noncash effects, we add back increases in current liabilities. Second, adding increases in current liabilities allows us to **include** the cash effects of other transactions that did not affect net income in the current period but did increase cash. For example, Cash and Unearned Revenue increase when the company receives cash in advance of providing services. Adding the increase in current liabilities captures these cash inflows.

Under Armour's Operating Cash Flows—Indirect Method

The preceding approach to preparing an operating cash flow schedule can be applied to Under Armour's information in Exhibit 12.3. By taking the amount of the change in each account marked by an O in Exhibit 12.3, we have prepared an operating cash flow schedule for Under Armour in Exhibit 12.4. Understanding the causes of increases or decreases in each current asset and current liability is the key to understanding the logic behind the items in the schedule. Take your time reading the following explanations and make sure you understand the reasons for each item.

Net Income + Depreciation   Net income and depreciation are always the first two lines to appear in a statement of cash flows prepared using the indirect method. They begin the process of converting net income to operating cash flows. They also begin the process of explaining the change in Cash by accounting for changes in the other balance sheet accounts. In the case of Under Armour, the $68 million of net income fully accounts for the change in Retained Earnings (the company had no dividends). Similarly, the $17 million of depreciation accounts for the change in Accumulated Depreciation (the company had no disposals).[2]

COACH'S TIP

The depreciation addback is not intended to suggest that depreciation creates an increase in cash. Rather, it's just showing that depreciation does not cause a decrease in cash. This is a subtle, but very important, difference in interpretation.

---

[2]Amortization and impairment losses (discussed in Chapter 9) are handled in exactly the same way as depreciation. Gains and losses on fixed asset disposals also are dealt with in a similar manner and are discussed in Chapter Supplement 12A.

EXHIBIT 12.4	Under Armour's Schedule of Operating Cash Flows	

Items	Amount (in millions)	Explanations
Net income	$ 68	Starting point, from the income statement
Items included in net income that do not involve cash		
+ Depreciation	17	Depreciation is a noncash expense
Changes in current assets and current liabilities		
– Increase in Accounts Receivable	(8)	Cash collections less than sales on account
– Increase in Inventories	(67)	Purchases greater than cost of goods sold
– Increase in Prepaid Expenses	(2)	Prepayments greater than related expenses
+ Increase in Accounts Payable	16	Purchases greater than payments to suppliers
+ Increase in Accrued Liabilities	13	Cash payments less than accrued expenses
Net cash flow provided by (used in) operating activities	$ 37	Overall increase in cash from operations

Decrease in Accounts Receivable

Accounts Receivable increases when sales are made on account and it decreases when cash is collected from customers. An overall increase in this account, then, implies that cash collections were less than sales on account. To convert from the higher sales number that is included in net income to the lower cash collected from customers, we subtract the difference ($8 million).

Another way to remember whether to add or subtract the difference is to think about whether the overall change in the account balance is explained by a debit or credit. If the change in the account is explained by a credit, the adjustment in the cash flow schedule is reported like a corresponding debit to cash (added). In Under Armour's case, the increase in Accounts Receivable is explained by a debit, so the adjustment in the cash flow schedule is reported like a credit to cash (a decrease), as follows:

CASH FLOWS FROM OPERATING ACTIVITIES	
Net income	68
– Accounts receivable increase	(8)
. . .	. . .
Net cash inflow	—

Accounts Receivable (A)		
Beg. bal.	94	
Increase	8	
End. bal.	102	

Increase in Inventory

The income statement reports the cost of goods sold during the period, but cash flow from operating activities must report cash purchases of inventory. As shown in the T-account on the left, purchases of goods increase the balance in inventory, and recording the cost of goods sold decreases the balance in inventory.

Inventories (A)	
Beg. bal.	
Purchases	Cost of goods sold
End. bal.	

Inventories (A)		
Beg. bal.	148	
Increase	67	
End. bal.	215	

Under Armour's $67 million inventory increase means that the cash outflow for inventory purchases is more than the cost of goods sold. The increase (the extra purchases) must be subtracted from net income to convert to cash flow from operating activities in Exhibit 12.4. (A decrease would be added.)

Increase in Prepaid Expenses

The income statement reports expenses of the period, but cash flow from operating activities must reflect the cash payments. Cash prepayments increase the balance in prepaid expenses, and recording of expenses decreases the balance in prepaid expenses.

Prepaid Expenses (A)			Prepaid Expenses (A)	
Beg. bal.			Beg. bal.	33
Cash prepayments	Used-up / expensed		Increase	2
End. bal.			End. bal.	35

Under Armour's $2 million increase in Prepaid Expenses means that cash prepayments this period were more than expenses. These extra cash prepayments must be subtracted in Exhibit 12.4. (A decrease would be added.)

Increase in Accounts Payable

Cash flow from operations must reflect cash purchases, but not all purchases are for cash. Purchases on account increase Accounts Payable and cash paid to suppliers decreases Accounts Payable.

Accounts Payable (L)			Accounts Payable (L)	
Cash payments	Beg. bal.		Beg. bal.	69
	Purchases on account		Increase	16
	End. bal.		End. bal.	85

Accounts Payable increased by $16 million, which means that purchases on account were greater than cash payments to suppliers. Thus, to show the lower cash outflow, the increase in Accounts Payable must be added back in Exhibit 12.4. (A decrease would be subtracted.)

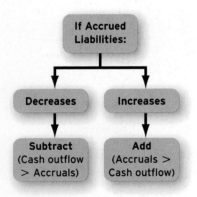

Increase in Accrued Liabilities

The income statement reports all accrued expenses, but the cash flow statement must reflect only the actual payments for expenses. Recording accrued expenses increases the balance in Accrued Liabilities and cash payments for the expenses decreases Accrued Liabilities.

Accrued Liabilities (L)			Accrued Liabilities (L)	
Cash payments	Beg. bal.		Beg. bal.	51
	Accrued expenses		Increase	13
	End. bal.		End. bal.	64

Under Armour's Accrued Liabilities increased by $13 million, which indicates that more expenses were accrued than paid. Consequently, this difference (representing less cash paid) must be added back in Exhibit 12.4. (A decrease would be subtracted.)

By scanning Exhibit 12.3 on page 556 you can see that you have now considered the changes in all balance sheet accounts that relate to operating activities (marked by the letter O). The last step in determining the net cash flow provided by (used in) operating activities is to calculate a total. As shown in Exhibit 12.4, the combined effects of all operating cash flows is a net inflow of $37 million.

Now that you have seen how to compute operating cash flows using the indirect method, take a moment to complete the following Self-Study Practice.

> ### 💡 How's it going? Self-Study Practice
>
> Indicate whether the following items taken from Brunswick Corporation's cash flow statement would be added (+), subtracted (−), or not included (0) in the reconciliation of net income to cash flow from operations.
>
> ☐ *a.* Decrease in inventories.   ☐ *d.* Increase in accounts receivable.
>
> ☐ *b.* Increase in accounts payable.   ☐ *e.* Increase in accrued liabilities.
>
> ☐ *c.* Depreciation expense.   ☐ *f.* Increase in prepaid expenses.
>
> *After you have finished, check your answers with the solution in the margin.*

Solution to Self-Study Practice
a. + , *b.* + , *c.* + , *d.* − , *e.* + , *f.* −

Under Armour's Investing Cash Flow Calculations

To prepare the investing section of the statement of cash flows, you must analyze accounts related to long-lived tangible and intangible assets.[3] Unlike the analysis of operating activities, where you were concerned only with the *net* change in selected balance sheet accounts, an analysis of investing (and financing) activities requires that you identify and separately report the causes of *both* increases and decreases in account balances. The following relationships are the ones that you will encounter most frequently:

> **Learning Objective 12-3**
> Report cash flows from investing activities.

Related Balance Sheet Accounts	Investing Activity	Cash Flow Effect
Property, Plant, and Equipment	Purchase of property, plant, and equipment for cash	Outflow
	Sale of property, plant, and equipment for cash	Inflow
Intangible Assets	Purchase of intangible assets	Outflow
	Sale of intangible assets	Inflow

Under Armour's balance sheet (Exhibit 12.3) shows two investing assets (noted with an I) that changed during the year: Equipment and Intangible and Other Assets.

Equipment To determine the cause of the change in the Equipment account, accountants would examine the detailed accounting records for equipment. Purchases of equipment increase the account, and disposals of equipment decrease it. The additional data in Exhibit 12.3 indicates that Under Armour purchased equipment for $30 million cash. This purchase is a cash outflow, which we subtract in the schedule of investing activities in Exhibit 12.5. In our example, this purchase fully accounts for the change in the Equipment balance, as shown in the Equipment T-account. Thus, we can assume that Under Armour did not dispose of any equipment during the year. Chapter Supplement 12A explains how disposals of property, plant, and equipment affect the statement of cash flows.

Equipment (A)			
Beg. bal.	133		
Purchases	30	Disposals	0
End. bal.	163		

---

[3] Investing activities also affect other assets described in Appendix D (investments in other companies). Although not shown here, the cash flows for investments are similar to those shown in this section for equipment and intangible assets.

EXHIBIT 12.5   **Under Armour's Schedule of Investing Cash Flows**

Items	Amount (in millions)	Explanations
Purchase of equipment	$(30)	Payment of cash for equipment
Purchase of intangible and other assets	(11)	Payment of cash for intangibles
Net cash provided by (used in) investing activities	(41)	Subtotal for the statement of cash flows

---

Intangible and Other Assets   A similar approach is used to determine cash flows associated with intangible assets. Analysis of Under Armour's detailed records indicate that the company did not have any reductions in its intangible assets as a result of disposals, impairments, or amortization during the year. However, Under Armour did purchase intangible assets for $11 million cash, as noted in the additional data in Exhibit 12.3. This cash outflow is subtracted in the schedule of investing activities in Exhibit 12.5.

Under Armour's Financing Cash Flow Calculations

Learning Objective 12-4
Report cash flows from financing activities.

This section of the cash flow statement includes changes in liabilities owed to owners (Dividends Payable) and financial institutions (Notes Payable and other types of debt), as well as changes in stockholders' equity accounts. Interest is considered an operating activity so it is excluded from financing cash flows. The following relationships are the ones that you will encounter most often:

COACH'S TIP

Dividends paid are financing cash flows. Dividends received, however, are operating cash flows.

Related Balance Sheet Accounts	Financing Activity	Cash Flow Effect
Notes Payable	Borrowing cash from bank or other financial institutions	Inflow
	Repayment of loan principal	Outflow
Bonds Payable	Issuance of bonds for cash	Inflow
	Repayment of bond face value	Outflow
Contributed Capital	Issuance of stock for cash	Inflow
	Repurchase of stock with cash	Outflow
Retained Earnings	Payment of cash dividends	Outflow

To compute cash flows from financing activities, you should review changes in all debt and stockholders' equity accounts. Increases and decreases must be identified and reported separately. Under Armour's balance sheet in Exhibit 12.3 indicates that Long-term Debt and Contributed Capital changed during the period as a result of financing cash flows (noted with an F).

Long-term Debt   The additional data in Exhibit 12.3 indicates that Long-term Debt was affected by both cash inflows and outflows, as shown in the T-account below. These cash flows are reported separately in the schedule of financing activities shown in Exhibit 12.6.

Long-term Debt (L)			
		Beg. bal.	25
Repayments	5	Borrowings	9
		End. bal.	29

Contributed Capital   Under Armour did not repurchase stock during the year, but it did issue stock for $3 million cash. This stock issuance fully accounts for the change in

EXHIBIT 12.6	Under Armour's Schedule of Financing Cash Flows

Items	Amount (in millions)	Explanations
Additional borrowings of long-term debt	$9	Cash received when new loan obtained
Payments on long-term debt	(5)	Cash paid on loan principal
Proceeds from stock issuance	3	Cash received from stockholders for new stock
Net cash provided by financing activities	7	Subtotal for the statement of cash flows

Contributed Capital, as shown in the following T-account. This cash inflow is listed in the schedule of financing activities in Exhibit 12.6.

Contributed Capital (SE)

	Beg. bal.	224
	Stock issued	3
	End. bal.	227

Retained Earnings   Net income increases Retained Earnings and any dividends decrease Retained Earnings. Net income has already been accounted for as an operating cash flow. In Under Armour's case, no dividends were declared or paid in 2010 (see the additional data in Exhibit 12.3). As shown in the following T-account, dividends would have decreased Retained Earnings, had they been declared; their payment would have been reported as a cash outflow in the financing section of the statement of cash flows.

Retained Earnings (SE)

		Beg. bal.	188
Dividends	0	Net income	68
		End. bal.	256

Under Armour's Statement of Cash Flows

Now that you have determined the cash flows for the three main types of business activities in Exhibits 12.4, 12.5, and 12.6, you can prepare the statement of cash flows in a proper format. Exhibit 12.7 shows the statement of cash flows for Under Armour using the indirect method. Notice that the $3 million subtotal for Net increase (decrease) in cash and cash equivalents combines cash flows from operating, investing, and financing activities to produce an overall net change in cash. This net change is added to the beginning cash balance to arrive at the ending cash balance, which is the same cash balance as reported on the balance sheet.

Supplemental Disclosures   In addition to their cash flows, all companies are required to report material investing and financing transactions that did not have cash flow effects (called **noncash investing and financing activities**). For example, the purchase of a $10,000 piece of equipment with a $10,000 note payable to the supplier does not cause either an inflow or an outflow of cash. As a result, these activities are not listed in the three main sections of the statement of cash flows. This important information is normally presented for users in a supplementary schedule to the statement of cash flows or in the financial statement notes. Supplementary information must also disclose (for companies using the indirect method) the amount of cash paid for interest and for income taxes. An example of this disclosure is shown at the bottom of Exhibit 12.7.

 COACH'S TIP

When doing homework problems, assume that all changes in noncurrent account balances are caused by cash transactions (unless the problem also describes changes caused by noncash investing and financing activities).

EXHIBIT 12.7 Under Armour's Statement of Cash Flows (Indirect Method)

UNDER ARMOUR, INC.
Statement of Cash Flows*
For the Year Ended December 31, 2010

(in millions)

Cash Flows from Operating Activities	
Net income	$ 68
Adjustments to reconcile net income to net cash provided by operating activities:	
Depreciation	17
Changes in current assets and current liabilities	
Accounts Receivable	(8)
Inventories	(67)
Prepaid Expenses	(2)
Accounts Payable	16
Accrued Liabilities	13
Net cash provided by (used in) operating activities	37
Cash Flows from Investing Activities	
Purchase of equipment	(30)
Purchase of intangible and other assets	(11)
Net cash provided by (used in) investing activities	(41)
Cash Flows from Financing Activities	
Additional borrowings of long-term debt	9
Payments on long-term debt	(5)
Proceeds from stock issuance	3
Net cash provided by (used in) financing activities	7
Net increase (decrease) in cash and cash equivalents	3
Cash and cash equivalents at beginning of period	187
Cash and cash equivalents at end of period	$190
Supplemental Disclosures	
Cash paid for interest	$ 1
Cash paid for income tax	39

*Certain amounts have been adjusted to simplify the presentation.

> **COACH'S TIP**
>
> If you have difficulty remembering the order in which to report operating (O), investing (I), and financing (F) cash flows, say to yourself, "O, IF only I could remember!"

Evaluate the Results

Learning Objective 12-5
Interpret cash flows from operating, investing, and financing activities.

Unlike the income statement, which summarizes its detailed information in one number (net income), the statement of cash flows does not provide a summary measure of cash flow performance. Instead, it must be evaluated in terms of the cash flow pattern suggested by the subtotals of each of the three main sections. As we discussed at the beginning of this chapter, expect different patterns of cash flows from operating, investing, and financing activities depending on how well established a company is. An established, healthy company will show positive cash flows from operations, which are sufficiently large to pay for replacing existing property, plant, and equipment and to pay dividends to stockholders. Any additional cash (called **free cash flow**) can (a) be used to expand the business through additional investing activities, (*b*) be used for other financing activities, or (*c*) simply build up the company's cash balance. After considering where the company stands in relation to this big picture, you should then look at the details within each of the three sections.

EVALUATING CASH FLOWS

Cash Flows from Operating Activities

The operating activities section indicates how well a company is able to generate cash internally through its operations and management of current assets and current liabilities. Most analysts believe this is the most important section of the statement because, in the long run, operations are the only continuing source of cash. Investors will not invest in a company if they do not believe that cash generated from operations will be available to pay dividends or expand the company. Similarly, creditors will not lend money or extend credit if they believe that cash generated from operations will be insufficient to repay them.

When evaluating the operating activities section of the statement of cash flows, consider the absolute amount of cash flow (is it positive or negative?), keeping in mind that operating cash flows have to be positive over the long run for a company to be successful. Also, look at the relationship between operating cash flows and net income.

All other things being equal, when net income and operating cash flows are similar, there is a high likelihood that revenues are realized in cash and that expenses are associated with cash outflows. Any major deviations should be investigated. In some cases, a deviation may be nothing to worry about, but in others it could be the first sign of big problems to come. Four potential causes of deviations to consider include:

1. **Seasonality.** As in Under Armour's case, seasonal variations in sales and inventory levels can cause the relationship between net income and cash flow from operations to fluctuate from one quarter to the next. Usually, this isn't a cause for alarm.

2. **The corporate life cycle (growth in sales).** New companies often experience rapid sales growth. When sales are increasing, accounts receivable and inventory normally increase faster than the cash flows being collected from sales. This often causes operating cash flows to be lower than the related net income. This isn't a big deal, provided that the company can obtain cash from financing activities until operating activities begin to generate more positive cash flows.

3. **Changes in revenue and expense recognition.** Most cases of fraudulent financial reporting involve aggressive revenue recognition (recording revenues before they are earned) or delayed expense recognition (failing to report expenses when they are incurred). Both of these tactics cause net income to increase in the current period, making it seem as though the company has improved its performance. Neither of these tactics, though, affects cash flows from operating activities. As a result, if revenue and expense recognition policies are changed to boost net income, cash flow from operations will be significantly lower than net income, providing one of the first clues that the financial statements might contain errors or fraud.

4. **Changes in working capital management.** Working capital is a measure of the amount by which current assets exceed current liabilities. If a company's current assets (such as accounts receivable and inventories) are allowed to grow out of control, its operating cash flows will decrease. More efficient management will have the opposite effect. To investigate this potential cause more closely, use the inventory and accounts receivable turnover ratios covered in Chapters 7 and 8.

Cash Flows from Investing Activities

Although it might seem counterintuitive at first, healthy companies tend to show negative cash flows in the investing section of the statement of cash flows. A negative total for this section means the company is spending more to acquire new long-term assets than it is taking in from selling its existing long-term assets. That's normal for any healthy, growing company. In fact, if you see a positive total cash flow in the investing activities section, you should be concerned because it could mean the company is selling

Lehman Brothers' Operating Cash Flows and the Financial Crisis

Lehman Brothers Holdings, Inc., was one of the largest and most profitable financial services companies in the world. But cash flow and working capital management problems led to the company's bankruptcy only a month before the stock market crash of 2008. The following comparison of Lehman's net income and net operating cash flows reveals the company's problems:

off its long-term assets just to generate cash inflows. If a company sells off too many long-term assets, it may not have a sufficient base to continue running its business effectively, which would likely lead to further decline in the future.

Cash Flows from Financing Activities

Unlike the operating and investing activities sections, where a healthy company typically shows positive and negative cash flows, respectively, the financing activities section does not have an obvious expected direction for cash flows. For example, a healthy company that is growing rapidly could need financing cash inflows to fund its expansion. In this case, the company could take out new loans or issue new shares, both of which would result in positive net cash flows from financing activities. Alternatively, a healthy company could use its cash resources to repay existing loans, pay dividends, or repurchase shares, all of which would result in negative net cash flows from financing activities. Thus, it's not possible to evaluate the company's financing cash flows by simply determining whether they are positive or negative on an overall basis. Rather, you will need to consider detailed line items within this section to assess the company's overall financing strategy (is the company moving toward greater reliance on risky debt financing?).

Overall Patterns of Cash Flows

Just as most products go through a series of developmental phases, most companies have lifecycles as well. The corporate lifecycle phases include an **introductory phase** when the company is being established, a **growth phase** when the company's presence expands, a **maturity phase** when the company stabilizes, and finally a **decline phase** when the company loses its way. During each of these phases, a company is likely to show different patterns of net cash flows from operating, investing, and financing activities. Exhibit 12.8 illustrates the cash flow patterns that suggest the lifecycle phase being experienced by a company. Although exceptions to these patterns can exist, they can help you to better understand and evaluate a company's cash flows.

As Exhibit 12.8 suggests, most companies in the introductory (start-up) phase experience negative net operating cash flows. Negative cash flows arise during this

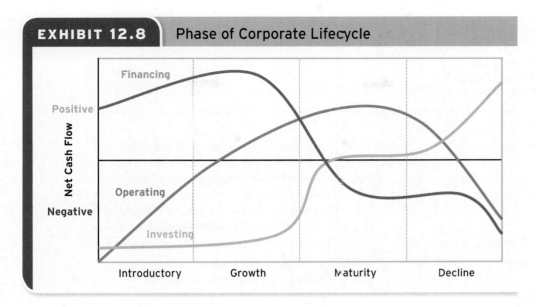

EXHIBIT 12.8 | **Phase of Corporate Lifecycle**

phase because companies pay cash out to employees and suppliers but haven't established a large enough customer base to generate sizable cash inflows from customers. Also during the introductory phase, these companies are spending significant amounts of cash on long-term assets (e.g., equipment and buildings), resulting in negative investing cash flows. To fund these negative investing and operating cash flows, companies in the introductory phase rely heavily on cash obtained through financing activities (e.g., borrowing from lenders and obtaining contributions from shareholders). If a company survives the introductory phase, it will enter a growth phase, which is similar to the introductory phase except that operating cash flows turn positive because the company has improved its cash inflows from customers. In the maturity phase, the company continues to enjoy positive operating cash flows, but no longer has opportunities for expanding the business, so it stops spending cash on investing activities and instead uses its cash for financing activities such as repaying lenders and returning excess cash to shareholders. Finally, during the decline phase, a company's operating cash flows again become negative, prompting lenders to demand repayment of loans (i.e., negative financing cash flows). To fund these repayments, the company sells off its long-term assets, resulting in significantly positive investing cash flows.

OPERATING CASH FLOWS REVISITED (DIRECT METHOD)

> **Learning Objective 12-6**
> Report and interpret cash flows from operating activities, using the direct method.

Earlier in this chapter, we discussed the indirect method of presenting a company's statement of cash flows. This method computes operating cash flows indirectly, by adding and subtracting items from Net Income. Because these items, by themselves, don't mean a lot, analyses of operating cash flows are limited to using just the overall Net Cash Provided by (Used for) Operating Activities. In contrast, the direct method of presentation provides more detailed information on each input into overall operating cash flows, which allows analysts to conduct more detailed analyses.

Exhibit 12.9 presents Under Armour's statement of cash flows using the direct method. Because this method lists each operating cash flow component, it allows more detailed analyses of operating cash flows. For example, the direct method would allow Under Armour's managers to determine that a 10 percent increase in product costs in 2010 would have required an additional cash outflow to inventory suppliers of $58.5 million (= 10% × $585 million). To cover these additional cash outflows, Under Armour could raise prices by 5.5 percent, which would generate a $58.9 million (= 5.5% × $1,070 million) cash inflow from customer collections.

The direct method also provides financial statement users with more information to identify potential relationships between cash inflows and outflows. An increase in some activities, such as sales, generally leads to an increase in cash inflows from customers and

EXHIBIT 12.9   Under Armour's Statement of Cash Flows (Direct Method)

UNDER ARMOUR, INC. Statement of Cash Flows For the Year Ended December 31, 2010		Explanations
(in millions)		
Cash Flows from Operating Activities		Cash flows related to day-to-day activities
Cash collected from customers	$1,070	Cash collected on account and from any cash sales
Cash paid to suppliers of inventory	(585)	Cash paid in the current period to acquire inventory
Cash paid to employees and suppliers of services	(408)	Cash paid for salaries, wages, utilities, rent, etc.
Cash paid for interest	(1)	Separate reporting of these items fulfills the role of
Cash paid for income tax	(39)	the supplemental disclosures in Exhibit 12.7
Net cash provided by (used in) operating activities	37	Indicates overall cash impact of operating activities
Cash Flows from Investing Activities		Cash flows related to long-term assets
Purchase of equipment	(30)	Cash was used to purchase equipment
Purchase of intangible and other assets	(11)	Cash was used to purchase intangibles
Net cash provided by (used in) investing activities	(41)	Indicates overall cash impact of investing activities
Cash Flows from Financing Activities		Cash flows from transactions with lenders, investors
Proceeds from long-term debt	9	Cash received from borrowing
Payments on long-term debt	(5)	Cash used to repay amounts previously borrowed
Proceeds from stock issuances	3	Cash received from issuing stock
Net cash provided by (used in) financing activities	7	Indicates overall cash impact of financing activities
Net Change in Cash and Cash Equivalents	3	$37 + $(41) + $7 = $3
Cash and cash equivalents, beginning of year	187	Cash balance at beginning of the period
Cash and cash equivalents, end of year	$ 190	Cash balance at end of the period (on balance sheet)

cash outflows to inventory suppliers. However, an increase in sales activity only loosely affects other cash outflows, such as interest paid on loans. Knowing the detailed components of operating cash flows allows analysts to more reliably predict a company's future cash flows.[4]

In the remainder of this section, we describe how to prepare the statement of cash flows using the direct method. We focus on preparing just the operating activities section. For instructions on preparing the investing and financing activities sections, which are identical under both the direct and indirect methods, see pages 561–564.

Reporting Operating Cash Flows with the Direct Method

The direct method presents a summary of all operating transactions that result in either a debit or a credit to cash. It is prepared by adjusting each revenue and expense on the income statement from the accrual basis to the cash basis. We will complete this process for all of the revenues and expenses reported in the Under Armour income statement in Exhibit 12.3 to show the calculations underlying the operating cash flows in Exhibit 12.9. Notice that, with the direct method, we work directly with each revenue and expense listed on the income statement and ignore any totals or subtotals (such as net income).

Converting Sales Revenues to Cash Inflows
When sales are recorded, Accounts Receivable increases, and when cash is collected, Accounts Receivable decreases. This means that if Accounts Receivable increases by $8 million, then cash collections were $8 million less than sales on account. To convert sales revenue to the cash collected, we need to subtract $8 million from Sales Revenue. The following flowchart shows this visually:

---

[4]Steven F. Orpurt and Yoonseok Zang, "Do Direct Cash Flow Disclosures Help Predict Future Operating Cash Flows and Earnings?" *The Accounting Review* 84, no. 3, 893–936 (May 2009).

Using information from Under Armour's income statement and balance sheet presented in Exhibit 12.3, we compute cash collected from customers as follows:

Net Sales	$1,078
− Increase in Accounts Receivable	(8)
Cash collected from customers	$1,070

Accounts Receivable (A)	
Beg. bal.	94
Increase	8
End. bal.	102

Converting Cost of Goods Sold to Cash Paid to Suppliers

Cost of Goods Sold represents the cost of merchandise sold during the accounting period, which may be more or less than the amount of cash paid to suppliers during the period. In Under Armour's case, Inventory increased during the year, implying the company bought more merchandise than it sold. If the company paid cash to suppliers of inventory, it would have paid more cash to suppliers than the amount of Cost of Goods Sold. So, the increase in Inventory must be added to Cost of Goods Sold to compute cash paid to suppliers.

Typically, companies buy inventory on account from suppliers (as indicated by an Accounts Payable balance on the balance sheet). Consequently, we need to consider more than just the change in Inventory to convert Cost of Goods Sold to cash paid to suppliers. The credit purchases and payments that are recorded in Accounts Payable must also be considered. Credit purchases increase Accounts Payable, and cash payments decrease it. The overall increase in Accounts Payable reported by Under Armour in Exhibit 12.3 indicates that cash payments were less than credit purchases, so the difference must be subtracted in the computation of total cash payments to suppliers.

In summary, to fully convert Cost of Goods Sold to a cash basis, you must consider changes in both Inventory and Accounts Payable as follows:

Using information from Exhibit 12.3, we compute cash paid to suppliers as follows:

Cost of Goods Sold	$534
+ Increase in Inventory	67
− Increase in Accounts Payable	(16)
Cash paid to inventory suppliers	$585

Inventories (A)	
Beg. bal.	148
Increase	67
End. bal.	215

Accounts Payable (L)	
Beg. bal.	69
Increase	16
End. bal.	85

Converting Operating Expenses to a Cash Outflow

The total amount of an expense on the income statement may differ from the cash outflow associated with that activity. Some amounts, like prepaid rent, are paid before they are recognized as expenses.

When prepayments are made, the balance in the asset Prepaid Expenses increases. When expenses are recorded, Prepaid Expenses decreases. When we see Under Armour's prepaids increase by $2 million during the year, it means the company paid more cash than it recorded as operating expenses. This amount must be added in computing cash paid to service suppliers for operating expenses.

Some other expenses, like wages, are paid for after they are incurred. In this case, when expenses are recorded, the balance in Accrued Liabilities increases. When payments are made, Accrued Liabilities decreases. When Under Armour's Accrued Liabilities increase by $13 million, it means the company paid that much less cash than it recorded as operating expenses. This amount must be subtracted when computing cash paid to employees and service suppliers for operating expenses.

Generally, operating expenses such as Selling, General, and Administrative Expenses can be converted from the accrual basis to the cash basis in the following manner:

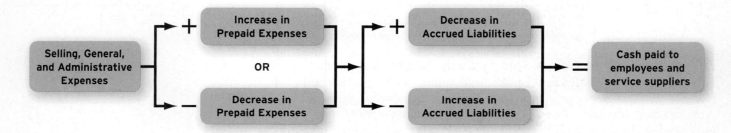

Using information from Exhibit 12.3, we can compute the total cash paid as follows:

Prepaid Expenses (A)		
Beg. bal.	33	
Increase	2	
End. bal.	35	

Accrued Liabilities (L)		
	Beg. bal.	51
	Increase	13
	End. bal.	64

Selling, General, and Administrative Expenses	$419
+ Increase in Prepaid Expenses	2
− Increase in Accrued Liabilities	(13)
Cash paid to employees and suppliers of services	$408

You don't have to convert Depreciation Expense on the income statement to the cash basis for the statement of cash flows because depreciation doesn't involve cash. It is merely reporting previously incurred costs as an expense in the current period. Noncash expenses like depreciation (or, similarly, revenues that don't affect cash) are omitted when the statement of cash flows is prepared using the direct method. Because of this, be sure to exclude any Depreciation Expense that might have been included in Selling, General, and Administrative Expenses.

The next account listed on the income statement in Exhibit 12.3 is Interest Expense of $1 million. Because the balance sheet does not report Interest Payable, we will assume all of the interest was paid in cash. Thus, interest expense equals interest paid.

Interest Expense	$1
No change in Interest Payable	0
Cash paid for interest	$1

The same logic can be applied to income taxes. Under Armour presents Income Tax Expense of $39 million. Exhibit 12.3 does not report an Income Tax Payable balance, so we assume income tax paid is equal to income tax expense.

Income Tax Expense	$39
No change in Income Tax Payable	0
Cash paid for income tax	$39

You have now seen, in this section, how to determine each amount reported in the operating activities section of a statement of cash flows prepared using the direct method. For a quick check on your understanding of this material, complete the following Self-Study Practice.

💡 How's it going?   Self-Study Practice

Indicate whether the following items taken from a cash flow statement would be added (+), subtracted (−), or not included (0) when calculating cash flow from operations using the direct method.

☐ *a.* Cash paid to suppliers.

☐ *b.* Payment of dividends to stockholders.

☐ *c.* Cash collections from customers.

☐ *d.* Purchase of plant and equipment for cash.

☐ *e.* Payments of interest to lenders.

☐ *f.* Payment of taxes to the government.

After you have finished, check your answers with the solution in the margin.

SUPPLEMENT 12A REPORTING DISPOSALS OF PROPERTY, PLANT, AND EQUIPMENT (INDIRECT METHOD)

Learning Objective 12-S1
Report cash flows from PPE disposals using the indirect method.

Whenever a company sells property, plant, and equipment (PPE), it records three things: (1) decreases in the PPE accounts for the assets sold, (2) an increase in the Cash account for the cash received on disposal, and (3) a gain if the cash received is more than the book value of the assets sold (or a loss if the cash received is less than the book value of the assets sold). The only part of this transaction that qualifies for the statement of cash flows is the cash received on disposal. This cash inflow is classified as an investing activity, just like the original equipment purchase.

🔨 **COACH'S TIP**

If you're a little rusty on the journal entry to record this disposal, it would be worth your time to review the material on pages 411–412 of Chapter 9.

Okay, that seems straightforward, so why do we have a separate chapter supplement for this kind of transaction? Well, there is one complicating factor. Gains and losses on disposal are included in the computation of net income, which is the starting point for the operating activities section when prepared using the indirect method. So, just as we had to add back the depreciation subtracted on the income statement, we also have to add back losses reported on disposals of PPE. As the following example shows, the flip side is true for gains on disposal (they are subtracted).

To illustrate, assume that Under Armour sold a piece of its manufacturing equipment for $7 million. The equipment originally cost $15 million and had $10 million of accumulated depreciation at the time of disposal. The disposal would have been analyzed and recorded as follows (in millions):

① Analyze

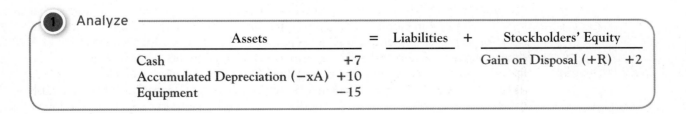

Assets		=	Liabilities	+	Stockholders' Equity	
Cash	+7				Gain on Disposal (+R)	+2
Accumulated Depreciation (−xA)	+10					
Equipment	−15					

2 Record

dr **Cash** (+A) 7
dr **Accumulated Depreciation** (−xA, +A) 10
  cr **Equipment** (−A) 15
  cr **Gain on Disposal** (+R, +SE) 2

The $7 million inflow of cash would be reported as an investing activity. The $10 million and $15 million are taken into account when considering changes in the Accumulated Depreciation and Equipment account balances. Lastly, the $2 million Gain on Disposal was included in net income, so we must remove (subtract) it in the operating activities section of the statement. Thus, the disposal would affect two parts of the statement of cash flows:

Cash flows provided by (used in) operating activities
Net income $68
  Adjustments to reconcile net income to net cash from operations:
    . . .
    Gain on disposal of property, plant, and equipment .... (2)
  . . .
Net cash provided by (used in) operating activities
Cash provided by (used in) investing activities
Additions to property, plant, and equipment
Cash received from disposal of property, plant, and equipment 7
. . .
Net cash provided by (used in) investing activities

Learning Objective 12-S2
Use the T-account approach for preparing an indirect method statement of cash flows.

SUPPLEMENT 12B T-ACCOUNT APPROACH (INDIRECT METHOD)

When we began our discussion of preparing the statement of cash flows, we noted that changes in cash must equal the sum of the changes in all other balance sheet accounts. Based on this idea, we used the following three steps to prepare the statement of cash flows:

1. Determine the change in each balance sheet account. From this year's ending balance, subtract this year's beginning balance (i.e., last year's ending balance).
2. Identify the cash flow category or categories to which each account relates. Use Exhibit 12.2 as a guide, but be aware that some accounts may include two categories of cash flows. Retained Earnings, for example, can include both financing cash flows (paying dividends) and operating cash flows (generating net income). Similarly, Accumulated Depreciation can be affected by operating activities (depreciation for using equipment in daily operations) as well as investing activities (disposing of equipment).
3. Create schedules that summarize operating, investing, and financing cash flows.

Instead of creating separate schedules for each section of the statement, many accountants prefer to prepare a single large T-account to represent the changes that have taken place in cash subdivided into the three sections of the cash flow statement. Such an account is presented in Panel A of Exhibit 12B.1. The cash account in Panel A shows increases in cash as debits and decreases in cash as credits. Note how each section matches the three schedules that we prepared for Under Armour's cash flows presented in Exhibits 12.4, 12.5, and 12.6. Panel B includes the same T-accounts for the noncash balance sheet accounts we used in our discussion of each cash flow statement section in

| EXHIBIT 12B.1 | T-Account Approach to Preparing the Statement of Cash Flows (Indirect Method) |

Panel A: Changes in Cash Account

Cash (A)				
Operating				
(1) Net Income	68		8	(3) Accounts Receivable
(2) Depreciation Expense	17		67	(4) Inventory
(6) Accounts Payable	16		2	(5) Prepaid Expense
(7) Accrued Liabilities	13			
Net cash flow provided by operating activities	37			
Investing				
			30	(8) Purchased Equipment
			11	(9) Purchased Intangibles
			41	Net cash used in investing activities
Financing				
(10) Additional borrowing of long-term debt	9		5	(11) Payment of long-term debt
(12) Proceeds from stock issuance	3			
Net cash provided by financing activities	7			
Net increase in cash and cash equivalents	3			

Panel B: Changes in Noncash Accounts

Accounts Receivable (A)			
Beg. bal.	94		
(3) Increase	8		
End. bal.	102		

Inventories (A)			
Beg. bal.	148		
(4) Increase	67		
End. bal.	215		

Prepaid Expenses (A)			
Beg. bal.	33		
(5) Increase	2		
End. bal.	35		

Accounts Payable (A)			
	Beg. bal.	69	
	(6) Increase	16	
	End. bal.	85	

Accrued Liabilities (L)			
	Beg. bal.	51	
	(7) Increase	13	
	End. bal.	64	

Equipment (A)			
Beg. bal.	133		
(8) Purchases	30	Disposals	0
End. bal.	163		

Accumulated Depreciation (xA)			
	Beg. bal.	70	
Disposals	0	(2) Depreciation	17
	End. bal.	87	

Intangible and Other Assets (A)			
Beg. bal.	32		
(9) Purchases	11	Disposals	0
End. bal.	43		

Long-term Debt (L)			
		Beg. bal.	25
(11) Payments	5	(10) Borrowings	9
		End. bal.	29

Contributed Capital (SE)			
	Beg. bal.	224	
Stock repurchased	0	(12) Stock issued	3
	End. bal.	227	

Retained Earnings (SE)			
	Beg. bal.	188	
Disposals	0	(1) Net income	68
	End. bal.	256	

the body of the chapter. Note how each change in the noncash balance sheet accounts has a number referencing the change in the cash account that it accompanies. The statement of cash flows presented in Exhibit 12.7 can be prepared in proper format based on the information in the cash flow T-account.

SUPPLEMENT 12C SPREADSHEET APPROACH (INDIRECT METHOD)

As situations become more complex, the analytical approach that we used to prepare the statement of cash flows for Under Armour becomes cumbersome and inefficient. In actual practice, many companies use a spreadsheet approach to prepare the statement of cash flows. The spreadsheet is based on the same logic that we used in the main body of the chapter. The spreadsheet's primary advantage is that it offers a more systematic way to keep track of information. You may find it useful even in simple situations.

Exhibit 12C.1 shows the Under Armour spreadsheet, which we created as follows:

1. Make four columns to record dollar amounts. The first column is for the beginning balances for items reported on the balance sheet, the next two columns reflect debit and credit changes to those balances, and the final column contains the ending balances for the balance sheet accounts.

2. Enter each account name from the balance sheet in the far left of the top half of the spreadsheet.

3. As you analyze changes in each balance sheet account, enter the explanation of each item to be reported on the statement of cash flows in the far left of the bottom half of the spreadsheet.

Changes in the various balance sheet accounts are analyzed in terms of debits and credits in the top half of the spreadsheet with the corresponding debits and credits being recorded in the bottom half of the spreadsheet in terms of their impact on cash flows. The changes in balance sheet accounts other than cash contribute to explaining the change in the Cash account.

Let's go through each of the entries on the spreadsheet for Under Armour shown in Exhibit 12C.1, starting with the first one shown in the bottom half of the spreadsheet (all amounts in millions).

a. Net income of $68 is shown as an inflow in the operating activities section, with the corresponding credit going to Retained Earnings in the top half of the spreadsheet (to show that net income increased Retained Earnings).

b. Depreciation Expense of $17 is added back to net income because this type of expense does not cause a cash outflow when it is recorded. The corresponding credit explains the increase in the Accumulated Depreciation account during the period.

c. The increase in Accounts Receivable means that cash collections from customers were less than sales on account. Net income includes the sales number, so to adjust down to the actual cash collected, we subtract the extra amount. This appears in our spreadsheet as if it is a credit to Cash and a corresponding debit to Accounts Receivable.

d. This entry reconciles the purchases of Inventory with Cost of Goods Sold. It is subtracted from net income because more inventory was purchased than was sold.

e. This entry reconciles the prepayment of expenses with their expiration. It is subtracted from net income because cash payments for new prepayments are more than the amounts that were reported as expenses when they expired.

f. This entry reconciles cash paid to suppliers with purchases on account. It is added because more was purchased on account than was paid in cash.

g. This entry reconciles the accrual of liabilities for operating expenses with payments for these expenses. The increase in Accrued Liabilities is added because the cash paid for accrued liabilities was less than the expenses accrued. The debit to Cash corresponds to the net credit to Accrued Liabilities.

h. This entry records the cash purchases of new equipment.

i. This entry records the cash purchase of intangibles.

j. This entry records cash provided by borrowing additional long-term debt.

EXHIBIT 12C.1 Spreadsheet to Prepare Statement of Cash Flows, Indirect Method

UNDER ARMOUR, INC.
Statement of Cash Flows Spreadsheet
For the Year Ended December 31, 2010

(in millions)	Beginning Balances, December 31, 2009	Debit		Credit		Ending Balances, December 31, 2010
Items from Balance Sheet						
Cash and Cash Equivalents (A)	187	(m)	3			190
Accounts Receivable (A)	94	(c)	8			102
Inventories (A)	148	(d)	67			215
Prepaid Expenses (A)	33	(e)	2			35
Equipment (A)	133	(h)	30			163
Accumulated Depreciation (xA)	70			(b)	17	87
Intangible and Other Assets (A)	32	(i)	11			43
Accounts Payable (L)	69			(f)	16	85
Accrued Liabilities (L)	51			(g)	13	64
Long-term Debt (L)	25	(k)	5	(j)	9	29
Contributed Capital (SE)	224			(l)	3	227
Retained Earnings (SE)	188			(a)	68	256

		Cash		
		Inflows	Outflows	Subtotals
Statement of Cash Flows				
Cash flows from operating activities:				
Net income	(a)	68		
Adjustments to reconcile net income to cash provided by operating activities:				
Depreciation	(b)	17		
Changes in current assets and current liabilities				
Accounts Receivable	(c)		8	
Inventories	(d)		67	
Prepaid Expenses	(e)		2	
Accounts Payable	(f)	16		
Accrued Liabilities	(g)	13		
				37
Cash flows from investing activities:				
Purchase of equipment	(h)		30	
Purchase of intangible and other assets	(i)		11	
				(41)
Cash flows from financing activities:				
Additional borrowings of long-term debt	(j)	9		
Payments of long-term debt	(k)		5	
Proceeds from stock issuance	(l)	3		
				7
Net increase in Cash and Cash Equivalents	(m)		3	
		126	126	3

k. This entry records cash used to repay long-term debt.

l. This entry records the cash received from issuing stock.

m. This entry shows that the change in cash (in the top part of the spreadsheet) is accounted for by the net cash flows listed in the bottom part of the spreadsheet.

Check to see that Debits = Credits in your spreadsheet, because if they don't, you've missed something along the way. The bottom part of the spreadsheet can be used to prepare the formal statement of cash flows shown in Exhibit 12.7.

REVIEW THE CHAPTER

DEMONSTRATION CASE A: INDIRECT METHOD

During a recent year (ended April 30), National Beverage Corp. reported net income of $24,742 (all numbers in thousands of dollars). The company also reported the following activities:

a. Purchased equipment for $6,491 in cash.

b. Issued stock for $645 in cash.

c. Depreciation of equipment was $8,891 for the year.

Its comparative balance sheet is presented below.

Balance Sheet Year Ended April 30		
(Dollars in Thousands)	Current Year	Prior Year
Assets		
Current assets:		
Cash and cash equivalents	$ 84,140	$ 51,497
Accounts receivable	53,735	49,186
Inventories	39,612	38,754
Prepaid expenses	5,552	15,009
Equipment	206,081	199,590
Accumulated Depreciation	(126,700)	(117,809)
Total assets	$ 262,420	$ 236,227
Liabilities and Stockholders' Equity		
Current liabilities:		
Accounts payable	$ 48,005	$ 49,803
Accrued liabilities	44,403	41,799
Total current liabilities	92,408	91,602
Stockholders' equity:		
Contributed capital	9,803	9,158
Retained earnings	160,209	135,467
Total stockholders' equity	170,012	144,625
Total liabilities and stockholders' equity	$ 262,420	$ 236,227

Required:

Based on this information, prepare the cash flow statement using the indirect method. Evaluate cash flows reported in the statement.

Suggested Solution

NATIONAL BEVERAGE CORP.
Statement of Cash Flows
Year Ended April 30

(Dollars in Thousands)

Cash flows from operating activities:	
Net income	$ 24,742
Adjustments to reconcile net income to net cash provided by operating activities:	
Depreciation	8,891
Accounts receivable	(4,549)
Inventory	(858)
Prepaid expenses	9,457
Accounts payable	(1,798)
Accrued liabilities	2,604
Net cash provided by operating activities	38,489
Cash flows from investing activities:	
Purchases of equipment	(6,491)
Net cash used in investing activities	(6,491)
Cash flows from financing activities:	
Proceeds from issuance of stock	645
Net cash provided by financing activities	645
Net increase in cash and cash equivalents	32,643
Cash and cash equivalents at beginning of period	51,497
Cash and cash equivalents at end of period	$ 84,140

National Beverage reported positive profits and even higher cash flows from operations for the year. This difference between the two is caused primarily by depreciation and decreases in prepaid expenses. This also suggests that National Beverage is carefully managing its current assets and current liabilities so that it has more than sufficient cash on hand to cover the costs of purchases of additional equipment without the need to borrow additional funds. This cash can be used for future expansion or to pay future dividends to stockholders.

DEMONSTRATION CASE B: DIRECT METHOD

During a recent quarter (ended March 29), Cybex International reported that its cash and cash equivalents had increased from $216 on December 31 to $469 on March 29 (all amounts in thousands). The company also indicated the following:

a. Paid $13,229 to suppliers for inventory purchases.
b. Borrowed $2,400 from one of the company's main stockholders.
c. Paid $554 in cash for purchase of property, plant, and equipment.
d. Reported sales on account of $20,608. The company reported Accounts Receivable of $13,628 at the beginning of the quarter and $12,386 at the end of the quarter.
e. Paid operating expenses to employees and suppliers of services totaling $6,188.
f. Cash payments for interest totaled $1,060.
g. Made payments of $2,625 for principal owed on long-term debt.
h. Paid $284 cash for other financing activities.
i. Paid $57 cash for income taxes.

Required:

Based on this information, prepare the cash flow statement using the direct method. Evaluate the cash flows reported in the statement.

Suggested Solution

CYBEX INTERNATIONAL
Statement of Cash Flows
For the Quarter Ended March 29

CYBEX

(in thousands)

Cash Flows from Operating Activities	
Cash collected from customers ($13,628 + $20,608 − $12,386)	$ 21,850
Cash paid to suppliers of inventory	(13,229)
Cash paid to employees and suppliers of services	(6,188)
Cash paid for interest	(1,060)
Cash paid for income taxes	(57)
Net cash flow provided by operating activities	1,316
Cash Flows from Investing Activities	
Additions to property, plant, and equipment	(554)
Net cash flow provided by (used in) investing activities	(554)
Cash Flows from Financing Activities	
Proceeds from borrowing from a related party (stockholder)	2,400
Repayment of long-term debt principal	(2,625)
Payments for other financing activities	(284)
Net cash flow provided by (used in) financing activities	(509)
Increase (decrease) in Cash and Cash Equivalents	253
Cash and Cash Equivalents, December 31	216
Cash and Cash Equivalents, March 29	$ 469

Cybex reported a net inflow of $1,316 cash from operating activities during the quarter. These cash flows were more than enough to pay for the property, plant, and equipment purchased this quarter. Some of the extra cash from operations that was not used to purchase property, plant, and equipment (also called free cash flow) could be used to pay down debt or to increase the company's cash balance. The financing activities section suggests that the company paid down a significant amount of long-term debt ($2,625), in part by borrowing funds from a related party ($2,400). Borrowing from a related party (particularly a major stockholder) is unusual, which would prompt analysts to investigate further. The company's quarterly report explains that its lenders had demanded immediate repayment of their loans because the company had violated its debt covenants. A major stockholder loaned money to the company so that it could make this repayment.

CHAPTER SUMMARY

LO 12-1   **Identify cash flows arising from operating, investing, and financing activities. p. 550**

- The statement has three main sections: Cash flows from operating activities, which are related to earning income from normal operations; Cash flows from investing activities, which are related to the acquisition and sale of productive assets; and Cash flows from financing activities, which are related to external financing of the enterprise.

- The net cash inflow or outflow for the period is the same amount as the increase or decrease in cash and cash equivalents for the period on the balance sheet. Cash equivalents are highly liquid investments purchased within three months of maturity.

Report cash flows from operating activities, using the indirect method. p. 557   LO 12-2

- The indirect method for reporting cash flows from operating activities reports a conversion of net income to net cash flow from operating activities.
- The conversion involves additions and subtractions for (1) noncash expenses (such as depreciation expense) and revenues that do not affect current assets or current liabilities, and (2) changes in each of the individual current assets (other than cash) and current liabilities (other than debt to financial institutions, which relates to financing).

Report cash flows from investing activities. p. 561   LO 12-3

- Investing activities reported on the cash flow statement include cash payments to acquire fixed assets and investments and cash proceeds from the sale of fixed assets and investments.

Report cash flows from financing activities. p. 562   LO 12-4

- Cash inflows from financing activities include cash proceeds from issuance of debt and common stock. Cash outflows include cash principal payments on debt, cash paid for the repurchase of the company's stock, and cash dividend payments. Cash payments associated with interest are a cash flow from operating activities.

Interpret cash flows from operating, investing, and financing activities. p. 564   LO 12-5

- A healthy company will generate positive cash flows from operations, some of which will be used to pay for purchases of property, plant, and equipment. Any additional cash (called free cash flow) can be used to further expand the business, pay down some of the company's debt, or simply build up the cash balance. A company is in trouble if it is unable to generate positive cash flows from operations in the long-run because eventually creditors will stop lending to the company and stockholders will stop investing in it.

Report and interpret cash flows from operating activities, using the direct method. p. 567   LO 12-6

- The direct method for reporting cash flows from operating activities accumulates all of the operating transactions that result in either a debit or a credit to cash into categories. The most common inflows are cash received from customers and dividends and interest on investments. The most common outflows are cash paid for purchase of services and goods for resale, salaries and wages, income taxes, and interest on liabilities. It is prepared by adjusting each item on the income statement from an accrual basis to a cash basis.

KEY TERMS

Cash Flows from Financing Activities p. 553
Cash Flows from Investing Activities p. 552
Cash Flows from Operating Activities (Cash Flows from Operations) p. 552
Direct Method p. 555
Indirect Method p. 555

See complete definitions in the glossary in the back of this text.

HOMEWORK HELPER

Helpful reminders

- Although some exceptions exist, operating activities typically affect current assets and current liabilities; investing activities typically affect noncurrent assets; and financing activities typically affect noncurrent liabilities and stockholders' equity accounts.

- The typical additions and subtractions that are required when using the indirect method to reconcile net income with cash flows from operating activities are as follows:

COACH'S TIP

Notice in this table that, to reconcile net income to cash flows from operations, you:
- add the change when the current asset decreases or current liability increases
- subtract the change when the current asset increases or current liability decreases

Item	Additions and Subtractions to Reconcile Net Income to Cash Flows From Operating Activities*	
	When Item Increases	When Item Decreases
Depreciation	+	n/a
Accounts Receivable	−	+
Inventory	−	+
Prepaid Expenses	−	+
Accounts Payable	+	−
Accrued Liabilities	+	−

* This summary excludes additions and subtractions for losses and gains arising on disposal of certain assets, which are discussed in Supplement 12A.

- The following adjustments are commonly made to convert income statement items to the related operating cash flow amounts for the direct method:

Income Statement Account	+/− Change in Balance Sheet Account(s)	= Operating Cash Flow
Sales Revenue	+ Decrease in Accounts Receivable (A) − Increase in Accounts Receivable (A)	= Cash collected from customers
Cost of Goods Sold	+ Increase in Inventory (A) − Decrease in Inventory (A) − Increase in Accounts Payable (L) + Decrease in Accounts Payable (L)	= Cash paid to suppliers of inventory
Other Expenses	+ Increase in Prepaid Expenses (A) − Decrease in Prepaid Expenses (A) − Increase in Accrued Expenses (L) + Decrease in Accrued Expenses (L)	= Cash paid to employees and suppliers of services (e.g., wages, rent, utilities)
Interest Expense	− Increase in Interest Payable (L) + Decrease in Interest Payable (L)	= Cash paid for interest
Income Tax Expense	− Increase in Income Taxes Payable (Deferred Taxes) (L) + Decrease in Income Taxes Payable (Deferred Taxes) (L)	= Cash paid for income tax

Frequent mistakes

- Do not merely report the net change in all balance sheet accounts. Some accounts (typically those affected by investing and financing activities) include both inflows and outflows of cash, which must be reported separately.

PRACTICE MATERIAL

QUESTIONS (⊖ Symbol indicates questions that require analysis from more than one perspective.)

1. Compare the purposes of the income statement, the balance sheet, and the statement of cash flows.

2. What information does the statement of cash flows report that is not reported on the other required financial statements?

3. What are cash equivalents? How are they reported on the statement of cash flows?

4. What are the major categories of business activities reported on the statement of cash flows? Define each of these activities.

5. What are the typical cash inflows from operating activities? What are the typical cash outflows from operating activities?

6. Describe the types of items used to compute cash flows from operating activities under the two alternative methods of reporting.

7. Under the indirect method, depreciation expense is added to net income to report cash flows from operating activities. Does depreciation cause an inflow of cash?

8. Explain why cash outflows during the period for purchases and salaries are not specifically reported on a statement of cash flows prepared using the indirect method.

9. Explain why a $50,000 increase in inventory during the year must be included in computing cash flows from operating activities under both the direct and indirect methods.

10. Loan covenants require that E-Gadget Corporation (EGC) generate $200,000 cash from operating activities each year. Without intervening during the last month of the current year, EGC will generate only $180,000 cash from operations. What are the pros and cons of each of the following possible interventions: (*a*) pressuring customers to pay overdue accounts, (*b*) delaying payment of amounts owing to suppliers, and (*c*) purchasing additional equipment to increase depreciation?

11. As a junior analyst, you are evaluating the financial performance of Digilog Corporation. Impressed by this year's growth in sales (20% increase), receivables (40% increase), and inventories (50% increase), you plan to report a favorable evaluation of the company. Your supervisor cautions you that those increases may signal difficulties rather than successes. When you ask what she means, she just says you should look at the company's statement of cash flows. What do you think you will find there? What are the cash flow effects when a company's receivables and inventories increase faster than its sales?

12. What are the typical cash inflows from investing activities? What are the typical cash outflows from investing activities?

13. What are the typical cash inflows from financing activities? What are the typical cash outflows from financing activities?

14. What are noncash investing and financing activities? Give one example. How are noncash investing and financing activities reported on the statement of cash flows?

15. (Supplement 12A) How is the sale of equipment reported on the statement of cash flows using the indirect method?

MULTIPLE CHOICE

1. Where is the overall change in cash shown in the statement of cash flows?
   a. In the top part, before the operating activities section.
   b. In one of the operating, investing, or financing activities sections.
   c. In the bottom part, following the financing activities section.
   d. None of the above.

2. In what order do the three sections of the statement of cash flows appear when reading from top to bottom?
   a. Financing, investing, operating.
   b. Investing, operating, financing.
   c. Operating, financing, investing.
   d. Operating, investing, financing.

3. Total cash inflow in the operating section of the statement of cash flows should include which of the following?
   a. Cash received from customers at the point of sale.
   b. Cash collections from customer accounts receivable.
   c. Cash received in advance of revenue recognition (unearned revenue).
   d. All of the above.

4. If the balance in Prepaid Expenses increased during the year, what action should be taken on the statement of cash flows when following the indirect method, *and why?*
   a. The change in the account balance should be subtracted from net income, because the net increase in Prepaid Expenses did not impact net income but did reduce the cash balance.
   b. The change in the account balance should be added to net income, because the net increase in Prepaid Expenses did not impact net income but did increase the cash balance.

   c. The net change in Prepaid Expenses should be subtracted from net income, to reverse the income statement effect that had no impact on cash.
   d. The net change in Prepaid Expenses should be added to net income, to reverse the income statement effect that had no impact on cash.

5. Which of the following would not appear in the investing section of the statement of cash flows?
   a. Purchase of inventory.
   b. Sale of investments.
   c. Purchase of land.
   d. All of the above would appear in the investing section of the statement of cash flows.

6. Which of the following items would not appear in the financing section of the statement of cash flows?
   a. The issuance of the company's own stock.
   b. The repayment of debt.
   c. The payment of dividends.
   d. All of the above would appear in the financing section of the statement of cash flows.

7. Which of the following is not added when computing cash flows from operations using the indirect method?
   a. The net increase in accounts payable.
   b. The net decrease in accounts receivable.
   c. The net decrease in inventory.
   d. All of the above should be added.

8. If a company engages in a material noncash transaction, which of the following is required?
   a. The company must include an explanatory narrative or schedule accompanying the statement of cash flows.
   b. No disclosure is necessary.

c. The company must include an explanatory narrative or schedule accompanying the balance sheet.

d. It must be reported in the investing and financing sections of the statement of cash flows.

9. The *total* change in cash as shown near the bottom of the statement of cash flows for the year should agree with which of the following?

a. The difference in Retained Earnings when reviewing the comparative balance sheet.

b. Net income or net loss as found on the income statement.

c. The difference in cash when reviewing the comparative balance sheet.

d. None of the above.

10. If a company's current assets (such as accounts receivable and inventories) are allowed to grow out of control, which of the following would occur?

a. Cash flows from investing activities would be reduced.

b. Cash flows from operating activities would be reduced.

c. Cash flows from financing activities would increase.

d. None of the above.

> For answers to the Multiple-Choice Questions **see page Q1** located in the last section of the book.

MINI-EXERCISES

LO 12-1, 12-5   M12-1 Identifying Companies from Cash Flow Patterns

Based on the cash flows shown, classify each of the following cases as a growing start-up company (S), a healthy established company (E), or an established company facing financial difficulties (F).

	Case 1	Case 2	Case 3
Cash provided by (used for) operating activities	$ 3,000	$(120,000)	$ 80,000
Cash provided by (used for) investing activities	(70,000)	10,000	(40,000)
Cash provided by (used for) financing activities	75,000	75,000	(30,000)
Net change in cash	8,000	(35,000)	10,000
Cash position at beginning of year	2,000	40,000	30,000
Cash position at end of year	$ 10,000	$ 5,000	$ 40,000

LO 12-1, 12-2   M12-2 Matching Items Reported to Cash Flow Statement Categories (Indirect Method)

The Buckle, Inc.

The Buckle, Inc., operates 420 stores in 41 states, selling brand name apparel like Lucky jeans and Fossil belts and watches. Some of the items included in its 2010 statement of cash flows presented using the indirect method are listed here. Indicate whether each item is disclosed in the operating activities (O), investing activities (I), or financing activities (F) section of the statement or use (NA) if the item does not appear on the statement.

_____ 1. Purchase of investments.

_____ 2. Proceeds from issuance of stock.

_____ 3. Purchase of property and equipment.

_____ 4. Depreciation.

_____ 5. Accounts payable (decrease).

_____ 6. Inventories (increase).

LO 12-2   M12-3 Determining the Effects of Account Changes on Cash Flows from Operating Activities (Indirect Method)

Indicate whether each item would be added (+) or subtracted (−) in the computation of cash flow from operating activities using the indirect method.

_____ 1. Depreciation.

_____ 2. Inventories decrease.

_____ 3. Accounts payable decrease.

_____ 4. Accounts receivable increase.

_____ 5. Accrued liabilities increase.

LO 12-2   M12-4 Computing Cash Flows from Operating Activities (Indirect Method)

For each of the following independent cases, compute cash flows from operating activities. Assume the list below includes all balance sheet accounts related to operating activities.

	Case A	Case B	Case C
Net income	$310,000	$ 15,000	$420,000
Depreciation expense	40,000	150,000	80,000
Accounts receivable increase (decrease)	100,000	(200,000)	(20,000)
Inventory increase (decrease)	(50,000)	35,000	50,000
Accounts payable increase (decrease)	(50,000)	120,000	70,000
Accrued liabilities increase (decrease)	60,000	(220,000)	(40,000)

M12-5 Computing Cash Flows from Operating Activities (Indirect Method)

LO 12-2

For the following two independent cases, show the cash flows from operating activities section of the 2013 statement of cash flows using the indirect method.

	Case A		Case B	
	2013	2012	2013	2012
Sales Revenue	$11,000	$9,000	$21,000	$18,000
Cost of Goods Sold	6,000	5,500	12,000	11,000
Gross Profit	5,000	3,500	9,000	7,000
Depreciation Expense	1,000	1,000	1,500	1,500
Salaries Expense	2,500	2,000	5,000	5,000
Net Income	1,500	500	2,500	500
Accounts Receivable	300	400	750	600
Inventories	750	500	730	800
Accounts Payable	800	700	800	850
Salaries Payable	1,000	1,200	200	250

M12-6 Computing Cash Flows from Investing Activities

LO 12-3

Based on the following information, compute cash flows from investing activities under GAAP.

Cash collections from customers	$800
Purchase of used equipment	200
Depreciation expense	200
Sale of investments	450
Dividends received	100
Interest received	200

M12-7 Computing Cash Flows from Financing Activities

LO 12-4

Based on the following information, compute cash flows from financing activities under GAAP.

Purchase of investments	$ 250
Dividends paid	1,200
Interest paid	400
Additional borrowing from bank	2,800

M12-8 Computing Cash Flows Under IFRS

LO 12-1

Using the data from M12-6, calculate the maximum investing cash inflows that could be reported under IFRS. Using data from M12-7 calculate the maximum financing cash flows that could be reported under IFRS.

M12-9 Reporting Noncash Investing and Financing Activities

LO 12-3, 12-4

Which of the following transactions would be considered noncash investing and financing activities?

_____ 1. Additional borrowing from bank.

_____ 2. Purchase of equipment with investments.

_____ 3. Dividends paid in cash.

_____ 4. Purchase of a building with a promissory note.

LO 12-5   **M12-10 Interpreting Cash Flows from Operating, Investing, and Financing Activities**

Quantum Dots, Inc., is a nanotechnology company that manufactures "quantum dots," which are tiny pieces of silicon consisting of 100 or more molecules. Quantum dots can be used to illuminate very small objects, enabling scientists to see the blood vessels beneath a mouse's skin ripple with each heartbeat, at the rate of 100 times per second. Evaluate this research-intensive company's cash flows, assuming the following was reported in its statement of cash flows.

	Current Year	Previous Year
Cash Flows from Operating Activities		
Net cash provided by (used for) operating activities	$ (50,790)	$ (46,730)
Cash Flows from Investing Activities		
Purchases of research equipment	(250,770)	(480,145)
Proceeds from selling all short-term investments	35,000	—
Net cash provided by (used for) investing activities	(215,770)	(480,145)
Cash Flows from Financing Activities		
Additional long-term debt borrowed	100,000	200,000
Proceeds from stock issuance	140,000	200,000
Cash dividends paid	—	(10,000)
Net cash provided by (used for) financing activities	240,000	390,000
Net increase (decrease) in cash	(26,560)	(136,875)
Cash at beginning of period	29,025	165,900
Cash at end of period	$ 2,465	$ 29,025

LO 12-1, 12-6   **M12-11 Matching Items Reported to Cash Flow Statement Categories (Direct Method)**

Prestige Manufacturing Corporation reports the following items in its 2013 statement of cash flows presented using the direct method. Indicate whether each item is disclosed in the operating activities (O), investing activities (I), or financing activities (F) section of the statement under GAAP or use (NA) if the item does not appear on the statement.

_____ 1. Payment for equipment purchase.   _____ 4. Proceeds from issuance of stock.

_____ 2. Repayments of bank loan.   _____ 5. Interest paid.

_____ 3. Dividends paid.   _____ 6. Receipts from customers.

LO 12-6   **M12-12 Computing Cash Flows from Operating Activities (Direct Method)**

For each of the following independent cases, compute cash flows from operating activities using the direct method. Assume the list below includes all items relevant to operating activities.

	Case A	Case B	Case C
Sales revenue	$50,000	$55,000	$96,000
Cost of goods sold	35,000	26,000	65,000
Depreciation expense	10,000	2,000	10,000
Other operating expenses	5,000	13,000	8,000
Net income	20,000	8,000	12,000
Accounts receivable increase (decrease)	(1,000)	4,000	3,000
Inventory increase (decrease)	2,000	0	(3,000)
Accounts payable increase (decrease)	0	2,500	(1,000)
Accrued liabilities increase (decrease)	1,500	(2,000)	1,000

LO 12-6   **M12-13 Computing Cash Flows from Operating Activities (Direct Method)**

Refer to the two cases presented in M12-5, and show the cash flow from operating activities section of the 2013 statement of cash flows using the direct method.

EXERCISES

 |ACCOUNTING

E12-1 Matching Items Reported to Cash Flow Statement Categories (Indirect Method)

LO 12-1, 12-2

NIKE, Inc., is the best-known sports shoe, apparel, and equipment company in the world because of its association with sports stars such as LeBron James and Serena Williams. Some of the items included in its recent statement of cash flows presented using the indirect method are listed here.

NIKE, Inc.

Indicate whether each item is disclosed in the operating activities (O), investing activities (I), or financing activities (F) section of the statement or use (NA) if the item does not appear on the statement.

_____ 1. Additions to long-term debt.

_____ 2. Depreciation.

_____ 3. Additions to property, plant, and equipment.

_____ 4. Increase (decrease) in notes payable. (The amount is owed to financial institutions.)

_____ 5. (Increase) decrease in other current assets.

_____ 6. Cash received from disposal of property, plant, and equipment.

_____ 7. Reductions in long-term debt.

_____ 8. Issuance of stock.

_____ 9. (Increase) decrease in inventory.

_____ 10. Net income.

E12-2 Understanding the Computation of Cash Flows from Operating Activities (Indirect Method)

LO 12-2

Suppose your company sells services of $180 in exchange for $110 cash and $70 on account.

Required:

1. Show the journal entry to record this transaction.
2. Identify the amount that should be reported as net cash flow from operating activities.
3. Identify the amount that would be included in net income.
4. Show how the indirect method would convert net income (requirement 3) to net cash flow from operating activities (requirement 2).
5. What general rule about converting net income to operating cash flows is revealed by your answer to requirement 4?

E12-3 Understanding the Computation of Cash Flows from Operating Activities (Indirect Method)

LO 12-2

Suppose your company sells services for $325 cash this month. Your company also pays $100 in wages, which includes $15 that was payable at the end of the previous month and $85 for wages of this month.

Required:

1. Show the journal entries to record these transactions.
2. Calculate the amount that should be reported as net cash flow from operating activities.
3. Calculate the amount that should be reported as net income.
4. Show how the indirect method would convert net income (requirement 3) to net cash flow from operating activities (requirement 2).
5. What general rule about converting net income to operating cash flows is revealed by your answer to requirement 4?

E12-4 Understanding the Computation of Cash Flows from Operating Activities (Indirect Method)

LO 12-2

Suppose your company sells services of $150 in exchange for $120 cash and $30 on account. Depreciation of $50 also is recorded.

Required:

1. Show the journal entries to record these transactions.
2. Calculate the amount that should be reported as net cash flow from operating activities.
3. Calculate the amount that should be reported as net income.
4. Show how the indirect method would convert net income (requirement 3) to net cash flow from operating activities (requirement 2).
5. What general rule about converting net income to operating cash flows is revealed by your answer to requirement 4?

LO 12-2   **E12-5** **Understanding the Computation of Cash Flows from Operating Activities (Indirect Method)**

Suppose your company sells goods for $300, of which $200 is received in cash and $100 is on account. The goods cost your company $125 in a previous period. Your company also recorded wages of $70, of which only $30 has been paid in cash.

Required:

1. Show the journal entries to record these transactions.
2. Calculate the amount that should be reported as net cash flow from operating activities.
3. Calculate the amount that should be reported as net income.
4. Show how the indirect method would convert net income (requirement 3) to net cash flow from operating activities (requirement 2).
5. What general rule about converting net income to operating cash flows is revealed by your answer to requirement 4?

LO 12-2, 12-5   **E12-6** **Preparing and Evaluating a Simple Statement of Cash Flows (Indirect Method)**

Suppose your company's income statement reports $160 of net income, and its comparative balance sheet indicates the following.

	Beginning	Ending
Cash	$ 35	$205
Accounts Receivable	75	175
Inventory	245	135
Total	355	$515
Wages Payable	$ 10	$ 50
Retained Earnings	345	465
Total	$355	$515

Required:

1. Prepare the operating activities section of the statement of cash flows, using the indirect method.
2. Identify the most important cause of the difference between the company's net income and net cash flow from operating activities.

LO 12-1, 12-2, 12-5   **E12-7** **Preparing and Evaluating a Simple Statement of Cash Flows (Indirect Method)**

Suppose the income statement for Goggle Company reports $95 of net income, after deducting depreciation of $35. The company bought equipment costing $60 and obtained a long-term bank loan for $70. The company's comparative balance sheet, at December 31, is presented on the following page.

	2012	2013	Change
Cash	$ 35	$ 240	
Accounts Receivable	75	175	
Inventory	260	135	
Equipment	500	560	
Accumulated Depreciation	(45)	(80)	
Total	$825	$1,030	
Wages Payable	$ 10	$ 50	
Long-term Debt	445	515	
Contributed Capital	10	10	
Retained Earnings	360	455	
Total	$825	$1,030	

Required:

1. Calculate the change in each balance sheet account, and indicate whether each account relates to operating, investing, and/or financing activities.
2. Prepare a statement of cash flows using the indirect method.
3. In one sentence, explain why an increase in accounts receivable is subtracted.
4. In one sentence, explain why a decrease in inventory is added.
5. In one sentence, explain why an increase in wages payable is added.
6. Are the cash flows typical of a start-up, healthy, or troubled company? Explain.

E12-8 Reporting Cash Flows from Operating Activities (Indirect Method)

LO 12-2

The following information pertains to Guy's Gear Company:

Sales		$80,000
Expenses:		
Cost of Goods Sold	$50,000	
Depreciation Expense	6,000	
Salaries Expense	12,000	68,000
Net Income		$12,000
Accounts Receivable decrease	$ 4,000	
Merchandise Inventory increase	8,000	
Salaries Payable increase	750	

Required:

Present the operating activities section of the statement of cash flows for Guy's Gear Company using the indirect method.

E12-9 Reporting and Interpreting Cash Flows from Operating Activities from an Analyst's Perspective (Indirect Method)

LO 12-2, 12-5

New Vision Company completed its income statement and balance sheet for 2013 and provided the following information:

Service Revenue		$66,000
Expenses:		
Salaries	$42,000	
Depreciation	7,300	
Utilities	6,000	
Other	1,700	57,000
Net Income		$ 9,000
Decrease in Accounts Receivable	$12,000	
Bought a small service machine	5,000	
Increase in Salaries Payable	9,000	
Decrease in Other Accrued Liabilities	4,250	

Required:

1. Present the operating activities section of the statement of cash flows for New Vision Company using the indirect method.
2. Of the potential causes of differences between cash flow from operations and net income, which are the most important to financial analysts?

LO 12-2, 12-5

E12-10 Reporting and Interpreting Cash Flows from Operating Activities from an Analyst's Perspective (Indirect Method)

Pizza International, Inc., operates 700 family restaurants around the world. The company's annual report contained the following information (in thousands):

Operating Activities			
Net loss	$(9,482)	Decrease in accounts payable	2,282
Depreciation	33,305	Decrease in accrued liabilities	719
Increase in receivables	170	Increase in income taxes payable	1,861
Decrease in inventories	643	Reduction of long-term debt	12,691
Increase in prepaid expenses	664	Additions to equipment	29,073

Required:

1. Based on this information, compute cash flow from operating activities using the indirect method.
2. What were the major reasons that Pizza International was able to report positive cash flow from operations despite having a net loss?
3. Of the potential causes of differences between cash flow from operations and net income, which are the most important to financial analysts?

LO 12-2

E12-11 Inferring Balance Sheet Changes from the Cash Flow Statement (Indirect Method)

Colgate-Palmolive

Colgate-Palmolive was founded in 1806. Its statement of cash flows reported the following information (in millions) for the year ended December 31, 2010:

Operating Activities	
Net Income	$2,313
Depreciation	376
Cash effect of changes in	
Accounts Receivable	40
Inventories	(10)
Accounts Payable	(65)
Other	557
Net Cash Provided by Operations	$3,211

Required:

Based on the information reported in the operating activities section of the statement of cash flows for Colgate-Palmolive, determine whether the following accounts increased or decreased during the period: Accounts Receivable, Inventories, and Accounts Payable.

LO 12-2

E12-12 Inferring Balance Sheet Changes from the Cash Flow Statement (Indirect Method)

Apple Inc.

The statement of cash flows for Apple Inc. contained the following information (in millions) for the year ended September 25, 2010:

Operating Activities	
Net Income	$14,013
Depreciation	1,027
Changes in current assets and current liabilities	
Accounts Receivable	(2,142)
Inventories	(596)
Accounts Payable	6,307
Unearned Revenue	1,217
Other adjustments	(1,231)
Net Cash Provided by Operations	$18,595

Required:

For each of the four current asset and liability accounts listed in the operating activities section of the statement of cash flows, determine whether the account balances increased or decreased during the period.

E12-13 Preparing and Evaluating a Statement of Cash Flows (Indirect Method) from Comparative Balance Sheets and Income Statements

LO 12-1, 12-2, 12-3, 12-4, 12-5

Consultex, Inc., was founded in 2010 as a small financial consulting business. The company had done reasonably well in 2010–2012, but started noticing its cash dwindle early in 2013. In January 2013, Consultex had paid $16,000 to purchase land and repaid $2,000 principal on an existing promissory note. In March 2013, the company paid $2,000 cash for dividends and $1,000 to repurchase Consultex stock that had previously been issued for $1,000. To improve its cash position, Consultex borrowed $5,000 by signing a new promissory note in May 2013 and also issued stock to a new private investor for $12,000 cash. Comparative balance sheets and income statements for the most recent fiscal year are presented below.

	CONSULTEX, INC. **Balance Sheet** **October 31**	
	2013	**2012**
Assets		
Cash	$11,000	$14,000
Accounts Receivable	14,000	12,000
Prepaid Rent	2,000	3,000
Land	26,000	10,000
Total Assets	$53,000	$39,000
Liabilities and Stockholders' Equity		
Wages Payable	$ 2,000	$ 3,000
Income Taxes Payable	1,000	1,000
Notes Payable (long-term)	15,000	12,000
Contributed Capital	20,000	9,000
Retained Earnings	15,000	14,000
Total Liabilities and Stockholders' Equity	$53,000	$39,000

	CONSULTEX, INC. **Income Statement** **For the Year Ended October 31**	
	2013	**2012**
Sales Revenue	$158,000	$161,000
Wages Expense	98,000	97,000
Rent Expense	36,000	30,000
Other Operating Expenses	19,700	20,000
Income before Income Tax Expense	4,300	14,000
Income Tax Expense	1,300	4,200
Net Income	$ 3,000	$ 9,800

Requirements:

1. Prepare a properly formatted Statement of Cash Flows for Consultex, Inc., for the year ended October 31, 2013 (using the indirect method).
2. What one thing can Consultex reasonably change in 2014 to avoid depleting its cash?

LO 12-2

E12-14 **Calculating and Understanding Operating Cash Flows Relating to Inventory Purchases (Indirect Method)**

The following information was reported by three companies. When completing the requirements, assume that any and all purchases on account are for inventory.

	Aztec Corporation	Bikes Unlimited	Campus Cycles
Cost of goods sold	$175	$175	$350
Inventory purchases from suppliers made using cash	200	0	200
Inventory purchases from suppliers made on account	0	200	200
Cash payments to suppliers on account	0	160	160
Beginning inventory	100	100	200
Ending inventory	125	125	250
Beginning accounts payable	0	80	80
Ending accounts payable	0	120	120

Required:

1. What amount did each company deduct on the income statement related to inventory?
2. What total amount did each company pay out in cash during the period related to inventory purchased with cash and on account?
3. By what amount do your answers in 1 and 2 differ for each company?
4. By what amount did each company's inventory increase (decrease)? By what amount did each company's accounts payable increase (decrease)?
5. Using the indirect method of presentation, what amount(s) must each company add (deduct) from net income to convert from accrual to cash basis?
6. Describe any similarities between your answers to requirements 3 and 5. Are these answers the same? Why or why not?

LO 12-3, 12-4

E12-15 **Reporting Cash Flows from Investing and Financing Activities**

Rowe Furniture Corporation is a Virginia-based manufacturer of furniture. In a recent quarter, it reported the following activities:

Net income	$ 4,135	Payments to reduce long-term debt	46
Purchase of property, plant, and equipment	871	Sale of investments	134
Borrowings under line of credit (bank)	1,417	Proceeds from sale of property and equipment	6,594
Proceeds from issuance of stock	11	Dividends paid	277
Cash received from customers	29,164	Interest paid	90

Required:

Based on this information, present the cash flows from investing and financing activities sections of the cash flow statement.

LO 12-3, 12-4, 12-5

E12-16 **Reporting and Interpreting Cash Flows from Investing and Financing Activities with Discussion of Management Strategy**

Gibraltar Industries, Inc.

Gibraltar Industries, Inc., is a manufacturer of steel products for customers such as Home Depot, Lowe's, Chrysler, Ford, and General Motors. In the year ended December 31, 2010, it reported the following activities:

Net income	$(91,068)	Proceeds from sale of property, plant, and equipment	$ 313
Purchase of property, plant, and equipment	8,470	Decrease in accounts receivable	4,115
Payments on notes payable (bank)	58,967	Proceeds from notes payable (bank)	8,559
Net proceeds from stock issuance	270	Payment of dividends	—
Depreciation	26,395	Other financing cash outflows	(1,114)

Required:

1. Based on this information, present the cash flows from the investing and financing activities sections of the cash flow statement.

2. Referring to your response to requirement 1, comment on whether you think Gibraltar's cash flows are typical of a healthy or struggling company.

E12-17 Interpreting the Cash Flow Statement

The Walt Disney Company reported the following in its 2010 annual report (in millions).

	2010	2009	2008
Net income	$ 4,313	$ 3,609	$ 4,729
Net cash provided by operating activities	6,578	5,319	5,701
Purchase of parks, resorts, and other property	(2,110)	(1,753)	(1,578)

Required:

1. Note that in all three years, net cash provided by operating activities is greater than net income. Given what you know about the Walt Disney Company from your own personal observations, provide one reason that could explain the sizable difference between net income and net cash provided by operating activities.

2. Based on the results for the three years, do you believe that Walt Disney Company needed external financing to purchase parks, resorts, and other property during these years?

E12-18 Comparing the Direct and Indirect Methods

To compare statement of cash flows reporting under the direct and indirect methods, enter check marks to indicate which line items are reported on the statement of cash flows with each method.

Cash Flows (and Related Changes)	Statement of Cash Flows Method	
	Direct	Indirect
1. Net income		
2. Receipts from customers		
3. Accounts receivable increase or decrease		
4. Payments to suppliers		
5. Inventory increase or decrease		
6. Accounts payable increase or decrease		
7. Payments to employees		
8. Wages payable, increase or decrease		
9. Depreciation expense		
10. Cash flows from operating activities		
11. Cash flows from investing activities		
12. Cash flows from financing activities		
13. Net increase or decrease in cash during the period		

E12-19 Reporting and Interpreting Cash Flows from Operating Activities from an Analyst's Perspective (Direct Method)

Refer to the information for New Vision Company in E12-9.

Required:

1. Present the operating activities section of the statement of cash flows for New Vision Company using the direct method. Assume that Other Accrued Liabilities relate to Other Expenses on the income statement.

2. Of the potential causes of differences between cash flow from operations and net income, which are the most important to financial analysts?

LO 12-5, 12-6

E12-20 Reporting and Interpreting Cash Flows from Operating Activities from an Analyst's Perspective (Direct Method)

Refer back to the information given for E12-10, plus the following summarized income statement for Pizza International, Inc. (in millions):

Revenues	$136,500
Cost of Sales	45,500
Gross Profit	91,000
Salary Expense	56,835
Depreciation	33,305
Other Expenses	7,781
Net Loss before Income Tax Expense	(6,921)
Income Tax Expense	2,561
Net Loss	$ (9,482)

Required:

1. Based on this information, compute cash flow from operating activities using the direct method. Assume that Prepaid Expenses and Accrued Liabilities relate to other expenses.

2. What were the major reasons that Pizza International was able to report positive cash flow from operations despite having a net loss?

3. Of the potential causes of differences between cash flow from operations and net income, which are the most important to financial analysts?

LO 12-S1

E12-21 (Supplement 12A) Determining Cash Flows from the Sale of Property

AMC Entertainment

AMC Entertainment operates 380 movie theaters in the United States, Canada, and Europe. During fiscal 2008, the company sold its Fandango assets for $20,360,000 cash and recorded a gain on disposal of $18,360,000, which was included in the company's net income of $43,445,000.

Required:

1. Show how the disposal would be reported on the statement of cash flows, using the following format (which assumes the indirect method):

(in thousands)	
Cash flows from operating activities	
Net income	$43,445
Gain on sale of property	
Cash flows from investing activities	
Proceeds from disposition of property	

2. Compute the book value of the Fandango assets that were sold.

LO 12-S1

E12-22 (Supplement 12A) Determining Cash Flows from the Sale of Equipment

During the period, Teen's Trends sold some excess equipment at a loss. The following information was collected from the company's accounting records:

From the income statement	
Depreciation expense	$ 500
Loss on sale of equipment	4,000
From the balance sheet	
Beginning equipment	12,500
Ending equipment	6,500
Beginning accumulated depreciation	2,000
Ending accumulated depreciation	2,200

No new equipment was bought during the period.

Required:

For the equipment that was sold, determine its original cost, its accumulated depreciation, and the cash received from the sale.

E12-23 (Supplement 12B) Preparing a Statement of Cash Flows, Indirect Method: T-Account Approach   LO 12-S2

Golf Universe is a regional and online golf equipment retailer. The company reported the following for the current year:

- Purchased a long-term investment for cash, $15,000.
- Paid cash dividend, $12,000.
- Sold equipment for $6,000 cash (cost, $21,000, accumulated depreciation, $15,000).
- Issued shares of no-par stock, 500 shares at $12 cash per share.
- Net income was $20,200.
- Depreciation expense was $3,000.

Its comparative balance sheet is presented below.

	Balances 12/31/2013	Balances 12/31/2012
Cash	$ 19,200	$ 20,500
Accounts receivable	22,000	22,000
Merchandise inventory	75,000	68,000
Investments	15,000	0
Equipment	93,500	114,500
Accumulated depreciation	(20,000)	(32,000)
Total	$204,700	$193,000
Accounts payable	$ 14,000	$ 17,000
Wages payable	1,500	2,500
Income taxes payable	4,500	3,000
Notes payable	54,000	54,000
Contributed capital	106,000	100,000
Retained earnings	24,700	16,500
Total	$204,700	$193,000

Required:

1. Following Supplement 12B, complete a T-account worksheet to be used to prepare the statement of cash flows for the current year.

2. Based on the T-account worksheet, prepare the statement of cash flows for the current year in proper format.

E12-24 (Supplement 12C) Preparing a Statement of Cash Flows, Indirect Method: Complete Spreadsheet   LO 12-S3

To prepare a statement of cash flows for Golf Champion Store, you examined the company's accounts, noting the following:

Purchased equipment, $20,000, and issued a promissory note in full payment.
Purchased a long-term investment for cash, $15,000.
Paid cash dividend, $12,000.
Sold equipment for $6,000 cash (cost, $21,000, accumulated depreciation, $15,000).
Issued shares of no-par stock, 500 shares at $12 cash per share.
Net income was $20,200.
Depreciation expense was $3,000.

You also created the following spreadsheet to use when preparing the statement of cash flows.

	Beginning Balances, December 31, 2012	Analysis of Changes		Ending Balances, December 31, 2013
		Debit	Credit	
Balance Sheet Items				
Cash	$ 20,500			$ 19,200
Accounts Receivable	22,000			22,000
Merchandise Inventory	68,000			75,000
Investments	0			15,000
Equipment	114,500			113,500
Accumulated Depreciation	32,000			20,000
Accounts Payable	17,000			14,000
Wages Payable	2,500			1,500
Income Taxes Payable	3,000			4,500
Notes Payable	54,000			74,000
Contributed Capital	100,000			106,000
Retained Earnings	16,500			24,700
		Inflows	Outflows	
Statement of Cash Flows				
Cash flows from operating activities				
Cash flows from investing activities				
Cash flows from financing activities				
Net increase (decrease) in cash				
Totals				

Required:

1. Complete the spreadsheet.
2. Prepare the 2013 statement of cash flows using the indirect method.

COACHED PROBLEMS

|ACCOUNTING

LO 12-1

CP12-1 Determining Cash Flow Statement Effects of Transactions

For each of the following transactions, indicate whether operating (O), investing (I), or financing activities (F) are affected and whether the effect is a cash inflow (+) or outflow (−), or (NE) if the transaction has no effect on cash.

TIP: Think about the journal entry recorded for the transaction. The transaction affects net cash flows if and only if the account Cash is affected.

_____ 1. Purchased new equipment by signing a promissory note.

_____ 2. Recorded and paid income taxes to the federal government.

_____ 3. Issued shares of stock for cash.

_____ 4. Prepaid rent for the following period.

_____ 5. Recorded an adjusting entry for expiration of a prepaid expense.

_____ 6. Paid cash to purchase new equipment.

_____ 7. Issued long-term debt for cash.

_____ 8. Collected payments on account from customers.

_____ 9. Recorded and paid salaries to employees.

LO 12-2

CP12-2 Computing Cash Flows from Operating Activities (Indirect Method)

The income statement and selected balance sheet information for Hamburger Heaven for the year ended December 31, 2013, are presented below.

Income Statement	
Sales Revenue	$2,060
Expenses:	
Cost of Goods Sold	900
Depreciation Expense	200
Salaries Expense	500
Rent Expense	250
Insurance Expense	80
Interest Expense	60
Utilities Expense	50
Net Income	$ 20

Selected Balance Sheet Accounts	2013	2012
Merchandise Inventory	$ 82	$ 60
Accounts Receivable	380	450
Accounts Payable	200	210
Salaries Payable	29	20
Utilities Payable	20	60
Prepaid Rent	2	10
Prepaid Insurance	14	5

TIP: Prepaid Rent decreased in 2013 because the amount taken out of Prepaid Rent (and sub-tracted from net income as Rent Expense) was more than the amount paid for rent in cash during 2013.

Required:

Prepare the cash flows from operating activities section of the 2013 statement of cash flows using the indirect method.

CP12-3 Preparing a Statement of Cash Flows (Indirect Method)   LO 12-2, 12-3, 12-4, 12-5

Hunter Company is developing its annual financial statements at December 31, 2013. The statements are complete except for the statement of cash flows. The completed comparative balance sheets and income statement are summarized:

	2013	2012
Balance Sheet at December 31		
Cash	$ 44,000	$ 18,000
Accounts Receivable	27,000	29,000
Merchandise Inventory	30,000	36,000
Property and Equipment	111,000	102,000
Less: Accumulated Depreciation	(36,000)	(30,000)
	$176,000	$155,000
Accounts Payable	$ 25,000	$ 22,000
Wages Payable	800	1,000
Note Payable, Long-Term	38,000	48,000
Contributed Capital	80,000	60,000
Retained Earnings	32,200	24,000
	$176,000	$155,000
Income Statement for 2013		
Sales	$100,000	
Cost of Goods Sold	61,000	
Other Expenses	27,000	
Net Income	$ 12,000	

Additional Data:

a. Bought equipment for cash, $9,000.
b. Paid $10,000 on the long-term note payable.
c. Issued new shares of stock for $20,000 cash.
d. Declared and paid a $3,800 cash dividend.
e. Other expenses included depreciation, $6,000; wages, $10,000; taxes, $3,000; other, $8,000.
f. Accounts Payable includes only inventory purchases made on credit. Because there are no liability accounts relating to taxes or other expenses, assume that these expenses were fully paid in cash.

Required:

1. Prepare the statement of cash flows for the year ended December 31, 2013, using the indirect method.
2. Use the statement of cash flows to evaluate Hunter's cash flows.
   TIP: The demonstration cases provide good examples of information to consider when evaluating cash flows.

LO 12-2, 12-3, 12-4, 12-5   **CP12-4 Preparing and Interpreting a Statement of Cash Flows (Indirect Method)**

Soft Touch Company was started several years ago by two golf instructors. The company's comparative balance sheets and income statement are presented below, along with additional information.

	2013	2012
Balance Sheet at December 31		
Cash	$13,500	$ 8,000
Accounts Receivable	2,500	3,500
Equipment	11,000	10,000
Less: Accumulated Depreciation	(3,000)	(2,500)
	$24,000	$19,000
Accounts Payable	$ 1,000	$ 2,000
Wages Payable	1,000	1,500
Long-term Bank Loan Payable	3,000	1,000
Contributed Capital	10,000	10,000
Retained Earnings	9,000	4,500
	$24,000	$19,000
Income Statement for 2013		
Lessons Revenue	$75,000	
Wages Expense	68,000	
Depreciation Expense	500	
Income Tax Expense	2,000	
Net Income	$ 4,500	

Additional Data:

a. Bought new golf clubs using cash, $1,000.
b. Borrowed $2,000 cash from the bank during the year.
c. Accounts Payable includes only purchases of services made on credit for operating purposes. Because there are no liability accounts relating to income tax, assume that Income Tax Expense was fully paid in cash.

Required:

1. Prepare the statement of cash flows for the year ended December 31, 2013, using the indirect method.
2. Use the statement of cash flows to evaluate the company's cash flows.
   TIP: The demonstration cases provide good examples of information to consider when evaluating cash flows.

LO 12-6   **CP12-5 Computing Cash Flows from Operating Activities (Direct Method)**

Refer to the information in CP12-2.

Required:

Prepare the cash flows from operating activities section of the 2013 statement of cash flows using the direct method.
TIP: Convert the cost of goods sold to cash paid to suppliers by adding the increase in inventory and subtracting the increase in accounts payable.

LO 12-3, 12-4, 12-5, 12-6   **CP12-6 Preparing and Interpreting a Statement of Cash Flows (Direct Method)**

Refer to CP12-4.

Required:

Complete requirements 1 and 2 using the direct method.

TIP: Remember to exclude depreciation expense when converting to the cash basis.

CP12-7 (Supplement 12A) Preparing and Interpreting a Statement of Cash Flows with Loss on Disposal (Indirect Method)

LO 12-S1

Assume the same facts as CP12-4, except for additional data item (*a*) and the income statement. Instead of item (*a*) from CP12-4, assume that the company bought new golf clubs for $3,000 cash and sold existing clubs for $1,000 cash. The clubs that were sold cost $2,000 and had Accumulated Depreciation of $500 at the time of sale. The income statement follows.

Income Statement for 2013	
Lessons Revenue	$75,000
Wages Expense	68,000
Depreciation Expense	1,000
Loss on Disposal of Equipment	500
Income Tax Expense	1,000
Net Income	$ 4,500

Required:

1. Prepare the statement of cash flows for the year ended December 31, 2013, using the indirect method.
2. Use the statement of cash flows to evaluate the company's cash flows.

GROUP A PROBLEMS

 |ACCOUNTING

PA12-1 Determining Cash Flow Statement Effects of Transactions

LO 12-1

Motif Furniture is an Austin-based furniture company. For each of the following first-quarter transactions, indicate whether operating (O), investing (I), or financing activities (F) are affected and whether the effect is a cash inflow (+) or outflow (−), or (NE) if the transaction has no effect on cash.

____ 1. Bought used equipment for cash.

____ 2. Paid cash to purchase new equipment.

____ 3. Declared and paid cash dividends to stockholders.

____ 4. Collected payments on account from customers.

____ 5. Recorded an adjusting entry to record accrued salaries expense.

____ 6. Recorded and paid interest on debt to creditors.

____ 7. Repaid principal on loan from bank.

____ 8. Prepaid rent for the following period.

____ 9. Made payment to suppliers on account.

PA12-2 Computing Cash Flows from Operating Activities (Indirect Method)

LO 12-2

The income statement and selected balance sheet information for Direct Products Company for the year ended December 31, 2013, is presented below.

Income Statement	
Sales Revenue	$48,600
Expenses:	
Cost of Goods Sold	21,000
Depreciation Expense	2,000
Salaries Expense	9,000
Rent Expense	4,500
Insurance Expense	1,900
Interest Expense	1,800
Utilities Expense	1,400
Net Income	$ 7,000

Selected Balance Sheet Accounts		
	2013	2012
Accounts Receivable	$560	$580
Merchandise Inventory	990	770
Accounts Payable	420	460
Prepaid Rent	25	20
Prepaid Insurance	25	28
Salaries Payable	100	60
Utilities Payable	20	15

Required:

Prepare the cash flows from operating activities section of the 2013 statement of cash flows using the indirect method.

LO 12-2, 12-3, 12-4, 12-5   **PA12-3 Preparing a Statement of Cash Flows (Indirect Method)**

XS Supply Company is developing its annual financial statements at December 31, 2013. The statements are complete except for the statement of cash flows. The completed comparative balance sheets and income statement are summarized:

	2013	2012
Balance Sheet at December 31		
Cash	$ 34,000	$ 29,000
Accounts Receivable	35,000	28,000
Merchandise Inventory	41,000	38,000
Property and Equipment	121,000	100,000
Less: Accumulated Depreciation	(30,000)	(25,000)
	$201,000	$170,000
Accounts Payable	$ 36,000	$ 27,000
Wages Payable	1,200	1,400
Note Payable, Long-Term	38,000	44,000
Contributed Capital	88,600	72,600
Retained Earnings	37,200	25,000
	$201,000	$170,000
Income Statement for 2013		
Sales	$120,000	
Cost of Goods Sold	70,000	
Other Expenses	37,800	
Net Income	$ 12,200	

Additional Data:

a. Bought equipment for cash, $21,000.
b. Paid $6,000 on the long-term note payable.
c. Issued new shares of stock for $16,000 cash.
d. No dividends were declared or paid.
e. Other expenses included depreciation, $5,000; wages, $20,000; taxes, $6,000; other, $6,800.
f. Accounts Payable includes only inventory purchases made on credit. Because there are no liability accounts relating to taxes or other expenses, assume that these expenses were fully paid in cash.

Required:

1. Prepare the statement of cash flows for the year ended December 31, 2013, using the indirect method.
2. Evaluate the statement of cash flows.

LO 12-2, 12-3, 12-4, 12-5   **PA12-4 Preparing and Interpreting a Statement of Cash Flows (Indirect Method)**

Heads Up Company was started several years ago by two hockey instructors. The company's comparative balance sheets and income statement follow, along with additional information.

	2013	2012
Balance Sheet at December 31		
Cash	$ 6,300	$4,000
Accounts Receivable	900	1,750
Equipment	5,500	5,000
Less: Accumulated Depreciation	(1,500)	(1,250)
	$11,200	$9,500
Accounts Payable	$ 500	$1,000
Wages Payable	500	750
Long-Term Bank Loan Payable	1,700	500
Contributed Capital	5,000	5,000
Retained Earnings	3,500	2,250
	$11,200	$9,500
Income Statement for 2013		
Lessons Revenue	$37,500	
Wages Expense	35,000	
Depreciation Expense	250	
Income Tax Expense	1,000	
Net Income	$ 1,250	

Additional Data:

a.   Bought new hockey equipment for cash, $500.
b.   Borrowed $1,200 cash from the bank during the year.
c.   Accounts Payable includes only purchases of services made on credit for operating purposes. Because there are no liability accounts relating to income tax, assume that this expense was fully paid in cash.

Required:

1.   Prepare the statement of cash flows for the year ended December 31, 2013, using the indirect method.
2.   Use the statement of cash flows to evaluate the company's cash flows.

PA12-5 Computing Cash Flows from Operating Activities (Direct Method)   LO 12-6

Refer to the information in PA12-2.

Required:

Prepare the cash flows from operating activities section of the 2013 statement of cash flows using the direct method.

PA12-6 Preparing and Interpreting a Statement of Cash Flows (Direct Method)   LO 12-3, 12-4, 12-5, 12-6

Refer to PA12-4.

Required:

Complete requirements 1 and 2 using the direct method.

PA12-7 (Supplement 12A) Preparing and Interpreting a Statement of Cash Flows with Loss on Disposal (Indirect Method)   LO 12-S1

Assume the same facts as PA12-4, except for the income statement and additional data item (a). The new income statement is shown on the following page. Instead of item (a) from PA12-4, assume that the company bought new equipment for $1,800 cash and sold existing equipment for $500 cash. The equipment that was sold had cost $1,300 and had Accumulated Depreciation of $250 at the time of sale.

Income Statement for 2013	
Lessons Revenue	$37,500
Wages Expense	35,000
Depreciation Expense	500
Loss on Disposal of Equipment	550
Income Tax Expense	200
Net Income	$ 1,250

Required:

1. Prepare the statement of cash flows for the year ended December 31, 2013, using the indirect method.
2. Use the statement of cash flows to evaluate the company's cash flows.

GROUP B PROBLEMS

LO 12-1

PB12-1 Determining Cash Flow Statement Effects of Transactions

For each of the following transactions, indicate whether operating (O), investing (I), or financing activities (F) are affected and whether the effect is a cash inflow (+) or outflow (−), or (NE) if the transaction has no effect on cash.

____ 1. Received deposits from customers for products to be delivered the following period.

____ 2. Principal repayments on loan.

____ 3. Paid cash to purchase new equipment.

____ 4. Received proceeds from loan.

____ 5. Collected payments on account from customers.

____ 6. Recorded and paid salaries to employees.

____ 7. Paid cash for building construction.

____ 8. Recorded and paid interest to debt holders.

LO 12-2

PB12-2 Computing Cash Flows from Operating Activities (Indirect Method)

The income statement and selected balance sheet information for Calendars Incorporated for the year ended December 31, 2013, is presented below.

Income Statement	
Sales Revenue	$78,000
Expenses:	
Cost of Goods Sold	36,000
Depreciation Expense	16,000
Salaries Expense	10,000
Rent Expense	2,500
Insurance Expense	1,300
Interest Expense	1,200
Utilities Expense	1,000
Net Income	$10,000

Selected Balance Sheet Accounts	2013	2012
Merchandise Inventory	$ 430	$ 490
Accounts Receivable	1,800	1,500
Accounts Payable	1,200	1,300
Salaries Payable	450	250
Utilities Payable	100	0
Prepaid Rent	80	100
Prepaid Insurance	70	90

Required:

Prepare the cash flows from operating activities section of the 2013 statement of cash flows using the indirect method.

PB12-3 Preparing a Statement of Cash Flows (Indirect Method)

LO 12-2, 12-3, 12-4, 12-5

Audio City, Inc., is developing its annual financial statements at December 31, 2013. The statements are complete except for the statement of cash flows. The completed comparative balance sheets and income statement are summarized below:

	2013	2012
Balance Sheet at December 31		
Cash	$ 60,000	$ 65,000
Accounts Receivable	15,000	20,000
Merchandise Inventory	22,000	20,000
Property and Equipment	223,000	150,000
Less: Accumulated Depreciation	(60,000)	(45,000)
	$260,000	$210,000
Accounts Payable	$ 8,000	$ 19,000
Wages Payable	2,000	1,000
Note Payable, Long-Term	60,000	75,000
Contributed Capital	100,000	70,000
Retained Earnings	90,000	45,000
	$260,000	$210,000
Income Statement for 2013		
Sales	$200,000	
Cost of Goods Sold	90,000	
Other Expenses	60,000	
Net Income	$ 50,000	

Additional Data:

a. Bought equipment for cash, $73,000.
b. Paid $15,000 on the long-term note payable.
c. Issued new shares of stock for $30,000 cash.
d. Dividends of $5,000 were paid in cash.
e. Other expenses included depreciation, $15,000; wages, $20,000; taxes, $25,000.
f. Accounts Payable includes only inventory purchases made on credit. Because a liability relating to taxes does not exist, assume that they were fully paid in cash.

Required:

1. Prepare the statement of cash flows for the year ended December 31, 2013, using the indirect method.
2. Evaluate the statement of cash flows.

PB12-4 Preparing and Interpreting a Statement of Cash Flows (Indirect Method)

LO 12-2, 12-3, 12-4, 12-5

Dive In Company was started several years ago by two diving instructors. The company's comparative balance sheets and income statement are presented below. Additional information is presented on the following page.

	2013	2012
Balance Sheet at December 31		
Cash	$ 3,200	$4,000
Accounts Receivable	1,000	500
Prepaid Expenses	100	50
	$ 4,300	$4,550
Wages Payable	$ 350	$1,100
Contributed Capital	1,200	1,000
Retained Earnings	2,750	2,450
	$ 4,300	$4,550
Income Statement for 2013		
Lessons Revenue	$33,950	
Wages Expense	30,000	
Other Operating Expenses	3,650	
Net Income	$ 300	

Additional Data:

a. Prepaid Expenses relate to rent paid in advance.
b. Other Operating Expenses were paid in cash.
c. An owner contributed capital by paying $200 cash in exchange for the company's stock.

Required:

1. Prepare the statement of cash flows for the year ended December 31, 2013, using the indirect method.
2. Use the statement of cash flows to evaluate the company's cash flows.

LO 12-6   **PB12-5 Computing Cash Flows from Operating Activities (Direct Method)**

Refer to the information in PB12-2.

Required:

Prepare the cash flows from operating activities section of the 2013 statement of cash flows using the direct method.

LO 12-3, 12-4, 12-5, 12-6   **PB12-6 Preparing and Interpreting a Statement of Cash Flows (Direct Method)**

Refer to PB12-4.

Required:

Complete requirements 1 and 2 using the direct method.

LO 12-1, 12-5   # SKILLS DEVELOPMENT CASES

S12-1 Finding Financial Information

Refer to the financial statements of The Home Depot in Appendix A at the end of this book, or download the annual report from the *Cases* section of the text's Web site at www.mhhe.com/phillips4e.

Required:

1. Which of the two basic reporting approaches for the cash flows from operating activities did The Home Depot use?
   a. Direct   **b.** Indirect
2. What amount of tax payments did The Home Depot make during the year ended January 30, 2011?
   a. $13,000,000   **c.** $1,935,000,000
   b. $108,000,000   **d.** $2,067,000,000
3. In the 2010–11 fiscal year, The Home Depot generated $4,585 million from operating activities. Indicate where this cash was spent by listing the two largest cash outflows.
   a. Amortization ($1,718,000,000) and Capital Expenditures ($1,096,000,000)
   b. Share Repurchase ($2,608,000,000) and Capital Expenditures ($1,096,000,000)
   c. Amortization ($1,718,000,000) and Share Repurchase ($2,608,000,000)
   d. Dividends ($1,569,000,000) and Share Repurchase ($2,608,000,000)

LO 12-1, 12-5   **S12-2 Comparing Financial Information**

Lowe's

Refer to the financial statements of The Home Depot in Appendix A and Lowe's in Appendix B at the end of this book, or download the annual reports from the *Cases* section of the text's Web site at www.mhhe.com/phillips4e.

Required:

1. Which of the two basic reporting approaches for the cash flows from operating activities did Lowe's use? Is this the same as what The Home Depot used?
2. What amount of cash did Lowe's receive from issuing long-term debt during the year ended January 28, 2011?

3. In the 2010–11 fiscal year, Lowe's generated $3,852 million from operating activities. Where did Lowe's spend this money? List the two largest cash outflows reported in the investing or financing activities sections. Do Lowe's uses differ significantly from The Home Depot's?

S12-3 Internet-Based Team Research: Examining an Annual Report

LO 12-5

As a team, select an industry to analyze. Using your Web browser, each team member should access the annual report or 10-K for one publicly traded company in the industry, with each member selecting a different company. (See S1-3 in Chapter 1 for a description of possible resources for these tasks.)

Required:

1. On an individual basis, each team member should write a short report that incorporates the following:
   a. Has the company generated positive or negative operating cash flows during the past three years?
   b. Has the company been expanding over the period? If so, what appears to have been the source of financing for this expansion (operating cash flow, additional borrowing, issuance of stock)?
   c. Compare and analyze the difference between net income and operating cash flows over the past three years.
2. Then, as a team, write a short report comparing and contrasting your companies using these attributes. Discuss any patterns across the companies that you as a team observe. Provide potential explanations for any differences discovered.

S12-4 Ethical Decision Making: A Real-Life Example

LO 12-1, 12-5

Enron

This case is based on a cash flow reporting fraud at Enron. The case is available online at www. mhhe.com/phillips4e. To complete this case, you will evaluate the statement of cash flow effects of misclassifying a loan as a sale.

S12-5 Ethical Decision Making: A Mini-Case

This case is available online at www.mhhe.com/phillips4e. To complete this case, you will evaluate two alternatives for increasing a sports club's reported operating cash flows.

LO 12-1, 12-5

S12-6 Critical Thinking: Interpreting Adjustments Reported on the Statement of Cash Flows from a Management Perspective (Indirect Method)

LO 12-2

QuickServe, a chain of convenience stores, was experiencing some serious cash flow difficulties because of rapid growth. The company did not generate sufficient cash from operating activities to finance its new stores, and creditors were not willing to lend money because the company had not produced any income for the previous three years. The new controller for QuickServe proposed a reduction in the estimated life of store equipment to increase depreciation expense; thus, "we can improve cash flows from operating activities because depreciation expense is added back on the statement of cash flows." Other executives were not sure that this was a good idea because the increase in depreciation would make it more difficult to report positive earnings: "Without income, the bank will never lend us money."

Required:

What action would you recommend for QuickServe? Why?

S12-7 Using a Spreadsheet that Calculates Cash Flows from Operating Activities (Indirect Method)

LO 12-2

You've recently been hired by B2B Consultants to provide financial advisory services to small business managers. B2B's clients often need advice on how to improve their operating cash flows and, given your accounting background, you're frequently called upon to show them how operating cash flows would change if they were to speed up their sales of inventory and their collections of accounts receivable or delay their payment of accounts payable. Each time you're asked to show the effects of these business decisions on the cash flows from operating activities, you get the uneasy feeling that you might inadvertently miscalculate their effects. To deal with this once and for all, you e-mail your friend Owen and ask him to prepare a template that automatically calculates the net operating cash flows from a simple comparative balance sheet. You received his reply today.

From:	Owentheaccountant@yahoo.com
To:	Helpme@hotmail.com
Cc:	
Subject:	Excel Help

Hey pal. I like your idea of working smarter, not harder. Too bad it involved me doing the thinking. Anyhow, I've created a spreadsheet file that contains four worksheets. The first two tabs (labeled BS and IS) are the input sheets where you would enter the numbers from each client's comparative balance sheets and income statement. Your clients are small, so this template allows for only the usual accounts. Also, I've assumed that depreciation is the only reason for a change in accumulated depreciation. If your clients' business activities differ from these, you'll need to contact me for more complex templates. The third worksheet calculates the operating cash flows using the indirect method and the fourth does this calculation using the direct method. I'll attach the screenshots of each of the worksheets so you can create your own. To answer "what if" questions, all you'll need to do is change selected amounts in the balance sheet and income statement.

Required:

Copy the account balances from the worksheets for the balance sheet and income statement into a spreadsheet file. Enter formulas into the balance sheet worksheet to compute the change in each account balance, and then enter the formulas for the statement of cash flows (indirect method only) into a third worksheet. From this third worksheet, report the net cash flow provided by (used in) operating activities.

S12-8 Using a Spreadsheet that Calculates Cash Flows from Operating Activities (Direct Method)

LO 12-6

Refer to the information presented in S12-7.

Required:

Complete the same requirements, except use the direct method only.

S12-9 Using a Spreadsheet to Answer "What If" Management Decisions (Indirect or Direct Method)

LO 12-5

Change the amounts for selected balance sheet accounts in the spreadsheets created for either S12-7 or S12-8 to calculate the net cash flows from operating activities if, just before the current year-end, the company's management took the actions listed in the following requirements. Consider each question independently, unless indicated otherwise.

Required:

1. What if the company collected $10,000 of the accounts receivable?
2. What if the company had paid down its interest payable by an extra $2,000?
3. What if the company waited an additional month before paying $6,000 of its accounts payable?
4. What if the company had reported $5,000 more depreciation expense?
5. What if all four of the above events had taken place at the same time?

CONTINUING CASES

Mc Graw Hill **connect**
|ACCOUNTING

CC12-1 Accounting for Cash Flows

LO 12-2, 12-3, 12-4, 12-5

During a recent year (ended December 31, 2014), Nicole's Getaway Spa (NGS) reported net income of $2,300. The company reported the following activities:

a. Increase in inventories of $400.
b. Depreciation of $3,000.
c. Increase of $2,170 in prepaid expenses.
d. Payments of $4,600 on long-term debt.
e. Purchased new spa equipment for $7,582.
f. Payments on accounts payable exceeded purchases by $320.
g. Collections on accounts receivable exceeded credit sales by $859.
h. Issued $10,000 of common stock.

Required:

Based on this information, prepare a statement of cash flows for the year ended December 31, 2014, using the indirect method. Assume the cash balance at December 31, 2013, was $7,000.

CC12-2 Wiki Art Gallery (WAG)

LO 12-2

Access the Wiki Art Gallery (WAG) instructional case in Connect, and read the case in sufficient depth to answer the following.

WAG reported $140,000 in total revenues in 2011. What amount of cash did WAG collect in 2011 from its customers (artwork buyers and artists)?

    a. $140,000.
    b. $78,400.
    c. $71,550.
    d. $61,650.

CHAPTER 13

Measuring and Evaluating Financial Performance

YOUR LEARNING OBJECTIVES

Understand the business

LO 13-1   Describe the purposes and uses of horizontal, vertical, and ratio analyses.

Study the accounting methods

LO 13-2   Use horizontal (trend) analyses to recognize financial changes that unfold over time.

LO 13-3   Use vertical (common size) analyses to understand important relationships within financial statements.

LO 13-4   Calculate financial ratios to assess profitability, liquidity, and solvency.

Evaluate the results

LO 13-5   Interpret the results of financial analyses.

LO 13-6   Describe how analyses depend on key accounting decisions and concepts.

Review the chapter

Supplemental materials

LO 13-S1   Describe how nonrecurring and other comprehensive income items are reported.

LO 13-S2   Describe significant differences between GAAP and IFRS.

FOCUS COMPANY: Lowe's

www.lowes.com

Measuring and evaluating financial performance is like judging gymnastics or figure skating at the Olympics. You have to know three things: (1) the general categories to evaluate for each event, (2) the particular elements to consider within each category, and (3) how to measure performance for each element. On the financial side, managers and analysts follow the same process. They evaluate general categories such as profitability, liquidity, and solvency, which are separated into particular elements such as gross profit margin and net profit margin. For each of these elements, managers and analysts measure performance by computing various percentages and ratios, which themselves are based on information reported in the financial statements.

In this chapter, we focus on Lowe's, the second largest home improvement retailer in the world. Lowe's is a giant with 1,750 stores and 230,000 employees. Yet the company's continued success still requires innovations to increase sales in existing markets and to successfully enter new markets. At the same time, Lowe's must control costs while maintaining a high level of customer service in its stores. Finally, Lowe's management must anticipate the actions of its larger rival, The Home Depot, and address changes in overall demand for building products over which it has little control.

How do managers, analysts, investors, and creditors assess Lowe's success in meeting these challenges? This is the purpose of financial statement analysis. Our discussion begins with an explanation of how to analyze financial statements to understand the financial results of a company's business activities. We conclude the chapter with a review of the key accounting decisions analysts consider when evaluating financial statements.

THIS IS NOW

This chapter synthesizes previous chapters by evaluating the financial statements and accounting decisions of a publicly traded company.

ORGANIZATION OF THE CHAPTER

Understand the business	Study the accounting methods	Evaluate the results	Review the chapter
• Horizontal, vertical, and ratio analyses	• Horizontal (trend) computations • Vertical (common size) computations • Ratio computations	• Interpreting horizontal and vertical analyses • Interpreting ratio analyses • Underlying accounting decisions and concepts	• Demonstration case • Chapter summary • Key terms • Homework helper • Practice material

Understand the Business

Learning Objective 13-1
Describe the purposes and uses of horizontal, vertical, and ratio analyses.

As you first learned in Chapter 1, the goal of accounting is to provide information that allows decision makers to understand and evaluate the results of business activities. Throughout the course, you have learned how financial statements are used in a variety of decisions. Managers analyze financial statements to evaluate past financial performance and make future decisions. Creditors use financial statements to assess compliance with loan covenants. And, of course, analysts use financial statements to generate advice for investors and others. You have learned that no single number fully captures the results of all business activities nor does it predict a company's success or failure. Instead, to understand and evaluate the results of business activities, you need to look at a business from many different angles. An understanding of whether a business is successful will emerge only after you have learned to combine all of your evaluations into a complete picture or story that depicts the company's performance. Our goal for this chapter is to demonstrate how you can do this, relying on horizontal, vertical, and ratio analyses to develop the "story" of how well a company has performed.

HORIZONTAL, VERTICAL, AND RATIO ANALYSES

Most good stories have a plot, which the reader comes to understand as it unfolds over time or as one event relates to another. This is the same way that financial analyses work. **Horizontal (trend) analyses are conducted to help financial statement users recognize important financial changes that unfold over time.** Horizontal analyses compare individual financial statement line items horizontally (from one period to the next), with the general goal of identifying significant sustained changes (trends). These changes are typically described in terms of dollar amounts and year-over-year percentages. For example, trend analyses could be used to determine the dollar amount and percentage by which Cost of Goods Sold increased this year, relative to prior years. **Vertical analyses focus on important relationships between items on the same financial statement.** These items are compared vertically (one account balance versus another) and are typically expressed as percentages to reveal the relative contributions made by each financial statement item. For example, vertical analyses could show that operating expenses consume one quarter of a company's net sales revenue. **Ratio analyses are conducted to understand relationships among various items reported in one or more of the financial statements.** Ratio analyses allow you to evaluate how well a company has performed given the level of other company resources. For example, while vertical analyses can show that Cost of Goods Sold consumes 65 percent of Net Sales and horizontal analyses can show that this percentage has increased over time, ratio analyses can relate these amounts to inventory levels to evaluate inventory management decisions.

Before we show you how to calculate horizontal, vertical, and ratio analyses (in the next section), we must emphasize that **no analysis is complete unless it leads to an interpretation that helps financial statement users understand and evaluate a company's financial results.** Without interpretation, these computations can appear as nothing more than a list of disconnected numbers.

Study the Accounting Methods

HORIZONTAL (TREND) COMPUTATIONS

Horizontal (trend) analyses help financial statement users to recognize financial changes that unfold over time. This approach compares individual financial statement items from year to year with the general goal of identifying significant sustained changes or trends. For example, trend analysis can be used to determine the dollar and percentage changes in the cost of goods sold this year relative to prior years. Because this type of analysis compares the results on each line of the financial statements across several years, trend analysis is also known as horizontal analysis. Because it compares results over a series of periods, it is sometimes called **time-series analysis.**

Regardless of the name, trend analyses are usually calculated in terms of year-to-year dollar and percentage changes. A year-to-year percentage change expresses the current year's dollar change as a percentage of the prior year's total by using the following calculation:

$$\text{Year-to-Year Change (\%)} = \frac{\text{Change This Year}}{\text{Prior Year's Total}} \times 100 = \frac{(\text{Current Year's Total} - \text{Prior Year's Total})}{\text{Prior Year's Total}} \times 100$$

To demonstrate how to calculate a trend, we analyze Lowe's financial statements. Summaries of Lowe's balance sheets and income statements from two recent years appear in Exhibits 13.1 and 13.2. Dollar and percentage changes from fiscal year 2009 to 2010[1] are shown to the right of the balance sheet and income statement. The dollar changes were calculated by subtracting the fiscal 2009 balances from the fiscal 2010 balances. The percentage changes were calculated by dividing those differences by the fiscal 2009 balances. For example, according to Exhibit 13.1, Cash increased by $20 (= $652 − $632) in fiscal 2010 relative to fiscal 2009 (all numbers in millions). That dollar amount represented an increase of 3.2% [= ($20 ÷ $632) × 100].

---

[1]Like many retail companies, Lowe's fiscal year ends at the end of January.

EXHIBIT 13.1   Horizontal (Trend) Analysis of Lowe's Summarized Balance Sheets   Lowe's

LOWE'S
Balance Sheets
(in millions)

	January 28, 2011 (Fiscal 2010)	January 29, 2010 (Fiscal 2009)	Increase (Decrease) Amount	Increase (Decrease) Percent*
Assets				
Current Assets				
Cash	$ 652	$ 632	$ 20	3.2%
Short-term Investments	471	425	46	10.8
Accounts Receivable	—	—	—	—
Inventories	8,321	8,249	72	0.9
Other Current Assets	523	426	97	22.8
Total Current Assets	9,967	9,732	235	2.4
Property and Equipment, Net	22,089	22,499	(410)	(1.8)
Other Assets	1,643	774	869	112.3
Total Assets	$33,699	$33,005	$ 694	2.1
Liabilities and Stockholders' Equity				
Current Liabilities	$ 7,119	$ 7,355	$(236)	(3.2)
Long-term Liabilities	8,468	6,581	1,887	28.7
Total Liabilities	15,587	13,936	1,651	11.8
Stockholders' Equity	18,112	19,069	(957)	(5.0)
Total Liabilities and Stockholders' Equity	$33,699	$33,005	$ 694	2.1

*Amount of Increase (Decrease) ÷ Fiscal 2009 × 100

EXHIBIT 13.2   Horizontal (Trend) Analysis of Lowe's Summarized Income Statements   Lowe's

LOWE'S
Income Statements
(in millions)

Year Ended:	January 28, 2011 (Fiscal 2010)	January 29, 2010 (Fiscal 2009)	Increase (Decrease) Amount	Increase (Decrease) Percent†
Net Sales Revenue	$48,815	$47,220	$1,595	3.4%
Cost of Sales	31,663	30,757	906	2.9
Gross Profit	17,152	16,463	689	4.2
Operating and Other Expenses	13,592	13,351	241	1.8
Interest Expense	332	287	45	15.7
Income Tax Expense	1,218	1,042	176	16.9
Net Income	$ 2,010	$ 1,783	$ 227	12.7
Earnings per Share	$ 1.42	$ 1.21	$ 0.21	17.4

†Amount of Increase (Decrease) ÷ Fiscal 2009 × 100

In a later section, we will explain and evaluate the underlying causes of significant changes in account balances. But before we leave this topic, we must note that not all large percentage changes will be significant. For example, the 22.8 percent increase in Other Current Assets is the third largest percentage change on the balance sheet (Exhibit 13.1) but the $97 increase is relatively small when compared to other changes, such as the $869 increase in Other Assets. To avoid focusing on unimportant changes, use the percentage changes to identify potentially significant changes but then check the dollar change to make sure that it too is significant.

VERTICAL (COMMON SIZE) COMPUTATIONS

A second type of analysis, **vertical (common size) analysis**, focuses on important relationships within a financial statement. When a company is growing or shrinking overall, it is difficult to tell from the dollar amounts whether the proportions within each statement category are changing. Common size financial statements provide this information by expressing each financial statement amount as a percentage of another amount on that statement. The usefulness of common size statements is illustrated by the fact that Lowe's presents its balance sheet and income statement in the common size format illustrated in Exhibits 13.3 and 13.4.

In a common size balance sheet, each asset appears as a percent of total assets, and each liability or stockholders' equity item appears as a percent of total liabilities and stockholders' equity. For example, in Exhibit 13.3, which presents Lowe's common size balance sheets, cash was 1.9 percent of total assets [= ($652 ÷ $33,699) × 100] at the end of fiscal 2010.

> **Learning Objective 13-3**
> Use vertical (common size) analyses to understand important relationships within financial statements.

> **YOU SHOULD KNOW**
>
> Vertical (common size) analyses: Expressing each financial statement amount as a percentage of another amount on the same financial statement.

EXHIBIT 13.3 Vertical (Common Size) Analysis of Lowe's Summarized Balance Sheets Lowe's

LOWE'S
Balance Sheets
(in millions)

	Fiscal 2010		Fiscal 2009	
	Amount	Percent	Amount	Percent
Assets				
Current Assets				
Cash	$ 652	1.9%	$ 632	1.9%
Short-term Investments	471	1.4	425	1.3
Inventories	8,321	24.7	8,249	25.0
Other Current Assets	523	1.6	426	1.3
Property and Equipment, Net	22,089	65.5	22,499	68.2
Other Assets	1,643	4.9	774	2.3
Total Assets	$33,699	100.0%	$33,005	100.0%
Liabilities and Stockholders' Equity				
Current Liabilities	$ 7,119	21.1%	$ 7,355	22.3%
Long-term Liabilities	8,468	25.2	6,581	19.9
Total Liabilities	15,587	46.3	13,936	42.2
Stockholders' Equity	18,112	53.7	19,069	57.8
Total Liabilities and Stockholders' Equity	$33,699	100.0%	$33,005	100.0%

| EXHIBIT 13.4 | Vertical (Common Size) Analysis of Lowe's Summarized Income Statements | Lowe's |

LOWE'S
Income Statements
(in millions)

	Fiscal 2010		Fiscal 2009	
	Amount	Percent	Amount	Percent
Net Sales Revenue	$48,815	100.0%	$47,220	100.0%
Cost of Sales	31,663	64.9	30,757	65.1
Gross Profit	17,152	35.1	16,463	34.9
Operating and Other Expenses	13,592	27.8	13,351	28.3
Interest Expense	332	0.7	287	0.6
Income Tax Expense	1,218	2.5	1,042	2.2
Net Income	$ 2,010	4.1%	$1,783	3.8%

The common size income statement reports each income statement item as a percentage of sales. For example, in Exhibit 13.4, cost of sales was equal to 64.9 percent of net sales revenue in 2010 [= ($31,663 ÷ $48,815) × 100].

RATIO COMPUTATIONS

Ratio analyses help financial statement users to understand relationships among various items reported in the financial statements. These analyses compare the amounts for one or more line items to the amounts for other line items in the same year. Ratio analyses are useful because they consider differences in the size of the amounts being compared, similar to common size statements. In fact, some of the most popular ratios, such as net profit margin and the debt-to-assets ratio, are taken directly from the common size statements. Ratios allow users to evaluate how well a company has performed given the level of its other resources.

Most analysts classify ratios into three categories:

1. **Profitability** ratios, which relate to the company's performance in the current period—in particular, the company's ability to generate income.

2. **Liquidity** ratios, which relate to the company's short-term survival—in particular, the company's ability to use current assets to repay liabilities as they become due.

3. **Solvency** ratios, which relate to the company's long-run survival—in particular, the company's ability to repay lenders when debt matures and to make the required interest payments prior to the date of maturity.

Exhibit 13.5 organizes the ratios introduced in previous chapters according to these three categories, and demonstrates their calculations for fiscal 2010 using data from Exhibits 13.1 and 13.2.

EXHIBIT 13.5	Common Ratios Used in Financial Statement Analysis

Profitability Ratios | **Lowe's Fiscal 2010**

(1) Net Profit Margin $= \dfrac{\text{Net Income}}{\text{Total Revenue}} \times 100$
(Ch. 5, p. 221)

$\dfrac{\$2,010}{\$48,815} \times 100 = 4.1\%$

(2) Gross Profit Percentage $= \dfrac{\text{Net Sales Revenue} - \text{Cost of Goods Sold}}{\text{Net Sales Revenue}} \times 100$
(Ch. 6, p. 270)

$\dfrac{\$48,815 - \$31,663}{\$48,815} \times 100 = 35.1\%$

(3) Asset Turnover $= \dfrac{\text{Total Revenue}}{\text{Average Total Assets}}$
(Ch. 5, p. 221)

$\dfrac{\$48,815}{(\$33,699 + \$33,005)/2} = 1.46$

(4) Fixed Asset Turnover $= \dfrac{\text{Total Revenue}}{\text{Average Net Fixed Assets}}$
(Ch. 9, p. 416)

$\dfrac{\$48,815}{(\$22,089 + \$22,499)/2} = 2.19$

(5) Return on Equity (ROE) $= \dfrac{\text{Net Income}}{\text{Average Stockholders' Equity}} \times 100$
(Ch. 11, p. 517)

$\dfrac{\$2,010}{(\$18,112 + \$19,069)/2} \times 100 = 10.8\%$

(6) Earnings per Share (EPS) $= \dfrac{\text{Net Income*}}{\text{Average Number of Common Shares Outstanding}}$
(Ch. 11, p. 517)

$\dfrac{\$2,010 - \$17}{1,401} = \$1.42$

(7) Price/Earnings Ratio $= \dfrac{\text{Stock Price**}}{\text{EPS}}$
(Ch. 11, p. 517)

$\dfrac{\$25.73}{1.42} = 18.1$

Liquidity Ratios

(8) Receivables Turnover $= \dfrac{\text{Net Sales Revenue}}{\text{Average Net Receivables}}$
(Ch. 8, p. 368)

n/a

Days to Collect $= \dfrac{365}{\text{Receivables Turnover Ratio}}$
(Ch. 8, p. 368)

n/a

(9) Inventory Turnover $= \dfrac{\text{Cost of Goods Sold}}{\text{Average Inventory}}$
(Ch. 7, p. 319)

$\dfrac{\$31,663}{(\$8,321 + \$8,249)/2} = 3.8$

Days to Sell $= \dfrac{365}{\text{Inventory Turnover Ratio}}$
(Ch. 7, p. 319)

$\dfrac{365}{3.8} = 96.1$

(10) Current Ratio $= \dfrac{\text{Current Assets}}{\text{Current Liabilities}}$
(Ch. 2, p. 65)

$\dfrac{\$9,967}{\$7,119} = 1.40$

(11) Quick Ratio $= \dfrac{\text{Cash} + \text{Short-term Investments} + \text{Accounts Receivable, Net}}{\text{Current Liabilities}}$
(Ch. 10, p. 464)

$\dfrac{\$652 + \$471 + \$0}{\$7,119} = 0.16$

Solvency Ratios

(12) Debt-to-Assets $= \dfrac{\text{Total Liabilities}}{\text{Total Assets}}$
(Ch. 5, p. 221)

$\dfrac{\$15,587}{\$33,699} = 0.46$

(13) Times Interest Earned $= \dfrac{\text{Net Income} + \text{Interest Expense} + \text{Income Tax Expense}}{\text{Interest Expense}}$
(Ch. 10, p. 464)

$\dfrac{\$2,010 + \$332 + \$1,218}{\$332} = 10.7$

* If a company has preferred stock or similar securities outstanding, dividends on these securities are subtracted from net income in the numerator to assess the earnings for each share of common stock. The dividends and average number of shares shown above were reported in Lowe's annual report.
** Stock price is the closing price reported for the day on which the company first reports its annual earnings in a press release.

Solution to Self-Study Practice
Gross Profit Percentage = ($68.0 − $44.7)/$68.0 × 100
= 34.3%
Net Profit Margin = $3.3/$68.0 × 100 = 4.9%
Sales Increase (Percentage) = ($68.0 − $66.2)/$66.2 × 100
= 2.7%

 How's it going? Self-Study Practice

For the year ended January 30, 2011, The Home Depot reported net income of $3.3 billion on sales of $68.0 billion. If the company's cost of sales that year was $44.7 billion, what was the company's gross profit percentage and net profit margin? If sales were $66.2 billion in the prior year, what was the year-over-year percentage increase in the most recent year?

$$\text{Gross Profit Percentage} = \frac{(\$\quad - \$\quad)\text{ billion}}{\$68.0\text{ billion}} \times 100 =$$

$$\text{Net Profit Margin} = \frac{\$3.3\text{ billion}}{} \times 100 =$$

$$\text{Sales Increase (Percentage)} = \frac{(\$\quad\quad - \$\quad\quad)\text{ billion}}{\$\quad\quad\text{ billion}} \times 100 =$$

After you have finished, check your answers with the solution in the margin.

Evaluate the Results

INTERPRETING HORIZONTAL AND VERTICAL ANALYSES

Learning Objective 13-5
Interpret the results of financial analyses.

As noted in the previous section, financial statement analyses are not complete unless they lead to interpretations that help users understand and evaluate a company's financial results. When interpreting analyses, your goals should be to understand what each analysis is telling you and then combine your findings into a coherent "story" that explains the results of the company's business activities. We demonstrate how to do this, beginning with interpretations of each set of analyses shown in Exhibits 13.1–13.5 and later concluding with an overall summary of Lowe's results.

Trends Revealed in Horizontal Analyses

Horizontal (trend) analysis of Lowe's balance sheet in Exhibit 13.1 shows that the company grew only a little in fiscal 2010. Overall, total assets increased a mere 2.1 percent. The most significant change indicated by the balance sheet is that the company began relying more on debt and less on equity financing. During 2010, Lowe's long-term liabilities increased by 28.7 percent, which resulted from issuing $2.0 billion in new bonds, as explained in its financial statement notes. Also, stockholders' equity decreased by 5.0 percent, largely the result of Lowe's repurchasing common shares that were immediately retired and returned to authorized and unissued status.

Horizontal analysis of Lowe's income statement in Exhibit 13.2 shows a 3.4 percent increase in Net Sales Revenue and a 2.9 percent increase in Cost of Sales, as a result of more customer transactions. The company explains in the Management's Discussion and Analysis (MD&A) section of its annual report that 2010 saw 20 million more sales transactions than 2009. It also explains that the company sold more seasonal products in 2010, leading to fewer inventory write-downs than in 2009, which had weakened the prior year's gross profit percentage. Operating expenses increased 1.8 percent in 2010 as a result of wage increases and higher fuel costs, which were partially offset by savings from better truck utilization. The MD&A reported that improvements in transportation use led the company to eliminate about 90 million road miles and save 16 million gallons of diesel fuel in 2010. Finally, 2010 expenses for interest and income taxes increased more than 15 percent each, as a direct result of carrying more debt and earning more income.

Relationships Noted in Vertical Analyses

Vertical (common size) analysis of Lowe's balance sheet in Exhibit 13.3 highlights key elements of the company. Its most significant assets have always been Inventories and Property and Equipment, with these assets representing 24.7 and 65.5 percent of Lowe's total assets. As noted in the horizontal analysis, the company's financing strategy shifted somewhat in 2010. As a result of the bond issuances and stock repurchases, debt and equity financing are nearly equally balanced (53.7 percent equity) at the end of Fiscal 2010.

Vertical analysis of Lowe's income statement in Exhibit 13.4 indicates that Cost of Sales and Operating Expenses are the most important determinants of the company's profitability. Cost of Sales consumed 64.9 percent of Sales in 2010 and Operating Expenses consumed an additional 27.8 percent. Much of the increase in the company's Net Income (from 3.8 percent of Sales in 2009 to 4.1 in 2010) is explained by greater control of these two categories of expenses, as suggested by the horizontal analyses.

These findings from the vertical analyses serve to underscore findings from the horizontal analyses. The emerging story is that Lowe's success depends on its ability to use significant investments in Inventory and Property and Equipment to generate sales. By focusing on greater sell-through of its products and more efficient operating practices, Lowe's was able to improve its net income in a recovering but still challenging economy.

Fiscal 2010

27.8
0.7
2.5
4.1
64.9

■ Cost of Sales
■ Operating Expenses
■ Interest Expense
■ Income Tax Expense
■ Net Income

INTERPRETING RATIO ANALYSES

As shown throughout other chapters in this book, benchmarks help when interpreting a company's ratios. These benchmarks can include the company's prior year results, as well as the results of close competitors or the average for the industry. In a competitive economy, companies strive to outperform one another, so comparisons against other companies can provide clues about who is likely to survive and thrive in the long run.

In the following analyses, we compare Lowe's financial ratios to the prior year and in some cases to those for The Home Depot and the home improvement industry as a whole. (Both Lowe's and The Home Depot's annual reports for fiscal 2010 are printed in Appendix A and B at the end of this book.)

> **⚲ COACH'S TIP**
>
> Industry averages are reported in the *Annual Statement Studies,* which are published by the Risk Management Association at statementstudies.org. You can obtain industry averages also from reuters.com/finance or google.com/finance, which were available free of charge at the time this book was written.

Profitability Ratios

The analyses in this section focus on the level of profits the company generated during the period. We will analyze ratios (1) through (7) from Exhibit 13.5. The first two profitability ratios come right from the common size income statement in Exhibit 13.4.

(1) Net Profit Margin Net profit margin represents the percentage of revenue that ultimately makes it into net income, after deducting expenses. Using the equation in Exhibit 13.5, the calculation of Lowe's net profit margin for each of the last two years yields:

Fiscal Year	2010	2009
Net profit margin = $\dfrac{\text{Net Income}}{\text{Total Revenue}} \times 100$	4.1%	3.8%

As discussed in the previous sections, the slowly improving economy helped boost Lowe's profits in 2010. Lowe's net profit margin increased from 3.8 percent in 2009 to 4.1 percent in 2010. The Home Depot's net profit margin saw a similar increase over this period, rising from 4.0 to 4.9 percent.

(2) Gross Profit Percentage The horizontal analysis indicated that Lowe's gross profit increased from 2009 to 2010 in terms of total dollars, but it did not indicate whether that increase was caused solely by greater total sales or also by more profit per sale. The gross profit percentage addresses these possibilities by indicating how much profit was made, on average, on each dollar of sales after deducting the cost of goods sold. Lowe's gross profit percentage for the last two years was:

Fiscal Year		2010	2009
Gross Profit Percentage $= \dfrac{\text{Net Sales} - \text{Cost of Goods Sold}}{\text{Net Sales}} \times 100 =$		35.1%	34.9%

This analysis shows that in 2010, after deducting the cost of merchandise sold, 35.1 cents of each sales dollar were left to cover other costs, such as employee wages, advertising, and utilities and to provide profits to the stockholders. The increase in the gross profit percentage from 2009 to 2010 (35.1% − 34.9%) means that Lowe's made 0.2¢ more gross profit on each dollar of sales in 2010 than in 2009. There are two potential explanations for this increase: (1) Lowe's charged higher selling prices without experiencing a corresponding increase in the cost of merchandise and (2) Lowe's obtained merchandise at a lower unit cost. The MD&A section of Lowe's annual report explains that the increase in gross profit percentage came from both higher selling prices and a decrease in product costs (fewer inventory write-downs).

(3) Asset Turnover   The asset turnover ratio indicates the amount of sales revenue generated for each dollar invested in assets during the period. Lowe's ratios for the two years were:

		2010	2009
Asset Turnover $= \dfrac{\text{Total Revenue}}{\text{Average Total Assets}} =$		1.46	1.44

The asset turnover ratio suggests that Lowe's assets generated sales more efficiently in 2010 than in the prior year. To understand why, it is helpful to focus on the key assets used to generate sales. For a retailer such as Lowe's, the key asset is store properties, which we can compare to sales using the fixed asset turnover ratio, discussed next.

(4) Fixed Asset Turnover   The fixed asset turnover ratio indicates how much revenue the company generates for each dollar invested in fixed assets, such as store buildings and the property they sit on. Lowe's fixed asset turnover ratios for the two years were:

		2010	2009
Fixed Asset Turnover $= \dfrac{\text{Total Revenue}}{\text{Average Net Fixed Assets}} =$		2.19	2.09

This analysis shows that Lowe's had $2.19 of sales in 2010 for each dollar invested in fixed assets. By looking at the components of this ratio, we can see that an increase in 2010 sales and a decrease in net fixed assets both contributed to the ratio's increase in 2010. Increased sales resulted from the slight improvement in the economy and decreased net fixed assets resulted from additional depreciation in 2010 coupled with a decision Lowe's made to limit new store openings in 2010.

Although Lowe's fixed asset turnover ratio improved in 2010, it is low compared to that of its main competitor, The Home Depot, whose fixed asset turnover ratio was 2.69 in 2010. In terms of using fixed assets to generate sales revenue, The Home Depot has a competitive advantage over Lowe's. In other words, Lowe's is operating less efficiently than its major competitor.

(5) Return on Equity (ROE)   The return on equity ratio compares the amount of net income to average stockholders' equity. Like the interest rate on your bank account, ROE reports the net amount earned during the period as a percentage of each dollar contributed by stockholders and retained in the business. Lowe's ROE ratios for the past two years were:

		2010	2009
Return on Equity (ROE) = $\dfrac{\text{Net Income}}{\text{Average Stockholders' Equity}} \times 100 =$		10.8%	9.6%

Lowe's ROE increase from 9.6 to 10.8 percent was inevitable, given our previous analyses. Specifically, horizontal analysis indicated that the company had decreased its stockholders' equity through a stock repurchase and it had increased its net income in 2010 through more profitable operations. Taken together, these results imply that net income as a percentage of average stockholders' equity was sure to rise in 2010. Despite this good news, Lowe's 10.8 percent ROE lagged behind The Home Depot's fiscal 2010 ROE of 17.4 percent.

(6) Earnings per Share (EPS)   Earnings per share (EPS) indicates the amount of earnings generated for each share of outstanding common stock. Consistent with the increase in ROE, the EPS ratio increased from $1.21 in 2009 to $1.42 in 2010, as shown below. This represents an increase of $0.21 per share ($1.42 − $1.21).

Fiscal Year		2010	2009
Earnings per Share (EPS) = $\dfrac{\text{Net Income}}{\text{Average Number of Common Shares Outstanding}}$		$1.42	$1.21

(7) Price/Earnings (P/E) Ratio   The P/E ratio relates the company's stock price to its EPS, as follows:

Fiscal Year	2010	2009
Price/Earnings Ratio = $\dfrac{\text{Stock Price}}{\text{EPS}}$	18.1	19.1

Using the going price for Lowe's stock when its 2010 and 2009 earnings were announced during the last week of February 2011 and 2010, the P/E ratio was 18.1 and 19.1, respectively. This means investors were willing to pay 18.1 times earnings to buy a share of Lowe's stock in early 2011 (versus 19.1 times earnings a year earlier). The decline from the prior year suggests investors were not as optimistic about the company's future prospects as they were a year earlier. Lingering concerns about the U.S. and European economies had dampened enthusiasm for Lowe's stock, as it had for many other companies. The Home Depot's P/E ratio also had fallen from 19.7 to 18.8.

Let's pause to summarize what we've learned so far. After struggling during the financial crisis of 2008 and 2009, Lowe's began to see improvement in 2010. Additional customer traffic resulted in both increased sales and a reduction in inventory write-downs, which contributed to increases in gross profit percentage and net profit margin. Greater sales revenue in 2010 combined with fewer store openings to also boost asset turnover ratios in 2010. These improved results were magnified in the ROE and EPS ratios because Lowe's reduced its stockholders' equity and the number of outstanding common shares in 2010 through stock repurchases. Despite these improvements in Lowe's 2010 results, the P/E ratio indicated that investors were not as optimistic as they had been in the prior year when Lowe's began its recovery. The company still was trailing The Home Depot on several key ratios and there were signs that the worldwide economy would dip back into another economic recession.

Liquidity Ratios

The analyses in this section focus on the company's ability to survive in the short term, by converting assets to cash that can be used to pay current liabilities as they come due. We interpret ratios (8) through (11) from Exhibit 13.5.

(8) Receivables Turnover Most home improvement retailers have low levels of accounts receivable relative to sales revenue because they collect the majority of their sales immediately in cash. Although the formula calls for net **credit** sales in the top of the ratio, companies rarely report their credit sales and cash sales separately. Consequently, financial statement users typically use total net sales revenue in the formula, which results in a receivables turnover ratio that is not terribly meaningful for businesses that make few sales on account. The formula is presented in Exhibit 13.5 simply to remind you of how it's calculated.

(9) Inventory Turnover The inventory turnover ratio indicates how frequently inventory is bought and sold during the year. The measure "days to sell" converts the inventory turnover ratio into the average number of days needed to sell each purchase of inventory.

Fiscal Year	2010	2009
$\text{Inventory Turnover} = \dfrac{\text{Cost of Goods Sold}}{\text{Average Inventory}}$	3.8	3.7
$\text{Days to Sell} = \dfrac{365}{\text{Inventory Turnover Ratio}}$	96.1	98.6

Consistent with the improving economy in 2010, Lowe's inventory turned over more frequently. On average, its inventory took 2.5 fewer days to sell (98.6 − 96.1). These results are a positive sign because almost every retailer's success depends on its ability to offer customers the right product when they need it at a price that beats the competition. Despite its improvement, Lowe's inventory turnover still trails The Home Depot (where inventory takes an average of 85 days to sell). The Home Depot enjoys a faster inventory turnover because it carries fewer big-ticket items than Lowe's. According to their 2010 annual reports, the average ticket price was $62.07 at Lowe's and $51.93 at The Home Depot.

Turnover ratios vary significantly from one industry to the next. Companies in the food industry (restaurants and grocery stores) have high inventory turnover ratios because their inventory is subject to spoilage. Companies that sell expensive merchandise (automobiles and high-fashion clothes) have much slower turnover because sales of those items are infrequent, but these companies must carry lots of inventory so that customers have a wide selection to choose from when they do buy.

(10) Current Ratio The current ratio compares current assets to current liabilities, as follows:

Fiscal Year	2010	2009
$\text{Current Ratio} = \dfrac{\text{Current Assets}}{\text{Current Liabilities}}$	1.40	1.32

The current ratio measures the company's ability to pay its current liabilities. Lowe's ratio increased slightly from 2009 to 2010, ending the year with a ratio of 1.40. In this industry, a current ratio greater than 1.0 is deemed acceptable. Most analysts would judge Lowe's ratio to be very strong, especially considering the company's ability to generate cash.

(11) Quick Ratio   The quick ratio compares the sum of cash, short-term investments, and accounts receivable to current liabilities as follows:

Fiscal Year		2010	2009
Quick Ratio = $\dfrac{\text{Cash + Short-term Investments + Accounts Receivable, Net}}{\text{Current Liabilities}}$		0.16	0.14

The quick ratio is a much more stringent test of short-term liquidity than is the current ratio. Lowe's quick ratio increased slightly in 2010, just as its current ratio did. The low quick ratio shown here is typical for industries where most customers buy with cash or credit card. These forms of payment result in very low levels of accounts receivable and the cash received from sales is often used immediately in other business activities. In industries where credit sales are common, the quick ratio may be much higher. For example, according to reuters.com, the average quick ratio in 2010 for the homebuilding industry was 0.80.

Solvency Ratios

The analyses in this section focus on Lowe's ability to survive over the long term—that is, its ability to repay debt at maturity and pay interest prior to that time. We interpret ratios (12) and (13) from Exhibit 13.5.

(12) Debt to Assets   The debt-to-assets ratio indicates the proportion of total assets that creditors finance. Remember that creditors must be paid regardless of how difficult a year the company may have had. The higher this ratio, the riskier is the company's financing strategy. Lowe's ratio for each of the two years was:

		2010	2009
Debt to Assets = $\dfrac{\text{Total Liabilities}}{\text{Total Assets}}$ =		0.46	0.42

Lowe's ratio of 0.46 in 2010 indicates that creditors contributed 46 percent of the company's financing, implying that stockholders' equity was the company's main source of financing at 54 percent (100 percent − 46 percent). The debt-to-assets ratio increased from 2009 to 2010, as a result of issuing new bonds and repurchasing common stock. The Home Depot, which had a debt-to-assets ratio of 53 percent in 2010, relies much more on debt financing.

(13) Times Interest Earned   The times interest earned ratio indicates how many times the company's interest expense was covered by its operating results. This ratio is calculated using accrual-based interest expense and net income before interest and income taxes, as follows:

		2010	2009
Times Interest Earned = $\dfrac{\text{Net Income + Interest Expense + Income Tax Expense}}{\text{Interest Expense}}$ =		10.7	10.8

A times interest earned ratio above 1.0 indicates that net income (before the costs of financing and taxes) is sufficient to cover the company's interest expense. Lowe's ratio of 10.7 indicates the company is generating more than enough profit to cover its interest expense.

COACH'S TIP

Instead of the debt-to-assets ratio, analysts might use a debt-to-equity ratio, which gives the same basic information as debt-to-assets. Debt-to-equity typically is calculated as total liabilities ÷ total stockholders' equity. As with debt-to-assets, the higher the debt-to-equity ratio, the more the company relies on debt (rather than equity) financing.

COACH'S TIP

If the company reports a net loss, rather than net income, include the loss as a negative number in the formula. A negative ratio indicates that the operating results (before the costs of financing and taxes) are insufficient to cover interest costs.

How's it going?   Self-Study Practice

Show the computations for the following two ratios for Lowe's for fiscal 2009. Use the information in Exhibits 13.1 and 13.2.

a. Times interest earned ratio

b. Current ratio

After you have finished, check your answers with the solution in the margin.

Learning Objective 13-6
Describe how analyses depend on key accounting decisions and concepts.

UNDERLYING ACCOUNTING DECISIONS AND CONCEPTS

Accounting Decisions

In the analyses just presented, we compared Lowe's results with those of The Home Depot. When appropriate, we discussed how differences in the two companies' strategies (for example, relying on debt versus equity financing) and business operations (for example, carrying big-ticket versus less expensive items) affected their financial ratios. We should also consider whether differences between the two companies' financial ratios might be caused by differences in their accounting decisions.

Information about a company's accounting decisions is presented in a note to the financial statements. Exhibit 13.6 shows the policies that three home improvement retailers follow in accounting for inventory and depreciation—two line items that can have a noticeable impact on a retailer's results. Take a moment to study the exhibit.

EXHIBIT 13.6	**Comparison of Accounting Methods**		
	Lowe's	The Home Depot	Builder's FirstSource
Inventory	FIFO	FIFO	Weighted Average Cost
Depreciation	Straight line Buildings: 5-40 yrs Equipment: 3-15 yrs	Straight line Buildings: 5-45 yrs Equipment: 2-20 yrs	Straight line Buildings: 20-40 yrs Equipment: 3-10 yrs

As you can see, the three companies follow similar but not identical policies. Lowe's and The Home Depot use the FIFO method of accounting for inventory and cost of goods sold; Builder's FirstSource uses the weighted average method. Although these two methods result in different numbers, the overall impact on the companies' financial ratios should be minor because inventory costs did not rise rapidly in 2010.

All three companies calculate depreciation using the straight-line method with a similar range of estimated useful lives for buildings and equipment. Because buildings and equipment make up such a large portion of each company's assets, these similarities go a long way toward making their financial results comparable. In conclusion, although the companies' accounting policies have some differences, they are unlikely to have a major impact on our comparisons.

Accounting Concepts

Before wrapping up this chapter, it's worth revisiting the accounting concepts that were introduced in previous chapters. At this stage of the course, you should have developed a fairly good understanding of the rules of accounting and be better able to appreciate

---

EXHIBIT 13.7 | Conceptual Framework for Financial Accounting and Reporting

Objective of External Financial Reporting
To provide useful financial information to external users for decision making (Ch.1)
- It must be relevant and a faithful representation of the business
- It is more useful if it is comparable, verifiable, timely, and understandable

Elements to Be Measured and Reported
- Assets, Liabilities, Stockholders' Equity, Revenues, Expenses, Dividends (Ch.1)

Concepts for Measuring and Reporting Information
- **Assumptions:** Unit of Measure (Ch.1), Separate Entity (Ch.1), Going Concern, Time Period (Ch. 3)
- **Principles:** Cost (Ch. 2), Revenue and Expense Recognition (Ch. 3), Full Disclosure

---

why accounting relies on these particular concepts. Exhibit 13.7 presents the conceptual framework for financial accounting and reporting that was first introduced in Chapter 1. The concepts that you have already learned about in prior chapters are highlighted in red in Exhibit 13.7.

As shown in Exhibit 13.7, the primary objective of financial accounting and reporting is to provide useful financial information for people external to a company to use in making decisions about the company. To be useful, this information must be relevant and faithfully represent the underlying business.

As Exhibit 13.7 indicates, only two accounting concepts have not been introduced in previous chapters, so we will explain them here. The **going-concern** (also called *continuity*) **assumption** quietly underlies accounting rules. It is the belief that any business will be capable of continuing its operations long enough to realize the economic benefits of its assets and meet its obligations in the normal course of business. If a company runs into severe financial difficulty (such as bankruptcy), this assumption may no longer be appropriate, leading to what is called a **going-concern problem.** If ever a company encounters a going-concern problem, it may need to adjust the amount and classification of items in its financial statements, which would be explained in the financial statement notes and to which the auditor's report would draw attention. Some of the factors that commonly contribute to going-concern problems are listed in Exhibit 13.8. Notice that some of the analyses presented earlier in this chapter are key inputs into determining whether a company has a going-concern problem.

One of the principles of accounting that was not previously explained is full disclosure. Simply put, according to the **full disclosure principle,** financial reports should present all information that is needed to properly interpret the results of the company's business activities. This doesn't mean that every single transaction needs to be explained in detail, but rather that adequate information needs to be presented to allow financial statement users to fairly interpret reports about the company's income, financial position, and cash flows.

> **YOU SHOULD KNOW**
>
> **Going-concern assumption:** A business is assumed to be capable of continuing its operations long enough to meet its obligations.

> **YOU SHOULD KNOW**
>
> **Full disclosure principle:** The financial statements should present information needed to understand the financial results of the company's business activities.

EXHIBIT 13.8 | Factors Contributing to Going-Concern Problems

Revealed by Financial Analyses	Revealed by Other Analyses
• Declining sales	• Overdependence on one customer
• Declining gross profit	• Insufficient product innovation/quality
• Significant one-time expenses	• Significant barriers to expansion
• Fluctuating net income	• Loss of key personnel without replacement
• Insufficient current assets	• Inability to negotiate favorable purchases
• Excessive reliance on debt financing	• Inadequate maintenance of long-lived assets
• Adverse financial commitments	• Loss of a key patent

Before closing the book on this topic (and possibly this course), take a moment to complete the following Self-Study Practice. It'll give you a good idea of whether you need a detailed review of the concepts introduced in earlier chapters or whether you're ready to move on to review and practice key aspects of this chapter.

 How's it going?   Self-Study Practice

Match each statement below to the concept to which it most closely relates.

1. Everything comes down to dollars and cents.
2. That's not our issue. It's for somebody else to report.
3. If it relates to this period's earnings, you'd better report it.
4. I've told you everything you could possibly want to know.
5. At that rate, you may not survive past the end of the year.
6. I know it's a long time, but let's break it down into stages.

(a) Separate entity
(b) Revenue and expense recognition
(c) Going concern
(d) Unit of measure
(e) Time period
(f) Full disclosure

After you have finished, check your answers with the solution in the margin.

Solution to Self-Study Practice
1. (d) 2. (a) 3. (b) 4. (f)
5. (c) 6. (e)

You have now seen enough to interpret most basic financial statements. When analyzing real-world financial statements, you will probably encounter nonrecurring or other special items reported in the income statement. These items are discussed in Chapter Supplement 13A.

SUPPLEMENT 13A NONRECURRING AND OTHER SPECIAL ITEMS

> **Learning Objective 13-S1**
> Describe how nonrecurring and other comprehensive income items are reported.

Nonrecurring Items

Until 2005, three different types of nonrecurring items were reported in income statements: discontinued operations, extraordinary items, and the cumulative effects of changes in accounting methods. Recently, however, **new accounting standards have nearly eliminated income statement reporting of extraordinary items and the cumulative effects of changes in accounting methods.** In fact, the definition of **extraordinary** has become so restricted that few events—not even BP's $20 billion of losses that arose from its April 2010 oil spill in the Gulf of Mexico—qualify as extraordinary. The cumulative effects of changes in accounting methods are reported as adjustments to Retained Earnings rather than as part of the income statement in the period when the change is made. (The technical procedures used to make these adjustments are discussed in intermediate accounting courses.) That leaves only one remaining nonrecurring item, discontinued operations.

> **YOU SHOULD KNOW**
>
> **Discontinued operations:** Result from the disposal of a major component of the business and are reported net of income tax effects.

Discontinued operations result from abandoning or selling a major business component. Because an abandoned or sold business unit will not affect financial results in future years, its results for the current year are reported on a separate line of the income statement following Income Tax Expense. This discontinued operations line includes any gain or loss on disposal of the discontinued operation as well as any operating income generated before its disposal. Because this appears below the Income Tax Expense line, any related tax effects are netted against (included with) the gains or losses on discontinued operations. Exhibit 13A.1 shows how The Home Depot reported discontinued operations in a recent year.

EXHIBIT 13A.1	Nonrecurring Items Reported Net of Tax on the Income Statement

THE HOME DEPOT, INC.
Condensed Income Statements
For the Year Ended January 31, 2010
(in millions)

Net Sales	$66,176
Cost of Sales	43,764
Gross Profit	22,412
Selling, General, and Administrative Expenses	15,902
Depreciation and Amortization Expense	1,707
Income from Operations	4,803
Interest and Other Expenses, Net	821
Income from Continuing Operations before Income Tax Expense	3,982
Income Tax Expense	1,362
Net Income from Continuing Operations	2,620
Earnings from Discontinued Operations, Net of Tax	41
Net Income	$ 2,661

Other Items in Comprehensive Income

In some cases, you may see that companies include additional items on their income statements after the net income line. These items may be added to or subtracted from net income to arrive at the amount of **Comprehensive Income**. As you can learn in detail in intermediate financial accounting courses, these items represent gains or losses relating to changes in the value of certain balance sheet accounts. While most gains and losses are included in the computation of net income, some (relating to changes in foreign currency exchange rates and the value of certain investments, for example) are excluded from net income and included only in comprehensive income. The main reason for excluding these gains and losses from net income is that the changes in value that created them may well disappear before they are ever realized when the company sells the related assets or discharges the related liabilities. For this reason, most analysts will consider the size of these special items in relation to net income. If the amount is not large, they will exclude the items in calculating profitability ratios.

> **YOU SHOULD KNOW**
>
> **Comprehensive Income** = Net Income + Other Comprehensive Income (OCI). OCI includes gains and losses arising from changes in the values of certain assets and liabilities (see Appendix D).

SUPPLEMENT 13B	REVIEWING AND CONTRASTING

IFRS AND GAAP

In this supplement, we review and contrast IFRS and GAAP, as they relate to topics raised in earlier chapters of the text. We begin with a theoretical discussion of similarities and differences between IFRS and GAAP that potentially affect the accounting rules for specific topics. We then follow with a summary of specific topic discussions.

> **Learning Objective 13-S2**
> Describe significant differences between GAAP and IFRS.

Overview

Generally speaking, IFRS and GAAP are similar. Both aim to guide businesses in reporting financial information that is relevant and that faithfully represents the underlying activities of businesses. At a basic level, these accounting rules describe (1) when an item should be recognized in the accounting system, (2) how that item should be classified (e.g., asset or expense, revenue or liability), and (3) the amount at which each item should be measured.

Although some exceptions exist, both IFRS and GAAP require that items be recorded only after an exchange between the company and another party. Initially, these items are recorded at the value they enter the company (called the *entry price* or *historical cost*). Later, this value may be revised (upwards or downwards) as a result of events or changes in circumstances. The new value may be (*a*) the entry price adjusted for items such as interest, depreciation, and amortization, (*b*) a current market price, or (*c*) another computed amount (such as the *fair value* or *exit price* that the company would receive or pay in the future for that item).

Many differences between IFRS and GAAP that we have noted in this book relate to cases where IFRS requires or allows companies to report items using values that differ from those required or allowed by GAAP. For example, in Chapter 9, we noted that IFRS allows companies to report fixed assets at fair values. Researchers studying a sample of European and Canadian companies found that financial ratios changed significantly when the companies switched from GAAP to IFRS.[2] Thus, it is useful for you to consider the effects of possible accounting differences when doing your own analyses. A summary of the differences introduced in this text is presented in the next section.

Specific Topics Integrated in Earlier Chapters

Chapter 1

- **Page 18.** Discusses the joint work of the Financial Accounting Standards Board and the International Accounting Standards Board to establish accounting rules and a unified conceptual framework.

Chapter 5

- **Pages 216–218.** Outlines financial statement presentation differences, including financial statement titles, ordering of accounts, and grouping of items. Illustrates a European company's statement of financial position and presents a glimpse into future possible directions for financial statement formatting. Applies ratio analysis to two U.S. companies and one European company.

Chapter 7

- **Page 314.** Explains that IFRS prohibits LIFO and discusses the potential tax impact of switching to IFRS.

Chapter 9

- **Page 401.** Discusses IFRS's accounting for component costs.
- **Page 416.** Discusses IFRS's accounting for R&D and revaluation at fair value.

Chapter 10

- **Page 455.** Discusses IFRS's current classification of long-term debt involving violated loan covenants.
- **Page 464.** Discusses IFRS's threshold for accruing contingent liabilities.

Chapter 11

- **Page 515.** Discusses classification of some preferred stock as a liability.

Chapter 12

- **Page 554.** Illustrates differences in classification of dividends and interest received and paid, under IFRS and GAAP.

---

[2]See Anna-Maija Lantto and Petri Sahlström, "Impact of International Financial Reporting Standard Adoption on Key Financial Ratios," *Accounting and Finance*, 49: 341–361, 2009; and Michel Blanchette, François-Eric Raciot, and Jean-Yves Girard, *The Effects of IFRS on Financial Ratios: Early Evidence in Canada*, CGA-Canada, 2011.

REVIEW THE CHAPTER

DEMONSTRATION CASE

The following information was taken from The Home Depot's annual report.

(in millions of dollars)	Year Ended January 30, 2011 (Fiscal 2010)	
Net Sales Revenue	$67,997	
Cost of Goods Sold	44,693	
Other Expenses	19,966	
Net Income	3,338	
	January 30, 2011 (Fiscal 2010)	January 31, 2010 (Fiscal 2009)
Inventory	$10,625	$10,188
Current Assets	13,479	13,900
Property and Equipment, Net	25,060	25,550
Total Assets	40,125	40,877
Current Liabilities	10,122	10,363
Total Liabilities	21,236	21,484
Total Stockholders' Equity	18,889	19,393

Required:

1. Conduct a horizontal analysis of Inventory, and a vertical analysis of the income statement items.
2. Compute the following ratios for The Home Depot for the year ended January 30, 2011.

   Fixed Asset Turnover   Days to Sell   Debt to Assets

   Return on Equity   Current Ratio
3. Interpret the meaning of the ratios you calculated in requirement 2.

Suggested Solution

1. | Horizontal Analysis | January 30, 2011 | January 31, 2010 | Increase | |
    | --- | --- | --- | --- | --- |
    | Inventory | $10,625 | $10,188 | $437 | 4.3% |

Vertical Analysis		
Net Sales Revenue	$67,997	100.0%
Cost of Goods Sold	44,693	65.7
Other Expenses	19,966	29.4
Net Income	$3,338	4.9%

2. Calculating ratios:

Fixed Asset Turnover = Net Sales Revenue/Average Net Fixed Assets
 = $67,997 ÷ [($25,060 + $25,550) ÷ 2]
 = 2.69

Return on Equity = Net Income/Average Stockholders' Equity
 = $3,338 ÷ [($18,889 + $19,393) ÷ 2]
 = 0.174 or 17.4%

Days to Sell = 365 ÷ Inventory Turnover Ratio
 = 365 ÷ (Cost of Goods Sold/Average Inventory)
 = 365 ÷ [$44,693 ÷ [($10,625 + $10,188) ÷ 2]]
 = 85

Current Ratio = Current Assets/Current Liabilities
 = $13,479 ÷ $10,122
 = 1.33

Debt-to-Assets = Total Liabilities/Total Assets
 = $21,236 ÷ $40,125
 = 0.53

3. Interpreting ratios

- The fixed asset turnover ratio of 2.69 means that, on average, The Home Depot generated $2.69 of sales for each dollar of fixed assets.

- The return on equity of 17.4 percent means that The Home Depot's net income for the year was 17.4 percent of the amount investors contributed to and left in the company.

- The days to sell ratio of 85 means that, on average, 85 days elapsed between the time The Home Depot acquired the inventory and the time the company sold it.

- The current ratio of 1.33 means that at year-end, The Home Depot had $1.33 of current assets for each dollar of current liabilities.

- The debt-to-assets ratio of 0.53 means that The Home Depot relied on short-term and long-term debt to finance 53 percent of its assets, implying that stockholders' equity financed 47 percent ($=100 - 53$) of its total assets.

CHAPTER SUMMARY

LO 13-1   **Describe the purposes and uses of horizontal, vertical, and ratio analyses. p. 608**

- Horizontal analyses (also called trend analyses) compare financial statement items to comparable amounts in prior periods with the goal of identifying sustained changes, or trends.

- Vertical analyses create common size financial statements that express each line of the income statement (or balance sheet) as a percentage of total sales (or total assets).

- Ratio analyses compare one or more financial statement items to an amount for other items for the same year. Ratios take into account differences in the size of amounts to allow for evaluations of performance given existing levels of other company resources.

LO 13-2   **Use horizontal (trend) analyses to recognize financial changes that unfold over time. p. 609**

- Trend analyses involve computing the dollar amount by which each account changes from one period to the next and expressing that change as a percentage of the balance for the prior period.

LO 13-3   **Use vertical (common size) analyses to understand important relationships within financial statements. p. 611**

- Vertical (common size) analyses indicate the proportions within each financial statement category.

LO 13-4   **Calculate financial ratios to assess profitability, liquidity, and solvency. p. 612**

- Financial ratios are commonly classified with relation to profitability, liquidity, or solvency. Exhibit 13.5 lists common ratios in these three categories and shows how to compute them.

- Profitability ratios focus on measuring the adequacy of a company's income by comparing it to other items reported on the financial statements.

- Liquidity ratios measure a company's ability to meet its current debt obligations.

- Solvency ratios measure a company's ability to meet its long-term debt obligations.

LO 13-5   **Interpret the results of financial analyses. p. 614**

- Financial analyses are not complete unless they lead to an interpretation that helps financial statement users understand and evaluate a company's financial results.

- An understanding of whether a business is successful emerges only after you have learned to combine analyses into a complete picture or story that depicts the company's performance.

- To assist in developing this picture or story, most analysts compare to benchmarks such as the company's performance in prior years or to competitors' performance in the current year.

Describe how analyses depend on key accounting decisions and concepts. p. 620   LO 13-6

- Before comparing across companies or time periods, users should determine the extent to which differences in accounting decisions (e.g., methods used to account for inventory, depreciation, contingent liabilities, etc.) might reduce comparability or consistency of the financial information being compared.

- Many accounting concepts were presented throughout earlier chapters, all of which aim to make accounting information more useful for creditors and investors. Two new concepts were explained in this chapter:

  - Going-concern (continuity) assumption—a business is assumed to continue to operate into the foreseeable future.

  - Full disclosure principle—a company's financial statements should provide all information that is important to users' decisions.

Accounting Decision Tools

See Exhibit 13.5 on page 613 for a summary

KEY TERMS

Comprehensive Income p. 623
Discontinued Operations p. 622
Full Disclosure Principle p. 621

Going-Concern Assumption p. 621
Horizontal (Trend) Analyses p. 609
Liquidity p. 612

Profitability p. 612
Solvency p. 612
Vertical (Common Size) Analyses p. 611

See complete definitions in the glossary in the back of this text.

HOMEWORK HELPER

Helpful reminders

- Ratios that include both income statement and balance sheet accounts require you to calculate an average for the balance sheet accounts rather than just use the end-of-period balance. An average ensures the balance sheet data cover the same period as the income statement data.
- To calculate averages for the current and prior years, you will need three years of balance sheet data. (The statement of stockholders' equity reports three years of stockholders' equity data. To calculate averages for other balance sheet accounts, you will need comparative balance sheets from at least two annual reports.)
- The pronoun for referring to a specific company is "its" not "their."

Frequent mistakes

- In calculating year-over-year percentages, divide the change in the account balance by its balance from the prior year, not the current year.

PRACTICE MATERIAL

QUESTIONS (⊖ Symbol indicates questions that require analysis from more than one perspective.)

1. What is the general goal of trend analysis?

2. How is a year-over-year percentage calculated?

3. What is ratio analysis? Why is it useful?

4. What benchmarks are commonly used for interpreting ratios?

5. Into what three categories of performance are most financial ratios reported? To what in particular do each of these categories relate?

6. Why are some analyses called *horizontal* and others called *vertical*?

7. Slow Cellar's current ratio increased from 1.2 to 1.5. What is one favorable interpretation of this change? What is one unfavorable interpretation of this change? ☻

8. From 2012 to 2013, Colossal Company's current ratio increased and its quick ratio decreased. What does this imply about the level of inventory and prepaids? ☻

9. From 2012 to 2013, Berry Barn reported that its Net Sales increased from $300,000 to $400,000, and its Gross Profit increased from $90,000 to $130,000. Was the Gross Profit increase caused by (a) an increase in sales volume only, (b) an increase in gross profit per sale only, or (c) a combination of both? Explain your answer. ☻

10. Explain whether the following situations, taken independently, would be favorable or unfavorable: (a) increase in gross profit percentage, (b) decrease in inventory turnover ratio, (c) increase in earnings per share, (d) decrease in days to collect, (e) increase in net profit margin, and (f) decrease in quick ratio.

11. What are the two essential characteristics of useful financial information? What other characteristics enhance the usefulness of financial information?

12. What is the primary objective of financial reporting?

13. What is the full disclosure principle?

14. What is the going-concern assumption? What is a going-concern problem? What factors can contribute to such a problem?

15. Techgear is an electronics company in the United States. It uses the LIFO inventory method. You plan to compare its ratios to Eurotext, but you are concerned because Eurotext uses IFRS. What accounting policy difference is certain to exist between the two companies? Of the ratios in Exhibit 13.5, name five that will be affected by this difference. ☻

16. (Supplement 13A) Name the most commonly reported nonrecurring item, and explain where and how it is reported on the income statement.

MULTIPLE CHOICE

1. Which of the following ratios is *not* used to analyze profitability?
   a. Net profit margin ratio.
   b. Gross profit percentage.
   c. Current ratio.
   d. Return on equity.

2. Which of the following would *not* directly change the receivables turnover ratio for a company?
   a. Increases in the selling prices of your inventory.
   b. A change in your credit policy.
   c. Increases in the cost you incur to purchase inventory.
   d. All of the above would directly change the receivables turnover ratio.

3. Which of the following ratios is used to analyze liquidity?
   a. Earnings per share.
   b. Debt-to-assets.
   c. Current ratio.
   d. Both b and c.

4. Analysts use ratios to
   a. Compare different companies in the same industry.
   b. Track a company's performance over time.
   c. Compare a company's performance to industry averages.
   d. All of the above describe ways that analysts use ratios.

5. Which of the following ratios incorporates stock market data?
   a. Inventory turnover.
   b. Earnings per share.
   c. Price/earnings ratio.
   d. All of the above.

6. Given the following ratios for four companies, which company is least likely to experience problems paying its current liabilities promptly?

	Current Ratio	Receivables Turnover Ratio
a.	1.2	7.0
b.	1.2	6.0
c.	1.0	6.0
d.	0.5	7.0

7. A decrease in Selling and Administrative Expenses would directly impact what ratio?
   a. Fixed asset turnover ratio.   c. Current ratio.
   b. Times interest earned.   d. Gross profit percentage.

8. A bank is least likely to use which of the following ratios when analyzing the likelihood that a borrower will pay interest and principal on its loans?
   a. Current ratio.   c. Times interest earned ratio.
   b. Debt-to-assets ratio.   d. Price/earnings ratio.

9. Which of the following accounting concepts do accountants and auditors assess by using financial analyses?
   a. Time period.   c. Full disclosure.
   b. Separate entity.   d. Going-concern assumption.

10. (Supplement 13A) Which of the following items is reported net of related income taxes?
    a. Gain or loss from discontinued operations.
    b. Gain or loss from disposal of property, plant, and equipment.
    c. Interest on long-term debt.
    d. Gain or loss from early extinguishment of debt.

For answers to the Multiple-Choice Questions **see page Q1** located in the last section of the book.

MINI-EXERCISES

McGraw Hill connect
|ACCOUNTING

M13-1 Calculations for Horizontal Analyses

LO 13-2

Using the following income statements, perform the calculations needed for horizontal analyses. Round percentages to one decimal place.

LOCKEY FENCING CORPORATION
Income Statements
For the Years Ended December 31

	2013	2012
Net Sales	$100,000	$75,000
Cost of Goods Sold	58,000	45,000
Gross Profit	42,000	30,000
Selling, General, and Administrative Expenses	9,000	4,500
Income from Operations	33,000	25,500
Interest Expense	3,000	3,750
Income before Income Tax	30,000	21,750
Income Tax Expense	9,000	6,525
Net Income	$ 21,000	$15,225

M13-2 Calculations for Vertical Analyses

LO 13-3

Refer to M13-1. Perform the calculations needed for vertical analyses. Round percentages to one decimal place.

M13-3 Interpreting Horizontal Analyses

LO 13-5

Refer to the calculations from M13-1. What are the two most significant year-over-year changes in terms of dollars and in terms of percentages? Give one potential cause of each of these changes.

M13-4 Interpreting Vertical Analyses

LO 13-5

Refer to the calculations from M13-2. Which of the ratios from Exhibit 13.5 have been included in these calculations? Have these two ratios improved or deteriorated in 2013 compared to 2012?

M13-5 Inferring Financial Information Using Gross Profit Percentage

LO 13-4

Your campus computer store reported Sales Revenue of $168,000. The company's gross profit percentage was 60.0 percent. What amount of Cost of Goods Sold did the company report?

M13-6 Inferring Financial Information Using Gross Profit Percentage and Year-over-Year Comparisons

LO 13-2, 13-4

A consumer products company reported a 25 percent increase in sales from 2012 to 2013. Sales in 2012 were $200,000. In 2013, the company reported Cost of Goods Sold in the amount of $150,000. What was the gross profit percentage in 2013? Round to one decimal place.

M13-7 Computing the Return on Equity Ratio

LO 13-4

Given the following data, compute the 2013 return on equity ratio (expressed as a percentage with one decimal place).

	2013	2012
Net income	$ 1,850	$ 1,600
Stockholders' equity	10,000	13,125
Total assets	24,000	26,000
Interest expense	400	300

LO 13-4, 13-5   **M13-8 Analyzing the Inventory Turnover Ratio**

A manufacturer reported an inventory turnover ratio of 8.6 during 2012. During 2013, management introduced a new inventory control system that was expected to reduce average inventory levels by 25 percent without affecting sales volume. Given these circumstances, would you expect the inventory turnover ratio to increase or decrease during 2013? Explain.

LO 13-4   **M13-9 Inferring Financial Information Using the Current Ratio**

Mystic Laboratories reported total assets of $11,200,000 and noncurrent assets of $1,480,000. The company also reported a current ratio of 1.5. What amount of current liabilities did the company report?

LO 13-4   **M13-10 Inferring Financial Information Using the P/E Ratio**

In 2012, Big W Company reported earnings per share of $2.50 when its stock was selling for $50.00. If its 2013 earnings increase by 10 percent and the P/E ratio remains constant, what will be the price of its stock? Explain.

LO 13-4, 13-5   **M13-11 Identifying Relevant Ratios**

Identify the ratio that is relevant to answering each of the following questions.

a. How much net income does the company earn from each dollar of sales?
b. Is the company financed primarily by debt or equity?
c. How many dollars of sales were generated for each dollar invested in fixed assets?
d. How many days, on average, does it take the company to collect on credit sales made to customers?
e. How much net income does the company earn for each dollar owners have invested in it?
f. Does the company have sufficient assets to convert into cash for paying liabilities as they come due in the upcoming year?

LO 13-4, 13-5   **M13-12 Interpreting Ratios**

Generally speaking, do the following indicate good news, or bad news?

a. Increase in times interest earned ratio.
b. Decrease in days to sell.
c. Increase in gross profit percentage.
d. Decrease in EPS.
e. Increase in asset turnover ratio.

LO 13-6   **M13-13 Analyzing the Impact of Accounting Alternatives**

Nevis Corporation operates in an industry where costs are falling. The company is considering changing its inventory method from FIFO to LIFO and wants to determine the impact that the change would have on selected accounting ratios in future years. In general, what impact would you expect on the following ratios: net profit margin, fixed asset turnover, and current ratio?

LO 13-6   **M13-14 Describing the Effect of Accounting Decisions on Ratios**

For each of the following three accounting choices, indicate the decision that will yield (a) a higher net profit margin and (b) a lower current ratio. If the decision does not affect the ratio, indicate "no effect."

1. Straight-line versus accelerated depreciation (in the first year of the asset's life).
2. FIFO versus LIFO (in periods of constantly rising costs and rising inventory levels).
3. Straight-line depreciation with a four-year useful life versus a seven-year useful life (no residual value).

EXERCISES

LO 13-2, 13-3, 13-5   **E13-1 Preparing and Interpreting a Schedule for Horizontal and Vertical Analyses**

Chevron Corporation

The average price of a gallon of gas in 2010 jumped $0.43 (18 percent) from $2.36 in 2009 (to $2.79 in 2010). Let's see whether these changes are reflected in the income statement of Chevron Corporation for the year ended December 31, 2010 (amounts in billions).

	2010	2009
Total Revenues	$205	$172
Costs of Crude Oil and Products	116	100
Other Operating Costs	57	53
Income before Income Tax Expense	32	19
Income Tax Expense	13	8
Net Income	$ 19	$ 11

Required:

1. Conduct a horizontal analysis by calculating the year-over-year changes in each line item, expressed in dollars and in percentages (rounded to one decimal place). How did the change in gas prices compare to the changes in Chevron's total revenues and costs of crude oil and products?

2. Conduct a vertical analysis by expressing each line as a percentage of total revenues (round to one decimal place). Excluding income tax and other operating costs, did Chevron earn more profit per dollar of revenue in 2010 compared to 2009?

E13-2 Computing and Interpreting Profitability Ratios

LO 13-4, 13-5

Use the information for Chevron Corporation in E13-1 to complete the following requirements.

Chevron Corporation

Required:

1. Compute the gross profit percentage for each year (rounded to one decimal place). Assuming that the change from 2009 to 2010 is the beginning of a sustained trend, is Chevron likely to earn more or less gross profit from each dollar of sales in 2011?

2. Compute the net profit margin for each year (expressed as a percentage with one decimal place). Given your calculations here and in requirement 1, explain whether Chevron did a better or worse job of controlling expenses other than the costs of crude oil and products in 2010 relative to 2009.

3. Chevron reported average net fixed assets of $100 billion in 2010 and $94 billion in 2009. Compute the fixed asset turnover ratios for both years (round to two decimal places). Did the company better utilize its investment in fixed assets to generate revenues in 2010 or 2009?

4. Chevron reported average stockholders' equity of $99 billion in 2010 and $89 billion in 2009. Compute the return on equity ratios for both years (expressed as a percentage with one decimal place). Did the company generate greater returns for stockholders in 2010 or 2009?

E13-3 Preparing and Interpreting a Schedule for Horizontal and Vertical Analyses

LO 13-2, 13-3, 13-5

According to the producer price index database maintained by the Bureau of Labor Statistics, the average cost of computer equipment fell 4.8 percent between 2009 and 2010. Let's see whether these changes are reflected in the income statement of Computer Tycoon Inc. for the year ended December 31, 2010.

	2010	2009
Sales Revenue	$100,000	$120,000
Cost of Goods Sold	60,000	71,500
Gross Profit	40,000	48,500
Selling, General, and Administrative Expenses	36,000	37,000
Interest Expense	500	475
Income before Income Tax Expense	3,500	11,025
Income Tax Expense	1,000	5,000
Net Income	$ 2,500	$ 6,025

Required:

1. Conduct a horizontal analysis by calculating the year-over-year changes in each line item, expressed in dollars and in percentages (rounded to one decimal place). How did the change in computer prices compare to the changes in Computer Tycoon's sales revenues?

2. Conduct a vertical analysis by expressing each line as a percentage of total revenues (round to one decimal place). Excluding income tax, interest, and operating expenses, did Computer Tycoon earn more profit per dollar of sales in 2010 compared to 2009?

LO 13-4, 13-5 **E13-4 Computing Profitability Ratios**

Use the information in E13-3 to complete the following requirements.

Required:

1. Compute the gross profit percentage for each year (rounded to one decimal place). Assuming that the change from 2009 to 2010 is the beginning of a sustained trend, is Computer Tycoon likely to earn more or less gross profit from each dollar of sales in 2011?

2. Compute the net profit margin for each year (expressed as a percentage with one decimal place). Given your calculations here and in requirement 1, explain whether Computer Tycoon did a better or worse job of controlling operating expenses in 2010 relative to 2009.

3. Computer Tycoon reported average net fixed assets of $54,200 in 2010 and $45,100 in 2009. Compute the fixed asset turnover ratios for both years (round to two decimal places). Did the company better utilize its investment in fixed assets to generate revenues in 2010 or 2009?

4. Computer Tycoon reported average stockholders' equity of $54,000 in 2010 and $40,800 in 2009. Compute the return on equity ratios for both years (expressed as a percentage with one decimal place). Did the company generate greater returns for stockholders in 2010 than in 2009?

LO 13-4, 13-5 **E13-5 Computing a Commonly Used Solvency Ratio**

Use the information in E13-3 to complete the following requirement.

Required:

Compute the times interest earned ratios for 2010 and 2009. In your opinion, does Computer Tycoon generate sufficient net income (before taxes and interest) to cover the cost of debt financing?

LO 13-4 **E13-6 Matching Each Ratio with Its Computational Formula**

Match each ratio or percentage with its formula by entering the appropriate letter for each numbered item.

Ratios or Percentages	Formula
_____ 1. Current ratio	A. Net income ÷ Total revenue
_____ 2. Net profit margin	B. (Net sales revenue − Cost of goods sold) ÷ Net sales revenue
_____ 3. Inventory turnover ratio	C. Current assets ÷ Current liabilities
_____ 4. Gross profit percentage	D. Cost of goods sold ÷ Average inventory
_____ 5. Fixed asset turnover	E. Net credit sales revenue ÷ Average net receivables
_____ 6. Return on equity	F. Net income ÷ Average number of common shares outstanding
_____ 7. Times interest earned	G. Total liabilities ÷ Total assets
_____ 8. Debt-to-assets ratio	H. (Net income + Interest expense + Income tax expense) ÷ Interest expense
_____ 9. Price/earnings ratio	I. Current market price per share ÷ Earnings per share
_____ 10. Receivables turnover ratio	J. Net income ÷ Average total stockholders' equity
_____ 11. Earnings per share	K. Total revenue ÷ Average net fixed assets

LO 13-4, 13-5 **E13-7 Computing and Interpreting Selected Liquidity Ratios**

Double West Suppliers (DWS) reported sales for the year of $300,000, all on credit. The average gross profit percentage was 40 percent on sales. Account balances follow:

	Beginning	Ending
Accounts receivable (net)	$45,000	$55,000
Inventory	60,000	40,000

Required:

1. Compute the turnover ratios for accounts receivable and inventory (round to one decimal place).
2. By dividing 365 by your ratios from requirement 1, calculate the average days to collect receivables and the average days to sell inventory (round to one decimal place).
3. Explain what each of these ratios and measures mean for DWS.

E13-8 Computing and Interpreting Liquidity Ratios

Cintas Corporation is the largest uniform supplier in North America, providing products and services to approximately 800,000 businesses of all types. Selected information from its 2010 annual report follows. For the 2010 fiscal year, the company reported sales revenue of $2.6 billion and Cost of Goods Sold of $1.5 billion.

LO 13-4, 13-5

Cintas Corporation

Fiscal Year	2010	2009
Balance Sheet (amounts in millions)		
Cash	$411	$130
Accounts Receivable, less allowance of $14 and $20	366	358
Inventories	169	202
Prepaid Expenses	13	17
Other Current Assets	566	563
Accounts Payable	72	70
Wages Payable	67	48
Income Tax Payable	–	10
Other Current Liabilities	245	173

Required:

Assuming that all sales are on credit, compute the current ratio (two decimal places), inventory turnover ratio (one decimal place), and accounts receivable turnover ratio (one decimal place) for 2010. Explain what each ratio means for Cintas.

E13-9 Computing the Accounts Receivable and Inventory Turnover Ratios

Procter & Gamble is a multinational corporation that manufactures and markets many products that you use every day. In 2010, sales for the company were $78,938 (all amounts in millions). The annual report did not report the amount of credit sales, so we will assume that all sales were on credit. The average gross profit percentage was 52.0 percent. Account balances follow:

LO 13-4, 13-5

P&G

	Beginning	Ending
Accounts receivable (net)	$5,836	$5,335
Inventory	6,880	6,384

Required:

1. Rounded to one decimal place, compute the turnover ratios for accounts receivable and inventory.
2. By dividing 365 by your ratios from requirement 1, calculate the average days to collect receivables and the average days to sell inventory.
3. Interpret what these ratios and measures mean for P&G.

LO 13-4, 13-5

Dollar General Corporation

E13-10 Inferring Financial Information from Profitability and Liquidity Ratios

Dollar General Corporation operates approximately 9,400 general merchandise stores that feature quality merchandise at low prices to meet the needs of middle-, low-, and fixed-income families in southern, eastern, and midwestern states. For the year ended January 28, 2011, the company reported average inventories of $1,643 (in millions) and an inventory turnover of 5.39. Average total fixed assets were $1,427 (million), and the fixed asset turnover ratio was 9.13.

Required:

1. Calculate Dollar General's gross profit percentage (expressed as a percentage with one decimal place). What does this imply about the amount of gross profit made from each dollar of sales?

   TIP: Work backward from the fixed asset turnover and inventory turnover ratios to compute the amounts needed for the gross profit percentage.

2. Is this an improvement from the gross profit percentage of 31.3 percent earned during the previous year?

LO 13-4, 13-5

E13-11 Analyzing the Impact of Selected Transactions on the Current Ratio

In its most recent annual report, Appalachian Beverages reported current assets of $54,000 and a current ratio of 1.80. Assume that the following transactions were completed: (1) purchased merchandise for $6,000 on account, and (2) purchased a delivery truck for $10,000, paying $1,000 cash and signing a two-year promissory note for the balance.

Required:

Compute the updated current ratio, rounded to two decimal places, after each transaction.

LO 13-4, 13-5

E13-12 Analyzing the Impact of Selected Transactions on the Current Ratio

In its most recent annual report, Sunrise Enterprises reported current assets of $1,090,000 and current liabilities of $602,000.

Required:

Determine for each of the following transactions whether the current ratio, and each of its two components, for Sunrise will increase, decrease, or have no change: (1) sold long-term assets for cash, (2) accrued severance pay for terminated employees, (3) wrote down the carrying value of certain inventory items that were deemed to be obsolete, and (4) acquired new inventory by signing an 18-month promissory note (the supplier was not willing to provide normal credit terms).

LO 13-4, 13-5

The Sports Authority, Inc.

E13-13 Analyzing the Impact of Selected Transactions on the Current Ratio

The Sports Authority, Inc., is a private full-line sporting goods retailer. Assume one of the Sports Authority stores reported current assets of $88,000 and its current ratio was 1.75, and then completed the following transactions: (1) paid $6,000 on accounts payable, (2) purchased a delivery truck for $10,000 cash, (3) wrote off a bad account receivable for $2,000, and (4) paid previously declared dividends in the amount of $25,000.

Required:

Compute the updated current ratio, rounded to two decimal places, after each transaction.

LO 13-4, 13-5

E13-14 Analyzing the Impact of Selected Transactions on the Current Ratio

A company has current assets that total $500,000, a current ratio of 2.00, and uses the perpetual inventory method. Assume that the following transactions are then completed: (1) sold $12,000 in merchandise on short-term credit for $15,000, (2) declared but did not pay dividends of $50,000, (3) paid prepaid rent in the amount of $12,000, (4) paid previously declared dividends in the amount of $50,000, (5) collected an account receivable in the amount of $12,000, and (6) reclassified $40,000 of long-term debt as a current liability.

Required:

Compute the updated current ratio, rounded to two decimal places, after each transaction.

E13-15 Analyzing the Impact of Alternative Inventory Methods on Selected Ratios LO 13-6

Company A uses the FIFC method to cost inventory, and Company B uses the LIFO method. The two companies are exactly alike except for the difference in inventory costing methods. Costs of inventory items for both companies have been falling steadily in recent years, and each company has increased its inventory each year. Ignore income tax effects.

Required:

Identify which company will report the higher amount for each of the following ratios. If it is not possible to identify which will report the higher amount, explain why.

1. Current ratio.
2. Debt-to-assets ratio.
3. Earnings per share.

COACHED PROBLEMS

|ACCOUNTING

CP13-1 Analyzing Comparative Financial Statements Using Horizontal Analyses LO 13-2, 13-5

The comparative financial statements prepared at December 31, 2013, for Golden Corporation showed the following summarized data:

	2013	2012	Increase (Decrease) in 2013 (versus 2012) Amount	Percentage
Income Statement				
Sales revenue	$180,000	$165,000		
Cost of goods sold	110,000	100,000		
Gross profit	70,000	65,000		
Operating expenses	53,300	50,400		
Interest expense	2,700	2,600		
Income before income taxes	14,000	12,000		
Income tax expense	4,000	3,000		
Net income	$ 10,000	$ 9,000		
Balance Sheet				
Cash	$ 4,000	$ 8,000		
Accounts receivable (net)	19,000	23,000		
Inventory	40,000	35,000		
Property and equipment (net)	45,000	38,000		
	$108,000	$104,000		
Current liabilities (no interest)	$ 16,000	$ 19,000		
Long-term liabilities (6% interest)	45,000	45,000		
Common stock (par $5)	30,000	30,000		
Additional paid-in capital	5,000	5,000		
Retained earnings	12,000	5,000		
	$108,000	$104,000		

Required:

1. Complete the two final columns shown beside each item in Golden Corporation's comparative financial statements. Round the percentages to one decimal place.

   TIP: Calculate the increase (decrease) by subtracting 2012 from 2013. Calculate the percentage by dividing the amount of increase (decrease) by the 2012 balance.

2. Use the horizontal (trend) analyses to identify (a) a large percentage change in one account that is accompanied by a small dollar change, and (b) a directional change in one account balance that is inconsistent with the direction of change in a related account balance.

LO 13-4, 13-5

CP13-2 Analyzing Comparative Financial Statements Using Selected Ratios

Use the data given in CP13-1 for Golden Corporation.

Required:

1. Compute the gross profit percentage for 2013 and 2012. Round the percentages to one decimal place. Is the trend going in the right direction?

2. Compute the net profit margin for 2013 and 2012. Round the percentages to one decimal place. Is the trend going in the right direction?

3. Compute the earnings per share for 2013 and 2012. Does the trend look good or bad? Explain.
   TIP: To calculate EPS, use the balance in Common Stock to determine the number of shares outstanding. Common Stock equals the par value per share times the number of shares.

4. Stockholders' equity totaled $30,000 at the end of 2011. Compute the return on equity (ROE) ratios for 2012 and 2013. Express the ROE as percentages rounded to one decimal place. Is the trend going in the right direction?

5. Net property and equipment totaled $35,000 at the end of 2011. Compute the fixed asset turnover ratios for 2013 and 2012. Round the ratios to two decimal places. Is the trend going in the right direction?

6. Compute the debt-to-assets ratios for 2013 and 2012. Round the ratios to two decimal places. Is debt providing financing for a larger or smaller proportion of the company's asset growth? Explain.

7. Compute the times interest earned ratios for 2013 and 2012. Round the ratios to one decimal place. Do they look good or bad? Explain.

8. After Golden released its 2013 financial statements, the company's stock was trading at $30. After the release of its 2012 financial statements, the company's stock price was $21 per share. Compute the P/E ratios for both years, rounded to one decimal place. Does it appear that investors have become more (or less) optimistic about Golden's future success?

LO 13-3, 13-5

CP13-3 Vertical Analysis of a Balance Sheet

Electronic Arts

Electronic Arts is a video game company that competes with Activision. A condensed balance sheet for Electronic Arts and a partially completed vertical analysis are presented below.

ELECTRONIC ARTS, INC.
Balance Sheet (summarized)
March 31, 2010
(in millions of U.S. dollars)

Cash and Short-term Investments	$1,273	27%	Accounts Payable	$ 91	2%
Accounts Receivable	206	4	Accrued Liabilities	717	d
Inventories	100	2	Long-term Debt	1,109	24
Other Current Assets	1,006	a	Total Liabilities	1,917	e
Intangibles	1,297	b	Contributed Capital	2,378	51
Property and Equipment	537	c	Retained Earnings	351	8
Other Assets	227	5	Total Stockholders' Equity	2,729	59
Total Assets	$4,646	100%	Total Liabilities & Stockholders' Equity	$4,646	100%

Required:

1. Complete the vertical analysis by computing each line item (*a*)–(*e*) as a percentage of total assets. Round to the nearest whole percentage.
   TIP: Inventories were 2 percent of total assets, computed as ($100 ÷ $4,646) × 100.

2. What percentages of Electronic Arts' assets relate to intangibles versus property and equipment? What business reasons would explain this relative emphasis?

LO 13-3, 13-5

CP13-4 Vertical Analysis of an Income Statement

Electronic Arts

A condensed income statement for Electronic Arts and a partially completed vertical analysis follow.

ELECTRONIC ARTS, INC.
Income Statement (summarized)
For the Year Ended March 31
(in millions of U.S. dollars)

	2010		2009	
Net Revenues	$3,654	100%	$ 4,212	100%
Cost of Goods Sold	1,866	a	2,127	50
Research and Development Expense	1,229	b	1,359	32
Sales and Marketing Expense	730	c	691	16
General and Administrative Expense	515	14	862	21
Income (Loss) from Operations	(636)	(19)	(827)	(19)
Other Revenue (Expenses)	(20)	(1)	(28)	(1)
Income (Loss) before Income Tax	(706)	(20)	(855)	(20)
Income Tax Recovery (Expense)	29	1	(233)	(6)
Net Income (Loss)	(677)	d%	$(1,088)	(26)%

Required:

1. Complete the vertical analysis by computing each line item (a)–(d) as a percentage of net revenues. Round to the nearest whole percentage.

   TIP: Research and Development was 32 percent of net revenues in 2009, which was computed as (1,359 ÷ 4,212) × 100.

2. Does Electronic Arts' 2010 Cost of Goods Sold, as a percentage of Net Revenues, represent better or worse performance as compared to 2009?

CP13-5 Interpreting Profitability, Liquidity, Solvency, and P/E Ratios

LO 13-4, 13-5

Kohl's Corporation is a national retail department store. The company's total revenues for the year ended January 29, 2010, were $18 billion. J.C. Penney is a similar size department store company with $18 billion of revenues. The following ratios for the two companies were obtained for that fiscal year from reuters.com/finance:

Kohl's Corporation
J.C. Penney

Ratio	Kohl's	J.C. Penney
Gross profit percentage	38.2%	39.2%
Net profit margin	6.0%	2.1%
Return on equity	14.0%	7.38%
EPS	$ 3.75	$ 1.57
Inventory turnover ratio	3.81	3.46
Current ratio	2.08	2.41
Debt to assets	0.96	0.98
P/E ratio	14.2	23.3

Required:

1. Which company appears more profitable? Describe the ratio(s) that you used to reach this decision.

2. Which company appears more liquid? Describe the ratio(s) that you used to reach this decision.

3. Which company appears more solvent? Describe the ratio(s) that you used to reach this decision.

4. Are the conclusions from your analyses in requirements 1–3 consistent with the value of the two companies, as suggested by their P/E ratios? If not, offer one explanation for any apparent inconsistency.

   TIP: Remember that the stock price in the top of the P/E ratio represents investors' expectations about future financial performance whereas the bottom number reports past financial performance.

LO 13-4, 13-5, 13-6   **CP13-6 Using Ratios to Compare Alternative Investment Opportunities**

The 2013 financial statements for Armstrong and Blair companies are summarized here:

	Armstrong Company	Blair Company
Balance Sheet		
Cash	$ 35,000	$ 22,000
Accounts Receivable, Net	40,000	30,000
Inventory	100,000	40,000
Property and Equipment, Net	180,000	300,000
Other Assets	45,000	408,000
Total Assets	$400,000	$800,000
Current Liabilities	$100,000	$ 50,000
Long-term Debt	60,000	370,000
Total Liabilities	160,000	420,000
Common Stock (par $10)	150,000	200,000
Additional Paid-in Capital	30,000	110,000
Retained Earnings	60,000	70,000
Total Liabilities and Stockholders' Equity	$400,000	$800,000
Income Statement		
Sales Revenue (1/3 on credit)	$450,000	$810,000
Cost of Goods Sold	(245,000)	(405,000)
Other Expenses	(160,000)	(315,000)
Net Income	$ 45,000	$ 90,000
Selected Data from 2012 Statements		
Accounts Receivable, Net	$ 20,000	$ 38,000
Inventory	92,000	45,000
Property and Equipment, Net	180,000	300,000
Long-term Debt	60,000	70,000
Total Stockholders' Equity	231,000	440,000
Other Data		
Estimated value of each share at end of 2013	$ 18	$ 27

The companies are in the same line of business and are direct competitors in a large metropolitan area. Both have been in business approximately 10 years, and each has had steady growth. One-third of both companies' sales are on credit. Despite these similarities, the management of each has a different viewpoint in many respects. Blair is more conservative, and as its president said, "We avoid what we consider to be undue risk." Both companies use straight-line depreciation, but Blair estimates slightly shorter useful lives than Armstrong. No shares were issued in 2013, and neither company is publicly held. Blair Company has an annual audit by a CPA but Armstrong Company does not. Assume the end-of-year total assets and net property and equipment balances approximate the year's average.

Required:

1. Calculate the ratios in Exhibit 13.5 for which sufficient information is available. Round all calculations to two decimal places.
   TIP: To calculate EPS, use the balance in Common Stock to determine the number of shares outstanding. Common Stock equals the par value per share times the number of shares.

2. A venture capitalist is considering buying shares in one of the two companies. Based on the data given, prepare a comparative written evaluation of the ratio analyses (and any other available information) and conclude with your recommended choice.
   TIP: Comment on how accounting differences affect your evaluations, if at all.

LO 13-5   **CP13-7 Analyzing an Investment by Comparing Selected Ratios**

You have the opportunity to invest $10,000 in one of two companies from a single industry. The only information you have follows. The word *high* refers to the top third of the industry; *average* is the middle third; *low* is the bottom third.

Ratio	Company A	Company B
Current	High	Average
Inventory turnover	Low	Average
Debt to assets	High	Average
Times interest earned	Low	Average
Price/earnings	Low	Average

Required:

Which company would you select? Write a brief explanation for your recommendation.

TIP: When interpreting ratios, think about how they are related to one another. For example, the current ratio and the inventory turnover ratio both include the Inventory balance. This means that the low inventory turnover ratio can help you to interpret the high current ratio.

GROUP A PROBLEMS

PA13-1 Analyzing Financial Statements Using Horizontal Analyses   LO 13-2, 13-5

The comparative financial statements prepared at December 31, 2013, for Pinnacle Plus showed the following summarized data:

	2013	2012	Increase (Decrease) in 2013 (versus 2012) Amount	Percentage
Income Statement				
Sales Revenue*	$110,000	$ 99,000		
Cost of Goods Sold	52,000	48,000		
Gross Profit	58,000	51,000		
Operating Expenses	36,000	33,000		
Interest Expense	4,000	4,000		
Income before Income Tax Expense	18,000	14,000		
Income Tax Expense (30%)	5,400	4,200		
Net Income	$ 12,600	$ 9,800		
Balance Sheet				
Cash	$ 49,500	$ 18,000		
Accounts Receivable, Net	37,000	32,000		
Inventory	25,000	38,000		
Property and Equipment, Net	95,000	105,000		
Total Assets	$206,500	$193,000		
Accounts Payable	$ 42,000	$ 35,000		
Income Tax Payable	1,000	500		
Note Payable, Long-term	40,000	40,000		
Total Liabilities	83,000	75,500		
Common Stock (par $10)	90,000	90,000		
Retained Earnings[†]	33,500	27,500		
Total Liabilities and Stockholders' Equity	$206,500	$193,000		

*One-half of all sales are on credit.
[†]During 2013, cash dividends amounting to $6,600 were declared and paid.

Required:

1. Complete the two final columns shown beside each item in Pinnacle Plus's comparative financial statements. Round the percentages to one decimal place.

2. Which account increased by the largest dollar amount? Which account increased by the largest percentage?

LO 13-4, 13-5   **PA13-2 Analyzing Comparative Financial Statements Using Selected Ratios**

Use the data given in PA13-1 for Pinnacle Plus.

Required:

1. Compute the gross profit percentage in 2013 and 2012. Round the percentages to one decimal place. Is the trend going in the right direction?
2. Compute the net profit margin for 2013 and 2012. Round the percentages to one decimal place. Is the trend going in the right direction?
3. Compute the earnings per share for 2013 and 2012. Does the trend look good or bad? Explain.
4. Stockholders' equity totaled $100,000 at the end of 2011. Compute the return on equity (ROE) ratios for 2013 and 2012. Express the ROE as percentages rounded to one decimal place. Is the trend going in the right direction?
5. Net property and equipment totaled $110,000 at the end of 2011. Compute the fixed asset turnover ratios for 2013 and 2012. Round the ratios to two decimal places. Is the trend going in the right direction?
6. Compute the debt-to-assets ratios for 2013 and 2012. Round the ratios to two decimal places. Is debt providing financing for a larger or smaller proportion of the company's asset growth? Explain.
7. Compute the times interest earned ratios for 2013 and 2012. Round the ratios to one decimal place. Do they look good or bad? Explain.
8. After Pinnacle Plus released its 2013 financial statements, the company's stock was trading at $18. After the release of its 2012 financial statements, the company's stock price was $15 per share. Compute the P/E ratios for both years, rounded to one decimal place. Does it appear that investors have become more (or less) optimistic about Pinnacle's future success?

LO 13-3, 13-5   **PA13-3 Vertical Analysis of a Balance Sheet**

A condensed balance sheet for Simultech Corporation and a partially completed vertical analysis are presented below.

SIMULTECH CORPORATION
Balance Sheet (summarized)
January 31, 2013
(in millions of U.S. dollars)

Cash and Short-term Investments	$ 433	29%	Current Liabilities	$ 409	27%
Accounts Receivable	294	19	Long-term Liabilities	495	33
Inventories	206	14	Total Liabilities	904	b
Other Current Assets	109	a	Contributed Capital	118	c
Property and Equipment	27	2	Retained Earnings	492	32
Other Assets	445	29	Total Stockholders' Equity	610	d
Total Assets	$1,514	100%	Total Liabilities & Stockholders' Equity	$1,514	100%

Required:

1. Complete the vertical analysis by computing each line item (a)–(d) as a percentage of total assets. Round to the nearest whole percentage.
2. What percentages of Simultech's assets relate to inventories versus property and equipment? What does this tell you about the relative significance of these two assets to Simultech's business?
3. What percentage of Simultech's assets is financed by total stockholder's equity? By total liabilities?

LO 13-3, 13-5   **PA13-4 Vertical Analysis of an Income Statement**

A condensed income statement for Simultech Corporation and a partially completed vertical analysis are presented below.

SIMULTECH CORPORATION
Income Statement (summarized)
(in millions of U.S. dollars)

	For the Years Ended			
	January 31, 2013		January 31, 2012	
Sales Revenues	$2,062	100%	$2,200	100%
Cost of Goods Sold	1,637	79	1,721	d
Selling, General, and Administrative Expenses	333	a	346	16
Other Operating Expenses	53	3	12	1
Interest Expense	22	b	26	1
Income before Income Tax Expense	17	1	95	e
Income Tax Expense	6	0	33	1
Net Income	$ 11	c%	$ 62	f%

Required:

1. Complete the vertical analysis by computing each line item (a)–(f) as a percentage of sales revenues. Round to the nearest whole percentage.

2. Does Simultech's Cost of Goods Sold for the year ended January 31, 2013, as a percentage of revenues, represent better or worse performance as compared to that for the year ended January 31, 2012?

3. Do the percentages for (c) and (f) that you calculated in 1 indicate whether Simultech's net profit margin has changed over the two years?

PA13-5 Interpreting Profitability, Liquidity, Solvency, and P/E Ratios

Coke and Pepsi are well-known international brands. Coca-Cola sells more than $35 billion worth of beverages each year while annual sales of Pepsi products exceed $43 billion. Compare the two companies as a potential investment based on the following ratios:

LO 13-4, 13-5

Coca-Cola Company
PepsiCo

Ratio	Coca-Cola	PepsiCo
Gross profit percentage	63.9%	54.1%
Net profit margin	33.6%	10.9%
Return on equity	37.7%	29.4%
EPS	$ 5.06	$ 3.91
Receivables turnover ratio	8.6	10.6
Inventory turnover ratio	5.1	8.9
Current ratio	1 17	1.11
Debt to assets	0 57	0.68
P/E ratio	12 6	16.2

Required:

1. Which company appears more profitable? Describe the ratio(s) that you used to reach this decision.

2. Which company appears more liquid? Describe the ratio(s) that you used to reach this decision.

3. Which company appears more solvent? Describe the ratio(s) that you used to reach this decision.

4. Are the conclusions from your analyses in requirements 1–3 consistent with the value of the two companies, as suggested by their P/E ratios? If not, offer one explanation for any apparent inconsistency.

LO 13-4, 13-5, 13-6   **PA13-6 Using Ratios to Compare Loan Requests from Two Companies**

The 2013 financial statements for Royale and Cavalier companies are summarized here:

	Royale Company	Cavalier Company
Balance Sheet		
Cash	$ 25,000	$ 45,000
Accounts Receivable, Net	55,000	5,000
Inventory	110,000	25,000
Property and Equipment, Net	550,000	160,000
Other Assets	140,000	57,000
Total Assets	$880,000	$292,000
Current Liabilities	$120,000	$ 15,000
Long-term Debt	190,000	55,000
Capital Stock (par $20)	480,000	210,000
Additional Paid-in Capital	50,000	4,000
Retained Earnings	40,000	8,000
Total Liabilities and Stockholders' Equity	$880,000	$292,000
Income Statement		
Sales Revenue	$800,000	$280,000
Cost of Goods Sold	(480,000)	(150,000)
Other Expenses	(240,000)	(95,000)
Net Income	$ 80,000	$ 35,000
Selected Data from 2012 Statements		
Accounts Receivable, Net	$ 47,000	$ 11,000
Long-term Debt	190,000	55,000
Property and Equipment, Net	550,000	160,000
Inventory	95,000	38,000
Total Stockholders' Equity	570,000	202,000
Other Data		
Per share price at end of 2013	$ 14.00	$ 11.00

These two companies are in the same business and state but different cities. One-half of Royale's sales and one-quarter of Cavalier's sales are on credit. Each company has been in operation for about 10 years. Both companies received an unqualified audit opinion on the financial statements. Royale Company wants to borrow $75,000 cash, and Cavalier Company is asking for $30,000. The loans will be for a two-year period. Both companies estimate bad debts based on an aging analysis, but Cavalier has estimated slightly higher uncollectible rates than Royale. Neither company issued stock in 2013. Assume the end-of-year total assets and net property and equipment balances approximate the year's average.

Required:

1. Calculate the ratios in Exhibit 13.5 for which sufficient information is available. Round all calculations to two decimal places.

2. Assume that you work in the loan department of a local bank. You have been asked to analyze the situation and recommend which loan is preferable. Based on the data given, your analysis prepared in requirement 1, and any other information (e.g., accounting policies and decisions), give your choice and the supporting explanation.

LO 13-5   **PA13-7 Analyzing an Investment by Comparing Selected Ratios**

You have the opportunity to invest $10,000 in one of two companies from a single industry. The only information you have is shown here. The word *high* refers to the top third of the industry; *average* is the middle third; *low* is the bottom third.

Ratio	Company A	Company B
Current	Low	High
Inventory turnover	High	Low
Debt to assets	Low	Average
Times interest earned	High	Average
Price/earnings	High	Average

Required:

Which company would you select? Write a brief explanation for your recommendation.

GROUP B PROBLEMS

PB13-1 Analyzing Financial Statements Using Horizontal and Ratio Analyses

LO 13-2, 13-4, 13-5

The comparative financial statements prepared at December 31, 2013, for Tiger Audio showed the following summarized data:

	2013	2012	Increase (Decrease) in 2013 (versus 2012)	
			Amount	Percentage
Income Statement				
Sales Revenue	$222,000	$185,000		
Cost of Goods Sold	127,650	111,000		
Gross Profit	94,350	74,000		
Operating Expenses	39,600	33,730		
Interest Expense	4,000	3,270		
Income before Income Tax Expense	50,750	37,000		
Income Tax Expense (30%)	15,225	11,100		
Net Income	$ 35,525	$ 25,900		
Balance Sheet				
Cash	$ 40,000	$ 38,000		
Accounts Receivable, Net	18,500	16,000		
Inventory	25,000	22,000		
Property and Equipment, Net	127,000	119,000		
Total Assets	$210,500	$195,000		
Accounts Payable	$ 27,000	$ 25,000		
Income Tax Payable	3,000	2,800		
Note Payable, Long-term	75,500	92,200		
Total Liabilities	105,500	120,000		
Capital Stock (par $1)	25,000	25,000		
Retained Earnings	80,000	50,000		
Total Liabilities and Stockholders' Equity	$210,500	$195,000		

Required:

1. Complete the two final columns shown beside each item in Tiger Audio's comparative financial statements. Round the percentages to one decimal place.
2. Which account increased by the largest dollar amount? Which account increased by the largest percentage?

PB13-2 Analyzing Comparative Financial Statements Using Selected Ratios

LO 13-4, 13-5

Use the data given in PB13-1 for Tiger Audio.

Required:

1. Compute the gross profit percentage in 2013 and 2012. Is the trend going in the right direction?
2. Compute the net profit margin for 2013 and 2012. Is the trend going in the right direction?
3. Compute the earnings per share for 2013 and 2012. Does the trend look good or bad? Explain.
4. Stockholders' equity totaled $65,000 at the end of 2011. Compute the return on equity ratios for 2013 and 2012. Is the trend going in the right direction?
5. Net property and equipment totaled $115,000 at the end of 2011. Compute the fixed asset turnover ratios for 2013 and 2012. Is the trend going in the right direction?
6. Compute the debt-to-assets ratios for 2013 and 2012. Is debt providing financing for a larger or smaller proportion of the company's asset growth? Explain.

7. Compute the times interest earned ratios for 2013 and 2012. Do they look good or bad? Explain.

8. After Tiger released its 2013 financial statements, the company's stock was trading at $17. After the release of its 2012 financial statements, the company's stock price was $12 per share. Compute the P/E ratios for both years. Does it appear that investors have become more (or less) optimistic about Tiger's future success?

LO 13-3, 13-5

PB13-3 Vertical Analysis of a Balance Sheet

A condensed balance sheet for Southwest Airlines and a partially completed vertical analysis are presented below.

SOUTHWEST AIRLINES
Balance Sheet (summarized)
December 31, 2010
(in millions of U.S. dollars)

Cash	$ 1,261	8%	Current Liabilities	$ 3,305	b%
Accounts Receivable	195	1	Long-term Liabilities	5,921	38
Inventory of Parts and Supplies	243	2	Total Liabilities	9,226	60
Other Current Assets	2,580	17	Contributed Capital	1,100	7
Property and Equipment, Net	10,578	a	Retained Earnings	5,137	33
Other Assets	606	4	Total Stockholders' Equity	6,237	c
Total Assets	$15,463	100%	Total Liabilities & Stockholders' Equity	$15,463	100%

Required:

1. Complete the vertical analysis by computing each line item (a)–(c) as a percentage of total assets. Round to the nearest whole percentage.

2. What percentages of Southwest's assets relate to inventory of parts and supplies versus property and equipment? What does this tell you about the relative significance of these two assets to Southwest's business?

3. What percentage of Southwest's assets is financed by total stockholders' equity? By total liabilities?

LO 13-3, 13-5

PB13-4 Vertical Analysis of an Income Statement

A condensed income statement for Southwest Airlines and a partially completed vertical analysis are presented below.

SOUTHWEST AIRLINES
Income Statement (summarized)
For the Year Ended December 31
(in millions of U.S. dollars)

	2010		2009	
Sales Revenues	$12,104	100%	$10,350	100%
Salaries, Wages, and Benefits	3,704	31	3,468	d
Fuel, Oil, Repairs, and Maintenance	3,620	a	3,044	29
Other Operating Expenses	3,792	b	3,576	35
Other Expenses (Revenues)	243	2	98	1
Income before Income Tax Expense	745	6	164	e
Income Tax Expense	286	2	65	1
Net Income	459	c%	99	f%

Required:

1. Complete the vertical analysis by computing each line item (a)–(f) as a percentage of sales revenues. Round to the nearest whole percentage.

2. Does the percentage that you calculated in 1(a) suggest that Southwest tried to increase its profit by cutting repairs and maintenance costs in 2010 compared to 2009?

3. Refer to the percentages that you calculated in 1(c) and (f). Is Southwest's net profit margin improving or declining?

PB13-5 Interpreting Profitability, Liquidity, Solvency, and P/E Ratios

LO 13-4, 13-5

Mattel, Inc.

Mattel and Hasbro are the two biggest makers of games and toys in the world. Mattel sells nearly $6 billion of products each year while annual sales of Hasbro products exceed $4 billion. Compare the two companies as a potential investment based on the following ratios:

Ratio	Mattel	Hasbro
Gross profit percentage	50.5%	57.2%
Net profit margin	11.7%	9.9%
Return on equity	26.1%	6.8%
EPS	$ 1.86	$ 2.74
Receivables turnover ratio	5.1	4.2
Inventory turnover ratio	6.3	4.7
Current ratio	2.39	3.09
Debt to assets	0.51	0.61
P/E ratio	13.2	16.1

Required:

1. Which company appears more profitable? Describe the ratio(s) that you used to reach this decision.

2. Which company appears more liquid? Describe the ratio(s) that you used to reach this decision.

3. Which company appears more solvent? Describe the ratio(s) that you used to reach this decision.

4. Are the conclusions from your analyses in requirements 1–3 consistent with the value of the two companies, as suggested by their P/E ratios? If not, offer one explanation for any apparent inconsistency.

PB13-6 Using Ratios to Compare Loan Requests from Two Companies

LO 13-4, 13-5, 13-6

The 2013 financial statements for Thor and Gunnar Companies are summarized here

	Thor Company	Gunnar Company
Balance Sheet		
Cash	$ 35,000	$ 54,000
Accounts Receivable, Net	77,000	6,000
Inventory	154,000	30,000
Property and Equipment, Net	770,000	192,000
Other Assets	196,000	68,400
Total Assets	$1,232,000	$350,400
Current Liabilities	$ 168,000	$ 18,000
Long-term Debt (12% interest rate)	266,000	66,000
Capital Stock (par $20)	672,000	252,000
Additional Paid-in Capital	70,000	4,800
Retained Earnings	56,000	9,600
Total Liabilities and Stockholders' Equity	$1,232,000	$350,400
Income Statement		
Sales Revenue	$1,120,000	$336,000
Cost of Goods Sold	(672,000)	(180,000)
Other Expenses	(336,000)	(114,000)
Net Income	$ 112,000	$ 42,000
Selected Data from 2012 Statements		
Accounts Receivable, Net	$ 65,800	$ 13,200
Inventory	133,000	45,600
Property and Equipment, Net	770,000	192,000
Long-term Debt (12% interest rate)	266,000	66,000
Total Stockholders' Equity	798,000	266,400
Other Data		
Per share price at end of 2013	$ 13.20	$ 19.60

These two companies are in the same business and state but different cities. One-half of Thor's sales and one-quarter of Gunnar's sales are on credit. Each company has been in operation for about 10 years. Both companies received an unqualified audit opinion on the financial statements. Thor Company wants to borrow $105,000, and Gunnar Company is asking for $36,000. The loans will be for a two-year period. Neither company issued stock in 2013. Assume the end-of-year total assets and net property and equipment balances approximate the year's average.

Required:

1. Calculate the ratios in Exhibit 13.5 for which sufficient information is available. Round all calculations to two decimal places.

2. Assume that you work in the loan department of a local bank. You have been asked to analyze the situation and recommend which loan is preferable. Based on the data given, your analysis prepared in requirement 1, and any other information, give your choice and the supporting explanation.

LO 13-5   **PB13-7 Analyzing an Investment by Comparing Selected Ratios**

You have the opportunity to invest $10,000 in one of two companies from a single industry. The only information you have is shown here. The word *high* refers to the top third of the industry; *average* is the middle third; *low* is the bottom third.

Ratio	Company A	Company B
EPS	High	High
Return on equity	High	Average
Debt to assets	High	Low
Current	Low	Average
Price/earnings	Low	High

Required:

Which company would you select? Write a brief explanation for your recommendation.

SKILLS DEVELOPMENT CASES

LO 13-4   **S13-1 Computing Ratios**

Compute the following ratios for The Home Depot's year ended January 30, 2011: fixed asset turnover, days to sell, and debt-to-assets. To calculate the ratios, use the financial statements of The Home Depot in Appendix A at the end of this book, or download them from the *Cases* section of the text's Web site at www.mhhe.com/phillips4e.

a. 2.69; 85; 0.53
b. 2.71; 85; 0.53
c. 2.69; 85; 1.12
d. 2.69; 87; 1.12

LO 13-5   **S13-2 Evaluating Financial Information**

Lumber Liquidators, Inc.
Lowe's

Lumber Liquidators, Inc., competes with Lowe's in product lines such as hardwood flooring, moldings, and noise-reducing underlay. The two companies reported the following financial results in fiscal 2010:

	Lumber Liquidators	Lowe's
Gross profit percentage	34.8%	35.1%
Net profit margin	4.2%	4.1%
Return on equity	14.6%	11.1%
Earnings per share	$ 0.96	$ 1.42

Required:

1. Explain how Lowe's could have a higher gross profit percentage than Lumber Liquidators but a nearly identical net profit margin. What does this suggest about the relative ability of the two companies to control operating expenses?

2. Explain how Lumber Liquidators could have a higher return on equity but lower earnings per share. What does this suggest about the companies' relative number of outstanding shares? What other explanations could account for this seemingly contradictory pattern?

S13-3 Internet-Based Team Research: Examining an Annual Report

LO 13-1, 13-2, 13-3, 13-4, 13-5, 13-6

As a team, select an industry to analyze. Using your Web browser, each team member should access the annual report or 10-K for one publicly traded company in the industry, with each member selecting a different company. (See S1-3 in Chapter 1 for a description of possible resources for these tasks.)

Required:

1. On an individual basis, each team member should write a short report that incorporates horizontal and vertical analyses and as many of the ratios from the chapter as are applicable given the nature of the selected company.

2. Then, as a team, write a short report comparing and contrasting your companies using these attributes. Discuss any patterns across the companies that you as a team observe. Provide potential explanations for any differences discovered. Consider the impact of differences in accounting policies.

S13-4 Ethical Decision Making: A Real-Life Example

LO 13-6

This case is available online at www.mhhe.com/phillips4e. To complete this case, you will consider the negative effects of auditors (a) failing to identify going-concern problems that exist and (b) reporting going-concern problems that do not exist.

S13-5 Ethical Decision Making: A Mini-Case

LO 13-4, 13-5

Capital Investments Corporation (CIC) requested a sizable loan from First Federal Bank to acquire a large piece of land for future expansion. CIC reported current assets of $1,900,000 (including $430,000 in cash) and current liabilities of $1,075,000. First Federal denied the loan request for a number of reasons, including the fact that the current ratio was below 2:1. When CIC was informed of the loan denial, the controller of the company immediately paid $420,000 that was owed to several trade creditors. The controller then asked First Federal to reconsider the loan application. Based on these abbreviated facts, would you recommend that First Federal approve the loan request? Why? Are the controller's actions ethical?

S13-6 Critical Thinking: Analyzing the Impact of Alternative Depreciation Methods on Ratio Analysis

LO 13-4, 13-5, 13-6

Speedy Company uses the double-declining-balance method to depreciate its property, plant, and equipment, and Turtle Company uses the straight-line method. The two companies are exactly alike except for the difference in depreciation methods.

Required:

1. Identify the financial ratios discussed in this chapter that are likely to be affected by the difference in depreciation methods.

2. Which company will report the higher amount for each ratio that you have identified in response to requirement 1? If you cannot be certain, explain why.

S13-7 Using a Spreadsheet to Calculate Financial Statement Ratios

LO 13-2 13-3

Enter the account names and dollar amounts from the comparative balance sheets in Exhibit 13.1 into a worksheet in a spreadsheet file. Create a second copy of the worksheet in the same spreadsheet file.

Required:

1. To the right of the comparative numbers in the first worksheet, enter the necessary formulas to compute the amount and percent change as shown in Exhibit 13.1.

2. To the right of each column in the second worksheet, enter the necessary formulas to create common size statements similar to those shown in Exhibit 13.3.

CONTINUING CASE

LO 13-4, 13-5   **CC13-1 Evaluating Profitability, Liquidity, and Solvency**

Looking back over the last few years it is clear that Nicole Mackisey has accomplished a lot running her business Nicole's Getaway Spa (NGS). Nicole is curious about her company's performance as she compares its financial statements.

	2015	2014	2013
Balance Sheet			
Cash	$ 6,700	$ 4,200	$ 3,800
Accounts Receivable, Net	2,000	2,500	1,800
Inventory	1,200	3,000	1,600
Prepaid Expenses	750	1,050	200
Other Current Assets	300	350	200
Total Current Assets	10,950	11,100	7,600
Property and Equipment, Net	64,000	79,000	27,000
Total Assets	$74,950	$90,100	$34,600
Current Liabilities	$ 8,000	$ 8,000	$ 9,000
Long-term Liabilities	35,000	50,000	14,000
Total Liabilities	43,000	58,000	23,000
Contributed Capital	25,000	30,000	10,900
Retained Earnings	6,950	2,100	700
Total Stockholders' Equity	31,950	32,100	11,600
Total Liabilities and Stockholders' Equity	$74,950	$90,100	$34,600
Income Statement			
Sales Revenue	$80,000	$56,000	$44,000
Cost of Goods Sold	65,000	48,000	35,000
Gross Profit	15,000	8,000	9,000
Operating Expenses	4,000	2,000	7,000
Income from Operations	11,000	6,000	2,000
Interest Expense	1,000	3,100	800
Income before Income Tax Expense	10,000	2,900	1,200
Income Tax Expense	3,050	800	500
Net Income	$ 6,950	$ 2,100	$ 700

Required:

1. Was NGS more profitable in 2014 or 2015? Use the gross profit percentage, return on equity, and asset turnover ratio to help in making a decision (round each ratio to two decimal places).

2. Was NGS more liquid in 2014 or 2015? Use the current ratio and quick ratio to help in making a decision (round each ratio to two decimal places).

3. Was NGS more solvent in 2014 or 2015? Use the debt-to-assets ratio and times interest earned ratio to help in making a decision (round each ratio to two decimal places).

APPENDIX A

Excerpts from the Fiscal 2010 Annual Report of The Home Depot, Inc.

Note: The materials in Appendix A are selected from the full Annual Report of The Home Depot, Inc., for fiscal year 2010, which ended January 30, 2011. The complete annual report is available from the textbook Web site at www.mhhe.com/phillips4e or from www.homedepotar.com/.

A2   Management's Reports

A3   Reports of Independent Registered Public Accounting Firm

A5   Financial Statements

A9   Excerpt from Notes to Consolidated Financial Statements

Management's Responsibility for Financial Statements

The financial statements presented in this Annual Report have been prepared with integrity and objectivity and are the responsibility of the management of The Home Depot, Inc. These financial statements have been prepared in conformity with U.S. generally accepted accounting principles and properly reflect certain estimates and judgments based upon the best available information.

The financial statements of the Company have been audited by KPMG LLP, an independent registered public accounting firm. Their accompanying report is based upon an audit conducted in accordance with the standards of the Public Company Accounting Oversight Board (United States).

The Audit Committee of the Board of Directors, consisting solely of independent directors, meets five times a year with the independent registered public accounting firm, the internal auditors and representatives of management to discuss auditing and financial reporting matters. In addition, a telephonic meeting is held prior to each quarterly earnings release. The Audit Committee retains the independent registered public accounting firm and regularly reviews the internal accounting controls, the activities of the independent registered public accounting firm and internal auditors and the financial condition of the Company. Both the Company's independent registered public accounting firm and the internal auditors have free access to the Audit Committee.

Management's Report on Internal Control over Financial Reporting

Our management is responsible for establishing and maintaining adequate internal control over financial reporting, as such term is defined in Rule 13a-15(f) promulgated under the Securities Exchange Act of 1934, as amended (the "Exchange Act"). Under the supervision and with the participation of our management, including our Chief Executive Officer and Chief Financial Officer, we conducted an evaluation of the effectiveness of our internal control over financial reporting as of January 30, 2011 based on the framework in *Internal Control—Integrated Framework* issued by the Committee of Sponsoring Organizations of the Treadway Commission (COSO). Based on our evaluation, our management concluded that our internal control over financial reporting was effective as of January 30, 2011 in providing reasonable assurance regarding the reliability of financial reporting and the preparation of financial statements for external purposes in accordance with U.S. generally accepted accounting principles. The effectiveness of our internal control over financial reporting as of January 30, 2011 has been audited by KPMG LLP, an independent registered public accounting firm.

/s/ FRANCIS S. BLAKE

Francis S. Blake
Chairman &
Chief Executive Officer

/s/ CAROL B. TOMÉ

Carol B. Tomé
Chief Financial Officer &
Executive Vice President—Corporate Services

Report of Independent Registered Public Accounting Firm

The Board of Directors and Stockholders
The Home Depot, Inc.:

We have audited The Home Depot Inc.'s internal control over financial reporting as of January 30, 2011, based on criteria established in *Internal Control—Integrated Framework* issued by the Committee of Sponsoring Organizations of the Treadway Commission (COSO). The Home Depot Inc.'s management is responsible for maintaining effective internal control over financial reporting and for its assessment of the effectiveness of internal control over financial reporting, included in the accompanying Management's Report on Internal Control Over Financial Reporting. Our responsibility is to express an opinion on the Company's internal control over financial reporting based on our audit.

We conducted our audit in accordance with the standards of the Public Company Accounting Oversight Board (United States). Those standards require that we plan and perform the audit to obtain reasonable assurance about whether effective internal control over financial reporting was maintained in all material respects. Our audit included obtaining an understanding of internal control over financial reporting, assessing the risk that a material weakness exists, and testing and evaluating the design and operating effectiveness of internal control based on the assessed risk. Our audit also included performing such other procedures as we considered necessary in the circumstances. We believe that our audit provides a reasonable basis for our opinion.

A company's internal control over financial reporting is a process designed to provide reasonable assurance regarding the reliability of financial reporting and the preparation of financial statements for external purposes in accordance with generally accepted accounting principles. A company's internal control over financial reporting includes those policies and procedures that (1) pertain to the maintenance of records that, in reasonable detail, accurately and fairly reflect the transactions and dispositions of the assets of the company; (2) provide reasonable assurance that transactions are recorded as necessary to permit preparation of financial statements in accordance with generally accepted accounting principles, and that receipts and expenditures of the company are being made only in accordance with authorizations of management and directors of the company; and (3) provide reasonable assurance regarding prevention or timely detection of unauthorized acquisition, use, or disposition of the company's assets that could have a material effect on the financial statements.

Because of its inherent limitations, internal control over financial reporting may not prevent or detect misstatements. Also, projections of any evaluation of effectiveness to future periods are subject to the risk that controls may become inadequate because of changes in conditions, or that the degree of compliance with the policies or procedures may deteriorate.

In our opinion, The Home Depot, Inc. maintained, in all material respects, effective internal control over financial reporting as of January 30, 2011, based on criteria established in *Internal Control—Integrated Framework* issued by the Committee of Sponsoring Organizations of the Treadway Commission.

We also have audited, in accordance with the standards of the Public Company Accounting Oversight Board (United States), the Consolidated Balance Sheets of The Home Depot, Inc. and subsidiaries as of January 30, 2011 and January 31, 2010, and the related Consolidated Statements of Earnings, Stockholders' Equity and Comprehensive Income, and Cash Flows for each of the fiscal years in the three-year period ended January 30, 2011, and our report dated March 24, 2011 expressed an unqualified opinion on those consolidated financial statements.

/s/ KPMG LLP

Atlanta, Georgia
March 24, 2011

Report of Independent Registered Public Accounting Firm

The Board of Directors and Stockholders
The Home Depot, Inc.:

We have audited the accompanying Consolidated Balance Sheets of The Home Depot, Inc. and subsidiaries as of January 30, 2011 and January 31, 2010, and the related Consolidated Statements of Earnings, Stockholders' Equity and Comprehensive Income, and Cash Flows for each of the fiscal years in the three-year period ended January 30, 2011. These Consolidated Financial Statements are the responsibility of the Company's management. Our responsibility is to express an opinion on these Consolidated Financial Statements based on our audits.

We conducted our audits in accordance with the standards of the Public Company Accounting Oversight Board (United States). Those standards require that we plan and perform the audit to obtain reasonable assurance about whether the financial statements are free of material misstatement. An audit includes examining, on a test basis, evidence supporting the amounts and disclosures in the financial statements. An audit also includes assessing the accounting principles used and significant estimates made by management, as well as evaluating the overall financial statement presentation. We believe that our audits provide a reasonable basis for our opinion.

In our opinion, the Consolidated Financial Statements referred to above present fairly, in all material respects, the financial position of The Home Depot, Inc. and subsidiaries as of January 30, 2011 and January 31, 2010, and the results of their operations and their cash flows for each of the fiscal years in the three-year period ended January 30, 2011, in conformity with U.S. generally accepted accounting principles.

We also have audited, in accordance with the standards of the Public Company Accounting Oversight Board (United States), The Home Depot, Inc.'s internal control over financial reporting as of January 30, 2011, based on criteria established in *Internal Control—Integrated Framework* issued by the Committee of Sponsoring Organizations of the Treadway Commission (COSO), and our report dated March 24, 2011 expressed an unqualified opinion on the effectiveness of the Company's internal control over financial reporting.

/s/ KPMG LLP

Atlanta, Georgia
March 24, 2011

THE HOME DEPOT, INC., AND SUBSIDIARIES
Consolidated Statements of Earnings

	Fiscal Year Ended[1]		
amounts in millions, except per share data	January 30, 2011	January 31, 2010	February 1, 2009
NET SALES	$67,997	$66,176	$71,288
Cost of Sales	44,693	43,764	47,298
GROSS PROFIT	23,304	22,412	23,990
Operating Expenses:			
Selling, General and Administrative	15,849	15,902	17,846
Depreciation and Amortization	1,616	1,707	1,785
Total Operating Expenses	17,465	17,609	19,631
OPERATING INCOME	5,839	4,803	4,359
Interest and Other (Income) Expense:			
Interest and Investment Income	(15)	(18)	(18)
Interest Expense	530	676	624
Other	51	163	163
Interest and Other, net	566	821	769
EARNINGS FROM CONTINUING OPERATIONS BEFORE PROVISION FOR INCOME TAXES	5,273	3,982	3,590
Provision for Income Taxes	1,935	1,362	1,278
EARNINGS FROM CONTINUING OPERATIONS	3,338	2,620	2,312
EARNINGS (LOSS) FROM DISCONTINUED OPERATIONS, NET OF TAX	—	41	(52)
NET EARNINGS	$ 3,338	$ 2,661	$ 2,260
Weighted Average Common Shares	1,648	1,683	1,682
BASIC EARNINGS PER SHARE FROM CONTINUING OPERATIONS	$ 2.03	$ 1.56	$ 1.37
BASIC EARNINGS (LOSS) PER SHARE FROM DISCONTINUED OPERATIONS	$ —	$ 0.02	$ (0.03)
BASIC EARNINGS PER SHARE	$ 2.03	$ 1.58	$ 1.34
Diluted Weighted Average Common Shares	1,658	1,692	1,686
DILUTED EARNINGS PER SHARE FROM CONTINUING OPERATIONS	$ 2.01	$ 1.55	$ 1.37
DILUTED EARNINGS (LOSS) PER SHARE FROM DISCONTINUED OPERATIONS	$ —	$ 0.02	$ (0.03)
DILUTED EARNINGS PER SHARE	$ 2.01	$ 1.57	$ 1.34

(1) Fiscal years ended January 30, 2011, January 31, 2010 and February 1, 2009 include 52 weeks.

See accompanying Notes to Consolidated Financial Statements.

THE HOME DEPOT, INC., AND SUBSIDIARIES
Consolidated Balance Sheets

amounts in millions, except share and per share data	January 30, 2011	January 31, 2010
ASSETS		
Current Assets:		
Cash and Cash Equivalents	$ 545	$ 1,421
Receivables, net	1,085	964
Merchandise Inventories	10,625	10,188
Other Current Assets	1,224	1,327
Total Current Assets	13,479	13,900
Property and Equipment, at cost:		
Land	8,497	8,451
Buildings	17,606	17,391
Furniture, Fixtures and Equipment	9,687	9,091
Leasehold Improvements	1,373	1,383
Construction in Progress	654	525
Capital Leases	568	504
	38,385	37,345
Less Accumulated Depreciation and Amortization	13,325	11,795
Net Property and Equipment	25,060	25,550
Notes Receivable	139	33
Goodwill	1,187	1,171
Other Assets	260	223
Total Assets	**$40,125**	**$40,877**
LIABILITIES AND STOCKHOLDERS' EQUITY		
Current Liabilities:		
Accounts Payable	$ 4,717	$ 4,863
Accrued Salaries and Related Expenses	1,290	1,263
Sales Taxes Payable	368	362
Deferred Revenue	1,177	1,158
Income Taxes Payable	13	108
Current Installments of Long-Term Debt	1,042	1,020
Other Accrued Expenses	1,515	1,589
Total Current Liabilities	10,122	10,363
Long-Term Debt, excluding current installments	8,707	8,662
Other Long-Term Liabilities	2,135	2,140
Deferred Income Taxes	272	319
Total Liabilities	21,236	21,484
STOCKHOLDERS' EQUITY		
Common Stock, par value $0.05; authorized: 10 billion shares; issued: 1.722 billion shares at January 30, 2011 and 1.716 billion shares at January 31, 2010; outstanding: 1.623 billion shares at January 30, 2011 and 1.698 billion shares at January 31, 2010	86	86
Paid-In Capital	6,556	6,304
Retained Earnings	14,995	13,226
Accumulated Other Comprehensive Income	445	362
Treasury Stock, at cost, 99 million shares at January 30, 2011 and 18 million shares at January 31, 2010	(3,193)	(585)
Total Stockholders' Equity	18,889	19,393
Total Liabilities and Stockholders' Equity	**$40,125**	**$40,877**

See accompanying Notes to Consolidated Financial Statements.

THE HOME DEPOT, INC., AND SUBSIDIARIES
Consolidated Statements of Stockholders' Equity and Comprehensive Income

amounts in millions, except per share data	Common Stock Shares	Amount	Paid-In Capital	Retained Earnings	Accumulated Other Comprehensive Income (Loss)	Treasury Stock Shares	Amount	Stockholders' Equity	Total Income Comprehensive
BALANCE, FEBRUARY 3, 2008	1,698	$85	$5,800	$11,388	$ 755	(8)	$ (314)	$17,714	
Net Earnings	—	—	—	2,260	—	—	—	2,260	$2,260
Shares Issued Under Employee Stock Plans	9	—	68	—	—	—	—	68	
Tax Effect of Sale of Option Shares by Employees	—	—	7	—	—	—	—	7	
Translation Adjustments	—	—	—	—	(831)	—	—	(831)	(831)
Cash Flow Hedges, net of tax	—	—	—	—	(1)	—	—	(1)	(1)
Stock Options, Awards and Amortization of Restricted Stock	—	—	176	—	—	—	—	176	
Repurchases of Common Stock	—	—	—	—	—	(3)	(70)	(70)	
Cash Dividends ($0.90 per share)	—	—	—	(1,521)	—	—	—	(1,521)	
Other	—	—	(3)	(34)	—	—	12	(25)	
Comprehensive Income									$1,428
BALANCE, FEBRUARY 1, 2009	1,707	$85	$6,048	$12,093	$(77)	(11)	$ (372)	$17,777	
Net Earnings	—	—	—	2,661	—	—	—	2,661	$2,661
Shares Issued Under Employee Stock Plans	9	1	57	—	—	—	—	58	
Tax Effect of Sale of Option Shares by Employees	—	—	(2)	—	—	—	—	(2)	
Translation Adjustments	—	—	—	—	426	—	—	426	426
Cash Flow Hedges, net of tax	—	—	—	—	11	—	—	11	11
Stock Options, Awards and Amortization of Restricted Stock	—	—	201	—	—	—	—	201	
Repurchases of Common Stock	—	—	—	—	—	(7)	(213)	(213)	
Cash Dividends ($0.90 per share)	—	—	—	(1,525)	—	—	—	(1,525)	
Other	—	—	—	(3)	2	—	—	(1)	2
Comprehensive Income									$3,100
BALANCE, JANUARY 31, 2010	1,716	$86	$6,304	$13,226	$362	(18)	$ (585)	$19,393	
Net Earnings	—	—	—	3,338	—	—	—	3,338	$3,338
Shares Issued Under Employee Stock Plans	6	—	42	—	—	—	—	42	
Tax Effect of Sale of Option Shares by Employees	—	—	2	—	—	—	—	2	
Translation Adjustments	—	—	—	—	206	—	—	206	206
Cash Flow Hedges, net of tax	—	—	—	—	(116)	—	—	(116)	(116)
Stock Options, Awards and Amortization of Restricted Stock	—	—	214	—	—	—	—	214	
Repurchases of Common Stock	—	—	—	—	—	(81)	(2,608)	(2,608)	
Cash Dividends ($0.945 per share)	—	—	—	(1,569)	—	—	—	(1,569)	
Other	—	—	(6)	—	(7)	—	—	(13)	(7)
Comprehensive Income									$3,421
BALANCE, JANUARY 30, 2011	1,722	$86	$6,556	$14,995	$445	(99)	$(3,193)	$18,889	

See accompanying Notes to Consolidated Financial Statements.

THE HOME DEPOT, INC., AND SUBSIDIARIES
Consolidated Statements of Cash Flows

	Fiscal Year Ended[1]		
amounts in millions	January 30, 2011	January 31, 2010	February 1, 2009
CASH FLOWS FROM OPERATING ACTIVITIES:			
Net Earnings	$3,338	$2,661	$2,260
Reconciliation of Net Earnings to Net Cash Provided by Operating Activities:			
Depreciation and Amortization	1,718	1,806	1,902
Impairment Related to Rationalization Charges	—	—	580
Impairment of Investment	—	163	163
Stock-Based Compensation Expense	214	201	176
Changes in Assets and Liabilities:			
(Increase) Decrease in Receivables, net	(102)	(23)	121
(Increase) Decrease in Merchandise Inventories	(355)	625	743
Decrease (Increase) in Other Current Assets	12	4	(7)
(Decrease) Increase in Accounts Payable and Accrued Expenses	(133)	59	(646)
Increase (Decrease) in Deferred Revenue	10	(21)	(292)
(Decrease) Increase in Income Taxes Payable	(85)	(174)	262
Increase (Decrease) in Deferred Income Taxes	104	(227)	(282)
(Decrease) Increase in Other Long-Term Liabilities	(61)	(19)	306
Other	(75)	70	242
Net Cash Provided by Operating Activities	4,585	5,125	5,528
CASH FLOWS FROM INVESTING ACTIVITIES:			
Capital Expenditures, net of $62, $10 and $37 of non-cash capital expenditures in fiscal 2010, 2009 and 2008, respectively	(1,096)	(966)	(1,847)
Proceeds from Sales of Property and Equipment	84	178	147
Purchases of Investments	—	—	(168)
Proceeds from Sales and Maturities of Investments	—	33	139
Net Cash Used in Investing Activities	(1,012)	(755)	(1,729)
CASH FLOWS FROM FINANCING ACTIVITIES:			
Repayments of Short-Term Borrowings, net	—	—	(1,732)
Proceeds from Long-Term Borrowings, net of discount	998	—	—
Repayments of Long-Term Debt	(1,029)	(1,774)	(313)
Repurchases of Common Stock	(2,608)	(213)	(70)
Proceeds from Sales of Common Stock	104	73	84
Cash Dividends Paid to Stockholders	(1,569)	(1,525)	(1,521)
Other Financing Activities	(347)	(64)	(128)
Net Cash Used in Financing Activities	(4,451)	(3,503)	(3,680)
(Decrease) Increase in Cash and Cash Equivalents	(878)	867	119
Effect of Exchange Rate Changes on Cash and Cash Equivalents	2	35	(45)
Cash and Cash Equivalents at Beginning of Year	1,421	519	445
Cash and Cash Equivalents at End of Year	$ 545	$1,421	$ 519
SUPPLEMENTAL DISCLOSURE OF CASH PAYMENTS MADE FOR:			
Interest, net of interest capitalized	$ 579	$ 664	$ 622
Income Taxes	$2,067	$2,082	$1,265

(1) *Fiscal years ended January 30, 2011, January 31, 2010 and February 1, 2009 include 52 weeks.*

See accompanying Notes to Consolidated Financial Statements

NOTES TO CONSOLIDATED FINANCIAL STATEMENTS

1. Summary of Significant Accounting Policies

Business, Consolidation and Presentation   The Home Depot, Inc. and its subsidiaries (the "Company") operate The Home Depot stores, which are full-service, warehouse-style stores averaging approximately 105,000 square feet in size. The stores stock approximately 30,000 to 40,000 different kinds of building materials, home improvement supplies and lawn and garden products that are sold to do-it-yourself customers, do-it-for-me customers and professional customers. At the end of fiscal 2010, the Company was operating 2,248 stores, which included 1,976 The Home Depot stores in the United States, including the Commonwealth of Puerto Rico and the territories of the U.S. Virgin Islands and Guam ("U.S."), 179 The Home Depot stores in Canada, 85 The Home Depot stores in Mexico and 8 The Home Depot stores in China. The Consolidated Financial Statements include the accounts of the Company and its wholly-owned subsidiaries. All significant intercompany transactions have been eliminated in consolidation.

Fiscal Year   The Company's fiscal year is a 52- or 53-week period ending on the Sunday nearest to January 31. Fiscal years ended January 30, 2011 ("fiscal 2010"), January 31, 2010 ("fiscal 2009") and February 1, 2009 ("fiscal 2008") include 52 weeks.

Use of Estimates   Management of the Company has made a number of estimates and assumptions relating to the reporting of assets and liabilities, the disclosure of contingent assets and liabilities, and reported amounts of revenues and expenses in preparing these financial statements in conformity with U.S. generally accepted accounting principles. Actual results could differ from these estimates.

Fair Value of Financial Instruments   The carrying amounts of Cash and Cash Equivalents, Receivables and Accounts Payable approximate fair value due to the short-term maturities of these financial instruments. The fair value of the Company's investments is discussed under the caption "Short-Term Investments" in this Note 1. The fair value of the Company's Long-Term Debt is discussed in Note 11.

Cash Equivalents   The Company considers all highly liquid investments purchased with original maturities of three months or less to be cash equivalents. The Company's cash equivalents are carried at fair market value and consist primarily of high-grade commercial paper, money market funds and U.S. government agency securities.

Short-Term Investments   Short-term investments are recorded at fair value based on current market rates and are classified as available-for-sale. The Company's short-term investments are included in Other Current Assets in the accompanying Consolidated Balance Sheets.

Accounts Receivable   The Company has an agreement with a third-party service provider who directly extends credit to customers, manages the Company's private label credit card program and owns the related receivables. The Company evaluated the third-party entities holding the receivables under the program and concluded that they should not be consolidated by the Company. The agreement with the third-party service provider expires in 2018, with the Company having the option, but no obligation, to purchase the receivables at the end of the agreement. The deferred interest charges incurred by the Company for its deferred financing programs offered to its customers are included in Cost of Sales. The interchange fees charged to the Company for the customers' use of the cards and the profit sharing with the third-party administrator are included in Selling, General and Administrative expenses ("SG&A"). The sum of the three is referred to by the Company as "the cost of credit" of the private label credit card program.

In addition, certain subsidiaries of the Company extend credit directly to customers in the ordinary course of business. The receivables due from customers were $42 million and $38 million as of January 30, 2011 and January 31, 2010, respectively. The Company's valuation reserve related to accounts receivable was not material to the Consolidated Financial Statements of the Company as of the end of fiscal 2010 or 2009.

Merchandise Inventories   The majority of the Company's Merchandise Inventories are stated at the lower of cost (first-in, first-out) or market, as determined by the retail inventory method. As the inventory retail value is adjusted regularly to reflect market conditions, the inventory valued using the retail method approximates the lower of cost or market. Certain subsidiaries, including retail operations in Canada, Mexico and China, and distribution centers, record Merchandise Inventories at the lower of cost or market, as determined by a cost method. These Merchandise Inventories represent approximately 20% of the total Merchandise Inventories balance. The Company evaluates the inventory valued using a cost method at the end of each quarter to ensure that it is carried at the lower of cost or market. The valuation allowance for Merchandise Inventories valued under a cost method was not material to the Consolidated Financial Statements of the Company as of the end of fiscal 2010 or 2009.

Independent physical inventory counts or cycle counts are taken on a regular basis in each store and distribution center to ensure that amounts reflected in the accompanying Consolidated Financial Statements for Merchandise Inventories are properly stated. During the period between physical inventory counts in stores, the Company accrues for estimated losses related to shrink on a store-by-store basis based on historical shrink results and current trends in the business. Shrink (or in the case of excess inventory, "swell") is the difference between the recorded amount of inventory and the physical inventory. Shrink may occur due to theft, loss, inaccurate records for the receipt of inventory or deterioration of goods, among other things.

Income Taxes   Income taxes are accounted for under the asset and liability method. The Company provides for federal, state and foreign income taxes currently payable, as well as for those deferred due to timing differences between reporting income and expenses for financial statement purposes versus tax purposes. Deferred tax assets and liabilities are recognized for the future tax consequences attributable to temporary differences between the financial statement carrying amounts of existing assets and liabilities and their respective tax bases. Deferred tax assets and liabilities are measured using enacted income tax rates expected to apply to taxable income in the years in which those temporary differences are expected to be recovered or settled. The effect of a change in income tax rates is recognized as income or expense in the period that includes the enactment date.

Depreciation and Amortization   The Company's Buildings, Furniture, Fixtures and Equipment are recorded at cost and depreciated using the straight-line method over the estimated useful lives of the assets. Leasehold Improvements are amortized using the straight-line method over the original term of the lease or the useful life of the improvement, whichever is shorter. The Company's Property and Equipment is depreciated using the following estimated useful lives:

	Life
Buildings	5–45 years
Furniture, Fixtures and Equipment	2–20 years
Leasehold Improvements	5–45 years

Capitalized Software Costs   The Company capitalizes certain costs related to the acquisition and development of software and amortizes these costs using the straight-line method over the estimated useful life of the software, which is three to six years. These costs are included in Furniture, Fixtures and Equipment in the accompanying Consolidated Balance Sheets. Certain development costs not meeting the criteria for capitalization are expensed as incurred.

Revenues   The Company recognizes revenue, net of estimated returns and sales tax, at the time the customer takes possession of merchandise or receives services. The liability for sales returns is estimated based on historical return levels. When the Company receives payment from customers before the customer has taken possession of the merchandise or the service has been performed, the amount received is recorded as Deferred Revenue in the accompanying Consolidated Balance Sheets until the sale or service is complete. The Company also records Deferred Revenue for the sale of gift cards and recognizes this revenue upon the redemption of gift cards in Net Sales. Gift card breakage income is recognized based upon historical redemption patterns and represents the balance of gift cards for which the Company believes the likelihood of redemption by the customer is remote. During fiscal 2010, 2009 and 2008, the Company recognized $46 million, $40 million and $37 million, respectively, of gift card breakage income. This income is included in the accompanying Consolidated Statements of Earnings as a reduction in SG&A.

Services Revenue   Net Sales include services revenue generated through a variety of installation, home maintenance and professional service programs. In these programs, the customer selects and purchases material for a project and the Company provides or arranges professional installation. These programs are offered through the Company's stores. Under certain programs, when the Company provides or arranges the installation of a project and the subcontractor provides material as part of the installation, both the material and labor are included in services revenue. The Company recognizes this revenue when the service for the customer is complete.

All payments received prior to the completion of services are recorded in Deferred Revenue in the accompanying Consolidated Balance Sheets. Services revenue was $2.7 billion, $2.6 billion and $3.1 billion for fiscal 2010, 2009 and 2008, respectively.

Self-Insurance   The Company is self-insured for certain losses related to general liability, workers' compensation, medical, product liability and automobile claims. The expected ultimate cost for claims incurred as of the balance sheet date is not discounted and is recognized as a liability. The expected ultimate cost of claims is estimated based upon analysis of historical data and actuarial estimates.

Prepaid Advertising   Television and radio advertising production costs, along with media placement costs, are expensed when the advertisement first appears. Amounts included in Other Current Assets in the accompanying Consolidated Balance Sheets relating to prepayments of production costs for print and broadcast advertising as well as sponsorship promotions were not material at the end of fiscal 2010 and 2009.

Vendor Allowances   Vendor allowances primarily consist of volume rebates that are earned as a result of attaining certain purchase levels and advertising co-op allowances for the promotion of vendors' products that are typically based on guaranteed minimum amounts with additional amounts being earned for attaining certain purchase levels. These vendor allowances are accrued as earned, with those allowances received as a result of attaining certain purchase levels accrued over the incentive period based on estimates of purchases.

Volume rebates and certain advertising co-op allowances earned are initially recorded as a reduction in Merchandise Inventories and a subsequent reduction in Cost of Sales when the related product is sold. Certain advertising co-op allowances that are reimbursements of specific, incremental and identifiable costs incurred to promote vendors' products are recorded as an offset against advertising expense. In fiscal 2010, 2009 and 2008, gross advertising expense was $864 million, $897 million and $1.0 billion, respectively, and is included in SG&A. Specific, incremental and identifiable advertising co-op allowances were $90 million, $105 million and $107 million for fiscal 2010, 2009 and 2008, respectively, and are recorded as an offset to advertising expense in SG&A.

Cost of Sales   Cost of Sales includes the actual cost of merchandise sold and services performed, the cost of transportation of merchandise from vendors to the Company's stores, locations or customers, the operating cost of the Company's sourcing and distribution network and the cost of deferred interest programs offered through the Company's private label credit card program.

The cost of handling and shipping merchandise from the Company's stores, locations or distribution centers to the customer is classified as SG&A. The cost of shipping and handling, including internal costs and payments to third parties, classified as SG&A was $438 million, $426 million and $501 million in fiscal 2010, 2009 and 2008, respectively.

Impairment of Long-Lived Assets   The Company evaluates its long-lived assets each quarter for indicators of potential impairment. Indicators of impairment include current period losses combined with a history of losses, management's decision to relocate or close a store or other location before the end of its previously estimated useful life, or when changes in other circumstances indicate the carrying amount of an asset may not be recoverable.

The assets of a store with indicators of impairment are evaluated by comparing its undiscounted cash flows with its carrying value. The estimate of cash flows includes management's assumptions of cash inflows and outflows directly resulting from the use of those assets in operations, including gross margin on Net Sales, payroll and related items, occupancy costs, insurance allocations and other costs to operate a store. If the carrying value is greater than the undiscounted cash flows, an impairment loss is recognized for the difference between the carrying value and the estimated fair market value. Impairment losses are recorded as a component of SG&A in the accompanying Consolidated Statements of Earnings. When a leased location closes, the Company also recognizes in SG&A the net present value of future lease obligations less estimated sublease income.

As part of its Rationalization Charges, the Company recorded no asset impairments in fiscal 2010 and 2009 and recorded $580 million of asset impairments in fiscal 2008. Also as part of its Rationalization Charges, the Company recorded no lease obligation costs in fiscal 2010 and recorded $84 million and $252 million of lease obligation costs in fiscal 2009 and 2008, respectively. See Note 2 for more details on the Rationalization Charges. The Company also recorded impairments and other lease obligation costs on other closings and relocations in the ordinary course of business, which were not material to the Consolidated Financial Statements in fiscal 2010, 2009 and 2008.

Goodwill and Other Intangible Assets   Goodwill represents the excess of purchase price over the fair value of net assets acquired. The Company does not amortize goodwill, but does assess the recoverability of goodwill in the third quarter of each fiscal year, or more often if indicators warrant, by determining whether the fair value of each reporting unit supports its carrying value. The fair values of the Company's identified reporting units were estimated using the present value of expected future discounted cash flows.

The Company amortizes the cost of other intangible assets over their estimated useful lives, which range up to 20 years, unless such lives are deemed indefinite. Intangible assets with indefinite lives are tested in the third quarter of each fiscal year for impairment, or more often if indicators warrant. Impairment charges related to goodwill and other intangible assets were not material for fiscal 2010, 2009 or 2008.

Comprehensive Income   Comprehensive Income includes Net Earnings adjusted for certain revenues, expenses, gains and losses that are excluded from Net Earnings under U.S. generally accepted accounting principles. Adjustments to Net Earnings and Accumulated Other Comprehensive Income consist primarily of foreign currency translation adjustments.

Foreign Currency Translation   Assets and liabilities denominated in a foreign currency are translated into U.S. dollars at the current rate of exchange on the last day of the reporting period. Revenues and expenses are generally translated using average exchange rates for the period and equity transactions are translated using the actual rate on the day of the transaction.

Other notes to the financial statements can be downloaded from the Web sites indicated on page A1.

APPENDIX B

Excerpts from the Fiscal 2010 Annual Report of Lowe's Companies, Inc.

Note: The materials in Appendix B are selected from the full Annual Report of Lowe's Companies, Inc., for fiscal year 2010, which ended January 28, 2011. The complete annual report is available from the textbook Web site at www.mhhe.com/phillips4e or from www.lowes.com/AboutLowes/AnnualReports/annual_report_10/index.html.

B2 Management's Report on Internal Control over Financial Reporting and Reports of Independent Registered Public Accounting Firm

B4 Financial Statements

B8 Excerpts from Notes to Consolidated Financial Statements

MANAGEMENT'S REPORT ON INTERNAL CONTROL OVER FINANCIAL REPORTING

Management of Lowe's Companies, Inc. and its subsidiaries is responsible for establishing and maintaining adequate internal control over financial reporting (Internal Control) as defined in Rule 13a-15(f) under the Securities Exchange Act of 1934, as amended. Our Internal Control was designed to provide reasonable assurance to our management and the Board of Directors regarding the reliability of financial reporting and the preparation and fair presentation of published financial statements.

All internal control systems, no matter how well designed, have inherent limitations, including the possibility of human error and the circumvention or overriding of controls. Therefore, even those systems determined to be effective can provide only reasonable assurance with respect to the reliability of financial reporting and financial statement preparation and presentation. Further, because of changes in conditions, the effectiveness may vary over time.

Our management, with the participation of the Chief Executive Officer and Chief Financial Officer, evaluated the effectiveness of our Internal Control as of January 28, 2011. In evaluating our Internal Control, we used the criteria set forth by the Committee of Sponsoring Organizations of the Treadway Commission (COSO) in *Internal Control—Integrated Framework*. Based on our management's assessment, we have concluded that, as of January 28, 2011, our Internal Control is effective.

Deloitte & Touche LLP, the independent registered public accounting firm that audited the financial statements contained in this report, was engaged to audit our Internal Control.

REPORT OF INDEPENDENT REGISTERED PUBLIC ACCOUNTING FIRM

To the Board of Directors and Shareholders of Lowe's Companies, Inc., Mooresville, North Carolina:

We have audited the accompanying consolidated balance sheets of Lowe's Companies, Inc. and subsidiaries (the "Company") as of January 28, 2011 and January 29, 2010, and the related consolidated statements of earnings, shareholders' equity, and cash flows for each of the three fiscal years in the period ended January 28, 2011. These financial statements are the responsibility of the Company's management. Our responsibility is to express an opinion on these financial statements based on our audits.

We conducted our audits in accordance with the standards of the Public Company Accounting Oversight Board (United States). Those standards require that we plan and perform the audit to obtain reasonable assurance about whether the financial statements are free of material misstatement. An audit includes examining, on a test basis, evidence supporting the amounts and disclosures in the financial statements. An audit also includes assessing the accounting principles used and significant estimates made by management, as well as evaluating the overall financial statement presentation. We believe that our audits provide a reasonable basis for our opinion.

In our opinion, such consolidated financial statements present fairly, in all material respects, the financial position of the Company at January 28, 2011 and January 29, 2010, and the results of its operations and its cash flows for each of the three fiscal years in the period ended January 28, 2011, in conformity with accounting principles generally accepted in the United States of America.

We have also audited, in accordance with the standards of the Public Company Accounting Oversight Board (United States), the Company's internal control over financial reporting as of January 28, 2011, based on the criteria established in *Internal Control—Integrated Framework* issued by the committee of Sponsoring Organizations of the Treadway Commission and our report dated March 28, 2011 expressed an unqualified opinion on the Company's internal control over financial reporting.

/s/ Deloitte & Touche LLP

Charlotte, North Carolina
March 28, 2011

REPORT OF INDEPENDENT REGISTERED PUBLIC ACCOUNTING FIRM

To the Board of Directors and Shareholders of Lowe's Companies, Inc., Mooresville, North Carolina:

We have audited the internal control over financial reporting of Lowe's Companies, Inc. and subsidiaries (the "Company") as of January 28, 2011, based on criteria established in *Internal Control -Integrated Framework* issued by the Committee of Sponsoring Organizations of the Treadway Commission. The Company's management is responsible for maintaining effective internal control over financial reporting and for its assessment of the effectiveness of internal control over financial reporting, included in the accompanying Management's Report on Internal Control Over Financial Reporting. Our responsibility is to express an opinion on the Company's internal control over financial reporting based on our audit.

We conducted our audit in accordance with the standards of the Public Company Accounting Oversight Board (United States). Those standards require that we plan and perform the audit to obtain reasonable assurance about whether effective internal control over financial reporting was maintained in all material respects. Our audit included obtaining an understanding of internal control over financial reporting, assessing the risk that a material weakness exists, testing and evaluating the design and operating effectiveness of internal control based on the assessed risk, and performing such other procedures as we considered necessary in the circumstances. We believe that our audit provides a reasonable basis for our opinion.

A company's internal control over financial reporting is a process designed by, or under the supervision of, the company's principal executive and principal financial officers, or persons performing similar functions, and effected by the company's board of directors, management, and other personnel to provide reasonable assurance regarding the reliability of financial reporting and the preparation of financial statements for external purposes in accordance with generally accepted accounting principles. A company's internal control over financial reporting includes those policies and procedures that (1) pertain to the maintenance of records that, in reasonable detail, accurately and fairly reflect the transactions and dispositions of the assets of the company; (2) provide reasonable assurance that transactions are recorded as necessary to permit preparation of financial statements in accordance with generally accepted accounting principles, and that receipts and expenditures of the company are being made only in accordance with authorizations of management and directors of the company; and (3) provide reasonable assurance regarding prevention or timely detection of unauthorized acquisition, use, or disposition of the company's assets that could have a material effect on the financial statements.

Because of the inherent limitations of internal control over financial reporting, including the possibility of collusion or improper management override of controls, material misstatements due to error or fraud may not be prevented or detected on a timely basis. Also, projections of any evaluation of the effectiveness of the internal control over financial reporting to future periods are subject to the risk that the controls may become inadequate because of changes in conditions, or that the degree of compliance with the policies or procedures may deteriorate.

In our opinion, the Company maintained, in all material respects, effective internal control over financial reporting as of January 28, 2011, based on the criteria established in *Internal Control—Integrated Framework* issued by the Committee of Sponsoring Organizations of the Treadway commission.

We have also audited, in accordance with the standards of the Public Company Accounting Oversight Board (United States), the consolidated financial statements as of and for the fiscal year ended January 28, 2011 of the Company and our report dated March 28, 2011 expressed an unqualified opinion on those financial statements.

/s/ Deloitte & Touche LLP

Charlotte, North Carolina
March 28, 2011

LOWE'S COMPANIES, INC.
Consolidated Statements of Earnings

(in millions, except per share and percentage data)

Fiscal years ended on	January 28, 2011	% Sales	January 29, 2010	% Sales	January 30, 2009	% Sales
Net sales	$48,815	100.00%	$47,220	100.00%	$48,230	100.00%
Cost of sales	31,663	64.86	30,757	65.14	31,729	65.79
Gross margin	17,152	35.14	16,463	34.86	16,501	34.21
Expenses:						
Selling, general and administrative	12,006	24.60	11,737	24.85	11,176	23.17
Depreciation	1,586	3.25	1,614	3.42	1,539	3.19
Interest—net	332	0.68	287	0.61	280	0.58
Total expenses	13,924	28.53	13,638	28.88	12,995	26.94
Pre-tax earnings	3,228	6.61	2,825	5.98	3,506	7.27
Income tax provision	1,218	2.49	1,042	2.20	1,311	2.72
Net earnings	$ 2,010	4.12%	$ 1,783	3.78%	$ 2,195	4.55%
Basic earnings per common share	$ 1.42		$ 1.21		$ 1.50	
Diluted earnings per common share	$ 1.42		$ 1.21		$ 1.49	
Cash dividends per share	$ 0.420		$ 0.355		$ 0.335	

See accompanying notes to consolidated financial statements.

LOWE'S COMPANIES, INC.
Consolidated Balance Sheets

(in millions, except par value and percentage data)	January 28, 2011	% Total	January 29, 2010	% Total
Assets				
Current assets:				
Cash and cash equivalents	$ 652	1.9%	$ 632	1.9%
Short-term investments	471	1.4	425	1.3
Merchandise inventory—net	8,321	24.7	8,249	25.0
Deferred income taxes—net	193	0.6	208	0.6
Other current assets	330	1.0	218	0.7
Total current assets	9,967	29.6	9,732	29.5
Property, less accumulated depreciation	22,089	65.5	22,499	68.2
Long-term investments	1,008	3.0	277	0.8
Other assets	635	1.9	497	1.5
Total assets	$33,699	100.0%	$33,005	100.0%
Liabilities and Shareholders' Equity				
Current liabilities:				
Current maturities of long-term debt	$ 36	0.1%	$ 552	1.7%
Accounts payable	4,351	12.9	4,287	13.0
Accrued compensation and employee benefits	667	2.0	577	1.7
Deferred revenue	707	2.1	683	2.1
Other current liabilities	1,358	4.0	1,256	3.8
Total current liabilities	7,119	21.1	7,355	22.3
Long-term debt, excluding current maturities	6,537	19.4	4,528	13.7
Deferred income taxes—net	467	1.4	598	1.8
Deferred revenue—extended protection plans	631	1.9	549	1.7
Other liabilities	833	2.5	906	2.7
Total liabilities	15,587	46.3	13,936	42.2
Commitments and contingencies				
Shareholders' equity:				
Preferred stock—$5 par value, none issued	—	—	—	—
Common stock—$.50 par value;				
Shares issued and outstanding				
January 28, 2011: 1,354				
January 29, 2010: 1,459	677	2.0	729	2.2
Capital in excess of par value	11	—	6	—
Retained earnings	17,371	51.5	18,307	55.5
Accumulated other comprehensive income	53	0.2	27	0.1
Total shareholders' equity	18,112	53.7	19,069	57.8
Total liabilities and shareholders' equity	$33,699	100.0%	$33,005	100.0%

See accompanying notes to consolidated financial statements.

LOWE'S COMPANIES, INC.
Consolidated Statements of Shareholders' Equity

(in millions)	Common Stock Shares	Amount	Capital in Excess of Par Value	Retained Earnings	Accumulated Other Comprehensive Income (Loss)	Total Shareholders' Equity
Balance February 1, 2008	1,458	$729	$ 16	$15,345	$ 8	$16,098
Comprehensive income:						
Net earnings				2,195		
Foreign currency translation					(13)	
Net unrealized investment losses					(1)	
Total comprehensive income						2,181
Tax effect of non-qualified stock options exercised and restricted stock vested			5			5
Cash dividends declared				(491)		(491)
Share-based payment expense			95			95
Repurchase of common stock	—	—	(8)			(8)
Conversion of debt to common stock	—	—	1			1
Issuance of common stock under share-based payment plans	12	6	168			174
Balance January 30, 2009	1,470	$735	$ 277	$17,049	$ (6)	$18,055
Comprehensive income:						
Net earnings				1,783		
Foreign currency translation					32	
Net unrealized investment gains					1	
Total comprehensive income						1,816
Tax effect of non-qualified stock options exercised and restricted stock vested			(6)			(6)
Cash dividends declared				(522)		(522)
Share-based payment expense			102			102
Repurchase of common stock	(22)	(11)	(490)	(3)		(504)
Issuance of common stock under share-based payment plans	11	5	123			128
Balance January 29, 2010	1,459	$729	$ 6	$18,307	$27	$19,069
Comprehensive income:						
Net earnings				2,010		
Foreign currency translation					28	
Net unrealized investment losses					(2)	
Total comprehensive income						2,036
Tax effect of non-qualified stock options exercised and restricted stock vested			(6)			(6)
Cash dividends declared				(588)		(588)
Share-based payment expense			115			115
Repurchase of common stock	(113)	(56)	(204)	(2,358)		(2,618)
Issuance of common stock under share-based payment plans	8	4	100			104
Balance January 28, 2011	1,354	$677	$ 11	$17,371	$53	$18,112

See accompanying notes to consolidated financial statements.

LOWE'S COMPANIES, INC.
Consolidated Statements of Cash Flows

(in millions) Fiscal years ended on	January 28, 2011	January 29, 2010	January 30, 2009
Cash flows from operating activities:			
Net earnings	$ 2,010	$ 1,783	$ 2,195
Adjustments to reconcile net earnings to net cash provided by operating activities:			
Depreciation and amortization	1,684	1,733	1,667
Deferred income taxes	(133)	(123)	69
Loss on property and other assets—net	103	193	89
Loss on redemption of long-term debt	—	—	8
Share-based payment expense	115	102	95
Changes in operating assets and liabilities:			
Merchandise inventory—net	(64)	(28)	(611)
Other operating assets	(142)	7	31
Accounts payable	60	175	402
Other operating liabilities	219	212	177
Net cash provided by operating activities	**3,852**	**4,054**	**4,122**
Cash flows from investing activities:			
Purchases of investments	(2,605)	(1,827)	(1,358)
Proceeds from sale/maturity of investments	1,822	1,784	1,425
Increase in other long-term assets	(97)	(62)	(56)
Property acquired	(1,329)	(1,799)	(3,266)
Proceeds from sale of property and other long-term assets	25	18	29
Net cash used in investing activities	**(2,184)**	**(1,886)**	**(3,226)**
Cash flows from financing activities:			
Net decrease in short-term borrowings	—	(1,007)	(57)
Net proceeds from issuance of long-term debt	1,985	10	15
Repayment of long-term debt	(552)	(37)	(573)
Proceeds from issuance of common stock under share-based payment plans	104	128	174
Cash dividend payments	(571)	(391)	(491)
Repurchase of common stock	(2,618)	(504)	(8)
Excess tax benefits of share-based payments	1	—	1
Net cash used in financing activities	**(1,651)**	**(1,801)**	**(939)**
Effect of exchange rate changes on cash	3	20	7
Net increase (decrease) in cash and cash equivalents	20	387	(36)
Cash and cash equivalents, beginning of year	632	245	281
Cash and cash equivalents, end of year	**$ 652**	**$ 632**	**$ 245**

See accompanying notes to consolidated financial statements.

NOTES TO CONSOLIDATED FINANCIAL STATEMENTS
YEARS ENDED JANUARY 28, 2011, JANUARY 29, 2010, AND JANUARY 30, 2009

NOTE 1: Summary of Significant Accounting Policies

Lowe's Companies, Inc. and subsidiaries (the Company) is the world's second-largest home improvement retailer and operated 1,749 stores in the United States, Canada and Mexico at January 28, 2011. Below are those accounting policies considered by the Company to be significant.

Fiscal Year   The Company's fiscal year ends on the Friday nearest the end of January. Each of the fiscal years presented contained 52 weeks. All references herein for the years 2010, 2009, and 2008 represent the fiscal years ended January 28, 2011, January 29, 2010, and January 30, 2009, respectively.

Principles of Consolidation   The consolidated financial statements include the accounts of the Company and its wholly-owned or controlled operating subsidiaries. All intercompany accounts and transactions have been eliminated.

Foreign Currency   The functional currencies of the Company's international subsidiaries are the local currencies of the countries in which the subsidiaries are located. Foreign currency denominated assets and liabilities are translated into U.S. dollars using the exchange rates in effect at the consolidated balance sheet date. Results of operations and cash flows are translated using the average exchange rates throughout the period. The effect of exchange rate fluctuations on translation of assets and liabilities is included as a component of shareholders' equity in accumulated other comprehensive income (loss). Gains and losses from foreign currency transactions, which are included in selling, general and administrative (SG&A) expense, have not been significant.

Use of Estimates   The preparation of the Company's financial statements in accordance with accounting principles generally accepted in the United States of America requires management to make estimates that affect the reported amounts of assets, liabilities, sales and expenses, and related disclosures of contingent assets and liabilities. The Company bases these estimates on historical results and various other assumptions believed to be reasonable, all of which form the basis for making estimates concerning the carrying values of assets and liabilities that are not readily available from other sources. Actual results may differ from these estimates.

Cash and Cash Equivalents   Cash and cash equivalents include cash on hand, demand deposits and short-term investments with original maturities of three months or less when purchased. Cash and cash equivalents are carried at amortized cost on the consolidated balance sheets. The majority of payments due from financial institutions for the settlement of credit card and debit card transactions process within two business days and are, therefore, classified as cash and cash equivalents.

Investments   As of January 28, 2011, investments consisted primarily of municipal obligations, floating rate municipal obligations, money market funds and mutual funds. The Company classifies as investments restricted balances pledged as collateral for the Company's extended protection plan program and for a portion of the Company's casualty insurance and Installed Sales program liabilities. Investments, exclusive of cash equivalents, with a stated maturity date of one year or less from the balance sheet date or that are expected to be used in current operations, are classified as short-term investments. The Company's trading securities are also classified as short-term investments. All other investments are classified as long-term.

The Company maintains investment securities in conjunction with certain employee benefit plans that are classified as trading securities. These securities are carried at fair value with unrealized gains and losses included in SG&A expense. All other investment securities are classified as available-for-sale and are carried at fair value with unrealized gains and losses included in accumulated other comprehensive income (loss) in shareholders' equity.

Merchandise Inventory Inventory is stated at the lower of cost or market using the first-in, first-out method of inventory accounting. The cost of inventory also includes certain costs associated with the preparation of inventory for resale, including distribution center costs, and is net of vendor funds.

The Company records an inventory reserve for the anticipated loss associated with selling inventories below cost. This reserve is based on management's current knowledge with respect to inventory levels, sales trends and historical experience. Management does not believe the Company's merchandise inventories are subject to significant risk of obsolescence in the near term, and management has the ability to adjust purchasing practices based on anticipated sales trends and general economic conditions. However, changes in consumer purchasing patterns could result in the need for additional reserves. The Company also records an inventory reserve for the estimated shrinkage between physical inventories. This reserve is based primarily on actual shrink results from previous physical inventories. Changes in the estimated shrink reserve may be necessary based on the timing and results of physical inventories.

Credit Programs The majority of the Company's accounts receivable arises from sales of goods and services to Commercial Business Customers. The Company has an agreement with GE Money Bank (GE) under which GE purchases at face value commercial business accounts receivable originated by the Company and services these accounts.

Sales generated through the Company's proprietary credit cards are not reflected in receivables. Under an agreement with GE, credit is extended directly to customers by GE. All credit program-related services are performed and controlled directly by GE.

The total portfolio of receivables held by GE, including both receivables originated by GE from the Company's proprietary credit cards and commercial business accounts receivable originated by the Company and sold to GE, approximated $5.8 billion at January 28, 2011, and $6.5 billion at January 29, 2010.

Property and Depreciation Property is recorded at cost. Costs associated with major additions are capitalized and depreciated. Capital assets are expected to yield future benefits and have useful lives which exceed one year. The total cost of a capital asset generally includes all applicable sales taxes, delivery costs, installation costs and other appropriate costs incurred by the Company, including interest in the case of self-constructed assets. Upon disposal, the cost of properties and related accumulated depreciation is removed from the accounts, with gains and losses reflected in SG&A expense on the consolidated statements of earnings.

Depreciation is provided over the estimated useful lives of the depreciable assets. Assets are depreciated using the straight-line method. Leasehold improvements and assets under capital lease are depreciated over the shorter of their estimated useful lives or the term of the related lease, which may include one or more option renewal periods where failure to exercise such options would result in an economic penalty in such amount that renewal appears, at the inception of the lease, to be reasonably assured. During the term of a lease, if leasehold improvements are placed in service significantly after the inception of the lease, the Company depreciates these leasehold improvements over the shorter of the useful life of the leasehold assets or a term that includes lease renewal periods deemed to be reasonably assured at the time the leasehold improvements are placed into service. The amortization of these assets is included in depreciation expense on the consolidated financial statements.

Long-Lived Asset Impairment/Exit Activities The carrying amounts of long-lived assets are reviewed whenever certain events or changes in circumstances indicate that the carrying amounts may not be recoverable.

Long-lived assets held-for-use includes operating stores as well as excess properties, such as relocated stores, closed stores and other properties that do not meet the held-for-sale criteria. A potential impairment has occurred for long-lived assets held-for-use if projected future undiscounted cash flows expected to result from the use and eventual disposition of the assets are less than the carrying amounts of the assets. An impairment loss is recorded for long-lived assets held-for-use when the carrying amount of the asset is not recoverable and exceeds its fair value.

Excess properties that are expected to be sold within the next 12 months and meet the other relevant held-for-sale criteria are classified as long-lived assets held-for-sale. An impairment loss is recorded for long-lived assets held-for-sale when the carrying amount of the asset exceeds its fair value less cost to sell. A long-lived asset is not depreciated while it is classified as held-for-sale.

For long-lived assets to be abandoned, the Company considers the asset to be disposed of when it ceases to be used. Until it ceases to be used, the Company continues to classify the asset as held-for-use and tests for potential impairment accordingly. If the Company commits to a plan to abandon a long-lived asset before the end of its previously estimated useful life, its depreciable life is re-evaluated.

Impairment losses are included in SG&A expense. The Company recorded long-lived asset impairment losses of $71 million during 2010, including $36 million for operating stores, $26 million for excess properties classified as held-for-use and $9 million, including costs to sell, for excess properties classified as held-for-sale. The Company recorded long-lived asset impairment losses of $114 million during 2009, including $53 million for operating stores, $40 million for excess properties classified as held-for-use and $21 million, including costs to sell, for excess properties classified as held-for-sale. The Company recorded long-lived asset impairment losses of $21 million during 2008, including $16 million for operating stores and $5 million for excess properties classified as held-for-use.

The net carrying amount of excess properties that do not meet the held-for-sale criteria is included in other assets (non-current) on the consolidated balance sheets and totaled $239 million and $205 million at January 28, 2011 and January 29, 2010, respectively.

When locations under operating leases are closed, a liability is recognized for the fair value of future contractual obligations, including future minimum lease payments, property taxes, utilities and common area maintenance, net of estimated sublease income. Amounts accrued were not material for any of the periods presented.

Leases For lease agreements that provide for escalating rent payments or free-rent occupancy periods, the Company recognizes rent expense on a straight-line basis over the non-cancelable lease term and option renewal periods where failure to exercise such options would result in an economic penalty in such amount that renewal appears, at the inception of the lease, to be reasonably assured. The lease term commences on the date that the Company takes possession of or controls the physical use of the property. Deferred rent is included in other liabilities (non-current) on the consolidated balance sheets.

Accounts Payable The Company has an agreement with a third party to provide an accounts payable tracking system which facilitates participating suppliers' ability to finance payment obligations from the Company with designated third-party financial institutions. Participating suppliers may, at their sole discretion, make offers to finance one or more payment obligations of the Company prior to their scheduled due dates at a discounted price to participating financial institutions. The Company's goal in entering into this arrangement is to capture overall supply chain savings, in the form of pricing, payment terms or vendor funding, created by facilitating suppliers' ability to finance payment obligations at more favorable discount rates, while providing them with greater working capital flexibility.

The Company's obligations to its suppliers, including amounts due and scheduled payment dates, are not impacted by suppliers' decisions to finance amounts under this arrangement. However, the Company's right to offset balances due from suppliers against payment obligations is restricted by this arrangement for those payment obligations that have been financed by suppliers. As of January 28, 2011 and January 29, 2010, $645 million and $602 million, respectively, of the Company's outstanding payment obligations had been placed on the accounts payable tracking system, and participating suppliers had financed $476 million and $253 million, respectively, of those payment obligations to participating financial institutions.

Other Current Liabilities   Other current liabilities on the consolidated balance sheets consist of:

(in millions)	January 28, 2011	January 29, 2010
Self-insurance liabilities	$ 311	$ 300
Accrued dividends	148	131
Accrued interest	115	102
Accrued property taxes	113	103
Sales tax liabilities	112	131
Other	559	489
Total	**$1,358**	**$1,256**

Self-Insurance   The Company is self-insured for certain losses relating to workers' compensation, automobile, property, and general and product liability claims. The Company has stop-loss coverage to limit the exposure arising from these claims. The Company is also self-insured for certain losses relating to extended protection plan and medical and dental claims. Self-insurance claims filed and claims incurred but not reported are accrued based upon management's estimates of the discounted ultimate cost for self-insured claims incurred using actuarial assumptions followed in the insurance industry and historical experience. Although management believes it has the ability to reasonably estimate losses related to claims, it is possible that actual results could differ from recorded self-insurance liabilities.

Income Taxes   The Company establishes deferred income tax assets and liabilities for temporary differences between the tax and financial accounting bases of assets and liabilities. The tax effects of such differences are reflected in the consolidated balance sheets at the enacted tax rates expected to be in effect when the differences reverse. A valuation allowance is recorded to reduce the carrying amount of deferred tax assets if it is more likely than not that all or a portion of the asset will not be realized. The tax balances and income tax expense recognized by the Company are based on management's interpretation of the tax statutes of multiple jurisdictions.

The Company establishes a liability for tax positions for which there is uncertainty as to whether or not the position will be ultimately sustained. The Company includes interest related to tax issues as part of net interest on the consolidated financial statements. The company records any applicable penalties related to tax issues within the income tax provision.

Revenue Recognition   The Company recognizes revenues, net of sales tax, when sales transactions occur and customers take possession of the merchandise. A provision for anticipated merchandise returns is provided through a reduction of sales and cost of sales in the period that the related sales are recorded. Revenues from product installation services are recognized when the installation is completed. Deferred revenues associated with amounts received for which customers have not yet taken possession of merchandise or for which installation has not yet been completed were $371 million and $354 million at January 28, 2011, and January 29, 2010, respectively.

Revenues from stored-value cards, which include gift cards and returned merchandise credits, are deferred and recognized when the cards are redeemed. The liability associated with outstanding stored-value cards was $336 million and $329 million at January 28, 2011, and January 29, 2010, respectively, and these amounts are included in deferred revenue on the consolidated balance sheets. The Company recognizes income from unredeemed stored-value cards at the point at which redemption becomes remote. The Company's stored-value cards have no expiration date or dormancy fees. Therefore, to determine when redemption is remote, the Company analyzes an aging of the unredeemed cards based on the date of last stored-value card use.

Cost of Sales and Selling, General and Administrative Expenses   The following lists the primary costs classified in each major expense category:

Cost of Sales

- Total cost of products sold, including:
  - Purchase costs, net of vendor funds;
  - Freight expenses associated with moving merchandise inventories from vendors to retail stores;
  - Costs associated with operating the Company's distribution network, including payroll and benefit costs and occupancy costs;
- Costs of installation services provided;
- Costs associated with delivery of products directly from vendors to customers by third parties;
- Costs associated with inventory shrinkage and obsolescence.

Selling, General and Administrative

- Payroll and benefit costs for retail and corporate employees;
- Occupancy costs of retail and corporate facilities;
- Advertising;
- Costs associated with delivery of products from stores to customers;
- Third-party, in-store service costs;
- Tender costs, including bank charges, costs associated with credit card interchange fees and amounts associated with accepting the Company's proprietary credit cards;
- Costs associated with self-insured plans, and premium costs for stop-loss coverage and fully insured plans;
- Long-lived asset impairment losses and gains/losses on disposal of assets;
- Other administrative costs, such as supplies, and travel and entertainment.

Advertising   Costs associated with advertising are charged to expense as incurred. Advertising expenses were $790 million, $750 million, and $789 million in 2010, 2009, and 2008, respectively.

Shipping and Handling Costs   The Company includes shipping and handling costs relating to the delivery of products directly from vendors to customers by third parties in cost of sales. Shipping and handling costs, which include third-party delivery costs, salaries, and vehicle operations expenses relating to the delivery of products from stores to customers, are classified as SG&A expense. Shipping and handling costs included in SG&A expense were $431 million, $371 million, and $378 million in 2010, 2009, and 2008, respectively.

Store Opening Costs   Costs of opening new or relocated retail stores, which include payroll and supply costs incurred prior to store opening and grand opening advertising costs, are charged to expense as incurred.

Comprehensive Income   The Company reports comprehensive income on its consolidated statements of shareholders' equity. Comprehensive income represents changes in shareholders' equity from non-owner sources and is comprised primarily of net earnings plus or minus unrealized gains or losses on available-for-sale securities, as well as foreign currency translation adjustments. Net unrealized gains, net of tax, on available-for-sale securities classified in accumulated other comprehensive income on the consolidated balance sheets were insignificant at January 28, 2011 and $2 million at January 29, 2010. Foreign currency translation gains, net of tax, classified in accumulated other comprehensive income were $53 million and $25 million at January 28, 2011 and January 29, 2010, respectively. The reclassification adjustments for gains/losses included in net earnings were not significant for any of the periods presented.

Other notes to the financial statements can be downloaded from the Web sites indicated on page B1.

APPENDIX C

Present and Future Value Concepts

The concepts of present value (PV) and future value (FV) are based on the time value of money. The **time value of money** is the idea that, quite simply, money received today is worth more than money to be received one year from today (or at any other future date), because it can be used to earn interest. If you invest $1,000 today at 10 percent, you will have $1,100 in one year. So $1,000 in one year is worth $100 less than $1,000 today because you lose the opportunity to earn the $100 in interest.

In some business situations, you will know the dollar amount of a cash flow that occurs in the future and will need to determine its value now. This type of situation is known as a **present value** problem. The opposite situation occurs when you know the dollar amount of a cash flow that occurs today and need to determine its value at some point in the future. These situations are called **future value** problems. The value of money changes over time because money can earn interest. The following table illustrates the basic difference between present value and future value problems:

	Now	Future
Present value	?	$1,000
Future value	$1,000	?

Present and future value problems may involve two types of cash flow: a single payment or an annuity (which is the fancy word for a series of equal cash payments). Combining two types of time value of money problems with two types of cash flows yields four different situations:

1. Future value of a single payment
2. Present value of a single payment
3. Future value of an annuity
4. Present value of an annuity

Most inexpensive handheld calculators and any spreadsheet program can perform the detailed arithmetic computations required to solve future value and present value problems. In later courses and in all business situations, you will probably use a calculator or computer to solve these problems. At this stage, we encourage you to solve problems using Tables C.1 through C.4 at the end of this appendix. We believe that using the tables will give you a better understanding of how and why present and future value concepts apply to business problems. The tables give the value of a $1 cash flow (single payment or annuity) for different periods (n) and at different interest rates (i). If a problem involves payments other than $1, multiply the value from the table by the amount of the payment.[1] In the final section of this appendix, we explain how to use Excel to compute present values.

Computing Future and Present Values of a Single Amount

FUTURE VALUE OF A SINGLE AMOUNT

In future value of a single amount problems, you will be asked to calculate how much money you will have in the future as the result of investing a certain amount in the present. If you were to receive a gift of $10,000, for instance, you might decide to put it in a savings account and use the money as a down payment on a house after you graduate. The future value computation would tell you how much money will be available when you graduate.

To solve a future value problem, you need to know three items:

1. Amount to be invested.
2. Interest rate (i) the amount will earn.
3. Number of periods (n) in which the amount will earn interest.

The future value concept is based on compound interest, which simply means that interest is calculated on top of interest. Thus, the amount of interest for each period is calculated using the principal plus any interest not paid out in prior periods. Graphically, the calculation of the future value of $1 for three periods at an interest rate of 10 percent may be represented as follows:

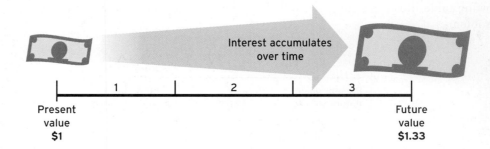

Assume that on January 1, 2013, you deposit $1,000 in a savings account at 10 percent annual interest, compounded annually. At the end of three years, the $1,000 will have increased to $1,331 as follows:

Year	Amount at Start of Year	+	Interest During the Year	=	Amount at End of Year
1	$1,000	+	$1,000 × 10% = $100	=	$1,100
2	1,100	+	1,100 × 10% = 110	=	1,210
3	1,210	+	1,210 × 10% = 121	=	1,331

---

[1]Present value and future value problems involve cash flows. The basic concepts are the same for cash inflows (receipts) and cash outflows (payments). No fundamental differences exist between present value and future value calculations for cash payments versus cash receipts.

We can avoid the detailed arithmetic by referring to Table C.1, Future Value of $1, on page C14. For $i = 10\%$, $n = 3$, we find the value 1.3310. We then compute the balance at the end of year 3 as follows:

$$\$1,000 \times 1.3310 = \$1,331$$

From Table C.1,
Interest rate = 10%
$n = 3$

Note that the increase of $331 is due to the time value of money. It is interest revenue to the owner of the savings account and interest expense to the bank.

PRESENT VALUE OF A SINGLE AMOUNT

The present value of a single amount is the worth to you today of receiving that amount sometime in the future. For instance, you might be offered an opportunity to invest in a financial instrument that would pay you $1,000 in 3 years. Before you decided whether to invest, you would want to determine the present value of the instrument.

To compute the present value of an amount to be received in the future, we must discount (a procedure that is the opposite of compounding) at i interest rate for n periods. In discounting, the interest is subtracted rather than added, as it is in compounding. Graphically, the present value of $1 due at the end of the third period with an interest rate of 10 percent can be represented as follows:

Assume that today is January 1, 2013, and you have the opportunity to receive $1,000 cash on December 31, 2015. At an interest rate of 10 percent per year, how much is the $1,000 payment worth to you on January 1, 2013? You could discount the amount year by year,[2] but it is easier to use Table C.2, Present Value of $1, on page C15. For $i = 10\%$, $n = 3$, we find that the present value of $1 is 0.7513. The present value of $1,000 to be received at the end of three years can be computed as follows:

$$\$1,000 \times 0.7513 = \$751.30$$

From Table C.2,
Interest rate = 10%
$n = 3$

It's important to learn not only how to compute a present value but also to understand what it means. The $751.30 is the amount you would pay now to have the right to receive $1,000 at the end of three years, assuming an interest rate of 10 percent. Conceptually, you should be indifferent between having $751.30 today and receiving $1,000 in three years. If you had $751.30 today but wanted $1,000 in three years, you would deposit the money in a savings account that pays 10% interest and it would grow to $1,000 in three years. Alternatively, if you had a contract that promised you $1,000

---

[2]The detailed discounting is as follows:

Periods	Interest for the Year	Present Value*
1	$1,000 − ($1,000 × 1/1.10) = $90.91	$1,000 − $90.91 = $909.09
2	$909.09 − ($909.09 × 1/1.10) = $82.65	$909.09 − $82.65 = $826.44
3	$826.44 − ($826.44 × 1/1.10) = $75.14[†]	$826.44 − $75.14 = $751.30

*Verifiable in Table C.2.
[†]Adjusted for rounding.

in three years, you could sell it to an investor for $751.30 in cash today because it would permit the investor to earn the difference in interest.

What if you could only earn 6 percent during the three-year period from January 1, 2013, to December 31, 2015? What would be the present value on January 1, 2013, of receiving $1,000 on December 31, 2015? To answer this we would take the same approach, using Table C.2, except that the interest rate would change to $i = 6\%$. Referring to Table C.2, we see the present value factor for $i = 6\%$, $n = 3$, is 0.8396. Thus, the present value of $1,000 to be received at the end of three years, assuming a 6 percent interest rate, would be computed as $1,000 \times 0.8396 = $839.60. Notice that when we assume a 6 percent interest rate the present value is greater than when we assumed a 10 percent interest rate. The reason for this difference is that, to reach $1,000 three years from now, you'd need to deposit more money in a savings account now if it earns 6 percent interest than if it earns 10 percent interest.

How's it going?   Self-Study Practice

1. If the interest rate in a present value problem increases from 8 percent to 10 percent, will the present value increase or decrease?

2. What is the present value of $10,000 to be received 10 years from now if the interest rate is 5 percent, compounded annually?

3. If $10,000 is deposited now in a savings account that earns 5 percent interest compounded annually, how much will it be worth 10 years from now?

After you have finished, check your answers with the solution in the margin.

Solution to Self-Study Practice
1. The present value will decrease.
2. $10,000 × 0.6139 = $6,139.
3. $10,000 × 1.6289 = $16,289.

The Power of Compounding

Compound interest is a remarkably powerful economic force. In fact, the ability to earn interest on interest is the key to building economic wealth. If you save $1,000 per year for the first 10 years of your career, you will have more money when you retire than you would if you had saved $15,000 per year for the last 10 years of your career. This surprising outcome occurs because the money you save early in your career will earn more interest than the money you save at the end of your career. If you start saving money now, the majority of your wealth will not be the money you saved but the interest your money was able to earn.

The table in the margin shows how a single investment of $1,000 today grows over time, at the investment community's historic average growth rate of 10 percent. Two important lessons are revealed in the table: (1) **you can earn a lot of interest through the effects of compounding** (in just 10 years, you will earn $1,600 interest on a $1,000 investment), and (2) **start early** (notice that the balance more than doubles every 10 years, so letting your investment sit an extra decade could make you twice as rich).

Period	Value
Now	$ 1,000
10 years	$ 2,600
20 years	$ 6,700
30 years	$ 17,400
40 years	$ 45,300
50 years	$117,400
60 years	$304,500
70 years	$789,700

Computing Future and Present Values of an Annuity

Instead of a single payment, many business problems involve multiple cash payments over a number of periods. An **annuity** is a series of consecutive payments characterized by

1. An equal dollar amount each interest period.

2. Interest periods of equal length (year, half a year, quarter, or month).

3. An equal interest rate each interest period.

YOU SHOULD KNOW

Annuity: A series of periodic cash receipts or payments that are equal in amount each interest period.

Examples of annuities include monthly payments on a car or house, yearly contributions to a savings account, and monthly pension benefits.

FUTURE VALUE OF AN ANNUITY

If you are saving money for some purpose, such as a new car or a trip to Europe, you might decide to deposit a fixed amount of money in a savings account each month. The future value of an annuity computation will tell you how much money will be in your savings account at some point in the future.

The future value of an annuity includes compound interest on each payment from the date of payment to the end of the term of the annuity. Each new payment accumulates less interest than prior payments, only because the number of periods remaining in which to accumulate interest decreases. The future value of an annuity of $1 for three periods at 10 percent may be represented graphically as

Future value
of an annuity
$3.31

Assume that each year for three years, you deposit $1,000 cash in a savings account at 10 percent interest per year. You make the first $1,000 deposit on December 31, 2013, the second one on December 31, 2014, and the third and last one on December 31, 2015. The first $1,000 deposit earns compound interest for two years (for a total principal and interest of $1,210); the second deposit earns interest for one year (for a total principal and interest of $1,100). The third deposit earns no interest because it was made on the day that the balance is computed. Thus, the total amount in the savings account at the end of three years is $3,310 ($1,210 + $1,100 + $1,000).

To calculate the future value of this annuity, we could compute the interest on each deposit, similar to what's described above. However, a faster way is to refer to Table C.3, Future Value of Annuity of $1, on page C16. For $i = 10\%$, $n = 3$, we find the value 3.3100. The future value of your three deposits of $1,000 each can be computed as follows:

From Table C.1,
Interest rate = 10%
$n = 3$

$$\$1,000 \times 3.3100 = \$3,310$$

PRESENT VALUE OF AN ANNUITY

The present value of an annuity is the value now of a series of equal amounts to be received (or paid out) for some specified number of periods in the future. It is computed by discounting each of the equal periodic amounts. A good example of this type of problem is a retirement program that offers employees a monthly income after retirement.

The present value of an annuity of $1 for three periods at 10 percent may be represented graphically as

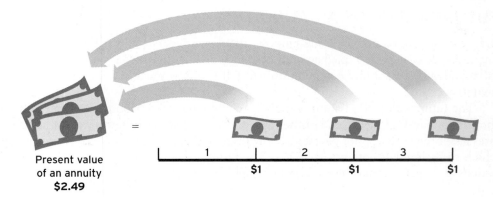

**Present value
of an annuity
$2.49**

Assume you are to receive $1,000 cash on each December 31, 2013, 2014, and 2015. How much would the sum of these three $1,000 future amounts be worth on January 1, 2013, assuming an interest rate of 10 percent per year? One way to determine this is to use Table C.2 to calculate the present value of each single amount as follows:

		FACTOR FROM TABLE C.2			
Year	**Amount**		**$i = 10\%$**		**Present Value**
1	$1,000	×	0.9091 ($n = 1$)	=	$ 909.10
2	$1,000	×	0.8264 ($n = 2$)	=	826.40
3	$1,000	×	0.7513 ($n = 3$)	=	751.30
			Total present value	=	$2,486.80

Alternatively, we can compute the present value of this annuity more easily by using Table C.4, Present Value of Annuity of $1 (on page C17), as follows:

From Table C.4,
Interest rate = 10%
$n = 3$

$1,000 × 2.4869 = $2,487 (rounded)

INTEREST RATES AND INTEREST PERIODS

The preceding illustrations assumed annual periods for compounding and discounting. Although interest rates are almost always quoted on an annual basis, many compounding periods encountered in business are less than one year. When interest periods are less than a year, the values of n and i must be restated to be consistent with the length of the interest compounding period.

To illustrate, 12 percent interest compounded annually for five years requires the use of $n = 5$ and $i = 12\%$. If compounding is quarterly, however, there will be four interest periods per year (20 interest periods in five years), and the quarterly interest rate is one quarter of the annual rate (3 percent per quarter). Therefore, 12 percent interest compounded quarterly for five years requires use of $n = 20$ and $i = 3\%$.

Accounting Applications of Present Values

Many business transactions require the use of future and present value concepts. In finance classes, you will see how to apply future value concepts. In this section, we apply present value concepts to three common accounting cases.

Case A—Present Value of a Single Amount

On January 1, 2013, General Mills bought some new delivery trucks. The company signed a note and agreed to pay $200,000 on December 31, 2014, an amount representing the cash equivalent price of the trucks plus interest for two years. The market interest rate for this note was 12 percent.

1. How should the accountant record the purchase?

Answer   This case requires the computation of the present value of a single amount. In conformity with the cost principle, the cost of the trucks is their current cash equivalent price, which is the present value of the future payment. The problem can be shown graphically as follows:

January 1, 2013	December 31, 2013	December 31, 2014
?		$200,000

The present value of the $200,000 is computed as follows:

> From Table C.2,
> Interest rate = 12%
> n = 2

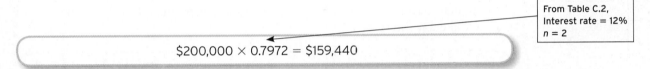

$200,000 × 0.7972 = $159,440

This transaction has the following financial effects, and would be recorded with the journal entry shown below.

Assets	=	Liabilities	+ Stockholders' Equity
Delivery Trucks +159,440		Note Payable +159,440	

dr Delivery Trucks (+A)	159,440	
cr Note Payable (+L)		159,440

2. How should the effects of interest be reported at the end of 2013 and 2014?

Answer   Interest expense would be calculated, reported, and recorded as follows:

<u>December 31, 2013</u>

> Interest = Principal × Rate × Time
>   = $159,440 × 12% × 12/12 = $19,132 (rounded)

Assets	=	Liabilities	+	Stockholders' Equity
		Note Payable +19,132		Interest Expense (+E) −19,132

dr Interest Expense (+E, −SE)	19,132	
cr Note Payable (+L)		19,132

COACH'S TIP

The interest is recorded in the Note Payable account because it would be paid as part of the note at maturity.

<u>December 31, 2014</u>

> Interest = Principal × Rate × Time
> = ($159,440 + $19,132) × 12% × 12/12 = $21,428 (rounded)

Assets	=	Liabilities	+	Stockholders' Equity
		Note Payable +21,428		Interest Expense (+E) −21,428

> dr Interest Expense (+E, −SE) 21,428
>   cr Note Payable (+L)   21,428

Note Payable (L)

	159,440	Jan. 1, 2013
	19,132	Interest 2013
	21,428	Interest 2014
200,000		Dec. 31, 2014

3. What is the effect of the $200,000 debt payment made on December 31, 2014?

Answer At this date the amount to be paid is the balance in Note Payable, after it has been updated for interest pertaining to 2014, as shown in the T-account in the margin. Notice that, just prior to its repayment, the balance for the note on December 31, 2014, is the same as the maturity amount on the due date.

The debt payment has the following financial effects, and would be recorded with the journal entry shown below.

Assets	=	Liabilities	+	Stockholders' Equity
Cash −200,000		Note Payable −200,000		

> dr Note Payable (−L) 200,000
>   cr Cash (−A)   200,000

Case B—Present Value of an Annuity

On January 1, 2013, General Mills bought new milling equipment. The company elected to finance the purchase with a note payable to be paid off in three years in annual installments of $163,686. Each installment includes principal plus interest on the unpaid balance at 11 percent per year. The annual installments are due on December 31, 2013, 2014, and 2015. This problem can be shown graphically as follows:

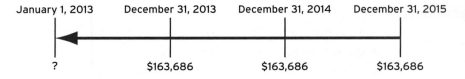

January 1, 2013   December 31, 2013   December 31, 2014   December 31, 2015

? $163,686 $163,686 $163,686

1. What is the amount of the note?

Answer The note is the present value of each installment payment, $i = 11\%$ and $n = 3$. This is an annuity because the note repayment is made in three equal installments. The amount of the note is computed as follows:

From Table C.4,
Interest rate = 11%
$n = 3$

> $163,686 × 2.4437 = $400,000 (rounded)

The acquisition on January 1, 2013, would be accounted for as follows:

Assets	=	Liabilities	+ Stockholders' Equity
Milling Equipment +400,000		Note Payable +400,000	

dr Milling Equipment (+A) 400,000
   cr Note Payable (+L)   400,000

2. How should the payments made at the end of each year be accounted for?

Answer:

December 31, 2013
Each payment includes both interest and principal. The interest part of the first payment is calculated as:

$$\text{Interest} = \text{Principal} \times \text{Rate} \times \text{Time}$$
$$= \$400,000 \times 11\% \times 12/12 = \$44,000$$

Now that we know the interest component, the principal portion of the first payment of \$163,686 can be calculated (\$163,686 − \$44,000 = \$119,686). Thus, the first payment on December 31, 2013, would be accounted for as:

Assets	=	Liabilities	+	Stockholders' Equity
Cash −163,686		Note Payable −119,686		Interest Expense (+E) −44,000

dr Interest Expense (+E, −SE) 44,000
dr Note Payable (−L) (\$163,686 − \$44,000) 119,686
   cr Cash (−A)   163,686

December 31, 2014
The interest portion of the second and third payments would be calculated in the same way, although notice that the principal balance in the Note Payable account changes after each payment.

$$\text{Interest} = \text{Principal} \times \text{Rate} \times \text{Time}$$
$$= [(\$400,000 - \$119,686) \times 11\% \times 12/12] = \$30,835 \text{ (rounded)}$$
$$\text{Principal} = \text{Payment} - \text{Interest}$$
$$= \$163,686 - \$30,835 = \$132,851$$

Assets	=	Liabilities	+	Stockholders' Equity
Cash −163,686		Note Payable −132,851		Interest Expense (+E) −30,835

dr Interest Expense (+E, −SE) 30,835
dr Note Payable (−L) 132,851
   cr Cash (−A)   163,686

<u>**December 31, 2015**</u>

Interest = Principal × Rate × Time
= [($400,000 − $119,686 − $132,851) × 11% × 12/12]
= $16,223 (adjusted for rounding of the present value factor)
Principal = Payment − Interest
= $163,686 − $16,223 = $147,463

Note Payable (L)			
		400,000	Jan. 1, 2013
Dec. 31, 2013	119,686		
Dec. 31, 2014	132,851		
Dec. 31, 2015	147,463		
		0	Dec. 31, 2015

Assets	=	Liabilities	+	Stockholders' Equity	
Cash −163,686		Note Payable −147,463		Interest Expense (+E)	−16,223

dr Interest Expense (+E, −SE)   16,223
dr Note Payable (−L)   147,463
   cr Cash (−A)   163,686

Case C—Present Value of a Single Amount and an Annuity (Bond Pricing)

On January 1, 2013, General Mills issued 100 four-year, $1,000 bonds. The bonds pay interest annually at a rate of 6 percent of face value. What total amount would investors be willing to pay for the bonds if they require an annual return of: (*a*) 4 percent, (*b*) 6 percent, or (*c*) 8 percent?

Answer   This case requires the computation of the present value of a single amount (the $100,000 face value paid at maturity) plus the present value of an annuity (the annual interest payments of $6,000). The problem can be shown graphically as follows:

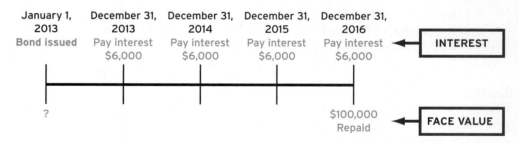

January 1, 2013	December 31, 2013	December 31, 2014	December 31, 2015	December 31, 2016	
Bond issued	Pay interest $6,000	Pay interest $6,000	Pay interest $6,000	Pay interest $6,000	◄— **INTEREST**
?				$100,000 Repaid	◄— **FACE VALUE**

COACH'S TIP

Each interest payment of $6,000 is calculated as: $100,000 × 6% × 12/12.

(a) 4 Percent Market Interest Rate

The present value of the $100,000 face value is computed as follows:

From Table C.2, Interest rate = 4% *n* = 4

$100,000 × 0.8548 = $85,480

The present value of the $6,000 annuity is computed as follows:

From Table C.4, Interest rate = 4% *n* = 4

$6,000 × 3.6299 = $21,780*

*Adjusted to accommodate rounding in the present value factor.

The present value of the total bond payments, computed using the discount rate of 4 percent, is $107,260 (= $85,480 + $21,780).

(b) 6 Percent Market Interest Rate

The present value of the $100,000 face value is computed as follows:

$$\$100,000 \times 0.7921 = \$79,210$$

> From Table C.2,
> Interest rate = 6%
> $n = 4$

The present value of the $6,000 annuity is computed as follows:

$$\$6,000 \times 3.4651 = \$20,790*$$

> From Table C.4,
> Interest rate = 6%
> $n = 4$

*Adjusted to accommodate rounding in the present value factor.

The present value of the total bond payments, computed using the discount rate of 6%, is $100,000 (= $79,210 + $20,790).

(c) 8 Percent Market Interest Rate

The present value of the $100,000 face value is computed as follows:

$$\$100,000 \times 0.7350 = \$73,503*$$

> From Table C.2,
> Interest rate = 8%
> $n = 4$

*Adjusted to accommodate rounding in the present value factor.

The present value of the $6,000 annuity is computed as follows:

$$\$6,000 \times 3.3121 = \$19,873$$

> From Table C.4,
> Interest rate = 8%
> $n = 4$

The present value of the total bond payments, computed using the discount rate of 8%, is $93,376 (= $73,503 + $19,873).

The following table summarizes these calculations:

> **COACH'S TIP**
>
> The present values in a, b, and c demonstrate the calculation of the bond issue prices used in Chapter 10.

	MARKET INTEREST RATES		
	4%	6%	8%
Present value of $100,000 face value (principal) paid four years from now	$ 85,480	$ 79,210	$ 73,503
Present value of $6,000 (interest) paid once a year for four years	21,780	20,790	19,873
Bond price	**$107,260**	**$100,000**	**$93,376**

Of course, these calculations are just the starting point for understanding how bond liabilities are determined and reported. You'll need to read Chapter 10 for information about how to account for bond liabilities.

PRESENT VALUE COMPUTATIONS USING EXCEL

While the present value tables are useful for educational purposes, most present value problems in business are solved with calculators or Excel spreadsheets. Because of the widespread availability of Excel, we will show you how to solve present value problems using Excel. Slightly different versions of Excel are available. The illustrations in this text are based on Microsoft Office 2007.

Present Value of a Single Payment

The calculation of a present value amount is based on a fairly simple mathematical formula:

$$PV = Payment/(1+i)^n$$

In this formula, *payment* is the cash payment made at some point in the future, *i* is the interest rate each period, and *n* is the number of periods in the problem. We could use this formula to solve all problems involving the present value of a single payment. It is, of course, easier to use a present value table (like the one at the end of this appendix) which is derived by solving the present value formula for various interest rates and numbers of periods. Unfortunately, a table that included all interest rates and numbers of periods actually encountered in business would be too large to work with. As a result, most accountants and analysts use Excel to compute a present value.

To compute the present value of a single payment in Excel, you enter the present value formula in a cell, using the format required by Excel. You should select a cell and enter the following formula:

$$= Payment/(1+i)\verb|^|n$$

To illustrate, if you want to solve for the present value of a $100,000 payment to be made in five years with an interest rate of 10%, you would enter the following in the function field:

$$= 100,000/(1.10)\verb|^|5$$

Based on this entry, Excel would compute the present value of $62,092.13. This answer is slightly different from the answer you would have if you used the present value tables at the end of this appendix. The tables are rounded based on four digits. Excel does not round and, therefore, provides a more accurate computation.

Present Value of an Annuity

The formula for computing the present value of an annuity is a little more complicated than the present value of a single payment. As a result, Excel has been programmed to include the formula so that you do not have to enter it yourself.

To compute the present value of an annuity in Excel, select a cell, click on the Formulas tab, and then click on the function button (f^x). The following dropdown box will appear:

Under the Select Category heading, you should pick "Financial," scroll down under "Select a Function," and click on PV. Then, click on "OK" and a new dropdown box will appear:

In this box, you should enter the interest rate, 10% in this example, under Rate. Notice that the rate must be entered as a decimal (i.e., 0.10). Enter the number of periods (20) under Nper. Excel has an unusual convention associated with the payment. It must be entered as a negative amount (−15,000) under Pmt. Do not include a comma or brackets with the amount you enter. When you click on OK, Excel will enter the present value in the cell you selected. In this example, the value determined by Excel is $127,703.46.

TABLE C.1 | Future Value of $1

Periods	2%	3%	3.75%	4%	4.25%	5%	6%	7%	8%
0	1.	1.	1.	1.	1.	1.	1.	1.	1.
1	1.02	1.03	1.0375	1.04	1.0425	1.05	1.06	1.07	1.08
2	1.0404	1.0609	1.0764	1.0816	1.0868	1.1025	1.1236	1.1449	1.1664
3	1.0612	1.0927	1.1168	1.1249	1.1330	1.1576	1.1910	1.2250	1.2597
4	1.0824	1.1255	1.1587	1.1699	1.1811	1.2155	1.2625	1.3108	1.3605
5	1.1041	1.1593	1.2021	1.2167	1.2313	1.2763	1.3382	1.4026	1.4693
6	1.1262	1.1941	1.2472	1.2653	1.2837	1.3401	1.4185	1.5007	1.5869
7	1.1487	1.2299	1.2939	1.3159	1.3382	1.4071	1.5036	1.6058	1.7138
8	1.1717	1.2668	1.3425	1.3686	1.3951	1.4775	1.5938	1.7182	1.8509
9	1.1951	1.3048	1.3928	1.4233	1.4544	1.5513	1.6895	1.8385	1.9990
10	1.2190	1.3439	1.4450	1.4802	1.5162	1.6289	1.7908	1.9672	2.1589
20	1.4859	1.8061	2.0882	2.1911	2.2989	2.6533	3.2071	3.8697	4.6610

Periods	9%	10%	11%	12%	13%	14%	15%	20%	25%
0	1.	1.	1.	1.	1.	1.	1.	1.	1.
1	1.09	1.10	1.11	1.12	1.13	1.14	1.15	1.20	1.25
2	1.1881	1.2100	1.2321	1.2544	1.2769	1.2996	1.3225	1.4400	1.5625
3	1.2950	1.3310	1.3676	1.4049	1.4429	1.4815	1.5209	1.7280	1.9531
4	1.4116	1.4641	1.5181	1.5735	1.6305	1.6890	1.7490	2.0736	2.4414
5	1.5386	1.6105	1.6851	1.7623	1.8424	1.9254	2.0114	2.4883	3.0518
6	1.6771	1.7716	1.8704	1.9738	2.0820	2.1950	2.3131	2.9860	3.8147
7	1.8280	1.9487	2.0762	2.2107	2.3526	2.5023	2.6600	3.5832	4.7684
8	1.9926	2.1436	2.3045	2.4760	2.6584	2.8526	3.0590	4.2998	5.9605
9	2.1719	2.3579	2.5580	2.7731	3.0040	3.2519	3.5179	5.1598	7.4506
10	2.3674	2.5937	2.8394	3.1058	3.3946	3.7072	4.0456	6.1917	9.3132
20	5.6044	6.7275	8.0623	9.6463	11.5231	13.7435	16.3665	38.3376	86.7362

TABLE C.2	Present Value of $1

Periods	2%	3%	3.75%	4%	4.25%	5%	6%	7%	8%
1	0.9804	0.9709	0.9639	0.9615	0.9592	0.9524	0.9434	0.9346	0.9259
2	0.9612	0.9426	0.9290	0.9246	0.9201	0.9070	0.8900	0.8734	0.8573
3	0.9423	0.9151	0.8954	0.8890	0.8826	0.8638	0.8396	0.8163	0.7938
4	0.9238	0.8885	0.8631	0.8548	0.8466	0.8227	0.7921	0.7629	0.7350
5	0.9057	0.8626	0.8319	0.8219	0.8121	0.7835	0.7473	0.7130	0.6806
6	0.8880	0.8375	0.8018	0.7903	0.7790	0.7462	0.7050	0.6663	0.6302
7	0.8706	0.8131	0.7728	0.7599	0.7473	0.7107	0.6651	0.6228	0.5835
8	0.8535	0.7894	0.7449	0.7307	0.7168	0.6768	0.6274	0.5820	0.5403
9	0.8368	0.7664	0.7180	0.7026	0.6876	0.6446	0.5919	0.5439	0.5002
10	0.8203	0.7441	0.6920	0.6756	0.6595	0.6139	0.5584	0.5083	0.4632
20	0.6730	0.5537	0.4789	0.4564	0.4350	0.3769	0.3118	0.2584	0.2145

Periods	9%	10%	11%	12%	13%	14%	15%	20%	25%
1	0.9174	0.9091	0.9009	0.8929	0.8850	0.8772	0.8696	0.8333	0.8000
2	0.8417	0.8264	0.8116	0.7972	0.7831	0.7695	0.7561	0.6944	0.6400
3	0.7722	0.7513	0.7312	0.7118	0.6931	0.6750	0.6575	0.5787	0.5120
4	0.7084	0.6830	0.6587	0.6355	0.6133	0.5921	0.5718	0.4823	0.4096
5	0.6499	0.6209	0.5935	0.5674	0.5428	0.5194	0.4972	0.4019	0.3277
6	0.5963	0.5645	0.5346	0.5066	0.4803	0.4556	0.4323	0.3349	0.2621
7	0.5470	0.5132	0.4817	0.4523	0.4251	0.3996	0.3759	0.2791	0.2097
8	0.5019	0.4665	0.4339	0.4039	0.3762	0.3506	0.3269	0.2326	0.1678
9	0.4604	0.4241	0.3909	0.3606	0.3329	0.3075	0.2843	0.1938	0.1342
10	0.4224	0.3855	0.3522	0.3220	0.2946	0.2697	0.2472	0.1615	0.1074
20	0.1784	0.1486	0.1240	0.1037	0.0863	0.0728	0.0611	0.0261	0.0115

TABLE C.3	Future Value of Annuity of $1

Periods*	2%	3%	3.75%	4%	4.25%	5%	6%	7%	8%
1	1.	1.	1.	1.	1.	1.	1.	1.	1.
2	2.02	2.03	2.0375	2.04	2.0425	2.05	2.06	2.07	2.08
3	3.0604	3.0909	3.1139	3.1216	3.1293	3.1525	3.1836	3.2149	3.2464
4	4.1216	4.1836	4.2307	4.2465	4.2623	4.3101	4.3746	4.4399	4.5061
5	5.2040	5.3091	5.3893	5.4163	5.4434	5.5256	5.6371	5.7507	5.8666
6	6.3081	6.4684	6.5914	6.6330	6.6748	6.8019	6.9753	7.1533	7.3359
7	7.4343	7.6625	7.8386	7.8983	7.9585	8.1420	8.3938	8.6540	8.9228
8	8.5830	8.8923	9.1326	9.2142	9.2967	9.5491	9.8975	10.2598	10.6366
9	9.7546	10.1591	10.4750	10.5828	10.6918	11.0266	11.4913	11.9780	12.4876
10	10.9497	11.4639	11.8678	12.0061	12.1462	12.5779	13.1808	13.8164	14.4866
20	24.2974	26.8704	29.0174	29.7781	30.5625	33.0660	36.7856	40.9955	45.7620

Periods*	9%	10%	11%	12%	13%	14%	15%	20%	25%
1	1.	1.	1.	1.	1.	1.	1.	1.	1.
2	2.09	2.10	2.11	2.12	2.13	2.14	2.15	2.20	2.25
3	3.2781	3.3100	3.3421	3.3744	3.4069	3.4396	3.4725	3.6400	3.8125
4	4.5731	4.6410	4.7097	4.7793	4.8498	4.9211	4.9934	5.3680	5.7656
5	5.9847	6.1051	6.2278	6.3528	6.4803	6.6101	6.7424	7.4416	8.2070
6	7.5233	7.7156	7.9129	8.1152	8.3227	8.5355	8.7537	9.9299	11.2588
7	9.2004	9.4872	9.7833	10.0890	10.4047	10.7305	11.0668	12.9159	15.0735
8	11.0285	11.4359	11.8594	12.2997	12.7573	13.2328	13.7268	16.4991	19.8419
9	13.0210	13.5975	14.1640	14.7757	15.4157	16.0853	16.7858	20.7989	25.8023
10	15.1929	15.9374	16.7220	17.5487	18.4197	19.3373	20.3037	25.9587	33.2529
20	51.1601	57.2750	64.2028	72.0524	80.9468	91.0249	102.4436	186.6880	342.9447

*There is one payment each period.

TABLE C.4   Present Value of Annuity of $1

Periods*	2%	3%	3.75%	4%	4.25%	5%	6%	7%	8%
1	0.9804	0.9709	0.9639	0.9615	0.9592	0.9524	0.9434	0.9346	0.9259
2	1.9416	1.9135	1.8929	1.8861	1.8794	1.8594	1.8334	1.8080	1.7833
3	2.8839	2.8286	2.7883	2.7751	2.7620	2.7232	2.6730	2.6243	2.5771
4	3.8077	3.7171	3.6514	3.6299	3.6086	3.5460	3.4651	3.3872	3.3121
5	4.7135	4.5797	4.4833	4.4518	4.4207	4.3295	4.2124	4.1002	3.9927
6	5.6014	5.4172	5.2851	5.2421	5.1997	5.0757	4.9173	4.7665	4.6229
7	6.4720	6.2303	6.0579	6.0021	5.9470	5.7864	5.5824	5.3893	5.2064
8	7.3255	7.0197	6.8028	6.7327	6.6638	6.4632	6.2098	5.9713	5.7466
9	8.1622	7.7861	7.5208	7.4353	7.3513	7.1078	6.8017	6.5152	6.2469
10	8.9826	8.5302	8.2128	8.1109	8.01C9	7.7217	7.3601	7.0236	6.7101
20	16.3514	14.8775	13.8962	13.5903	13.2944	12.4622	11.4699	10.5940	9.8181

Periods*	9%	10%	11%	12%	13%	14%	15%	20%	25%
1	0.9174	0.9091	0.9009	0.8929	0.8850	0.8772	0.8696	0.8333	0.8000
2	1.7591	1.7355	1.7125	1.6901	1.6681	1.6467	1.6257	1.5278	1.4400
3	2.5313	2.4869	2.4437	2.4018	2.3612	2.3216	2.2832	2.1065	1.9520
4	3.2397	3.1699	3.1024	3.0373	2.9745	2.9137	2.8550	2.5887	2.3616
5	3.8897	3.7908	3.6959	3.6048	3.5172	3.4331	3.3522	2.9906	2.6893
6	4.4859	4.3553	4.2305	4.1114	3.9975	3.8887	3.7845	3.3255	2.9514
7	5.0330	4.8684	4.7122	4.5638	4.4226	4.2883	4.1604	3.6046	3.1611
8	5.5348	5.3349	5.1461	4.9676	4.7988	4.6389	4.4873	3.8372	3.3289
9	5.9952	5.7590	5.5370	5.3282	5.1317	4.9464	4.7716	4.0310	3.4631
10	6.4177	6.1446	5.8892	5.6502	5.4262	5.2161	5.0188	4.1925	3.5705
20	9.1285	8.5136	7.9633	7.4694	7.0248	6.6231	6.2593	4.8696	3.9539

*There is one payment each period.

KEY TERMS

Annuity p. C4

Future Value p. C1

Present Value p. C1

Time Value of Money p. C1

See complete definitions in the glossary in the back of this text.

PRACTICE MATERIAL

QUESTIONS

1. Explain the concept of the time value of money.

2. Explain the basic difference between future value and present value.

3. If you deposited $10,000 in a savings account that earns 10 percent, how much would you have at the end of 10 years? Use a convenient format to display your computations.

4. If you hold a valid contract that will pay you $8,000 cash 10 years from now and the going rate of interest is 10 percent, what is its present value? Use a convenient format to display your computations.

5. What is an annuity?

6. Use Tables C.1 to C.4 to complete the following schedule:

	Table Values		
	$i = 5\%$, $n = 4$	$i = 10\%$, $n = 7$	$i = 14\%$, $n = 10$
FV of $1			
PV of $1			
FV of annuity of $1			
PV of annuity of $1			

7. If you deposit $1,000 at the end of each period for 10 interest periods and you earn 8 percent interest, how much would you have at the end of period 10? Use a convenient format to display your computations.

MULTIPLE CHOICE

1. You are saving up for a Mercedes-Benz SLR McLaren, which currently sells for nearly half a million dollars. Your plan is to deposit $15,000 at the end of each year for the next 10 years. You expect to earn 5 percent each year. How much will you have saved after 10 years, rounded to the nearest 10 dollars?

   a. $150,000.
   b. $188,670.
   c. $495,990.
   d. None of the above.

2. Which of the following is a characteristic of an annuity?

   a. An equal dollar amount each interest period.
   b. Interest periods of equal length.
   c. An equal interest rate each interest period.
   d. All of the above are characteristics of an annuity.

3. Which of the following is most likely to be an annuity?

   a. Monthly payments on a credit card bill.
   b. Monthly interest earned on a checking account.
   c. Monthly payments on a home mortgage.
   d. Monthly utility bill payments.

4. Assume you bought a state of the art entertainment system, with no payments to be made until two years from now, when you must pay $6,000. If the going rate of interest on most loans is 5 percent, which table in this appendix would you use to calculate the system's equivalent cost if you were to pay for it today?

   a. Table C.1 (Future Value of $1)
   b. Table C.2 (Present Value of $1)

   c. Table C.3 (Future Value of Annuity of $1)
   d. Table C.4 (Present Value of Annuity of $1)

5. Assuming the facts in question 4, what is the system's equivalent cost if you were to pay for it today?

   a. $5,442
   c. $11,100
   b. $6,615
   d. $12,300

6. Assume you bought a car using a loan that requires payments of $3,000 to be made at the end of every year for the next three years. The loan agreement indicates the annual interest rate is 6 percent. Which table in this appendix would you use to calculate the car's equivalent cost if you were to pay for it in full today?

   a. Table C.1 (Future Value of $1)
   b. Table C.2 (Present Value of $1)
   c. Table C.3 (Future Value of Annuity of $1)
   d. Table C.4 (Present Value of Annuity of $1)

7. Assuming the facts in question 6, what is the car's equivalent cost if you were to pay for it today? Round to the nearest hundred dollars.

   a. $2,600
   b. $3,600
   c. $8,000
   d. $9,600

8. Which of the following statements is true?

   a. When the interest rate increases, the present value of a single amount decreases.

   b. When the number of interest periods increases, the present value of a single amount increases.

   c. When the interest rate increases, the present value of an annuity increases.

   d. None of the above are true.

9. Which of the following describes how to calculate a bond's issue price?

Face Value	Interest Payments
a. Present value of single amount	Future value of annuity
b. Future value of single amount	Present value of annuity

c. Present value of single amount	Present value of annuity
d. Future value of single amount	Future value of annuity

10. If interest is compounded quarterly, rather than yearly, how do you adjust the number of years and annual interest rate when using the present value tables?

Number of years	Annual interest rate
a. Divide by 4	Divide by 4
b. Divide by 4	Multiply by 4
c. Multiply by 4	Divide by 4
d. Multiply by 4	Multiply by 4

Solutions to Multiple-Choice Questions can be found on **page Q1.**

MINI-EXERCISES

ACCOUNTING

MC-1 Computing the Present Value of a Single Payment

What is the present value of $500,000 to be paid in 10 years, with an interest rate of 8 percent?

MC-2 Computing the Present Value of an Annuity

What is the present value of 10 equal payments of $15,000, with an interest rate of 10 percent?

MC-3 Computing the Present Value of a Complex Contract

As a result of a slowdown in operations, Mercantile Stores is offering to employees who have been terminated a severance package of $100,000 cash; another $100,000 to be paid in one year; and an annuity of $30,000 to be paid each year for 20 years. What is the present value of the package, assuming an interest rate of 8 percent?

MC-4 Computing the Future Value of an Annuity

You plan to retire in 20 years. Calculate whether it is better for you to save $25,000 a year for the last 10 years before retirement or $15,000 for each of the 20 years. Assume you are able to earn 10 percent interest on your investments.

EXERCISES

connect
ACCOUNTING

EC-1 Computing Growth in a Savings Account: A Single Amount

On January 1, 2013, you deposited $6,000 in a savings account. The account will earn 10 percent annual compound interest, which will be added to the fund balance at the end of each year.

Required: (round to the nearest dollar):

1. What will be the balance in the savings account at the end of 10 years?
2. What is the interest for the 10 years?
3. How much interest revenue did the fund earn in 2013? 2014?

EC-2 Computing Deposit Required and Accounting for a Single-Sum Savings Account

On January 1, 2013, Alan King decided to transfer an amount from his checking account into a savings account that later will provide $80,000 to send his son to college (four years from now). The savings account will earn 8 percent, which will be added to the fund each year-end.

Required (show computations and round to the nearest dollar):

1. How much must Alan deposit on January 1, 2013?
2. Give the journal entry that Alan should make on January 1, 2013, to record the transfer.

3. What is the interest for the four years?

4. Give the journal entry that Alan should make on (*a*) December 31, 2013, and (*b*) December 31, 2014.

EC-3 Recording Growth in a Savings Account with Equal Periodic Payments

On each December 31, you plan to transfer $2,000 from your checking account into a savings account. The savings account will earn 9 percent annual interest, which will be added to the savings account balance at each year-end. The first deposit will be made December 31, 2013 (at the end of the period).

Required (show computations and round to the nearest dollar):

1. Give the required journal entry on December 31, 2013.
2. What will be the balance in the savings account at the end of the 10th year (i.e., 10 deposits)?
3. What is the total amount of interest earned on the 10 deposits?
4. How much interest revenue did the fund earn in 2014? 2015?
5. Give all required journal entries at the end of 2014 and 2015.

EC-4 Computing Growth for a Savings Fund with Periodic Deposits

On January 1, 2013, you plan to take a trip around the world upon graduation four years from now. Your grandmother wants to deposit sufficient funds for this trip in a savings account for you. On the basis of a budget, you estimate that the trip currently would cost $15,000. Being the generous and sweet lady she is, your grandmother decided to deposit $3,500 in the fund at the end of each of the next four years, starting on December 31, 2013. The savings account will earn 6 percent annual interest, which will be added to the savings account at each year-end.

Required (show computations and round to the nearest dollar):

1. How much money will you have for the trip at the end of year 4 (i.e., after four deposits)?
2. What is the total amount of interest earned over the four years?
3. How much interest revenue did the fund earn in 2013, 2014, 2015, and 2016?

EC-5 Computing Value of an Asset Based on Present Value

You have the chance to purchase an oil well. Your best estimate is that the oil well's net royalty income will average $25,000 per year for five years. There will be no residual value at that time. Assume that the cash inflow occurs at each year-end and that considering the uncertainty in your estimates, you expect to earn 15 percent per year on the investment. What should you be willing to pay for this investment right now?

EC-6 Computing Bond Issue Proceeds and Issue Price

Your company plans to issue bonds later in the upcoming year. But with the economic uncertainty and varied interest rates, it is not clear how much money the company will receive when the bonds are issued. The company is committed to issuing 2,000 bonds, each of which will have a face value of $1,000, a stated interest rate of 8 percent paid annually, and a period to maturity of 10 years.

Required:

1. Compute the bond issue proceeds assuming a market interest rate of 8 percent. (When computing proceeds, round the present value of the face amount and the annual interest payment to the nearest hundred dollars.) Also, express the bond issue price as a percentage by comparing the total proceeds to the total face value.

2. Compute the bond issue proceeds assuming a market interest rate of 7 percent. (When computing proceeds, round the present value of the face amount and the annual interest payment to the nearest hundred dollars.) Also, express the bond issue price as a percentage by comparing the total proceeds to the total face value.

3. Compute the bond issue proceeds assuming a market interest rate of 9 percent. (When computing proceeds, round the present value of the face amount and the annual interest payment to the nearest hundred dollars.) Also, express the bond issue price as a percentage by comparing the total proceeds to the total face value.

COACHED PROBLEM

CPC-1 **Comparing Options Using Present Value Concepts**

After hearing a knock at your front door, you are surprised to see the Prize Patrol from a large, well-known magazine subscription company. It has arrived with the good news that you are the big winner, having won "$20 million." You discover that you have three options: (1) you can receive $1 million per year for the next 20 years, (2) you can have $8 million today, or (3) you can have $2 million today and receive $700,000 for each of the next 20 years. Your financial adviser tells you that it is reasonable to expect to earn 10 percent on investments. Which option do you prefer? What factors influence your decision?

TIP: All three scenarios require you to determine today's value of the various payment options. These are present value problems.

GROUP A PROBLEM

PAC-1 **Comparing Options Using Present Value Concepts**

After completing a long and successful career as senior vice president for a large bank, you are preparing for retirement. After visiting the human resources office, you have found that you have several retirement options: (1) you can receive an immediate cash payment of $1 million, (2) you can receive $60,000 per year for life (your remaining life expectancy is 20 years), or (3) you can receive $50,000 per year for 10 years and then $70,000 per year for life (this option is intended to give you some protection against inflation). You have determined that you can earn 8 percent on your investments. Which option do you prefer and why?

GROUP B PROBLEM

PBC-1 **Comparing Options Using Present Value Concepts**

After incurring a serious injury caused by a manufacturing defect, your friend has sued the manufacturer for damages. Your friend received three offers from the manufacturer to settle the lawsuit: (1) receive an immediate cash payment of $100,000, (2) receive $6,000 per year for life (your friend's remaining life expectancy is 20 years), or (3) receive $5,000 per year for 10 years and then $7,000 per year for life (this option is intended to compensate your friend for increased aggravation of the injury over time). Your friend can earn 8 percent interest and has asked you for advice. Which option would you recommend and why?

Investments in Other Corporations

Online at www.mhhe.com/phillips4e.

Appendix Introduction

Along with financial hardship, the financial crisis that began in 2008 generated a great deal of criticism of accounting rules applied to Investments in Other Corporations. As you will read in Appendix D (online), these rules use fair values when accounting for certain types of investments. Critics complained that use of fair values had forced companies to report losses simply because the economic crisis had caused reductions in their investment values. Critics argued that these losses did not accurately reflect reality and that each reported loss caused further reductions in investment value, like the downward spiral of a toilet flush. Supporters of the accounting rules countered that the accounting rules did not cause the economic crisis. Rather, the accounting rules merely exposed the underlying economic problems that existed.

To download a copy of Appendix D, go to www.mhhe.com/phillips4e. The following topics are discussed in the appendix.

An Overview	**Accounting for Passive Investments**	**Accounting for Influential Investments**
• Reasons companies invest • Identifying investment types and accounting methods	• Debt investments held to maturity: Amortized cost method • Available-for-sale securities: Fair value method • Comparison of available-for-sale and trading securities	• Investments for significant influence: Equity method • Investments with controlling interests: Consolidated statements

Solutions to Multiple-Choice Questions

Chapter 1
1. b 2. a 3. c 4. c 5. a 6. c 7. c 8. d 9. b 10. d

Chapter 2
1. d 2. a 3. d 4. a 5. d 6. c 7. a 8. d 9. d 10. b

Chapter 3
1. b 2. b 3. d 4. b 5. a 6. c 7. c 8. a 9. b 10. c

Chapter 4
1. b 2. a 3. d 4. c 5. d 6. d 7. a 8. c 9. c 10. a

Chapter 5
1. b 2. b 3. c 4. a 5. b 6. a 7. b 8. d 9. c 10. d

Chapter 6
1. b 2. d 3. d 4. c 5. c 6. a 7. b 8. c 9. c 10. b

Chapter 7
1. c 2. d 3. d 4. b 5. d 6. d 7. c 8. c 9. c 10. b

Chapter 8
1. d 2. b 3. b 4. d 5. c 6. d 7. c 8. b 9. d 10. d

Chapter 9
1. d 2. d 3. c 4. c 5. d 6. a 7. d 8. b 9. d 10. b

Chapter 10
1. c 2. b 3. c 4. a 5. c 6. b 7. c 8. c 9. d 10. c

Chapter 11
1. a 2. d 3. d 4. a 5. c 6. b 7. c 8. c 9. d 10. a

Chapter 12
1. c 2. d 3. d 4. a 5. a 6. d 7. d 8. a 9. c 10. b

Chapter 13
1. c 2. c 3. c 4. d 5. c 6. a 7. b 8. d 9. d 10. a

Appendix C
1. b 2. d 3. c 4. b 5. a 6. d 7. c 8. a 9. c 10. c

Appendix D
Included in the online appendix

A

Account A standardized format that organizations use to accumulate the dollar effects of transactions on each financial statement item. (10)

Accounting A system of analyzing, recording, and summarizing the results of a business's operating, investing, and financing activities and then reporting them to decision makers. (5)

Accounting Period The time period covered by the financial statements.

Accounting Process The process used by businesses to analyze, record, and summarize transactions and adjustments, prepare financial statements, and prepare the records for the next cycle.

Accounts Payable Amounts owed by the business to suppliers for past transactions.

Accounts Receivable (Trade Receivables, Receivables) Amounts owed to the business by customers for past transactions. (357)

Accrual Basis Accounting Recording revenues when earned and expenses when incurred, regardless of the timing of cash receipts or payments. (98)

Accrued Expenses See *Accrued Liabilities*. (450)

Accrued Liabilities Previously unrecorded expenses that need to be adjusted at the end of the accounting period to reflect the amount incurred and its related liability account. (450)

Accrued Revenues Previously unrecorded revenues that need to be adjusted at the end of the accounting period to reflect the amount earned and its related receivable account.

Acquisition Cost Cash equivalent amount paid or to be paid for an asset.

Adjusted Trial Balance A list of all accounts and their adjusted balances to check on the equality of recorded debits and credits. (158)

Adjusting Journal Entries Entries necessary at the end of each accounting period to measure all revenues and expenses of that period. (148)

Adjustments See *Adjusting Journal Entries*. (148)

Aging of Accounts Receivable Method Using the age of each accounts receivable to estimate uncollectible amounts. (361)

Allowance for Doubtful Accounts (Allowance for Bad Debts, Allowance for Uncollectible Accounts, Reserve for Bad Debts) Contra-asset account containing the estimated dollar value of uncollectible accounts receivable.

Allowance Method Bases bad debt expense on an estimate of uncollectible accounts. (358)

Amortization (1) For intangible assets, this is the systematic and rational allocation of the cost of an intangible asset over its useful life. (2) For bonds payable, this involves allocating any premium or discount over the life of the bond. (415)

Annuity A series of periodic cash receipts or payments that are equal in amount each interest period. (C4)

Assets Probable future economic benefits owned by the business as a result of past transactions. (46)

Asset Turnover Ratio Indicates how well assets are being used to generate revenues. (222)

Audit An examination of a company's financial statements (and management's report on internal control effectiveness) with the goal of detecting misstatements.

Audit Report Describes the auditors' opinion of the fairness of the financial statement presentations and management's assessment of internal control effectiveness.

Authorized Shares Maximum number of shares of a corporation's capital stock that can be issued. (505)

Available-for-Sale Securities All passive investments other than trading securities (classified as either short term or long term). (D5)

Average Cost Method See *Weighted Average Cost Method*. (310)

B

Bad Debt Expense (Doubtful Accounts Expenses, Uncollectible Accounts Expense, Provision for Uncollectible Accounts) Expense associated with estimated uncollectible accounts receivable. (358)

Balance When used as a noun, balance is the dollar amount recorded in an account; when used as a verb, balance is the act of ensuring total assets equal total liabilities plus stockholders' equity.

Balance Sheet (Statement of Financial Position) Reports the amount of assets, liabilities, and stockholders' equity of an accounting entity at a point in time. (12)

Bank Reconciliation Process of using both the bank statement and the cash accounts of a business to determine the appropriate amount of cash in a bank account, after taking into consideration delays or errors in processing cash transactions. (258)

Bank Statement Monthly report from a bank that shows deposits recorded, checks cleared, other debits and credits, and a running bank balance.

Basic Accounting Equation (Balance Sheet Equation) Assets = Liabilities + Stockholders' Equity. (8)

Board of Directors A group of people elected by the stockholders of a company to oversee the decisions made by officers and managers of the company.

Bond Certificate The bond document that each bondholder receives.

Bond Discount The difference between issue price and face value when a bond is sold for less than face value.

Bond Premium The difference between issue price and face value when a bond is sold for more than face value.

Bond Principal The amount (1) payable at the maturity of the bond and (2) on which the periodic cash interest payments are computed.

Book Value See *Carrying Value, Net Book Value.*

C

Callable Bonds Bonds that may be called for early repayment at the option of the company that issued the bond.

Capitalize To record a cost as an asset rather than an expense. (400)

Carrying Value See *Book Value, Net Book Value.*

Cash Money or any instrument that banks will accept for deposit and immediate credit to the company's account, such as a check, money order, or bank draft. (263)

Cash Basis Accounting Recording revenues when cash is received and expenses when cash is paid. (97)

Cash Equivalents Short-term, highly liquid investments purchased within three months of maturity. (263)

Cash Flows from Financing Activities Cash inflows and outflows related to external sources of financing (owners and lenders). (553)

Cash Flows from Investing Activities Cash inflows and outflows related to the purchase or sale of long-lived productive assets. (552)

Cash Flows from Operating Activities (Cash Flows from Operations) Cash inflows and outflows directly related to earnings from normal operations. (552)

Certificate of Deposit A savings certificate, generally issued by commercial banks, entitling the holder to receive interest after a specified maturity date.

Chart of Accounts A summary of all account names and corresponding account numbers used to record financial results in the accounting system. (49)

Classified Balance Sheet A balance sheet that classifies assets and liabilities into current and other (long-term) categories. (63)

Closing Entries Made at the end of the accounting period to transfer balances in temporary accounts to *Retained Earnings* and to establish a zero balance in each of the temporary accounts.

Closing Journal Entries See *Closing Entries.*

Common Stock The basic voting stock issued by a corporation. (503)

Comparable Information Information that can be compared across businesses because similar accounting methods have been applied.

Comparative Financial Statements Report numbers for two or more time periods to make it easy for users to compare account balances from one period to the next. (210)

Comprehensive Income Includes net income plus net unrealized gains or losses on securities available for sale and other adjustments (related to pensions and foreign currency translation) which are directly credited or debited to the stockholders' equity accounts. (623)

Conservatism An accounting practice to not overstate assets and revenues or understate liabilities and expenses.

Consistent Information Information that can be compared over time because similar accounting methods have been applied.

Consolidated Financial Statements The financial statements of two or more companies that have been combined into a single set of financial statements as if the companies were one. (D14)

Contingent Liability Potential liability that has arisen as the result of a past event; not a liability until some future event occurs. (463)

Continuity Assumption See *Going-Concern Assumption.* (621)

Contra-Account An account that is an offset to, or reduction of, another account. (153)

Contract Rate See *Stated Interest Rate.* (457)

Contributed Capital The result of owners providing to the business cash (and sometimes other assets).

Convertible Bonds Bonds that may be converted to other securities of the issuer (usually common stock).

Copyright A form of protection provided to the original authors of literary, musical, artistic, dramatic, and other works of authorship. (413)

Corporation A business organized as a legal entity separate and distinct from its owners under state law.

Cost The amount of resources that a company sacrifices to obtain goods or services; often said to be incurred when the company pays cash or uses credit to acquire the item.

Cost of Goods Sold (CGS) Equation Expresses the relationship between inventory on hand, purchased, and sold;
$BI + P - EI = CGS$ or
$BI + P - CGS = EI$ (308)

Cost Principle Requires assets to be recorded at the historical cash-equivalent cost, which is the amount paid or payable on the date of the transaction. (47)

Coupon Rate See *Stated Interest Rate.* (457)

Credit When used as a noun, credit is the right side of an account; when used as a verb, credit is the act of recording the credit portion of a journal entry to a particular account. (56)

Creditor Any business or individual to whom the company owes money.

Cross-Sectional Analysis Compares one company's financial results to that of other companies competing in the same industry. (219)

Cumulative Dividend Preference Preferred stock feature that requires specified current dividends not paid in full to accumulate for every year in which they are not paid. These cumulative preferred dividends must be paid before any common dividends can be paid. (516)

Cumulative Effects of Changes in Accounting Methods Amounts reflected on the income statement for adjustments made to balance sheet accounts when applying new accounting principles.

Current Assets Assets that will be used up or turned into cash within 12 months or the next operating cycle, whichever is longer. (64)

Current Dividend Preference The feature of preferred stock that grants priority to preferred dividends over common dividends. (515)

Current Liabilities Short-term obligations that will be paid in cash (or fulfilled with other current assets) within 12 months or the next operating cycle, whichever is longer. (64, 448)

Current Ratio Ratio of current assets to current liabilities, used to evaluate liquidity.

D

Days to Collect Measure of the average number of days from the time a sale is made on account to the time it is collected. (368)

Days to Sell Measure of the average number of days from the time inventory is bought to the time it is sold. (319)

Debit When used as a noun, debit is the left side of an account; when used as a verb, debit is the act of recording the debit portion of a journal entry to a particular account. (56)

Debt Covenants See *Loan Covenants*. (205)

Debt-to-Assets Ratio Measures the proportion of total assets financed by debt, computed as total liabilities divided by total assets. (222)

Declaration Date The date on which the board of directors officially approves a dividend. (510)

Declining-Balance Depreciation Method Allocates the cost of an asset over its useful life based on a multiple of (often two times) the straight-line rate. (407)

Deferred Expenses Previously acquired assets that need to be adjusted at the end of the accounting period to reflect the amount of expense incurred in using the asset to generate revenue.

Deferred Revenues Previously recorded liabilities that need to be adjusted at the end of the period to reflect the amount of revenue earned.

Deferred Tax Items Caused by reporting revenues and expenses according to GAAP on a company's income statement at a time that differs from their reporting on the tax return.

Depletion Process of allocating a natural resource's cost over the periods of its extraction or harvesting. (420)

Depreciable Cost The portion of the asset's cost that will be used up during its life. It is calculated as asset cost minus residual value, and it is allocated to depreciation expense throughout the asset's life. (405)

Depreciation Process of allocating the cost of buildings and equipment over their productive lives using a systematic and rational method of allocation. (153, 404)

Direct Method A method of presenting the operating activities section of the statement of cash flows, in which each line of the income statement is reported in terms of gross cash receipts and payments. (555)

Direct Write-Off Method Records bad debt expense only when accounts are written-off; not allowed under GAAP. (371)

Discontinued Operations Financial results from the disposal of a major component of the business. (622)

Discount For bonds, occurs when the issue price is less than the face value.

Alternatively used in the context of sales discounts and purchase discounts. (457)

Discount Rate The interest rate used to compute present values.

Dividends Payments a company periodically makes to its stockholders as a return on their investment.

Dividends in Arrears Dividends on cumulative preferred stock that have not been declared in prior years. (516)

E

Earnings Forecasts Predictions of earnings for future accounting periods.

Earned To have done what is necessary to obtain the right to receive payment.

EBITDA Abbreviation for "earnings before interest, taxes, depreciation, and amortization," which is a measure of operating performance that some managers and analysts use in place of net income. (420)

Effective-Interest Method of Amortization Amortizes a bond discount or premium on the basis of the market interest rate.

Effective Interest Rate Another name for the market rate of interest on a bond.

Electronic Funds Transfer Funds transferred into or out of your account.

Equity Method Used when an investor can exert significant influence over an investee. It requires the investor to record its share of net income and dividends reported by the investee.

Estimated Useful Life Expected service life of a long-lived asset to the present owner.

Expenditures Outflows of cash for any purpose.

Expense Recognition Principle Expenses are recorded when incurred in earning revenue; also called "matching." (100)

Expenses Decreases in assets or increases in liabilities from ongoing operations, incurred to generate revenues during the current period. (95)

Extraordinary Items Gains and losses that are both unusual in nature and infrequent in occurrence.

Extraordinary Repairs Infrequent expenditures that increase an asset's economic usefulness in the future, and that are capitalized. (404)

F

Face Value (Par Value) The amount of a bond payable at its maturity; used to compute interest payments.

Factoring An arrangement where receivables are sold to another company (called a *factor*) for immediate cash (minus a factoring fee). (370)

Fair Value Method Reports securities at their current market value.

Financial Accounting Standards Board (FASB) The private sector body given the primary responsibility to work out the concepts and detailed rules that become generally accepted accounting principles.

Financial Statements Reports that summarize the financial results of business activities.(6)

Financial Statement Users People who base their decisions, in part, on information reported in a company's financial statements.

Financing Activities Related to exchanging money with lenders or owners.

Finished Goods Inventory Manufactured goods that are completed and ready for sale.

First-In, First-Out (FIFO) Method Assumes that the first goods purchased (the first in) are the first goods sold. (310)

Fiscal Any matters relating to money; typically used to describe a specified period of time used for financial reporting.

Fixed Assets Tangible assets that are fixed in place, such as land, buildings, and production equipment.

FOB Destination Term of sale indicating that goods are owned by the seller until delivered to the customer. (265)

FOB Shipping Point Term of sale indicating that goods are owned by the customer the moment they leave the seller's premises. (265)

Form 10-K The annual report that publicly traded companies must file with the SEC.

Form 10-Q The quarterly report that publicly traded companies must file with the SEC.

Franchise A contractual right to sell certain products or services, use certain trademarks, or perform activities in a certain geographical region. (414)

Free Cash Flow Computed as Cash Flows from Operating Activities–Dividends–Capital Expenditures.

Full Disclosure Principle States that relevant information should be disclosed in either the main financial statements or the notes to the financial statements. (621)

Future Value The sum to which an amount will increase as the result of compound interest.

G

Generally Accepted Accounting Principles (GAAP) The rules used in the United States to calculate and report information in the financial statements. (18)

Going-Concern Assumption States that businesses are assumed to continue to operate into the foreseeable future. (621)

Goods Available for Sale The sum of beginning inventory and purchases for the period. (308)

Goodwill (Cost in Excess of Net Assets Acquired) For accounting purposes, the excess of the purchase price of a business over the market value of the business's assets and liabilities. (404)

Gross Profit (Gross Margin, Margin) Net sales less cost of goods sold. (269)

Gross Profit Percentage Indicates how much above cost a company sells its products; calculated as Gross Profit divided by Net Sales. (270)

H

Historical Cost Principle See *Cost Principle*. (47)

Horizontal (Trend) Analyses Trend comparisons across time, often expressing changes in account balances as a percentage of prior year balances. (609)

I

Impairment Occurs when the cash to be generated by an asset is estimated to be less than the carrying value of that asset and requires that the carrying value of the asset be written down. (411)

Imprest System A process that controls the amount paid to others by limiting the total amount of money available for making payments to others. (257)

Income from Operations (Operating Income) Equals net sales less cost of goods sold and other operating expenses.

Income Statement (Statement of Income, Statement of Profit and Loss, Statement of Operations) Reports the revenues less the expenses of the accounting period. (10)

Incur To make oneself subject to; typically refers to expenses, which are incurred by using up the economic benefits of assets or becoming obligated for liabilities, resulting in a decrease in the company's resources in the current period.

Indirect Method A method of presenting the operating activities section of the statement of cash flows, in which net income is adjusted to compute cash flows from operating activities. (555)

Intangible Assets Assets that have special rights but not physical substance.

Interest Formula $I = P \times R \times T$, where I = interest calculated; P = principal; R = annual interest rate; and T = time period covered in the interest calculation (number of months out of 12). (364)

Internal Controls Processes by which a company provides reasonable assurance regarding the reliability of the company's financial reporting, the effectiveness and efficiency of its operations, and its compliance with applicable laws and regulations. (250)

International Financial Reporting Standards (IFRS) The rules used internationally to calculate and report information in the financial statements. (18, 216)

Inventory Tangible property held for sale in the normal course of business or used in producing goods or services for sale.

Inventory Turnover The process of buying and selling inventory. (319)

Investing Activities Involve buying or selling long-lived items such as land, buildings, and equipment.

Investments in Associated (or Affiliated) Companies Investments in stock held for the purpose of influencing the operating and financing strategies for the long term.

Issue Price The amount of money that a lender pays (and the company receives) when a bond is issued. (457)

Issued Shares Total number of shares of stock that have been sold; equals shares outstanding plus treasury shares held. (505)

J

Journal A record of each day's transactions. (56)

Journal Entry An accounting method for expressing the effects of a transaction on accounts in a debits-equal-credits format. (57)

Journalize The process of noting a transaction in the journal in the debits-equal-credits journal entry format.

L

Last-In, First-Out (LIFO) Method Assumes that the most recently purchased units (the last in) are sold first. (310)

Ledger A collection of records that summarizes the effects of transactions entered in the journal. (56)

Lender A creditor that has loaned money to the company.

Liabilities Probable debts or obligations of the entity that result from past transactions, which will be fulfilled by providing assets or services. (46)

Licensing Right The limited permission to use property according to specific terms and conditions set out in a contract. (413)

Line Item An account name or title reported in the body of a financial statement; can represent a single account or the total of several accounts.

Line of Credit A prearranged agreement that allows a company to borrow any amount of money at any time, up to a prearranged limit. (465)

Liquidity The ability to pay current obligations. (612)

Loan Covenants Terms of a loan agreement that, if broken, entitle the lender to renegotiate terms of the loan, including its due date. (205)

Long-Lived Assets Tangible and intangible resources owned by a business and used in its operations over several years. (398)

Long-Term Assets Resources that will be used up or turned into cash more than 12 months after the balance sheet date.

Long-Term Liabilities All of the entity's obligations that are not classified as current liabilities.

Lower of Cost or Market (LCM) Valuation method departing from the cost principle; recognizes a loss when asset value drops below cost. (314)

M

Manufacturing Company A company that sells goods that it has made itself. (250)

Market Interest Rate The current rate of interest that exists when a debt is incurred. Also called *yield*, *discount rate*, or *effective interest rate*. (459)

Matching See *Expense Recognition Principle*. (100)

Material Misstatements Amounts that are large enough to influence a user's decision. (213)

Maturity Date The date on which a bond is due to be paid in full. (457)

Merchandise Inventory Goods held for resale in the ordinary course of business.

Merchandising Company A company that sells goods which have been obtained from a supplier. (250)

Multistep Income Statement Reports alternative measures of income by calculating subtotals for core and peripheral business activities. (269)

N

Net To combine by subtracting one or more amounts from another.

Net Assets Shorthand term used to refer to assets minus liabilities. (414)

Net Book Value (Book Value, Carrying Value) The amount at which an asset or liability is reported after deducting any contra-accounts.

Net Income Equal to revenues minus expenses. (96)

Net Income before Income Taxes Revenues and gains minus losses and all expenses except income tax expense.

Net Profit Margin Profit earned from each dollar of revenue. (112)

Net Profit Margin Ratio Indicates how much profit is earned from each dollar of revenue. (223)

Net Sales Total sales revenue minus Sales Returns and Allowances and Sales Discounts.

Noncash Investing and Financing Activities Transactions that do not have direct cash flow effects; reported as a supplement to the statement of cash flows in narrative or schedule form.

Noncumulative Preferred Stock Preferred stock that does not have cumulative dividend rights, such that dividend rights do not carry over from one year to the next.

Noncurrent Long-term; assets and liabilities that do not meet the definition of current. (64)

No-Par Value Stock Capital stock that has no specified par value. (506)

Notes (Footnotes) Provide supplemental information about the financial condition of a company, without which the financial statements cannot be fully understood.

Notes Receivable Written promises that require another party to pay the business under specified conditions (amount, time, interest). (357)

NSF Checks (Not Sufficient Funds) Checks written for an amount greater than the funds available to cover them. (260)

O

Obsolescence The process of becoming out of date or falling into disuse.

Operating Activities The day-to-day events involved in running a business.

Operating Cycle (Cash-to-Cash Cycle) The time and activities needed for a company to sell goods and services to customers, collect cash from customers, and pay cash to suppliers.

Ordinary Repairs and Maintenance Expenditures for the normal operating upkeep of long-lived assets, recorded as expenses. (403)

Outstanding Shares Total number of shares of stock that are owned by stockholders on any particular date. (505)

P

Paid-In Capital (Additional Paid-In Capital, Contributed Capital in Excess of Par) The amount of contributed capital less the par value of the stock.

Par Value (1) For shares of stock, this is a legal amount per share established by the board of directors; it establishes the minimum amount a stockholder must contribute and has no relationship to the market price of the stock. (2) For bonds, see *Face Value*. (506)

Parent Company The entity that gains a controlling influence over another company (the subsidiary). (D14)

Partnerships Business organizations owned by two or more people. Each partner often is personally liable for debts that the partnership cannot pay.

Patent A right to exclude others from making, using, selling, or importing an invention. (413)

Payment Date The date on which a cash dividend is paid to the stockholders of record. (510)

Percentage of Credit Sales Method Bases bad debt expense on the historical percentage of credit sales that result in bad debts. (361)

Periodic Inventory System A system in which ending inventory and cost of goods sold are determined only at the end of the accounting period based on a physical inventory count. (264)

Permanent Accounts The balance sheet accounts that carry their ending balances into the next accounting period. (163)

Perpetual Inventory System A system in which a detailed inventory record is maintained by recording each purchase and sale of inventory during the accounting period. (263)

Post-Closing Trial Balance Prepared as the last step in the accounting cycle to check that debits equal credits and

that all temporary accounts have been closed. (165)

Preferred Stock Stock that has specified rights over common stock. (514)

Premium For bonds, occurs when the issue price is greater than the face value. (457)

Prepaid Expenses A general account name used to describe payments made in advance of receiving future services; typically includes prepaid rent, prepaid insurance, and other specific types of prepayments.

Present Value The current value of an amount to be received in the future; a future amount discounted for compound interest. (457)

Press Release A written public news announcement normally distributed to major news services.

Private Company A company that has its stock bought and sold privately.

Profit An alternative term for net income.

Profitability Extent to which a company generates income. (612)

Public Company A company that has its stock bought and sold on public stock exchanges.

Public Company Accounting Oversight Board Makes the rules used by auditors of public companies.

Purchase Discount Cash discount received for prompt payment of an account. (317)

Purchase Returns and Allowances A reduction in the cost of purchases associated with unsatisfactory goods. (317)

Q

Qualified Audit Opinion Indicates that either the financial statements do not follow GAAP or the auditors were not able to complete the tests needed to determine whether the financial statements follow GAAP. (214)

Quick Ratio The ratio of liquid assets to current liabilities. Liquid assets include cash and cash equivalents, short-term investments, and accounts receivable (net of doubtful accounts). (464)

R

Ratio (Percentage) Analysis An analytical tool that measures the proportional relationship between two financial statement amounts.

Raw Materials Inventory Items acquired for the purpose of processing into finished goods.

Receivables Turnover The process of selling and collecting on an account. The receivables turnover ratio determines how many times this process occurs during the period on average. (368)

Record Date The date on which the corporation prepares the list of current stockholders as shown on its records. Dividends are paid only to the stockholders who own stock on that date. (510)

Relevant Information Information that can influence a decision. It is timely and has predictive and/or feedback value.

Reliable Information Information that is accurate, unbiased, and verifiable.

Research and Development Costs Expenditures that may someday lead to patents, copyrights, or other intangible assets, but the uncertainty about their future benefits requires that they be expensed. (414)

Residual (or Salvage) Value Estimated amount to be recovered, less disposal costs, at the end of the company's estimated useful life of an asset. (405)

Revenue Recognition Principle Revenues are recorded when goods or services are delivered, there is evidence of an arrangement for customer payment, the price is fixed or determinable, and collection is reasonably assured. (98)

Revenue Recognition Policy An accounting policy that describes when a company reports revenue from providing services or goods to customers.

Revenues Increases in assets or settlements of liabilities arising from ongoing operations. (95)

S

Sales (or Cash) Discount Cash discount offered to customers to encourage prompt payment of an account receivable. (267)

Sales Returns and Allowances Reduction of sales revenues for return of or allowances for unsatisfactory goods. (266)

Sarbanes-Oxley Act (SOX) A set of laws established to strengthen corporate reporting in the United States. (19, 207)

Securities and Exchange Commission (SEC) The U.S. government agency that determines the financial statements that public companies must provide to stockholders and the rules that they must use in producing those statements.

Segregation of Duties An internal control that involves separating employees' duties so that the work of one person can be used to check the work of another person. (252)

Separate-Entity Assumption States that business transactions are separate from and should exclude the personal transactions of the owners. (8)

Service Company A company that sells services rather than physical goods. (250)

Shrinkage The cost of inventory lost to theft, fraud, and error. (264)

Single-Step Income Statement Reports net income by subtracting a single group of expenses from a single group of revenues. (210)

Sole Proprietorship A business organization owned by one person who is liable for debts the business cannot pay.

Solvency Ability to survive long enough to repay lenders when debt matures. (612)

Specific Identification Method A method of assigning costs to inventory, which identifies the cost of each specific item purchased and sold. (309)

Stated Interest Rate The rate of cash interest per period specified in a bond contract. Also called *coupon rate* or *contract rate*. (457)

Statement of Cash Flows Reports inflows and outflows of cash during the accounting period in the categories of operating, investing, and financing. (13)

Statement of Retained Earnings Reports the way that net income and the distribution of dividends affected the financial position of the company during the accounting period. (11)

Stock Dividend Declared by the board of directors to distribute to existing stockholders additional shares of a corporation's own stock. (511)

Stock Split An increase in the total number of authorized shares by a specified ratio; does not decrease retained earnings. (513)

Stockholders' Equity (Owners' Equity or Shareholders' Equity) The financing provided by the owners and the operations of the business. (46)

Straight-Line Method of Amortization Method of amortizing a bond discount or premium that allocates an equal dollar amount to each interest period. (466)

Straight-Line Depreciation Method Allocates the depreciable cost of an asset in equal periodic amounts over its useful life. (406)

Subsidiary Company A business that is controlled by another company (the parent). (D14)

T

10-K See *Form 10-K*.

10-Q See *Form 10-Q*.

T-Account A simplified version of a ledger account used for summarizing transaction effects and determining balances for each account. (58)

Tangible Assets Assets that have physical substance.

Technology Assets Capitalized computer software and Web development costs; an intangible asset. (413)

Temporary Accounts Income statement accounts that are closed to *Retained Earnings* at the end of the accounting period. (163)

Tests of Liquidity Ratios that measure a company's ability to meet its currently maturing obligations.

Tests of Profitability Ratios that compare income with one or more primary activities.

Tests of Solvency Ratios that measure a company's ability to meet its long-term obligations.

Ticker Symbol The one- to four-letter abbreviation used to identify a company on a public securities exchange.

Time Period Assumption The assumption that allows the long life of a company to be reported in shorter time periods. (96)

Time-Series Analysis Compares a company's results for one period to its own results over a series of time periods. (219)

Times Interest Earned Ratio Determines the extent to which earnings before taxes and financing costs are sufficient to cover interest expense incurred on debt. (465)

Time Value of Money The idea that money received today is worth more than the same amount received in the future because money received today

can be invested to earn interest over time.

Trademark An exclusive legal right to use a special name, image, or slogan. (413)

Trading Securities All investments in stocks or bonds that are held primarily for the purpose of active trading (buying and selling) in the near future (classified as short term). (D5)

Transaction An exchange or an event that has a direct economic effect on the assets, liabilities, or stockholders' equity of a business. (48)

Transaction Analysis The process of studying a transaction to determine its economic effect on the business in terms of the accounting equation.

Treasury Stock A corporation's own stock that has been issued but was subsequently reacquired by and is still being held by the corporation. (505)

Trial Balance A list of all accounts with their balances to provide a check on the equality of the debits and credits. (108)

U

Unearned Revenue A liability representing a company's obligation to provide goods or services to customers in the future. (99)

Unit of Measure Assumption States that accounting information should be measured and reported in the national monetary unit. (10)

Units-of-Production Depreciation Method Allocates the depreciable cost of an asset over its useful life

based on its periodic output in relation to its total estimated output. (407)

Unqualified Audit Opinion Auditors' statements that the financial statements are fair presentations in all material respects in conformity with GAAP. (214)

Unrealized Holding Gains and Losses Amounts associated with price changes of securities that are currently held.

Useful Life The expected service life of an asset to the present owner. (405)

V

Vertical (Common Size) Analysis Expresses each financial statement amount as a percentage of another amount on the same financial statement. (611)

Voucher System A process for approving and documenting all purchases and payments on account. (256)

W

Weighted Average Cost Method Uses the weighted average unit cost of goods available for sale for calculations of both the cost of goods sold and ending inventory. (310)

Work in Process Inventory Goods in the process of being manufactured.

Write-Off The removal from an uncollectible account and its corresponding allowance from the accounting records. (359)

Y

Yield See *Market Interest Rate*. (459)

Chapter 1

Chapter 1 Opener: © National Geographic/SuperStock; p. 4 (both) © The McGraw-Hill Companies, Inc./ Brian Moeskau, photographer; p. 21: © Rubberball/Getty Images.

Chapter 2

Chapter 2 Opener: © Jijo Kunily/ Alamy; Exhibit 2.1 (cash): © Comstock/ PunchStock; Exhibit 2.1 (stock certificate): © David A. Tietz/Editorial Image, LLC; Exhibit 2.2 (oven): Courtesy of Toastmaster; Exhibit 2.2 (check): © David A. Tietz/Editorial Image, LLC; Exhibit 2.2 (pan): © Jaimie Duplass/ Alamy; Exhibit 2.2 (invoice due): © Studio 101/Alamy; p. 53 (restaurant): © Creatrixcordis/iStock; p. 55 (invoice paid): © Studio 101/Alamy; p. 56 (manufacturing equipment): © Corbis Premium RF/Alamy; p. 69 (truck): © GeoStock/Photodisc/Getty Images.

Chapter 3

Chapter 3 Opener: © Ted Pink/Alamy.

Chapter 4

Chapter 4 Opener: © Nick Dolding/The Image Bank/Getty Images; p. 155:

© Bernd Euler/VISUM/The Image Works; p. 173: AP Photo/Steve Helber.

Chapter 5

Chapter 5 Opener: © Ethan Miller/Getty Images; p. 225: © Sean Gallup/Getty Images.

Chapter 6

Chapter 6 Opener: Paul Taggart/ Bloomberg via Getty Images; p. 263 (top): © Royalty-Free/Corbis; p. 263 (bottom): © Jill Battaglia/iStock Photo; p. 278 (left): Paul Taggart/Bloomberg via Getty Images; p. 278 (right): © Comstock/PunchStock.

Chapter 7

Chapter 7 Opener: © David Paul Morris/Bloomberg via Getty Images.

Chapter 8

Chapter 8 Opener: © Danita Delimont/ Alamy.

Chapter 9

Chapter 9 Opener: © Robin Smith/ Stone/Getty Images; p. 416 (top): Courtesy of Cedar Point; p. 416 (bottom left): Courtesy of Cedar Point;

p. 416 (bottom right): © Rolf Haid/ epa/Corbis; p. 419: © Bill Aron/Photo Researchers, Inc.

Chapter 10

Chapter 10 Opener: © Laura Dwight/ PhotoEdit.

Chapter 11

Chapter 11 Opener: Courtesy of National Beverage Corporation; p. 530: © The McGraw-Hill Companies, Inc./ David A. Tietz, photographer.

Chapter 12

Chapter 12 Opener: © Scott Boehm/ Getty Images.

Chapter 13

Chapter 13 Opener: © Kevork Djansezian/Getty Images; Appendix D: © Bloomberg/Bloomberg via Getty Images.

A

A. T. Cross Company, 383–384
Aaron's, Inc., 538
Abercrombie & Fitch, 96, 137–138, 176
Activision, 203, 544–545
Activision Blizzard, Inc., 226, 537, 551
 balance sheet, comparative, 210, 211, 218
 comparison to common benchmarks, 219–220
 description and history, 203
 economic crisis, 219
 financial reporting environment, 205–209
 financial statement ratio analysis, 220–224
 financial statement release, 214–215
 financial statement users, 204–205
 income statement, comparative, 210–212
 income statement, multiple-step, 210–212
 independent external audit, 213–214
 international financial reporting standards (IFRS), 216–218
 statement of stockholders' equity, 212
Adelphia Communications, 42
Adidas, 10, 271
Aéropostale, Inc., 508
Ahlers Clocks, 481
Alaska Airlines, 420
Amazon.com, 348
AMC Entertainment, Inc., 495, 592
American Airlines, 126–127, 154
American Eagle Outfitters, 281
 balance sheet reporting of inventory, 307–309
 description and history, 305
 errors in ending inventory, 324–325
 income statement reporting of inventory, 307–309
 inventory costing methods, 309–314
 inventory management decisions, 306
 inventory transaction recording, 315–318
 inventory turnover analysis, 318–320
 inventory types, 306–307
 lower of cost or market, 314–315
 periodic inventory system, 325–326
 perpetual inventory system, 321–324
American Express, 127, 370
American Golf Corporation, 428–429
American Greetings Corporation, 480
Apple Inc., 21, 29, 126–127, 152, 176, 434–435, 588–589
Arctic Cat, 340
Arthur Andersen, 20, 226
Atari Incorporated, 236
AT&T Corp., 126–127, 410
Aurora Foods Inc., 244

B

Bank of America, 96, 212
Bausch & Lomb, 209
Bayer, 427
Benetton, 216
Best Buy Co. Inc., 238, 343, 455
Black & Decker, 534
Borders, 348
Brand Affinity Technologies, 148
British Airways, 401
Brunswick Corporation, 489, 553, 561
The Buckle, Inc., 582
Builder's FirstSource, 620

C

Caffe D'Amore, 393
California Pizza Kitchen, 66, 112
Callaway Golf, 245
Capital One, 212
Cargill, 5
Car Max, 309
Carnival Corporation, 113–114
Caterpillar, Inc., 321, 369, 378, 476–477
Cedar Fair, L. P., 443
 depletion expense, 420–421
 depreciation expense, 418–420, 421–422
 description and history, 397
 fixed asset turnover analysis, 416–417
 intangible assets, 398, 413–415
 long-lived asset classification, 398–399
 tangible assets, 398, 399–412
Chevron Corporation, 630–631
Chick-Fil-A, 5
Chiquita Brands, 148
Cinemark Holdings, Inc., 33
Cintas Corporation, 633
Circuit City Stores, Inc., 167, 223, 448, 502
Coach, Inc., 180–181
Coca-Cola Company, 35–36, 387, 501, 509, 641
Coca-Cola Enterprises, 376
Coinstar, Inc., 38–39, 200
Colgate-Palmolive, 588
Columbia Sportswear, 234
Computer Associates (CA), 97
Costco, 229, 250
Cybex International, 577–578

D

Deere & Company, 321
Dell Corporation, 96, 127, 509
Delta Airlines, 176, 427
Despair.com, 81-82
DHB Industries, Inc., 316, 338-339
Dillard's, Inc., 240, 332, 334
DIRECTV, 454
Discover Card, 370
Dollar General Corporation, 634
Domino's Pizza, 66, 112
Dow Jones & Company, 154
Dreyer's Grand Ice Cream, 216
DSW Inc., 31-32

E

eBay, 411
Electronic Arts, Inc., 30, 42, 219-220, 221, 222-223, 636-637
Elizabeth Arden, Inc., 91
Enron, 20, 207, 209, 226, 251, 603
Escalade, Inc., 201
Ethan Allen Interiors, Inc., 87
Euro Disney, 416
ExxonMobil Corp., 410, 420

F

Facebook, 514
Famous Footwear, 300
FedEx Corporation, 3, 46, 212, 382-383, 427, 433-434
Fitch, 447
Ford Motor Company, 403, 482
Fortune Brands, Inc., 281-282, 530

G

GameStop Corp., 238, 343
The Gap, Inc., 335
General Electric, 503
General Mills, 28
   balance sheet, 449
   bond amortization, 466-474
   contingent liabilities, 463-464
   current liabilities, 448, 449-456
   description and history, 447
   long-term liabilities, 456-463
   quick ratio, 464-465
   times interest earned ratio, 465
General Motors Corporation, 429-430, 448, 527

Gibraltar Industries, Inc., 590-591
Goldman Sachs, 21
Goodyear, 250
Google, Inc., 21, 29, 96, 208, 413, 514
Grant (W. T.) Company, 551
Greek Peak, 129
Green Bay Packers, Inc., 9
GSD + M, 176

H

H. J. Heinz Company, 21, 209
Half Price Books, 75
Harley-Davidson Motorcycles, 319, 320
Harman International Industries, 345-346
Hasbro, Inc., 74, 236, 385, 431, 645
Heelys, Inc., 386
Heinz (H. J.) Company, 21, 209
Hershey Foods Corporation, 245-246
Hewlett-Packard, 369
H&M, 216, 238-239
The Home Depot, Inc., 40-41, 89, 90, 140-141, 199-200, 214, 243-244, 299-300, 351, 391, 441-442, 497, 543-544, 602-603, 607, 614, 615-618, 620, 622-623, 625-626, 646, A1-A12
   balance sheets, A6
   management's reports, A2
   notes to financial statements, A9-A12
   statements of cash flows, A8
   statements of earnings, A5
   stockholders' equity and comprehensive income, A7

I

IBM, 176
IKEA, 216
Infogrames, 236
Intamin, 401
Intel Corporation, 29, 388
International Airlines Group, 401
International Flavors and Fragrances, 148
International Paper, 420

J

JCPenney Company, Inc., 284-285, 637
(John) Deere & Company, 321
Johnson & Johnson, 427, 463
John Wiley & Sons, Inc., 225-226

K

K12, Inc., 60
Kellogg Company, 360, 369
The Knot, Inc., 331
Kohl's Corporation, 240, 375, 637
KPMG, 226
Kraft Foods Inc., 385-386, 486
Krispy Kreme Doughnuts, 375, 414
K-Swiss Inc., 32-33, 369

L

Land O' Lakes, Inc., 481
La-Z-Boy Incorporated, 237
LEGO, 10, 416
Lehman Brothers Holdings, Inc., 66, 566
Levi Strauss, 234
Life Time Fitness, 36-37
Live Nation Entertainment, 148, 455
Lowe's Companies, Inc., 41, 90, 141, 199-200, 244, 299, 351,
    391, 497, 544, 602-603, 646-647, B1-B12
  accounting decisions and concepts, 620-622
  balance sheets, B5
  description and history, 607
  horizontal (trend) analysis, 608-611, 614
  management's reports, B2
  nonrecurring items, 622-623
  notes to financial statements, B8-B12
  other special items, 622-623
  ratio computations, 609, 612-613, 615-619
  reviewing and contrasting IFRS and GAAP, 623-624
  statements of cash flows, B7
  statements of earnings, B4
  statements of shareholders' equity, B6
  vertical analysis, 609, 611-612, 615
Lumber Liquidators, 646-647
Luxottica Group, 281

M

Mack Trucks, 216
Macromedia, Inc., 492-493
Macy's, 334, 355, 356
Mad Catz Interactive, Inc., 235, 363, 367
MasterCard, 370
Mattel, Inc., 9, 250, 385, 645
McDonald's Corporation, 241, 319, 320, 413, 482
McGraw-Hill Education, 127
MCI, 367, 391-392

Microsoft Corporation, 382
MicroStrategy, 20
Moody's, 447

N

National Beverage Corp., 528, 576-577
  common stock transactions, 504-511
  corporate ownership, 502-503
  description and history, 501
  earnings per share (EPS), 517-518
  equity versus debt financing, 503-504
  owners' equity, 519-523
  preferred stock, 514-516
  price/earnings (P/E) ratio, 519
  retained earnings, 516
  return on equity, 518
  stock dividends, 511-513
  stock splits, 513
NBA Players, 21
Nestlé, 10
Netflix, Inc., 74, 96
New Bakery Company, 403
NIKE, Inc., 54, 80, 585
Nintendo of America, 21, 209
Northwest Airlines, 427
Nutek, Inc., 434

O

Oakley, Inc., 28, 273-274, 287-288
Office Max, 75

P

Papa John's International, 10, 50n, 65, 66, 99, 112, 236, 239
Paramount Parks, 401, 414
PayPal, 370
PC Mall, Inc., 334
Penney (JC) Company, Inc., 637
PepsiCo, 387, 501, 517, 518, 519, 641
Pfizer, 212
Phar Mor, 352
Pioneer Corporation, 345-346
Pixar, 157
Pizza Aroma, 203, 398, 551
  accounting cycle, 48-54
  accounting ethics, 19-20
  accounting for business decisions, 5-7

Pizza Aroma–*Cont.*
  accrual adjustments, 147-148, 155-157
  accrual basis accounting, 98-101
  adjusted financial results, 166
  adjusting journal entries, 148-158
  assessing ability to pay, 64-65
  balance sheet, 12-13, 15, 16, 46-54, 63-67, 161-162
  basic accounting equation, 7-9, 49-54
  cash basis accounting, 97-98
  chart of accounts, 49-50
  closing temporary accounts, 162-166
  debit/credit framework, 56-63
  deferral adjustments, 147, 149-154
  description and history, 3, 45, 93, 145
  dividend accounts, 163
  expanded accounting equation, 102-108
  external users of financial statements, 6-7, 18-19
  financing activities and balance sheet accounts, 46-48
  generally accepted accounting principles (GAAP) and, 18-19
  income statement, 10-11, 15, 16, 159-161
  income statement accounts, 95-96, 163-164
  income statement limitations, 112-113
  investing activities and balance sheet accounts, 46-48
  matching principle, 102-108
  net profit margin, 111-112
  notes to financial statements, 14
  operating activities, 46-48, 94-95
  organizational forms, 4-5
  relationships among financial statements, 15-16
  review of revenues and expenses, 110-111
  statement of cash flows, 13-14, 15, 16, 162
  statement of retained earnings, 11-12, 15, 16, 159-161
  transaction analysis for balance sheet, 49-54, 60-63
  transaction analysis for income statement, 103-108
  transaction recording and summary, 54-63
  trial balance
    adjusted, 158-159
    post-closing, 165-166
    unadjusted, 108-110, 159
  using financial statements, 17
Pizza Hut, 96
Polaris Industries Inc., 340, 360
Procter & Gamble, 21, 27, 176, 633

R

RadioShack Corporation, 236-237
Reader's Digest Association, 485
Red Bull, 48
Regal Entertainment Group, 240-241
Regis Corporation, 192-193

Rent-A-Center, Inc., 538
Research in Motion (RIM), 315, 333
Reuters, 41, 216
Rocky Mountain Chocolate Factory, Inc., 245-246, 373

S

Safety-Kleen Corp., 200
Saks, 320
Sam's Club, 229, 267-268
Schutt Sports, 176
Sears Holding Corporation, 382
Singapore Airlines, 420
Six Flags, 397, 417, 418, 419, 443
Skechers, 369
Sonic Corporation, 384, 433
Southwest Airlines, Inc., 30-31, 96, 420, 644
Speedo International, 480
Sports Authority, Inc., The, 634
Standard & Poor's, 447
Starbucks Corporation, 48, 88-89, 454
Sunglass Hut, 273-274
Sysco, 129

T

Take-Two Interactive, 207
Target Corporation, 21, 96, 262, 355, 357, 389-390, 483
Tech Data Corporation, 35
Texas Instruments, 271, 321
Tiger Woods Foundation, 176
Time-Warner, Inc., 125-126, 236
T-Mobile, 127, 154
Toll Brothers, 309
Tootsie Roll Industries, 28, 245-246
The Toro Company, 74-75
Toyota, 216
Trump Entertainments Resorts, Inc., 77

U

Ubisoft, 221, 223
Under Armour Inc., 21-23, 271
  business activities and cash flows, 550
  cash flow classification, 551-554
  cash flow evaluation, 566-567
  description and history, 549
  direct method for determining cash flows, 555-557, 567-571
  financing activities, 553, 562-563, 566

indirect method for determining cash flows, 557-560,
    571-576
investing activities, 552-553, 561-562, 565-566
operating activities, 552, 558-560, 565-566, 567-571
sales of property, plant, and equipment, 571-572
spreadsheet approach to statement of cash flows, 574-576
statement of cash flows preparation, 555-564
US Airways, 420

V

Verizon, 207, 400, 442
VF Corporation (VFC), 376
  accounts receivable, 357-360
  bad debts, 357-364
  description and history, 355
  direct write-off method, 371
  interest revenue, 364-367
  notes receivable, 364-367
  pros and cons of extending credit, 356-357
  receivables turnover analysis, 368-370
Visa, 370
Vivendi, 217, 218, 223
Vivendi Games, 203, 215
Volcom, Inc., 82-83, 188-189, 239

W

W. T. Grant Company, 551
Walgreens, 310, 390

Walmart, 287, 320, 355, 356, 389-390, 398
  cash controls and reporting, 253-263
  description and history, 249
  gross profit analysis, 269-271
  income statement, multistep, 270
  internal control, 251-253
  inventory controls and reporting, 263-269
  merchandise sales controls and reporting, 263-269
  net sales, 269
  operating cycles, 250
Walt Disney Company, 397, 591
Warnaco Group Inc., 480
Waste Management, Inc., 127, 427
Wolverine World Wide, Inc., 128, 287
Worldcom, 20, 141, 207, 400, 442
WorldGym, 250

X

Xerox Corporation, 388

Y

Yahoo! Finance, 216, 417, 457, 518
Yahoo! Inc., 237-238
YUM Brands, Inc., 241

Subject Index

A

Accountants
  career options for, 20-21
  certification of, 19
Accounting
  for business decisions, 5-7
  careers in, 20-21
  defined, 5
  ethical issues in. *See* Accounting fraud; Ethical issues
  external users of information, 6-7, 17, 18-19, 204-205
  internal users of information, 6, 205
  key features of, 47-48
  legal issues in. *See* Legal issues
  system overview, 6
Accounting concepts, 620-622
Accounting cycle, 49-56. *See also* Operating cycle
  adjusted trial balance, 158-162
  analysis in. *See* Analysis of accounting transactions
  closing temporary accounts, 55, 162-166
  defined, 55
  overview, 49, 166
  post-closing trial balance, 165-166
  recording in. *See* Recording accounting transactions
  review of, 56-63
  summarizing in. *See* Summarizing accounting transactions
  unadjusted trial balance, 108-110, 149, 150
Accounting equations
  balance sheet, 12-13, 554
  basic accounting equation, 7-9, 12-13, 16, 46, 49, 102
  cost of goods sold, 308-309
  expanded, 102-108
  income statement, 10-11, 16, 102-108
  statement of cash flows, 16
  statement of retained earnings, 16
Accounting fraud, 206-208, 209, 251. *See also* Ethical issues
  capitalizing expenses, 400
  character to rationalize and conceal, 207, 208
  conditions for, 206-207
  incentive to commit, 206-207
  inventory and, 316
  lack of internal controls and, 263
  opportunity to commit, 207, 208
  preventing, 19-20, 207-208
Accounting period, adjusting entries at end of, 55, 146
Accounting process, elements of, 55
Account(s)
  balance sheet, 12-13, 46-49
  calculating balances, 108

  defined, 10
  income statement, 10-11, 95-96, 102-108, 111-112
Accounts payable
  on balance sheet, 13
  as current liability, 449
  incurring cost to be paid later, 107
  inventory purchase and, 315-318
  operating activities and, 560
Accounts receivable, 356-364
  aging, 361-362
  allowance method for bad debts, 358-360, 362
  bad debts and, 357-364, 371
  on balance sheet, 13
  credit card sales, 370
  days to collect, 368, 369, 613
  defined, 357
  factoring, 370
  operating activities and, 559
  pros and cons of extending credit, 356-357
  providing services on credit, 104
  receivables turnover analysis, 368-370, 613, 618
  receiving payment on account, 104
Accrual adjustments
  accounts affected by, 148
  nature of, 147-148, 155
  role of, 147-148, 155
  sample entries, 155-157
Accrual basis accounting, 98-101
  accrued liabilities. *See* Accrued liabilities
  accruing interest earned, 365-366
  adjustments. *See* Accrual adjustments
  defined, 98
  expense recognition in, 100-101, 111, 358, 565
  liabilities. *See* Accrued liabilities
  manipulation of, 551
  matching principle in, 100-101, 146, 157, 358, 420-421
  revenue recognition in, 98-99, 110-111, 565
Accrued liabilities, 449-453
  defined, 450
  expense recognition, 100-101, 111, 358, 565
  income taxes, 452
  interest expense, 452-453, 456-463
  operating activities and, 560
  payroll deductions, 450-451
  unearned revenue, 99, 103, 455-456
Accumulated deficit, 516
Accumulated depreciation, 153-154, 266-267, 404-405, 408, 412
Acquisition
  of intangible assets, 414

of inventory, 315-318
of tangible assets, 400-403
Additional paid-in capital, 506
Adjusted trial balance, 158-162
  defined, 158-159
  financial statements and, 159-162
  sample entries, 159, 160
  T-accounts, 158-162
Adjusting journal entries, 146, 148-158
Adjustments to financial statements, 144-174
  accrual adjustments, 147-148, 155-157
  adjusted financial results, 166
  adjusted trial balance, 158-162
  balance sheet, 161-162
  closing temporary accounts, 162-166
  deferral adjustments, 147, 149-154
  defined, 146
  at end of accounting period, 55, 146
  income statement, 159-161
  journal entries, 148-158
  making required adjustments, 148-158
  need for, 146-158
  statement of cash flows and notes, 162
  statement of retained earnings, 159-161
Aging of accounts receivable method, 361-362
AICPA (American Institute of Certified Public Accountants),
    Code of Professional Conduct, 19
Allowance for doubtful accounts, 362, 367
Allowance method, for bad debts, 358-360, 362
American Institute of Certified Public Accountants (AICPA),
    Code of Professional Conduct, 19
Amortization, 415
  discount on bonds payable, 461, 466-467, 469-471,
    473-474
  effective-interest, 467-474
  of liabilities, 466-474
  premium on bonds payable, 460-461, 468-469, 472-473
  simplified effective-interest, 471-474
  straight-line, 461, 466-467
Analysis of accounting transactions, 49-64
  accounting transactions, nature of, 48
  adjustments, 148-158
  balance sheet concepts and values in, 49-54
  debit/credit framework in, 57, 102-108
  financial ratios and. See Ratio analysis
  financing from lender, 51, 61
  financing from stockholders, 50, 60
  income statement concepts and values in, 103-108
  incurring costs to be paid later, 107
  investing in equipment, 50-51, 52, 61-62, 561-562
  nature of, 49

ordering supplies, 52-53, 62
paying cash in advance, 106
paying cash to employees, 105, 256-257
paying supplier, 53, 62, 107, 569
providing services for cash, 103
providing services on credit, 104
receiving cash for future services, 103
receiving payment on account, 104
receiving supplies, 53-54, 62
transaction analysis, 49-54
Annual interest rate, 364
Annual report
  examples, A1-A12, B1-B12
  filing of, 215
  typical elements of financial section, 215
Annuity
  defined, C4
  future value of, C5, C16
  present value of, C5-C6, C8-C11, C12-C13, C17
Arrears, dividends in, 516
Asset impairment losses, 411
Asset(s). See also Intangible assets; Tangible assets
  in accounting equation, 8
  adjusting entries for, 146
  on balance sheet, 13, 46, 64. See also Balance sheet
  in basic business model, 220-221
  basket purchase of, 401
  current, 64, 557-558
  defined, 8, 46
  long-lived. See Long-lived assets
Asset turnover ratio, 221, 222-223, 416-417, 613, 616
Association of Certified Fraud Examiners, 253
Audit committee, 208
Authorized shares, 505-507

B

Bad debt expense
  adjusting for estimated bad debts, 358-359
  aging of accounts receivable method for estimating,
    361-362
  allowance method for estimating, 362
  collection of previously written off account, 363
  direct write-off method, 359-360, 363-364, 371
  estimating, 357-364, 367, 371
  percentage of credit sales method for estimating, 361
  pros and cons of extending credit, 356-357
  revising estimates for, 363
Balance sheet, 12-13, 44-71
  accounts on, 13, 46-49
  adjusted trial balance and, 161-162

Balance sheet–*Cont.*
  assessing ability to pay, 64-65
  basic equation for, 7-9, 13, 16, 46, 49, 102
  bond liability reporting, 459
  bond premium reporting, 466
  business activities and, 46-49
  chart of accounts, 49-50
  classified, 63-65
  comparative, 210, 211
  concepts and values on, 65-67
  defined, 12
  dividend effects, 511
  equation for, 13
  inventory on, 307-309
  preparing, 63-64
  relationship with other financial statements, 15, 553, 554-555
  summary, 16
Bank reconciliation, 257-263
  bank statement in, 258-260
  defined, 258
  need for, 259-262
  procedures, 260-262
Bank(s)
  as creditors, 7, 51, 61
  financing from, 7, 51, 61
  procedures concerning, 257-263
Bank statement, 258-260
  checks cleared, 258-259
  deposits made, 259
Basic accounting equation, 7-9, 13, 16, 46, 49, 102
Basket purchase of assets, 401
Beginning inventory, 308
Benchmarks
  cross-sectional analysis, 219-220
  for financial statements, 219-220
  for inventory turnover, 319-320
  for receivables turnover, 369-370
  time-series analysis, 219-220, 609
Bond amortization, 460-461, 466-467, 469-474
Bonding employees, 253
Bonds payable, 456-463, 466-474
  bonds, defined, 456
  certificate, sample, 456
  discount amortization, 457-459, 461, 466-467, 469-471, 473-474
  initial issuance, 457-460
  interest owed and paid, 460-461
  issued above or below face value, 457-459, 460-461, 466-467, 468-469, 472-474
  issued at face value, 458, 460
  premium amortization, 460-461, 468-469, 472-473
  pricing, 457
  retirements, 462-463
  times interest earned ratio, 465, 613, 619
  types of, 463
Book (carrying) value, 153, 405
Brand managers, 21
Brooks, David H., 316
Buildings. *See also* Long-lived assets; Property, plant, and equipment
  acquisition of, 400
  as tangible asset, 400
Business decisions
  accounting decisions in trend analysis, 620
  accounting for, 5-7
  constraints on, 620-622
  inventory, 306
  liabilities. *See* Liabilities
  long-lived assets, 418-420
  recording, 66
Business organization. *See* Organizational forms
Business partners, incentive to commit fraud and, 206

C

Callability, of long-term debt, 463
Capital accounts
  contributed capital, 102, 212, 504, 562-563
  partnership, 522-523
  sole proprietorship, 520
Capital expenditures, extraordinary repairs, replacements, and additions as, 404
Capitalization
  defined, 400
  of tangible asset costs, 400
Careers in accounting, 20-21
Carrying (book) value, 153, 405
Cash
  adjusting entries impact on, 158
  on balance sheet, 13
  bank reconciliations, 258-260
  controlling and reporting, 253-263
  defined, 263
  dividend declaration, 511
  in financial statement reporting, 263
  internal control over, 253-263
  paying in advance, 106
  paying to employees, 105, 256-257
  paying to supplier, 107
  pros and cons of extending credit, 356-357
  providing services for, 103
  in purchase of tangible assets, 402

receiving for future services, 103
receiving payment on account, 104
timing of reporting expenses versus cash receipts, 101
timing of reporting revenue versus cash receipts, 98-99, 110-111
Cash basis accounting, 97-98
Cash dividends. *See also* Stock dividends
  in arrears, 516
  balance sheet effects, 511
  closing temporary accounts, 163, 164
  on common stock, 509-511
  cuts in taxes, 509
  declaration, 510-511
  declared and paid, 158, 510-511
  dividends, defined, 9
  nature of, 503
  payment, 158, 510-511
  on preferred stock, 514, 515-516
  record date, 510
  on statement of retained earnings, 11-12
Cash equivalents
  defined, 263
  in financial statement reporting, 263
Cash flow. *See also* Statement of cash flows
  classifying cash flows, 551-554
  converting operating expenses to cash outflow, 569-57
  converting revenues to cash inflows, 568-569
  from financing, 14, 553, 562-563, 566, 571-576
  inventory reporting method and, 313
  from investment, 14, 552-553, 561-562, 565-566, 571-572
  from operations, 14, 552, 555-560, 565-567
  overall patterns, 566-567
Cash payments, 256-257
  by check for purchases on account, 256
  to employees versus electronic funds transfer, 256-257
Cash receipts, 253-255
  by mail, 255
  in person, 253-255
  via electronic funds transfer, 255
Certification of accountants, 19, 213-214
Channel stuffing, 368
Character
  encouraging good, 208
  to rationalize and conceal fraud, 207
Charter, partnership, 521
Chart of accounts, 49-50
  balance sheet, 49-50
  defined, 49
Checks, 258-259, 260, 261
Chief executive officer (CEO)
  financial statement responsibility of, 19

internal controls, 19, 251
release of financial statements, 214-215
role of, 205
Chief financial officer (CFO)
  financial statement responsibility of, 19
  internal controls, 19, 251
  role of, 205
Classified balance sheet, 63-65
  assessing ability to pay, 64-65
  components, 63-64
Closing processes
  at end of accounting period, 55
  temporary accounts, 162-166
Code of Professional Conduct (AICPA), 19
Collusion, 253
Common-size analysis. *See* Vertical analysis
Common stock, 504-514
  authorization, 505-507
  benefits of owning, 503
  defined, 503
  dividends. *See* Cash dividends; Stock dividends
  issuance, 5
  preferred stock versus, 514
  reissuance of, 508-509
  repurchase, 507
  stock splits, 513
  treasury stock, 504, 505, 507-509
Comparative financial statements, 210, 211
Compensation analysts, 21
Compounding, power of, C4
Compound interest, C4
Comprehensive income, 623
Conservatism principle, accounts receivable and, 358
Consignment inventory, 306-307
Consistency, in inventory reporting, 314
Consolidated financial statements, examples, A5-A12, B4-B12
Construction in progress, 399
Contingent liabilities, 463-464
Contra-accounts
  accumulated depreciation, 153-154, 266-267, 404-405, 408, 412
  allowance for doubtful accounts, 362
  defined, 153
  equity, 5C7, 508
  Treasury stock, 507, 508
Contributed capital, 102, 212, 504, 562-563
Control. *See* Internal control
Convertible bonds, 463
Copyright, 413
Corporate bonds, 463
Corporate life cycle, 565, 566-567

Corporations. *See also* Common stock; Stockholders' equity
  extent of use, 5
  nature of, 5
  organization structure, 503
  ownership characteristics, 502-503
Cost of goods sold (CGS)
  converting to cash paid to suppliers, 569
  errors in ending inventory, 324-325
  first-in, first-out (FIFO) method and, 310, 311, 322
  last-in, first-out (LIFO) method and, 310, 311-312, 322-323
  periodic inventory system, 264, 316, 325-326
  perpetual inventory system, 263, 264-266, 315-318, 321-324, 326
  reporting, 308-309
  weighted average cost method, 310, 312, 323
Cost of goods sold (COGS) equation, 308-309
Cost principle, 13, 47, 420-421
CPA (Certified Public Accountant), 19, 213-214
Credit
  credit card sales, 370
  defined, 56, 102
  extending, pros and cons of, 356-357
  providing services on, 104
  in purchase of tangible assets, 402-403
Credit balance, 59
Credit crisis of 2008-2009. *See* Financial crisis of 2008-2009
Creditors
  accounting fraud and, 20
  banks as, 7, 51, 61
  as external users of financial information, 7, 17, 205
  nature of, 7
  types of, 7
Credit ratings, 448
Credit terms, in benchmarks for receivables turnover, 369
Cross-sectional analysis, 219-220
Cumulative dividend preference, 516
Currency, and unit of measure assumption, 10
Current assets
  defined, 64
  operating activities and, 557-558
Current dividend preference, 515-516
Current liabilities, 449-456
  accounts payable, 449
  accrued liabilities, 449-453
  current portion of long-term debt, 454
  defined, 64, 448
  notes payable, 452-453
  operating activities and, 558
  sales tax payable, 455

  unearned revenue, 99, 103, 455-456
Current ratio, 65, 613, 618-619
Customers
  customer business developers, 21
  as external users of accounting information, 7

D

Days to collect, 368, 369, 613
Days to sell, 319, 321, 613
Debentures, 463
Debit, defined, 56, 102
Debit balance, 59
Debit/credit framework, 56-63, 102-111
Debt. *See also* Long-term liabilities
  defined, 46
  early retirement, 462-463
  nonliability of corporate shareholders for, 502
Debt financing, equity financing versus, 46, 503-504
Debt-to-assets ratio, 221, 222, 224, 613, 619
Declaration date of dividend, 510-511
Decline phase, 566-567
Declining-balance depreciation method, 406, 407-408, 409, 410-411, 419
Deferral adjustments
  accounts affected by, 149-154
  nature of, 147
  role of, 147, 149
  sample entries, 149-154
Deferred Income Tax, 410-411
Depletion, 420-421
Deposits in transit, 261
Deposits made, 259
Depreciable cost, 405-411
Depreciation, 404-411
  accumulated, 153-154, 404-405, 412
  asset impairment losses, 411
  book (carrying) value, 153, 405
  calculating, 405-411
  changes in estimates, 421-422
  declining-balance method, 406, 407-408, 409, 410-411, 419
  deferral adjustments for, 153-154
  defined, 153, 404
  in determining operating cash flows, 557, 558, 570
  differences, impact of, 418-420
  disposal of tangible assets, 405, 411-412
  partial-year calculations, 410-411
  straight-line method, 406-407, 409, 410-411, 419
  tax, 410-411
  units-of-production method, 406, 407, 409
Direct method

defined, 555
    of reporting operating activities, 555-557, 567-571
    of writing off bad debt expense, 359-360, 363-364, 371
Directors
    audit committee requirement, 208
    declaration of dividends, 509-511
    as internal users of financial information, 6, 205
Direct write-off method for bad debts, 359-360, 363-364, 371
Discontinued operations, 622
Discount
    accounting for bonds issued at, 457-459, 461, 466-467,
        469-471, 473-474
    amortization of bonds issued at, 461, 466-467, 469-471,
        473-474
    purchase, 317-318
    sales, 267-268
Disposal
    gain/loss on, 412
    of intangible assets, 415-416
    of tangible assets, 405, 411-412
    useful lives, 405
Dividend declared account, 510-511
Dividends. See Cash dividends; Stock dividends
Documenting procedures, internal control and, 47, 251, 252,
        257, 269
Double-declining balance depreciation method, 408, 409
Doubtful accounts, allowance for, 362
Duality of effects, 49

E

Early retirement of debt, 462-463
Earnings per share (EPS), 517-518, 613, 617
EBITDA (earnings before interest, taxes, depreciation, and
        amortization), 420
EDGAR (Electronic Data Gathering and Retrieval Service),
        215
Edison, Thomas, 503
Effective-interest amortization, 467-474
    of bonds issued at discount, 469-471, 473-474
    of bonds issued at premium, 468-469, 472-473
    simplified, 471-474
Electronic Data Gathering and Retrieval Service (EDGAR),
        215
Electronic funds transfer (EFT)
    bank reconciliation and, 260, 261
    cash paid to employees via, 256-257
    cash received via, 255
Employees
    accrued income taxes, 452
    accrued payroll deductions, 450-451

cash paid to, 105, 256-257
    incentives to commit fraud and, 206-208
    inventory shrinkage and, 264-265
    opportunity to commit fraud, 207
    rationalizing and concealing fraud, 207
    stock used to compensate, 507
    wages expense, 105, 155-156
Ending inventory, 308, 311-312, 324-325
Equations. See Accounting equations
Equipment. See also Long-lived assets; Property, plant,
        and equipment
    acquisition of, 400
    on balance sheet, 13
    depreciation for use of, 153-154
    investing in, 50-51, 52, 61-62, 561-562
    on statement of cash flows, 561-562
    as tangible asset, 400
Equity, defined, 46
Equity financing. See also Common stock; Preferred
        stock
    debt financing versus, 46, 503-504
    incentive to commit fraud and, 206
    nature of, 46
Errors
    bank reconciliation and, 259, 260, 261-262
    in ending inventory, 324-325
Estimates
    bad debt expense, 357-364, 367, 371
    depreciation, 421-422
    prospective change in, 421-422
    revising, 363
Ethical issues. See also Accounting fraud
    control over cash, 263
    ethics, defined, 19
    nature of accounting ethics, 19-20
    stock options, 507
    time period assumption, 97
Expanded accounting equation, 102-108
Expense recognition ("matching") principle, 100-101, 146,
        157, 358, 420-421, 565
Expenses
    in accrual basis accounting, 100-101, 110-111, 358, 565
    adjusting entries for, 146
    in cash basis accounting, 97-98
    changes in recognition, 565
    converting to cash outflow, 569-571
    defined, 8-9, 95
    on income statement, 10-11, 95-96, 102-108, 111
    incurring cost to be paid later, 107
    review of, 110-111
    as subcategory of retained earnings, 102
    time period assumption, 96

External audits of financial statements, 208, 213-214
External exchanges, in accounting cycle, 48
External users of accounting information
  accounting system and, 6
  concepts for external reporting, 18
  types of, 7, 17, 204-205
Extraordinary repairs and maintenance, 404

F

Face value
  bonds issued above, 457-458, 460-461, 466, 472-473
  bonds issued at, 458, 460
  bonds issued below, 457-459, 461, 466-467, 469-471,
    473-474
  defined, 457
Factoring receivables, 370
Federal Insurance Contributions Act (FICA), 450-451
Federal Unemployment Tax Act (FUTA), 451
FICA taxes, 450-451
Financial accounting
  in accounting system, 6-7
  government regulation of, 19, 205, 207-208, 213-214, 251
Financial Accounting Standards Board (FASB), 18-19, 216. See
    also Generally accepted accounting principles (GAAP)
Financial analysts, 21
Financial crisis of 2008-2009, 219
  Circuit City failure, 167, 223, 448, 502
  current ratios before and after, 66
  days to collect before and after, 369
  days to sell before and after, 321
  fixed asset turnover before and after, 418
  gross profit percentage before and after, 271
  Lehman Brothers' operating cash flows, 566
  liabilities in, 448
  lines of credit, 465
  net profit margin before and after, 112
Financial fraud. See Accounting fraud; Ethical issues
Financial performance, 606-627
  horizontal analysis, 608-611
  ratio analysis. See Ratio analysis
  vertical analysis, 609, 611-612, 615
Financial ratios. See Ratio analysis
Financial statements, 9-17
  accounting concepts underlying, 620-622
  accounting decisions underlying, 620
  adjusted trial balance and, 159-162
  adjustments to. See Adjustments to financial statements
  balance sheet. See Balance sheet
  comparative, 210, 211
  comparison to common benchmarks, 219-220
  defined, 6-7
  ethical issues and. See Ethical issues
  examples, A5-A12, B4-B12
  faithful representation of information, 18
  financial reporting environment, 19, 205-209, 209-216
  format of, 210-212, 217-218, 556
  income statement. See Income statement
  independent external audits, 208, 213-214
  inventory costing method impact on, 307-309, 312-313
  legal issues and. See Legal issues
  notes to, 14
  quarterly reports, 215
  ratio analysis. See Ratio analysis
  relationships among, 15
  release of, 214-215
  relevance to users, 18
  reliability of, 18-19. See also Generally accepted
    accounting principles (GAAP)
  reporting in the U.S., 209-216
  SEC filings, 215, 216
  statement of cash flows. See Statement of cash flows
  statement of retained earnings. See Statement of retained
    earnings
  summary, 16
  useful financial information, 17-20
  users, needs of, 6-7, 17, 205
  using, 17
Financing activities
  on balance sheet, 46-48
  defined, 14
  indirect method of reporting, 571-576
  on statement of cash flows, 14, 553, 562-563, 566,
    571-576
Finished goods inventory, 306
First-in, first-out (FIFO) inventory costing method, 310, 311,
    322
Fixed assets. See Tangible assets
Fixed asset turnover ratio, 416-417, 613, 616
FOB destination, 265, 307, 316-317
FOB shipping point, 265, 307, 316-317
Foreign exchange, unit of measure assumption and, 10
Form 8-K, 215
Form 10-K, 215
Form 10-Q, 215
Franchise, 413-414
Fraud. See Accounting fraud
Full disclosure principle, 621
Future value
  of an annuity, C5, C16
  defined, C1
  of a single amount, C2-C3
  tables for determining, C14, C16

G

Generally accepted accounting principles (GAAP)
  accrual basis accounting, 98
  classification choices, 554
  for contingent liabilities, 463, 464
  defined, 18
  direct write-off method for bad debts, 371
  external audits, 208, 213-214
  format of financial statements, 217
  International Financial Reporting Standards (IFRS) versus,
      18-19, 216-218, 314, 416, 464, 554, 557, 623-624
  preferred stock as stockholders' equity, 515
Gift cards, redemption of, 154
Going concern assumption, 621
Going-concern problem, 621
Goods available for sale, 308
Goods in transit, 307
Goodwill, 414
Government
  as external user of accounting information, 7, 205
  regulation of financial reporting, 19, 205, 207-208, 213-
      214, 251
Greed, in accounting fraud, 207
Gross earnings, 450
Gross profit, defined, 265-266
Gross profit analysis, 269-271
Gross profit percentage, 270-271, 320, 613, 615-616
Growth investment, 509
Growth phase, 566-567

H

Headd, Brian, 11n
Hensley, Laurie, 3-7, 10-11, 18-20, 45-48, 145
Hermanson, Dana R., 207n
Hollinger, Richard, 265n
Horizontal analysis, 608-611
  computations, 609-611
  defined, 608
  examples of, 610
  trends revealed in, 614
Hotlines, anonymous, 253

I

Impairment
  asset impairment losses, 411
  defined, 411
Imprest system, 257

Income before income tax expense, 212
Income from operations, 210-212
Income statement, 92-118
  accounts on, 10-11, 95-96, 102-108, 111-112
  accrual basis accounting. See Accrual basis accounting
  adjusted trial balance and, 159-161
  basic equation for, 10-11, 16, 102-108
  cash basis accounting, 97-98
  closing temporary accounts, 163-164
  comparative, 210, 211
  concepts and values, 103-108
  defined, 10
  equations for, 10-11, 16, 102-108
  expanded accounting equation, 102-108
  expense accounts, 10-11, 95-96, 102-108, 111
  interest expense reporting on, 459
  inventory and, 307-309
  limitations of, 112-113
  multistep, 210-212, 269, 270
  operating transactions. See Operating activities
  relationship with other financial statements, 15, 553,
      554-555
  revenue accounts. See Revenue(s)
  single-step, 210
  summary, 16
  time period assumption, 96, 97
  unadjusted trial balance, 108-110, 149, 150
  unit of measure assumption in, 10
Income taxes. See also Internal Revenue Service (IRS)
  accrued, 452
  deferred, 410-411
  direct write-off method for bad debts, 371
  dividend policy affected by tax rules, 509
  employee taxes withheld, 452
  income before income tax expense, 212
  incurred but not yet recorded, 156-157
  inventory reporting method and, 313
  tax depreciation, 410-411
Independent verification, internal control and, 251,
      252, 258
Indirect method
  defined, 555
  of reporting investing activities, 571-572
  of reporting operating activities, 557-560, 571-572
Industry analysis. See also Benchmarks; Horizontal
      analysis
  cross-sectional analysis, 219-220
  gross profit percentage, 270-271, 320
  inventory turnover, 319-320
  operating results, 271
  receivable turnover, 369-370
Initial public offerings (IPOs), 5, 506

Intangible assets, 413–415, 562
  acquisition, 414
  defined, 398, 413
  disposal, 415–416
  types of, 398, 413–415
  use, 415
Interest expenses
  accrued, 452–453
    on bonds payable, 460–461
    on notes payable, 453
  incurred but not yet recorded, 156
  long-term liabilities, 456–463
Interest formula, 364
Interest periods, time value of money and, C6
Interest rates
  calculating interest on notes receivable, 364
  relationship to bond prices, 459
  stated, 457
  time value of money and, C6
Interest revenue
  accruing interest earned, 365–366
  bank reconciliation and, 260, 261
  calculating, 364
  compound interest, C4
  interest formula, 364
  recording, 365–367
  reporting, on notes receivable, 365–367
  timelines for, 365
Internal control, 19, 248–276
  over cash, 253–263
  common control principles, 251–252
  defined, 250
  gross profit analysis, 269–271
  independent verification and, 251, 252, 258
  over inventory, 263–269
  lack of, 263
  limitations of, 252–253
  nature of, 251
  principles of, 251–252
Internal events, in accounting cycle, 48
Internal Revenue Service (IRS), 205, 410–411. *See also*
    Income taxes
Internal users of accounting information
  accounting system and, 6
  types of, 6, 205
International Accounting Standards Board (IASB), 18
International Financial Reporting Standards (IFRS)
  accounting for tangible and intangible assets, 410
  accrual basis accounting, 98
  classification choices, 554
  component allocation in basket purchases, 401

  defined, 18
  direct write-off method for bad debts, 371
  format of financial statements, 217
  generally accepted accounting principles (GAAP) versus,
      18–19, 216–218, 314, 416, 464, 554, 557, 623–624
  globalization process and, 216–218
  inventory accounting methods, 314
  LIFO reporting not allowed, 314
  loan covenants, violated, 455
  lower of cost or market inventory reporting, 314
  preferred stock as stockholders' equity, 515
Introductory phase, 566–567
Inventory, 304–329
  balance sheet reporting, 307–309
  comparison to benchmarks, 319–320
  consignment, 306–307
  cost flow computations, 309–315
  costing/valuation methods, 321–324
  days to sell, 319, 321, 613
  defined, 306
  financial statement effects of costing methods, 307–309,
      312–313, 323–324
  finished goods, 306
  first-in, first-out (FIFO), 310, 311, 322
  income statement reporting, 307–309
  internal control over, 263–269
  last-in, first-out (LIFO), 310, 311–312, 322–323
  lower of cost or market (LCM), 314–315
  management decisions, 306
  merchandise, 306
  operating activities and, 559
  periodic inventory system, 264, 316, 325–326
  perpetual inventory system, 263, 264–266, 316–318, 321–324
  purchase-related transactions, 308, 315–318
  raw materials, 306
  sales-related transactions, 265–269, 306–307
  shrinkage, 264–265
  type of business and, 306–307
  weighted average costing method, 310, 312, 323
  work in process, 306
Inventory costing methods, 309–315
  cost flow assumptions, 309–315
  lower of cost or market, 314–315
  specific identification, 309–310
Inventory turnover, 318–320, 613, 618
Investing activities
  on balance sheet, 46–48
  defined, 14
  indirect method of reporting, 571–572
  on statement of cash flows, 14, 552–553, 561–562, 565–
      566, 571–572

Investment analysts, 21
Investors
  as external users of financial information, 7, 17, 205
  investor information Web sites, 215, 216
  nature of, 7
  stock exchanged between, 506
  types of, 7
Issued shares
  defined, 505
  repurchase of, 507
  stock exchanged between investors, 506
  stock used to compensate employees, 507
Issue price
  bonds issued above face value, 457-458, 460-461, 466, 472-473
  bonds issued at face value, 458, 460
  bonds issued below face value, 457-459, 461, 466-467, 469-471, 473-474
  defined, 457

J

Job security, incentive to commit fraud and, 207
Journal entries
  accrual adjustments, 155-157
  adjusting, 146, 148-158
  allowance method for doubtful accounts, 362
  balance sheet accounts, 57-58, 59-60, 60-63
  closing temporary accounts, 162-166
  debit/credit framework in, 57-63
  deferral adjustments, 149-154
  defined, 57
  formal journal page, 57
  income statement accounts, 103-108
  periodic inventory system, 316, 325-326
  perpetual inventory system, 266, 316-318, 326, 327
  posting to ledger, 58
  repurchase of stock, 507
  stock dividends, 512
  for tangible asset acquisition, 402
Journals
  debit/credit framework for, 56-63
  defined, 56

L

Labor relations managers, 21
Land. See also Long-lived assets; Property, plant, and equipment
  acquisition of, 400

land improvements versus, 399
  as tangible asset, 400
Largay, James A., III, 551n
Last-in, first-out (LIFO) inventory costing method, 310, 311-312, 322-323
Least and latest rule, 411
Ledger
  debit/credit framework for, 56-63
  defined, 56
  posting from journal to, 58
Ledger accounts
  summarizing in, 58-60
  T-account simplified format for, 59-60
Legal issues
  internal controls, 19, 251, 252
  organizational forms, 4-5, 502-503, 519-523
  reporting requirements for corporations, 18-19, 207-208
Lenders, financing from, 51, 61
Leone, M., 216n
Liabilities, 446-479
  in accounting equation, 8
  accounting for, 466-474
  accrued. See Accrued liabilities
  adjusting entries for, 146, 155-156
  amortization of, 466-474
  on balance sheet, 13, 46, 64. See also Balance sheet
  in basic business model, 220-221
  contingent, 463-464
  current, 64, 448, 449-456
  decisions related to, 448
  defined, 8, 46
  financial analysis tools, 464-465
  long-term, 456-463, 503-504, 562
  long-term, current portion, 454
  measuring, 449
  noncurrent, 64
  reporting bond liabilities, 459
  role of, 448
Licensing rights, 413
LIFO Conformity Rule, 314
Limited liability companies (LLCs), 521
  extent of use, 5
  nature of, 5
Limited liability partnerships (LLPs), 521
Limited life
  amortization and, 415
  depreciation and, 153-154, 404-411
Line of credit, 465
Liquidity ratios
  current ratio, 65, 613, 618-619
  days to collect, 368, 369, 613

Liquidity ratios—*Cont.*
　days to sell, 319, 321, 613
　defined, 612
　inventory turnover, 318-320, 613, 618
　list of, 613
　quick ratio, 464-465, 613, 619
　receivables turnover, 368-370, 613, 618
Loan covenants
　accounting fraud and, 206
　defined, 205
　incentive to commit fraud and, 206
　violated, 455
Long-lived assets, 396-426
　amortization of. *See* Amortization
　defined, 398
　depreciation of. *See* Depreciation
　intangible, 398, 413-416, 562
　management decisions concerning, 418-420
　natural resources, 420-421
　tangible, 398, 399-413
　turnover analysis, 416-417
Long-term liabilities, 456-463
　bonds payable, 456-463, 466-474
　current portion of long-term debt, 454
　equity financing versus, 46, 503-504
　nature of, 456
　on statement of cash flows, 562
Lower of cost or market (LCM) inventory valuation,
　　314-315

M

MACRS (Modified Accelerated Cost Recovery System), 410n
Maintenance costs
　accounting policy, 403-404
　extraordinary repairs, 404
　ordinary, 403-404
Management's Discussion and Analysis (MD&A), 614, 616
Managerial accounting, 6
Managers
　counteracting incentives to commit fraud, 207-208
　decisions concerning long-lived assets, 418-420
　encouraging honesty in employees, 208
　incentives to commit fraud, 206-207
　as internal users of financial information, 6, 205
　opportunity to commit fraud, 207
　rationalizing and concealing fraud, 207
　reducing opportunities for fraud, 208
　use of financial statements, 205
Manufacturing companies
　common control principles, 251-252

　defined, 250
　gross profit percentage, 270-271, 320
　inventory of, 306-307
　operating activities and cycles, 271
Market interest rate, 459
Matching principle, 100-101, 146, 157
　accounts receivable and, 358
　depletion of natural resources, 420-421
Materiality principle, 213
Material misstatements, 213
Maturity date
　bond retirement on, 462
　bonds payable, 457
　defined, 364
　notes receivable, 364
Maturity phase, 566-567
Medicare, FICA taxes withheld, 450-451
Merchandising companies
　common control principles, 251-252
　controlling and reporting sales, 263-269
　defined, 250
　gross profit percentage, 271
　inventory of, 306
　operating activities and cycles, 271
　sales tax payable, 455
Misstatements, material, 213
Mistakes. *See* Errors
Modified Accelerated Cost Recovery System
　　(MACRS), 410n
Multistep income statement, 210-212, 269, 270
Municipal bonds, 463

N

Natural resources, 420-421
Net assets, 414
Net book value (carrying value), 153, 405
Net income. *See also* Income statement
　defined, 96
　in determining operating cash flows, 557, 558
　limitations of income statement, 112-113
　nature of, 9, 11
Net profit margin ratio, 111-112, 221, 223, 613, 615
Net sales, 269
New issues
　bonds, 457-460
　common stocks, 5, 506
　preferred stocks, 515
Noncurrent liabilities, 64
Nonrecurring items, 622-623
No-par value stock, 506

Notes payable
  on balance sheet, 13
  creation, 452
  as current liability, 452-453
  defined, 51
Notes receivable, 364-367
  defined, 357
  establishing, 365
  interest revenue and, 364-367
  pros and cons of extending credit, 356-357
  recording, 365-367
  uncollectible, accounting for, 367
Notes to the financial statements, 14
NSF (not sufficient funds) checks, 260, 261

O

1/15, n/16, 369
Operating activities, 94-95
  on balance sheet, 46-48
  converting operating expenses to cash outflow, 569-571
  current assets and, 558
  current liabilities and, 558
  defined, 14, 94
  direct method of reporting, 555-557, 567-571
  on income statement, 94-95
  indirect method of reporting, 557-560, 571-576
  interpreting cash flows from, 555-560
  merchandising company, 271
  on statement of cash flows, 14, 552, 555-560, 565-567
Operating cycle
  activities, 94-95, 251
  control over cash, 253-263
  control over inventory, 263-269
  defined, 250
  gross profit percentage, 270-271, 320
  type of business, 250
Ordinary repairs and maintenance, 403-404
Organizational forms, 4-5
  corporation, 5, 502-503
  limited liability company (LLC), 5, 521
  partnership, 4, 6, 521, 522-523
  sole proprietorship, 4, 5, 519-521
Orpurt, Steven F., 568n
Outsourcing specialists, 21
Outstanding checks, 261
Outstanding shares, 505
Overriding controls, 253
Owners' equity. See also Stockholders' equity
  for partnership, 521, 522-523
  for sole proprietorship, 519-521

P

Pacioli, Luca, 18
Partnerships, 521, 522-523
  extent of use, 5
  nature of, 4, 521
  owner's equity for, 521, 522-523
Par value, 506
Passive investments, D1
Patent, 413
Payment date of dividend, 510-511
Payroll, accrued, 450-451
Payroll deductions, 450-451
Payroll taxes, accrued, 450-451
Percentage of credit sales method, for estimating bad debts, 361
Periodic inventory system
  inventory control in, 264
  journal entries, 316, 325-326
  nature of, 264
Permanent accounts, 163
Perpetual inventory system, 264-266, 321-324
  inventory control in, 263
  journal entries, 266, 315-318, 326, 327
  nature of, 263
Petty cash, 263
Physical flow of goods, 310
Post-closing trial balance, 165-166
Preemptive rights, of common stockholders, 503
Preferred stock, 514-516
  common stock versus, 514
  defined, 514
  dividends, 514, 515-516
  issuance, 515
Preliminary release of financial information, 214
Premium
  accounting for bonds issued at, 457-458, 460-461, 466, 472-473
  amortization of bonds issued at, 460-461, 468-469, 472-473
Prepaid expenses
  deferral adjustments and, 147, 152
  operating activities and, 560
  paying cash in advance, 106
Present value
  of an annuity, C5-C6, C8-C11, C12-C13, C17
  of bond payments, 467-471
  computations using Excel, C11-C13
  defined, 457, C1
  of a single amount, C3-C4, C7-C8, C10-C11, C12
  tables for determining, C15, C17

Price/earnings (P/E) ratio, 517, 518, 519, 613, 617-618
Principal
  defined, 364
  recording for notes payable, 453
  recording for notes receivable, 366-367
Prior accounting period, time-series analysis, 219-220
Private accountants, 5
Private companies, 5
Production managers, 21
Profitability ratios, 615-618
  asset turnover, 221, 222-223, 416-417, 613, 616
  defined, 612
  earnings per share (EPS), 517-518, 613, 617
  fixed asset turnover, 416-417, 613, 616
  gross profit percentage, 270-271, 320, 613, 615-616
  list of, 613
  net profit margin, 111-112, 221, 223, 613, 615
  price/earnings (P/E) ratio, 517, 518, 519, 613, 617-618
  return on equity (ROE), 517, 518, 613, 617
Profit(s)
  in cash basis accounting, 97
  generation of, 9
Property, plant, and equipment, 398. See also Equipment;
      Long-lived assets; Tangible assets
  buildings, 400
  land, 399, 400
  reporting sales of, 571-572
Pro rata basis, 511-512
Public accountants, 5
Public companies, 5, 19-20
Public Company Accounting Oversight Board (PCAOB), 19
Purchase discounts, inventory, 317-318
Purchase returns and allowances, 317
Purchase(s)
  inventory, 308, 315-318
  of tangible asset for cash, 402
  of tangible asset on credit, 402-403

Q

Qualified audit opinion, 214
Quarterly report, release of, 215
Quick ratio, 464-465, 613, 619

R

Ratio analysis, 220-224
  basic business model, 220-221
  computations, 612-613
  defined, 609
  impact of transactions on ratios, 224

interpreting, 615-619
  liquidity ratios. See Liquidity ratios
  nature of, 609
  profitability ratios. See Profitability ratios
  solvency ratios. See Solvency ratios
Raw materials inventory, 306
Receivables turnover analysis, 368-370, 613, 618
Reconciliation. See Bank reconciliation
Record date of dividend, 510
Recording accounting transactions
  adjusting entries, 146, 148-158
  balance sheet concepts and values in, 65-67
  debit/credit framework for, 57-58
  income statement concepts and values in, 103-108
  inventory, 315-318
  nature of, 49, 54-56, 57-58
Recovery, 363
Reissuance of common stock, 508-509
Release of financial information
  financial statement release, 214-215
  investor information Web sites, 215, 216
  preliminary, 214
Rent
  benefits expiring during period, 151-153
  prepaid, 106, 147
Repurchase of stock, 507
Research and development expenses, 414
Residual claims, of common stockholders, 503
Residual value, 405, 408
Responsibility, internal control and, 251, 252
Restricted access, internal control and, 252, 257
Retailers, 250
Retained earnings, 504, 516. See also Statement
      of retained earnings
  on balance sheet, 13
  cash dividends and, 511
  distributions to shareholders, 509-511
  dividend declaration, 510-511
  in expanded accounting equation, 102
  expense as subcategory of, 102
  revenue as subcategory of, 102
  on statement of cash flows, 563
  stock splits and, 513
Retirement of bonds payable, 462-463
Return on equity (ROE), 517, 518, 613, 617
Revenue expenditures, ordinary repairs and maintenance
      as, 403-404
Revenue principle, 146
Revenue recognition principle, 98-99, 110-111, 565
Revenue(s)
  in accrual basis accounting, 98-99, 110-111, 565
  adjusting entries for, 148

in basic business model, 221
in cash basis accounting, 97-98
converting to cash inflows, 568-569
credit card sales, 370
credit sales, pros and cons of, 356-357
defined, 8, 95
earned but not yet recorded, 155
on income statement, 10-11, 95, 102-108
operating activities and, 567-571
review of, 110-111
as subcategory of retained earnings, 102
time period assumption, 96, 97
unearned, 99, 103, 455-456
Risk Management Association, 615
Rosa, Mauricio, 3-7, 10-11, 13, 18-20, 45-48, 60-61, 93, 95,
   145, 166
Rule of accrual, 98

S

Sales, inventory, 265-269, 306-307
Sales discounts, inventory, 267-268
Sales returns and allowances, 266-267, 269
Sales revenue. *See* Revenue(s)
Sales tax payable, 455
Salvage value, 405, 408
Sarbanes-Oxley Act of 2002 (SOX), 19, 207-208, 251
Seasonality, cash flows from operating activities and, 565
Secured bonds, 463
Securities and Exchange Commission (SEC), 19
   Electronic Data Gathering and Retrieval Service
      (EDGAR), 215
   external audit requirement, 208, 213-214
   filings with, 215, 216
   regulation of public company financial reporting, 205
   repurchase of stock and, 507
   Rule 5-03, 411n
Segregation of duties
   defined, 252
   internal control and, 251, 252
Separate entity assumption, 8
Serial bonds, 463
Service charges, bank reconciliation and, 260, 261
Service companies
   common control principles, 251
   defined, 250
Services
   future, receiving cash for, 103
   gift cards redeemed for, 154
   providing for cash, 103
   providing on credit, 104

Shrinkage, inventory, 264-265
Simplified effective-interest amortization, 471-474
Single amount
   future value, C2-C3
   present value, C3-C4, C7-C8, C10-C11, C12
Single-step income statement, 210
Social Security, FICA taxes withheld, 450-451
Sole proprietorships
   extent of use, 5
   nature of, 4, 519
   owner's equity for, 519-521
Solvency ratios
   debt-to-assets, 221, 222, 224, 613, 619
   defined, 612
   list of, 613
   times interest earned ratio, 465, 613, 619
SOX. *See* Sarbanes-Oxley Act of 2002 (SOX)
Specific identification inventory costing method, 309-310
Spreadsheet analysis
   to prepare statement of cash flows, 574-576
   present value computations, C11-C13
   to record and summarize transactions, 54-56
Stated interest rate, 457
Statement of cash flows, 13-14, 548-579
   adjusted trial balance and, 162
   basic equation for, 16
   categories of business activities, 14, 550
   classifying cash flows, 551-554
   defined, 13
   direct method of reporting, 555-557, 567-571
   evaluating cash flows, 565-567
   financing activities, 14, 553, 562-563, 566, 571-576
   format, 564, 568
   indirect method of reporting, 557-560, 571-576
   investing activities, 14, 552-553, 561-562, 565-566,
      571-572
   operating activities, 14, 552, 555-560, 565-567
   preparing, 555-564, 574-576
   relationship with other financial statements, 15, 553,
      554-555
   spreadsheet in preparation of, 574-576
   summary, 16
   supplemental disclosure, 563
Statement of retained earnings, 11-12
   adjusted trial balance and, 159-161
   basic equation for, 16
   defined, 11
   relationship with other financial statements, 15, 554
   summary, 16
Statement of stockholders' equity, 212
State Unemployment Tax Act (SUTA), 451
Stickney, Clyde P., 551n

Stock certificates, 512
Stock dividends, 511–513, 514
Stockholders
  financing from, 50, 60
  as investors, 7
  ownership characteristics, 502–503
Stockholders' equity, 500–526. *See also* Owners' equity;
    Statement of retained earnings
  in accounting equation, 8–9
  adjusting entries, 158
  on balance sheet, 13, 46. *See also* Balance sheet
  in basic business model, 221
  common stock. *See* Common stock
  components of, 8–9
  corporate ownership, concept of, 502–503
  defined, 8, 46
  distributions to shareholders, 509–511
  dividends. *See* Cash dividends; Stock dividends
  equity versus debt financing, 503–504
  financial ratios, 517–519
  preferred stock, 514–516
  retained earnings. *See* Retained earnings
  statement of, 212
Stock options, 507
Stock splits, 513
Straight-line amortization method
  of bonds issued at discount, 466–467
  of bonds issued at premium, 461, 466
  defined, 466
Straight-line depreciation method, 406–407, 409, 410–411, 419
Strips, 463
Subsidiary accounts, 359
Summarizing accounting transactions
  adjusting entries, 148–158
  debit/credit framework for, 58–60
  income statement concepts and values in, 103–108
  nature of, 49, 54–56, 58–60
Suppliers
  as creditors, 7
  paying, 53, 62, 107, 569
Supplies
  on balance sheet, 13
  ordering, 52–53, 62
  paying cash in advance, 106
  receiving, 53–54, 62
  used during period, 149–151

T

T-accounts
  accrual adjustments, 155–157

adjusted trial balance, 158–162
  balance sheet transactions, 59–63
  debit/credit framework for, 58–60
  deferral adjustments, 149–154
  defined, 58
  income statement transactions, 103–108
  to prepare statement of cash flows, 572–573
  simplified format for ledger accounts, 59–60
  unadjusted trial balance, 108–110
Tangible assets, 399–413
  acquisition, 400–403
  defined, 398
  depreciation, 404–411. *See also* Depreciation
  disposal, 405, 408, 411–412
  maintenance costs, 403–404
  types of, 398, 399
  use, 403–411
Tax depreciation, 410–411
Taxes. *See also* Income taxes
  FICA, 450–451
  sales tax payable, 455
  unemployment, 451
Temporary accounts
  closing, 162–166
  defined, 163
Time lags
  bank reconciliation and, 259–260
  receivables turnover analysis, 368–370
  resetting the clock for doubtful accounts, 367
Timelines, interest period, 365
Time period assumption
  defined, 96
  ethical issues in, 97
Times accounts receivable, 368–370
Time-series analysis, 219–220, 609
Times interest earned ratio, 465, 613, 619
Time value of money
  annuity, C4–C6, C8–C11, C12–C13, C16, C17
  defined, C1
  future value, C1, C2–C3, C5, C14, C16
  interest periods in, C6
  interest rates in, C6
  present value, C1, C3–C4, C5–C6, C7–C13, C15, C17
  single amount, C2–C4, C7–C8, C10–C11, C12, C14–C15
Timing
  of reporting expenses versus cash receipts, 101
  of reporting revenue versus cash receipts, 98–99, 110–111
Trademark, 413
Transactions
  analysis of, in accounting cycle, 49–54
  basic accounting equation and, 49

defined, 48
 duality of effects, 49
 types of events, 48
Transportation cost, inventory, 316–317
Treasury bonds, 463
Treasury stock, 504, 507–509
 contra-accounts, 507, 508
 defined, 505
 reissuance of, 508–509
 repurchase of stock, 507
Trend analysis. *See* Horizontal analysis
Trial balance
 adjusted, 158–162
 defined, 108
 post-closing, 165–166
 unadjusted, 108–110, 149, 150
Turnover analysis
 asset, 221, 222–223, 416–417, 613, 616
 fixed asset, 416–417, 613, 616
 inventory, 318–320, 613, 618
 receivables, 368–370, 613, 618

U

Unadjusted trial balance, 108–110, 149
 debit/credit framework and, 108–110
 sample, 110, 150
Uncollectible accounts
 aging of accounts receivable method for estimating, 361–362
 allowance method for estimating, 362, 367
 direct write-off method, 359–360, 363–364, 371
 percentage of credit sales method for estimating, 361
 revising estimates for, 363
 segregating collections and write-offs, 371
Uncollectible notes, 367
Unearned revenue, 99, 103, 455–456
Unearned subscriptions, deferral adjustments and, 147
Unemployment taxes, 451
Uniform Partnership Act, 521
U.S. Patent and Trademark Office, 413
Unit of measure assumption, 10
Units-of-production depreciation method, 406, 407, 409
Unlimited life, amortization and, 415

Unqualified audit opinion, 213–214
Useful life, 405

V

Vacation, mandatory, 253
Verification of transactions. *See* Independent verification
Vertical analysis, 611–612
 computations, 611–612
 defined, 609, 611
 examples of, 611–612
 relationships noted in, 615
Voting power, stock options and, 507
Voting rights
 common stock, 503
 preferred stock, 514
Voucher system
 defined, 256
 overview of, 257

W

Wages expense
 incurred but not yet recorded, 155–156
 paying cash to employees, 105
Wealth, incentive to commit fraud and, 207
Weighted average inventory costing method, 310, 312, 323
Wholesalers, 250
Wolfe, David T., 207n
Working capital management, 565
Work in process inventory, 306
Write-off
 defined, 359
 direct write-off method for bad debts, 359–360, 363–364, 371

X

XBRL tagging system, 216

Z

Zang, Yoonseok, 568n
Zero-coupon bonds, 463

Common Ratios Used in Financial Statement Analysis

Profitability Ratios

(1) Net Profit Margin = $\dfrac{\text{Net Income}}{\text{Total Revenue}} \times 100$
(Ch. 5, p. 221)

(2) Gross Profit Percentage = $\dfrac{\text{Net Sales Revenue} - \text{Cost of Goods Sold}}{\text{Net Sales Revenue}} \times 100$
(Ch. 6, p. 270)

(3) Asset Turnover = $\dfrac{\text{Total Revenue}}{\text{Average Total Assets}}$
(Ch. 5, p. 221)

(4) Fixed Asset Turnover = $\dfrac{\text{Total Revenue}}{\text{Average Net Fixed Assets}}$
(Ch. 9, p. 416)

(5) Return on Equity (ROE) = $\dfrac{\text{Net Income}}{\text{Average Stockholders' Equity}} \times 100$
(Ch. 11, p. 517)

(6) Earnings per Share (EPS) = $\dfrac{\text{Net Income*}}{\text{Average Number of Common Shares Outstanding}}$
(Ch. 11, p. 517)

(7) Price/Earnings Ratio = $\dfrac{\text{Stock Price**}}{\text{EPS}}$
(Ch. 11, p. 517)

Liquidity Ratios

(8) Receivables Turnover = $\dfrac{\text{Net Sales Revenue}}{\text{Average Net Receivables}}$
(Ch. 8, p. 368)

Days to Collect = $\dfrac{365}{\text{Receivables Turnover Ratio}}$
(Ch. 8, p. 368)

(9) Inventory Turnover = $\dfrac{\text{Cost of Goods Sold}}{\text{Average Inventory}}$
(Ch. 7, p. 319)

Days to Sell = $\dfrac{365}{\text{Inventory Turnover Ratio}}$
(Ch. 7, p. 319)

(10) Current Ratio = $\dfrac{\text{Current Assets}}{\text{Current Liabilities}}$
(Ch. 2, p. 65)

(11) Quick Ratio = $\dfrac{\text{Cash} + \text{Short-term Investments} + \text{Accounts Receivable, Net}}{\text{Current Liabilities}}$
(Ch. 10, p. 464)

Solvency Ratios

(12) Debt-to-Assets = $\dfrac{\text{Total Liabilities}}{\text{Total Assets}}$
(Ch. 5, p. 221)

(13) Times Interest Earned = $\dfrac{\text{Net Income} + \text{Interest Expense} + \text{Income Tax Expense}}{\text{Interest Expense}}$
(Ch. 10, p. 464)

* If a company has preferred stock or similar securities outstanding, dividends on these securities are subtracted from net income in the numerator to assess the earnings for each share of common stock.
** Stock price is the closing price reported for the day on which the company first reports its annual earnings in a press release.

Chapter Title	Chapter Focus Company	Company Logo	Type of Company	Contrast Companies	Key Ratios
1 Business Decisions and Financial Accounting	**Pizza Aroma**	PIZZA AROMA	Restaurant	Under Armour, Inc. Southwest Airlines Regal Entertainment	
2 The Balance Sheet	**Pizza Aroma**	PIZZA AROMA	Restaurant	Domino's Pizza Hasbro, Inc. Half Price Books, Inc. Starbucks Corporation	Current Ratio
3 The Income Statement	**Pizza Aroma**	PIZZA AROMA	Restaurant	Papa John's Domino's Pizza Carnival Corporation H & R Block, Inc.	Net Profit Margin
4 Adjustments, Financial Statements, and Financial Results	**Pizza Aroma**	PIZZA AROMA	Restaurant	Coach, Inc. Delta Airlines Apple, Inc. Volcom, Inc.	
5 Financial Reporting and Analysis	**Activision, Inc.**	ACTIVISION	Video game developer	Electronic Arts Inc. Ubisoft John Wiley & Sons	Debt-to-Assets Asset Turnover Net Profit Margin
6 Internal Control, Cash, and Merchandise Sales	**Walmart Stores, Inc.**	Walmart	Discount retail store	Oakley Texas Instruments Under Armour, Inc. JCPenney, Inc. Fortune Brands	Gross Profit Percentage